中国世界贸易组织年鉴

李岚清

主　管：中华人民共和国商务部
主　办：中国世界贸易组织研究会
合　办：对外经济贸易大学
北京市国际服务贸易事务中心
上海WTO事务咨询中心
深圳市公平贸易促进署
武汉大学WTO学院
国际贸易和可持续发展中心

2015
总第9期

中国商务出版社
CHINA COMMERCE AND TRADE PRESS

图书在版编目（CIP）数据

中国世界贸易组织年鉴．2015/中国世界贸易组织研究会编．—北京：中国商务出版社，2016.5

ISBN 978-7-5103-1493-3

Ⅰ.①中… Ⅱ.①中… Ⅲ.①世界贸易组织–影响–中国经济–2015–年鉴 Ⅳ.①F743-54②F12-54

中国版本图书馆CIP数据核字（2016）第107202号

中国世界贸易组织年鉴 2015

ZHONGGUO SHIJIE MAOYI ZUZHI NIANJIAN 2015

中国世界贸易组织研究会 编

出　　版：中国商务出版社

地　　址：北京市东城区安外东后巷28号　　邮　　编：100710

责任部门：经管与人文社科事业部（010-64255862　cctpress@163.com）

责任编辑：李彩娟　孙　梅

网　　址：http：//www.cctpress.com

邮　　箱：cctp@cctpress.com

排　　版：北京通润四达企业形象策划有限责任公司

印　　刷：北京墨阁印刷有限公司

开　　本：890毫米×1240毫米　1/16

印　　张：50.75（正文）　5.25（彩插）　　字　　数：1620千字

版　　次：2016年5月第1版　　印　　次：2016年5月第1次印刷

书　　号：ISBN 978-7-5103-1493-3

定　　价：480.00元

凡所购本版图书有印装质量问题，请与本社综合业务部联系（电话：010－64212247）

《中国世界贸易组织年鉴》编委会组织机构

主　编

孙振宇　第十一届全国政协委员、商务部前副部长、中国首任常驻世界贸易组织代表团常驻代表、特命全权大使、中国世界贸易组织研究会会长

副 主 编

俞晓松　中国世界贸易组织研究会高级顾问、中国国际贸易促进委员会前会长、中国世界贸易组织研究会竞争政策与法律专业委员会主席

张志刚　中共中国商业联合会委员会党委书记、中国世界贸易组织研究会高级顾问、商务部前副部长

徐秉金　中国世界贸易组织研究会高级顾问、中国欧洲经济技术合作协会会长、原对外贸易经济合作部部长助理、原国家机电办主任

李恩恒　中国常驻世界贸易组织代表团前副代表、中国世界贸易组织研究会前副会长

王琴华　商务部产业司前司长、中国世界贸易组织研究会前副会长

王成安　中国—葡语国家经贸合作论坛（澳门）前秘书长、中国世界贸易组织研究会副会长、中国世界贸易组织研究会竞争政策与法律专业委员会执行主席

薛荣久　对外经济贸易大学教授、中国世界贸易组织研究会副会长

郑志海　原对外贸易经济合作部研究院院长、中国世界贸易组织研究会前副会长

吴家煌　中国入世市场准入谈判代表、中国世界贸易组织研究会前副会长

执 行 主 编

陈　鹏　中国世界贸易组织研究会副会长兼秘书长、商务部配额许可证事务局前局长、中国国际贸易学会前副会长

施建军　对外经济贸易大学校长、教授、中国世界贸易组织研究会副会长

霍建国　商务部国际贸易经济合作研究院前院长、中国世界贸易组织研究会副会长

梁惊原　北京市国际服务贸易事务中心常务副主任

高　瞻　深圳市公平贸易促进署署长

余敏友　武汉大学 WTO 学院院长、教授

梅林德　国际贸易和可持续发展中心（ICTSD）总裁

委　员

（以下按姓氏笔画排序）

王世春　联合国工发组织总干事办公室主任

王利群　中国钢铁工业协会副会长

王俊文　中国国际贸易学会会长

王洛林　商务部经贸政策咨询委员会前主任

王　晖　海峡两岸经贸交流协会副会长

尹宗华　中国国际贸易促进委员会副会长

吕克俭　中国驻日本使馆经济商务处前公使、商务部亚洲司前司长

任鸿斌　商务部世界贸易组织司司长兼中国政府世界贸易组织通报咨询局局长

刘有厚　驻欧盟经济商务参赞处前公使衔参赞

刘　佐　中国税务报社总编辑

孙永福　商务部欧洲司前司长

杜　墨　中国保险监督管理委员会国际部国际规则处处长

李月芬　南方中心经济和发展金融特别顾问

李　永　中国世界贸易组织研究会外经贸咨询顾问委员会委员、中国国际贸易学会中美欧经济战略研究中心共同主席

岑兆琦　中国世界贸易组织研究会竞争政策与法律专业委员会副秘书长

何　宁　中国驻美国使馆经济商务处前公使、商务部美大司前司长

汪　敏　大益爱心基金会秘书长，北京中联智库咨询公司董事长，原中国青年企业家协会副会长、秘书长

沙开清　国家知识产权局办公室综合信息处处长

张丽萍　联合国贸易和发展会议高级经济事务官员

张晓婉　农业部农业贸易促进中心研究员

陈　星　中央人民政府驻澳门特别行政区联络办公室经济部副部长、贸易处负责人

陈婧丹　中国民用航空局政策法规司政策处

林桂军　对外经济贸易大学副校长

周宏达　中国证监会国际合作部副处长

周冠山　海关总署国际合作司前司长

赵龙跃　南开大学教授、南开大学中国国际发展研究中心主任

赵　宏　商务部国际贸易经济合作研究院副院长、商务部世界贸易组织司前世界贸易组织谈判专员

赵明霞　中国纺织工业联合会产业部处长

赵忠秀　对外经济贸易大学副校长

胡　铁　中国世界贸易组织研究会竞争政策与法律专业委员会副秘书长

侯　颖　中国钢铁工业协会高级分析师、市场调研部副主任、教授级高级工程师

姜　波　中国保险监督管理委员会国际部主任

钱建初　中国商务出版社常务副社长、总编辑
郭俊峰　商务部西亚非洲司前副司长
唐　炜　中国国际贸易中心股份有限公司总经理
崔明谟　中国国际经济合作学会会长
屠新泉　对外经济贸易大学中国WTO研究院执行院长
隆国强　国务院发展研究中心副主任
蒋璇芳　中国钢铁工业协会市场调研部进出口处副处长
韩铁城　中国驻法国使馆经济商务参赞处前公使衔参赞
戴云楼　中国驻美国使馆经济商务参赞处前公使衔参赞

指导单位

世界贸易组织秘书处
联合国贸易和发展会议
商务部国际贸易经济合作研究院
北京大学
武汉大学
上海对外经贸大学
中华人民共和国常驻世界贸易组织代表团
联合国工业发展组织
清华大学
对外经济贸易大学
南开大学

编辑部

总编辑：刘学煌
副总编辑：宫和平　崔　凡　杨凤鸣　杨　芳
编　　辑：（以下按姓氏笔画排序）
王　项　王　惠　王加伟　王劲松　孙靓莹　李雪峰　杨　旸　杨永坤　吴洪岗
宋春峰　张春霞　庞　嫣　侯虓昆　程志刚　蔡立华　蔡尚融　蔡凌鹏　戴　臻

序

2015年12月19日，世界贸易组织第十届部长级会议在内罗毕落幕。会议就多哈回合农业出口竞争、最不发达国家议题达成共识，承诺全面取消农产品出口补贴，并达成了近十八年来首个关税减让协议《信息技术协定》扩围协议。然而，美欧等发达成员与发展中成员对于多哈回合的分歧也明朗化。

2001年12月，中国成为世贸组织大家庭的一员。十四年来，我们与其他成员共商共建共享多边贸易体制，成为多边体制的受益者。中国对外贸易额增长6.8倍，年均增幅16%；国内生产总值增长5.1倍，年均增幅14%。中国经济总量已稳居世界第二位，产业向中高端水平迈进，全球价值链地位有所提高。

十四年来，中国的开放发展惠及世界。2001—2014年，全球货物贸易额增长2.1倍，年均增幅9%。尤其在2008年国际金融危机后，中国对全球经济走出泥淖做出了巨大贡献。中国不断深化对外开放，成为全球第一货物贸易大国和主要对外投资大国，成为120多个国家和地区的最大贸易伙伴，进口总额占全球比重超过10%，为贸易伙伴创造了2000万个就业机会。

作为多边体制的积极参与者、建设者和贡献者，我们在维护多边体制、履行贸易大国义务方面任重而道远。如何坚持多哈授权与框架、坚决维护发展利益，同时又能统筹协调投资、电子商务、中小企业等前瞻性新议题，需要与各方一道继续深入探索。我们将借助G20、APEC等国际平台，加强多双边协调沟通，继续在多边这个主渠道发挥引领作用。

由中国世界贸易组织研究会编辑出版的《中国世界贸易组织年鉴2015》，围绕当前国际形势下多边贸易体制的新挑战、多哈回合谈判的新进展、中国在WTO中的新动态、中国学术界的最新研究等内容，进行了全面、客观、系统的介绍。希望这部工具书能较全面地宣传 WTO 的规则，为社会各界研究世界贸易组织多边贸易体制和中国经贸发展提供有益的参考和借鉴。

中国世界贸易组织研究会名誉会长
中华人民共和国商务部前部长 陈德铭

2015 年 12 月

编辑说明

《中国世界贸易组织年鉴（2015）》（以下简称“本年鉴”）是中华人民共和国商务部主管，由中国世界贸易组织研究会组织国内外权威部门和专家、学者参与编撰出版的大型工具书，集政策性、研究性、实用性、史料性为一体，是国内外追踪研究WTO及相关问题，全面了解加入WTO后中国对外开放新形势和新变化的年度出版物。

2015年，世界贸易组织二十岁了。二十年来，世界贸易组织取得了巨大成就，同时也面临着诸多挑战。2015年12月19日，第十届部长级会议在内罗毕落幕。会议就多哈回合农业出口竞争、最不发达国家议题达成共识，承诺全面取消农产品出口补贴，并达成了近18年来首个关税减让协议，即《信息技术协定》扩围协议。然而，美欧等发达成员与发展中成员关于多哈回合谈判的分歧也愈加明朗化。

WTO二十年造就了强有力的多边贸易体制，这二十年也促进了中国的发展与进步。如何依托多边贸易体系，推进全球经济增长？作为世贸组织的核心成员，WTO的未来与中国密不可分。TPP已完成谈判并达成协定，亚太区域如何促进区域内的贸易投资一体化？此外，诸如中国“市场经济地位”条款到期的具体问题等亦会影响中国的经济贸易发展。面对当前国际经贸格局的变化，中国如何加快构建开放型经济新体制，从上海自贸试验区的探索可以窥知一二。本年鉴的专文对上述问题分别进行了阐述。

在内容框架体系方面，本年鉴不断完善，框架体系不断充实调整，目前包括：专文、WTO事务、中国与WTO、中国大陆与港澳台、中国与WTO主要成员经贸关系、与WTO有关的政策与管理措施、中国地方WTO事务、WTO学术成果、与WTO有关的法规及政策、贸易统计数据等篇目。

本年鉴在编撰过程中，得到了商务部、国务院，其他相关经济贸易主管部门以及我国常驻世界贸易组织代表团和广大作者、译者的积极支持和帮助，在此谨表示衷心的感谢！

本年鉴所涉及单位名称、作者姓名及职务均以截稿日期为准。我们真诚希望社会各界继续对年鉴的编辑和出版工作给予关心和支持，对不足之处敬请提出批评和改进意见，以使本刊日臻完善。

通信地址：北京市朝阳区惠新东街10号，对外经济贸易大学行政楼125室

邮政编码：100029

电　　话：0086-10-8425 5121

传　　真：0086-10-8425 5121

E-mail：cwtoyearbook@163. com

《中国世界贸易组织年鉴》编辑部

2016年3月

目　录

- 学术论文

➢ 中国与世界贸易组织

● 中国商务统计

附　录

CONTENTS

2015 | 中国世界贸易组织年鉴支持单位

SUPPORTS OF CHINA WORLD TRADE ORGANIZATION YEARBOOK

DTW 大田物流 Logistics	NU SKIN 优异·你看得见 大中华区副总裁：李潮东	青岛市商务局 Bureau of Commerce,Qingdao
CEDZ 常熟经济技术开发区	山东兖州工业园区	CETZ 重庆经济技术开发区 CHONGQING ECONOMIC&TECHNOLOGICAL DEVELOPMENT ZONE 党工委书记、主任——王俊
成都经济技术开发区	邹平经济技术开发区 Zouping Economic and Technological Development Zone	江苏沛县经济开发区
中国—中东欧国家投资贸易博览会 CHINA-CEEC INVESTMENT AND TRADE EXPO	MEDA 绵阳国家级经济技术开发区 Mianyang Economic and Technical Development Area	潍坊滨海经济技术开发区 Weifang Binhai Economic and Techoiogical Development Zone

中车大同电力机车有限公司
CRRC DATONG CO., LTD.

自主化HXD2型电力机车
Self-determination HXD2 Electric Locomotive

中车大同电力机车有限公司是中国最重要的电力机车研发和生产基地之一。公司始建于1954年，历经蒸汽机车和内燃机车时代，目前专注于电力机车领域。

公司是中国电力机车产品品种最为齐全的厂家，产品覆盖直流传动和交流传动两大技术领域，是中国铁路干线电力机车的主要供货商之一。一直以来，公司以强大的技术实力和生产能力为平台，以客户需求为导向，不断实现产品创新（部分产品如图片所示）。

2010年，公司自主研发的“中白货运1型”大功率交流传动电力机车出口白俄罗斯，成为中国首家成功向欧洲市场出口电力机车整车的企业。以此为契机，2013年公司再次获得白俄罗斯铁路联盟的18台中白六轴大功率交流传动电力机车订单。

未来，公司将继续与国内外客户携手并肩，实现共赢互惠。

CRRC Datong Co., Ltd. is one of the most important bases for electric locomotive research and development in China. It was established in 1954 and experienced the period of steam locomotive and diesel locomotive. At present, it devotes to electric locomotive field.

Datong Company is the supplier which has the most complete electric locomotive products in China. Its products cover AC and DC driven locomotive technical fields. It is one of the most important suppliers of electric locomotive for Chinese mainline railways. Datong Company has a strong platform based on technical ability and production capacity, which is oriented by customers’ requirements and promotes to fulfill products upgrade (partial products see the pictures).

In 2010, Datong Company researched and developed “BKT-1” high power AC driven electric locomotive and exported it to Belarus successfully, which realizes a break for exporting the complete locomotive to European countries. Being highly praised by Belarus customers, Datong Company signed a contract of 18 BKT six axle high-power AC electric locomotives with the Belarusian Union of Railways in 2013.

In future, Datong Company will continually cooperate with our customers at home and abroad to realize final win-win.

HXD2型电力机车
HXD2 electric locomotive

30t轴重电力机车
30t Axle Load Electric Locomotive

中白货运1型电力机车
“BKT-1” electric locomotive

地址：中国山西省大同市前进街1号，037038
电话：+86 352 7162829
传真：+86 352 7162246

Address: No.1 Qianjin Street Datong, Shanxi Province, China, 037038
Tel: +86 352 7162829
Fax: +86 352 7162246

萍乡经济技术开发区

Pingxiang Economic and Technological Development Zone

一、电子商务产业基地

该项目由开发区管委会投资3亿元兴建，选址电商大厦，由一个现代化集中办公楼及数千平方米的集中仓储物流中心组成。目前，江西康洁企创有限公司投资1.2亿元开发电商大厦，主要是管理电商大厦与电子商务的运营，并且与入驻电商大厦的企业进行对接。

二、玉湖新区城市综合体

该项目由开发区投资30亿元兴建，选址湖新区玉湖路两侧，位于新市政府中心区域，占地580亩。规划目标是建成集娱乐、休闲、购物于一体的高档商业中心，全面提升玉湖新城的城市形象和品位；进一步完善开发区现代服务功能，提高城市档次，改善居民精神文化生活，并带动相关产业发展，预计投资回收期为4至6年。

三、洪山片区城市综合体

该项目由开发区投资20亿元兴建，选址萍乡经济开发区洪山大道边洪山片区，占地520亩，主要建设文化商业步行街、3D国际影视城、书城、国际商贸酒店、写字楼、公司总部基地等商住项目和商贸开发等项目。项目建设计划在4至5年内完成，可进一步完善开发区现代服务功能，提升服务水平，加速文化产业的集聚。

杭南长高铁萍乡北站

热闹的工业园区

四、萍实湿地公园新区项目

田中新区位于玉湖新区西侧，高铁萍乡北站、田中生态湖、聚龙公园、奥体中心、毛家湾文化村等项目均坐落在这里。田中新区总占地面积31500亩，近期可建设开发土地约3000亩，将逐步打造成集商业金融、生态居住、教育科研、休闲旅游为一体的城市门户展示区。

五、城乡一体化项目

位于田中新区西面的上柳源管理处和清泉管理处之间，区域内规划项目用地总面积为4200亩。这里依山傍水，鸟语花香，尚是一块有望大展宏图的处女地项目。按照新型城镇化要求，将布局一个集养老休闲、民俗文化为一体的综合型开发项目。开发区将此项目列为首批采用PPP模式建设的项目。

六、新三板工业园

位于萍乡经济开发区原三田煤矿改造区，占地面积1200亩，计划引进50至60家能够在新三板上市的企业入驻，主要为科技型中小企业提供融资、上市的平台，以促进开发区新型科技企业快速发展。已签约新三板工业园入园协议的项目有联友建材、应陶康顺、新胜新材料、瑞发科技等。目前在进行现有“新三板”上市企业的初步筛选，将符合开发区产业发展政策、与开发区现有产业关联度高、能够形成产业集群的企业优先筛选出来，以提高招商引资的针对性与实效性。下一步将继续引进已在新三板上市或能够在新三板上市的企业入驻园区，将其真正打造成一个具有竞争力的特色园区。

建设中的田中生态湿地公园

DTW 大田物流
Logistics
OKAIR
IBC
BULK

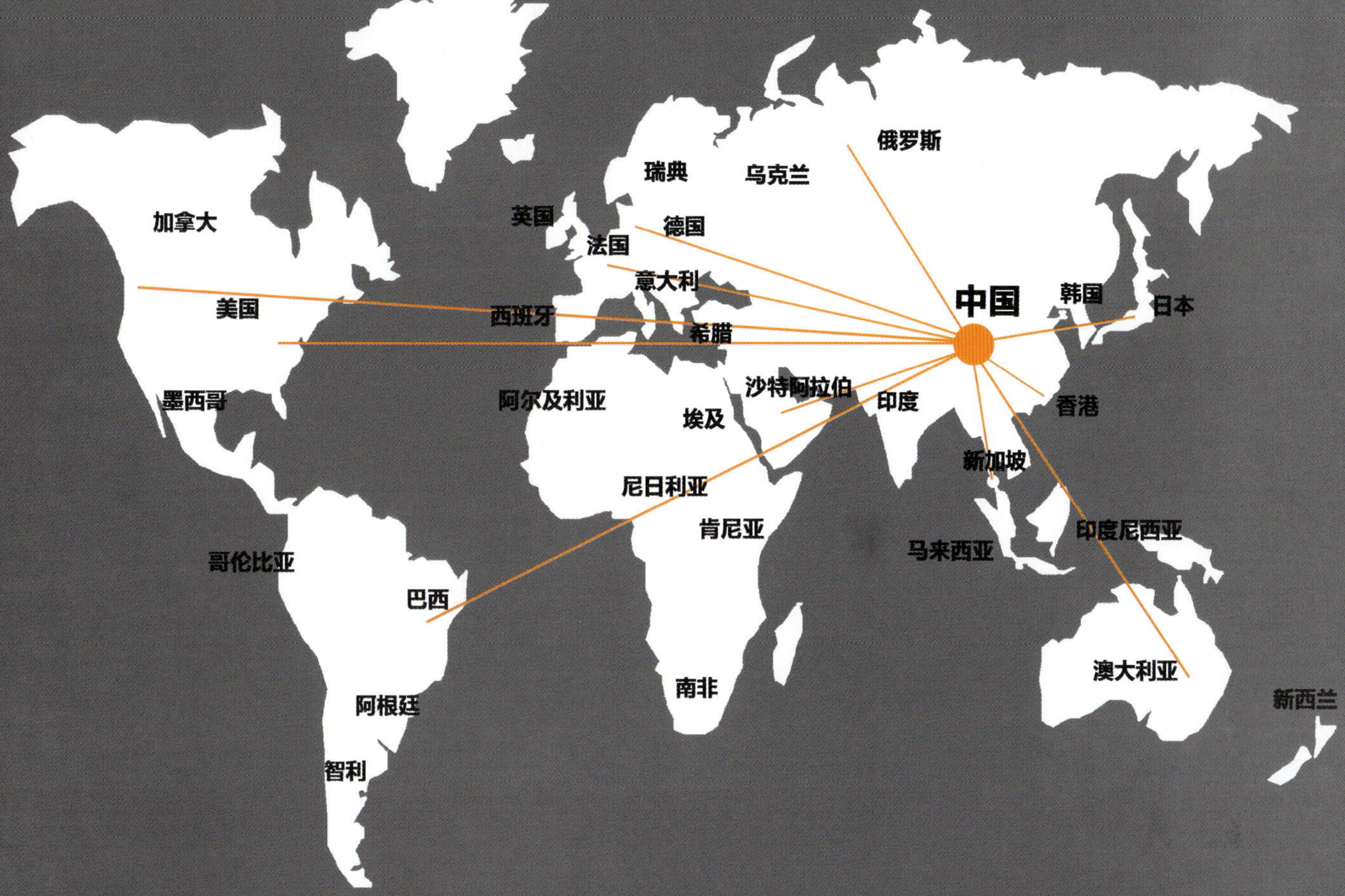

助力跨境电商

服务全球伙伴

开封经济技术开发区

Kaifeng Economic and Technological Development Zone

开封经济技术开发区位于八朝古都开封的西部，面积287平方公里，人口28万，1992年成立，2010年升级为国家经济技术开发区，开发区定位是建设内陆开发开放高地，打造“三化”协调发展先导区，形成中原经济区核心增长板块和最具活力的发展区域。近年来，开封经济技术开发区抢抓河南自由贸易试验区建设、中原经济区建设、郑汴一体化发展等重大机遇，逐步确立了汽车及零部件、空分及特色装备制造、电子商务、文化旅游、生物医药、电子信息六大产业体系，产业发展呈现出弯道超车、蓄势崛起的良好态势。面对新常态要有新作为，开封经济技术开发区将继续发挥自身独特的区位、产业、资源、政策优势，努力建设成为开封引领新型城镇化建设的龙头、推动经济发展的核心增长极、向河南新兴副中心城市迈进的排头兵。

Located in the west part of Kaifeng, an ancient capital of 8 dynasties, Kaifeng Economic and Technological Development Zone was founded in 1992. Upgraded into national level in 2010, Kaifeng Economic and Technological Development Zone now covers 287 km^2 with a total population of 280,000.In recent years, aiming at constructing an inland highland for opening-up and development, a pilot zone for coordinated development of new industrialization, new urbanization and modernization of agriculture, as well as serving as the key growth pole and the most dynamic section for Central China Economic Area, Kaifeng Economic and Technological Development Zone is making the best use of several major opportunities such as the construction of Henan Free Trade Zone, Central China Economic Area and the integration of Zhengzhou and Kaifeng to set up 6 industrial complex including automobile and car part, air separation equipment and other feathered machine building industry, E-commerce, cultural tourism, bio-pharmaceuticals and electronic information, all of which are on the verge of quick rise.Facing the New Normal, Kaifeng Economic and Technological Development Zone is determined to make new achievements. Giving full play of its advantages in location, industry, resources and policies, Kaifeng Economic and Technological Development Zone is striving to build itself as the usher of Kaifeng's new urbanization and key growth pole of economic development on its way to Henan province's sub center.

唐山市曹妃甸经济技术开发区

唐山曹妃甸经济技术开发区地处环渤海经济圈的核心位置。开发建设曹妃甸是国家做出的重大战略部署，是河北省实施“沿海强省”战略和唐山实现转型升级的重要支撑。自开发建设以来，先后有 60 多位党和国家领导人到这里视察指导工作，明确提出：“要努力把唐山建成东北亚区域合作的窗口城市、环渤海地区的新型工业化基地、首都经济圈的重要支点。” 按照《曹妃甸循环经济示范区产业发展总体规划》，曹妃甸将建设成为能源、矿石等大宗货物的集疏港，新型工业化基地，商业性能源储备基地，以及国家级循环经济示范区。在《京津冀协同发展规划纲要》中，曹妃甸将成为国家战略部署中重要承载地，以建设环渤海地区集疏运综合港口、新型工业化基地、宜居宜业的现代化新城为目标，打造成为首都战略功能区和协同发展示范区。

曹妃甸拥有五大独特优势：一是港口条件得天独厚。曹妃甸因海而生，因港而兴，港产联动，是世界一流的临港

首钢京唐钢铁厂

华润曹妃甸热电厂

产业聚集地。港口特点可概括为水深、港阔、地广。二是区位交通畅达全球。曹妃甸是“一带一路”和京津冀协同发展的重要连接点。《京津冀协同发展规划纲要》明确提出打造世界一流石化基地，建设国家原油战略储备库，京冀共建曹妃甸现代产业发展试验区，将天津滨海新区政策延伸至曹妃甸。曹妃甸成为疏解非首都核心功能、推进北京产业转移、承担国家重大科技项目的重要平台。三是资源能源十分丰富。曹妃甸腹地唐山是一个资源性城市，为全国焦煤主要产区，是全国三大铁矿区之一。曹妃甸地区拥有年产 200 万吨原盐的亚洲最大盐场，石油储量达 10 亿吨以上，天然气储量 780 亿立方米以上。全区规划总装机容量达到 460 万千瓦，为河北省装机容量最大。四是生态环境优美独特。曹妃甸还有一大宝贵的自然资源——湿地。湿地具有调节气候、净化污染、蓄养植被以及教育科研等诸多功能，是物种丰富的“博物馆”，也被称为“地球之肾”。五是腹地产业支撑有力。曹妃甸的直接腹地唐山市具有 130 多年工业历史，被誉为“中国近代工业的摇篮”。

中石化原油储备基地

综合保税区

NU SKIN
眺望未来，
生活一切如新

人才
文化
产品
事业

2014 APEC
贸易部长会议发表《青岛声明》

2014 APEC Ministers Responsible for Trade Meeting Adopt Qingdao Statement

2014年5月17—18日，2014年亚太经合组织（APEC）贸易部长会议在青岛召开，来自21个成员的贸易部长和WTO等5个国际组织代表团围绕主要议题展开探讨，推动相关领域合作并共同发表APEC贸易部长《青岛声明》，重申对多边贸易体制的支持，同意制订《APEC推动实现亚太自贸区路线图》，加强区域经济一体化。

这是APEC贸易部长会议2001年在上海举办之后，时隔13年第二次在我国举办，也是青岛历史上承办的最高级别的国际会议。这是对这座城市开放和国际化城市环境的最好认可。亚太经合组织秘书处执行主任艾伦•博拉德给予青岛筹备工作很高的评价，他说，“青岛不负众望地交出了一张令人满意的答卷。”作为见证APEC经济体之间思想碰撞的地方城市，青岛已然在亚太共同发展的蓝图上镌刻下重要一笔，而这座城市细致入微的服务，也深深地打动了与会代表，成为青岛不断向前发展的软实力。

On May 17-18, the 2014 Meeting of APEC Ministers Responsible for Trade was held in Qingdao. Ministers from 21 members and five international organizations such as WTO discussed the topics, promoted the cooperation in relevant fields, and issued Qingdao Statement. The participants reiterated the supports to the multilateral trading system, and agreed the enactment of Road Map of Establishing Free Trade Area of the Asia-Pacific (FTAAP), so as to advance regional economic integration.

In 2001, APEC MRT Meeting was hosted in Shanghai. After 13 years, the meeting in Qingdao is the 2nd time held in China. It is also the highest level international meeting in Qingdao in its history. The meeting is the best recognition of the openness and internationalization of the city. Alan Bollard, Executive Director of Asia Pacific Economic Cooperation (APEC) Secretariat, spoke highly of the preparatory work. He said that Qingdao has handed over a satisfactory answer as expected. As a place witnessed the meeting of minds of APEC members, Qingdao has engraved an important mark for the joint development of Asia-Pacific region. The considerate services of Qingdao has impressed all participants and become a soft power for its development.

潍坊滨海经济技术开发区

Weifang Binhai Economic and Techoiogical Development Zone

潍坊滨海经济技术开发区成立于1995年8月，2010年升级为国家经济技术开发区。开发区陆域面积677平方公里，海域面积510平方公里，先后被确定为“国家科技兴贸创新基地”、“国家生态工业示范园区”、“国家职业教育创新发展试验区”、“全国科技兴海示范区”和“山东科学发展园区、循环经济示范区”。

滨海区位于山东半岛北部、渤海湾南岸，地处环渤海经济圈的咽喉地带，是连接长三角与京津地区的重要节点，也是省会都市圈的出海口、济青一体化的支撑点、对接东北亚的保税港、海洋产业群的聚集地，地缘优势明显。区内的潍坊港为国家一类开放口岸、地区性重要港口，2015年将建成亿吨大港。2014年底，由交通运输部与山东省、辽宁省共同推进的鲁辽陆海联运滚装甩挂运输大通道实现首航，潍坊至营口这条渤海湾“黄金水道”正式贯通，首开中国海上绿色货滚甩挂运输通道。

开发区海岸线长69公里，有浅海滩涂20多万亩，集约用海面积100多平方公里，可直接开发利用的工矿存量用地近500多平方公里，办理土地手续方便快捷，发展空间非常广阔。

目前已有海化集团、潍柴大机、瑞驰汽车、海王化工、中棉集团、新和成药业、中化弘润石化、颐杰鸿丰重型钢构等一大批骨干企业投产达效，盐化油化一体化、新能源汽车、机器人、高档游艇、中速机、港口建设等1000多个大项目正在建设。下一步，将着力打造汽车制造、动力机械、工程机械、海洋化工四个产业城，临港物流、滨海旅游两个产业基地，加快形成过万亿的蓝色高端产业体系。

“蓝黄”两大国家战略在滨海交汇融合，为滨海带来千载难逢的发展机遇

“Blue and Yellow ” nationl strategies overlapping in BEDA,brings golden development opportunities to BEI

国电集团风电场

Guodian Coastal Wind Power Project

中海油山东海化集团石化项目

Petrochemical Project of Shandong Haihua Group of CNOOC

瑞驰新能源汽车装配线

Assembly Line of Ruichi New Energy Automobile

Established in August 1995, Weifang Binhai Economic and Technological Development Area(BEDA) upgraded to a national economic and technological development area in 2010. Covering a land area of 677 square kilometers and a sea area of 510 square kilometers, BEDA has been continuously accredited as National Innovation Base for Rejuvenating Trade through Science and Technology, National Demonstration Eco-Industry Park, National Vocational Education Innovation Zone, National Demonstration Zone Invigorating the Sea by Science and Technology and Scientific Development Park and Circular Economy Demonstration zone in Shandong Province.

BEDA is located in the northern part of Shandong Peninsula. It has obvious geography advantages, such as the throat of Bohai Economy Circle, the important connecting place of Yangtze River Delta and Beijing-Tianjin Region, the estuary of the provincial Capital City Circle, the supporting point of Jinan-Qingdao Integration, the boned port connecting with Northeast Asia and the gathering place of marine industrial groups. Weifang Harbor, a national first class open port and regional important harbor with all berths opening to the world. The start-up of the Lu-Liao land and the marine joint “Drop and Pull” Transport Project, which is cooperated by the Ministry of Transport, Shandong Province and Liaoning Province, would make Weifang Harbor a 100 million harbor by 2015.

The coastline of BEDA stretches a distance of 69 kilometers with more than 200,000 Mu offshore lands. BEDA possesses a large state-owned land for industrial use with an area of nearly 500 square kilometers. The land can be transacted conveniently which would guarantee the setting down of the projects and provide broad development space for the enterprises in the area.

Currently, there are more than 100 backbone enterprises, including Haihua, Weichai Heavy Machine, Rainchst, Haiwang, Xinhecheng Pharmacy, etc, putting into application and making benefits. And there are many big projects under construction, like petrochemical & salinization integration, new energy automobiles, robots, high-end yachts, medium-speed engines, port construction and so on. In the next step, BEDA will strive to build four industrial cities, such as automobile manufacturing, power machinery, engineering machinery and marine chemical, to build two industrial bases, such as port logistics and coastal tourism, so as to accelerate shaping the blue high-end industrial system with value more than 1 billion RMB.

潍柴滨海产业园

Weichai Binhai Industrial Park

太阳都市花园鸟瞰

曜晖太阳能公司生产车间

太阳纸业年产 25 万吨铜版纸生产线

华勤轿车胎工厂

山东兖州工业园区

兖州是古九州之一，现辖 7 镇 3 个街道办事处，面积 535 平方公里，人口 54.9 万，名列全省三十强县市和全国百强县。2014 年济宁市兖州区完成外贸进出口 19.77 亿美元，同比增长 4.7%，实现逆势上扬，呈现总量高、增幅高、质量高的良好局面；完成利用外资 1.7 亿美元，同比增长 12.9%，外资实现平稳增长；新批外商投资项目 3 个，新批境外投资项目 2 个，外派劳务 404 人。

坚持“工业立区、工业强区”不动摇，一手抓传统产业改造升级，一手抓新兴产业招大引强，培育了造纸包装、橡胶轮胎、机械制造、食品加工、精细化工、医疗器械六大优势主导产业；大力实施“三创工程”，推进大型企业创千亿、骨干企业创百亿、中小企业创亿元，规模以上工业企业发展到 210 家；全面展开了医药产业园、多式联运物流园、华勤工业城、精细化工园、信息产业园等六大特色产业园建设。

加大出口基地建设。兖州区已建成橡胶制品和纸制品两个外贸转型升级专业型示范基地，进出口总额占比达 90%以上。为进一步发挥各类出口基地的示范带动作用，利用好基地的各项优惠政策，兖州工业园区正积极申报济宁市首批省级加工贸易梯度转移重点承接地，省级出口农产品质量安全示范区的创建工作也在积极推进中。

全力扩大开放招商引资，成功举办了两届“百家名企走进兖州经贸洽谈”等招商活动。截至目前，共有美国国际纸业、德国大陆、意大利倍耐力、新加坡丰益集团等 16 家世界 500 强企业落户兖州，太阳纸业、华勤集团、森林木业、益宝生物等 23 家本土企业成功“走出去”，全方位、多层次、宽领域的对外开放新格局已基本形成。

Yanzhou is one of nine ancient counties, 7 towns, 3 street offices, with an area of 535 square kilometers, population of 549,000, which is the province's thirty-strong counties and the hundred counties. In 2014, Yanzhou completed import and export 1.977 billion US dollars, with an increase of 4.7%, showing a high total increase, high quality and good situation; complete utilization of foreign investment 170 million US dollars, with a steady growth of 12.9% increase; the number of newly approved foreign investment projects is 3, newly approved foreign investment projects is 2, the number of expatriate labor is 404.

Unswervingly adhere to “industry makes areas strong”, grasping the traditional and new industry upgrade, cultivate paper packaging, rubber tire, machinery manufacturing, food processing, fine chemical industry and medical equipment six advantage leading industries. Vigorously implement “three creative engineering”, to promote large enterprises to create hundred billion Yuan, backbone enterprises to create tens of billions Yuan, small and medium-sized enterprises create one hundred million Yuan, industrial enterprises above designated size increase to 210. The six major characteristics Parks of Pharmaceutical Industry Park, Multimodal Logistics Park, Hixih Industrial City, Fine Chemical Industry Park, Information Industry Park, are under construction.

Increase the building of export bases. Yanzhou has built 2 foreign trade transformation and upgrading professional bases of rubber products and paper products bases, whose import and export volume accounted for more than 90%, which played a huge role. To further enhance all types of demonstration effect of export bases, the use of the preferential policies, Yanzhou Industrial Park is actively declare Jining City, the first provincial-level key undertaking gradient transfer of processing trade. The work of provincial agricultural products export quality and safety demonstration area is under building.

Efforts to expand open investment, Yanzhou successfully held two "hundred famous enterprises into the Yanzhou with trade negotiations" and other investment activities. So far, there are 16 Fortune 500 companies located in Yanzhou, American International Paper, German Continental, Italy Pirelli, Italy, Singapore Wilmar Group. Sun Paper, Hixih Group, forest wood, Yibao Biological and other 23 local businesses succeed to "go out". An all-round, multi-level and wide-ranging pattern has been basically formed.

太阳工业园

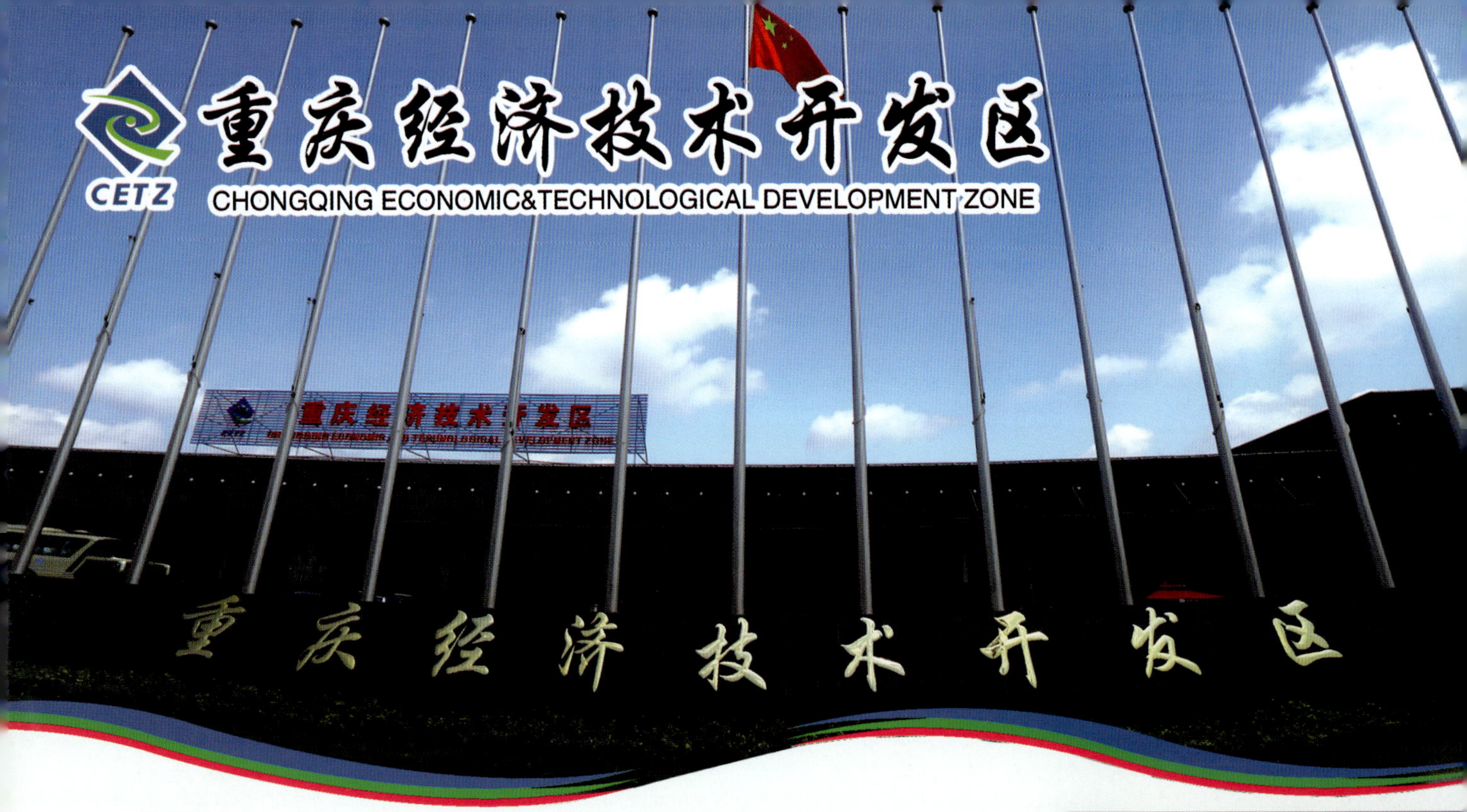

一、发展历史

重庆经济技术开发区于1993年经国务院批准成立，是西部地区成立最早的国家经济技术开发区之一。开发区设立以来，先后带动完成了近90平方公里的开发建设任务，成为重庆乃至西部地区重要的经济发展引擎。

二、区位优势

在城市发展方面，重庆经开区占据重庆主城区东南门户，位于重庆半小时核心经济圈内，区域面积约60平方公里，可建设用地50平方公里，是重庆东南片区发展核心区域，距重庆政治经济中心渝中半岛仅有10分钟车程，区位优势非常突出。

三、产业发展概况

重庆经开区正在努力打造“现代信息技术、现代服务业、高端装备制造”三大主导产业，重点发展移动通讯终端与物联网产业集群，已经形成良好的产业基础。

现代信息技术业。重点发展智能终端设备制造和物联网技术应用，拥有9家国家、部（省）级科研机构，西部唯一的移动通讯检测中心——工信部电信研究院西部分院，国家新型工业化产业（物联网）示范基地、国家电子信息产业基地、移动通信高新技术产业化基地、中国移动物联网基地。正在努力打造“中国西部手机之都”，已成功引进了维沃通讯、国虹科技、国信通、宝捷讯、百立丰等手机生产企业。世界IT产业巨头微软在经开区成立了云计算服务基地、全球软件服务外包交付中心，信息服务产业正在蓬勃发展。还引进了北大方正、北京讯美、中感科技、台湾智捷、深圳物联通等物联网企业。

高端装备制造业。重点发展制冷设备、数控机床、电机电子等产业。拥有中国最大的制冷产品制造商美的集团；拥有国内第三轴承生产企业长江轴承；中国最大的流体机械生产厂、机械工业500强通用工业。代表中国齿轮制造高水平的重庆机床集团也在区内建立了生产基地。

现代服务业。努力打造以现代物流业、总部经济、专业市场集群为主的现代服务业，拥有国家级物流枢纽东港集装箱码头，拥有西部最大的综合批发市场朝天门国际商贸城，拥有国家海关总署获批设立的A型保税物流中心重庆经开区法斯特保税物流中心。此外还布局了迎龙医药城、佛罗伦萨小镇重庆奥特莱斯、普洛斯（中国）、新天泽国际总部基地等知名物流与商贸项目，引进了金科、同景、中铁等知名房地产开发企业和高盛、凯华、中天资本等金融企业。

地址：重庆市南岸区江桥路1号

电话：023-62457762

成都经济技术开发区建设发展情况

The Development and Construction Situation of Chengdu Economic & Technological Development zone

一、 经开区建设发展现状

基本情况：成都经开区是以汽车及关键零部件为主导的先进制造业基地，2000年被正式批准为国家经济技术开发区，2005年被批准为国家（成都）电子元器件产业园，2010年被批准为国家汽车产业新型工业化产业示范基地创建单位，是四川省重点打造的两大千亿产业园区之一，2010年被成都市委、市政府确定为汽车产业综合功能区的主体区。

主导产业：成都经开区已基本形成百万整车生产平台。一汽大众、一汽丰田、沃尔沃、吉利汽车、大运汽车等重大整车项目建成投产，瑞华特电动汽车、一汽新能源客车、川汽新能源客车等新能源汽车项目加快发展，卡特彼勒、普什重机、神钢大吨位起重机等工程机械项目扩能增效，东风神龙汽车加快建设，初步形成了“十车七机”产业体系。已建、再建、拟建总产能达到125万台，百万辆整车生产平台成功搭建，可生产轿车、客车、越野车、商务车、SUV、载重车、专用车等多种车型，成为成都市乃至四川省最重要的汽车产业聚集区和核心区。

二、基本思路和奋斗目标

基本思路：抓住机遇，深入实施区域互动和追赶跨越战略，以汽车产业综合功能区为主体，以汽车制造为基础，以新能源汽车和汽车研发为突破口，以汽车服务链深度创新为核心，强化建厂建链，做大产业规模，强化“两个高端”，加快培育核心竞争力，加快建设“西部第一、全国一流、世界知名”的成都国际汽车城。

近期目标：到2020年，汽车整车产量达到125万台，本地配套率达60%以上，建成全国一流的汽车产业城，进入全国汽车产业集群格局中的一级体系，建成功能齐备，产城相融、城乡一体的现代都市区。

远期目标：再用20年时间进入国际汽车集群高端行列，成为四川加快“西部经济发展高地”和成都建设“世界生态田园城市”的重要支撑，最终建成“成都国际汽车城”。

一汽大众成都轿车基地

沃尔沃成都轿车基地

神龙汽车奠基仪式

一汽丰田柯斯达总装生产线

1.Current status of construction

Overview

Chengdu Economic and Technological Development Zone is the advanced manufacturing industry base which takes automobile and key parts as the leading industry. It is approved as the state-level Economic and Technological Development Zone in 2000, is approved as the national (Chengdu) Electronic Components Industrial Park in 2005, is approved as the a national new industrialization demonstration base (automobile industry) creating unit in 2010, and it is one of the two one-hundred-billion industrial parks, is approved by Chengdu as the main part of comprehensive functional area of automobile industry.

Current status of leading industry: The million vehicle production platform is basically formed. Major vehicle projects such as FAW Volkswagen, FAW Toyota, Volvo, Geely Automobile, Dayun Automobile have been put into operation. New energy automobile projects such as Ruihuate Pure Electric Automobile, FAW New Energy Bus, Sichuan Automobile New Energy Bus have accelerated development, engineering machinery projects such as Caterpillar, Push heavy machine, Kobelco large tonnage crane have expand the production capability and efficiency, DPC (Dongfeng Peugeot Citroen) project is speeding up the construction, the "ten buses seven machines" industrial system is initially formed. The built construction and the proposed construction as well as the expansion construction capacity have reached 1,250,000 units, one million vehicles production platform have been successfully built, which can produce car, bus, off-road vehicle, commercial vehicle, SUV, truck, special vehicles and other models, and become the most important gathering and core region of auto industry of Sichuan province.

2.Basic ideas and Goals

Basic ideas: We should seize the opportunity and firmly implement the strategy of regional interaction and pursuant & span-type development, dominated by auto industry comprehensive functional areas, based on auto manufacture, using new–energy auto and auto R&D as a breakthrough point, with auto service chain deep innovation at the core, intensifying plant & link building, making big industry scale, strengthening “two high-ends”, accelerating the cultivation of core competitiveness, only in this way, can we accelerate the construction of Chengdu International Auto City with the title of” The best in the West, The first class in the whole nation and The first tier in the world”.

Short-term target: to fulfill the target of annual output of 1.25 million whole vehicles and local supplying rate of more than 60%, to build the first rate auto industry city, to be listed in the first level system of the auto industry cluster around China, to establish the fully functioned, industry and city combined and rural-urban balanced modern town in 2020.

Long-term target: To enter the international high-end car cluster in 20 years, to become the important support for Sichuan’s speeding up to build “the Western highland of economic development” and Chengdu’s speeding up to build “the ecological garden city of the world”, and eventually to create the “Chengdu international auto city”.

邹平经济技术开发区

Zouping Economic and Technological Development Zone

邹平经济技术开发区地处黄河三角洲高效生态经济区和山东半岛蓝色经济辐射区，是山东省首家设在县级区域内的国家经济技术开发区。邹平经开区规划面积108平方公里，已开发面积50平方公里，建成面积40平方公里，入区企业达630余家，区内从业人员13.5万人。

自建区以来，邹平经开区大力实施环境立区、工业兴区、科技强区“三大战略”，狠抓项目建设、招商引资、高新技术、基础设施、优化环境“五大重点”，已发展成为以纺织服装、食品医药、新型材料为主导产业，集仓储、物流、研发、商贸于一体的综合性经济技术开发区，拥有全球最大的棉纺织生产基地、亚洲最大的葡萄糖生产基地、全国重要的铝材精深加工制造基地和山东省首家设在县级区域的保税物流中心（B型）。

2014年，邹平经开区完成工业总产值2253亿元，实现地方财政收入19.2亿元；实现进出口总额15.2亿美元，合同利用外资4亿美元，实际利用外资3.1亿美元；完成固定资产投资68亿元。

魏桥创业集团办公大楼外景

鲁中运达保税物流中心

大商集团邹平新玛特购物广场

Located in the efficient ecological economic zone in Yellow River Delta Region and covered by the Shandong Peninsular Blue Economic Zone, Zouping Economic and Technological Development Zone (“Zone”) is Shandong Province’s first state-level economic and technological development zone established in a county. With a planned total area of 108 square kilometers, the Zone has developed 50 square kilometers with 40 square kilometers completed. Now more than 630 enterprises have settled in the Zone, with 135,000 employees.

Since its inception, the Zone has been implementing its “three-pronged strategies”: environmental protection, industrials and technology. It also focuses on the “five priorities”: project construction, investment attraction, high-tech, infrastructure, and environment improvement. The Zone has established itself into a comprehensive economic and technological zone with textile & apparels, food & medicines and new materials as major industries, integrating such functionalities as warehousing, logistics, R&D and trade. It boasts of the world’s largest cotton & textile production base, Asia’s largest glucose production base, an important deep processing and manufacturing base of aluminum profiles and Shandong Province’s first bonded logistic center (B-type) set up in a county.

In 2014, the Zone realized gross industrial output of RMB225.3bn; local fiscal revenues of RMB1.92bn; total exports and imports of US$1.52bn; contracted utilized foreign investment of US$400mn, and actually utilized foreign investment of US$310mn; and fixed asset investment of RMB6.8bn.

地址:邹平经济技术开发区会仙二路17号
邮编:256200
传真:0543-2100017
联系热线:0543-2100015

邹平经济技术开发区管委会

江苏沛县经济开发区

江苏沛县经济开发区是省级开发区，规划面积70平方公里，特色是“中国新型铝材产业基地”、“全国农产品加工创业基地”。2014年被列为省行政审批制度改革试点园区。

目前，沛县经济开发区已入驻企业327家，其中国内外著名企业投资项目80余家，上市公司投资项目14家。开发区规划建设了3个特色产业园区和 2个创业平台即科技创业园、电商产业园。其中江苏新型铝材产业园是江苏省批准的唯一发展新型铝材加工产业的特色园区，现已形成了中煤、华西、佛山三大百亿元铝加工产业板块。高新技术产业园重点发展光伏、光电、风能、光电子四大产业，光伏产业已形成了“多晶硅铸锭-切片-太阳能电池片-太阳能电池组件-太阳能光伏电站”为主的完整产业链。江苏绿色食品产业园则是江苏省首家绿色食品产业园，形成了生态肉鸭、果品蔬菜、饮料食品加工三大产业链条。

沛县经济开发区
电商产业园开业仪式

Jiangsu Pei County Economic Development Zone is a provincial development zone which covers a planned area of 70 square kilometers. It is the State-level New-type Aluminum Material Industrial Base and the National Agricultural Products Processing and Entrepreneurial Base. Jiangsu Pei County Economic Development Zone is listed as provincial administrative examination and approval system reform pilot park in 2014.

At present, Jiangsu Pei County Economic Development Zone has been settled in 327 enterprises, of which, more than 80 domestic and foreign famous enterprises investment projects and the listing corporation invested 14 projects. It planning and construction of 3 characteristics of industrial parks and 2 business platforms of the science and Technology innovation park and the electricity business park. Among them, Jiangsu new type aluminum industrial park is the only one which has the development of new type aluminum processing industry approved by Jiangsu Province. Which has the formation of three tens of billions of dollars of aluminum processing industry sector of china-coal, Huaxi, Foshan. High-tech Industrial Park focuses on the development of photovoltaic, photoelectricity, wind power, optoelectronics of four major industries. PV industry has formed a completed industrial chain of a polycrystalline silicon ingot-polycrystalline silicon slice-solar cells-solar cell components-solar photovoltaic power plant. Jiangsu Green food-processing industrial park is the first which applied for Jiangsu Green Food Processing Industrial Park with three agricultural chains of eco-duck processing, fruits and vegetables processing and beverage food processing.

伏产业园

江苏新型铝材产业园

中国首届
煤电铝高层论坛

生态园区

联系电话：0516-69090005　传真：0516-69090555
网址：http://www.pxkfq.gov.cn/
邮编：221600
邮箱：pxkfq97@163.com
地址：江苏省沛县汉源大道101号

Tel ： 0516-69090005　Fax ： 0516-69090555
Website ： http://www.pxkfq.gov.cn/
Zip Code ：221600
E-mail ： pxkfq97@163.com
Add ： No.101 hanyuan Rode, Pei County, Jiangsu

扩大开放合作　共建一带一路

中国—中东欧国家投资贸易博览会
CHINA-CEEC INVESTMENT AND TRADE EXPO

中国—中东欧国家投资贸易博览会

中国•宁波

首届中国—中东欧国家投资贸易博览会（以下简称中东欧博览会）是《中国—中东欧国家合作贝尔格莱德纲要》确定的重要内容之一，于2015年6月8日至12日在中国宁波成功举办，是中国与中东欧国家首个以投资贸易为主题的综合性博览会。

中东欧博览会由中国商务部和浙江省人民政府共同主办，由商务部相关司局、宁波市人民府、浙江省商务厅共同承办。

中东欧博览会以“扩大开放合作、共建一带一路,促进中国与中东欧国家共同发展”为主题，通过举办投资洽谈、贸易展览、会议论坛、人文交流等系列活动，努力将中东欧博览会打造成为中国与中东欧国家开展经贸文化交流合作的重要平台。

THE 1ST CHINA-CENTRAL AND EASTERN EUROPEAN COUNTRIES INVESTMENT AND TRADE EXPO (HEREINAFTER REFERRED TO AS CHINA-CEEC EXPO) IS AN IMPORTANT PART OF THE BELGRADE GUIDELINES FOR COOPERATION BETWEEN CHINA AND CEE COUNTRIES, WHICH WAS HELD ON JUNE 8 TO JUNE 12, 2015 IN NINGBO. THIS IS THE FIRST COMPREHENSIVE EXPOSITION THEMED WITH INVESTMENT AND TRADE BETWEEN CHINA AND CENTRAL AND EASTERN EUROPEAN COUNTRIES。

THE MAIN HOSTS OF CHINA-CEEC EXPO ARE MINISTRY OF COMMERCE OF THE PEOPLE'S REPUBLIC OF CHINA AND PEOPLE'S GOVERNMENT OF ZHEJIANG PROVINCE, AND THE ORGANIZERS ARE RELEVANT DEPARTMENTS AND BUREAUS UNDER THE MINISTRY OF COMMERCE, PEOPLE'S GOVERNMENT OF NINGBO AND DEPARTMENT OF COMMERCE OF ZHEJIANG PROVINCE.

THEMED WITH "PROMOTING OPENING & COOPERATION AND JOINTLY DEVELOPING ONE BELT ONE ROAD", CEEC EXPO SET ITS ACTIVITIES IN FOUR ASPECTS: INVESTMENT SYMPOSIUMS, TRADING EXHIBITIONS, CONFERENCES & FORUMS, AND CULTURAL EXCHANGES. IT IS ONE OF THE MOST IMPORTANT PLATFORMS FOR ECONOMIC AND TRADE COOPERATION BETWEEN CHINA AND CEEC.

中东欧国家特色产品展

中东欧博览会官方网站：HTTP://WWW.CCEECEXPO.ORG/

绵阳国家级经济技术开发区

Mianyang Economic and Technical Development Area

一、园区简介

位　　置：四川省绵阳市（地级市）　创建时间：2000年8月

规划面积：70km²　　　　　升级时间(国家级)：2012年10月

园区特色：绵阳国家经济技术开发区是国家批准建设的绵阳科技城的城市副中心，绵阳市特色产业园区和新型工业集中区，四川省优秀工业园区、四川省新型工业示范基地。

环境建设：园区日供水能力近3万吨，日供气量170万立方米，日处理污水能力22万吨，已建成110KV变电站5座、220KV变电站1座。道路骨架网络、给排水管网、燃气、电力、通讯、宽带、有线电视网等全面配套，产业承载功能齐备。

二、主导产业

电子信息产业：规划面积约7平方公里，是园区主导产业，重点发展平板整机、移动终端设备、电子材料和元器件项目，具有机加、钣金、模具、表处理、元器件、整机等完整产业链。

化工环保产业：规划面积约5平方公里，重点发展天然气化工、精细化工、环保材料、环保示范工程基地项目，代表企业有四川美丰、东材科技、利尔化学、禾大西普等。

食品及机械加工产业：规划面积约7平方公里，重点发展食品饮料、汽车零配件项目，代表企业有华润啤酒、丰谷酒业、蓝剑饮品、好圣汽车零部件等。

1. Brief Introduction

Location: Mianyang City, Sichuan Province

Founded in: August 8, 2000

Upgrading Date (State-level): October 10, 2012

Planning Area: 70 km²

Features of the Zone: Mianyang Economic and Technological Development Area (MEDA) was approved by the State Council to build itself into the sub-centre of Mianyang, a special industry park and new industrial cluster in Mianyang, as well as a premier industrial park and new industrial demonstration base in Sichuan.

Environmental Construction: MEDA has a daily capacity of supplying 30,000 tons of water, providing 1.7 million m^3 of natural gas, and treating 220,000 tons of waste water. In addition, one 220KV transformer sub-station and five 110 KV transformer sub-stations have been built in MEDA. In this way, a comprehensive network of supporting facilities, including roads, water supply and drainage, gas, electric power, communication, broadband and CATV, has been put in place in the area.

2. Leading Industries

Electronic Information Industry: The electronic information industry within MEDA is planned to cover an area of about 7 km², focusing on the development of flat panel TV, smart mobile terminals, electronic material and electronic components. A comprehensive industry chain ranging from machinery, sheet metal, molding, surface treatment, components and parts, and electronic equipment has been made available in the area.

Chemical and Environmental Protection Industries: The chemical and environmental protection industries cluster within MEDA is planned to cover an area of about 5 km², focusing on the development of natural gas, fine chemicals, eco-friendly material industries, as well as the demonstration of environmental protection projects. The key enterprises in these industries that have established presence within MEDA include Lier Chemical Co., Ltd, Sichuan Meifeng Chemical Industry Co., Ltd, Sichuan Dongfang Insulating Material Co., Ltd, and Croda Sipo (Sichuan) Co., Ltd.

Food and Machinery Processing Industries: The food and machinery processing industries cluster within MEDA is planned to cover an area of about 7km², focusing on the development of food and beverage, and auto parts. The key enterprises in these industries that have established presence within MEDA include China Resources Breweries (Mianyang) Co., Ltd, Mianyang For good Distillery, Sichuan Blue Sword Drink & Food Co., Ltd, and Sichuan Haosheng Auto Parts Manufacture Co., Ltd.

雪宝乳业
Sichuan Mianyang Xuebao Dairy Co.,Ltd.

丰谷酒业
Mianyang Forgood Distillery

好圣汽车零部件
Sichuan Haosheng Auto Parts Manufacture Co.,Ltd.

日普精化
Sichuan Nipo Fine Chemical Co.,Ltd.

地　址：四川省绵阳市经开区三江大道39号

电　话：0816-8130110　　传　真：0816-8130110

邮　箱：25757204@qq.com

网　址：http://www.meda.gov.cn

Address：39 Sanjiang Avenue,Mianyang Economic and Technological Development Area,Sichuan,P.R.China

Tel：86-816-8130110　　Fax：86-816-8130110

E-mail：25757204@qq.com

Website： http://www.meda.gov.cn

烟 台 港
Yantai Port

港口基本概况

烟台港自古就是中国北方沿海的重要通商口岸。作为海上丝绸之路的重要起点，自1861年8月开埠，至今已有150余年的历史。

烟台港位于东北亚国际经济圈的核心地带，是中国沿海25个重要枢纽港口之一，也是中国沿海南北大通道的重要枢纽和贯通日韩至欧洲的新欧亚大陆桥的重要节点。现辖芝罘湾港区、西港区、龙口港区和蓬莱港区四大港区，参股运营莱州华电煤炭码头，控股建设并运营潍坊寿光港区；拥有各类泊位98个，其中万吨级以上深水泊位59个，码头岸线总长19041米，铁路专线34.9公里，库场总面积736.5万平方米。2014年，烟台港完成货物吞吐量2.36亿吨，集装箱吞吐量达到235万标箱。

商品车全景

集疏运优势

铁路：烟台港铁路运输优势明显，港口通过蓝烟铁路和德龙烟铁路与山东、河北、山西等内陆腹地相连接。

公路：烟台港各港区通过疏港公路直接与沈海高速（G15）、荣乌高速(G18)相连，进而融入山东及全国公路网，运输条件优越。

水路：烟台港已开通至韩国、日本、东南亚各国乃至欧美的班轮航线，目前已与世界上100多个国家和地区的150多个港口保持着通航和贸易往来。

航空: 位于西港区后方的烟台蓬莱国际机场已于2015年5月正式通航，可满足年旅客吞吐量1000万到1200万人次需要。

烟台港西港区油轮靠泊

未来，烟台港将利用各项优惠政策，加大投资规模，完善港口功能，将西港区建设成为中国北方重要的能源进出口、仓储中转基地和辐射中国北方乃至东北亚地区的矿石中转分拨基地，发展成为以油品、矿石、煤炭、铝矾土、化肥、钢铁、再生资源等大宗散货为主的综合性专业化中心港区。

Overview of Yantai Port

Port of Yantai is one of the main trading harbors in the North of China since ancient times. As an important starting point of Maritime Silk Route, it was opened to the outside world for trading in August 1861 and has a history of over 150 years up to now.

Situated in the core area of Northeast Asia International Economic Circle, Port of Yantai is not only one of the 25 Chinese key pivotal ports, but also a major hinge along the coastal north-south thoroughfare of China, as well as one of the important links along the new Eurasian continental bridge (connecting Japan and South Korea with Europe). At present, the Port of Yantai consists of four port areas, namely Zhifu Bay Port Area, Western Port Area, Longkou Port Area and Penglai Port Area. In addition, Yantai Port Group has invested as a shareholder in the operation of Laizhou Huadian Coal Terminal, and invested as a controlling shareholder in the construction and operation of Shouguang Port Area in Weifang City of Shandong Province. Now there are 98 various berths (including 59 deep water-depth ones of over 10,000 DWT), with a total quay line of 19,041m, a specialized railway line of 34.9 km and the storage yards of 7.365 million square meters in total. The cargo-handling of Yaitai port was 236 million tons and the container traffic turned out to be 2.356 million TEUs in 2014.

集装箱堆场

Transportation Advantage

Railway: Port of Yantai enjoys unique advantage in railway transportation. Through Lancun-Yantai Railway and Dezhou-Longkou-Yantai Railway lines, the port is directly linked with the interior hinterlands in Shandong, Hebei and Shanxi Province.

Highway: Through the port excess road, all the port areas of Yantai are directly linked with Shenyang-Haikou Expressway (G15) and Rongcheng-Wuhai Expressway (G18), and then integrated in the highway networks of Shandong Province and the whole country, enjoying perfect transportation conditions.

Waterway: Port of Yantai has opened regular shipping lines with South Korea, Japan and countries in Southeast Asia, Europe and America. Nowadays Yantai Port has established shipping and trading links with over 150 ports in more than 100 countries and regions all over the world.

Aviation: Yantai Penglai International Airport, which is located in the backup area of Western Yantai Port Area, has been completed for operation in May 2015, with a capability of 10-12 million passengers per annum.

烟台港西港区管道和油罐

In the future, Yantai Port Group will make full utilization of various preferential policies, intensify investment on improvement of port function, and eventually establish the Western Port Area into a base for energy import/export, storage and transferring businesses in the north of China, an ore transshipment and distribution base in the north of China and even in the Northeast Asia, as well as a comprehensive and professional central port area for oil products, ore, coal, bauxite, fertilizer, steel and renewable resources.

TEL：0535-6742134 Postcode：264000 E-mail：ytport@yantaiport.com.cn

中国水电基础局有限公司

印尼芝拉扎火电基础工程项目

新加坡地铁环线多美歌和艺术博物馆站

三峡二期上游围堰防渗墙施工

山西太原平阳景苑
高层建筑项目开挖后的楼座灌注桩

中国水电基础局有限公司（以下简称基础局）始建于1959年，隶属于中国电力建设集团有限公司，主要从事大中型水利水电工程与各类土木工程的总承包以及铁路交通、市政公用、矿山环保、核电火电、机场码头等领域地基与基础工程的设计与施工，兼顾投资与装备制造业务。

自1970年首次走出国门，基础局参与中国援建阿尔巴尼亚毛泽东水电站施工以来，先后在亚、非、欧、南美的22个国家承揽实施海外项目46个。近年来，基础局加快转型升级，积极转变经济发展方式，努力做优做强海外业务，坚持以基础施工为主导，积极向综合型发展，以水利水电工程施工为平台，向市政、港口、桥梁、公路、火电等领域延伸，以厂矿运营管理为依托，涉足相关业务领域。

基础局已通过了质量、环境和职业健康安全体系认证和水利部安全生产标准化一级达标评审验收，是天津市高新技术企业，拥有国家资质认定（计量认证）试验中心，荣获鲁班奖、詹天佑奖、大禹奖等各类奖项73项，拥有实用新型专利24项，软件著作权10项，是多项行业标准、国家级工法、省部级工法的主编单位，多次荣获天津市“五一”劳动奖章和文明单位称号。

Sinohydro Foundation Engineering Co., Ltd. (hereinafter called Sinohydro Foundation), initially founded in 1959, an important subsidiary of POWERCHINA, majorly providing the general contracting services of large, medium, and small-scale water resources and hydropower projects, and qualified in construction and design of various civil works, railway traffic, municipal public works, mining, environments, nuclear power, thermal power, airport and wharf etc. It also has been accessed to capital investment and equipment manufacturing area.

Sinohydro Foundation has, which executed its international business since 1970 to construct the Maozedong hydropower station in Albania, undertaken 46 oversea projects in 22 countries throughout Asia, Africa, European and South America. For the past few years, Sinohydro Foundation has speeded up the transformation and upgrading program, and initiatively to seek the new economy pattern to develop our oversea business. The foundation construction is fundamental to our firm's business and forming an integrated development model is always the culture and integral to every discipline of the firm. Sinohydro Foundation undertakes not only the hydro power and water resource works, but also to the wide variety of related projects such as public works, port, road and bridge, thermal power etc.

Additionally, our company has achieved the certification of ISO system, ranking # 1 level of AQ/T9006-2010 acceptance system, awarded as high-tech enterprises, National May Day Labor Prize, Civilized enterprises of Tianjin and owned a state-level aptitude test center. The company has been honored 73 prizes including the Luban Prize, Zhan Tianyou Prize and Dayu Prize etc. It is the chief editor of 10 such industrial standards, technical guidelines and national level engineering methods as we owned 24 national technical patents, 10 computer software copyrights.

西藏旁多水利枢纽防渗墙施工

瑞丽

——国家重点开发开放试验区

瑞丽国家重点开发开放试验区位于云南省德宏傣族景颇族自治州内，是党中央、国务院推进西部大开发，扩大沿边开放而确定的首批三个国家重点开发开放试验区之一，于2010年8月提出设立，2012年7月正式获批，2012年9月挂牌成立，按照《云南瑞丽重点开发开放试验区建设总体规划》中提出的“一核两翼”空间布局，以瑞丽市为核心，芒市、陇川县为两翼，总面积2133平方公里。瑞丽是中国17个国际陆港城市之一，紧邻缅甸的木姐、九谷和南坎，历来是中缅友好交往合作的窗口和桥梁。“我住江之头，君住江之尾，彼此情无限，共饮一江水”。穿境蜿蜒而过的瑞丽江，记载着中缅两国人民源远流长的“胞波”情。

经过中缅两国多年携手共建，德宏州已成为我国对缅贸易最大的陆路口岸，对缅贸易总量占云南省对缅贸易的70%，占全国对缅贸易的近30%。贸易方式由最初的边民互市发展为一般贸易、边境贸易、过境贸易、加工贸易、劳务合作等。出口商品结构从日用百货为主，逐步向以机电等高新技术产品转变，天然气进口、电力进出口和加工贸易成为对外贸易新的强劲增长点。瑞丽、木姐口岸车水马龙，资金、商品、信息、人才纷纷汇聚，快速流动。随着国家“一带一路”重大战略部署，特别是孟中印缅经济走廊建设的推进，瑞丽试验区的区位优势更加凸显，从开放的“末梢”变成了前沿，从交通的末端变成了枢纽，成为我国进入南亚、东南亚最便捷的陆路通道和走向印度洋的战略支点。瑞丽试验区正在围绕建设“沿边特区、开放前沿、美丽德宏”总目标，按照“通道枢纽、产业基地、交流平台”三个功能定位，积极打好“沿边开放、民族团结、生态环境”三张优势牌，实施“基础设施、产业培育、精准脱贫”三大攻坚战，全力打造瑞丽试验区升级版，努力成为“一带一路”建设的关键一环、面向南亚东南亚辐射中心的重要节点、孟中印缅经济走廊的先行区。

一寨两国 两国共饮一井水

珠宝产业

唐山中国陶瓷博览会

唐山中国陶瓷博览会自1998年举办以来，受到海内外各界朋友特别是陶瓷界朋友的欢迎，展位数由首届的350个发展到第十七届的近千个，专业参会客商由首届的2800人发展到第十七届的4000余人。参展瓷区除了唐山、景德镇、淄博、醴陵、宜兴、潮州、德化等国内著名陶瓷产区，还有来自美国、英国、法国、日本、意大利、德国、韩国、香港、澳门、台湾等国家及地区的陶瓷及相关产品的厂商、经销商参加。唐山中国陶瓷博览会已成功加入国际展览业协会（UFI）和国际展览与项目协会（IAEE）并取得其认证。

第十八届唐山中国陶瓷博览会于2015年9月16-20日在唐山国际会展中心举行，共设国际标准展位900个。展馆按国际展馆设计，配有签约厅、多功能厅、洽谈室、放映厅、大小会议室等服务设施。国内外陶瓷及相关产品企业，各类陶瓷采供商和有意在唐山投资兴业、观光考察的各界贵宾受邀参加了博览会。

诚挚的欢迎国内外的朋友在每年的9月16日至20日，来唐山参加陶瓷博览会，来唐山参观考察。

Since its debut in 1998, China Ceramic Fair Tangshan has been favorably received by people of all walks of life. The number of exhibition booths had increased to 1,000 in the Seventeenth Fair from 350 of the First one. 2,800 business people attended the First Fair, and in the Seventeenth one, more than 4,000 participated. Attracted to the Fair were not only producers from some famous domestic ceramic production areas, such as Tangshan, Jingdezhen, Zibo, Liling, Yixing, Chaozhou and Dehua etc, but also producers and dealers of ceramics and related products from the USA, UK, France, Japan, Italy, Germany, ROK, Hong Kong, Macau, Taiwan, and other countries and regions. Some world-famous ceramic purchasers and suppliers had also taken part in the fair. China ceramic fair Tangshan has been successfully to join UFI and IAEE and obtain the certification.

The Eighteenth China Ceramic Fair Tangshan was held in the Tangshan International Convention and Exhibition Center during September 16-20, 2015. The center was installed with 900 exhibition booths, which were designed in accordance with the international standard. Other facilities include the signing room, the multifunctional hall, the negotiation rooms, the projection hall and meeting rooms of different capacities. The representatives of both domestic and overseas producers of ceramics and related products, purchasing and supplying agents of ceramic products and people of all circles who are interested in doing business and sight-seeing in Tangshan were invited to the occasion.

Sincerely welcome friends both at home and abroad on 20th September 16 solstice each year, to the tangshan ceramic fair, visit to tangshan.

沈阳鼓风机集团核电泵业有限公司

Shenyang Blower Works Group Nuclear Pump Co., Ltd

沈阳鼓风机集团核电泵业有限公司（以下简称“沈鼓核电”）成立于2010年2月，为沈阳鼓风机集团股份有限公司（以下简称“沈鼓集团”）子公司，前身为沈阳水泵股份有限公司。为了强化企业管理，提高泵类产品的专业化制造水平，沈鼓集团斥巨资建造了拥有精良设备的现代化泵类产品生产制造基地，于2011年5月竣工，并于同月顺利完成了沈鼓核电的整体搬迁工作。

沈鼓核电主营各种泵类产品，涵盖51个系列597种泵类产品及备件。主要产品有：火电站用高压锅炉给水泵机组、冷凝泵、斜流泵；核电用核主泵，核二、三级泵，常规岛用泵；军工船用泵和核潜艇用泵。其他用途的还有：输油管理线泵、高压注水泵、强制循环泵等。产品主要用于核电站、火电站，国防建设、民用排水、石油化工、环境保护等各大领域。产品还销往巴基斯坦、印度、泰国、伊朗等二十多个国家和地区。各类产品市场占有率达到80%以上。

高压锅炉给水泵（超临界火电机组）

LDTN型凝结水泵（超临界火电机组）

核二级安全壳喷淋泵（百万千瓦核电机组）

沈鼓核电坐落于沈阳经济技术开发区，年产值6.8亿元，年设计生产能力500台套。公司现有在岗员工621人，其中专业技术人员和管理人员344人，专业技术和管理人员中具有中、高级专业职称的184人；在生产制造领域，拥有技术工人277人，其中具有技师、高级技师资格的81人，高级技工131人。

公司拥有2.65米立式车铣中心、数控卧车、试验台架等先进的机加、检验设备98台，用于大、中、小型泵类产品的生产制造。公司内GB/T19001-2008、ASME、 HAF三大质量管理体系同时运行，可满足民品、核电产品的管理需要。公司拥有优秀的技术、管理团队，经验丰富的技术工人和各类先进的加工、检验、试验设备，以先进的加工方法、一流的服务确保产品质量，满足用户对产品功能及附加的各类特殊要求。公司还可提供泵类产品的技术开发、技术服务、技术咨询、技术转让，以及安装调试、维修、备品备件的制造、产品使用培训等服务。

公司将竭诚为用户服务，提供令顾客满意的高质量的泵类产品，力争为国家经济的发展、国防力量的强大、人类社会的进步创造更多的价值，做出更大的贡献。

核二级余热排出泵（百万千瓦核电机组）

核二级电动辅助给水泵（百万千瓦核电机组）

地址：沈阳经济技术开发区开发大路16号甲
电话：024-25800456　　传真：024-25800868
邮箱：hdzjlb@shengu.com.cn　　邮编：110869
网址：www.shengu.com.cn

中国水利水电第十三工程局有限公司
STECOL CORPORATION

中国水利水电第十三工程局有限公司（以下简称公司）始建于1962年，是世界500强企业——中国电力建设集团有限公司旗下特级企业，是一家以国内外工程承包为主、具有丰富的海内外工程项目综合经营管理能力的国有大型建筑施工企业。公司总部位于天津滨海高新区，注册资本金9.13亿元，总资产104亿元，2015年度营业收入112亿元。

公司具有水利水电、市政公用、公路、房屋建筑、机电安装工程施工总承包一级资质，以及铁路、公路路基与路面、电力、矿山、土石方、管道工程、钢结构、地基与基础工程等多项总承包或专业承包资质，通过了质量、环境和职业健康安全管理体系认证。

公司下设二十多个分支机构，经营区域遍及全国除港澳台外所有省、市、自治区，海外则形成了以亚洲、非洲为主，辐射东欧、南美、大洋洲的市场格局，涉及英、法、俄、葡、阿拉伯语五大语系地区，先后在三十多个国家开展工程承包业务，施工合同总额超过百亿美元。

公司积极践行“为股东创效益、为社会担责任、为员工谋幸福”的核心价值观，多年保持了国家AAA信用企业荣誉，承建工程多次获得鲁班奖、“国家优质工程奖”、“全国市政金杯示范工程奖”，企业荣获“全国文明单位”、“中国建筑业竞争力百强企业”、“全国优秀施工企业”等多项殊荣。

STECOL CORPORATION (also known as Sinohydro Tianjin Engineering Co., Ltd.) was founded in 1962. It is a top qualification enterprise under Power Construction Corporation of China (POWERCHINA), a Fortune 500 company. Focusing on engineering and construction works, STECOL has become an international contractor rich with integrated project management experience. Headquartered in Tianjin Binhai High-tech Area, the company has a registered capital of CNY 913 million, a total asset of CNY 10.4 billion, and a turnover of CNY 11.2 billion (2015 figure).

STECOL has qualifications of first-class general contractor in water resources/hydropower works, municipal works, roads, buildings, electro-mechanical installation, and other qualifications as general or specialized contractor in railways, Highway subgrade and pavement, electric power, mining, earthworks, pipeline, steel structures and foundation works, all covered by the integrated QEHS management system certification.

With more than 20 branches, the company has expanded its business to all provinces and autonomous regions of mainland China, while its overseas business, traditionally concentrated in Asia and Africa, is growing to reach East Europe, South America, and Oceania, with projects amounting to USD 10 billion in total, distributed in 30 countries and five major language areas (English, French, Russia, Portuguese, Arabian).

The company has been actively pursuing its values of “create benefit for shareholders, shoulder responsibility for society, seek well-being for employees”. Over the years, it has maintained the AAA credit rating with banks, and its projects have won numerous awards in China, such as Luban Award (the highest quality award for a building project in the country), National Premium Quality Project, National Municipal Gold Cup Project. Honor titles won by the company include: National Civilized Unit, Top 100 Competent Construction Enterprise, National Excellent Construction Enterprise, etc.

京沪高铁项目

肯尼亚内罗毕-锡卡公路项目

卡塔尔多哈路赛项目

波兰弗罗茨瓦夫防洪工程-完工后南船闸通航

地址：天津市华苑产业区榕苑路2号　邮编：300384
值班电话：022-58569000　传真：022-58569002
网址：http://www.stecol.cn/

公司参建的安徽临淮岗洪水控制工程荣获2007年度“中国建筑工程鲁班奖”

湖北荆门国家高新技术产业开发区

——创业高地 科技新城

荆门九派通众创空间

荆门高新区 2000 年设立省级高新区，2013 年晋级为国家高新技术产业开发区。现有中集集团、福耀集团、中兴集团等 500 强企业落户园区，中航工业、格林美、华工科技、亿纬锂能、李宁公司等国内外知名品牌上市企业汇集于此，形成了装备制造、再生资源利用和再制造、生物医药、新能源新材料、电子信息五大主导产业，构建了“六个一”工作机制，即：一个产业、一个产业链行动计划、一张产业链招商地图、一支专业招商队伍、一个承载园区、一支基金。

融资渠道多样。通过建立产业发展基金、科技金融基金，以及“助保贷”、“政银通宝”等政企银合作融资平台，为科技型中小企业拓宽融资渠道。通过出台鼓励新三板、新四板挂牌融资政策，推进上海股权托管交易中心和前海股权交易中心在高新区落户。目前已有 11 家企业在上海股权托管交易中心集中挂牌，资本市场的“荆门高新区板块”已初具雏形。

创新创业平台完善。“荆门九派通”众创空间、荆门高新区荆楚理工学院大学生创新创业园、海归创业园和荆门创新创业中心等平台已初具规模。现已建成聚盛国家级科技企业孵化器、荆门百盟•慧谷科技企业加速器、荆门台银两岸三地华中创业中心等科技创新载体，产品检验检测中心、产学研网络服务平台、大型科研仪器设备共享网络平台等科技创新平台，中航通用飞机设计研究院、东光物联网技术研究院等一批省级以上科研机构。

市委常委、高新区党工委书记李涛

高新区管委会主任许道伦

行政审批办事大厅

政务环境舒心。创造性地推行“123”行政审批和服务模式，建立并联审批“绿色通道”和“中介服务直通车”，推行“一枚印章”管审批，行政审批园区办结，为园区企业提供便捷、高效、优质服务。

服务团队贴心。实行领导包联责任制和驻点秘书制度，选派部门负责人担任落户项目服务秘书。对企业项目建设开展“一对一”的“保姆式”服务，协调解决项目建设中遇到的各种问题。

营商环境倾心。市委、市政府相继出台《支持荆门国家高新技术产业发展的意见》“黄金 18 条”和《支持“大众创业、万众创新”的意见》等含金量极高的扶持政策，高新区也相继配套《科技领军与高端人才创业扶持政策》、《海归创业园扶持发展办法》、《创客与创客空间扶持发展办法》、《科技型中小企业培育发展办法》和《大学生创新创业园扶持政策》等政策文件，从政策上优待企业家，把优质资源配置给优质项目，全力打造高新技术产业发展政策高地。

地址：湖北省荆门市兴隆大道 238 号荆门高新区管委会　电话：0724-2498286　传真：0724-2498780

常熟经济技术开发区

常熟经济技术开发区成立于1992年8月，2010年11月升级为国家经济技术开发区。目前已有20多个国家和地区投资的外资企业近600家，外商总投资276亿美元，注册外资121亿美元。2015年上半年，实现地区生产总值371.4亿元，工业总产值1279.7亿元，工业产品销售收入1233.9亿元，财政收入73.8亿元，社会固定资产投资173.4亿元，进出口总额51.7亿美元。

经济转型成效显著：近年来，开发区围绕汽车及零部件、装备制造、新能源、创新创意、现代物流五大产业招商引资，先后引进了总投资150亿元的观致汽车、总投资175亿元的奇瑞捷豹路虎汽车等一大批项目。紧紧依托港区优势和出口加工区拓展保税物流功能的有利条件，形成了重大装备制造产业园、国际物流园等载体，并正在规划建设汽车产业园。

城市森林公园

观致3-都市SUV

车辆驶下生产线

科技创新全面发展：着力推进“常熟科创园”建设，已引进海内外人才创新创业项目150多个，涉及高端装备制造、医疗器械及生物医药、节能环保新能源新材料、新一代信息技术等。目前，已有8人列入国家“千人计划”，44人次列入江苏省“双创”人才和苏州市“姑苏人才计划”，9家大学研究院（所）入驻运行。

传统产业不断提升：电力能源、高档造纸、精细化工、特殊钢铁和汽车零部件五大传统产业在提档升级、延伸产业链、扩大市场占有率等方面取得突破。开发区已发展成为国内最大的高档文化用纸和氟化物生产基地，华东地区重要的火力发电、子午线轮胎生产、钢铁加工及钢材进出口基地。

滨江新城日趋完善：着力推进城市功能项目的开发建设，累计完成基础设施建设投资17亿元。随着新一轮的基础设施及配套项目的推进，一座现代化、国际化、生态化的滨江新城正在加速崛起。

港口物流发展迅猛：区内国家一类对外开放口岸常熟港已建成20个码头、59个泊位，其中万吨级泊位24个，逐步形成了钢材、纸浆、木材及化工品等特色货种，2015年上半年完成货物吞吐量4346万吨。

酒店主楼

新城

第一篇　专　　文

WTO 二十年：强有力的 WTO 和强大的中国

世界贸易组织总干事 罗伯托·阿泽维多

世界贸易组织成立二十年来，世界的发展已经超出了我们的认知。我们的人际交流、信息收集、娱乐购物以及工作和生活的方式已经发生了根本改变。但是在这引人注目的变革中，WTO 却一直稳居全球商业活动的中心地位。

过去的二十年，如大多数组织一样，WTO 既取得了巨大的成就，也经历了一些挫折。然而，鉴于全球经济联系的日益紧密和贸易关系的日益复杂，我认为很难想象一个没有多边一致框架的世界贸易，而这正是 WTO 的特质。

正如中国比多数成员更为了解的，自 1995 年正式运行以来，过去二十年间 WTO 一直在发展壮大。迄今已迎接了 33 个新成员——但是不言而喻，没有哪一个成员加入的影响能大于中国加入世界贸易组织。毫不夸张地说，无论是对于 WTO 还是对于中国自身来说，中国的入世改变了游戏规则。

对于 WTO 而言，中国入世是我们迈向实现覆盖全球目标的巨大一步。如今的世界贸易组织管辖了 98%的全球贸易。中国的加入意味着，世界上最大经济体之一的中国与 WTO 其他 160 个成员——无论大小——共同遵守着相同的多边规则。此外，中国加入后对 WTO 各领域工作的积极参与，也强化了 WTO 的体制基础。

对于中国来说，我认为中国的加入收获巨大。这里我将强调以下四点：

第一，我认为加入世界贸易组织有助于巩固中国自 1978 年启动的国内改革，而且向世界传达了一种讯息，即中国在现代化和经济开放的道路上可以走多远。

第二，加入世界贸易组织给中国提供了参与制定 21 世纪贸易体制规则的机遇。中国为推动 2013 年巴厘部长级会议的成功，的的确确发挥了领导作用，这次会议通过了包括《贸易便利化协议》在内的一系列历史性决议。经济学家们测算，《贸易便利化协议》将削减进出口成本，创造每年 1 万亿美元的全球收益。

第三，加入世界贸易组织使中国得以适用 WTO 争端解决机制——这使得中国自感其 WTO 项下权益受到侵害时，可以利用该机制进行保护。加入前，一些人曾对中国将如何应对争端解决机制心存疑虑。随后的事实证明这些担忧是毫无必要的。今天中国是利用该机制最为积极的成员之一，中国作为起诉方或应诉方已经参与了 50 起争端案件。

第四，加入世界贸易组织使中国享有了所有 WTO 成员获得的非歧视待遇和互惠市场准入的权利，从而支撑了中国的贸易潜力并进而促进其经济增长。或许这一点对改善人民生活具有最重要的意义。

中国的加入极大地加强了外国投资者对于中国市场的信心。随着中国国内改革的实施和入世谈判步伐的加快，外商对华直接投资开始急剧上升。1991 年改革初期，外商对华直接投资总量为 210 亿美元，到 2001 年中国加入前夕，总量已增加至 1580 亿美元，且呈持续上升态势。截至 2013 年，外商对华直接投资总存量已经超过了 6900 亿美元。

中国的贸易数字也有着相似的增长轨迹。2001 年，中国对外出口约为 2650 亿美元。2014 年，这一数额已经超过 2.3 万亿美元，中国已经成长为世界最大的货物贸易出口方。众多中国经济学家认为，作为中国向世界扩大开放的组成部分，贸易的激增是中国取得 5 亿人脱贫的惊人成功的主要因素。

中国加入世界贸易组织的收益也惠及其他的 WTO 成员。因为人们多把注意力集中在中国作为出口大国的崛起方面，因而对中国的进口方面少有关注。中国的进口总额自 2001 年的 2430 亿美元跃升至 2013 年的 2 万亿美元。如果没有过去六七年间中国进口的激增，全球经济很可能陷入更深的衰退之中。

如今，WTO 成员戮力合作以促进全球范围的增长与发展。新一届部长级会议在内罗毕举行，这也是 WTO 首次在非洲召开部长级会议。农业、工业品和服务等领域的众多重要问题仍然有待解决，如果能够达成协议，将对中国有着巨大的意义。我们将倾尽全力争取这些谈判的积极成果。毫无疑问，中国将会发挥重要的作用。截至今年，中国已经在相当高的程度上参与了为数可观的工作。

WTO 谈判领域远不止这些。WTO 在努力推动新的《环境产品协议》和扩围《信息技术产品协议》谈判。这些行动有着巨大的经济潜力，中国均参与其中。例如，自 1997 年协议达成以来，《信息技术产品协议》支撑了信息技术产品全球贸易的繁荣，而该协议的扩围谈判更是着眼于总贸易额可达约 1 万亿美元的范围广泛的众多新产品。因此今后一段时间，将是 WTO 很有意思的一个发展阶段。

回顾 WTO 短短二十年的历史，我们可以总结一些真正的成就。世界贸易组织已经成为全球经济体制的有力支柱和维护该体制稳定性、可预测性和开放性的可靠力量。中国加入世界贸易组织是迄今 WTO 历史上决定性的时刻之一，它促进了中国和 WTO 的进一步强大。我期待中国在进一步强化 WTO 以及在今后岁月促成新的贸易协议方面发挥全面的作用。我相信这符合大家的共同利益。

附原文：

TWENTY YEARS ON：A STRONG WTO AND A STRONG CHINA DG ARTICLE FOR THE 'CHINA WTO YEARBOOK'

Roberto Azevêdo，Director-General，WTO

In the 20 years since the World Trade Organization first opened its doors，the world has evolved almost beyond recognition. The way we communicate，gather information，entertain ourselves，shop and work has changed fundamentally. But throughout this remarkable transformation，the WTO has remained steadfastly at the centre of global commercial activity.

Over the past two decades the WTO has，like most organizations，had its successes and its setbacks. Yet，given the ever more interconnected nature of the global economy and the increasingly complex nature of trading relationships，I think it is now impossible to imagine a world without a multilaterally-agreed framework for world trade—and that is what the WTO represents.

As China knows better than most，the WTO has expanded over these 20 years. Since 1995，we have welcomed 33 new Members—but surely none of these accessions has had a greater global impact than that of China. It is no overstatement to say that China's accession to the WTO has been a game changer，for the WTO and for China.

For the WTO，China's membership was a huge step towards achieving our goal of universal coverage. Today the Organization accounts for 98% of global trade. China's accession meant that one of the world's biggest economies now plays by the same multilaterally agreed rule book as our other 160 members—big and small. Moreover，the WTO is strengthened in an institutional sense by China's active participation in all area of our work.

For China，I think that WTO membership has brought a range of benefits. I will highlight just four here.

First，I think membership helped to underpin the domestic reform programmes begun in 1978—and sent a message to the world of just how far China had come in modernizing and opening its economy.

Second，membership provided China with a seat at the table in crafting the rules and disciplines that will shape the trading system in the 21st century. Indeed，China played a leading role in delivering a successful Bali ministerial conference in 2013，when a series of historic decisions were taken，including the Trade Facilitation Agreement. This Agreement will cut the costs of exporting and importing to such an extent that economists say it can add ＄1 trillion annually to global output.

Third，membership provided access to the WTO's unique Dispute Settlement System—giving China the ability to defend itself if it believes its rights under the WTO agreements are being infringed. Before China joined the WTO some wondered how the country would respond to the dispute system. These doubts were soon proved unnecessary. Today China is one of the most active users of the system，having taken part in nearly 50 disputes as a complainant or respondent.

Fourth，by guaranteeing China the non-discriminatory treatment and reciprocal market access that is the right of all WTO members, membership bolstered China's trading potential and therefore supported its economic growth. This is perhaps the most important point, because it is the one which has had the greatest impact on helping to improve people's lives.

Joining the WTO greatly enhanced the confidence of foreign investors in the Chinese market. As China's domestic reforms were implemented and accession negotiations gathered pace, the stock of Foreign Direct Investment (FDI) began to rise sharply. In 1991 when the reforms were in their initial stages, the total stock of FDI in China was around $21 billion. By 2001, just before the accession was completed, the stock had risen to $158 billion—and it continued to rise. By 2013 it had reached over $690 billion.

China's trade figures have followed a similar trajectory. In 2001, China's exports to the rest of the world were around $265 billion. By 2014, that figure had risen to over $2.3 trillion and China had become the world's largest exporter of merchandise. Many Chinese economists believe the surge in trade, as part of China's broader campaign of greater openness to the world, was a major factor in the country's phenomenal success in lifting 500 million people out of poverty.

The benefits of China's membership extend to other WTO members, too. For all the attention given to China's rise as an export power, commentators have focused less on the question of China's imports. From $243 billion in 2001, imports into China leapt to almost $2 trillion last year. Without this surge of imports into China over the last six or seven years, it is very likely the global recession would have been even deeper.

Today, WTO members are working together to try to deliver a new boost for growth and development around the world. Our next ministerial conference will be held in Nairobi in December this year—the first time a WTO ministerial conference has been held in Africa. There are a series of big issues on the table including agriculture, industrial goods and services—so an agreement here would have huge significance for China. We will do everything we can to achieve a positive outcome to these negotiations, and I have no doubt that China will play a central role. The level of engagement so far this year has been remarkable.

But this isn't the only area of negotiations at the WTO. Efforts are under way to reach a new Environmental Goods Agreement and to expand the Information Technology Agreement. China is involved in both of these initiatives—and they have significant economic potential. For example, the original Information Technology Agreement helped to support the boom in global trade in IT products that we have seen since the agreement was finalized in 1997. The negotiations to expand this agreement are looking at including a wide range of new products with a global trade value of roughly $1 trillion. So the coming months will be a very interesting period at the WTO.

Looking back over the short history of the WTO, I think we can point to some real achievements. The organization has become firmly established as a pillar of the global economic architecture, and a force for stability, predictability and openness. China's membership has been one of the defining moments of the story so far, making both China and the WTO stronger. I look forward to China playing its full role in strengthening the organization yet further and helping to strike new trade agreements in the months and years to come. I believe that this is in all of our interests.

依托多边贸易体系，推进全球经济增长

世界贸易组织副总干事 易小准

位于瑞士日内瓦莱蒙湖畔的世界贸易组织于1995年1月1日正式开始运作，负责管理世界贸易秩序。今年是世贸组织成立二十周年，世贸组织秘书处及成员以各种形式纪念该组织推动贸易发展促进世界经济增长，帮助开展稳定、自由、公平的贸易，解决贸易争端等方面的贡献。20年来，世贸组织作为具有法人地位的国际组织，日益受到国际关注，尽管由于多哈回合谈判迟迟没能结束而受到一些质疑，但世贸组织将继续在全球经济治理和国际经济格局变化中扮演不可替代的重要角色。

一、20年来世贸组织积极发挥多方面功能

世贸组织成立20周年了，但世人常常忽视了多边贸易体制对世界经济增长和提升就业的重要意义。事实上，世贸组织成立以来，有效发挥了政策审议、争端解决、贸易谈判、贸易发展等方面作用，使多边贸易体制成为历史上最全面和最重要的全球经济合作制度。

第一，世贸组织不断推动贸易自由化进程。

当前世贸组织涵盖了约98%的全球贸易，有力地稳定了全球经济增长。作为多边贸易体制的代表和监管者，20年来世贸组织致力于促进世界贸易自由化。在各谈判方的共同努力下，当前各世贸组织成员的平均实施关税已降至不足5%，近2/3的世界贸易是在零关税下实现的。世贸组织禁止其成员使用非关税壁垒，尤其是以配额和许可证为主要方式的数量限制，但允许使用关税进行保护。诸如海关手续的繁文缛节、技术标准限制等许多非关税壁垒正在全球进行统一和简化。特别值得注意的是，在数字网络新时代，从电子商务到电子医疗、电子学习，这些新的服务行业正在跨境免税交易。一定程度上可以说，世界经济正在日益接近全球的自由贸易。

第二，世贸组织吸纳了更多有广泛代表性的成员。

目前，世贸组织有161个成员，其中五分之一为过去20年里新加入成员，中国和俄罗斯的加入是世贸组织功能转变的重要标志。在冷战时期的关贸总协定时代，发达国家占主导地位。目前，世贸组织五分之四的成员为发展中国家，它们日益活跃地参与世贸组织多边贸易事务，在世贸组织管理体制、贸易谈判议程制订以及多边协议谈判中发挥着关键作用。在世界经济史上，这是第一次世界上所有的主要经济体都成为多边贸易体系的一部分。

第三，世贸组织为各成员提供了处理贸易纠纷的平台。

当世贸组织各成员之间出现贸易纠纷时，世贸组织让各成员相互倾听对方的意见，力促双方达成共识，并确保各方遵守协议。世贸组织要求其成员将各自有关对外贸易的各项法律、法规、行政规章、司法判决等迅速加以公布，以使其他成员的政府和贸易经营者能够及时了解，各成员签署的影响国际贸易政策的协定和条约也应加以公布。如果世贸组织各成员之间无法就其贸易争端达成谅解，世贸组织争端解决机制将发挥作用。短短20年间，该机制以公平、公开、透明的方式成功处理了近500个贸易争端案件，要求各成员的贸易经营者不得采取不公正的贸易手段，进行（或扭曲）国际贸易竞争，尤其不能采取倾销和补贴的方式在他国销售产品。世贸组织成员之间如需解决贸易争端和冲突，不应倚强欺弱大打贸易战，而应提交给世贸组织的“国际贸易法院”，这代表了全球经济关系的一个巨变。

第四，世贸组织在反对保护主义方面发挥了核心作用。

1929 年至 1933 年大危机期间，由于各国之间报复性的贸易限制措施，导致世界贸易下降了三分之二。而 2008 年国际金融危机以来，世贸组织呼吁各成员冷静克制使用贸易保护措施，避免重蹈历史错误。同时，世贸组织成员意识到遵守规则是一项义务，从而顶住了保护主义压力，使贸易保护措施未能泛滥。

第五，世贸组织帮助发展中国家融入多边贸易体制。

在复杂的多边贸易体制中，更加重视发展中成员的经济发展需求。世贸组织是发展中国家和最不发达国家占有一席之地的主要国际舞台，这些国家对全球贸易问题享有平等的发言权，成员无论大小强弱，都可以表达自身诉求。世贸组织为这些发展中成员提供了特殊和差别待遇，帮助其改善参与全球贸易的能力。与其前身关贸总协定相比，世贸组织更加重视培训、技术援助和能力建设。世贸组织不仅通过本身的工作安排（如新设立的“贸易便利化基金”）来加强发展中成员的发展能力，还通过加强与其他机构（如促贸援助倡议等）的合作来满足发展中成员的各种技术援助需求。世贸组织不仅关注市场和贸易开放，也帮助发展中国家从中受益，这标志着世贸组织的角色和思维方式发生了又一个变化。

第六，世贸组织体现了较大的包容性。

世贸组织秘书处与各成员保持密切的业务联系与沟通，部长级会议发挥了越来越积极的作用，提供了更多的政治指导。世贸组织各个层级的高官会和技术层级的工作磋商等机制起到了政策协调作用，成为在世贸组织争端解决机制之外的重要政策沟通渠道。事实上，成员政府、私营部门的代表不断增进互动交流，加强政策连续性，这是世贸组织推进的制度变革，同时成为全球经济治理的重要内容。

由于世贸组织充分发挥了上述功能，多边贸易体制更具弹性，促进了国际贸易不断扩大和世界市场的深化整合。2000 年以来，随着发展中国家的贸易快速增长，世界贸易增加了一倍以上。发展中国家占世界贸易份额从 1995 年的不到 25%，升至 2014 年的 43%以上。即使遭遇到 2008 年的国际金融危机和随后的经济复苏放缓，世界并没有爆发贸易大战，更没有出现类似 20 世纪 30 年代那种高强度的贸易保护主义。

二、世贸组织将在多边贸易体制中继续发挥引领作用

众所周知，多哈回合谈判经过多年停滞后，又开始前进了。2013 年 12 月世贸组织第九届部长级会议在巴厘岛取得成功。会议成果包括棉花、粮食安全“一揽子”措施，支持最不发达国家和《贸易便利化协定》。现在面临的挑战是，只有在三分之二的世贸组织成员核准后，《贸易便利化协定》才能生效，各成员才能享受该协定带来的新增 1 万亿美元和 2100 万就业机会的经济收益。此外，世贸组织各成员针对多哈回合的重大未决议题重新展开磋商，包括农业、工业和服务业等棘手的议题都回到谈判桌上。

当然，随着世贸组织成员的不断扩大和各方利益存在的重大分歧，世贸组织多边谈判进展不会一帆风顺。展望未来，只要各方致力于构建公正、透明、包容的多边贸易体制，世贸组织将继续发挥应有作用，为世界经济实现强劲、平衡和可持续增长做出更大贡献。

三、中国与世贸组织互动更为紧密

在过去 20 年中，中国已成长为世界第二大经济体、第一大货物贸易国、第三大引资国和对外投资国，这些炫目的成就在多边贸易体制下才有可能实现。中国希望世界贸易进一步自由化，希望就投资、环境、电子商务、竞争政策等新议题展开多边讨论，并参与这些领域全球贸易规则的制订。但这些目标均需依托多边贸易体制来实现。

对今天的世贸组织而言，要想达成任何协议，制订或者修改任何规则，中国的参与和支持都是不可或缺的。反过来看，中国要想成功跨越“中等收入陷阱”，实现十三亿人口伟大复兴的中国梦，没有一个高效、公平的多边贸易体制做保障，也将是不可想象的。

因此，中国作为最大的、发展最快的发展中国家，应当旗帜鲜明地高举多边主义大旗，坚定推进多边贸易自由化，以十三亿中国人改革开放的决心和成果，赢得大多数世贸组织成员的支持和信任，引领多边贸易体制走出困境，迈向新的辉煌。

世界贸易组织的未来与中国

中国常驻世界贸易组织大使 俞建华

今年是世界贸易组织成立20周年。20年来，世贸组织走过了一条不平凡的道路，在推动自由贸易，抵制保护主义，加强全球治理方面做出了重要贡献，显示了多边贸易体制强大的生命力。加入世贸组织后的14年是中国改革开放后发展最快的阶段，中国已成为多边贸易体制的重要参与者和建设者。面对新一轮国际规则重构大潮，世贸组织当前和未来面临着诸多问题和挑战，亟须与时俱进，革故鼎新。中国将发挥负责任大国作用，为构建更加开放、公平、包容的多边贸易体制做出积极贡献。

一、世贸组织成立20年来的成就与作用

从9.11事件到国际金融危机，从互联网兴起到全球价值链布局，过去的20年，国际政治经济格局风云变幻、科学技术日新月异，以世贸组织为核心的多边贸易体制也经受住了各种考验，为确保各国开展自由贸易、抵御保护主义提供了强有力的制度保障。

第一，不断加强多边贸易体制。多边贸易体制是第二次世界大战后国际秩序的一部分，世贸组织作为唯一规范全球贸易的国际组织，其规则得到了广泛认可和应用。20年间，全球货物贸易总额翻了四番，达到19万亿美元，成员的平均实施关税降低了15%。中国、俄罗斯、沙特阿拉伯、塞舌尔等33个国家和单独关税区陆续加入世贸组织，其中有9个是在金融危机后加入的，还有22个经济体正在申请谈判加入。迄今世贸组织拥有161个成员，涵盖了98%的全球贸易，多边贸易体制的代表性和普遍性进一步得到提高。20年来，世贸组织努力扩大自身影响力，与世界银行、国际货币基金等其他国际组织一同参与20国集团（G20）主导的全球治理；积极向社会公众开放，重大会议活动向全球进行网络直播，每年主办"公共论坛"及世贸组织"开放日"等，打造了该组织亲民惠民的良好社会形象。

第二，维护开放公平的贸易环境。20年来，世贸组织共受理了近500起争端案件，绝大多数裁决得到执行，公平合理地解决成员贸易纠纷，维护了成员之间权利与义务的平衡。同期，世贸组织对150个成员进行了405次贸易政策审议，通过对被审议成员经贸政策定期"体检"，成员集体对被审议成员进行"会诊"，确保了成员经贸政策的合规性。特别是世贸组织在应对2008年国际金融危机方面独树一帜，发挥了重要作用。在危机爆发的第一时间，世贸组织便对G20成员的贸易与投资措施进行监督，定期出台监督报告。迄今报告已发布13期，有效遏制了贸易保护主义，避免了重蹈历史覆辙，保障了全球经济走向复苏。此外，世贸组织下属各机构对成员执行义务的监督提高了透明度，确保了世贸规则的有效实施。

第三，有力推动全球贸易开放。贸易是经济增长的发动机。世贸组织成立以来的20年也是不断推动贸易开放的20年。2001年启动的多哈回合，一波三折，艰苦谈判14年，锲而不舍，旨在进一步打开全球市场，制定新的贸易规则。2013年世贸组织在其第九届部长级会议上达成了《贸易便利化协定》，这是世贸组织成立以来第一个多边协定，将为全球经济带来一万亿美元的收益。2014年7月中旬，《信息技术协定》扩围谈判取得重大突破，有望成为世贸组织成立后18年来第一个关税减让协议。同时，世贸组织还在积极推动《环境产品协定》等诸边谈判，将进一步促进全球贸易的自由化和便利化。

第四，坚持倡导发展目标。世贸组织成立20年来，新兴经济体和发展中国家群体性崛起，发展中国家

在全球贸易中已占半壁江山。为顺应这一现实，世贸组织十分重视发展问题。在多边贸易谈判史上，多哈回合第一次把发展作为主题，在各议题上给予发展中成员特殊与差别待遇。世贸组织还与其他国际组织一道，大力开展“促贸援助”活动，加大对发展中国家提供技术援助，提高最不发达国家参与国际贸易的能力；通过修改知识产权协定条款确保发展中国家在公共健康面临威胁时获得廉价治疗药品等；香港部长宣言决定给予最不发达国家出口产品免关税、免配额的优惠待遇（双免）等。

二、世贸组织当前和未来面临的几个问题

当前，国际经贸格局发生深刻变化，多哈谈判久拖不决，各种区域贸易安排风生水起，世贸组织在全球治理中的地位和作用受到严重冲击，一些人担心世贸组织走向衰落，更多人则希望多边贸易体制能够重获新生。站在时代的十字路口，世贸组织面临着诸多挑战和问题，也面临着选择和希望。

第一，如何进一步推进全球贸易开放？国际贸易的历史充满了贸易开放与保护主义之间的博弈。随着全球化的发展，贸易保护主义势力也在加强，保护主义的方式和花样层出不穷。经过多轮贸易谈判，各国农业、工业和服务业等领域可供开放的市场越来越小，剩下的都是具有较大难度的议题，直接触及各国政治经济中枢。而多哈谈判是迄今议题最广泛、参加成员最多、利益格局最复杂的一轮谈判，上述新情况使多哈谈判变得更加困难。

第二，世贸组织如何反映国际力量“东升西降”的现实？过去二十年，发达国家与发展中国家的力量对比发生了深刻的变化。20 年前，发展中国家占世界经济的 35%，如今已接近 50%，而世贸现行规则并没有反映这一变化，存在着许多“规则赤字”和“发展赤字”。发展中国家希望世贸规则反映其力量上升的趋势，获得更多的话语权，而发达国家并不愿放弃现有体制和规则下的既有优势。他们开始加快推进各类区域贸易谈判，在多边谈判中要求新兴经济体承担更大的责任，同时减少自身责任。

第三，世贸组织如何适应时代和产业的需求？进入 21 世纪，随着科技的迅猛发展，经济生产和贸易领域出现许多新业态新模式，产业界更多关注全球价值链、互联网经济、跨国投资、竞争政策等，发达国家打着公平竞争的旗号，提出劳工标准、环保、政府采购等议题。然而，现有世贸规则制定于 20 年前，许多规则落后于国际经贸现实，无法回应产业的新需求。正因为如此，多哈回合成为产业界支持程度最低的一轮多边谈判。

第四，世贸组织如何应对区域化势头？进入 21 世纪以来，各种区域、双边和诸边经贸安排越来越多，越做越大，水平参差不齐，规则千奇百怪，彼此相互排斥，扭曲了市场竞争，影响了全球价值链的延伸，削弱了规则的统一性和有效性，导致全球规则碎片化。这种“区域醉氧、多边缺氧”的局面反映了各国政策的务实取向，是“理想主义与现实主义的结合”。然而，对于多边贸易体制来说，如何应对这种碎片化趋势，已成为当务之急。

面对上述形势，世贸组织亟须发扬自身比较优势，与时俱进，开拓进取，主动适应世界经济发展趋势和全球价值链合作的新要求，在全球治理中发挥更大的作用。一是坚持贸易自由化、便利化，抵制保护主义，推动尽快完成多哈回合谈判，进一步促进农业、工业及服务业的开放。二是坚持发展目标，切实解决发展中成员特别是最不发达成员的关注，推动构建反映成员利益诉求的包容性多边贸易体系。三是应对 21 世纪的挑战，探讨投资、电子商务、环境、非关税壁垒等新议题。四是坚持多边贸易体制主渠道作用，整合区域、双边和诸边贸易开放安排，形成合力，推动全球经济治理。

三、中国将在世贸组织中发挥更积极的作用

加入世贸组织后的 14 年是中国改革开放后发展最快的阶段，为中国带来了更多的市场准入机会和稳定的外贸环境，极大地推进了中国的经贸管理体制改革，催生出巨大的发展红利。14 年过去了，中国已成为全球第一大货物贸易方，95%的贸易是与世贸组织成员间开展的。中国在世贸组织中的地位迅速提升，全面积极地参与了各方面活动，成为各方瞩目的决定性力量。我们应按照“四个全面”的战略布局，发挥负责任大国作用，更好地参与引领全球经贸规则重构，努力推动构建机会平等、规则平等、权利平等的包容性多边

贸易体系。

第一，参与引领多边贸易体制建设。中国是多边贸易体制的参与者、受益者和建设者，将始终坚持和维护多边贸易体制，与各方一道共同努力建设开放型世界经济。当前多哈回合已到最后关键阶段，各方希望尽快完成谈判，但谈判涉及各成员核心利益，难以推动，需全体成员齐心协力，共克难关。中国作为负责任大国，应发挥“促谈、促和、促成”作用，既要推动全球贸易进一步开放，促使规则更加公平，更要维护发展中成员的正当权益，积极推动多哈谈判尽早取得平衡有利的成果。

第二，高举多边主义旗帜，坚持“两条腿走路”。发挥多边贸易体制主渠道作用，多边与区域双边贸易安排“双轮驱动”。在双边自贸区谈判中要放眼21世纪，参与高水平规则的制定，同时要注意遵守世贸组织规则，推动各自贸区之间互通互联，在各个自贸区最大公约数基础上多边化，以实现区域与多边的融合。

第三，进一步实现内外统筹，把多边工作与促进市场化改革结合起来。以贸易自由化便利化促进国内改革开放，把多边、区域工作放在国内改革的大环境下予以统筹谋划，保证谈判成果为我所用，推动完成产业转型升级，简化经贸管理程序，改善营商环境，完善市场在资源配置中的决定作用。

第四，妥善处理与主要大国及发展中国家关系。中美均是世贸组织核心成员，在多边中妥善处理好中美关系也将有利于推动双边工作顺利开展。同时，中国作为最大的发展中国家，在世贸组织中要坚持发展目标，推动多边贸易体制和规则顺应发展中国家力量上升的趋势，通过向最不发达国家提供“双免”、向“促贸援助”倡议捐款、分享加入世贸组织成功经验，为其他发展中国家特别是最不发达国家参与并受益于多边贸易体制做出力所能及的贡献。

今天，中国与世贸组织紧密相连，世贸组织需要中国发挥建设性的积极作用，中国也需要通过深入参与多边规则的制定来实现自身发展。中国将更积极主动地提出中国方案，发出中国声音，与各方一道推动多边贸易体制不断进取，继往开来，开创新的未来。

利用 APEC 平台推进 FTAAP 建设

中国世界贸易组织研究会会长
商务部前副部长 孙振宇

APEC 推动亚太区域市场开放的成就

亚洲太平洋经济合作组织（Asia-Pacific Economic Cooperation，简称 APEC）自 1989 年成立至今已经走过 26 年。这 26 年来，APEC 作为介于论坛与制度化合作（硬组织）之间的一种“软组织”运作形式，以独特的“APEC 方式”①，逐步灵活地推动亚太区域贸易和投资自由化进程，持续不断地使 APEC 在推动区域经济一体化，促进区域经济增长，共同繁荣与稳定上的努力取得了很大的进展。

在这一进程中，考虑到亚太经合组织是一个“由发达经济、新工业经济和发展中经济组成的经济多样化的地区”，APEC 为 21 个成员确定了有区别的时间表：发达成员经济体实现自由和开放贸易与投资目标不迟于 2010 年，发展中成员经济体实现该目标不迟于 2020 年——茂物目标（Bogor Goals）。

APEC 实现茂物目标的两个轮子是贸易与投资自由化、便利化和经济技术合作。通过关税的多边减让、单边行动和放松管制，APEC 成员已经在简单平均关税税率方面取得了相当可观的成绩，削减了非关税壁垒，促进了服务贸易与投资的自由化。通过《贸易便利化行动计划 I 和 Ⅱ》（Trade Facilitation Action Plan I Ⅱ，TFAP），以及《投资便利化行动计划》（Investment Facilitation Action Plan，IFAP），极大地促进了 APEC 的贸易与投资便利化。并通过开展合作项目推动了 APEC 成员之间的经济技术合作。

如果 2020 年茂物目标能够全面实现，应当可以极大地促进区域贸易与投资自由化。即使没有百分之百实现茂物目标，2020 年后 APEC 成员也将制定出相应的方案，加倍努力以推动区域经济一体化。

如果 2020 年茂物目标不能完全实现，一个主要因素将可能是前述自由化进程的非约束性，虽然这一原则为 APEC 取得前期成果发挥了重要作用，但由于“APEC 方式”的非强制性自愿参与的原则，将影响到茂物目标的全面实现。这就促使其成员在继续参与和推进 APEC“茂物目标”的同时，采取区域、次区域或双边自贸协定的方式，以便实现更高水平的贸易与投资自由化。

亚太区域经济一体化面临的挑战

目前的现实是，WTO 所有成员都宣称支持多边贸易体制，反对国际贸易规则的碎片化和“意大利面碗”效应。同时，大多数成员尤其是主要的贸易国家，正在努力商谈区域或双边的 RTA/FTAs。最近 TPP 谈判的达成，已经引起学者和专家的普遍关注，纷纷议论这将对中国，对所有新兴经济体成员，以及对整个多边贸易体制形成的挑战。

在我看来，当前这种局面产生的主要原因如下：第一，由于 2008 年的全球金融危机，美国政府领导人

① 1996 年在马尼拉年会上，成员就“APEC 方式”达成共识 。“APEC 方式”是 APEC 区别于目前国际上任何区域经济集团的独特的运行方式。其特点是：承认多样性，强调灵活性、渐进性和开放性；遵守相互尊重、平等互利、协商一致、自主自愿的原则；单边行动和集体行动相结合，在集体制定的共同目标指引下，APEC 各成员根据各自不同的情况做出自己的努力。

的更迭，以及WTO决策机制中的“协商一致”原则和多哈回合“一揽子”谈判的原则，导致谈判效率低下，使整个多边谈判陷入僵局；第二，主要贸易大国把重点放到区域和双边的RTA/FTAs谈判上，试图通过区域与双边谈判带来快速的贸易和投资自由化的成果；第三，试图通过RTA/FTAs的相关协议为未来多边平台新规则的谈判提供范例，从而主导今后多边贸易规则的制定。

目前的TPP、TTIP和RCEP谈判，以及许多其他的RTAs和FTAs谈判客观上对于多边贸易体制起到了一定补充作用。尤其是如果这些成员能接受Richard Baldwin教授的建议，将“区域主义多边化”作为最终目标。

TPP谈判的达成将会对RCEP谈判进程以及FTAAP谈判的启动起到一定的推动作用。从目前形势来看，由于美国进入大选期，TPP在其12个成员内完成国内程序是有难度的。如果TPP今年底明年初不能获得美国国会的通过，可能会为FTAAP谈判的启动注入新的动力。

自21世纪初，APEC区域内的RTA/FTAs开始蓬勃发展。截至2014年底APEC成员之间一共建立了54个RTA/FTAs，包含APEC成员对外建立并生效的则高达148个。随着金融危机以来世界和亚太地区政治经济格局的演变，各种新的亚太多边合作机制纷纷出台，并在覆盖地域上和APEC形成了高度的重叠，从而对APEC的地位和亚太地区的一体化进程造成了前所未有的挑战。APEC扮演着协调者和规范者的角色，始终积极推动RTA/FTAs的良性发展，并力争消除或减少RTA/FTAs可能导致的负面影响。

APEC通过“最佳范例”和“示范条款”对区域内的RTA/FTAs进行协调。但这些措施协调效果仍然有限。因而，APEC推动亚太自贸区（FTAAP）将会是一个必然的选择，因为只有制度化的合作才能确保最有效地实现亚太地区的一体化进程。

利用APEC平台推进FTAAP实现的关键要素

APEC成员通过不断强化的全球供应链和价值链而紧密地联系起来，这为进一步促进区域经济一体化提供了良好的基础。面临世界经济下滑和金融动荡，亚太区域的经济体亟须通过APEC平台推进FTAAP。FTAAP提出已经近10年了，现在正在做实质性的准备。据了解这一工作正在顺利进行。

我们期待CTI主席之友为FTAAP的实现给出具体的步骤和建议。我个人认为，FTAAP的实现必须处理好三方面内容：FTAAP协定的实质内容及其范围的界定；FTAAP的具体路线图；为达成协定所需克服的主要障碍。

在第一个问题上，我们必须考虑协定覆盖的范围，如协定在多大程度上涵盖“边境”“边境后”和“跨境”议题？除了贸易规则的传统议题，应该包括多少新议题？如何界定所有领域中的贸易和投资自由化的雄心水平？

在第二个问题上，我们必须探索出构建FTAAP最为有效的方式。这有几种可能：第一，可以将本区域内现存的RTA/FTAs作为FTAAP的构建基础，探寻满足新时代挑战的可能步骤；第二，可以鼓励成员加快CJK、RCEP的谈判，并将这些谈判与TPP合并以便被所有APEC成员接受；第三，我们先聚焦于2020年茂物目标的实现，制定出一个更富雄心的后巴厘方案，制定全新的FTAAP的目标。我确信实现FTAAP还有其他的可能途径，CTI主席之友将会提出具体的建议。

就第三个问题，我认为主要的障碍是给FTAAP制定多高的雄心水平。考虑到亚太区域经济体的多样性，FTAAP如何确保所有成员的利益？成员如何制定统一的规则以使美国、日本、澳大利亚和加拿大这样的发达国家，以及中国、印度尼西亚、老挝和柬埔寨这样的发展中国家，都可以接受并遵守这些规则？具体而言，成员在新一代议题上的处理能力，如IPR保护、国有企业、环境和劳工、电子商务等议题如何处理？FTAAP可以为最不发达国家和其他的发展中国家提供怎样灵活的待遇？

在我看来，解决这些挑战的适当方案，将是成功达成FTAAP的关键。而这些适当方案需要亚太区域内各国家和地区的通力合作，并在APEC平台上推进。

美国应按期中止对中国的“替代价格”条款

中国世界贸易组织研究会副会长
对外经济贸易大学教授
薛荣久

2015 年中期以来，美国政府掀起决定中国市场经济地位的活动，以摆脱理应按期中止的《中国加入世界贸易组织议定书》第 15 条中“替代价格”条款的义务。笔者认为，美国作为世贸组织成员，必须履行按期中止该项条款的义务，中国有权享受该项条款按期中止的权利，对不履行该项条款按时中止义务的成员采取必要的维权措施。

《中国加入世贸组织议定书》第 15 条明确规定相关成员方应尽的义务

所谓市场经济地位问题，来自《中国加入世界贸易组织议定书》第 15 条，出现在中国货物出口商品遭遇进口国反倾销和反补贴时选用价格可比性的条款中。该条款内容如下：

第 15 条　确定补贴和倾销时的价格可比性

GATT 1994 第 6 条、《关于实施 1994 年关税与贸易总协定第 6 条的协定》（“《反倾销协定》”）以及《SCM 协定》应适用于涉及原产于中国的进口产品进入一 WTO 成员的程序，并应符合下列规定：

（a）在根据 GATT 1994 第 6 条和《反倾销协定》确定价格可比性时，该 WTO 进口成员应依据下列规则，使用接受调查产业的中国价格或成本，或者使用不依据与中国国内价格或成本进行严格比较的方法：

（i）如受调查的生产者能够明确证明，生产该同类产品的产业在制造、生产和销售该产品方面具备市场经济条件，则该 WTO 进口成员在确定价格可比性时，应使用受调查产业的中国价格或成本；

（ii）如受调查的生产者不能明确证明生产该同类产品的产业在制造、生产和销售该产品方面具备市场经济条件，则该 WTO 进口成员可使用不依据与中国国内价格或成本进行严格比较的方法。

（b）在根据《SCM 协定》第二、三及五部分规定进行的程序中，在处理第 14 条（a）项、（b）项、（c）项和（d）项所述补贴时，应适用《SCM 协定》的有关规定；但是，如此种适用遇有特殊困难，则该 WTO 进口成员可使用考虑到中国国内现有情况和条件并非总能用做适当基准这一可能性的确定和衡量补贴利益的方法。在适用此类方法时，只要可行，该 WTO 进口成员在考虑使用中国以外的情况和条件之前，应对此类现有情况和条件进行调整。

（c）该 WTO 进口成员应向反倾销措施委员会通知依照（a）项使用的方法，并应向补贴与反补贴措施委员会通知依照（b）项使用的方法。

（d）一旦中国根据该 WTO 进口成员的国内法证实其是一个市场经济体，则（a）项的规定即应终止，但截至加入之日，该 WTO 进口成员的国内法中须包含有关市场经济的标准。**无论如何，（a）项（ii）目的规定应在加入之日后 15 年终止。**此外，如中国根据该 WTO 进口成员的国内法证实一特定产业或部门具备市场经济条件，则（a）项中的非市场经济条款不得再对该产业或部门适用。①

从上可知，因市场经济条件带来的“替代价格”只适用于中国加入世贸组织 15 年过渡期内出现的反倾销和反补贴。对中国而言，这个条款是有前提条件的。第一，受到反倾销投诉的中国出口产品原则上可用世贸组织反倾销协议确定中国出口价格；第二，在中国出口企业不能证明该产品是在市场经济条件下生产时，则以替代价格确定该产品的出口价格；第三，无论如何，该规定在中国加入世贸组织之日后 15 年终止。按时终止替代价格条款，对中国来讲是理所当然应该享受的权利，对世贸组织其他成员则是应尽的义务，不存在中国是否为市场经济地位的再认定问题。

美国妄以中国市场经济地位议题摆脱理应届时终止该条款的义务

对“无论如何，(a) 项 (ii) 目的规定应在加入之日后 15 年终止”的规定条款，美国并不甘心，开始掀起决定中国市场经济地位的活动，以节外生枝，摆脱应按期履行的义务。

首先，美国是第 15 条款的始作俑者，应率先按约终止“替代价格”条款。

在中国加入世贸组织谈判中，美国借口中国市场经济条件的不完善，坚持对出口产品施以替代价格判定中国产品是否倾销，经过中国力争，最终决定中国出口产品倾销和补贴的价格确定的折中办法和“替代价格”条款终止的时间。

“长期以来，美国根据其国内立法，对中国实施与 WTO 协定不符的反倾销调查方法，包括采用第三国家价格比较的方法确定倾销幅度。这使美国可以较容易地针对中国产品采取反倾销措施，给中国产品对美国的出口造成威胁。中国在谈判中要求美国修改国内立法，对中国适用 WTO《反倾销协定》。美国出于制约中国出口产品竞争力目的，要求永久保留其歧视性的国内措施，遭到中方的拒绝。经过长期谈判，美国同意和中方讨论‘日落条款’，即在一定的过渡期后取消现行做法。美国要求过渡期为 20 年，中国则要求尽快取消。最终双方达成协议，**美国将于 2015 年取消这种视中国为非市场经济体制的反倾销调查方法，对中国适用 WTO《反倾销协定》的规定。**”②

通过与美国等国的谈判，2001 年中国加入世界贸易组织决定书中，明确写着 2016 年年底以“替代价格”确定反倾销依据价格的做法，无论如何都要终止的条款。临近终止年份，美国不仅想要毁约，并向欧盟施加压力，把应按期履约偷换为中国是否达到市场经济地位的命题，用心可谓良苦。

其次，中国加入世贸组织议定书对双方均有约束，对中国与他方都有权利和义务。

就第 15 条而言，中国的义务是在过渡期内执行条款规定，同时也享有相应的权利，包括替代价格在 2016 年年底无论如何都要终止。在 15 年过渡期内以替代价格作为判定中国出口产品倾销依据的价格条款的世贸组织成员，在过渡期终止时，都要毫无疑义地自动终止替代价格做法。

中国要理直气壮维护“价格替代”条款按时中止的权利

第一，揭露美国鼓噪中国市场经济地位的卑劣用心。首先，迄今为止，尚无世界公认的市场经济地位认定的标准。2008 年美国发生的金融危机表明美国市场经济体系的缺陷，美国没有资格给中国确定市场经济地位。其次，中国加入世贸组织后中国市场经济体系的高度发展举世公认。

第二，中国坚持美国等成员应履行中国加入世贸组织议定书中的承诺，拒绝并揭露了美国在中国市场经济地位上鼓噪的企图。如果拒不履行他们在中国加入世贸组织议定书中承诺的“无论如何”要终止“替代价格”做法的义务，中国可以诉诸世贸组织。

第三，中国有权利公开表示从 2017 年开始，在中国出口产品遭遇国外反倾销，确定中国出口产品依据价格时按世贸组织反倾销协议行事，即以中国国内价格为依据价格，不再接受以“替代价格”作为反倾销依据价格的做法。

第四，中国有权根据世贸组织相关成员履行“替代价格”依约届时终止义务的态度和决定，做出相应的维权措施。对不履行义务者采取上诉世贸组织获取相应报复措施的权利；对主动履行义务者的理智行为表示恰如其分的欢迎态度。

第五，中国出口企业要做好完全运用世贸组织《反倾销协议》的准备，不要产生反倾销案随着“替代价格”条款终止而减少的迷思。在经济政治发展不平衡规律作用下，贸易保护主义的动力始终存在。为了与崛起的中国竞争，反倾销仍将是相关国家对中国采用的重要手段之一。因此，中国企业要练好内功，做好长期应对反倾销投诉和采取反倾销措施的各种准备。

注：

①石广生主编. 中国加入世贸组织法律文件导读. 北京：人民出版社，2002，p16－17. 黑字为作者所加。

②石广生主编. 张向晨，索必成著. 中国加入世界贸易组织谈判历程. 北京：人民出版社，2011 年，p285. 黑字为作者所加。

加快构建开放型经济新体制：来自上海自贸试验区的探索

上海 WTO 事务咨询中心理事长兼总裁 王新奎

上海自贸试验区的设立，是中国在全球经济和中国经济进入重大转折的关键阶段所做出的重大战略部署，对中国今后很长一段时期内的转型与发展都会产生深远的影响。

设立上海自贸试验区是中国适应经济全球化新趋势的需要

自 2010 年起，经济全球化的新趋势集中表现为全球贸易和投资规则重构的进程明显加快。目前，这一重构构成主要有以下几方面的趋势性特点：

首先，规则谈判的主要平台已经从 WTO 多边贸易体制谈判平台转向以美欧发达国家，特别是以美国为主导的跨太平洋伙伴关系协议（TPP）和跨大西洋贸易与投资伙伴协议（TTIP）为代表的区域性贸易安排谈判平台。

其次，规则谈判的重心已经从过去的以贸易领域的边境措施为主转向以投资领域的境内措施为主，并出现了数字贸易自由化、竞争中立、公平贸易等所谓 21 世纪新议题。

最后，规则重构的机制强化。具体表现在两个方面，一是减让表承诺越来越多地采取“负面清单”的表述方式，提高了承诺的透明度和约束力；二是在最终的协议中越来越多地引进争端解决机制，特别是投资者对政府的争端解决机制安排，提高了对贸易和投资市场准入承诺的监督度和执行力。

经过三十多年的改革开放，中国已经崛起为全球最大贸易体和第二大经济体。成为推动经济全球化的一支不可或缺的重要力量。全球贸易与投资重构的以上发展趋势，标志着中国的对外开放环境已经发生了重大的变化。

设立上海自贸试验区是中国实施以开放促改革战略的需要

中国作为一个经济总量规模巨大，但整体国家实力还处于发展中经济体水平的情况下，要适应经济全球化的新趋势，成为推动经济全球化和参与全球规则重构的一支重要力量，面临着以下三方面的挑战：

第一，中国必须有实施双向、全方位的对外开放战略。与过去中国实施的单向的有选择的对外开放战略相比，实施这一战略有一系列的平衡关系需要我们去把握，如：货物贸易开放和服务贸易开放的平衡，贸易开放和投资开放的平衡，经济开放和社会开放的平衡，等等。

第二，中国必须按全球高标准的贸易和投资规则的要求，不断深化国内经济体制的改革。中国所主张的规则不但要为国际社会所接受，而且要在自己的国家内高标准地实践。因此，提升参与全球贸易投资规则重构的软实力，中国首先必须按国际高标准在国内逐步建立起国际化、法治化、市场化，公平高效的营商环境。

第三，中国必须具有承受世界经济周期性波动冲击的整体经济实力，具有全球视野的政府宏观经济调控能力以及企业微观跨国经营能力。如果中国的政府宏观经济调控不具备国际视野，企业也不具备跨国经营能力，中国就无法承受实施全方位对外开放战略带来的风险。

设立上海自贸试验区是实施全面依法治国战略的需要

首先，中国主要通过制造业和货物贸易的扩大开放来参与经济全球化，实施与扩大开放有关的改革措施一般采取有形的特殊经济区的监管模式，因为货物贸易的有形性质决定了可通过边境措施加以有效管理。但在当前及今后很长一段时期内，中国将越来越多地通过服务业和服务贸易的扩大开放来参与经济全球化，服务业和服务贸易的无形性质决定了很难对其实行有形的特殊经济区的管理模式。对服务业和服务贸易探索建立无形的制度平台管理方式已势在必行。

其次，当前中国所处的改革开放的内外环境已经完全不同于 21 世纪初加入世界贸易组织前后，故不可能继续采取二十世纪八九十年代自下而上、先破后立的改革推进方式，改革必须在现有的法制框架内进行。但与此同时，处在当前的经济全球化发展新趋势和国内经济发展转型的大背景下，又要求在改革开放上能够大胆闯、大胆试，不断提供可复制和可推广的经验，于是必然面对如何处理大胆闯、大胆试与依法改革之间的关系问题。

最后，在今后相当长的一段时期内，中国以双边、诸边和区域性贸易和投资安排的方式参与全球贸易和投资规则重构，将成为推进双向开放战略的主要方式，对外开放的广度和深度将会大大增加。诸如反垄断、安全审查和司法救济等新的法治领域将不断出现。因此，中国对国际贸易与外国投资境内监管的法律和程序向国际通行做法逐步靠拢将不可避免。

上海自贸试验区，以开放促改革的压力测试平台

通过设立特殊经济区域进行试验来推动改革开放，获得经验后，再进一步复制和推广，是我国三十多年来改革开放实践的成功经验。根据适应经济全球化发展新趋势和实施以开放促改革战略的需要，在国务院印发的《中国（上海）自由贸易试验区总体方案》中确定了设立上海自贸试验区的以下基本原则：

（1）功能定位上的国家战略的原则。总体方案明确指出设立上海自贸试验区是一项国家战略。上海自贸试验区的这一新的功能定位改变了长期以来国家设立特殊经济区域的主要功能是推动地方经济发展的传统做法。

（2）目标定位上的改革原则。总体方案明确指出，设立上海自贸试验区的目的是通过扩大对外开放促进政府行政管理体制、外商投资管理体制，以及投资及贸易便利化的改革，并没有提出扩大出口、引进外资、促进 GDP 增长等传统的经济增长目标。上海自贸试验区的这一新的目标定位体现了新时期中国发展转型和结构调整的要求。

（3）机制定位上的可复制、可推广原则。总体方案明确要求，在上海自贸试验区不搞政策洼地，所有改革成果均要求达到在其他特殊经济区域或全国范围内可复制、可推广的标准。上海自贸试验区的这一机制定位改变了长期以来中国设立特殊经济区域的传统运作模式，体现了以开放促进改革的基本要求。

（4）法律地位定位上的“因地调整原则”。总体方案明确要求，在上海自贸试验区实施的各项改革措施，凡是与现行法律不符的，应由全国人大决定是否在上海自贸试验区暂停实施（法律），或授权国务院暂停实施（法规）。上海自贸试验区的这一法律地位定位，体现了全面依法治国的要求。

（5）操作定位上的风险可控原则。总体方案要求上海自贸试验区的各项改革措施要在法治的框架内实施，做到风险可控，成熟一项，实施一项。上海自贸试验区的这一操作定位体现了设立自由贸易试验区这一国家战略的长期性和全局性。

按上述基本原则，总体方案为上海自贸试验区确定了在全国人大法律授权期限内（三年）的第一阶段主要改革任务，具体包括：

第一，改革政府对市场准入的管理方式。要求政府对市场准入的管理从以事前审批为主改为以事中、事后监管为主，这一改革措施提高了政府在市场准入管理上的公平性。

第二，改革对外国投资市场准入的管理方式。要求对外国投资实行准入前国民待遇和“负面清单”管理。这一改革要求提高了政府在外国投资市场准入管理上的透明度。

第三，在提高投资便利化程度方面，通过设立 FTZ 账户系统，为国内和国际投资的双向流动提供通道和监管平台；通过对境外投资管理改审批制为备案制，放宽对境外投资的限制；通过鼓励人民币对外投资，加快人民币国际化的步伐。在提高贸易便利化程度方面，通过建立电子围网管理系统，海关管理从传统的卡口管理为主改为以状态管理为主，并为通关的单一窗口管理创造了基本的条件。

上海自贸试验区自 2013 年 9 月设立至今已经有一年半的时间。人们似乎未曾见到以往特殊经济区设立以后司空见惯的塔吊林立、万商云集的盛况。但以上海自贸试验区的设立为标志，全国范围内一股通过制度创新加快构建开放型经济新体制的热潮已经初见端倪。

上海自贸试验区运行一年来的实践证明，首先，社会各界对新时期特殊经济区域的功能定位已经形成共识。从最近国务院新批准的天津、广东和福建自贸试验区的总体方案来看，已经改变了各行政区域相互竞争，竞相要中央给予特殊政策，用招商引资的方式推动本行政区域经济增长的传统做法。

其次，社会各界对新时期特殊经济区域的机制定位已经形成共识。到 2014 年底，在上海自贸试验区先行实施的改革措施大部分已在全国范围内复制和推广。可以预见，随着新设自贸试验区的不断增加，可供复制和推广的改革措施的内容会进一步丰富，数量会进一步增加，改革的红利会因改革的规模效应而不断增加。

最后，社会各界对新时期特殊经济区域的目标定位已经形成共识。以转变政府职能按国际高标准改革投资准入管理体制为突破口来释放市场活力，以推进投资和贸易的便利化来提高市场的效率，改革的红利也会因改革的质量效应而不断增加。

2015 年，上海自贸试验区扩区和广东、福建、天津自贸试验区的设立，标志着作为中国改革开放高地的自贸试验区板块已经初具雏形。特别是上海自贸试验区扩区以后，不但试验区覆盖的地域面积大大扩大，而且区域内经济活动的密度空前增加，这将使上海自贸试验区在中国加快构建开放型经济新体制过程中的地位和作用不断提升，从这个意义上来说，上海自贸试验区的建设任重而道远。

第二篇　WTO 事务

● WTO运行总体情况（2014）

一、WTO秘书处人员与预算（2014）

（一）WTO秘书处人员

WTO秘书处总部设在日内瓦，2014年有634名日常工作人员，统一受新任总干事巴西人罗伯托·卡瓦略·阿泽维多（Roberto Carvalho de Azevêdo）的领导。总干事的任期始于2013年9月1日，他的领导班子包括四位副总干事——尼日利亚人尤诺夫·阿加（Yonov Frederick Agah），德国人卡尔·布劳纳（Karl Brauner），美国人戴维·沙克（David Shark）和中国人易小准——任期开始于2013年10月1日。WTO一切决策权归其全体成员，秘书处没有任何决策权。

WTO秘书处的主要职责是为各理事会和委员会提供技术和专业支持，为发展中国家成员提供技术援助，监督和分析全球贸易发展动态，为公众和媒体提供信息，组织召开部长级会议。此外，秘书处提供争端解决程序中的一定形式的法律支持服务，并为申请加入WTO的政府提供咨询服务。

WTO秘书处致力于吸收优秀的工作人员，并力争其来源更加多样化。2014年秘书处人员共来自于78个WTO成员。其中，专业人员大多由经济学家、法学家和其他国际贸易政策方面的专家组成。此外，还有大量负责提供支持性服务的员工，包括信息技术人员、统计人员、财务人员、人力资源及语言服务人员。

2014年WTO秘书处的专业人员比重为58%，支持性服务人员比重为42%。女职员人数超过男职员，其中女职员330人，男职员304人。专业人员中，女性职员占41%，男性职员占59%。WTO工作语言是英语、法语和西班牙语。

人力资源部门继续应对秘书处不断变化的需求。提高员工的工作绩效最终实现最佳产出，这是制订一些关键的人力资源计划的主要动力。各项计划之间强大的管理系统已经实施，确保集体讨论通过WTO领导对员工的期望和员工一年一度的集体绩效和成果以确定谁最值得奖励。WTO员工委员会由所有职员选举产生，以确保所有职员的利益。

为应对预算和行政管理的挑战，2014年1月总干事阿泽维多主持启动了一项机构审议程序。该程序旨在有效提供WTO成员未来面对的挑战和确定的优先事项，以及改善秘书处若干关键领域的政策和程序。2014年9月，总干事向预算、财务和管理委员会提交了反映机构审议进展的中期报告。

由于持续大量的争端，法律部门的工作量大大增加。因此，总干事调整资源，为法律部门增加了15个新职位，包括6个高级职位和9个初级职位。考虑到WTO成员的限制，包括对预算的全面封顶，该措施是通过使用秘书处其他突出的高级职位预算来实现的。

根据《关于争端解决规则与程序的谅解》，WTO秘书处专门设立上诉机构，负责处理争端解决专家组裁决的上诉事宜。上诉机构设有独立秘书处，由7名在法律和国际贸易领域拥有特别威望的专家组成，每位专家的每届任期4年，且可以连任一届。

表 1　WTO 秘书处组织机构

总干事 罗伯托·卡瓦略·阿泽维多（Roberto Carvalho de Azevêdo）	总干事办公室 理事会与贸易谈判委员会部 内部审计部 信息与媒体联系部 上诉机构秘书处向总干事报告非争端的行政事务 增强综合框架秘书处向总干事报告行政事务
副总干事 尤诺夫·阿加（Yonov Frederick Agah）	贸易政策审议部 发展部 培训与技术援助研究所
副总干事 卡尔·布劳纳（Karl Brauner）	法律事务部 规则部 行政与综合服务部 人力资源部
副总干事 戴维·沙克（David Shark）	农业与货物贸易部 贸易与环境部 加入部 信息技术解决方案部 语言、文件与信息管理部
副总干事 易小准（Xiaozhun Yi）	市场准入部 服务贸易部 知识产权部 经济研究与统计部

资料来源：WTO Annual Report 2015，Figure 1，WTO Secretariat organization chart，截至 2014 年 12 月 31 日。

表 2　WTO 秘书处日常工作人数统计，按性别、地区和成员

地　区	成　员	女　性	男　性	小　计
北美洲	加拿大	5	16	21
	墨西哥	2	5	7
	美国	19	12	31
合计		26	33	59
南/中美洲	阿根廷	4	7	11
	巴巴多斯	0	1	1
	玻利维亚	1	1	2
	巴西	4	7	11
	智利	2	0	2
	哥伦比亚	4	6	10
	哥斯达黎加	1	1	2
	古巴	1	0	1
	厄瓜多尔	1	1	2
	危地马拉	2	0	2
	洪都拉斯	2	0	2
	巴拉圭	1	0	1
	秘鲁	3	4	7
	圣卢西亚	0	1	1
	特立尼达和多巴哥	1	0	1
	乌拉圭	0	5	5
	委内瑞拉	1	4	5
合计		28	38	66

续 表

地区	成员	女性	男性	小计
欧洲	阿尔巴尼亚	1	0	1
	奥地利	2	3	5
	比利时	3	2	5
	保加利亚	0	4	4
	克罗地亚	1	0	1
	丹麦	1	1	2
	爱沙尼亚	1	0	1
	芬兰	2	3	5
	法国	97	72	169
	德国	5	14	19
	希腊	3	2	5
	匈牙利	0	1	1
	爱尔兰	10	1	11
	意大利	9	10	19
	荷兰	2	4	6
	挪威	0	2	2
	波兰	2	2	4
	葡萄牙	1	3	4
	罗马尼亚	2	0	2
	俄罗斯	1	0	1
	西班牙	26	13	39
	瑞典	1	2	3
	瑞士	21	12	33
	土耳其	2	1	3
	英国	43	13	56
合计		236	165	401
非洲	贝宁	0	2	2
	乍得	0	1	1
	科特迪瓦	0	1	1
	刚果（金）	1	1	2
	埃及	3	2	5
	加纳	0	1	1
	几内亚	0	1	1
	肯尼亚	1	0	1
	马拉维	0	1	1
	毛里求斯	0	2	2
	摩洛哥	1	2	3
	尼日利亚	0	2	2
	卢旺达	0	1	1
	塞内加尔	0	1	1
	南非	0	1	1
	坦桑尼亚	1	0	1
	突尼斯	2	3	5
	乌干达	3	0	3
	赞比亚	1	0	1
	津巴布韦	2	0	2
合计		15	22	37

续 表

地　区	成　员	女　性	男　性	小　计
亚洲	孟加拉国	0	1	1
	中国	6	7	13
	印度	2	11	13
	日本	2	2	4
	约旦	1	0	1
	韩国	4	0	4
	马来西亚	0	2	2
	巴基斯坦	0	3	3
	菲律宾	5	8	13
	斯里兰卡	0	2	2
	泰国	0	1	1
合计		20	37	57
大洋洲	澳大利亚	4	8	12
	新西兰	1	1	2
合计		5	9	14

资料来源：WTO Annual Report 2015，Figure 4，WTO staff on regular budget by gender and nationality，截至 2014 年 12 月 31 日。

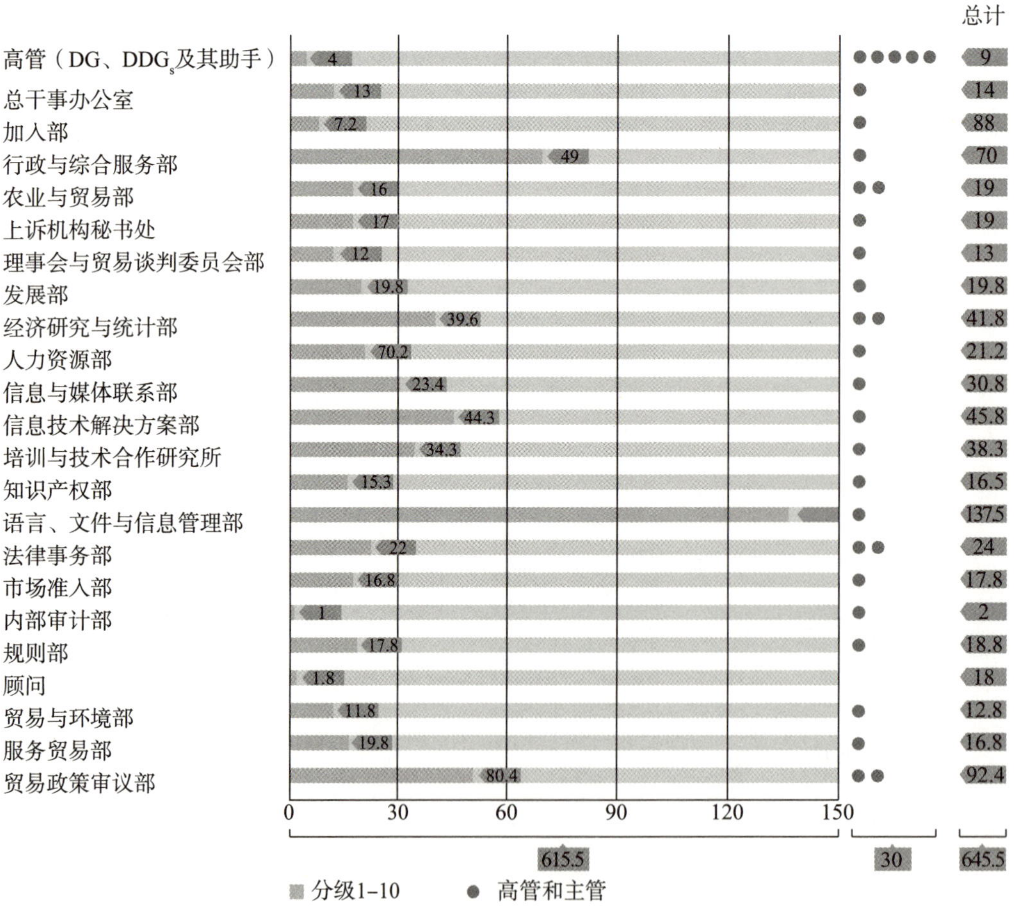

图 1　WTO 秘书处各部门职位分布

资料来源：WTO Annual Report 2015，Figure 4，WTO staff on regular budget by gender and nationality，截至 2014 年 12 月 31 日。

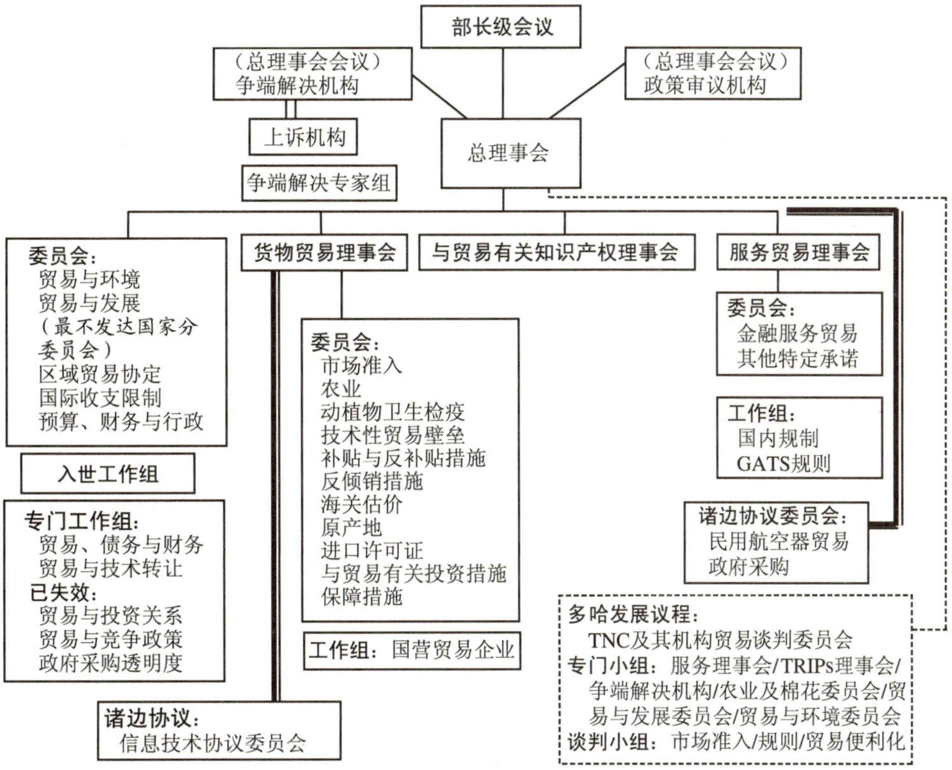

图2 WTO组织结构

注：——向总理事会（或其下属机构）报告　▭向争端解决机构报告
-----诸边贸易协议委员会将其活动通知总理事会或货物理事会（虽然只有部分WTO成员签署这些协议）
▬贸易谈判委员会向总理事会报告

资料来源：http://www.wto.org/english/thewto_e/whatis_e/tif_e/org2_e.htm，访问日期 2015 年 10 月 31 日。

（二）WTO 秘书处经费

WTO 秘书处年度经费绝大部分来自于所有成员所承担的会费。依据过去五年货物、服务和知识产权贸易的可用数据，每个成员的会费取决于其在国际贸易中所占的份额。此外，WTO 秘书处年度经费还来源于其他收入，主要包括租金及纸质和电子出版物的销售收入。WTO 还管理大量的由成员出资的信托基金。这些资金主要用于特定的活动，如旨在使最不发达国家成员和发展中国家成员更好地利用 WTO 以及自多边贸易体制中获取更大利益的技术合作与培训项目。

表 3　　2014 年 WTO 秘书处的合并开支

单位：千瑞士法郎

项　目	预算	开支	结余
人员支出（包括员工薪酬、退休金和就业后福利、健康和伤残保险，家庭和国际利益）	131 415	122 280	9 136
临时补助（包括短期工作人员、专家人员和上诉机构成员费用）	17 167	17 390	−223
一般服务（包括电信和邮政、合约服务和维护、能源和供应、文献出版）	15 801	12 944	2 857
旅行和招待	7 481	5 970	1 511
执行伙伴（包括任何由 WTO 部分/联合/全部资助的活动或事件，但由第三方来组织）	273	200	73
资本支出（包括固定资产的采购和设备租赁）	2 967	1 661	1 306
财务支出（包括银行和利息费用、房屋贷款偿还）	1 230	1 224	6
国际贸易中心和特殊储备的捐款（包括受理上诉机构运作基金和部长级会议劳动基金）	20 870	20 870	0
合计	197 204	182 540	14 664

资料来源：WTO Annual Report 2015，Table 1，Consolidated expenditure 2014。

表 4　　2014 年度 WTO 成员承担的会费

成　员	瑞士法郎	占比（%）
阿尔巴尼亚	54 740	0.03
安哥拉	490 705	0.25
安提瓜和巴布达	29 325	0.02
阿根廷	780 045	0.40
亚美尼亚	33 235	0.02
澳大利亚	2 584 510	1.32
奥地利	2 258 025	1.16
巴林	175 950	0.09
孟加拉国	244 375	0.13
巴巴多斯	29 325	0.02
比利时	4 158 285	2.13
伯利兹	29 325	0.02
贝宁	29 325	0.02
玻利维亚	68 425	0.04
博茨瓦纳	60 605	0.03
巴西	2 381 190	1.22
文莱	64 515	0.03
保加利亚	336 260	0.17
布基纳法索	29 325	0.02
布隆迪	29 325	0.02
柬埔寨	74 290	0.04
喀麦隆	64 515	0.03
加拿大	5 253 085	2.69
佛得角	29 325	0.02
中非	29 325	0.02
乍得	37 145	0.02
智利	778 090	0.40
中国	15 921 520	8.14
哥伦比亚	488 750	0.25
刚果（布）	56 695	0.03
哥斯达黎加	146 625	0.08
科特迪瓦	105 570	0.05
克罗地亚	287 385	0.15
古巴	146 625	0.08

续　表

成　员	瑞士法郎	占比（%）
塞浦路斯	117 300	0.06
捷克	1 429 105	0.73
刚果（金）	87 975	0.05
丹麦	1 728 220	0.88
吉布提	29 325	0.02
多米尼克	29 325	0.02
多米尼加	154 445	0.08
厄瓜多尔	215 050	0.11
埃及	572 815	0.29
萨尔瓦多	80 155	0.04
爱沙尼亚	179 860	0.09
欧盟	0	0.00
斐济	29 325	0.02
芬兰	1 129 990	0.58
法国	7 988 130	4.09
加蓬	43 010	0.02
冈比亚	29 325	0.02
格鲁吉亚	54 740	0.03
德国	16 410 270	8.39
加纳	117 300	0.06
希腊	868 020	0.44
格林纳达	29 325	0.02
危地马拉	136 850	0.07
几内亚	29 325	0.02
几内亚比绍	29 325	0.02
圭亚那	29 325	0.02
海地	29 325	0.02
洪都拉斯	87 975	0.05
中国香港	4 952 015	2.53
匈牙利	1 202 325	0.62
冰岛	78 200	0.04
印度	3 853 305	1.97
印度尼西亚	1 634 380	0.84
爱尔兰	2 128 995	1.09

续 表

成 员	瑞士法郎	占比（%）
以色列	842 605	0.43
意大利	6 443 680	3.30
牙买加	66 470	0.03
日本	8 850 285	4.53
约旦	158 355	0.08
肯尼亚	109 480	0.06
韩国	5 526 785	2.83
科威特	637 330	0.33
吉尔吉斯斯坦	35 190	0.02
老挝	29 325	0.02
拉脱维亚	156 400	0.08
莱索托	29 325	0.02
列支敦士登	46 920	0.02
立陶宛	287 385	0.15
卢森堡	785 910	0.40
中国澳门	211 140	0.11
马达加斯加	29 325	0.02
马拉维	29 325	0.02
马来西亚	2 181 780	1.12
马尔代夫	29 325	0.02
马里	29 325	0.02
马耳他	80 155	0.04
毛里塔尼亚	29 325	0.02
毛里求斯	58 650	0.03
墨西哥	3 376 285	1.73
摩尔多瓦	39 100	0.02
蒙古	39 100	0.02
黑山	29 325	0.02
摩洛哥	373 405	0.19
莫桑比克	43 010	0.02
缅甸	68 425	0.04
纳米比亚	50 830	0.03
尼泊尔	35 190	0.02
荷兰	5 986 210	3.06

续 表

成 员	瑞士法郎	占比（%）
新西兰	432 055	0.22
尼加拉瓜	46 920	0.02
尼日尔	29 325	0.02
尼日利亚	752 675	0.39
挪威	1 657 840	0.85
阿曼	328 440	0.17
巴基斯坦	349 945	0.18
巴拿马	199 410	0.10
巴布亚新几内亚	44 965	0.02
巴拉圭	99 705	0.05
秘鲁	375 360	0.19
菲律宾	666 655	0.34
波兰	2 207 195	1.13
葡萄牙	922 760	0.47
卡塔尔	551 310	0.28
罗马尼亚	713 575	0.37
俄罗斯	4 226 710	2.16
卢旺达	29 325	0.02
圣基茨和尼维斯	29 325	0.02
圣卢西亚	29 325	0.02
圣文森特和格林纳丁斯	29 325	0.02
萨摩亚	29 325	0.02
沙特阿拉伯	2 326 450	1.19
塞内加尔	44 965	0.02
塞拉利昂	29 325	0.02
新加坡	4 508 230	2.31
斯洛伐克	782 000	0.40
斯洛文尼亚	357 765	0.18
所罗门群岛	29 325	0.02
南非	1 069 385	0.55
西班牙	4 590 340	2.35
斯里兰卡	140 760	0.07
苏里南	29 325	0.02
斯威士兰	29 325	0.02

续 表

成 员	瑞士法郎	占比（%）
瑞典	2 365 550	1.21
瑞士	2 873 850	1.47
中国台北	3 032 205	1.55
塔吉克斯坦	29 325	0.02
坦桑尼亚	78 200	0.04
泰国	2 207 195	1.13
马其顿	58 650	0.03
多哥	29 325	0.02
汤加	29 325	0.02
特立尼达和多巴哥	119 255	0.06
突尼斯	244 375	0.13
土耳其	1 908 080	0.98
乌干达	46 920	0.02
乌克兰	809 370	0.41
阿联酋	2 385 100	1.22
英国	7 954 895	4.07
美国	22 298 730	11.41
乌拉圭	103 615	0.05
瓦努阿图	29 325	0.02
委内瑞拉	725 305	0.37
越南	856 290	0.44
赞比亚	62 560	0.03
津巴布韦	39 100	0.02
合计	195 500 000	100.00

资料来源：https：//www. wto. org/english/thewto _ e/secre _ e/contrib14 _ e. htm ，访问日期2015年10月31日 。

二、WTO主要活动（2014）

（一）技术援助和培训

WTO与贸易有关的技术援助计划旨在提高成员对WTO活动的了解程度，各项培训都尽可能地满足成员方的实际要求。WTO成员任何时候都可以向秘书处提出技术援助的相关请求，这可以确保技术援助能及时集中反映成员方的要求，特别是发展中成员和最不发达成员的诉求。

2014年，WTO在日内瓦以及全球其他地区共举行了324次技术援助和培训活动，这一数字高于2013年的279次，但低于2012年的343次。虽然过去两年的活动次数有所减少，但由于电子课程等形式（WTO online，https：//ecampus. wto. org）的引入，对于最不发达国家和非洲国家的持续关注，使得受益人数反而增加。2014年受益人数为15000，比2012年增长了6.4%。

这些活动近一半（47%）使最不发达国家受益，包括在最不发达国家举行的也包括最不发达国家成员参与的。甚至一些活动是针对最不发达国家成员设计或最不发达国家成员优先参与。如为期三周的培训最不发达国家人员的活动，既有介绍性课程也有高阶课程。

这些活动绝大多数是与其他国际组织、区域组织和次区域组织共同举办的。国家层面的活动主要是多重议题的简报会，重点围绕世界贸易组织所管辖的协定协议或多哈回合谈判，包括农业、非农市场准入、卫生与植物卫生措施、与贸易相关的知识产权协定等领域。而且为了满足WTO成员的不同需求，这些活动35%都是在国家层面开展的。为了方便与区域合作伙伴及利益相关者的沟通，WTO还持续推动具体议题的区域性论坛。其中20%针对非洲国家，16%为亚洲和太平洋地区，10%为拉丁美洲，8%为阿拉伯和中东地区，9%为中东欧和中亚（具体参见表5）。

表5　　2014年与贸易有关的技术援助活动分布（按地区统计）

地　区	国　别		区　域		全　球		其他（会议等）		合　计	
非洲	41	31%	15	25%	0	0%	9	24%	65	20%
阿拉伯和中东地区	15	11%	8	13%	0	0%	3	8%	26	8%
亚太地区	28	21%	15	25%	0	0%	9	24%	52	16%
中东欧和中亚	19	15%	7	11%	0	0%	4	11%	30	9%
加勒比地区	6	5%	3	5%	0	0%	0	0%	9	3%
拉丁美洲地区	22	17%	10	16%	0	0%	1	3%	33	10%
次区域合计	131	100%	58	95%	0	0%	26	68%	215	66%
全球	0	0%	3	5%	94	100%	12	32%	109	34%
合计	131	100%	61	100%	94	100%	38	100%	324	100%

资料来源：WTO Annual Report 2015，CH7 Table 1 Trade-related technical assistance by region in 2014。

这些活动的直接目标是促使参与者更好地了解所涉及议题的WTO基本原则。多哈回合谈判的一些特定谈判领域，目的是让参加者掌握其谈判立场所需要的技能和专业知识，以便于其国家在多哈回合谈判达成时取得积极的成果。2014年设立和更新了8个WTO信息咨询中心，以便能依据受益人的需求，更好地调整项目活动。其中，3个在非洲地区，3个在亚太地区，2个在加勒比和拉丁美洲地区。这些信息咨询中心配有信息设备、书籍、CD、DVD和其他WTO相关文件。

技术援助和培训最为重要的是确保有及时充分的资金。金融援助项目主要来自多哈发展议程全球信托基金（Doha Development Agenda Global Trust Fund，DDAGTF）。这是一个由WTO成员发起的自愿的基金窗口。2014年和2015年共收到捐助额达2590万瑞士法郎。2014年共收到来自13个成员的捐助额780万瑞士法郎。这几年捐助数额和成员数均呈下降趋势。

（二）WTO各理事会活动

1. *总理事会*

自上次年度报告起，总理事会一共举行了5次会议，分别为2014年3月14日，5月12日，7月24—25日，10月21日，12月10—11日。这些会议的纪要都包括在文件WT/GC/M/150；WT/GC/M/151；WT/GC/M/152；WT/GC/M/153；WT/GC/M/154；以及WT/GC/M/155中。

2014年，总理事会负责2013年12月巴厘部长级会议的执行情况。2014年7月，WTO成员在相关决议执行的时机问题上出现分歧而陷入僵局。然而，11月会议上僵局被打破，总理事会通过了《贸易便利化协议》，就食品安全的公共储备、后巴厘问题达成一致。2014年12月总理事会通过了塞舌尔的入世“一揽子”协议，同时决定2015年12月15—18日在肯尼亚的内罗毕召开第10届部长级会议。

表6　　正在申请加入WTO的国家谈判进展情况

	申请日期	工作组成立日期	达成备忘录日期	首次/最后一次日期（工作组会议）	工作组会议次数	货物贸易承诺		服务贸易承诺		起草工作组报告日期
						初始	最终	初始	最终	
阿富汗	2004.11	2004.12	2009.03	2011.01/2013.07	4	2012.11		2012.06		2014.03
阿尔及利亚	1987.06	1987.06	1996.07	1998.04/2014.03	12	2002.02	2013.11	2002.03	2013.10	2014.02
安道尔	1997.07	1997.07	1999.03	1999.10	1	1999.09		1999.09		
阿塞拜疆	1997.06	1997.07	1999.04	2002.06/2015.02	12	2005.05	2014.11	2005.05	2015.02	2015.01
巴哈马	2001.05	2001.07	2009.04	2010.09/2012.06	2	2012.03		2012.03	2013.08	
白俄罗斯	1993.09	1993.10	1996.01	1997.06/2005.05	7	1998.03	2006.05	2000.02	2006.09	2012.11
不丹	1999.09	1999.10	2003.02	2004.11/2008.01	4	2005.08	2007.11	2005.08	2007.11	2007.12
波黑	1999.05	1999.07	2002.1	2003.11/2013.06	12	2004.10	2007.02	2004.10	2007.02	2013.05
科摩罗	2007.02	2007.10	2013.10							
赤道几内亚	2007.02	2008.02								
埃塞俄比亚	2003.01	2003.02	2007.01	2008.05/2012.05	3	2012.02				2012.03
伊朗	1996.07	2005.05	2009.11							
伊拉克	2004.09	2004.12	2005.09	2007.04/2008.04	2					
黎巴嫩	1999.01	1999.04	2001.06	2002.10/2009.10	7	2003.11	2004.06	2003.12	2004.06	2009.10
利比里亚	2007.06	2007.12	2011.04	2012.07/2015.05	2	2014.11		2014.11		2015.03
利比亚	2004.06	2004.07								
圣多美和普林西比	2005.01	2005.05								
塞尔维亚	2004.12	2005.02	2005.03	2005.10/2013.06	13	2006.04	2008.11	2006.10	2008.11	2012.10
苏丹	1994.10	1994.10	1999.01	2003.07/2004.03	2	2004.07	2006.10	2004.06	2006.10	2004.09
叙利亚	2001.10	2010.05								
乌兹别克斯坦	1994.12	1994.12	1998.10	2002.07/2005.10	3	2005.09		2005.09		

资料来源：http：//www.wto.org/english/thewto_e/acc_e/status_e.htm，截至2015年10月31日。

2. 货物贸易理事会

（1）进口许可程序委员会

进口许可程序委员会2014年度报告考察期为2013年10月5日至2014年10月20日。考察期间，进口许可程序委员会分别于2014年4月15日和10月20日举行了两次会议。在4月15日的会议上，委员会任命来自莱索托的Tsotetsi Makong先生为委员会主席，同时选举来自芬兰的Juha Niemi先生为副主席。

根据《进口许可程序协议》第1.4（a）条和第8.2（b）条，报告考察期内进口许可程序委员会共从18个成员收到25次通报：喀麦隆，厄瓜多尔，以色列，吉尔吉斯共和国，老挝，马达加斯加，墨西哥，巴拉圭，秘鲁，摩洛哥，菲律宾，俄罗斯，萨摩亚，台湾、澎湖、金门、马祖单独关税区，斯里兰卡，特立尼达和多巴哥，乌克兰，土耳其。

根据《进口许可程序协议》第5条第5.1～5.4段，进口许可程序委员会共从9个成员收到18次通报：印度尼西亚，以色列，老挝，马来西亚，墨西哥，巴拉圭，俄罗斯，沙特阿拉伯，乌克兰。

根据《进口许可程序协议》第7.3条，进口许可程序委员会共从46个成员收到58次通报：阿尔巴尼亚，澳大利亚，布基纳法索，加拿大，喀麦隆，中国，哥斯达黎加，科特迪瓦，古巴，欧盟，冈比亚，格鲁吉亚，海地，洪都拉斯，中国香港，印度，印度尼西亚，以色列，牙买加，日本，科威特州，老挝，中国澳门，前南斯拉夫马其顿共和国，马来西亚，马里，毛里求斯，墨西哥，新西兰，尼加拉瓜，巴拿马，巴拉圭，阿曼，秘鲁，菲律宾，卡塔尔，俄罗斯，台湾、澎湖、金门和马祖单独关税区，斯里兰卡，瑞士，塔吉克斯坦，特立尼达和多巴哥，乌克兰，美国，土耳其，越南。

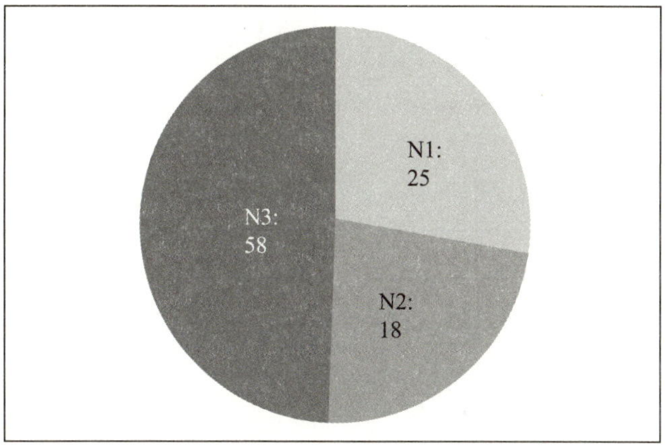

图3 审查期间通报的成员数和通报次数

注：N1：根据第1.4（a）条和第8.2（b）条，相关的法律、法规和行政程序及其变更的通报。

N2：根据第5.1～5.4条，相关实施程序及其变更的通报。

N3：根据第7.3条，相关调查问卷回复的通报。

资料来源：Report（2014）of the committee on import licensing to the council for trade in goods，G/L/1078.

（2）补贴与反补贴措施委员会

补贴与反补贴措施委员会2014年度报告考察期为2013年10月22日至2014年10月28日。考察期内，补贴与反补贴措施委员会分别于2014年4月29日和10月28日举行了两次常规会议和两次特别会议。考察初期，来自澳大利亚的Marcus Bartley Johns先生为委员会主席，来自埃及的Hamed El Etreby先生为副主席。

在2013年4月29日的常规会议上，委员会选举了来自巴西的Eduardo Minoru Chikusa先生为委员会主席，同时选举了挪威的Vegard Emaus先生为副主席。

截至2014年10月28日，共有40[①]个WTO成员向委员会通报了其所发起的反补贴调查措施，有22个成员做了无反补贴调查措施通报。在半年度报告中，2013年7月1日至2013年12月31日期间，有14个成员通报其所发起的反补贴调查措施，70个成员做了无反补贴调查措施通报，共有47个成员未履行通报义务；2014年1月1日至2014年6月30日期间，有16个成员通报其所发起的反补贴调查措施，55个成员做了无反补贴调查措施通报，共有61个成员未履行通报义务。

表7　　全球发起反补贴调查案件数（按被调查国/地区）

被调查国/地区	1995	1996	1997	1998	1999	2000	2001	2002	2003	2004	2005	2006	2007	2008	2009	2010	2011	2012	2013	2014	合计
阿根廷						3	1					1	1		1			1		1	9
澳大利亚					1																1
奥地利								1													1
比利时				1																	1
巴西			1	1	1	1	2					1									7

① 欧盟作为一个成员计数。

续 表

被调查国/地区	1995	1996	1997	1998	1999	2000	2001	2002	2003	2004	2005	2006	2007	2008	2009	2010	2011	2012	2013	2014	合计
加拿大		1	1	1			2	2		1											8
智利			1		1		1														3
中国										3		2	8	11	13	6	9	10	14	14	90
哥伦比亚									1												1
捷克					1																1
丹麦				1																	1
厄瓜多尔																			1		1
欧盟	3	1	1	1	1			1	2						1	1		1	1		14
马其顿					1																1
法国				2	2		2					1									7
德国			1				2														3
希腊			1						1												2
匈牙利							1														1
印度	1		3	6	5	7	8	2	8	1	1	1	1	2	1	1	5	2	6	4	65
印度尼西亚				1	5	1	2				1	1			1		2	2	2	1	19
伊朗															1						1
以色列						1															1
意大利	3	2	1	3	1		1	1	1												13
韩国				5	4	1	1	2		1	1	1			1		1	1	1	4	24
马来西亚					2						1			1	1				1	2	8
墨西哥																				1	1
荷兰							1													1	2
挪威		1																			1
阿曼																	2	1		2	5
巴基斯坦						1									1			1		1	4
秘鲁			1																		1
菲律宾					1															1	2
波兰					1				1												2
俄罗斯																				1	1
沙特阿拉伯				1													1				2
新加坡					1																1
南非		2	1	1	1	1													1		7
西班牙			1	1					1												3
中国台北			1		5					1									1	1	9
泰国	1				5	1				1	1				1		2		1	1	14
特立尼达和多巴哥			1				1													1	3

续 表

被调查国/地区	1995	1996	1997	1998	1999	2000	2001	2002	2003	2004	2005	2006	2007	2008	2009	2010	2011	2012	2013	2014	合计
土耳其	1						1												2	5	9
乌克兰																				2	2
阿联酋															1		1	1			3
英国							1														1
美国	1				1	1					1		1	2	4	1	1	2			15
委内瑞拉			1		1																2
越南															1		1	1	2	2	7
合计	10	7	16	25	41	18	27	9	15	8	6	8	11	16	28	9	25	23	33	45	380

注：调查类型：最初；自 1995 年 1 月 1 日至 2014 年 12 月 31 日。

资料来源：http：//www. wto. org/english/tratop _ e/scm _ e/scm _ e. htm，访问日期 2015 年 10 月 31 日。

表 8　　全球发起反补贴调查案件数（按发起调查的成员）

发起调查的成员	1995	1996	1997	1998	1999	2000	2001	2002	2003	2004	2005	2006	2007	2008	2009	2010	2011	2012	2013	2014	合计
阿根廷	1	1	1																		3
澳大利亚			1		1			1	3			1		2	1	1	2	2	1	2	18
巴西							1		1				1				3	1	2	1	10
加拿大	3				3	4	1		1	4	1	2	1	3	1	1	2	6	4	12	49
智利					4							1	1								6
中国															3	1		2	1		7
哥斯达黎加									1												1
埃及				4																6	10
欧盟		1	4	8	19		6	3	1		3	1		2	6	3	4	6	5	2	74
印度															1					1	2
以色列	2																				2
日本										1											1
拉脱维亚									1												1
墨西哥			1						1								3		1		6
新西兰	1	4	1																		6
巴基斯坦																	2				2
秘鲁			1			1		1					1		2			1		1	8
俄罗斯																				1	1
南非			1	1	2	6	1							2							13
土耳其														1							1
乌克兰																				1	1
美国	3	1	6	12	11	7	18	4	5	3	2	3	7	6	14	3	9	5	19	18	156
委内瑞拉					1				1												2
合计	10	7	16	25	41	18	27	9	15	8	6	8	11	16	28	9	25	23	33	45	380

注：调查类型：最初；自 1995 年 1 月 1 日至 2014 年 12 月 31 日。

资料来源：http：//www. wto. org/english/tratop _ e/scm _ e/scm _ e. htm，访问日期 2015 年 10 月 31 日。

表 9　　全球发起反补贴调查案件数（按产品类别）

HS 编码	1995	1996	1997	1998	1999	2000	2001	2002	2003	2004	2005	2006	2007	2008	2009	2010	2011	2012	2013	2014	合计
Ⅰ活动物，动物产品	1	1	1	1	4	1			1	1			1		1					2	15
Ⅱ植物产品		1				2	1	2			1	1				1					9
Ⅲ动、植物油、脂、蜡			1					1	5						1						8
Ⅳ食品；饮料，酒，醋；烟草	8	4	2	5	2			1	1			1							8	1	33
Ⅴ矿产品							4							1		1	1	2			9
Ⅵ化学工业及其相关工业的产品	1		2		1		2		4			1	1	3	4		3	3	6	5	36
Ⅶ树脂、塑料及其制品；橡胶及其制品				4	7	2	2			2	2		2	1	4		2		2	7	37
Ⅸ木材，软木制品；篮筐		1					1			1						1		1			5
Ⅹ纸、纸板及其制品											2	3	1	1	2	1	2				12
Ⅺ纺织原料及纺织制品				2	5	1	2	1					2		1		3	2	3		22
Ⅻ鞋、帽；羽毛；人造花；风扇						1															1
ⅩⅢ石料、石膏的制品；陶瓷产品；玻璃			1		1										1				2		5
ⅩⅤ贱金属及其制品			7	12	20	11	14	1	3	3		2	3	7	11	4	10	11	12	24	155
ⅩⅥ机器和电气设备			1	1	1		1	3	1	1	1		1	3	2	1	2	3		3	25
ⅩⅦ车辆、航空器和船舶			1												1		2	1		2	7
ⅩⅩ 杂项制品																				1	1
总计	10	7	16	25	41	18	27	9	15	8	6	8	11	16	28	9	25	23	33	45	380

注：调查类型：最初；自 1995 年 1 月 1 日至 2014 年 12 月 31 日。

资料来源：http：//www. wto. org/english/tratop _ e/scm _ e/scm _ e. htm，访问 日期 2015 年 10 月 31 日。

表 10　　全球实施反补贴措施案件数（按被调查国/地区）

被调查国/地区	1995	1996	1997	1998	1999	2000	2001	2002	2003	2004	2005	2006	2007	2008	2009	2010	2011	2012	2013	2014	合计
阿根廷	1						3														4
澳大利亚						1															1
奥地利	1																				1
比利时					1																1
巴西	4					2		2													8
加拿大								2	1												3
中国											2		1	10	6	10	5	8	10	4	56
哥伦比亚										1											1
科特迪瓦	1																				1
欧盟	1	2		2		1			1	1	1					1	1			1	12

续 表

被调查国/地区	1995	1996	1997	1998	1999	2000	2001	2002	2003	2004	2005	2006	2007	2008	2009	2010	2011	2012	2013	2014	合计
法国					2	1	1	1					1								6
德国							1	1													2
匈牙利								1													1
印度	1			2	4	4	3	5	1	6		1		1	2		1	2	1	2	36
印度尼西亚	1				1	2	1		1			1				1					8
伊朗																1					1
以色列	1																				1
意大利	2	2		1	3			1													9
韩国					2	1		1	2		1	1							1		9
马来西亚	1					2															3
墨西哥																				1	1
荷兰							1														1
挪威			1																		1
巴基斯坦							1									1					2
菲律宾	1					1															2
南非			2		1		1														4
西班牙				1																	1
斯里兰卡	1																				1
中国台北						3														1	4
泰国						2	1														3
土耳其		1																		2	3
阿联酋																1					1
英国							1														1
美国						1									1	3	2			1	8
委内瑞拉	3																				3
越南																1			1		2
合计	19	5	3	6	14	21	14	14	6	8	4	3	2	11	9	19	9	10	13	12	202

注：调查类型：最初；自1995年1月1日至2014年12月31日。

资料来源：http：//www. wto. org/english/tratop _ e/scm _ e/scm _ e. htm，访问日期2015年10月31日。

表11　　全球实施反补贴措施案件数（按发起调查的成员）

发起调查的成员	1995	1996	1997	1998	1999	2000	2001	2002	2003	2004	2005	2006	2007	2008	2009	2010	2011	2012	2013	2014	合计
阿根廷		2		2																	4
澳大利亚						1							1			1	1	2	3		9
巴西	5									1				1							7
加拿大	1					5	1			1	2		1	3	1	1	1	4	3		24
智利						2															2

续 表

发起调查的成员	1995	1996	1997	1998	1999	2000	2001	2002	2003	2004	2005	2006	2007	2008	2009	2010	2011	2012	2013	2014	合计
中国																2	2			2	6
哥斯达黎加										1											1
欧盟			1	2	3	10		2	3	2	1				1	3	2		3	2	35
日本												1									1
墨西哥	7										1							2		1	11
新西兰		1	2	1																	4
秘鲁	1						1		1							2					5
南非						1	2	2													5
土耳其															1						1
美国	5	2		1	11	2	10	10	2	2		2		7	6	10	3	2	4	7	86
委内瑞拉										1											1
合计	19	5	3	6	14	21	14	14	6	8	4	3	2	11	9	19	9	10	13	12	202

注：调查类型：最初；自 1995 年 1 月 1 日至 2014 年 12 月 31 日。

资料来源：http：//www. wto. org/english/tratop _ e/scm _ e/scm _ e. htm，访问日期 2015 年 10 月 31 日。

表 12 **全球实施反补贴措施案件数（按产品类别）**

HS 编码	1995	1996	1997	1998	1999	2000	2001	2002	2003	2004	2005	2006	2007	2008	2009	2010	2011	2012	2013	2014	合计
Ⅰ活动物，动物产品			1			2	1									1					5
Ⅱ植物产品	5			1			1		1								1				9
Ⅲ动、植物油、脂、蜡				1					1	1	1					1					5
Ⅳ食品；饮料，酒，醋；烟草	2	5	2	1		1				1			1							1	14
Ⅴ矿产品							4								1		1				6
Ⅵ化学工业及其相关工业的产品				1		1		2		1				1	2	2		2	1	4	17
Ⅶ树脂、塑料及其制品；橡胶及其制品					1	4	1	1						2	1	4					14
Ⅸ木材，软木制品；篮筐								1			1						1				3
Ⅹ纸、纸板及其制品												2		1		2	1				6
Ⅺ纺织原料及纺织制品						3	1	1		1				1		1					8
XIII石料、石膏的制品；陶瓷产品；玻璃																1				2	3
XV贱金属及其制品	12			2	13	10	6	9	1	3	1		1	4	3	7	4	6	9	5	96
XVI机器和电气设备									3	1	1	1		2	2			1	3		14
XVII车辆、航空器和船舶																	1	1			2
合计	19	5	3	6	14	21	14	14	6	8	4	3	2	11	9	19	9	10	13	12	202

注：调查类型：最初；自 1995 年 1 月 1 日至 2014 年 12 月 31 日。

资料来源：http：//www. wto. org/english/tratop _ e/scm _ e/scm _ e. htm，访问日期 2015 年 10 月 31 日。

（3）反倾销措施委员会

反倾销措施委员会2014年度报告考察期为2013年10月23日至2014年10月29日。考察期间，反倾销措施委员会分别于2014年4月30日和10月29日举行了两次常规会议。

考察初期，来自泰国的Parima Damrithamanji女士为委员会主席，来自新西兰的Alana Hudson女士为委员会副主席。在2014年4月30日会议上，委员会选举了来自英国的Andrew Staines先生为委员会主席，来自埃及的Hamed El-Etreby先生为委员会副主席。

截至2014年10月29日，共有76个WTO成员对其国内的反倾销立法做了通报，其中有37个成员做了无反倾销立法的通报。此外，还有19个成员未尽到通报义务。在半年度报告中，2013年7月1日至2013年12月31日期间，有34个成员通报了其反倾销的行动，23个成员通报其无反倾销行动，共有14个成员未履行通报义务；2014年1月1日至2014年6月30日期间，有34个成员通报了其反倾销的行动，15个成员通报其无反倾销行动，共有15个成员未履行通报义务。

表13　全球发起反倾销调查案件数（按被调查国/地区）

被调查国/地区	1995	1996	1997	1998	1999	2000	2001	2002	2003	2004	2005	2006	2007	2008	2009	2010	2011	2012	2013	2014	合计
阿尔及利亚					1			1													2
阿根廷	1			1	4	2	5	3	1	3	4	3	1	2	2	2	1	2	5	2	44
亚美尼亚														1							1
澳大利亚	1		2	2	3	4	1	3	2			1	2	2			1	1	1		26
奥地利		2	3		3	3		1		1		1		2		2	1	1			20
巴林					1																1
孟加拉							1						1								2
白俄罗斯					3	4	3	2	1	2			1	2		1	3				22
比利时	1	2	3	3	1		5	1	3	2					3	1	1		2	1	29
波黑	1												1			1					3
巴西	8	10	5	6	13	9	13	3	3	10	4	7	2	3	12	3	3	2	6		122
保加利亚		3	2	1	1	1	2		1		1	1		1			1				15
加拿大	2	1	3	4		1	7	5	4	2	1	1	2	2	1	2	1		2		41
智利	2	2	2	2	1	6	4	4			1	1		1	1	2		2	2		33
中国	20	43	33	27	43	43	55	50	53	49	53	73	61	78	78	44	51	60	75	63	1 052
哥伦比亚		1		2			1	1											3		8
哥斯达黎加				2																	2
克罗地亚	1			1	1	1					1										5
古巴		1			1																2
捷克	1	1		2	7	3	2	1	1				1				1		1		21
丹麦	1	1		2	2							1						1	1		9
多米尼加							1						1			1					3
厄瓜多尔								1		1				1							3
埃及	1	2	1	2		1	3					2						1	1	5	19
萨尔瓦多															2	1					3
爱沙尼亚			1			1	1	1									1				5
欧盟		1	2	4	7	9	9	10	10	3	5	3	2	4	6	9	3	5	8	8	108
法罗群岛								2													2

续 表

被调查国/地区	1995	1996	1997	1998	1999	2000	2001	2002	2003	2004	2005	2006	2007	2008	2009	2010	2011	2012	2013	2014	合计
芬兰			1	1	2		1	2	2	2	1		1			2		2		1	18
马其顿	1		1	1	1		2	1				1						1			9
法国		4	4	10	7	2	3	2	3	1	1	1	1	1	1	2			1	3	47
格鲁吉亚								1													1
德国	7	9	13	8	11	6	9	7	3	2	2	2	4	1	3	3	2	3	7	4	106
希腊			3			1	1		1					1	1				1		9
危地马拉		1					1				1				1	1					5
洪都拉斯				1																	1
中国香港	1	4	2	3	2	1	3	3			2	2	3	3	2		1		1	1	34
匈牙利	2		2	2	4		4	1								1				1	17
印度	3	11	8	13	13	10	12	16	14	8	14	6	4	6	7	4	7	10	11	15	192
印度尼西亚	7	7	9	5	20	13	18	12	8	8	14	9	5	11	10	4	5	6	7	5	183
伊朗		1	2		2	3	2	2	1	2			1	3	1	2		1	1		24
爱尔兰			2	1					1	2											6
以色列		1	2	1		1	2						1	1	1		2		1	3	16
意大利	6	5	5	5	2	5	8	3	4	1	1			2	2	1	2	3	3	1	59
日本	5	6	14	14	22	12	14	13	16	9	7	9	4	3	5	5	5	6	11	7	187
约旦							1														1
哈萨克斯坦	3	1	2	4		3	3	6				2		1			1				26
肯尼亚																1	1				2
朝鲜							1									1					2
韩国	14	11	15	27	35	23	23	23	17	24	12	10	13	9	8	9	11	22	25	18	349
科威特														1		1					2
吉尔吉斯																				1	1
拉脱维亚			2	1	1	3															7
利比亚						1	1														2
列支敦士登			1																		1
立陶宛			1		4	1	1	3									1				11
卢森堡							2			1											3
中国澳门	1							1				1		1	1		1				6
马拉维					1																1
马来西亚	2	3	5	4	7	9	6	4	8	6	14	5	7	10	7	4	2	3	9	10	125
墨西哥	3	5	2	9	4	1	4	1	4	3	1	2	2		5	5	3	3	6	3	66
摩尔多瓦						2	1							1							4
莫桑比克			1																		1
尼泊尔							2														2
荷兰	6	1	5	3	2	3	4	1		2					1	1			2	1	32
新西兰	1	1			2		3	1					1	1	1						11
尼加拉瓜		1																			1

续 表

被调查国/地区	1995	1996	1997	1998	1999	2000	2001	2002	2003	2004	2005	2006	2007	2008	2009	2010	2011	2012	2013	2014	合计
尼日利亚									1												1
挪威		1				1	1	1		1				1		1				1	8
阿曼							1								1	2	2	1		2	9
巴基斯坦		2	1		1		1	2	2		1				1	1	1	2	1	4	20
巴拉圭			1												1						2
秘鲁	1					1								2					2		6
菲律宾	2					1	1	1	1	2		3		1					2	2	16
波兰	2	3	3	5	3	5	1	4	1	2						1	2		1		33
葡萄牙		2		2		1	1									1			2	1	10
卡塔尔							1														1
罗马尼亚	1	2	1	5	4	4	5	8	2		2			2		1	1	1			39
俄罗斯	2	7	7	13	18	12	9	20	2	8	4	5	6	2	4	2	3	3	5	4	136
沙特阿拉伯		1		3	2	3	1	1	2		1	1		4	2	2	1	2	5	2	33
塞尔维亚																		1			1
塞尔维亚和黑山					1		1				1										3
新加坡	2		4		5		12	9	1	1	1	6	2		1	1		2	1	5	53
斯洛伐克		1	1	1	3	1	2	1		1											11
斯洛文尼亚	1			1																	2
南非	2	6	4	5	4	6	9	10	4		2	2	1	3	1	1	1	2	3	2	68
西班牙	2	4	7	7	5	6	4	2	4	1			1	1		2	1		4	3	54
斯里兰卡										1			1	2			1			1	6
瑞典	1	2	5		1		2	1		1	1	1		1		1	1		3	1	22
瑞士		2	1		1				1			1			1	1		1		1	10
中国台北	4	9	16	10	22	14	19	16	13	21	13	13	6	11	12	5	9	22	17	13	265
泰国	8	9	5	2	19	12	17	12	7	9	13	8	9	13	8	5	8	10	14	9	197
特立尼达和多巴哥			2				1													1	4
土耳其	2	3	1	2	6	7	5	4	4	1		2	3	4	2	4	4	5	5	8	72
乌克兰	2	3	4	9	9	7	6	8	3	1	5	4	1	2	3	2		3	3	4	79
阿联酋			1			2	2		3	2			3		1	4	3	1	3	3	28
英国	6	4	6	4	2	9	6	2		1	1			3					3		47
美国	12	21	15	16	14	13	15	11	21	14	12	11	7	8	14	19	10	9	13	11	266
乌拉圭	1				1					1			1						2		6
乌兹别克斯坦	2									1											3
委内瑞拉		1	1	4	2	2	4	3	1								2		2		22
越南			1		1	1		3		7	3	2	2	3	3	1	3	8	3	5	46
南斯拉夫	1	1			1																3
津巴布韦	1			1																	2
合计	157	226	246	264	359	296	372	311	234	220	200	203	165	218	217	173	165	208	287	236	4 757

注：调查类型：最初；自 1995 年 1 月 1 日至 2014 年 12 月 31 日。

资料来源：http：//www. wto. org/english/tratop _ e/adp _ e/adp _ e. htm，访问日期 2015 年 10 月 31 日。

表 14　　全球发起反倾销调查案件数（按发起调查的成员）

发起调查的成员	1995	1996	1997	1998	1999	2000	2001	2002	2003	2004	2005	2006	2007	2008	2009	2010	2011	2012	2013	2014	合计
阿根廷	27	22	14	6	24	41	28	10	1	12	9	10	7	19	28	14	7	12	19	6	316
澳大利亚	5	17	44	13	24	15	24	16	8	9	7	11	2	6	9	7	18	12	20	22	289
巴西	5	18	11	18	16	11	17	8	4	8	6	12	13	24	9	37	16	47	54	35	369
保加利亚								1													1
加拿大	11	5	14	8	18	21	25	5	15	11	1	7	1	3	6	2	2	11	17	13	196
智利	4	3		2		5						1	1	1	1	1	1	1	4		25
中国				3	2	11	14	30	22	27	24	10	4	14	17	8	5	9	11	7	218
哥伦比亚	4	1	1	6	2	3	6			2	2	9	1	6	5	2	4	2	11	6	73
哥斯达黎加		4	1	1							1	1			2						10
捷克				2	1																3
多米尼加																1			2		3
厄瓜多尔				1												2					3
埃及			7	14	7	3	7	3	1		12	9	2		2	1	2	1	2	9	82
欧盟	33	25	41	22	65	32	28	20	7	30	24	35	9	19	15	15	17	13	4	14	468
危地马拉		1																		1	2
洪都拉斯																3					3
印度	6	21	13	28	64	41	79	81	46	21	28	31	47	55	31	41	19	21	29	38	740
印度尼西亚		11	5	8	8	3	4	4	12	5		5	1	7	7	3	6	7	14	12	122
以色列	5	6	3	7		1	4			1	4			1	6	6	1	2	1		48
牙买加						1	1	1	1						1	1					6
日本							2						4					1		1	8
约旦												1									1
韩国	4	13	15	3	6	2	4	9	18	3	4	7	15	5		3		2	8	6	127
拉脱维亚							1	6													7
立陶宛					1	6															7
马来西亚	3	2	8	1	2		1	5	6	3	4	8						11	8	8	70
墨西哥	4	4	6	12	11	6	6	10	14	6	6	6	3	1	2	2	6	4	6	14	129
摩洛哥																	1	2	3	1	7
新西兰	10	4	5	1	4	9	1	2	5	5		1	6			1	2		1		57
尼加拉瓜				2																	2
巴基斯坦								1	3	3	13	4		3	26	11	7	5	6		82
巴拿马				2											4						6
巴拉圭					1					1											2
秘鲁	2	8	2	3	8	1	8	13	4	7	4	3	2		4		1	1	1		72
菲律宾	1	1	2	3	6	2		1	1						1				1		19
波兰			1		7			3	1												12

续 表

发起调查的成员	1995	1996	1997	1998	1999	2000	2001	2002	2003	2004	2005	2006	2007	2008	2009	2010	2011	2012	2013	2014	合计
俄罗斯											2	4	1	4	8		10	1	1	7	38
斯洛文尼亚					1																1
南非	16	34	23	41	16	21	6	4	8	6	23	3	5	3	3		4	1	10	2	229
中国台北			1	6		4	3		2			5			1	2		9	3		36
泰国		1	3				3	21	3	3		3	2	1	1	2	13	5			61
特立尼达和多巴哥		1		4	3	1	1		2											1	13
土耳其			4	1	8	7	15	18	11	25	12	8	6	23	6	2	2	14	6	12	180
乌克兰							2	3	2	6	2	1	5	7	2	2	6	3	2	2	45
美国	14	22	15	36	47	47	77	35	37	26	12	8	28	16	20	3	15	11	39	19	527
乌拉圭			1			1	4									1					7
委内瑞拉	3	2	6	10	7	1	1	1													31
越南																			4		4
合计	157	226	246	264	359	296	372	311	234	220	200	203	165	218	217	173	165	208	287	236	4 757

注：调查类型：最初；自 1995 年 1 月 1 日至 2014 年 12 月 31 日。

资料来源：http：//www. wto. org/english/tratop _ e/adp _ e/adp _ e. htm，访问日期 2015 年 10 月 31 日。

表 15　　全球发起反倾销调查案件数（按产品类别）

HS 编码	1995	1996	1997	1998	1999	2000	2001	2002	2003	2004	2005	2006	2007	2008	2009	2010	2011	2012	2013	2014	合计
...																			1		1
Ⅰ活动物，动物产品	1	2	2	6	8	3	2	10	2	10			1	1	3		2		4	1	58
Ⅱ植物产品		5	2	4	1	7	8	3	1	6	4	3	1	5	1	1	1	1	2	4	60
Ⅲ动、植物油、脂、蜡							4	2	2	1	2	3								1	15
Ⅳ食品；饮料、酒及醋；烟草	13	6	4	8	2	3	2	3		1	1	7			2	1	5		6	1	65
Ⅴ矿产品	1	4	3	4	9	9	16	8	5	1		2	2	2	1	4	2	2		1	76
Ⅵ化学工业及其相关产品	31	42	21	24	74	63	67	96	73	49	37	39	56	34	47	44	29	34	48	53	961
Ⅶ树脂、塑料及其制品；橡胶及其制品	20	26	36	33	40	24	56	40	24	44	37	24	16	21	31	24	13	40	41	45	635
Ⅷ生皮、毛皮及制品；马具和旅行用品		3									2										5
Ⅸ木材，软木制品；篮筐	1	4	11	3	1	5	4		11	11	3	2	1	9	7	5	13	1	5	1	98
Ⅹ纸、纸板及其制品	3	14	36	7	18	5	7	7	20	8	6	17	19	2	8	20	11	6	12	3	229
Ⅺ纺织原料及纺织制品	1	23	8	28	36	17	27	7	14	21	27	17	12	39	20	7	2	12	21	7	346
Ⅻ鞋、帽；羽毛，人造花，风扇	6	1		4	2	3	2	3			4	3		1	3						32
ⅩⅢ石料、石膏的制品；陶瓷产品；玻璃	3	11	11	12	8	6	6	11	11	8	10	12	3	4	11	12	14	13	23	5	194

续 表

HS 编码	1995	1996	1997	1998	1999	2000	2001	2002	2003	2004	2005	2006	2007	2008	2009	2010	2011	2012	2013	2014	合计
XIV珠宝，贵金属和金属，硬币							1														1
XV贱金属及其制品	43	39	64	111	111	109	137	96	53	38	39	31	23	70	52	43	58	76	97	89	1 379
XVI机器和电气设备	24	33	34	10	30	30	24	9	12	16	16	30	28	16	22	10	8	18	21	17	408
XVII车辆、航空器和船舶	3	3	1		4	5		2	2	2	4	2	1	3	3	1	6	4		5	51
XVIII仪器，钟表，录音机和复读机	1	5	9	5	2		3	3	2	1	1	5		6	3	1	1		1	2	51
XX 杂项制品	6	5	4	5	13	7	6	11	2	3	7	6	2	5	3			1	5	1	92
总计	157	226	246	264	359	296	372	311	234	220	200	203	165	218	217	173	165	208	287	236	4 757

注：调查类型：最初；自 1995 年 1 月 1 日至 2014 年 12 月 31 日。

资料来源：http：//www. wto. org/english/tratop _ e/adp _ e/adp _ e. htm，访问日期 2015 年 10 月 31 日。

表 16 全球实施反倾销措施案件数（按被调查国/地区）

被调查国/地区	1995	1996	1997	1998	1999	2000	2001	2002	2003	2004	2005	2006	2007	2008	2009	2010	2011	2012	2013	2014	合计
阿尔及利亚						1			1												2
阿根廷	3				1	1	3	1	1		2	1	2		1	1	2	1	1		21
亚美尼亚															1						1
澳大利亚			1	1	2	2			1	2				2		1					12
奥地利	1			3		2							1		2			1			10
孟加拉国							1							1							2
白俄罗斯		1				3	4	3	1	1	1			1	1			2			18
比利时		1		4	5			2	2		1				1		1	1			18
波黑		1															1				2
巴西	9	10	7	6	5	8	2	6	4	3	5	5	2	2	3	4	2		3	3	89
保加利亚	2		1		2	1	1	2		1		1	1			1		1			14
加拿大	1			3	1			4	4	1			1	2	1			1		2	21
智利		1	1	3			4	4	1	1		1	1				1		2	1	21
中国	27	16	33	24	21	31	31	36	40	44	42	37	46	54	57	56	37	35	52	40	759
哥伦比亚	1				1																2
克罗地亚		2				1		1			1										5
古巴						1															1
捷克	1	1	1		1	4	1	3	1	1					1						15
丹麦	1			1		1	1													2	6
多米尼加								1													1
厄瓜多尔	1								1		1										3
埃及			2		2									1						1	6
爱沙尼亚					1			1	1												3

续 表

被调查国/地区	1995	1996	1997	1998	1999	2000	2001	2002	2003	2004	2005	2006	2007	2008	2009	2010	2011	2012	2013	2014	合计
欧盟			1	1	4	4	8	6	7	6	3	3	1	3	1	4	4	8	4	6	74
法罗群岛										1											1
芬兰				1	1	2			1	2	2	1		1				2	1	1	15
马其顿		1			1		1		1					1							5
法国	1	1	2	5	7	3	4	1	1		2				2		1				30
格鲁吉亚									1												1
德国	4	2	2	7	5	7	1	6	4			2		3	4			1	3	2	53
希腊				2				1	1						1				1		6
危地马拉									1												1
洪都拉斯					1																1
中国香港		3	1	1	1	1	1	2	2				1	1	2	3		1			20
匈牙利		1			2	2		2	1								1				9
印度	4	1	5	7	9	7	6	6	7	10	2	12	3	6	4	2	3	3	6	6	109
印度尼西亚		2	4	7	4	11	5	9	12	2	7	10	3	6	7	8	4	2	7	4	114
伊朗						1	2		1	2	1				1			2	1		11
爱尔兰					2							1									3
以色列	1				1		1	1	1							1		2			8
意大利	2	2	1	7	5	1	2	4	2		1				1		2		3	2	35
日本	5	6	5	9	11	22	9	5	11	6	7	8	4	3		2	3	5	5	8	134
约旦								1													1
哈萨克斯坦			2	2	4		1	2	7				1	1							20
肯尼亚																		1			1
韩国	4	6	3	15	15	23	12	13	22	13	8	10	6	8	7	4	4	10	18	12	213
科威特																1					1
拉脱维亚				1	1		4		1												7
利比亚								1													1
列支敦士登			1																		1
立陶宛					1	1		1													3
中国澳门														1		2		1			4
马拉维							1														1
马来西亚	3	3	3	4	3	4	1	4	3	6	3	6	5	2	7	3	5	2	1	5	73
墨西哥		3	4	1	3	4	1	4		3	2	1	2	1	1	2		2	3	6	43
摩尔多瓦	1						2	1													4
尼泊尔								2													2
荷兰	2		1	2	1	3	1	2	2		1				1	1					17
新西兰				1			1		1							1					4
尼日利亚										1											1
挪威			1							1		1					1				4

续 表

被调查国/地区	1995	1996	1997	1998	1999	2000	2001	2002	2003	2004	2005	2006	2007	2008	2009	2010	2011	2012	2013	2014	合计
阿曼								1								1		1	1		4
巴基斯坦	1		1				1		1	2								1		2	9
巴拉圭	1				1											1					3
秘鲁															1						1
菲律宾			1			1		1	1			3									7
波兰	1	1	3	2	4	2	4	1	1	1	1							1			22
葡萄牙			1	1	1			1												1	5
卡塔尔								1													1
罗马尼亚	2	1	1	2	2	4	1	4	5	2	1	1			1		1		1		29
俄罗斯	8	3	9	5	16	8	8	4	13	5	6	3	1	6		3	1	3	3	1	106
沙特阿拉伯				1	1	1	1	1			1		1		1	2			1	2	13
塞尔维亚																			1		1
塞尔维亚和黑山						1	1					1									3
新加坡				3		3		7	7	1		2	4	3		1		1	1		33
斯洛伐克			1		2	1		2	1		1										8
斯洛文尼亚		1																			1
南非	2	3	2	2	3	4	3	7	8					4		2	1		2	2	45
西班牙	3			4	4	3	3	3		1	1			1	1		1			2	27
斯里兰卡										1					1				1		3
瑞典				4	1	1			1		1	1		1	1			1		2	14
瑞士				1						1			1								3
中国台北	2	2	7	12	8	17	8	13	11	10	8	7	7	9	7	8	5	9	12	11	173
泰国	5	8	2	5	1	12	8	8	8	6	6	8	4	4	10	7	7	3	9	8	129
特立尼达和多巴哥			1	1				1													3
土耳其	1	1	1	2	4	3	3	3	2	2				3		1	2	2	3	2	35
乌克兰	5	1	3	5	7	8	7	5	6		1	3	2		1	1	1	2	1	3	62
阿联酋							1	1		1	1	1		1	1		1	3	2	2	15
英国	3	1	2	3	3	1	2	5	1			1			2	1					25
美国	8	4	9	12	8	13	4	10	6	10	13	9	4	7	5	7	7	9	5	12	162
乌拉圭							1				1			1							3
乌兹别克斯坦										1											1
委内瑞拉	4	1		1		2		1	2	1									1		13
越南				1		1	1		1	2	4	2	2	2	4	2			6	6	34
南斯拉夫		1																			1
津巴布韦			1																		1
合计	120	92	127	185	190	238	169	218	223	154	138	142	106	142	143	134	99	120	161	157	3 058

注：调查类型：最初；自 1995 年 1 月 1 日至 2014 年 12 月 31 日。

资料来源：http：//www. wto. org/english/tratop _ e/adp _ e/adp _ e. htm，访问日期 2015 年 10 月 31 日。

表 17　　全球实施反倾销措施案件数（按发起调查成员）

发起调查的成员	1995	1996	1997	1998	1999	2000	2001	2002	2003	2004	2005	2006	2007	2008	2009	2010	2011	2012	2013	2014	合计
阿根廷	13	20	11	12	9	16	14	22	19	1	8	4	8	5	16	15	8	9	9	9	228
澳大利亚	1	1	1	20	6	5	11	9	10	4	3	5	1	3	2	2	5	10	9	14	122
巴西	3	6	2	14	5	9	13	5	2	5	3		9	11	16	5	13	14	30	32	197
加拿大	7		7	10	10	14	19		5	8	4		3	3	2	3	1	10	7	6	119
智利	2		2	2									1		1	1		1			10
中国				3	2	5		5	33	14	16	24	12	4	12	15	6	5	8	12	176
哥伦比亚	1	1	1		6	2				1	1	1	7		3				6	4	34
哥斯达黎加									1				2								3
捷克						1															1
多米尼加																	1			1	2
埃及				5	14	1	2	7	4	1		12	2	3		1	1		1		54
欧盟	15	23	23	28	18	41	13	25	2	10	20	12	12	15	9	5	11	3	12	1	298
危地马拉			1																		1
印度	7	2	8	22	23	55	38	64	52	29	18	16	24	31	30	32	26	30	12	15	534
印度尼西亚			4	2	7		1		1	8	4	2		5	1	5	2	4	5	3	54
以色列	1			6	4		1	2		1		3	1			2	1		1		23
牙买加							1	2		1											4
日本	1							2						4							7
韩国		5	10	8		5		1	4	10	3	8		12	4		2		5	5	82
拉脱维亚								1	1												2
立陶宛							7														7
马来西亚		2	2	4	1	1		1	7		7								11	2	38
墨西哥	16	4	7	7	7	6	3	4	7	7	8	5			1	2	1	4	2	8	99
摩洛哥																		1	1	4	6
新西兰	3	4		1			2	1		2	4	2	3				2				24
尼加拉瓜					1																1
巴基斯坦								1	2	4	1	7	4		6	5	7	6	7		50
巴拉圭					1					1											2
秘鲁	2	2	3		3	4	1	7	7	8	3	4	1		2	1	1		1		50
菲律宾		2	1	1	3	4															11
波兰				1		6			2												9
俄罗斯												1	1	4	1	10	1	4	6		28
新加坡	2																				2
南非		8	18	13	36	13	5	15	1	4		7	1	3	3	1		1	2	1	132
中国台北			1	5	1	1		2				1	1			2	1		2		17
泰国			1	2				1	20	1	2		1		3		3	2	7	4	47
特立尼达和多巴哥				2		1	2		1	1											7

续 表

发起调查的成员	1995	1996	1997	1998	1999	2000	2001	2002	2003	2004	2005	2006	2007	2008	2009	2010	2011	2012	2013	2014	合计
土耳其	11				1	8	2	11	28	16	9	21	6	11	9	10	2	1	8	9	163
乌克兰							1	2	2	2	6	2	1	5	7			7	2	1	38
美国	33	12	20	16	24	31	33	27	12	14	18	5	5	23	15	17	4	7	7	22	345
乌拉圭				1														1			2
委内瑞拉	2		4		8	9		1		1											25
越南																				4	4
合计	120	92	127	185	190	238	169	218	223	154	138	142	106	142	143	134	99	120	161	157	3 058

注：调查类型：最初；自 1995 年 1 月 1 日至 2014 年 12 月 31 日。

资料来源：http：//www. wto. org/english/tratop _ e/adp _ e/adp _ e. htm，访问日期 2015 年 10 月 31 日。

表 18　　全球实施反倾销措施案件数（按产品类别）

HS 编码	1995	1996	1997	1998	1999	2000	2001	2002	2003	2004	2005	2006	2007	2008	2009	2010	2011	2012	2013	2014	合计
Ⅰ活动物，动物产品	2		1	2	1	3	7		1	2	6	1				1		1			28
Ⅱ植物产品	4	1	1	4	3	1	3	3	1		2	5	3	1	2	2		1			37
Ⅲ动、植物油、脂、蜡								1			1										2
Ⅳ食品；饮料、酒及醋，烟草	6	6	1	3	1	1	4	1	1			5	3				2			2	36
Ⅴ矿产品		1	2	3	1	5	11	8	2	7			1	1	2		3		3		50
Ⅵ化学工业及其相关工业的产品	19	12	22	15	15	49	38	57	68	46	31	27	28	46	18	32	28	36	22	31	640
Ⅶ树脂、塑料及其制品；橡胶及其制品	10	11	13	14	27	26	11	25	48	22	23	28	7	25	13	15	12	8	30	21	389
Ⅷ生皮、毛皮及其制品；马具和旅行用品			1									1									2
Ⅸ木材，软木制品；篮筐	1		1	6	7	1		3		4	5	5		3	6		2	1	5	1	51
Ⅹ纸、纸板及其制品	2		2	29	5	10	2	6	10	4	10	7	4	11		2	4	13	1	4	126
Ⅺ纺织原料及纺织制品	4	8	9	2	21	26	9	30	2	14	13	23	17	10	30	17	2	3	5	8	253
Ⅻ鞋、帽；羽毛，人造花，风扇	1		3	3		7	2	1				2	1		1	2					23
XIII石料、石膏的制品；陶瓷产品；玻璃	3	3	1	6	5	7	1	2	10	4	5	7	5	4	4	5	13	8	11	19	123
XV 贱金属及其制品	49	24	46	64	85	83	65	59	65	39	24	16	11	28	29	40	21	40	69	61	918
XVI机器和电气设备	9	17	16	30	4	14	11	15	8	6	12	9	15	12	27	14	7	7	11	8	252
XVII车辆、航空器和船舶	1	5	1	1	1		1		2	2	1		5		1	2	2	1	3		29
XVIII仪器，钟表，录音机和复读机	2	1			11		1		1	1	3		4		5	1	3	1		1	35
XX 杂项制品	7	3	7	3	3	5	3	7	4	3	2	6	2	1	5	1			1	1	64
合计	120	92	127	185	190	238	169	218	223	154	138	142	106	142	143	134	99	120	161	157	3 058

注：调查类型：最初；自 1995 年 1 月 1 日至 2014 年 12 月 31 日。

资料来源：http：//www. wto. org/english/tratop _ e/adp _ e/adp _ e. htm，访问日期 2015 年 10 月 31 日。

（4）保障措施委员会

保障措施委员会 2014 年度报告考察期为 2013 年 10 月 23 日至 2014 年 10 月 27 日。考察期内，保障措施委员会分别于 2014 年 4 月 28 日和 2013 年 10 月 27 日举行了两次常规会议。

2014 年 4 月 28 日会议上，委员会选举了 Kim Kampel 女士为委员会主席，选举了 Mitsuhiro Fukuyama 先生为副主席。

截至 2014 年 10 月 27 日，共有 111 个 WTO 成员对其国内的保障措施的立法和规章做了通报。此外，还有 22 个成员未尽到通报义务。

表 19　　全球发起保障措施调查案件数

发起调查的成员	1995	1996	1997	1998	1999	2000	2001	2002	2003	2004	2005	2006	2007	2008	2009	2010	2011	2012	2013	2014	2015	合计
阿根廷	0	0	1	1	0	1	1	0	0	1	0	1	0	0	0	0	0	0	0	0	0	6
澳大利亚	0	0	0	1	0	0	0	0	0	0	0	0	1	0	0	0	0	0	2	0	0	4
巴西	0	1	0	0	0	0	1	0	0	0	0	0	0	1	0	0	0	1	0	0	0	4
保加利亚*	0	0	0	0	0	1	1	3	1	0	0	0	0	0	0	0	0	0	0	0	0	6
加拿大	0	0	0	0	0	0	0	1	0	0	2	0	0	0	0	0	0	0	0	0	0	3
智利	0	0	0	0	2	3	2	2	0	1	0	1	0	0	1	0	0	1	2	0	0	15
中国	0	0	0	0	0	0	0	1	0	0	0	0	0	0	0	0	0	0	0	0	0	1
中国台北	0	0	0	0	0	0	0	0	0	0	0	0	0	0	0	0	0	0	1	0	0	1
哥伦比亚	0	0	0	0	1	0	0	0	0	2	0	0	0	0	0	0	0	0	4	0	0	7
哥斯达黎加	0	0	0	0	0	0	0	1	0	0	0	0	0	0	0	0	0	1	0	1	0	3
克罗地亚	0	0	0	0	0	0	0	0	0	0	0	0	0	0	1	0	0	0	0	0	0	1
捷克*	0	0	0	0	1	2	1	5	0	0	0	0	0	0	0	0	0	0	0	0	0	9
多米尼加	0	0	0	0	0	0	0	0	0	0	0	0	0	0	3	2	0	0	0	0	0	5
厄瓜多尔	0	0	0	0	2	0	0	1	4	0	0	0	0	0	0	1	0	0	0	1	0	9
埃及	0	0	0	1	1	1	0	0	0	0	0	0	0	1	0	0	1	4	0	2	1	12
萨尔瓦多	0	0	0	0	0	3	0	0	0	0	0	0	0	0	0	0	0	0	0	0	0	3
爱沙尼亚*	0	0	0	0	0	0	0	0	1	0	0	0	0	0	0	0	0	0	0	0	0	1
欧盟*	0	0	0	0	0	0	0	1	1	1	1	0	0	0	0	1	0	0	0	0	0	5
匈牙利	0	0	0	0	0	0	0	1	2	0	0	0	0	0	0	0	0	0	0	0	0	3
印度	0	0	1	5	3	2	0	2	1	1	0	0	0	1	10	1	1	1	3	7	0	39
印度尼西亚	0	0	0	0	0	0	0	0	0	1	1	1	0	2	0	7	4	7	0	3	0	26
以色列	0	0	0	0	0	0	0	0	0	0	0	0	0	0	1	0	1	0	0	0	0	2
牙买加	0	0	0	0	0	0	0	0	1	0	0	0	0	0	0	0	0	0	0	0	0	1
日本	0	0	0	0	0	1	0	0	0	0	0	0	0	0	0	0	0	0	0	0	0	1
约旦	0	0	0	0	0	1	0	8	0	0	1	1	1	2	0	1	0	1	0	1	0	17
韩国	1	2	0	0	1	0	0	0	0	0	0	0	0	0	0	0	0	0	0	0	0	4
吉尔吉斯斯坦	0	0	0	0	0	0	0	0	0	0	0	0	0	0	2	1	0	0	1	0	0	4
拉脱维亚*	0	0	0	0	1	0	0	1	0	0	0	0	0	0	0	0	0	0	0	0	0	2
立陶宛*	0	0	0	0	0	0	1	0	0	0	0	0	0	0	0	0	0	0	0	0	0	1
马来西亚	0	0	0	0	0	0	0	0	0	0	0	0	0	0	0	0	1	0	0	1	0	2
墨西哥	0	0	0	0	0	0	0	1	0	0	0	0	0	0	0	1	0	0	0	0	0	2

续 表

发起调查的成员	1995	1996	1997	1998	1999	2000	2001	2002	2003	2004	2005	2006	2007	2008	2009	2010	2011	2012	2013	2014	2015	合计
摩尔多瓦	0	0	0	0	0	0	0	0	1	1	0	0	0	0	0	0	0	0	0	0	0	2
摩洛哥	0	0	0	0	0	2	0	0	0	0	1	0	0	0	1	1	0	1	0	1	0	7
巴基斯坦	0	0	0	0	0	0	0	0	0	0	1	0	0	0	0	0	0	0	0	0	0	1
巴拿马	0	0	0	0	0	0	0	0	0	0	0	1	0	0	0	0	0	0	0	0	0	1
秘鲁	0	0	0	0	0	0	0	0	0	1	0	0	0	0	1	0	0	0	0	0	0	2
菲律宾	0	0	0	0	0	0	3	0	3	0	0	1	0	1	1	0	0	0	2	0	0	11
波兰*	0	0	0	0	0	1	0	4	0	0	0	0	0	0	0	0	0	0	0	0	0	5
俄罗斯	0	0	0	0	0	0	0	0	0	0	0	0	0	0	0	0	1	3	0	0	0	4
斯洛伐克*	0	0	0	0	1	1	0	1	0	0	0	0	0	0	0	0	0	0	0	0	0	3
斯洛文尼亚*	0	0	0	1	0	0	0	0	0	0	0	0	0	0	0	0	0	0	0	0	0	1
南非	0	0	0	0	0	0	0	0	0	0	0	0	1	0	0	0	0	1	1	0	0	3
泰国	0	0	0	0	0	0	0	0	0	0	0	0	0	0	0	1	0	2	0	1	0	4
突尼斯	0	0	0	0	0	0	0	0	0	0	0	2	0	0	0	0	0	0	0	2	0	4
土耳其	0	0	0	0	0	0	0	0	0	5	0	5	3	1	1	0	1	0	1	3	1	21
乌克兰	0	0	0	0	0	0	0	0	0	0	0	0	2	1	2	3	2	0	1	0	0	11
美国	1	2	1	1	2	2	1	0	0	0	0	0	0	0	0	0	0	0	0	0	0	10
委内瑞拉	0	0	0	0	0	4	1	1	0	0	0	0	0	0	0	0	0	0	0	0	0	6
越南	0	0	0	0	0	0	0	0	0	0	0	0	0	0	1	0	0	1	0	0	0	2
合计	2	5	3	10	15	25	12	34	15	14	7	13	8	10	25	20	12	24	18	23	2	297

注：自 1995 年 1 月 1 日至 2015 年 4 月 30 日。

* 欧共体 2004 年 5 月 1 日，2007 年 1 月 1 日和 2013 年 7 月 1 日东扩。所有新加入的国家加入前作为 WTO 成员统计数字仍有效。欧盟整体的数字：(a) 1995 年 1 月 1 日至 2004 年 4 月 30 日以 15 国为准；(b) 2004 年 5 月 1 日至 2006 年 12 月 31 日以 25 国为准；(c) 2007 年 1 月 1 日至 2013 年 6 月 30 日以 27 国为准；(d) 2013 年 7 月 1 日后以 28 国为准。

资料来源：http://www.wto.org/english/tratop_e/safeg_e/safeg_e.htm，访问日期 2014 年 10 月 31 日。

表 20　　全球发起保障措施调查案件数（按产品类别）

产品类别	1995	1996	1997	1998	1999	2000	2001	2002	2003	2004	2005	2006	2007	2008	2009	2010	2011	2012	2013	2014	2015	合计
Ⅰ	0	1	0	3	2	3	0	1	1	1	0	1	1	0	2	1	0	1	1	0	0	19
Ⅱ	1	1	1	0	2	3	2	1	0	2	1	0	0	0	1	0	0	3	2	1	0	21
Ⅲ	1	0	0	0	0	1	0	1	0	0	0	0	0	0	0	0	0	1	0	0	0	4
Ⅳ	0	0	0	0	1	4	3	3	3	0	1	0	0	1	1	0	0	3	3	0	1	24
Ⅴ	0	0	0	0	0	0	1	0	1	0	0	1	0	1	0	1	1	0	0	0	0	6
Ⅵ	0	0	1	3	4	5	0	8	2	2	1	1	1	2	6	2	1	3	3	3	0	48
Ⅶ	0	0	0	2	1	3	0	0	1	0	0	1	1	0	1	0	3	1	1	1	0	16
Ⅷ	0	0	0	0	0	0	0	0	0	0	0	0	1	0	0	0	0	0	0	0	0	1
Ⅸ	0	0	0	1	0	0	0	2	0	0	0	0	0	0	1	0	0	0	0	2	0	6
Ⅹ	0	0	0	0	0	1	0	0	1	0	0	0	0	0	4	1	0	0	1	4	0	12
Ⅺ	0	0	0	0	0	1	0	0	0	1	0	0	0	2	3	4	2	3	0	1	0	17

续 表

产品类别	1995	1996	1997	1998	1999	2000	2001	2002	2003	2004	2005	2006	2007	2008	2009	2010	2011	2012	2013	2014	2015	合计
XII	0	0	1	0	1	1	0	1	0	0	1	2	0	0	0	0	0	0	0	0	0	7
XIII	0	0	0	0	0	0	1	2	5	3	1	2	1	1	3	2	1	1	1	1	1	26
XV	0	0	0	0	2	2	4	12	1	0	0	0	1	2	3	7	3	6	6	8	0	57
XVI	0	0	0	0	1	0	0	3	0	3	0	4	1	1	0	1	0	1	0	2	0	17
XVII	0	1	0	0	1	1	0	0	0	0	1	1	0	0	0	1	1	0	0	0	0	7
XVIII	0	0	0	0	0	0	0	0	0	2	0	0	1	0	0	0	0	1	0	0	0	4
XX	0	2	0	1	0	0	1	0	0	0	1	0	0	0	0	0	0	0	0	0	0	5
合计	2	5	3	10	15	25	12	34	15	14	7	13	8	10	25	20	12	24	18	23	2	297

注：自 1995 年 1 月 1 日至 2015 年 4 月 30 日。

资料来源：http：//www. wto. org/english/tratop _ e/safeg _ e/safeg _ e. htm，访问日期 2015 年 10 月 31 日。

表 21　　全球实施保障措施案件数

发起调查的成员	1996	1997	1998	1999	2000	2001	2002	2003	2004	2005	2006	2007	2008	2009	2010	2011	2012	2013	2014	2015	合计
阿根廷	0	1	0	0	0	2	0	0	0	0	0	1	0	0	0	0	0	0	0	0	4
亚美尼亚	0	0	0	0	0	0	0	0	0	0	0	0	0	0	0	0	0	0	2	0	2
巴西	0	1	0	0	0	0	1	0	0	0	0	0	0	0	0	0	0	0	0	0	2
保加利亚*	0	0	0	0	0	0	2	0	0	0	0	0	0	0	0	0	0	0	0	0	2
智利	0	0	0	0	2	1	2	0	0	1	1	0	0	0	0	0	1	0	0	0	8
中国	0	0	0	0	0	0	1	0	0	0	0	0	0	0	0	0	0	0	0	0	1
哥伦比亚	0	0	0	0	0	0	0	0	0	0	0	0	0	0	0	0	0	0	1	0	1
哥斯达黎加	0	0	0	0	0	0	0	0	0	0	0	0	0	0	0	0	0	0	0	1	1
克罗地亚*	0	0	0	0	0	0	0	0	0	0	0	0	0	1	0	0	0	0	0	0	1
捷克*	0	0	0	1	0	1	1	2	0	0	0	0	0	0	0	0	0	0	0	0	5
多米尼加	0	0	0	0	0	0	0	0	0	0	0	0	0	0	2	0	0	0	0	0	2
厄瓜多尔	0	0	0	0	0	1	0	1	1	0	0	0	0	0	1	0	0	0	0	0	4
埃及	0	0	0	1	1	1	0	0	0	0	0	0	1	0	0	0	1	0	0	1	6
欧盟*	0	0	0	0	0	0	1	0	1	1	0	0	0	0	0	0	0	0	0	0	3
匈牙利*	0	0	0	0	0	0	0	3	0	0	0	0	0	0	0	0	0	0	0	0	3
印度	0	0	4	1	1	0	2	0	0	1	0	0	0	3	0	1	2	0	4	0	19
印度尼西亚	0	0	0	0	0	0	0	0	0	0	1	0	0	2	0	7	1	1	2	2	16
约旦	0	0	0	0	0	1	1	2	0	1	0	1	0	0	1	0	0	1	0	1	9
韩国	0	1	0	0	1	0	0	0	0	0	0	0	0	0	0	0	0	0	0	0	2
吉尔吉斯斯坦	0	0	0	0	0	0	0	0	0	0	0	0	0	1	0	0	0	1	0	0	2
拉脱维亚*	0	0	0	1	0	0	0	1	0	0	0	0	0	0	0	0	0	0	0	0	2
立陶宛*	0	0	0	0	0	0	1	0	0	0	0	0	0	0	0	0	0	0	0	0	1
摩尔多瓦	0	0	0	0	0	0	0	0	1	0	0	0	0	0	0	0	0	0	0	0	1
摩洛哥	0	0	0	0	0	1	0	0	0	0	1	0	0	0	0	0	0	1	0	0	3

续 表

发起调查的成员	1996	1997	1998	1999	2000	2001	2002	2003	2004	2005	2006	2007	2008	2009	2010	2011	2012	2013	2014	2015	合计
巴拿马	0	0	0	0	0	0	0	0	0	0	0	1	0	0	0	0	0	0	0	0	1
菲律宾	0	0	0	0	0	0	1	1	3	0	0	0	0	1	0	1	0	0	0	0	7
波兰*	0	0	0	0	0	0	0	4	0	0	0	0	0	0	0	0	0	0	0	0	4
俄罗斯	0	0	0	0	0	0	0	0	0	0	0	0	0	0	0	0	1	1	1	0	3
斯洛伐克*	0	0	0	0	0	1	0	1	0	0	0	0	0	0	0	0	0	0	0	0	2
南非	0	0	0	0	0	0	0	0	0	0	0	1	0	0	0	0	0	0	1	0	2
泰国	0	0	0	0	0	0	0	0	0	0	0	0	0	0	0	1	0	1	1	0	3
土耳其	0	0	0	0	0	0	0	0	0	2	4	1	4	1	0	1	0	0	1	0	14
乌克兰	0	0	0	0	0	0	0	0	0	0	0	0	1	1	0	0	0	1	1	0	4
美国	1	0	1	1	2	0	1	0	0	0	0	0	0	0	0	0	0	0	0	0	6
越南	0	0	0	0	0	0	0	0	0	0	0	0	0	0	0	0	0	1	0	0	1
合计	1	3	5	5	7	9	14	15	6	6	7	5	6	10	4	11	6	8	14	5	147

注：自 1995 年 1 月 1 日至 2015 年 4 月 30 日。

* 欧共体 2004 年 5 月 1 日，2007 年 1 月 1 日和 2013 年 7 月 1 日东扩。所有新加入的国家加入前作为 WTO 成员统计数字仍有效。欧盟整体的数字：(a) 1995 年 1 月 1 日至 2004 年 4 月 30 日以 15 国为准；(b) 2004 年 5 月 1 日至 2006 年 12 月 31 日以 25 国为准；(c) 2007 年 1 月 1 日至 2013 年 6 月 30 日以 27 国为准；(d) 2013 年 7 月 1 日后以 28 国为准。

资料来源：http：//www. wto. org/english/tratop _ e/safeg _ e/safeg _ e. htm，访问日期 2015 年 10 月 31 日。

表 22　　全球实施保障措施案件数（按产品类别）

产品类别	1996	1997	1998	1999	2000	2001	2002	2003	2004	2005	2006	2007	2008	2009	2010	2011	2012	2013	2014	2015	合计
Ⅰ	0	1	0	2	0	2	0	1	0	1	1	0	0	1	0	0	0	0	0	0	9
Ⅱ	0	0	1	0	2	2	1	0	0	2	0	0	0	1	0	0	1	1	1	1	13
Ⅲ	0	0	0	0	0	0	0	0	0	0	0	0	0	0	0	0	0	1	0	0	1
Ⅳ	0	0	0	1	0	3	3	2	2	0	0	0	0	1	0	0	0	0	1	0	13
Ⅴ	0	0	0	0	0	0	0	1	0	0	1	0	0	0	0	0	0	0	0	0	2
Ⅵ	0	0	3	2	1	1	3	5	0	2	0	1	0	5	0	1	2	0	4	0	30
Ⅶ	0	0	1	0	0	0	0	0	0	0	0	1	0	0	0	1	0	0	0	0	3
Ⅷ	0	0	0	0	0	0	0	0	0	0	0	0	1	0	0	0	0	0	0	0	1
Ⅸ	0	0	0	0	0	0	0	1	0	0	0	0	0	0	0	0	0	0	0	0	1
Ⅹ	0	0	0	0	0	0	0	0	0	0	0	0	0	0	0	1	0	0	0	1	2
Ⅺ	0	0	0	0	1	0	0	0	0	0	0	0	2	0	2	3	1	0	0	0	9
Ⅻ	0	1	0	0	0	0	0	0	0	0	1	1	0	0	0	0	0	0	0	0	3
ⅩⅢ	0	0	0	0	0	0	1	1	4	0	2	0	0	0	2	1	0	1	2	0	14
ⅩⅤ	0	0	0	0	2	0	5	3	0	0	0	0	1	2	0	4	2	4	4	3	30
ⅩⅥ	0	0	0	0	1	0	1	1	0	0	2	1	1	0	0	0	0	0	1	0	8
ⅩⅦ	0	0	0	0	0	1	0	0	0	0	0	1	0	0	0	0	0	1	1	0	4
ⅩⅧ	0	0	0	0	0	0	0	0	0	1	0	0	1	0	0	0	0	0	0	0	2
ⅩⅩ	1	1	0	0	0	0	0	0	0	0	0	0	0	0	0	0	0	0	0	0	2
合计	1	3	5	5	7	9	14	15	6	6	7	5	6	10	4	11	6	8	14	5	147

注：自 1995 年 1 月 1 日至 2015 年 4 月 30 日。

资料来源：http：//www. wto. org/english/tratop _ e/safeg _ e/safeg _ e. htm，访问日期 2015 年 10 月 31 日。

3. 服务贸易理事会

服务贸易理事会于2013年10月29日和2014年2月26日、5月8日、6月20日、9月17日共举行了五次正式会议，重点审议和解决了下列问题：第一，审议成员方根据《服务贸易总协定》第3条第3款，第5条第7款，第7条第4款所通报的服务贸易措施；第二，《服务贸易总协定》通报义务的相符性讨论；第三，有关电子商务的工作计划；第四，最不发达国家服务豁免；第五，部门和模式讨论的后续行动；第六，服务贸易的最新发展；第七，I-TIP Services数据库；第八，部分成员的服务贸易限制措施；第九，服务贸易与规则的发展；第十，附属机构的工作。

服务贸易理事会下属委员会和工作组活动如下：

(1) 金融服务贸易委员会

年度报告期内，金融服务贸易委员会举行了五次正式会议，分别为2013年10月28日、2014年2月26日、5月6日、6月19日和9月18日。委员会讨论了下列议题：对加入GATS第5议定书的监管、金融服务贸易和发展、金融服务监管、金融服务分类的技术问题等。

(2) 特定承诺委员会

自2013年度报告以来，国内规制工作组举行了四次正式会议，分别为2013年10月29日和2014年2月25日、5月7日、9月18日。特定承诺委员会重点讨论两方面议题：分类问题和减让表问题。

(3) 国内规制工作组

自2013年度报告以来，国内规制工作组举行了四次正式会议和数次非正式会议，分别为2013年10月28日和2014年2月25日、5月7日、9月17日。工作组工作中心仍是国内规制协议文本草稿的修订与讨论。重点讨论了技术问题，有关服务提供模式和部门的监管问题，以及区域贸易协定中的国内规制问题。

(4) GATS规则工作组

自2013年度报告以来，2013年10月29日和2014年2月25日、5月7日、9月18日，GATS规则工作组举行了四次正式会议。工作重点仍然是紧急保障措施、政府采购和补贴三个问题。

4. 知识产权理事会

自2013年度报告以来，知识产权理事会共举行三次正式会议，分别为2014年2月25—26日、6月11日和10月28—29日。这三次会议内容可参见IP/C/M/75和IP/C/M/75/Add.1，IP/C/M/76和IP/C/M/76/Add.1，IP/C/M/77和IP/C/M/77/Add.1。其中2月的会议由洪都拉斯大使Dacio Castillo主持，后续会议由博茨瓦纳大使Alfredo Suescum主持。

这些会议向所有的WTO成员、其他政府和观察员以及具有该理事会观察员地位的某些国际政府间组织开放。理事会继续讨论了通报和成员相关法律框架的审议、《与贸易有关的知识产权协定》与《生物多样性公约》的关系以及对传统知识和历史传说的保护、非违反之诉和情势之诉、技术合作和能力建设问题等。

● 多哈回合谈判进展（2014）

2014 多哈谈判的整体概况

2013 年 12 月在巴厘岛举行的第九届部长级会议的成功，为 2014 年多哈发展回合谈判提供了新的动力。所谓的“巴厘一揽子”，就是在贸易便利化、农业议题、棉花和有助于最不发达国家发展的一些领域达成了一揽子协议。这一成果被认为是世界贸易组织自 1995 年成立以来所达成的第一个重要的协定，同时也是多哈回合谈判成功结束的重要里程碑。“巴厘一揽子”表明 WTO 有能力达成促进全球经济发展，尤其是有助于发展中国家和最不发达国家经济发展的协议。

为了夯实巴厘会议成功所倚重的政治动力，部长们指示贸易谈判委员会在 2014 年年底前准备一份解决多哈发展回合谈判剩余议题的清晰的工作方案，指明工作方案的重点为“巴厘一揽子”协议和其他有助于多哈发展回合成功结束的主要议题。部长们给出了最明确的期限，即 2014 年 7 月 31 日前将《贸易便利化协议》纳入 WTO 的法律框架并完成成员国内的审核程序。

启动“后巴厘”工作

按照部长们的指令，贸易谈判委员会于 2014 年 2 月启动了两项工作：一是推动所达成的决议和协议的执行，二是准备多哈发展回合剩余议题的工作方案。公众将巴厘决议视为对多边贸易体制的可信度的考验。很多工作超出了贸易谈判委员会的范围，但为了确保所有相关领域的议题有所进展并保持一致性，贸易谈判委员会主席、总干事阿泽维多号召要通力协作，监测并报告所有领域议题的进展。

关于在 2014 年年底提出“后巴厘”工作方案的目标，贸易谈判委员会主席和各谈判小组主席启动了与各成员的对话，共同探讨可能推进的议题以及结束多哈回合的可行路径。这一磋商程序采取了各种不同的方式，并试图找出形成方案的各种要素。

其中，农业、非农市场准入和服务议题是该方案核心，这一认知日益清晰。一些其他的要素也纳入讨论，包括以发展为中心，注重结果的可行性，认识到多哈发展回合中的主要议题是互相联系密不可分的，以及创新性和开放性，包容性和透明度，保持一种紧迫感等。总干事、贸易谈判委员会主席阿泽维多要求所有成员要现实。他告诫所有成员“这并不是要结束所有回合的一轮谈判……而是贸易自由化持续性进程的一步……我们应当立足于在大部分或全部多哈回合谈判领域取得一定的进程。让我们将所有内容都放在台面上，来看看我们可以把每一个谈判领域推进到哪一步。”

意外但暂时的挫折

各成员的注意力集中在暑休前取得实质性进展。然而，随着期限的临近，相对于其他议题来说，一些成员提高了对贸易便利化进展的关注，包括对于食品安全公共储备的永久性解决方案。《贸易便利化协议》的实施对于该领域的进展有政治性影响，部长们将最后一次的实施期限放在了 2017 年。尽管进行了多方努力，各成员并没能弥补分歧，因而错过了 2014 年 7 月 1 日的截止日期。

这冻结了“后巴厘”工作，包括结束多哈发展回合的工作方案的准备。2014 年 7 月 31 日的贸易谈判委员会非正式会议上，主席阿泽维多要求成员们考虑应对这些变化情况的策略。

一系列密集磋商在暑休后启动，试图找到僵局的破解之策。这些磋商主要发生在 WTO 成员，各机构和谈判机构主席、谈判委员会主席和总理事会主席之间。WTO 各成员所面临的问题是，如果《贸易便利化协议》和公共储备问题没有得到解决，如何实施“巴厘一揽子协议”以及如何确定“后巴厘”工作方案。

突破

2014年11月，就公共储备和贸易便利化达成的谅解为打破僵局提供了机会。贸易谈判委员会主席和总理事会主席与各代表团进一步磋商，力图将这一双边谅解推广至多边，使所有成员都接受。经过密集磋商和讨论后，WTO成员于11月27日总理事会特别会议上通过了三个决议：食品安全的公共储备；《贸易便利化协议》纳入WTO协定附件1A；后巴厘工作立即恢复，并将最后期限延展至2015年7月31日。

就公共储备而言，WTO成员承诺加速时间框架，争取在2015年12月找到该议题的永久性解决方案。在永久性解决方案之前一个和平条款生效。在这一和平条款下，假使其他条件也满足，WTO成员将不会挑战在巴厘决议前存在的为传统主食作物提供粮食安全的公共储备的国内支持承诺。就贸易便利化而言，将《贸易便利化协议》纳入WTO协定是认证程序的开始。就后巴厘工作而言，WTO成员一致同意立即恢复工作，就所有巴厘决议的实施努力取得建设性进展，同时将后巴厘工作方案的提出日期延至2015年7月。

后巴厘工作方案谈判重启

这些决议的通过使具体实施工作和后巴厘工作方案的准备工作都重回到正轨。考虑到重要性，谈判委员会主席指示谈判小组的主席立即重启相关工作，为2015年1月的多项工作做好准备。

2014年12月总理事会会议上，谈判委员会主席报告了谈判小组的相关活动。他欢迎WTO成员们重新投入谈判中，并强调了他所认为的谈判成功的关键“要素”。这些要素是：保持紧迫性，合理务实，关注可行性，所有代表团必须有较深入的参与度，包括高层领导的参与，从而可做出重要的政治呼吁。他还强调各成员对于谈判的参与必须广泛，确保发展中国家的需求必须是谈判的核心。农业、非农市场准入和服务仍然是谈判的核心议题，同时WTO成员也需要考虑核心领域以外的其他议题。

谈判委员会主席宣布2015的谈判工作将继续并根据需要紧密推进。他指出2015年是WTO的大年，鼓励所有代表团努力使这一年值得铭记。

农业谈判情况

• 按照巴厘部长级会议的指示，2014年上半年，农业谈判集中在提出推进多哈回合谈判达成的农业部分的工作方案。WTO成员优先考虑巴厘会议上没有达成相关成果的法律约束问题，如出口竞争和棉花问题。因为谈判僵局，工作于下半年停滞。总理事会11月会议打破僵局后，该工作于12月恢复。

2014年上半年，农业谈判小组主席John Adank召开了一系列非正式磋商会议以找出WTO成员之间的分歧，为农业议题后巴厘工作方案的提出扫除障碍。显然多哈发展回合农业议题中的所有相关因素是相互关联的，需要通过一揽子的方式打包解决。

出口竞争（出口补贴和具同等效果的出口措施），该领域被认为是WTO成员具有成熟想法的可达成相关协议的潜在着陆区。国内补贴和市场准入这两个支柱是需要深入讨论的。为推进这些讨论，2014年7月15日，谈判小组主席散发了对于这两个领域的调查问卷，7月23日的非正式会议上对于调查的问题WTO成员给出了初步回应。

会议集中讨论了2008年时的谈判草案是否应该继续成为谈判的重点。一些谈判集团，如进口食品的发展中国家组成的G-33坚持这些草案文本。一些集团则认为虽然这些文件是继续谈判的最合适的基础性文件，但仍应该有更多可能的选择。一些WTO成员认为草案文本Rev. 4过于复杂。

应一些WTO成员的要求，秘书处举行了两次技术研讨会（一次是国内支持，一次是市场准入），以帮助这些成员更好地理解谈判中的技术内容。

然而，2014年7月的僵局后，WTO成员将焦点转向“巴厘一揽子”中的贸易便利化议题，以及食品安全的公共储备议题，所有的努力也集中在解决这两个议题上。2014年总理事会11月会议找到解决方案，理事会呼吁立即恢复此前有关“巴厘一揽子”决议的实施工作以及多哈发展回合相关议题的后巴厘工作方案的相关工作。后巴厘工作方案提出的截止日期为2015年7月。2014年12月的农业谈判委员会特别会议重启了农业领域的谈判。

食品公共储备

2013年12月巴厘部长级会议，部长们一致同意维持发展中国家粮食安全的公共储备机制，维持《农业协议》所规定的农业补贴限制。这一妥协旨在解决两方的关注，一是支持食品安全国家的关注，二是那些担心没有约束的食品储备和随后放出将会压低价格进而影响农民收入和其他国家的食品安全的相关国家和地区的关注。永久性解决方案的时限为 2017 年。

2014 年早期，一些 WTO 成员提出反对意见，认为永久性解决方案的时间拖得太久。这一不同意见直接导致了 7 月时所有谈判的冻结。最终总理事会于 11 月下旬达成一致，声明 WTO 成员将努力于 2015 年 12 月前就这一问题达成永久性解决方案。WTO 成员还指出在农业谈判委员会专门会议上找出永久解决方案，这一问题将被加速解决并独立于多哈农业谈判的其他议题之外。在永久解决方案达成前，这一暂时的解决方案将会一直有效。

棉花

在巴厘岛，部长们一致同意 WTO 成员开展一年两次的专门研讨，从出口竞争、国内支持和棉花贸易关税及非关税措施的角度关注贸易发展。这些有关棉花的研讨应该在农业谈判的背景下开展，要以增加透明度和强化监管为目标。决议以贝宁、布基纳法索、乍得和马里（棉花四国）联合提出的提案为基础。

2014 年在棉花领域的两次讨论都是与贸易有关的发展问题。第一次于 6 月召开，检视了 WTO 成员在棉花问题上与贸易相关的政策和相关发展的变化情况。由秘书处根据成员所通报的事实信息和数据，以及就出口补贴、国内支持和市场准入所提交的其他通报，汇总而成的基础性文件通报了此次讨论的情况。第二次讨论于 11 月召开，秘书处更新和修正的基础性文件以及国际棉花咨询委员会就国际棉花市场所做的情况说明通报了第二次讨论的情况。

棉花四国注意到最近棉花价格的下降正在伤害其生产商的利益，呼吁尽快完成谈判以解决贸易扭曲政策。不同的成员通报了其与棉花相关的政策信息，遗憾的是，一些成员没有更新其相关的政策信息，迟迟未提交相关的通报。另外该领域相关的政策进展情况还可以从调查问卷、政策审议报告和国际棉花咨询委员会的信息中获取。谈判主席还指出棉花问题是后巴厘工作进程的一个关键因素。

非农产品市场准入的谈判情况

• 非农产品市场准入（NAMA）谈判由于巴厘 WTO 第九届部长级大会通过的《贸易便利化协议》的实施陷入僵局而有所放缓，从而使多哈回合的几乎所有工作陷入瘫痪。然而，这一僵局于 11 月被打破，谈判小组主席 Remigi Winzap 大使宣称他将于 2015 年以不同的形式恢复磋商。

在 3 月和 7 月的谈判小组会议上，谈判小组主席 Remigi Winzap 大使指出 WTO 成员尚未就如何推进谈判达成一致。WTO 成员在是否以 2008 年 NAMA 草案模式（Rev. 3）为谈判基础仍然存在分歧。Winzap 主席进一步指出，那些认为 Rev. 3 可以作为进一步谈判基础的成员已经做好心理准备去承认这并不是“板上钉钉”的。那些反对将 Rev. 3 作为进一步谈判基础的成员则准备承认已投入的大量努力，并纳之为谈判基础之一。

Winzap 主席督促 WTO 成员反思“考虑到过去的经验、目前的现实情况和手边可能的工具手段，如何以及在什么样的情况下 WTO 成员能够达成一个有意义的 NAMA 谈判的结果。”他观察到相比于 2011 年的情况，一个积极的方面是就 NAMA 的讨论已经重新开始，WTO 成员开始合力寻找解决方案。他指出：很清楚，WTO 成员不得不以“整体”态度来考虑多哈回合的两大支柱——NAMA 和农业问题。Winzap 主席说：“农业领域的雄心与 NAMA 领域的雄心是相伴而生的，NAMA 的雄心必须为农业的雄心买单。”

应谈判小组的请求，WTO 秘书处给出了三份文件以协助其工作。这些文件都包括 WTO 成员提交的有关非农贸易情况、最近的 NAMA 情况和进口关税数据，以及与最新的协调关税制度相匹配的成员关税减让表的具体情况。

由于贸易便利化领域的僵局，2014 年下半年 NAMA 领域并没有进一步的磋商进展。这一僵局与巴厘部长级会议上做出的与食品安全相关的政府公共储备的另一个决议相关。11 月的总理事会就食品安全决议的实施达成了一致，为将《贸易便利化协议》纳入 WTO 的规则体制扫清了道路，这一僵局也得以打破。

服务谈判的情况

• 2014，服务贸易理事会讨论了后巴厘工作方案，提出了一些指导性原则。然而由于 2014 年下半年贸易便利化领域的僵局，多哈回合谈判的多数领域的谈判都有所停滞。国内规则谈判小组继续就许可证、资格要求和程序以及技术标准领域展开讨论，而且还就区域贸易协定中的国内规则问题展开了讨论。《服务贸易总协定》规则工作组就区域和双边贸易协定中的紧急保障条款进行了讨论，同时进一步探索了《政府采购协定》与《服务贸易总协定》之间的关系和互补性。

2014年，服务贸易理事会召开了两次特别会议，主要讨论服务领域的后巴厘工作方案的程序问题和实质问题。WTO成员提出了几个指导性原则，如平衡（服务部门之间，以及与其他部门之间），雄心（市场开放或其他承诺的程度），与农业、非农领域的对称性，发展维度的重要性。

WTO成员强调聚焦于哪些是“可行的”，并在透明度和包容性的基础上推进。在WTO成员提交其修正的服务出价之前，考虑需要完成哪些工作以推进未来服务贸易谈判，而许多成员强调这需要引进新的方式。

一种建议是从区域贸易协定有关服务贸易的内容中汲取灵感，许多成员已经在区域贸易协定中做出了比GATS中的服务承诺更为开放的市场准入承诺。另一种建议是增加所涉及的服务部门，如与数字经济、电子商务、供应链、贸易便利化，或与发展中国家利益相关的服务部门。

然而，由于2014年7月底前适用《贸易便利化协议》失败后，下半年服务贸易部门谈判也显著放缓了。2014年11月总理事会达成《贸易便利化协议》后，服务贸易理事会于12月召开了一次非正式会议，讨论多哈回合服务贸易谈判在2015年7月的工作方案。许多成员强调后巴厘服务贸易部门的谈判进展取决于农业和非农市场准入的谈判进展。

同时，巴厘部长宣言中有关最不发达国家服务贸易出口的决议进展良好。

此外，23个成员参加了诸边的服务贸易协定谈判（TISA），并向服务贸易理事会定期通报其谈判进展。

国内规制

国内规则谈判小组的工作是提出相关的规则，以确保许可证、资格要求和程序以及技术标准不会对服务贸易带来不必要的壁垒。2014年，国内规则谈判小组继续探讨许可证、资格要求和程序以及技术标准等的技术问题。WTO成员完成了“供讨论的潜在技术问题清单”中的3个问题的审查。在这些讨论结果的基础上，主席散发了有关信息以及审查过程中成员观点变化情况的文件。

在讨论中，WTO成员曾试图澄清使用某些国内监管的概念和术语，因为它们涉及监管框架和实践。一些成员也反映了对于同一行业的国内规制进展的启示。

为了便于讨论，WTO秘书处准备了三个背景说明：普遍适用措施、服务部门和提供模式的监管问题、服务的技术标准。

这些讨论进一步阐明了所讨论的规则如何涉及并影响国家层面的监管措施。

在秘书处背景说明“服务部门和提供模式的监管问题”的帮助下，WTO成员也完成了监管问题的讨论。作为讨论的一部分，WTO成员专门讨论了发展中成员在服务部门监管方面所面临的挑战。未来将在WTO秘书处准备的背景说明“发展中国家成员服务部门监管面临的挑战”的基础上进一步讨论。

虽然有关国内规制的讨论并没有取得特别的结论，正如WTO成员所指出的，这一工作是一种有益的经验交流，有助于WTO成员更好地理解国内规制与市场准入之间的关系。

2014年该领域启动了新的讨论内容即区域贸易协定中的国内规制问题。这一讨论的目的是使成员有机会分享其在不同的区域贸易协定中的国内规制的不同规定，同时也可提请大家注意其与GATS第VI：4条下的规制谈判的共性与区别。大量的区域贸易协定的信息表明国内规制条款是以GATS所承诺的义务及以在GATS第VI：4条下的规制谈判为基础的。大量的案例都是在水平承诺或部门承诺的基础上增加了部分修正或额外的承诺。2015年这一讨论仍将继续。

《服务贸易总协定》规则

《服务贸易总协定》规则工作组的任务是对GATS第10条（紧急保障措施）、第13条（政府采购）和第15条（补贴）进行谈判。然而，在前些年，WTO成员集中在对这三个领域的技术讨论。

就紧急保障措施（ESM）而言，在“ESM之友”（由文莱、柬埔寨、印度尼西亚、马来西亚、缅甸、菲律宾、泰国、越南，以及2014年9月加入的老挝组成）提交方案之后，工作组讨论区域和双边贸易协定中的紧急保障措施条款。应WTO成员的要求，WTO秘书处准备并更新了向WTO通报的122个区域贸易协定中有关保障措施的或保障措施类的条款说明。

就政府采购而言，工作组讨论了WTO工作人员的工作文件草案“服务贸易和政府采购承诺的关系：相关的WTO协定和最近的RTAs视角”。这是由秘书处知识产权部门中从事《政府采购协定》的员工和服务贸易部门的员工基于其个人能力所准备的文件。经过两轮的讨论，代表团们提供了有益的改善建议，也将提供最终的工作文件，以便在2015年进行更深入的审查。

就服务补贴而言，应WTO成员的要求，秘书处发布了修订的背景说明“服务部门的补贴——WTO政府审议中的信息”，提供了更新的经验数据，以及个别服务部门的支持措施。

与贸易有关的知识产权问题的谈判情况

• 与贸易有关的知识产权理事会特别会议已恢复工作，但有关葡萄酒和烈酒的地理标志注册和通报的谈判仍然处于僵局。寻找一个共同的解决方法仍然具有挑战性。与贸易有关的知识产权理事会常规会议，对发达国家成员向最不发达国家成员技术转移的激励措施进行了第十二次年度审议。巴厘部长级会议确认了与贸易有关的知识产权理事会提出的延长《与贸易有关的知识产权协定》（TRIPs）非违反之诉和情势之诉的暂停期。但与贸易有关的知识产权理事会继续在新的通报的基础上考虑这一问题。

地理标志注册的谈判

借助于巴厘部长级会议对于多哈回合的推动作用，地理标志注册谈判的工作开始有所恢复。然而，在地理标志注册谈判问题上并没有取得实质性进展。地理标志注册的法律效果，以及是否要向所有WTO成员适用或仅仅向签字方适用，这两个问题至今仍有分歧。分歧在于产品的覆盖范围，以及如谈判任务所显示的，注册应仅限于葡萄酒和烈酒还是也适用于其他产品，如食品和农产品。

葡萄酒和烈酒地理标志注册旨在便利地理标志的保护。这些标识（地名或有时与地方相关的其他条件或体征）用于识别产品的位置，以确认或区分其特定品质、声誉或其他特性。苏格兰粗呢、香槟酒和龙舌兰酒是众所周知的例子。自1996年以来，《与贸易有关的知识产权协定》即在进行地理标志注册谈判。

2014年4月，在一系列春季磋商后，主席散发了自2011年“复合文本草案”后第一份《与贸易有关的知识产权协定》特别会议报告。这份报告表明找到一种解决方法的尝试仍然存在挑战性，尤其是两个与TRIPs相关的实施问题的广泛相关性，即地理标志的外延以及《与贸易有关的知识产权协定》与《生物多样性公约》的关系问题。

考虑到这些问题及其程序的复杂性，磋商集中在考虑如何在后巴厘工作方案中体现地理标志注册问题。在12月召开的第二次非正式特别会议上，代表团们重申将在2015年7月会议前确定工作方案，以确定如何完成多哈回合任务并覆盖所有的谈判团体。TRIPs谈判，意味着如何确定葡萄酒和烈酒地理标志注册问题。然而，代表团们并没有提供新的想法，他们指出在农业、非农市场准入和服务谈判结果尚不明确之前，TRIPs不应进行实质性对话。

突出的实施问题的磋商

实施加强或过度保护其他产品的外延问题，现在加强保护一般用在葡萄酒和烈酒上，2014年WTO成员没有就这一问题继续磋商。WTO成员在将地理标识注册保护外延至其他产品是否可以促进此类产品的贸易，以及是否产生不必要的法律和商业负担方面还存在分歧。“地理标志注册外延”就是与贸易相关的知识产权的“突出的实施问题”中的首要问题。总干事在2005年香港部长宣言号召就与贸易相关的知识产权的两个“突出的实施问题”的首要问题即“地理标识的外延”进行磋商。

第二个问题是，《与贸易有关的知识产权协定》和生物多样性公约的关系，《与贸易有关的知识产权协定》是否应采取措施促进生物多样性目标的实现，同时享受遗产资源被用于研究和产业所带来的好处。现在已有成员提案要求修订《与贸易有关的知识产权协定》，要求专利权人披露提供遗传资源和相关传统知识的来源和国家。自总干事拉米提交2009年3月至2011年4月期间的书面报告后没有进一步的磋商。这一问题曾在2014与贸易有关的知识产权总理事会上由几个成员提出，但并没有取得任何进展。

技术转移的激励措施

2014年10月与贸易有关的知识产权理事会常规会议上，对发达国家成员向最不发达国家成员技术转移的激励措施进行第十二次年度审议，《与贸易有关的知识产权协定》要求发达国家对公司给予向最不发达国家转让技术的激励措施。2003年理事会决定建立这样一个审查机制，要求发达国家提供关于激励措施实施的详细信息。

WTO秘书处组织了第七次年度专题讨论会，发达国家成员和最不发达国家成员之间深入讨论这些激励措施实施的程度。这些讨论包括基于最不发达国家提议的协调报告模式，秘书处努力改善大量有用可得信息的准入，以及大量的需求改善的信息工具。

知识产权保护非违反之诉争端

2013年巴厘部长级会议决定延长《与贸易有关的知识产权协定》（TRIPs）“非违反之诉”的暂停期后，TRIPs理事会继续讨论在TRIPs下这些“非违反之诉”的优点。在知识产权相关的“非违反之诉”是否要纳入WTO的争端解决机制。在是否接受这类投诉以及是否把这类投诉作为争端的法律基础方面成员还存在争议。

一般而言，提交到WTO争端解决机制的争端不仅包括违反了协议，还包括并未违反协议但根据协议可预期利益可能被破坏。然而，就知识产权保护方面的争端来说，就启动此类“非违反之诉和情势之诉”，《与贸易有关的知识产权协定》规定了知识产权加强保护的五年过渡期。这个过渡期条款规定还被一系列的部长级会议延长。

在巴厘部长级会议的筹备阶段，WTO成员已经打算在2014年早期通过一系列的密集工作来审查这类范畴和模式，也希望可以就目前“非违反之诉”的过渡期以部长级会议年年延期的方式中探寻到最终的解决方案。

6月的会议上，TRIPs理事会已经提前提交了一份就此问题的说明，详细阐述了将此类诉讼适用于TRIPs的背景与条件。TRIPs理事会指示继续审查此类争端的范畴和模式，并为2015年召开的下一届部长级会议提出建议。

贸易与发展的谈判情况

• 巴厘部长级会议就发展中国家成员特殊与差别待遇的监管机制达成一致后，贸易与发展委员会召开特别会议，集中对未来的工作提出建议。

监管机制启动后，今年开始进行广泛磋商以确定成员就如何推进特别会议的工作意见。监管机制问题为分析和审查WTO多边协定、部长宣言和总理事会决议所涵盖的特殊与差别待遇实施的各个方面提供了很好的机会。关于构建监管体制的提案最初是在2002年贸易与发展委员会特别会议上由非洲集团提交的。当年总理事会同意设立该机制，并指示委员会特别会议确定该机制的功能、结构和参照条件。

一些成员表示他们希望将全面审查所有S&D提案作为特别会议工作的一部分。2015年2月，这些成员提交了25个S&D条款，他们期望贸易与发展委员会的特别会议可以解决这些问题并作为后巴厘工作方案的一部分。他们承诺在第二个阶段提交实质提案以解释其合理性并明确每一条款的问题。考虑到2015年7月底的最后期限，主席督促WTO成员尽快提供具体的文本提案，以便贸易与发展委员会的特别会议可以进行实质性讨论。

就如何推进这些工作以便最终确定工作方案以及重启特别协定议案的实质工作的问题，正在征求意见。

贸易和技术转移的谈判情况

• 贸易和技术转移工作组召开了一个一天的论坛以讨论贸易与技术转移的关系。同样的主题在其3次正式会议上也进行了讨论，同时探讨增加向发展中国家转移技术。

贸易和技术转移工作组继续讨论“环境技术扩散”的挑战与机遇，其与可持续发展的关系及其与第九届部长级会议指示的一致性。12月份的巴厘部长级会议，部长们决定为完成多哈部长宣言的任务，贸易和技术转移工作组仍需要做更多的工作，尤其是强化向发展中国家的技术转移方面。部长们指示工作组继续努力以便全面实施《多哈部长宣言》的要求。

6月的研讨会上，来自公、私部门、政府间组织和学术界的专家们讨论了贸易与技术转移的关系。与会者审视了技术转移为何是增加劳动生产率、促进经济增长和发展的关键因素。贸易曾经被视作技术转移的重要因素，也是机器、设备和服务进口中技术转移的直接工具，也是对外投资中技术转移的间接工具。

虽然贸易协定被视作是潜在的促进技术转移的因素，至少其通过减少政策不确定性发挥作用，但是与会的专家强调贸易协定只是影响技术转移的因素之一。重复强调教育的重要性和熟练的人力资源的可用性和东道国适当的体制和政策环境，对于技术转移和吸收/适应的重要程度。与会者强调了研究和开发（研发）机构和知识中心在促进技术和创新方面的作用。

演讲者指出最贫穷的国家没有从技术转移中受益，他们认为应该通过提供更好的技术适应的投资机会，通过培育其与发展中国家和发达国家研究机构的联系程度，以改善向不发达国家的技术转移。

贸易和环境的谈判情况

• 贸易和环境委员会召开特别会议于 2014 年进行了许多磋商以讨论多哈回合谈判中环境章节的前景和其在后巴厘工作方案中的优先性。WTO 秘书处将在 2015 年初组织一次信息说明会，涵盖多哈回合中有关贸易与环境的所有方面。

2014 年上半年就如何推进贸易和环境委员会特别会议的工作进行磋商。在 12 月的信息说明会上，WTO 成员讨论了下一步工作，认为 2015 年将是环境工作重要的一年。

几个 WTO 成员强调在贸易和环境问题上传达与其他发展问题，如 2015 年后期的发展议程中的可持续发展提案以及 12 月将在巴黎举行的联合国气候变化大会，释放一致的适当的信号。

其他成员认识到多哈贸易与环境议题在后巴厘工作方案中的重要性，强调先解决多哈议程中的其他关键议题——农业、非农市场准入和服务贸易——将有助于可持续发展问题的解决。

目前达成一致的是 WTO 秘书处将在 2015 年初组织一场信息说明会，以检视多哈谈判中的环境章节的内容。这些谈判包括现有 WTO 规则和《多边环境协定》（MEAs）的关系，WTO 和多边环境机构秘书处之间的日常信息交流，以及消除环境产品和服务中的关税和非关税壁垒。

贸易便利化的谈判情况

• 2013 年 12 月召开的 WTO 第九届部长级会议完成贸易便利化谈判后，新成立贸易便利化筹备委员会对《贸易便利化协议》进行法律审核，并起草修正条款以将《贸易便利化协议》纳入 WTO 的法律框架。总理事会 11 月会议上 WTO 成员通过了修正条款，为协议的实施扫清了道路。贸易便利化筹备委员会成立并帮助发展中国家成员和最不发达国家成员实施《贸易便利化协议》。

贸易便利化筹备委员会完成了 2013 年 12 月巴厘部长级会议所交代的任务。这些任务包括对《贸易便利化协议》进行法律审议，批准修正条款，接受 WTO 成员在《贸易便利化协议》勘正的承诺通报。前两个任务已经于 2014 年完成，第三个任务也取得了较大进展。

巴厘部长级会议上部长们为协议的实施制定了路线图，总理事会将于 2014 年 7 月 31 日前批准修正条款。但是虽然按时完成了协议文本的法律审议，但由于一些成员将此议题与多哈回合的其他议题进行捆绑，致使在最终期限前并没有批准修正条款。

后来经过一系列密集的磋商，2014 年 11 月 27 日总理事会特别会议上通过了修正条款。《贸易便利化协议》正式纳入 WTO 的法律框架。WTO 成员开始其国内批准程序。中国香港是第一个完成批准程序的成员，于 12 月 8 日向 WTO 秘书处交存其接受书。

《贸易便利化协议》以其实施方式为发展中国家和最不发达国家开辟了新天地。在 WTO 的历史上首次规定，实施条款的能力与时限与一个国家的能力相关联。另外，协议中还规定应该帮助相关国家和地区提供能力建设援助。WTO 成员还设立了贸易便利化协议筹备委员会以帮助发展中国家和最不发达国家。

《贸易便利化协议》概述

该协定共有三个主要部分。

第一部分包括加快过境货物的流动、放行和清关，以及货物运输。这部分旨在澄清和改善 GATT 1994 的相关条款：第 5 条过境自由、第 8 条进出口规费和手续、第 10 条贸易法规的公布和实施。

第二部分包括向发展中国家和最不发达国家提供特殊与差别待遇的条款，这部分旨在帮助这些国家尽快实施该协定，提供能力建议援助。

每一发展中国家和最不发达国家成员应各自自行指定下列 A、B、C 类分别包含的条款。B 类和 C 类条款，成员必须提供实施期限。

➢A 类包含一发展中或最不发达国家成员指定的自本协定生效时起立即实施的条款，或对于最不发达国家成员在生效后 1 年内实施的条款。

➢B 类包含一发展中或最不发达国家成员指定的在本协定生效后的一过渡期结束后的日期起实施的条款。

➢C 类包含一发展中或最不发达国家成员指定的在本协定生效后的一过渡期结束后的日期起实施的、同时要求通过提供能力建设援助和支持以获得实施能力的条款。

第三部分包括在 WTO 设立永久的贸易便利化委员会，要求每一成员应建立并/或设立一国家贸易便利化委员会或指定一现有机制以促进国内协调和本协定条款的实施。还包括最后条款。

WTO 规则的谈判情况

• 规则谈判组继续其技术活动，最显著的是技术谈判小组在 WTO 成员反倾销实践领域交换信息。随着 2014 年尾声的临近，谈判组开始考虑 WTO 规则谈判在巴厘部长宣言所号召的工作方案中的角色。11 月总理事会将 2015 年 7 月作为涉及所有多哈回合内容的后巴厘工作方案的最后期限。

2012 年 10 月公开的非正式磋商代表团之间交换不同的意见后，来自牙买加的 Wayne McCook 大使总结成员之间缺乏重启谈判的欲望，除非多哈回合的方向和范围得到确认。这一状况持续到 2014 年。随着今年尾声的临近，响应巴厘部长级会议上部长们的指示，谈判组开始反思其作用，如果存在一些领域，如在反倾销、补贴、反补贴措施和区域贸易协定领域，这些领域中的后巴厘工作方案 WTO 规则谈判可以起到什么作用。

技术谈判小组在 WTO 成员反倾销实践领域交换信息。技术谈判小组于 2014 年 4 月和 10 月召开了会议，WTO 成员在如日落复审、价格承诺和调查的产品范围等议题交换了信息。

争端解决谈判情况

• 2014 年，谈判试图就讨论的所有 12 个领域都取得现实的和可实现的结果。新的谈判在 2013 年 6 月达成的“水平程序”基础上推进，这是感兴趣的参与方探索结束所有讨论内容的可能解决方式。

现阶段，探索各种可能解决方案的概念性因素并不能反映 WTO 成员立场的一致性。所有的参与者也不认为这些因素可以作为充分的或可接受的各方整体利益的平衡。想要聚合不同的立场仍有大量的工作要完成，而且每个不同的议题面临的问题也不同。在一些领域，已经达成了一些基本的原则，这反映在法律文本草案中，如一致同意的解决方案，严格机密信息的保护等。在另一些领域，足以形成最终方案基础的要素仍需要再确认，以目前的工作为基础，这些要素还需要在法律文本上转化及表达出来。

所讨论的 12 个议题包括：发展中国家利益（包括特殊和差别待遇）；有效执行；灵活性和成员控制；一致同意的解决方案；专家组构成；后报复问题；发回重审；适用顺序；严格机密信息；第三方权利；时间性规定；透明度和法庭之友陈述。

《政府采购协议》的谈判情况

• 在其三分之二的成员完成国内批准程序后，修订的《政府采购协议》于 2014 年 4 月 6 日正式实施。修订后的《政府采购协议》扩大国际政府采购市场准入机会，大约每年为 800 亿～1000 亿美元。

修订后的《政府采购协议》，扩大了覆盖范围，增加了约 500 个采购实体，包括地方政府及其附属机构，还覆盖了服务领域的政府采购。修订后的《政府采购协议》将会带来大约每年 800 亿～1000 亿美元的市场准入机会。

新的文本纳入了政府采购实践的发展，如电子设备的广泛使用，同时强化了《政府采购协议》对于改善良好管理和抗争腐败的作用。

修订后的《政府采购协议》，对发展中国家的加入提供了灵活性，增加了过渡期，以便于其加入更加具有竞争性的政府采购体制。修订后的《政府采购协议》，强化了可持续采购实践，强化了自然资源和环境保护的内容。

2012 年 3 月 30 日，WTO《政府采购协议》各方正式适用修订后的案文，包括 15 位成员（欧盟和其 28 个成员视为整体），批准成员数达到三分之二即可生效。2015 年 2 月，其中 12 个成员已经完成国内批准程序。这些成员是：列支敦士登、挪威、加拿大、中国台北、美国、中国香港、欧盟（及其 28 个成员）、冰岛、新加坡、以色列、日本、荷兰王国的阿鲁巴。

修订的《政府采购协议》于 2014 年正式实施，完成了巴厘部长级会议时所确定的希望两年内实施的目标。

修订的《政府采购协议》的实施，引发了政府采购委员会在几个领域的新的工作计划。这些工作计划代表了谈判的一个成果，将解决一些重要的问题，如便利中小企业对于政府采购的参与，促进可持续采购实践，改善该协议统计数据的收集和报告。与这些计划相关的工作预计在 2015 年内加速。

（张上冉译，杨凤鸣校）

●向争端解决机构请求磋商的案件（2014）

一、俄罗斯——影响自欧盟进口的生猪、猪肉及其他猪产品的措施：欧盟请求磋商

此文件自 2014 年 4 月 8 日，在欧盟代表团和俄罗斯代表团及争端解决机构主席间进行沟通，现根据 DSU 第 4 条第 4 款的规定予以散发。

受我方政府授权，根据《关于争端解决规则与程序的谅解》（简称“DSU”）第 1 条和第 4 条，GATT 1994 第 23 条，以及《实施卫生与植物卫生措施协议》（简称“SPS 协议”）第 11 条，就俄罗斯基于偶发的非洲猪瘟个案而采取的影响自欧盟进口的生猪及其基因材料、猪肉，猪肉产品以及其他一些商品（统称为涉案产品）措施，我代表团请求与俄罗斯进行磋商。

争议产生之背景及涉案之卫生措施

2014 年 1 月 24 日，立陶宛东南部出现两起野猪感染非洲猪瘟的案例，俄罗斯随即于 2014 年 1 月 27 日停止从欧盟全境进口部分涉案产品。同年 2 月 17 日和 2 月 19 日，波兰东部地区再出现两起野猪感染非洲猪瘟之案例。下列证据，连同其他情况，证明俄罗斯事实上采纳、维持和/或实施了进口禁令或进口限制措施。

2014 年 1 月 29 日，俄罗斯兽医和植物卫生监督联邦服务处发布了编号为 FS-SA-7/1275 和 FS-SA-8/1277 的两则行政通知。

依据俄罗斯在 2014 年 2 月 10 日向 WTO 做出的通报（编号为 G/SPS/N/RUS/48），俄罗斯在 2014 年 1 月 25 日对立陶宛采取了紧急措施，对“生猪及其基因材料，未经至少 72℃加热 30 分钟或以上的猪肉产品、包括屠宰野猪产品、角蹄和皮革、肠原料、猪鬃、猪饲料、狩猎样品、曾用于养殖、运输、屠宰和切割猪的设备”实施临时进口限制措施（相关措施文件为 FS-EN-8/1023）。欧盟于 2014 年 2 月 19 日向 WTO 全体成员通报了俄罗斯对立陶宛所采取的措施（通报编号为 G/SPS/GEN/1305）。

俄罗斯在 2014 年 3 月 4 日向 WTO 做出的第二份通报（编号为 G/SPS/N/RUS/49）显示，俄罗斯于 2014 年 2 月 27 日对波兰实施了类似的紧急措施（相关文件为 FS-EN-8/1023）。欧盟于 2014 年 3 月 11 日向 WTO 全体成员通报了俄罗斯对波兰采取的措施（通报编号为 G/SPS/GEN/1313）。

2014 年 3 月 14 日，在上述通报之后，俄罗斯向 WTO 全体成员发出通报（通报编号为 G/SPS/GEN/1315）作为回应。

在四起非洲猪瘟案例发生后，欧盟立即采取了行动，通过立陶宛和波兰的国内措施，划定疫区以防止非洲猪瘟向其他地区扩散。这些措施均符合欧盟法律以及世界动物卫生组织订立的国际标准。俄罗斯对这些措施均已知晓，并参与了专家会议。

俄罗斯有关当局曾试图为其拒绝从欧盟领土范围内进口辩护，认为在立陶宛和波兰发生了四起非洲猪瘟案例的情况下，自欧盟出口至俄罗斯的涉案产品所附的兽医出口许可证之措辞表明其不允许对来自欧盟非疫区的出口发出更正许可证。欧盟当局立即向俄罗斯当局提供了所有其请求的相关信息。欧盟还主动提供了其他额外的信息。另外，在 2014 年 2 月到 3 月间，欧盟和俄罗斯当局之间还举行了一系列双边会谈，欧盟在会谈中向俄方提供了进一步的信息和说明。尽管欧盟提供了上述的信息和说明，俄罗斯依然拒绝认可欧盟对隔离疫区所采取的行动，并继续维持其措施，拒绝恢复自欧盟非疫区以及自立陶宛和波兰的进口。

2014 年 1 月 8 日，乌克兰通报在临近俄罗斯边境的卢甘斯克 Stanychno-Luganskyi 区域，一个名为 Pischane 的猎场中发现野猪感染非洲猪瘟的

案例。俄罗斯依据兽医和植物卫生监督联邦服务处与 2014 年 1 月 15 日发布的编号为 FS-NW-8/528 之行政通知，仅对来自该地区的生猪和猪肉产品之进口采取限制措施。该决定的发布距离立陶宛发现非洲猪瘟个案仅数天，其详情见诸俄罗斯向 WTO 发出的编号为 G/SPS/N/RUS/46 之通报。

同样地，尽管自 2013 年 6 月起白俄罗斯已经确认并通报了其境内两个区域发现了非洲猪瘟，俄罗斯依然同意向来自白俄罗斯的进口放宽某些进口限制，俄罗斯依据兽医和植物卫生监督联邦服务处与 2014 年 1 月 27 日发布的编号为 FS-EN-8/1093 的行政通知，允许来自白俄罗斯莫吉廖夫州猪场和肉类处理公司的生猪和猪肉产品进入流通。

在欧盟采取启动 WTO 磋商程序之行动后，俄罗斯当局在 2014 年 4 月 2 日宣布，从 2014 年 4 月 7 日起，将采取临时性限制措施，并将禁令范围扩大至除了经过加热处理（在不低于 70 摄氏度环境下处理 20 分钟以上）的即用型猫粮和狗粮外，其他来自立陶宛和波兰的包含猪肉的加工成品（相关文件编号为 FS-EN-8/5084）。在该公告发布后，俄罗斯随即对其两份原始通报做出修正（编号为 G/SPS/N/RUS/48/Add. 2 and G/SPS/N/RUS/49/Add. 1），以宣布扩大已生效之禁令范围。这些修正包括一份来自俄罗斯兽医和植物卫生监督联邦服务处的行政通知（该通知编号为 ref. FS-EN-8/5081）。

涉案措施包括俄罗斯通过作为与不作为的方式，在事实和法律上，在措施本身和措施适用层面上，对来自欧盟或其内部（除了依欧盟法律要求适用防治非洲猪瘟保护措施的地区外）的生猪及其基因材料、猪肉、猪肉产品和包括上述某些其他商品采取、维持和适用的进口限制措施。涉案措施也包括俄罗斯对欧盟及其成员国采取的区别于对白俄罗斯和乌克兰采取的措施的歧视性待遇。另外，涉案措施还包括 2014 年 4 月 7 日实施的与立陶宛、波兰和欧盟相关的措施。

涉案措施违反了俄罗斯在 SPS 协议和 GATT 1994 下承担的义务。

SPS 协议第 2. 2 条

俄罗斯未曾保证，现在也没有保证这些涉案措施仅在为保护人类、动物或植物的生命或健康所必需的限度内实施。俄罗斯对欧盟非疫区采取的进口限制，以及对所有涉案产品采取的进口限制并非必须。

俄罗斯未曾保证，现在也没有保证涉案措施是基于科学原理制定的。俄罗斯对欧盟非疫区采取的进口限制，以及对所有涉案产品采取的进口限制并没有科学依据。

俄罗斯未曾保证，现在也没有保证在无充分的科学证据情况下不再维持涉案措施。

SPS 协议第 3. 1 条、第 3. 2 条和第 3. 3 条

俄罗斯并没有依据 SPS 协议第 3. 1 条、第 3. 2 条之规定，根据现有的国际标准、指南或建议制定这些措施，或以符合国际标准、指南或建议的方式制定这些措施。另外，俄罗斯并无科学理由使其措施偏离相关国际标准、指南或建议，涉案措施也并非俄罗斯维持卫生保护水平的结果，因此涉案措施违反了 SPS 协议第 3. 3 条之规定。

SPS 协议第 5. 1 条和第 5. 2 条

俄罗斯未能依据 SPS 协议第 5. 1 条的要求，保证涉案措施的制定以对人类、动物或植物的生命或健康所进行的适合有关情况的风险评估为基础，并考虑有关国际组织制定的风险评估技术。俄罗斯并没有提供或提及任何此类风险评估。

俄罗斯在采纳、维持和/或实施涉案措施时，并没有考虑：可获得的科学证据；有关工序和生产方法；有关检查、抽样和检验方法；特定病害或虫害的流行；病虫害非疫区的存在；有关生态和环境条件；以及检疫或其他处理方法。俄罗斯并没有提供其已依据 SPS 协议第 5. 2 条之规定将上诉事项纳入考虑范围之证据。如果俄罗斯恰当地将上诉因素纳入考量，其必定也会得出涉案措施不必要和不合理之结论。

SPS 协议第 5. 7 条

仅就与立陶宛和波兰相关的涉案措施而言，俄罗斯在 2014 年 3 月 14 日向 WTO 全体成员发出的通报（通报编号为 G/SPS/GEN/1315）表明，其认为基于 SPS 协议第 5. 7 条之规定，这些措施是合理的。

就涉案措施而言，俄罗斯并没有遵循 SPS 协议第 5. 7 条的任何规定。在本争议中，俄罗斯在相关科学证据并不充分的情况下，错误地采取了有关措施。从表面上看，涉案措施并非临时性的。俄罗斯并没有将其措施建立在可获得的相关信息的基础上，包括来自有关国际组织以及其他成员实施的卫生与植物卫生措施的信息。虽然俄罗斯已经获得进行更加客观的风险评估所需的信息，但其并没有，同时也没有证据表明，卫生措施在合理期限内得到了审议。

SPS协议第6.1条、第6.2条和第6.3条

俄罗斯未曾保证，现在也没有保证其按照SPS第6.1条之要求，使涉案措施适应产品的产地和目的地的卫生特点。俄罗斯在评估疫区的卫生特点时，并没有考察包括下列要素在内的因素：非洲猪瘟的流行程度（4宗野猪感染案例均发生在靠近欧盟东部外缘边界地区），欧盟采取的根除和控制计划（欧盟马上依据世界动物卫生组织所制定的国际标准进行处理），以及有关国际组织可能制定的适当标准或指南。

就涉案措施而言，俄罗斯并不承认病虫害非疫区和低度流行区的概念，从而违反了SPS协议第6.2条。此外，俄罗斯也没有把对这些地区采取涉案措施的决定建立在地理、生态系统、流行病监测以及卫生与植物卫生控制的有效性等因素之上。在欧盟已经采取了适当的区域隔离措施情况下，俄罗斯仍拒绝承认除限制区域外的其他欧盟属地为非疫区。

就SPS协议第6.3条而言，欧盟认为其已经向俄罗斯提供了必要的证据，并客观地证明了欧盟（除撒丁岛、立陶宛和波兰受非洲猪瘟影响而采取的限制措施的地区）是病虫害非疫区或低度流行区。为此，欧盟已经对俄罗斯给予了在应俄方要求的情况下，俄方能进行检查、检验及其他有关程序的机会。

SPS协议第5.3条、第5.4条和第5.6条

在评估对动物的健康构成的风险并确定为实现适当的卫生保护水平以防止此类风险所采取的措施时，俄罗斯没有考虑SPS协议第5.3条规定下的所有相关经济因素，包括采用替代方法控制风险的相对成本效益。

在确定适当的卫生保护水平时，俄罗斯并没有考虑或没有恰当地考虑SPS协议第5.4条所规定的，将对贸易的消极影响减少到最低程度的目标。

在制定和维持涉案措施时，俄罗斯并没有依据SPS协议第5.6条之规定保证此类措施对贸易的限制不超过为达到适当的卫生保护水平所要求的限度，并考虑其技术和经济可行性。俄罗斯并没有考虑其他更具有技术和经济可行性，且在达到俄罗斯适当的卫生保护水平的同时也能减少对贸易的限制之措施。

可替代措施是指将依据《世界动物卫生组织陆生动物卫生法典关于区划和生物安全隔离区划规定》（第4.3章）以及SPS协议第6条之规定纳入考虑范围之措施。俄罗斯应该承认欧盟属地（除受非洲猪瘟影响而采取的限制措施的地区）为非疫区。可替代措施同样应将涉案产品范围缩小。

SPS协议第2.3条和第5.5条

俄罗斯并没有依SPS协议第2.3条之规定，保证涉案措施不在情形相同或相似的成员之间，包括在成员自己领土和其他成员的领土之间构成任意或不合理的歧视。进一步说，俄罗斯涉案措施的实施方式构成了对国际贸易的交相限制。另外，俄罗斯并没有避免其认为适当的保护水平在不同的情况下存在任意或不合理的差异，如此类差异造成对国际贸易的歧视或变相限制，这违反了SPS协议第5.5条之要求。

俄罗斯在拒绝承认欧盟及其成员国（包括立陶宛和波兰的非疫区）在属地上所做之区划的同时，承认乌克兰和白俄罗斯所做的区划，违反了其在SPS协议第2.3条和第5.5条下之义务。

此外，俄罗斯以禁止自欧盟进口所有涉案产品的方式作为对欧盟两个成员国中偶发的非洲猪瘟个案的回应。相比之下，在俄罗斯爆发非洲猪瘟时，俄罗斯并没有向所有国内涉案产品关闭整个俄罗斯市场。基于此，俄罗斯违反了SPS协议第2.3条和第5.5条。

在此背景下，我们应注意到俄罗斯并未对非洲猪瘟病毒在其领土内的扩散进行有效的控制：自非洲猪瘟于2007年出现在高加索地区以来，该病毒向西和向北扩散，野猪和家猪都受到该病毒影响。依据俄罗斯向世界动物卫生组织的通报，自2007年以来，一共有约600个关于野猪感染非洲猪瘟的报告案例以及接近400起国内企业爆发非洲猪瘟的报告，大量家猪感染了非洲猪瘟病毒。在立陶宛和波兰发生的四起野猪感染个案中发现的病毒类型，与俄罗斯领土内发现的非洲猪瘟病毒种类非常相似。在欧盟发生的个案位于与白俄罗斯接壤的地区，而由于俄罗斯病毒扩散，白俄罗斯同样也出现了疫情。

最后，包括对不同的产品而言，俄罗斯未能避免其认为适当的保护水平在不同的情况下存在任意或不合理的差异。此类差异造成对国际贸易的歧视或变相限制，从而再次违反了 SPS 协议第 2.3 条和第 5.5 条。

SPS 协议第 8 条和附件 C 第 1（a）条、第 1（b）条和第 1（c）条

自 2014 年 2 月初，欧盟多次与俄罗斯接触，意图就俄罗斯针对欧盟区域条件所采取的涉案措施进行讨论。欧盟当局迅速向俄罗斯当局提供其请求的所有信息，并主动地提供了进一步的信息。另外，在 2014 年 2 月到 3 月间，欧盟和俄罗斯当局之间还举行了一系列双边会谈，欧盟还在会谈中向俄方提供了进一步的信息和说明。尽管欧盟提供了上述信息和说明，俄罗斯并未能修改涉案措施以允许恢复自欧盟非疫区进口涉案产品，以及/或已经过恰当处理或加工的产品。

由此导致的不合理迟延，除了在其他方面，主要体现在：

• 俄罗斯兽医和植物卫生监督联邦服务处于 2014 年 3 月 12 日发布的编号为 FS-SD-4/3620 的行政通知；

• 未对欧盟当局于 2014 年 1 月 31 日和 2 月 14 日向其发出的召开紧急会议的邀请做出答复；

• 请求欧盟对与本争议并不相关的问题做出回答（如在非疫区中被依据产量和生物安全评级之企业的信息，以及所有成员国中外国捕猎者的数量和出身）；

• 双方曾于 2014 年 2 月 21 日约定将在 2014 年 2 月 25 日召开技术会议，但俄罗斯未能如期提供签证，导致该会议延期至 2014 年 3 月 7 日进行。因此，俄罗斯违反了附件 C 关于控制、检查和批准程序，从而未能遵循 SPS 第 8 条的要求，违反了 SPS 协议。

此外，就其检验程序以及保证卫生措施的实施而言，俄罗斯未能保证其遵循 SPS 协议附件 C 第 1（a）条，使此类程序的实施和完成不受到不适当的迟延，且对进口产品实施的方式不严于国内同类产品。

另外，就 SPS 协议附件 C 第 1（b）条而言，俄罗斯未能保证公布每一程序的标准处理期限，或应请求，告知申请人预期的处理期限；未能保证主管机构在接到申请后迅速审查文件是否齐全，并以准确和完整的方式通知申请人所有不足之处；未能保证尽快以准确和完整的方式向申请人传达程序的结果，以便在必要时采取纠正措施；未能保证即使在申请存在不足之处时，如申请人提出请求，主管机构也应尽可能继续进行该程序；以及未能应请求，将程序所进行的阶段通知申请人，并对任何迟延做出说明。

而且，就 SPS 协议附件 C 第 1（c）条而言，俄罗斯未能保证有关信息的要求仅限于控制、检查和批准程序所必需的限度。

SPS 协议第 7 条和附件 B 第 1 段、第 5 段和第 6 段

俄罗斯于 2014 年 1 月 25 日对立陶宛采取某些涉案措施（相关文件编号为 ref. FS-EN-8/1032）。俄罗斯直到 2014 年 2 月 10 日，即已经实施这些措施后的第 16 天，才对这些所谓“紧急措施”做出通报。而其他与欧盟相关的涉案措施，俄罗斯从未向 WTO 做出通报。这违反了 SPS 协议中有关透明度的要求。

具体言之，俄罗斯未能依照附件 B 的规定通知其卫生与植物卫生措施的变更，并提供有关其卫生与植物卫生措施的信息，这违反了 SPS 协议第 7 条的规定。此外，俄罗斯未能保证迅速公布所有已采用的卫生法规，以使欧盟及其成员国知晓。

同时，俄罗斯未能通过秘书处通知其他成员涉案措施将要涵盖的产品以及已经涵盖的产品，并对拟议措施的目的和理由做出简要说明，包括提前发布紧急问题之性质，以留出修订和考虑相关评论的机会。此外，俄罗斯未能提供涉案措施的副本，并标明与国际标准、指南或建议有实质性偏离的部分。同时，俄罗斯也未能无歧视地给予其他成员合理的时间以提出书面意见，应请求讨论这些意见，并对这些书面意见和讨论的结果予以考虑。

GATT 1994 第 1 条第 1 款、第 3 条第 4 款以及第 11 条第 1 款

基于上述原因，涉案措施同样违反了俄罗斯在 GATT 1994 下承担的义务。具体而言，是 GATT 第 1 条第 1 款（最惠国待遇原则）、第 3 条第 4 款（内部监管的国民待遇）以及第 11 条第 1 款（数量限制的一般取消）。

俄罗斯的措施对产自欧盟及其成员国的生猪、鲜猪肉和其他涉案产品出口至向俄罗斯带来不利影响。这些措施显然剥夺或减损了欧盟及其成员国依据引述的协议所能直接或间接获得的利益。

本磋商请求包括涉案的措施，以及对这些措施所做的任何修订、增补、展期和替代措施，更新措施和落实措施，包括但不限于双方在本磋商请求所指的讨论中所提及的所有此类措施。

针对上述问题，欧盟保留在磋商过程中提出更多的涉案措施以及依据涵盖协议的其他条款增加诉求的权利。

欧盟期待俄方对本请求的回复，并愿安排一个彼此可以接受的日期和地点举行磋商。

（钟楹译，戴臻校）

二、欧盟及其成员国——对能源部门采取的某些措施：俄罗斯请求磋商

此文件自 2014 年 4 月 30 日，在俄罗斯代表团和欧盟及其成员国代表团及争端解决机构主席间进行沟通，现根据 DSU 第 4 条第 4 款的规定予以散发。

受我方政府授权，根据 DSU 第 1 条和第 4 条，《服务与贸易总协定》（简称 GATS）第 23 条，GATT 1994 第 23 条，《补贴与反补贴措施协议》（简称“SCM”协议）第 4.1 条、第 7.1 条和第 30 条，以及《与贸易有关的投资措施协议》第 8 条，就欧盟及包括克罗地亚、匈牙利和立陶宛在内的欧盟成员国，以落实欧盟的法律和决定以及《成立能源共同体协定》（简称欧盟第三次能源改革方案）为目的，在其领土范围内通过所谓“欧盟第三次能源改革方案指令和细则”实施的限制和要求，特别是对与天然气或电力的生产、供应和传送相关的垂直一体化经营中的货物和服务之价格进行分拆处理，对第三国许可要求采取歧视性待遇，以及在授予传送服务经营者在天然气和电力网络容量上的准入要求等方面的问题，我代表团请求与欧盟及其成员国进行磋商。

俄罗斯认为，欧盟第三次能源改革方案中之规定违反了欧盟及其成员国在 WTO 协定中的多项义务和具体承诺。这特别体现在（但不仅限于）下列措施中：

同一人或多人不能在作为燃气/电力的生产者或供应商的同时，处理其产品的运输或传送。同一人或多人不能在对任何生产或供应职能中享有直接或间接之控制权的同时，对传送系统经营者或传送系统享有直接和间接的控制权或其他任何权利。反之亦然。当一个从事国内燃气生产的外国人意图获得或行使对传送系统或传送系统经营者之控制权时，该禁令同样适用。

欧盟第三次能源改革方案之要求对数种不同类型的管道网络给予豁免，因为天然气的“传送”被定义为“从向客户输送的角度出发，天然气运输所用之网络，主要包括高压管道，而非上游管道或高压管道中主要用于对天然气进行本地分配的部分。”

以下三种分拆制度均可实现该禁令：所有权分拆，建立独立系统经营者或建立独立传送经营者。这些制度的限制性各不相同，因此欧盟内部不同地方实施不同制度。除了在欧盟领土内部实施的具有不同程度限制性的多种制度外，欧盟第三次能源改革方案也规定，依据获得欧盟内部传送系统控制权的日期的不同，相关政府可采取不同的分拆制度。

此外，欧盟法律也规定了多项对分拆要求的豁免、例外和免除情况。这特别体现在对于某些类型的基础设施给予的豁免。比如，欧盟可随意向新的大型基础设施就分拆之要求给予部分或全部豁免。授予豁免之决定是依据个案的不同情况做出的。

分拆要求并不适用于新兴市场和孤立市场，也不适用于较小的天然气企业。

限制性程度最高的分拆要求——所有权分拆——不适用于为向客户输送天然气而通过本地或区域管道网络进行天然气运输的个人。

对于传送系统所有人或经营者的许可，在涉及外国个人或多人控制的情况下会增加额外的要求。当这些经营者被认为会对欧盟成员国以及欧盟整体的能源供应安全带来威胁时，他们将不会获得许可。由外国个人或多人控制的传送系统所有者和经营者之许可程序与由欧盟个人或多人控制的传送系统所有者和经营者之许可程序并不相同，前者的负担更为繁重。

除其他事项外，欧盟第三次能源改革方案要求传送系统所有者或经营者须在法定关税基础上，非歧视性地向所有网络用户提供服务；该方案还要求传送系统所有者或经营者向第三方提供稳定且可中断的接入服务。然而，就这些和其他对传送和分配系统准入进行管制的要求而言，欧盟第三次能源改

革方案同样规定了豁免、例外和免除情形，包括与分拆要求规定相似的豁免、例外和免除规定。

欧盟第三次能源改革方案对电力生产者或供应商以及电力运输和传送做出相同规定，并在这些部门产生相同的结果。

欧盟第三次能源改革方案中与第三方准入相关的要求降低了进口商在传输能力中可用的容量，且损害了已经签署的长期燃气供应合同。与此同时，该方案还对豁免、例外和免除情形做出规定，使燃气在通过某些基础设施运输时，能获得比其通过附有第三方准入要求的基础设施进口获得更有利的待遇。

进口的燃气在欧盟领土内的内部销售、推销、购买、运输、分配或使用都受到额外要求的限制。然而，对于包括生物气在内的国产天然气，并没有同样要求的限制。另外，国产生物气还享有额外的特惠待遇，意图取代进口天然气。

欧盟及其成员国采取上述措施所依据的法律文件，包括但不限于：

• 2009 年 7 月 13 日欧洲议会和欧洲理事会第 2009/73/EC 号关于天然气内部市场一般规则及撤销第 2003/55/EC 号指令之指令；

• 2003 年 6 月 26 日欧洲议会和欧洲理事会第 2003/55/EC 号关于天然气内部市场一般规则及撤销第 98/30/EC 号指令之指令；

• 2009 年 7 月 13 日欧洲议会和欧洲理事会第 2009/72/EC 号关于电力内部市场一般规则及撤销第 2003/54/EC 号指令之指令；

• 2009 年 7 月 13 日欧洲议会和欧洲理事会第 713/2009 号关于建立能源监管者合作机构之条例；

• 2009 年 7 月 13 日欧洲议会和欧洲理事会第 714/2009 号关于跨边境电力交换网络准入之条件及撤销第 1228/2003 号条例之条例；

• 2009 年 7 月 13 日欧洲议会和欧洲理事会第 715/2009 号关于天然气传送网络准入条件及撤销第 1775/2005 号条例之条例；

• 2010 年 10 月 20 日欧洲议会和欧洲理事会第 994/2010 号关于燃气供应保障安全措施及撤销欧洲理事会第 2004/67/EC 号指令之条例；

• 2013 年 4 月 17 日欧洲议会和欧洲理事会第 347/2013 号关于全欧能源基础设施指南、撤销第 1364/2006/EC 号决定，以及对第 No713/2009 号、第 714/2009 号和第 715/2009 号条例进行修订之条例；

• 2011 年 6 月 12 日欧盟委员会对第 715/2009 号条例之意见；

• 2005 年 10 月 25 日《成立能源共同体协定》；

• 2009 年 4 月 23 日欧洲议会和欧洲理事会第 2009/28/EC 号关于提倡使用可再生能源及修订并撤销第 2001/77/EC 号和第 2003/30/EC 指令之指令；

• 2011 年 6 月 30 日立陶宛共和国关于修订天然气法之法案，编号为 XI-1564；

• 2011 年 6 月 30 日立陶宛共和国关于实施修订天然气法之法案，编号为 No. XI-1565；

• 2011 年 10 月 28 日立陶宛共和国第 1239 号关于批准对违反立陶宛天然气法要求之天然气企业之行为和控制权进行分拆计划之决议；

• 2011 年 10 月 28 日立陶宛共和国第 1239 号决议通过的对违反立陶宛天然气法要求之天然气企业之行为和控制权进行分拆计划（2011 年第 130—6170 号官方通报）；

• 2011 年匈牙利政府第 29 号关于修订燃气供应法之法令；

• 2008 年匈牙利政府第 40 号关于天然气供应之法令；

• 爱沙尼亚政府天然气法令，天然气修正法，法的修正，RT I，28.06.2012，2；国家电子杂志，MNE（2012）52911；

• 克罗地亚政府能源法令（第 120/12 号官方通报）；

• 2012 年 11 月 11 日克罗地亚政府关于能源活动监管法令；

• 2012 年 1 月 8 日比利时（联邦）政府关于修订 1965 年 4 月 12 日联邦燃气法之法令；

• 2011 年 7 月 8 日比利时（佛兰德斯）政府关于修订 2009 年 5 月 8 日能源法之法令；

• 2011 年 7 月 20 日比利时（布鲁塞尔首都地区）政府关于修订 2004 年 4 月 1 日燃气法之法令；

• 比利时（瓦隆）政府关于实施燃气指令的多项修订法令和政府命令；

• 2011 年英国政府关于电力和燃气（内部市场）之规定；

• 德国政府电力供应法，（能源经济法），条例草案第2条和1.61.2012的行为，BGBI I S.74；

• 2010年9月3日德国燃气网络准入命令；

• 欧盟成员国依据燃气指令所做出的许可决定以及欧盟委员会对这些决定的意见；

• 2013年5月16日欧盟委员会关于对跨亚得里亚海管道在第2009/73/EC号指令第9条、第32条、第41条第6款，第41条第8款和第41条第10款下有关第三方准入、关税管理和所有权分拆之要求给予豁免之决定；

• 2013年6月6日能源监管机构对TAP AG之豁免申请做出的最终联合意见；

• 欧盟委员会关于依据第2009/73/EC号指令第36条对加塞列内连线管道给予豁免之决定；

• 欧盟委员会关于对加塞列内连线管道在第2009/73/EC号指令第9条下之所有权分拆要求给予豁免之决定；

• 欧盟委员会关于奥地利、罗马尼亚、匈牙利和保加利亚当局做出的、与纳布科管道相关的豁免决议之决定；

• 欧盟委员会关于德国当局和/捷克共和国当局做出的、与欧洲管道相关的豁免决议之决定；

• 欧盟委员会关于国家当局所做出的与LNG Grain（UK），South Hook（UK），Rovigo（IT），Dragon（UK），LNG Brindisi（IT），Gate Terminal（NL），LionGas（NL），LNG Eemshaven（NL），LNG Livorno（IT），LNG Shannon（IE），LNG Dunkerque（FR），LNG Porto Empedocle（IT）和National Grid Grain LNG（UK）相关的豁免决议之决定；

以及所做的任何修订、增补、展期和替代措施、更新措施、相关措施或落实措施；还有依欧盟第三次能源改革方案所做出的决定或落实措施，与其他被欧盟成员国采纳但未在此请求中明确，且俄罗斯在磋商中请求欧盟委员会给予协助予以明确的落实措施或决定，或者双方在磋商过程中所提及的此类措施。

因此，欧盟及其成员国违反了欧盟在GATS下第2条、第6条第16条和第17条，GATT 1994第1条、第3条、第10条和第11条，SCM协议第3条，《与贸易有关的投资措施协议》第8条以及《马拉喀什建立世界贸易组织协定》（简称《马拉喀什协定》）第16条第4款下所承担的义务。

本措施请求所引之措施显然剥夺或减损了俄罗斯依据引述的协议所能直接或间接获得的利益。

俄罗斯保留针对上述事项列举更多措施，以及依据涵盖协议的其他条款增加主张的权利。

俄方期待欧盟及其成员国对该请求做出回复，并商定一个彼此可以接受的日期进行磋商。

（钟楹译，戴臻校）

三、印度尼西亚——涉及园艺产品、动物和动物产品的进口措施：新西兰请求磋商

此文件自2014年5月8日，在新西兰代表团和印度尼西亚代表团及争端解决机构主席间进行沟通，现根据DSU第4条第4款的规定予以散发。

受我方政府授权，根据DSU第1条和第4条、GATT 1994第22条、《农业协议》第19条、《进口许可程序协议》第6条和《装船前检验协议》第7条和第8条的规定，就印度尼西亚对进口到印度尼西亚的园艺产品①、动物和动物产品②实施的特定措施，我代表团请求与印度尼西亚共和国（简称印度尼西亚）政府进行磋商。

如下所述，印度尼西亚：（1）实施禁止或限制园艺产品、动物和动物产品进口的措施；（2）对这些产品实施不正当的和限制贸易的非自动进口许可要求；（3）对进口产品给予较来自其本国的同类产品更低的待遇；（4）实施不合理和歧视性的装船前检验要求；以及（5）未能通知和公布关于其进口

---

① 相关的印度尼西亚措施把园艺界定为“关于水果、蔬菜、植物药材和花艺栽培的所有事物”，把园艺产品界定为“源于新鲜或加工过的园艺植物的所有产品”，详见《贸易部第16/2013号条例》（MOT Regulation 16/2013）第1条第1款和第2款，由《贸易部第47/2013号条例》（MOT Regulation 47/2013）的第14条修订。

② 相关的印度尼西亚措施把动物产品界定为“源于动物的新鲜和/或加工过的所有材料，这些材料用于食用、药物、农业和/或其他满足人类需求和福祉的其他目的”。详见《贸易部第47/2013号条例》（MOT Regulation 47/2013）第1条第5款的规定。印度尼西亚的涉案措施还覆盖了“兽体、肉类、可食用的内脏和/或其他衍生品”，详见《贸易部第84/2013号条例》（MOT Regulation 84/2013）。

许可措施的充分信息。

关于园艺产品，印度尼西亚的非自动进口许可体制涉及至少三个要素：（1）由贸易部指定作为园艺产品的生产进口商（“PI”）或注册进口商（RI）；（2）由农业部颁发的园艺产品进口推荐书（RIPH）；以及（3）由贸易部颁发的进口许可。对生产进口商（PI）和注册进口商（RI）的指定限制了对可能进口的园艺产品的使用。进口推荐书（RIPH）和进口许可的有效期为六个月①。对这些文件的申请只能在该年的两个时间段进行提交，这些文件的颁布亦是如此②。进口许可特别说明了一个进口商可在那些期间进口的园艺产品的总数量以及原产国。

关于动物和动物产品，印度尼西亚的非自动进口许可体制涉及至少四个要素：（1）满足农业部对进口商的要求；（2）由贸易部指定的动物和动物产品的注册进口商（RI）③；（3）由农业部颁发的推荐书；以及（4）由贸易部颁发的进口许可推荐书限制了进口产品的数量、类型、原产国和预期用途。它们具有明确的有效期，有效期截止到现年年底，并且也许只能适用于该年的四个时间段④。进口许可的有效期为 3 个月，进口许可的申请和许可的颁发只能在该年的四个时间段之间。进口许可特别说明了持有者在特定期限内可能进口的产品的总数量和原产国。

印度尼西亚的进口许可制度并非一项自动的许可机制，并且无法作为贯彻 WTO 规则的非自动许可机制而得以正当化。

印度尼西亚的非自动进口许可制度在下述几方面禁止和限制了进口：

• 关于园艺产品，RIPH 认证不允许超过 6 个月之前采摘的用于消费的新鲜园艺产品进口。

• 关于动物和动物产品，任何未列入进口许可法规附件的动物产品都可能完全不被允许进口。

• 关于园艺产品、动物和动物产品，进口商只能在进口前可能长达数月的特定期间内申请进口许可，并且，一旦颁发许可，该进口许可还对该特定期间内进口的产品的种类、数量、原产地和状态进行限制。

• 进口商必须提前预测其希望在给定期间内进口的产品数量，进而申请特定数量，这将记录在他们进口许可中三个月或六个月的期间内。如果实际进口的数量少于记录数量的一定比例，进口商将面临其 RI/PI 资格被中止或撤销的风险。

• 禁止或限制进口涉及一定预期内使用、销售、购买和/或分销形式的园艺产品、动物和动物产品。

• 在国内生产足以充分地满足国内市场时，禁止园艺产品、动物和动物产品的进口。

• 当特定园艺产品、动物和动物产品的价格降至内阁机构（无论“园艺产品价格监督小组”还是“牛肉价格监督小组”）制定的参考价格以下时，这些产品将被禁止或限制进口。

• 基于上述原因和制度的复杂性，印度尼西亚的进口许可制度是对进口的一项限制，并非尽可能简单，而是比绝对必要的限度更具行政负担性，不必要地要求接洽一家以上的行政机构，并且具有贸易限制性。

与其进口许可体制相联系，印度尼西亚还采纳了限制进口园艺产品、动物和动物产品的国内销售、标价出售、购买、分销或使用的措施，这使得进口产品的待遇低于国内同类产品的待遇。例如，印度尼西亚的措施把进口园艺产品的国内销售仅限于分销商，并限定进口牛肉的销售只能用于工业、酒店、餐厅和餐饮业。印度尼西亚对国内同类产品并未施加类似的限制。

---

① 对于辣椒和青葱而言，进口许可（Import Approval）的有效期为 3 个月，详见《贸易部第 16/2013 号条例》（MOT Regulation 16/2013），由《贸易部第 47/2013 号条例》（MOT Regulation 47/2013）的第 14 条修订，但没有明确规定进口推荐书（RIPH）的有效期，详见《贸易部第 86/2013 号条例》（MOT Regulation 86/2013）。

② 辣椒和青葱的申请时间段不一样，详见《贸易部第 16/2013 号条例》（MOT Regulation 16/2013），由《贸易部第 47/2013 号条例》（MOT Regulation 47/2013）的第 14 条修订。

③ 关于附件 2 所列的动物和动物产品，这一要求似乎只适用于作为商业经营者（business operators）的进口商，并不适用于其他类别的进口商，例如社会团体或国有企业。详见《贸易部第 46/2013 号条例》（MOT Regulation 46/2013）第 4 条、第 9 条和第 10 条；《贸易部第 84/2013 号条例》（MOT Regulation 84/2013）第 22 条。

④ 时间表似乎只适用于作为商业经营者（business operators）的进口商，并不适用于其他类别的进口商。

印度尼西亚的措施包含了装船前检验要求。这样的要求对贸易构成不必要的限制，因为同样的信息已经通过植物卫生证书提供，同样，印度尼西亚把装船前检验活动的监管限于一个在新西兰的必维国际检验集团。印度尼西亚未能确保装船前检验活动不会造成不合理的迟延、以非歧视的方式实施并且对所有出口商都以平等的基准适用。

最后，新西兰理解印度尼西亚的进口许可体制不符合《进口许可程序协议》第 5 条项下的通知义务，也不符合《进口许可程序协议》第 3 条项下的公布要求。

印度尼西亚用以实施和监管上述措施的法律文件包括但不限于以下文件：

- 《印度尼西亚共和国 2014 年第 7 号贸易法》；
- 《印度尼西亚共和国 2010 年第 13 号园艺法》；
- 《农业部 86/ Permentan/OT. 140/8/2013 号关于园艺产品的进口推荐条例》，该条例废除并取代了《农业部 47/Permentan/OT. 140/4/2013 号关于园艺产品的进口推荐条例》，且该条例废除并取代了《农业部 60/ Permentan/OT. 140/9/2012 号条例》(简称“《农业部 60/2012 号条例》”)；
- 《贸易部 16/M-DAG/PER/4/2013 号关于园艺产品进口条款条例》，该条例废除并取代了《贸易部 30/M-DAG/PER/5/2012 号关于进口园艺产品条款条例》和《贸易部 60/M-DAG/PER/9/2012 关于对〈贸易部 30/MDAG/PER/5/2012 号关于园艺产品进口条款条例〉的第二次修正案的条例》；
- 《贸易部 47/M-DAG/PER/8/2013 号关于对〈贸易部 16/M-DAG/PER/4/2013 号关于园艺产品进口条款条例〉的修正案的条例》；
- 《印度尼西亚共和国第 18/2009 号畜牧业和动物健康法》；
- 《农业部 84/Permentan/PD. 410/8/2013 号关于进口兽体、肉类、内脏和/或其他衍生品至印度尼西亚共和国领土内的条例》，该条例废除并取代了《农业部 50/Permentan/OT. 140/9/2011 号关于进口兽体、肉类、可食用的内脏和/或加工产品至印度尼西亚领土内的许可推荐的条例》，《农业部 50/2011 号条例》被《农业部 63/Permentan/OT. 140/5/2013 号关于对〈农业部 50/Permentan/OT. 140/9/2011 号关于兽体、肉类、内脏和/或其衍生品进入印度尼西亚领土的进口许可推荐条例〉的修正案的条例》；
- 《贸易部 46/M-DAG/PER/8/2013 号动物与动物产品进出口条款条例》(简称“《贸易部 46/2013 号条例》”)，该条例废除并取代了《贸易部 22/MDAG/PER/5/2013 号动物与动物产品进出口条例》，而该条例废除并取代了《贸易部 24/M-DAG/PER/9/2011 号动物与动物产品进出口条款条例》。
- 《印度尼西亚共和国第 18/2012 号食品法》；以及
- 《印度尼西亚共和国第 19/2013 号保护农民与向农民赋权法》；

以及任何关于上述法律文件的修正案，取代上述法律法规的法律文件，与上述法律文件相关的措施或实施措施。

印度尼西亚的措施显然与印度尼西亚在下列涵盖协定的条款项下所承担的义务不符：

(1) GATT 1994 第 3 条第 4 款、第 10 条第 1 款和第 11 条第 1 款；

(2)《农业协议》第 4.2 条；

(3)《进口许可程序协议》第 1.2 条、第 1.5 条、第 1.6 条、第 2.2 条、第 3.2 条、第 3.3 条、第 5.1 条、第 5.2 条；以及

(4)《装船前检验协议》第 2.1 条、第 2.15 条。

我方期待收到贵方对此请求做出的回复，并确定一个彼此方便的日期与地点进行磋商。根据美国就相同的措施提出的磋商请求，我方建议于 2014 年 5 月 8 日与美国共同（与贵方）进行磋商。

（梁意译，孙靓莹校）

四、印度尼西亚——园艺产品、动物和动物产品的进口：美国请求磋商

此文件自 2014 年 5 月 8 日，在美国代表团和印度尼西亚代表团及争端解决机构主席间进行沟通，现根据 DSU 第 4 条第 4 款的规定予以散发。

受我方政府授权，根据 DSU 第 1 条和第 4 条、GATT 1994 第 22 条、《农业协议》第 19 条、《进口许可程序协议》第 6 条，以及《装船前检验协

议》第 7 条和第 8 条，就印度尼西亚对园艺产品[①]、动物和动物产品[②]进口采取的特定措施，我代表团请求与印度尼西亚共和国进行磋商。

如下所述，印度尼西亚：（1）实施禁止或限制园艺产品、动物和动物产品进口的措施；（2）对这些产品实施不正当的和限制贸易的非自动进口许可要求；（3）对进口产品给予较来自其本国的同类产品更低的待遇；（4）实施不合理和歧视性的装船前检验要求；以及（5）未能通知和公布关于其进口许可措施的充分信息。

关于园艺产品，印度尼西亚的非自动进口许可体制涉及至少三个要素：（1）由贸易部指定作为园艺产品的生产进口商（“PI”）或注册进口商（RI）；（2）由农业部颁发的园艺产品进口推荐书（RIPH）；以及（3）由贸易部颁发的进口许可。对生产进口商（PI）和注册进口商（RI）的指定限制了对可能进口的园艺产品的使用。进口推荐书（RIPH）和进口许可的有效期为六个月[③]。对这些文件的申请只能在该年的两个时间段进行提交，这些文件的颁布亦是如此[④]。进口许可特别说明了一个进口商可在那些期间进口的园艺产品的总数量以及原产国。

关于动物和动物产品，印度尼西亚的非自动进口许可体制涉及至少四个要素：（1）满足农业部对进口商的要求；（2）由贸易部指定的动物和动物产品的注册进口商（RI）[⑤]；（3）由农业部颁发的推荐书；以及（4）由贸易部颁发的进口许可。推荐书限制了进口产品的数量、类型、原产国和预期用途。它们具有明确的有效期，有效期截止到现年年底，并且也许只能适用于该年的四个时间段[⑥]。进口许可的有效期为 3 个月，进口许可的申请和许可的颁发只能在该年的四个时间段之间。进口许可特别说明了持有者在特定期限内可能进口的产品的总数量和原产国。

印度尼西亚的进口许可制度并非一项自动的许可机制，并且无法作为贯彻 WTO 规则的非自动许可机制而得以正当化。

印度尼西亚的非自动进口许可制度在下述几方面禁止和限制了进口：

• 关于园艺产品，RIPH 认证不允许超过 6 个月之前采摘的用于消费的新鲜园艺产品进口。

• 关于动物和动物产品，任何未列入进口许可法规附件的动物产品都可能完全不被允许进口。

• 关于园艺产品、动物和动物产品，进口商只能在进口前可能长达数月的特定期间内申请进口许可，并且，一旦颁发许可，该进口许可还对该特定期间内进口的产品的种类、数量、原产地和状态进行限制。

• 进口商必须提前预测其希望在给定期间内进口的产品数量，进而申请特定数量，这将记录在他们进口许可中三个月或六个月的期间内。如果实际进口的数量少于记录数量的一定比例，进口商将面临其 RI/PI 资格被中止或撤销的风险。

• 禁止或限制进口涉及一定预期内使用、销

---

① 相关的印度尼西亚措施把园艺界定为“关于水果、蔬菜、植物药材和花艺栽培的所有事物”，把园艺产品界定为“源于新鲜或加工过的园艺植物的所有产品”，详见《贸易部第 16/2013 号条例》（MOT Regulation 16/2013）第 1 条第 1 款和第 2 款，由《贸易部第 47/2013 号条例》（MOT Regulation 47/2013）的第 14 条修订。

② 相关的印度尼西亚措施把动物产品界定为“源于动物的新鲜和/或加工过的所有材料，这些材料用于食用、药物、农业和/或其他满足人类需求和福祉的其他目的”。详见《贸易部第 47/2013 号条例》（MOT Regulation 47/2013）第 1 条第 5 款的规定。印度尼西亚的涉案措施还覆盖了“兽体、肉类、可食用的内脏和/或其他衍生品”，详见《贸易部第 84/2013 号条例》（MOT Regulation 84/2013）。

③ 对于辣椒和青葱而言，进口许可（Import Approval）的有效期为 3 个月，详见《贸易部第 16/2013 号条例》（MOT Regulation 16/2013），由《贸易部第 47/2013 号条例》（MOT Regulation 47/2013）的第 14 条修订，但没有明确规定进口推荐书（RIPH）的有效期，详见《贸易部第 86/2013 号条例》（MOT Regulation 86/2013）。

④ 辣椒和青葱的申请时间段不一样，详见《贸易部第 16/2013 号条例》（MOT Regulation 16/2013），由《贸易部第 47/2013 号条例》（MOT Regulation 47/2013）的第 14 条修订。

⑤ 关于附件 2 所列的动物和动物产品，这一要求似乎只适用于是商业经营者（business operators）的进口商，并不适用于其他类别的进口商，例如社会团体或国有企业。详见《贸易部第 46/2013 号条例》（MOT Regulation 46/2013）第 4 条、第 9 条和第 10 条；《贸易部第 84/2013 号条例》（MOT Regulation 84/2013）第 22 条。

⑥ 时间表似乎只适用于是商业经营者（business operators）的进口商，并不适用于其他类别的进口商。

售、购买和/或分销形式的园艺产品、动物和动物产品。

• 在国内生产足以充分地满足国内市场时，禁止园艺产品、动物和动物产品的进口。

• 当特定园艺产品、动物和动物产品的价格降至内阁机构（无论“园艺产品价格监督小组”还是“牛肉价格监督小组”）制定的参考价格以下时，这些产品将被禁止或限制进口①。

• 基于上述原因和制度的复杂性，印度尼西亚的进口许可制度是对进口的一项限制，并非尽可能简单，而是比绝对必要的限度更具行政负担性，不必要地要求接洽一家以上的行政机构，并且具有贸易限制性。

与其进口许可体制相联系起来，印度尼西亚还采纳了限制进口园艺产品、动物和动物产品的国内销售、标价出售、购买、分销或使用的措施，这使得进口产品的待遇低于国内同类产品的待遇。例如，印度尼西亚的措施把进口园艺产品的国内销售仅限于分销商，并限定进口牛肉的销售只能用于工业、酒店、餐厅和餐饮业。印度尼西亚对国内同类产品并未施加类似限制。

印度尼西亚的措施包括装船前检验规定。印度尼西亚未能确保该装船前检验行为不会引起不合理的迟延、以非歧视方式进行且平等地适用于所有出口商。

最后，关于其进口许可制度，美国认为印度尼西亚违反了《装船前检验协议》第5条项下的通知义务和《进口许可程序协议》第3条项下的公布要求。

印度尼西亚据以实施和管理上述措施的法律文件，包括但不限于下列法规：

• 与贸易有关的印度尼西亚共和国2014年第7号法律（“贸易法”）；

• 与园艺有关的印度尼西亚共和国2010年第13号法律（“园艺法”）；

• 《农业部有关园艺产品进口建议的第86/Permentan/OT. 140/8/2013号条例》（“MOA条例86/2013”），废止并替代了《农业部有关园艺产品进口的第47/Permentan/OT. 140/4/2013号条例》（“MOA条例47/2013”），该条例又废止并替代了《农业部第60/Permentan/OT. 140/9/2012号条例》（“MOA条例60/2012”）；

• 《贸易部有关园艺产品进口的第16/M-DAG/PER/4/2013号条例》（“MOT条例16/2013”），废止并替代了《贸易部有关园艺产品进口的第30/M-DAG/PER/5/2012号条例》（“MOT条例30/2012”）和《关于〈第30/M-DAG/PER/5/2012号有关园艺产品进口的贸易部条例〉（“MOT条例60/2012”）之第二修正案的第60/M-DAG/PER/9/2012号贸易部法规》；

• 《有关修改〈贸易部涉及园艺产品进口的第16/M-DAG/PER/4/2013号条例〉（“MOT条例47/2013”）的第47/M-DAG/PER/8/2013号法规》；

• 与畜牧业和动物健康有关的印度尼西亚共和国第18/2009号法律（“动物法”）；

• 《农业部有关畜体、肉类、内脏及/或其衍生物进口至印度尼西亚共和国境内的第84/Permentan/PD. 410/8/2013号条例》（“MOA条例84/2013”），废止和替代了《农业部第50/Permentan/OT. 140/9/2011号有关建议批准畜体、肉类、食用内脏及/或其加工制品进口至印度尼西亚境内的条例》（“MOA条例50/2011”）。该50/2011号条例已经农业部第63/Permentan/OT. 140/5/2013号法规修改，即《有关修改〈第50/Permentan/OT. 140/9/2011号涉及建议批准畜体、肉类、内脏及/或其衍生品进口至印度尼西亚共和国境内的条例〉（“MOA Regulation 63/2013”）的农业部法规》；

• 第46/M-DAG/PER/8/2013号有关动物和动物产品进出口规定的贸易部条例（“MOT条例46/2013”），废止和替代了第22/M-DAG/PER/5/2013号有关动物和动物产品进出口的贸易部条例（“MOT条例22/2013”），该条例又废止和替代了第24/M-DAG/PER/9/2011号有关动物和动物产品进出口的贸易部条例（“MOT条例24/2011”）；

• 与食品有关的印度尼西亚共和国第18/2012

① 这些包括动物和动物产品在内的产品被列在《贸易部第46/2013号条例》（MOT Regulation 46/2013）的附件1中，园艺产品则被列在《贸易部第16/2013号条例》（MOT Regulation 16/2013），由《贸易部第47/2013号条例》（MOT Regulation 47/2013）的第14条B款修订。

号法律（“食品法”）；以及

• 与保护和赋权农民有关的印度尼西亚共和国第 19/2013 号法律（“农民法”），包括任何修订、替代前述措施，与前述措施相关或具体的执行措施。

欧盟的措施显然与其在下列 WTO 条款中的承诺不相符：

（1）GATT 1994 第Ⅲ：4 条，第Ⅹ：1 条和第Ⅺ：1 条；

（2）《农业协议》第 4.2 条；

（3）《进口许可程序协议》第 1.2 条、第 1.5 条、第 1.6 条、第 2.2 条、第 3.2 条、第 3.3 条、第 5.1 条及第 5.2 条；以及

（4）《装船前检验协议》第 2.1 条和第 2.15 条。

我们期待贵方对此请求做出的回复，并确定一个彼此可以接受的日期和地点进行磋商。鉴于新西兰就同一事项于 2014 年 5 月 8 日提出磋商，我们建议与新西兰一同举行磋商。

（马兰译，邓晓虹校）

五、俄罗斯——对自德国和意大利进口的轻型商用车采取反倾销措施：欧盟请求磋商

此文件自 2014 年 5 月 21 日，在欧盟代表团和俄罗斯代表团及争端解决机构主席间进行沟通，现根据 DSU 第 4 条第 4 款的规定予以散发。

受我方政府授权，根据 DSU 第 1 条和第 4 条，GATT 1994 第 23 条第 1 款，以及《关于实施 1994 年关税与贸易总协定第 6 条的协定》（简称《反倾销协议》）第 17.2 条和 17.3 条，就俄罗斯依据欧亚经济委员会学院于 2013 年 5 月 14 日发布的第 113 号决定向自德国和意大利进口的轻型商用车征收的反倾销税，以及包括该学院内部市场保护部所发布的所有附录、通知和报告所列明措施，我代表团请求与俄罗斯进行磋商。

涉案措施与俄罗斯在下列 GATT 1994 以及《反倾销协议》条款中所承担的义务不相符：

1.《反倾销协议》第 2.2 条，第 2.3 条，第 2.4 条，第 6.8 条，第 6.10 条，第 9.2 条，第 9.3 条和附录 2。因为俄罗斯未能依据这些条款所规定的义务，基于所有可获信息确定正常价值、出口价格和每一个已知出口商的倾销幅度；同时俄罗斯也未能对正常价值和出口价格做出公平比较。

2.《反倾销协议》第 3.1 条，第 3.2 条，第 3.4 条和第 3.5 条。因为俄罗斯对损害的确定并非建立于肯定性证据之上，且未对在调查期间倾销进口产品的数量和倾销进口产品对国内市场同类产品价格的影响，及这些进口产品随之对相似产品国内生产者产生的影响做出客观审查。俄罗斯同时未能基于肯定性证据对损害因素和指标之趋势进行客观审查。

3.《反倾销协议》第 3.1 条和第 3.2 条。因为俄罗斯未能在对肯定性证据进行客观审查的基础上考虑倾销进口产品是否大幅增加，俄罗斯也未能在对肯定性证据进行客观审查的基础上考虑倾销进口产品是否大幅削低国内价格，或是否会在很大程度上抑制在其他情况下国内市场本应发生的价格上升。

4.《反倾销协议》第 3.1 条和第 3.4 条。因为俄罗斯对损害的确定并非建立于肯定性证据之上，也未能对这些进口产品随之对相似产品国内生产者产生的影响做出客观审查，同时俄罗斯也未能评估或是忽略了那些表明国内产业并未受损的、与产业状况相关的经济因素和指标。

5.《反倾销协议》第 3.1 条和第 3.5 条。因为俄罗斯未能基于肯定性证据对被调查的进口产品与宣称的国内产业损害之间的因果关系进行客观审查。俄罗斯也未能基于肯定性证据，对除被调查的进口产品外损害国内产业的其他因素进行客观审查，因此俄罗斯将其他因素引起的损害错误地归结于被调查的进口产品中。

6.《反倾销协议》第 4.1 条。因为俄罗斯错误地界定国内产业。

7.《反倾销协议》第 6.2 条和第 6.4 条。因为俄罗斯未能在整个调查期间向所有利害关系方提供为自身利益进行辩护的充分机会。同时，俄罗斯也未能向所有利害关系方披露与其陈述相关的、涉及倾销和损害确定的所有信息，包括用于确定倾销幅度，以及被调查的进口产品对相似产品在国内市场价格产生之影响的信息。

8.《反倾销协议》第 6.5 条。因为俄罗斯在没有正当理由的情况下，将国内生产者提供的信息视为机密。

9.《反倾销协议》第 6.5.1 条。因为俄罗斯未

能要求国内生产者提供足够详细，以便利害关系方能够合理了解以机密形式提交的信息的实质内容之非机密摘要。

10.《反倾销协议》第 6.9 条。因为俄罗斯未能将考虑中的、构成是否实施最终反倾销措施决定依据的基本事实，包括作为确定存在倾销情况之依据的基本事实以及作为计算倾销幅度和损害确定之依据的基本事实，通知所有利害关系方。

11.《反倾销协议》第 12.2 条和第 12.2.2 条。因为俄罗斯未能详细提供调查主管机关就其认为重要的所有事实问题和法律问题所得出的调查结果和结论，以及导致实施最终措施所有相关的事实问题和法律问题及理由的相关信息。

12. 由于俄罗斯对自德国和意大利进口的轻型商用车采取的反倾销措施违反了上述《反倾销协议》条款，因此俄罗斯也违反了《反倾销协议》第 1 条和第 18.4 条，以及 GATT 1994 第 6 条规定的义务。

俄罗斯的措施显然剥夺或减损了欧盟依据引述的协议所能直接或间接获得的利益。欧盟因此要求俄罗斯遵守其加入 WTO 的承诺，并尽早对该情况做出修正。

针对上述问题，欧盟保留在磋商过程中提出更多的涉案措施以及依据涵盖协议的其他条款增加诉求的权利。

欧盟期待俄方依正当程序对此磋商请求做出回复。欧盟愿与俄方商定一个彼此可以接受的日期进行磋商。

（钟楹译，邓晓虹校）

六、欧盟——对源自印度尼西亚的生物柴油实施反倾销措施：印度尼西亚请求磋商

此文件自 2014 年 6 月 10 日，在印度尼西亚代表团和欧盟代表团及争端解决机构主席间进行沟通，现根据 DSU 第 4 条第 4 款的规定予以散发。

受我方政府授权，根据 DSU 第 1 条和第 4 条、GATT 1994 第 22.1 条，以及《反倾销协议》第 17.2 条和第 17.3 条，就印度尼西亚认为与欧盟在 WTO 协定相关条款项下的义务不符的下列措施，包括任何后续的修改、替代和关联措施以及执行措施，我代表团请求与欧盟进行磋商：

1. 关于防止非欧共体成员国倾销进口的 2009 年 11 月 30 日第 1225/2009 号理事会条例（EC）（即“基本反倾销法规”），第 2.5 条和第 2.6（b）条，包括任何后续修改、替代、执行措施和相关文件或惯例。

2. 欧盟对尤其源自印度尼西亚的生物柴油的进口实施的反倾销措施，以及潜在调查。

（一）有关《基本反倾销法规》的诉求

A.《基本倾销法规》第 2 条第 5 款第 2 段规定，“如果与受调查的产品的生产和销售相关的成本没有合理反映在有关当事人的记录中，应该以同一国内的其他生产商或出口商的成本为基础调整或确定上述成本，若无法得知或使用此类信息，应参照任何其他合理的基础，包括来自其他典型市场的信息。”印度尼西亚认为《基本倾销法规》第 2 条第 5 款本身与《反倾销协议》、GATT 1994 和《马拉喀什协定》的下列条款不符：

1.《反倾销协议》第 2.2 条和 GATT 1994 第 VI：1 条。因为前述条款不允许以和原产国生产不相关的其他数据或信息为基础调整或确定生产成本。

2.《反倾销协议》第 2.2 条和第 2.2.1.1 条、GATT 1994 第 VI：1 条。因为前述条款要求，如果受调查的出口商或生产商存有的记录符合出口国的会计通则，并合理反映与有关产品的生产和销售相关的成本，则成本费用通常应根据该记录计算；并且不允许由其他成本调整或替代受调查生产商实际发生的成本，无非是因为其被认为人为地低廉、萧条和扭曲。而且，因为前述条款要求成本与有关产品的生产和销售相关。

3.《反倾销协议》第 9.3. 条。由于未能根据《反倾销协议》第 2.2 条和第 2.2.1.1 条推定正常价值，如果依据《反倾销协议》第 2 款的规则正确计算，欲实施的反倾销税额会超过倾销幅度。

4.《马拉喀什协定》第 XVI：4 条和《反倾销协议》第 18.4 条。鉴于欧盟目前尚未采取全部措施确保其法律、法规和行政程序与 GATT 1994 和《反倾销协议》的规定相符。

B.《基本反倾销法规》第 2 条第 6 款（b）项规定，如果销售费、一般费用和管理费以及利润的数额无法根据与受调查的出口商或生产商在正常贸易过程中相同产品的生产和销售有关的实际数据加以确定，可以根据“原产国国内市场中受调查出口商或生产商在正常贸易过程中，适用于相同大类产

品的生产和销售的实际金额。”印度尼西亚认为基本反倾销法规第2条第6款（b）项本身与《反倾销协议》和《马拉喀什协定》的下列条款不符：

1.《反倾销协议》第2.2.2（i）条。因为该条款并未要求以原产国国内市场中受调查出口商或生产商在正常贸易过程中，与相同大类产品的生产和销售相关的实际发生和实现的金额来确定管理费、销售费和一般费用以及利润数额。

2.《马拉喀什协定》第XVI：4条和《反倾销协议》第18.4.条。鉴于欧盟目前尚未采取全部措施确保其法律、法规和行政程序与《反倾销协议》的规定相符。

（二）有关对印度尼西亚的生物柴油施加的反倾销措施以及潜在调查的诉求

印度尼西亚认为欧盟对尤其是源自印度尼西亚的生物柴油施加的反倾销措施和潜在调查与《反倾销协议》和GATT 1994的下列规定不符：

1.《反倾销协议》第2.2条和第2.2.1.1条。因为欧盟错误地判定存在与受调查印度尼西亚生产商生产生物柴油过程中使用的原材料成本有关的特殊市场情况，将其作为调整生物柴油生产成本的根据。

2.《反倾销协议》第2.1条、第2.2条、第2.2.1.1条和GATT 1994第VI：1条。因为在为受调查印度尼西亚生产商推定正常价值时，欧盟没有依据这些生产商保存的记录来计算生物柴油的生产成本，并且因为欧盟因此未能适当地计算生产成本，亦未能为这些生产商适当地推定正常价值。

3.《反倾销协议》第2.1条和第2.2条。因为欧盟未能以源自原产国如印度尼西亚的生物柴油的生产成本为依据，为受调查生产商推定正常价值。

4.《反倾销协议》第2.1条、第2.2条和第2.2.1.1条，GATT 1994第VI：1条。由于在为受调查生产商推定正常价值时，欧盟计入了未能合理反映与印度尼西亚生物柴油的生产和销售相关的成本；并且，对其中的一些生产商而言，调整是以在生物柴油的生产中未曾实际使用的原料为基础，所以欧盟调整实际生产成本的方法不合理，且无法使生物柴油的生产成本得以合理反映。欧盟因此未能适当地计算生产成本，亦未能适当地为这些生产商推定正常价值。

此外，如前2至4项诉求所述，印度尼西亚认为适用于反倾销措施下潜在调查的《基本倾销法规》第2条第5款与《反倾销协议》第2.1条、第2.2条、第2.2.1.1条和GATT 1994第VI：1条不符。

5.《反倾销协议》第2.1条、第2.2条、第2.2.2条和第2.2.2（3）条。由于为受调查的印度尼西亚生产商推定正常价值时，欧盟没有按第2.2.2（3）条的规定设立利润上限；欧盟未依据合理方法确定利润金额；并且，欧盟不适当地拒绝根据一些印度尼西亚出口商或生产商在印度尼西亚国内市场上生产和销售相同大类产品所承担和实现的实际费用数额来计算利润金额。因此，欧盟未能适当地为这些生产商推定正常价值。

6.《反倾销协议》第2.4条。由于特别基于下列原因，在比较正常价值和出口价格时，欧盟未能对包括税收差异在内的影响价格可比性的差异留出适当的余地：

（1）对一项内含基于原材料参考价格的生产成本的推定正常价值与出口价格进行比较，该出口价格反映出受调查印度尼西亚生产商实际承担的该原材料成本，而原材料的参考价格反过来取决于该原材料的国际价格，包含其出口税；

（2）在向欧盟的出口额中扣除一印度尼西亚生产商通过其位于第三国的关联公司产生的所谓的佣金和溢价；

（3）未能以相关的欧盟进口商在调查期间获取的实际利润为根据，对归属于同印度尼西亚出口商关联的欧盟进口商的利润留出余地；拒绝实际应计利润；拒绝特定印度尼西亚生产商提供的与生物柴油的欧盟进口商的名义利润率水平相关的确凿证据。

7.《反倾销协议》第2.3条和第2.4条。因为欧盟未以进口的生物柴油首次转售给欧盟境内的独立买主的价格为依据，为一家受调查的印度尼西亚生产商推算出口价格。或者因为欧盟没有在该印度尼西亚生产商收到的“重复计算”生物柴油的溢价基础上，而对出口价格做出调整。

8.《反倾销协议》第9.3条、GATT 1994第VI：2条。因为欧盟施加和征收的反倾销税超过了本应依据《反倾销协议》第2条确定的倾销幅度。

9.《反倾销协议》第3.1条和第3.2条。因为欧盟在确定对其产业造成的损害时，没有对与声称的倾销的进口产品数量、倾销的进口产品对国内生物柴油市场中的价格所造成的影响，以及这些声称的倾销的进口产品对国内生物柴油生产商所造成的后续影响这三方面相关的确凿证据进行客观的审查。第一，关于倾销的进口产品数量，欧盟未能进行客观审查，因为没有在其分析中考虑由欧盟产业制造的倾销的进口产品的庞大数量，也没有考虑到在调查结束时进口数量的逆转趋势。第二，鉴于欧盟尤其未能在物理性能和模型匹配方面确保价格的可比性，并且以抽样的欧盟生产商的部分和未经解释的销售额为依据确定降价幅度，欧盟做出的关于倾销的进口产品对价格（包括降价）的影响的裁决，并非依据对记录在案证据的客观审查而做出。

10.《反倾销协议》第3.1条和第3.4条。因为欧盟对损害的确定没有依据确凿的证据做出，未能对倾销的进口产品对国内同类产品生产商造成的后续影响，尤其是与欧盟产业的市场份额、市场容量和产能利用率相关的影响进行客观审查。并且，欧盟未能对损害因素间的整体发展和相互作用综合考虑并做出适当评估。

11.《反倾销协议》第3.1条和第3.5条。鉴于欧盟未能基于全部相关证据，客观地确定倾销的进口产品是否通过倾销效果正在引起损害，亦未能基于确凿证据，对除声称的倾销进口产品之外的在同一时间损害欧盟产业的其他因素进行客观审查，而将这些其他因素造成的损害归咎于倾销的进口产品。欧盟未能以确凿证据为依据，对声称倾销的进口产品和对其国内产业造成的损害之间的因果关系进行客观审查。其他因素尤其包括，“重复计算”制度对欧盟国内生物柴油需求的影响，欧盟及其成员国对生物柴油支持的减少、欧盟产业产能过剩、欧盟制造的生物柴油进口，以及欧盟产业缺乏原材料的垂直整合和准入这些方面造成的影响。

12.《反倾销协议》第6.5条和第6.5.1条。因为第一，欧盟将起诉状及原告在调查过程中所做陈词里的特定信息视为保密，但未证明有“正当理由”；第二，欧盟未能遵循相关规定提供充分详尽的非机密性摘要，以使人能够合理地理解被原告呈交的涉及起诉状几个附件和在调查中所提交宏观经济数据的机密资料的实质，亦未能使人合理地理解抽样的欧盟生产商所做问卷回答中的特定信息，或合理解释特殊保密信息不能做非保密性摘要的原因。

13.《反倾销协议》第6.9条。因为欧盟未能通告利益方其考虑中的重要事实，该重要事实构成决定是否适用最终措施的依据，包括判定倾销是否存在、损害和因果关系，以及倾销和损害幅度的计算等重要事实，因而损害了印度尼西亚生产商为自身利益辩护的权利。

14.《反倾销协议》第7.1条、第7.2条、第9.2条和第9.3条。因为欧盟错误地向一受调查印度尼西亚生产商施加和征收了超过已确定倾销幅度的临时税，后在临时阶段予以改正。

15.《反倾销协议》第15条。因为欧盟未能积极考虑两家受调查印度尼西亚生产商的承诺，因而欧盟在对印度尼西亚生物柴油进口产品适用反倾销税之前，未曾探讨建设性补偿的可能性。并且，欧盟未能对印度尼西亚作为发展中成员的特殊情况给予特别考虑。

鉴于上述诉求，印度尼西亚认为欧盟同时违反了GATT 1994第VI条和《反倾销协议》第1条。

欧盟的措施显然剥夺或减损了印度尼西亚依据引述的协议所能直接或间接获得的利益。

印度尼西亚保留在磋商过程中提出与上述事项相关的其他措施和诉求的权利，包括任何修正、替代、扩张及实施的措施或其他相关问题。

我们期待贵方对此请求做出的回复，并确定一个彼此方便的日期和形式进行磋商。

（马兰译，李雪峰校）

七、印度尼西亚——在“美国丁香烟案”中援引DSU第22条第2款：欧盟请求磋商

此文件自2014年6月13日，在欧盟代表团和印度尼西亚代表团及争端解决机构主席间进行沟通，现根据DSU第4条第4款的规定予以散发。

受我方政府授权，根据DSU第1条和第4条，GATT 1994第22条第1款的规定，就印度尼西亚在美国丁香烟案（DS406）中在合规性和仲裁小组程序下单方援引DSU第22条第2款，并在该程序中排除第三方的行为，我代表团请求与印度尼西亚进行磋商。我方认为该做法与DSU第21条第5款、第22条第2款、第23条第1款和第23条第2款（a）项不符，同时与DSU第10条第1至3款

不符。上诉机构已明确指出：

……在取得 DSB 对中止减让的授权之前，一成员方必须启动认为另一成员方采取的措施违反了 WTO 项下协定的争端解决程序。当涉案措施被专家组（和上诉机构，如上诉）认定与 WTO 项下协定不符，并且采取该措施的成员方未能在合理期限内执行专家组（或上诉机构）的裁决，或需要采取某项措施以使之相符合，而该项措施被专家组（和上诉机构）在合规程序中认定未能使被诉成员方达到合规程度时，发起争端解决程序的成员方将仅仅被授权中止减让。换言之，在依据第 23 条第 1 款的规定而广泛诉诸并遵守 DSU 的规则和程序后，该成员方根据 DSB 的授权只能中止减让。

（一）争端背景

2012 年 4 月 24 日，争端解决机构（DSB）在其会议中采纳了美国—影响丁香烟生产和销售的措施（WT/DS406/AB/R）一案的上诉机构报告和经上诉机构修改后的专家组报告（WT/DS406/R）。遵从专家组和上诉机构的执行建议，DSB 要求美国促使其在上诉机构报告和经上诉机构修改的专家组报告中认定的与 TBT 协议不符的措施符合该协定项下的义务。依据 DSU 第 21 条第 3 款（b）项，印度尼西亚和美国一致同意美国使其措施合规的合理期限为 15 个月，自 2012 年 4 月 24 日起至 2013 年 7 月 24 日止。

2013 年 7 月 23 日，美国通知 DSB 和 WTO 全体成员，依其之见，美国已经依照原始程序遵守 DSB 的建议和裁决。印度尼西亚于 2013 年 8 月 12 日通知 DSB 和 WTO 全体成员，印度尼西亚认为，美国未能在合理期间内将其与适用协定不符的措施合规化，也未能在合理期间内遵守 DSB 的建议和裁决，并且未达成使其满意的补偿。因此，根据 DSU 第 21 条第 5 款规定，在是否存在为遵守建议和裁决所采取的措施或此类措施是否与适用协定相一致的问题上，美国和印度尼西亚存在分歧。第 21 条第 5 款规定，此争端也应通过援用这些争端解决程序加以决定，包括只要可能即求助于原专家组。

尽管对合规性存在分歧，印度尼西亚于 2013 年 8 月 12 日依据 DSU 第 22 条第 2 款，请求 DSB 授权中止对美国实施适用协定项下的减让或其他义务。美国反对印度尼西亚提议的中止程度，并主张第 22 条第 3 款规定的原则和程序未得到遵守。DSB 同意该事项涉及 DSU 第 22 条第 6 款规定的仲裁程序。

在 2013 年 8 月 23 日的 DSB 会议上，欧盟代表做出如下陈述：

欧盟注意到，美国声称其已采取措施遵守 DSB 的建议和裁决。欧盟也注意到印度尼西亚不同意美国已使其措施符合 TBT 协议。由此看来，在 DSU 第 21 条第 5 款含义内，“在是否存在为遵守建议和裁决所采取的措施或此类措施是否与适用协定相一致的问题上存在分歧”。欧盟意在回顾，根据该条款，“此争端也应通过援用这些争端解决程序加以决定，包括只要可能即求助于原专家组”。若在是否存在为遵守 WTO 规则所采取的措施或此类措施是否与适用规则相一致的问题上存在分歧，一旦对该声称的遵守行为有多边决定，在 DSU 项下减让或其他义务可以被中止。欧盟希望美国和印度尼西亚能确保本争端中关于合规和义务减让的 DSU 程序能被有效执行，并遵守正确的顺序。最后欧盟旨在回顾，欧盟作为第三方参与了本争端的专家组和上诉程序，因此根据 DSU 第 10 条第 1、2、3 款，保留其作为第三方参与任何后续程序的权利，包括关于在是否存在为遵守建议和裁决所采取的措施或此类措施是否与适用协定相一致的问题上存在的任何分歧。

通过 2013 年 9 月 2 日的沟通，WTO 成员被通知，依据 DSU 第 22 条第 6 款，涉及合规/仲裁小组的事项将由原专家组审查。

通过 2013 年 9 月 4 日的沟通，欧盟请求在合规/仲裁小组的工作程序和时间表中提供适当条款，以促进欧盟在本争端中实施第三方权利。

经 2013 年 12 月 18 日沟通，合规/仲裁小组告知欧盟其决议，考虑到印度尼西亚表达的观点，在合规/仲裁小组程序中不给予欧盟第三方权利。

合规/仲裁小组未通告 WTO 成员该合规/仲裁小组程序已中止。

在 2014 年 1 月 22 日的 DSB 会议中，欧盟做出声明称其第三方权利已遭侵害，并且所发生的事实与 DSU 第 22 条第 2 款、第 23 条第 1 款和第 23 条第 2 款（a）项不符，其后就此进行了讨论。欧盟随后请求传阅沟通文件以解释其观点，各方也就此在随后 2014 年 2 月 26 日的 DSB 定期会议上进行了讨论。

在合规/仲裁小组程序中（2013 年 12 月 19 日），美国提交的第一份书面陈述以 55 页中的 39 页篇幅解释了美国已经全面执行 DSB 的建议和裁决。同样，美国在实体会议（2014 年 3 月 11 日）之前对合规/仲裁小组问题的答复，美国的开场口头陈词（2014 年 3 月 7 日）和美国在实体会议（2014 年 4 月 10 日）之后对合规/仲裁小组问题的答复，上述所有都证明进行了合法程序。

（二）涉案措施

本案的涉案措施为，在印度尼西亚与美国未就合规事项达成一致的情况下，印度尼西亚直接援引并要求适用 DSU 第 22 条第 2 款规定，这一点已经 WT/DS406/12 案证实；以及其对发起和寻求第 21 条第 5 款项下的合规程序的不作为和对在合规仲裁小组程序结果出炉之前要求和促使中止仲裁小组程序的不作为。

本案的涉案措施也包括，由于印度尼西亚的请求，欧盟被非法地从合规/仲裁小组程序中排除。印度尼西亚的请求系欧盟被排除的一个真实且实质性的原因，这一点已经合规/仲裁小组程序 2013 年 12 月 18 日下发的文件证实。

任何可归咎于 WTO 成员的作为或不作为均为 WTO 争端解决所称的措施。欧盟所提及的措施系可归咎于印度尼西亚的作为或不作为。

WTO 成员依据 DSU 提起诉讼并不需要证明其在不符合 WTO 规定的事实上有特殊的利益。基于下述原因，本案的涉案措施为不符合 WTO 规定的措施。无论如何，在本案中，欧盟是原仲裁小组程序的第三方，也是原上诉程序的第三方。另外，欧盟也参与香烟的生产、贸易和监管，包括本案中提到的几种香烟。而且，欧盟对适用协定的正确及一致性的解释和适用有系统性的利益，特别是在任何中止减让及其对欧盟的潜在影响方面，包括贸易偏转和贸易转移效应。我们对这些合规/仲裁小组程序有密切的利益。

（三）涉案措施与 WTO 规则不相符

DSU 第 21 条第 5 款意指在是否存在为遵守建议和裁决所采取的措施或此类措施是否与适用协定相一致的问题上存在分歧的情形。在此情形下，该条规定了应援引 DSU 争端解决程序的无条件义务（“此争端也应通过援用这些争端解决程序加以决定，包括只要可能即求助于原专家组”）。

第 21 条第 5 款和第 22 条表明，第 22 条是以存在不符情形为前提条件，对此上诉机构指出必须基于一项多边的决议。由此而论，印度尼西亚依据第 22 条第 2 款请求 DSB 授权中止对美国实施适用协定项下的减让或其他义务，连同其有所疏漏而未依据第 21 条第 5 款启动和进行合规程序、亦未请求和获得仲裁小组程序的中止，这些依法都应以美国未能在第 21 条第 3 款规定的合理期间内使其被认定与适用协定不一致的措施符合该协定或建议和裁决这一命题为前提条件。然而，本案中未曾就合规问题达成任何多边决定。相反，如上所述，依据 DSU 第 21 条第 5 款，在是否存在为遵守建议和裁决所采取的措施或此类措施是否与适用协定相一致的问题上，美国和印度尼西亚存在分歧。

DSU 第 22 条第 6 款是以本条第 2 款所述情形为前提。第 2 款所指情形包括有关成员未能使其措施符合，以及存在分歧时应就此达成一项多边决定。DSU 第 22 条第 7 款规定，应确定中止的程度是否等于利益丧失或减损的程度，确定在适用协定项下是否允许拟议的中止减让，以及确定 DSU 第 22 条第 3 款所列原则和程序是否被得到遵循。既然如此，这些任务仍应由原仲裁小组进行。因此，第 22 条第 3 款至第 8 款整体都是以存在不符情形为前提条件。它们都直接或间接涉及由不符引起的权利丧失或减损。若在已达合规的情形下，DSB 欲依据 DSU 第 22 条第 7 款，通过反向一致或自动地授权中止减让，将必然违反 DSU 第 22 条第 5 款。

对此欧盟指出，上诉机构认为是否一项与适用协定不符的措施已被移除这一问题，依据 DSU 第 22 条第 8 款，应以一项多边决定为必要条件。特别是，上诉机构做出了如下裁决：

> 第 21 条第 5 款规定了特殊程序来确定在为执行 DSB 的建议和裁决而采取的措施与适用协定是否一致这个问题上存在分歧。因此，第 21 条第 5 款项下的小组程序是解决第 2003/74/EC 号指令是否已实质一致，及因而第 22 条第 8 款规定的解除中止减让的条件是否满足的适当程序。……
>
> ……第 21 条第 5 款系强制性义务。……
>
> 综上，我们认为依据第 21 条第 5 款，正如本案中在遭受中止减让的一成员已采取执行措施，但

在第 22 条第 8 款项下对“该被认定为与适用协定不一致的措施是否已被移除”这一问题存在分歧时，在 DSU 程序框架内，小组程序是正确的行动步骤。因此，我们同意欧盟的观点，即对第 2003/74/EC 号指令是否已经实质一致存在分歧时，第 21 条第 5 款中的小组程序是应被遵循的程序。……

本上诉机构认为，第 23 条第 1 款规定了当 WTO 成员寻求纠正违反适用协定的情形时，应援用 DSU 规则和程序这一基本义务。第 23 条在两方面约束着 WTO 成员的行为。第一，第 23 条第 1 款将 WTO 争端解决机制确立为解决 WTO 争端的唯一场所，并要求遵守 DSU 的规则。第二，第 23 条第 2 款禁止一 WTO 成员的特定单方行为。因此，一成员不能单方面地：（1）对违反义务已发生、利益已丧失或减损或适用协定任何目标的实现已受到妨碍做出确定；（2）确定执行的合理期限；或（3）确定中止减让及减让水平。

……在取得 DSB 对中止减让的授权之前，一成员必须启动认为另一成员方采取的措施违反了 WTO 项下协定的争端解决程序。当涉案措施被专家组（和上诉机构，如上诉）认定与 WTO 项下协定不符，并且采取该措施的成员方未能在合理期限内执行专家组（或上诉机构）的裁决，或需要采取某项措施以使之相符合，而该项措施被专家组（和上诉机构）在合规程序中认定未能使被诉成员方达到合规程度时，发起争端解决程序的成员方将仅仅被授权中止减让。换言之，在依据第 23 条第 1 款的规定而广泛诉诸并遵守 DSU 的规则和程序后，该成员方根据 DSB 的授权只能中止减让。

据此，印度尼西亚依据第 22 条第 2 款所做出的决定和请求，连同其有所疏漏而未依据第 21 条第 5 款启动和进行合规程序，亦未请求并导致中止仲裁小组程序而使合规小组程序的结果悬而未决，这些都分别与上述对应条款不符。并且，由于在对一致性有所争议时，印度尼西亚采取了单方行为而未对不符性达成多边决定，前述行为还与 DSU 第 21 条第 5 款、第 23 条第 1 款和第 23 条第 2 款（a）项不符。

此外，印度尼西亚请求欧盟被非法地从合规/仲裁小组程序中排除系欧盟被排除的真实且实质性的原因，该点与以下不符：由于印度尼西亚没有保证其他成员的利益被充分考虑，与 DSU 第 10 条第 1 款不符；由于欧盟对合规/仲裁小组裁定的事项有实质性利益且已将该利益通告 DSB，却无法有机会申辩或提交书面陈词，与 DSU 第 10 条第 2 款不符；以及，由于欧盟未收到且不会收到首次会议上该案当事人提交的所有陈词，与第 10 条第 3 款不符。

基于上述原因，印度尼西亚的措施显然剥夺或减损了欧盟依据引述的协定和条款所能直接或间接获得的利益。

欧盟保留在磋商中提出有关以上事项的额外措施及诉求之权利。

欧盟期待贵方对此请求做出的回复，并确定一个彼此可以接受的日期和形式进行磋商。

（马兰译，李雪峰校）

八、加拿大——对自台、澎、金、马单独关税区进口的加拿大碳钢焊接管采取反倾销措施：台、澎、金、马单独关税区请求磋商

此文件自 2014 年 11 月 7 日，在台、澎、金、马单独关税区代表团和加拿大代表团及争端解决机构主席间进行沟通，现根据 DSU 第 4 条第 4 款的规定予以散发。

台、澎、金、马独立关税区于 2014 年 6 月 25 日，就加拿大对包括台、澎、金、马单独关税区在内的多地进口之碳钢焊接管所采取的临时性最终反倾销措施以及为采取这些措施所进行的调查（WT/DS482/1，G/L/1073，G/ADP/D105/1），请求与加拿大进行磋商。

2014 年 7 月 24 日，台、澎、金、马单独关税区与加拿大就上述措施进行了磋商。

在该轮磋商后，台、澎、金、马单独关税区就加拿大对包括台、澎、金、马单独关税区在内的多地进口之碳钢焊接管所采取的反倾销措施提出额外的诉求。作为涉案的反倾销措施以及为采取这些措施所进行的调查的某些方面之法律依据，相关立法规定显然违反了 GATT 1994 以及《反倾销协议》多个条款的规定。

因此，受我方政府授权，根据 DSU 第 1 条和第 4 条，GATT 1994 第 22 条，以及《反倾销协议》第 17 条，我代表团请求与加拿大进行磋商。

虽然双方已于2014年6月25日依据原始磋商请求举行了磋商，但本次磋商请求作为对原始磋商请求之补充，应被视为原始磋商请求之组成部分，而非对原始磋商请求的替代。

加拿大对自包括台、澎、金、马单独关税区在内的多地进口之碳钢焊接管所采取的临时性最终反倾销措施以及为采取这些措施所进行的调查，除了违反在原始磋商请求上所列之义务外，还违反了《反倾销协议》的下列条款：

1.《反倾销协议》第7.1条第（ii）项，因为加拿大在没有对倾销得出初步肯定裁定的情况下，对倾销幅度在微量范围内的出口商关于碳钢焊接管的进口采取了临时性反倾销措施。

2.《反倾销协议》第7.5条和第9.2条，因为加拿大对倾销幅度在微量范围内的出口商的进口实施并收取临时性最终反倾销税。

3.《反倾销协议》第6.8条和附录2，因为加拿大在利用可获得的事实以确定"其他所有出口商"的倾销幅度时，并没有遵循相关条款规定的条件。

4.《反倾销协议》第6.8条和附录2，因为加拿大利用可获得的事实计算对合作生产者出口的新产品类型的进口所收取的反倾销税。

5.《反倾销协议》第2.2条，因为加拿大以《反倾销协议》第2.2条不能预见的方式计算合做出口商的新产品类型的正常价值。

6.《反倾销协议》第9.3条，因为加拿大对合作出口商关于新产品类型的进口所征收的反倾销税额超过他们在《反倾销协议》第2条下所确定的倾销幅度。

此外，台、澎、金、马单独关税区认为加拿大《特别进口措施法》（SIMA）以及《特别进口措施细则》（SIMR）本身违反了《反倾销协议》下列条款的规定：

特别是《特别进口措施法》第2条第1款，第30.1条，第35条第1款和第2款，第38条第1款以及第41条第1款，连同所有修订案、实施措施或相关措施，本身都违反了下列规定：

1.《反倾销协议》第5.8条，因为上述条款规定只有在出口国作为整体的幅度属微量时才停止调查，而非依《反倾销协议》第5.8条之规定，在单个出口商的倾销幅度为微量时停止。

2.《反倾销协议》第7.1条第（ii）项，因为上述条款要求对倾销幅度在微量范围内的出口商的进口采取临时反倾销措施。

3.《反倾销协议》第7.5条和第9.2条，因为上述条款要求向倾销幅度在微量范围内出口商的进口采取并收取临时性最终反倾销税。

此外，连同上述条款，《特别进口措施法》第42条第1款，第42条第6款和第43条第1款，《特别进口措施细则》第37条第1款，以及所有实施措施或相关措施，本身违反了《反倾销协议》第3.1条、第3.2条、第3.4条、第3.5条和第3.7条的规定，因为加方在确定损害时将倾销幅度在微量范围内的出口商的进口也纳入在内。

因此上述措施违反了《反倾销协议》第1条和第18条，以及GATT 1994第6条。

台、澎、金、马单独关税区保留在磋商阶段对上述问题，包括所有修正案、替代方案、展期、实施措施或其他相关措施，采取进一步措施和提出其他诉求的权利。

台、澎、金、马单独关税区期待收到加拿大对此请求的回复，并确定双方均方便的磋商日期和地点。

（钟楹译，黄满盈校）

九、中国——对自加拿大进口的纤维素纸浆采取的反倾销措施：加拿大请求磋商

此文件自2014年10月15日，在加拿大代表团和中国代表团及争端解决机构主席间进行沟通，现根据DSU第4条第4款的规定予以散发。

受我方政府授权，根据DSU第1条和第4条、GATT 1994第22条第1款和《反倾销协议》第17.2条和第17.3款的规定，就中国对自加拿大进口的纤维素纸浆采取的反倾销措施，即包含其附件（"初步裁定"）在内的《商务部公告2013年第75号》（2013年11月6日发布）和包含其附件（"最终裁定"）在内的《商务部公告2014年第18号》，我代表团请求与中华人民共和国（简称"中国"）进行磋商。

这些措施显然与中国在《反倾销协议》和GATT 1994下述条款项下所承担的义务不符：

1.《反倾销协议》第2.2条和第2.2.1.1条，因为中国未能根据出口商或生产商的记录计算成

本，这些记录合理地反映了生产和销售的相关成本；中国也未能根据成本在调查期间受到启动运行的影响这一情况来适当地调整成本。

2.《反倾销协议》第 2.2 条和第 2.2.2 条，因为中国未能根据受到调查的同类产品出口商和生产商在一般贸易过程中的生产和销售的实际数据来确定管理、销售和一般成本的数额。

3.《反倾销协议》第 2.1 条和第 2.4 条，因为中国未能在出口价格和正常价值之间进行公平比较，例如，中国不恰当地扣除出口价格的特定费用，并且在计算出口价格时不排除特定的销售。

4.《反倾销协议》第 3.1 条和第 3.2 条，因为中国对损害的确定并非基于肯定性证据，未能包括对倾销进口产品的数量进行客观审查，也未能就那些进口对同类产品的国内市场价格的影响进行客观审查；中国未能适当地考虑是否已经存在倾销进口产品显著增加的情形，也未能适当考虑与国内同类产品的价格相比是否存在由倾销进口导致的显著价格削减，又或者是否这种进口的影响达到了显著压低价格或显著阻止价格上涨（若非倾销进口，价格已经上涨）的程度。

5.《反倾销协议》第 3.1 条和第 3.4 条，因为中国对损害的确定并非基于肯定性证据，没有包括就倾销进口对同类产品的国内生产商的影响进行客观审查，未能对影响国内产业状况的所有有关经济因素和指标进行适当的评估。

6.《反倾销协议》第 3.1 条和第 3.5 条，因为中国未能通过基于肯定性证据的客观审查来证明倾销进口和对国内产业的损害之间存在因果关系；中国也未能基于肯定性证据对倾销进口产品以外的所有已知因素进行客观审查，这些倾销进口产品以外的所有已知因素同时也损害着国内产业，并且不恰当地把这些因素引起的损害归因于倾销进口产品。

7.《反倾销协议》第 3.1 条和第 4.1 条，因为中国做出损害的决定没有恰当地界定国内产业，并因而未能根据肯定性证据和对有关生产同类产品的国内产业的事实进行客观审查来做出决定。

8.《反倾销协议》第 6.2 条，因为中国未能给予利害关系方充分的机会去维护自身利益。

9.《反倾销协议》第 6.1 条和第 6.8 条以及《反倾销协议》附件 2 的第 3 段，因为中国在决定倾销幅度时，未能给予加拿大出口商或生产商充分的机会去书面提供它们认为与调查有关的所有相关证据，未能考虑可核实的、适当提交的且及时提供的信息的所有信息。

10.《反倾销协议》第 6.8 条以及《反倾销协议》附件 2 的第 7 段，因为中国不恰当地依赖用以确定加拿大纤维素纸浆生产商倾销幅度的事实，而这是因为没有确立单独倾销幅度。

11.《反倾销协议》第 6.9 条，因为在没有确立单独倾销幅度的情况下，中国未能把考虑中的、构成是否对加拿大纤维素纸浆生产商实施最终反倾销措施决定的依据的基本事实通知所有利害关系方。

12.《反倾销协议》第 6.10 条、第 6.10.2 条和第 9.4 条，因为中国没有为最初没被选上但自愿及时提交必要信息的生产商或出口商确定单独倾销幅度，而它们所提交的信息在调查期间被中国列入考虑范围。

13.《反倾销协议》第 8.1 条和第 8.3 条，因为中国不恰当地拒绝出口商在肯定的初步裁决之后提出的价格承诺。

14.《反倾销协议》第 12.2 条和第 12.2.2 条，因为中国未能提供公告，这一公告应列出关于事实问题和法律问题以及得出实施最终（反倾销）措施的理由的所有相关信息。

15.《反倾销协议》第 1 条，由于违反《反倾销协议》的上述条款进而违反 GATT 1994 第 6 条。

因此，中国的措施显然剥夺或减损了加拿大根据上述所引协议所直接或间接获得的利益。

加拿大保留在磋商期间进一步举证事实/采取措施以及提起法律申诉的权利。

加拿大期待收到中国对此请求做出的回复，并确定一个彼此方便的日期进行磋商。

（梁意译，李雪峰校）

十、印度尼西亚——与鸡肉和鸡肉产品进口相关的措施：巴西请求磋商

此文件自 2014 年 10 月 16 日，在巴西代表团和印度尼西亚代表团及争端解决机构主席间进行沟通，现根据 DSU 第 4 条第 4 款的规定予以散发。

受我方政府授权，根据 DSU 第 1 条和第 4 条，GATT 1994 第 22 条，SPS 协议第 11 条，《进口许

可程序协议》第6条，《技术性贸易壁垒协议》（简称“TBT协议”）第14条，《农业协议》第19条，以及《装船前检验协议》第8条，就印度尼西亚对家鸡肉和家鸡产品（下文简称“鸡肉和鸡肉产品”）实施的措施，我代表团请求与印度尼西亚进行磋商。

过去五年中，巴西一直致力于进入印度尼西亚的家禽市场，尤其是鸡肉和鸡肉产品市场。尽管巴西竭尽全力，印度尼西亚仍采取并维持了有效禁止巴西鸡肉和鸡肉产品进入印度尼西亚市场的禁止性规则和程序。

2009年，巴西向印度尼西亚政府提交了其家禽肉的健康认证提案。一年后，又提交了关于火鸡和鸭肉的特别提案。尽管巴西政府立即提供了所有要求的信息，并且主动提供额外信息，迄今为止上述提案均未得到印度尼西亚当局的批准。印度尼西亚未曾采取任何有效措施批准上述文件，也未曾提出一项能够表明因任何科学原因而无法批准的风险评估。相反，印度尼西亚看似以毫不相关的卫生问题作为健康认证得以批准的条件，并且缺乏科学依据。

对健康认证不予批准并非唯一令人担忧的措施。巴西有理由相信，在授予健康认证后，其鸡肉和鸡肉产品仍将面临严重的准入壁垒。

印度尼西亚的卫生条例（第84/2013条例）包含一份可能进口至其境内的动物产品的正面清单，在其进口许可条例（46/2013）中也有所反映。在这两份清单中，对新鲜和冷冻的未切鸡肉的描述与鸭肉相同。据此，根本无法确定鸡肉是否被允许进口。此外，印度尼西亚似乎不允许已切鸡肉的进口，无论新鲜还是冷冻。

巴西同时有理由相信，印度尼西亚的特定措施，尤其与鸡肉和鸡肉产品进口的海运和检疫相关的措施，对巴西出口造成了不必要的限制和差别对待，并且未基于相关的国际标准、指南或建议。与此同时，其他一些法规也可能进一步限制巴西出口鸡肉和鸡肉产品。

巴西鸡肉和鸡肉产品能否被允许进口，在此种复杂而不透明的体系中，仍将受制于多个机构的批准和多重许可的获取。同时，印度尼西亚对鸡肉和鸡肉产品实施了一项非自动的进口许可制度，由于其以不相一致并且不可预测的方式实施并执行该项非自动的许可制度，对进口的准入造成了不适当的负担和限制，因此不正当地限制了贸易。

进口商必须从贸易部获得由贸易部长自由裁量而签发的进口识别号码（API）。同时，必须在财政部下设的海关和关税总署登记。此外，鸡肉和鸡肉产品的进口商必须通过印度尼西亚贸易部获得能够作为“特定产品”进口商的认证资格（即“特定产品的注册进口商”）。这些许可都有非常严格的截止日期和非常短的申请期限，并可能限制进口货物的入境港。

鸡肉和鸡肉产品的进口均要求首先获得农业部的建议，而这些建议对限制前述产品的数量、目的地和/或用途有明显的灵活性。这一要求还有严格的截止日期和很短的申请期限，并且看似未被以透明的方式执行。

此外，印度尼西亚似乎实施了装船前检验要求，这将引起不合理的迟延，并且以歧视的方式施行。

最后，印度尼西亚的法律授权了与价格政策和进口管理相关的措施，可能为管理“战略物资”（鸡肉和鸡肉产品属于这一概念）的内部供应而施加限制。

印度尼西亚施加及执行的影响巴西在WTO项下权利的措施，包括但不限于下列措施，以及条例、补充规定和/或修正案：

• 与贸易相关的印度尼西亚共和国法律，2014年第7号（“贸易法”）；

• 印度尼西亚饲养和动物健康法，2009年第18号；

• 《农业部有关畜体、肉、内脏和/或此种已加工产品进口至印度尼西亚境内的第84/Permentan/PD.410/8/2013条例》，被农业部《第96/Permentan/PD.410/9/2013号条例》和《第110/Permentan/OT.410/9/2014号条例》修改（简称“MoA条例84/2013”）；

• 《贸易部有关动物和动物产品进出口的第46/M-DAG/PER/8/2013号条例》，被贸易部《第57/M-DAG/PER/9/2013号条例》和《第17/M-DAG/PER/3/2014号条例》修改（简称“MoT条例46/2013”）；

• 《贸易部有关特定产品进口的第83/M-DAG/PER/12/2012号条例》，被《贸易部第61/

M-DAG/PER/9/2013 号条例》修改（简称“MoT 条例 83/2012”）；

•《贸易部有关进口商识别码的第 27/M-DAG/PER/5/2012 号条例》，被贸易部《第 59/M-DAG/PER/9/2012 号条例》和《第 84/M-DAG/PER/12/2012 号条例》修改（简称“MoT 条例 27/2012”）；

•《贸易部有关进口一般规定的第 54/M-DAG/PER/10/2009 号条例》（简称“MoT 条例 54/2009”）；

•《财政部有关进口商注册的第 454/KMK.04/2002 号命令》（简称“MoF 命令 454/2002”）。

巴西认为，上述措施与印度尼西亚在下列协定条款项下应承担的义务不符：

（1）SPS 协议第 2.2 条、第 2.3 条、第 3.1 条、第 5 条、第 5.1 条、第 5.2 条、第 5.5 条、第 5.6 条、第 8 条以及附件 C；

（2）TBT 协议第 2.1 条、第 2.2 条、第 2.4 条、第 5.1 条和第 5.2 条；

（3）《农业协议》第 4.2. 条和第 14 条；

（4）《进口许可程序协议》第 1.3 条、第 3.2 条和第 3.3 条；

（5）《装船前检验协议》第 2.1 条和第 2.15 条；

（6）GATT 1994 第 3.4 条、第 10.3 条和第 11.1 条。

巴西保留在磋商过程中提出后续事实和法律主张的权利。特别是，巴西注意到印度尼西亚议会于 2014 年 10 月 14 日批准了 2009 年第 18 号饲养和动物健康法的修正案，目前尚未开始实施。巴西特别保留在磋商和争议事项相关的后续程序中提出上述立法变化的权利。

我们期待贵方对此请求做出的回复，并确定一个彼此方便的日期进行磋商。

（马兰译，李雪峰校）

十一、俄罗斯——对某些农产品和制造成品之关税待遇：欧盟请求磋商

此文件自 2014 年 10 月 31 日，在欧盟代表团和争端解决机构主席间进行沟通，现根据 DSU 第 4 条第 4 款的规定予以散发。

受我方政府授权，根据 DSU 第 1 条和第 4 条，GATT 1994 第 22 条，以及《关于实施 1994 年关税与贸易总协定第 7 条的协议》(《海关估价协议》）第 19 条，就俄罗斯对某些农产品和制成品给予的关税待遇，我代表团请求与俄罗斯进行磋商。这些措施对涉案产品自欧盟向俄罗斯之出口产生负面影响。

俄罗斯违反 GATT 1994 附表中承诺和减让表之义务，对多种货物征收进口税。这特别体现在俄罗斯以数种不同方式征收超过约束税率之税款。

首先，对于包括纸和纸板的某些产品，俄罗斯依据下文所列之法律文件所征收的从价税率超过从价约束税率。举例来说，俄方在五个税目（4810 22 900 0，4810 29 300 0，4810 92 300 0，4810 13 800 9 和 4810 19 900 0）下设置了 15%或 10%的税率，这明显超出这些税目 5%的约束税率。

其次，对于包括棕榈油及其分提产品、冰箱及组合冰箱——冷冻箱在内的某些其他产品，这些法律文件规定了与减让表中规定不相一致的税种和税的结构。涉案的按数量征收的关税之结构和安排，导致这些货物在海关估价低于某一水平时被征收高于减让表规定之税款。举例来说，这些措施与下列税目相关：1511 90 190 2，1511 90 990 2（棕榈油）以及 8418108001，8418102001，8418211000（冰箱及组合冰箱——冷冻箱）。

最后，对于某些原产自欧盟的货物，俄罗斯政府未能依据进口商品的真实价值进行海关估价。

俄罗斯实施的措施特别体现在下列法律文件之中：

通过欧亚经济委员会董事局于 2012 年 7 月 16 日发布的第 54 号决定——《关于对白俄罗斯共和国、哈萨克斯坦共和国和俄罗斯关税同盟共同关税条例》（2012 年 8 月 23 日生效）批准的《白俄罗斯共和国、哈萨克斯坦共和国和俄罗斯关税同盟的共同关税》以及下列修订案：

•欧亚经济委员会董事局于 2014 年 1 月 29 日发布的第 9 号决定——《关于确定某些纸和纸板在关税同盟共同关税中的税率的决定》；

•欧亚经济委员会董事局于 2014 年 5 月 26 日发布的第 77 号决定，对关税同盟对外经济活动单项商品关税税则分类表进行了修订，同时对某些货物在关税同盟下的单一关税做出了与俄罗斯对

WTO的减让承诺相一致的修改，另外该决定还批准了欧亚经济委员会理事会的决定草案；

• 欧亚经济委员会董事局于2014年7月16日发布的第52号决定——《关于依据俄罗斯对WTO承担之义务确定某些货物在关税同盟共同关税中之税率的决定》。

对于上述的每一项措施，本请求同样包含对其做出的任何修订、替代、延长、实施措施，或由欧亚经济委员会下属机构和（或）俄罗斯政府立法机关或行政部门采取的其他相关措施。

这些措施违反了俄罗斯在引述协议下的义务，特别是：

• GATT 1994第2条第1款（a）和（b）项；

• GATT 1994第7条；

• 《海关估价协议》第1条到第7条以及附录1。

俄罗斯的措施显然剥夺或减损了欧盟依据引述协议所能直接或间接获得的利益。

欧盟保留在磋商阶段对上述问题依据引述协议的其他条款采取进一步措施和提出其他诉求的权利。

欧盟期待俄方依正当程序对此磋商请求做出回复。欧盟愿与俄方商定一个彼此可以接受的日期进行磋商。

（钟楹译，孙靓莹校）

十二、欧盟——对自巴基斯坦进口的聚对苯二甲酸乙二醇酯采取的反补贴措施：巴基斯坦请求磋商

此文件于2014年11月5日送达WTO，在巴基斯坦代表团和欧盟代表团及争端解决机构主席间进行沟通，现根据DSU第4条第4款的规定予以散发。

依据DSU第4条，SCM协议第30条以及GATT 1994第23条第1款，就欧盟对自巴基斯坦进口的某些聚对苯二甲酸乙二醇酯采取的临时和最终反补贴措施，以及为采取这些措施所进行的调查的某些方面，巴基斯坦代表团请求与欧盟代表团进行磋商。

巴基斯坦特别关注涉案措施的下述几个方面：

1. 欧盟认定巴基斯坦税法中的最终税制构成基于出口表现的可采取反补贴措施的补贴。巴方认为欧盟的观点与SCM协议第1条、第3条和第19条，以及GATT 1994第6条不符。特别是：

（1）欧盟认定巴基斯坦最终税制构成了政府本应征收收入的豁免，这违反了SCM协议中第1.1（a）（1）（ii）条和第3.1（a）条以及GATT 1994第6条之规定。欧盟将最终税制中的课税待遇假定为普通税制下的课税待遇，并错误地把两种税制下纳税义务的所有不同都归结为政府本应征收收入的豁免；以及

（2）欧盟拒绝用由巴基斯坦出口商缴纳的出口发展费抵消其主张的出口补贴，这违反了SCM协议第1.1（a）（1）（ii）条，第3.1（a）条和第19.3条，以及GATT 1994第6条之规定。

2. 欧盟将制造业债券计划视为基于出口表现的可采取反补贴措施的补贴。该认定与SCM协议第1条、第3条与附件Ⅰ、附件Ⅱ和附件Ⅲ，以及GATT 1994第6条不符。特别是：

（1）欧盟认定制造业债券计划是对进口费用的豁免或退税，且数额超出了对出口产品生产所用进口成分所征收的费用，这违反了GATT 1994第6条，SCM协议第1.1（a）（1）（i）条、第1.1（a）（1）（ii）条，以及第3.1（a）条本身以及其与附件Ⅰ（h）、附件Ⅰ（i）、附件Ⅱ（I）（2）、附件Ⅱ（Ⅱ）（1）、附件Ⅱ（Ⅱ）（2）、附件Ⅲ（Ⅱ）（2）和附件Ⅲ（Ⅱ）（3）的联合规定；以及

（2）欧盟认定制造业债券计划中的整个退税安排（而非退税安排中超出部分），构成出口补贴。这违反了GATT 1994第6条，SCM协议第1.1（a）（1）（i）条、第1.1（a）（1）（ii）条，以及第3.1（a）条本身以及其与附件Ⅰ（h）、附件Ⅰ（i）、附件Ⅱ（Ⅰ）（2）、附件Ⅱ（Ⅱ）（2）、附件Ⅲ（Ⅰ）和附件Ⅲ（Ⅱ）（3）的联合规定。

3. 欧盟将出口导向长期融资项目视为基于出口表现的可采取反补贴措施的补贴，并在计算补贴幅度时将其包含在内。该认定与SCM协议第1条、第3条、第14条和第19条，以及GATT 1994第6条不符。特别是：

（1）欧盟未能对其在本案中适用相关措施做出合理解释，并且在调查期间计算补贴数额时选择了错误的利率基准。这违反了SCM协议第1.1（a）（1）（i）条、第1.1（a）（1）（iv）条、第3.1（a）条、第14（b）条和第19.3条，以及GATT 1994

第 6 条；以及

（2）欧盟在分配补贴数额时违反了 SCM 协议第 1.1（b）条、第 3.1（a）条、第 14（b）条和第 19.3 条，以及 GATT 1994 第 6 条。

4. 欧盟将有关设施、机械和装备进口的制造业债券项目视为基于出口表现的可采取反补贴措施的补贴，并在计算补贴幅度时将其包含在内。该认定与 SCM 协议第 1 条、第 3 条、第 14 条和第 19 条，以及 GATT 1994 第 6 条不符。特别是：

（1）欧盟未能对其在本案中适用相关措施做出合理解释，并且在调查期间计算补贴数额时选择了错误的利率基准。这违反了 SCM 协议第 1.1（a）（1）（i）条、第 1.1（a）（1）（iv）条、第 3.1（a）条、第 14（b）条和第 19.3 条，以及 GATT 1994 第 6 条。

（2）欧盟在分配补贴数额时违反了 SCM 协议第 1.1（b）条、第 3.1（a）条、第 14（b）条和第 19.3 条，以及 GATT 1994 第 6 条。

5. 欧盟认定其国内产业受到的实质性损害与其指控的受补贴进口之间存在因果关系。欧盟这一认定未能明确已知因素的损害作用，比如从他处的进口、来自未被包含在国内产业中的国内生产者的竞争、经济下滑以及低油价等，都错误地未被纳入对其宣称的受补贴进口的考虑中，这违反了 SCM 第 15.5 条。

6. 欧盟未能向巴基斯坦出口商提供欧盟对其进行核实访问的结果，也未能向所有利益关联方提供其审议的重要事实，这违反了 SCM 协议第 12.6 条和第 12.8 条。同时，在核实访问期间，欧盟未能对问题做出彻底和客观的评估，包括未能对事实做出合理的认定，这违反了 SCM 协议第 12.6 条与附件 VI（1）—（8）。

7. 欧盟未能对其基于最终税制、制造业债券计划、出口导向长期融资项目和有关设施、机械和装备进口的制造业债券项目所得出的存在补贴情况的判定、解释和结论提供足够详细的充分信息，这违反了 SCM 协议第 22.3 条和第 22.4 条。

巴基斯坦还认为上述欧盟的认定可能违反了 SCM 协议第 10 条、第 19.1 条和第 32 条，以及上述的其他条款。

除上文所列的法律文件外，本磋商请求还包括就所有的修订、展期、相关的文件或实践、所有的审查程序的结果，以及依据（包括欧洲法院程序在内的）所有欧盟法律规定的程序对原措施进行的任何修改，进行磋商。巴基斯坦保留在磋商过程中增加其他法律诉求或提出其他事项的权利。

巴基斯坦期待收到欧盟方面对本请求的回复。巴方愿在双方同意的时间和地点进行磋商。

（钟楹译，邓晓虹校）

十三、美国——对大型民用航空器采取的有条件税收优惠：欧盟请求磋商

此文件自 2014 年 12 月 19 日，在欧盟代表团和美国代表团及争端解决机构主席间进行沟通，现根据 DSU 第 4 条第 4 款的规定予以散发。

受我方政府授权，根据 SCM 协议第 4.1 条和第 30 条，GATT 1994 第 23 条第 1 款，以及 DSU 第 4 条，就华盛顿州对大型民用航空器的发展、制造和销售采取的有条件税收优惠，我代表团请求与美国进行磋商。

（一）背景

为吸引波音公司在该州生产其新 777 型大型民用航空器，华盛顿在 2013 年 11 月修改并大幅度提高其航空与航天工业税收优惠政策，为波音公司提供了数十亿美元额外补贴。此修订同时明确将全部或部分税收优惠的存续建立于两个基础之上：（1）波音公司将新型或其他型号的商用航空器的机翼生产以及最后组装程序选址在华盛顿州；（2）波音公司将该型号的商用航空器的所有机翼组装和最后组装生产排他性地保留在华盛顿州。

（二）涉案措施

本请求所涉措施是华盛顿州通过第 5952 号参议院替代议案（2013 年第 3 次法律特别会议第 2 号议案）规定的对民用航空器提供的税收优惠政策。具体而言，这些税收优惠措施包含在华盛顿州修订法典（RCW）以下章节中：82.04.260（11）（对商用飞机生产与销售适用之特惠性营业及开业许可税）；82.04.4463（对商用飞机生产设施给予财产税以及租赁消费税减免）；82.04.4461（对航空与航天新产品给予税收减免）；82.08.975（对电脑硬件、软件及外围设备给予销售税豁免）；82.08.980（对建筑服务和材料给予税收豁免）；82.29A.137（租赁消费税的豁免）以及 84.36.655（租赁财产税的豁免）。此外，由于税收减免措施是

否适用取决于第 5952 号参议院替代议案第 2 节、第 5 节及第 6 节［被包含在 RCW 82.32.850 和 82.04.260（11）（e）（ii）中］所规定的条件是否得到满足，因此本请求也包含这些条款。

除上述措施外，本请求还包括对这些措施的修订、补充、展期和替代措施、更新措施、相关措施或落实措施。

（三）诉求的法律依据

这些措施构成了 SCM 协议第 1 条和第 2 条下的专向性补贴。具体而言，这些措施构成了 SCM 协议第 1.1（a）（1）（ii）条下“政府本应征收收入的豁免”，以及第 1.1（b）条下的“给予的某种利益”。基于下文阐述的理由，这些补贴措施具有 SCM 协议第 2.3 条下的专向性。

欧盟注意到这数十亿美元的补贴措施建立于使用在华盛顿州生产的航空器零部件的基础之上。具体而言，第 5952 号参议院替代议案第 2 节、第 5 节及第 6 节［被包含在 RCW 82.32.850 和 82.04.260（11）（e）（ii）中］的规定，构成 SCM 协议下第 3.1（b）条下“将进口替代作为唯一或多种条件之一而提供的补贴”。因此，欧盟认为这些措施构成了 SCM 协议第 3.1（b）条和第 3.2 条下所禁止的“禁止性补贴”。

（四）有关可得到证据的说明

依据 SCM 协议第 4.2 条的规定，一份对所涉及的补贴的存在和性质做出说明的可得到的证据将附于本请求最后部分。

欧盟期待美方对此磋商请求做出回复，并愿与美方商定一个彼此可以接受的日期进行磋商。依据 SCM 协议第 4.12 条以及 DSU 第 4.3 条的规定，收到磋商请求的成员国须在收到该请求 5 天之内做出回复。出于对年末假期的考虑，欧盟愿意将美方回复的最后期限延长至 2015 年 1 月 7 日。

附录：有关可得到证据之说明

依据 SCM 协议第 4.2 条之规定，欧盟现附上一份可得到证据，以说明所涉及的补贴的存在和性质。欧盟保留对此说明在未来根据需要进行增补或修改的权利。

• 第 5952 号参议院替代议案（2013 年第 3 次法律特别会议第 2 号议案）（华盛顿州）

• 最终法案报告，第 5952 号参议院替代议案最终印件

• 州税局关于第 5952 号参议院议案（航空航天税收优惠）的财税注释

• 华盛顿州立法机构法案信息，编号：SB 5952-2013-14，访问地址：http://apps.leg.wa.gov/billinfo/summary.aspx?bill=5952

• 华盛顿州税局局长卡洛 G. 亨特于 2014 年 7 月 10 日发给华盛顿州法典改编者凯尔·泰森的“有关 SSB 5952 应急措施之照会”

• 华盛顿州修订法典（2014）：82.04.260（11）；82.04.4461；82.04.4463；82.08.975；82.08.980；82.12.975；82.12.980；82.29A.137；82.32.850；84.36.655

• 2013 年 11 月 17 日波音新闻，“波音 777X 项目以创纪录订单及购买承诺开局”，访问地址：http://www.ustr.gov/sites/default/files/DS353.US_.Sub1_.Non_.BCI_.Fin_.Public.pdf

• 2013 年 6 月 27 日，美国关于美国——大型民用航空器案第一次书面意见（非商业机密信息版）

• 2013 年 11 月 9 日州长杰伊·英思利新闻，“立法机构批准 777X 税收优惠一揽子计划之关键部分”

• 2014 年 1 月 4 日波音新闻，“波音对 IAM751 合同展期投票声明”

• 2014 年 2 月 18 日波音新闻，“波音将新 777X 复合机翼中心设在华盛顿州埃弗里特”

（钟楹译，邓晓虹校）

十四、美国——对自韩国进口的石油工业用管材采取的反倾销措施：韩国请求磋商

此文件自 2014 年 12 月 22 日，在韩国代表团和美国代表团及争端解决机构主席间进行沟通，现根据 DSU 第 4 条第 4 款的规定予以散发。

受我方政府授权，根据 DSU 第 4 条，GATT 1994 第 22 条，以及《反倾销协议》第 17 条，就下述美国所采取的反倾销措施，我代表团谨代表韩国政府请求与美国进行磋商。

（一）美国对自韩国进口的石油工业用管材适用的反倾销措施，在适用层面上：

韩国希望与美方就其对自韩国进口的石油工业用管材适用的下列反倾销措施（Inv. No. A-580-870）进行磋商：

1.《关于自韩国进口的石油工业用管材以低于公平价值销售的最终决定：对低于公平价值销售的最终决定和对关键事实的否定性最终决定》，编号为 79 Fed. Reg. 41983，2014 年 7 月 18 日。

2.《关于自韩国进口的石油工业用管材低于公平价值之调查的最终肯定性决定之争议和决定备忘录》，2014 年 7 月 10 日，访问地址：http：//enforcement. trade. gov/frn/summary/korea-south/2014-16874-1. pdf。

3.《对自印度、韩国、中国台北、土耳其及越南进口的石油工业用管材征收反倾销税的指令》，编号为 9 Fed. Reg. 53691，2014 年 9 月 10 日。

4. 在名称包含自韩国进口的石油工业用管材之程序中所采纳的所有相关措施，包括调查本身、行政复查、新发货商审查、情势变更审查、日落审查以及程序中的其他环节。

韩国认为这些措施违反了美国在 GATT 1994 和《反倾销协议》下列条款中所承担的义务，这些条款包括但不仅限于：

1.《反倾销协议》第 2.2.2 条，因为美国商务部在计算韩国应诉企业的推算价值利润时：

a. 错误地理解并使用“同一大类产品”一词，拒绝在计算推算价值利润的调查中利用强制和自愿应诉企业提交的真实利润数据；

b. 不恰当地依据与一个并不在韩国生产和销售石油工业用管材的生产商相关的信息计算推算价值利润；以及

c. 未能确保其计算的利润率不超过其他出口商或生产者在原产国国内市场销售同一大类产品通常所得的利润。

2.《反倾销协议》第 2.2 条，因为比照石油工业用管材在全球范围内，包括美国本土的利润幅度，美国商务部对韩国应诉企业推算价值利润的计算并不合理；

3.《反倾销协议》第 2.4 条，因为美国商务部未能在作为推算价值来源的生产者所生产的产品与由应诉企业生产的产品中设定合理空间，导致其无法在出口价格和正常价值间做公平比较。

4.《反倾销协议》第 2.2.2 条，因为美国商务部并没有使用应诉企业在母国市场销售的真实数据来确定用于计算正常价值的利润率。

5.《反倾销协议》第 2.2.2 条，因为美国商务部并没有使用应诉企业在第三国市场销售的真实数据来确定用于计算正常价值的利润率。

6.《反倾销协议》第 2.2 条，就计算正常价值而言，美国商务部忽视了应诉企业向第三国销售相似产品的情况。

7.《反倾销协议》第 2.3 条，因为美国商务部不恰当地认定韩国应诉企业 NEXTEEL 与一个非关联的供货商和非关联的客户存在关联关系。美国商务部做出这一认定的部分原因是该供货商与该客户存在关联关系。依据该错误的认定，美国商务部认为 NEXTEEL 向客户出口的价格不可靠。

《反倾销协议》第 2.2.1.1 条，因为美国商务部在错误地认为 NEXTEEL 与供货商存在关联关系之基础上，依据非关联供货商的记录计算 NEXTEEL 的成本。

8.《反倾销协议》第 6.2 条、第 6.4 条和第 6.9 条，因为美国商务部并没有告知利害关系方其同意在法定限期期满后仍接受申请者提交的推算价值利润数据的决定，同时美国商务部也没有将其接收的、来自美国政府其他部门和美国行业代表处的通讯告知利害关系方。此外，美国商务部在发布其最终决定前并没有向应诉企业提供充分的机会以便其对新信息做出回应。

9.《反倾销协议》第 6.1 条，包括第 6.10.1 条和第 6.10.2 条，因为美国商务部不合理地仅选择 2 家强制性应诉企业，且没有由三家未被选中的企业所提交的自愿答复。举例而言，SeAH 是唯一一家在美国进行深加工和创造额外附加价值的韩国出口公司，尽管 SeAH 拥有同其他韩国石油工业用管材生产商完全不同的销售渠道（不仅能出售给分销商，还可以直接向最终用户出售产品），但其依然未被选中为自愿应诉企业。

10.《反倾销协议》第 12.2.2 条，因为美国商务部的最终决定以及争议和决定备忘录中都没有对应诉企业提出的问题和主张做出充分的解释。这些问题包括美国商务部计算推算价值理论问题，以及包括 NEXTEEL 与其顾客存在关联关系、美国商务部接受不适时的信息以及美国商务部对关联方投入的分析在内的其他问题和主张。

11. GATT 1994 第 1 条，因为与同被调查的来自其他国家的相似产品相比，韩国石油工业用管材在美国商务部在发布初裁决定后的行动受到了更不利的待遇。

12. GATT 1994第10.3条，因为美国商务部并没有以统一、公平和合理的方式执行其规定，这体现在美国商务部允许申请者在提交新事实信息的法定期限届满后仍提交新的推测价值利润数据。

（二）美国对自韩国进口的石油工业用管材适用的反倾销措施，在措施本身的层面上：

韩国同时希望与美国就其所采用的方法进行磋商，即在应诉企业的国内市场销售无法用于计算正常价值的情况下，若应诉企业向第三国市场的出口低于应诉企业向美国出售的百分之五，则美国商务部擅自忽视该应诉企业向第三国市场的出口，包括但不限于上述针对来自韩国的石油工业用管材所采取的反倾销程序。这些方法由以下措施所确立：

1.《1930年海关法》，包括第771（35）（A）条、第777A（c）条和第777A（d）条［19 U.S.C. §§1677（35）（A）和1677f-1（c）］；

2.《乌拉圭回合协议法》下的《行政行为说明》，编号为H.R. Doc. No. 103-316，vol. I；

3. 美国商务部实施细则，19 C.F.R. Part 351，包括第351.404（b）（1）段和第351.404（b）（2）段；

4.《美国商务部进口管理反倾销说明》，包括所有修订版本以及其援引的计算机程序；

5. 在反倾销调查、行政复议和其他反倾销程序的其他环节中，为批准和实施所谓“可行性测试”所采取的所有其他相关和后续措施。

美国商务部以未能达到“可行性测试”百分之五的标准为由忽视应诉企业向第三国的销售情况，韩国认为这一方法违反了《反倾销协议》第2.2条，因为该方法与考察相似产品向第三国市场销售的价格是否具有代表性这一问题并不相关。

由于美国所采取的涉案措施违反了上述《反倾销协议》和GATT 1994的规定，这些措施因此也违反了《反倾销协议》第1条与GATT 1994第6条。与此同时，由于美国尚未采取行动以保证其法律、法规和行政程序与GATT 1994和《反倾销协议》的规定相符，因此这些措施也违反了《马拉喀什协定》第16.4条和《反倾销协议》第18.4条。

此外，美国的措施显然剥夺或减损了韩国依据引述的协议所能直接或间接获得的利益。

韩国保留在磋商过程中以及建立专家组的请求中提出其他事实和法律争议问题的权利。

韩国期待美方依正当程序，以与DSU第4.3条规定相一致的方式对此磋商请求做出回复，并安排一个彼此可以接受的日期和地点举行磋商。

（钟楹译，孙靓莹校）

附录 1：1995—2014 年争端解决机构受理的案件①

第 一 部 分
请求磋商；成立专家组；达成解决方案

序号	案件	请求磋商	收到磋商请求（日-月-年）	加入磋商请求	请求成立专家组（日-月-年）	专家组成立（日-月-年）	双边达成解决方案（日-月-年）
1	马来西亚—聚乙烯和聚丙烯进口禁令	新加坡 WT/DS1/1	10-01-1995		17-03-1995 新加坡 WT/DS1/2 WT/DSB/M/6 （请求撤回）		
2	美国—精炼汽油及传统汽油标准	委内瑞拉 WT/DS2/1	24-01-1995		27-03-1995 委内瑞拉 WT/DS2/2	10-04-1995 WT/DSB/M/3	
3	韩国—对于农业产品检测及检验措施	美国 WT/DS3/1	04-04-1995	日本 WT/DS3/2			
4	美国—精炼汽油及传统汽油标准	巴西 WT/DS4/1	10-04-1995		22-05-1995 巴西 WT/DS4/2	31-05-1995 WT/DSB/M/5	
5	韩国—韩国产品保质期措施	美国 WT/DS5/1	03-05-1995	加拿大 WT/DS5/2 日本 WT/DS5/4			31-07-1995 WT/DS5/5 和 Corr. 1 24-11-1995 Add. 1 22-04-1996 Add. 1/Rev. 1 22-04-1996 Add. 2 22-04-1996 Add. 3 19-07-1996 Add. 4 20-09-1996 Add. 5
6	美国—在 1974 年贸易法第 301 及 304 节中来自日本汽车征收进口税	日本 WT/DS6/1	17-05-1995	欧共体 WT/DS6/2 澳大利亚 WT/DS6/3			19-07-1995 WT/DSB/M/6

① 此统计截至 2014 年 10 月 31 日。案件可分为五个部分：第一部分包括从最初提出磋商请求到成立专家组，再到争议各方形成双方满意的解决方法的案件；第二部分包括从成立专家组到通过专家组报告，再到提起上诉和通过上诉机构报告的案件；第三部分包括从通过专家组/上诉机构报告到执行争端解决机构建议和裁决的案件；第四、五部分分别包括援引《关于争端解决规则与程序的谅解》第 21.5 条和第 22 条再次提请申诉的案件。

续 表

序号	案件	请求磋商	收到磋商请求（日-月-年）	加入磋商请求	请求成立专家组（日-月-年）	专家组成立（日-月-年）	双边达成解决方案（日-月-年）
7	欧共体—扇贝的贸易描述	加拿大 WT/DS7/1	19-05-1995	智利 WT/DS7/2 爱尔兰 WT/DS7/3 日本 WT/DS7/4 秘鲁 WT/DS7/5	10-07-1995 加拿大 WT/DS7/7 和 Corr. 1	19-07-1995 WT/DSB/M/6	19-07-1996 WT/DS7/12
8	日本—对酒精饮料征税	欧共体 WT/DS8/1	21-06-1995	美国 WT/DS8/2 加拿大 WT/DS8/3	15-09-1995 欧共体 WT/DS8/5	27-09-1995 WT/DSB/M/7	
9	欧共体—谷类进口税	加拿大 WT/DS9/1	30-06-1995		15-09-1995 加拿大 WT/DS9/2	11-10-1995 WT/DSB/M/8	
10	日本—对酒精饮料征税	加拿大 WT/DS10/1	07-07-1995	美国 WT/DS10/2 欧共体 WT/DS10/3	15-09-1995 加拿大 WT/DS10/5	27-09-1995 WT/DSB/M/7	
11	日本—对酒精饮料征税	美国 WT/DS11/1	07-07-1995		15-09-1995 美国 WT/DS11/2 和 Corr. 1	27-09-1995 WT/DSB/M/7	
12	欧共体—扇贝的贸易描述	秘鲁 WT/DS12/1	18-07-1995	加拿大 WT/DS12/3 智利 WT/DS12/2 和 Rev. 1 日本 WT/DS12/5	15-09-1995 秘鲁 WT/DS12/6 附录 22-09-1995 秘鲁 WT/DS12/7	11-10-1995 WT/DSB/M/8	19-07-1996 WT/DS12/12
13	欧共体—对谷物征收进口税	美国 WT/DS13/1	19-07-1995		29-09-1995 美国 WT/DS13/2 22-11-1996 WT/DS13/2/Add. 1 13-02-1997 WT/DS13/5 27-03-1997 WT/DS13/6		02-05-1997 WTDS13/8（请求撤回）

续 表

序号	案件	请求磋商	收到磋商请求（日-月-年）	加入磋商请求	请求成立专家组（日-月-年）	专家组成立（日-月-年）	双边达成解决方案（日-月-年）
14	欧共体—扇贝的贸易描述	智利 WT/DS14/1	24-07-1995	加拿大 WT/DS14/2 秘鲁 WT/DS14/3 日本 WT/DS14/4	15-09-1995 智利 WT/DS14/5 附录 27-09-1995 智利 WT/DS14/6 附录	11-10-1995 WT/DSB/M/8	19-07-1996 WT/DS14/11
15	日本—影响电信设备购买措施	欧共体 WT/DS15/1	18-08-1995	美国 WT/DS15/2			
16	欧共体—对于香蕉进口、销售及分销的规定	危地马拉 洪都拉斯 墨西哥 美国 WT/DS16/1	28-09-1995	圣卢西亚 WT/DS16/2 哥伦比亚 WT/DS16/3 多米尼加 WT/DS16/4 委内瑞拉 WT/DS16/5 尼加拉瓜 WT/DS16/6 哥斯达黎加 WT/DS16/7			08 11 2012 WT/DS16/8
17	欧共体—稻米进口征税	泰国 WT/DS17/1	05-10-1995				
18	澳大利亚—影响鲑鱼进口措施	加拿大 WT/DS18/1	05-10-1995		10-03-1997 WT/DS18/2	10-04-1997 WT/DSB/M/31	
19	波兰—汽车进口管理体制	印度 WT/DS19/1	28-09-1995				11-09-1996 WT/DS19/2
20	韩国—罐装水措施	加拿大 WT/DS20/1	08-11-1995	美国 WT/DS20/2 欧共体 WT/DS20/4			24-04-1996 WT/DS20/6
21	澳大利亚—影响鲑鱼进口措施	美国 WT/DS21/1	20-11-1995	加拿大 WT/DS21/2	11-05-1999 美国 WT/DS21/4	16-06-1999 WT/DSB/M/64	27-10-2000 WT/DS21/10
22	巴西—影响可可粉措施	菲律宾 WT/DS22/1	30-11-1995		08-02-1996 菲律宾 WT/DS22/5	05-03-1996 WT/DSB/M/12	
23	委内瑞拉—对工业用管材的反倾销调查	墨西哥 WT/DS23/1	05-12-1995				26-05-1997 WT/DS23/3 （调查终止）
24	美国—对棉质及人造纤维质内衣进口的限制	哥斯达黎加 WT/DS24/1	22-12-1995		27-02-1996 哥斯达黎加 WT/DS24/2	05-03-1996 WT/DSB/M/12	

续 表

序号	案件	请求磋商	收到磋商请求（日-月-年）	加入磋商请求	请求成立专家组（日-月-年）	专家组成立（日-月-年）	双边达成解决方案（日-月-年）
25	欧共体—乌拉圭回合稻米协议实施	乌拉圭 WT/DS25/1	14-12-1995				
26	欧共体—与肉及肉类制品相关措施（荷尔蒙）	美国 WT/DS26/1	26-01-1996	新西兰 WT/DS26/2 澳大利亚 WT/DS26/3 加拿大 WT/DS26/4	25-04-1996 美国 WT/DS26/6	20-05-1996 WT/DSB/M/17	
27	欧共体—对于香蕉进口、销售及分销的规定	厄瓜多尔 危地马拉 洪都拉斯 墨西哥 美国 WT/DS27/1	05-02-1996	多米尼加 WT/DS27/2 圣卢西亚 WT/DS27/3 尼加拉瓜 WT/DS27/4 牙买加 WT/DS/27/5	12-04-1996 厄瓜多尔 危地马拉 洪都拉斯 墨西哥 美国 WT/DS27/6	08-05-1996 WT/DSB/M/16	08-11-2012 WT/DS27/98
28	日本—关于音像制品措施	美国 WT/DS28/1	09-02-1996	欧共体 WT/DS28/2			24-01-1997 WT/DS28/4
29	土耳其—对于纺织品和服装限制措施	中国香港 WT/DS29/1	12-02-1996	欧共体 WT/DS29/2 马来西亚 菲律宾 泰国 WT/DS29/3 秘鲁 WT/DS29/4 印度 WT/DS29/5 巴西 WT/DS29/7 加拿大 WT/DS29/8			
30	巴西—对来自斯里兰卡的可可粉和可可奶进口征收补贴税	斯里兰卡 WT/DS30/1	23-02-1996				
31	加拿大—关于杂志的特定措施	美国 WT/DS31/1	11-03-1996		24-05-1996 美国 WT/DS31/2	19-06-1996 WT/DSB/M/19	
32	美国—影响女士及女童羊毛外套进口措施				15-03-1996 印度 WT/DS32/1	17-04-1996 WT/DSB/M/14	30-04-1996 WT/DS32/2 （根据争端解决机构1996年4月17日决定终止进一步行动）

续 表

序号	案件	请求磋商	收到磋商请求（日-月-年）	加入磋商请求	请求成立专家组（日-月-年）	专家组成立（日-月-年）	双边达成解决方案（日-月-年）
33	美国—影响羊毛衬衫及女上衣进口的措施				15-03-1996 印度 WT/DS33/1 和 Corr. 1	17-04-1996 WT/DSB/M/14	
34	土耳其—对于纺织品及服装进口的限制	印度 WT/DS34/1	21-03-1996		02-02-1998 WT/DS34/2	13-03-1998 WT/DSB/M/43	06-07-2001 WT/DS34/14
35	匈牙利—对于农产品出口补贴	阿根廷 澳大利亚 加拿大 新西兰 泰国 美国 WT/DS35/1	27-03-1996	日本 WT/DS35/2	10-01-1997 澳大利亚 WT/DS35/4 10-01-1997 新西兰 WT/DS/35/5 10-01-1997 美国 WT/DS35/6 10-01-1997 阿根廷 WT/DS35/7	25-02-1997 WT/DSB/M/29	30-07-1997 WT/DSB/M/36
36	巴基斯坦—制药及农业化学产品的专利保护	美国 WT/DS36/1	30-04-1996	欧共体 WT/DS36/2	04-07-1996 美国 WT/DS36/3		07-03-1997 WT/DS36/4
37	葡萄牙—工业产权法案专利权保护	美国 WT/DS37/1	30-04-1996				15-10-1996 WT/DS37/2 和 Corr. 1
38	美国—古巴自由民主团结法	欧共体 WT/DS38/1	03-05-1996		08-10-1996 欧共体 WT/DS38/2 14-10-1996 Corr. 1	20-11-1996 WT/DSB/M/26 根据 DSU 第 12.12 条 1998 年 4 月 22 日 专家组解散	
39	美国—对来自欧共体的产品提高关税	欧共体 WT/DS39/1	18-04-1996		24-06-1996 欧共体 WT/DS39/2		
40	韩国—电信采购部门的法律、法规及实践	欧共体 WT/DS40/1	09-05-1996				29-10-1997 WT/DS40/2
41	韩国—关于农产品检验措施	美国 WT/DS41/1	24-05-1996				
42	日本—音像制品相关措施	欧共体 WT/DS42/1	28-05-1996	美国 WT/DS42/2			7-11-1997 WT/DS42/4
43	土耳其—对外国电影收入征税	美国 WT/DS43/1	12-06-1996		10-01-1997 美国 WT/DS43/2	25-02-1997 WT/DSB/M/29	24-07-1997 WT/DS43/3

续 表

序号	案件	请求磋商	收到磋商请求（日-月-年）	加入磋商请求	请求成立专家组（日-月-年）	专家组成立（日-月-年）	双边达成解决方案（日-月-年）
44	日本—影响消费者照相软片及相纸的措施	美国 WT/DS44/1	13-06-1996		20-09-1996 美国 WT/DS44/2	16-10-1996 WT/DSB/M/24	
45	日本—影响分销服务的措施	美国 WT/DS45/1 和 Add. 1	13-06-1996				
46	巴西—航空器出口融资计划	加拿大 WT/DS46/1	19-06-1996		17-09-1996 加拿大 WT/DS46/2 04-10-1996 WT/DS46/4 13-07-1998 WT/DS46/5	23-07-1998 WT/DSB/M/47	
47	土耳其—对于纺织品及服装进口的限制	泰国 WT/DS47/1	20-06-1996				
48	欧共体—影响家畜及肉类措施（荷尔蒙）	加拿大 WT/DS48/1	28-06-1996	澳大利亚 WT/DS48/2 美国 WT/DS48/3 新西兰 WT/DS48/4	17-09-1996 加拿大 WT/DS48/5	16-10-1996 WT/DSB/M/24	
49	美国—对来自墨西哥的新鲜或冷藏西红柿的反倾销调查	墨西哥 WT/DS49/1	01-07-1996				
50	印度—对于药物及农业化学产品专利权保护	美国 WT/DS50/1 美国 WT/DS50/11	02-07-1996	欧共体 WT/DS50/2 欧共体 WT/DS50/12	08-11-1996 美国 WT/DS50/4	20-11-1996 WT/DSB/M/26	
51	巴西—特定汽车投资措施	日本 WT/DS51/1	30-07-1996	韩国 WT/DS51/2 欧共体 WT/DS51/3 美国 WT/DS51/4 加拿大 WT/DS51/6			
52	巴西—影响汽车部门贸易及投资措施	美国 WT/DS52/1	09-08-1996	加拿大 WT/DS52/2 日本 WT/DS52/3 韩国 WT/DS52/4 欧共体 WT/DS52/5			
53	墨西哥—进口海关估价	欧共体 WT/DS53/1	27-08-1996	挪威 WT/DS53/2 瑞士 WT/DS53/3			

续 表

序号	案件	请求磋商	收到磋商请求（日-月-年）	加入磋商请求	请求成立专家组（日-月-年）	专家组成立（日-月-年）	双边达成解决方案（日-月-年）
54	印度尼西亚—影响汽车工业特定措施	欧共体 WT/DS54/1	03-10-1996	美国 WT/DS54/2 日本 WT/DS54/3 韩国 WT/DS54/4 加拿大 WT/DS54/5	12-05-1997 欧共体 WT/DS54/6	12-06-1997 欧共体 WT/DSB/M/34	
55	印度尼西亚—影响汽车工业特定措施	日本 WT/DS55/1	04-10-1996	美国 WT/DS55/2 欧共体 WT/DS55/3 韩国 WT/DS55/4 加拿大 WT/DS55/5	18-04-1997 日本 WT/DS55/6 WT/DS64/4	12-06-1997 WT/DSB/M/34	
56	阿根廷—影响鞋类、纺织品、服装和其他项目进口的措施	美国 WT/DS56/1	04-10-1996	匈牙利 WT/DS56/2 欧共体 WT/DS56/3	10-01-1997 美国 WT/DS56/5	25-02-1997 WT/DSB/M/29	
57	澳大利亚—纺织品、服装及鞋类进口信贷计划	美国 WT/DS57/1	07-10-1996				
58	美国—对特定虾类及虾类产品进口限制	印度 马来西亚 巴基斯坦 泰国 WT/DS58/1	08-10-1996	中国香港 WT/DS58/2 欧共体 WT/DS58/3 日本 WT/DS58/4 澳大利亚 WT/DS58/5	10-01-1997 马来西亚 泰国 WT/DS58/6 07-02-1997 巴基斯坦 WT/DS58/7 04-03-1997 印度 WT/DS58/8	25-02-1997 WT/DSB/M/29 （马来西亚、 泰国、 巴基斯坦） 10-04-1997 WT/DSB/M/31 印度	
59	印度尼西亚—影响汽车工业的特定措施	美国 WT/DS59/1	08-10-1996	日本 WT/DS59/2 欧共体 WT/DS59/3 韩国 WT/DS59/4 加拿大 WT/DS59/5	13-06-1997 美国 WT/DS59/6	30-07-1997 WT/DSB/M/36	
60	危地马拉—对来自墨西哥的波兰特水泥的反倾销调查	墨西哥 WT/DS60/1	17-10-1996		13-02-1997 墨西哥 WT/DS60/2	20-03-1997 WT/DSB/M/30	
61	美国—对特定虾类及虾类产品进口限制	菲律宾 WT/DS61/1	25-10-1996	澳大利亚 WT/DS61/2 日本 WT/DS61/3			

续 表

序号	案件	请求磋商	收到磋商请求（日-月-年）	加入磋商请求	请求成立专家组（日-月-年）	专家组成立（日-月-年）	双边达成解决方案（日-月-年）
62	欧共体—对某些计算机设备的海关分类	美国 WT/DS62/1	08-11-1996	韩国 WT/DS62/2 加拿大 WT/DS62/3	13-02-1997 美国 WT/DS62/4	25-02-1997 WT/DSB/M/29	
63	美国—对于前民主德国的尿素进口采取反倾销措施	欧共体 WT/DS63/1	28-11-1996				
64	印度尼西亚—影响汽车工业的特定措施	日本 WT/DS64/1	29-11-1996	美国 WT/DS64/2 欧共体 WT/DS64/3	18-04-1997 日本 WT/DS55/6 WT/DS64/4	12-06-1997 WT/DSB/M/34	
65	巴西—影响汽车部门贸易及投资措施	美国 WT/DS65/1	10-01-1997				
66	日本—影响猪肉进口措施	欧共体 WT/DS66/1	15-01-1997	加拿大 WT/DS66/2			
67	英国—对某些计算机设备的海关分类	美国 WT/DS67/1	14-02-1997	韩国 WT/DS67/2	10-03-1997 美国 WT/DS67/3	20-03-1997 争端解决机构决定此问题交由1997年2月25日成立的专家组决定 WT/DSB/M/30	
68	爱尔兰—对某些计算机设备的海关分类	美国 WT/DS68/1	14-02-1997		10-03-1997 美国 WT/DS68/2	20-03-1997 争端解决机构决定此问题交由1997年2月25日成立的专家组决定 WT/DSB/M/30	
69	欧共体—影响特定家禽产品进口的措施	巴西 WT/DS69/1	24-02-1997		12-06-1997 巴西 WT/DS69/2	30-07-1997 WT/DSB/M/36	
70	加拿大—影响民用航空器出口的措施	巴西 WT/DS70/1	10-03-1997		13-07-1998 巴西 WT/DS70/2	23-07-1998 WT/DSB/M/47	
71	加拿大—影响民用航空器出口的措施	巴西 WT/DS71/1	10-03-1997				
72	欧共体—影响黄油产品的措施	新西兰 WT/DS72/1	24-03-1997		7-11-1997 新西兰 WT/DS72/2	18-11-1997 WT/DSB/M/39	11-11-1999 WT/DS72/7
73	日本—导航卫星政府采购	欧共体 WT/DS73/1	26-03-1997	美国 WT/DS73/2			19-02-1998 WT/DS73/5
74	菲律宾—影响猪肉及家禽措施	美国 WT/DS74/1	01-04-1997	欧共体 WT/DS74/2 加拿大 WT/DS74/3			13-03-1998 WT/DS74/5 WT/DS102/6

续 表

序号	案件	请求磋商	收到磋商请求（日-月-年）	加入磋商请求	请求成立专家组（日-月-年）	专家组成立（日-月-年）	双边达成解决方案（日-月-年）
75	韩国—对酒精类饮料征税	欧共体 WT/DS75/1	02-04-1997	美国 WT/DS75/2 加拿大 WT/DS75/3	15-09-1997 欧共体 WT/DS75/6	16-10-1997 WT/DSB/M/38	
76	日本—影响农产品措施	美国 WT/DS76/1	07-04-1997		06-10-1997 美国 WT/DS76/2	18-11-1997 WT/DSB/M/39	23-08-2001 WT/DS76/12
77	阿根廷—影响纺织品及服装措施	欧共体 WT/DS77/1	21-04-1997	美国 WT/DS77/2	15-09-1997 欧共体 WT/DS77/3 06-10-1997 Rev. 1 16-10-1997 Rev. 1/Corr. 1	16-10-1997 WT/DSB/M/38 29-07-1998 WT/DS77/5 专家组暂停其程序	
78	美国—扫帚进口的保障措施	哥伦比亚 WT/DS78/1	28-04-1997				
79	印度—对于药物及农业化学产品专利权保护	欧共体 WT/DS79/1	28-04-1997		15-09-1997 欧共体 WT/DS79/2	16-10-1997 WT/DSB/M/38	
80	比利时—影响商业电话目录服务的措施	美国 WT/DS80/1	02-05-1997				
81	巴西—影响汽车部门贸易及投资措施	欧共体 WT/DS81/1	07-05-1997				
82	爱尔兰—影响版权及邻接权的措施	美国 WT/DS82/1	14-05-1997		12-01-1998 美国 WT/DS82/2		06-11-2000 WT/DS82/3
83	丹麦—影响知识产权实施的措施	美国 WT/DS83/1	14-05-1997				07-06-2001 WT/DS83/2
84	韩国—对酒精饮料征税	美国 WT/DS84/1	23-05-1997	加拿大 WT/DS/84/2 欧共体 WT/DS84/3	15-09-1997 美国 WT/DS84/4	16-10-1997 WT/DSB/M/38	
85	美国—影响纺织品及服装产品的措施	欧共体 WT/DS85/1	22-05-1997	瑞士 WT/DS85/2 洪都拉斯 WT/DS85/3 中国香港 WT/DS85/4 巴基斯坦 WT/DS85/5 印度 WT/DS85/6 日本 WT/DS85/7 多米尼加 WT/DS85/8			11-02-1998 WT/DS85/9

续 表

序号	案件	请求磋商	收到磋商请求（日-月-年）	加入磋商请求	请求成立专家组（日-月-年）	专家组成立（日-月-年）	双边达成解决方案（日-月-年）
86	瑞典—影响知识产权实施的措施	美国 WT/DS86/1	28-05-1997				02-12-1998 WT/DS86/2
87	智利—对酒精饮料征税	欧共体 WT/DS87/1	04-06-1997	秘鲁 WT/DS87/2 美国 WT/DS87/3 墨西哥 WT/DS87/4	06-10-1997 欧共体 WT/DS87/5	18-11-1997 WT/DSB/M/39	
88	美国—影响政府采购措施	欧共体 WT/DS88/1	20-06-1997	日本 WT/DS88/2	09-09-1998 欧共体 WT/DS88/3	21-10-1998 WT/DSB/M/49 14-02-2000 WT/DS88/6 专家组建立的授权取消	
89	美国—对于来自韩国彩色电视接收机进口征收反倾销税	韩国 WT/DS89/1 和 Corr. 1	10-07-1997	墨西哥 WT/DS89/2 泰国 WT/DS89/3 日本 WT/DS89/4 中国香港 WT/DS89/5 欧共体 WT/DS89/6	07-11-1997 韩国 WT/DS89/7 28-11-1997 WT/DS89/7/ Corr. 1		05-01-1998 WT/DS89/8 18-09-1998 WT/DS89/9 （请求撤回）
90	印度—对于农产品、纺织品及工业品的数量限制	美国 WT/DS90/1	15-07-1997	日本 WT/DS90/2 欧共体 WT/DS90/3 加拿大 WT/DS90/4 澳大利亚 WT/DS90/5 瑞士 WT/DS90/6 新西兰 WT/DS90/7	06-10-1997 美国 WT/DS90/8 07-11-1997 WT/DS90/8/ Corr. 1	18-11-1997 WT/DSB/M/39	
91	印度—对于农产品、纺织品及工业品的数量限制	澳大利亚 WT/DS91/1	16-07-1997	日本 WT/DS91/2 美国 WT/DS91/3 欧共体 WT/DS91/4 加拿大 WT/DS91/5 瑞士 WT/DS91/6 新西兰 WT/DS91/7			17-03-1998 WT/DS91/8 17-08-1998 WT/DS91/8 Corr. 1

续 表

序号	案件	请求磋商	收到磋商请求（日-月-年）	加入磋商请求	请求成立专家组（日-月-年）	专家组成立（日-月-年）	双边达成解决方案（日-月-年）
92	印度—对于农产品、纺织品及工业品的数量限制	加拿大 WT/DS92/1	16-07-1997	日本 WT/DS92/2 美国 WT/DS92/3 欧共体 WT/DS92/4 澳大利亚 WT/DS92/5 瑞士 WT/DS92/6 新西兰 WT/DS92/7			18-03-1998 WT/DS92/8 25-09-1998 WT/DS92/8/Corr. 1
93	印度—对于农产品、纺织品及工业品的数量限制	新西兰 WT/DS93/1	16-07-1997	日本 WT/DS93/2 美国 WT/DS93/3 欧共体 WT/DS93/4 加拿大 WT/DS93/5 澳大利亚 WT/DS93/6 瑞士 WT/DS93/7			01-12-1998 WT/DS93/8
94	印度—对于农产品、纺织品及工业品的数量限制	瑞士 WT/DS94/1 和 Corr. 1	17-07-1997	日本 WT/DS94/2 美国 WT/DS94/3 欧共体 WT/DS94/4 加拿大 WT/DS94/5 澳大利亚 WT/DS94/6 新西兰 WT/DS94/7			23-02-1998 WT/DS94/9 18-09-1998 WT/DS94/9/Corr. 1
95	美国—影响政府采购措施	日本 WT/DS95/1	18-07-1997	欧共体 WT/DS95/2	09-09-1998 日本 WT/DS95/3	21-10-1998 WT/DSB/M/49 14-02-2000 WT/DS95/6 建立专家组的授权取消	

续 表

序号	案件	请求磋商	收到磋商请求（日-月-年）	加入磋商请求	请求成立专家组（日-月-年）	专家组成立（日-月-年）	双边达成解决方案（日-月-年）
96	印度—对于农产品、纺织品及工业品的数量限制	欧共体 WT/DS96/1	18-07-1997	日本 WT/DS96/2 美国 WT/DS96/3 加拿大 WT/DS96/4 澳大利亚 WT/DS96/5 瑞士 WT/DS96/6 新西兰 WT/DS96/7			07-04-1998 WT/DS96/8 28-09-1998 WT/DS96/8/Corr. 1
97	美国—对来自智利的鳟鱼进口实施反补贴税调查	智利 WT/DS97/1	05-08-1997				
98	韩国—对于特定奶制品进口保障措施	欧共体 WT/DS/98/1	12-08-1997	澳大利亚 WT/DS98/2	12-01-1998 欧共体 WT/DS98/4	23-07-1998 WT/DSB/M/47	
99	美国—对来自韩国1兆及以上的计算机动态随机存取存储器芯片征收反倾销税	韩国 WT/DS99/1 和 Corr. 1&2	14-08-1997		07-11-1997 韩国 WT/DS99/2	16-01-1998 WT/DSB/M/40	25-10-2000 WT/DS99/12
100	美国—影响家禽产品进口措施	欧共体 WT/DS100/1	18-08-1997				
101	墨西哥—对来自美国的高果糖玉米糖浆开展反倾销调查	美国 WT/DS101/1	04-09-1997				
102	菲律宾—影响猪肉及家禽产品措施	美国 WT/DS102/1	07-10-1997	加拿大 WT/DS102/3 欧共体 WT/DS102/4			13-03-1998 WT/DS74/5 WT/DS102/6
103	加拿大—影响牛奶进口及奶制品出口的措施	美国 WT/DS103/1	08-10-1997	日本 WT/DS103/2 澳大利亚 WT/DS103/3	03-02-1998 WT/DS103/4	25-03-1998 WT/DSB/M/44	09-05-2003 WT/DS103/33
104	欧共体—影响融化干酪出口的措施	美国 WT/DS104/1	08-10-1997	日本 WT/DS104/2 澳大利亚 WT/DS104/3 加拿大 WT/DS104/4			

续 表

序号	案件	请求磋商	收到磋商请求（日-月-年）	加入磋商请求	请求成立专家组（日-月-年）	专家组成立（日-月-年）	双边达成解决方案（日-月-年）
105	欧共体—对于香蕉进口、销售及分销区域的规定	巴拿马 WT/DS105/1 和 Add. 1&2	24-10-1997	哥伦比亚 WT/DS105/2 和 Add. 1 危地马拉 WT/DS105/3 多米尼加 WT/DS105/4 墨西哥 WT/DS105/5 哥斯达黎加 WT/DS105/6 洪都拉斯 WT/DS105/7 和 Add. 1 厄瓜多尔 WT/DS105/8 美国 WT/DS105/9 科特迪瓦 WT/DS105/10			08-11-2012 WT/DS105/11
106	澳大利亚—对汽车皮革生产和采购补助	美国 WT/DS106/1	10-11-1997		12-01-1998 美国 WT/DS106/2	22-01-1998 WT/DSB/M/41	11-06-1998 WT/DS126/2 （专家组要求撤销）
107	巴基斯坦—影响皮革出口措施	欧共体 WT/DS107/1	07-11-1997				
108	美国—“海外销售公司”的税收	欧共体 WT/DS108/1 和 Add. 1	18-11-1997		09-07-1998 欧共体 WT/DS108/2	22-09-1998 WT/DSB/M/48	
109	智利—对酒精饮料征税	美国 WT/DS109/1 和 Corr. 1	11-12-1997	秘鲁 WT/DS109/2 墨西哥 WT/DS/109/3			
110	智利—对酒精饮料征税	欧共体 WT/DS110/1	15-12-1997	美国 WT/DS110/2 墨西哥 WT/DS110/3	13-03-1998 WT/DS110/4	25-03-1998 WT/DSB/M/44	
111	美国—落花生进口关税率配额	阿根廷 WT/DS111/1	19-12-1997	加拿大 WT/DS111/2 日本 WT/DS111/3			
112	秘鲁—对来自巴西的公交车进口的反补贴税调查	巴西 WT/DS112/1	23-12-1997				

续 表

序号	案件	请求磋商	收到磋商请求（日-月-年）	加入磋商请求	请求成立专家组（日-月-年）	专家组成立（日-月-年）	双边达成解决方案（日-月-年）
113	加拿大—影响奶制品出口措施	新西兰 WT/DS113/1	29-12-1997	美国 WT/DS113/2 日本 WT/DS113/3	12-03-1998 WT/DS113/4	25-03-1998 WT/DSB/M/44	09-05-2003 WT/DS113/33
114	加拿大—药物产品专利权保护	欧共体 WT/DS114/1	19-12-1997	美国 WT/DS114/2 澳大利亚 WT/DS114/3 瑞士 WT/DS114/4	12-11-1998 WT/DS114/5	01-02-1999 WT/DSB/M/54	
115	欧共体—影响版权及邻接权的措施	美国 WT/DS115/1	06-01-1998		12-01-1998 美国 WT/DS115/2		06-11-2000 WT/DS115/3
116	巴西—影响进口付款条件的措施	欧共体 WT/DS116/1	08-01-1998	瑞士 WT/DS116/2 日本 WT/DS116/3 澳大利亚 WT/DS116/4 美国 WT/DS116/5 韩国 WT/DS116/6			
117	加拿大—影响企业分销服务的措施	欧共体 WT/DS117/1	20-01-1998				
118	美国—港口维护税	欧共体 WT/DS118/1	06-02-1998	加拿大 WT/DS118/2 日本 WT/DS118/3 挪威 WT/DS118/4			
119	澳大利亚—涂层非木纸反倾销措施	瑞士 WT/DS119/1	20-02-1998	日本 WT/DS119/2 欧共体 WT/DS119/3			13-05-1998 WT/DS119/4
120	印度—影响特定商品出口措施	欧共体 WT/DS120/1	11-03-1998		13-10-2000 欧共体 WT/DS120/2		
121	阿根廷—鞋类产品进口保障措施	欧共体 WT/DS121/1	06-04-1998	美国 WT/DS121/2	11-06-1998 欧共体 WT/DS121/3	23-07-1998 WT/DSB/M/47	
122	泰国—对波兰出口的铁或非合金钢的角铁、型材、轧材及工字梁的反倾销税案	波兰 WT/DS122/1	06-04-1998		15-10-1999 波兰 WT/DS122/2	19-11-1999 WT/DSB/M/71	

续 表

序号	案件	请求磋商	收到磋商请求（日-月-年）	加入磋商请求	请求成立专家组（日-月-年）	专家组成立（日-月-年）	双边达成解决方案（日-月-年）
123	阿根廷—鞋类产品进口保障措施	印度尼西亚 WT/DS123/1	22-04-1998	美国 WT/DS123/2	16-04-1999 WT/DS123/3 10-05-1999 印度尼西亚要求从争端解决机构议程中撤回上诉，并保留其在以后的争端解决机构会议上做出上诉的权利（WT/DS123/4）		
124	欧共体—动画片及电视节目知识产权保护的实施	美国 WT/DS124/1	30-04-1998				20-03-2001 WT/DS124/2
125	希腊—动画片及电视节目知识产权保护的实施	美国 WT/DS125/1	04-05-1998				20-03-2001 WT/DS125/2
126	澳大利亚—汽车皮革生产和出口的补贴	美国 WT/DS126/1	04-05-1998		11-04-1998 美国 WT/DS126/2	22-06-1998 WT/DSB/M/46	24-07-2000 WT/DS126/11
127	比利时—构成补贴的特定进口税	美国 WT/DS127/1	05-05-1998				
128	荷兰—构成补贴的特定进口税	美国 WT/DS128/1	05-05-1998				
129	希腊—构成补贴的特定进口税	美国 WT/DS129/1	05-05-1998				
130	爱尔兰—构成补贴的特定进口税	美国 WT/DS130/1	05-05-1998				
131	法国—构成补贴的特定进口税	美国 WT/DS131/1	05-05-1998				
132	墨西哥—对来自美国的高果糖玉米糖浆开展反倾销调查	美国 WT/DS132/1	08-05-1998		14-10-1998 美国 WT/DS132/2	25-11-1998 WT/DSB/M/51	
133	斯洛伐克—关于牛的运输及奶制品进口的措施	瑞士 WT/DS133/1	07-05-1998	美国 WT/DS133/2			
134	欧共体—对于稻米的特定进口税的限制	印度 WT/DS134/1 和 Corr. 1	27-05-1998				
135	欧共体—影响石棉及石棉产品的措施	加拿大 WT/DS135/1	28-05-1998	巴西 WT/DS135/2	09-10-1998 加拿大 WT/DS135/3	25-11-1998 WT/DSB/M/51	
136	美国—1916 年反倾销法案	欧共体 WT/DS136/1	04-06-1998		12-11-1998 欧共体 WT/DS136/2	01-02-1999 WT/DSB/M/54	

续 表

序号	案件	请求磋商	收到磋商请求（日-月-年）	加入磋商请求	请求成立专家组（日-月-年）	专家组成立（日-月-年）	双边达成解决方案（日-月-年）
137	欧共体—影响从加拿大进口松木的措施	加拿大 WT/DS137/1	17-06-1998				
138	美国—对来自英国的热轧铅铋碳钢产品征收反补贴税	欧共体 WT/DS138/1	12-06-1998	加拿大 WT/DS138/2	14-01-1999 WT/DS138/3 25-01-1999 WT/DS138/3 和 Corr. 1	17-02-1999 WT/DSB/M/55 和 Corr. 1	
139	加拿大—特定汽车工业措施	日本 WT/DS139/1	03-07-1998		13-11-1998 WT/DS139/2	01-02-1999 WT/DSB/M/54	
140	欧共体—对来自印度未漂平纹棉布进行反倾销调查	印度 WT/DS140/1	03-08-1998	巴基斯坦 WT/DS140/2			
141	欧共体—对来指印度棉布床单进口征收反倾销税	印度 WT/DS141/1	03-08-1998	巴基斯坦 WT/DS141/2	08-09-1999 印度 WT/DS141/3	27-10-1999 WT/DSB/M/70	
142	加拿大—特定汽车工业措施	欧共体 WT/DS142/1	17-08-1998		14-01-1999 WT/DS142/2	01-02-1999 WT/DSB/M/54	
143	斯洛伐克—影响从匈牙利小麦进口关税的措施	匈牙利 WT/DS143/1	18-09-1998（20 天）		09-10-1998 匈牙利 WT/DS143/2		
144	美国—影响从加拿大进口牛、羊和谷物的特定措施	加拿大 WT/DS144/1	25-09-1998				
145	阿根廷—对来自欧共体的面筋征收反补贴税	欧共体 WT/DS145/1 和 Rev. 1	23-09-1998				
146	印度—影响汽车部门的措施	欧共体 WT/DS146/1 和 Corr. 1	06-10-1998	日本 WT/DS146/2 美国 WT/DS146/3	13-10-2000 欧共体 WT/DS146/4	17-11-2000 WT/DSB/M/92	
147	日本—影响皮革的关税配额及补贴	欧共体 WT/DS147/1	08-10-1998				
148	捷克—影响从匈牙利小麦进口关税的措施	匈牙利 WT/DS148/1	12-10-1998（20 天）				
149	印度—进口限制	欧共体 WT/DS149/1	28-10-1998	美国 WT/DS149/2 日本 WT/DS149/3 瑞士 WT/DS149/4 澳大利亚 WT/DS149/5			

续 表

序号	案件	请求磋商	收到磋商请求（日-月-年）	加入磋商请求	请求成立专家组（日-月-年）	专家组成立（日-月-年）	双边达成解决方案（日-月-年）
150	印度—影响关税措施	欧共体 WT/DS150/1	31-10-1998	美国 WT/DS150/2 加拿大 WT/DS150/3 日本 WT/DS150/4 瑞士 WT/DS150/5 澳大利亚 WT/DS150/6			
151	美国—影响纺织品及服装产品的措施（Ⅱ）	欧共体 WT/DS151/1	19-11-1998	多米尼加 WT/DS151/2 中国香港 WT/DS151/3 巴基斯坦 WT/DS151/4 洪都拉斯 WT/DS151/5 日本 WT/DS151/6 瑞士 WT/DS151/7 萨尔瓦多 WT/DS151/8 印度 WT/DS151/9			24-07-2000 WT/DS151/10
152	美国—1974年贸易法案第301—310部分	欧共体 WT/DS152/1	25-11-1998	多米尼加 WT/DS152/2 巴拿马 WT/DS152/3 危地马拉 WT/DS152/4 墨西哥 WT/DS152/5 牙买加 WT/DS152/6 洪都拉斯 WT/DS152/7 日本 WT/DS152/8 哥伦比亚 WT/DS152/9 厄瓜多尔 WT/DS152/10	02-02-1999 欧共体 WT/DS152/11	02-03-1999 WT/DSB/M/56	

续 表

序号	案件	请求磋商	收到磋商请求（日-月-年）	加入磋商请求	请求成立专家组（日-月-年）	专家组成立（日-月-年）	双边达成解决方案（日-月-年）
153	欧共体—制药及农业化学产品的专利保护	加拿大 WT/DS153/1	02-12-1998	美国 WT/DS153/2 澳大利亚 WT/DS153/3 瑞士 WT/DS153/4			
154	欧共体—影响咖啡差别及优惠待遇的措施	巴西 WT/DS154/1	07-12-1998	哥伦比亚 WT/DS154/2 秘鲁 WT/DS154/3 哥斯达黎加 WT/DS154/4 玻利维亚 WT/DS154/5			
155	阿根廷—影响牛皮出口及成皮进口的措施	欧共体 WT/DS155/1	23-12-1998		04-06-1999 欧共体 WT/DS155/2	26-07-1999 WT/DSB/M/65	
156	危地马拉—对来自墨西哥的波兰特水泥的反倾销措施	墨西哥 WT/DS156/1 和 Corr. 1&2	05-01-1999		15-07-1999 墨西哥 WT/DS156/2 05-08-1999 WT/DS156/2 和 Corr. 1	22-09-1999 WT/DSB/M/68	
157	阿根廷—从意大利进口钻头的采取反倾销措施	欧共体 WT/DS157/1	14-01-1999				
158	欧共体—对于香蕉进口、销售及分销的规定	危地马拉，洪都拉斯，墨西哥，巴拿马和美国 WT/DS158/1	20-01-1999	厄瓜多尔 WT/DS158/2 伯利兹 WT/DS158/3			08-11-2012 WT/DS158/4
159	匈牙利—对来自捷克的钢铁产品进口的保障措施	捷克 WT/DS159/1	21-01-1999				
160	美国—美国版权法第 110（5）节	欧共体 WT/DS160/1	26-01-1999	澳大利亚 WT/DS160/2 加拿大 WT/DS160/3 瑞士 WT/DS160/4	16-04-1999 欧共体 WT/DS160/5	26-05-1999 WT/DSB/M/62	

续 表

序号	案件	请求磋商	收到磋商请求（日-月-年）	加入磋商请求	请求成立专家组（日-月-年）	专家组成立（日-月-年）	双边达成解决方案（日-月-年）
161	韩国—影响新鲜、冷藏、冷冻牛肉进口措施	美国 WT/DS161/1	01-02-1999	新西兰 WT/DS161/2 澳大利亚 WT/DS161/3 加拿大 WT/DS161/4	16-04-1999 美国 WT/DS161/5	26-05-1999 WT/DSB/M/62	
162	美国—1916 反倾销法案	日本 WT/DS162/1	10-02-1999	欧共体 WT/DS162/2	04-06-1999 日本 WT/DS162/3	26-07-1999 WT/DSB/M/65	
163	韩国—影响政府采购措施	美国 WT/DS163/1	16-02-1999	欧共体 WT/DS163/2 日本 WT/DS163/3	11-05-1999 美国 WT/DS163/4	16-06-1999 WT/DSB/M/64	
164	阿根廷—影响鞋类进口措施	美国 WT/DS164/1	01-03-1999	欧共体 WT/DS164/2	20-05-1999 美国 WT/DS164/3 15-07-1999 WT/DS164/4	26-07-1999 WT/DSB/M/65	
165	美国—对来自欧共体特定产品的进口措施	欧共体 WT/DS165/1	04-03-1999	多米尼加 WT/DS165/2 日本 WT/DS165/3 洪都拉斯 WT/DS165/4 危地马拉 WT/DS165/5 厄瓜多尔 WT/DS165/6 巴拿马 WT/DS165/7 和 Corr. 1	11-05-1999 欧共体 WT/DS165/8	16-06-1999 WT/DSB/M/64	
166	美国—对来自欧共体面筋进口的保障措施	欧共体 WT/DS166/1	17-03-1999	澳大利亚 WT/DS166/2	04-06-1999 欧共体 WT/DS166/3	26-07-1999 WT/DSB/M/65	
167	美国—对来自加拿大活牛的反补贴税调查	加拿大 WT/DS167/1	19-03-1999	墨西哥 WT/DS167/2			
168	南非—对来自印度某些药品征收反倾销税	印度 WT/DS168/1	01-04-1999				

续 表

序号	案件	请求磋商	收到磋商请求（日-月-年）	加入磋商请求	请求成立专家组（日-月-年）	专家组成立（日-月-年）	双边达成解决方案（日-月-年）
169	韩国—影响新鲜、冷藏及冷冻牛肉进口的措施	澳大利亚 WT/DS169/1	13-04-1999	新西兰 WT/DS169/2 美国 WT/DS169/3 加拿大 WT/DS169/4 和 Corr. 1	15-07-1999 澳大利亚 WT/DS169/5	26-07-1999 WT/DSB/M/65	
170	加拿大—专利保护条款	美国 WT/DS170/1	06-05-1999		15-07-1999 美国 WT/DS170/2	22-09-1999 WT/DSB/M/68	
171	阿根廷—对药品的专利权保护及对农业化学品测试数据保护	美国 WT/DS171/1	06-05-1999	瑞士 WT/DS171/2			31-05-2002 WT/DS171/3
172	欧共体—航班管理系统开发有关措施	美国 WT/DS172/1	21-05-1999				
173	法国—航班管理系统开发有关措施	美国 WT/DS173/1	21-05-1999				
174	欧共体—农产品和食品的商标及地理标识保护	美国 WT/DS174/1 和 Add. 1	01-06-1999 04-04-2003	加拿大 WT/DS174/3 澳大利亚 WT/DS174/4 墨西哥 WT/DS174/5 新西兰 WT/DS174/6 斯里兰卡 WT/DS174/7 印度 WT/DS174/8 阿根廷 WT/DS174/9 匈牙利 WT/DS174/10 马耳他 WT/DS174/11 保加利亚 WT/DS174/12 捷克 WT/DS174/13 塞浦路斯 WT/DS174/14 斯洛文尼亚 WT/DS174/15 土耳其 WT/DS174/16 罗马尼亚 WT/DS174/17 斯洛伐克 WT/DS174/18	18-08-2003 美国 WT/DS174/20	02-10-2003 WT/DSB/M/156	

续 表

序号	案件	请求磋商	收到磋商请求（日-月-年）	加入磋商请求	请求成立专家组（日-月-年）	专家组成立（日-月-年）	双边达成解决方案（日-月-年）
175	印度—影响汽车部门投资和贸易的措施	美国 WT/DS175/1	02-06-1999	日本 WT/DS175/2 欧共体 WT/DS175/3	18-05-2000 美国 WT/DS175/4	27-07-2000 WT/DSB/M/86	
176	美国—1998 年全面拨款法第 211 部分	欧共体 WT/DS176/1	08-07-1999		07-07-2000 欧共体 WT/DS176/2	26-09-2000 WT/DSB/M/89	
177	美国—对来自新西兰的新鲜、冷藏及冷冻羔羊肉采取保障措施	新西兰 WT/DS177/1	16-07-1999	澳大利亚 WT/DS177/2 加拿大 WT/DS177/3	15-10-1999 新西兰 WT/DS177/4	19-11-1999 WT/DSB/M/71	
178	美国—对来自澳大利亚羔羊肉进口的保障措施	澳大利亚 WT/DS178/1 和 Corr. 1	23-07-1999	新西兰 WT/DS178/2 和 Corr. 1 欧共体 WT/DS178/3 加拿大 WT/DS178/4	15-10-1999 澳大利亚 WT/DS178/5 和 Corr. 1	19-11-1999 WT/DSB/M/71	
179	美国—来自韩国的不锈钢卷板和不锈钢条的反倾销措施	韩国 WT/DS179/1	30-07-1999		15-10-1999 韩国 WT/DS179/2	19-11-1999 WT/DSB/M/71	
180	美国—特定糖浆税则归类	加拿大 WT/DS180/1	06-09-1999				
181	哥伦比亚—对来自泰国的纯聚酯长丝布进口的保障措施				08-09-1999 泰国 WT/DS181/1 撤销请求 27-10-1999 WT/DSB/M/70		
182	厄瓜多尔—对来自墨西哥的灰水泥的反倾销措施	墨西哥 WT/DS182/1 和 Corr. 1	05-10-1999				
183	巴西—对于进口许可证及最低进口价格的措施	欧共体 WT/DS183/1	14-10-1999	美国 WT/DS183/2			
184	美国—对来自日本的热轧薄板卷产品征收反倾销税	日本 WT/DS184/1	18-11-1999		11-02-2000 日本 WT/DS184/2	20-03-2000 WT/DSB/M/77	

续 表

序号	案件	请求磋商	收到磋商请求（日-月-年）	加入磋商请求	请求成立专家组（日-月-年）	专家组成立（日-月-年）	双边达成解决方案（日-月-年）
185	特立尼达和多巴哥—影响从哥斯达黎加进口的意大利面的措施	哥斯达黎加 WT/DS185/1	18-11-1999				
186	美国—1930关税法及修正，第337部分	欧共体 WT/DS186/1	12-01-2000	加拿大 WT/DS186/2 日本 WT/DS186/3			
187	特立尼达和多巴哥—对来自哥斯达黎加的通心粉和意大利面进口的临时反倾销措施	哥斯达黎加 WT/DS187/1	17-01-2000				
188	尼加拉瓜—洪都拉斯和哥伦比亚进口措施	哥伦比亚 WT/DS188/1	17-01-2000		28-03-2000 哥伦比亚 WT/DS188/1 和 Corr. 1	18-05-2000 WT/DSB/M/80	
189	阿根廷—对从德国进口动画板和意大利进口的瓷砖采取明确反倾销措施	欧共体 WT/DS189/1	26-01-2000		15-09-2000 欧共体 WT/DS189/2 07-11-2000 WT/DS189/3	17-11-2000 WT/DSB/M/92	
190	阿根廷—对于原产巴西的特定机织棉布的过渡期保障措施				11-02-2000 巴西 WT/DS190/1	20-03-2000 WT/DSB/M/77	27-06-2000 WT/DS190/2
191	厄瓜多尔—来自墨西哥水泥的明确反倾销措施	墨西哥 WT/DS191/1	15-03-2000				
192	美国—对来自巴基斯坦精梳棉纱线的过渡期保障措施	N. A.	N. A.	N. A.	03-04-2000 巴基斯坦 WT/DS192/1	19-06-2000 WT/DSB/M/84	
193	智利—影响剑鱼的运输及进口措施	欧共体 WT/DS193/1	19-04-2000		06-11-2000 欧共体 WT/DS193/2	12-12-2000 WT/DSB/M/94 23-03-2001 WT/DS193/3 终止成立专家组	
194	美国—作为出口限制的补贴	加拿大 WT/DS194/1	19-05-2000		24-07-2000 加拿大 WT/DS194/2	11-09-2000 WT/DSB/M/88	

续 表

序号	案件	请求磋商	收到磋商请求（日-月-年）	加入磋商请求	请求成立专家组（日-月-年）	专家组成立（日-月-年）	双边达成解决方案（日-月-年）
195	菲律宾—影响汽车部门投资和贸易的措施	美国 WT/DS195/1	23-05-2000		13-10-2000 美国 WT/DS195/3	17-11-2000 WT/DSB/M/92	
196	阿根廷—对于专利及测试数据的特定保护措施	美国 WT/DS196/1	30-05-2000	欧共体 WT/DS196/2 瑞士 WT/DS196/3			31-05-2002 WT/DS196/4
197	巴西—最低进口价格措施	美国 WT/DS197/1	30-05-2000	欧共体 WT/DS197/2			
198	罗马尼亚—最低进口价格措施	美国 WT/DS198/1	30-05-2000				26-09-2001 WT/DS198/2
199	巴西—影响专利保护措施	美国 WT/DS199/1	30-05-2000	欧共体 WT/DS/199/2	08-01-2001 美国 WT/DS199/3	01-02-2001 WT/DSB/M/98	05-07-2001 WT/DS199/4
200	美国—1974 贸易法案及修正案第 306 节	欧共体 WT/DS200/1	05-06-2000	厄瓜多尔 W/DS200/2 牙买加 WT/DS200/3 日本 WT/DS200/4 多米尼加 WT/DS200/5 洪都拉斯 WT/DS200/6 危地马拉 WT/DS200/7 加拿大 WT/DS200/8 巴拿马 WT/DS200/9 澳大利亚 WT/DS200/10 圣卢西亚 WT/DS200/11			
201	尼加拉瓜—影响从洪都拉斯和哥伦比亚进口的措施	洪都拉斯 WT/DS201/1	06-06-2000	欧共体 WT/DS201/2			
202	美国—自韩国进口的圆焊碳质条形管的保障措施	韩国 WT/DS202/1	13-06-2000	欧共体 WT/DS202/2 日本 WT/DS202/3	15-09-2000 韩国 WT/DS202/4	23-10-2000 WT/DSB/M/91	

续 表

序号	案件	请求磋商	收到磋商请求（日-月-年）	加入磋商请求	请求成立专家组（日-月-年）	专家组成立（日-月-年）	双边达成解决方案（日-月-年）
203	墨西哥—影响活猪贸易的措施	美国 WT/DS203/1	10-07-2000				
204	墨西哥—影响电信服务的措施	美国 WT/DS204/1 和 Add. 1	17-08-2000		10-11-2000 美国 WT/DS204/2 18-02-2002 WT/DS204/3	17-04-2002 WT/DSB/M/123	
205	埃及—豆油罐装金枪鱼进口限令	泰国 WT/DS205/1	22-09-2000				
206	美国—对来自印度钢板的反倾销及反补贴措施	印度 WT/DS206/1	04-10-2000		07-06-2001 印度 WT/DS206/2	24-07-2001 WT/DSB/M/107	
207	智利—对特定农产品的综合价格制度及保障措施	阿根廷 WT/DS207/1	05-10-2000		19-01-2001 阿根廷 WT/DS207/2	12-03-2001 WT/DSB/M/101	
208	土耳其—对于钢铁管配件征收反倾销税	巴西 WT/DS208/1	09-10-2000				
209	欧共体—影响速溶咖啡措施	巴西 WT/DS209/1	12-10-2000	厄瓜多尔 WT/DS209/2			
210	比利时—建立稻米海关税的管理办法	美国 WT/DS210/1	12-10-2000		19-01-2001 美国 WT/DS210/2 01-03-2001 WT/DS201/2/Rev. 1	12-03-2001 WT/DSB/M/101	18-12-2001 WT/DS210/6
211	埃及—对来自土耳其钢筋采取反倾销措施	土耳其 WT/DS211/1	06-11-2000		04-05-2001 土耳其 WT/DS211/2 11-05-2001 WT/DS/211/2/Corr. 1	20-06-2001 WT/DSB/M/106	
212	美国—对于特定来自欧共体产品的反补贴措施	欧共体 WT/DS212/1 和 Add. 1	10-11-2000	巴西 WT/DS212/2 和 Add. 1 以色列 WT/DS212/3	10-08-2001 欧共体 WT/DS212/4	10-09-2001 WT/DSB/M/109	
213	美国—对特定来自德国的耐腐蚀扁钢征收反补贴税	欧共体 WT/DS213/1 和 Add. 1	10-11-2000	印度 WT/DS213/2	10-08-2001 欧共体 WT/DS213/3	10-09-2001 WT/DSB/M/109	
214	美国—对钢盘条和圆缝碳质钢管的保障措施	欧共体 WT/DS214/1	01-12-2000	加拿大 WT/DS214/2 印度 WT/DS214/3	10-08-2001 WT/DS214/4	10-09-2001 WT/DSB/M/109	
215	菲律宾—对来自韩国的聚乙烯树脂采取反倾销措施	韩国 WT/DS215/1	15-12-2000				

续 表

序号	案件	请求磋商	收到磋商请求（日-月-年）	加入磋商请求	请求成立专家组（日-月-年）	专家组成立（日-月-年）	双边达成解决方案（日-月-年）
216	墨西哥—对电力传输器采取临时反倾销措施	巴西 WT/DS216/1	20-12-2000	欧共体 WT/DS216/2 美国 WT/DS216/3			
217	美国—2000 年持续性倾销及补贴补偿法	澳大利亚、巴西、智利、欧共体、印度、印度尼西亚、日本、韩国和泰国 WT/DS217/1	21-12-2000	阿根廷 WT/DS217/2 加拿大 WT/DS217/3 墨西哥 WT/DS217/4 和 Add. 1	13-07-2001 澳大利亚、巴西、智利、欧共体、印度、印度尼西亚、日本、韩国和泰国 WT/DS217/5	23-08-2001 WT/DSB/M/108	
218	美国—对来自巴西的特定碳钢制品的反补贴税	巴西 WT/DS218/1	21-12-2000	欧共体 WT/DS218/2			
219	欧共体—对来自巴西的可锻铸铁管接头征收反倾销税	巴西 WT/DS219/1	21-12-2000		08-06-2001 巴西 WT/DS219/2	24-07-2001 WT/DSB/M/107	
220	智利—对特定农产品相关的综合价格制度及保障措施	危地马拉 WT/DS220/1	05-01-2001				
221	美国—乌拉圭回合协议第 129（C）（1）节	加拿大 WT/DS221/1	17-01-2001	印度 WT/DS221/2 欧共体 WT/DS221/3	13-07-2001 加拿大 WT/DS221/4	23-08-2001 WT/DSB/M/108	
222	加拿大—地区航空器的出口信贷保证	巴西 WT/DS222/1	22-01-2001		01-03-2001 巴西 WT/DS222/2	12-03-2001 WT/DSB/M/101	
223	欧共体—来自美国的玉米黄浆饲料的关税率配额	美国 WT/DS223/1	25-01-2001				
224	美国—美国专利权	巴西 WT/DS224/1	31-01-2001	印度 WT/DS224/2			
225	美国—对从意大利进口无缝管征收反倾销税	欧共体 WT/DS225/1	05-02-2001	日本 WT/DS225/2			
226	智利—对食用油混合物的临时保障措施	阿根廷 WT/DS226/1	19-02-2002				
227	秘鲁—对香烟征税	智利 WT/DS227/1 和 Corr. 1&2	01-03-2001		03-05-2001 智利 WT/DS227/2 此上诉于 2001 年 7 月 12 日被正式撤回 WT/DS227/3	20-06-2001 WT/DSB/M/106	

续 表

序号	案件	请求磋商	收到磋商请求（日-月-年）	加入磋商请求	请求成立专家组（日-月-年）	专家组成立（日-月-年）	双边达成解决方案（日-月-年）
228	智利—对糖类的保障措施	哥伦比亚 WT/DS228/1	15-03-2001	古巴 WT/DS228/2 危地马拉 WT/DS228/3 尼加拉瓜 WT/DS228/4 哥斯达黎加 WT/DS228/5 萨尔瓦多 WT/DS228/6			
229	巴西—对来自印度的麻袋征收反倾销税	印度 WT/DS229/1	09-04-2001				
230	智利—关于糖类的保障措施和程序修改	哥伦比亚 WT/DS230/1	17-04-2001	危地马拉 WT/DS230/2 哥斯达黎加 WT/DS230/3 古巴 WT/DS230/4 尼加拉瓜 WT/DS230/5			
231	欧共体—沙丁鱼贸易描述	秘鲁 WT/DS231/1	20-03-2001	委内瑞拉 WT/DS231/2 智利 WT/DS231/3 美国 WT/DS231/4 厄瓜多尔 WT/DS231/5	07-06-2001 秘鲁 WT/DS231/6	24-07-2001 WT/DSB/M/107	25-07-2003 WT/DS231/18
232	墨西哥—影响火柴的进口措施	智利 WT/DS232/1 要求磋商的申请撤回 WT/DS232/3 (02-02-2004)	17-05-2001	欧共体 WT/DS232/2			
233	阿根廷—影响药类产品进口的措施	印度 WT/DS233/1	25-05-2001				

续 表

序号	案件	请求磋商	收到磋商请求（日-月-年）	加入磋商请求	请求成立专家组（日-月-年）	专家组成立（日-月-年）	双边达成解决方案（日-月-年）
234	美国—2000 年持续性倾销及补贴补偿法案	加拿大和墨西哥 WT/DS234/1	21-05-2001	日本 WT/DS234/2 欧共体 WT/DS234/3 巴西 WT/DS234/4 印度尼西亚 WT/DS234/5 韩国 WT/DS234/6 印度 WT/DS234/7 危地马拉 WT/DS234/8 泰国 WT/DS234/9 澳大利亚 WT/DS234/10 智利 WT/DS234/11	10-08-2001 加拿大 WT/DS234/12 10-08-2001 墨西哥 WT/DS234/13	10-09-2001 争端解决机构决定于 2001 年 8 月 23 日成立专家组，应澳大利亚、巴西、智利、欧共体、印度、印度尼西亚、日本、韩国和泰国的要求。此案件也可参见加拿大和墨西哥申请 WT/DSB/M/109	
235	斯洛伐克—糖类进口的保障措施	波兰 WT/DS235/1	11-07-2001				11-01-2002 WT/DS235/2
236	美国—对来自加拿大的特定软木的初步判决	加拿大 WT/DS236/1	21-08-2001		26-10-2001 加拿大 WT/DS236/2	05-12-2001 WT/DSB/M/114	12-10-2006 WT/DS236/5/Add. 1
237	土耳其—新鲜水果的特定进口程序	厄瓜多尔 WT/DS237/1	31-08-2001	欧共体 WT/DS237/2	14-06-2002 厄瓜多尔 WT/DS237/3	29-07-2002 WT/DSB/M/130	22-11-2002 WT/DS237/4
238	阿根廷—桃脯进口的保障措施	智利 WT/DS238/1	14-09-2001		06-12-2002 智利 WT/DS238/2	18-01-2002 WT/DSB/M/117	
239	美国—对从巴西进口硅金属征收反倾销税	巴西 WT/DS239/1 和 Rev. 1	18-09-2001 01-11-2001	泰国 WT/DS239/2 欧共体 WT/DS239/3			
240	罗马尼亚—小麦及小麦粉进口禁令	匈牙利 WT/DS240/1 WT/DS240/1/Add. 1	18-10-2001 30-10-2001		28-11-2001 匈牙利 WT/DS240/2 2001 年 12 月 20 日撤销建立专家组请求 WT/DS240/3		
241	阿根廷—对来自巴西家禽征收反倾销税	巴西 WT/DS241/1	07-11-2001	欧共体 WT/DS241/2	26-02-2002 巴西 WT/DS241/3	17-04-2002 WT/DSB/M/123	

续 表

序号	案件	请求磋商	收到磋商请求（日-月-年）	加入磋商请求	请求成立专家组（日-月-年）	专家组成立（日-月-年）	双边达成解决方案（日-月-年）
242	欧共体—普惠制	泰国 WT/DS242/1	07-12-2001	哥斯达黎加 WT/DS242/2 危地马拉 WT/DS242/3 尼加拉瓜 WT/DS242/4 洪都拉斯 WT/DS242/5 哥伦比亚 WT/DS242/6			
243	美国—纺织品及服装原产地证明	印度 WT/DS243/1	11-01-2002	孟加拉国 WT/DS243/2 欧共体 WT/DS243/3	08-05-2002 印度 WT/DS243/5 07-06-2002 WT/DS243/5/Rev. 1	24-06-2002 WT/DSB/M/128	
244	美国—对来自日本的耐腐蚀钢板反倾销税日复审	日本 WT/DS244/1	30-01-2002	欧共体 WT/DS244/2 印度 WT/DS244/3	05-04-2002 日本 WT/DS244/4	22-05-2002 WT/DSB/M/124 和 Corr. 1	
245	日本—影响苹果进口措施	美国 WT/DS245/1	01-03-2002		08-05-2002 美国 WT/DS245/2	03-06-2002 WT/DSB/M/125	30-08-2005 WT/DS245/21
246	欧共体—给予发展中国家的优惠关税条件	印度 WT/DS246/1	05-03-2002	委内瑞拉 WT/DS246/2 哥伦比亚 WT/DS246/3	06-12-2002 印度 WT/DS246/4	27-01-2003 WT/DSB/M/142	
247	美国—对来自加拿大的软木进口的临时反倾销措施	加拿大 WT/DS247/1	06-03-2002				12-10-2006 WT/DS247/2 23-02-2007 WT/DS247/2/Add. 1
248	美国—对于特定钢铁制品进口的保障措施	欧共体 WT/DS248/1	07-03-2002	日本 WT/DS248/2 瑞士 WT/DS248/3 韩国 WT/DS248/4 挪威 WT/DS248/5 委内瑞拉 WT/DS248/6 加拿大 WT/DS248/7 墨西哥 WT/DS248/8 中国 WT/DS248/9 新西兰 WT/DS248/10	08-05-2002 欧共体 WT/DS248/12	03-06-2002 WT/DSB/M/125	

续 表

序号	案件	请求磋商	收到磋商请求（日-月-年）	加入磋商请求	请求成立专家组（日-月-年）	专家组成立（日-月-年）	双边达成解决方案（日-月-年）
249	美国—对于特定钢铁产品的保障措施	日本 WT/DS249/1	20-03-2002	挪威 WT/DS249/2 新西兰 WT/DS249/3 墨西哥 WT/DS249/4	24-05-2002 日本 WT/DS249/6	14-06-2002 争端解决机构同意在 2002 年 6 月 3 日成立专家组来调查欧共体提请的上诉，同时也就日本提请的类似案件上诉做相应调查 WT/DSB/M/127	
250	美国—美国佛罗里达州对橙、柚加工产品的补贴性特许权税	巴西 WT/DS250/1	20-03-2002		19-08-2002 巴西 WT/DS250/2	01-10-2002 WT/DSB/M/133	28-05-2004 WT/DS250/3
251	美国—对于特定钢铁产品进口的保障措施	韩国 WT/DS251/1	20-03-2002	挪威 WT/DS251/2 日本 WT/DS251/3 新西兰 WT/DS251/4 墨西哥 WT/DS251/5	24-05-2002 韩国 WT/DS251/7	14-06-2002 争端解决机构同意在 2002 年 6 月 3 日成立专家组来调查欧共体提请的上诉，同时也就韩国提请的类似案件上诉做相应调查 WT/DSB/M/127	
252	美国—对于特定钢铁产品进口的保障措施	中国 WT/DS252/1	26-03-2002	日本 WT/DS252/2 新西兰 WT/DS252/3	27-05-2002 中国 WT/DS252/5	24-06-2002 争端解决机构同意在 2002 年 6 月 3 日成立专家组来调查欧共体提请的上诉，同时也就中国提请的类似案件上诉做相应调查 WT/DSB/M/128	
253	美国—对于特定钢铁产品进口的保障措施	瑞士 WT/DS253/1	03-04-2002	新西兰 WT/DS253/2 日本 WT/DS253/3	04-06-2002 瑞士 WT/DS253/5	24-06-2002 争端解决机构同意在 2002 年 6 月 3 日成立专家组来调查欧共体提请的上诉，同时也就瑞士提请的类似案件上诉做相应调查 WT/DSB/M/128	

续 表

序号	案件	请求磋商	收到磋商请求（日-月-年）	加入磋商请求	请求成立专家组（日-月-年）	专家组成立（日-月-年）	双边达成解决方案（日-月-年）
254	美国—对于特定钢铁产品进口的保障措施	挪威 WT/DS254/1	04-04-2002	新西兰 WT/DS254/2 日本 WT/DS254/3	04-06-2002 挪威 WT/DS254/5	24-06-2002 争端解决机构同意在2002年6月3日成立专家组来调查欧共体提请的上诉，同时也就挪威提请的类似案件上诉做相应调查 WT/DSB/M/128	
255	秘鲁—对特定进口产品的税收措施	智利 WT/DS255/1	22-04-2002	美国 WT/DS255/2	14-06-2002 智利 WT/DS255/3 25-09-2002 WT/DS255/5（此事件撤回）		
256	土耳其—对来自匈牙利的宠物食品进口禁令	匈牙利 WT/DS256/1	03-05-2002				
257	美国—对来自加拿大的特定软木的最终反补贴税决定	加拿大 WT/DS257/1	03-05-2002		19-07-2002 加拿大 WT/DS257/2 19-08-2002 WT/DS257/3	01-10-2002 WT/DSB/M/133	12-10-2006 WT/DS257/26 23-02-2007 WT/DS257/26/Add. 1
258	美国—对于特定钢铁产品进口的保障措施	新西兰 WT/DS258/1	14-05-2002	欧共体 WT/DS258/2 日本 WT/DS258/3 韩国 WT/DS258/4 挪威 WT/DS258/5 中国 WT/DS258/6 墨西哥 WT/DS258/7	28-06-2002 新西兰 WT/DS258/9	08-07-2002 争端解决机构同意在2002年6月3日成立专家组来调查欧共体提请的上诉，同时也就新西兰提请的类似案件上做相应调查 WT/DSB/M/129	

续 表

序号	案件	请求磋商	收到磋商请求（日-月-年）	加入磋商请求	请求成立专家组（日-月-年）	专家组成立（日-月-年）	双边达成解决方案（日-月-年）
259	美国—对特定钢铁产品进口采取保障措施	巴西 WT/DS259/1	21-05-2002	欧共体 WT/DS259/2 日本 WT/DS259/3 韩国 WT/DS259/4 挪威 WT/DS259/5 中国 WT/DS259/6 墨西哥 WT/DS259/7	22-07-2002 巴西 WT/DS259/10	29-07-2002 争端解决机构同意在2002年6月3日成立专家组来调查欧共体提请的上诉，同时也就巴西提请的类似案件上诉做相应调查 WT/DSB/M/130	
260	欧共体—对于特定钢铁产品进口的临时保障措施	美国 WT/DS260/1	30-05 2002	日本 WT/DS260/2	19-08-2002 美国 WT/DS260/4	16-09-2002 WT/DSB/M/132	
261	乌拉圭—特定产品的税收待遇	智利 WT/DS261/1	18-06-2002	欧共体 WT/DS261/2 墨西哥 WT/DS261/3	03-04-2003 智利 WT/DS261/4	19-05-2003 WT/DSB/M/150	08-01-2004 WT/DS261/7
262	美国—对来自德国和法国的特定钢铁产品的反倾销和反补贴税的日落复审	欧共体 WT/DS262/1	25-07-2002	加拿大 WT/DS262/2 日本 WT/DS262/3			
263	欧共体—影响酒类进口的措施	阿根廷 WT/DS263/1	04-09-2002				
264	美国—对来自加拿大的木材的最终倾销决定	加拿大 WT/DS264/1	13-09-2002		06-12-2002 加拿大 WT/DS264/2	08-01-2003 WT/DSB/M/140	12-10-2006 WT/DS264/29 23-02-2007 Add. 1

续 表

序号	案件	请求磋商	收到磋商请求（日-月-年）	加入磋商请求	请求成立专家组（日-月-年）	专家组成立（日-月-年）	双边达成解决方案（日-月-年）
265	欧共体—糖类出口补贴	澳大利亚 WT/DS265/1	27-09-2002	毛里求斯 WT/DS265/2 巴西 WT/DS265/3 瑞士 WT/DS265/4 斐济 WT/DS265/5 圭亚那 WT/DS265/6 伯利兹 WT/DS265/7 牙买加 WT/DS265/8 印度 WT/DS265/9 津巴布韦 WT/DS265/10 马拉维 WT/DS265/11 加拿大 WT/DS265/12 肯尼亚 WT/DS265/13 巴巴多斯 WT/DS265/14 科特迪瓦 WT/DS265/15 刚果 WT/DS265/16 马达加斯加 WT/DS265/17 哥伦比亚 WT/DS265/18 圣基茨和尼维斯 WT/DS265/19	09-07-2003 澳大利亚 WT/DS265/21	29-08-2003 WT/DSB/M/155	

续 表

序号	案件	请求磋商	收到磋商请求（日-月-年）	加入磋商请求	请求成立专家组（日-月-年）	专家组成立（日-月-年）	双边达成解决方案（日-月-年）
266	欧共体—糖类出口补贴	巴西 WT/DS266/1	27-09-2002	澳大利亚 WT/DS266/2 毛里求斯 WT/DS266/3 印度 WT/DS266/4 瑞士 WT/DS266/5 斐济 WT/DS266/6 圭亚那 WT/DS266/7 伯利兹 WT/DS266/8 牙买加 WT/DS266/9 津巴布韦 WT/DS266/10 马拉维 WT/DS266/11 加拿大 WT/DS266/12 肯尼亚 WT/DS266/13 巴巴多斯 WT/DS266/14 科特迪瓦 WT/DS266/15 刚果 WT/DS266/16 马达加斯加 WT/DS266/17 哥伦比亚 WT/DS266/18 圣基茨和尼维斯 WT/DS266/19	09-07-2003 巴西 WT/DS266/21	29-08-2003 WT/DSB/M/155	
267	美国—陆地棉补贴	巴西 WT/DS267/1	27-09-2002	津巴布韦 WT/DS267/2 印度 WT/DS267/3 阿根廷 WT/DS267/4 加拿大 WT/DS267/5	06-02-2003 巴西 WT/DS267/7	18-03-2003 WT/DSB/M/145	16-10-2014 WT/DS267/46
268	美国—对来自阿根廷的石油管材的反倾销措施日落复审	阿根廷 WT/DS268/1	07-10-2002		03-04-2003 阿根廷 WT/DS268/2	19-05-2003 WT/DSB/M/150	

续 表

序号	案件	请求磋商	收到磋商请求（日-月-年）	加入磋商请求	请求成立专家组（日-月-年）	专家组成立（日-月-年）	双边达成解决方案（日-月-年）
269	欧共体—对冷冻无骨鸡块的关税分类	巴西 WT/DS269/1	11-10-2002	美国 WT/DS269/2	19-09-2003 巴西 WT/DS269/3	07-11-2003 WT/DSB/M/157	
270	澳大利亚—影响新鲜水果和蔬菜进口的特定措施	菲律宾 WT/DS270/1	18-10-2002	欧共体 WT/DS270/2 泰国 WT/DS270/3	07-07-2003 菲律宾 WT/DS270/5/Rev. 1	29-08-2003 WT/DSB/M/155	
271	澳大利亚—影响菠萝进口的措施	菲律宾 WT/DS271/1	18-10-2002	欧共体 WT/DS271/2 泰国 WT/DS271/3			
272	秘鲁—对来自阿根廷的植物油征收临时	阿根廷 WT/DS272/1	21-10-2002				
273	韩国—影响商船贸易的措施	欧共体 WT/DS273/1	21-10-2002		11-06-2003 欧共体 WT/DS273/2	21-07-2003 WT/DSB/M/153	
274	美国—对于特定钢铁产品进口的保障措施	台、澎、金、马单独关税区 WT/DS274/1	01-11-2002	日本 WT/DS274/2			
275	委内瑞拉—对特定农产品进口许可证措施	美国 WT/DS275/1	07-11-2002	欧共体 WT/DS275/2 加拿大 WT/DS275/3 新西兰 WT/DS275/4 阿根廷 WT/DS275/5 哥伦比亚 WT/DS275/6 智利 WT/DS275/7			
276	加拿大—对于小麦出口措施和谷物进口待遇	美国 WT/DS276/1	17-12-2002	日本 WT/DS276/2 墨西哥 WT/DS276/3 欧共体 WT/DS276/4 澳大利亚 WT/DS276/5	06-03-2003 美国 WT/DS276/6 30-06-2003 美国 WT/DS276/9	31-03-2003 WT/DSB/M/146 11-07-2003 WT/DSB/M/152	
277	美国—对来自加拿大的软木的国际贸易商会调查	加拿大 WT/DS277/1	20-12-2002		03-04-2003 加拿大 WT/DS277/2	07-05-2003 WT/DSB/M/149	12-10-2006 WT/DS277/20
278	智利—果糖进口的保障措施	阿根廷 WT/DS278/1	20-12-2002				

续 表

序号	案件	请求磋商	收到磋商请求（日-月-年）	加入磋商请求	请求成立专家组（日-月-年）	专家组成立（日-月-年）	双边达成解决方案（日-月-年）
279	印度—2002 年至 2007 年进出口政策中进口限制的持续	欧共体 WT/DS279/1	23-12-2002	美国 WT/DS279/2			
280	美国—对来自墨西哥的钢板的反补贴税	墨西哥 WT/DS280/1	21-01-2003		04-08-2003 墨西哥 WT/DS280/2	29-08-2003 WT/DSB/M/155	
281	美国—对来自墨西哥水泥的反倾销措施	墨西哥 WT/DS281/1	31-01-2003		29-07-2003 墨西哥 WT/DS281/2	29-08-2003 WT/DSB/M/155	16-05-2007 WT/DS281/8
282	美国—对来自墨西哥的石油工业用管材的反倾销措施	墨西哥 WT/DS282/1	18-02-2003		29-07-2003 墨西哥 WT/DS282/2	29-08-2003 WT/DSB/M/155	
283	欧共体—糖类出口补贴	泰国 WT/DS283/1	14-03-2003		09-07-2003 泰国 WT/DS283/2	29-08-2003 WT/DSB/M/155	
284	墨西哥—阻碍来自尼加拉瓜黑豆进口的特定措施	尼加拉瓜 WT/DS284/1	17-03-2003	美国 WT/DS284/2 加拿大 WT/DS284/3			
285	美国—影响博彩业跨境提供的措施	安提瓜和巴布达 WT/DS285/1 和 WT/DS285/1/Add. 1	13-03-2003 01-04-2003		12-06-2003 安提瓜和巴布达 WT/DS285/2	21-07-2003 WT/DSB/M/153	
286	欧共体—冷冻无骨鸡的关税分类	泰国 WT/DS286/1	25-03-2003	巴西 WT/DS286/2 美国 WT/DS286/3	27-10-2003 泰国 WT/DS286/5	21-11-2003 争端解决机构同意在 11 月 7 日成立专家组对巴西（WT/DS269/3）做出的上诉进行调查，同时也调查泰国（WT/DSB/M/15）就同一事件提出的投诉	
287	澳大利亚—进口检疫制度	欧共体 WT/DS287/1	03-04-2003	智利 WT/DS287/2 加拿大 WT/DS287/3 印度 WT/DS287/4 菲律宾 WT/DS287/5	29-08-2003 欧共体 WT/DS287/7 和 14-10-2003 WT/DS287/7 Rev. 1		09-03-2007 WT/DS287/8
288	南非—对来自土耳其毛毯的反倾销措施	土耳其 WT/DS288/1	09-04-2003				
289	捷克—对来自波兰的猪肉进口的额外关税	波兰 WT/DS289/1	16-04-2003				

续 表

序号	案件	请求磋商	收到磋商请求（日-月-年）	加入磋商请求	请求成立专家组（日-月-年）	专家组成立（日-月-年）	双边达成解决方案（日-月-年）
290	欧共体—农产品和食品的商标及地理标识保护	澳大利亚 WT/DS290/1	17-04-2003	马耳他 WT/DS290/2 保加利亚 WT/DS290/3 捷克 WT/DS290/4 塞浦路斯 WT/DS290/5 美国 WT/DS290/6 斯洛文尼亚 WT/DS290/7 新西兰 WT/DS290/8 土耳其 WT/DS290/9 墨西哥 WT/DS290/10 阿根廷 WT/DS290/11 匈牙利 WT/DS290/12 哥伦比亚 WT/DS290/13 罗马尼亚 WT/DS290/14 斯洛伐克 WT/DS290/15 台、澎、金、马单独关税区 WT/DS290/16	18-08-2003 澳大利亚 WT/DS290/18	02-10-2003 WT/DSB/M/156	
291	欧共体—影响生物科技产品审批及营销的措施	美国 WT/DS291/1	13-05-2003	秘鲁 WT/DS291/2 哥伦比亚 WT/DS291/3 墨西哥 WT/DS291/4 澳大利亚 WT/DS291/5 新西兰 WT/DS291/6 阿根廷 WT/DS291/7 巴西 WT/DS291/8 加拿大 WT/DS291/9 印度 WT/DS291/10 智利 WT/DS291/11	07-08-2003 WT/DS291/23	29-08-2003 WT/DSB/M/155	

续 表

序号	案件	请求磋商	收到磋商请求（日-月-年）	加入磋商请求	请求成立专家组（日-月-年）	专家组成立（日-月-年）	双边达成解决方案（日-月-年）
292	欧共体—影响生物科技产品审批及营销的措施	加拿大 WT/DS292/1	13-05-2003	墨西哥 WT/DS292/2 美国 WT/DS292/3 澳大利亚 WT/DS292/4 阿根廷 WT/DS292/5 巴西 WT/DS292/6 印度 WT/DS292/7 新西兰 WT/DS292/8	07-08-2003 WT/DS292/17	29-08-2003 WT/DSB/M/155	15-07-2009 WT/DS292/40
293	欧共体—影响生物科技产品批准及营销的措施	阿根廷 WT/DS293/1	14-05-2003	墨西哥 WT/DS293/2 美国 WT/DS293/3 澳大利亚 WT/DS293/4 巴西 WT/DS293/5 加拿大 WT/DS293/6 印度 WT/DS293/7 新西兰 WT/DS293/8	07-08-2003 阿根廷 WT/DS293/17	29-08-2003 WT/DSB/M/155	19-03-2010 WT/DS293/41
294	美国—计算倾销差额（归零法）的法律、规则及方法	欧共体 WT/DS294/1 和 WT/DS294/1/Add. 1	12-06-2003 08-09-2003	印度 WT/DS294/2 韩国 WT/DS294/3 日本 WT/DS294/4 墨西哥 WT/DS294/5 和 WT/DS294/6	05-02-2004 欧共体 WT/DS294/7	19-03-2004 WT/DSB/M/166	
295	墨西哥—对于牛肉及稻米反倾销措施	美国 WT/DS295/1	16-06-2003		19-09-2003 美国 WT/DS295/2		
296	美国—对于来自韩国的可计算机动态随机存取存储器芯片（DRAMS）征收反补贴税调查	韩国 WT/DS296/1 和 WT/DS296/1/Add. 1	30-06-2003 18-08-2003		19-11-2003 韩国 WT/DS296/2	23-01-2004 WT/DSB/M/163	

续 表

序号	案件	请求磋商	收到磋商请求（日-月-年）	加入磋商请求	请求成立专家组（日-月-年）	专家组成立（日-月-年）	双边达成解决方案（日-月-年）
297	克罗地亚—影响活体动物及肉产品进口的措施	匈牙利 WT/DS297/1	09-07-2003				30-01-2009 WT/DS297/2
298	墨西哥—对于海关估价及其他特定用途的定价方法	危地马拉 WT/DS298/1 撤销要求磋商的请求 WT/DS298/2 (29-08-2005)	22-07-2003				
299	欧共体—对来自韩国的计算机动态随机存取存储器芯片采取反补贴措施	韩国 WT/DS299/1 和 WT/DS299/1/Rev. 1/Add. 1	25-07-2003 25-08-2003		19-11-2003 韩国 WT/DS299/2	23-01-2004 WT/DSB/M/163	
300	多米尼加—影响香烟进口的措施	洪都拉斯 WT/DS300/1	28-08-2003				
301	欧共体—影响商船贸易的措施	韩国 WT/DS301/1	03-09-2003	中国 WT/DS301/2	05-02-2004 韩国 WT/DS301/3	19-03-2004 WT/DSB/M/163	
302	多米尼加—影响香烟进口和国内销售的措施	洪都拉斯 WT/DS302/1	08-10-2003	危地马拉 WT/DS302/2 尼加拉瓜 WT/DS302/3	08-12-2003 洪都拉斯 WT/DS302/5	09-01-2004 WT/DSB/M/162	
303	厄瓜多尔—对中密度板进口的保障措施	智利 WT/DS303/1	24-11-2003				
304	印度—对来自欧共体的特定产品进口的反倾销措施	欧共体 WT/DS304/1 和 Corr. 1	08-12-2003	土耳其 WT/DS304/2 台、澎、金、马单独关税区 WT/DS304/3			
305	埃及—影响纺织品及服装进口措施	美国 WT/DS305/1	23-12-2003	欧共体 WT/DS305/2			20-05-2005 WT/DS305/4
306	印度—对来自孟加拉电池采取反倾销措施	孟加拉 WT/DS306/1	28-01-2004	欧共体 WT/DS306/2			20-02-2006 WT/DS306/3
307	欧共体—对商船的补贴	韩国 WT/DS307/1	13-02-2004				

续 表

序号	案件	请求磋商	收到磋商请求（日-月-年）	加入磋商请求	请求成立专家组（日-月-年）	专家组成立（日-月-年）	双边达成解决方案（日-月-年）
308	墨西哥—对于非酒精饮料及其他饮料征税	美国 WT/DS308/1	16-03-2004	加拿大 WT/DS308/2	10-06-2004 美国 WT/DS308/4	06-07-2004 WT/DSB/M/172	
309	中国—对集成电路的增值税	美国 WT/DS309/1	18-03-2004	欧共体 WT/DS309/2 日本 WT/DS309/3 墨西哥 WT/DS309/4 台、澎、金、马单独关税区 WT/DS309/5			05-10-2005 WT/DS309/8
310	美国—国际贸易委员会对来自加拿大的硬粒赤春小麦的决定	加拿大 WT/DS310/1	08-04-2004		10-06-2004 加拿大 WT/DS310/2 2004年7月20日加拿大请求将成立专家组的要求从争端解决机构议程中撤出，保留其在未来会议中对该项请求的权利（WT/DSB/M/173）		
311	美国—对来自加拿大软木的反补贴税复审	加拿大 WT/DS311/1	14-04-2004				12-10-2006 WT/DS311/2 23-02-2007 WT/DS311/2/Add. 1
312	韩国—对来自印度尼西亚特定纸张征收反倾销税	印度尼西亚 WT/DS312/1	04-06-2004		16-08-2004 印度尼西亚 WT/DS312/2	27-09-2004 WT/DSB/M/176	
313	欧共体—对来自印度的扁钢和非合金钢产品采取反倾销措施	印度 WT/DS313/1	05-07-2004				22-10-2004 WT/DS313/2
314	墨西哥—对来自欧共体的橄榄油采取临时反补贴措施	欧共体 WT/DS314/1	18-08-2004				

续 表

序号	案件	请求磋商	收到磋商请求（日-月-年）	加入磋商请求	请求成立专家组（日-月-年）	专家组成立（日-月-年）	双边达成解决方案（日-月-年）
315	欧共体—特定海关措施	美国 WT/DS315/1	21-09-2004	澳大利亚 WT/DS315/2 日本 WT/DS315/3 巴西 WT/DS315/4 阿根廷 WT/DS315/5 台、澎、金、马单独关税区 WT/DS315/6 印度 WT/DS315/7	13-01-2005 美国 WT/DS315/8	21-03-2005 WT/DSB/M/186	
316	欧共体及其某些成员国—影响大型民用航空器贸易的措施	美国 WT/DS316/1 WT/DS316/1/Add. 1	06-10-2004 31-01-2006		31-05-2005 美国 WT/DS316/2 11-04-2006 美国 WT/DS316/6	20-07-2005 WT/DSB/M/194 09-05-2006 WT/DSB/M/211 和 Corr. 1	
317	美国—影响大型民用航空器贸易的措施	欧共体 WT/DS317/1 WT/DS317/1/Add. 1	06-10-2004 27-06-2005		31-05-2005 欧共体 WT/DS317/2 20-01-2006 欧共体 WT/DS317/5	20-07-2005 WT/DSB/M/194 17-02-2006 WT/DSB/M/205	
318	印度—对来自台、澎、金、马单独关税区特定产品的反倾销措施	台、澎、金、马单独关税区 WT/DS318/1	28-10-2004				
319	美国—1930年关税法案第776节	欧共体 WT/DS319/1	05-11-2004				
320	美国—继续中止在荷尔蒙案件中的义务	欧共体 WT/DS320/1	08-11-2004	加拿大 WT/DS320/2 澳大利亚 WT/DS320/3 墨西哥 WT/DS320/4	13-01-2005 欧共体 WT/DS320/6	17-02-2005 WT/DSB/M/183	
321	加拿大—欧共体继续中止在荷尔蒙案件中义务	欧共体 WT/DS321/1	08-11-2004	澳大利亚 WT/DS321/2 墨西哥 WT/DS321/3 美国 WT/DS321/4	13-01-2005 欧共体 WT/DS321/6	17-02-2005 WT/DSB/M/183	

续 表

序号	案件	请求磋商	收到磋商请求（日-月-年）	加入磋商请求	请求成立专家组（日-月-年）	专家组成立（日-月-年）	双边达成解决方案（日-月-年）
322	美国—与归零法及日落复审相关的措施	日本 WT/DS322/1	24-11-2004	印度 WT/DS322/2 挪威 WT/DS322/3 阿根廷 WT/DS322/4 台、澎、金、马单独关税区 WT/DS322/5 欧共体 WT/DS322/6 墨西哥 WT/DS322/7	04-02-2005 日本 WT/DS322/8	28-02-2005 WT/DSB/M/185	
323	日本—干紫菜和味付紫菜进口配额	韩国 WT/DS323/1	01-12-2004		04-02-2005 韩国 WT/DS323/2	21-03-2005 WT/DSB/M/186	23-01-2006 WT/DS323/5
324	美国—对来自泰国虾的临时反倾销措施	泰国 WT/DS324/1	09-12-2004	日本 WT/DS324/2 巴西 WT/DS324/3 欧共体 WT/DS324/4 中国 WT/DS324/5 印度 WT/DS324/6 厄瓜多尔 WT/DS324/7			
325	美国—对来自墨西哥的不锈钢的反倾销措施	墨西哥 WT/DS325/1	05-01-2005	日本 WT/DS325/2 欧共体 WT/DS325/3			
326	欧共体—对于鲑鱼的保障措施	智利 WT/DS326/1 撤回磋商请求 WT/DS326/4 (12-05-2005)	08-02-2005	挪威 WT/DS326/2			
327	埃及—对来自巴基斯坦火柴的反倾销措施	巴基斯坦 WT/DS327/1	21-02-2005		09-06-2005 巴基斯坦 WT/DS327/2	20-07-2005 WT/DSB/M/194	27-03-2006 WT/DS327/3
328	欧共体—对于鲑鱼的保障措施	挪威 WT/DS328/1	01-03-2005	智利 WT/DS328/2			
329	巴拿马—对于特定奶类产品的关税分类	墨西哥 WT/DS329/1	16-03-2005				20-09-2005 WT/DS329/2

续 表

序号	案件	请求磋商	收到磋商请求（日-月-年）	加入磋商请求	请求成立专家组（日-月-年）	专家组成立（日-月-年）	双边达成解决方案（日-月-年）
330	阿根廷—对于橄榄油、面筋及桃子的反补贴税	欧共体 WT/DS330/1	29-04-2005				
331	墨西哥—对来自危地马拉的钢管征收反倾销税	危地马拉 WT/DS331/1	17-06-2005		.06-02-2006 危地马拉 WT/DS331/2	17-03-2006 WT/DSB/M/207	
332	巴西—影响翻新轮胎进口的措施	欧共体 WT/DS332/1	20-06-2005	阿根廷 WT/DS332/2	17-11-2005 欧共体 WT/DS332/4	20-01-2006 WT/DSB/M/203	
333	多米尼加—影响从自哥斯达黎加进口的外汇费用	哥斯达黎加 WT/DS333/1	12-09-2005	危地马拉 WT/DS333/2 萨尔瓦多 WT/DS333/3			
334	土耳其—影响稻米进口的措施	美国 WT/DS334/1	02-11-2005	澳大利亚 WT/DS334/2 泰国 WT/DS334/3	06-02-2006 美国 WT/DS334/4	17-03-2006 WT/DSB/M/207	
335	美国—对来自厄瓜多尔的虾的反倾销措施	厄瓜多尔 WT/DS335/1	17-11-2005	欧共体 WT/DS335/2 印度 WT/DS335/3 巴西 WT/DS335/4 泰国 WT/DS335/5	08-06-2006 厄瓜多尔 WT/DS335/6	19-07-2006 WT/DSB/M/217	
336	日本—对来自韩国的计算机动态随机存取存储器芯片的反补贴措施	韩国 WT/DS336/1	14-03-2006	美国 WT/DS336/2 欧共体 WT/DS336/3	18-05-2006 韩国 WT/DS336/5	19-06-2006 WT/DSB/M/215	
337	欧共体—对来自挪威的养殖鲑鱼的反倾销措施	挪威 WT/DS337/1 和 WT/DS337/1/Add. 1	17-03-2006 27-03-2006		29-05-2006 挪威 WT/DS337/2	22-06-2006 WT/DSB/M/216	
338	加拿大—对来自美国谷物玉米征收临时的反倾销税和反补贴税	美国 WT/DS338/1	17-03-2006				

续 表

序号	案件	请求磋商	收到磋商请求（日-月-年）	加入磋商请求	请求成立专家组（日-月-年）	专家组成立（日-月-年）	双边达成解决方案（日-月-年）
339	中国—影响汽车零部件进口的措施	欧共体 WT/DS339/1	30-03-2006	美国 WT/DS339/2 日本 WT/DS339/3 澳大利亚 WT/DS339/4 墨西哥 WT/DS339/5 加拿大 WT/DS339/6	15-09-2006 欧共体 WT/DS339/8	26-10-2006 WT/DSB/M/221	
340	中国—影响汽车零部件进口的措施	美国 WT/DS340/1	30-03-2006	日本 WT/DS340/2 欧共体 WT/DS340/3 澳大利亚 WT/DS340/4 墨西哥 WT/DS340/5 加拿大 WT/DS340/6	15-09-2006 美国 WT/DS340/8	26-10-2006 WT/DSB/M/221	
341	墨西哥—对来自欧共体的橄榄油采取反补贴措施	欧共体 WT/DS341/1	31-03-2006		07-12-2006 欧共体 WT/DS341/2	23-01-2007 WT/DSB/M/225	
342	中国—影响汽车零部件进口的措施	加拿大 WT/DS342/1	13-04-2006	美国 WT/DS342/2 澳大利亚 WT/DS342/3 日本 WT/DS342/4 欧共体 WT/DS342/5 墨西哥 WT/DS342/6	15-09-2006 加拿大 WT/DS342/8	26-10-2006 WT/DSB/M/221	
343	美国—影响来自泰国虾的措施	泰国 WT/DS343/1 和 Corr. 2	24-04-2006	印度 WT/DS343/2 日本 WT/DS343/3 巴西 WT/DS343/4 中国 WT/DS343/5	15-09-2006 泰国 WT/DS343/7	26-10-2006 WT/DSB/M/221	

续 表

序号	案件	请求磋商	收到磋商请求（日-月-年）	加入磋商请求	请求成立专家组（日-月-年）	专家组成立（日-月-年）	双边达成解决方案（日-月-年）
344	美国—对来自墨西哥不锈钢的反倾销措施	墨西哥 WT/DS344/1	26-05-2006	日本 WT/DS344/2	12-10-2006 墨西哥 WT/DS344/4	26-10-2006 WT/DSB/M/221	08-04-2013 WT/DS344/26
345	美国—涉及反倾销及反补贴税的商品海关保证金	印度 WT/DS345/1	06-06-2006	泰国 WT/DS345/2 中国 WT/DS345/3 巴西 WT/DS345/4	13-10-2006 印度 WT/DS345/6	21-11-2006 WT/DSB/M/222	
346	美国—对来自阿根廷的工业用管材的反倾销行政复审	阿根廷 WT/DS346/1	20-06-2006				
347	欧共体及其某些成员国—影响大型民用航空器贸易的措施（二诉）	美国 WT/DS347/1	31-01-2006		11-04-2006 美国 WT/DS347/3	09-05-2006 WT/DSB/M/211 和 Corr. 1 根据 DSU 第 12.12 条 2007 年 10 月 7 日专家组解散	
348	哥伦比亚—来自巴拿马特定产品进口的海关措施	巴拿马 WT/DS348/1	20-07-2006	危地马拉 WT/DS348/2 中国 WT/DS348/3 菲律宾 WT/DS348/4 中国香港 WT/DS348/5 巴基斯坦 WT/DS348/6 WT/DS348/7 泰国 WT/DS348/8			01-12-2006 WT/DS348/10
349	欧共体—影响新鲜及冷藏大蒜的关税配额措施	阿根廷 WT/DS349/1	06-09-2006				
350	美国—继续使用归零法	欧共体 WT/DS350/1 和 WT/DS350/1/Add. 1	02-10-2006 09-10-2006	日本 WT/DS350/2 泰国 WT/DS350/3 巴西 WT/DS350/4 印度 WT/DS350/5	10-05-2007 欧共体 WT/DS350/6	04-06-2007 WT/DSB/M/233	
351	智利—对于特定奶制品的临时保障措施	阿根廷 WT/DS351/1	25-10-2006		8-03-2007 阿根廷 WT/DS351/2 WT/DS356/2	24-04-2007 WT/DSB/M/230	

续 表

序号	案件	请求磋商	收到磋商请求（日-月-年）	加入磋商请求	请求成立专家组（日-月-年）	专家组成立（日-月-年）	双边达成解决方案（日-月-年）
352	印度—影响来自欧共体葡萄酒和烈性酒进口和销售的措施	欧共体 WT/DS352/1	20-11-2006	美国 WT/DS352/2 澳大利亚 WT/DS352/3	23-03-2007 欧共体 WT/DS352/4	24-04-2007 WT/DSB/M/230 17-07-2008 建立专家组的授权取消（WT/DS352/7）	
353	美国—影响大型民用航空器贸易的措施（二诉）	欧共体 WT/DS353/1 WT/DS317/1/Add. 2			欧共体 WT/DS353/2/Corr. 1 WT/DS317/5/Add. 1/Corr. 1		
354	加拿大—对葡萄酒和啤酒的税收减免	欧共体 WT/DS354/1	29-11-2006				17-12-2008 WT/DS354/2
355	巴西—对产自阿根廷特定树脂征收反倾销税	阿根廷 WT/DS355/1	26-12-2006		07-06-2007 阿根廷 WT/DS355/2	24-07-2007 WT/DSB/M/236 05-02-2009 建立专家组的授权取消 WT/DS355/6	
356	智利—对特定奶制品实施保障措施	阿根廷 WT/DS356/1	28-12-2006		8-03-2007 阿根廷 WT/DS351/2 WT/DS356/2	24-04-2007 WT/DSB/M/230	
357	美国—对玉米和其他农产品的补贴和国内支持	加拿大 WT/DS357/1	08-01-2007	澳大利亚 WT/DS357/2 危地马拉 WT/DS357/3 巴西 WT/DS357/4 阿根廷 WT/DS357/5 欧共体 WT/DS357/6 乌拉圭 WT/DS357/7 尼加拉瓜 WT/DS357/8 泰国 WT/DS357/9	07-06-2007 加拿大 WT/DS357/11 15-11-2007 撤回请求 WT/DS357/13 08-11-2007 加拿大 WT/DS357/12 和 Corr. 1	17-12-2007 WT/DSB/M/243	

续 表

序号	案件	请求磋商	收到磋商请求（日-月-年）	加入磋商请求	请求成立专家组（日-月-年）	专家组成立（日-月-年）	双边达成解决方案（日-月-年）
358	中国—国内税收和其他支付的退还、抵免、减免措施	美国 WT/DS358/1	02-02-2007	欧共体 WT/DS358/2 澳大利亚 WT/DS358/3 日本 WT/DS358/4 墨西哥 WT/DS358/5	12-07-2007 美国 WT/DS358/13	31-08-2007 WT/DSB/M/238	
		WT/DS358/1/Add. 1	27-04-2007	墨西哥 WT/DS358/7 欧共体 WT/DS358/8 澳大利亚 WT/DS358/9 日本 WT/DS358/10 加拿大 WT/DS358/11			
359	中国—国内税收和其他支付的退还、抵免、减免措施	墨西哥 WT/DS359/1	26-02-2007	欧共体 WT/DS359/2 澳大利亚 WT/DS359/3 日本 WT/DS359/4 美国 WT/DS359/5	12-07-2007 墨西哥 WT/DS359/13	31-08-2007 WT/DSB/M/238	
		WT/DS359/1/Add. 1	04-05-2007	澳大利亚 WT/DS359/7 欧共体 WT/DS359/8 加拿大 WT/DS359/9 日本 WT/DS359/10 美国 WT/DS359/11			
360	印度—对来自美国的进口产品征收“附加税”和“超额附加税”	美国 WT/DS360/1	06-03-2007	欧共体 WT/DS360/2 澳大利亚 WT/DS360/3	24-05-2007 美国 WT/DS360/5	20-06-2007 WT/DSB/M/234	
361	欧共体—香蕉进口制度	哥伦比亚 WT/DS361/1	21-03-2007				08-11-2012 WT/DS361/3

续 表

序号	案件	请求磋商	收到磋商请求（日-月-年）	加入磋商请求	请求成立专家组（日-月-年）	专家组成立（日-月-年）	双边达成解决方案（日-月-年）
362	中国—影响知识产权保护和执法的措施	美国 WT/DS362/1	10-04-2007	日本 WT/DS362/2 欧共体 WT/DS362/3 加拿大 WT/DS362/4 墨西哥 WT/DS362/5	21-08-2007 美国 WT/DS362/7	25-09-2007 WT/DSB/M/239	
363	中国—影响某些出版物和视听娱乐产品贸易权和分销权的措施	美国 WT/DS363/1 WT/DS363/1/Add. 1	10-04-2007 10-07-2007	欧共体 WT/DS363/2 欧共体 WT/DS363/4	10-10-2007 美国 WT/DS363/5	27-11-2007 WT/DSB/M/242	
364	欧共体—香蕉进口制度	巴拿马 WT/DS364/1	22-06-2007				08-11-2012 WT/DS364/3
365	美国—对农产品的国内支持和出口信贷担保	巴西 WT/DS365/1	11-07-2007	加拿大 WT/DS365/2 危地马拉 WT/DS365/3 哥斯达黎加 WT/DS365/4 欧共体 WT/DS365/5 墨西哥 WT/DS365/6 澳大利亚 WT/DS365/7 阿根廷 WT/DS365/8 泰国 WT/DS365/9 印度 WT/DS365/10 尼加拉瓜 WT/DS365/11	08-11-2007 巴西 WT/DS365/13	17-12-2007 WT/DSB/M/243	
366	哥伦比亚—指示性价格和入境港口的限制	巴拿马 WT/DS366/1	12-07-2007	危地马拉 WT/DS366/2 洪都拉斯 WT/DS366/3 台、澎、金、马单独关税区 WT/DS366/4	14-09-2007 巴拿马 WT/DS366/6	22-10-2007 WT/DSB/M/241	

续表

序号	案件	请求磋商	收到磋商请求（日-月-年）	加入磋商请求	请求成立专家组（日-月-年）	专家组成立（日-月-年）	双边达成解决方案（日-月-年）
367	澳大利亚—影响来自新西兰苹果进口的措施	新西兰 WT/DS367/1	31-08-2007	欧共体 WT/DS367/2 美国 WT/DS367/3	06-12-2007 新西兰 WT/DS367/5	21-01-2008 WT/DSB/M/245	
368	美国—对来自中国的铜版纸征收临时反倾销和反补贴税	中国 WT/DS368/1	14-09-2007				
369	欧共体—禁止海豹产品进口和销售的措施	加拿大 WT/DS369/1	25-09-2007		11-02-2011 加拿大 WT/DS369/2	25-03-2011 WT/DSB/M/294	
370	泰国—对来自欧共体特定商品的海关估价制度	欧共体 WT/DS370/1	25-01-2008	菲律宾 WT/DS370/2 美国 WT/DS370/3			
371	泰国—对来自菲律宾烟草所采取的海关和财政措施	菲律宾 WT/DS371/1	07-02-2008	欧共体 WT/DS371/2	29-09-2008 菲律宾 WT/DS371/3	17-11-2008 WT/DSB/M/259	
372	中国—影响金融信息服务和外资金融信息服务提供商的措施	欧共体 WT/DS372/1	03-03-2008	美国 WT/DS372/2			
373	中国—影响金融信息服务和外资金融信息服务提供商的措施	美国 WT/DS373/1	03-03-2008	欧共体 WT/DS373/2			
374	南非—对未涂层纸采取反倾销措施	印度尼西亚 WT/DS374/1 撤回磋商请求 WT/DS374/2（2008年11月20日）	09-05-2008				
375	欧共体及其成员—对特定信息技术产品的关税措施	美国 WT/DS375/1	28-05-2008	泰国 WT/DS375/2 日本 WT/DS375/3 新加坡 WT/DS375/4 菲律宾 WT/DS375/5 台、澎、金、马单独关税区 WT/DS375/6 中国 WT/DS375/7	18-08-2008 美国 WT/DS375/8 WT/DS376/8 WT/DS377/6	23-09-2008 WT/DSB/M/256	

续 表

序号	案件	请求磋商	收到磋商请求（日-月-年）	加入磋商请求	请求成立专家组（日-月-年）	专家组成立（日-月-年）	双边达成解决方案（日-月-年）
376	欧共体及其成员—对特定信息技术产品的关税措施	日本 WT/DS376/1	28-05-2008	泰国 WT/DS376/2 台、澎、金、马单独关税区 WT/DS376/3 新加坡 WT/DS376/4 菲律宾 WT/DS376/5 美国 WT/DS376/6 中国 WT/DS376/7	18-08-2008 日本 WT/D376/8 WT/DS375/8 WT/DS377/6	23-09-2008 WT/DSB/M/256	
377	欧共体及其成员—对特定信息技术产品的关税措施	台、澎、金、马单独关税区 WT/DS377/1	12-06-2008	美国 WT/DS377/2 中国 WT/DS377/3 日本 WT/DS377/4	18-08-2008 台、澎、金、马单独关税区 WT/DS377/6 WT/DS375/8 WT/DS376/8	23-09-2008 WT/DSB/M/256	
378	中国—影响金融信息服务和外资金融信息服务提供商的措施	加拿大 WT/DS378/1	20-06-2008	美国 WT/DS378/2			
379	美国—对来自中国的特定产品征收反倾销税和反补贴税	中国 WT/DS379/1	19-09-2008		09-12-2008 中国 WT/DS379/2	20-01-2009 WT/DSB/M/263	
380	印度—对进口葡萄酒与烈酒采取的某些税收和其他措施	欧共体 WT/DS380/1 WT/DS380/1/Add. 1 WT/DS380/1/Add. 2	22-09-2008 15-12-2008 04-05-2009	澳大利亚 WT/DS380/2 美国 WT/DS380/3 美国 WT/DS380/4 美国 WT/DS380/5			
381	美国—对金枪鱼和金枪鱼产品的进口、营销和销售采取的措施	墨西哥 WT/DS381/1	24-10-2008	欧共体 WT/DS381/2 澳大利亚 WT/DS381/3	09-03-2009 墨西哥 WT/DS381/4	20-04-2009 WT/DSB/M/267	
382	美国—对从巴西进口的特定橙汁采取的反倾销行政复审和其他措施	巴西 WT/DS382/1 WT/DS382/1/Add. 1	27-11-2008 22-05-2009	日本 WT/DS382/2 日本 WT/DS382/3	20-08-2009 巴西 WT/DS382/4	25-09-2009 WT/DSB/M/274	14-02-2013 WT/DS382/12（双方达成满意的解决方案）

续 表

序号	案件	请求磋商	收到磋商请求（日-月-年）	加入磋商请求	请求成立专家组（日-月-年）	专家组成立（日-月-年）	双边达成解决方案（日-月-年）
383	美国—对从泰国进口的聚乙烯包装袋采取的反倾销措施	泰国 WT/DS383/1	26-11-2008		09-03-2009 泰国 WT/DS383/2	20-03-2009 WT/DSB/M/266	
384	美国—对特定国家原产地标签要求	加拿大 WT/DS384/1 WT/DS384/1/Add. 1	01-12-2008 07-05-2009	尼加拉瓜 WT/DS384/2 墨西哥 WT/DS384/3 墨西哥 WT/DS384/5 秘鲁 WT/DS384/6	07-10-2009 加拿大 WT/DS384/8	19-11-2009 WT/DSB/M276	
385	欧共体—对从印度进口的聚对苯二甲酸乙二醇酯（PET）征收反倾销和反补贴税的期终复审	印度 WT/DS385/1	04-12-2008				
386	美国—对特定国家原产地标签要求	墨西哥 WT/DS386/1 WT/DS386/1/Add. 1	17-12-2008 07-05-2009	加拿大 WT/DS386/2 加拿大 WT/DS386/4 秘鲁 WT/DS386/5	13-10-2009 墨西哥 WT/DS386/7和Corr. 1	19-11-2009 WT/DSB/M/276	
387	中国—援助、贷款和其他鼓励措施	美国 WT/DS387/1	19-12-2008	墨西哥 WT/DS387/2 欧共体 WT/DS387/3 加拿大 WT/DS387/4 澳大利亚 WT/DS387/5 土耳其 WT/DS387/6 哥伦比亚 WT/DS387/7 危地马拉 WT/DS387/8 厄瓜多尔 WT/DS387/9 新西兰 WT/DS387/10			

续 表

序号	案件	请求磋商	收到磋商请求（日-月-年）	加入磋商请求	请求成立专家组（日-月-年）	专家组成立（日-月-年）	双边达成解决方案（日-月-年）
388	中国—援助、贷款和其他鼓励措施	墨西哥 WT/DS388/1	19-12-2008	欧共体 WT/DS388/2 加拿大 WT/DS388/3 澳大利亚 WT/DS388/4 土耳其 WT/DS388/5 美国 WT/DS388/6 哥伦比亚 WT/DS388/7 危地马拉 WT/DS388/8 厄瓜多尔 WT/DS388/9 新西兰 WT/DS388/10			
389	欧共体—对从美国进口的鸡肉及其产品采取的特定措施	美国 WT/DS389/1	16-01-2009	澳大利亚 WT/DS389/2	08-10-2009 美国 WT/DS389/4	19-11-2009 WT/DSB/M/276	
390	中国—援助、贷款和其他鼓励措施	危地马拉 WT/DS390/1	19-01-2009	欧共体 WT/DS390/2 澳大利亚 WT/DS390/3 墨西哥 WT/DS390/4 美国 WT/DS390/5 土耳其 WT/DS390/6 厄瓜多尔 WT/DS390/7 哥伦比亚 WT/DS390/8 加拿大 WT/DS390/9 新西兰 WT/DS390/10			
391	韩国—对从加拿大进口牛肉及其产品采取的措施	加拿大 WT/DS391/1	09-04-2009	欧共体 WT/DS391/2	09-07-2009 加拿大 WT/DS391/3	31-08-2009 WT/DSB/M/273	19-06-2012 WT/DS391/9
392	美国—对从中国进口的鸡肉采取的特定措施	中国 WT/DS392/1	17-04-2009		23-06-2009 中国 WT/DS392/2	31-07-2009 WT/DSB/M/272	
393	智利—对从阿根廷进口面粉采取的反倾销措施	阿根廷 WT/DS393/1	14-05-2009				

续 表

序号	案件	请求磋商	收到磋商请求（日-月-年）	加入磋商请求	请求成立专家组（日-月-年）	专家组成立（日-月-年）	双边达成解决方案（日-月-年）
394	中国—与限制原材料出口有关的措施	美国 WT/DS394/1	23-06-2009	欧共体 WT/DS394/2 土耳其 WT/DS394/3 加拿大 WT/DS394/4 墨西哥 WT/DS394/5	04-11-2009 美国 WT/DS394/7	21-12-2009 WT/DSB/M/277	
395	中国—与限制原材料出口有关的措施	欧共体 WT/DS395/1	23-06-2009	土耳其 WT/DS395/2 美国 WT/DS395/3 加拿大 WT/DS395/4 墨西哥 WT/DS395/5	04-11-2009 欧共体 WT/DS395/7	21-12-2009 WT/DSB/M/277	
396	菲律宾—对蒸馏酒征收国内税	欧共体 WT/DS396/1	29-07-2009	美国 WT/DS396/2	10-12-2009 欧盟 WT/DS396/4	19-01-2010 WT/DSB/M/278	
397	欧共体—对从中国进口的钢铁紧固件采取最终反倾销措施	中国 WT/DS397/1	31-07-2009		12-10-2009 中国 WT/DS397/3	23-10-2009 WT/DSB/M/275	
398	中国—与限制原材料出口有关的措施	墨西哥 WT/DS398/1	21-08-2009	欧共体 WT/DS398/2 美国 WT/DS398/3 哥伦比亚 WT/DS398/4 加拿大 WT/DS398/5	04-11-2009 墨西哥 WT/DS398/6	21-12-2009 WT/DSB/M/277	
399	美国—对从中国进口汽车轮胎采取的限制措施	中国 WT/DS399/1	14-09-2009		09-12-2009 中国 WT/DS399/2	19-01-2010 WT/DSB/M/278	
400	欧共体—限制海豹产品进口及营销的限制措施	加拿大 WT/DS400/1 WT/DS400/1/Add. 1	02-11-2009 18-10-2010	冰岛 WT/DS400/2 挪威 WT/DS400/3	11-02-2011 加拿大 WT/DS400/4	25-03-2011 WT/DSB/M/294	
401	欧共体—限制海豹产品进口及营销的限制措施	挪威 WT/DS401/1 WT/DS401/1/Add. 1	05-11-2009 19-10-2010	冰岛 WT/DS401/2 加拿大 WT/DS401/3 加拿大 WT/DS401/4	14-03-2011 挪威 WT/DS401/5	21-04-2011 争端解决机构同意在2011年3月25日会议上，设立专家组以调查加拿大的投诉（WT/DS400/4）和挪威的投诉（WT/DSB/M/295）	

续 表

序号	案件	请求磋商	收到磋商请求（日-月-年）	加入磋商请求	请求成立专家组（日-月-年）	专家组成立（日-月-年）	双边达成解决方案（日-月-年）
402	美国—对自韩国产品的反倾销措施适用归零法	韩国 WT/DS402/1	24-11-2009	日本 WT/DS402/2	08-04-2010 韩国 WT/DS402/3	18-05-2010 WT/DSB/M/283	
403	菲律宾—对蒸馏酒精征税	美国 WT/DS403/1	14-01-2010	欧盟 WT/DS403/2	26-03-2010 美国 WT/DS403/4	20-04-2010 争端解决机构同意在 2010 年 1 月 19 日会议上成立专家组来调查欧盟提请的上诉，同时也就美国提请的类似案件上诉做相应调查 WT/DSB/M/282	
404	美国—对自越南进口的虾采取反倾销措施	越南 WT/DS404/1	01-02-2010	日本 WT/DS404/2 欧盟 WT/DS404/3 泰国 WT/DS404/4	07-04-2020 越南 WT/DS404/5	18-05-2010 WT/DSB/M/283	
405	欧盟—对自中国进口的鞋采取反倾销措施	中国 WT/DS405/1	04-02-2010		08-04-2010 中国 WT/DS405/2	18-05-2010 WT/DSB/M/283	
406	美国—影响丁香香烟生产和销售的措施	印度尼西亚 WT/DS406/1	07-04-2010		09-06-2010 印度尼西亚 WT/DS406/2	20-07-2010 WT/DSB/M/285	03-10-2014 WT/DS406/17
407	中国—对自欧盟的钢铁坚固件征收临时反倾销税	欧盟 WT/DS407/1	07-05-2010				
408	欧盟及其成员—运输中的癫痫仿制药	印度 WT/DS408/1	11-05-2010	加拿大 WT/DS408/2 巴西 WT/DS408/3 厄瓜多尔 WT/DS408/4 土耳其 WT/DS408/5 中国 WT/DS408/6 日本 WT/DS408/7			

续 表

序号	案件	请求磋商	收到磋商请求（日-月-年）	加入磋商请求	请求成立专家组（日-月-年）	专家组成立（日-月-年）	双边达成解决方案（日-月-年）
409	欧盟及其成员—运输中的癫痫仿制药	巴西 WT/DS409/1	12-05-2010	加拿大 WT/DS409/2 厄瓜多尔 WT/DS409/3 印度 WT/DS409/4 土耳其 WT/DS409/5 中国 WT/DS409/6 日本 WT/DS409/7			
410	阿根廷—对来自秘鲁的紧固件及链条实施反倾销措施	秘鲁 WT/DS410/1	19-05-2010				
411	亚美尼亚—影响香烟和酒精输入和进口的措施	乌克兰 WT/DS411/1	20-07-2010		06-10-2010 乌克兰 WT/DS411/2/Rev. 1		
412	加拿大—影响再生能源部门的措施	日本 WT/DS412/1	13-09-2010	美国 WT/DS412/2 欧盟 WT/DS412/3	01-06-2011 日本 WT/DS412/5	20-07-2011 WT/DSB/M/300	
413	中国—影响电子支付服务的措施	美国 WT/DS413/1	15-09-2010		11-02-2011 美国 WT/DS413/2	25-03-2011 WT/DSB/M/294	
414	中国—对自美国进口的取向电工钢征收反补贴税和反倾销税	美国 WT/DS414/1	15-09-2010		11-02-2011 美国 WT/DS414/2	25-03-2011 WT/DSB/M/294	
415	多米尼加—聚丙烯管状织物包装袋进口的保障措施	哥斯达黎加 WT/DS415/1	15-10-2010	巴拿马 WT/DS415/2 萨尔瓦多 WT/DS415/3 洪都拉斯 WT/DS415/4 危地马拉 WT/DS415/5	15-12-2010 哥斯达黎加 WT/DS415/7	07-02-2011 WT/DSB/M/292	
416	多米尼加—聚丙烯管状织物包装袋进口的保障措施	危地马拉 WT/DS416/1	15-10-2010	巴拿马 WT/DS416/2 哥斯达黎加 WT/DS416/3 厄瓜多尔 WT/DS416/4 洪都拉斯 WT/DS416/5	15-12-2010 危地马拉 WT/DS416/7	07-02-2011 WT/DSB/M/292	

续 表

序号	案件	请求磋商	收到磋商请求（日-月-年）	加入磋商请求	请求成立专家组（日-月-年）	专家组成立（日-月-年）	双边达成解决方案（日-月-年）
417	多米尼加—聚丙烯管状织物包装袋进口的保障措施	洪都拉斯 WT/DS417/1	18-10-2010	巴拿马 WT/DS417/2 和 Corr. 1 哥斯达黎加 WT/DS417/3 萨尔瓦多 WT/DS417/4 危地马拉 WT/DS417/5	20-12-2010 洪都拉斯 WT/DS417/7	07-02-2011 WT/DSB/M/292	
418	多米尼加—聚丙烯管状织物包装袋进口的保障措施	萨尔瓦多 WT/DS418/1	19-10-2010	巴拿马 WT/DS418/2 哥斯达黎加 WT/DS418/3 洪都拉斯 WT/DS418/4 危地马拉 WT/DS418/5	20-12-2010 萨尔瓦多 WT/DS418/7	07-02-2011 WT/DSB/M/292	
419	中国—有关风能设备的措施	美国 WT/DS419/1	22-12-2010	欧盟 WT/DS419/2 日本 WT/DS419/3			
420	美国—对自韩国进口的耐腐蚀碳钢板采取反倾销措施	韩国 WT/DS420/1	31-01-2011	日本 WT/DS420/2 墨西哥 WT/DS420/3	15-09-2011 韩国 WT/DS420/4 09-02-2012 韩国 WT/DS420/5	22-02-2012 WT/DSB/M/312	
421	摩尔多瓦-影响货物进口及国内销售的措施（环保税）	乌克兰 WT/DS421/1	17-02-2011	欧盟 WT/DS421/2	12-05-2011 乌克兰 WT/DS421/4	17-06-2011 WT/DSB/M/298	
422	美国—对自中国进口的冷冻暖水虾采取反倾销措施	中国 WT/DS422/1 WT/DS422/1/Add. 1	28-02-2011 27-07-2011	日本 WT/DS422/2	13-10-2011 中国 WT/DS422/3	25-10-2011 WT/DSB/M/305	
423	乌克兰—蒸馏酒征税	摩尔多瓦 WT/DS423/1	02-03-2011	欧盟 WT/DS423/2	01-06-2011 摩尔多瓦 WT/DS423/4	20-07-2011 WT/DSB/M/300	
424	美国—对自意大利进口的不锈钢薄板和卷材不锈钢薄板和卷材采取反倾销措施	欧盟 WT/DS424/1	01-04-2011	日本 WT/DS424/2			
425	中国—对从欧盟进口的X射线安全检查设备征收最终反倾销税	欧盟 WT/DS425/1	25-07-2011		08-12-2011 欧盟 WT/DS425/2	20-01-2012 WT/DSB/M/311	

续 表

序号	案件	请求磋商	收到磋商请求（日-月-年）	加入磋商请求	请求成立专家组（日-月-年）	专家组成立（日-月-年）	双边达成解决方案（日-月-年）
426	加拿大—上网电价补贴计划相关措施	欧盟 WT/DS426/1 WT/DS426/1/Add. 1	11-08-2011 22-08-2011	美国 WT/DS426/2 日本 WT/DS426/3	09-01-2012 欧盟 WT/DS426/5	20-01-2012 WT/DSB/M/311	
427	中国—对自美国的白羽肉鸡产品采取反倾销和反补贴措施	美国 WT/DS427/1	20-09-2011		08-12-2011 美国 WT/DS427/2	20-01-2012 WT/DSB/M/311	
428	土耳其—对来自印度的进口棉纱（不包括缝纫线）采取保障措施	印度 WT/DS428/1	13-02-2012				
429	美国—对源自越南的某些暖水虾的反倾销措施	越南 WT/DS429/1	22-02-2012		17-01-2013 越南 WT/DS429/2/Rev. 1 和 Corr. 2	27-02-2013 WT/DSB/M/329	
430	印度—影响某些农产品进口的措施	美国 WT/DS430/1	06-03-2012	哥伦比亚 WT/DS430/2	11-05-2012 美国 WT/DS430/3	25-06-2012 WT/DSB/M/318	
431	中国—影响稀土、钨、钼出口的措施	美国 WT/DS431/1	13-03-2012	欧盟 WT/DS431/2 日本 WT/DS431/3 加拿大 WT/DS431/4	27-06-2012 美国 WT/DS431/6	23-07-2012 WT/DSB/M/320	
432	中国—影响稀土、钨、钼出口的措施	欧盟 WT/DS432/1	13-03-2012	日本 WT/DS432/2 美国 WT/DS432/3 加拿大 WT/DS432/4	27-06-2012 欧盟 WT/DS432/6	23-07-2012 WT/DSB/M/320	
433	中国—影响稀土、钨、钼出口的措施	日本 WT/DS433/1	13-03-2012	欧盟 WT/DS433/2 美国 WT/DS433/3 加拿大 WT/DS433/4	27-06-2012 日本 WT/DS433/6	23-07-2012 WT/DSB/M/320	
434	澳大利亚—影响烟草制品包装使用商标及其他简单包装要求的措施	乌克兰 WT/DS434/1	13-03-2012	危地马拉 WT/DS434/2 乌拉圭 WT/DS434/3 巴西 WT/DS434/4 挪威 WT/DS434/5 欧盟 WT/DS434/6 新西兰 WT/DS434/7 加拿大 WT/DS434/8 尼加拉瓜 WT/DS434/9	14-08-2012 乌克兰 WT/DS434/11	28-09-2012 WT/DSB/M/322	

续 表

序号	案件	请求磋商	收到磋商请求（日-月-年）	加入磋商请求	请求成立专家组（日-月-年）	专家组成立（日-月-年）	双边达成解决方案（日-月-年）
435	澳大利亚—影响烟草制品包装使用商标及其他简单包装要求的措施	洪都拉斯 WT/DS435/1 Corr. 1	04-04-2012	巴西 WT/DS435/2 Corr. 1 津巴布韦 WT/DS435/3 Corr. 1 新西兰 WT/DS435/4 Corr. 1 尼加拉瓜 WT/DS435/5 Corr. 1 危地马拉 WT/DS435/6 Corr. 1 乌拉圭 WT/DS435/7 Corr. 1 欧盟 WT/DS435/8 Corr. 1 乌克兰 WT/DS435/9 Corr. 1 加拿大 WT/DS435/10 Corr. 1 萨尔瓦多 WT/DS435/11 Corr. 1 挪威 WT/DS435/12 Corr. 1 菲律宾 WT/DS435/13 Corr. 1 印度尼西亚 WT/DS435/14 Corr. 1	15-10-2012 洪都拉斯 WT/DS435/16	25-09-2013 WT/DSB/M/337	
436	美国—对源自印度的某些热轧碳钢产品的反补贴措施	印度 WT/DS436/1 Rev. 1	12-04-2012 24-04-2012	加拿大 WT/DS436/2	12-07-2012 印度 WT/DS436/3	31-08-2012 WT/DSB/M/321	
437	美国—对来自中国的某些产品的反补贴税的措施	中国 WT/DS437/1	25-05-2012		20-08-2012 中国 WT/DS437/2	28-09-2012 WT/DSB/M/322	

续 表

序号	案件	请求磋商	收到磋商请求（日-月-年）	加入磋商请求	请求成立专家组（日-月-年）	专家组成立（日-月-年）	双边达成解决方案（日-月-年）
438	阿根廷—影响货物进口的措施	欧盟 WT/DS438/1	25-05-2012	土耳其 WT/DS438/2 美国 WT/DS438/3 乌克兰 WT/DS438/4 日本 WT/DS438/5 加拿大 WT/DS438/6 危地马拉 WT/DS438/7 澳大利亚 WT/DS438/8 墨西哥 WT/DS438/9	06-12-2012 欧盟 WT/DS438/11	28-01-2013 WT/DSB/M/328	
439	南非—对来自巴西的冷冻鸡征收反倾销税	巴西 WT/DS439/1	21-06-2012				
440	中国—对美部分进口汽车实施反倾销和反补贴措施	美国 WT/DS440/1	05-07-2012		17-09-2012 美国 WT/DS440/2	23-10-2012 WT/DSB/M/323	
441	澳大利亚—影响烟草制品包装使用商标、地理标志及其他简单包装要求的措施	多米尼加 WT/DS441/1	18-07-2012	乌拉圭 WT/DS441/2 新西兰 WT/DS441/3 洪都拉斯 WT/DS441/4 尼加拉瓜 WT/DS441/5 危地马拉 WT/DS441/6 萨尔瓦多 WT/DS441/7 欧盟 WT/DS441/8 巴西 WT/DS441/9 乌克兰 WT/DS441/10 南非 WT/DS441/11 加拿大 WT/DS441/12 挪威 WT/DS441/13	09-11-2012 多米尼加 WT/DS441/15	25-04-2014 WT/DSB/M/344	
442	欧盟—对印度尼西亚脂肪醇的进口反倾销措施	印度尼西亚 WT/DS442/1	27-07-2012		01-05-2013 印度尼西亚 WT/DS442/2	25-06-2013 WT/DSB/M/333	

续 表

序号	案件	请求磋商	收到磋商请求（日-月-年）	加入磋商请求	请求成立专家组（日-月-年）	专家组成立（日-月-年）	双边达成解决方案（日-月-年）
443	欧盟及其成员国—生物柴油进口的某些措施	阿根廷 WT/DS443/1	17-08-2012	澳大利亚 WT/DS443/2 印度尼西亚 WT/DS443/3	06-12-2012 阿根廷 WT/DS443/5		
444	阿根廷—影响货物进口的措施	美国 WT/DS444/1	21-08-2012	墨西哥 WT/DS444/2 土耳其 WT/DS444/3 欧盟 WT/DS444/4 澳大利亚 WT/DS444/5 日本 WT/DS444/6 加拿大 WT/DS444/7 危地马拉 WT/DS444/8	06-12-2012 美国 WT/DS444/10	28-01-2013 WT/DSB/M/328	
445	阿根廷—影响货物进口的措施	日本 WT/DS445/1	21-08-2012	墨西哥 WT/DS445/2 土耳其 WT/DS445/3 欧盟 WT/DS445/4 澳大利亚 WT/DS445/5 加拿大 WT/DS445/6 危地马拉 WT/DS445/7 美国 WT/DS445/8	06-12-2012 日本 WT/DS445/10	28-01-2013 WT/DSB/M/328	
446	阿根廷—影响货物进口的措施	墨西哥 WT/DS446/1	24-08-2012	土耳其 WT/DS446/2 澳大利亚 WT/DS446/3 日本 WT/DS446/4 加拿大 WT/DS446/5 欧盟 WT/DS446/6 危地马拉 WT/DS446/7 美国 WT/DS446/8	21-11-2012 墨西哥 WT/DS446/10		

续 表

序号	案件	请求磋商	收到磋商请求（日-月-年）	加入磋商请求	请求成立专家组（日-月-年）	专家组成立（日-月-年）	双边达成解决方案（日-月-年）
447	美国—影响源自阿根廷动物，肉类和其他动物制品进口的措施	阿根廷 WT/DS447/1 Corr-1	30-08-2012		06-12-2012 阿根廷 WT/DS447/2	28-01-2013 WT/DSB/M/328	
448	美国—影响新鲜柠檬进口的措施	阿根廷 WT/DS448/1 Corr-1	03-09-2012		06-12-2012 阿根廷 WT/DS448/2		
449	美国—对自中国的某些产品的反补贴和反倾销措施	中国 WT/DS449/1	17-09-2012		19-11-2012 中国 WT/DS449/2	17-12-2012 WT/DSB/M/327	
450	中国—影响汽车与汽车零部件产业的若干措施	美国 WT/DS450/1	17-09-2012	欧盟 WT/DS450/2			
451	中国—影响纺织品服装产品生产与出口的措施	墨西哥 WT/DS451/1	15-10-2012	欧盟 WT/DS451/2 危地马拉 WT/DS451/3 澳大利亚 WT/DS451/4 美国 WT/DS451/5 巴西 WT/DS451/6 秘鲁 WT/DS451/7 洪都拉斯 WT/DS451/8 哥伦比亚 WT/DS451/9			
452	欧盟及其成员国—影响可再生能源生产部门的措施	中国 WT/DS452/1	05-11-2012	日本 WT/DS452/2 澳大利亚 WT/DS452/3 阿根廷 WT/DS452/4			
453	阿根廷—与货物和服务贸易相关的措施	巴拿马 WT/DS453/1	12-12-2012	美国 WT/DS453/2 欧盟 WT/DS453/3	13-05-2013 巴拿马 WT/DS453/4	25-06-2013 WT/DSB/M/333	

续 表

序号	案件	请求磋商	收到磋商请求（日-月-年）	加入磋商请求	请求成立专家组（日-月-年）	专家组成立（日-月-年）	双边达成解决方案（日-月-年）
454	中国—对日本进口的高性能不锈钢无缝钢管（HP-SSST）征收反倾销税	日本 WT/DS454/1	20-12-2012	欧盟 WT/DS454/2	11-04-2013 日本 WT/DS454/4	24-05-2013 WT/DSB/M/332	
455	印度尼西亚—园艺产品、动物及动物产品进口	美国 WT/DS455/1	10-01-2013	欧盟 WT/DS455/2 加拿大 WT/DS455/3 澳大利亚 WT/DS455/4	14-03-2013 美国 WT/DS455/7	24-04-2013 WT/DSB/M/331	
456	印度—有关太阳能电池和太阳能模块的相关措施	美国 WT/DS456/1	06-02-2013	日本 WT/DS456/2 澳大利亚 WT/DS456/3	14-04-2014 美国 WT/DS456/5	23-05-2014 WT/DSB/M/345	
457	秘鲁—某些农产品进口的附加税	危地马拉 WT/DS457/1	12-04-2013		13-06-2013 危地马拉 WT/DS457/2	23-07-2013 WT/DSB/M/334	
458	澳大利亚—关于烟草制品和包装的商标、地理标志和其他简单包装措施	古巴 WT/DS458/1	03-05-2013	加拿大 WT/DS458/2 新西兰 WT/DS458/3 挪威 WT/DS458/4 乌克兰 WT/DS458/5 洪都拉斯 WT/DS458/6 欧盟 WT/DS458/7 多米尼加 WT/DS458/8 乌拉圭 WT/DS458/9 巴西 WT/DS458/10 危地马拉 WT/DS458/11 尼加拉瓜 WT/DS458/12	04-04-2014 古巴 WT/DS458/14	25-04-2014 WT/DSB/M/344	
459	欧盟及部分成员国—对生物柴油进口营销采取的部分措施及支持生物柴油产业的措施	阿根廷 WT/DS459/1	15-05-2013				

续 表

序号	案件	请求磋商	收到磋商请求（日-月-年）	加入磋商请求	请求成立专家组（日-月-年）	专家组成立（日-月-年）	双边达成解决方案（日-月-年）
460	中国—对欧盟高性能不锈钢无缝钢管（HP-SSST）征收反倾销税	欧盟 WT/DS460/1	13-06-2013	日本 WT/DS460/2	16-08-2013 欧盟 WT/DS460/4	30-08-2013 WT/DSB/M/336	
461	哥伦比亚—与纺织品、服装和鞋类产品进口有关的措施	巴拿马 WT/DS461/1	18-06-2013	危地马拉 WT/DS461/2	19-08-2013 巴拿马 WT/DS461/3	25-09-2013 WT/DSB/M/337	
462	俄罗斯—机动车的回收费	欧盟 WT/DS462/1	09-07-2013	美国 WT/DS462/2 日本 WT/DS462/3 中国 WT/DS462/4 土耳其 WT/DS462/5 乌克兰 WT/DS462/6	10-10-2013 欧盟 WT/DS462/8	25-11-2013 WT/DSB/M/339	
463	俄罗斯—对机动车征收回收费	日本 WT/DS463/1	24-07-2013	美国 WT/DS463/2 土耳其 WT/DS463/3 欧盟 WT/DS463/4 乌克兰 WT/DS463/5 中国 WT/DS463/6			
464	美国—对韩国产大型家用洗衣机采取反倾销和反补贴措施	韩国 WT/DS464/1	29-08-2013	中国 WT/DS464/2 日本 WT/DS464/3	05-12-2013 韩国 WT/DS464/4	22-01-2014 WT/DSB/M/341	
465	印度尼西亚—园艺产品、动物及动物产品的进口	美国 WT/DS465/1	30-08-2013	新西兰 WT/DS465/2 加拿大 WT/DS465/3 欧盟 WT/DS465/4 泰国 WT/DS465/5 澳大利亚 WT/DS465/6			

续 表

序号	案件	请求磋商	收到磋商请求（日-月-年）	加入磋商请求	请求成立专家组（日-月-年）	专家组成立（日-月-年）	双边达成解决方案（日-月-年）
466	印度尼西亚—园艺产品、动物及动物产品进口	新西兰 WT/DS466/1	30-08-2013	美国 WT/DS466/2 加拿大 WT/DS466/3 欧盟 WT/DS466/4 泰国 WT/DS466/5 澳大利亚 WT/DS466/6			
467	澳大利亚—关于烟草制品和包装的商标、地理标志和其他简单包装措施	印度尼西亚 WT/DS467/1	20-09-2013	危地马拉 WT/DS467/2 尼加拉瓜 WT/DS467/3 新西兰 WT/DS467/4 乌拉圭 WT/DS467/5 欧盟 WT/DS467/6 挪威 WT/DS467/7 加拿大 WT/DS467/8 多米尼加 WT/DS467/9 巴西 WT/DS467/10 洪都拉斯 WT/DS467/11 乌克兰 WT/DS467/12 古巴 WT/DS467/13	03-03-2014 印度尼西亚 WT/DS467/15	26-03-2014 WT/DSB/M/343	
468	乌克兰—有关小轿车的最终保障措施		30-10-2013	欧盟 WT/DS468/2 俄罗斯 WT/DS468/3	13-02-2014 日本 WT/DS468/5	26-03-2014 WT/DSB/M/343	
469	欧盟—针对亚特兰大—斯坎迪亚鲱鱼的措施	丹麦代表法罗群岛 WT/DS469/1	04-11-2013		08-01-2014 丹麦代表法罗群岛 WT/DS469/2	26-02-2014 WT/DSB/M/343	21-08-2014 WT/DS469/3（联合通报，解决）
470	巴基斯坦—对产自印度尼西亚的部分纸制品的反倾销和反补贴措施	印度尼西亚 WT/DS470/1	27-11-2013		12-05-2014 印度尼西亚 WT/DS470/2		

续 表

序号	案件	请求磋商	收到磋商请求（日-月-年）	加入磋商请求	请求成立专家组（日-月-年）	专家组成立（日-月-年）	双边达成解决方案（日-月-年）
471	部分方法及其在涉及中国的反倾销诉讼中的运用	中国 WT/DS471/1	03-12-2013	日本 WT/DS471/2 俄罗斯 WT/DS471/3 乌克兰 WT/DS471/4	13-02-2014 中国 WT/DS471/5 和 Corr. 1	26-03-2014 WT/DSB/M/343	
472	关于税收和收费的部分措施	欧盟 WT/DS472/1	19-12-2013	日本 WT/DS472/2 阿根廷 WT/DS472/3 美国 WT/DS472/4	31-10-2014 欧盟 WT/DS472/5		
473	欧盟—对产自阿根廷的生物柴油的反倾销措施	阿根廷 WT/DS473/1	19-12-2013	俄罗斯 WT/DS473/2 印度尼西亚 WT/DS473/3	13-03-2014 阿根廷 WT/DS473/5	25-04-2014 WT/DSB/M/344	
474	欧盟—成本调整方法论和部分对产自俄罗斯的进口品的反倾销措施	俄罗斯 WT/DS474/1	23-12-2013	中国 WT/DS474/2 印度尼西亚 WT/DS474/3	04-06-2014 俄罗斯 WT/DS474/4	22-07-2014 WT/DSB/M/348	
275	俄罗斯—影响自欧盟进口的生猪、猪肉及其他猪产品的措施	欧盟 WT/DS475/1	08-04-2014		27-06-2014 欧盟 WT/DS475/2	22-07-2014 WT/DSB/M/348	
476	欧盟及其成员国—对能源部门采取的某些措施	俄罗斯 WT/DS476/1	30-04-2014				
477	印度尼西亚—涉及园艺产品、动物和动物产品的进口措施	新西兰 WT/DS477/1	08-05-2014	美国 WT/DS477/2 泰国 WT/DS477/3 欧盟 WT/DS477/4 加拿大 WT/DS477/5 台、澎、金、马单独关税区 WT/DS477/6 澳大利亚 WT/DS477/7			

续 表

序号	案件	请求磋商	收到磋商请求（日-月-年）	加入磋商请求	请求成立专家组（日-月-年）	专家组成立（日-月-年）	双边达成解决方案（日-月-年）
478	印度尼西亚—园艺产品、动物和动物产品的进口	美国 WT/DS478/1	08-05-2014	新西兰 WT/DS478/2 泰国 WT/DS478/3 欧盟 WT/DS478/4 加拿大 WT/DS478/5 台、澎、金、马单独关税区 WT/DS478/6 澳大利亚 WT/DS478/7			
479	俄罗斯—对自德国和意大利进口的轻型商用车采取反倾销措施	欧盟 WT/DS479/1	21-05-2014		15-09-2014 欧盟 WT/DS479/2	20-10-2014 WT/DSB/M/351	
480	欧盟—对源自印度尼西亚的生物柴油实施反倾销措施	印度尼西亚 WT/DS480/1	10-06-2014				
481	印度尼西亚—在“美国丁香烟案”中援引 DSU 第 22 条第 2 款	欧盟 WT/DS481/1	13-06-2014	澳大利亚 WT/DS481/2 巴西 WT/DS481/3			
482	加拿大—对自台、澎、金、马单独关税区进口的加拿大碳钢焊接管采取反倾销措施	台、澎、金、马单独关税区 WT/DS482/1	25-06-2014				
483	中国—对自加拿大进口的纤维素纸浆采取的反倾销措施	加拿大 WT/DS483/1	15-10-2014				
484	印度尼西亚—与鸡肉和鸡肉产品进口相关的措施	巴西 WT/DS484/1	16-10-2014	美国 WT/DS484/2 新西兰 WT/DS484/3 台、澎、金、马单独关税区 WT/DS484/4 澳大利亚 WT/DS484/5 欧盟 WT/DS484/6			

续 表

序号	案件	请求磋商	收到磋商请求（日-月-年）	加入磋商请求	请求成立专家组（日-月-年）	专家组成立（日-月-年）	双边达成解决方案（日-月-年）
485	俄罗斯—对某些农产品和制造成品之关税待遇	欧盟 WT/DS485/1	31-10-2014				
486	欧盟—对自巴基斯坦进口的聚对苯二甲酸乙二醇酯采取的反补贴措施	巴基斯坦 WT/DS486/1	28-10-2014				

第二部分
散发及通过专家组及上诉机构报告

序号	案件	专家组成立（日-月-年）	散发专家组报告（日-月-年）	通知上诉（日-月-年）	通过专家组报告（日-月-年）	散发上诉机构报告（日-月-年）	通过上诉机构报告（日-月-年）
1	美国—精炼及传统汽油标准	10-04-1995 委内瑞拉 WT/DS2 31-05-1995 巴西 WT/DS4	29-01-1996 WT/DS2/R	21-02-1996 美国 WT/DS2/6	20-05-1996 WT/DS2/9	29-04-1996 WT/DS2/AB/R	20-05-1996 WT/DS2/9
2	日本—对酒精饮料征税	27-09-1995 欧共体 WT/DS8 加拿大 WT/DS10 美国 WT/DS11	11-07-1996 WT/DS8/R WT/DS10/R WT/DS11/R	08-08-1996 日本 WT/DS8/9 WT/DS10/9 WT/DS11/6	01-11-1996 WT/DS8/11 WT/DS10/11 WT/DS11/8	04-10-1996 WT/DS8/AB/R WT/DS10/AB/R WT/DS11/AB/R	01-11-1996 WT/DS8/11 WT/DS10/11 WT/DS11/8
3	欧共体—扇贝的贸易描述	19-07-1995 加拿大 WT/DS7	05-08-1996 WT/DS7/R	N. A.	N. A.	N. A.	N. A.
4	欧共体—扇贝的贸易描述	11-10-1995 秘鲁 WT/DS12 智利 WT/DS14	05-08-1996 WT/DS12/R WT/DS14/R	N. A.	N. A.	N. A.	N. A.
5	巴西—影响可可粉的措施	05-03-1996 菲律宾 WT/DS22	17-10-1996 WT/DS22/R	16-12-1996 菲律宾 WT/DS22/8	20-03-1997 WT/DS22/11/Rev. 2	21-02-1997 WT/DS22/AB/R	20-03-1997 WT/DS22/11/Rev. 2
6	美国—对于棉质及人造纤维内衣的进口限制	05-03-1996 哥斯达黎加 WT/DS24	08-11-1996 WT/DS24/R	11-11-1996 哥斯达黎加 WT/DS24/5	25-02-1997 WT/DS24/8	10-02-1997 WT/DS24/AB/R	25-02-1997 WT/DS24/8
7	美国—影响从印度进口羊毛衬衫和女上衣进口的措施	17-04-1996 印度 WT/DS33	06-01-1997 WT/DS33/R	24-02-1997 印度 WT/DS33/3	23-05-1997 WT/DS33/5	25-04-1997 WT/DS33/AB/R 和 Corr. 1	23-05-1997 WT/DS33/5

续 表

序号	案件	专家组成立（日-月-年）	散发专家组报告（日-月-年）	通知上诉（日-月-年）	通过专家组报告（日-月-年）	散发上诉机构报告（日-月-年）	通过上诉机构报告（日-月-年）
8	加拿大—关于杂志的特定措施	19-06-1996 美国 WT/DS31	14-03-1997 WT/DS31/R 和 Corr. 1	29-04-1997 加拿大 WT/DS31/5	30-07-1997 WT/DS31/7	30-06-1997 WT/DS31/AB/R	30-07-1997 WT/DS31/7
9	欧共体—香蕉进口、销售和分销	08-05-1996 厄瓜多尔、危地马拉、洪都拉斯、墨西哥、美国 WT/DS27	22-05-1997 WT/DS27/R/ECU WT/DS27/R/GTM WT/DS27/R/HND WT/DS27/R/MEX WT/DS27/R/美国 A	11-06-1997 欧共体 WT/DS27/9	25-09-1997 WT/DS27/12	09-09-1997 WT/DS27/AB/R	25-09-1997 WT/DS27/12
10	欧共体—关于肉类及肉制品措施（荷尔蒙）	20-05-1996 美国 WT/DS26 16-10-1996 加拿大 WT/DS48	18-08-1997 WT/DS26/R/美国 A WT/DS48/R/CAN	24-09-1997 欧共体 WT/DS26/9 WT/DS48/7	13-02-1998 WT/DS26/13 WT/DS48/11	16-01-1998 WT/DS26/AB/R WT/DS48/AB/R	13-02-1998 WT/DS26/13 WT/DS48/11
11	印度—对于药品及农业化学品的专利权保护	20-11-1996 美国 WT/DS50	05-09-1997 WT/DS50/R	15-10-1997 印度 WT/DS50/6	16-01-1998 WT/DS50/9	19-12-1997 WT/DS50/AB/R	16-01-1998 WT/DS50/9
12	阿根廷—影响鞋类、纺织品、服装和其他项目的进口措施	25-02-1997 美国 WT/DS56	25-11-1997 WT/DS56/R	21-01-1998 阿根廷 WT/DS56/8	22-04-1998 WT/DS56/11	27-03-1998 WT/DS56/AB/R 20-04-1998 WT/DS56/AB/R/Corr. 1	22-04-1998 WT/DS56/11
13	欧共体—特定计算机设备的海关分类	25-02-1997 美国 WT/DS62 30-03-1997 WT/DS67 WT/DS68	05-02-1998 WT/DS62/R WT/DS67/R WT/DS68/R	24-03-1998 欧共体 WT/DS62/8 WT/DS67/6 WT/DS68/5	22-06-1998 WT/DS62/11 WT/DS64/9 WT/DS68/8	05-06-1998 WT/DS62/AB/R WT/DS67/AB/R WT/DS68/AB/R	22-06-1998 WT/DS62/11 WT/DS67/9 WT/DS68/10
14	欧共体—影响特定家禽产品进口的措施	30-07-1997 巴西 WT/DS69	12-03-1998 WT/DS69/R	29-04-1998 巴西 WT/DS69/4	23-07-1998 WT/DS69/7	13-07-1998 WT/DS69/AB/R	23-07-1998 WT/DS69/7
15	日本—对进口胶卷相纸的限制	16-10-1996 美国 WT/DS44	31-03-1998 WT/DS44/R	N. A.	22-04-1998 WT/DS44/5	N. A.	N. A.

续 表

序号	案件	专家组成立（日-月-年）	散发专家组报告（日-月-年）	通知上诉（日-月-年）	通过专家组报告（日-月-年）	散发上诉机构报告（日-月-年）	通过上诉机构报告（日-月-年）
16	美国—对特定虾及虾类产品进口限制	25-02-1997 马来西亚， 泰国， 巴基斯坦 10-04-1997 印度 WT/DS58	15-05-1998 WT/DS58/R 09-11-1998 WT/DS58/R/ Corr-. 1	13-07-1998 美国 WT/DS58/11	06-11-1998 WT/DS58/14	12-10-1998 WT/DS58/AB/R	06-11-1998 WT/DS58/14
17	澳大利亚—影响鲑鱼进口的措施	10-04-1997 加拿大 WT/DS18	12-06-1998 WT/DS18/R 13-07-1998 WT/DS18/R/ Corr. 1	22-07-1998 澳大利亚 WT/DS18/5	06-11-1998 WT/DS18/11	20-10-1998 WT/DS18/AB/R	06-11-1998 WT/DS18/11
18	危地马拉—对来自墨西哥的波兰特水泥的反倾销调查	20-09-1997 墨西哥 WT/DS60	19-06-1998 WT/DS60/R	04-08-1998 危地马拉 WT/DS60/9	25-11-1998 WT/DS60/12	02-11-1998 WT/DS60/AB/R	25-11-1998 WT/DS60/12
19	印度尼西亚—影响汽车工业的特定措施	12-06-1998 日本 WT/DS55 WT/DS64 欧共体 WT/DS54 30-06-1997 美国 WT/DS59	02-07-1998 WT/DS54/R WT/DS55/R WT/DS59/R WT/DS64/R 和 Corr. 2	N. A.	23-07-1998 WT/DS54/10 WT/DS55/10 WT/DS59/9 WT/DS64/8	N. A.	N. A.
20	印度—对于药品及农业化学品的专利权保护	16-10-1997 欧共体 WT/DS79	24-08-1998 WT/DS79/R	N. A.	22-09-1998 WT/DS79/5 和 Corr. 1	N. A.	N. A.
21	韩国—对酒精饮料征税	16-10-1997 欧共体 WT/DS75 美国 WT/DS84	17-09-1998 WT/DS75/R WT/DS84/R	20-10-1998 韩国 WT/DS75/9 WT/DS84/7	17-02-1999 WT/DS75/12 WT/DS84/10	18-01-1999 WT/DS75/AB/R WT/DS84/AB/R	17-02-1999 WT/DS75/12 WT/DS84/10
22	日本—影响农产品的措施	18-11-1997 美国 WT/DS76	27-10-1998 WT/DS76/R	24-11-1998 日本 WT/DS76/5	19-03-1999 WT/DS76/8	22-02-1999 WT/DS76/AB/R	19-03-1999 WT/DS76/8
23	美国—对来自韩国的1兆或以上的计算机动态随机存取存储器芯片征收反倾销税	16-01-1998 韩国 WT/DS99	29-01-1999 WT/DS99/R	N. A.	19-03-1999 WT/DS99/5	N. A.	N. A.
24	印度—对于农产品、纺织品和工业产品进口的数量限制	18-11-1997 美国 WT/DS90	06-04-1999 WT/DS90/R	25-05-1999 印度 WT/DS90/11	22-09-1999 WT/DS90/14	23-08-1999 WT/DS90/AB/R	22-09-1999 WT/DS90/14

续 表

序号	案件	专家组成立（日-月-年）	散发专家组报告（日-月-年）	通知上诉（日-月-年）	通过专家组报告（日-月-年）	散发上诉机构报告（日-月-年）	通过上诉机构报告（日-月-年）
25	巴西—对于航空器出口融资	23-07-1998 加拿大 WT/DS46	14-04-1999 WT/DS46/R	03-05-1999 巴西 WT/DS46/8	20-08-1999 WT/DS46/10	02-08-1999 WT/DS46/AB/R	20-08-1999 WT/DS46/10
26	加拿大—影响民用航空器措施	23-07-1998 巴西 WT/DS70	14-04-1999 WT/DS70/R	03-05-1999 加拿大 WT/DS70/4	20-08-1999 WT/DS70/6	02-08-1999 WT/DS70/AB/R	20-08-1999 WT/DS70/6
27	加拿大—影响牛奶进口及奶制品出口的措施	25-03-1998 美国 WT/DS103 新西兰 WT/DS113	17-05-1999 WT/DS103/R WT/DS113/R	15-07-1999 加拿大 WT/DS103/6 WT/DS113/6	27-10-1999 WT/DS103/11 WT/DS113/11	13-10-1999 WT/DS103/AB/R WT/DS113/AB/R	27-10-1999 WT/DS103/11 WT/DS113/11
28	澳大利亚—对于汽车皮革制造商和生产商提供的补贴	22-06-1998 美国 WT/DS126	25-05-1999 WT/DS126/R	N. A.	16-06-1999 WT/DS126/5	N. A.	N. A.
29	土耳其—对于纺织品和服装进口的限制	13-03-1998 印度 WT/DS34	31-05-1999 WT/DS34/R	26-07-1999 土耳其 WT/DS34/6	19-11-1999 WT/DS34/11	22-10-1999 WT/DS34/AB/R	19-11-1999 WT/DS34/11
30	智利—对酒精饮料征税	18-11-1997 欧共体 WT/DS87 25-03-1998 欧共体 WT/DS110	15-06-1999 WT/DS87/R WT/DS110/R	13-09-1999 智利 WT/DS87/8 WT/DS110/7	12-01-2000 WT/DS87/12 WT/DS110/11	13-12-1999 WT/DS87/AB/R WT/DS110/AB/R	12-01-2000 WT/DS87/12 WT/DS110/11
31	韩国—对于特定奶制品进口的保障措施	22-07-1998 欧共体 WT/DS98	21-06-1999 WT/DS98/R	15-09-1999 韩国 WT/DS98/7	12-01-2000 WT/DS98/10	14-12-1999 WT/DS98/AB/R	12-01-2000 WT/DS98/10
32	阿根廷—对鞋类产品进口的保障措施	23-07-1998 欧共体 WT/DS121	25-06-1999 WT/DS121/R	15-09-1999 阿根廷 WT/DS121/6 和 Corr. 1	12-01-2000 WT/DS121/9	14-12-1999 WT/DS121/AB/R	12-01-2000 WT/DS121/9
33	欧共体—影响黄油产品的措施	18-11-1997 新西兰 WT/DS72	24-11-1999 WT/DS72/R	N. A.	N. A.	N. A.	N. A.
34	美国—"海外销售公司"税收待遇	22-09-1998 欧共体 WT/DS108	08-10-1999 WT/DS108/R	26-11-1999 美国 WT/DS108/7	20-03-2000 WT/DS108/10	24-02-2000 WT/DS108/AB/R	20-03-2000 WT/DS108/10
35	美国—1974 年贸易法第 301-310 节	02-03-1999 欧共体 WT/DS152	22-12-1999 WT/DS152/R	N. A.	27-01-2000 WT/DS152/14	N. A.	N. A.
36	美国—对来自英国的热轧钢铅铋碳钢产品征收反补贴税	17-02-1999 欧共体 WT/DS138	23-12-1999 WT/DS138/R	27-01-2000 美国 WT/DS138/5	07-06-2000 WT/DS138/9 和 Corr. 1	10-05-2000 WT/DS138/AB/R	07-06-2000 WT/DS138/9 和 Corr. 1

续 表

序号	案件	专家组成立（日-月-年）	散发专家组报告（日-月-年）	通知上诉（日-月-年）	通过专家组报告（日-月-年）	散发上诉机构报告（日-月-年）	通过上诉机构报告（日-月-年）
37	墨西哥—对来自美国的高果糖玉米浆进行反倾销调查	25-11-1998 美国 WT/DS132 和 Corr. 1	28-01-2000 WT/DS132/R	N. A.	24-02-2000 WT/DS132/4 和 Corr. 1	N. A.	N. A.
38	加拿大—影响汽车工业的特定措施	01-02-1999 日本 WT/DS139 01-02-1999 欧共体 WT/DS142	11-02-2000 WT/DS139/R WT/DS142/R	02-03-2000 加拿大 WT/DS139/5 WT/DS142/5	19-06-2000 WT/DS139/8 WT/DS142/8	31-05-2000 WT/DS139/R WT/DS142/R	19-06-2000 WT/DS139/8 WT/DS142/8
39	加拿大—药品的专利权保护	04-02-1999 欧共体 WT/DS114	17-03-2000 WT/DS114/R	N. A.	07-04-2000 WT/DS114/9	N. A.	N. A.
40	美国—1916 年反倾销法	01-02-1999 欧共体 WT/DS136	31-03-2000 WT/DS136/R 和 Corr. 1	29-05-2000 美国 WT/DS136/5	26-09-2000 WT/DS136/8	28-08-2000 WT/DS136/AB/R	26-09-2000 WT/DS136/8
41	韩国—影响政府采购措施	16-06-1999 美国 WT/DS163	01-05-2000 WT/DS163/R	N. A.	19-06-2000 WT/DS163/7	N. A.	N. A.
42	加拿大—专利保护条款	22-09-1999 美国 WT/DS170	05-05-2000 WT/DS170/R	19-06-2000 加拿大 WT/DS170/4	12-10-2000 WT/DS170/7	18-09-2000 WT/DS170/AB/R	12-10-2000 WT/DS170/7
43	美国—1916 年反倾销法	26-07-1999 日本 WT/DS162	29-05-2000 WT/DS162/R 和 25-09-2000 Add. 1	29-05-2000 美国 WT/DS162/6	26-09-2000 WT/DS162/11	28-08-2000 WT/DS162/AB/R	26-09-2000 WT/DS162/11
44	美国—美国版权法第 110（5）节	26-05-1999 欧共体 WT/DS160	15-06-2000 WT/DS160/R	N. A.	27-07-2000 WT/DS160/8	N. A.	N. A.
45	美国—对来自欧共体特定产品的进口措施	16-06-1999 欧共体 WT/DS165	17-07-2000 WT/DS165/R 和 Add. 1	12-09-2000 欧共体 WT/DS165/10	10-01-2001 WT/DS165/13	11-12-2000 WT/DS165/AB/R	10-01-2001 WT/DS165/13
46	韩国—影响新鲜、冷藏及冷冻牛肉进口的措施	26-05-1999 美国 WT/DS161 26-07-1999 澳大利亚 WT/DS169	31-07-2000 WT/DS161/R WT/DS169/R	11-09-2000 韩国 WT/DS161/8 WT/DS169/8	10-01-2001 WT/DS161/11 WT/DS169/11	11-12-2000 WT/DS161/AB/R WT/DS169/AB/R	10-01-2001 WT/DS161/11 WT/DS169/11

续 表

序号	案件	专家组成立（日-月-年）	散发专家组报告（日-月-年）	通知上诉（日-月-年）	通过专家组报告（日-月-年）	散发上诉机构报告（日-月-年）	通过上诉机构报告（日-月-年）
47	美国—对来自欧共体面筋进口的保障措施	26-07-1999 欧共体 WT/DS166	31-07-2000 WT/DS166/R	26-09-2000 美国 WT/DS166/7	19-01-2001 WT/DS166/10	22-12-2000 WT/DS166/AB/R	19-01-2001 WT/DS166/10
48	欧共体—影响石棉及含石棉产品的措施	25-11-1998 加拿大 WT/DS135	18-09-2000 WT/DS135/R 和 Add. 1	23-10-2000 加拿大 WT/DS135/8	05-04-2001 WT/DS135/12	12-03-2001 WT/DS135/AB/R	05-04-2001 WT/DS135/12
49	危地马拉—对来自墨西哥的灰波兰特水泥采取反倾销措施	22-09-1999 墨西哥 WT/DS156	24-10-2000 WT/DS156/R	N. A.	17-11-2000 WT/DS156/4	N. A.	N. A.
50	美国—对来自韩国的不锈钢卷板和不锈钢条采取反倾销措施	19-11-1999 韩国 WT/DS179	22-12-2000 WT/DS179/R	N. A.	01-02-2001 WT/DS179/4	N. A.	N. A.
51	阿根廷—影响牛皮出口和成皮进口的措施	26-07-1999 欧共体 WT/DS155	19-12-2000 WT/DS155/R 和 Corr. 1	N. A.	16-02-2001 WT/DS155/5	N. A.	N. A.
52	欧共体—对于来自印度棉质床单进口征收反倾销税	27-10-1999 印度 WT/DS141	30-10-2000 WT/DS141/R	01-12-2000 欧共体 WT/DS141/6	12-03-2001 WT/DS141/9	01-03-2001 WT/DS141/AB/R	12-03-2001 WT/DS141/9
53	泰国—对波兰出口的铁或非合金钢的角铁、型材、轧材及工字梁的反倾销税案	19-11-1999 波兰 WT/DS122	28-09-2000 WT/DS122/R	23-10-2000 泰国 WT/DS122/4	05-04-2001 WT/DS122/7	12-03-2001 WT/DS122/AB/R	05-04-2001 WT/DS122/7
54	美国—对来自新西兰和澳大利亚的新鲜、冷藏和冷冻羔羊肉进口采取保障措施	19-11-1999 新西兰 WT/DS177 澳大利亚 WT/DS178	21-12-2000 WT/DS177/R WT/DS178/R	31-01-2001 美国 WT/DS177/7 WT/DS178/8	16-05-2001 WT/DS177/10 WT/DS178/11	01-05-2001 WT/DS177/AB/R WT/DS178/AB/R	16-05-2001 WT/DS177/10 WT/DS178/11
55	美国—对来自日本的某些热轧钢产品采取反倾销措施	20-03-2000 日本 WT/DS184	28-02-2001 WT/DS184/R	25-04-2001 美国 WT/DS184/5	23-08-2001 WT/DS184/8	24-07-2001 WT/DS184/AB/R	23-08-2001 WT/DS184/8
56	美国—对来自巴基斯坦棉纱采取过渡性保障措施	19-06-2000 巴基斯坦 WT/DS192	31-05-2001 WT/DS192/R	09-07-2001 美国 WT/DS192/4	05-11-2001 WT/DS192/7	08-10-2001 WT/DS192/AB/R	05-11-2001 WT/DS192/7
57	美国—对于作为出口限制的补贴措施	11-09-2000 加拿大 WT/DS194	29-06-2001 WT/DS194/R	N. A.	23-08-2001 WT/DS194/4	N. A.	N. A.

续 表

序号	案件	专家组成立（日-月-年）	散发专家组报告（日-月-年）	通知上诉（日-月-年）	通过专家组报告（日-月-年）	散发上诉机构报告（日-月-年）	通过上诉机构报告（日-月-年）
58	美国—1998年全面拨款法第211节	26-09-2000 欧共体 WT/DS176	06-08-2001 WT/DS176/R	04-10-2001 欧共体 WT/DS176/5	01-02-2002 WT/DS176/9	02-01-2002 WT/DS176/AB/R	01-02-2002 WT/DS176/9
59	阿根廷—影响从意大利进口地板砖的措施	17-11-2000 欧共体 WT/DS189	28-09-2001 WT/DS189/R	N. A.	05-11-2001 WT/DS189/6	N. A.	N. A.
60	美国—自韩国进口的圆焊碳质条形管的保障措施	23-10-2000 韩国 WT/DS202	29-10-2001 WT/DS202/R	19-11-2001 美国 WT/DS202/9	08-03-2002 WT/DS202/13	15-02-2002 WT/DS202/AB/R	08-03-2002 WT/DS202/13
61	印度—影响汽车部门的措施	27-07-2000 美国 WT/DS175 17-11-2000 欧共体 WT/DS146	21-12-2001 WT/DS146/R 和 Corr. 1 WT/DS175/R 和 Corr. 1	31-01-2002 印度 WT/DS146/8 WT/DS175/8	05-04-2002 WT/DS146/11 WT/DS175/11	19-03-2002 WT/DS146/AB/R WT/DS175/AB/R	05-04-2002 WT/DS146/11 WT/DS175/11
62	加拿大—地区性航空器的出口信贷保证	12-03-2001 巴西 WT/DS222	28-01-2002 WT/DS222/R 和 Corr. 1	N. A.	19-02-2002 WT/DS222/6	N. A.	N. A.
63	智利—对特定农产品相关的综合价格制度及保障措施	12-03-2001 阿根廷 WT/DS207	03-05-2002 WT/DS207/R	24-06-2002 智利 WT/DS207/5	23-10-2002 WT/DS207/8	23-09-2002 WT/DS207/AB/R	23-10-2002 WT/DS207/8
64	欧共体—沙丁鱼贸易描述	24-07-2001 秘鲁 WT/DS231	29-05-2002 WT/DS231/R 和 Corr. 1	28-06-2002 欧共体 WT/DS231/11	23-10-2002 WT/DS231/15	26-09-02	23-10-2002 WT/DS231/15
65	美国—对来自印度的钢板采取反倾销及反补贴措施	24-07-2001 印度 WT/DS206	28-06-2002 WT/DS206/R 和 Corr. 1	N. A.	29-07-2002 WT/DS206/5	N. A.	N. A.
66	美国—对于来自德国的某些耐腐蚀碳钢板产品征收反补贴税	10-09-2001 欧共体 WT/DS213	03-07-2002 WT/DS213/R 和 Corr. 1	30-08-2002 美国 WT/DS213/6	19-12-2002 WT/DS213/9	28-11-2002 WT/DS213/AB/R 和 Corr. 1	19-12-2002 WT/DS213/9
67	美国—乌拉圭回合协议法案第129（C）（1）节	23-08-2001 加拿大 WT/DS221	15-07-2002 WT/DS221/R 和 Corr. 1	N. A.	30-08-2002 WT/DS221/7	N. A.	N. A.

续 表

序号	案件	专家组成立（日-月-年）	散发专家组报告（日-月-年）	通知上诉（日-月-年）	通过专家组报告（日-月-年）	散发上诉机构报告（日-月-年）	通过上诉机构报告（日-月-年）
68	美国—对来自欧共体某些产品采取反补贴措施	10-09-2001 欧共体 WT/DS212	31-07-2002 WT/DS212/R	09-09-2002 美国 WT/DS212/7	08-01-2003 WT/DS212/11	09-12-2002 WT/DS212/AB/R	08-01-2003 WT/DS212/11
69	埃及—对来自土耳其钢筋采取反倾销措施	20-06-2001 土耳其 WT/DS211	08-08-2002 WT/DS211/R	N. A.	01-10-2002 WT/DS211/5	N. A.	N. A.
70	美国—2000 年持续性倾销及补贴补偿法案	23-08-2001 澳大利亚 巴西 智利 欧共体 印度 印度尼西亚 日本 韩国 泰国 WT/DS217 10-09-2001 加拿大 墨西哥 WT/DS234	16-09-2002 WT/DS217/R WT/DS234/R	18-10-2002 美国 WT/DS217/8 WT/DS234/16	27-01-2003 WT/DS217/11 WT/DS234/19	16-01-03	27-01-2003 WT/DS217/11 WT/DS234/19
71	美国—对来自加拿大特定软木的初步决定	05-12-2001 加拿大 WT/DS236	27-09-2002 WT/DS236/R	N. A.	01-11-2002 WT/DS236/4	N. A.	N. A.
72	阿根廷—对于桃脯进口的保障措施	18-01-2002 智利 WT/DS238	14-02-2003 WT/DS238/R	N. A.	15-04-2003 WT/DS238/5	N. A.	N. A.
73	欧共体—对来自巴西的可锻铸铁管接头征收反倾销税	24-07-2001 巴西 WT/DS219	07-03-2003 WT/DS219/R	23-04-2003 巴西 WT/DS219/7	18-08-2003 WT/DS219/10	22-07-2003 WT/DS219/AB/R	18-08-2003 WT/DS219/10
74	阿根廷—对来自巴西的家禽征收反倾销税	17-04-2002 巴西 WT/DS241	22-04-2003 WT/DS241/R	N. A.	19-05-2003 WT/DS241/6	N. A.	N. A.
75	美国—纺织品及服装原产地证明	24-06-2002 印度 WT/DS243	20-06-2003 WT/DS243/R 和 Corr. 1	N. A.	21-07-2003 WT/DS243/8	N. A.	N. A.

续 表

序号	案件	专家组成立（日-月-年）	散发专家组报告（日-月-年）	通知上诉（日-月-年）	通过专家组报告（日-月-年）	散发上诉机构报告（日-月-年）	通过上诉机构报告（日-月-年）
76	美国—对特定钢铁产品进口采取保障措施	03-06-2002 欧共体 WT/DS248 14-06-2002 日本 WT/DS249 14-06-2002 韩国 WT/DS251 24-06-2002 中国 WT/DS252 24-06-2002 瑞士 WT/DS253 24-06-2002 挪威 WT/DS254 08-07-2002 新西兰 WT/DS258 29-07-2002 巴西 WT/DS259	11-07-2003 WT/DS248/R 和 Corr. 1 WT/DS249/R 和 Corr. 1 WT/DS251 和 Corr. 1 WT/DS252 和 Corr. 1 WT/DS253 和 Corr. 1 WT/DS254 和 Corr. 1 WT/DS254 和 Corr. 1 WT/DS258 和 Corr. 1 WT/DS259 和 Corr. 1	11-08-2003 美国 WT/DS248/17 WT/DS249/11 WT/DS251/12 WT/DS252/10 WT/DS253/10 WT/DS254/10 WT/DS258/14 WT/DS259/13	10-12-2003 WT/DS248/20 WT/DS249/14 WT/DS251/15 WT/DS252/13 WT/DS253/13 WT/DS254/13 WT/DS258/17 WT/DS259/16	10-11-2003 WT/DS248/AB/R WT/DS249/AB/R WT/DS251/AB/R WT/DS252/AB/R WT/DS253/AB/R WT/DS254/AB/R WT/DS258/AB/R WT/DS259/AB/R	10-12-2003 WT/DS248/20 WT/DS249/14 WT/DS251/15 WT/DS252/13 WT/DS253/13 WT/DS254/13 WT/DS258/17 WT/DS259/16
77	日本—影响苹果进口的措施	03-06-2002 美国 WT/DS245	15-07-2003 WT/DS245/R	28-08-2003 日本 WT/DS245/5	10-12-2003 WT/DS245/8	26-11-2003 WT/DS245/AB/R	10-12-2003 WT/DS245/8
78	美国—对来自日本的耐腐蚀碳钢板产品的反倾销税日落复审	22-05-2002 日本 WT/DS244	14-08-2003 WT/DS244/R	15-09-2003 日本 WT/DS244/7	09-01-2004 WT/DS244/10	15-12-2003 WT/DS244/AB/R	09-01-2004 WT/DS244/10
79	美国—对来自加拿大的软木最终反补贴税决定	01-10-2002 加拿大 WT/DS257	29-08-2003 WT/DS257/R 和 Corr. 1	21-10-2003 美国 WT/DS257/8	17-02-2004 WT/DS257/11	19-01-2004 WT/DS257/AB/R	17-02-2004 WT/DS257/11
80	欧共体—发展中国家优惠关税授予条件	27-01-2003 印度 WT/DS246	01-12-2003 WT/DS246/R	08-01-2004 欧共体 WT/DS246/7	20-04-2004 WT/DS246/10	07-04-2004 WT/DS246/AB/R	20-04-2004 WT/DS246/10
81	美国—对加拿大软木的国际贸易委员会调查	07-05-2003 加拿大 WT/DS277	22-03-2004 WT/DS277/R	N. A.	26-04-2004 WT/DS277/5	N. A.	N. A.
82	墨西哥—影响电信服务的措施	17-04-2002 美国 WT/DS204	02-04-2004 WT/DS204/R	N. A.	01-06-2004 WT/DS204/8	N. A.	N. A.
83	美国—对加拿大软木的最终倾销决定	08-01-2003 加拿大 WT/DS264	13-04-2004 WT/DS264/R	13-05-2004 美国 WT/DS264/6	31-08-2004 WT/DS264/9	11-08-2004 WT/DS264/AB/R	31-08-2004 WT/DS264/9

续 表

序号	案件	专家组成立（日-月-年）	散发专家组报告（日-月-年）	通知上诉（日-月-年）	通过专家组报告（日-月-年）	散发上诉机构报告（日-月-年）	通过上诉机构报告（日-月-年）
84	加拿大—关于小麦出口和谷物进口的措施	31-03-2003 美国 WT/DS276	06-04-2004 WT/DS276/R	01-06-2004 美国 WT/DS276/15	27-09-2004 WT/DS276/18	30-08-2004 WT/DS276/AB/R	27-09-2004 WT/DS276/18
85	美国—对来自阿根廷石油工业用管材的反倾销措施日落复审	19-05-2003 阿根廷 WT/DS268	16-07-2004 WT/DS268/R	31-08-2004 美国 WT/DS268/5	17-12-2004 WT/DS268/8	29-11-2004 WT/DS268/AB/R	17-12-2004 WT/DS268/8
86	美国—陆地棉补贴	18-03-2003 巴西 WT/DS267	08-09-2004 WT/DS267/R 和 Corr. 1	18-10-2004 美国 WT/DS267/17	21-03-2005 WT/DS267/20	03-03-2005 WT/DS267/AB/R	21-03-2005 WT/DS267/20
87	韩国—影响商船贸易的措施	21-07-2003 欧共体 WT/DS273	07-03-2005 WT/DS273/R	N. A.	11-04-2005 WT/DS273/8	N. A.	N. A.
88	欧共体—农产品和食品的商标及地理标识保护	02-10-2003 美国 WT/DS174 澳大利亚 WT/DS290	15-03-2005 WT/DS174/R 和 Add. 1，2 & 3 WT/DS290/R 和 Add. 1，2 & 3	N. A.	20-04-2005 WT/DS174/23 WT/DS290/21	N. A.	N. A.
89	美国—影响博彩业跨境交付的措施	21-07-2003 安提瓜和巴布达 WT/DS285	10-11-2004 WT/DS285/R	07-01-2005 美国 WT/DS285/6	20-04-2005 WT/DS285/10	07-04-2005 WT/DS285/AB/R	20-04-2005 WT/DS285/10
90	欧共体—糖类出口补贴	29-08-2003 澳大利亚 WT/DS265 巴西 WT/DS266 泰国 WT/DS283	15-10-2004 WT/DS265/R WT/DS266/R WT/DS283/R	13-01-2005 欧共体 WT/DS265/25 WT/DS266/25 WT/DS283/6	19-05-2005 WT/DS265/29 WT/DS266/29 WT/DS283/10	28-04-2005 WT/DS265/AB/R WT/DS266/AB/R WT/DS283/AB/R	19-05-2005 WT/DS265/29 WT/DS266/29 WT/DS283/10
91	多米尼加—影响香烟进口和国内销售的措施	09-01-2004 洪都拉斯 WT/DS302	26-11-2004 WT/DS302/R	24-01-2004 多米尼加 WT/DS302/8	19-05-2005 WT/DS302/12	25-04-2005 WT/DS302/AB/R	19-05-2005 WT/DS302/12
92	欧共体—影响商船贸易的措施	19-03-2004 韩国 WT/DS301	22-04-2005 WT/DS301/R	N. A.	20-06-2005 WT/DS301/6	N. A.	N. A.
93	美国—对来自韩国的计算机动态随机存取存储器芯片进行反补贴税调查	19-11-2003 韩国 WT/DS296	21-02-2005 WT/DS296/R	29-03-2005 美国 WT/DS296/5	20-07-2005 WT/DS296/10	27-06-2005 WT/DS296/AB/R	20-07-2005 WT/DS296/10

续 表

序号	案件	专家组成立（日-月-年）	散发专家组报告（日-月-年）	通知上诉（日-月-年）	通过专家组报告（日-月-年）	散发上诉机构报告（日-月-年）	通过上诉机构报告（日-月-年）
94	欧共体—对于来自韩国的计算机动态随机存取存储器芯片采取补贴措施	23-01-2004 韩国 WT/DS299	17-06-2005 WT/DS299/R	N. A.	03-08-2005 WT/DS299/6	N. A.	N. A.
95	欧共体—冷冻无骨鸡的关税分类	07-11-2003 巴西 WT/DS269 21-11-2003 泰国 WT/DS286	30-05-2005 WT/DS269/R WT/DS286/R	13-06-2005 欧共体 WT/DS269/6 WT/DS286/8	27-09-2005 WT/DS269/10 WT/DS286/12	12-09-2005 WT/DS269/AB/R WT/DS286/AB/R	27-09-2005 WT/DS269/10 WT/DS286/12
96	墨西哥—对于牛肉和稻米的反倾销措施：针对稻米的上诉	07-11-2003 美国 WT/DS295	06-06-2005 WT/DS295/R	20-07-2005 墨西哥 WT/DS295/6	20-12-2005 WT/DS295/9	29-11-2005 WT/DS295/AB/R	20-12-2005 WT/DS295/9
97	美国—对来自墨西哥的石油工业用管材反倾销措施	29-08-2003 墨西哥 WT/DS282	20-06-2005 WT/DS282/R	04-08-2005 墨西哥 WT/DS282/6	28-11-2005 WT/DS282/10	02-11-2005 WT/DS282/AB/R	28-11-2005 WT/DS282/10
98	韩国—对来自印度尼西亚特定纸张进口征收反倾销税	27-09-2004 印度尼西亚 WT/DS312	28-10-2005 WT/DS312/R	N. A.	28-11-2005 WT/DS312/5	N. A.	N. A.
99	墨西哥—对非酒精饮料及其他饮料征税	06-07-2004 美国 WT/DS308	07-10-2005 WT/DS308/R	06-12-2005 墨西哥 WT/DS308/10	24-03-2006 WT/DS308/13	06-03-2006 WT/DS308/AB/R	24-03-2006 WT/DS308/13
100	美国—计算倾销差额（归零法）的法律、规则及方法	19-03-2004 欧共体 WT/DS294	31-10-2005 WT/DS294/R	17-01-2006 欧共体 WT/DS294/12	09-05-2006 WT/DS294/17	18-04-2006 WT/DS294/AB/R	09-05-2006 WT/DS294/17
101	日本—干紫菜和味付紫菜进口配额	21-03-2005 韩国 WT/DS323	01-02-2006 WT/DS323/R	N. A.	N. A.	N. A.	N. A.
102	欧共体—特定海关措施	21-03-2005 美国 WT/DS315	16-06-2006 WT/DS315/R	14-08-2006 美国 WT/DS315/11	11-12-2006 WT/DS315/15	13-11-2006 WT/DS315/AB/R	11-12-2006 WT/DS315/15
103	美国—关于归零法及日落复审措施	28-02-2005 日本 WT/DS322	20-09-2006 WT/DS322/R	11-10-2006 日本 WT/DS322/12	23-01-2007 WT/DS322/15	09-01-2007 WT/DS322/AB/R	23-01-2007 WT/DS322/15

续 表

序号	案件	专家组成立（日-月-年）	散发专家组报告（日-月-年）	通知上诉（日-月-年）	通过专家组报告（日-月-年）	散发上诉机构报告（日-月-年）	通过上诉机构报告（日-月-年）
104	欧共体—影响生物科技产品审批及营销的措施	29-08-2003 美国 WT/DS291 加拿大 WT/DS292 阿根廷 WT/DS293	29/09-2006 WT/DS291/R WT/DS292/R WT/DS293/R		21-11-2006 WT/DS291/33 WT/DS292/27 WT/DS293/27	N. A.	N. A.
105	美国—对来自厄瓜多尔的虾的反倾销措施	19-07-2006 厄瓜多尔 WT/DS335	30-01-2007 WT/DS335/R	N. A.	20-02-2007 WT/DS335/9	N. A.	N. A.
106	墨西哥—对来自危地马拉的钢管征收反倾销税	17-03-2006 危地马拉 WT/DS331	08-06-2007 WT/DS331/R	N. A.	24-07-2007 WT/DS331/5	N. A.	N. A.
107	巴西—影响翻新轮胎进口的措施	20-01-2006 欧共体 WT/DS332	12-06-2007 WT/DS332/R	03-09-2007 欧共体 WT/DS332/9	17-12-2007 WT/DS332/12	03-12-2007 WT/DS332/AB/R	17-12-2007 WT/DS332/12
108	日本—对来自韩国的计算机动态随机存取存储器芯片的反补贴措施	19-06-2006 韩国 WT/DS336	13-07-2007 WT/DS336/R	30-08-2007 日本 WT/DS336/8	17-12-2007 WT/DS336/12	28-11-2007 WT/DS336/AB/R 和 Corr. 1	17-12-2007 WT/DS336/12
109	土耳其—影响稻米进口的措施	17-03-2006 美国 WT/DS334/4	21-09-2007 WT/DS334/R	N. A.	22-10-2007 WT/DS334/8	N. A.	N. A.
110	欧共体—对产自挪威的养殖鲑鱼采取反倾销措施	22-06-2006 挪威 WT/DS337	16-11-2007 WT/DS337/R	N. A.	15-01-2008 WT/DS337/6	N. A.	N. A.
111	美国—对来自墨西哥的不锈钢采取最终反倾销措施	21-10-2006 墨西哥 WT/DS344	20-12-2007 WT/DS344/R	31-01-2008 墨西哥 WT/DS344/7	20-05-2008 WT/DS344/10	30-04-2008 WT/DS344/AB/R	20-05-2008 WT/DS344/10
112	美国—对来自泰国的虾采取的措施	26-10-2006 泰国 WT/DS343	29-02-2008 WT/DS343/R	17-04-2008 泰国 WT/DS343/10	01-08-2008 WT/DS343/14	16-07-2008 WT/DS343/AB/R	01-08-2008 WT/DS343/14
113	美国—海关保税指令	21-11-2006 印度 WT/DS345	29-02-2008 WT/DS345/R	17-04-2008 印度 WT/DS345/9	01-08-2008 WT/DS345/13	16-07-2008 WT/DS345/AB/R	01-08-2008 WT/DS345/13
114	美国—欧共体要求取消报复措施：荷尔蒙争端	17-02-2005 欧共体 WT/DS320	31-03-2008 WT/DS320/R	29-05-2008 欧共体 WT/DS320/12	14-11-2008 WT/DS320/18	16-10-2008 WT/DS320/AB/R	14-11-2008 WT/DS320/18

续 表

序号	案件	专家组成立（日-月-年）	散发专家组报告（日-月-年）	通知上诉（日-月-年）	通过专家组报告（日-月-年）	散发上诉机构报告（日-月-年）	通过上诉机构报告（日-月-年）
115	加拿大—欧共体要求取消报复措施：荷尔蒙争端	17-02-2005 欧共体 WT/DS321	31-03-2008 WT/DS321/R	29-05-2008 欧共体 WT/DS321/12	14-11-2008 WT/DS321/16	16-10-2008 WT/DS321/AB/R	14-11-2008 WT/DS321/16
116	印度—对来自美国的进口产品征收“附加税”和“超额附加税”	20-06-2007 美国 WT/DS360	09-06-2008 WT/DS360/R	01-08-2008 美国 WT/DS360/8	17-11-2008 WT/DS360/12	30-10-2008 WT/DS360/AB/R	17-11-2008 WT/DS360/12
117	中国—影响汽车零部件进口的措施	26-10-2006 欧共体 WT/DS339 美国 WT/DS340 加拿大 WT/DS342	18-07-2008 WT/DS339/R WT/DS340/R WT/DS342/R 和 Add. 1 & 2	15-09-2008 中国 WT/DS339/12 WT/DS340/12 WT/DS342/12	12-01-2009 WT/DS339/14 WT/DS340/14 WT/DS342/14	15-12-2008 WT/DS339/AB/R WT/DS340/AB/R WT/DS342/AB/R	12-01-2009 WT/DS339/14 WT/DS340/14 WT/DS342/14
118	墨西哥—对来自欧共体的橄榄油采取反补贴措施	23-01-2007 欧共体 WT/DS341	04-09-2008 WT/DS341/R	N. A.	21-10-2008 WT/DS341/5	N. A.	N. A.
119	美国—与归零法和日落复审相关的措施	04-06-2007 欧共体 WT/DS350	01-10-2008 WT/DS350/R	06-11-2008 欧共体 WT/DS350/11	19-02-2009 WT/DS350/15	04-02-2009 WT/DS350/AB/R	19-02-2009 WT/DS350/15
120	中国—影响知识产权保护和执法的措施	25-09-2007 美国 WT/DS362	26-01-2009 WT/DS362/R	N. A.	20-03-2009 WT/DS362/10	N. A.	N. A.
121	哥伦比亚—对港口入境的价格限制要求	22-10-2007 巴拿马 WT/DS366	27-04-2009 WT/DS366/R 和 Corr. 1	N. A.	20-05-2009 WT/DS366/9	N. A.	N. A.
122	中国—影响知识产权保护和执法的措施	27-11-2007 美国 WT/DS363	12-08-2009 WT/DS363/R 和 Corr. 1	22-09-2009 WT/DS363/10	19-01-10 WT/DS363/14	21-12-2009 WT/DS363/AB/R	19-01-10 WT/DS363/14
123	美国—对自泰国的 PE 塑胶购物袋采取反倾销措施	20-03-2009 泰国 WT/DS383	22-01-10 WT/DS383/R	N. A.	18-02-10 WT/DS383/5	N. A.	N. A.
124	欧共体及其部分成员—影响大型民用飞机贸易的措施	20-07-2005 美国 WT/DS316	30-06-10 WT/DS316/R	21-07-10 欧盟 WT/DS316/12	01-06-11 WT/DS316/16	18-05-11 WT/DS316/AB/R	01-06-11 WT/DS316/16
125	澳大利亚—影响自新西兰进口苹果的措施	21-01-2008 新西兰 WT/DS367	09-08-2010 WT/DS367/R	31-08-2010 澳大利亚 WT/DS367/13	01-06-2011 WT/DS316/16	18-05-2011 WT/DS316/AB/R	01-06-2011 WT/DS316/16

续 表

序号	案件	专家组成立（日-月-年）	散发专家组报告（日-月-年）	通知上诉（日-月-年）	通过专家组报告（日-月-年）	散发上诉机构报告（日-月-年）	通过上诉机构报告（日-月-年）
126	欧共体及其成员国—部分信息技术产品的关税待遇	23-09-2008 美国 WT/DS375 日本 WT/DS376 台、澎、金、马单独关税区 WT/DS377	16-08-2010 WT/DS375/R WT/DS376/R WT/DS377/R	N. A.	21-09-2010 WT/DS375/13 WT/DS376/13 WT/DS377/11	N. A.	N. A.
127	美国—影响自中国进口家禽的措施	31-07-2009 中国 WT/DS392	29-09-2010 WT/DS392/R	N. A.	25-10-2010 WT/DS392/5	N. A.	N. A.
128	美国—对自中国进口的产品征收确定性反倾销税和反补贴税	20-01-2009 中国 WT/DS379	22-10-2010 WT/DS379/R	01-12-2010 中国 WT/DS379/6	25-03-2011 WT/DS379/9	11-03-2011 WT/DS379/AB/R	25-03-2011 WT/DS379/9
129	泰国—对自菲律宾进口香烟的关税和财政措施	17-11-2008 菲律宾 WT/DS371	15-11-2010 WT/DS371/R	22-02-2011 泰国 WT/DS371/8	15-07-2011 WT/DS371/11	17-06-2011 WT/DS371/AB/R	15-07-2011 WT/DS371/11
130	欧共体—对从中国进口的钢铁紧固件采取最终反倾销措施	23-10-2009 中国 WT/DS397	03-12-2010 WT/DS397/R	25-03-2011 欧盟 WT/DS397/7	28-07-2011 WT/DS397/11	15-07-2011 WT/DS397/AB/R	28-07-2011 WT/DS397/11
131	美国—对从中国进口汽车轮胎采取的限制措施	19-01-2010 中国 WT/DS399	13-12-2010 WT/DS399/R	24-05-2011 中国 WT/DS399/6	05-10-2011 WT/DS399/9	05-09-2011 WT/DS399/AB/R	05-10-2011 WT/DS399/9
132	美国—对自韩国产品的反倾销措施适用归零法	18-05-2010 韩国 WT/DS402	18-01-2011 WT/DS402/R	N. A.	24-02-2011 WT/DS402/5	N. A.	N. A.
133	美国—对从巴西进口的特定橙汁采取的反倾销行政复审和其他措施	25-09-2009 巴西 WT/DS382	25-03-2011 WT/DS382/R	N. A.	17-06-2011 WT/DS382/8	N. A.	N. A.
134	美国—影响大型民用航空器贸易的措施（二诉）	17-02-2006 欧共体 WT/DS353	31-03-2011 WT/DS353/R	01-04-2011 欧盟 WT/DS353/8	23-03-2012 WT/DS353/13	12-03-2012 WT/DS353/AB/R	23-03-2012 WT/DS353/13
135	中国—与限制原材料出口有关的措施	21-12-2009 美国 WT/DS394 欧共体 WT/DS395 墨西哥 WT/DS398	05-07-2011 WT/DS394/R WT/DS395/R WT/DS398/R	31-08-2011 中国 WT/DS394/11 WT/DS395/11 WT/DS398/10	22-02-2012 WT/DS394/16 WT/DS395/15 WT/DS398/14	30-01-2012 WT/DS394/AB/R WT/DS395/AB/R WT/DS398/AB/R	22-02-2012 WT/DS394/16 WT/DS395/15 WT/DS398/14

续 表

序号	案件	专家组成立（日-月-年）	散发专家组报告（日-月-年）	通知上诉（日-月-年）	通过专家组报告（日-月-年）	散发上诉机构报告（日-月-年）	通过上诉机构报告（日-月-年）
136	美国—对自越南进口的虾采取反倾销措施	18-05-2010 越南 WT/DS404	11-07-2011 WT/DS404/R	N. A.	02-09-2011 WT/DS404/9	N. A.	N. A.
137	菲律宾—对蒸馏酒精征税	19-01-2010 欧盟 WT/DS396 20-04-2010 美国 WT/DS403	15-08-2011 WT/DS396/R WT/DS403/R	23-09-2011 菲律宾 WT/DS396/7 WT/DS403/7	20-01-2012 WT/DS396/11 WT/DS403/11	21-12-2011 WT/DS396/AB/R WT/DS403/AB/R	20-01-2012 WT/DS396/11 WT/DS403/11
138	美国—影响丁香香烟生产和销售的措施	20-07-2010 印度尼西亚 WT/DS406	02-09-2011 WT/DS406/R	05-01-2012 美国 WT/DS406/6	24-04-2012 WT/DS406/9	04-04-2012 WT/DS406/AB/R	24-04-2012 WT/DS406/9
139	美国—对金枪鱼和金枪鱼产品的进口、营销和销售采取的措施	20-04-2009 墨西哥 WT/DS381	15-09-2011 WT/DS381/R	20-01-2012 美国 WT/DS381/10	13-06-2012 WT/DS381/15	16-05-2012 WT/DS381/AB/R	13-06-2012 WT/DS381/15
140	欧盟—对自中国进口的鞋采取反倾销措施	18-05-2010 中国 WT/DS405	28-10-2011 WT/DS405/R	N. A.	22-02-2012 WT/DS405/6	N. A.	N. A.
141	多米尼加—聚丙烯管状织物包装袋进口的保障措施	07-02-2011 哥斯达黎加 WT/DS415 危地马拉 WT/DS416 洪都拉斯 WT/DS417 萨尔瓦多 WT/DS418	31-01-2012 WT/DS415/R WT/DS416/R WT/DS417/R WT/DS418/R Add. 1	N. A.	22-02-2012 WT/DS415/11 WT/DS416/11 WT/DS417/11 WT/DS418/11	N. A.	N. A.
142	美国—对特定国家原产地标签要求	19-11-2009 加拿大 WT/DS384 墨西哥 WT/DS386	18-11-2011 WT/DS384/R WT/DS386/R	23-03-2012 美国 WT/DS384/12 WT/DS386/11	23-07-2012 WT/DS384/18 WT/DS386/17	29-06-2012 WT/DS384/AB/R WT/DS386/AB/R	23-07-2012 WT/DS384/18 WT/DS386/17
143	美国—对自中国进口的冷冻暖水虾采取反倾销措施	25-10-2011 WT/DS422	08-06-2012 WT/DS422/R Add. 1	N. A.	23-07-2012 WT/DS422/6	N. A.	N. A.
144	中国—对自美国进口的取向电工钢征收反补贴税和反倾销税	25-03-2011 WT/DS414	15-06-2012 WT/DS414/R Add. 1	20-07-2012 中国 WT/DS414/5	16-11-2012 WT/DS414/8	18-10-2012 WT/DS414/AB/R	16-11-2012 WT/DS414/8
145	中国—影响电子支付服务的措施	25-03-2011 WT/DS413	16-07-2012 WT/DS413/R Add. 1	N. A.	31-08-2012 WT/DS413/6	N. A.	N. A.

续 表

序号	案件	专家组成立（日-月-年）	散发专家组报告（日-月-年）	通知上诉（日-月-年）	通过专家组报告（日-月-年）	散发上诉机构报告（日-月-年）	通过上诉机构报告（日-月-年）
146	中国—对从欧盟进口的 X 射线安全检查设备征收最终反倾销税	20-01-2012 欧盟 WT/DS425	26-02-13 WT/DS425/R 和 Add. 1	N. A.	24-04-13 WT/DS425/6	N. A.	N. A.
147	加拿大—影响再生能源部门的措施/加拿大—上网电价补贴计划相关措施	20-07-2011 日本 WT/DS412 20-01-2012 欧盟 WT/DS426	19-12-2012 WT/DS412/R WT/DS426/R 和 Add. 1	05-02-2013 加拿大 WT/DS412/10 WT/DS426/9	24-05-2013 WT/DS412/14 WT/DS426/13	06-05-2013 WT/DS412/AB/R WT/DS426/AB/R	24-05-2013 WT/DS412/14 WT/DS426/13
148	中国 —对自美国的白羽肉鸡产品采取反倾销和反补贴措施	20-01-2012 美国 WT/DS427	02-08-2013 WT/DS427/R 和 Add. 1	N. A.	25-09-2013 WT/DS427/5	N. A.	N. A.
149	欧共体—限制海豹产品进口及营销的限制措施	25-03-2011 加拿大 WT/DS400 21-04-2011 挪威 WT/DS401	25-11-2013 WT/DS400/R WT/DS401/R 和 Add. 1	24-01-2014 加拿大 WT/DS400/8 挪威 WT/DS401/9	18-06-2014 WT/DS400/13 WT/DS401/14	22-05-2014 WT/DS400/AB/R WT/DS401/AB/R	18-06-2014 WT/DS400/13 WT/DS401/14
150	中国—对美部分进口汽车实施反倾销和反补贴措施	23-10-2012 美国 WT/DS440	23-05-2014 WT/DS440/R 和 Add. 1	N. A.	18-06-2014 WT/DS440/5	N. A.	N. A.
151	美国—对自中国的某些产品的反补贴和反倾销措施	17-12-2012 中国 WT/DS449	27-03-2014 WT/DS449/R Add. 1	08-04-2014 中国 WT/DS449/6	22-07-2014 WT/DS449/10	07-07-2014 WT/DS449/AB/R 和 Corr. 1	22-07-2014 WT/DS449/10
152	中国—影响稀土、钨、钼出口的措施	23-07-2012 美国 WT/DS431 欧盟 WT/DS432 日本 WT/DS433	26-03-2014 WT/DS431/R WT/DS432/R WT/DS433/R 和 Add. 1	08-04-2014 美国 WT/DS431/9 25-04-2014 中国 WT/DS432/9 WT/DS433/9	29-08-2014 WT/DS431/14 WT/DS432/12 WT/DS433/12	07-08-2014 WT/DS431/AB/R WT/DS432/AB/R WT/DS433/AB/R	29-08-2014 WT/DS431/14 WT/DS432/12 WT/DS433/12
153	美国—对源自印度的某些热轧碳钢产品的反补贴措施	31-08-2012 印度 WT/DS436	14-07-2014 WT/DS436/R 和 Add. 1	08-08-2014 印度 WT/DS436/6			
154	美国—对来自中国的某些产品的反补贴税的措施	28-09-2012 中国 WT/DS437	14-07-2014 WT/DS437/R 和 Add. 1	22-08-2014 中国 WT/DS437/7			

续 表

序号	案件	专家组成立（日-月-年）	散发专家组报告（日-月-年）	通知上诉（日-月-年）	通过专家组报告（日-月-年）	散发上诉机构报告（日-月-年）	通过上诉机构报告（日-月-年）
155	阿根廷—影响货物进口的措施	28-01-2013 欧盟 WT/DS438 美国 WT/DS444 日本 WT/DS445	22-08-2014 WT/DS438/R WT/DS444/R WT/DS445/R 和 Add. 1	26-09-2014 阿根廷 WT/DS438/15 WT/DS444/14 WT/DS445/14			
156	印度—影响某些农产品进口的措施	25-06-2012 美国 WT/DS430	14-10-2014 WT/DS430/R 和 Add. 1				

第三部分
执行争端解决机构建议

序号	案件	通过专家组及上诉机构报告（日-月-年）	通知执行争端解决机构建议的意向（日-月-年）	确定合理时限（日-月-年）	根据 DSU 第 21.3 条确定的合理期限	根据 DSU 第 21.6 条争端解决机构对执行的监督
1	美国—精炼及传统汽油标准	20-05-1996 WT/DS2/9	19-06-1996 WT/DSB/M/19	03-12-1996 WT/DSB/M/27	20-05-1996 至 20-08-1997 （15 个月）	WT/DS2/10 和 Add. 1-Add. 7
2	日本—对酒精饮料征税	01-11-1996 WT/DS8/11 WT/DS10/11 WT/DS11/8	20-11-1996 WT/DSB/M/26	14-02-1997 WT/DS8/15 WT/DS10/15 WT/DS11/13 （通过仲裁）	14-02-1997 至 14-05-1998 （15 个月）	WT/DS8/18 WT/DS10/18 WT/DS11/16 和 Add. 1-Add. 2
3	美国—对于棉质及人造纤维内衣的进口限制	25-02-1997 WT/DS24/8	20-03-1997 WT/DSB/M/30	N. A.	N. A.	此措施于 1997 年 3 月 28 日到期 WT/DSB/M/31
4	巴西—影响可可粉的措施	20-03-1997 WT/DS22/11/ Rev. 2	N. A.	N. A.	N. A.	N. A.
5	美国—影响从印度进口羊毛衬衫和女上衣进口的措施	23-05-1997 WT/DS33/5	N. A.	N. A.	N. A.	该限制于 1996 年 12 月 3 日废除 WT/DSB/M/33
6	加拿大—关于杂志的特定措施	30-07-1997 WT/DS31/7	29-08-1997 WT/DS31/8	15-09-1997	30-07-1997 至 30-10-1998 （15 个月）	WT/DS31/9 和 Add. 1-Add. 5
7	欧共体—香蕉进口、销售和分销	25-09-1997 WT/DS27/12	16-10-1997 WT/DSB/M/38	07-01-1998 WT/DS27/15 （通过仲裁）	25-09-1997 至 01-01-1999 （15 个月零 1 周）	WT/DS27/17 和 Add. 1-Add. 3 WT/DS27/51 和 Add. 1-Add. 25
8	印度—对于药品及农业化学品的专利权保护	16-01-1998 WT/DS50/9	13-02-1998 WT/DSB/M/42	21-04-1998 WT/DSB/M/45	16-01-1998 至 19-04-1999 （15 个月）	WT/DS50/10 和 Add. 1-Add. 4

续 表

序号	案件	通过专家组及上诉机构报告（日-月-年）	通知执行争端解决机构建议的意向（日-月-年）	确定合理时限（日-月-年）	根据 DSU 第 21.3 条确定的合理期限	根据 DSU 第 21.6 条争端解决机构对执行的监督
9	欧共体—关于肉及肉制品措施（荷尔蒙）	13-02-1998 WT/DS26/13 WT/DS48/11	13-03-1998 WT/DSB/M/43	29-05-1998 WT/DS26/15 WT/DS48/13 （通过仲裁）	13-02-1998 至 13-05-1999 （15 个月）	WT/DS26/17 WT/DS48/15 和 Add. 1-Add. 4
10	阿根廷—影响鞋类、纺织品、服装和其他项目的进口措施	22-04-1998 WT/DS56/11	08-05-1998 WT/DS56/12	15-06-1998 WT/DSB/M/46	22-04-1998 至 19-10-1998 （有 180 天的调查期限来决定纺织品和服装的特殊税） 22-04-1998— 01-01-1999 （有 242 天的调查期限决定统计税）	WT/DS56/15 和 Add. 1-Add. 4
11	日本—对进口胶卷相纸的限制	22-04-1998 WT/DS44/5	N. A.	N. A.	N. A.	N. A.
12	欧共体—特定计算机设备的海关分类	22-06-1998 WT/DS62/11 WT/DS67/9 WT/DS68/8	N. A.	N. A.	N. A.	N. A.
13	欧共体—影响特定家禽产品进口的措施	23-07-1998 WT/DS69/7	27-08-1998 WT/DS69/8	20-10-1998 WT/DS69/9	直至 31-03-1999	
14	印度尼西亚—影响汽车工业的特定措施	23-07-1998 WT/DS54/10 WT/DS55/10 WT/DS59/9 WT/DS64/8	21-08-1998 WT/DS54/12 WT/DS55/11 WT/DS59/10 WT/DS64/9	07-12-1998 WT/DS54/15 WT/DS55/14 WT/DS59/13 WT/DS64/12 （通过仲裁）	23-07-1998 至 23-07-1999 （12 个月）	WT/DS54/17 WT/DS55/16 WT/DS59/15 WT/DS64/14 和 Add. 1
15	印度—对于药品及农业化学品的专利权保护	22-09-1998 WT/DS79/5 和 Corr. 1	21-10-1998 WT/DSB/M/49	24-11-1998 WT/DSB/M/51	直至 19-04-1999	WT/DS79/6
16	美国—对特定虾及虾类产品进口限制	06-11-1998 WT/DS58/14	25-11-1998 WT/DSB/M/51	21-01-1999 WT/DSB/M/54	06-11-1998 至 06-12-1999 （13 个月）	WT/DS58/15
17	澳大利亚—影响鲑鱼进口的措施	06-11-1998 WT/DS18/11	25-11-1998 WT/DSB/M/51	23-02-1999 WT/DS18/9 （通过仲裁）	06-11-1998 至 06-07-1999 （8 个月）	（见第四部分）
18	危地马拉—对来自墨西哥的波兰特水泥的反倾销调查	25-11-1998 WT/DS60/12	N. A.	N. A.	N. A.	N. A.

续 表

序号	案件	通过专家组及上诉机构报告（日-月-年）	通知执行争端解决机构建议的意向（日-月-年）	确定合理时限（日-月-年）	根据DSU第21.3条确定的合理期限	根据DSU第21.6条争端解决机构对执行的监督
19	韩国—对酒精饮料征税	17-02-1999 WT/DS75/12 WT/DS84/10	19-03-1999 WT/DSB/M/57	04-06-1999 WT/DS75/16 WT/DS84/14 （通过仲裁）	17-02-1999至 31-01-2000 （11个月零2周）	WT/DS75/18 WT/DS84/16
20	日本—影响农产品的措施	19-03-1999 WT/DS76/8	15-04-1999 WT/DSB/M/58	15-06-1999 WT/DS76/9	19-03-1999至 31-12-1999 （9个月零12天）	WT/DS76/11和 Add. 1-Add. 16 日本和美国已通知争端解决机构，他们已达成双方满意的解决方案 WT/DS76/12
21	美国—对来自韩国的1兆或以上的计算机动态随机存取存储器芯片征收反倾销税	19-03-1999 WT/DS99/5	15-04-1999 WT/DSB/M/58	19-05-1999 WT/DSB/M/65	19-03-1999至 19-11-1999 （8个月）	WT/DS99/6
22	澳大利亚—对于汽车皮革制造商和生产商提供的补贴	16-06-1999 WT/DS126/5	06-07-1999 WT/DS126/6		根据《补贴与反补贴协议》第4.7条，专家组建议于报告批准日起90天内撤销此措施	WT/DS126/7 （见第四部分）
23	巴西—对于航空器出口资金融通	20-08-1999 WT/DS46/10	13-09-1999 WT/DS46/11		根据《补贴与反补贴协议》第4.7条，专家组建议于报告批准日起90天内撤销此措施	WT/DS46/12 （见第四部分）
24	加拿大—影响民用航空器措施	20-08-1999 WT/DS70/6	06-09-1999 WT/DS70/1		根据《补贴与反补贴协议》第4.7条，专家组建议于报告批准日起90天内撤销此措施	WT/DS70/8 （见第四部分）
25	印度—对于农产品、纺织品和工业产品进口的数量限制	22-09-1999 WT/DS90/14	14-10-1999 WT/DSB/M/69	28-12-1999 WT/DS90/15	直至01-04-2000及01-04-2001	WT/DS90/16 和 Add. 1-Add. 7
26	加拿大—影响牛奶进口及奶制品出口的措施	27-10-1999 WT/DS103/11 WT/DS113/11	19-11-1999 WT/DSB/M/71	22-12-1999 WT/DS103/10 WT/DS113/10	此实施阶段最迟不迟于2000年12月31日	WT/DS103/12— WT/DS113/12 和 Add. 1-Add. 6 （见第四部分）

续 表

序号	案件	通过专家组及上诉机构报告（日-月-年）	通知执行争端解决机构建议的意向（日-月-年）	确定合理时限（日-月-年）	根据DSU第21.3条确定的合理期限	根据DSU第21.6条争端解决机构对执行的监督
27	土耳其—对于纺织品和服装进口的限制	19-11-1999 WT/DS34/11	15-12-1999 WT/DS34/9	07-01-2000 WT/DS34/10	19-02-2001	WT/DS34/12 和 Add. 1-Add. 8 就土耳其所采取的措施达成一致的通知 WT/DS34/14
28	智利—对酒精饮料征税	12-01-2000 WT/DS87/12 WT/DS110/11	11-02-2000 WT/DSB/M/75	23-05-2000 WT/DS87/15 WT/DS110/4（通过仲裁）	12-01-2000 至 21-03-2001（14 个月零 9 天）	WT/DS87/17 和 Add. 1 & 2
29	韩国—对于特定奶制品进口的保障措施	12-01-2000 WT/DS98/10	11-02-2000 WT/DSB/M/75	21-03-2000 WT/DS98/11	直至 20-05-2000	WT/DS98/12
30	阿根廷—对鞋类产品进口的保障措施	12-01-2000 WT/DS121/9	11-02-2000 WT/DSB/M/75	N. A.	N. A.	N. A.
31	美国—1974 年贸易法第 301-310 部分	27-01-2000 WT/DS152/14	N. A.	N. A.	N. A.	N. A.
32	墨西哥—对来自美国的高果糖玉米浆进行反倾销调查	24-02-2000 WT/DS132/4 和 Corr. 1	20-03-2000 WT/DSB/M/77	10-04-2000 WT/DS132/5	24-02-2000 至 22-09-2000（6 个月零 29 天）	（见第四部分）
33	美国—“海外销售公司”税收待遇	20-03-2000 WT/DS108/10	07-04-2000 WT/DSB/M/78	20-03-2000（报告批准）	直至 01-10-2000 相应时间延至 01-11-2000	（见第四部分）
34	加拿大—药品的专利权保护	07-04-2000 WT/DS114/9	25-04-2000 WT/DSB/M/79	18-08-2000 WT/DS114/13（通过仲裁）	直至 07-10-2000	相关规定于 07-10-2000 公布
35	美国—对来自英国的热轧铅铋碳钢产品征收反补贴税	07-06-2000 WT/DS138/9 和 Corr. 1	05-07-2000 WT/DSB/M/85	N. A.	N. A.	N. A.
36	加拿大—影响汽车工业的特定措施	19-06-2000 WT/DS139/8 WT/DS142/8	27-07-2000 WT/DSB/M/86	04-10-2000 WT/DS139/12 WT/DS142/12（通过仲裁）	直至 19-02-2001	此措施于 18-02-2001 废止 WT/DSB/M/101
37	韩国—影响政府采购措施	19-06-2000 WT/DS163/7	N. A.	N. A.	N. A.	N. A.

续 表

序号	案件	通过专家组及上诉机构报告（日-月-年）	通知执行争端解决机构建议的意向（日-月-年）	确定合理时限（日-月-年）	根据DSU第21.3条确定的合理期限	根据DSU第21.6条争端解决机构对执行的监督
38	美国—美国版权法第110（5）节	27-07-2000 WT/DS160/8	24-08-2000 WT/DS160/9	15-01-2001 WT/DS160/12（通过仲裁）	直至27-07-2001 相应时间顺延直至美国国会结束或31-12-2001（WT/DS160/14）	WT/DS160/18 和Add. 1-Add. 16（见第四部分）在23-06-2003各方达成了相互满意的临时性协议（WT/DS160/23）相应地现状报告重新开始 WT/DS160/24 和Add. 1-Add. 22
39	美国—1916年反倾销法	26-09-2000 WT/DS136/8 WT/DS162/11	23-10-2000 WT/DSB/M/91	28-02-2001 WT/DS136/11 WT/DS162/14（通过仲裁）	直至26-07-2001 相应时间顺延直至美国国会结束或31-12-2001（WT/DS136/13 WT/DS162/16）	WT/DS136/14 WT/DS162/17 和Add. 1-Add. 31（见第四部分）
40	加拿大—专利保护条款	12-10-2000 WT/DS170/7	23-10-2000 WT/DSB/M/91	28-02-2001 WT/DS170/10（通过仲裁）	直至12-08-2001	加拿大宣布执行建议至12-08-2001止 WT/DSB/M/107
41	危地马拉—对来自墨西哥的灰波兰特水泥采取反倾销措	17-11-2000 WT/DS156/4	12-12-2000 WT/DSB/M/94	N. A.	N. A.	反倾销税至02-10-2000止 WT/DSB/M/94
42	韩国—影响新鲜、冷藏及冷冻牛肉进口的措施	10-01-2001 WT/DS161/11 WT/DS169/11	01-02-2001 WT/DSB/M/98	19-04-2001 WT/DS161/12 WT/DS169/12	直至10-09-2001	韩国宣布执行建议至10-09-2001止 WT/DSB/M/110
43	美国—对来自欧共体面筋进口的保障措施	19-01-2001 WT/DS166/10	03-04-2001 WT/DSB/M/99	04-04-2001 WT/DS166/12	直至02-06-2001	
44	美国—来自韩国的不锈钢卷板和不锈钢条的反倾销措施	01-02-2001 WT/DS179/4	01-03-2001 WT/DSB/M/100	26-04-2001 WT/DS179/5	直至01-09-2001	美国宣布执行建议至01-09-2001止 WT/DSB/M/109
45	阿根廷—影响牛皮出口和成皮进口的措施	16-02-2001 WT/DS155/5	12-03-2001 WT/DSB/M/101	31-08-2001 WT/DS155/10（通过仲裁）	直至28-02-2002	WT/DS155/12 争端解决机构注意到欧共体和阿根廷之间根据《关于争端解决规则与程序的谅解》第21和22条达成的协议 WT/DSB/M/121

续 表

序号	案件	通过专家组及上诉机构报告（日-月-年）	通知执行争端解决机构建议的意向（日-月-年）	确定合理时限（日-月-年）	根据 DSU 第 21.3 条确定的合理期限	根据 DSU 第 21.6 条争端解决机构对执行的监督
46	欧共体—对来自印度的棉质床单进口征收反倾销税	12-03-2001 WT/DS141/9	05-04-2001 WT/DSB/M/103	26-04-2001 WT/DS141/10	直至 14-08-2001	见第四部分
47	泰国—对波兰出口的铁或非合金钢的角铁、型材、轧材及工字梁的反倾销税案	05-04-2001 WT/DS122/7	26-04-2001 WT/DSB/M/104	25-05-2001 WT/DS122/8	直至 20-10-2001	WT/DS122/9 WT/DS122/11 （双方达成协议，此项不再出现在争端解决机构的日程中）
48	欧共体—影响石棉及含石棉产品的措施	05-04-2001 WT/DS135/12	N. A.	N. A.	N. A.	N. A.
49	美国—对来自新西兰和澳大利亚的新鲜、冷藏和冷冻羔羊肉进口采取保障措施	16-05-2001 WT/DS177/10 WT/DS178/11	20-06-2001 WT/DS177/11 WT/DS178/12	31-08-2001 决定于 15-11-2001 停止该措施 WT/DS177/12 WT/DS178/13	直至 15-11-2001	14-11-2001 美国宣布已完成必要的法律步骤来实施8月31日的决定 WT/DSB/M/113
50	美国—对来自日本的某些热轧钢产品采取反倾销措施	23-08-2001 WT/DS184/8	10-09-2001 WT/DSB/M/109	19-02-2002 WT/DS184/13 （通过仲裁）	23-08-2001 至 23-11-2002 （15 个月） 相应的，时间顺延直至 31-12-2003 或直至美国国会休会日，选两者较前者 （WT/DS184/16） 相应地，时间被修改，于 31-07-2004 到期 （WT/DS184/17） 相应地，时间被修改，于 31-07-2005 到期 （WT/DS184/18）	WT/DS184/15 和 Add. 1-Add. 47
51	美国—对于作为出口限制的补贴措施	23-08-2001 WT/DS194/4	N. A.	N. A.	N. A.	N. A.
52	美国—对来自巴基斯坦棉纱采取过渡性保障措施	05-11-2001 WT/DS192/7	21-11-2001 WT/DSB/M/113	N. A.	N. A.	美国宣布此措施于 01-11-2001 被废除 WT/DSB/M/113
53	阿根廷—对来自意大利的地板砖进口的反倾销措施	05-11-2001 WT/DS189/6	05-12-2001 WT/DSB/M/114	18-12-2001 WT/DS189/7	05-11-2001 至 05-04-2002 WT/DS189/7	WT/DS189/8

续 表

序号	案件	通过专家组及上诉机构报告（日-月-年）	通知执行争端解决机构建议的意向（日-月-年）	确定合理时限（日-月-年）	根据 DSU 第 21.3 条确定的合理期限	根据 DSU 第 21.6 条争端解决机构对执行的监督
54	美国—1998 年全面拨款法第 211 节	01-02-2002 WT/DS176/9	19-02-2002 WT/DSB/M/120	28-03-2002 WT/DS176/10	直至 31-12-2002 或美国国会休会日，不迟于 03-01-2003 相应地，时间被修改，于 30-06-2003 到期（WT/DS176/12） 时间再次被修改为 31-12-03 到期（WT/DS176/13） 相应地，时间被修改，于 31-12-2004 到期（WT/DS176/14） 相应地，时间被修改，于 30-06-2005 到期（WT/DS176/15）	WT/DS176/11 和 Add. 1-Add. 47
55	加拿大—地区性航空器的出口信贷保证	19-02-2002 WT/DS222/6	08-03-2002 WT/DSB/M/121		专家组建议从报告通过后的 90 天内撤销此措施（截止 20-05-2002）	（见第四部分）
56	美国—对产自韩国的环状焊接碳素钢管实施保障措施	08-03-2002 WT/DS202/13	05-04-2002 WT/DSB/M/122	29-07-2002 WT/DS202/18	直至 01-09-2002	在 18-03-2003 争端解决机构会议上，美国宣布此措施已于 01-03-2003 终止 WT/DSB/M/145
57	印度—影响汽车部门的措施	05-04-2002 WT/DS146/11 WT/DS175/11	02-05-2002 WT/DS146/12 WT/DS175/12	18-07-2002 WT/DS146/13 WT/DS175/13	05-04-2002 至 05-09-2002（5 个月）	在 11-11-2002 争端解决机构会议上，印度宣布其已执行了争端解决机构的建议 WT/DSB/M/136
58	美国—对来自印度的钢板采取反倾销及反补贴措施	29-07-2002 WT/DS206/5	27-08-2002 WT/DS206/6	01-10-2002 WT/DS206/7	20-07-2002 至 29-12-2002（5 个月） 相应地，时间被修改为 31-01-2003 到期（WT/DS206/8）	在 19-02-2003 争端解决机构会议上，美国宣布已按争端解决机构建议来执行 WT/DSB/M/143

续 表

序号	案件	通过专家组及上诉机构报告（日-月-年）	通知执行争端解决机构建议的意向（日-月-年）	确定合理时限（日-月-年）	根据 DSU 第 21.3 条确定的合理期限	根据 DSU 第 21.6 条争端解决机构对执行的监督
59	美国—乌拉圭回合协议第 129（c）（1）	30-08-2002 WT/DS221/7	N. A.	N. A.	N. A.	N. A.
60	埃及—对来自土耳其钢筋采取反倾销措施	01-10-2002 WT/DS211/5	23-10-2002 WT/DSB/M/134	14-11-2002 WT/DS211/6	01-10-2002 至 31-07-2003（9 个月）	WT/DS211/7 和 Add. 1-Add. 3（在 29-08-2003 争端解决机构会议上，埃及宣布已按争端解决机构建议执行）
61	智利—对特定农产品相关的综合价格制度及保障措施	23-10-2002 WT/DS207/8	11-11-2002 WT/DSB/M/136	17-03-2003 WT/DS207/13（通过仲裁）	23-10-2002 至 23-12-2003（14 个月）	WT/DS207/15 和 Add. 7（见第四部分）
62	欧共体—沙丁鱼贸易描述	23-10-2002 WT/DS231/15	11-11-2002 WT/DSB/M/136	19-12-2002 WT/DS231/16	23-10-2002 至 23-04-2003 相应地，时间被修改于 01-07-2003 到期（WT/DS231/17）	WT/DS231/18（双方同意的解决方案）
63	美国—对来自加拿大特定软木的初步决定	01-11-2002 WT/DS236/4	28-11-2002 WT/DSB/M/137	N. A.	N. A.	N. A.
64	美国—对来自德国的特定耐腐蚀碳钢板征收反补贴税	19-12-2002 WT/DS213/9	17-01-2003 WT/DSB/M/141	N. A.	N. A.	在 20-04-2004 争端解决机构会议上，美国宣布已按争端解决机构建议执行（WT/DSB/M/167）
65	美国—对于特定来自欧共体产品的反补贴措施	08-01-2003 WT/DS212/11	27-01-2003 WT/DSB/M/142	10-04-2003 WT/DS212/12	08-01-2003 至 08-11-2003（10 个月）	WT/DS212/13 WT/DS212/19（见第四部分）

续 表

序号	案件	通过专家组及上诉机构报告（日-月-年）	通知执行争端解决机构建议的意向（日-月-年）	确定合理时限（日-月-年）	根据DSU第21.3条确定的合理期限	根据DSU第21.6条争端解决机构对执行的监督
66	美国—2000年持续性倾销及补贴补偿法案	27-01-2003 WT/DS217/11 WT/DS234/19	27-01-2003 WT/DSB/M/142 19-02-2003 WT/DSB/M/143 26-02-2003 WT/DSB/M/144	13-06-2003 WT/DS217/14 WT/DS234/22 （通过仲裁）	27-01-03至 27-12-2003 （11个月） 在与澳大利亚，印度尼西亚和泰国有关的争议中，实施期间被修改至27-12-2004到期 （WT/DS217/17，18，19） 相应地，美国就此事项分别与下列国家达成程序谅解 澳大利亚 （WT/DS217/44） 泰国 （WT/DS217/45） 印度尼西亚 （WT/DS217/46）	WT/DS217/16 WT/DS234/24 和 Add.1—Add.24 （见第四部分）
67	阿根廷—对于桃脯进口的保障措施	15-04-2003 WT/DS238/5	14-05-2003 WT/DS238/6 19-05-2003 WT/DSB/M/150	30-05-2003 WT/DS238/7	直至31-12-2003	在23-01-2004争端解决机构会议上，阿根廷宣布已按争端解决机构建议执行 （WT/DSB/M/163）
68	阿根廷—对来自巴西的家禽征收反倾销税	19-05-2003 WT/DS241/6	N.A.	N.A.	N.A.	N.A.
69	美国—纺织品及服装原产地证明	21-07-2003 WT/DS243/8	N.A.	N.A.	N.A.	N.A.
70	欧共体—对来自巴西的可锻铸铁管接头征收反倾销税	18-08-2003 WT/DS219/10	15-09-2003 WT/DS219/11 02-10-2003 WT/DSB/M/156	01-10-2003 WT/DS219/12	18-08-2003至 19-03-2004 （7个月）	17-03-2004，欧共体就其执行争端解决机构建议提供信息 （WT/DS219/13）
71	日本—影响苹果进口的措施	10-12-2003 WT/DS245/8	09-01-2004 WT/DSB/M/162	30-01-2004 WT/DS245/9	10-12-2003至 30-06-2004 （6个月零20天）	（见第四部分）

续 表

序号	案件	通过专家组及上诉机构报告（日-月-年）	通知执行争端解决机构建议的意向（日-月-年）	确定合理时限（日-月-年）	根据 DSU 第 21.3 条确定的合理期限	根据 DSU 第 21.6 条争端解决机构对执行的监督
72	美国—对特定钢铁产品进口采取保障措施	10-12-2003 WT/DS248/20 WT/DS249/14 WT/DS251/15 WT/DS252/13 WT/DS253/13 WT/DS254/13 WT/DS258/17 WT/DS259/16	N. A.	N. A.	N. A.	在 10-12-2003 的争端解决机构会议上，美国宣布其总统已经下令停止与此争议相关的 10 项保障措施（WT/DSB/M/160）
73	美国—对来自日本的耐腐蚀碳钢板产品的反倾销税日落复审	09-01-2004 WT/DS244/10	N. A.	N. A.	N. A.	N. A.
74	美国—对来自加拿大的软木最终反补贴税决定	17-02-2004 WT/DS257/11	05-03-2004 WT/DS257/12	28-04-2004 WT/DS257/13	17-02-2004 至 17-12-2004（10 个月）	WT/DS257/14 和 Add. 1（见第四部分）
75	欧共体—发展中国家优惠关税授予条件	20-04-2004 WT/DS246/10	19-05-2004 WT/DSB/M/169	20-09-2004 WT/DS246/14（通过仲裁）	20-04-2004 至 01-07-2005（14 个月 零 11 天）	WT/DS246/16 和 Add. 1-Add. 3
76	美国—国际贸易委员会对加拿大软木的调查	26-04-2004 WT/DS277/R	19-05-2004 WT/DSB/M/169	01-10-2004 WT/DS277/7	26-04-2004 至 26-01-2005（9 个月）	在 25-01-2005 的争端解决机构会议上，美国说明其已按争端解决机构在此争端中的建议执行（见第四部分）
77	墨西哥—影响电信服务的措施	01-06-2004 WT/DS204/8	01-06-2004 WT/DS204/7	01-06-2004 WT/DS204/7	从报告通过之日起的 13 个月内；也就是说在 2005 年 7 月底前	WT/DS204/9 和 Add. 1-Add. 8
78	美国—对加拿大软木的最终倾销决定	31-08-2004 WT/DS264/9	27-09-2004 WT/DSB/M/176	06-12-2004 WT/DS264/12	31-08-2004 至 15-04-2005 相应地，时间被修改于 02-05-2005 到期（WT/DS264/15）	在 19-05-2005 的争端解决机构会议上，美国说明其已按争端解决机构的建议和规则执行 WT/DSB/M/189)（见第四部分）
79	加拿大—关于小麦出口和谷物进口的措施	27-09-2004 WT/DS276/18	18-10-2004 WT/DSB/M/177	15-11-2004 WT/DS276/19	27-09-2004 至 01-08-2005（10 个月零 5 天）	WT/DS276/20 和 Add. 1-Add. 3

续 表

序号	案件	通过专家组及上诉机构报告（日-月-年）	通知执行争端解决机构建议的意向（日-月-年）	确定合理时限（日-月-年）	根据DSU第21.3条确定的合理期限	根据DSU第21.6条争端解决机构对执行的监督
80	美国—对来自阿根廷石油工业用管材的反倾销措施日落复审	17-12-2004 WT/DS268/8	14-01-2005 WT/DSB/M/181	07-06-2005 WT/DS268/12 （通过仲裁）	17-12-2004至 17-12-2005 （12个月）	在20-12-2005的争端解决机构会议上美国说明其已按争端解决机构的建议和规则执行 （见第四部分）
81	美国—陆地棉补贴	21-03-2005 WT/DS/267/20	20-04-2005 WT/DSB/M/188		根据《补贴与反补贴协议》第4.7条，专家组建议此措施自报告被批准后的6个月内或在2005年7月1日之前撤销 （以较早的为准）	（见第四部分）
82	韩国—影响商船贸易的措施	11-04-2005 WT/DS273/8			根据《补贴与反补贴协议》第4.7条，专家组建议此措施自报告被批准后的90天内撤销	
83	欧共体—农产品和食品的商标及地理标识保护	20-04-2005 WT/DS174/23 WT/DS290/21	19-05-2005 WT/DSB/M/189	09-06-2005 WT/DS174/24 WT/DS290/22	实施时间至03-04-2006为止（11个月零2周）	WT/DS174/25 WT/DS290/23 和 Add. 1-Add. 3
84	美国—影响博彩业跨境交付的措施	20-04-2005 WT/DS285/10	19-05-2005 WT/DSB/M/189	19-08-2005 WT/DS285/13 （通过仲裁）	20-04-2005至 03-04-2006 （11个月零2周）	WT/DS285/15 和 Add. 1 （见第四部分）
85	欧共体—糖类出口补贴	19-05-2005 WT/DS265/29 WT/DS266/29 WT/DS283/10	13-06-2005 WT/DSB/M/191	28-10-2005 WT/DS265/33— WT/DS266/33— WT/DS283/14 （通过仲裁）	19-05-05至 22-05-2006 （12个月零3天）	WT/DS265/35 WT/DS266/35 WT/DS283/16 和 Add. 1
86	多米尼加—影响香烟进口和国内销售的措施	19-05-2005 WT/DS302/12	13-06-2005 WT/DSB/M/191	16-08-2005 WT/DS302/17	19-05-2005之后的24个月：也就是在19-05-2007之前	
87	欧共体—影响商船贸易的措施	20-06-2005 WT/DS301/6	20-07-2005 WT/DSB/M/194			

续 表

序号	案件	通过专家组及上诉机构报告（日-月-年）	通知执行争端解决机构建议的意向（日-月-年）	确定合理时限（日-月-年）	根据 DSU 第 21.3 条确定的合理期限	根据 DSU 第 21.6 条争端解决机构对执行的监督
88	美国—对来自韩国的计算机动态随机存取存储器芯片的反补贴税调查	20-07-2005 WT/DS296/10	03-08-2005 WT/DSB/M/195	07-11-2005 WT/DS296/11	20-07-2005 至 08-03-2006 （7 个月零 16 天）	在 14-03-2006 的争端解决机构会议上美国说明其已按争端解决机构的建议和规则执行（WT/DSB/M/206）
89	欧共体—对来自韩国的计算机动态随机存取存储器芯片的反补贴措施	03-08-2005 WT/DS299/6	31-08-2005 WT/DSB/M/196	12-10-2005 WT/DS299/7	03-08-2005 至 03-04-2006 （8 个月）	WT/DS299/8 WT/DS299/9
90	欧共体—冷冻无骨鸡的关税分类	27-09-2005 WT/DS269/10 WT/DS286/12	18-10-2005 WT/DSB/M/199	20-02-2006 WT/DS269/13— WT/DS286/15 （通过仲裁）	27-09-2005 至 27-06-2006 （9 个月）	WT/DS269/15 WT/DS286/17 和 Add. 1
91	美国—对来自墨西哥的石油工业用管材反倾销措施	28-11-2005 WT/DS282/10	20-12-2005 WT/DSB/M/202	15-02-2006 WT/DS282/11	28-11-2005 至 28-05-2006 （6 个月）	（见第四部分）
92	韩国—对来自印度尼西亚特定纸张进口征收反倾销税	28-11-2005 WT/DS312/5	20-12-2005 WT/DSB/M/202	10-02-2006 WT/DS312/6	28-11-2005 至 28-07-2006 （8 个月）	（见第四部分）
93	墨西哥—对于牛肉和稻米的反倾销措施：对于稻米的上诉	20-12-2005 WT/DS295/9	19-01-2006 WT/DS295/10	18-05-2006 WT/DS295/12	20-12-2005 至 20-08-2006 [8 个月，考虑到专家组报告第 8.1 和 8.3 段和上诉机构报告第 350（b）和（c）段] 20-12-2005 至 20-12-2006 [12 个月，考虑到专家组报告第 8.5 段和上诉机构报告第 350（d）段]	WT/DS295/13 和 Add. 1

续　表

序号	案件	通过专家组及上诉机构报告（日-月-年）	通知执行争端解决机构建议的意向（日-月-年）	确定合理时限（日-月-年）	根据 DSU 第 21.3 条确定的合理期限	根据 DSU 第 21.6 条争端解决机构对执行的监督
94	墨西哥—对于非酒精饮料及其他饮料征税	24-03-2006 WT/DS308/13	21-04-2006 WT/DSB/M/210	03-07-2006 WT/DS308/15	24-03-2006 至 01-01-2007 （9 个月零 8 天） 或者如果墨西哥国会在 2006 年 12 月 1—31 日间制定法律停止此措施 24-03-2006 至 31-01-2007 （10 个月零 7 天）	WT/DS308/16
95	美国—计算倾销差额（归零法）的法律、规则及方法	09-05-2006 WT/DS294/17	30-05-2006 WT/DSB/M/213	28-07-2006 WT/DS294/19	09-05-2006 至 09-04-2007 （11 个月）	WT/DS294/20 和 Add. 1-Add. 6 （见第四部分） WT/DS294/34 和 Add. 1-Add. 6 随后的报告： WT/DS294/38 和 Add. 1-Add. 20
96	欧共体—影响生物科技产品审批及营销的措施	21-11-2006 WT/DS291/33 WT/DS292/27 WT/DS293/27	19-12-2006 WT/DSB/M/224	21-06-2007 WT/DS291/35	21-11-2006 至 21-11-2007 （12 个月） 期限延长 WT/DS292/34，35，36，37，38 & 39（Corr. 1） （加拿大） 和 WT/DS293/34，35，36，37，38，39 & 40 （阿根廷）	WT/DS291/37 和 Add. 1-Add. 57 WT/DS292/31 和 Add. 1-Add. 18 WT/DS293/31 和 Add. 1-Add. 26 （见第四部分）
97	欧共体—特定海关措施	11-12-2006 WT/DS315/15	19-12-2006 WT/DSB/M/224			
98	美国—关于归零法及日落复审措施	23-01-2007 WT/DS322/15	20-02-2007 WT/DSB/M/226	04-05-2007 WT/DS322/20	23-01-2007 至 24-12-2007 （11 个月）	WT/DS322/22 和 Add. 1-Add. 2 （见第四部分） WT/DS322/36 和 Add. 1-Add. 29
99	美国—对来自厄瓜多尔虾征收反倾销税	20-02-2007 WT/DS335/9	20-03-2007 WT/DSB/M/228	26-03-2007 WT/DS335/10	20-02-2007 至 20-08-2007 （6 个月）	2007 年 8 月，美国宣布已按争端解决机构建议和裁决执行 WT/DSB/M/238

续 表

序号	案件	通过专家组及上诉机构报告（日-月-年）	通知执行争端解决机构建议的意向（日-月-年）	确定合理时限（日-月-年）	根据 DSU 第 21.3 条确定的合理期限	根据 DSU 第 21.6 条争端解决机构对执行的监督
100	墨西哥-对来自危地马拉的钢管征收反倾销税	24-07-2007 WT/DS331/5	23-08-2007 WT/DS331/6	25-09-2007 WT/DS331/7	24-07-2007 至 24-01-2008 （6 个月）	2008 年 1 月 24 日，墨西哥宣布已按争端解决机构建议和裁决执行 WT/DSB/M/248
101	土耳其—影响大米进口的措施	22-10-2007 WT/DS334/8	20-11-2007 WT/DS334/10	09-04-2008 WT/DS334/12	22-10-2007 至 22-04-2008 （6 个月）	WT/DS334/14
102	巴西—影响翻新轮胎进口的措施	17-12-2007 WT/DS332/12	15-01-2008 WT/DSB/M/244	29-08-2008 WT/DS332/16 （通过仲裁）	17-12-2007 至 11-12-2008 （12 个月）	WT/DS332/19 和 Add. 1-Add. 6
103	日本—对来自韩国的动态随机存储器征收反补贴税	17-12-2007 WT/DS336/12	15-01-2008 WT/DSB/M/244	05-05-2008 WT/DS336/16 （通过仲裁）	17-12-2007 至 01-09-2008 （8 个月零 2 星期）	（见第四部分）
104	欧共体—对产自挪威人工养殖的鲑鱼采取反倾销措施	15-01-2008 WT/DS337/6	08-02-2008 WT/DSB/M/246	06-05-2008 WT/DS337/8	15-01-2008 至 15-11-2008 （10 个月）	争端解决机构于 2008 年 8 月 1 日开会宣布撤销该措施，于 2008 年 7 月 20 日生效 WT/DSB/M/254
105	美国—对产自墨西哥的不锈钢采取最终反倾销措施	20-05-2008 WT/DS344/10	02-06-2008 WT/DSB/M/251	31-10-2008 WT/DS344/15 （通过仲裁）	20-05-2008 至 30-04-2009 （11 个零 10 天）	（见第四部分）
106	美国—与来自泰国虾有关的措施	01-08-2008 WT/DS343/14	29-08-2008 WT/DSB/M/255	31-10-2008 WT/DS343/16	01-08-2008 至 01-04-2009 （8 个月）	在 2009 年 4 月 20 日争端解决机构会议上，美国说明其已按争端解决机构的建议和规则执行 WT/DSB/M/267
107	美国—海关保税指令	01-08-2008 WT/DS345/13	29-08-2008 WT/DSB/M/255	31-10-2008 WT/DS345/15	01-08-2008 至 01-04-2009 （8 个月）	在 2009 年 4 月 20 日争端解决机构会议上，美国说明其已按争端解决机构的建议和规则执行 WT/DSB/M/267

续 表

序号	案件	通过专家组及上诉机构报告（日-月-年）	通知执行争端解决机构建议的意向（日-月-年）	确定合理时限（日-月-年）	根据DSU第21.3条确定的合理期限	根据DSU第21.6条争端解决机构对执行的监督
108	墨西哥—对从欧共体进口的橄榄油采取最终反补贴措施	21-10-2008 WT/DS341/5	17-11-2008 WT/DSB/M/259			在2008年12月11日争端解决机构会议上，墨西哥说明其已按争端解决机构的建议和规则执行 WT/DSB/M/260
109	美国-欧共体继续要求中止在荷尔蒙案件中的义务	14-11-2008 WT/DS320/18	11-12-2008 WT/DSB/M/260			
110	加拿大—欧共体继续要求中止在荷尔蒙案件中的义务	14-11-2008 WT/DS321/16	11-12-2008 WT/DSB/M/260			
111	中国—影响汽车零部件进口的措施	12-01-2009 WT/DS339/14 WT/DS340/14 WT/DS342/14	11-02-2009 WT/DSB/M/264	27-02-2009 WT/DS339/15 WT/DS340/15 WT/DS342/15	12-01-2009至 01-09-2009 （7个月零20天）	在2009年8月31日争端解决机构会议上，中国说明其已使其措施与争端解决机构的建议和裁决一致 WT/DSB/M/273
112	美国—继续存在和运用归零法	19-02-2009 WT/DS350/15	20-03-2009 WT/DSB/M/266	02-06-2009 WT/DS350/17	19-02-2009至 19-12-2009 （10个月）	WT/DS350/18 和Add.1-Add.10
113	中国-影响知识产权保护和执法的措施	20-03-2009 WT/DS362/10	20-04-2009 WT/DSB/M/267	29-06-2009 WT/DS362/13	20-03-2009至 20-03-2010 （12个月）	WT/DS362/14 和Add.1 & Add.2 2010年4月20日争端解决机构会议上，中国说明其已使其措施与争端解决机构的建议和裁决一致 （WT/DSB/M/282）
114	哥伦比亚—对港口入境的价格限制要求	20-05-2009 WT/DS366/9	19-06-2009 WT/DSB/M/270	02-10-2009 WT/DS366/13	20-05-2009至 04-02-2010 （8个月零15天）	WT/DS366/15
115	中国—影响出版物和视听娱乐产品的贸易权和分销服务措施	19-01-2010 WT/DS363/14	18-02-2010 WT/DSB/M/279	12-07-2010 WT/DS363/16	19-01-2010至 19-03-2011 （14个月）	WT/DS363/17 和Add.1-Add.15

续 表

序号	案件	通过专家组及上诉机构报告（日-月-年）	通知执行争端解决机构建议的意向（日-月-年）	确定合理时限（日-月-年）	根据 DSU 第 21.3 条确定的合理期限	根据 DSU 第 21.6 条争端解决机构对执行的监督
116	美国—对自泰国的 PE 塑胶购物袋采取反倾销措施	18-02-2010 WT/DS383/5	19-03-2010 WT/DSB/M/280	31-03-2010 WT/DS383/6	18-02-2010 至 18-08-2010 （6 个月）	2010 年 8 月 31 日争端解决机构会议上，美国说明其已使其措施与争端解决机构的建议和裁决一致（WT/DSB/M/286）
117	欧盟及其成员国—某些信息技术产品的关税待遇	21-09-2010 WT/DS375/13 WT/DS376/13 WT/DS377/11	13-10-2010 WT/DS375/14 WT/DS376/14 WT/DS377/12	20-12-2010 WT/DS375/16 WT/DS376/16 WT/DS377/14	21-09-2010 至 30-06-2011 （9 个月零 9 天）	WT/DS375/18 WT/DS376/18 WT/DS377/16
118	澳大利亚—影响自新西兰进口苹果的措施	17-12-2010 WT/DS367/17	10-01-2011 WT/DS367/18	31-01-2011 WT/DS367/19	直至 17-08-2011	WT/DS367/20
119	美国—对自韩国产品的反倾销措施适用归零法	24-02-2011 WT/DS402/5	25-03-2011 WT/DSB/M/294	17-06-2011 WT/DS402/6	(i) 9 个月， 直至 24-11-2011 (ii) 8 个月， 直至 24-10-2011	
120	美国—对来自中国的特定产品征收反倾销税和反补贴税	25-03-2011 WT/DS379/6	21-04-2011 WT/DSB/M/295	08-07-2011 WT/DS379/11	25-03-2011 至 25-02-2012 （11 个月）	WT/DS379/12 和 Add. 1-Add. 7
121	欧共体及其某些成员国—影响大型民用航空器贸易的措施	01-06-2011 WT/DS316/16	17-06-2011 WT/DSB/M/298		根据《补贴与反补贴协议》第 7.9 条，此措施自报告被批准后的 6 个月内撤销（01-12-2011）	（见第四部分）
122	美国—对从巴西进口的特定橙汁采取的反倾销行政复审和其他措施	17-06-2011 WT/DS382/8	17-06-2011 WT/DSB/M/298	17-06-2011 WT/DS382/9	17-06-2011 至 17-03-2012 （9 个月）	WT/DS382/10 和 Add. 1-Add. 10
123	泰国—对来自菲律宾烟草所采取的海关和财政措施	15-07-2011 WT/DS371/11	11-08-2011 WT/DS371/12	23-09-2011 WT/DS371/14	15-07-2011 至 15-05-2012 （10 个月） 15-07-2011 至 15-10-2012 （15 个月）	WT/DS371/15 和 Add. 1-Add. 6
124	欧共体—对从中国进口的钢铁紧固件采取最终反倾销措施	28-07-2011 WT/DS397/11	18-08-2011 WT/DS397/12	19-01-2012 WT/DS397/14	28-07-2011 至 12-10-2012 （14 个月零 2 周）	WT/DS397/15 和 Add. 1-Add. 3
125	美国—对自越南进口的虾采取反倾销措施	02-09-2011 WT/DS404/9	27-09-2011 WT/DSB/M/303	31-10-2011 WT/DS404/10	02-09-2011 至 02-07-2012 （10 个月）	WT/DS404/11 和 Add. 1-Add. 5

续 表

序号	案件	通过专家组及上诉机构报告（日-月-年）	通知执行争端解决机构建议的意向（日-月-年）	确定合理时限（日-月-年）	根据 DSU 第 21.3 条确定的合理期限	根据 DSU 第 21.6 条争端解决机构对执行的监督
126	美国—对从中国进口汽车轮胎采取的限制措施	05-10-2011 WT/DS399/9	N. A.	N. A.	N. A.	N. A.
127	菲律宾—对蒸馏酒精征税	20-01-2012 WT/DS396/11 WT/DS403/11	15-02-2012 WT/DS396/12 WT/DS403/12	20-04-2012 WT/DS396/14 WT/DS403/14	20-01-2012 至 08-03-2013 （13 个月零 16 天）	WT/DS396/15 WT/DS403/15
128	欧盟—对自中国进口的鞋采取反倾销措施	22-02-2012 WT/DS405/6	23-03-2012 WT/DSB/M/313	23-05-2012 WT/DS405/7	22-02-2012 至 11-10-2012 （7 个月零 19 天）	
129	多米尼加—聚丙烯管状织物包装袋进口的保障措施	22-02-2012 WT/DS415/11 WT/DS416/11 WT/DS417/11 WT/DS418/11	23-03-2012 WT/DSB/M/313	13-04-2012 WT/DS415/12 WT/DS416/12 WT/DS417/12 WT/DS418/12	RPT 2012 年 4 月 21 日结束 WT/DS415/13 WT/DS416/13 WT/DS417/13 WT/DS418/13 （保障措施 2012 年 4 月 21 日取消）	
130	中国—与限制原材料出口有关的措施	22-02-2012 WT/DS394/16 WT/DS395/15 WT/DS398/14	23-03-2012 WT/DSB/M/313	24-05-2012 WT/DS394/18 WT/DS395/17 WT/DS398/16	22-02-2012 至 31-12-2012 （10 个月零 9 天）	WT/DS394/19 WT/DS395/18 WT/DS398/17 和 Add. 1
131	美国—影响大型民用航空器贸易的措施（二诉）	23-03-2012 WT/DS353/13	13-04-2012 WT/DSB/M/314		SCM 协议相符 23-09-2012	WT/DS353/15
132	美国—影响丁香香烟生产和销售的措施	24-04-2012 WT/DS406/9	24-05-2012 WT/DSB/M/316	14-06-2012 WT/DS406/10	24-04-2012 至 24-07-2013 （15 个月）	WT/DS406/11 和 Add. 1-Add. 7
133	美国—对金枪鱼和金枪鱼产品的进口，营销和销售采取的措施	13-06-2012 WT/DS381/15	25-06-2012 WT/DSB/M/318	17-09-2012 WT/DS381/17	13-06-2012 至 13-07-2013 （13 个月）	WT/DS381/18 和 Add. 1-Add. 3
134	美国—对自中国进口的冷冻暖水虾采取反倾销措施	23-07-2012 WT/DS422/6	23-07-2012 WT/DSB/M/320	27-07-2012 WT/DS422/7	23-07-2012 至 23-03-2013 （8 个月）	WT/DS422/8 和 Add. 1
135	美国—对特定国家原产地标签要求	23-07-2012 WT/DS384/18 WT/DS386/17	21-08-2012 WT/DS384/19 WT/DS386/18	04-12-2012 WT/DS384/24— WT/DS386/23 （仲裁）	23-07-2012 至 23-05-2013 （10 个月）	24-05-2013 美国关于 DSB 建议实施声明 （WT/DSB/M/332）
136	中国—影响电子支付服务的措施	31-08-2012 WT/DS413/6	28-09-2012 WT/DSB/M/322	22-11-2012 WT/DS413/8	31-08-2012 至 31-07-2013 （11 个月）	WT/DS413/9 和 Add. 1

续 表

序号	案件	通过专家组及上诉机构报告（日-月-年）	通知执行争端解决机构建议的意向（日-月-年）	确定合理时限（日-月-年）	根据 DSU 第 21.3 条确定的合理期限	根据 DSU 第 21.6 条争端解决机构对执行的监督
137	中国—对自美国进口的取向电工钢征收反补贴税和反倾销税	16-11-2012 WT/DS414/8	30-11-2012 WT/DSB/M/326	03-05-2013 WT/DS414/12 （仲裁）	16-11-12 至 31-07-2013 （8 个月零 15 天）	30-08-2013 中国关于 DSB 建议实施声明 WT/DSB/M/336
138	中国—对从欧盟进口的 X 射线安全检查设备征收最终反倾销税	24-04-2013 WT/DS425/6	24-05-2013 WT/DSB/M/332	19-07-2013 WT/DS425/8	24-04-2013 至 19-02-2014 （9 个月零 25 天）	WT/DS425/9
139	加拿大—影响再生能源部门的措施/加拿大—上网电价补贴计划相关措施	24-05-2013 WT/DS412/14 WT/DS426/13	20-06-2013 WT/DS412/15 WT/DS426/14 25-06-2013 WT/DSB/M/333	29-07-2013 WT/DS412/16 WT/DS426/16	24-05-2013 至 24-03-2014 （10 个月） 随后时间被延长至 05-06-2014 （WT/DS412/18） （WT/DS426/18）	WT/DS412/17 WT/DS426/17 和 Add. 1-Add. 3 WT/DS412/19 WT/DS426/19
140	中国—对自美国的白羽肉鸡产品采取反倾销和反补贴措施	25-09-2013 WT/DS427/5	22-10-2013 WT/DSB/M/338	19-12-2013 WT/DS427/7	25-09-2013 至 09-07-2014 （9 个月零 14 天）	WT/DS427/8
141	欧共体—限制海豹产品进口及营销的限制措施	18-06-2014 WT/DS400/13 WT/DS401/14	10-07-2014 WT/DSB/M/347	05-09-2014 WT/DS400/15 WT/DS401/16	18-06-2014 至 18-10-15 （16 个月）	
142	美国—对自中国的某些产品的反补贴和反倾销措施	22-07-2014 WT/DS449/10	21-08-2014 WT/DS449/11 WT/DSB/M/349			
143	中国—影响稀土、钨、钼出口的措施	29-08-2014 WT/ DS431/14 WT/DS432/12 WT/DS433/12	26-09-2014 WT/DSB/M/350			

第四部分

援引《关于争端解决规则与程序的谅解》第 21.5 条

序号	案件	援引第 21.5 条（日-月-年）	提交原专家组（日-月-年）	散发专家组报告（日-月-年）	通知上诉（日-月-年）	散发上诉机构报告（日-月-年）	通过专家组和/或上诉机构报告（日-月-年）
1	欧共体—香蕉进口、销售和分销	15-12-1998 欧共体 WT/DS27/40 18-12-1998 厄瓜多尔 WT/DS27/41	12-01-1999 WT/DSB/M/53 欧共体、 厄瓜多尔	12-04-1999 WT/DS27/ RW/ECU WT/DS27/ RW/EEC 和 Corr. 1	N. A.	N. A.	06-05-1999 WT/DSB/M/61 （WT/DS27/ RW/ECU）

续 表

序号	案件	援引第21.5条（日-月-年）	提交原专家组（日-月-年）	散发专家组报告（日-月-年）	通知上诉（日-月-年）	散发上诉机构报告（日-月-年）	通过专家组和/或上诉机构报告（日-月-年）
2	澳大利亚—影响鲑鱼进口的措施	28-07-1999 加拿大 WT/DS18/14	28-07-1999 WT/DSB/M/66	18-02-2000 WT/DS18/RW	N. A.	N. A.	20-03-2000 WT/DSB/M/77
3	澳大利亚—对于汽车皮革制造商和生产商提供的补贴	04-10-1999 美国 WT/DS126/8	14-10-1999 WT/DSB/M/69	21-01-2000 WT/DS126/RW 和 Corr. 1	N. A.	N. A.	11-02-2000 WT/DSB/M/75
4	巴西—对于航空器出口融资	26-11-1999 加拿大 WT/DS46/13	09-12-1999 WT/DSB/M/72	09-05-2000 WT/DS46/RW	22-05-2000 巴西 WT/DS46/17	21-07-2000 WT/DS46/ AB/RW	04-08-2000 WT/DSB/M/87
5	加拿大—影响民用航空器措施	23-11-1999 巴西 WT/DS70/9	09-12-1999 WT/DSB/M/72	09-05-2000 WT/DS70/RW	22-05-2000 巴西 WT/DS70/12	21-07-2000 WT/DS70/ AB/RW	04-08-2000 WT/DSB/M/87
6	美国—对自韩国计算机动态随机存取存储器芯片征收反倾销税	07-04-2000 韩国 WT/DS99/8	25-04-2000 WT/DSB/M/79	07-11-2000 WT/DS99/RW （双方达成协议）	N. A.	N. A.	N. A.
7	美国—对特定虾及虾类产品进口限制	13-10-2000 马来西亚 WT/DS58/17	23-10-2000 WT/DSB/M/91	15-06-2001 WT/DS58/RW	23-07-2001 马来西亚 WT/DS58/20	22-10-2001 WT/DS58/ AB/RW	21-11-2001 WT/DSB/M/113
8	墨西哥—对来自美国的高果糖玉米浆开展反倾销调查	13-10-2000 美国 WT/DS132/6	23-10-2000 WT/DSB/M/91	22-06-2001 WT/DS132/RW	24-07-2001 墨西哥 WT/DS132/10	22-10-2001 WT/DS132/ AB/RW	21-11-2001 WT/DSB/M/113
9	美国—“海外销售公司”税收待遇	07-12-2000 欧共体 WT/DS108/16	20-12-2000 WT/DSB/M/95	20-08-2001 WT/DS108/RW	15-10-2001 美国 WT/DS108/21	14-01-2002 WT/DS108/ AB/RW	29-01-2002 WT/DSB/M/118
10	巴西—对于航空器出口资金融通：加拿大再次援引 DSU 第21.5条	19-01-2001 加拿大 WT/DS46/26	16-02-2001 WT/DSB/M/99	26-07-2001 WT/DS46/ RW/2	N. A.	N. A.	23-08-2001 WT/DSB/M/108
11	加拿大—影响牛奶进口及奶制品出口的措施	16-02-2001 美国 WT/DS103/16 16-02-2001 新西兰 WT/DS113/16	01-03-2001 WT/DSB/M/100	11-07-2001 WT/DS103/RW WT/DS113/RW	04-09-2001 加拿大 WT/DS103/20 WT/DS113/20	03-12-2001 WT/DS103/ AB/RW WT/DS113/ AB/RW	18-12-2001 WT/DSB/M/116
12	加拿大—影响牛奶进口及奶制品出口的措施：美国和新西兰再次引用第21.5条	06-12-2001 美国 WT/DS103/23 06-12-2001 新西兰 WT/DS113/23	18-12-2001 WT/DSB/M/116	26-07-2002 WT/DS103/ RW/2 WT/DS113/ RW/2	23-09-2002 加拿大 WT/DS103/28 WT/DS113/28	20-12-2002 WT/DS103/ AB/RW2 WT/DS113/ AB/RW2	17-01-2003 WT/DSB/M/141

续 表

序号	案件	援引第 21.5 条（日-月-年）	提交原专家组（日-月-年）	散发专家组报告（日-月-年）	通知上诉（日-月-年）	散发上诉机构报告（日-月-年）	通过专家组和/或上诉机构报告（日-月-年）
13	欧共体—对于来自印度棉质床单进口征收反倾销税	07-05-2002 印度 WT/DS141/13/Rev. 1	22-05-2002 WT/DSB/M/124 和 Corr. 1	29-11-2002 WT/DS141/RW	08-01-2003 印度 WT/DS141/16	08-04-2003 WT/DS141/AB/RW	24-04-2003 WT/DSB/M/148
14	美国—对来自欧共体特定产品反补贴措施	17-03-2004 欧共体 WT/DS212/14	27-09-2004 WT/DS212/15 WT/DSB/M/176	17-08-2005 WT/DS212/RW	N. A.	N. A.	27-09-2005 WT/DSB/M/198
15	智利—对特定农产品相关的综合价格制度及保障措施	19-05-2004 阿根廷 WT/DS207/17	20-01-2006 WT/DS207/18 WT/DSB/M/203	08-12-2006 WT/DS207/RW	05-02-2007 智利 WT/DS207/22	07-05-2007 WT/DS207/AB/RW	22-05-2007 WT/DSB/M/232
16	日本—影响苹果进口的措施	19-07-2004 美国 WT/DS245/11	30-07-2004 WT/DSB/M/174	23-06-2005 WT/DS245/RW	N. A.	N. A.	20-07-2005 WT/DSB/M/194
17	美国—对来自加拿大的软木最终反补贴税决定	04-01-2005 加拿大 WT/DS257/15	14-01-2005 WT/DSB/M/181	01-08-2005 WT/DS257/RW	06-09-2005 美国 WT/DS257/22	05-12-2005 WT/DS257/AB/RW	20-12-2005 WT/DSB/M/202
18	美国—“海外销售公司”税收待遇：欧共体再次援引第 21.5 条	14-01-2005 欧共体 WT/DS108/29	17-02-2005 WT/DSB/M/183	30-09-2005 WT/DS108/RW2	14-11-2005 美国 WT/DS108/32	13-02-2006 WT/DS108/AB/RW2	14-03-2006 WT/DS108/36
19	美国—国际贸易委员会对加拿大软木的调查	15-02-2005 加拿大 WT/DS277/8	25-02-2005 WT/DSB/M/184	15-11-2005 WT/DS277/RW	13-01-2006 加拿大 WT/DS277/16	13-04-2006 WT/DS277/AB/RW	09-05-2006 WT/DS277/19
20	美国—对加拿大软木的最终倾销决定	19-05-2005 加拿大 WT/DS264/16	01-06-2005 WT/DSB/M/190	03-04-2006 WT/DS264/RW	17-05-2006 加拿大 WT/DS264/25	15-08-06 WT/DS264/AB/RW	01-09-2006 WT/DS264/28
21	欧共体—香蕉进口制度及 ACP-EC 合作伙伴协定	30-11-2005 洪都拉斯 WT/DS27/62 30-11-2005 巴拿马 WT/DS27/63 30-11-2005 尼加拉瓜 WT/DS27/64					
22	美国—对来自阿根廷石油工业用管材的反倾销措施日落复审	26-01-2006 阿根廷 WT/DS268/15	17-03-2006 WT/DS268/16 WT/DSB/M/207	30-11-2006 WT/DS268/RW	12-01-2007 美国 WT/DS268/19	12-04-2007 WT/DS268/AB/RW	11-05-2007 WT/DSB/M/231
23	美国—影响博彩业跨境交付的措施	08-06-2006 安提瓜和巴布达 WT/DS285/17	19-07-2006 WT/DS285/18 WT/DSB/M/217	30-03-2007 WT/DS285/RW	N. A.	N. A.	22-05-2007 WT/DSB/M/232

续 表

序号	案件	援引第21.5条（日-月-年）	提交原专家组（日-月-年）	散发专家组报告（日-月-年）	通知上诉（日-月-年）	散发上诉机构报告（日-月-年）	通过专家组和/或上诉机构报告（日-月-年）
24	美国—陆地棉补贴	18-08-2006 巴西 WT/DS267/30	28-09-2006 WT/DSB/M/220	18-12-2007 WT/DS267/RW 和 Corr. 1	12-02-2008 美国 WT/DS267/33	02-06-2008 WT/DS267/AB/RW	20-06-2008 WT/DSB/M/252
25	美国—对来自墨西哥的石油工业用管材反倾销措施	21-08-2006 墨西哥 WT/DS282/13	24-04-2007 WT/DS282/14 WT/DSB/M/230 06-07-2008 专家组建立的授权取消 WT/DS282/17				
26	韩国—对来自印度尼西亚特定纸张进口征收反倾销税	26-10-2006 印度尼西亚 WT/DS312/8	23-01-2007 WT/DS312/9 WT/DSB/M/225	28-09-2007 WT/DS312/RW	N. A.	N. A.	22-10-2007 WT/DS312/12
27	欧共体—关于香蕉进口、销售和分销的制度	16-11-2006 厄瓜多尔 WT/DS27/65	20-03-2007 WT/DS27/80 WT/DSB/M/228	07-04-2008 WT/DS27/RW2/ECU	28-08-2008 欧共体 WT/DS27/89	26-11-2008 WT/DS27/AB/RW2/ECU	11-12-2008 WT/DSB/M/260
28	欧共体—关于香蕉进口、销售和分销的制度	29-06-2007 美国 WT/DS27/83	12-07-2007 WT/DSB/M/235	19-05-2008 WT/DS27/RW/美国 A 和 Corr. 1	28-08-2008 欧共体 WT/DS27/90	26-11-2008 WT/DS27/AB/RW/美国 A 和 Corr. 1	22-12-2008 WT/DSB/M/261
29	美国—计算倾销幅度的法律、法规和方法（“归零法”）	09-07-2007 欧共体 WT/DS294/22	25-09-2007 WT/DS294/25 WT/DSB/M/239	17-12-2008 WT/DS294/RW	13-02-2009 欧共体 WT/DS294/28	14-05-2009 WT/DS294/AB/RW 和 Corr. 1	11-06-2009 WT/DSB/M/269
30	美国—与归零法和日落复审相关的措施	07-04-2008 日本 WT/DS322/27	18-04-2008 WT/DSB/M/249	24-04-2009 WT/DS322/RW	20-05-2009 美国 WT/DS322/32	18-08-2009 WT/DS322/AB/RW	31-08-2009 WT/DSB/M/273
31	日本—对来自韩国的动态随机存储器征收反补贴税	09-09-2008 韩国 WT/DS336/19	23-09-2008 WT/DSB/M/256 2009年3月4日，韩国要求专家组中止工作 WT/DS336/22 05-03-2010 专家组建立的授权取消 WT/DS336/23				
32	欧共体—与肉及肉制品有关的措施（荷尔蒙）	22-12-2008 欧共体 WT/DS26/23					
33	欧共体—与肉及肉制品有关的措施（荷尔蒙）	22-12-2008 欧共体 WT/DS48/21					

续 表

序号	案件	援引第 21.5 条（日-月-年）	提交原专家组（日-月-年）	散发专家组报告（日-月-年）	通知上诉（日-月-年）	散发上诉机构报告（日-月-年）	通过专家组和/或上诉机构报告（日-月-年）
34	美国—对从墨西哥进口的不锈钢采取最终反倾销措施	19-08-2009 墨西哥 WT/DS344/18	21-09-2010 WT/DS344/20 WT/DSB/M/287	06-05-2013 WT/DS344/RW WT/DS344/26 （见第一部分）	N. A.	N. A.	N. A.
35	欧盟及其部分成员国—影响大型民用航空器贸易的措施	30-03-2012 美国 WT/DS316/23	13-04-2012 WT/DS316/23 WT/DSB/M/314				
36	美国—影响大型民用航空器贸易的措施（二诉）	25-09-2012 欧盟 WT/DS353/16	23-10-2012 WT/DS353/18 WT/DSB/M/323				
37	美国—对特定国家原产地标签要求	19-08-2013 加拿大 WT/DS384/26 墨西哥 WT/DS386/25	25-09-2013 WT/DSB/M/337	20-10-2014 WT/DS384/RW WT/DS386/RW 和 Add. 1			
38	欧共体—对从中国进口的钢铁紧固件采取最终反倾销措施	30-10-2013 中国 WT/DS397/17	18-12-2013 WT/DS397/18 WT/DSB/M/340				
39	美国—对金枪鱼和金枪鱼产品的进口、营销和销售采取的措施	14-11-2013 墨西哥 WT/DS381/20	22-01-2014 WT/DSB/M/341				
40	中国—对自美国进口的取向电工钢征收反补贴税和反倾销税	13-01-2014 美国 WT/DS414/15	26-02-2014 WT/DS414/16 WT/DSB/M/342				

第五部分
援引《关于争端解决规则与程序的谅解》第 22 条

序号	案件	援引第 22 条	在第 22.6 下进行仲裁	仲裁人报告	由争端解决机构授权中止减让
1	欧共体—香蕉进口、销售和分销	14-01-1999 美国 WT/DS27/43	29-01-1999 欧共体 WT/DS27/46	09-04-1999 WT/DS27/ARB	根据美国要求 （WT/DS27/49） 于 1999 年 4 月 19 日 争端解决机构会议上授权 （WT/DSB/M/59）

续 表

序号	案件	援引第22条	在第22.6下进行仲裁	仲裁人报告	由争端解决机构授权中止减让
2	欧共体—香蕉进口、销售和分销	08-11-1999 厄瓜多尔 WT/DS27/52	19-11-1999 欧共体 WT/DS27/53	24-03-2000 WT/DS27/ARB/ECU	根据厄瓜多尔要求 (WT/DS27/54) 于2000年5月18日 争端解决机构会议上授权 (WT/DSB/M/80)
3	欧共体—关于肉及肉制品措施(荷尔蒙)	17-05-1999 美国 WT/DS26/19 20-05-1999 加拿大 WT/DS48/17	02-06-1999 欧共体 WT/DS26/20 WT/DS48/18	12-07-1999 WT/DS26/ARB WT/DS48/ARB	根据美国要求 (WT/DS26/21)和 加拿大要求(WT/DS48/19) 于1999年7月26日 争端解决机构会议上授权 (WT/DSB/M/65)
4	澳大利亚—影响鲑鱼进口的措施	15-07-1999 加拿大 WT/DS18/12	27-07-1999 澳大利亚 WT/DS18/13	N. A.	N. A.
5	巴西—对于航空器出口融资	10-05-2000 加拿大 WT/DS46/16	22-05-2000 巴西 WT/DS46/18	28-08-2000 WT/DS46/ARB	根据加拿大要求 (WT/DS46/25) 于2000年12月12日 争端解决机构会议上授权 (WT/DSB/M/94)
6	美国—"海外销售公司"税收待遇	17-11-2000 欧共体 WT/DS108/13	28-11-2000 美国 WT/DS108/17	30-08-2002 WT/DS108/ARB	根据欧共体要求 (WT/DS108/26) 于2003年5月7日的 争端解决机构会议上授权 (WT/DSB/M/149)
7	加拿大—影响牛奶进口及奶制品出口的措施	16-02-2001 美国 WT/DS103/17 16-02-2001 新西兰 WT/DS113/17	28-02-2001 加拿大 WT/DS103/18 WT/DS113/18	双方达成一致 (WT/DS103/33, WT/DS113/33) 仲裁于2003年 5月9日终止	
8	美国—1916年反倾销法	07-01-2002 欧共体 WT/DS136/15 07-01-2002 日本 WT/DS162/18	17-01-2002 美国 WT/DS136/16 WT/DS162/19	24-02-2004 WT/DS136/ARB	
9	美国—美国版权法第110(5)节	07-01-2002 欧共体 WT/DS160/19	17-01-2002 美国 WT/DS160/20	N. A.	N. A.
10	加拿大—地区性航空器的出口信贷保证	23-05-2002 巴西 WT/DS222/7 和Corr. 1	21-06-2002 加拿大 WT/DS222/8	17-02-2003 WT/DS222/ARB	根据巴西要求 (WT/DS222/10) 于2003年3月18日 争端解决机构会议上授权 (WT/DSB/M/145)

续 表

序号	案件	援引第22条	在第22.6下进行仲裁	仲裁人报告	由争端解决机构授权中止减让
11	美国—2000年持续性倾销及补贴补偿法案	15-01-2004 巴西 WT/DS217/20 智利 WT/DS217/21 欧共体 WT/DS217/22 印度 WT/DS217/23 日本 WT/DS217/24 韩国 WT/DS217/25 加拿大 WT/DS234/25 墨西哥 WT/DS234/26 和 Corr. 1	23-01-2004 美国 WT/DS217/26 WT/DS217/27 WT/DS217/28 WT/DS217/29 WT/DS217/30 WT/DS217/31 WT/DS234/27 WT/DS234/28	31-08-2004 WT/DS217/ ARB/BRA WT/DS217/ ARB/CHL WT/DS217/ ARB/EEC WT/DS217/ ARB/IND WT/DS217/ ARB/JPN WT/DS217/ ARB/KOR WT/DS234/ ARB/CAN WT/DS234/ ARB/MEX	根据巴西要求 (WT/DS217/38); 欧共体(WT/DS217/39); 印度(WT/DS217/40); 日本(WT/DS217/41); 韩国(WT/DS217/42); 加拿大(WT/DS234/31); 墨西哥(WT/DS234/32), 于2004年11月26日 在争端解决机构会议上授权 (WT/DSB/M/178) 根据智利(WT/DS217/43) 要求,于2004年12月17日 在争端解决机构会议上授权 (WT/DSB/M/180)
12	日本—影响苹果进口的措施	19-07-2004 美国 WT/DS245/12	29-07-2004 日本 WT/DS245/13	双方达成一致 (WT/DS245/21) 仲裁于2005年 8月30日终止	
13	美国—对来自加拿大的软木最终反补贴税决定	04-01-2005 加拿大 WT/DS257/16	13-01-2005 美国 WT/DS257/17	双方达成一致 (WT/DS257/26) 仲裁于2006年 10月12日终止	
14	美国—国际贸易委员会对加拿大软木的调查	15-02-2005 加拿大 WT/DS277/9	23-02-2005 美国 WT/DS277/10	双方达成一致 (WT/DS277/20) 仲裁于2006年 10月12日终止	
15	美国—对加拿大软木的最终倾销决定	19-05-2005 加拿大 WT/DS264/17	31-05-2005 美国 WT/DS264/19	双方达成一致 (WT/DS264/29) 仲裁于2006年 10月12日终止	
16	美国—陆地棉补贴(I)	05-07-2005 巴西 WT/DS267/21	14-07-2005 美国 WT/DS267/23	31-08-2009 WT/DS267/ARB/1	根据巴西请求 (WT/DS267/41) 于2009年11月19日 争端解决机构会议上授权 (WT/DSB/M/276)
17	美国—陆地棉补贴(Ⅱ)	06-10-2005 巴西 WT/DS267/26	17-10-2005 美国 WT/DS267/27	31-08-2009 WT/DS267/ARB/2 和 Corr. 1	根据巴西请求 (WT/DS267/42) 于2009年11月19日 争端解决机构会议上授权 (WT/DSB/M/276)

续 表

序号	案件	援引第22条	在第22.6下进行仲裁	仲裁人报告	由争端解决机构授权中止减让
18	美国—对来自阿根廷石油工业用管材的反倾销措施日落复审	21-05-2007 阿根廷 WT/DS268/24	01-06-2007 美国 WT/DS268/25		
19	美国—影响博彩业跨境交付的措施	21-06-2007 安提瓜和巴布达 WT/DS285/22	23-07-2007 美国 WT/DS285/23	21-12-2007 WT/DS285/ARB	根据安提瓜和巴布达请求（WT/DS285/25）于2013年1月28日争端解决机构会议上授权（WT/DSB/M/328）
20	美国—与归零法和日落复审相关的措施	10-01-2008 日本 WT/DS322/23 10-01-2008 日本 WT/DS322/24	18-01-2008 美国 WT/DS322/25		
21	欧共体—影响生物科技产品审批和营销的措施	17-01-2008 美国 WT/DS291/39	06-02-2008 欧共体 WT/DS291/40		
22	美国—计算倾销幅度的法律、法规和方法（“归零法”）	29-01-2010 欧盟 WT/DS294/35 22-06-12 WT/DS294/45 （欧盟根据DSU第22.2条撤销）	12-02-2010 美国 WT/DS294/36		
23	欧盟及其部分成员国—影响大型民用航空器贸易的措施	09-12-2011 美国 WT/DS316/18	22-12-2011 欧盟 WT/DSB/M/309		
24	美国—影响大型民用航空器贸易的措施（二诉）	27-09-2012 欧盟 WT/DS353/17	22-10-2012 WT/DS353/19		
25	美国—影响丁香香烟生产和销售的措施	12-08-2013 印度尼西亚 WT/DS406/12 08-10-2014 WT/DS406/18 （印度尼西亚根据DSU第22.2条撤销）	22-08-2013 WT/DS406/13 WT/DSB/M/335 （见第一部分）		

附录 2：1995—2014 年上诉机构受理的案件①

1. 上诉案件数量（1995—2014 年）

年份	数量	最初上诉程序	第 21.5 条上诉程序
1995	0	0	0
1996	4	4	0
1997	6	6	0
1998	8	8	0
1999	9	9	0
2000	13	11	2
2001	9	5	4
2002	7	6	1
2003	6	5	1
2004	5	5	0
2005	10	8	2
2006	5	3	2
2007	4	2	2
2008	13	10	3
2009	3	1	2
2010	3	3	0
2011	9	9	0
2012	5	5	0
2013	1	1	0
2014	9	8	1
合计	129	109	20

2. 被上诉的专家组报告比率（1995—2014 年）②

批准年份	所有专家组报告			非第 21.5 条专家组报告			第 21.5 条专家组报告		
	批准的专家组报告	被上诉的专家组报告	被上诉比率	批准的专家组报告	被上诉的专家组报告	被上诉比率	批准的专家组报告	被上诉的专家组报告	被上诉比率
1996	2	2	100%	2	2	100%	0	0	—
1997	5	5	100%	5	5	100%	0	0	—
1998	12	9	75%	12	9	75%	0	0	—
1999	10	7	70%	9	7	78%	1	0	0
2000	19	11	58%	15	9	60%	4	2	50%
2001	17	12	71%	13	9	69%	4	3	75%
2002	12	6	50%	11	5	45%	1	1	100%
2003	10	7	70%	8	5	63%	2	2	100%
2004	8	6	75%	8	6	75%	0	0	—
2005	20	12	60%	17	11	65%	3	1	33%

① 1995 年无专家组报告。
② 1995 年无专家组报告。

续 表

批准年份	所有专家组报告			非第21.5条专家组报告			第21.5条专家组报告		
	批准的专家组报告	被上诉的专家组报告	被上诉比率	批准的专家组报告	被上诉的专家组报告	被上诉比率	批准的专家组报告	被上诉的专家组报告	被上诉比率
2006	7	6	86%	4	3	75%	3	3	100%
2007	10	5	50%	6	3	50%	4	2	50%
2008	11	9	82%	8	6	75%	3	3	100%
2009	8	6	75%	6	4	67%	2	2	100%
2010	5	2	40%	5	2	40%	0	0	—
2011	8	5	63%	8	5	63%	0	0	—
2012	18	11	61%	18	11	61%	0	0	—
2013	4	2	50%	4	2	50%	0	0	—
2014	15	13	87%	13	11	85%	2	2	100%
合计	201	136	68%	172	115	67%	29	21	72%

3. 上诉机构报告所涉及的WTO协议（1995—2014年）①

年份	DSU	WTO协议	GATT1994	农业	SPS	ATC	TBT	TRIMs	反倾销	进口许可证	SCM	保障措施	GATS	TRIPs
1996	0	0	2	0	0	0	0	0	0	0	0	0	0	0
1997	4	1	5	1	0	2	0	0	0	1	1	0	1	1
1998	7	1	4	1	2	0	0	0	1	1	0	0	0	0
1999	7	1	6	1	1	0	0	0	0	0	2	1	0	0
2000	8	1	7	2	0	0	0	0	2	0	5	2	1	1
2001	7	1	3	1	0	1	1	0	4	0	1	2	0	0
2002	8	2	4	3	0	0	1	0	1	0	3	1	1	1
2003	4	2	3	0	1	0	0	0	4	0	1	1	0	0
2004	2	0	5	0	0	0	0	0	2	0	1	0	0	0
2005	9	0	5	2	0	0	0	0	2	0	4	0	1	0
2006	5	0	3	0	0	0	0	0	3	0	2	0	0	0
2007	5	0	2	1	0	0	0	0	2	0	1	0	0	0
2008	8	1	9	1	2	0	0	0	3	0	3	0	0	0
2009	3	0	4	0	0	0	0	0	3	0	0	0	1	0
2010	1	0	0	0	1	0	0	0	0	0	0	0	0	0
2011	7	1	6	0	0	0	0	0	1	0	2	0	0	0
2012	9	0	7	0	0	0	4	0	1	0	2	0	0	0
2013	0	0	2	0	0	0	0	2	0	0	2	0	0	0
2014	6	4	7	0	0	0	2	0	0	0	3	0	0	0
合计	100	15	84	13	7	3	8	2	29	2	33	7	5	3

① 1995年上诉。

4. 上诉案件中的参与方及第三方（1995—2014 年）

（1）统计概况

WTO 成员	上诉方	其他上诉方	被上诉方	第三方	合计
安提瓜和巴布达	0	1	1	0	2
阿根廷	2	3	5	18	28
澳大利亚	2	2	6	40	50
巴林	0	0	0	1	1
巴巴多斯	0	0	0	1	1
伯利兹	0	0	0	4	4
贝宁	0	0	0	1	1
委内瑞拉	0	0	1	6	7
玻利维亚	0	0	0	1	1
巴西	5	7	12	32	56
喀麦隆	0	0	0	3	3
加拿大	14	9	22	29	74
乍得	0	0	0	2	2
智利	3	0	2	12	17
中国	14	3	9	40	66
哥伦比亚	0	0	0	20	20
哥斯达黎加	1	0	0	3	4
科特迪瓦	0	0	0	4	4
古巴	0	0	0	4	4
多米尼克	0	0	0	4	4
多米尼加	1	0	1	4	6
厄瓜多尔	0	2	2	12	16
埃及	0	0	0	2	2
萨尔瓦多	0	0	0	4	4
欧盟	21	18	44	63	146
斐济	0	0	0	1	1
加纳	0	0	0	2	2
格林纳达	0	0	0	1	1
危地马拉	1	1	1	8	11
圭亚那	0	0	0	1	1
洪都拉斯	0	2	2	3	7
中国香港	0	0	0	8	8
冰岛	0	0	0	2	2
印度	7	2	8	41	58
印度尼西亚	0	1	1	4	6
以色列	0	0	0	1	1

续 表

WTO成员	上诉方	其他上诉方	被上诉方	第三方	合计
牙买加	0	0	0	5	5
日本	6	5	13	60	84
肯尼亚	0	0	0	1	1
韩国	3	4	6	31	44
科威特	0	0	0	1	1
马达加斯加	0	0	0	1	1
马来西亚	1	0	1	0	2
马拉维	0	0	0	1	1
毛里求斯	0	0	0	2	2
墨西哥	5	4	7	35	51
纳米比亚	0	0	0	1	1
新西兰	0	3	6	13	22
尼加拉瓜	0	0	0	4	4
尼日利亚	0	0	0	1	1
挪威	2	1	3	25	31
阿曼	0	0	0	3	3
巴基斯坦	0	0	2	3	5
巴拿马	0	0	0	3	3
巴拉圭	0	0	0	5	5
秘鲁	0	0	1	7	8
菲律宾	3	0	3	1	7
波兰	0	0	1	0	1
俄罗斯	0	0	0	7	7
塞内加尔	0	0	0	1	1
圣卢西亚	0	0	0	4	4
沙特	0	0	0	11	11
圣基茨和尼维斯	0	0	0	1	1
圣文森特和格林纳丁斯	0	0	0	3	3
苏里南	0	0	0	3	3
斯威士兰	0	0	0	1	1
瑞士	0	1	1	0	2
中国台北	0	0	0	38	38
坦桑尼亚	0	0	0	1	1
泰国	3	2	5	20	30
特立尼达和多巴哥	0	0	0	1	1
土耳其	1	0	0	15	16
美国	34	24	75	35	168
越南	0	0	0	7	7
合计	129	95	241	733	1 198

（2）年度详细信息

1996 年

案件	上诉方	其他上诉方	被上诉方	第三方
美国—汽油 WT/DS2/AB/R	美国	—	巴西 委内瑞拉	欧共体 挪威
日本—含酒精饮料 II WT/DS8/AB/R WT/DS10/AB/R WT/DS11/AB/R	日本	美国	加拿大 欧共体 日本 美国	—

1997 年

案件	上诉方	其他上诉方	被上诉方	第三方
美国—内衣裤 WT/DS24/AB/R	哥斯达黎加	—	美国	印度
巴西—可可粉 WT/DS22/AB/R	菲律宾	巴西	巴西 菲律宾	欧共体 美国
美国—羊毛衬衫及女上衣 WT/DS33/AB/R 和 Corr. 1	印度	—	美国	—
加拿大—期刊 WT/DS31/AB/R	加拿大	美国	加拿大 美国	—
欧共体—香蕉Ⅲ WT/DS27/AB/R	欧共体	厄瓜多尔 危地马拉 洪都拉斯 墨西哥 美国	厄瓜多尔 欧共体 危地马拉 洪都拉斯 墨西哥 美国	伯利兹 喀麦隆 哥伦比亚 哥斯达黎加 科特迪瓦 多米尼加 多米尼克 加纳 格林纳达 牙买加 日本 尼加拉瓜 圣卢西亚 圣文森特和格林纳丁斯 塞内加尔 苏里南 委内瑞拉
印度—专利权（美国） WT/DS50/AB/R	印度	—	美国	欧共体

1998 年

案件	上诉方	其他上诉方	被上诉方	第三方
欧共体—荷尔蒙 WT/DS26/AB/R WT/DS48/AB/R	欧共体	加拿大 美国	加拿大 欧共体 美国	澳大利亚 新西兰 挪威
阿根廷—纺织品及服装 WT/DS56/AB/R 和 Corr. 1	阿根廷	—	美国	欧共体
欧共体—计算机设备 WT/DS62/AB/R WT/DS67/AB/R WT/DS68/AB/R	欧共体	—	美国	日本
欧共体—家禽 WT/DS69/AB/R	巴西	欧共体	巴西 欧共体	泰国 美国
美国—虾 WT/DS58/AB/R	美国	—	印度 马来西亚 巴基斯坦 泰国	澳大利亚 厄瓜多尔 欧共体 中国香港 墨西哥 尼日利亚
澳大利亚—鲑鱼 WT/DS18/AB/R	澳大利亚	加拿大	澳大利亚 加拿大	欧共体 印度 挪威 美国
危地马拉—水泥 I WT/DS60/AB/R	危地马拉	—	墨西哥	美国

1999 年

案件	上诉方	其他上诉方	被上诉方	第三方
韩国—含酒精饮料 WT/DS75/AB/R WT/DS84/AB/R	韩国	—	欧共体 美国	墨西哥
日本—农产品 II WT/DS76/AB/R	日本	美国	日本 美国	巴西 欧共体
巴西—航行器 WT/DS46/AB/R	巴西	加拿大	巴西 加拿大	欧共体 美国
加拿大—航行器 WT/DS70/AB/R	加拿大	巴西	巴西 加拿大	欧共体 美国

续 表

案件	上诉方	其他上诉方	被上诉方	第三方
印度—数量限制 WT/DS90/AB/R	印度	—	美国	—
加拿大—奶制品 WT/DS103/AB/R WT/DS113/AB/R 和 Corr. 1	加拿大	—	新西兰 美国	—
土耳其—纺织品 WT/DS34/AB/R	土耳其	—	印度	中国香港 日本 菲律宾
智利—含酒精饮料 WT/DS87/AB/R WT/DS110/AB/R	智利	—	欧共体	墨西哥 美国
阿根廷—鞋类（欧共体） WT/DS121/AB/R	阿根廷	欧共体	阿根廷 欧共体	印度尼西亚 美国
韩国—奶制品 WT/DS98/AB/R	韩国	欧共体	韩国 欧共体	美国

2000 年

案件	上诉人	其他上诉人	被上诉人	第三方
美国—海外销售公司 WT/DS108/AB/R	美国	欧共体	欧共体 美国	加拿大 日本
美国—热轧铅铋碳钢制品案 II WT/DS138/AB/R	美国	—	欧共体	巴西 墨西哥
加拿大—汽车 WT/DS139/AB/R	加拿大	欧共体 日本	加拿大 欧共体 日本	韩国 美国
巴西—航空器 （第 21.5 条—加拿大） WT/DS46/AB/RW	巴西	—	加拿大	欧共体 美国
加拿大—航空器 （第 21.5 条—巴西） WT/DS70/AB/RW	巴西	—	加拿大	欧共体 美国
美国—1916 年法案 WT/DS136/AB/R WT/DS162/AB/R	美国	欧共体 日本	欧共体 日本 美国	欧共体 印度 日本 墨西哥
加拿大—专利权保护 WT/DS170/AB/R	加拿大	—	美国	—
韩国—对牛肉的多种标准 WT/DS161/AB/R WT/DS169/AB/R	韩国	—	澳大利亚 美国	加拿大 新西兰

续 表

案件	上诉人	其他上诉人	被上诉人	第三方
美国—特定欧共体产品 WT/DS165/AB/R	欧共体	美国	欧共体 美国	多米尼克 厄瓜多尔 印度 牙买加 日本 圣卢西亚
美国—麦麸 WT/DS166/AB/R	美国	欧共体	欧共体 美国	澳大利亚 加拿大 新西兰

2001 年

案件	上诉方	其他上诉方	被上诉方	第三方
欧共体—棉质床单 WT/DS141/AB/R	欧共体	印度	欧共体 印度	埃及 日本 美国
欧共体—石棉 WT/DS135/AB/R	加拿大	欧共体	加拿大 欧共体	巴西 美国
泰国—工字梁 WT/DS122/AB/R	泰国	—	波兰	欧共体 日本 美国
美国—羔羊 WT/DS177/AB/R WT/DS178/AB/R	美国	澳大利亚 新西兰	澳大利亚 新西兰 美国	欧共体
美国—热轧钢 WT/DS184/AB/R	美国	日本	日本 美国	巴西 加拿大 智利 欧共体 韩国
美国—棉纱 WT/DS192/AB/R	美国	—	巴基斯坦	欧共体 印度
美国—虾 （第 21.5 条—马来西亚） WT/DS58/AB/RW	马来西亚	—	美国	澳大利亚 欧共体 中国香港 印度 日本 墨西哥 泰国
墨西哥—玉米浆（第 21.5 条—美国） WT/DS132/AB/RW	墨西哥	—	美国	欧共体
加拿大—奶制品 （第 21.5 条—新西兰和美国） WT/DS103/AB/RW WT/DS113/AB/RW	加拿大	—	新西兰 美国	欧共体

2002 年

案件	上诉方	其他上诉方	被上诉方	第三方
美国—211 拨款法 WT/DS176/AB/R	欧共体	美国	欧共体 美国	—
美国—海外销售公司 （第 21.5 条—欧共体） WT/DS108/AB/RW	美国	欧共体	欧共体 美国	澳大利亚 加拿大 印度 日本
美国—直线管 WT/DS202/AB/R	美国	韩国	韩国 美国	澳大利亚 加拿大 欧共体 日本 墨西哥
印度—汽车 II WT/DS146/AB/R WT/DS175/AB/R	印度	—	欧共体 美国	韩国
智利—综合价格制度 WT/DS207/AB/R 和 Corr. 1	智利	—	阿根廷	澳大利亚 巴西 哥伦比亚 厄瓜多尔 欧共体 巴拉圭 美国 委内瑞拉
欧共体—沙丁鱼 WT/DS231/AB/R	欧共体	—	秘鲁	加拿大 智利 厄瓜多尔 美国 委内瑞拉
美国—碳钢 WT/DS213/AB/R 和 Corr. 1	美国	欧共体	欧共体 美国	日本 挪威
美国—特定欧共体产品补偿措施 WT/DS212/AB/R	美国	—	欧共体	巴西 印度 墨西哥
加拿大—奶制品 （第 21.5 条—新西兰和美国 II） WT/DS103/AB/RW2 WT/DS113/AB/RW2	加拿大	—	新西兰 美国	阿根廷 澳大利亚 欧共体

2003 年

案件	上诉方	其他上诉方	被上诉方	第三方
美国—抵消法案 （伯德修正案） WT/DS217/AB/R WT/DS234/AB/R	美国	—	澳大利亚 巴西 加拿大 智利 欧共体 印度 印度尼西亚 日本 韩国 墨西哥 泰国	阿根廷 哥斯达黎加 中国香港 以色列 挪威
欧共体—棉质床单 （第 21.5 条—印度） WT/DS141/AB/RW	印度	—	欧共体	日本 韩国 美国
欧共体—管道配件 WT/DS219/AB/R	巴西	—	欧共体	智利 日本 墨西哥 美国
美国—钢铁保障措施 WT/DS248/AB/R WT/DS249/AB/R WT/DS251/AB/R WT/DS252/AB/R WT/DS253/AB/R WT/DS254/AB/R WT/DS258/AB/R WT/DS259/AB/R	美国	巴西 中国 欧共体 日本 韩国 新西兰 挪威 瑞士	巴西 中国 欧共体 日本 韩国 新西兰 挪威 瑞士 美国	加拿大 古巴 墨西哥 中国台北 泰国 土耳其 委内瑞拉
日本—苹果 WT/DS245/AB/R	日本	美国	日本 美国	澳大利亚 巴西 欧共体 新西兰 中国台北
美国—不锈钢日落复审 WT/DS244/AB/R	日本	—	美国	巴西 智利 欧共体 印度 韩国 挪威

2004 年

案件	上诉方	其他上诉方	被上诉方	第三方
美国—软木 IV WT/DS257/AB/R	美国	加拿大	加拿大 美国	欧共体 印度 日本

续 表

案件	上诉方	其他上诉方	被上诉方	第三方
欧共体—歧视性关税 WT/DS246/AB/R	欧共体	—	印度	玻利维亚 巴西 哥伦比亚 哥斯达黎加 古巴 厄瓜多尔 圣萨尔瓦多 危地马拉 洪都拉斯 毛里求斯 尼加拉瓜 巴基斯坦 巴拿马 巴拉圭 秘鲁 美国 委内瑞拉
美国—软木 V WT/DS264/AB/R	美国	加拿大	加拿大 美国	欧共体 印度 日本
加拿大—小麦出口和谷物进口 WT/DS276/AB/R	美国	加拿大	加拿大 美国	澳大利亚 中国 欧共体 墨西哥 中国台北
美国—石油国家工业用管材日落复审 WT/DS268/AB/R	美国	阿根廷	阿根廷 美国	欧共体 日本 韩国 墨西哥 中国台北

2005 年

案件	上诉方	其他上诉方	被上诉方	第三方
美国—细绒棉 WT/DS267/AB/R	美国	巴西	巴西 美国	阿根廷 澳大利亚 贝宁 加拿大 乍得 中国 欧共体 印度 新西兰 巴基斯坦 巴拉圭 中国台北 委内瑞拉

续 表

案件	上诉方	其他上诉方	被上诉方	第三方
美国—博彩业 WT/DS285/AB/R 和 Corr. 1	美国	安提瓜和巴布达	安提瓜和巴布达 美国	加拿大 欧共体 日本 墨西哥 中国台北
欧共体—糖类 出口补贴 WT/DS265/AB/R WT/DS266/AB/R WT/DS283/AB/R	欧共体	澳大利亚 巴西 泰国	澳大利亚 巴西 欧共体 泰国	巴巴多斯 伯利兹 加拿大 中国 哥伦比亚 科特迪瓦 古巴 斐济 圭亚那 印度 牙买加 肯尼亚 马达加斯加 马拉维 毛里求斯 新西兰 巴拉圭 圣基茨和尼维斯 瑞士 坦桑尼亚 特立尼达和多巴哥 美国
多米尼加—烟草进口和销售 WT/DS302/AB/R	多米尼加	洪都拉斯	多米尼加 洪都拉斯	中国 萨尔瓦多 欧共体 危地马拉 美国
美国—对计算机动态随机存取存储器芯片反补贴税调查案 WT/DS296/AB/R	美国	韩国	韩国 美国	中国 欧共体 日本 中国台北
欧共体—鸡块 WT/DS269/AB/R WT/DS286/AB/R 和 Corr. 1	欧共体	巴西 泰国	巴西 欧共体 泰国	中国 美国
墨西哥—稻米反倾销措施 WT/DS295/AB/R	墨西哥	—	美国	中国 欧共体

续 表

案件	上诉方	其他上诉方	被上诉方	第三方
美国—石油工业用管材反倾销措施 WT/DS282/AB/R	墨西哥	美国	墨西哥 美国	阿根廷 加拿大 中国 欧共体 日本 中国台北
美国—软木 IV （第 21.5 条—加拿大） WT/DS257/AB/RW	美国	加拿大	加拿大 美国	中国 欧共体

2006 年

案件	上诉方	其他上诉方	被上诉方	第三方
美国—海外销售公司 （第 21.5 条—欧共体 II） WT/DS108/AB/RW2	美国	欧共体	欧共体 美国	澳大利亚 巴西 中国
墨西哥—不含酒精饮料税 WT/DS308/AB/R	墨西哥	—	美国	加拿大 中国 欧共体 危地马拉 日本
美国—软木 VI （第 21.5 条—加拿大） WT/DS277/AB/RW 和 Corr. 1	加拿大	—	美国	中国 欧共体
美国—归零法（欧共体） WT/DS294/AB/R 和 Corr. 1	欧共体	美国	美国 欧共体	阿根廷 巴西 中国 中国香港 印度 日本 韩国 墨西哥 挪威 中国台北
美国—软木 V （第 21.5 条—加拿大） WT/DS264/AB/RW	加拿大	—	美国	中国 欧共体 印度 日本 新西兰 泰国
欧共体—特定海关事项案 WT/DS315/AB/R	美国	欧共体	欧共体 美国	阿根廷 澳大利亚 巴西 中国 中国香港 印度 日本 韩国 中国台北

2007年

案件	上诉方	其他上诉方	被上诉方	第三方
美国—归零法（日本） WT/DS322/AB/R	日本	美国	美国 日本	阿根廷 中国 欧共体 中国香港 印度 韩国 墨西哥 新西兰 挪威 泰国
美国—石油工业用管材日落复审（第 21.5 条—阿根廷） WT/DS268/AB/RW	美国	阿根廷	阿根廷 美国	中国 欧共体 日本 韩国 墨西哥
智利—价格综合制度（第 21.5 条—阿根廷）WT/DS207/AB/RW	智利	阿根廷	阿根廷 智利	澳大利亚 巴西 加拿大 中国 哥伦比亚 欧共体 秘鲁 泰国 美国
日本—计算机动态随机存取存储器 芯片（韩国） WT/DS336/AB/R 和 Corr.1	日本	韩国	韩国 日本	欧共体 美国
巴西—翻新轮胎 WT/DS332/AB/R	欧共体	—	巴西	阿根廷 澳大利亚 中国 古巴 危地马拉 日本 韩国 墨西哥 巴拉圭 中国台北 泰国 美国

2008 年

案件	上诉方	其他上诉方	被上诉方	第三方
美国—不锈钢（墨西哥） WT/DS344/AB/R	墨西哥	—	美国	智利 中国 欧共体 日本 泰国
美国—高地棉 （第 21.5 条—巴西） WT/DS267/AB/RW	美国	巴西	巴西 美国	阿根廷 澳大利亚 加拿大 乍得 中国 欧共体 印度 日本 新西兰 泰国
美国—虾（泰国） WT/DS343/AB/R	泰国	美国	美国 泰国	巴西 智利 中国 欧共体 印度 日本 韩国 墨西哥 越南
美国—海关保税指令 WT/DS345/AB/R	印度	美国	美国 印度	巴西 中国 欧共体 日本 泰国
美国—要求取消报复措施 WT/DS320/AB/R	欧共体	美国	美国 欧共体	澳大利亚 巴西 中国 印度 墨西哥 新西兰 挪威 中国台北
加拿大—要求取消报复措施 WT/DS321/AB/R	欧共体	加拿大	加拿大 欧共体	澳大利亚 巴西 中国 印度 墨西哥 新西兰 挪威 中国台北

续 表

案件	上诉方	其他上诉方	被上诉方	第三方
印度—进口附加税 WT/DS360/AB/R	美国	印度	印度 美国	澳大利亚 智利 欧共体 日本 越南
欧共体—香蕉 III (第 21.5 条—厄瓜多尔 II) WT/DS27/AB/RW2/ECU 和 Corr. 1	欧共体	厄瓜多尔	厄瓜多尔 欧共体	伯利兹 巴西 喀麦隆 哥伦比亚 科特迪瓦 多米尼克 多米尼加 加纳 牙买加 日本 尼加拉瓜 巴拿马 圣卢西亚 圣文森特和格林纳丁斯 苏里南 美国
欧共体—香蕉 III (第 21.5 条—美国) WT/DS27/AB/RW/USA 和 Corr. 1	欧共体	—	美国	伯利兹 巴西 喀麦隆 哥伦比亚 科特迪瓦 多米尼克 多米尼加 厄瓜多尔 牙买加 日本 墨西哥 尼加拉瓜 巴拿马 圣卢西亚 圣文森特和格林纳丁斯 苏里南
中国—汽车零部件(欧共体) WT/DS339/AB/R	中国	—	欧共体	阿根廷 澳大利亚 巴西 日本 墨西哥 中国台北 泰国

续 表

案件	上诉方	其他上诉方	被上诉方	第三方
中国—汽车零部件（美国） WT/DS340/AB/R	中国	—	美国	阿根廷 澳大利亚 巴西 日本 墨西哥 中国台北 泰国
中国—汽车零部件（加拿大） WT/DS342/AB/R	中国	—	加拿大	阿根廷 澳大利亚 巴西 日本 墨西哥 中国台北 泰国

2009 年

案件	上诉方	其他上诉方	被上诉方	第三方
美国—归零法 WT/DS350/AB/R	欧共体	美国	欧共体 美国	巴西 中国 埃及 印度 日本 韩国 墨西哥 挪威 中国台北 泰国
美国—归零法（欧共体） （第 21.5 条—欧共体） WT/DS294/AB/RW 和 Corr. 1	欧共体	美国	欧共体 美国	印度 日本 韩国 墨西哥 挪威 中国台北 泰国
美国—归零法（日本） （第 21.5 条—日本） WT/DS322/AB/RW	美国	—	日本	中国 欧共体 中国香港 韩国 墨西哥 挪威 中国台北 泰国
中国—出版物和视听产品 WT/DS363/AB/R	中国	美国	中国 美国	澳大利亚 欧共体 日本 韩国 中国台北

2010年

案件	上诉方	其他上诉方	被上诉方	第三方
澳大利亚—苹果 WT/DS367/AB/R	澳大利亚	新西兰	新西兰 澳大利亚	智利 欧盟 日本 巴基斯坦 中国台北 美国

2011年

案件	上诉方	其他上诉方	被上诉方	第三方
美国—反倾销和反补贴税（中国） WT/DS379/AB/R	中国	—	美国	阿根廷 澳大利亚 巴林 巴西 加拿大 欧盟 印度 日本 科威特 墨西哥 挪威 沙特 中国台北 土耳其
欧盟及其部分成员国—大型民用航空器 WT/DS316/AB/R	欧盟	美国	美国 欧盟	澳大利亚 巴西 加拿大 中国 日本 韩国
泰国—香烟（菲律宾） WT/DS371/AB/R	泰国	—	菲律宾	澳大利亚 中国 欧盟 印度 中国台北 美国
欧共体— 坚固件（中国） WT/DS397/AB/R	欧盟	中国	中国 欧盟	巴西 加拿大 智利 哥伦比亚 印度 日本 挪威 中国台北 泰国 土耳其 美国

续 表

案件	上诉方	其他上诉方	被上诉方	第三方
美国—轮胎（中国） WT/DS399/AB/R	中国	—	美国	欧盟 日本 中国台北 土耳其 越南
菲律宾—蒸馏酒精（欧盟） WT/DS396/AB/R	菲律宾	欧盟	欧盟 菲律宾	澳大利亚 中国 印度 墨西哥 中国台北 泰国
菲律宾—蒸馏酒精（美国） WT/DS403/AB/R	菲律宾	—	美国	澳大利亚 中国 哥伦比亚 印度 墨西哥 中国台北 泰国

2012 年

案件	上诉方	其他上诉方	被上诉方	第三方
中国—原材料（美国） WT/DS394/AB/R	中国	美国	中国 美国	阿根廷 巴西 加拿大 智利 哥伦比亚 厄瓜多尔 印度 日本 韩国 挪威 沙特 中国台北 土耳其
中国—原材料（欧盟） WT/DS395/AB/R	中国	欧盟	中国 欧盟	阿根廷 巴西 加拿大 智利 哥伦比亚 厄瓜多尔 印度 日本 韩国 挪威 沙特 中国台北 土耳其

续 表

案件	上诉方	其他上诉方	被上诉方	第三方
中国—原材料（墨西哥） WT/DS398/AB/R	中国	墨西哥	中国 墨西哥	阿根廷 巴西 加拿大 智利 哥伦比亚 厄瓜多尔 印度 日本 韩国 挪威 沙特 中国台北 土耳其
美国—大型民用航空器（2诉） WT/DS353/AB/R	欧盟	美国	美国 欧盟	澳大利亚 巴西 加拿大 中国 日本 韩国
美国—丁香香烟 WT/DS406/AB/R	美国	—	印度尼西亚	巴西 哥伦比亚 多米尼加 欧盟 危地马拉 墨西哥 挪威 土耳其
美国—金枪鱼 II（墨西哥） WT/DS381/AB/R	美国	墨西哥	墨西哥 美国	阿根廷 澳大利亚 巴西 加拿大 中国 厄瓜多尔 危地马拉 日本 韩国 新西兰 中国台北 泰国 土耳其 委内瑞拉

续 表

案件	上诉方	其他上诉方	被上诉方	第三方
美国—原产地标签（加拿大） WT/DS384/AB/R	美国	加拿大	加拿大 美国	阿根廷 澳大利亚 巴西 中国 哥伦比亚 欧盟 危地马拉 印度 日本 韩国 新西兰 秘鲁 中国台北
美国—原产地标签（墨西哥） WT/DS386/AB/R	美国	墨西哥	墨西哥 美国	阿根廷 澳大利亚 巴西 中国 哥伦比亚 欧盟 危地马拉 印度 日本 韩国 新西兰 秘鲁 中国台北
中国—取向电工钢 WT/DS414/AB/R	中国	———	美国	阿根廷 欧盟 洪都拉斯 印度 日本 韩国 沙特 越南

2013 年

案件	上诉方	其他上诉方	被上诉方	第三方
加拿大—影响可再生能源部门的措施 WT/DS412/AB/R	加拿大	日本	日本 加拿大	澳大利亚 巴西 中国 萨尔瓦多 欧盟 洪都拉斯 印度 韩国 墨西哥 挪威 沙特 中国台北 美国

续 表

案件	上诉方	其他上诉方	被上诉方	第三方
加拿大—有关上网电价补贴措施 WT/DS426/AB/R	加拿大	欧盟	欧盟 加拿大	澳大利亚 巴西 中国 萨尔瓦多 印度 日本 韩国 墨西哥 挪威 沙特 中国台北 土耳其 美国

2014 年

案件	上诉方	其他上诉方	被上诉方	第三方
欧共体—限制海豹产品进口及营销的限制措施 WT/DS400/AB/R	加拿大 挪威	欧盟	加拿大 挪威 欧盟	阿根廷 中国 哥伦比亚 厄瓜多尔 冰岛 日本 墨西哥 俄罗斯 美国
欧共体—限制海豹产品进口及营销的限制措施 WT/DS401/AB/R	加拿大 挪威	欧盟	加拿大 挪威 欧盟	阿根廷 中国 哥伦比亚 厄瓜多尔 冰岛 日本 墨西哥 纳米比亚 俄罗斯 美国
美国—对来自中国的某些产品的反补贴税的措施 WT/DS437/AB/R	中国	美国	中国 美国	澳大利亚 加拿大 欧盟 印度 日本 俄罗斯 土耳其 越南

续 表

案件	上诉方	其他上诉方	被上诉方	第三方
中国—影响稀土、钨、钼出口的措施 WT/DS431/AB/R	美国	中国	美国 中国	阿根廷 澳大利亚 巴西 加拿大 中国台北 哥伦比亚 欧盟 印度 印度尼西亚 韩国 日本 挪威 阿曼 秘鲁 俄罗斯 沙特 土耳其 越南
中国—影响稀土、钨、钼出口的措施 WT/DS432/AB/R	中国		欧盟	阿根廷 澳大利亚 巴西 加拿大 中国台北 哥伦比亚 印度 印度尼西亚 日本 韩国 挪威 阿曼 秘鲁 俄罗斯 沙特 土耳其 美国 越南
中国—影响稀土、钨、钼出口的措施 WT/DS433/AB/R	中国		日本	阿根廷 澳大利亚 巴西 加拿大 中国台北 哥伦比亚 印度 印度尼西亚 韩国 挪威 阿曼 秘鲁 俄罗斯

续 表

案件	上诉方	其他上诉方	被上诉方	第三方
美国—对源自印度的某些热轧碳钢产品的反补贴措施 WT/DS436/AB/R	印度	美国	印度 美国	澳大利亚 加拿大 中国 欧盟 沙特 土耳其
美国—对自中国的某些产品的反补贴和反倾销措施 WT/DS449/AB/R and Corr. 1	中国	美国	中国 美国	澳大利亚 巴西 加拿大 欧盟 印度 日本 韩国 挪威 俄罗斯 沙特 土耳其 越南

5. WTO争端解决报告及裁决（1995—2013）

简要标题	案件标题全称及出处
阿根廷—陶瓷	专家组报告，阿根廷—对于从意大利进口地板瓷砖的明确反倾销措施，WT/DS189/R，2001年11月5日通过，DSR 2001：XII，6241
阿根廷—鞋类（欧共体）	上诉机构报告，阿根廷—鞋类进口安全标准措施，WT/DS121/AB/R，2000年1月12日通过，DSR 2000：I，515
阿根廷—鞋类（欧共体）	专家组报告，阿根廷—鞋类进口安全标准措施，WT/DS121/R，2000年1月12日通过，上诉机构报告修正，WT/DS121/AB/R，DSR 2000：II，575
阿根廷—皮革	专家组报告，阿根廷—影响牛皮出口及成皮进口措施，WT/DS155/R和Corr. 1，2001年2月16日通过，DSR 2001：V，1779
阿根廷—皮革［第21.3（c）条］	仲裁决议，阿根廷—影响牛皮出口及成皮进口措施—在DSU第21.3（c）条下的仲裁，WT/DS155/10，2001年8月31日，DSR 2001：XII，6013
阿根廷—进口措施	上诉机构报告，阿根廷—影响货物进口的措施，WT/DS438/AB/R/WT/DS444/AB/R/WT/DS445/AB/R，2015年1月26日通过
阿根廷—进口措施	专家组报告，阿根廷—影响货物进口的措施，WT/DS438/AB/R/WT/DS444/AB/R/WT/DS445/AB/R和Add. 1，2015年1月26日通过，由上诉机构报告WT/DS438/AB/R/WT/DS444/AB/R/WT/DS445/AB/R修正（WT/DS438/R）和支持（WT/DS444/R/WT/DS445/R）
阿根廷—家禽反倾销税	专家组报告，阿根廷—对来自巴西家禽的明确反倾销措施，WT/DS241/R，2003年5月19日通过DSR 2003：V，1727
阿根廷—桃脯	专家组报告，阿根廷—对进口桃脯的明确保障措施，WT/DS238/R，2003年4月15日通过，DSR 2003：Ⅲ，1037
阿根廷—纺织品及服装	上诉机构报告，阿根廷—影响鞋类、纺织品、服装和其他项目的进口措施，WT/DS56/AB/R和Corr. 1，1998年4月22日通过，DSR 1998：Ⅲ，1003

续 表

简要标题	案件标题全称及出处
阿根廷—纺织品及服装	专家组报告，阿根廷—影响鞋类、纺织品、服装和其他项目的进口措施，WT/DS56/R，1998 年 4 月 22 日通过，上诉机构报告修正，WT/DS56/AB/R，DSR 1998：III，1033
澳大利亚—苹果	上诉机构报告，澳大利亚—影响自新西兰苹果进口的措施，WT/DS367/AB/R，2010 年 12 月 17 日通过，DSR 2010：V，2175
澳大利亚—苹果	专家组报告，澳大利亚—影响自新西兰苹果进口的措施，WT/DS367/R，2010 年 12 月 17 日通过，上诉机构报告修正，WT/DS367/AB/R，DSR 2010：VI，2371
澳大利亚—汽车皮革Ⅱ	专家组报告，澳大利亚—对汽车皮革生产商及出口商的补贴，WT/DS126/R，1999 年 6 月 16 日，DSR 1999：III，951
澳大利亚—汽车皮革Ⅱ （第 21.5 条—美国）	专家组报告，澳大利亚—对汽车皮革生产商及出口商的补贴—根据 DSU 第 21.5 条，WT/DS126/RW 和 Corr. 1，通过 2000 年 2 月 11 日通过，DSR 2000：III，1189
澳大利亚—鲑鱼	上诉机构报告，澳大利亚—影响鲑鱼进口措施，WT/DS18/AB/R，1998 年 11 月 6 日通过，DSR 1998：VIII，3327
澳大利亚—鲑鱼	专家组报告，澳大利亚—影响鲑鱼进口措施，WT/DS18/R 和 Corr. 1，1998 年 11 月 6 日通过，上诉机构报告修正，WT/DS18/AB/R，DSR 1998：VIII，3407
澳大利亚—鲑鱼 [第 21.3（c）条]	仲裁决议，澳大利亚 — 影响鲑鱼进口措施—第 21.3（c）条下的仲裁，WT/DS18/9，1999 年 2 月 23 日，DSR 1999：I，267
澳大利亚—鲑鱼 （第 21.5 条—加拿大）	专家组报告，澳大利亚—影响鲑鱼进口措施—根据加拿大 DSU 第 21.5 条，WT/DS18/RW，2000 年 3 月 20 日通过，DSR 2000：IV，2031
巴西—民用航空器	上诉机构报告，巴西—民用航空器出口资助计划，WT/DS46/AB/R，1999 年 8 月 20 日通过，DSR 1999：III，1161
巴西—民用航空器	专家组报告，巴西—民用航空器出口补贴计划，1999 年 8 月 20 日通过，上诉机构报告修正，WT/DS46/AB/R，DSR 1999：III，1221
巴西—民用航空器 （第 21.5 条—加拿大）	上诉机构报告，巴西—民用航空器出口补贴计划—加拿大引用 DSU 第 21.5 条，WT/DS46/AB/RW，2000 年 8 月 4 日通过，DSR 2000：VIII，4067
巴西—民用航空器 （第 21.5 条—加拿大）	专家组报告，巴西—民用航空器出口补贴计划—加拿大引用 DSU 第 21.5 条，WT/DS46/RW，2000 年 8 月 4 日，上诉机构报告修正，WT/DS46/AB/RW，DSR 2000：IX，4093
巴西—民用航空器 （第 21.5 条—加拿大 II）	专家组报告，巴西—民用航空器出口补贴计划—加拿大再次引用 DSU 第 21.5 条，WT/DS46/RW/2，2001 年 8 月 23 日通过，DSR 2001：X，5481
巴西—民用航空器 （第 22.6 条—巴西）	仲裁决定，巴西—民用航空器出口补贴计划—巴西根据 DSU 第 22.6 条及 SCM 协议第 4.11 条提出仲裁，WT/DS46/ARB，2000 年 8 月 28 日，DSR 2002：I，p. 19
巴西—可可粉	上诉机构报告，巴西—影响可可粉措施 WT/DS22/AB/R，1997 年 3 月 20 日通过，DSR 1997：I，167
巴西—可可粉	专家组报告，巴西—影响可可粉措施，WT/DS22/R，1997 年 3 月 20 日通过，得到上诉机构报告支持，WT/DS22/AB/R，DSR 1997：I，p. 189
巴西 — 翻新轮胎	上诉机构报告，巴西—影响翻新轮胎进口的措施，WT/DS332/AB/R，2007 年 12 月 17 日通过，DSR 2007：IV，p. 1527

续 表

简要标题	案件标题全称及出处
巴西 — 翻新轮胎	专家组报告，巴西—影响翻新轮胎进口的措施，WT/DS332/R，2007年12月17日通过，上诉机构报告修正，WT/DS332/AB/R，DSR 2007：V，p. 1649
巴西 — 翻新轮胎［第21.3（c）条］	仲裁决定，巴西—影响翻新轮胎进口的措施—DSU第21.3（c）条下的仲裁，WT/DS332/16，2008年8月29日，DSR 2008：XX，p. 8581
加拿大—民用航空器	上诉机构报告，加拿大—影响民用航空器出口措施，WT/DS70/AB/R，1999年8月20日通过，DSR 1999：III，p. 1377
加拿大—民用航空器	专家组报告，加拿大—影响民用航空器出口措施，WT/DS70/R，1999年8月20日通过，得到上诉机构报告支持，WT/DS70/AB/R，DSR 1999：IV，p. 1443
加拿大—民用航空器（第21.5条—巴西）	上诉机构报告，加拿大—影响民用航空器出口措施—巴西引用DSU第21.5条，WT/DS70/AB/RW，2000年8月4日通过，DSR 2000：IX，p. 4299
加拿大—民用航空器（第21.5条—巴西）	专家组报告，加拿大—影响民用航空器出口措施—巴西引用DSU第21.5条，WT/DS70/RW，2000年8月4日通过，上诉机构报告修正，WT/DS70/AB/RW，DSR 2000：IX，p. 4315
加拿大—民用航空器信贷保证	专家组报告，加拿大—地区民用航空器出口信贷保证，WT/DS222/R和Corr. 1，2002年2月19日，DSR 2002：III，p. 849
加拿大—民用航空器信贷保证（第22.6条—加拿大）	仲裁决定，加拿大—地区民用航空器出口信贷保证—加拿大引用DSU第22.6条SCM协议第4.11条，WT/DS222/ARB，2003年2月17日，DSR 2003：III，p. 1187
加拿大—汽车	上诉机构报告，加拿大—影响汽车工业特定措施，WT/DS139/AB/R，WT/DS142/AB/R，2000年6月19日通过，DSR 2000：VI，p. 2985
加拿大—汽车	专家组报告，加拿大—影响汽车工业特定措施，WT/DS139/R，WT/DS142/R，2000年6月19日，上诉机构报告修正，WT/DS139/AB/R，WT/DS142/AB/R，DSR 2000：VII，p. 3043
加拿大—汽车［第21.3（c）条］	仲裁决定，加拿大—影响汽车工业特定措施—DSU第21.3（c）条下的仲裁WT/DS139/12，WT/DS142/12，2000年10月4日，DSR 2000：X，p. 5079
加拿大—要求取消报复措施	上诉机构报告，加拿大—欧共体要求取消报复措施—荷尔蒙争端，WT/DS321/AB/R，2008年11月14日通过，DSR 2008：XIV，p. 5373
加拿大—要求取消报复措施	专家组报告，加拿大—欧共体要求取消报复措施—荷尔蒙争端，WT/DS321/AB/R和Add. 1—Add. 7，2008年11月14日通过，上诉机构报告修正，WT/DS321/AB/R，DSR 2008：XV，p. 5757
加拿大—奶制品	上诉机构报告，加拿大—影响牛奶进口及奶制品出口的措施，WT/DS103/AB/R，WT/DS113/AB/R及Corr. 1，引自1999年10月27日DSR 1999：V，p. 2057
加拿大—奶制品	专家组报告，加拿大—影响牛奶进口及奶制品出口的措施，WT/DS103/R，WT/DS113/R，1999年10月27日通过，上诉机构报告修正，WT/DS103/AB/R，WT/DS113/AB/R，DSR 1999：VI，p. 2097
加拿大—奶制品（第21.5条—新西兰和美国）	上诉机构报告，加拿大—影响牛奶进口及奶制品出口的措施—新西兰和美国引用DSU第21.5条，WT/DS103/AB/RW，WT/DS113/AB/RW，2001年12月18日通过，DSR 2001：XIII，p. 6829
加拿大—奶制品（第21.5条—新西兰和美国）	专家组报告，加拿大—影响牛奶进口及奶制品出口的措施—新西兰和美国引用DSU第21.5条，WT/DS103/RW，WT/DS113/RW，2001年12月18日通过，上诉机构报告驳回，WT/DS103/AB/RW，WT/DS113/AB/RW，DSR 2001：XIII，p. 6865

续 表

简要标题	案件标题全称及出处
加拿大—奶制品 (第 21.5 条—新西兰和美国 II)	上诉机构报告，加拿大—影响牛奶进口及奶制品出口的措施—新西兰和美国引用 DSU 第 21.5 条，WT/DS103/AB/RW2，WT/DS113/AB/RW2，2003 年 1 月 17 日通过，DSR 2003：I，p. 213
加拿大—奶制品 (第 21.5 条—新西兰和美国 II)	专家组报告，加拿大—影响牛奶进口及奶制品出口的措施—新西兰和美国引用 DSU 第 21.5 条，WT/DS103/RW2，WT/DS113/RW2，2003 年 1 月 17 日通过，上诉机构报告修正，WT/DS103/AB/RW2，WT/DS113/AB/RW2，DSR 2003：I，p. 255
加拿大—专利条款	上诉机构报告，加拿大—专利保护条款，WT/DS170/AB/R，2000 年 10 月 12 日通过，DSR 2000：X，p. 5093
加拿大—上网电价计划	专家组报告，加拿大—有关上网电价计划，WT/DS426/R 和 Add. 1，2012 年 12 月 19 日在 WTO 成员中散发【上诉中】
加拿大—专利条款	专家组报告，加拿大—专利保护条款，WT/DS170/R，2000 年 10 月 12 日通过，得到上诉机构报告支持，WT/DS170/AB/R，DSR 2000：XI，p. 5121
加拿大—专利条款 [第 21.3（c）条]	仲裁决定，加拿大—专利保护条款—DSU 第 21.3（c）条下仲裁，WT/DS170/10，2001 年 2 月 28 日，DSR 2001：V，p. 2031
加拿大—杂志	上诉机构报告，加拿大—相关杂志特定措施，WT/DS31/AB/R，1997 年 7 月 30 日通过，DSR 1997：I，p. 449
加拿大—杂志	专家组报告，加拿大—相关杂志特定措施，WT/DS31/R 和 Corr. 1，1997 年 7 月 30 日 通过，上诉机构报告修正，WT/DS31/AB/R，DSR 1997：I，p. 481
加拿大—药品专利	专家组报告，加拿大—药品专利保护，WT/DS114/R，2000 年 4 月 7 日通过，DSR 2000：V，p. 2289
加拿大—药品专利 [第 21.3（c）条]	仲裁决定，加拿大—药品专利保护—根据 DSU 第 21.3（c）进行的仲裁，WT/DS114/13，2000 年 8 月 18 日，DSR 2002：I，p. 3
加拿大—可再生能源/加拿大— 影响上网电价补贴的措施	上诉机构报告，加拿大—影响可再生能源生产部门的措施/加拿大— 影响上网电价补贴的措施，WT/DS412/R/WT/DS426/R，2013 年 5 月 24 日通过
加拿大—可再生能源/加拿大— 影响上网电价补贴的措施	专家组报告，加拿大—影响可再生能源生产部门的措施/加拿大— 影响上网电价补贴的措施，WT/DS412/R/WT/DS426/R/和 Add. 1，2013 年 5 月 24 日通过，上诉机构报告修正，WT/DS412/AB/R/WT/DS426/AB/R
加拿大—小麦出口和谷物进口	上诉机构报告，加拿大—小麦出口和谷物进口措施，WT/DS276/AB/R，2004 年 9 月 27 日通过，DSR 2004：VI，p. 2739
加拿大—小麦出口和谷物进口	专家组报告，加拿大—小麦出口和谷物进口措施，WT/DS276/R，2004 年 9 月 27 日通过，得到上诉机构报告支持，WT/DS276/AB/R，DSR 2004：VI，p. 2817
智利—酒精饮料	上诉机构报告，智利—酒精饮料税，WT/DS87/AB/R，WT/DS110/AB/R，2000 年 1 月 12 日通过，DSR 2000：I，p. 281
智利—酒精饮料	专家组报告，智利—酒精饮料税，WT/DS87/R，WT/DS110/R，2000 年 1 月 12 日通过，上诉机构报告修正，WT/DS87/AB/R，WT/DS110/AB/R，DSR 2000：I，p. 303
智利—酒精饮料 [第 21.3（c）条]	仲裁决定，智利—酒精饮料税—在 DSU 第 21.3（c）条下仲裁，WT/DS87/15，WT/DS110/14，2000 年 5 月 23 日，DSR 2000：V，p. 2583

续 表

简要标题	案件标题全称及出处
智利—综合价格制度	上诉机构报告，智利—与特定农产品有关的综合价格制度和保障措施 WT/DS207/AB/R，2002年10月23日通过，DSR 2002：VIII，3045 (Corr. 1，DSR 2006：XII，p. 5473)
智利—综合价格制度	专家组报告，智利—与特定农产品有关的综合价格制度和保障措施，WT/DS207/R，2002年10月23日通过，上诉机构报告修正，WT/DS207AB/R，DSR 2002：VIII，p. 3127
智利—综合价格制度 [第21.3（c）条]	仲裁决定，智利—与特定农产品有关的综合价格制度和保障措施 —在DSU第21.3（c）条下仲裁，WT/DS207/13，2003年3月17日，DSR 2003：III，p. 1237
智利—综合价格制度 （第21.5条—阿根廷）	上诉机构报告，智利—与特定农产品有关的综合价格制度和保障措施—阿根廷引自DSU第21.5条，WT/DS207/RW，2007年5月22日通过，DSR 2007：II，p. 513
智利—综合价格制度 （第21.5条—阿根廷）	专家组报告，智利—与特定农产品有关的综合价格制度和保障措施—阿根廷引自DSU第21.5条，WT/DS207/RW和Corr. 1，2007年5月22日通过，得到上诉机构报告的支持，WT/DS207/AB/RW，DSR 2007：II III，p. 613
中国—汽车零部件	上诉机构报告，中国—影响汽车零部件进口的措施，T/DS339/AB/R，WT/DS340/AB/R，WT/DS342/AB/R，2009年1月12日通过，DSR 2009：I，p. 3
中国—汽车零部件	专家组报告，中国—影响汽车零部件进口的措施，WT/DS339/R，WT/DS340/R，WT/DS342/R和Add. 1和Add. 2，2009年1月12日通过，得到（WT/DS339/R）支持，由上诉机构报告WT/DS339/AB/R，WT/DS340/AB/R，WT/DS342/AB/R，DSR 2009：I，p. 119— DSR 2009：II，625修正（WT/DS340/R/WT/DS342/R）
中国—汽车（美国）	专家组报告，中国—对自美国进口的某些汽车实施反倾销和反补贴措施，WT/DS440/R和Add. 1，2014年6月18日通过
中国—肉鸡产品	专家组报告，中国 — 对自美国的白羽肉鸡产品采取反倾销和反补贴措施，WT/DS427/R和Add. 1，2013年9月25日通过
中国—电子支付服务	专家组报告，中国—影响电子支付服务的措施，WT/DS413/R和Add. 1，2012年8月31日通过，DSR 2012：X，p. 5305
中国—取向电工钢	上诉机构报告，对自美国进口的取向电工钢征收反补贴税和反倾销税，WT/DS414/AB/R，2012年11月16日通过，DSR 2012：XII，p. 6251
中国—取向电工钢	专家组报告，对自美国进口的取向电工钢征收反补贴税和反倾销税，WT/DS414/R，2012年11月16日通过，上诉机构报告WT/DS414/AB/R支持，DSR 2012：XII，p. 6369
中国—取向电工钢 [第21.3（c）条]	仲裁裁决，中国—对自美国进口的取向电工钢征收反补贴税和反倾销税—在DSU第21.3（c）条下的仲裁，WT/DS414/12，2013年5月3日
中国 —高性能不锈钢无缝钢管（日本）/中国 —高性能不锈钢无缝钢管（欧盟）	专家组报告，中国 —对日本高性能不锈钢无缝钢管（HP—SSST）征收反倾销税/中国 —对欧盟高性能不锈钢无缝钢管（HP—SSST）征收反倾销税，WT/DS454/R/WT/DS460/R/和Add. 1，2015年2月13日向WTO成员散发，[等待通过/上诉]
中国—知识产权	专家组报告，中国—影响知识产权保护和执法的措施，WT/DS362/R，2009年3月20日通过，DSR 2009：V，p. 2097

续 表

简要标题	案件标题全称及出处
中国—出版物和视听产品	上诉机构报告，中国—影响特定出版物和视听产品贸易和分销权的措施，WT/DS363/AB/R，2010 年 1 月 19 日通过，DSR 2010：I，p. 3
中国—出版物和视听产品	专家组报告，中国—影响特定出版物和视听产品贸易和分销权的措施，WT/DS363/R 和 Corr. 1，2010 年 1 月 19 日通过，上诉机构报告修正，WT/DS363/AB/R，DSR 2010：II，p. 261
中国—稀土	上诉机构报告，中国—影响稀土、钨、钼出口的措施，WT/DS431/AB/R/WT/DS432/AB/R/WT/DS433/AB/R，2014 年 8 月 29 日通过
中国—稀土	专家组报告，中国—影响稀土、钨、钼出口的措施，WT/DS431/R/WT/DS432/R/WT/DS433/R/和 Add. 1，2014 年 8 月 29 日通过，由上诉机构报告支持 WT/DS431/AB/R/WT/DS432/AB/R/WT/DS433/AB/R
中国—原材料出口	上诉报告，中国—不同原材料的出口措施，WT/DS394/R，WT/DS395/R，WT/DS398/R，2012 年 2 月 22 日通过，DSR 2012：VII，p. 3295
中国—原材料出口	专家组报告，中国—不同原材料的出口措施，WT/DS394/R/WT/DS395/R/WT/DS398/R/和 Corr. 1，2012 年 2 月 22 日通过，上诉机构执行修正，WT/DS394/AB/R/WT/DS395/AB/R/WT/DS398/AB/R，DSR 2012：VII，p. 3501
中国—X 射线设备	专家组报告，中国 — 对从欧盟进口的 X 射线安全检查设备征收最终反倾销税，WT/DS425/R 和 Add. 1，2013 年 4 月 24 日通过
哥伦比亚—港口入境	专家组报告，哥伦比亚—对港口入境的价格限制要求，WT/DS366/R 和 Corr. 1，2009 年 5 月 20 日通过，DSR 2009：VI，p. 2535
哥伦比亚—港口入境 [第 21. 3（c）条]	仲裁报告，哥伦比亚—对港口入境的价格限制要求—在 DSU 第 21. 3（c）条下的仲裁，WT/DS366/13，2009 年 10 月 2 日，DSR 2009：IX，p. 3819
多米尼加—香烟的进口和销售	上诉机构报告，多米尼加—影响香烟进口及国内销售的措施，WT/DS302/AB/R，2005 年 5 月 19 日通过，DSR 2005：XV，p. 7367
多米尼加—香烟的进口和销售	专家组报告，多米尼加—影响香烟进口及国内销售的措施，WT/DS302/R，2005 年 5 月 19 日通过，上诉机构报告修正，WT/DS302/AB/R，DSR 2005：XV，p. 7425
多米尼加—香烟的进口和销售 [第 21. 3（c）条]	仲裁报告，多米尼加—影响香烟进口及国内销售的措施—在 DSU 第 21. 3（c）条下的仲裁 WT/DS302/17，2005 年 8 月 29 日，DSR 2005：XXIII，p. 11665
多米尼加—保障措施	专家组报告，多米尼加—聚丙烯管状织物包装袋进口的保障措施，WT/DS415/R，WT/DS416/R，WT/DS417/R，WT/DS418/R 和 Add. 1，2012 年 2 月 22 日通过，DSR 2012：XIII，p. 6775
欧共体—科托努协议	仲裁决定，欧共体—科托努协议—根据 2001 年 11 月 14 日决定提请仲裁，WT/L/616，2005 年 8 月 1 日，DSR 2005：XXIII，p. 11669
欧共体—科托努协议 II	仲裁决定，欧共体—科托努协议—根据 2001 年 11 月 14 日决定提请仲裁，WT/L/625，2005 年 10 月 27 日，DSR 2005：XXIII，p. 11703
欧共体—生物科技产品批准及营销	专家组报告，欧共体—影响生物科技产品批准及营销的措施，WT/DS291/R，WT/DS292/R，WT/DS293/R，Corr. 1 和 Add. 1，2，3，4，5，6，7，8 和 9，2006 年 11 月 21 日通过，DSR 2006：III—VIII，p. 847
欧共体—石棉	上诉机构报告，欧共体—影响石棉及含石棉产品的措施，WT/DS135/AB/R，2001 年 4 月 5 日通过，DSR 2001：VII，p. 3243

续 表

简要标题	案件标题全称及出处
欧共体—石棉	专家组报告，欧共体—影响石棉及含石棉产品的措施，WT/DS135/R 和 Add. 1，2001年4月5日通过，上诉机构报告修正，WT/DS135/AB/R，DSR 2001：VIII，p. 3305
欧共体—香蕉 III	上诉机构报告，欧共体—香蕉进口、销售及分销区域，WT/DS27/AB/R，1997年9月25日通过，DSR 1997：II，p. 591
欧共体—香蕉 III（厄瓜多尔）	专家组报告，欧共体—香蕉进口，销售及分销区域，厄瓜多尔提出上诉，WT/DS27/R/ECU，1997年9月25日通过，上诉机构报告修正，WT/DS27/AB/R，DSR 1997：III，p. 1085
欧共体—香蕉 III（危地马拉和洪都拉斯）	专家组报告，欧共体—香蕉进口，销售及分销区域，危地马拉和洪都拉斯上诉，WT/DS27/R/GTM，WT/DS27/R/HND，1997年9月25日通过，上诉机构报告修正，WT/DS27/AB/R，DSR 1997：II，p. 695
欧共体—香蕉 III（墨西哥）	专家组报告，欧共体—香蕉进口，销售及分销区域，墨西哥上诉，WT/DS27/R/MEX，1997年9月25日通过，上诉机构报告修正，WT/DS27/AB/R，DSR 1997：II，p. 803
欧共体—香蕉 III（美国）	专家组报告，香蕉进口、销售及分销区域，美国上诉，WT/DS27/R/USA，1997年9月25日通过，上诉机构报告修正，WT/DS27/AB/R，DSR 1997：II，p. 943
欧共体—香蕉 III [第21.3（c）条]	仲裁决定，欧共体—香蕉进口，销售及分销区域—在DSU第21.3（c）条下仲裁，WT/DS27/15，1998年1月7日，DSR 1998：I，p. 3
欧共体—香蕉 III （第21.5条—欧共体）	专家组报告，欧共体—香蕉进口、销售及分销区域，墨西哥上诉—欧共体根据DSU第21.5条提出，WT/DS27/RW/EEC 和 Corr. 1，1999年4月12日，未通过，DSR 1999：II，p. 783
欧共体—香蕉 III （第21.5条—厄瓜多尔）	专家组报告，欧共体—香蕉进口，销售及分销区域—厄瓜多尔根据DSU第21.5条提出，WT/DS27/RW/ECU，1999年5月6日通过，DSR 1999：II，p. 803
欧共体—香蕉 III （第21.5条—厄瓜多尔）/ 欧共体—香蕉 III （第21.5条—美国）	上诉机构报告，欧共体—香蕉进口、销售及分销区域—厄瓜多尔根据DSU第21.5条第二次提出上诉，WT/DS27/AB/RW2/ECU，和 Corr. 1，2008年12月11日通过。/欧共体—香蕉进口、销售及分销区域—美国根据DSU第21.5条提出上诉，WT/DS27/AB/RW/USA 和 Corr. 1，2008年12月22日通过，DSR 2008：XVIII，p. 7165
欧共体—香蕉 III （第21.5条—厄瓜多尔 II）	专家组报告，欧共体—香蕉进口、销售及分销区域—厄瓜多尔根据DSU第21.5条第二次提出上诉，WT/DS27/RW2/ECU，2008年12月11日通过。上诉机构报告修正，WT/DS27/AB/RW2/ECU，DSR 2008：XVIII，p. 7329
欧共体—香蕉 III （第21.5条—美国）	专家组报告，欧共体—香蕉进口，销售及分销区域—美国根据DSU第21.5条提出上诉，WT/DS27/RW/USA 和 Corr. 1，2008年12月22日通过，得到上诉机构报告的支持，WT/DS27/AB/RW/USA，DSR 2008：XIX，p. 7761
欧共体—香蕉 III（厄瓜多尔） （第22.6条—欧共体）	仲裁判决，欧共体—香蕉进口，销售及分销区域—欧共体根据DSU第22.6条提出仲裁，WT/DS27/ARB/ECU，2000年3月24日，DSR 2000年：V，p. 2237
欧共体—香蕉 III（美国） （第22.6条—欧共体）	仲裁判决，欧共体—香蕉进口，销售及分销区域—欧共体根据DSU第22.6条提出仲裁，WT/DS27/ARB，1994年4月9日，DSR 1999：II，p. 725
欧共体—棉质床单	上诉机构报告，欧共体—对来自印度的进口棉质床单征收反倾销税，WT/DS141/AB/R，2001年3月12日通过，DSR 2001：V，p. 2049

续 表

简要标题	案件标题全称及出处
欧共体—棉质床单	专家组报告，欧共体—对来自印度的进口棉质床单征收反倾销税，WT/DS141/R，2001 年 3 月 12 日通过，上诉机构报告修正，WT/DS141/AB/R，DSR 2001：VI，p. 2077
欧共体—棉质床单（第 21.5 条—印度）	上诉机构报告，欧共体—对来自印度的进口棉质床单征收反倾销税—由印度根据 DSU 第 21.5 条提出，WT/DS141/AB/RW，2003 年 4 月 24 日通过，DSR 2003：III，p. 965
欧共体—棉质床单（第 21.5 条—印度）	专家组报告，欧共体—对来自印度的进口棉质床单征收反倾销税—印度根据 DSU 第 21.5 条提出，WT/DS141/RW，2003 年 4 月 24 日通过，上诉机构报告修正，WT/DS141/AB/RW，DSR 2003：IV，p. 1269
欧共体—黄油	专家组报告，欧共体—影响黄油产品的措施，WT/DS72/R，1999 年 11 月 24 日 ，未采纳
欧共体—鸡块	上诉机构报告，欧共体—冷冻无骨鸡块海关分类，WT/DS269/AB/R，WT/DS286/AB/R，和 Corr. 1，引自 2005 年 9 月 27 日，DSR 2005：XIX，p. 9157
欧共体—鸡块（巴西）	专家组报告，欧共体—冷冻无骨鸡块海关分类，巴西上诉，WT/DS269/R，引自 2005 年 9 月 27 日，上诉机构报告修正，WT/DS269/AB/R，WT/DS286/AB/R，DSR 2005：XIX，p. 9295
欧共体—鸡块（泰国）	专家组报告，欧共体—冷冻无骨鸡块海关分类，泰国，WT/DS286/R，2005 年 9 月 27 日通过，上诉机构报告修正，WT/DS269/AB/R，WT/DS286/AB/R，DSR 2005：XX，p. 9721
欧共体—鸡块［第 21.3（c）条］	仲裁决定，欧共体—冷冻无骨鸡块海关分类—在 DSU 第 21.3（c）条下仲裁，WT/DS269/13，WT/DS286/15，2006 年 2 月 20 日
欧共体—商船	专家组报告，欧共体—影响商船贸易的措施，WT/DS301/R，2005 年 6 月 20 日通过，DSR 2005：XV，p. 7713
欧共体—计算机设备	上诉机构报告，欧共体—特定计算机设备海关分类，WT/DS62/AB/R，WT/DS67/AB/R，WT/DS68/AB/R，1998 年 6 月 22 日通过，DSR 1998 年：V，p. 1851
欧共体—计算机设备	专家组报告，欧共体—特定计算机设备海关分类，WT/DS62/R，WT/DS67/R，WT/DS68/R，1998 年 6 月 22 日通过，上诉机构报告修正，WT/DS62/AB/R，WT/DS67/AB/R，WT/DS68/AB/R，DSR 1998：V，p. 1891
欧共体—芯片的反补贴措施	专家组报告，欧共体—对来自韩国的芯片的反补贴措施 WT/DS299/R，2005 年 8 月 3 日通过，DSR 2005：XVIII，p. 8671
欧共体—糖类出口补贴	上诉机构报告，欧共体—糖类出口补贴，WT/DS265/AB/R，WT/DS266/AB/R，WT/DS283/AB/R，2005 年 5 月 19 日通过 ，DSR 2005：XIII，p. 6365
欧共体—糖类出口补贴（澳大利亚）	专家组报告，欧共体—糖类出口补贴，由澳大利亚上诉 WT/DS265/R，2005 年 5 月 19 日通过，上诉机构报告修正，WT/DS265/AB/R，WT/DS266/AB/R，WT/DS283/AB/R，DSR 2005：XIII，p. 6499
欧共体—糖类出口补贴（巴西）	专家组报告，欧共体—糖类出口补贴，由巴西上诉，WT/DS266/R，2005 年 5 月 19 日通过，上诉机构报告修正，WT/DS265/AB/R，WT/DS266/AB/R，WT/DS283/AB/R，DSR 2005：XIV，p. 6793
欧共体—糖类出口补贴（泰国）	专家组报告，欧共体—糖类出口补贴，由泰国上诉，WT/DS283/R，2005 年 5 月 19 日通过，上诉机构报告修正，WT/DS265/AB/R，WT/DS266/AB/R，WT/DS283/AB/R，DSR 2005：XIV，p. 7071

续 表

简要标题	案件标题全称及出处
欧共体—糖类出口补贴[第21.3(c)条]	仲裁决定，欧共体—糖类出口补贴—在DSU第21.3(c)条下仲裁，WT/DS265/33，WT/DS266/33，WT/DS283/14，2005年10月28日，DSR 2005：XXIII，p. 11581
欧共体—紧固件（中国）	上诉机构报告，欧共体—对自中国进口的钢铁紧固件实施肯定性反倾销措施，WT/DS397/AB/R，2011年7月28日通过，DSR 2011：VII，p. 3995
欧共体— 紧固件（中国）	专家组报告，欧共体— 对自中国进口的钢铁紧固件实施肯定性反倾销措施，WT/DS397/R和Corr. 1，2011年7月28日通过，上诉机构报告修正，WT/DS397/AB/R，DSR 2011：VIII，p. 4289
欧共体— 荷尔蒙	上诉机构报告，欧共体— 肉类及肉制品措施（荷尔蒙），WT/DS26/AB/R，WT/DS48/AB/R，1998年2月13日通过，DSR 1998：I，p. 135
欧共体—荷尔蒙（加拿大）	专家组报告，欧共体—对于肉及肉制品相关措施（荷尔蒙），由加拿大上诉，WT/DS48/R/CAN，1998年2月13日通过，上诉机构报告修正，WT/DS26/AB/R，WT/DS48/AB/R，DSR 1998：II，p. 235
欧共体—荷尔蒙（美国）	专家组报告，欧共体—对于肉及肉制品相关措施（荷尔蒙），由美国上诉，WT/DS26/R/USA，1998年2月13日通过，上诉机构报告修正，WT/DS26/AB/R，WT/DS48/AB/R，DSR 1998：III，p. 699
欧共体—荷尔蒙[第21.3(c)条]	仲裁决定，欧共体—对于肉及肉制品相关措施（荷尔蒙）—在DSU第21.3(c)条下仲裁，WT/DS26/15，WT/DS48/13，1998年5月29日，DSR 1998：V，p. 1833
欧共体—荷尔蒙（加拿大）(第22.6条—欧共体)	仲裁判决，欧共体—对于肉及肉制品相关措施（荷尔蒙），最初由加拿大上诉—由欧共体根据DSU第22.6条提出，WT/DS48/ARB，1999年7月12日，DSR 1999：III，p. 1135
欧共体—荷尔蒙（美国）(第22.6条—欧共体)	仲裁判决，欧共体—对于肉及肉制品相关措施（荷尔蒙），最初由美国上诉—溯及欧共体根据DSU第22.6条的仲裁，WT/DS26/ARB，1999年7月12日，DSR 1999：III，p. 1105
欧共体—IT产品	专家组报告，欧共体及其成员国—信息技术产品的关税待遇，WT/DS375/R，WT/DS376/R，WT/DS377/R，2010年9月21日通过，DSR 2010：III，p. 933
欧共体—家禽	上诉机构报告，欧共体—影响特定家禽产品进口的措施，WT/DS69/AB/R，1998年7月23日通过，DSR 1998：V，p. 2031
欧共体—家禽	专家组报告，欧共体—影响特定家禽产品进口的措施，WT/DS69/R，1998年7月23日通过，上诉机构报告修正，WT/DS69/AB/R，DSR 1998：V，p. 2089
欧共体—鲑鱼（挪威）	专家组报告，欧共体—对产自挪威养殖鲑鱼采取反倾销措施，WT/DS337/R和Corr. 1，2008年1月15日通过，DSR 2008：I，p. 3
欧共体—沙丁鱼	上诉机构报告，欧共体—沙丁鱼贸易描述，WT/DS231/AB/R，2002年10月23日通过，DSR 2002：VIII，p. 3359
欧共体—沙丁鱼	专家组报告，欧共体—沙丁鱼贸易描述，WT/DS231/R和Corr. 1，2002年10月23日通过，上诉机构报告修正，WT/DS231/AB/R，DSR 2002：VIII，p. 3451
欧共体—扇贝（加拿大）	专家组报告，欧共体—扇贝贸易描述—由加拿大请求，WT/DS7/R，1996年8月日，未通过，DSR 1996：I，p. 89

续 表

简要标题	案件标题全称及出处
欧共体—扇贝（秘鲁和智利）	专家组报告，欧共体—对于扇贝的贸易描述—由秘鲁和智利申请，WT/DS12/R，WT/DS14/R，1996年8月5日，未通过，DSR 1996：I，p. 93
欧共体—海豹产品	上诉机构报告，欧共体—限制海豹产品进口及营销的限制措施，WT/DS400/AB/R/WT/DS401/AB/R，2014年6月18日通过
欧共体—海豹产品	专家组报告，欧共体—限制海豹产品进口及营销的限制措施，WT/DS400/R/WT/DS401/R/和 Add. 1，2014年6月18日通过，由上诉机构报告修正 WT/DS400/AB/R/WT/DS401/AB/R
欧共体—特定海关事项案	上诉机构报告，欧共体—客户对特殊规格要求案，WT/DS315/AB/R，2006年12月11日，DSR 2006：IX，p. 3791
欧共体—特定海关事项案	专家组报告，欧共体—客户对特殊规格要求案，WT/DS315/R，2006年12月11日，上诉机构报告修正，WT/DS315/AB/R，DSR 2006：IX X，p. 3915
欧共体—关税优惠	上诉机构报告，欧共体—给予发展中国家关税优惠的条件，WT/DS246/AB/R，2004年4月20日通过，DSR 2004：III，p. 925
欧共体—关税优惠	专家组报告，欧共体—给予发展中国家关税优惠的条件，WT/DS246/R，引自2004年4月20日，上诉机构报告修正，WT/DS/246/AB/R，DSR 2004：III，p. 1009
欧共体—关税优惠 [第21.3（c）条]	仲裁决定，欧共体—给予发展中国家关税优惠的条件—在DSU第21.3（c）条下仲裁，WT/DS246/14，2004年9月20日，DSR 2004：IX，p. 4313
欧共体—商标和地理标识（澳大利亚）	专家组报告，欧共体—对于农产品及粮食商标和地理标识的保护，由澳大利亚上诉，WT/DS290/R，2005年4月20日通过，DSR 2005：X，p. 4603
欧共体—商标和地理标识（美国）	专家组报告，欧共体—对于农产品及粮食商标和地理标识的保护，由美国上诉，WT/DS174/R，2005年4月20日通过，DSR 2005：VIII，p. 3499
欧共体—管材配件	上诉机构报告，欧共体—对来自巴西的可锻铸铁管路连接件反倾销税，WT/DS219/AB/R，2003年8月18日通过，DSR 2003：VI，p. 2613
欧共体—管材配件	专家组报告，欧共体—对来自巴西的可锻铸铁管路连接件反倾销税，WT/DS219/R，2003年8月18日通过，上诉机构报告修正，WT/DS219/AB/R，DSR 2003：VII，p. 2701
欧共体和其成员国—大型民用航空器	上诉机构报告，欧共体及其成员国—影响大型民用航空器贸易的措施，WT/DS316/AB/R，2011年6月1日通过，DSR 2011：I，p. 7
欧共体和其成员国—大型民用航空器	上专家组报告，欧共体及其成员国—影响大型民用航空器贸易的措施，WT/DS316/R，2011年6月1日通过，上诉机构报告修正，WT/DS316/AB/R，DSR 2011：II，p. 685
埃及—钢筋	专家组报告，埃及—对于来自土耳其的钢筋的明确反倾销措施，WT/DS211/R，2002年10月1日通过，DSR 2002：VII，p. 2667
欧盟—鞋类（中国）	专家组报告，欧盟—自中国进口的部分鞋实施反倾销措施，WT/DS405/R，2012年2月22日通过，DSR 2012：IX，p. 4585
危地马拉—水泥 I	上诉机构报告，危地马拉—对来自墨西哥的水泥进行反倾销调查，WT/DS60/AB/R，1998年11月25日通过，DSR 1998：IX，p. 3767
危地马拉—水泥 I	专家组报告，危地马拉—对来自墨西哥的水泥进行反倾销调查，WT/DS60/R，1998年11月25日通过，上诉机构报告修正，WT/DS60/AB/R，DSR 1998：IX，p. 3797

续 表

简要标题	案件标题全称及出处
危地马拉—水泥 II	专家组报告，危地马拉—对来自墨西哥的水泥采取反倾销措施，WT/DS156/R，2000年11月17日通过，DSR 2000：XI，p. 5295
印度—进口附加税	上诉机构报告，印度—对来自美国的商品征收进口附加税，WT/DS360/AB/R，2008年11月17日通过，DSR 2008：XX，p. 8223
印度—进口附加税	专家组报告报告，印度—对来自美国的商品征收进口附加税，WT/DS360/R，2008年11月17日通过，上诉机构报告驳回，WT/DS360/AB/R，DSR 2008：XX，p. 8317
印度—农产品	专家组报告，印度—影响某些农产品进口的措施，WT/DS430/R和Add. 1，2014年10月14日向WTO成员散发［等待通过/上诉］
印度—汽车	上诉机构报告，印度—影响汽车部门措施，WT/DS146/AB/R，WT/DS175/AB/R，2002年4月5日通过，DSR 2002：V，p. 1821
印度—汽车	专家组报告，印度—影响汽车部门措施，WT/DS146/R，WT/DS175/R和Corr. 1，2002年4月5日通过，DSR 2002：V，p. 1827
印度—专利权（欧共体）	专家组报告，印度—对于药品及农业化学产品的专利保护，由欧共体上诉，WT/DS79/R，1998年9月22日通过，DSR 1998：VI，p. 2661
印度—专利权（美国）	上诉机构报告，印度—对于药品及农业化学产品的专利保护，WT/DS50/AB/R，1998年1月16日通过，DSR 1998：I，p. 9
印度—专利权（美国）	专家组报告，印度—对于药品及农业化学产品的专利保护，由美国上诉，WT/DS50/R，1998年1月16日通过，上诉机构报告修正，WT/DS50/AB/R，DSR 1998：I，p. 41
印度—数量限制	上诉机构报告，印度—对于农产品、纺织品及工业产品进口的数量限制，WT/DS90/AB/R，1999年9月22日通过，DSR 1999：IV，p. 1763
印度—数量限制	专家组报告，印度—对于农产品、纺织品及工业产品进口的数量限制，WT/DS90/R，1999年9月22日通过，得到上诉机构报告支持，WT/DS90/AB/R，DSR 1999：V，p. 1799
印度尼西亚—汽车	专家组报告，印度尼西亚—影响汽车工业的特定措施，WT/DS54/R，WT/DS55/R，WT/DS59/R，WT/DS64/R和Corr. 1，2，3和4，1998年7月23日通过，DSR 1998：VI，p. 2201
印度尼西亚—汽车［第21.3（c）条］	仲裁决定，印度尼西亚—影响汽车工业的特定措施—在DSU第21.3（c）条下仲裁，WT/DS54/15，WT/DS55/14，WT/DS59/13，WT/DS64/12，1998年12月7日通过DSR 1998：IX，p. 4029
日本—农产品 II	上诉机构报告，日本—影响农产品措施，WT/DS76/AB/R，1999年3月19日通过，DSR 1999：I，p. 277
日本—农产品 II	专家组报告，日本—影响农产品措施，WT/DS76/R，1999年3月19日通过，上诉机构报告修正，WT/DS76/AB/R，DSR 1999：I，p. 315
日本—酒精饮料 II	上诉机构报告，日本—对酒精饮料征税 WT/DS8/AB/R，WT/DS10/AB/R，WT/DS11/AB/R，1996年11月1日通过，DSR 1996：I，p. 97
日本—酒精饮料 II	专家组报告，日本—对酒精饮料征税，WT/DS8/R，WT/DS10/R，WT/DS11/R，1996年11月1日通过，上诉机构报告修正，WT/DS8/AB/R，WT/DS10/AB/R，WT/DS11/AB/R，DSR 1996：I，p. 125
日本—酒精饮料 II［第21.3（c）条］	仲裁决定，日本—对酒精饮料征税—在DSU第21.3（c）条下仲裁，WT/DS8/15，WT/DS10/15，WT/DS11/13，1997年2月14日，DSR 1997：I，p. 3

续 表

简要标题	案件标题全称及出处
日本—苹果	上诉机构报告，日本— 影响苹果进口措施，WT/DS245/AB/R，2003 年 12 月 10 日通过，DSR 2003：IX，p. 4391
日本—苹果	专家组报告，日本—影响苹果进口措施，WT/DS245/R，2003 年 12 月 10 日通过，得到上诉机构报告支持，WT/DS245/AB/R，DSR 2003：IX，p. 4481
日本—苹果（第 21.5 条—美国）	专家组报告，日本—影响苹果进口措施—由美国根据 DSU 第 21.5 条提出，WT/DS245/RW，2005 年 7 月 20 日通过，DSR 2005：XVI，p. 7911
日本—动态存储器（韩国）	上诉机构报告，日本—对产自韩国动态存储器征收反补贴税，WT/DS336/AB/R 和 Corr. 1，2007 年 12 月 17 日通过，DSR 2007：VII，p. 2703
日本—动态存储器（韩国）	专家组报告，日本—对产自韩国动态存储器征收反补贴税，WT/DS336/R，2007 年 12 月 17 日通过，上诉机构报告修正，WT/DS336/AB/R，DSR 2007：VII，p. 2805
日本—动态存储器（韩国）[第 21.3（c）条]	仲裁决定，日本—对产自韩国动态存储器征收反补贴税—DSU 第 21.3（c）条下的仲裁，WT/DS336/16，2008 年 5 月 5 日，DSR 2008：XX，p. 8553
日本—胶卷	专家组报告，日本—影响消费冲印胶卷和纸张的措施，WT/DS44/R，1998 年 4 月 22 日通过，DSR 1998：IV，p. 1179
日本—紫菜配额	专家组报告，日本—干紫菜和味付紫菜进口配额 WT/DS323/R，2006 年 2 月 1 日，未通过
韩国—酒精饮料	上诉机构报告，韩国—酒精饮料征税，WT/DS75/AB/R，WT/DS84/AB/R，1999 年 2 月 17 日通过，DSR 1999：I，p. 3
韩国—酒精饮料	专家组报告，韩国—酒精饮料征税，WT/DS75/R，WT/DS84/R，1999 年 2 月 17 日通过，上诉机构报告修正，WT/DS75/AB/R，WT/DS84/AB/R，DSR 1999：I，p. 44
韩国—酒精饮料 [第 21.3（c）条]	仲裁决定，韩国—酒精饮料征税—在 DSU 第 21.3（c）条下仲裁，WT/DS75/16，WT/DS84/14，1999 年 6 月 4 日，DSR 1999：II，p. 937
韩国—牛肉（加拿大）	专家组报告，韩国—影响自加拿大进口牛肉和肉制品的措施，WT/DS391/R，2012 年 7 月 3 日未通过
韩国—特定纸张	专家组报告，韩国—对特定来自印度尼西亚进口产品征收反倾销税，WT/DS312/R，2005 年 11 月 28 日通过，DSR 2005：XXII，p. 10637
韩国—特定纸张（第 21.5 条—印度尼西亚）	专家组报告，韩国—对特定来自印度尼西亚进口产品征收反倾销税—由印度尼西亚根据 DSU 第 21.5 条提出，WT/DS312/RW，2007 年 10 月 22 日通过，DSR 2007：VIII，p. 3369
韩国—商船	专家组报告，韩国—影响商船贸易的措施，WT/DS273/R，2005 年 4 月 11 日通过，DSR 2005：VII，p. 2749
韩国—奶制品	上诉机构报告，韩国—进口特定奶制品的明确保障措施，WT/DS98/AB/R，2000 年 1 月 12 日通过，DSR 2000：I，p. 3
韩国—奶制品	专家组报告，韩国—进口特定奶制品的明确保障措施 WT/DS98/R 和 Corr. 1，2000 年 1 月 12 日通过，上诉机构报告修正，WT/DS98/AB/R，DSR 2000：I，p. 49
韩国—政府采购	专家组报告，韩国—影响政府采购措施，WT/DS163/R，2000 年 6 月 19 日通过，DSR 2000：VIII，p. 3541
韩国—牛肉多种措施	上诉机构报告，韩国—影响鲜肉、冷藏肉和冷冻肉的措施，WT/DS161/AB/R，WT/DS169/AB/R，2001 年 1 月 10 日通过，DSR 2001：I，p. 5

续 表

简要标题	案件标题全称及出处
韩国—牛肉多种措施	专家组报告，韩国—影响鲜肉、冷藏肉和冷冻肉的措施，WT/DS161/R，WT/DS169/R，2001年1月10日通过，上诉机构报告修正，WT/DS161/AB/R，WT/DS169/AB/R，DSR 2001：I，p. 59
墨西哥—稻米反倾销措施	上诉机构报告，墨西哥—对于牛肉和稻米的明确反倾销措施，对于稻米的上诉，WT/DS295/AB/R，2005年12月20日通过，DSR 2005：XXII，p. 10853
墨西哥—稻米反倾销措施	专家组报告，墨西哥—对于牛肉和稻米的明确反倾销措施，对于稻米的上诉，WT/DS295/R，2005年12月20日通过，上诉机构报告修正，WT/DS295/AB/R，DSR 2005：XXIII，p. 11007
墨西哥—玉米糖浆	专家组报告，墨西哥—对于来自美国的高果糖玉米糖浆的反倾销调查 WT/DS132/R 和 Corr. 1，2000年2月24日通过，DSR 2000：III，p. 1345
墨西哥—玉米糖浆（第21.5条—美国）	上诉机构报告，墨西哥—对于来自美国的高果糖玉米糖浆的反倾销调查—由美国根据DSU第21.5条提请，WT/DS132/AB/RW，2001年11月21日通过，DSR 2001：XIII，p. 6675
墨西哥—玉米糖浆（第21.5条—美国）	专家组报告，墨西哥—对于来自美国的高果糖玉米糖浆的反倾销调查—由美国根据DSU第21.5条提请，WT/DS132/RW，2001年11月21日通过，得到上诉机构报告支持，WT/DS132/AB/RW，DSR 2001：XIII，p. 6717
墨西哥—橄榄油	专家组报告，墨西哥—对来自欧共体的橄榄油征收最终反补贴税，WT/DS341/R，2008年10月21日通过，DSR 2008：IX，p. 3179
墨西哥—钢管	专家组报告，墨西哥—对产自危地马拉钢管征收反倾销税，WT/DS331/R，2007年7月24日通过，DSR 2007：IV，p. 1207
墨西哥—非酒精饮料征税	上诉机构报告，墨西哥—对于非酒精饮料及其他饮料的征税措施，WT/DS308/AB/R，2006年3月24日通过，DSR 2006：I，p. 3
墨西哥—非酒精饮料征税	专家组报告，墨西哥—对于非酒精饮料及其他饮料的征税措施，WT/DS308/R，2006年3月24日通过，上诉机构报告修正，WT/DS308/AB/R，DSR 2006：I，p. 43
墨西哥—电信	专家组报告，墨西哥—影响电信服务的措施，WT/DS204/R，2004年6月1日通过，DSR 2004：IV，p. 1537
秘鲁—农产品	专家组报告，秘鲁—某些农产品进口的附加税，WT/DS457/R 和 Add. 1，2014年11月27日向WTO成员散发，[等待通过/上诉]
菲律宾—蒸馏酒精	上诉机构报告，菲律宾—对蒸馏酒精征税，WT/DS396/AB/R/WT/DS403/AB/R，2012年1月20日通过，DSR 2012：VIII，p. 4163
菲律宾—蒸馏酒精	专家组报告，菲律宾—对蒸馏酒精征税，WT/DS396/AB/R/WT/DS403/AB/R，2012年1月20日通过，上诉机构报告修正，WT/DS396/AB/R/WT/DS403/AB/R，DSR 2012：VIII，p. 4271
泰国—香烟（菲律宾）	上诉机构报告，泰国—对自菲律宾进口香烟的海关和行政措施，WT/DS371/AB/R，2011年7月15日通过，DSR 2011：IV，p. 2203
泰国—香烟（菲律宾）	专家组报告，泰国—对自菲律宾进口香烟的海关和行政措施，WT/DS371/R，2011年7月15日通过，上诉机构报告修正，WT/DS371/AB/R，DSR 2011：IV，p. 2299
泰国—H型钢	上诉机构报告，泰国—对波兰出口的铁或非合金钢的角铁、型材、轧材及H型钢的反倾销税案，WT/DS122/AB/R，2001年4月5日通过，DSR 2001：VII，2 p. 701

续 表

简要标题	案件标题全称及出处
泰国—H 型钢	专家组报告，泰国—对波兰出口的铁或非合金钢的角铁、型材、轧材及 H 型钢的反倾销税案，WT/DS122/R，2001 年 4 月 5 日通过，上诉机构报告修正，WT/DS122/AB/R，DSR 2001：VII，p. 2741
土耳其—大米	专家组报告，土耳其—影响大米进口的措施，WT/DS334/R，2007 年 10 月 22 日通过，DSR 2007：VI，p. 2151
土耳其—纺织品	上诉机构报告，土耳其—对于纺织品及服装进口的限制，WT/DS34/AB/R，1999 年 11 月 19 日通过，DSR 1999 年：VI，p. 2345
土耳其—纺织品	专家组报告，土耳其—对于纺织品及服装进口的限制，WT/DS34/R，1999 年 11 月 19 日通过，上诉机构报告修正，WT/DS34/AB/R，DSR 1999：VI，p. 2363
美国—1916 年法案	上诉机构报告，美国—1916 年反倾销法案，WT/DS136/AB/R，WT/DS162/AB/R，2000 年 9 月 26 日通过，DSR 2000：X，p. 4793
美国—1916 年法案（欧共体）	专家组报告，美国—1916 年反倾销法案，由欧共体上诉，WT/DS136/R 和 Corr. 1，2000 年 9 月 26 日通过，得到上诉机构报告支持，WT/DS136/AB/R，WT/DS162/AB/R，DSR 2000 年：X，p. 4593
美国—1916 年法案（日本）	专家组报告，美国—1916 年反倾销法案，由日本上诉，WT/DS162/R 和 Add. 1，2000 年 9 月 26 日通过，得到上诉机构报告支持，WT/DS136/AB/R，WT/DS162/AB/R，DSR 2000：X，p. 4831
美国—1916 年法案 [第 21. 3（c）条]	仲裁决定，美国—1916 年反倾销法案—在 DSU 第 21. 3（c）条下仲裁，WT/DS136/11，WT/DS162/14，2001 年 2 月 28 日，DSR 2001：V，p. 2017
美国—1916 年法案（欧共体）（第 22. 6 条—美国）	仲裁判决，美国—1916 年反倾销法案，最初由欧共体上诉—由美国根据 DSU 第 22. 6 条的仲裁，WT/DS136/ARB，2004 年 2 月 24 日，DSR 2004：IX，p. 4269
美国—反倾销税和反补贴税（中国）	上诉机构报告，美国—对自中国的产品征收肯定反倾销税和反补贴税，WT/DS379/AB/R，2011 年 3 月 25 日，DSR 2011：V，p. 2869
美国—反倾销税和反补贴税（中国）	专家组报告，美国—对自中国的产品征收肯定反倾销税和反补贴税，WT/DS379/R，2011 年 3 月 25 日，上诉机构报告修正，WT/DS379/AB/R，DSR 2011：VI，p. 3143
美国—石油国家工业用管的反倾销措施	上诉机构报告，美国—对来自墨西哥石油国家工业用管的反倾销措施，WT/DS282/AB/R，2005 年 11 月 28 日通过，DSR 2005：XX，p. 10127
美国—石油国家工业用管的反倾销措施	专家组报告，美国—对来自墨西哥石油国家工业用管的反倾销措施，WT/DS282/R，2005 年 11 月 28 日通过，上诉机构报告修正，WT/DS282/AB/R，DSR 2005：XXI，p. 10225
美国—PET 包装袋反倾销措施	专家组报告，美国—对自泰国进口的 PET 包装袋采取反倾销措施，WT/DS383/R，2010 年 2 月 18 日通过，DSR 2010：IV，p. 1841
美国—碳钢	上诉机构报告，美国—对于来自德国的特殊耐腐蚀碳钢板的反补贴税，WT/DS213/AB/R 和 Corr. 1，2002 年 12 月 19 日通过，DSR 2002：IX，p. 3779
美国—碳钢	专家组报告，美国—对于来自德国的特殊耐腐蚀碳钢板的反补贴税，WT/DS213/R 和 Corr. 1，2002 年 12 月 19 日通过，上诉机构报告修正，WT/DS213/AB/R 和 Corr. 1，DSR 2002：IX，p. 3833
美国—碳钢（印度）	上诉机构报告，美国—对源自印度的某些热轧碳钢产品的反补贴措施，WT/DS436/AB/R，2014 年 12 月 19 日通过

续 表

简要标题	案件标题全称及出处
美国—碳钢（印度）	专家组报告，美国—对源自印度的某些热轧碳钢产品的反补贴措施，WT/DS436/R 和 Add. 1，2014 年 12 月 19 日通过，由上诉机构报告 WT/DS436/AB/R 修正
美国—特定欧共体产品	上诉机构报告，美国—特定从欧共体产品的进口措施 WT/DS165/AB/R，2001 年 1 月 10 日通过，DSR 2001：I，p. 373
美国—特定欧共体产品	专家组报告，美国—特定从欧共体产品的进口措施，WT/DS165/R 和 Add. 1，2001 年 1 月 10 通过，上诉机构报告修正，WT/DS165/AB/R，DSR 2001：II，p. 413
美国—丁香香烟	上诉机构报告，美国—影响丁香香烟生产和销售的措施，WT/DS406/AB/R，2012 年 4 月 24 日通过，DSR 2012：XI，p. 5751
美国—丁香香烟	专家组报告，美国—影响丁香香烟生产和销售的措施，WT/DS406/R，2012 年 4 月 24 日通过，上诉机构报告修正，WT/DS406/AB/R，DSR 2012：XI，p. 5865
美国—要求取消报复措施	上诉机构报告，美国—欧共体要求取消报复措施—荷尔蒙争端，WT/DS320/AB/R，2008 年 11 月 14 日通过，DSR 2008：X，p. 3507
美国—要求取消报复措施	专家组报告，美国—欧共体要求取消报复措施—荷尔蒙争端，WT/DS320/R 和 Add. 1—Add. 7，2008 年 11 月 14 日通过，上诉机构报告修正，WT/DS320/AB/R，DSR 2008：XI，3891
美国—归零法	上诉机构报告，美国—继续采用归零法则，WT/DS350/AB /R，2009 年 2 月 19 日通过，DSR 2009：III，p. 1291
美国—归零法	专家组报告，美国—继续采用归零法则，WT/DS350/R，2009 年 2 月 19 日通过，上诉机构报告修正，WT/DS350/AB/R，DSR 2009：III，p. 1481
美国—原产地标签	专家组报告，美国—部分原产地标签规定，WT/DS384/R/WT/DS384/AB/R/WT/DS386/AB/R，2012 年 7 月 23 日通过，DSR 2012：V，p. 2449
美国—原产地标签	专家组报告，美国—部分原产地标签规定，WT/DS384/R/WT/DS384/AB/R/WT/DS386/AB/R，2012 年 7 月 23 日通过，上诉机构报告修正，WT/DS384/AB/R/WT/DS386/AB/R，DSR 2012：VI，p. 2745
美国—原产地标签 [第 21. 3（C）条]	专家组报告，美国—部分原产地标签规定—在 DSU 第 21. 3（c）条下仲裁，WT/DS384/24，WT/DS386/23，2012 年 12 月 4 日，DSR 2012：XIII，p. 7173
美国—原产地标签 （第 21. 5 条— 加拿大和墨西哥）	专家组报告，美国 —部分原产地标签规定—加拿大和墨西哥根据 DSU 第 21. 5 条起诉，WT/DS384/RW/WT/DS386/RW/和 Add. 1，2014 年 10 月 20 日向 WTO 成员散发［等待通过/上诉］
美国—不锈钢日落复审	上诉机构报告，美国—对于来自日本的特殊耐腐蚀碳钢板反倾销税的日落复审，WT/DS244/AB/R，2004 年 1 月 9 日通过，DSR 2004：I，p. 3
美国—不锈钢日落复审	专家组报告，美国—对于来自日本的特殊耐腐蚀碳钢板反倾销税的日落复审，WT/DS244/R，2004 年 1 月 9 日通过，上诉机构报告修正，WTDS244/AB/R，DSR 2004：I，p. 85
美国—棉纱	上诉机构报告，美国—对来自巴基斯坦棉纱的过渡期保障措施 WT/DS192/AB/R，2001 年 11 月 5 日通过，DSR 2001：XII，p. 6027
美国—棉纱	专家组报告，美国—对来自巴基斯坦棉纱的过渡期保障措施，WT/DS192/R，2001 年 11 月 5 日通过，上诉机构报告修正，WT/DS192/AB/R，DSR 2001：XII，p. 6067

续 表

简要标题	案件标题全称及出处
美国—反补贴和反倾销措施（中国）	上诉机构报告，美国—对自中国的某些产品的反补贴和反倾销措施，WT/DS449/AB/R 和 Corr. 1，2014 年 7 月 22 日通过
美国—反补贴和反倾销措施（中国）	专家组报告，美国—对自中国的某些产品的反补贴和反倾销措施，WT/DS449/R 和 Add. 1，2014 年 7 月 22 日通过，由专家组报告修正 WT/DS449/AB/R
美国—对计算机动态随机存取存储器芯片进行反补贴税调查	上诉机构报告，美国—对来自韩国的计算机动态随机存取存储器芯片进行反补贴税调查，WT/DS296/AB/R，2005 年 7 月 20 日通过，DSR 2005：XVI，p. 8131
美国—对计算机动态随机存取存储器芯片进行反补贴税调查	专家组报告，美国—对来自韩国的计算机动态随机存取存储器芯片进行反补贴税调查，WT/DS296/R，2005 年 7 月 20 日通过，上诉机构报告修正，WT/DS296/AB/R，DSR 2005：XVII，p. 8243
美国—反补贴措施（中国）	上诉机构报告，美国—对来自中国的某些产品的反补贴税的措施，WT/DS437/AB/R，2015 年 1 月 16 日通过
美国—反补贴措施（中国）	专家组报告，美国—对来自中国的某些产品的反补贴税的措施，WT/DS437/R 和 Add. 1，2015 年 1 月 16 日通过，由上诉机构报告修正 WT/DS437/AB/R
美国—对特定欧共体产品贴税措施	上诉机构报告，美国—对特定欧共体产品贴税措施，WT/DS212/AB/R，2003 年 1 月 8 日通过，DSR 2003：I，p. 5
美国—对特定欧共体产品贴税措施	专家组报告，美国—对特定欧共体产品贴税措施，WT/DS212/R，2003 年 1 月 8 日通过，上诉机构报告修正，WT/DS212/AB/R，DSR 2003：I，p. 73
美国—对特定欧共体产品贴税措施（第 21. 5 条—欧共体）	专家组报告，美国—对特定欧共体产品贴税措施—由欧共体根据 DSU 第 21. 5 条提出，WT/DS212/RW，2005 年 9 月 27 日通过，DSR 2005：XVIII，p. 8950
美国—海关保税指令	专家组报告，美国—对征收反倾销和反补贴产品实行海关保税，WT/DS345/R，2008 年 8 月 1 日通过，上诉机构报告修正，WT/DS343/AB/R，WT/DS345/AB/R，DSR 2008：VIII，p. 2925
美国—计算机动态随机存取存储器芯片	专家组报告，美国—对来自韩国 1 兆或以上的计算机动态随机存取存储器芯片征收反倾销税，WT/DS99/R，1999 年 3 月 19 日通过，DSR 1999：II，p. 521
美国—计算机动态随机存取存储器芯片（第 21. 5 条—韩国）	专家组报告，美国—对来自韩国 1 兆或以上的计算机动态随机存取存储器芯片征收反倾销税—韩国根据 DSU 第 21. 5 条提出上诉，WT/DS99/RW，2000 年 11 月 7 日未通过
美国—出口限制	专家组报告，美国—作为补贴的出口限制措施 WT/DS194/R 和 Corr. 2，2001 年 8 月 23 日通过，DSR 2001：XI，p. 5767
美国—海外销售公司	上诉机构报告，美国—“海外销售公司”税收待遇，WT/DS108/AB/R，2000 年 3 月 20 日通过，DSR 2000：III，p. 1619
美国—海外销售公司	专家组报告，美国 —“海外销售公司”税收待遇，WT/DS108/R，2000 年 3 月 20 日，上诉机构报告修正，WT/DS108/AB/R，DSR 2000：IV，p. 1675
美国—海外销售公司（第 21. 5 条—欧共体）	上诉机构报告，美国 —“海外销售公司”税收待遇—由欧共体根据 DSU 第 21. 5 条提出，WT/DS108/AB/RW，2002 年 1 月 29 日通过，DSR 2002：I，p. 55
美国—海外销售公司（第 21. 5 条—欧共体）	专家组报告，美国—“海外销售公司”税收待遇—由欧共体根据 DSU 第 21. 5 条提出，WT/DS108/RW，2002 年 1 月 29 日通过，上诉机构报告修正，WT/DS108/AB/RW，DSR 2002：I，p. 119

续 表

简要标题	案件标题全称及出处
美国—海外销售公司（第21.5条—欧共体 II）	上诉机构报告，美国—“海外销售公司”税收待遇—由欧共体根据DSU第21.5条提出，WT/DS108/AB/RW2，2006年3月14日通过，DSR 2006：XI，p.4721
美国—海外销售公司（第21.5条—欧共体 II）	专家组报告，美国“海外销售公司”税收待遇—由欧共体根据DSU第21.5条提出，WT/DS108/RW2，2006年3月14日通过，得到上诉机构报告支持，WT/DS108/AB/RW2，DSR 2006：XI，p.4761
美国—海外销售公司（第22.6条—美国）	仲裁结论，美国—美国“海外销售公司”税收待遇—美国根据DSU第22.6条和SCM协议第4.11条做出的仲裁，WT/DS108/ARB，2002年8月30日，DSR 2002：VI，p.2517
美国—博彩业	上诉机构报告，美国—影响博彩业跨境提供服务的措施WT/DS285/AB/R，2005年4月20日通过，DSR 2005：XII，5663（Corr.1，DSR 2006：XII，p.5475）
美国—博彩业	专家组报告，美国—影响博彩业跨境提供服务的措施，WT/DS285/R，2005年4月20日通过，上诉机构报告修正，WT/DS285/AB/R，DSR 2005：XII，p.5797
美国—博彩业［第21.3（c）条］	仲裁决定，美国—影响博彩业跨境提供服务的措施—在DSU第21.3（c）条下仲裁，WT/DS285/13，2005年8月19日，DSR 2005：XXIII，p.11639
美国—博彩业（第21.5条—安提瓜和巴布达）	专家组报告，美国—影响博彩业跨境提供服务的措施—由安提瓜和巴布达根据第21.5条提出，WT/DS285/RW，2007年5月22日通过，DSR 2007：VIII，p.3105
美国—博彩业（第22.6条—美国）	仲裁决定，美国—影响博彩业跨境提供服务的措施——由美国根据DSU第22.6条提交仲裁，WT/DS285/ARB，2007年12月21日，DSR 2007：X，p.4163
美国—汽油	上诉机构报告，美国—精炼汽油及传统汽油标准WT/DS2/AB/R，1996年5月20日通过，DSR 1996：I，p.3
美国—汽油	专家组报告，美国—精炼汽油及传统汽油标准，WT/DS2/R，1996年5月20日通过，上诉机构报告修正，WT/DS2/AB/R，DSR 1996：I，p.29
美国—热轧钢	上诉机构报告，美国—对来自日本的热轧薄板卷产品征收反倾销税，WT/DS184/AB/R，2001年8月23日通过，DSR 2001：X，p.4697
美国—热轧钢	专家组报告，美国—对来自日本的热轧薄板卷产品征收反倾销税，WT/DS184/R，2001年8月23日通过，上诉机构报告修正，WT/DS184/AB/R，DSR 2001：X，p.4769
美国—热轧钢［第21.3（c）条］	仲裁决定，美国—对来自日本的热轧薄板卷产品征收反倾销税—在DSU第21.3（c）条下仲裁，WT/DS184/13，2002年2月19日，DSR 2002：IV，p.1389
美国—羔羊	上诉机构报告，美国—对来自新西兰和澳大利亚的新鲜、冷藏和冷冻羔羊肉进口保障措施，WT/DS177/AB/R，WT/DS178/AB/R，2001年5月16日通过，DSR 2001：IX，p.4051
美国—羔羊	专家组报告，美国—对来自新西兰和澳大利亚的新鲜、冷藏和冷冻羔羊肉进口保障措施，WT/DS177/R，WT/DS178/R，2001年5月16日通过，上诉机构报告修正，WT/DS177/AB/R，WT/DS178/AB/R，DSR 2001：IX，p.4107
美国—大型民用航空器（第2次起诉）	上诉机构报告，美国—影响大型民用航空器贸易的措施（第2次起诉），WT/DS353/AB/R，2012年3月23日通过，DSR 2012：I，p.7

续 表

简要标题	案件标题全称及出处
美国—大型民用航空器（第 2 次起诉）	专家组报告，美国—影响大型民用航空器贸易的措施（第 2 次起诉），WT/DS353/R，2012 年 3 月 23 日通过，上诉机构报告修正，WT/DS353/AB/R，DSR 2012：II，p. 649
美国—热轧铅铋碳钢制品案 II	上诉机构报告，美国—对于原产英国的某些热轧铅铋碳钢制品进行反补贴税，WT/DS138/AB/R，2000 年 6 月 7 日通过，DSR 2000：V，p. 2595
美国—热轧铅铋碳钢制品案 II	专家组报告，美国—对于原产英国的某些热轧铅铋碳钢制品进行反补贴税，WT/DS138/R 和 Corr. 2，2000 年 6 月 7 日通过，得到上诉机构报告支持，WT/DS138/AB/R，DSR 2000：VI，p. 2623
美国—直线管	上诉机构报告，美国—对来自韩国的圆焊碳质条形管进口的保障措施，WT/DS202/AB/R，2002 年 3 月 8 日通过，DSR 2002：IV，p. 1403
美国—直线管	专家组报告，美国—对来自韩国的圆焊碳质条形管进口的保障措施 WT/DS202/R，2002 年 3 月 8 日通过，上诉机构报告修正，WT/DS202/AB/，DSR 2002：IV，p. 1473
美国—直线管 [第 21.3（c）条]	仲裁员报告，美国—对来自韩国的圆焊碳质条形管进口的保障措施—在 DSU 第 21.3（c）条下仲裁，WT/DS202/17，2002 年 7 月 26 日，DSR 2002：V，p. 2061
美国—补偿法案 （伯德修正案）	上诉机构报告，美国—2000 年对持续倾销和补贴的补偿法案，WT/DS217/AB/R，WT/DS234/AB/R，2003 年 1 月 27 日通过，DSR 2003：I，p. 375
美国—补偿法案 （伯德修正案）	专家组报告，美国—2000 年对持续倾销和补贴的补偿法案，WT/DS217/R，WT/DS234/R，2003 年 1 月 27 日通过，上诉机构报告修正，WT/DS217/AB/R，WT/DS234/AB/R，DSR 2003：II，p. 489
美国—补偿法案 （伯德修正案） [第 21.3（c）条]	仲裁决定，美国—2000 年对持续倾销和补贴的补偿法案—在 DSU 第 21.3（c）条下仲裁，WT/DS217/14，WT/DS234/22，2003 年 6 月 13 日，DSR 2003：III，p. 1163
美国—补偿法案 （伯德修正案）（巴西） （第 22.6 条—美国）	仲裁决定，美国—2000 年对持续倾销和补贴的补偿法案，最初由巴西上诉—溯及美国根据 DSU 第 22.6 条仲裁，WT/DS217/ARB/BRA，2004 年 8 月 31 日，DSR 2004：IX，p. 4341
美国—补偿法案 （伯德修正案）（加拿大） （第 22.6 条—美国）	仲裁决定，美国—2000 年对持续倾销和补贴的补偿法案，由加拿大上诉—溯及美国根据 DSU 第 22.6 条仲裁，WT/DS234/ARB/CAN，2004 年 8 月 31 日，DSR 2004：IX，p. 4425
美国—补偿法案 （伯德修正案）（智利） （第 22.6 条—美国）	仲裁决定，美国—2000 年对持续倾销和补贴的补偿法案，由智利上诉—溯及美国根据 DSU 第 22.6 条仲裁，WT/DS217/ARB/CHL，2004 年 8 月 31 日，DSR 2004 年：IX，p. 4511
美国—补偿法案 （伯德修正案）（欧共体） （第 22.6 条—美国）	仲裁决定，美国—2000 年对持续倾销和补贴的补偿法案，由欧共体上诉—溯及美国根据 DSU 第 22.6 条仲裁，WT/DS217/ARB/EEC，2004 年 8 月 31 日，DSR 2004：IX，p. 4591
美国—补偿法案 （伯德修正案）（印度） （第 22.6 条—美国）	仲裁决定，美国—2000 年对持续倾销和补贴的补偿法案最初由印度上诉—溯及美国根据 DSU 第 22.6 条仲裁 WT/DS217/ARB/IND，2004 年 8 月 31 日，DSR 2004：X，p. 4691
美国—补偿法案 （伯德修正案）（日本） （第 22.6 条—美国）	仲裁决定，美国—2000 年对持续倾销和补贴的补偿法案最初由日本上诉—溯及美国根据 DSU 第 22.6 条仲裁 WT/DS217/ARB/JPN，2004 年 8 月 31 日，DSR 2004：X，p. 4771

续 表

简要标题	案件标题全称及出处
美国—补偿法案 (伯德修正案)(韩国) (第 22.6 条—美国)	仲裁决议，美国—2000 年对持续倾销和补贴的补偿法案最初由韩国上诉—溯及美国根据 DSU 第 22.6 条仲裁，WT/DS217/ARB/KOR，2004 年 8 月 31 日，DSR 2004：X，p. 4851
美国—补偿法案 (伯德修正案)(墨西哥) (第 22.6 条—美国)	仲裁决议，美国—2000 年对持续倾销和补贴的补偿法案最初由墨西哥上诉—溯及美国根据 DSU 第 22.6 条仲裁，WT/DS234/ARB/MEX，2004 年 8 月 31 日，DSR 2004：X，p. 4931
美国—石油工业用管材日落复审	上诉机构报告，美国—对来自阿根廷石油工业用管材反倾销措施日落复审，WT/DS268/AB/R，2004 年 12 月 17 日通过，DSR 2004：VII，p. 3257
美国—石油工业用管材日落复审	专家组报告，美国—对来自阿根廷石油工业用管材反倾销措施日落复审 WT/DS268/R 和 Corr. 1，2004 年 12 月 17 日通过，上诉机构报告修正，W/DS/268/AB/R，DSR 2004：VIII，p. 3421
美国—石油工业用管材日落复审 [第 21.3（c）条]	仲裁决议，美国—对来自阿根廷石油工业用管材反倾销措施日落复审—在 DSU 第 21.3（c）条下仲裁，WT/DS268/12，2005 年 6 月 7 日，DSR 2005：XXIII，p. 11619
美国—石油工业用管材日落复审 (第 21.5 条—阿根廷)	专家组报告，美国—对来自阿根廷石油工业用管材反倾销措施日落复审—由阿根廷根据 DSU 第 21.5 条提出，WT/DS268/RW，2007 年 5 月 11 日通过，DSR 2007：IX，p. 3523
美国—石油工业用管材日落复审 (第 21.5 条—阿根廷)	专家组报告，美国—对来自阿根廷石油工业用管材反倾销措施日落复审—由阿根廷根据 DSU 第 21.5 条提出，WT/DS268/RW，2007 年 5 月 11 日通过，上诉机构报告修正，WT/DS268/AB/RW，DSR 2007：IX X，p. 3609
美国—果汁（巴西）	专家组报告，美国—对自巴西进口的果汁采取反倾销行政复审及其他措施，WT/DS382/R，2011 年 6 月 17 日报告，DSR 2011：VII，p. 3753
美国—家禽（中国）	专家组报告，美国—影响自中国进口家禽的措施，WT/DS392/R，2010 年 10 月 25 日通过，DSR 2010：V，p. 1909
美国—美国版权法第 110 节第 5 段	专家组报告，美国版权法第 110 节第 5 段，WT/DS160/R，2000 年 7 月 27 日通过，DSR 2000：VIII，p. 3769
美国—美国版权法第 110 节第 5 段 [第 21.3（c）条]	仲裁决议，美国—美国版权法第 110 节第 5 段—在 DSU 第 21.3（c）条下仲裁，WT/DS160/12，2001 年 1 月 15 日 DSR 2001：II，p. 657
美国—美国版权法第 110 节第 5 段（第 25 条）	仲裁决议，美国—美国版权法第 110 节第 5 段—在 DSU 第 25 条下仲裁，WT/DS160/ARB25/1，2001 年 11 月 9 日，DSR 2001：II，p. 667
美国—乌拉圭回合农业协议第 129（c）节（1）段	专家组报告，美国—乌拉圭回合农业协议第 129（c）节（1）段，WT/DS221/R，引自 2002 年，8 月 30 日 DSR 2002：VII，p. 2581
美国—综合拨款法第 211 节	上诉机构报告，美国—1998 年综合拨款法第 211 节，WT/DS176/AB/R，2002 年 2 月 1 日通过，DSR 2002：II，p. 589
美国—综合拨款法第 211 节	专家组报告，美国—1998 年综合拨款法第 211 节，WT/DS176/R，2002 年 2 月 1 日通过，上诉机构报告修正，WT/DS176/AB/R，DSR 2002：II，p. 683
美国—贸易法的 301 条款	专家组报告，美国—1974 年综合拨款法第 211 节，WT/DS152/R，2000 年 1 月 27 日通过，DSR 2000：II，p. 815
美国—虾	上诉机构报告，美国—特定虾及虾类产品进口限制，WT/DS58/AB/R，1998 年 11 月 6 日通过，DSR 1998 年：VII，p. 2755

续 表

简要标题	案件标题全称及出处
美国—虾	专家组报告，美国—特定虾及虾类产品进口限制，WT/DS58/R 和 Corr. 1，1998 年 11 月 6 日通过，上诉机构报告修正，WT/DS58/AB/R，DSR 1998：VII，p. 2821
美国—虾 （第 21.5 条—马来西亚）	上诉机构报告，美国—特定虾及虾类产品进口限制—由马来西亚根据 DSU 第 21.5 条提出，WT/DS58/AB/RW，2001 年 11 月 21 日通过，DSR 2001：XIII，p. 6481
美国—虾 （第 21.5 条—马来西亚）	专家组报告，美国—特定虾及虾类产品进口限制—由马来西亚根据 DSU 第 21.5 条提出，WT/DS58/RW，2001 年 11 月 21 日通过，得到上诉机构报告支持，WT/DS58/AB/RW，DSR 2001：XIII，p. 6529
美国—虾（厄瓜多尔）	专家组报告，美国—对产自厄瓜多尔虾采取反倾销，WT/DS335/R，2007 年 2 月 20 日通过，DSR 2007：II，p. 425
美国—虾（泰国）/ 美国—海关保税指令	上诉机构报告，美国—与从泰国进口虾有关的措施/ 美国—对征收反倾销和反补贴的商品实行海关保税指令，WT/DS343/AB/R，WT/DS345/AB/R，2008 年 8 月 1 日通过，DSR 2008：VII，2385/DSR 2008：VIII，p. 2773
美国—虾（泰国）	专家组报告，美国—与从泰国进口虾有关的措施，WT/DS343/R，2008 年 8 月 1 日通过，上诉机构报告修正，WT/DS343/AB/R，WT/DS345/AB/R，DSR 2008：VII，p. 2539
美国—虾（越南）	专家组报告，美国—对自越南进口虾实施反倾销措施，WT/DS404/R，2011 年 9 月 2 日通过，DSR 2011：X，p. 5301
美国—软木 III	专家组报告，美国—对来自加拿大的特定软木产品的初步裁定，WT/DS236/R，2002 年 11 月 1 日通过，DSR 2002：IX，p. 3597
美国—软木 IV	上诉机构报告，美国—对来自加拿大的特定软木的最后反补贴税决定，WT/DS257/AB/R，2004 年 2 月 17 日通过，DSR 2004 年：II，p. 571
美国—软木 IV	专家组报告，美国—对来自加拿大的特定软木的最后反补贴税决定，WT/DS257/R 和 Corr. 1，2004 年 2 月 17 日通过，上诉机构报告修正，WT/DS257/AB/R，DSR 2004：II，p. 641
美国—软木 IV （第 21.5 条—加拿大）	上诉机构报告，美国—对来自加拿大的特定软木的最后反补贴税决定—由加拿大根据 DSU 第 21.5 条提出，WT/DS257/AB/RW，2005 年 12 月 20 日通过，DSR 2005：XXIII，p. 11357
美国—软木 IV （第 21.5 条—加拿大）	专家组报告，美国—对来自加拿大的特定软木的最后反补贴税决定—由加拿大根据 DSU 第 21.5 条提出，WT/DS257/RW，2005 年 12 月 20 日通过，上诉机构报告驳回，WT/DS257/AB/RW，DSR 2005：XXIII，p. 11401
美国—软木 V	上诉机构报告，美国—对来自加拿大软木的最终倾销判决，WT/DS264/AB/R，2004 年 8 月 31 日通过，DSR 2004：V，p. 1875
美国—软木 V	专家组报告，美国—对来自加拿大软木的最终倾销判决，WT/DS264/R，2004 年 8 月 31 日通过，上诉机构报告修正，WT/DS264/AB/R，DSR 2004：V，p. 1937
美国—软木 V [第 21.3（c）条]	仲裁员报告，美国—对来自加拿大软木的最终倾销判决—在 DSU 第 21.3（c）条下仲裁，WT/DS264/13，2004 年 12 月 13 日，DSR 2004：X，p. 5011
美国—软木 V （第 21.5 条—加拿大）	上诉机构报告，美国—对来自加拿大软木的最终倾销判决—由加拿大根据 DSU 第 21.5 条提出，WT/DS264/AB/RW，2006 年 9 月 1 日通过，DSR 2006：XII，p. 5087

续 表

简要标题	案件标题全称及出处
美国—软木 V（第 21.5 条—加拿大）	专家组报告，美国—对来自加拿大软木的最终倾销判决—由加拿大根据 DSU 第 21.5 条提出，WT/DS264/RW，2006 年 9 月 1 日通过，得到上诉机构报告支持，WT/DS264/AB/RW，DSR 2006：XII，p. 5147
美国—软木 VI	专家组报告，美国—国际贸易委员会对来自加拿大软木的调查，WT/DS277/R，2004 年 4 月 26 日通过，DSR 2004：VI，p. 2485
美国—软木 VI（第 21.5 条—加拿大）	上诉机构报告，美国—国际贸易委员会对来自加拿大软木的调查—由加拿大根据 DSU 第 21.5 条提出，WT/DS277/AB/RW，2006 年 5 月 9 日通过，和 Corr. 1，DSR 2006：XI，p. 4865
美国—软木 VI（第 21.5 条—加拿大）	专家组报告，美国—国际贸易委员会对来自加拿大软木的调查—由加拿大根据 DSU 第 21.5 条提出，WT/DS277/RW，2006 年 5 月 9 日通过，上诉机构报告修正，WT/DS277/AB/RW，DSR 2006：XI，p. 4935
美国—不锈钢（韩国）	专家组报告，美国—对来自韩国的不锈钢卷板和不锈钢条的反倾销措施，WT/DS179/R，2001 年 2 月 1 日 通过，DSR 2001：IV，p. 1295
美国—不锈钢（墨西哥）	上诉机构报告，美国—对来自墨西哥的不锈钢采取最终反倾销措施，WT/DS344/AB/R，2008 年 5 月 20 日通过，DSR 2008：II，p. 513
美国—不锈钢（墨西哥）	专家组报告，美国—对来自墨西哥的不锈钢采取最终反倾销措施，WT/DS344/R，2008 年 5 月 20 日通过，上诉机构报告修正，WT/DS344/AB/R，DSR 2008：II，p. 599
美国—不锈钢（墨西哥）[第 21.3（c）条]	仲裁决议，美国—对来自墨西哥的不锈钢采取最终反倾销措施—第 DSU 21.3（c）条下的仲裁，WT/DS344/15，2008 年 10 月 31 日，DSR 2008：XX，p. 8619
美国—不锈钢（墨西哥）（第 21.5 条）	专家组报告，美国—对来自墨西哥的不锈钢采取最终反倾销措施，墨西哥诉诸 DSU 第 21.5 条，WT/DS344/RW，2013 年 5 月 6 日，未通过
美国—钢板	专家组报告，美国—对来自印度钢板的反倾销及反补贴措施，WT/DS206/R 和 Corr. 1，2002 年 7 月 29 日通过，DSR 2002：VI，p. 2073
美国—钢铁保障措施	上诉机构报告，美国—对于特定钢制品进口的保障措施，WT/DS248/AB/R，WT/DS249/AB/R，WT/DS251/AB/R，WT/DS252/AB/R，WT/DS253/AB/R，WT/DS254/AB/R，WT/DS258/AB/R，WT/DS259/AB/R，2003 年 12 月 10 日通过，DSR 2003：VII，p. 3117
美国—钢铁保障措施	专家组报告，美国——对于特定钢制品进口的保障措施，WT/DS248/R，WT/DS249/R，WT/DS251/R，WT/DS252/R，WT/DS253/R，WT/DS254/R，WT/DS258/R，WT/DS259/R，和 Corr. 1，2003 年 12 月 10 日通过，上诉机构报告修正，WT/DS248/AB/R，WT/DS249/AB/R，WT/DS251/AB/R，WT/DS252/AB/R，WT/DS253/AB/R，WT/DS254/AB/R，WT/DS258/AB/R，WT/DS259/AB/R，DSR 2003：VIII，p. 3273
美国—纺织品原产地规则	专家组报告，美国—纺织品及服装产品原产地规则，WT/DS243/R 和 Corr. 1，2003 年 7 月 23 日通过，DSR 2003：VI，p. 2309
美国—金枪鱼 II（墨西哥）	上诉机构报告，美国—有关金枪鱼及其产品进口、市场和销售的措施，WT/DS381/AB/R，2012 年 6 月 13 日通过，DSR 2012：IV，p. 1837
美国—金枪鱼 II（墨西哥）	专家组报告，美国—有关金枪鱼及其产品进口、市场和销售的措施，WT/DS381/R，2012 年 6 月 13 日通过，由上诉机构报告修正 WT/DS381/AB/R，DSR 2012：IV，p. 2013

续 表

简要标题	案件标题全称及出处
美国—轮胎（中国）	上诉机构报告，美国—影响自中国进口的客车和轻卡车轮胎的措施，WT/DS399/AB/R，2011 年 10 月 5 日通过，DSR 2011：IX，p. 4811
美国—轮胎（中国）	专家组报告，美国—影响自中国进口的客车和轻卡车轮胎的措施，WT/DS399/R，2011 年 10 月 5 日通过，上诉机构报告支持 WT/DS399/AB/R，DSR 2011：IX，p. 4945
美国—内衣	上诉机构报告，美国—对于棉质及人造纤维内衣进口的限制，WT/DS24/AB/R，1997 年 2 月 25 日通过，DSR 1997：I，p. 11
美国—内衣	专家组报告，美国—对于棉质及人造纤维内衣进口的限制，WT/DS24/R，1997 年 2 月 25 日通过，上诉机构报告修正，WT/DS24/AB/R，DSR 1997：I，p. 31
美国—棉花	上诉机构报告，美国—对于棉花的补贴，WT/DS267/AB/R，2005 年 3 月 21 日通过，DSR 2005：I，p. 3
美国—棉花	专家组报告，美国—对于棉花的补贴，WT/DS267/R 和 Corr. 1，2005 年 3 月 21 日通过，上诉机构报告修正，WT/DS267/AB/R，DSR 2005：II，p. 299
美国—棉花 （第 21. 5 条—巴西）	专家组报告，美国—对于棉花的补贴　由巴西根据 DSU 第 21. 5 条提出，WT/DS267/RW 和 Corr. 1，2008 年 6 月 20 日通过，DSR 2008：III，p. 809
美国—棉花 （第 21. 5 条—巴西）	上诉机构报告，美国—对于棉花的补贴—由巴西根据 DSU 第 21. 5 条提出，WT/DS267/AB/RW 和 Corr. 1，2008 年 6 月 20 日通过，上诉机构报告修正，WT/DS267/AB/RW，DSR 2008：III，p. 997
美国—棉花 （第 22. 6 条—美国 I）	仲裁决议，美国—对于棉花的补贴—由美国根据 DSU 第 22. 6 条和《补贴和反补贴协议》第 4. 11 条提出，WT/DS267/ARB/1，2009 年 8 月 31 日通过，DSR 2009：IX，p. 3871
美国—棉花 （第 22. 6 条—美国 II）	仲裁决议，美国—对于棉花的补贴—由美国根据 DSU 第 22. 6 条和《补贴和反补贴协议》第 7. 10 条提交仲裁，WT/DS267/ARB/2 和 Corr. 1，2009 年 8 月 31 日通过，DSR 2009：IX，p. 4083
美国—面筋粉	上诉机构报告，美国—对来自欧共体的面筋粉进口的明确保障措施，WT/DS166/AB/R，2001 年 1 月 19 日通过，DSR 2001：II，p. 717
美国—面筋粉	专家组报告，美国—对来自欧共体的面筋粉进口的明确保障措施，WT/DS166/R，2001 年 1 月 19 日通过，上诉机构报告修正，WT/DS166/AB/R，DSR 2001：III，p. 779
美国—羊毛衬衫及女上衣	上诉机构报告，美国—影响从印度进口的羊毛恤衫及衬衫措施，WT/DS33/AB/R 和 Corr. 1，1997 5 月 23 日通过，DSR 1997：I，p. 323
美国—羊毛衬衫及女上衣	专家组报告，美国—影响从印度进口的羊毛恤衫及衬衫措施，WT/DS33/R，1997 年 5 月 23 日通过，得到上诉机构报告支持，WT/DS33/AB/R，DSR 1997：I，p. 343
美国—归零法（欧共体）	上诉机构报告，美国—计算倾销差额（归零法）的法律、规则及方法，WT/DS294/AB/R，2006 年 5 月 9 日通过，和 Corr. 1，DSR 2006：II，p. 417
美国—归零法（欧共体）	专家组报告，美国—计算倾销差额（归零法）的法律、规则及方法，WT/DS294/R，引自 2006 年 5 月 9 日，上诉机构报告修正，WT/DS294/AB/R，DSR 2006：II，p. 521
美国—归零法（欧共体） （第 21. 5 条—欧共体）	上诉机构报告，美国—计算倾销差额（归零法）的法律、规则及方法—由欧共体根据第 21. 5 条提出上诉，WT/DS294/AB/RW 和 Corr. 1，2009 年 6 月 11 日通过，DSR 2009：VII，p. 2911

续 表

简要标题	案件标题全称及出处
美国—归零法（欧共体）（第21.5条—欧共体）	专家组报告，美国—计算倾销差额（归零法）的法律、规则及方法—由欧共体根据第21.5条提出上诉，WT/DS294/RW，2009年6月11日通过，上诉机构报告修正，WT/DS294/AB/RW，DSR 2009：VII，p.3117
美国—归零法（日本）	上诉机构报告，美国—与归零法有关的措施及日落复审，WT/DS322/AB/R，2007年1月23日通过，DSR 2007：I，p.3
美国—归零法（日本）	专家组报告，美国—与归零法有关的措施及日落复审，WT/DS322/R，2007年1月23日通过，上诉机构报告修正，WT/DS322/AB/R，DSR 2007：I，p.97
美国—归零法（日本）[第21.3（c）条]	仲裁报告，美国—与归零法有关的措施及日落复审，WT/DS322/21，2007年5月11日，DSR 2007：X，p.4160
美国—归零法（日本）（第21.5条—日本）	上诉机构报告，美国—与归零法和日落复审有关的措施—由日本根据第21.5条提出上诉，WT/DS322/AB/RW，2009年8月31日通过，DSR 2009：VIII，p.3441
美国—归零法（日本）（第21.5条—日本）	专家组报告，美国—与归零法和日落复审有关的措施—由日本根据第21.5条提出上诉，WT/DS322/RW，2009年8月31日通过，得到上诉机构报告支持，WT/DS322/AB/RW，DSR 2009：VIII，p.3553
美国—归零法（韩国）	专家组报告，美国—对自韩国进口的产品实施反倾销使用归零法，WT/DS402/R，2011年2月24日通过，DSR 2011：X，p.5239

● 贸易政策审议（2014）

汤加贸易政策审议

1. 汤加王国是位于南太平洋的群岛国家，有约 10 万居民，还有大约同等数量的汤加人居住在国外，主要分布在新西兰、澳大利亚和美国。人均收入为 4500 美元，汤加被列为中等收入的发展中国家。侨民汇款是推动当地经济的重要力量，这也解释了为什么在任何一年其商品进口超过出口至少 10 倍。汤加主要进口燃油（来自新加坡）和粮食（来自新西兰和斐济），占总进口额的 50%以上。汤加的主要出口市场在太平洋沿岸地区，以初级农产品（主要是南瓜、块根作物、椰子）和海洋产品为主。由于旅游收入，服务贸易更加平衡了。

2. 汤加在 2006 年社会动荡之后着手进行政治改革。2010 年，汤加人民第一次选出了汤加立法议会的大部分成员。自 2011 年 2 月新内阁组成，已经推动了一些改组。商务部、旅游部和劳动部仍然负责对外贸易政策问题，直到 2012 年中期，贸易大臣调整到外交部且没有相应的人员转移。原贸易部仍负责与贸易有关的事项，如经营许可证、外商投资、知识产权保护、进口许可证、出口促进、保护消费者权益，以及价格管制等。

3. 这是汤加的首次贸易政策审议。2007 年 7 月汤加加入世贸组织，在短期过渡期执行 WTO《海关估价协议》和《与贸易有关的知识产权协定》，以及一些削减关税的协议。汤加约束其所有的关税税目，最终约束税率均没有超过 20%。另一方面，由于汤加以统一税率（15%）的关税结构为目标，它没有加入任何的部门举措，不参加《信息技术协议》或《民用航空器贸易协议》。汤加在 GATS 框架下对 90 个（总部门数为 160）服务业分部门承担具体承诺。自从加入 WTO，汤加已提交了 17 个与其承诺相关的通报，涵盖内容包括农业支持、企业许可程序、贸易救济和知识产权立法等。2009 年，WTO 知识产权理事会审议了汤加的知识产权立法。

4. 虽然自 2007 年以来汤加的关税和贸易措施发生了一些变化，但整体系统是相当稳定的。目前汤加的关税有六档。因此，当 2008 年 1 月 1 日新关税生效时没有实现预期的单一税率关税，60%的税目目前面临 15%的进口关税，其他进口商品的税率在 0 到 20%之间。简单的平均关税目前是 11.5%，远低于 17.6%的平均最终约束税率。汤加基本完成了从 HS2007 到 HS2012 的升级。在这种情况下，当局意识到，需要对 22 个税号的实施税率予以纠正，目前的实施税率（20%），超过了约束税率（15%）。

5. 汤加不通过关税配额规范市场准入，也不对任何贸易伙伴提供优惠关税。90%的海关估价案例中利用交易价格，重新确认价格往往是由于无证托运。大部分商品可以不受任何限制地进行交易。虽然很难建立一个关于汤加实施的非关税措施的详尽清单，但当涉及需要保护人类、动物或植物的生命或健康、公共道德、国家安全、文化遗产、即将用竭的自然资源的保护和维护知识产权时，贸易限制措施会受到激励。汤加不对任何商品征收出口税。

6. 汤加不断增长的财政收入份额来源于国内消费税和广泛的消费税。汤加对酒精饮料、烟草、石油产品都征收国内消费税。自 2013 年 8 月，还对努力劝阻的某些“非健康”的食品如动物脂肪和加糖软饮料征税。消费税按照15%的单一税率征收，但对一些公共、医疗和金融服务实施豁免。对电力、某些活动物，以及各种农业投入品实施零税率。在2012至2013年度，政府从消费税（进口产品和国内产品）筹集了近5500万潘加的财政收入，国内消费税近3000万潘加，加上1470万潘加的进口关税。

7. 流入汤加的外国直接投资水平有所变化，近几年平均在2000万潘加左右。汤加的投资体制的法律依据为《外国投资法2002》《外国投资实施细则2006》《营业执照法2002》以及《营业执照规定》。在汤加注册成立的企业，只要外方投资不超过25%或者不控制超过企业有表决权股份的25%就被认为是汤加本国企业。外商投资法规列出了对国内和国外投资者禁止从事某些活动，同时也规定了只为汤加投资者保留的某些活动。WTO目前正在审议外商投资法规，包括保留名单。2011年，为了重振渔业，汤加水域重新对外国金枪鱼渔船开放。2012年简化了营业执照条例，允许一个单一的许可足以让个人和企业从事多个商业活动。精简后的营业执照条例更容易申请，处理速度更快，费用有所降低，特别是电子注册。

8. 政府以直接支付、补贴和信贷措施等形式对农业和工业部门的支持是非常有限的。2012年，为了给农产品出口商提供短期优惠贷款，设立了一个100万潘加的农产品市场推广基金。就放弃的收入而言，免税在其中发挥了显著的作用。在过去，根据《1978年产业发展的激励机制（IDI）法案》，对进口资本品、材料和零部件分别给予关税和税务豁免。该法案在2007年被废止。但是，汤加的关税规定了对某些用途或用户实施关税豁免，例如对于啤酒制造商和其他酒精饮料。2013年6月约有40项用于渔业部门的材料和设备被添加到豁免清单。投资人也可以通过申请，获得投资品消费税豁免权。汤加还通过燃料优惠支持发电、航空运输、国内运输和商业捕鱼。据有关部门介绍，2010到2011年度海关免税总额达2390万潘加，其他免税额达670万潘加。国内生产的啤酒，某些烈酒和烟草产品也得益于国内消费税制度，因为该制度可以区分原装进口的商品和本地生产的商品。

9. 汤加的经济基于农业、渔业、面向国内的小规模的制造业和旅游业。其GDP大约为5亿美元，是世贸组织成员中经济规模最小的国家之一。国有企业存在于多个行业，包括电信、水电、交通、银行等行业。银行和外汇交易受中央银行（汤加国家储备银行）监督，但保险业和其他金融服务供应商不受任何机构监管。同样，汤加还未在电信部门建立独立监管机构。总体而言，汤加的法律和监管框架正面临着现代化和简化改革，其中涉及农业及相应的SPS措施、空中和海上运输及电信等方面。

10. 汤加是太平洋岛国论坛的成员，积极参与了基于南太平洋区域贸易和经济合作协定（SPARTECA）地区，太平洋岛国贸易协定（PICTA），更紧密经贸关系太平洋协定（PACER），“PACER＋”，以及非论坛国家的扩大贸易的倡议。汤加与欧盟和太平洋非加太集团关于经济伙伴协定的谈判始于2004年。虽然在各种谈判领域取得了进展，预期也得到了提升，但到目前为止并没有新的协议达成，而原定的最后期限早已过去。PICTA下的优惠交易对汤加还没有开始，只有非互惠SPARTECA似乎对汤加的出口（新西兰和澳大利亚）提供实实在在的关税优惠。尽管来自汤加的出口可能符合欧盟、美国和日本的普惠制资格，但这些优惠还没有被广泛使用。因此，WTO框架规则和最惠国关税继续为汤加的贸易和经济政策提供基本参数。

（苏日译，戴臻校）

马来西亚贸易政策审议

经济环境

1. 报告审议期间，马来西亚务实的经济管理和调整适当的宏观经济政策，使得其整体经济表现强劲。由于外部盈余下降，马来西亚经济继续经历一次显著的外部再平衡；同时，为了到2020年把马来西亚建设成为一个高收入国家，其政策继续确保可持续和包容性增长。尽管在2008到2012年期间，马来西亚全要素生产率（TFP）增长放缓；但其比较优势似乎从电子产品和电子制造转向加工商品和天然气，因此马来西亚仍然具有外部竞争力。

2. 马来西亚经济从2009年的经济紧缩中迅速恢复，并且经济增长率更加可持续和温和，特别是经济增长引擎明显从以出口为导向的制造业转向国内服务。强劲的国内需求抵消了外部疲软和燃料4.1%（2009—2012）的年平均增长率所带来的影响。在2012年下降至低于其2010年1.7%（亚太地区最低之一）的水平之前，由于临时性的供方及成本相关因素的影响，马来西亚的低通货膨胀率从2009年至2011年大幅上升。此外，其较低的官方失业率在2012年进一步下降至3%。

3. 报告审议期间，一个稍微宽松的货币政策继续保持支持经济增长与控制通货膨胀之间的平衡。自2011年5月以来基准利率一直维持在3%不变，抵制区域同行之间降低利率的态势。实际有效汇率在2009年9月和2010年4月之间强劲升值后，在2011年和2012年仅有轻微波动。同其各种资本市场和金融部门的发展计划相一致，马来西亚放宽或取消了一些外汇政策。其财政赤字逐渐从2009年占GDP的6.7%下降到2012年的4.5%，而政府债务估计已经上升至其自己规定的上限即国内生产总值的55%。马来西亚目前正在进行财政整顿、税收改革和支出合理化计划。几个关键措施已经实施，以改善公共财政状况，包括恢复补贴合理化。期待已久的商品及服务税（GST）将在2015年4月份实施。

4. 虽然有显著收缩，但马来西亚贸易和经常账户余额仍保持盈余。马来西亚充足的外汇储备在2009年至2011年间稳步上升，之后围绕一个相对平缓的趋势发展，如：在2013年11月15日，马来西亚外汇储备为1367亿美元（9.7个月的进口，3.7倍的短期外债）。在审议（除2012年）期间，马来西亚外债（短期）稳步上升。

5. 马来西亚的经济仍然是很强的外向型经济，其中货物和服务贸易占国内生产总值的162.4%。虽然相对多元化，但马来西亚相当大一部分外贸日益趋向于区域内贸易（亚太）；虽然商品的份额在贸易总额中占比上升，但制造业仍是主要的贸易商品来源。

6. 2008至2012年间，马来西亚的外国直接投资存量上升了58.8%，与其相对应的对外直接投资存量也以相同的速度增长，并继续主要投资于制造业和服务业活动。欧盟和新加坡仍然是主要的外国直接投资股东。外国直接投资流入在2012年有所放缓，反映出不确定的全球经济前景和马来西亚作为劳动密集型产业基地吸引力正在减弱。

7. 自2009年以来，马来西亚已在其服务领域的自由化方面做出了很大努力，消除或减少了一系列服务部门外资参股的限制。在剩下整个经济部门的外国直接投资上限完整列表不可用的同时，在本次审议的背景下，外国直接投资的限制领域被确定为：渔业、能源、电信、航空和海上运输。在公私合作项目中，外商参与只在某些特定情况下可以考虑。总体上，投资环境一定程度上仍然受到有利于土著社群和马来西亚人的政策的影响。

贸易政策框架

8. 马来西亚贸易政策的方向仍集中于确保马来西亚到2020年成为一个自力更生、工业化的国家。除此之外，重点被放在马来西亚企业融入全球价值链，并发展与新市场的商业关系上面。自2010年以来，负责制定贸易政策的机构没有改变。各种新的与贸易有关的法律已经生效：检疫及检查服务法案、战略贸易法案、竞争法以及价格控制及反暴利法。

9. 马来西亚继续新的区域贸易协定（RTAs）谈判，有双边的，也有与其东盟伙伴一起的。审议期间，马来西亚有七个新的区域贸易协定生效。其中三个是东盟与第三国（澳大利亚、新西兰、印度、韩国）的协定，四个是双边协定（与智利、印度、新西兰、澳大利亚）。马来西亚已经签署并批准了伊斯兰会议组织（TPS-OIC）和发展八大优惠关税安排（D8-PTA）的贸易优惠体系，预计将很快生效。马来西亚与土耳其、欧盟和欧洲自由贸易联盟的区域贸易协定谈判也正在进行中。马来西亚也是跨太平洋伙伴关系（TPP）谈判以及东盟地区经济伙伴关系（RCEP）谈判的参与者。

10. 在东盟层面，努力都集中在 2015 年实现东盟经济共同体；审议期间三个新的东盟协定生效：东盟货物贸易协议（ATIGA）、2012 年东盟全面投资协定（ACIA）、东盟海关协议。此外，服务贸易、金融服务和航空运输在东盟内的自由化也更进一步。东盟地区全面伙伴关系的谈判正在进行中。

11. 报告审议期间，马来西亚都没有卷入任何新的 WTO 争端解决案件，无论是作为原告还是被告。马来西亚一直以来保持对世界贸易组织的动态通报，且在一些领域内表现优异，但在另一些领域（如关税配额、对农业的国内支持）也存在较长时间的提交迟滞。自 2010 年以来，为了改善其商业环境，马来西亚进行了许多改革，包括缩短海关许可证的处理时间，消除和简化许可要求，以及减少施工许可证批准所需时间。此外，关于法规制定和实施的国家政策于 2013 年颁布，要求联邦政府机构遵循影响商业、贸易和投资的法规制定的特定步骤。为了以更迅速更简单的方式评估和核准投资项目，马来西亚在 2010 年设立了一个国家投资委员会（NCI）；并于同年开始实施马来西亚企业标识（MyCoID）计划，以简化与多个政府机构的业务往来。

贸易政策发展

12. 关税仍然是主要的贸易政策工具之一，尽管它只是一个较小的税收来源（占 2012 年税收总额的 1.3%）。采用 2012 协调制度税则目录后，通过减少税目数量（9.3%），马来西亚的关税得到了简化。关税涉及税率的多样性（从价税 19 种，特别关税 19 种，复合关税 11 种，选择关税 2 种），自 2009 年以来其数量几乎没有变化。作为在报告审议期间单边削减关税的结果，马来西亚平均适用最惠国税率从 2009 年的 7.4%下降至 5.6%（2013 年）。关税分散减少了，虽然关税升级依然明显。虽然非从价税往往隐藏了更高的税率峰值，关税税率区间仍为 0 到 90%，2013 年 80%的商品税率为 10%或更低。虽然 80%以上的关税税率是受约束的，但实际适用税率和约束最惠国税率之间的平均差距已经上升至少 10 个百分点，从而使适用关税的提高存在相当大的余地，虽然报告审议期间这似乎并没有发生。适用最惠国税率的简单平均值与来自不同特惠协定或 FTA 贸易伙伴进口商品的平均特惠税率之间的差距也减少了。

13. 贸易便利化加强了，特别是通过进一步将海关通关时的控制转向通关后的稽查控制；马来西亚跨境贸易的便利程度在国际上排名较高。

14. 实行进口禁令大多是由于国家安全、宗教和环境的原因。马来西亚的税目有相当一部分仍受制于进口许可（大部分是非自动的）并且继续被用作贸易和产业政策的工具，特别是被用于调节进口流量以及促进战略产业。虽然马来西亚采取的反倾销行动明显减少，在 2007 至 2011 年都没有案件发生；但在 2012 年，马来西亚对几乎所有来源于亚洲的进口钢盘条、双向拉伸聚丙烯薄膜、热轧卷板展开了调查。

15. 对某些特定商品（如木材、棕榈原油）的出口税（在 2012 年占税收总收入的 1.5%）和（或）出口限制，除其他外，继续阻碍某些商品和必需品的出口并降低它们的国内价格，从而保证充足的国内供应以及有关产品的下游加工。实行价格控制的必需品（如面粉、柴油、汽油 RON 95、液化石油气、糖和食用油），其中四种享受补贴，除非获得批准，这些产品禁止出口。实行进口关税豁免或对用于生产出口产品的进口中间产品实行退税，避免了对进口关税再次征收出口税。对某些干鲜水果、干鲜花卉、观赏植物和观赏鱼以及制成品以法定所得税豁免的形式予以支持，法定所得税豁免范围为其增加值的 10%～50%，增加值取决于除其他外的生产活动中的价值或（和）所有权的增加。类似的相当于其出口增加值 50%的法定所得税豁免也适用于选定服务部门的公司。其他的支持措施依然存在，如出口加工区涉及当地含量要求（自 2011 年）、优惠信贷、保险、担保以及政府资助的推广和营销援助。

16. 涉及补助、税收优惠、低息贷款的措施继续支持生产及各种农产品和制成品贸易，鼓励中小企业、研发和环保活动。马来西亚仍然是该地区以及世界范围内补贴最高的经济体之一。马来西亚推出旨在对汽油、炊事用气、电以及道路通行费方面的补贴制度的改革，但迄今为止成果有限；2013 年 10 月份马来西亚再次强调了这些努力。

17. 为了实现到 2020 年成为发达国家的目标，标准的完善和发展活动在马来西亚仍占优先地位。报告审议期间，马来西亚的强制性标准以及与国际标准接轨的比重持续上升。在 SPS 领域，监管和制度进行了改进。除其他外，重点进一步放在清真认证和生物安全问题上。

18. 虽然由于一些发展，与政府有联系的公司（GLCs）面临的竞争挑战有所加强，但国家对经济的参与在许多领域仍然存在（如石油、天然气、关键的战略性公用事业和服务）。为提高工作效率而付出的努力在某些情况下似乎已见成效。优惠的政府采购程序以及扩大对销贸易/抵消要求继续被用作产业政策的一种工具，以有利于当地企业；只有商品和服务在本地不能提供时，才会邀请国际招标。政联公司，并非受公共部门的采购规则和法规的约束，而是被鼓励从当地企业购买。马来西亚于 2012 年成为世界贸易组织政府采购协议的观察员，正努力增强其采购程序的透明度和“廉洁公约”。

19. 报告审议期间，管理竞争政策的法律和制度框架发生了显著变化，其中也涵盖了政联公司，但不包括某些特定的反竞争行为、协议或由其独自立法所涵盖的活动（如能源和通信）。对基本货物和服务的价格和供应的控制得到了加强，食糖价格补贴被取消，汽油价格补贴被减少。消费者保护在多个领域（广告、个人数据保护、信用卡销售、消费者赔偿）得到了加强。特别是通过提高这些领域的标准，在进一步完善法人治理结构的监管框架方面取得了实质性进展。

20. 马来西亚通过大力修订其专利、工业设计、版权和商标法律法规，完善了知识产权制度，并扩大其国际承诺。新举措（如车品牌 BOB 方案）促进了其积极执法方式的推进。

部门政策发展

21. 农业（包括林业和渔业）的贡献保持在大约占 GDP 的十分之一。虽然主要农产品的自足率在报告期内基本保持稳定，然而，连续采用新技术推动了其全要素生产率的增长。新的农业政策支持涉农食品产业的发展，重点特别放在促进生物技术以及高附加值的农业。马来西亚对农业继续保持相对自由的贸易体制，最惠国关税率普遍较低，在 2013 年平均为 2.9%（WTO 定义）。然而，对特定农产品实施的非从价税税率峰值继续允许更高的关税保护（酒精饮料、烟草废料的从价税等值达到 1439.2%）。与农业市场多边准入承诺相关的关税配额仍在实施，配额内税率为 0～25%（圆卷心菜），配额外税率为 20%～90%（圆卷心菜）。政府还实施措施以支持某些农产品的国内加工（例如非自动出口许可证和出口关税），以及促进出口（如通过企业税收减免），对棕榈原油出口关税大大减少，以提高其出口竞争力，并减少国内库存。马来西亚继续提供越来越多的特定产品支持（如水稻的价格支持）和主要集中在水稻有关活动的普遍支持（如化肥补贴和软贷款）。水稻是一种战略作物，为此当局调整其做法，确保水稻的可用性、可及性和负担能力，而不仅是自给自足。它仍是唯一可适用国家稻米有限公司垄断、非自动进口/出口许可证，以及价格和供给控制的项目。尽管采取了预防措施，如对许可的限制，鱼的生产还是远远超出了指标。马来西亚实施了渔业投入控制制度和某些资源的保护以及环境可持续性措施。渔业的国内支持包括额外的柴油燃料补贴（直到 2011 年 5 月底，对拖网渔船的补贴超过 70 GRT）。

22. 采矿业（包括燃料）和采石业对 GDP 的贡献在 2012 年小幅下降至 10.4%。矿业产品仍然适用相对较高的关税保护即从 0 到 50%（普通硅酸盐水泥）、出口许可证及出口税，从而协助下游产品的加工。

23. 审议期间，马来西亚通过增加可再生能源在一次性能源总供给中的份额，努力减少对石油和天然气的依赖，以应付能源需求的增长。然而，尽管有这些努力，可再生能源的贡献仍然微不足道。马来西亚还采取了一些行动以提高能源利用效率。对所有消费者的能源补贴仍然是一个主要的长期的财政、预算、发展、环境甚至政治问题。通过政联公司PETRONAS在石油、天然气和电力行业的国家参与，仍然是政府预算的最大贡献者。它允许，特别是通过政府实施的低天然气价格，对发电机进行补贴，因而使最终用户受益。此外，电费取决于不同的用户类别和消费，从而允许在不同消费群体中的交叉补贴；例如，商业和农业活动的平均电费比工业和住宅用电要高。

24. 尽管制造业占国内生产总值的份额在评估期间略有下降，但其就业比例保持相对稳定。全要素生产率增长方面，制造业排名第三，在建设和服务之后。除了汽车产品的明显例外，制造业在贸易和外商投资方面仍比较开放。由于命名的变化，自2009年以来，马来西亚进口工业产品的平均最惠国关税从8%下降到6.2%（2013年）。这一水平是影响农产品平均关税水平（WTO定义）的两倍多。政府采购合同中对当地产品的优惠措施，重要商品的出口许可证和出口关税，企业出口税的豁免，以及产品和贸易上一些关税和非关税措施，继续为制造业活动提供支持。虽然在2010年对自东盟成员国的进口关税降至零，但汽车行业仍然受到17.3%的平均最惠国关税保护，位居HS所有部分的榜首。非关税措施，如宪报刊登的价格体系和“批准许可证”进口许可制度依然存在，后者应在不久的将来（2015，2020）被废除。此外，一系列税收措施（例如，影响超大型车辆的高消费税，对销售“国产车”进行有针对性的消费税豁免，以及对国内组装的四轮驱动车辆的减税，并加强对出口所获法定收入的税的豁免），以及国家汽车政策框架内的非税收措施（软贷款和赠款）仍在起作用。

25. 服务部门仍然是经济中一个非常有活力的部分，2009—2012年年增长率平均为5.9%。2012年，在GDP和就业中所占份额略超过50%，并吸引了经济核准投资的最大份额。政府继续自主开放一系列服务部门的外资股权限制，2012年在17个服务分部门开始部分或完全解除外资股权限制，这些分部门分属6个行业：专业服务、通信服务、分销服务、教育服务、环境服务，以及与健康相关的社会服务。审议期间，马来西亚开始了金融服务立法的全面现代化和简化。新的法律已经取消了在银行和保险行业外国直接投资的上限。现在，保险和银行业务牌照的发放基于审慎和“马来西亚最佳利益”的标准。马来西亚正在寻求促使自己成为一个伊斯兰金融、医疗保健和教育服务中心，以及一个空运和海运的交通枢纽。

前景展望

26. 总的来说，马来西亚的经济基本面依然良好。尽管从全球金融危机中有力复苏，马来西亚经济仍然容易通过国际贸易、大宗商品价格和金融渠道受到全球经济增长和风险规避的外来冲击。公平和可持续的增长依赖于实现多样化以及提高全要素生产率，加强结构改革，尤其是在解决财政整顿、税收改革和支出合理化问题方面。以上这些以及相关的改革将提高马来西亚经济的灵活性及其应对不断加强的外部竞争的能力。

（梁小雨译，戴臻校）

缅甸贸易政策审议

1. 被孤立于大部分全球经济之外多年，2010年以来的改革为缅甸重新融入国际社会铺平了道路。因此，实际GDP增长一直在上升，估计在2011—2012年度上升5.9%，2012—2013年度为6.4%。在2012年3月底，缅甸的人均GDP在900美元左右。

2. 缅甸在其宏观经济政策方面开展了一系列改革。2012年4月1日，缅甸中央银行以本国货币有管理的浮动汇率取代了钉住汇率（特别提款权）。在改革之前，缅甸实行多重汇率制度，包括官方汇率和非正规平行市场汇率。此前，缅甸的货币政策由财政赤字的融资需求所决定，这导致了高通胀。为了给央行提供更大的操作自主权和完善货币传导机制，新的中央银行法于2013年7月11日颁布。新的法律规定了中央银行的自主权，使其能够独立于财政部进行运作。

3. 2011—2012年度，缅甸的商品出口约占国内生产总值的16%，主要出口产品包括天然气、玉石、木材和木制品以及鱼类和甲壳类动物。其商品进口也占国内生产总值的约16%，进口的主要产品包括石油产品、钢铁及其制品。2011—2012年度，缅甸的主要出口目的地为泰国、中国和印度，其主要进口供应商是中国、新加坡和泰国。

4. 缅甸有很大的增长潜力，因为其拥有年轻的劳动力，丰富的自然资源，并且靠近一个快速增长、充满活力的经济地区。然而，缅甸经济现代化和实现政府“促进包容性广泛性增长和减少贫困”的目标仍面临很大障碍。其中包括缺少能力和基础设施。

5. 缅甸是世界贸易组织的创始成员，这是它的第一次贸易政策审议。缅甸认为，多边贸易体制可以为缅甸的出口和克服供应方面的限制带来广泛的机会。与此同时，缅甸的贸易政策在很大程度上受到其在东盟的参与，以及东盟与第三国的自由贸易协定的影响。缅甸期望从欧盟和挪威恢复普惠制中受益。缅甸一直以来没有参加过WTO的任何争端解决程序，不论是作为原告、被告还是第三方。

6. 在经济改革的背景下，政府已采取措施以开放经济，并不断修改与贸易有关的立法。缅甸正在准备《竞争法》《消费者权益保护法》和全面的知识产权立法等。认识到经济的持续和可持续发展需要外国的资本和技术，政府在2012年颁布了新的外商投资法，除了限制或禁止的活动，一般允许外国直接投资。根据该法，出口所获累计利润可享受税收优惠，外国公司必须雇用当地劳动力并随着时间的推移增加本地员工的比例。

7. 缅甸18.5%的税目受协调制度八位编码水平的约束。所有的农业税目（WTO定义）都受HS约束，相比较而言，非农业税目只有5.7%。最终约束关税范围为0（如电气机械及运输设备）至550%（如化学品、饮料、烟草和谷物及制品）。2013年平均最惠国关税为5.5%。缅甸对所有贸易伙伴都至少给予最惠国待遇。缅甸还没有应用WTO《海关估价协议》的规定。在缅甸没有反倾销、反补贴、保障措施和补贴立法。

8. 2012年，缅甸开始改革其非自动进口许可证制度。以前，所有商品的进口商进口前要求有非自动进口许可证，而且花上几个星期才能获得进口许可证。在2013年4月，166项产品（在HS八位编码水平上超过1928个税号）的进口许可要求被取消。缅甸没有实施关税配额。缅甸尚未向世贸组织做出有关其国营贸易活动的通报。

9. 缅甸既不是世界贸易组织《政府采购协定》的成员，也不是其观察员。

10. 大部分产品的出口需要出口许可证。近日，缅甸开始改革其出口许可制度，从2013年起，152种商品不再需要出口许可证。缅甸还在2011年改革了其出口税制。改革前，出口商在货物出口前需支付8%的商业税和2%的所得税。目前，只对五种商品（宝石、天然气、原油、柚木和木材）的出口征收商业税。

11. 税收约占政府总收入的90%，其中最大的来源是商业税。然而，有70种物品，若是在国内生产的，则免征商业税；若是进口的，则需征5%

的税。这体现出对国内生产的商品和进口商品的差别对待。

12. 据当局称，2011—2012年度，私营部门占GDP的比重约为91%。目前，有41家国有经济企业。

13. 2012—2013年度，农业约占GDP的30%。农业劳动生产率不到其他经济部门的三分之一，可能是由于农场小、机械少以及该部门高劳动/低资本的结构。主要农作物有水稻、玉米、豆子和豆类、甘蔗以及棉花。缅甸是一个粮食净出口国。2013年，缅甸对农产品（HS01-24）和工业产品（HS25-97）的简单适用最惠国关税分别为9.0%和4.8%。

14. 缅甸生产的大部分的天然气出口到中国。缅甸不出口石油或石油产品。煤炭出口量不到其生产量的10%。约占GDP20%的制造业有所增长，但与农业和服务业相比，其增长仍相对较小。

15. 服务约占缅甸GDP的38%。主要服务活动包括贸易和运输/通信。缅甸是服务的净进口国。在《服务贸易总协定》背景下，缅甸在旅游和与旅游相关的服务以及运输服务方面做出了具体承诺，而它并没有做出水平承诺或列出任何最惠国豁免条款。总体上，服务业的特征是国家通过国有企业进行参与，以及对私营部门和外国参与的限制。尽管外国直接投资不是完全被禁止的，但没有任何一家外国公司经营银行或保险业务（除了外资银行的代表处）。政府正在正式发放两个新的全国性基础电信许可证，两间持牌机构都将涉及外国公司。在民用航空和海上运输方面，任何公司都没有被授予专属权利。在酒店及相关业务中允许外国资本参与高达100%的外国直接投资。

（梁小雨译，戴臻校）

阿曼贸易政策审议

经济发展

1. 自从2008年阿曼最后一次贸易政策审议以来，阿曼的经济运行良好，实体经济增长稳健，通货膨胀较低，财政政策合理可靠，对外账户表现强劲。高涨的油价、日益增长的石油开采量，以及一个开放透明的对外贸易体制，保证了阿曼的经济可以持续增长。

2. 审议期间阿曼的通货膨胀率有所下降，2012年已经低于3%。同时自从阿曼最后一次贸易政策审议以来，外籍劳工的数量大幅上升，至今已接近170万。汇率方面，阿曼里亚尔已经盯住了美元。国际收支方面，货物贸易存在大量盈余，服务贸易以及经常转移却存在赤字。国外投资集中于石油和天然气行业，出口则主要是各种烃类，而且大部门都出口到亚洲市场。同时阿曼进口的产成品种类较多，主要来自于中东以及亚洲国家。

贸易政策框架

3. 工贸部（MOCI）对阿曼的贸易政策制定负全部责任。由各部委代表、海关当局以及私营部门共同组成的国家委员会（NC）负责一切与WTO有关的事宜。首先相关部委负责起草贸易议案，再由内阁向国会及专家递交，最后苏丹负责以皇家法令或者苏丹法令的形式发布。

4. 阿曼的主要经济目标由长期发展策略（1996—2020）以及连续的五年规划所制定。主要包括支持经济增长、多样化生产以避免单一依靠石油的出口模式、为阿曼居民创造更多的就业机会。此外，预算方面实现平衡、增加GDP、保持较低的通货膨胀也是经济目标。新的五年规划（2016—2020）以及长期发展策略（2040版）正在制定当中。

5. 自从2000年加入WTO以来，阿曼给予其所有的贸易伙伴最惠国待遇。同时阿曼在多哈回合谈判中表现活跃并对非农市场准入以及服务领域表现出很大的兴趣。在WTO中阿曼从来没有直接与其他成员发生争端，但却在一系列的案件中以第三方的身份介入。

6. 阿曼是海湾合作委员会的成员之一，其他成员包括巴林、科威特、卡塔尔、沙特阿拉伯王国、阿拉伯联合酋长国。海湾委员会成员间1983年建立了自贸区，2008年1月又进一步建立了服务业的共同市场。除了少数产品，海湾合作委员会各成员都实行统一关税制度。针对应急措施、兽医检疫、植物检疫等一系列问题建立了共同法。阿曼也是泛阿拉伯自贸区协议成员之一，2005年1月1日，该协议下成员间大多数贸易壁垒已经被取消。

7. 阿曼同美国间的自贸协议于2009年1月开始实施，在其他的海湾合作委员会成员中，只有巴林同美国签署了自贸协议。海湾合作委员会决定将来所有的地区性协议都以团体的形式参与协商。新加坡同海湾合作委员会之间的自贸区已经在2013年9月正式生效。泛阿拉伯自贸区协议成员也与海湾合作委员会相互签署了自贸区协议，但直至2014年1月仍未生效。同时，海湾合作委员会与其他国家间的协商正在进行中。

8.《境外资本投资法》规定，所有的境外投资必须由商贸部审核通过。所有对资本少于或等于15万阿曼里亚尔的公司的境外投资都将被禁止。在这一限值之上，境外投资者可以持股最高达49%。实际上，自贸区内这一比例可能高达70%甚至是100%。经过内阁许可，境外投资者可以对资本超过50万阿曼里亚尔的企业全资控股。但是境外资本却受限不可以在某几个行业投资。对于境外投资者，虽然允许拥有土地所有权，但是长期的或者基于项目的土地使用却倾向于采取租赁的形式。投资激励包括税收豁免、水电天然气以及土地使用的补贴等形式。阿曼国有的中小型企业也有资格获得由阿曼发展银行这家国有银行提供的软贷款。

贸易政策工具及惯例

9. 自2003年1月以来，海湾合作委员会成员对大部分产品都适用0%～5%不等的外部关税。

此外，阿曼对含酒精饮料及猪肉制品适用100%关税。阿曼对于其给予最惠国待遇的贸易成员平均适用5.5%的关税。阿曼已经对其100%的关税进行约束，最高升幅达200%。除了含酒精饮料以及烟草制品，其他来自海湾合作委员会成员以及泛阿拉伯自贸区协议成员的产品都实施无关税政策，新加坡和美国的进口产品也获得了特惠待遇。阿曼的平均约束关税为：农业产品28%，非农产品11.6%。商业发票以及原产地认可必须由原产地的阿曼领事馆或者阿拉伯大使馆认证通过。商品通常会在24小时之内清关。其他的关税或是税费为零。

10. 阿曼不会对进口产品适用任何其他关税，同时也不会适用增值税以及销售税。但会采用一系列的进口限制或者是进口禁止，主要是出于安全、健康、道德等因素的考虑。同时阿曼不赞成使用进口许可证来限制进口行为。阿曼也没有采取过反倾销、反补贴等保护措施。尽管阿曼采用了海湾合作委员会关于应急贸易救济的原则，但却并没有使用过任何应急贸易救济方面的措施。阿曼的技术规则和标准也日趋与海湾合作委员会保持一致。其10000多条标准中只有12条为国内独有，同时海湾合作委员会和阿曼的标准通常基于国际标准制定。

11. 阿曼并不适用任何出口关税，对于几种生鲜或者是冷冻鱼类会存在暂时性的出口禁止。同时阿曼也不会对出口进行补贴，但却设立了三个自由贸易区来促进出口。投资促进及出口发展机构会出台一些促进出口及开拓市场的措施。

12. 2008年关于政府采购的新法规生效，主要以公开招标的方式确定政府采购。阿曼是《政府采购协议》的观察员之一。关于知识产权的新法案延长了版权保护的期限，这一法案也在2008年生效。

13. 国有制在阿曼经济中广泛存在，尤其在石油和天然气、空运及海运、公共品、邮政服务、通信以及某些制造业尤其严重。自2008年最后一次贸易政策审议以来，阿曼的私有制进程停滞不前。

14. 阿曼的消费者保护机构在2011年建立。尽管阿曼正在考虑出台竞争法，但至今其国内并没有相关法律。然而，消费者保护机构呼吁政府限制垄断以及市场过分集中。此外，金融服务业以及通信业的行业机构可能会支持反竞争行为。

部门政策

15. 农业和渔业占阿曼GDP的比重刚刚超过1%，但是却涉及37%的经济活跃人口，这些人口通常是在温饱水平线上。生产围绕着家畜和大枣。政府的长期目标是将农业占GDP的份额提升到3%以上，农业的份额提升到2%以上。由于农业生产方面的挑战以及强劲的人口增长，阿曼实际上是农业产品净进口国。

16. 来自石油和天然气的收入占政府总收入的85%以及商品出口的70%，近年来原油对阿曼GDP的贡献率每年都有较大幅度的波动，大约在36%到49%之间。2007至2012年间石油生产和出口大幅上涨，同时天然气出口使得阿曼的经济受石油冲击减小。部分国有产油企业最大储油量可以达到全国产油量的80%。然而根据最近的发现，估计到2030年阿曼的石油储量将被大部分耗尽。其他诸如采矿以及采石活动对阿曼GDP的贡献率仅仅在0.3%左右。

17. 阿曼的制造业主要是能源密集型行业，并且在政府的多样化策略中起了重要作用。生产通常在免税区或者是特殊工业区进行。制造业出口额在2006到2012年间翻了两番。随着需求的增加，发电量也大幅上涨。

18. 服务业大约占阿曼GDP的35%，在许多服务领域，阿曼遵守了关贸总协定下的相关承诺。服务业很多分部门由国有企业控制，同时阿曼日益成为服务业净出口国。

展望

19. 在很大程度上，阿曼的经济前景取决于世界石油市场的发展。中期来看，公共投资可以保持相对高的增长率。政府的多样化及私有化政策以及人口因素将对其未来的发展起重要作用。

（王达译，戴臻校）

巴林贸易政策审议

经济环境

1. 自2007年上次审议以来，巴林王国的经济持续增长，尽管在此期间遭遇了全球金融危机、2011年紧张的国内局势、2012年的石油减产。2013年巴林经济增长主要由石油产业驱动，实际国内生产总值增长率预期可以达到4.8%。审议期间，巴林的经常账户出现盈余，2012年贸易盈余从2007年的28.65亿美元增加到67.95亿美元。年平均通货膨胀率仍然保持较低水平，大约在2%左右。受房租下降影响较大，2011年通货膨胀率大幅下降直至−0.4%，但在下半年通胀恢复到正常水平。

2. 自2008年以来，巴林实施了促进发展策略，尤其是旨在减少对石油和天然气高度依赖的2030经济愿景，因此需要多部门共同努力。以金融业主导的服务业对2012年巴林实际国内生产总值的贡献率为58%，基于比较优势建立的能源密集型产业（主要是电解铝及石油化学）对实际国内生产总值的贡献率为15.2%。

制度框架

3. 贸易政策的出台和实施由巴林工贸部（MOIC）负责。工贸部会向相关部门咨询，包括经济发展委员会在内的其他的机构直接或间接地对贸易政策的出台起到影响。甚至私人企业也可以通过商贸部的内阁对贸易政策的制定造成影响。在工贸部许可的范围内，全国委员会及其子委员会负责处理与WTO相关的问题。

4. 为了保持与WTO的义务相一致，巴林对其法律进行了审议与修改。自从其最后一次贸易政策审议以来，巴林出台了几部新的法律，包括《民航法》(2013)、涵盖反倾销反补贴在内的贸易救济法、安保条例（2011)，以及其他与政府采购和海上运输相关的法律。

5. 巴林是WTO创始成员之一，也是《信息技术协议》的签约方之一，同时也是《政府采购协议》观察员之一。巴林并没有直接或间接地牵扯到任何争端解决中。巴林对其所有的贸易伙伴都给予了最惠国待遇。在某些WTO协议下，巴林很难满足一系列的通报要求，尤其是与贸易有关的知识产权协议。

6. 巴林是海湾合作委员会的成员国之一，还加入了泛阿拉伯自由贸易委员会。在海湾贸易委员会的框架下，巴林与欧洲自由贸易联盟以及新加坡签订了自由贸易协定。同时巴林与一些国家如美国签署了双边自由贸易协议。巴林是海湾地区第一个与其他国家签订双边贸易协议的国家，紧随其后的是阿曼。海湾贸易委员会的国家元首们把这些协议看成是一种例外，之后的贸易协议都必须以集体的形式协商。2014年1月海湾贸易委员会评估了将来与其他国家和地区签订自由贸易协议的可能性。

贸易政策工具

7. 自2003年1月1日，巴林实施了海湾贸易委员会框架下的共同关税原则。2013年巴林对其最惠国待遇的贸易伙伴的平均关税为5.1%。除烟草外所有关税为从价税，同时对进口产品没有征收关税配额、公害率，及其他任何税目。对于海湾贸易委员会成员共同关税的例外包括酒精（125%）、烟草（替代关税，100%从价税）。根据WTO定义，农产品平均实施7.5%关税，非农产品平均实施4.6%关税。而根据国际标准工业分类法定义(第二版)，关税保护最低的部门是农业（为3%)，其次是采矿业和采石业（4.9%)，制造业(5.2%)。

8. 总体来说，巴林的关税政策向积极方面发展，对于初加工产品平均关税为3.9%，半成品平均关税4.8%，产成品平均关税为5.5%。巴林已经对其70.6%的关税项目进行约束，大多数关税的上限为35%；然而对于烟草和酒精制品，约束关税分别为100%和200%，这给关税水平的上涨留下了充足空间。巴林没有采取任何反倾销、反补贴及保障措施。税收减让可以作为投资促进手段来使用（在选择性的基础上）。

9. 所有与进口产品有关的文件都必须被原产国的巴林使馆所认证，同时巴林会出于健康、安全以及道德等原因对进出口产品实施非关税措施。在标准制定以及技术规则方面，巴林在很大程度上与其他海湾贸易委员会国家保持一致。

10. 在2010年，巴林建立了新的政府采购体制，且仍对其本国产品及海湾贸易委员会其他成员国的产品分别提供10%和5%的价格优惠。巴林本身没有竞争性法规，但是电信及金融部门却不存在垄断。

部门政策

11. 巴林的经济持续受石油及相关产业支配，尽管巴林的石油和天然气储备有限。纵览其2030年经济愿景，政府努力使经济多元化发展，尤其是借助金融业及制造业。2012年，石油分部门生产总值占国内生产总值的24.6%以及政府收入的75%。

12. 在巴林的经济份额中，农业只占了相当小的一部分，大约0.3%。由于缺少耕地以及充足的水供给，巴林实际上是食品净进口国。通过省补贴以及对农民优先贷款对农业进行补贴。农产品方面，巴林对其给予最惠国待遇的贸易伙伴实施平均为3%的单一关税。

13. 审议期间制造业持续增长，成为自碳氢化工和金融服务之后对经济产出贡献最大的行业。作为其多样化进程的一部分，巴林专注于高附加值、能源密集型产业，比如电解铝、石油化工、金属产品、钢产品等。这些行业由最大的国有企业控制，最明显的是巴林铝业（ALBA）和海湾石化工业公司（GPIC)。巴林允许外资对工业公司控股最高达100%。其对最惠国贸易伙伴生产的制成品平均单一关税为5.2%。

14. 巴林的服务业持续扩张，2012年为国内生产总值贡献率达58%。然而整个行业受金融危机及2011年国内紧张局势影响较大。作为巴林多样化发展的基石，金融业由巴林中央银行管理得井井有条。近年来，巴林专注于发展其伊斯兰银行以及保险行业，试图在海湾地区高度竞争的大环境下建立起一个利基市场。然而，银行业的规模仍然保持着关键的结构脆弱性。2013年8月，零售银行及批发银行的资产分别为国内生产总值的248%和390%。

15. 通信市场自2003年已经完成自由化，一家名为Viva Bahrain的移动运营商于2009年进入市场，成为由国家部分控股的BATELCO和Zain Bahrain之后的第三大运营商。作为通信市场的管理者，通信监管当局（TRA）阶段性的对市场进行审查以确保没有显著垄断的出现。

16. 巴林的交通运输行业已经在交通运输部的管理下进行了现代化改造，交通运输部负责巴林的交运基建系统，包括航空、港口、海运、陆地运输。一项涉及民航及海运的重要法规已经生效，在其帮助下空运及海运规则与国际实践保持一致。经历了巨额亏损后，2007年，海湾航空这家巴林航空领域的老大哥最终被国有企业Mumtalakat收购。

17. 巴林的旅游业利用了该国的文化和历史遗产，同时也吸收了其运动及商业旅游的潜在优势。但旅游业受2011年国内紧张局势影响较大，到访人数暴跌32.7%，2012年有所回升。2010年，文化部下属的旅游业部门负责巴林旅游活动的管理，同时该行业允许外资企业100%控股。

（王达译，戴臻校）

卡塔尔贸易政策审议

1. 自上次审议以来，卡塔尔经济显著增长。按实际价值计算，其GDP大部分时间保持在12%至26%的两位数增幅。就人均国内生产总值而言，卡塔尔位居世界第二。随着对经济多样化的强调，卡塔尔在以知识为基础的基础设施方面着手投资，其中包括改善教育、基础设施和医疗保健。

2. 审议期间，强劲而不断增长的货物贸易顺差驱使当前账户不断上扬，并在2012年达到峰值2240亿里亚尔。服务贸易收支仍保持在略有逆差的水平。近年来，由于卡塔尔的海外投资不断增加，其资本和金融项目一般数额大且处于逆差，但在此期间（除2011年外），国际收支仍保持顺差。

3. 显著的出口增长主导了贸易发展，并于2012年创下了48406.5亿里亚尔的最高水平。自2007年以来，由于包括相关较强能源价格在内的石油和天然气的强劲出口，出口几乎翻了三倍。非能源出口也在此期间扩大，2012年占总出口的12%。尽管增速慢于出口，但进口也在增长且日趋多样化。其中，机械和交通运输设备进口占据主导地位，反映了资本投资和配套基础设施建设的发展。

4. 2013年新埃米尔接任，新政府也相应组建，然而主要的政策转向或转变却并未发生。卡塔尔依旧鼓励开放贸易和投资环境。同时政府还计划通过降低准入门槛，强化竞争以创建更加有竞争力的经济体。作为国家发展战略的一部分，卡塔尔《服务贸易总协定》进一步深化服务贸易自由化。

5. 自2001年签署GCC经济协议以来，卡塔尔和其他海湾合作委员会成员一直致力于实现更高程度的合作，特别是2003年建立了关税同盟。目前，在海湾委员会成员间有一个共同的对外关税(CET)，但内部的边防哨所之间仍在进行操作，并且每个海湾合作委员会成员通过其各自的海关管理尚保有自主性。虽然最惠国贸易对于卡塔尔进口和出口仍然占主导地位，但在该期间内海湾合作委员会贸易增加，目前已占卡塔尔进口的约15%、出口的7%。海湾合作委员会之间的主要贸易伙伴是阿联酋和沙特阿拉伯王国。

6. 根据卡塔尔的外商投资法律，外国投资者一般仅限于49%的少数股权，但经授权后，在某些领域（农业、工业、卫生、教育、旅游、开发和利用自然资源、能源和矿业、咨询服务、技术服务、IT服务、文化服务、体育服务、休闲服务、分销服务）也可以允许有100%的外资持股，外国投资者也被赋予了一定权力如基金的无限制转让和抵制征用的保证。卡塔尔利用双边投资协定来鼓励投资，目前有22个此类协议。

7. 审议期间海关的发展集中在建立通关单一窗口项目。自从2011年将其渐进引进以来，单一窗口使得通关时间降低到15分钟，检查率低至5%，并且为交易者提供了高品质的增值服务。超过90%的已登记的进口商和出口商使用该系统来促进贸易。预期在未来它将被整合到一个较宽的GCC级单窗口系统中。

8. 在进口保护方面，关税仍然很低，卡塔尔保持很少的非关税贸易壁垒。截至2013年，由于有几个峰值，其简单平均关税税率为4.7%，大多数关税为5%，低于海湾合作委员会共同的对外关税水平。关税峰值出现在烟草产品的20个税号和钢铁产品的6个税号，钢铁关税目前超过世贸组织约束值。此外，还有27个税号违禁品和50个税号需要特殊的进口手续。卡塔尔没有任何关于进口许可证、装运前预检验，或应急措施（反倾销、反补贴措施以及保障措施）的立法。

9. 审议期间，为提升多样化出口基础，卡塔尔建立了它的第一个出口发展机构。并在2012年创制了出口发展战略，它包括评估企业的出口准备的规定和设置卡塔尔的出口目标。还有一些应用于出口的规则或措施，卡塔尔对出口确实不征税，征费或采用许可。此外，很少有限制或禁令，但进口的禁令也同样适用于出口。

10. 尽管政府大力支持私营部门投资和商业机构，卡塔尔经济仍严重依赖国有企业。根据2009年的一项研究，公共和混合部门产值约占国内生产总值的60%。在卡塔尔，建立企业受几项法律的规制，包括投资法，它决定了企业实体的类型和外国所有权的份额，因此许多企业的建立必须有一个卡塔尔合作伙伴。2010年对法律的修订放松了若干对于独资和有限责任公司的规定。一个工业项目的立项，需要相关当局签发许可证。

11. 在知识产权保护方面，为了使一些关于专利、商标、地理标志和集成电路的必要规则归位，卡塔尔在2002—2006年颁布了若干法律，但许多此类法律尚未实施，因为必要的执行法规尚未签署。

12. 能源部门，特别是天然气仍然是卡塔尔工业产出和贸易的支柱。由于储量居世界第三，审议期间卡塔尔产出持续增加并且在2012年出口达到了最高水平。由于大部分天然气以液化天然气出口，所以有容量的限制和投资必要的基础设施，以保持出口水平不断提高。此外，2005年暂停对卡塔尔最大天然气田的进一步开发已被继续延期，这将潜在限制未来产出增长。

13. 审议期间，卡塔尔的银行和保险业经历了一些成长和发展，特别是始于2005年的卡塔尔金融中心（QFC）的建立，以及伊斯兰金融分部门的发展。为吸引国际银行公司、保险业务以及相关金融服务入驻卡塔尔，该中心在自由贸易区内的规定之下发挥效力。为了创建一个为卡塔尔金融服务的监管机构，2012年发起了一系列改革，但仍有一些部门和单行法规供该中心操作。

14. 近年来，多元化投资在一些服务行业如交通运输、建筑、旅游业已经帮助提振经济，并且预计在2022年世界杯筹备阶段将继续下去，因为卡塔尔将扩充酒店，发展铁路网络，并投资于大型基础设施建设项目。在教育和医疗保健领域的投资，将作为卡塔尔2030年国家远景规划的一部分，开发卡塔尔以知识为基础的经济。

（娄承蓉译，戴臻校）

加纳贸易政策审议

1. 加纳上次贸易政策审议是在 2008 年 5 月，自此以后，该国凭借运转良好的民主制度，丰富的自然资源和良好的治理吸引了外国投资，并促进了强劲的经济增长。它的社会政策集中于卫生和教育以及消除贫困。这些努力已显著地提高了加纳的人均收入（2012 年约为 1600 美元）和人类发展指数。然而，超过四分之一的人口仍然生活在 1.25 美元/天的贫困线以下。因此，挑战在于保持目前的经济扩张，以及减少不平等现象，确保将更多的经济利益惠及穷人。

2. 加纳的宏观经济表现相当混杂。最近几年，继大量的货币贬值和通货膨胀率年均超过 10%之后，扩张性财政和货币政策再次引发了不可持续的财政赤字。尤其是，加纳没有达到几个主要的趋同标准，该标准适用于在六个不参与西非货币联盟的西非经济共体成员之间拟建的西非国家经济共同体西非货币区（WAMZ）。在 WAMZ 框架之下，加纳的塞地将被捆绑为一个共同的区域货币。2013 年 7 月，政府试图通过增加税收特别是贸易来缓和日益增加的财政赤字。国际贸易税收份额已经上升到国内生产总值的 4%，超过财政收入的三分之一，从而显现出为了为财政融资政府对国际贸易税收的依赖。

3. 加纳的贸易动态扩展。基本上由三个主要的初级商品（黄金、原油及未加工的可可粉）构成的出口，审议期间翻了三倍多，并在 2012 年受强大的国际价格和产量增加的影响达到 140 亿美元，而进口则增长更快，达 170 亿美元。2012 年，外国直接投资由 2007 年不到 40 亿美元猛增至 160 亿美元。这些投资已大多流入金矿和石油行业。吸引投资到其他经济部门仍然是一个政策挑战，虽然加纳曾成功地改善其企业经营环境并取得了部分成就包括新的商业法庭、土地管理改革和新企业注册手续等；还有创新进程也得到了发展，以帮助执行知识产权。

4. 加纳在全国范围内对信息通信技术进行了大量投资，特别是在光纤宽带方面，以提高其互联网连接速度。配备计算机的学校数量持续上升，宽带价格显著下降，加纳的移动通信成本是非洲最低的几个国家之一。政府还致力于改进道路网络及其安全性。加纳已通过法律，以促进中小型企业私人信贷的便利化，而这也经常被列为阻碍撒哈拉以南非洲生产和贸易的一个主要障碍。结果是借贷双方的合法权益均得以改善，交易也更为安全。

5. 2013 年修订的投资法提高了最低资本，它是指外国人必须投资到高于加纳 1994 年《服务贸易总协定》中的水平承诺，不包括来自国外的竞争新活动。这可能会主要影响小型投资者，特别是那些来自西非国家经济共同体（西非共同体）其他成员的。根据该法，人员和资本的自由流动已经完全确立。2013 年，西非经共体结束了该地区共同对外关税（CET）的谈判，那些与欧盟签订经济伙伴协定的国家是加纳的主要贸易伙伴。总体而言，西非经共体一体化进程缓慢。

6. 自上次贸易政策审议以来，加纳已经修改了其运输系统的几个特点，结果是中转量几乎翻了一倍，表明交易者对适当的贸易便利化措施做出了迅速的赞成的回应。但是，对于跨境贸易，仍然需要做出相当大的努力，以便使进出口手续一致符合现代经济标准。具体问题包括：通关进程缓慢，扫描器故障或低效率应用，多重目的地检验机构的海关官员重复化以及频繁的货物实体检验。此外，港口业务拥挤且昂贵，造成了货物长期积压和额外的港口费用，同时众多的合规性检查机构进一步减慢了进程并增加了成本。正如近年来增长相对缓慢的货运业务所显示的，这些问题构成了目前制约加纳公司竞争力的主要瓶颈。

7. 由于健康、安全和机密等原因，处于边界位置的合格评定程序需要合理化，特别是那些“高风险货物”（HRGs）。海关对高风险货物的分类始于 20 世纪 90 年代，但分类是有问题的，因为有些产品要被食品药品管理局以及加纳标准局检查两次。虽然加纳已在 2012 年实现 SPS 立法现代化，1973 年标准法案并未对推荐性标准和技术法规做出明显区分：受管制产品的加纳产品标准接受技术法规和进口检查。

8. 加纳的最惠国关税于2008年至2013年间被频繁修改，期间其平均水平为12.8%，包含0%、5%、10%、20%的段位，最后两个适用于40%以上的税目。继加纳在2012年采用HS税则归类之后，2013年，本该低于GATT/WTO标准的关税份额从14.7%上升到总税目的16.3%，但仍然是相当低的。加纳还有在非农及大多数农产品关税水平为零的束缚，但在现实中许多其他税费（ODCs）被应用在所有的进口上，且其数目和发生率也随之增加。同时，普遍存在的关税和加纳法规中其他进口税可豁免制度有效地让许多运营商不支付关税、ODCs、增值税或其他税项。每年约25%的其他进口关税是因各种各样的豁免而流失。这反映了加纳经济结构和关税制度之间的不协调。西非国家经济共同体CET的应用可以稳定加纳的关税制度并解决部分不协调的状况。

9. 为了多元化加纳的出口基础，促进非传统产品出口，几种方案已经就绪。主要项目包括出口企业市场准入便利化，出口产品开发的技术咨询服务，贸易信息服务以及与出口相关的人力资源开发。其主要实体是加纳出口促进管理局（GEPA），资金主要来源于出口发展和农业投资基金，本身资金向所有非石油进口征收0.5%。为识别和支持新出口产品，GEPA与在日内瓦的UNCTAD/WTO国际贸易中心密切合作。同时，如有出口退税的要求则需要花很长的时间来支付，而2012年出口加工区的出口为以往累计进出口水平三倍的事实也表明，其制度需要重新进行审议。

10. 自2007年以来农业已经大规模增长，通过适当的政策支撑可可的生产环境和不断增长的世界价格。加纳是全球第二大可可生产商，每年出口超过20亿。可可的采购、定价和出口均由政府垄断，这一点至今尚未通知WTO。其他农产品的国内价格动态增长，成比例地提高了农民的名义收入。加纳实现了将政府支出的10%分配给农业的新伙伴关系目标，这使得粮食产量相应增加，且快于人口增长。平均水平接近16%的关税是主要的贸易政策工具。除进口外，对某些出口商品增值税的豁免，也是贸易政策的主要工具。

11. 与此相反，渔业和畜牧业分部门的经济增长一直低迷。近年来，林地和伐木业更是显著负增长，特别是在2011年和2012年采取了限制非法活动，试图阻止乱砍滥伐的措施之后。加纳正在谋求进口木材以利用其闲置的木材加工能力。受非法捕捞、缺乏船只注册和适度许可框架的影响，若想渔业部门增长，就必须大量投资。原则上，要求外商参与渔业部门时以与当地合作伙伴合资的形式，而在实际上大多数捕鱼业是外商独资。

12. 加纳也拥有丰富的金矿藏，受大幅增长的产量尤其是世界价格的影响，2012年的出口价值近50亿美元，约为2007年的三倍。然而2013年，黄金价格下跌了25%以上，同石油部门一样，凸显出收入稳定机制的必要。小规模开采行业员工总数超过50万人。虽然非加纳人不允许从事小规模开采，但自2008年以来，没有许可证的外来矿工为开采金矿而大量涌入，2013年5月有数百人被捕并被逐出加纳。

13. 自2010年石油生产开始，加纳的经济不断上扬，这触发了第四个国家能源监管机构的建立。为了管理石油收入，以负责、透明、清晰和可持续的方式为公民增益，加纳还设置了两个石油主权财富基金。当需要促进就业时，新的“本地拥有本土参与的石油行业—政策框架”要求运营商在所有的业务中，包括石油区的奖励、油田牌照、钻井、采油升降许可证、航空、交通、餐饮等，优先考虑那些拥有必要的资质、能力和经验的加纳人。外国人如要参与，则必须与加纳人合作。后者应履行至少5%的股权，接受部长的自由裁量权审议，并不得转让给非加纳人。

14. 加纳政府还于2014年1月宣布，这个本土参与政策会延展至整个能源分部门。同时，2013年，国有炼油厂的生产陷入停滞，部分原因是出于投资考虑，还有因政府期望重新分配收入，理顺价格波动而施加的低价格。对此，政府提高了石油产品炼油前价格及其效用，以使其与进口成本相匹配，从而逐步淘汰化石燃料补贴。下游石油工业已被进一步解除管制，包括采购、仓储、批量分布的石油产品。这将提高市场效率，但燃料短缺直到2014年初依旧持续。自2008年以来，尽管国内停电频繁，但加纳已成为电力净出口国且仍在不断增长。发电装机总量从2004年的1800兆瓦提高到约2828兆瓦；发电业开放竞争，但输配电则为垄断。

管制电价在 2007 年和 2013 年间翻了四番，其中 2013 年增幅最大。

15. 制造业部门的业绩有好有坏，既有农业加工业扩展也有拜倒在加纳国营冶炼厂的铝产量。为保证本地钢厂投入，对废金属的出口禁令已到位，而进口禁令归位则是为了提升当地制药能力。在 2011 年，加纳出台了详细的国家产业政策。

16. 服务行业的一些市场准入限制到位，主要集中在某些海上运输、贸易以及某些零售业。公路运输的自由环境有助于促进贸易和吸引投资。同样，一个宽松的制度也普遍存在于航空运输部门，其中几条从加纳到其他国家的航线服务由第三方国家来提供，这在很大程度上解释了分部门的活力。在金融服务业，自 2007 年以来大量新的外资银行已经加入了加纳银行，并且国家参与程度在削弱，与之相关的不良贷款率也在下降。

17. 总之，由于丰富的原料、良好的治理和政策改革，作为非洲撒哈拉以南地区最佳投资地之一，加纳引人注目。其中有前景的行业主要有农业—食品加工、石油下游产业、天然气、矿物加工业以及能源和采矿相关的服务分行业。如果当局着手收紧货币和财政政策，并彻底调整进口政策，其发展前景将被进一步夯实。加纳某些支持经济改革的活动表明，如果正确的政策落实，其他部门也可以发展得很好。

（娄承蓉译，戴臻校）

东加勒比国家组织贸易政策审议

1. WTO成员中，属于东加勒比国家组织（OECS）的包括坐落在小安的列斯群岛的六个主权国家：安提瓜和巴布达、多米尼加、格林纳达、圣基茨和尼维斯、圣卢西亚、圣文森特和格林纳丁斯。OECS中的WTO成员都是很小很容易受到冲击的经济体，其人均GDP从6300美元（圣文森特和格林纳丁斯）到13000美元（安提瓜和巴布达）不等。这些国家所在地区容易受到自然灾害的影响，主要是飓风的影响。OECS中的WTO成员经济主要依赖旅游业，旅游业占GDP比重从格林纳达的24.2%到安提瓜和巴布达的接近75%。在很小范围和不同程度上，金融服务部门对GDP和就业也做出了重要贡献，建筑业也是如此。对大多数OECS的WTO成员，农业、制造业对GDP的贡献甚微，而多米尼加的农业、圣基茨和尼维斯的制造业则是例外。

2. 它们微弱的经济基础、自然灾害的影响以及高度依赖进口使得OECS的WTO成员易受外部冲击的侵害。事实上，在此次贸易审议期间，国际金融危机连带自然灾害严重影响了此地区的经济。因此，OECS在2011年稍微转好之前的2009—2010年，GDP缩减10%，2012年再次缩减。GDP下降主要是因为来自北美和欧洲的游客减少，以及人均花费的下降。此外，OECS的WTO成员遭受这一地区金融部门问题的影响，包括CL金融集团的破产（特立尼达和多巴哥）通过它的子公司CLIXO和BAICO引发了传播效应。这两家当地银行和一家大的离岸金融机构的破产重创了安提瓜和巴布达的金融部门。2013年主要是由于服务业出口的上升，GDP才有所回升。2013年发布的预测共同实际增长率为1.2%。总而言之，2007—2013年，OECS中WTO成员的经济基本是停滞的。

3. OECS中WTO成员有共同的货币政策和中央银行，即东加勒比中央银行（ECCB），东加勒比元持续盯住美元。ECCB同时也经营区域市场的政府债券。ECCB的任务是保持通胀率可控，而通胀率由消费者价格指数（CPI）来衡量。CPI从2008年的6.5%降低到2009年的不到1%，反映了需求的下降，2010年和2011年有所回升，但是2012年和2013年下降主要是由于商品价格的降低，同时反映出被抑制的总需求。

4. 已修订的《巴斯特尔协议》建立了OECS经济联盟的基础，其经济联盟需要在OECS层面上让财政政策逐步协调。然而至今，每个OECS的WTO成员大体上还是独立制定财政政策。尽管OECS的WTO成员认为它们2009年总体财政赤字的上升是全球金融危机的结果，但是OECS国家的财政表现也有很大不同。糟糕的财政情况主要是因为收入的下降和持续性的高水平花费。为了应对此次危机，OECS的WTO成员实行了财政改革和巩固的方案。关于税收改革，方法包括取消消费税而代之以增值税（VAT）（圣基茨和尼维斯、圣卢西亚、多米尼加），使燃油税合法化（圣卢西亚、安提瓜和巴布达），改革消费税（圣基茨和尼维斯、安提瓜和巴布达、多米尼加、圣文森特和格林纳丁斯）。与此同时，债务重组战略已开始寻求债务减免。目前来看，采取的这些措施似乎是有效的，OECS的WTO成员的总体财政赤字从2009年的占GDP4.6%下降至2012年占GDP的2.4%。公共债务占GDP的比重已经从上次贸易审议时的100%下降至83%。

5. OECS的WTO成员持续以周期性储蓄小于投资为特征，这需要充足的资本流向外部经常账户中的财政赤字部门。经常账户赤字连同资产负债表赤字在2008年达到顶峰，约占GDP的30%，2012年占GDP的17%，此后一直在下降。主要是因为进口的下降和旅游收入的恢复。OECS的WTO成员在商品贸易方面有很大的赤字，而它们的服务业则有盈余。2012年，商品贸易余额的总赤字占GDP的32%，服务贸易余额的盈余占GDP的14%。

6. 贸易在OECS的WTO成员中扮演着主要角色，接近于它们加总GDP的100%，因此这些国家是商品的净进口国和服务的净出口国。在此次贸易政策审议期间，出口额依然相对稳定，但是进口额大幅下降，只占危机前水平的接近 80%。OECS 的 WTO 成员的主要贸易伙伴是美国、欧盟、特立尼达拉和多巴哥岛、巴巴多斯以及加拿大。

7. 自从上次审议后一个重要的发展情况是 2010 年 6 月签署的已修订的《巴斯特尔协议》建立了 OECS 经济联盟。此协议呼吁商品、人口、资本和服务的自由流动。虽然此经济联盟 2011 年 1 月就已成立，但尚未全面实施，因为还有很多工作需要做，需要协调程序、体系和关税日程。

8. 在 2008 年 10 月 OECS 的 WTO 成员与欧盟签署了《加勒比—欧盟经济伙伴协定（EPA)》，这是它们第一次和欧盟达成一个互惠自由贸易协定，据此，OECS 的 WTO 成员对欧洲的大部分贸易承诺了一个安排日程上的逐步的税收缩减。对 OECS 的 WTO 成员来说，主要的挑战与该协定的实施有关，特别是处理改革需要确保国内立法部门遵从《加勒比—欧盟经济伙伴协定（EPA)》的要求。若要做到这些，OECS 的 WTO 成员需要处理在以前贸易政策审议中成员提出的各种问题。

9. 在此次审议期间，作为事件的结果，现在 OECS 的 WTO 成员的国际贸易承诺围绕四个同心圆：(1) OECS 经济联盟；(2) 加勒比共同市场和加勒比单个市场和经济（CSME)；(3) 加勒比欧盟经济伙伴协定（EPA）和其他类似的未来协定；(4) 多边贸易体系。

10. 虽然它们参与了加勒比共同市场，OECS 的 WTO 成员也与加拿大、哥伦比亚、古巴、哥斯达黎加、多米尼加共和国、委内瑞拉签订了双边贸易协定。

11. 自从 2007 年上次审议之后，OECS 的 WTO 成员的贸易政策协调度增加，贸易协调度包括区域内的应急措施、竞争性政策和财政政策。OECS 的 WTO 成员的立法的相似性方便了示范立法的运用。这种示范法律的运用提高了国家间的透明度和相似度。尤其在服务领域最为明显，例如：在电信行业，国家法律遵循东加勒比电信管理局（ECTEL）模型；在银行业领域，由东加勒比中央银行设计的单一银行制度已经实施。然而，即使是根据一般示范法律，国内法律也必须由国家立法部门起草和通过。此外，更为常见的是，在区域和多边层面上，整合改变的决定是缓慢的，因为除了一部新法律的批准和发行，条例的实施还必须在每个国家做出准备。因为整个进程并未完成，因此有时候实施并非是有效的。对于一些 WTO 协定的细则的实施也是如此。希望在 OECS 经济联盟的完全合并中，这种状况可以改变。在五个区域内法律的起草和实施许可已经移交给 OECS。

12. 在它们参与多边贸易体系时，OECS 的 WTO 成员就 WTO 要求的灵活性不断强调它们的地位，声称 WTO 应考虑它们作为小的易受冲击的经济体的发展需要。它们也提倡加强保护机制，包括技术合作，来帮助履行其对 WTO 的承诺，引导制度、法律、经济的调整，这些是贸易自由化所需要的。

13. 遵从通报义务对 OECS 的 WTO 成员仍然是一个挑战，即使在某些（比如补贴）领域它们已经做出努力去跟随通报日期的步伐。而在农业、卫生和动植物检验检疫措施方面则缺乏通报。这也部分反映了人力资源限制的重要性，凸显了 OECS 的 WTO 成员之间在贸易政策制定和实施方面持续寻求更高程度合作的重要性。

14. OECS 的 WTO 成员的投资体制大体是开放的，主要的例外是需要获得转让土地所有权许可证，外国投资才可以享受国民待遇。在审议期间，安提瓜和巴布达、格林纳达、圣卢西亚废止它们的财政刺激法案，代之以更为广阔的刺激程序，这种程序并未提供明确的出口补贴也未施加本地内容要求。在其他三个 OECS 国家，这种程序也在进行中。

15. 在审议期间，OECS 的 WTO 成员已经持续引进方法来使贸易便利化。多米尼加、格林纳达、圣卢西亚、圣文森特和格林纳丁斯使用不同版本的海关数据和管理自动化系统（ASYCUDA）来进行海关处理和清关，而安提瓜和巴布达以及圣基茨和尼维斯则仍在向 ASYCUDA 系统转移的过程中。海关清关时间从五个小时（安提瓜和巴布达）到两天（圣文森特和格林纳丁斯）不等。OECS 的 WTO 成员使用交易价作为海关估值，除了格林纳达使用的是最小进口价格。

16. OECS 的 WTO 成员持续依赖国际贸易税收，主要是关税、海关服务费、消费税和环保费，这些比上次审议时的依赖程度有所减少。在 2012

年，OECS的WTO成员收取的国际贸易税收约占总税收的33%，在此次审议期间大多数OECS的WTO成员着手推进改革，目的在于降低对贸易税收的依赖度，主要是引进增值税（VAT），以适用于货物和服务业。增值税率各个国家不等，从10%～17%。增值税的实施是上次贸易政策审议时所推荐的。

17. OECS的WTO成员采用加勒比共同市场的共同对外关税，除了免责条款外。几乎所有的税收细目绑定在每个国家，平均适用的最惠国待遇税收仍然在11%。根据WTO定义，OECS对农产品平均进口关税是19.1%，大大超出非农产品的关税（9.4%）。在此次审议期间，所有的OECS的WTO成员转向应用编码HS2007的商品目录。然而，就税收结构和税收水平而言，即使是根据加勒比共同市场的共同外部关税，关税也因国家的不同而有很大差别。因此，主要的协调还需要实施。只有很少关税细目使用从量税，没有国家采用关税税率配额。海关服务费从多米尼加的3%到安提瓜和巴布达的10%不等。唯一在其WTO关税进程中记入海关服务费的国家是圣基茨和尼维斯。海关服务费适用于所有进口商品，包括从其他OECS的WTO成员的进口。

18. OECS的WTO成员在与第三方贸易时使用进口许可。大多数许可证自动发放；但非自动发放的许可证依然使用，这些主要是影响农业以及与农业有关的商品。OECS的WTO成员的一些特定商品，非自动发放的许可证的许可与国内购买的此种商品相关。

19. 独立的标准体现了每个OECS的WTO成员的功能。就其选取的标准和技术要求所需的结构、标准、程序，OECS的WTO成员是很相似。技术规定和标准采取国际标准，格林纳达、圣基茨和尼维斯、圣卢西亚进行认证。在审议期间，安提瓜和巴布达以及格林纳达通过了度量衡的立法程序。

20. 在此次审议期间，没有一个OECS成员向WTO卫生与植物卫生委员会通知任何措施。OECS的WTO成员没有任何卫生与植物卫生措施的详细目录。自从上次审议以来，安提瓜和巴布达以及圣基茨和尼维斯已起草出适合卫生与植物卫生措施的法律。

21. 因为一些免责条款，OECS的WTO成员并未使用出口许可。只有安提瓜和巴布达在一些商品中施加出口税。

22. 传统上，出口商品受益于税收刺激。OECS的WTO成员的六个国家已经就补贴与反补贴措施向WTO委员会通报了它们的财政刺激法案，即提供出口补贴。这种财政刺激方案在一定时间减轻了关税和所得税，深化了投资的规模出口目录。安提瓜和巴布达、格林纳达、圣卢西亚已经废除了这些法案，其余三个国家在2015年底WTO总理事会规定的截止日期之前也在废除进程中。安提瓜和巴布达、圣卢西亚、圣文森特和格林纳丁斯设立了自由贸易区，在此区域内，免除企业的关税和其他进口税。

23. OECS的WTO成员没有国家程序来处理出口信用、保险、担保。对制造业出口商品的保险业务由东加勒比中央银行提供，包括政治和商业风险，于2009年终止。

24. OECS的WTO成员实施了一些刺激方案来鼓励和提升国内和国外投资。在此次审议期间，安提瓜和巴布达起草了新的刺激程序来代替它们的财政刺激法案。主要的改变是更改了出现在以往法律中的出口补贴要素，以便从2015年使出口补贴逐步淘汰。其余OECS成员也在相应地改变它们的财政刺激法律的进程中。此外，特定部门刺激也都在适当给予。例如，一些国家通过酒店援助法案对旅游部门给予刺激，农业和小型企业也受到刺激措施的影响。

25. 没有一个OECS的WTO成员有适当的功能性竞争政策立法。然而2008年1月成立、总部坐落于苏里南的加勒比竞争委员会，在加勒比共同市场层面上负责竞争问题和执法。此外，OECS国家统一在2015年前简化东加勒比竞争局面。

26. 所有OECS的WTO成员对一些产品以最高价格和最高涨幅的方式来采取价格控制。从多米尼加的5种产品到圣文森特和格林纳丁斯的100个项目，产品覆盖包括基本的食物项目、燃料和天然气、肥料和某些建筑材料。营销机构在所有的OECS的WTO成员运作，主要在农业领域。

27. 没有一个OECS的WTO成员参加WTO的政府采购协定。在审议期间，安提瓜和巴布达、多米尼加、圣基茨和尼维斯通过了关于政府采购的新法律；这种法律至今在安提瓜和巴布达并未实行。OECS的WTO成员一般提供公开的和选择性的投标。公开投标一般用于较大的工程和需要捐赠者的规则的时候。当地或区域的供应商不允许有偏好，除了多米尼加。

28. OECS的WTO成员在知识产权方面有了重大进展。多米尼加在上次审议时已起草了有关知识产权的法律，但是这个法律并未付诸实施；法律在此次审议阶段生效。格林纳达在2011和2012年引进版权、专利和商标法，草拟了地理标识的法律，设计了集成电路的图纸，保护物种多样性、未披露信息也在考虑中。然而，即使出现这些进展，仍需进一步的努力才可以在国家立法中充分体现知识产权协定。

29. 农业在OECS的WTO成员中与以前相比扮演了更微小的角色，农业部门受逐渐减少的香蕉产量、自然灾害（例如格林纳达的肉豆蔻），以及圣基茨和尼维斯的糖产业的消亡的影响。相对重要的部门在OECS国家间差别也很大，从安提瓜和巴布达的几乎没有到多米尼加的较多。保护的程度也有所差别，一些国家寻求非关税壁垒来保护它们的生产者。在大多数OECS国家中工业活动仅限于生产饮料、洗涤剂和其他一些轻工业；圣基茨和尼维斯是个例外，那里在发展电子部件行业。

30. 服务业特别是旅游业及相关产业总体来说是GDP的主要贡献者。OECS的WTO成员的服务业各个部门大体对贸易和外国投资开放。所有的OECS的WTO成员都有国内和离岸金融服务活动。在审议期间，OECS的WTO成员的金融部门已经受到国际金融危机的影响。对安提瓜和巴布达的影响是最大的。这个国家的斯坦福国际银行的倒闭被预测为消耗GDP的20%。在审议期间，受到全球危机的影响，OECS的WTO成员已经对单个单位的陆上和离岸部门加强监管。（除了国内银行，它们是由东加勒比中央银行监管的。）

31. OECS中的五个国家（除了安提瓜和巴布达）有共同的电信政策。东加勒比电信管理局（ECTEL）是它们的管理机构，它协调着五个国家的国家电信监管委员会（NTRCs）。即使实行自由化，市场还是由一些参与者控制，电信费与国际比较仍然很高。在安提瓜和巴布达，国家垄断提供了国内固定路线服务，而一个私营操控者则提供国内长距离固定路线服务。

32. 在海上运输中，所有OECS的WTO成员设置条件为外国拥有国旗的船只。没有一个OECS的WTO成员对国际乘客和货物海上运输服务实行限制。没有政府或其他货物为国内船只或者政府拥有或操作的船只保留。商业港口是政府拥有的，一般来说由国有港口当局管理。空运政策在OECS层面由国内航空管理会制定。OECS的WTO成员的所有的主要机场和海港分别由各自的政府拥有，由国有当局管理。

33. 在大多数OECS的WTO成员中，旅游业直接或间接占GDP很大比重。从旅游业到建筑业、分销服务业、电力行业、农业和制造业有很重要的外溢效应。寄宿旅客的主要来源国仍然是加勒比国家、美国、英国、加拿大。在国家层面制定旅游政策。所有的OECS成员对旅馆业的发展提供财政刺激，包括关税和公司所得税的免除。

（刘欣译，戴臻校）

中国贸易政策审议

1. 审议期间（2012—2014），中国经济经历了稳定的增长。2012年与2013年实际GDP增长率均为7.7%，预计2014年该增长率为7.5%。推动中国经济增长的动因是以个人消费为主的强劲的国内需求。政府通过扩张性的财政政策、增加收入及增加信贷供应等方式刺激内需。又通过包括结构化减税在内的具体措施继续促进消费扩张。中国强劲的内需（包括进口）持续为全球经济做着贡献。由于商品价格下降，工资适度增长及对国内食品及能源价格的进一步控制，2012年和2013年的消费品价格上涨较2011年的5.4%有所下降。

2. 中国传统的对外经常账户顺差显示国民储蓄超过投资。过去几年中，消费的快速增长在某种程度上降低了中国的储蓄—投资缺口。这表现为较低的经常账户盈余（从占2010年GDP的4%降为2013年的2%），然而储蓄和投资水平仍然非常高，分别占国内生产总值的50%和47%。

3. 审议期间，中国继续实施积极的财政政策，财政支出较收入有更快的增长。财政赤字在2012年达到了GDP的1.7%，预计2013年会达到GDP的1.9%。虽然中央政府债务水平仍属适度，占2012年GDP的14.9%，但政府总债务水平却相当高，截至2012年底达到GDP的39.4%。中国继续促进民营经济在经济中的参与程度。民营企业、个体工业和个体工商户的数量都在不断增加。然而，国家在经济中的参与程度仍然相对较高，作为公共部门控制固定资产投资约40%，占出口总额的约三分之二。

4. 审议期间，为了应对通货膨胀压力和保持经济发展势头，中国的货币政策主要以微调措施为主。在2013年，包括进一步深化利率市场化在内的若干政策变化被提出，金融机构现在允许自主确定贷款利率。

5. 中国人民银行（PBC）采取一篮子货币作为参考，继续保持“有管理的浮动汇率制度”。审议期间，银行间即期外汇市场人民币/美元汇率的变动幅度扩大了两倍，从2012年的0.5%到1%，从2014年3月的1%到2%。更为灵活的汇率，反映了经济基本面的发展，对促进进口消费增长具有重要作用。事实上，从2005年汇率改革到2013年底，人民币无论是在名义或是在实际上都经历了大幅升值。人民银行在增强人民币汇率弹性的同时采取了促进外汇交易的措施。简化了经常项目跨境人民币业务流程，同时提出了逐步使人民币可兑换一定的资本账户交易的政策。另外，取消了外汇账户开立的一些限制要求。

6. 中国已成为世界上最大的贸易国（不包括欧盟内部贸易）。审议期间，中国货物出口和进口规模迅速扩大，其中2013年出口总额达2.21万亿美元，进口额达1.95万亿美元。然而在2013年，商品出口和进口份额在GDP中的比重却分别下降到24%和21.3%（从2010年的26.7%和23.7%）。同年，工业品出口占总出口额的94%，仍然在中国出口中占主导地位。在工业品中，办公设备、电信设备、纺织品和服装仍然是中国的主要出口产品。行业内贸易在中国越来越重要，2013年工业品进口占总进口额58%。中国的主要进口工业品有办公设备、通信设备和化工品。在2013年，燃料和其他矿物产品占中国进口量的近30%，而农产品进口占总量的约8%。

7. 2013年，中国主要向欧盟、美国、中国香港、日本、韩国以及东盟国家出口商品，主要从欧盟、韩国、日本、中国台北、美国、澳大利亚以及东盟国家进口商品。服务贸易占中国出口总额的8.7%，进口总额的14.4%。

8. 中国仍然是吸收外国直接投资的大国。2013年FDI流入达到1176亿美元。吸引FDI的主要部门有制造业、房地产、批发和零售贸易。外资来源仍然集中于中国香港。2013年，香港对华投资占全部FDI总额的62.4%。紧随其后的是新加坡、日本、欧盟、英属维尔京群岛、韩国、美国和中国台北。2012年，中国对外直接投资总额达701亿美元，其中三分之二的份额流入其主要投资对象香港。

9. 商务部（MOFCOM）仍然主要负责拟订和执行全国经济中与贸易相关的政策。国家发改委（NDRC）主要负责拟订社会发展政策。其他参与贸易政策制定和执行的部委有：农业部、环境保护部、财政部、工业和信息化部、国土资源部和交通运输部。审议期间，中国成立了全面深化改革领导小组，负责改革总体设计。通过允许市场在资源分配方面发挥更加决定性的作用、改革国有企业和鼓励私人所有权等方式，深化经济体制改革。通过加速实施自由贸易协定和发展中国（上海）自由贸易试验区和开放边境地区，使贸易和投资体制更加开放和可预测。

10. 2001 年 12 月 11 日中国正式成为 WTO 成员。中国是诸边政府采购协定（GPA）的观察员，并正在谈判加入其中。中国是一个诸边民用飞机贸易协议的观察员，也是信息技术协议（ITA）的参与者。中国对世界贸易组织的通报涵盖了广泛的协议，然而在补贴方面的通报似乎有必要更新。2012 至 2013 年，中国作为原告参与了 4 起争端解决案例，作为被告参与了 8 起案例，另外在 15 例案例中作为第三方。

11. 中国与 20 多个国家和地区缔结了 12 个自由贸易协定。中国与智利、哥斯达黎加、新西兰、巴基斯坦、秘鲁和新加坡签订的自由贸易协定已经生效。自从上次贸易政策审议后，中国已与瑞士、冰岛缔结自由贸易协定，但还没有生效。中国目前正在与海湾合作委员会（GCC）国家、澳大利亚、挪威、韩国和日本等国就自由贸易协定进行谈判。在原中国内地与香港、澳门签署《关于建立更紧密经贸关系的安排》的基础上又签署了《补充协议》。中国授予最不发达国家的单边优惠政策幅度自上一次审议有很大提高。

12. 中国的贸易和投资政策是通过一系列法律工具，以允许或禁止的方式来进行管理和微调的，其中包括中央政府五年计划，行业和省级五年计划以及不同的产业目录表。这些计划和目录指导了整体政策的实施，并列出了能够获得优惠待遇或者鼓励性投资的行业。由于这些目录表时有重叠甚至冲突，所以关于这些不同目录应该如何被解读并不明确。这反映了不同层面中的不同议程目标。而不同层级的监管又为解决中国具体的政策措施增加了一重难度。

13. 中国鼓励外国直接投资，以及中外合资企业，特别鼓励研发活动。FDI 流入中国具有战略利益的领域。中国鼓励 FDI 流入诸如高端制造业、高新技术产业、服务业、新能源和节能环保产业。中国积极引导外资流向中西部地区。外商投资项目可能受益于相对宽松的政策环境。外商投资项目可分为四类：鼓励、允许、限制、禁止。鼓励类的项目有资格享受相关法律、法规规定的优惠待遇，而限制类的项目必须进行更彻底的审查和批准。

14. 为吸引 FDI，中国简化和放宽了资本直接投资的规则和限制。例如，外商投资企业现在允许向境外股东发放贷款，并允许其持有某些领域内国有企业的股票。国内银行向外资企业发放贷款没有限制。2013 年 12 月，为了便于外商投资固定资产投资项目的成立，中国对相关审批程序进行了修改。根据要求的注册方式，目前有两类投资项目：一是核准类，二是备案类。《政府核准的投资项目目录》列出了需要核准的固定资产投资项目，在目录中未列出的项目，只需备案。

15. 2013 年 8 月，国务院正式批准设立中国（上海）自由贸易试验区。这一试点项目将测试服务贸易和资本账户交易的进一步自由化。上海自贸区旨在通过简化海关手续和允许区内货物便捷流转促进贸易便利化，同时自贸区也以简化投资手续为目标。另外，自贸区对外资企业授予准入前国民待遇。对于投资项目采用了负面清单的方法。那些列入清单的项目要求核准。关于试行办法提出的放开服务、电信及所有权条件等方面在八项增值服务上有不同程度的放宽。在金融服务领域，在开发区注册的外国投资者被允许参与国内期货交易，允许其在国内和国外的证券和期货市场投资，并在国内市场上发行以人民币计价的债券。在开发区内也开放了保险和保险中介服务。

16. 为了增强竞争力，中国还在开发区外采取了逐步推进服务自由化的措施。例如，在电信领域中国采取了扩大普遍服务地域范围的措施。在金融服务方面，采取了对国外供应商开放第三方强制汽车保险市场的措施。在航空运输领域内，唯一的主要发展是在计算机订座服务方面，期待已久的调控除明确了各有关行为者的法律责任外并不涉及任何新的自由化。中国为了应对系统性风险，如不良贷款和房地产资产泡沫，对金融服务领域采取了审慎措施，特别是在遵守巴塞尔委员会建议和反洗钱监管方面。

17. 自2006年开始中国便在货物贸易领域推出一系列改革促进贸易便利化，例如，引入无纸化通关手续。然而，尽管有这些努力，海关程序在全国范围内仍需要协调统一。此外，迄今为止没有一项关于货物许可和限制方面的便利化措施得到实施。

18. 关税制度自上次贸易政策审议以来没有太大变化。2013年中国的最惠国关税主要包括从价税率（总税目的99.5%）。非从价税率包括具体和备用税率以及配方税（Formula Duties）。2013年中国应用的平均最惠国税率为9.4%。这一数字自2011年几乎没有改变，2009年该数字为9.5%。对农产品（世贸组织定义）仍然实施较高的关税，为14.8%，较2009年和2011年略有下滑。2009年以来，非农业产品的平均关税维持在8.6%。

19. 中国会以维护国家安全、社会公德、人类及动物和植物的健康、环境保护、国际收支和遵守国际承诺为由采取进口许可证、限制和禁止等措施。中国使用自动和非自动授权。受限制的任何商品都将被有关机构纳入其出具的产品目录。然而，这些列表可以在必要时进行调整。有关机构也可以临时限制或禁止不包含在目录中的进口货物。

20. 审议期间中国没有修改与贸易救济措施有关的主要立法。对外贸易法通过相关的规定和一系列规则为反倾销调查和应采取措施提供了法律框架。其中一些法律法规为临时的。审议期间，中国面临的反倾销调查的数目略有下降，从2010年12月的117起下降到2013年12月31日的113起。化工产品占62.8%，其中22.1%涉及树脂、塑料和橡胶。来自16个国家或地区的进口受到影响。反倾销调查的最终裁决从2010年的15起，下降到2011年6起、2012年5起、2013年8起。然而，措施实施的平均时长增加至略超过六年，因为在此期间进行的所有日落复审都使得关税仍然有效。反倾销调查的启动从2011年的5个增至2012年的9个再到2013年的11个。在2011年和2013年间发起的22项调查中，约60%的调查都引起了临时性措施的形成。

21. 2012年中国展开三起反补贴调查，涉及原产于美国的四门轿车、越野车，原产于欧盟和美国的太阳能级多晶硅。2011年与2013年中国没有发起任何调查。截至2013年12月31日，有3项反补贴措施仍对来自欧盟和美国的进口产品产生影响。自上一次的贸易审查以来，中国还未开始依照WTO保障协议发起任何保障措施调查。

22. 自上次审议以来，程序设定的标准、技术法规和SPS措施都没有发生变化。省级政府采取的措施及其对贸易的影响无资料可供考察。

23. 出口限制是中国贸易体制的一个重要特点。中国对某些出口产品征税，对某些产品实施配额甚至禁止的措施。"法定"商品清单和临时出口税每年都会颁发。适用临时出口税的商品同时也可能适用特别出口关税。特别出口关税按季度征收，并且可能大大高于临时税率。2013年特别出口关税税率为75%，而临时税率在5%到35%的区间内。2013年出口税适用的税目约占所有HS 8位关税税目的4.2%。因为中国在某些产品的出口上是大国，所以对这些产品征税，可能对这些产品的国际价格产生影响。

24. 与进口的情况相同，商务部联合其他相关部门颁布限制或禁止出口货物目录。受出口限制的产品需要有出口许可证才可以出口。这些限制措施主要是为了保护环境和自然资源。但是，在实践中，影响出口的这些措施，已被用作鼓励或抑制出口的政策工具，用来满足产业发展目标。

25. 中国对出口和不同经济行业的支持程度并不明确，也没有向本次贸易审议秘书处提供相关具体信息。此外，中国向世界贸易组织供应链管理委员会提供的涵盖2005—2008年间的最近通报（2011年）以及向农业委员会提供的最新通报（2014年）中声称，包括2012年，它没有保持出口补贴。

26. 中国为了实现不同的经济和社会目标，对行业、区域和企业保留了大量的支持计划。不同的支持计划相互交织，既包括那些旨在实现主要政策目标（即经济增长）的计划，也包括那些旨在促进具体行业发展的计划。这些方案的实施并不总是透明的，往往是内部行政措施的结果。内部行政措施也并不总是容易识别的，而且一般只在中国才可行。因此秘书处并不会得到关于这些方案的完整的鉴定报告。此外由于预算是不公开的，因此无法确定支出。支持措施也会通过金融机构来提供。

27. 中国还对特定行业的投入、土地和技术进行补贴。受补贴的企业被中央和省级政府认为是具有重要的战略意义，或者被认为振兴它们符合国家发改委提出的关于调整和改造全国老工业基地（2013—2022）的号召。根据这一计划，国有企业和被青睐的企业可以直接以低于成本的价格互相购买投入品。这对企业的竞争力会产生影响。

28. 信贷政策在中国仍然非常重要。政府通过加快农村金融产品和服务创新、提高对中小型企业的金融服务以及防止和缓解地方债等措施，不断努力加强信贷政策和产业政策之间的协调。中国人民银行（PBC）引导金融机构加大对诸如科技创新领域、战略性新兴产业和服务业的金融支持。金融机构也被引导到铁路、航运、火电和钢铁等领域，并鼓励使用信用产品灵活地支持有潜力的出口型企业。信贷政策也在促进区域发展战略的实施过程中起到指导作用。

29. 农业继续得到支持，以保证农民收入、发展农村地区、确保国内市场粮食安全及农产品的价格稳定。支持该行业的四项主要补贴有：推广使用优良品种和种子补贴、购置农机具补贴、农业投入综合补贴和给农民的直接补贴。

30. 审议期间，随着经济自由化，中国开始实施上次审议过程中提及的有关竞争性政策的规定。该规定旨在加强履约和制止垄断行为。中国为了增强透明度而采取的措施包括实施反垄断审查（反托拉斯审查）和审查外国公司对涉及“国家安全”（国家安全审查）的国内企业的兼并与收购行为。针对主导地位者价格滥用、价格相关的行政垄断和价格垄断，该规定也提出了相应措施。中国的竞争法涵盖了所有类型的企业，然而对于中国经济与国家安全至关重要的国有企业却被授予免于法律规定的权利，或者被授予合法独家生产和销售的权利。竞争法还规定，当集中程度超过一定临界值时必须通报并接受反垄断审查。

31. 中国对商品和服务的价格管制被认为会对国民经济和人民生活产生直接影响。价格管制通过中央和省级两个层级进行设置。价格管制采取“政府定价”或“政府指导价格”两种方式。在“政府定价”中政府设定固定价格。而在“政府指导价格”中政府规定一个波动范围，在此范围内价格可以出现波动。政府定价或政府指导价根据产品或服务的类型而异。其定价基于以下因素：市场情况、社会平均成本、对居民生活水平的影响，也会考虑经济、区域性、季节性等因素。虽然各省制定价格的方法大同小异，但根据各省的特定情况价格水平可能不同。

32. 根据政府采购法，政府必须采购本国货物、工程和服务。但存在某些例外：采购物品无法在中国获得、缺乏可用性合理的商业条款、采购物品在国外使用，或者有其他法律和行政法规专门规定。政府采购可以集中或分散。2013 年中央预算的采购门槛是价值 50 万元人民币的货物服务和价值 60 万元人民币的建设项目。2012 年，集中采购占政府采购的 87.6%。在集中采购目录中未列出，但其价值超过某一门槛值的分散采购项目，是由各级政府具体规定、由采购代理机构自身来执行的。中国使用以下五种方法采购货物、服务和工程：公开招标，邀请招标，竞争性谈判，询价和单一来源采购。

33. 审议期间，中国继续实施旨在改善其知识产权保护监管环境的措施，包括修改相关法律法规和部门规章制度。在审议期间的一个主要变化是 2013 年 8 月公布了商标法第三次修正案 ，该法案自 2014 年 5 月 1 日起施行。在 2012 年中国还颁布了《发明专利申请优先审查管理办法》。尽管当局为打击侵权付出了努力，但知识产权保护仍是中国面临的一大挑战。

（苏日译）

巴拿马贸易政策审议

1. 自2007年以来，巴拿马的经济增长一直令人印象深刻，这主要归功于其动态投资和稳定的宏观经济环境。总的来说，巴拿马的贸易投资管理体制是相当开放的，并在2007—2013年期间继续拓展，主要是通过巴拿马参与优惠贸易协定，在立法改革领域如海关、知识产权、政府采购及其他与贸易相关的领域起到了催化剂的作用。作为其发展战略的一部分，巴拿马也保持激励机制以吸引外国直接投，其中包括一些特殊经济区，如科隆自由区（ZLC）。由于自身第三产业和它的地理位置的比较优势，巴拿马已经能够巩固在金融、港口、运输、仓储、分销服务和经过巴拿马运河的运输服务的出口大国地位。最近几年在大型公共基础设施投资是意欲将巴拿马转变成一个区域性物流中心。另一方面，尽管他们已经受到政府的支持和保护，农业份额和制造业在国内生产总值的比重都有所下降。

2. 这种经济的快速增长带来了人均名义国内生产总值的激增（在2013年为11075美元）和贫困率、失业率的下降。然而，仍存在相当的社会和区域不平等和熟练劳动力明显短缺的问题。从外商直接投资的显著增加情况来看，在过去几年里，该激励计划在吸引投资方面似乎已见成效。然而，特殊经济区和整体经济的联系需要加强，而前者对就业和当地价值增值的贡献需要加以改进。在适当情况下，重新评估和合理的激励机制将是明智的，这样做能够缩小大部分强大的经济区和部门与经济的其他部分之间的差距，并分配更多资源给诸如改善教育质量等问题的社会项目，以满足可持续的经济增长对熟练劳动力的需求和依赖。效率和经济竞争力也将通过解决电力短缺的问题来改进。

经济环境

3. 2007年至2013年，巴拿马经济年均增长率为8%，是拉丁美洲高增长率的国家之一。这种快速增长主要得益于私人消费、公共投资和私人投资的扩张，尤其是大型基础设施项目的实施。服务业是国家经济结构的重心，占国内生产总值的70%并提供了三分之二的就业机会。

4. 自2009年以来，由于支出水平尤其是资本支出水平的提高，公共财政出现赤字。虽然赤字一直温和，一直保持在每年批准的法律规定的范围之内，但在很多情况下不得不放松了这些限制。随着经济周期和可能的外部冲击的出现，主要财政政策的挑战是维持规则，以巩固公共财政和提振信心，缓和由于缺乏对监察政策的处理而变得更为紧迫的客观的心理状态（巴拿马使用美元作为法定货币）。公共债务占国内生产总值的比重在审议期间有所下降，而在2013年这一比重达到了36.8%。2013年，由于信贷繁荣，强劲的国内需求以及高涨的国际燃料和食品价格共同作用，已经把通胀压力维持在4%左右，高于美国同期水平。

5. 国际货物贸易和服务将以国内生产总值的166%的比重继续在巴拿马经济中起关键作用。2007—2013年期间，由于在商品贸易负平衡，巴拿马国际收支余额的经常账户出现赤字。另一方面，由于巴拿马运河、运输服务、港口服务和旅游业带来的收入增加，巴拿马服务贸易的结余保持乐观并持续增长。农产品和食品已经成为巴拿马的商品出口的支柱（占出口总数的56%，不计复出口的ZLC），相对地反映出巴拿马制造业的规模还很小。制成品和燃料占进口额的88%。虽然其相对重要性已经下降，但是美国仍然是占其巴拿马出口和进口总额20%以上的主要贸易伙伴，其他主要合作伙伴分别为欧盟、加拿大、中美洲国家、墨西哥、哥伦比亚和中国。审议期间，流入巴拿马的外国直接投资继续增长，2012年达到国内生产总值的7.6%。在过去的几年中巴拿马最终通过的优惠贸易协定有望促进对外贸易的多元化并吸引更多的外国直接投资。

贸易和投资政策框架

6. 巴拿马的贸易政策的主要关注点和目标是增加外国直接投资和出口。对于巴拿马，开放的进程与实现这些目标齐头并进，而且它不仅关注缔结贸易协定而且致力于提高竞争力，改善环境和加强基础设施建设。它正在寻求吸引高附加值的投资，这些投资能够促进人力资源培训并将技术向主要经济部门（金融服务、物流、旅游和农业）转移。为此，巴拿马设了投资与出口促进局（PROINVEX）作为投资者的一个窗口。为了提高体积、质量和出口供应的多样性，巴拿马专注于出口到某些市场，这些市场能够承担得起优先获取的商品和服务，并出口高附加值的非传统产品，例如非传统农业水产品。

7. 对于巴拿马，巩固多边贸易体系是非常重要的，这样能够在与这些成员建立区域或双边的贸易关系的同时，促进成员间出口和投资的增长。2007 到 2014 年间有 13 个区域贸易协定生效。其中包括巴拿马加入拉丁美洲一体化协会、中美洲经济一体化秘书处，巴拿马和美国结盟协定之间的贸易促销协议以及与欧盟和中美洲的合作协议。与哥伦比亚（2013 年）和墨西哥（2014 年）签订协议后，巴拿马希望加入包括哥伦比亚、智利、秘鲁和墨西哥这些国家在内的太平洋联盟。

8. 巴拿马通过引入一个电子处理的启动通知简化了设立公司的程序设置。巴拿马法律赋予外国投资者及其所参与的企业国民待遇。巴拿马没有外汇控制。巴拿马给予外国投资者由资本、股息、利息而产生的投资收益可以自由汇回和免税汇出的权力。任何投资金额 200 万美元及以上的投资可从投资稳定法中获益。投资者的投资不需要任何事先授权，除非其受益于激励计划或希望从事的活动需要特许经营、牌照、许可证或其他类型的授权。

贸易政策措施

9. 巴拿马继续将其海关制度现代化，为此巴拿马通过了一项新的法律，更新其计算机系统，并建立了国家海关总署。其他贸易便利化措施包括引入预先裁定，设置出口的单一窗口，以及开展授权经济运营计划。关税是主要的贸易政策工具。审议期间几乎所有的从价税和关税税率都从 37%减少至 29%。平均最惠国关税从 8.5%降至 7.6%，但农产品（WTO 定义）13.7%的平均关税仍然超过其他产品关税（6.4%）的两倍以上。在 59 种产品中，所施加的税率都超过 WTO 约束税率。2013 年，在巴拿马加入中美洲经济一体化秘书处后，适用中美洲进口税，当然有少数例外。根据其贸易协定，巴拿马从二十多个贸易伙伴的进口产品适用优惠关税。

10. 巴拿马对进口的海关服务征收行政费用和计算机系统使用费，二者都基于特定数额。另外，进口还会受转让动产服务税费、选择性消费税和石油衍生燃料消费税等的影响。某些产品（电子、机动车辆）消除的关税会因选择性消费税的增加而抵消。巴拿马对进口产品征收国内税时给予其国民待遇，但对包含进口乙醇的混合燃料适用税率高于包含国内乙醇的混合燃料，对进口的机动车（新车和二手车），会根据其使用年限征收最低的选择性消费税。

11. 审议期间，巴拿马努力为适用卫生与植物检疫（SPS）措施而培育其体制和技术能力。然而，巴拿马仍然需要在诸如风险分析、人员培训、国家卫生与植物检疫委员会评审的创建、认证以及通知程序领域做出改进。2007 年到 2013 年，巴拿马向世贸组织通报 8 项卫生与植物检疫措施，其中 5 次为紧急措施。巴拿马有 88 项技术法规，主要涉及食品，其中自 2007 年以来只有 6 项曾向 WTO 通报。通过改善其卫生与植物检疫系统和技术法规，提高透明度，巴拿马将更加能够有效地利用优惠协定所提供的贸易机会。

12. 尽管在审议期间巴拿马很少使用应急措施，但在 2009 年它确实采用了用于进行反倾销、反补贴和保障措施特保调查的程序规则的规定。

13. 一些海洋物种、易燃易爆品和武器的出口要符合特殊程序。出于对可持续性和促进国内价值增值的考虑，巴拿马禁止出口厚木板或积木或简单刨平的木板。除了从本地出口木材制品，巴拿马没有适用任何出口税。国内不征收出口税。

14. 巴拿马向 WTO 通报三大出口补贴计划，并收到世界贸易组织的延长消除补贴的允许，延长截止日期为 2015 年 12 月 31 日。2009 年，巴拿马取消了税收减免证书，并于 2010 年推出了产业振兴证书，取代了正式的国家行业注册。2011 年，巴拿马还通过了自由贸易区的第 32 号法令，出口补贴的税收优惠不再适用。2012 年，第 32 号法律下的自由区的份额不到出口总额（包括转口）的 2%。此外，由另一种法律管辖的科隆自由区（ZLC），是世界上第二大的自由区，处理本国

66%的对外贸易。成立于科隆自由区的公司的很多税种得以豁免，包括进口税、再出口税、制造业商品税、股息遣返税，以及其他国内税。此外，还有许多奖励计划，例如对跨国公司、微型和小型企业的总部和具体部门（农业和旅游业）的奖励计划。在适当情况下，提高其效率和透明度，使激励结构更加均匀，避免资源分配扭曲，将是值得进行的成本效益分析和合理化的激励方案。

15. 2007年，巴拿马通过了一个新的竞争和消费者保护法（45号法律），除其他事项外，引进经济效率标准，将操纵市场列为相对垄断的做法，推出了支付信息的计划，同时增加罚金。虽然第45号法使竞争政策可以更有力地执行，但仍有特定的市场，特别是货物市场集中度高。在消费者保护政策方面，当局对燃料、药品和商品的基本价格进行监督。由于电能的分配和销售费率，旅客的陆路运输价格受到管制。巴拿马向WTO通报其没有国营贸易的企业。

16. 巴拿马已进行了其政府采购法律法规的数量改革和澄清。这些大多是涉及程序问题，并对投标人有利。然而，诉诸特别程序仍然是常见的。2013年8月，经过数年的谈判，巴拿马宣布不加入WTO《政府采购协议》。尽管如此，它采用了双边协议的政府采购承诺，在某些情况下关于采购甚至可以与巴拿马运河管理局进行协商。当局已经宣布打算在双边基础上继续进行进入政府采购市场的谈判。

17. 2012年，巴拿马整顿其知识产权立法，使其与最新的国际法律相协调。修订涵盖很多方面，包括所有知识产权、延长保护条款、健全行政规定、对执法提供更强的规则，以及处罚的加重。即使是通过巴拿马过境、进口，或假冒、篡改、仿制产品的出口，仍被定义为构成刑事犯罪。

18. 巴拿马经济部门仍然是明显的二元结构，其标志是充满活力和竞争力的服务业并存，服务业主要是围绕巴拿马运河和ZLC活动的发展，相比之下生产力较低的农业生产部门，尽管有国家的支持，其经济形势处在温和状态，并且其份额一直在下降。

19. 农业在GDP中的相对份额在2007年至2013年间持续下降，但它仍占劳动人口的16.4%。在2013年，农业部门（WTO定义）的平均关税为13.7%，高于整体平均水平，且产品中具有最高关税的是农产品。在巴拿马的承诺减让表中，农产品平均关税配额填充率从60%变化到100%，此外因为供应短缺，自主关税配额被开启。巴拿马的国内支持属于绿箱措施。2007年至2012年间在“发展规划”的名义下国内支持大幅增加。

20. 2013年，制造业占巴拿马国内生产总值的5.1%，雇用劳动力占总劳动力的7.7%。该部门正在集中于一小部分的活动的开展，如食品饮料、出版印刷、非金属矿物制品的制造。各种财政和金融激励生产活动的发展。主要进口产品包括燃料、矿物油和机械，主要出口产品为贵金属、铸铁和钢。

21. 电力市场是分散的并受到监管。生产活动主要是私人企业在自由竞争的条件下进行，而传输活动掌控在国家企业手中，由三个半公开的上市公司负责独家特许地区的分布。巴拿马与中美洲电网相连接。相对于需求，装机容量利润率较窄，虽然有所改善，但仍不足以满足其一年四季的需求。国家正在分配补贴，以减轻最终用户电价增加的影响。巴拿马不会生产任何的烃类产品，但有大量的存储容量和丰富的港口基础设施。2013年，鉴于其领土内确定存量的商业开发，巴拿马采取了一些措施，以促进勘探工作。

22. 这些服务部门对巴拿马的经济起基础性作用，约占GDP的70%，总就业的三分之二和出口总额的36%。巴拿马已经巩固了其作为金融、港口、物流和旅游服务的主要出口国的地位。在《服务贸易总协定》（GATS）的11个部门做出了市场准入和国民待遇的承诺。金融领域的承诺是广泛的，在电信和运输部门是有限的，对海运服务没有承诺。实践中，巴拿马GATS承诺的范围已大大超过其当前对外国服务供应商的开放。

23. 通信服务部门，2009年两家移动运营商进入市场加剧了竞争，这有利于价格的降低和服务质量的改善。私营通信公司的外国投资没有限制。2008年，巴拿马通过《普遍服务和访问法》，2009年通过《号码携带规定》。GATS项下巴拿马只针对增值服务做出了具体承诺，而没有适用基本电信参考文件。

24. 巴拿马有一个多元化竞争的金融机构。银行体系是健全的：资本和流动性水平是相当高的，而且在最近几年出现了信贷繁荣。外资银行设置子公司或分公司的申请可以通过。审议期间，巴拿马修改了银行法来加强监管，以使其符合国际标准，提高透明度，遏制逃税行为，保护消费者的利益。此外，金融集团都受到监管，而且为促进负责监督该部门各机构之间的合作，巴拿马成立了金融协调委员会。

25. 外国保险公司可以设置公共有限责任公司或分支机构。在巴拿马的人身和财产保险政策，只能在全国设立的保险公司适用。2012 年，巴拿马通过了一个新的保险法，除其他事项外，这项法律扩大了部门的监督机构的职责，更新了最低资本金、偿付能力和准备金的规定范围，并通过授权金融企业和贸易公司保险销售。倘若这些公司一直在注册地经营，那么外国的再保险公司可以给定居在巴拿马的公司提供再保险服务。2011 年，巴拿马创建了具有广泛的管理和监督职责的证券市场监管机构。

26. 托库门国际机场是中美洲最繁忙的机场和支线航空运输枢纽。从 2007 年到 2013 年，旅客人数的年平均增长率为 12.8%，载客量增长率为 21%、货邮容量增长率为 5.2%。国际运输经营者的外国投资未受限制，但沿海运输业务保留，原则上至少公司 60%份额的沿海运输业务要掌握在巴拿马手中。根据法律规定，托库门机场管理公司为 100%国有公司。国际客运和货运航空经营证书颁发给双边协议下的外国公司。

27. 2009 年批准的巴拿马国家海事战略旨在将该国变成一个具有卓越的竞争力的海运和物流业务的综合中心。巴拿马拥有广泛的港口网络，可提供广泛的船舶服务。巴拿马拥有港口，但其管理可以外包给拥有特许权的私人公司，其最大的港口就是由私人管理的。在提供配套的航运服务时，有的企业对外国资本参与有所限制，而且 90%的从事此类服务的船只的船员必须是巴拿马国民。在 2012 年，海运业对 GDP 的贡献达 2.3%。巴拿马拥有世界上最大的商船队，截至 2013 年 6 月 30 日登记的船只数达到 8221 艘。在注册方面没有国籍的限制。巴拿马正寻求通过对新建船舶的登记发放各种折扣来恢复它的舰队。

28. 2012 年巴拿马运河对 GDP 的贡献为 3.2%。巴拿马运河是世界海上运输的神经中枢，除了来自通行费的贡献，它还催生各种经济活动。在审议期间，巴拿马运河管理局（ACP）改变其收费政策，使通行费与路径所提供的价值相符合。为使船舶业务与更大的草案相适应，2007 年，已开始动工建立第三套关卡来扩大运河规模。在 2014 年 2 月，在解决了有关成本超过融资等几个问题时，巴拿马运河管理局与建筑公司达成了 2015 年 12 月完成这个项目的概念性协议的一致目标。

29. 旅游业是外汇的主要引擎，在 2012 年占 GDP 的 12%。尤其是在巴拿马城，旅游业的投资在 2007—2012 年期间大幅增加。在同一时期，巴拿马拓展了对旅游投资给予税收优惠的范围，解除了对不再被视为零售业的旅游经营者和旅行社业务外资参与的限制，并加强了部门制度支持体系。

30. 巴拿马宪法保留了收到最终文件三年后，因出生或入籍的外籍巴拿马公民从事零售业的权利。从 2007 年到 2012 年，零售业以 8.5%的速度增长，2012 年其市场份额占 GDP 总额的 3.8%。在与美国的自贸协定下，巴拿马通过建立多个不被视为零售业的服务企业开辟了这一零售部门。

（孔艺晓译，戴臻校）

中国台北贸易政策审议

经济环境

1. 台湾、澎湖、金门和马祖单独关税区（以下简称“中国台北”）仍然是世界上最重要的经济和贸易实体之一。2012 年，在购买力平价 GDP 排名中，中国台北居世界第 19 位，同时是世界第 18 大出口经济体、第 18 大进口经济体。由于自然资源的匮乏，岛屿经济体进口主要是为满足其能源和原材料需求；其出口主要是制成品，满足了半导体、平板显示器、精密机床和其他大量产品的世界需求。

2. 经济增长严重依赖货物和服务的出口，几乎占 GDP 的 73%。由于 2008—2009 年的全球经济危机带来的全球性需求剧减，突显了依靠相对有限的制成品出口所带来的风险，促使当局寻求经济增长的新引擎和经济的多样化。

3. 2013 年经济增长 2.1%，之后随着 OECD 国家可能的强劲增长率，出口导向的经济从中期来看将从坚挺的外部需求获益。外部需求变动带来的经济脆弱性的主要风险在中期。政府的财政状况意味着，用于对抗外部需求变动的财政资源是有限的。

4. 中国台北与中国大陆的经济联系日益密切，政府亦希望该联系更加紧密，尤其是通过《海峡两岸经济合作框架协议》（以下简称“ECFA”）的谈判来推进海峡两岸经济关系的自由化。ECFA 可以促进服务部门的增长，这主要得益于两岸直航后所吸引的大陆赴台游客的增多。游客数量的增加预计将支撑就业，从而刺激居民消费继续作为经济增长的驱动力。

5. 最近几年发布的世界竞争力报告，由于信息技术制造产业的优势，中国台北是极具竞争力和发展潜力的。然而，政府面临巨大的经济挑战，制定了一系列经济改革方案：签署自由贸易协定；改革税制、土地监管、服务部门和医疗部门；开放海峡两岸经济政策，追求战略性改革，其中较为典型的是“经济倍增计划”（Economic Power-Up）和启动自由经济示范区。

6. 中国台北仍然是对外净投资者，对外直接投资流量是本地区吸引外国直接投资流量的近三倍。中国是其目前资本外流的主要目的地。虽然中国台北的外国直接投资占 GDP 的比率根据区域标准仍然较低，但是大多数行业仍然对外国直接投资开放。

贸易政策框架

7. 贸易政策的制定和实施结构仍然没有变化，“经济事务部”仍然担负主要的行政职责。高层的政策协调是由“总统”主持的“全球经济和贸易战略委员会”（Committee of Global Economic and Trade Strategy）来确保的。

8. 中国台北整体贸易政策目标仍然是，通过积极参与 WTO 多边贸易体制，通过日益增多的自由贸易协定和经济合作协定的谈判，加强贸易便利化和促进活动，消除海外市场的贸易壁垒等，从而逐渐融入全球经济一体化。自 2010 年与中国大陆签署 ECFA 后，政府开始寻求与其他未建交国家商签贸易协定，且已经于 2013 年与新西兰和新加坡成功签署了经济合作协定。其他经济体的类似协定将可能于中期跟进。目前政府希望加入美国主导的《跨太平洋伙伴关系协定》（TPP）和以东盟为基础的《区域全面经济伙伴关系》（RCEP）的谈判。推进 FTAs 的签署将能够支撑未来几年对于地区经济开放的尝试。

主要的贸易政策发展

9. 关税仍然是中国台北的主要贸易政策工具，约占税收总额的 5%。与贸易相关的税收（包括）占总税收的比重从 2009 年的 22.8%上升至 2013 年的 26.8%；审议期间商业税在整个与贸易相关的税收中占比高达三分之二。

10. 自上次审议以来，关税税率几乎没有变化。仍然包括从价税、特别税和选择税。2013 年，从价税覆盖了所有税目的 98.2%，强化了关税结构的透明度。然而，仍然有 150 种利率范围：86

种从价税，16 种特别税，48 种选择税。由于涉及多重税率，关税仍然比较复杂。非从价税，尤其是对农产品征收的非从价税，往往隐瞒相对较高的从价税等值。

11. 2013 年关税包括 8728 个八位税目：其中，30.2%的税目免税，52.6%的税目税率低于 10%；4.4%的税目为“低率”税率。2013 年适用的简单平均最惠国税率，包括非从价税的从价等值，为 7.8%，与 2009 年相同，审议期间没有任何关税削减。按照 WTO 的规定，中国台北的平均适用关税农产品为 22.1%，非农产品为 5.0%。关税配额主要适用于农产品，在总税目中的占比由 2009 的 1.2%下降至 2013 年的 0.8%。所有关税税目为约束税率。适用税率与 8.1%简单平均约束税率相近或一致，可以说中国台北的关税是可预见的。

12. 就贸易便利化而言，海关采用单一窗口系统以加快清关，引入官方经济运行体系以便利满足特定条件的贸易商。自 2010 年审议以来，中国台北进口禁令的范围有所扩大，从 63 种十位 HS 编码商品扩大到了 70 种。中国台北没有实施对进口进行数量限制的政策。但是，出于安全和/或商业考虑，中国台北仍然对约 2172 个税号实行禁止从中国大陆进口的政策，低于 2009 年的 2243 个税号。

13. 审议期间应急措施的法律和行政框架基本稳定。中国台北自 2003 年共适用了 12 项反倾销措施，主要影响钢铁、纺织和化学产业。中国台北从未使用过反补贴或保障措施，但在三种产品上仍然保持着五项反倾销措施。对农产品适用特别保障措施。

14. 政府采购体制没有重大变化。非中国台北的供应商在政府采购总额中所占份额从 2008 年的 28%跌至 2009 年的 10.6%，2012 年又上升至 26.5%。由于延长了政府采购招标的时间限制，GPA 成员资格对政府采购体制的运行带来影响。中国台北参与并为 GPA 的谈判做出了贡献，谈判成果于 2014 年 4 月 6 日生效。根据政府统计，这将每年增加 30 亿新台币的市场准入机会。

15. 各种形式的援助，包括生产补贴从而贸易补贴，继续向农业、渔业和工业产品或活动提供。继续为部分行业提供税收优惠的产业升级条例到期后，政府实施了一项新的、表面上非针对特定行业的奖励计划——“产业创新条例”，旨在促进创新和技术研发。

16. 政府所有企业（国有企业）持续在几个部门中占据垄断地位，尤其是电力、石油、邮政服务、公用事业、电信、银行和陆地运输等部门。除了航空航天部门，始于 1992 年的私有化进程已经陷入停滞或再评估的状态。政府所有企业的贸易活动涉及最重要的作物水稻。

17. 就出口措施而言，以维护治安、公共安全和保护环境为由，中国台北继续对出口实施禁令和许可证的措施。政府也继续提供免税、退税、自由区的便捷和优势措施。出口加工区（EPZs）和自由贸易园区（FTZs）为企业提供相似的奖励措施。企业可以在自由贸易园区内从事包括交易、收集、转运、货运代理、报关、装配、包装、修理、制造、测试和技术服务等活动。企业可以在出口加工区从事包括制造业、金融服务、管理服务、信息和通信等活动。当局指出，自由贸易园区主要的目标是建立一个全球物流产业，而出口加工区的重点放在促进投资和发展产业。除了进口关税豁免，出口加工区和自由贸易园区的进口免征边境上的其他间接税费。

18. 由于 2011 年对《公平贸易法》的修订和 2012 年公平贸易委员会独立地位的授予，中国台北的竞争政策框架有着显著的变化。某些活动，如进口卡特尔可以不适用《公平贸易法》。价格管制适用于一些公用事业服务，包括能源和电讯服务，以及价格稳定委员会监察某些商品及产品的价格，以期在必要时协调供应与需求。

19. 知识产权相关立法的变更：《著作权法》2010 年和 2014 年的修订，《著作权中介团体条例》2010 年的修订，新《商标法》2012 年生效，《专利法》2014 年最新的修订，《营业秘密法》2013 年的修订。当局一直在努力缩短专利审查程序。在执法方面，进口商品侵犯商标和版权的案件似乎一直在下降。当局认识到知识产权保护是经济发展和整体竞争力的重要贡献，也是吸引外国投资的一个重要方面。在边境的知识产权执法由海关负责，可依法暂停涉嫌侵犯知识产权货物放行。

20. 审议期间，SPS 和标准制度基本保持不变。适用强制性技术法规的产品通过市场监察活动而非事先准入控制进行商品检验。SPS 的边境检查程序已经简化。“国内”标准（包括“国家”标准和专业标准）是自愿的，除了技术法规。标准政策旨在促进标准化；追求产品、流程和服务的质量改善；提高生产率；确保生产、运输、销售和消费的充分性，以促进公共安全。

21. 根据有关部门的规定，所有的技术法规都符合国际标准。技术法规是合格证书签发的基础，是强制性的，主要适用于电子产品、化工产品、机器设备、农产品等。依技术法规规定，产品必须进行商品检验并合格后才可投放市场。进口品、出口品和国内生产的货物都需要进行检查。截至2014年2月，除1853个农产品和渔产品外，1137个商品受到强制检查，其中包括756个化工产品和381个机械、电气和电子产品。当局维持一个网站，向公众开放，以便公众查询商品检验的受检产品。

部门政策发展

22. 中国台北的经济结构自上一次审议以来几乎没有明显变化。尽管农业在经济中的作用一直受到限制和减少，农业占GDP的比重不足2%，农业仍然是政府援助的主要对象，包括边境保护和国内支持。自上次审议以来，农业部门的法律和司法框架没有显著变化。中国台北严重依赖食品进口，食品贸易呈现逆差。在生产的总价值方面，主要为水果、生猪饲养和蔬菜。水稻占农业生产总值的比重有限，仍然是政府援助的主要对象，包括通过关税、关税配额、特殊保障措施、“国家”贸易安排进行的边境保护，并包括直接补贴、价格支持、利息补贴等形式的国内支持。农产品的平均适用最惠国税（WTO定义），包括从价税等值，为22.1%，与2010年相同，非农产品平均适用的最惠国税只有5%。

23. 经济严重依赖能源进口，燃料进口占总进口额的比重由2009年的21%上升至2013年的25%，而能源供应总量的98%依靠进口。能源产品进口关税相对较低，平均为1.5%。部分能源产品需要进口和/或出口许可证。政府还提供了补贴，鼓励在山区和海岛地区的石油设施的建立和运作。

24. 审议期间，制造业占GDP的25%，占商品出口总额的88%。尽管政府的目标是优化和调整制造业，但似乎已经无法充分地解决发展问题，如过多地集中在信息和通信技术，相对较低的附加值和产品创新不足。

25. 服务业仍然是经济中最大的部门，约占GDP的66%，解决了59%的就业。政府确定的某些服务行业为“关键”产业，作为进一步发展的主要焦点。尽管如此，主要服务部门的立法或司法框架没有发生重大变化，而且没有明显的自由化措施，以进一步开放非本地服务供应商的市场准入。

26. 中国台北的服务贸易总协定的承诺，覆盖160个服务部门中的120个部门。服务承诺表列出了陆运和航空运输服务并购的最惠国待遇豁免，由互惠待遇和/或双边安排来规范。市场准入限制主要包括金融服务（包括银行、保险、资产管理），电信服务（包括卫星通信、陆地移动通信、广播、电视），以及一些专业服务（如法律服务、会计、税务）等。

27. 政府已选定十个重点服务行业和其他行业，作为促进其产业发展政策的重点。待定的十个服务行业是：医疗旅游、音乐和数字内容、国际物流、高新技术和创新型产业筹资、城市复兴、美食的国际推广、会展业（会议、奖励旅游、大型企业会议、展览）、WiMAX技术、中文电子商务、海外学生扩招。在这些行业的行动计划中，还制定了若干关键战略，包括拓展国际市场，培养具有外语和国际市场营销专长的人才，并提供贷款、指导和援助，以帮助海外市场扩张。

重要的服务分部门的发展中，通信部门迅速扩张，审议期间以平均每年20%的速度增长，是GDP增速的近10倍。2013年通信服务的总收入占GDP的3%，其中移动服务占最大比重。旅游业也得到了快速发展，是政府推动经济发展的关键性新兴产业之一。2012年有730万个国际旅行者，比2011年增长了20%。游客的最大来源地是中国，其次是日本和中国香港。旅游业的快速增长反映了两岸的航班增加，对中国游客开放了团体游和自由行，以及与日本和韩国启动的开放天空机制。在金融服务方面，政府股份占总银行资产的比重审议期间从52%增加至59%。银行部门的特点是超过400家机构被列为银行。只有39家是商业银行，但这些银行持有的总资产高达76%。

（张上冉译，杨凤鸣校）

蒙古贸易政策审议

1. 从2005年贸易政策审议后，蒙古继续保持一般开放程度的贸易体制。蒙古的经济增长显著。随着人均国内生产总值上升，失业率不升反降，而且人类发展指数的排名有所提升。由于矿产储量大以及毗邻中国这个大市场，蒙古的经济很可能会继续成长。然而，增长速度有所波动，并可能随着矿产资源的投资、价格和出口量的变化而持续波动。自2005年以来，实际GDP增长从2009年的－1.3%变化为2011年的17.5%。显然，蒙古是在投资、出口和政府收入波动管理的主要政策层面上面临挑战的国家之一。

2. 尽管数据有一些问题，但显而易见的是，出口和进口在审议期间大幅增加，同时出口额达到44亿美元，并且2012年进口额达到67亿美元。矿产对经济的重要性也有所增加，2012年出口量超过84%是矿物，几乎全部都出口到中国。

3. 当局意识到狭窄的经济基础导致了问题的出现。基于千年发展目标，2008年综合国家发展战略指出，虽然矿藏被开采，蒙古也追求多元化的政策；该战略提出了若干优先领域，包括以外销为主、私营部门主导的科技含量高、起驱动作用的制造业和服务业，如信息通信、生物和纳米技术、交通运输、物流、金融中介服务以及农产品再加工等。特别引起注意的是在支付战略上，促进中小企业生产进口替代产品的同时支持先进技术进口。

4. 外国投资对矿产的利用开采以及其他部门的发展相当重要。然而，外国直接投资所占国内生产总值的比重从2011年的53%下降为2013年的20%。从某种程度上说，这是因为需求下降，以及2012年在对业务实体具有战略重要性的行业监管工作中外国投资的法律机制还具有不确定性因素。为了解决这些问题并改善投资环境，2012年法案和1993年的外国投资法被《2013年投资法》（适用于外国和国内投资）所取代，它简化了投资和注册要求，并在几个方面提供了更高的法律准确性，包括对外商投资实体及外国政府拥有的法人实体的定义。

5. 除了新的对投资法，2013年还通过了其他一些法律。除其他事项外，这些法案旨于改善投资环境，促进财政稳定，其中包括《财政稳定法》《综合预算法》《社会福利法》。这些立法的变化，以及所采取的蒙古银行（中央银行）来稳定本国货币，控制通胀，提高商业的监管银行的方法，应有助于改善国外和国内投资。

6. 当局已采取了强化通关手续的一些措施，包括对海关法、关税法和2008年关税的修订，除其他的事情，允许清关后进行海关监管，以及推出海关自动化信息系统，允许提交电子文件和电子付款。

7. 在1997年加入世界贸易组织的时候，蒙古对其所有的关税都有约束，其中大多数税率是在20%，尽管在大多数情况下，实际利用的税率要低得多。然而，对于约60个税目，适用5%的实际关税比0%的约束税率要大得多。基于对国民健康和国家安全的考虑，也通过了一些针对乙醇等进口产品的禁令。此外，包括饲养动物等各种各样的产品，受非自动许可出口或进口的制约。出口税适用于小范围的产品，虽然在2009年他们将生原绒从中删除。作为出口多样化努力的一部分，蒙古开发银行成立于2011年，提供出口金融服务（包括装运前和装运后融资、出口保理、出口信用担保，以及出口信用保险）。

8. 蒙古继续开发和应用新标准，其中很多都是强制性的技术要求，总共超过六千条，达不到国际标准的一半。

9. 尽管蒙古经济本质上是市场驱动和被私有化，在经济的许多不同领域仍有约100个政府直接管理的或公私合营的国有企业参与。当局称这些企业都没有任何特别权利。在2005年到2011年间，约90个单位被私有化，其中几个包括国家航空公司（MIAT）和一些电厂企业的私有化被延期。

10. 审议期间，蒙古关于知识产权的法律也出现了一些变化，如在2006年著作权法和专利法的修订，在2010年商标和地理标志法案被修订，作物及种子品种法修订于2011年。不过自2010年以来，在监管等其他指标的数量方面，执法行动有所下降，如果是由于执法力度的减弱以及缺乏有效遵守，这样效果便并不明显。

11. 虽然矿产的投资和贸易主导了外商直接投资和出口，农业仍占就业的三分之一和国内生产总值的15%。蒙古的农业形势很特别，由于可供作物生长的季节短以及冬日严寒，游牧成了主要的农业活动。在回答关于对进口的依赖的担忧时，政府已出台了一些方案来促进部分大宗产品（小麦和马铃薯）的生产并且已初见成效，这些产品的进口都有所下降。但是目前尚不清楚，是否这些产品进口依存度减少是以其他产品进口的增加为代价的，如对大米的进口已经增加。蒙古的主要出口产品仍是羊绒、绵羊和山羊的皮革。

12. 相比于蒙古经济的规模，矿产部门的潜力非常大，在过去数年及未来几年矿产的投资总额相当于年度GDP多倍。与2004年相比，2012年煤的数量以及铁矿石的生产和输出大幅增加，与此同时随着价格的增长出口值也有显著的增加。由于在奥尤陶勒盖铜的生产量增加，陶勒盖的扩张，煤炭产量增加，出口金额和数量将进一步增加。然而，鉴于未使用的采矿许可证，为了保持其有效性，2010年蒙古暂停对新勘探许可证的发放，直至通过有关矿产品的新法律。

13. 蒙古的人口密度很低且气候恶劣，意味着像电力、电信和运输等基础设施项目都非常重要而且花费巨大。尽管还需要更多，蒙古在每个领域已经有相当大的投资，特别是在公路和铁路运输的建设上。

14. 在过去几年中，银行和金融业经历了几次巨变。尽管在开发和应用规范方面已有改进，分别在2008年，2009年和2013年，国家还是不得不接管了三个银行，他们的运营性质已改为蒙古国家银行的国有体制。蒙古仍然有13个注册的商业银行，这是一个很大的规模，即使商业银行在金融公司的总资产中占95%的份额。

15. 总体而言，蒙古在提高国民生活水平以及矿产的投资和贸易方面取得了长足的进展。然而，伴随立法而生的管理资源的膨胀，体制挑战问题出现，基础设施投资需求的增加是政府面临的最大挑战。与此同时，蒙古的地理和气候状况使得完成这些任务要比其他国家更困难。

（孔艺晓译，戴臻校）

毛里求斯贸易政策审议

1. 毛里求斯是一个小岛国，生活水平相对较高，联合国开发计划署认为它是高度发展国家。毛里求斯充分利用非互惠性的贸易优惠、良好的经济政策、对人力资本的大量投资以及稳定的社会政治，改善其经济竞争力，吸引了大量外国直接投资流入，增强了经济韧性。服务业占国内生产总值的72%，构成出口的重要组成部分，在经济中扮演着重要的角色。毛里求斯正在努力进一步提高服务贸易规模并创造更多的就业机会，以缓解部分由于非优惠税率优惠减少所带来的高失业率。

2. 毛里求斯的政府治理、竞争力和商业环境在各种各样的国际排名中都比较靠前。在非洲，它一直是表现最好的国家之一。其投资体制是开放和透明的。审议期间，旅游业的外国股权上限已放开，但在下列领域依然保留：电视广播、制糖和潜水中心。外国律师事务所只能从事外国法或国际法相关业务或者提供非诉法律服务，但法律服务领域有望进一步放开。外国人的财产所有权也受到限制。努力改善贸易和投资环境的措施包括：对大型投资项目快速审批，加强对投资者的法律保护。

3. 尽管全球经济危机，欧盟的进口需求走弱，审议期间，毛里求斯的经济表现基本良好。蓬勃发展的旅游业和持续增长的建筑业推动了 GDP 的增长。此外，宏观经济政策上的支撑，如财政刺激和稳健的货币政策，对避免经济衰退起了重要的作用。

4. 毛里求斯的对外贸易地位比较重要，进出口总额占 GDP 的 115%。审议期间出现经常账户赤字是由于大规模货物贸易赤字超过了服务贸易和收入项目盈余。服装、纺织品和糖是毛里求斯重要的出口商品，主要出口市场是欧盟；而石油和食品是重要的进口产品，主要来自欧盟、印度和中国。

5. 毛里求斯给予所有的贸易伙伴以最惠国待遇，它从未参与任何 WTO 争端解决案件，无论是作为原告还是被告。同时，在 WTO 保持良好记录，在一些项目上表现突出。

6. 最近毛里求斯采取了削减关税、减少进口许可、削减补贴计划等几项措施来进一步促进经济开放。随着关税的削减，毛里求斯的平均最惠国关税率从 2007 年的 6.6%下降到 2014 年的 2.3%。按照海关分类，最显著的关税降低是在鞋子和首饰、武器和弹药、加工食物和纺织品领域。随着这些关税的削减，88.8%的商品的最惠国关税为 0。关税保护水平最高的是服装行业，关税税率高达488%（从价税)。毛里求斯非常开放的治理机制与有限覆盖的高关税上形成了鲜明的对比。

7. 虽然在审议期间进出口许可证已经减少了很多，进口许可制度依然被用来保护国内生产商的一些农产品如茶、鸡肉和猪肉。洋葱和土豆的进口是通过农产品市场委员会进行进口配额管理来控制的。

8. 鉴于近 90%的最惠国关税是 0，毛里求斯能协商的范围是有限的。毛里求斯参与了五个区域贸易协定，共有 24 个合作伙伴。在审议期间最重要的突破是毛里求斯与土耳其的区域贸易协定，欧盟与来自非洲东部和南部国家及毛里求斯临时经济伙伴关系协定。与南部非洲发展共同体、东部和南部非洲共同市场的融合得到加强，更广泛的区域一体化的努力正在进行中。优先进入主要市场如欧盟和美国，对毛里求斯的出口表现一直都至关重要，尤其是对它的糖和纺织品而言。关税在政府的收入来源中占比很小且在不断降低，而其他税收收入——如增值税和消费税却在增加。

9. 通关时间已经显著缩短，授权经济运营商计划于 2008 年推出。自 2013 年以来，立法上的变动授权由海关预先裁决关税和原产地的相关问题，并在税务机关引入了涉及关税纠纷的非诉讼的独立上诉机构。毛里求斯是世贸组织成员中已经就贸易便利化协议 A 类项目做出承诺的国家。

10. 2010 年，毛里求斯颁布了一部涉及反倾销和反补贴的贸易法案。这是它首次针对该领域立法，然而因为该法案存在一些不合适的地方，修正案也在制定之中。同时保障措施立法和实施条例正在起草过程中。到目前为止，毛里求斯没有进行过反倾销或反补贴的调查。

11. 从上次审议以来，毛里求斯在标准设置和技术法规方面的立法和制度框架没有变化。技术规范由政府部门或者相应领域的监管部门制定和实施，其中一些是基于自愿的标准。虽然这些机构在起草过程中经常咨询一些利益相关者，技术法规的开发和实施过程中的协调与磋商环节依然有改善的空间。审议期间相关的世贸组织委员会并没有对毛里求斯的技术法规或SPS措施表现出特别的关切。

12. 毛里求斯有着各种激励措施，尤其是在促进商业发展、鼓励中小企业发展、支持房地产行业增长、鼓励与工作相关的培训和吸引离岸公司方面。上次审查期间采取的许多旨在促进出口的激励措施已经停止。为支持制造业、农业和渔业的发展采取了关税和增值税免税以及降低电子产品关税等措施。毛里求斯继续运营一个自由港计划来为国际贸易提供有竞争力的物流和分销平台，新的战略意图是鼓励有附加值的生产活动，如处理和简单组装商品，鼓励制造企业出口产品到非洲。自由港内经营的企业不需要缴纳企业所得税，同时还可享受其他财政和非财政激励。在特殊外汇信贷条件下，企业可以通过商业银行利用转贷将汇率风险最小化。创业毛里求斯（EM）和中小企业发展局（SMEDA）两个机构还运作了一系列项目来支持毛里求斯的企业参与交易会，开发出口市场及营销和推广活动。

13. 一项新的政府采购法案在2008年生效。采购是由不同的政府部门进行的。中央采购委员会负责批准所有超过一定额度的合同和公共/私营伙伴关系的建立。投标方可能被限制为毛里求斯的公民或在毛里求斯注册的经营实体，对国内商品、服务或承包商有一定程度的价格偏好。2012年，政府采购支出总额96.79亿，国内公司获得了大部分的采购合同。毛里求斯没有参加《政府采购协议》。

14. 国家通过各种半国营经济实体来干预经济活动。国家直接持有一些毛里求斯公司的股权，涉及电信、航空运输和金融服务部门。它也通过其投资部门——国有投资公司投资于各种各样的毛里求斯的企业。2012年，毛里求斯政府和几家商业银行联手组建了一个私募股权基金投资于毛里求斯中小企业的股票或资本。该基金将收购与资本回报率及风险水平相称的约1000万卢比到5000万卢比的股权，其目的是收购少数股权然后在五年内退出。

15. 两个半国营的实体参与农产品的进口：农业营销委员会（AMB）和国家贸易公司（STC）。AMB的角色是确保某些基本食品供应稳定并且价格可以负担得起。AMB是大蒜的唯一进口商，自2008年以来洋葱、姜黄和小豆蔻的进口垄断已经放开。国家贸易公司是唯一被授权的石油产品、液化石油气和面粉的进口商。

16. 一个新的竞争法在2009年11月生效。法案授权新成立的毛里求斯竞争委员会（CCM）调查合谋协议，审核涉嫌滥用垄断地位情况和合并所导致的实质性竞争减少，但是该法案不适用于石油产品。竞争委员会迄今为止的大多数调查都是针对垄断情况的评估。第一次针对卡特尔的调查是在2014年，调查对象是啤酒行业。竞争委员会有权针对个别经济领域竞争的有效性进行一般性研究。到目前为止，已经针对水泥和药品启动了两项研究，前项使得水泥的进口和装袋自由化。审议期间，针对商业和工业使用的12公斤液化石油气钢瓶价格管制解除，但仍然维持对其他一些产品的价格管制。

17. 毛里求斯正在寻求大范围的改革知识产权（IP）的立法，目标在于将知识产权与经济和社会发展相结合，促进创新和创造力的释放。2009年建立了知识产权发展计划（IPDP）。作为实施知识产权发展计划的第一步，2014年国民议会通过新的版权法案。工业产权法案将涉及商标、专利、工业设计、植物育种者的权利、地理标志、集成电路设计和实用新型，后4项目前不受现行立法的保护。政府还打算强化知识产权管理制度框架。正在进行中的立法仅仅允许受专利权保护的平行进口。

18. 甘蔗是毛里求斯的主要经济作物。审议期间，农业生产的主要趋势是持续下降，特别是甘蔗、烟草生产的急剧减少。另一方面，牛奶、猪肉和某些粮食作物的生产持续增长。2011年毛里求斯开始生产大米，主要用于出口。在审议期间，毛里求斯的农业政策一直集中在应对其食糖出口欧盟市场配额终止带来的挑战。这一领域的政府战略主要集中在：将甘蔗生产分为精制糖、电力和乙醇、重组糖产业，并通过各种奖励措施鼓励其他农产品的生产和出口。为了食品安全，许多农产品出口依然需要许可证。

19. 毛里求斯拥有世界上最大的专属经济区

(EEZs)；近 90%的年总捕鱼量由持有执照的外国船只占据。毛里求斯希望从海洋资源获取更大利益，主要方式包括发展水产养殖业，增加国家船队的捕捞能力。毛里求斯有一个海鲜中心，主要是海鲜加工活动和相关的服务。

20. 与上次审议相比，能源部门的结构在很大程度上仍然没有明显变化。石油产品是由国家贸易公司进口，并出售给四个石油公司在国内市场分销。中央电力局对电力传输和配电仍具有垄断性，它还与其他独立电力生产商一起从事发电。电费根据客户的类型不同而不同，低税率适用于工业和农业用电者。能源政策的一个新的重点是减少对进口化石燃料的依赖，利用可再生能源并以更有效率的方式利用能源资源。

21. 毛里求斯的制造业发展是基于双管齐下的战略，发展所谓的出口导向型企业（eoes），出口驱动外向型经济发展；这些企业主要是由享受优惠税率向美国和欧盟出口服装的企业组成。面向国内市场的产业主要是加工食品、饮料和烟草。因为毛里求斯出口加工区方案被放弃，2006 年出口导向型企业不再享受任何特殊优待或奖励。

22. 金融服务仍然是经济的一大支柱，贡献了超过 10%的国内生产总值，并对外国投资开放。银行服务占主导地位，政府在各金融服务企业中都有股份。全球金融危机没有导致毛里求斯银行倒闭。审议期间，其立法和监管都有所变化，以加强监督和透明度，打击非法活动。保险业有规模较大的并购，因为需要将长期的和一般的保险业务分开以满足新要求。地方资产不允许外国的保险公司投保。不过自 2013 年以来，这一限制并没有适用于出口保险的保险合同。

23. 政府的目标是让毛里求斯成为区域性的信息和通信技术中心，使该产业成为一个主要的经济支柱。在这样的背景下，已采取或正在酝酿着提高电信行业竞争力的措施，这个领域此前是由毛里求斯电信主导的，以及为宽带发展创造最有利的环境。政府拥有毛里求斯电信公司 59%的股权。审议期间，该产业的主要发展趋势是移动通讯用户和互联网用户持续增长以及国际带宽容量的指数性增长。

24. 国家在提供港口、机场运营和服务方面继续保持强势地位。它还拥有毛里求斯旗舰运输公司——毛里求斯航空的大量股份。政府对海运部门的战略是将其主要港口发展成为区域海运、物流和商务枢纽；在航空运输领域，毛里求斯为航空枢纽战略重点发展客运、货运、培训以及维护、一般修理和大修。毛里求斯将继续实施更自由的空域政策，并且正在抛弃只允许计划航班的政策。

25. 旅游政策的目的是促使毛里求斯成为一个上佳的旅游目的地。审议期间，政府已更新了针对非公民在旅游相关领域的投资政策，促成了与美国签署的双边投资协议，在汽车租赁、旅行社和旅游运营商部分对外国投资的限制已被解除。外商在酒店和餐馆上的直接投资只要是该项目能带来附加值，并且与毛里求斯旅游质量目标相符就会被放行。此外还通过特定的计划，鼓励对酒店和别墅的外国直接投资。

（陈雨译，魏亿亮校）

吉布提贸易政策审议

1. 吉布提的经济主要是靠服务业，商品生产份额非常小。制造业和农业部门一直表现疲弱，沉重的税收和生产要素（劳动力和能源）的高成本是主要原因。鉴于其对进口的严重依赖，国际贸易在吉布提扮演着重要的角色。商品和服务贸易占其国内生产总值的94%。

2. 由于其对基本商品的价格补贴政策和基于国家货币局安排的外汇制度，吉布提法郎（DF）采取盯住美元的固定汇率，1美元兑177.721吉布提法郎，自2006以来通货膨胀率控制在平均不到5%。由于中央银行没有给财政赤字买单的权力，进口成为通货膨胀的主要来源。预算赤字是由不力的税收征管、大额度的税收减免和非预算支出所导致的，过去主要靠国内支付欠账来弥补，现在是收紧预算并纳入国际货币基金组织的稳定方案。

3. 受大量投资流入的影响，特别是针对港口基础设施的投资，2006—2009年年均国内生产总值的增长率约为5%。受世界经济危机的影响，这一势头在2010年和2011年有所放缓。但2012年经济增长再次复苏，主要依赖港口、公路和酒店基础设施的投资恢复，以及埃塞俄比亚强劲的经济增长——该国90%的货物通过吉布提港过境。在吸引外国直接投资的同时，吉布提的优势还在于个人安全具有较高保障、战略性的地理位置和稳定的货币等。

4. 一般而言，吉布提的贸易政策旨在促进生产系统的多样化，私营部门对国内生产总值的贡献更多（不包括港口相关的经济活动），第二产业的份额增加，促进了企业规范化和商业体制改革。2010年，吉布提通过了一个国家贸易发展战略且已被部分实施。这一战略的成果包括：海关所使用的软件升级；统计数据的改进；为方便企业设立所做的努力；立法改革，特别是引入了商业代码。吉布提通过加大机构改革力度来加强公共部门与私营部门的沟通，以及参与区域和多边机制。然而，它仍然难以履行其对世贸组织的通报义务。

5. 吉布提是东南非共同市场（COMESA）的成员，并参与大陆规模的整合中。它还参加了欧洲联盟与东部和南部非洲国家之间建立经济伙伴关系的谈判。审议期间，在东南非共同市场的支持下，吉布提—亚的斯亚贝巴—南苏丹走廊启动了一个虚拟的贸易便利化制度安排。一旦这项工作完成，系统将能实时跟踪货物在整个走廊的位置。

6. 吉布提给予所有的贸易伙伴至少是最惠国待遇。进口货物可能会征收内部消费税（TIC）、增值税（VAT）、消费税、特殊团结税、石油产品税、营业执照费和一般团结税。2008年采用的增值税将逐步消除TIC，它对国内生产的商品豁免征税，以使其成为实质上的关税。大量的免税和豁免使得政府收入在2013年减少了1000亿吉布提法郎。这些豁免的根据是投资规定和海关税则、自贸区协议以及与某些公司的特殊协议。

7. 虽然吉布提没有关于标准化的立法，但在质量控制和标准局的指导下，最近通过了有关食品的技术法规。由于其技术手段非常有限，检查程序一般无法深入评估是否符合这些技术法规。自2011年以来，吉布提成立的国家食品法典委员会（CNCA）负责调整其SPS措施与国际标准保持一致。无论进口的还是本地生产的水和其他食品都要进行微生物和理化分析。

8. 为了促进出口，吉布提继续保持其自由港制度，公司享有免除直接和间接税长达50年。然而，自由港内的经济活动仍然不畅。2014成立了一个公共—私人对话委员会，以确定私营部门发展所受的限制，并提出解决方案。

9. 吉布提没有向WTO通报任何国营贸易企业，吉布提电信和吉布提电力等都是国有企业，在各自的领域中享有专营权。此外，吉布提的国有企业依然在经济中仍占主导地位，主要是在农业、采矿业、酒店业、金融服务、电信、运输和仓储服务领域。

10. 2008年吉布提通过了一种新的竞争法和消费者保护法，但并没有把国有企业包括在内。吉布提在竞争有限的领域进行价格管制。因此，邮政和电信、电力、水务和城市交通服务受国家管制。价格控制也适用于接收其他国家援助的产品，如面包、面粉和煤油。

11. 2009 年吉布提通过了一项新的政府采购守则，以简化对投标的选择标准、规范，获得政府采购的程序、上诉程序，以及不遵守守则条文的情况下的罚款的规定。根据守则，公开招标是采购的首选程序。在只有数量有限的供应商提供服务的情况下，遵循限制性投标程序，同时应确保有适当的竞争。法律为吉布提当地企业，以及与这些企业相关的外国人、使用吉布提生产的商品和服务的企业设置了一定的优惠幅度。

12. 审议期间，吉布提进行了关于保护知识产权的若干改革。2006 年，吉布提通过了著作权保护与相关权利保护的法律，2009 年通过了工业产权法。此外，它在 2012 年签署了针对视听表演《北京条约》，2013 年签署了《马拉喀什协议》。吉布提法律禁止伪造和假冒商品及其贸易或任何其他仿冒品交易，并对假冒和盗版行为实施刑事制裁。

13. 吉布提有巨大的农业潜力，但因为取水困难，缺乏培训，以及政府政策原因，仍然未被充分开发。农业部门受关注的重点是：通过农业协会和合作社提供燃料税减免，赠送种子和设备，以及为牲畜养殖户提供免费的牲畜。

14. 尽管盐是吉布提的主要矿业资源，采矿技术的缺乏和较低的产品附加值使得工业开发困难重重。

15. 吉布提电力（EDD），作为一家国有企业，在发电和分销上仍具有垄断地位。2011 年以来，吉布提电网已与埃塞俄比亚电网互联，吉布提的总用电量的 50%从埃塞俄比亚进口。这种互联使吉布提大大减少了石油产品进口，降低了电价。

16. 制造业仍处于萌芽阶段。出现了一些小的生产单位，主要是农产品和水泥生产商和其他手工业。

17. 在 2014 年，吉布提有 11 家银行机构，2006 年时只有两家，这足以证明其经济增长，且服务部门总体来说充满活力，这受益于其资本的自由流动和有限的外汇管制。2011 年新的银行法生效，金融机构的最低资本要求为 10 亿吉布提法郎，而且范围扩展到附属金融机构（尤其是转账中介）和伊斯兰金融机构。

18. 国有独资的吉布提电信（DT）是该国唯一的电信运营商（互联网、移动和固定电话服务）。国际长途电话质量较差，2012 年吉布提电信费率大幅下调。

19. 交通运输部门具有创造就业和减少贫困的巨大潜力。然而，缺乏持续的针对运输服务和物流的发展战略是一个严重的障碍。吉布提的地理位置决定了其海上运输在周边国家的国际贸易中的重要性。它与埃塞俄比亚接壤的地理位置使其成为埃塞俄比亚的一个海港，埃塞俄比亚的经济增长非常迅速。服务于埃塞俄比亚的运输产业促进了理货、船代、酒店、运输和餐饮行业的发展。由于铁路网络陈旧，埃塞俄比亚货物过境吉布提港口的散货通过陆路运输，几乎完全由埃塞俄比亚公司承运。

20. 目前正在拟订针对空运的发展计划，部分是为了促进旅游业的发展，但是这将面临邻近国家的竞争，吉布提自身发展战略实施水平不高也会带来一定的负面影响。

（陈雨译，魏亿亮校）

中国香港贸易政策审议

1. 2010年和2013年期间（审议期间），香港经济平均年增长率为3.1%（按照2012年价格计算），主要由内部强劲的需求驱动，伴随着脆弱的全球经济复苏。香港是世界上最市场化和最开放的经济体之一，2013年贸易额与GDP的比率高达458%，在经济自由程度、竞争力、经商的容易程度等一些指标上排在世界前列。它也有一个非常自由的外国投资制度。

2. 经历了全球金融动荡（2008—2009年）后，因外部需求疲软，政府实施反周期措施以维护金融稳定和刺激当地的经济。在2010年和2011年经济迅速反弹，并在2012年经历了一个短暂的放缓后，2013年经济增长达到2.9%。当时预测2014年经济增长为3.75%。

3. 审议期间，香港继续加强与中国大陆的经济和金融方面的联系，特别是通过更紧密经贸关系安排协议（CEPA）。CEPA提供了很多的贸易机会，香港的服务供应商和香港本身作为中国内地对外贸易的重要中介的地位得以巩固。香港作为一个国际金融中心，也得益于中国内地资本账户的逐步开放、人民币的国际化。同理，加强金融一体化让香港的金融机构更多地受到大陆的影响。总体来说，香港的经济前景越来越与中国大陆的经济表现交织在一起。

4. 香港具有一个健全的经济基础，如健康的财政平衡、大规模的外汇储备、灵活的市场和良好的金融体系，使它能够迅速适应具有挑战性的外部环境，并使其免于全球金融危机的影响。审慎的财政政策是其宏观经济框架的一个关键特征，使香港在审议期间保持了公共财政顺差（尽管它有所下降）。货币政策继续关注汇率稳定，通过自1983年盯住美元的汇率得以实现。2010年以来的低利率导致信贷快速扩张，有助于刺激国内需求。在2010—2011年快速增长后，通货膨胀率在2012和2013年降低到刚刚超过4%的水平，政府利用针对需求方的审慎的措施给房地产市场降温，并抑制进口食品价格的上涨。然而，其通胀仍高于美国，导致当地货币对美元实际升值。

5. 尽管有健全的宏观经济框架，香港仍面临着一系列的政策挑战，包括需要在人口老龄化条件下保持财政可持续性；解决收入不平等和社会福利、医疗和教育需求；确保适当的可负担得起的住房供应以及房地产市场的稳定；控制通货膨胀。

6. 服务业仍然占主导地位的经济，占国内生产总值的93%，占总就业人数的88%（2012年）。审议期间最有活力的部门是批发和零售业，住宿和餐饮业，这得益于充满活力的入境旅游，以及金融保险。因为其以服务业为导向的定位，香港依赖进口产品来满足国内消费。这反映了货物贸易持续的赤字，已经超过了在服务贸易上的大量盈余，服务贸易盈余主要来自于运输、旅游和金融服务的出口。鉴于香港是世界上最大的自由贸易区，转口贸易是商品贸易的驱动力，而中国大陆则是其主要的贸易伙伴，占香港转口贸易的55%和商品进口的48%（2013年）。

7. 香港坚定支持多边贸易体制、多哈发展议程的完成和巴厘一揽子计划的实施。香港承诺加入《贸易便利化协定》后将立即实施，且不使用任何灵活安排。香港是WTO《信息技术协议》、修改后的《政府采购协议》（GPA）的缔约方，并参与其他多边协议，如服务贸易协议（TISA）和最近开始的WTO成员环保产品对话。审议期间，或许香港最显著的政策发展在于积极参与自由贸易协定（FTA）。自2010年以来，香港已经签署了与新西兰、欧洲自由贸易联盟成员国、智利（前两个已经生效）的自由贸易协定。它也签署了CEPA的五个补充协议，目前正在谈判的自由贸易协定是与东盟国家的FTA。香港当局表示，只要是与WTO相一致，有助于多边贸易自由化，香港愿意参与各种双边、多边、区域自由贸易协定。

8. 2012年第一个全面的竞争法的实施，在香港的经济政策改革中是一个里程碑式的进步。竞争条例适用于所有的经济部门，为应对不同类型的反竞争行为提供了一个法律框架，并遵循国际最佳惯例。然而，合并控制权仅限于电讯部门，而法定机构则获豁免。一个具有充分调查权的竞争事务委员会，负责相关执法工作，促进竞争准则的发展。竞争法庭负责裁决工作和授权救济措施，包括罚款和救济。

9. 香港实行在最惠国待遇基础上免关税制度，但一半以上的税则仍游离在WTO之外。鉴于香港的自由港的地位，海关手续是世界上最容易最快的，几乎所有的报关单和相关文件都是电子化处理。香港在过去几年实施措施，以促进贸易和加强其作为运输枢纽的角色，包括正式引入许可经济营运商计划，联运转运促进方案和降低报关费。海关估价只用于征收四种产品（酒类、烟草、碳氢油、甲醇）的消费税和机动车首次注册税。

10. 非关税措施很少，进口禁令和许可证仅仅适用于安全、健康和环境方面的问题，或者用于遵守国际义务。2011年针对“非敏感市场”和纺织品转运的许可和通知要求取消。根据相关的立法改革要求，在2014年底之前，有计划地消除剩余的对纺织品贸易的要求。香港没有对应急措施和保障措施立法。

11. TBT和SPS系统是透明且简单的。新的食品安全条例在2012年2月生效，它建立了一个食品进口商和分销商的注册机制，要求食品贸易商在一定时期内保持良好的交易记录，以提高食品的可追溯性。

12. 香港没有出口关税。出口禁止范围和需要许可证出口的货物范围与相应的进口许可范围基本上是一致的，并基于相同的原因。2013年，为保证产品的本地供应，针对0—3岁的婴幼儿配方奶粉的出口实行许可证管理。如果货物被出口，将退还消费税。政府支持出口商，主要通过出口信用保险和提供出口促销活动的资金。2012年6月，香港推出一项旨在发展品牌、升级转型及拓展内销市场的专项基金（BUD），向在本地注册的以中国大陆市场为目标的中小企业提供出口援助。

13. 香港维持了一个简单的税收结构，税基窄而且税率低。即便如此，政府依然采取了一些税收优惠措施，包括购买环保的商用车和知识产权相关的支出税收优惠。非税收优惠，主要是支持中小企业和研发活动，以提供贷款、贷款担保和现金补助形式进行，但援助规模不大。

14. 香港是加入修订后的政府采购协议的首个WTO成员，并通过增加新的政府实体和服务类型来提高其承诺水平。知识产权制度在很大程度上仍然保持不变，但仍有重要的持续性措施来修改版权和专利权的立法。香港提高公众意识和知识产权执法的行动获得了国际认可，并且它还采取积极的措施来对抗数字环境中侵犯知识产权行为的全球性挑战。

15. 农业和渔业部门占比很小，仅占其生产总值和总就业人数的0.1%。制造业持续萎缩，占其生产总值不到2%。香港没有直接采取任何政策工具来扭转这一趋势。中国内地是制成品出口的最大市场，但在CEPA框架下“当地商品出口”到中国内地的尚不到“当地出口”总数的50%。

16. 香港是一个地区性甚至全球性金融服务、海运和航空运输的中心。香港的GATS承诺并不广泛，但制度是相当宽松的，这体现在hkc－efta自由贸易协定中规定的负面清单上。该协定包含非常少的保留条款，特别是对未来的措施上，大部分是纯粹预防性的，到目前为止都没有切实应用过。这份协议所规定的制度应用相当广泛。

17. 自2003年以来电信制度逐步开放。从运营商的数量来看，市场竞争程度很高，至少固定电信服务，按照国际电信联盟的价格基准进行国际范围内的比较衡量是这样的。当地三家企业占据移动电话市场的主导地位，它们赢得了最近的4G/LTE频段国际拍卖，同固定电信市场类似。

18. 在金融服务领域，香港是一个充满活力的区域和全球金融中心（如IPO市场）。三家本地银行占据了本地市场的主导地位，金融部门的最大一部分是专门为海外服务，特别是向中国大陆，几乎所有主要的全球参与者都有参与。实行的制度是相当宽松的，已进一步放宽对外资银行设立本地注册银行的设立条件。除此之外，金融服务的市场准入制度并没有实质性的改变，自上次审议以来所采取的大部分措施都是基于当地监管和审慎要求。

19. 香港是世界第四大港口（仅次于上海、新加坡和深圳），并且是第四大船舶注册地（在巴拿马、利比里亚和马绍尔群岛之后）。良好的经营条件和海事相关服务让香港吸引了来自全球各地的船东投资，这也解释了为什么在册运力的非常大的部分是外资独资控制的。此外，香港船东拥有挂着非香港旗的一个庞大的舰队。航运政策自由，没有限制在陆上活动和建设，没有货载分摊制度。没有支持或补贴，但对挂香港旗的船舶国际交易的收入免征所得税。大多数集装箱码头基本上是由当地的私人公司管理，但通过租赁协议，外国投资也大量存在。

20. 香港对签订了双边航空运输协定的国家的管理制度相对宽松。然而，因为香港拥有世界第一的航空货运机场，考虑到这是具有战略意义的产业，并且还有容量和土地的限制，对于某些辅助服务（如货物装卸和维修服务），香港采取了较不自由的体制，采用了数量有限的许可证制度。

21. 分销是香港主要的经济部门，占就业人数的近10%和GDP的近5%。香港的GATS承诺的配送服务仅限于零售服务并且具有相对自由的制度（对属于模式3市场准入没有限制）。香港签署的自由贸易协定覆盖了几乎所有的部门且仅保留了非常有限的保留条款。除分区和城市规划用途外，营业活动基本上是不受管制的。许多外国经销商也进入了这个市场，但超市市场很大程度上是由地方利益主导的。传统的露天生鲜食品市场（菜市场）仍然是香港分销系统的重要组成部分。

（王达译，覃松校）

美国贸易政策审议

1. 美国经济已基本上从2007—2009年的衰退中恢复过来。尽管受到欧盟市场疲软的进口需求拖累，但GDP增长一直保持稳定。在大部分的审议期间，占美国GDP主要部分的私人消费继续扩张，受益于劳动力市场的稳步提升、个人可支配收入的增长、因股市上涨和房价上涨盘活的家庭财富。私人国内投资和出口也表现良好，决定了整体的增长表现。

2. 最近美国页岩油和天然气产量的爆发已经影响到经济的各个方面。它降低了能源价格，并有助于降低生产成本。在制造业，这已经成为一个重要的创造就业的部门。由于石油贸易逆差的减少，2013年的赤字水平达到四年来的低点，之前石油贸易产生的逆差占货物和服务贸易总贸易逆差的一半。在审议期间，商品贸易继续扩大，出口在2013年达到历史最高水平，进口五年来首次下降。美国仍然是世界领先的服务出口国，其贸易顺差在审议期间有所增加。

3. 宏观经济政策继续积极支持美国经济，促进经济增长和减少失业。其采取的措施包括纠正在经济衰退期间普遍存在的扩张性政策所导致的巨额财政赤字；尽管非常规货币政策仍在继续实施，2013年12月美联储宣布将开始缩减其量化宽松措施。

4. 美国仍然是世界上最大的外国直接投资的流入国，虽然在过去两年里流入量已经下降。为了抵消这种趋势，政府维持或继续开展新计划以促进对外投资。2011年的“选择美国”计划继续吸引和留住投资，2012年的“美国制造”计划的目的是加快内包，即带回投资和工作。

5. 审议期间美国贸易政策最重要的变化之一是2014年2月7日颁布的新农业法案。这是商品农业政策方面相当大的变化。两个长期存在的针对乳品市场的支持政策（价格支持和出口补贴）已被取消。新农业法案取消了已脱钩的直接支付制度，该制度是乌拉圭回合谈判结束以来美国农业政策的基石，改革基于商品价格和收入的支持计划。新农业法案取消了农业的直接支付，而代之以与当前价格相联系的“差额支付工具”，如价格损失保险计划和农业风险保障计划。2014年农业法案继续完成从传统的商品、储备和灾害支付向农业保险补助金的长期政策转变。

6. 尽管美国的主要贸易政策框架一直没有大的变化，当局已经采取一些举措来提高贸易执法，主要依靠跨部门的贸易执法中心，同时通过建立专门的力量和相关的政策或策略打击贩卖野生动物和钓鱼欺诈。自2007年以来“贸易促进权”仍然没有生效。审议期间虽然国会做了一些努力，目前尚未形成立法。

7. 美国继续在最惠国待遇条款下进行绝大部分贸易，但是约有22%的进口可以归入自贸区或单方面优惠制度。在审议期间，通过自由贸易协定的进口小幅上涨，而那些通过单方面优惠制度进入的则在下降，部分原因是GSP、ATPA/ATPDEA在2013年7月过期。到目前为止，国会没有重新授权这些项目，审议期间也没有新的自由贸易协定结束谈判。

8. 在影响进口的政策方面，促进贸易发展的措施包括逐步实施单一窗口申请、简化进入范围扩大，以及新设或扩大可信任交易项目。关于进口禁令或限制，在审议期间实施了一些新措施。审议期间的关税、原产地规则、进口许可证、海关估价和其他收费的法律和法规框架没有变化。

9. 关于出口的进展包括正在进行中的出口控制改革（ECR）倡议，旨在创建一个新的出口控制系统，有一个单独控制机构和一个统一的控制清单；建立NEI/NEXT项目来替代国家出口计划（NEI），为继续支持和促进出口提供一个战略框架。美国继续维持一系列支持出口的机构或项目，如进出口银行出口信贷和海外投资公司提供发展筹资。

10. 在审议期间，有关贸易救济的监管制度基本没有太大变化，改变之处有四点：针对目的性倾销的管理、有关补贴的内部治理、复审程序中的受访人的选择以及针对非市场经济国家的处理惯例。反倾销和反补贴调查有所增加，尤其是在2013年针对钢铁产品的调查。另一方面，保障措施处于休眠状态，没有政策改变，也没有进行过调查。

11. 美国目前正在回顾其技术性贸易壁垒的监管实践，针对的是技术法规中自愿共识标准的使用和联邦采购。在2011年生效的食品药品管理局食品安全现代化法案是一项关于食品安全和动物饲料安全的重大改革，美国食品药品管理局正在制定法规实施这项新法律的一些关键要素。

12. 美国保持其在知识产权相关贸易的领先位置，2012年其特许权使用费收入占全球的43%。虽然美国知识产权产业是世界上最为成熟完善的，由于知识产权具有动态变化的特点，在审议期间依然有许多发展，其中包括21项立法变化、专利监管改革，减少盗窃美国商业秘密的行为的策略，以及2013年知识产权执法共同战略计划。

13. 服务业在美国经济中继续扮演着重要角色，在审议期间美国进行了一些服务部门的改革，建立了一系列加强金融服务的审慎标准，包括流动性、风险管理和资本管理，以加强对金融机构的监管。根据新规定，持有美国资产至少500亿美元的外国银行要为其在美国的金融业务建立中间控股公司，除少量例外情况，需满足与可比规模的美国银行相同的资本、流动性以及其他一些标准。国内银行将在2015年1月前、外国银行要在2016年1月前达到这些标准。在过去几年中，美国金融公司加强了它们的地位。尽管如此，在某些领域，包括针对“太大而不能倒闭”的银行（它们获得了大约700亿美元的援助）的监管仍然需要改进。

14. 在审议期间，美国取消了国际结算政策，以促使其国际长途规则更加现代化，进一步降低国际长途价格，以增加竞争。还采取了措施来改革普遍服务和跨运营商补偿系统，以使语音和宽带服务包括固定网和移动网能够让用户负担得起。此外，新的开放互联网政策预计在2014年底获得通过，以提高透明度为目标，强调并澄清了无阻断法则，并要求固定宽带（以后也包括移动宽带）运营商确保他们的做法是合情合理的。

15. 过去几年中，海上运输的体制和法律框架并没有改变。货物和旅客的沿海贸易仍然是由1920年的商船法案27条来规范（琼斯法）。美国资助各种海上安全计划，旨在保护美国国旗的船队和造船厂，如船舶保安计划。港口基础设施项目也有资格获得支持。美国将通过增加2020个主要港口的货物吞吐能力来解决港口拥挤问题。

16. 美国是目前世界上最大的医疗卫生服务市场，2010年总支出超过25亿美元。私人医疗支出约为12亿美元，人均支出约为8000美元。健康保险市场也是世界上最大的，因为它占健康支出的比重要比其他发达国家的公共社会保障体系占主导地位的比重大得多。最近主要的监管发展是2010年的患者保护与平价医疗法案，计划在2010年与2015年之间生效。它的目的是大大扩大覆盖人群的数量，并改善投保人的保障范围。因此，它会影响医疗保健和健康保险服务的供给和需求，从而对贸易产生影响。美国是WTO成员中少数对GATS中健康服务领域做出承诺的国家。

17. 美国视听产业是世界上规模最大的，电影制作和发行收入约460亿美元（2011年），电视产业（包括广播电视台、有线电视、卫星电视和网络视频发行）收入1610亿美元，电台产业收入180亿美元，音乐产业（唱片录制和分销）收入80亿美元。出口在很大程度上超过进口，与相应的对外销售（美国子公司的销售额）相比，外国在美国子公司的销售额要高得多。视听服务贸易相关的方面的政策是相当稳定的，审议期间的唯一进展是联邦通信委员会（FCC）放松对外资持股的政策，这与GATS和FTA的承诺一致。

（王达译，覃松校）

第三篇　中国与 WTO

● 中国 WTO 事务综述（2014）

中国是经济全球化的积极参与者和坚定支持者。2014年，我国适应经济全球化新形势，积极完善互利共赢、多元平衡、安全高效的开放型经济体系，充分利用世界贸易组织多边贸易体制平台，积极参与规则制定，妥善处理贸易纠纷，更好地参与国际经济合作，为实现经济社会和谐发展营造了良好的外部环境。

（一）坚持多边贸易体制主渠道地位，努力推动多哈回合谈判。中国积极落实在二十国集团（G20）、亚太经合组织（APEC）等场合做出的承诺，充分利用谈判核心成员和APEC东道主优势，发挥促和、促谈、促成作用，全面参与并积极推动多哈回合谈判，落实“巴厘一揽子”协议其他成果，维护多边贸易体制。加强与主要成员的沟通协调，团结和维护发展中成员，主动发出中国声音，提出中国思路，推动美国和印度就粮食安全问题达成和解，为通过《贸易便利化协定》议定书发挥了建设性作用。与此同时，积极宣讲“巴厘一揽子”协议成果，协调国内开展落实工作，及时通报《贸易便利化协定》实施措施。

（二）加快推进各项诸边谈判，深度参与贸易自由化进程。为积极参与《信息技术协定》扩围谈判，相关部门认真研究，精心准备谈判方案，同时加强与主要成员沟通，并与美国达成双边共识，打破《信息技术协定》扩围谈判僵局，为尽快恢复并最终结束谈判奠定了基础。高度重视环境产品谈判对建设生态文明、保护环境、促进产业升级的重要意义，积极参与《环境产品协定》谈判，加强产业调研，组建专家团队，与主要成员保持沟通，争取谈判主动权。此外，积极推进加入《政府采购协定》谈判，并按期提出第六次出价。

（三）成功完成世贸组织对华贸易政策审议。首次以货物贸易第一大国身份，接受世贸组织贸易政策审议。国内各有关部门加大协调力度，周密准备精心策划，撰写《中国政府政策声明》等书面材料逾45万字，回答世贸成员问题1700多个。通过正面舆论宣传，摆事实、讲道理，阐明中国坚持改革开放的决心，反对个别成员将审议政治化，增进了成员对我贸易投资政策的理解，充分展现了自信开放、重信守诺的大国形象，得到世贸组织多数成员的高度评价。同时，深度参与对美贸易政策审议，广泛征求国内政府部门、产业、学界意见诉求，充分表达关注，彰显贸易大国能力水平。

（四）主动运用世贸组织规则，妥善处理贸易争端。积极主动利用争端解决机制，维护我重要贸易利益。在2014年专家组和上诉机构散发的裁决报告中，我国作为争端方案件（按事项计算）占比分别达到40%和60%，起诉案件取得重要成果。特别是在两起诉美案件裁决中，美方对中国产品实施的大量反倾销、反补贴措施被认定违反世贸规则，商务部高虎城部长发表谈话敦促美方纠正滥用贸易救济规则的错误做法。首次根据《争端解决谅解》第21.5条启动执行争议程序，挑战欧盟执行紧固件案裁决情况，参与争端解决程序进一步深化。积极参与争端解决规则谈判、上诉机构成员遴选以及解决争端解决机制工作负担问题磋商等各项工作，在改进和完善争端解决机制方面发挥作用。

（五）开展贸易政策合规审查工作，引导技术壁垒相关讨论。贯彻落实十八届三中全会依法治国精神，扎实开展贸易政策合规工作，加快建设法治中国，完善法治化国际化营商环境。国务院办公厅颁布了合规工作相关文件，有序指导全国合规工作顺利开展。同时，商务部建立起横向联系各部门、纵向指导各地方的贸易政策合规工作机制，为稳步推进合规工作提供了重要保障。密切关注国际贸易技术壁垒新动向，及时提出具体贸易关注。引导成员就“私营标准”定义展开讨论并形成提案。联合发展中成员形成了“良好规制实践”议题的案文。

（商务部世界贸易组织司）

● 贸易争端与救济措施

中国参与世贸组织争端解决情况

2014年，世贸组织成员新发起争端解决案件共计14起。其中，中国作为当事方的案件1起（中国为被诉方），占当年全部新发起案件的7%。以下就2014年中国作为当事方参与的世贸组织争端解决案件情况做一简要介绍。

一、中国作为起诉方参与世贸组织争端解决案件新情况

（一）中国诉欧盟碳钢紧固件反倾销措施案（DS397）

1. 执行之诉涉案措施与主要诉求

本案涉案措施是欧盟对原产于中国的碳钢紧固件产品反倾销措施的复审决定。

中国认为，欧盟为执行诉欧盟紧固件反倾销措施案裁决所采取的措施违反了《关于实施1994年关税与贸易总协定第6条的协定》（《反倾销协定》）和《1994年关税与贸易总协定》（《1994年关贸总协定》）的诸多条款，包括：

（1）《反倾销协定》第6.4条和第6.2条。因为欧盟未及时向利害关系方提供机会，使其了解与其案件陈述有关的、不属于第6.5条规定的机密性质，且主管机关在反倾销调查中使用的特别是与印度生产商销售的产品有关的所有信息，因而未向利害关系方提供为其利益进行辩护的充分机会。

（2）《反倾销协定》第6.5条。因为欧盟在无正当理由的情况下认定印度生产商销售的产品相关的信息为“保密”信息，以及《反倾销协定》第6.5.1条，因为欧盟未要求印度同类生产商就保密基础上提供的信息提供足够详细的非保密摘要，以便能够合理了解以机密形式提交的信息的实质内容。

（3）《反倾销协定》第2.4条。因为欧盟未向所涉各方指明为保证进行公平比较所必需的信息，特别是欧盟未提供确定正常价值时使用的印度生产商销售的产品信息，并且未向当事方指明主张调整所需的信息。

（4）《反倾销协定》第2.4条。因为欧盟未保证中国出口生产商所生产的标准紧固件的出口价格未与特殊紧固件的正常价值进行比较。

（5）《反倾销协定》第2.4条与《1994年关税与贸易总协定》第6.1条。因为欧盟未对影响价格可比性的差异进行调整。

（6）《反倾销协定》第2.1条、第2.4条、第2.4.2条和第9.3条及《1994年关税与贸易总协定》第6.1条和第6.2条。因为欧盟未根据所有可比的出口交易计算倾销幅度并在此基础之上征收反倾销税。

（7）《反倾销协定》第4.1条和第3.1条。因为欧盟在重新定义国内产业时仅仅使用了原审《立案公告》第6条（b）项（i）规定的截止日之前登记的欧盟生产商的数据，因而未纠正该方法所造成的自我选择过程。

2. 争端进程

2009年7月31日，就欧盟对中国碳钢紧固件产品的反倾销措施，中国对欧盟提起世贸组织争端解决机制项下的磋商请求。2009年10月23日，专家组设立。2010年12月3日，世贸组织公布专家组报告。欧盟和中国分别于2011年3月25日和

30日提起上诉。2011年7月15日，世贸组织公布上诉机构报告。2011年7月28日，世贸组织争端解决机构（DSB）通过了本案专家组报告和上诉机构报告。

2012年3月6日至2012年10月10日，欧盟对原产于中国的碳钢紧固件产品的反倾销仲裁措施进行复审。2012年9月3日，欧盟公布的第765/2012号条例修改了《欧盟理事会关于防范非欧盟成员国进口产品倾销的第384/96号条例》第9(5)条，于2012年9月6日起开始实施。中国认为欧盟的复审决定仍涉嫌违反世贸组织规则，于2013年10月30日按照《关于争端解决规则与程序的谅解》（DSU）第21.5条的规定将欧盟的执行措施起诉至世贸组织。2014年2月18日，执行专家组设立。截至2014年底，本案仍在执行专家组审理阶段。

（二）中国诉美国反补贴措施案（DS437）

1. 涉案措施与主要诉求

本案涉案措施包括：（1）美国对中国22类输美产品发起的反补贴调查；（2）美国商务部认定"公共机构"时适用的"可反驳推定"，即美国商务部认为，一家企业所有权的多数由政府持有这一事实即足以认定该企业为《补贴与反补贴措施协定》（《补贴协定》）第1.1条意义上的"公共机构"，除非一方能够证明政府持有多数所有权并不导致对企业的"控制"。

中国认为，美国的下列措施违反了《1994年关贸总协定》和《补贴协定》有关条款：

（1）美国声称中国通过国有企业以低于充分回报的价格提供原材料产品，将其视为补贴并发起反补贴调查，违反《补贴协定》第1.1条、第2条、第11.1条至第11.3条和第14条（d）项。

（2）美国声称中国以低于充分回报的价格提供土地使用权，并将其认定为补贴，违反《补贴协定》第2条。

（3）美国声称中国维持出口限制，将其视为补贴并发起反补贴调查，违反《补贴协定》第1.1条(a)项（1）以及第11.1条至第11.3条。

（4）使用"可获得不利事实"做出不利推断，违反《补贴协定》第12.7条。

（5）美国适用"可反驳推定"认定"公共机构"，违反《补贴协定》第1.1条、第10条和第32.1条以及《1994年关税与贸易总协定》第6条。

2. 争端进程

2012年5月25日，中国就涉案措施对美国提起世贸组织争端解决机制项下的磋商请求。2012年9月28日，世贸组织争端解决机构正式设立了专家组，澳大利亚、巴西、加拿大、欧盟、印度、日本、韩国、挪威、俄罗斯、土耳其、越南和沙特阿拉伯共12个世贸组织成员保留各自的第三方权利。

2014年7月14日，世贸组织公布专家组报告。2014年8月22日，中国提起上诉。2014年8月27日，美国提起交叉上诉。上诉机构已于2014年12月18日发布报告。

3. 专家组主要裁决

专家组认为，美国商务部将国有企业推定为公共机构的做法以及在涉案反补贴措施中的适用违反《补贴协定》第1.1条。美国在认定补贴事实专向性应考虑因素、土地专向性认定、基于出口限制反补贴立案的做法违反《补贴协定》第2.2条、第2.4条和第11.3条。专家组未支持中方关于补贴专向性、外部基准及使用可获得不利事实等方面的主张。

4. 上诉机构主要裁决

（1）针对外部基准问题，上诉机构推翻了专家组关于外部基准的裁决，并裁定美国商务部在涉案反补贴调查中拒绝采用国内私营部门的价格作为计算利益的基准价格的做法违反了美国在《补贴协定》第14条（d）项和第1.1条（b）项下的义务。

（2）针对补贴专向性问题，上诉机构维持了专家组关于美国商务部仅依据第2.1条（c）项分析专向性符合《补贴协定》的认定；推翻了专家组关于中国未能证明美国商务部未指明"补贴计划"的做法违反了美国在《补贴协定》第2.1条下的义务的认定；但是，上诉机构认为专家组未审查关于补贴计划是否存在的大部分证据，双方也未就此问题展开充分抗辩，故而裁定其无法完成对此的法律分析；上诉机构推翻了专家组关于中国未能证明美国商务部未指明"授予机关"的做法违反了美国在《补贴协定》第2.1条义务的认定；但是，上诉机构认为专家组已经认定美国商务部未考虑第2.1条(c)项最后一句规定的两项要素即"授予机关管辖范围内经济活动的多样性"与"实施补贴计划的持续时间”违反了该条款，该认定与美国商务部指明“授权机关的管辖范围”相关联。由此，上诉机构认为其完成法律分析对于解决双方争端并无助益，因此未完成对此的法律分析。

（3）针对使用可获得不利事实问题，上诉机构推翻了专家组关于中国未能证明美国商务部未采用在案可获得事实的做法违反了美国在《补贴协定》第12.7条下的义务的认定；但是，上诉机构认为其已经认定专家组违反了《争端解决谅解》第11条，争端各方未就可获得事实有关问题充分发表意见，在此情况下完成法律分析将有损正当程序；同时，就此问题完成法律分析对解决双方争端并无助益，因为中国所挑战的42处使用可获得不利事实的情形是美国商务部用以支持其公共机构、利益、专向性和出口限制等方面的裁定，而对于这些裁定，专家组和上诉机构已经分别做出违反认定，且美国对专家组的认定并未提出上诉，故而上诉机构无须完成对此的法律分析。

（三）中国诉美国关税法修订案世贸争端案（DS449）

1. 涉案措施与主要诉求

本案的涉案措施包括：（1）2012年3月13日公布的美国《1930年关税法》修订案（GPX立法）；（2）2006年11月20日至2012年3月13日，美国对中国24类产品发起的反倾销和反补贴调查以及相关后续行动。

中国认为，美国上述措施违反了《1994年关贸总协定》、《补贴协定》和《反倾销协定》有关条款：

（1）GPX立法第1节规定美国《1930年关税法》中的反补贴条款可以追溯性地适用于2006年11月20日或之后发起的所有反补贴调查以及相关后续行动，违反《1994年关贸总协定》第10条。

（2）对于2006年11月20日至2012年3月13日期间发起的反倾销和反补贴调查或复审，美国商务部缺乏识别和避免双重救济的法定权力，事实上也没有调查并避免这些调查或复审中的双重救济，违反《1994年关贸总协定》第6条、《补贴协定》第10条、第15条、第19条、第21条、第32条以及《反倾销协定》第9条和第11条。

2. 争端进程

2012年9月17日，中国就涉案措施对美国提起世贸组织争端解决机制项下的磋商请求。2012年11月30日，中国请求设立专家组。2012年12月17日，世贸组织争端解决机构设立了专家组。澳大利亚、加拿大、欧盟、日本、土耳其和越南6个世贸组织成员保留各自的第三方权利。

2014年3月27日，世贸组织公布专家组报告。2014年4月8日，中国提出上诉。2014年4月17日，美国提出交叉上诉。上诉机构报告于2014年7月7日公布，7月22日通过。合理执行期为12个月零2周，至2015年8月5日。

3. 专家组主要裁决

专家组的主要裁决如下：

（1）美国商务部在2006年至2012年间对华发起的25起反倾销反补贴调查中，同时征收反倾销税（基于“非市场经济”方法）和反补贴税，未能进行避免双重救济的税额调整，违反了《补贴协定》第10条、第19.3条和第32.1条。

（2）专家组多数意见认为，美国GPX立法不违反《1994年关税与贸易总协定》第10条规定。

4. 上诉机构主要裁决

上诉机构的主要裁决为：美商务部在2006年至2012年间对华发起的25起双反调查中，同时征收反倾销税（基于“非市场经济”方法）和反补贴税，却未进行避免重复征税的税额调整，构成“双重救济”，违反了世贸规则。专家组在分析美国GPX立法是否符合《1994年关贸总协定》第10条时，适用了错误的法律解释，但由于专家组基于错误的法律解释未能审查美国反补贴法所有相关要素，上诉机构无法完成分析。

（四）中国诉欧盟及其特定成员国光伏补贴措施案（DS452）

1. 涉案措施与主要诉求

本案的涉案措施为意大利、希腊的光伏补贴措施。意大利、希腊有关法律规定，如果光伏发电项目的主要零部件原产于欧盟国家或欧洲经济区国家，该项目生产的电力即可获得一定金额或比例的上网电价补贴。

中国认为，上述补贴措施违反了世贸组织协定关于国民待遇（《1994年关贸总协定》第3条、《与贸易有关的投资措施协定》第2条）和最惠国待遇（《1994年关贸总协定》第1条）的规定，构成了世贸组织协定禁止的进口替代补贴［《补贴协定》第 3.1 条（b）项〕，并严重影响中国光伏产品出口，损害了中国作为世贸组织成员的正当权益。

2. 争端进程

2012 年 11 月 5 日，中国就涉案措施对欧盟提起世贸组织争端解决机制项下的磋商请求。目前，本案仍处于磋商阶段。

（五）中国诉美国反倾销措施案（DS471）

1. 涉案措施与主要诉求

本案的涉案措施为美国对中国铝型材、铜版纸、非公路用轮胎、石油管材、金刚石锯片等 13 种产品采取的反倾销措施。

中国认为，美国上诉措施违反了《1994 年关税与贸易总协定》和《反倾销协定》有关条款：

（1）美国在某些涉及“目标倾销”指控的反倾销调查中，为确定产品整体的倾销幅度，将每笔交易计算的加权平均正常价格与交易价格的比较结果进行叠加，并采用“归零法”（以下简称目标倾销方法）；同时，扩大目标倾销方法的适用范围，违反《反倾销协定》第 2.4.2 条。

（2）在行政复审中使用目标倾销方法，违反《反倾销协定》第 9.3 条和《1994 年关贸总协定》第 6.2 条。

（3）在与进口自被美国认为是非市场经济国家的产品有关的反倾销程序中，美国推定所有生产商和出口商构成一个受该国政府普遍控制的单一实体，并对该实体裁定一个单一的倾销幅度或一个单一的反倾销税率，违反《反倾销协定》第 6.10 条、第 9.2 条、第 9.4 条。

（4）美国在计算单一倾销幅度或反倾销税率中，未要求生产商和出口商提供必要信息，未提供抗辩权，并在此基础上使用可获得事实，违反《反倾销协定》第 6.1 条、第 6.8 条、第 9.4 条和附件 2 的相关规定。

（5）美国在反倾销调查中使用可获得不利事实，违反《反倾销协定》第 6.8 条和附件 2 的相关规定。

2. 争端进程

2013 年 12 月 3 日，中国就涉案措施对美国提起世贸组织争端解决机制项下的磋商请求。2014 年 1 月，中美双方在日内瓦进行了磋商。2014 年 3 月 26 日，世贸组织争端解决机构设立专家组审理本案。目前，本案正在专家组审理过程中。

（六）中国诉欧盟禽肉管理措施案（DS492）

1. 涉案措施与主要诉求

本案涉案措施为欧盟对禽肉产品的关税减让修改和配额分配措施。

2006 年 6 月 7 日，欧盟对世贸组织成员方发出通告，表示将对 021099 39、1602 31 和 1602 3219 三个税号的禽肉产品的关税减让进行修改。随后，欧盟依据《1994 年关税与贸易总协定》第 28 条，与巴西、泰国进行了谈判，并于 2006 年底达成协议。欧盟将绝大部分关税配额分配给巴西、泰国，而包括中国在内的其他世贸成员方只能分享很少量的关税配额，配额外税率远远超过修改前的约束税率。

2009 年 6 月 11 日，欧盟再次对世贸组织成员方发出通告，表示将对 1602 2010 等八个税号的禽肉产品的关税减让进行修改。随后，欧盟依据《1994 年关税与贸易总协定》第 28 条，与巴西、泰国进行了谈判，并于 2012 年 6 月达成协议。欧盟再次将绝大部分关税配额分配给巴西、泰国，而包括中国在内的其他世贸成员方只能分享很少量的关税配额，配额外税率远远超过修改前的约束税率。

欧盟认为中国在两次谈判中均不具有主要或实质供应利益，未与中国进行谈判。

中方认为，上述措施违反了《1994 年关贸总协定》第 1.1、2.1、2.2、8.1、8.2 及 28 条。

2. 争端进程

2015 年 4 月 8 日，中国就涉案措施对美国提起世贸组织争端解决机制项下的磋商请求。5 月 26 日，中欧双方举行磋商，但未能实现和解。6 月 8 日，中方向世贸组织争端解决机构提交了设立专家组的请求，7 月 20 日，专家组正式设立。

二、中国作为被诉方参与世贸组织争端解决案件新情况

（一）美国诉中国取向性硅电钢反倾销和反补贴措施案（DS414）

1. 涉案措施与主要诉求

本案涉案措施为中国对从美国进口的取向性硅电钢征收反倾销税和反补贴税的措施（商务部 2010 年第 21 号公告及其附件）。

美国认为，中国上述措施违反了相关协定的下

列条款：

（1）《反倾销协定》第3.1条和第3.2条，以及《补贴协定》第15.1条和第15.2条，因为中方没有基于对案卷材料的客观审查和肯定性证据，认定倾销和补贴进口产品大幅压低价格或者在很大程度上抑制在其他情况下本应发生的价格增长。

（2）《反倾销协定》第3.1条和第3.4条，以及《补贴协定》第15.1条和第15.4条，因为倾销和补贴进口产品对国内产业造成了负面影响这一裁定没有基于对案卷材料的客观审查和肯定性证据，包括对影响产业状况的所有相关经济因素和指标的评估。

（3）《反倾销协定》第3.1条和第3.5条，以及《补贴协定》第15.1条和第15.5条，因为（a）中国对被调查进口产品和国内产业损害之间所谓的因果关系分析没有基于对案卷材料的客观审查和肯定性证据，包括对调查机关获得的所有有关证据的审查，以及对除倾销和补贴进口产品以外其他同时损害国内产业的任何已知因素的审查；以及（b）中国没有遵守不得将其他因素造成的损害归因于倾销和补贴进口产品的义务。

（4）《反倾销协定》第6.9条以及《补贴协定》第12.8条，因为中国未能披露再裁定所依据的"基本事实"。

（5）《反倾销协定》第12.2条和第12.2.2条，以及《补贴协定》第22.3条和第22.5条，因为中国没有详细提供调查机关就其认为重要的所有事实问题和法律问题所得出的调查结果和结论，以及接受或拒绝有关论据或请求事项的理由。

（6）由于上述对《反倾销协定》的违反，所以违反了《反倾销协定》第1条。

（7）由于上述对《补贴协定》的违反，所以违反了《补贴协定》第10条。

（8）由于上述对《反倾销协定》和《补贴协定》的违反，所以违反了《1994年关贸总协定》第6条。

2. 争端进程

2010年9月15日，美国就中国对自美国进口的取向性硅电钢采取的反倾销反补贴措施对中国提起世贸组织争端解决机制项下的磋商请求。2011年3月25日，专家组设立。2012年6月15日，世贸组织公布专家组报告。2012年7月20日，中国提起上诉。2012年10月18日，世贸组织公布上诉机构报告。2012年11月16日，世贸组织争端解决机构通过了本案专家组报告和上诉机构报告。

2012年11月30日，中国在世贸组织争端解决机构会议上通报了执行意向。2013年2月8日，美国请求就合理执行期进行仲裁。2013年5月3日，仲裁员裁决合理执行期至2013年7月31日止。7月31日，中国公布再调查公告，依据世贸裁决对涉案措施进行了调整。2014年1月13日，美国将我执行措施诉诸世贸执行专家组。3月17日，专家组组成。截至2014年底，本案正在执行专家组审理阶段。

（二）欧盟诉中国X射线安检设备最终反倾销措施案（DS425）

1. 涉案措施与主要诉求

本案涉案措施为中国对原产于欧盟的X射线安全检查设备征收反倾销税的措施（中华人民共和国商务部2011年第1号公告及其附件）。

欧盟认为，中国上述措施违反《1994年关贸总协定》和《反倾销协定》的有关条款：

（1）未提供适当非保密摘要，违反《反倾销协定》第6.5.1条。

（2）未及时向所有利害关系方提供可得知所有与抗辩其利益相关非保密信息的机会，违反《反倾销协定》第6.1条、第6.2条、第6.4条和第6.5条。

（3）未在终裁前披露实施反倾销措施所依据的基本事实，违反《反倾销协定》第6.9条。

（4）未在终裁公告中进行充分披露，违反《反倾销协定》第12.2.2条。

（5）未对出口价格和正常价值进行公平比较，违反《反倾销协定》第2.4条和《1994年关贸总协定》第6.1条。

（6）未基于肯定性证据对倾销进口的价格影响进行客观分析，违反《反倾销协定》第3.1条和第3.2条。

（7）未依据肯定性证据客观审查倾销进口产品对国内产业的影响，违反《反倾销协定》第3.1条和第3.4条。

（8）因果关系判断错误，违反《反倾销协定》第3.5条和《1994年关贸总协定》第6.6条（a）项。

2. 争端进程

2011年7月25日，欧盟就中国对自欧盟进口X射线安全检查设备采取的反倾销措施对中国提出世贸组织争端解决机制下的磋商请求。2012年1月20日，专家组设立。2013年2月26日，世贸组织公布专家组报告。2013年4月24日，世贸组织争端解决机构通过了专家组报告。2013年7月，中国与欧盟就合理执行期达成一致，为9个月25天，至2014年2月19日止。中国已在2014年2月18日取消涉案措施。

（三）美国诉中国白羽肉鸡反倾销和反补贴措施案（DS427）

1. 涉案措施与主要诉求

本案涉案措施为中国对原产于美国的白羽肉鸡征收反倾销税和反补贴税的措施（商务部2010年第8、26、51、52号公告及其附件）。

美方认为，中国上述措施违反了《1994年关贸总协定》、《反倾销协定》和《补贴协定》的有关条款：

（1）未以调查的美国生产商保留的记录作为基础计算成本，违反《反倾销协定》第2.2条。

（2）未适当地分配生产成本，违反《反倾销协定》第2.2.1.1条。

（3）未要求申请人提供非保密摘要，违反《反倾销协定》第6.4条、第6.5.1条和《补贴协定》第12.3条、第12.4.1条。

（4）不适当地以可获得事实为基础做出裁定，违反了《反倾销协定》第6.8条、附件2相关规定和《补贴协定》第12.7条。

（5）征收反补贴税超过了补贴额，违反《1994年关税与贸易总协定》第6.3条和《补贴协定》第19.4条。

（6）对被调查进口产品影响和因果关系分析未依据肯定性证据进行客观审查，未就影响产业状况的所有因素、指标和相关证据进行审查，违反《反倾销协定》第3.1条、第3.2条、第3.4条、第3.5条和《补贴协定》第15.1条、第15.2条、第15.4条、第15.5条。

（7）不恰当地定义国内产业且未能进行适当调查或客观审查，违反《反倾销协定》第3.1条、第4.1条、第5.1条和《补贴协定》第11.1条、第15.1条、第16.1条。

（8）未披露裁定所依据的基本事实，违反《反倾销协定》第6.9条和《补贴协定》第12.8条。

（9）未详细提供采取措施所依据事实和法律的相关信息，包括采纳或拒绝相关抗辩的理由，违反《反倾销协定》第12.2条、第12.2.1条、第12.2.2条和《补贴协定》第22.3条、第22.4条、第22.5条。

（10）未向利害相关方提供完全的抗辩机会，违反《反倾销协定》第6.2条。

2. 争端进程

2011年9月20日，美国就中国对于原产于美国的白羽肉鸡征收反倾销税和反补贴税的措施对中国提出世贸组织争端解决机制下的磋商请求。2012年1月20日，专家组设立。专家组报告已于2013年8月2日公布，于9月25日通过。合理执行期为9个月14天，至2014年7月9日止。中国已进行了再调查并重新做出裁决。

3. 专家组主要裁决

专家组在国内产业定义、冷藏费的调整是否符合公平比较要求、是否在同一贸易水平上进行价格比较等方面驳回了美国诉求，支持了美国其他诉求。

（四）美国、欧盟、日本诉中国稀土、钨、钼出口管理措施案（DS431/432/433）

1. 涉案措施与主要诉求

本案涉案措施主要包括：

（1）中国对于稀土、钨和钼相关产品征收的出口税。

（2）中国对于稀土、钨和钼相关产品采取的出口配额等数量限制措施。

（3）中国对稀土和钼出口企业施加的出口业绩和注册资本要求。

起诉方指控中国上述措施违反了：（1）《1994年关贸总协定》第11条；（2）《中国加入议定书》第11.3条以及被并入到《中国加入议定书》的《中国加入工作组报告》第83段、第84段、第162段和第165段。

2. 争端进程

2012年3月13日，美国、欧盟和日本分别就涉案措施对中国提出世贸组织争端解决机制下的磋商请求。2012年7月23日，世贸组织争端解决机构设立了单一专家组审理本案。巴西、加拿大、哥伦比亚、印度、韩国、挪威、阿曼、沙特阿拉伯、中国台北、越南、阿根廷、澳大利亚、秘鲁、俄罗斯、印度尼西亚和土耳其共16个世贸组织成员保留各自的第三方权利。

世贸组织于2014年3月26日公布了专家组报告。美国于4月8日提出上诉。中国于4月17日对美提出交叉上诉，于4月25日对欧盟、日本提出上诉。8月7日，世贸组织公布上诉机构报告。8月29日，世贸组织争端解决机构通过了上诉机构报告和专家组报告。合理执行期为8个月零3天，至2015年5月2日。

3. 专家组主要裁决

专家组认为，我对稀土、钨、钼相关产品采取的出口关税、出口配额措施以及对稀土、钼相关产品出口配额的管理和分配措施不符合《1994年关贸总协定》和《中华人民共和国加入议定书》相关规定，且不符合《1994年关贸总协定》规定的例外情形。

同时，专家组驳回了欧盟关于我对申请钼出口配额企业的“出口业绩”要求歧视外国企业的主张。

4. 上诉机构主要裁决

上诉机构支持了中方对《1994年关贸总协定》第20条的部分法律解释，维持了专家组关于中方涉案产品的出口关税、出口配额措施不符合世贸组织规则和中方加入世贸组织承诺的裁决。

（五）美国诉中国汽车“双反”案（DS440）

1. 涉案措施与主要诉求

本案涉案措施为中国对美国某些汽车征收反倾销税和反补贴税措施。

美国认为上述措施违反了《1994年关贸总协定》、《反倾销协定》和《补贴协定》的下述条款：

（1）《反倾销协定》第5.3条和第5.4条以及《补贴协定》第11.3条和第11.4条，因为：中国在发起反倾销和反补贴调查之前没有审查同类产品国内生产商所表达的支持或反对申请的程度；中国在支持申请的国内生产商占国内产业生产的同类产品总产量不到25%的情况下发起了调查；中国没有审查申请人提交的证据的准确性和充分性。①

（2）《补贴协定》第11.3条，因为反补贴调查申请书没有包含申请人可以合理获得的信息，因此，申请书中没有足够的证据证明就涉案部分项目发起反补贴调查具有正当理由。

（3）《反倾销协定》第6.5.1条和《补贴协定》第12.4.1条，因为中国没有要求申请人对其声称的保密信息提供充分的非保密摘要。

（4）《反倾销协定》第6.9条，因为中国没有充分披露用于确定反倾销税率的计算方法和数据。

（5）《反倾销协定》第12.2条和第12.2.2条，因为对于中国认为重要的所有事实和法律问题，中国没有提供足够详细的关于这些事实和法律问题的认定和结论。中国也没有对接受或拒绝相关主张或诉求说明理由。

（6）《反倾销协定》第6.8条、第6.9条、第12.2条、第12.2.2条和附件2第1段以及《补贴协定》第12.7条、第12.8条、第22.3条和第22.5条，因为：中国不恰当地依据可获得事实认定了“所有其他企业”的反倾销和反补贴税率；中国没有披露支撑其“所有其他企业”税率认定的基本事实；对于中国认为重要的所有事实和法律问题，中国没有在其“所有其他企业”税率决定中足够详细地阐述关于这些事实和法律问题的认定和结论；就“所有其他企业”税率而言，中国未能提供导致采取最终措施的事实、法律和理由的所有相关信息。

（7）《反倾销协定》第3.1条和第4.1条以及《补贴协定》第15.1条和第16.1条，因为中国使用不恰当的国内产业定义做出了损害认定，由此导致其裁定没有肯定性证据的支持或者未能对生产被调查进口产品的国内产业相关事实进行客观审查。

（8）《反倾销协定》第3.1条和第3.2条以及《补贴协定》第15.1条和第15.2条，因为中国对于受调查进口产品对同类产品价格影响的分析没有依据对于案卷和肯定性证据的客观审查。

（9）《反倾销协定》第3.1条、第3.4条和第3.5条以及《补贴协定》第15.1条、第15.4条和第15.5条，因为中国对于声称的因果关系的分析没有依据对于案卷和肯定性证据的客观审查，包括审查影响产业状况的所有相关经济因素和指标，审

---

① 美国在其第一次书面陈述中明确放弃了此项诉求。

查调查当局面前的所有相关证据，或者审查声称的倾销和补贴进口产品之外的、正在同时损害国内产业的任何已知因素；中国没有满足下列非归因分析要求，即其他因素造成的损害不得归因于声称的倾销和补贴进口产品。

(10)《反倾销协定》第 6.2 条，因为中国没有给予利害关系方充分的抗辩机会。

(11) 由于违反了前述《反倾销协定》和《补贴协定》相关条款，美国认为中国也违反了《反倾销协定》第 1 条、《补贴协定》第 10 条和《1994 年关贸总协定》第 6 条。

2. 争端进程

2012 年 7 月 5 日，美国就涉案措施对中国提起世贸组织争端解决机制项下的磋商请求。2012 年 9 月 17 日，美国请求设立专家组。世贸组织争端解决机构于 2012 年 10 月 23 日设立了专家组。哥伦比亚、欧盟、印度、日本、韩国、阿曼、沙特阿拉伯和土耳其 8 个世贸组织成员保留各自的第三方权利。总干事于 2013 年 2 月 11 日指定了专家组成员。2013 年 12 月 14 日，中国终止了涉案措施；2014 年 5 月 23 日，世贸组织公布专家组报告。

3. 专家组主要裁决

专家组在国内产业的定义、对美国其他出口商反倾销税率及反补贴税率的披露及公告等方面驳回了美国诉求，支持了美国的其他诉求。

(六) 美国诉中国汽车及汽车零部件补贴政策案 (DS450)

1. 涉案措施与主要诉求

本案的涉案措施是 71 个关于汽车及零部件出口基地、汽车及零部件出口基地企业的中央和地方政府文件。

美国认为，中国通过上述措施设立了汽车及汽车零部件“出口基地”，并向位于这些“出口基地”或者被指定为“出口基地企业”的汽车及汽车零部件企业提供优惠服务，违反了《补贴协定》第 3 条。此外，美国还认为中国违反了相关透明度义务。

2. 争端进程

2012 年 9 月 17 日，美国就汽车及汽车零部件补贴政策对中国提出世贸组织争端解决机制下的磋商请求。2012 年 11 月 6 日至 7 日，中方与美方在日内瓦进行了首次磋商。本案目前仍处于磋商阶段。

(七) 墨西哥诉中国服装与纺织品案 (DS451)

1. 涉案措施与主要诉求

本案的涉案措施为中国对服装与纺织品生产商和出口商以及棉花和化纤产业供应商的多种补贴措施。具体包括以下类型：(1) 免除某些企业的税收；(2) 减免和退还某类企业以及特定地区企业所购买的设备的进口税和增值税；(3) 低于充分对价提供土地使用权和电价；(4) 国有银行向某些产业提供低息贷款；(5) 棉花和化纤生产、销售和运输环节扶持措施；(6) 政府提供的现金支付。

墨西哥认为上述措施涉及禁止性补贴和可诉补贴，后者正在通过替代和阻碍墨西哥产品进入美国，在同一市场造成显著价格削减、价格抑制、价格压低以及销售损失，对墨西哥利益造成严重损害或者严重损害威胁。墨西哥认为涉案措施违反了：(1)《补贴协定》第 3.1 条 (a) 项和 (b) 项、第 5 条 (c) 项、第 6.3 条 (b) 项和 (c) 项、第 6.4 条和第 6.5 条；(2)《1994 年关贸总协定》第 3.4 条；(3)《农业协定》第 3 条、第 9 条和第 10 条；(4)《中国加入议定书》第 I 部分第 1.2 段并入的《中国加入工作组报告》相关条款。

2. 争端进程

2012 年 10 月 15 日，墨西哥就涉案措施对中国提起世贸组织争端解决机制项下的磋商请求。欧盟、澳大利亚、危地马拉、巴西、秘鲁、美国、洪都拉斯、哥伦比亚 8 个世贸组织成员先后请求加入磋商。2013 年 6 月 4 日，双方开始磋商。目前，案件仍处于磋商阶段。

(八) 日本、欧盟诉中国无缝钢管反倾销措施案 (DS454/DS460)

1. 涉案措施与主要诉求

本案涉案措施是中国对自日本、欧盟进口的无缝钢管采取的反倾销措施。

日本认为，中方涉案措施违反了《1994 年关贸总协定》和《反倾销协定》的下述有关条款：

(1) 中国未依据肯定性证据客观审查数量影响和价格影响、对国内产业影响和因果关系等，违反《反倾销协定》第 3.1 条、第 3.2 条、第 3.4 条和第 3.5 条。

(2) 未满足保密信息披露要求，违反《反倾销协定》第 6.5 条和第 6.5.1 条。

（3）不恰当地依据可获得事实计算其他所有日本公司的倾销幅度，违反《反倾销协定》第6.8条和附件2第1段。

（4）未能向所有利害关系方充分披露相关基本事实，违反《反倾销协定》第6.9条。

（5）临时措施实施超过4个月，违反《反倾销协定》第7.4条。

（6）未详细提供调查结果和结论以及实施最终反倾销措施所依据的事实和法律的有关信息，违反《反倾销协定》第12.2条和第12.2.2条。

（7）以上不符措施违反《反倾销协定》第1条和《1994年关贸总协定》第6条。

欧盟认为，中国上述措施违反了《1994年关贸总协定》和《反倾销协定》的下述有关条款：

（1）未依据相关数据确定生产成本等，违反《反倾销协定》第2.2条。

（2）未基于公平比较证明倾销幅度的存在，违反《反倾销协定》第2.4条和第2.4.2条。

（3）未依据肯定性证据客观审查数量影响和价格影响、对国内生产者产生的影响和因果关系等，违反《反倾销协定》第3.1条、第3.2条、第3.4条和第3.5条。

（4）未向所有利害关系方披露所有信息，违反《反倾销协定》第6.4条。

（5）未满足非保密信息披露要求，违反《反倾销协定》第6.5条和第6.5.1条。

（6）拒绝考虑在实地核查期间提供的信息，违反《反倾销协定》第6.7条和附件1第7段。

（7）未考虑可核实的、与倾销幅度裁定有关的所有信息，违反了《反倾销协定》第6.8条和附件2第3段。

（8）不适当地使用可获得的事实裁定所有其他欧盟企业的倾销幅度，违反《反倾销协定》第6.8条和附件2第1段。

（9）未通知所有利害关系方实施最终反倾销措施所依据的基本事实，违反《反倾销协定》第6.9条。

（10）临时措施实施超过4个月，违反《反倾销协定》第7.4条。

（11）未详细提供调查结果和结论以及实施最终反倾销措施所依据的事实和法律的有关信息，违反《反倾销协定》第12.2条和第12.2.2条。

（12）以上不符措施违反《反倾销协定》第1条和《1994年关税与贸易总协定》第6条。

2. 争端进程

2012年12月20日，日本就中国对自日本进口的无缝钢管采取的反倾销措施对中国提起世贸组织争端解决机制下的磋商请求。2013年1月18日，欧盟作为第三方加入磋商。5月24日，专家组设立。

2013年6月13日，欧盟就相同涉案措施对中国提起世贸组织争端解决机制下的磋商请求。8月30日设立专家组。两案由同一专家组程序进行审理。2015年2月13日专家组向成员散发专家组报告。2015年5月20日，中方提出上诉（DS460），日本于同一天提出上诉（DS454）。截至2015年6月30日，本案仍在上诉机构审理阶段。

3. 专家组主要裁决

专家组在使用可获得事实、损害裁定、充分披露相关事实方面驳回了欧盟的请求，在终裁公告或单独报告中是否充分详细地说明处理方法及是否根据正常贸易过程中生产和销售同类产品的实际数据裁定相应费用问题方面未做出裁定，同时支持了欧盟的其他诉求。

（九）加拿大诉中国浆粕反倾销措施案（DS483）

1. 涉案措施与主要诉求

本案涉案措施是中国对原产于加拿大的浆粕实施的反倾销措施。

加拿大认为，涉案措施与中国于《1994年关贸总协定》和《反倾销协定》下列条款项下的义务不符：

（1）《反倾销协定》第2.2条和第2.2.1.1条，因为中国在为加拿大的生产商确定结构正常价值时，未能以生产商保存的、合理反映浆粕生产和销售成本的记录为基础计算成本，还未能对在调查期间支出受投产影响的情况做出适当调整。

（2）《反倾销协定》第2.2条和第2.2.2条，因为中国在为加拿大的生产商确定结构正常价值时，未能依据生产者在正常贸易过程中生产和销售浆粕的实际数据确定管理、销售和一般费用的金额。

（3）《反倾销协定》第2.1条和第2.4条，因为中国未能对出口价格和正常价值进行公平比较，例如从出口价格中不恰当地扣除了某些费用，以及在计算出口价格时没有适当考虑产品物理特征方面的差异。

（4）《反倾销协定》第 3.1 条和第 3.2 条，因为中国对损害的确定未能依据肯定性证据进行，也未能对倾销进口产品的数量和倾销进口产品对国内市场同类产品价格的影响进行客观审查。中国没有适当地考虑是否存在以下情形：（a）倾销进口商品是否大幅增加；（b）与国内同类产品的价格相比，倾销进口产品是否大幅削低价格，或此类进口产品的影响是否是大幅压低价格，或是否是在很大程度上抑制在其他情况下本应发生的价格增加。

（5）《反倾销协定》第 3.1 条和第 3.4 条，因为中国对损害的确定未能依据肯定性证据进行，未能对倾销进口产品对国内同类产品生产商产生的影响进行客观审查，还未能适当评估所有影响产业状况的有关经济因素和指标。

（6）《反倾销协定》第 3.1 条和第 3.5 条，因为中国未能：（a）通过依据肯定性证据进行的客观审查证明倾销进产品与对国内产业损害之间存在因果关系；（b）依据肯定性证据客观审查除倾销进口产品外的、同时正在损害国内产业的任何其他已知因素，并且不恰当地将这些其他因素造成的损害归因于倾销进口产品。

（7）《反倾销协定》第 3.1 条和第 4.1 条，因为中国做出的损害裁定不恰当地界定了国内产业，导致未能在依据肯定性证据对生产同类产品的国内产业进行客观审查的基础上做出裁定。

（8）《反倾销协定》第 6.2 条，因为中国未能向利害关系方提供为其利益进行辩护的充分机会。

（9）《反倾销协定》第 6.1 条和第 6.8 条以及附件 2 的第 3 段，因为中国在计算倾销幅度时，未能给予加拿大生产商充分机会以书面形式提出其认为与所涉调查有关的所有证据，还未能考虑所有可核实的、适当提交且及时提供的信息。

（10）《反倾销协定》第 6.8 条和附件 2 的第 7 段，因为中国不恰当地依据可获得的事实确定未获得单独倾销幅度的加拿大浆粕出口商或生产商的倾销幅度。

（11）《反倾销协定》第 6.9 条，因为中国未能将其考虑的、构成是否向未获得单独倾销幅度的加拿大浆粕出口商实施最终反倾销措施决定依据的基本事实通知所有利害关系方。

（12）《反倾销协定》第 6.10 条、第 6.10.2 和第 9.4 条，因为对最初未被抽中，但及时提交了可供调查过程中进行考虑的必要信息的出口商或生产商，中国未能对其单独确定倾销幅度。

（13）《反倾销协定》第 12.2 条和第 12.2.2 条，因为中国未能提供包括所有导致实施最终措施的有关事实问题和法律问题及理由等相关信息的足够详细的公告。

（14）中国对原产于加拿大的浆粕实施的反倾销措施由于违反了上述《反倾销协定》条款，进而违反了《反倾销协定》第 1 条和《1994 年关贸总协定》第 6 条。

2. 争端进程

2014 年 10 月 15 日，加拿大就涉案措施对中国提起世贸组织争端解决机制项下的磋商请求。2015 年 2 月 12 日，加拿大提出设立专家组请求。3 月 10 日，世贸组织争端解决机构宣布设立专家组。截至 2015 年 6 月 30 日，本案尚在专家组审理阶段。

（商务部条约法律司）

贸易救济工作概况

2014年，全球经济不景气发达，经济体经济运行分化加剧，发展中经济体增长放缓，世界经济复苏依旧艰难曲折。由于各国经济发展艰难，我国遭遇的贸易摩擦案件持续高发，涉案数量和金额均有上升；同时，我国企业面临的进口产品竞争加剧，维护国内产业安全形势严峻。

一、针对中国的贸易摩擦总体情况

2014年，我国共遭遇来自22个国家（地区）的贸易救济调查97起，包括反倾销61起、反补贴14起，保障措施22起，涉案金额104.9亿美元。

2014年我国遭遇的贸易摩擦呈现以下特点：一是贸易保护升温，美国、澳大利亚、印度和巴西等主要贸易伙伴均强化贸易救济执法，针对我国的案件数量和涉案金额增加。二是贸易摩擦呈多点多发态势，亚洲、北美、拉美、欧洲、非洲和大洋洲等各大洲均有贸易救济案件发生。除美国、欧盟、加拿大、印度、土耳其和巴西等传统上立案较多的国家（地区）之外，哥伦比亚、危地马拉、厄瓜多尔、摩洛哥和突尼斯等国家也对我国产品发起调查。三是发展中国家与我国的贸易摩擦数量继续增加，案件总量达66起，涉案金额达42.6亿美元，分别占总量和总额的68%和40.6%。四是对我产业影响范围广，五金、矿产、化工、机电、轻工、纺织、医保、食土类产品均有涉案，其中涉及钢铁类产品案件27起，涉案金额23.2亿美元。五是高科技产品成为摩擦新焦点，光伏产品、风力发电机组、手机等相继遭到贸易救济调查。六是大要案增多，1亿美元以上案件达到30起，推升全年涉案金额突破百亿美元。

二、贸易摩擦应对工作

2014年，我国应对贸易摩擦的重点工作如下：

（一）妥善处理欧盟无线通信设备等系列重大贸易摩擦

2013年5月，欧盟委员会通报称拟对我国无线通信设备启动“双反”调查，经与欧方多轮艰苦谈判，欧方最终放弃“双反”调查，维护了我国无线通信设备的重要出口市场，消除了影响中欧经贸关系的重大隐患；中欧光伏价格承诺协议平稳执行，欧委会再度下调最低限价。

（二）积极应对与美、澳等国的大要案

在应对美国对我国轮胎等其他产品的系列贸易救济案件中，取得良好效果，在应对部分重点补贴项目上实现突破，另有一些案件最终以无损害结案。针对澳大利亚拟对我光伏产品发起的“双反”调查，双边多渠道开展交涉磋商，最终澳方放弃反补贴调查，只发起反倾销调查。在政府、商会及企业的共同努力下，澳调查机关最终做出建议终止调查的决定。

（三）努力化解与发展中国家的贸易摩擦

我们坚持把对话磋商作为解决与发展中国家贸易摩擦的主渠道，推动马来西亚、欧亚经济委员会和印度放弃对我国螺纹钢、油井管和电厂设备等产品的反补贴调查；通过有效抗辩，印度放弃对我国光伏产品征收反倾销税；推动巴西、秘鲁、阿根廷、巴基斯坦等国调查机关接受我国企业价格承诺或终止调查，妥善执行中国—墨西哥鞋类产品出口协议。

三、依法开展贸易救济调查

我国产业处于结构调整和转型升级的关键时期，钢铁、化工等传统制造业低成本优势正在减弱，高端装备制造业等战略新兴产业受到国外竞争对手打压，少数产业弱势弱质问题凸显，竞争力亟待提升。随着市场开放加快，国内产业面临进口冲击压力加大，部分企业经营困难，对贸易救济诉求增多。依法运用贸易救济措施维护公平市场环境、提升我国产业竞争力的任务艰巨。

2014年4月，商务部整合原进出口公平贸易局和产业损害调查局部分业务职能，组建贸易救济调查局，统一承担与进出口公平贸易相关的各项职能。

（一）完善规章制度，提高依法行政水平

贸易救济调查局成立后，着力提高贸易救济调查制度的规范性、透明度和有效性，决定对我贸易救济领域 24 项部门规章进行修订。目前，已形成《反倾销和反补贴调查听证会规则（修订稿）》、《反倾销问卷调查规则（修订稿）》和《倾销及倾销幅度期中复审规则（修订稿）》三部部门规章的修订稿，并于 2015 年 8 月 25 日就上述三部规章修订稿对外公开征求意见。

（二）依法开展贸易救济调查，维护产业合法权益

按照世贸组织标准统计，2014 年我国对外发起反倾销调查 7 起，涉案产品包括光纤预制棒、血液透析机和甲基丙烯酸甲酯，涉案金额 9.68 亿美元，涉及美国、日本、欧盟、新加坡和泰国 5 个国家。另外，完成 4 起复审调查，终止 2 起反倾销措施。妥善执行争端解决案件，如白羽肉鸡、取向电工钢等 WTO 争端案件裁决。

（三）创新结案方式，推动中外产业合作

我国对欧盟葡萄酒发起的反倾销反补贴调查，受到双方各界的高度关注。后双方业界以对话、合作等方式达成和解，中欧葡萄酒业界最终签署了谅解与合作备忘录，双方实现了互利共赢。

四、积极参与多双边规则谈判与交流合作

近年来，美欧等西方国家欲主导国际贸易领域规则重构，树立国际贸易规则“新标杆”，对广大发展中国家特别是新兴经济体可能产生不利影响。在贸易救济规则领域，美国、欧盟、澳大利亚等纷纷修订其国内法规，并积极在国际层面推动有关规则的修订和调整。2014 年，为有效维护我国的规则利益，中国亦积极参与多双边规则谈判与交流工作。

一是积极参与世贸组织“两反一保”委员会春季和秋季例会以及技术专家组会，就个别成员方的部分规则和实践提出看法并深入交流，有效回应其他成员方对我方调查案件的关注。同时，认真履行世贸组织框架下反倾销、反补贴和保障措施的通报义务。

二是参与中韩、中澳等自贸协定谈判中的贸易救济规则谈判。在中韩自贸协定中，中韩双方相互承诺在反倾销调查中禁用歧视性的“替代国”做法，实现贸易救济规则领域的重大突破。

三是与欧盟、澳大利亚、阿根廷、巴西等八个国家（地区）举行贸易救济合作机制会议，参加第二届金砖国家贸易救济研讨会，加强与贸易伙伴调查机关的交流以增进互信，并就部分重点案件进行沟通以推动其妥善解决。

2015 年，我们将继续妥善处理与贸易伙伴之间的贸易摩擦，依法开展贸易救济调查，维护我国产业的安全和权益，为构建开放型经济新体制，培育我国产业国际竞争优势添活力、增动力。

（商务部贸易救济调查局局长　王贺军）

全球及中国反倾销措施情况

在经济全球化及区域经济一体化发展过程中，国际竞争日益激烈，贸易摩擦日益增多，贸易救济措施案件数量居高不下。其中，反倾销措施运用最为频繁。根据 WTO 数据统计，1995 年至 2014 年间，各成员发起的反倾销调查已有 4757 起，发起反倾销调查最多的为印度、美国和欧盟，分别为 740 起、527 起和 468 起。

一、WTO 成员反倾销实施情况

根据 WTO 数据，2014 年世贸成员共发起反倾销案件 236 起，其中，印度、巴西和澳大利亚发起最多，分别为 38 起、35 起和 22 起；从被调查国家/地区来看，中国、韩国以及印度涉案最多，分别为 63 起、18 起和 15 起。

二、与中国有关的反倾销措施情况

根据 WTO 数据，中国已连续 20 年成为遭受反倾销调查最多的国家。2010—2014 年，中国遭受反倾销调查数量分别为 44 起、51 起、60 起、72 起和 63 起，遭遇调查数量居高不下。2014 年，中国共对外发起反倾销调查 7 起，产品涉及光纤制品、机电设备和化工产品。

涉案产品	涉案国家	立案时间
光纤预制棒	美国、日本	2014 年 3 月 19 日
血液透析仪	欧盟、日本	2014 年 6 月 13 日
甲基丙烯酸甲酯	新加坡、泰国、日本	2014 年 8 月 8 日

三、全球反倾销实践动向

在传统的关税和非关税措施被限制和取消之后，反倾销已成为贸易保护的有效手段而被广泛应用。近年，全球经济虽走出低谷但尚未摆脱金融危机后遗症，各国继续实施贸易保护政策的动力仍在，反倾销措施亦不断被各国采用。除发达国家外，发展中国家对反倾销措施的使用亦日趋频繁。2011—2014 年，WTO 成员发起的反倾销调查数量一直高位运行，分别为 165 起、209 起、283 起以及 236 起。其中巴西和印度使用最为频繁，2011—2014 年的四年间，巴西共发起反倾销调查 152 起，印度发起 107 起。另外，各国采取反倾销措施的力度亦不断加大，如通过不断日落复审，某些反倾销措施可持续十余年甚至数十年。同时，近年来一些国家频繁发起“双反”调查，即对一产品同时进行反倾销反补贴调查，叠加使用以增加贸易救济的力度。

随着实践的深入，如何加强反倾销措施的使用纪律，防止反倾销措施沦为贸易保护主义手段，逐渐成为国际贸易领域的重要议题。由于多哈回合规则谈判处于停滞状态，世贸组织争端解决机制成为目前反倾销规则澄清的重要手段。2014 年，成员国之间发起的涉及反倾销措施的争端案件共 5 起，专家组和上诉机构对因果关系、可获得事实以及调查程序的透明度等规则都做出了进一步澄清。

（商务部贸易救济调查局）

全球及中国反补贴措施情况

目前，反补贴调查的发起者主要集中在发达国家。1995—2014年期间，WTO成员共发起反补贴调查案件380起。其中，美国、欧盟和加拿大发起措施最多，分别为156起、74起和49起，占全球反补贴调查案件发起数量的41.1%、19.5%和12.9%。被调查成员主要为发展中成员，其中中国和印度遭受反补贴调查最多，分别为90起和65起。

一、2014年WTO成员反补贴立案情况

根据WTO统计数据，2014年WTO成员共发起反补贴案件45起，其中美国、加拿大和埃及发起最多，分别为18起、12起和6起；中国、土耳其涉案最多，分别为14起和5起。

二、与中国有关的反补贴措施情况

2003年以前，中国从未遭受国外反补贴调查。2004年4月13日起，加拿大在不到半年的时间内连续对中国出口烧烤架、碳钢及不锈钢紧固件、复合地板发起反倾销和反补贴调查。这三起案件开启了国外对我出口产品发起反补贴调查并被征收反补贴税的历史。2014年，中国遭遇反补贴调查数量再创新高，达14起，占全球反补贴案件发起总量的三成多。中国已连续9年成为全球反补贴调查的最大目标国。

为限制受补贴产品的进口，保护国内生产商的利益，使国内产业获得公平竞争的市场环境，中国自2009年启动第一起反补贴调查，迄今对外发起7起反补贴调查，详见下表：

三、全球反补贴实践动向

金融危机后，贸易保护主义重新掀起浪潮。近年来，全球经济复苏乏力，反补贴措施使用频率居高不下。根据WTO统计数据，2010年至2014年，全球反补贴案件数量分别为9起、25起、23起、33起、45起，调查数量呈上升之势。其中，中国、印度等新兴发展中国家是反补贴调查的主要对象，而中国已连续9年成为全球反补贴调查最大的目标国。2014年，美国、加拿大和埃及是全球反补贴调查的最主要使用国，共发起反补贴调查36起，占全球反补贴调查总数的80%。值得注意的是，俄罗斯、乌克兰历史上首次发起反补贴调查。

涉案产品	涉案国家	立案时间
取向电工钢	美国	2009年6月1日
白羽肉鸡产品	美国	2009年9月27日
排气量在2.0升及2.0升以上的小轿车和越野车	美国	2009年11月6日
马铃薯淀粉案	欧盟	2010年8月30日
太阳能级多晶硅	美国	2012年7月20日
太阳能级多晶硅	欧盟	2012年11月1日
葡萄酒	欧盟	2013年7月1日

（商务部贸易救济调查局）

全球及中国保障措施情况

除反倾销和反补贴调查外，保障措施调查也是不少WTO成员频繁使用的贸易保护工具。据统计，1995年至2014年间，WTO各成员发起的保障措施调查共295起，发起最为频繁的为印度、印度尼西亚和土耳其，分别为39起、23起和17起。

一、2014年WTO成员保障措施实施情况

根据世贸组织统计，2014年WTO成员共发起23起保障措施调查。发起成员以发展中成员为主，其中印度发起7起，印度尼西亚、土耳其各发起3起。

二、与中国有关的保障措施情况

2014年中国未发起保障措施调查。WTO成员共发起21起涉及中国的保障措施调查，其中印度7起、土耳其4起（世贸组织少统计1起）、印度尼西亚3起、埃及2起、突尼斯2起，马来西亚、泰国、摩洛哥各1起。

三、全球保障措施实践动向

与针对不公平进口的反倾销、反补贴措施相比，保障措施是可以针对正常贸易下进口所采取的措施，保护力度强，对贸易的负面影响大，故《保障措施协定》为保障措施的实施设定了更高的门槛、更高的要求，因此各国对保障措施一直持谨慎使用态度。然而近年来，保障措施的使用亦呈大幅上升趋势。据世贸组织统计，2008—2014年期间，世贸组织成员国共发起保障措施调查131起，占世贸组织有统计数据（1995年）以来保障措施发起数量的40%以上。发起保障措施调查的成员主要为发展中国家。2008年至2014年间，印度共发起24起，印度尼西亚共发起23起，埃及共发起8起。这说明发展中国家为应对金融危机冲击，加大贸易保护力度，更倾向于选择保护力度强的保障措施手段。

（商务部贸易救济调查局）

● 政策审议

释放改革开放积极信号　彰显遵信守诺大国形象
——中国接受世贸组织第五次贸易政策审议

2014年7月1日至3日，世界贸易组织（以下简称世贸组织）在瑞士日内瓦对我国进行了第五次贸易政策审议。商务部王受文部长助理率领由商务部、发展改革委、财政部、农业部、人民银行、海关总署、税务总局、质检总局、统计局组成的代表团出席。中国常驻世贸组织大使俞建华参加了审议会议。

一、总体情况

此次审议是党中央、国务院新一届领导履职后，我国首次接受贸易政策审议，对此国务院领导高度重视。2012年6月第四次审议后，我国已成为全球第一大货物贸易国，此次贸易政策审议受到各方高度关注。审议会议前，共有31个成员向我国提交了1700多个书面问题，涉及我国经济贸易体制和政策措施的各个方面。审议会上，美国、欧盟、日本、俄罗斯、巴西、印度、南非等47个成员发言，对我国深化改革开放、拉动全球经济增长、参与多边贸易体制等方面进行了较为全面客观的评价，也对我经济贸易体制和政策中的具体问题表达了关注。

本次审议总体基调积极，气氛平和，成员的评论和提问大都客观中肯，未出现以往审议中发达成员质疑我政策方向，批评指责我国改革开放进程“停滞”的情形。原因主要包括以下几个方面：

（一）党的十八届三中全会关于全面深化改革的决定得到了国际社会广泛认同。党的十八届三中全会做出全面深化改革的重大决定，中央做出的包括建立上海自由贸易试验区在内的一系列重大决策，对外释放了我国主动扩大开放的积极信号，使世贸组织其他成员清楚地看到我国改革开放的方向，有效打消了各种疑虑。

（二）中国经济发展给许多贸易伙伴带来了实实在在的利益。近年来，我国与世贸组织其他成员的经贸联系日益密切，政策外溢性日益凸显。我国已经是128个成员最大的贸易伙伴，我国经济发展有力带动了其他成员特别是发展中国家和自贸协定伙伴的经济复苏和增长。同时，我国坚持正确的义利观，在世贸组织和南南合作框架下发挥了积极的作用。因此，我国在此次审议会议上得到大多数发展中国家、最不发达国家和所有自贸协定伙伴的积极支持。

（三）会前准备充分，为此次审议创造了良好的条件。根据国务院领导同志的指示精神，我国有关部门和中国常驻世贸组织代表团高度重视，提前准备，密切合作，对成员可能重点关注的问题进行了梳理并准备了答复口径。审议会议前，在各部门大力支持下，我国及时向世贸组织提交了《中国政府政策声明》。《政策声明》是此次审议的基础材料，也是各成员发言的重要依据。针对成员提出的1700多个书面问题，各有关部门加班加点，及时认真予以答复。中国常驻世贸组织代表团广泛做了相关成员的工作，促其在审议中对我国做出客观、公正的评价。

二、成员对中国的主要评价

（一）充分肯定中国对世界经济增长的贡献

审议讨论引导人瑞典大使表示，中国正在“塑造”全球经济。欧盟、马来西亚、韩国、津巴布韦、泰国等成员表示，中国经济增长举世瞩目，给其他成员带来了很多机会。美国表示，中国的经济增长和崛起对世界经济和世贸组织产生了重要影响。韩国表示，中国经济健康与世界经济健康是同义词。津巴布韦表示，中国已成为世界经济发展的引擎。加拿大认为中国经济的成败就是世界经济的成败。

审议会议主席认为，中国的经济以前一直是出口导向，近年来转向通过国内需求推动，创新驱动型的增长模式有助于实现可持续发展目标。我国自贸协定伙伴国智利、东盟、新加坡、新西兰等成员表示，其与中国的自贸协定推动了双边经贸关系的发展。瑞士、冰岛欢迎与我国的自贸协定生效，澳大利亚希望年底结束与我国的自贸谈判。

（二）积极评价我国全面深化改革开放的决定

美国在发言中肯定了中国进一步深化改革开放的大方向。东盟、巴基斯坦等积极评价“一路一带”的建设作用。新加坡赞赏我国在行政管理体制、工商登记、财税金融体制改革以及扶持中小微企业发展方面所做的努力，认为中国政府向所有贸易伙伴释放了积极明确的改革信号。冰岛认为中国正致力于为全球提供一个透明、稳定、无歧视并且以法治为基础的贸易环境，能使其他成员从中国的成功中获益。土耳其表示，中国政府努力在政府与市场之间达到平衡，在发挥市场作用的同时提高政府效率。澳大利亚认为中国的改革措施有助于加强市场竞争、公平对待国有企业和非公有制部门。巴巴多斯表示，中国调整发展模式，不断深化改革，使市场在资源配置中发挥关键作用。

（三）高度评价中国上海自由贸易试验区建设

澳大利亚、津巴布韦、巴巴多斯、多米尼加、新加坡、哥伦比亚等成员认为上海自由贸易试验区展现了中国政府对外开放的决心。新加坡认为中国将通过上海自由贸易试验区进一步推进服务贸易对外开放，并对资本直接投资方面的各种简化规则和放宽限制表示欢迎。澳大利亚认为上海自由贸易试验区将为中国政府进一步改革开放树立良好模型。

（四）充分肯定我国坚定维护多边贸易体制

东盟表示，中国积极参与多边贸易体制，支持多哈回合谈判，推动实现“平衡、普惠和共赢的多边贸易体制”。欧盟认为中国已是多边贸易体制的真正支持者。日本、秘鲁等成员欢迎我国提前通报《贸易便利化协定》落实措施。安提瓜和巴布达、巴巴多斯等成员感谢中国在世贸组织框架下对其提供援助。智利赞赏中国在亚太经合组织贸易部长会议期间，推动发表了单独声明支持多边贸易体制并坚决反对贸易保护主义。

（五）高度赞赏我国以实际行动推动“南南合作”

尼泊尔表示，中国对其他发展中国家和最不发达国家提供援助，增加其在中国市场的份额，连续五年中国成为最不发达国家最大的出口市场；世贸组织第九届部长会期间，中国宣布对非洲棉花出口提供援助和支持。安提瓜和巴布达对中国推动南南合作表示感谢。哥伦比亚、南非感谢中国2013年对建立外交关系的最不发达国家95%的税目给予免关税免配额待遇，大幅增加对最不发达国家的单边优惠。

三、成员的主要关注

（一）关于尽快落实十八届三中全会决定

成员希望我国尽快出台全面深化改革的具体措施，制定路线图和时间表，继续扩大开放，特别是服务贸易开放，并希望上海自由贸易试验区尽快形成可复制、可推广的经验，在全国其他地区实施。

（二）关于透明度问题

部分成员认为中国一些政策措施在出台时，没有公开征求意见，没有通过统一平台发布，也没有翻译成世贸组织官方语言。

（三）关于政府干预微观经济活动

个别成员认为中国仍然强调政府在经济发展中的作用，不少政府部门较多采用补贴等各种激励措施，扶持国内产业，可能导致产能过剩、信贷扩张，并引发与其他成员贸易摩擦。

（四）关于国有企业特殊待遇

个别成员认为中国国有企业改革虽已取得一些进展，但国有企业仍然可以从政府获得廉价原材料、土地和资金，并且在反垄断、许可、批准程序等方面也能享受优惠，不利于创造公平竞争的环境。

（五）关于海关执法统一性

部分成员认为中国海关估价、关税征收、进出境检验检疫等方面的执法缺乏统一性，需进一步协调规范。海关货物检查的效率有待提高，海关程序应进一步简化。

（六）关于标准和检验检疫措施

美国、日本、欧盟、挪威、韩国、阿根廷等成员认为，中国标准应更多与国际标准接轨；标准制定过程中，应允许外资企业充分参与；检验检疫措施缺乏科学依据，对贸易构成了壁垒。

（七）关于知识产权保护

欧盟、美国等认为，中国知识产权保护取得了可喜的进展，但仍需加大执法力度。中国推行强制性技术转让，对商业秘密保护不足，已成为阻碍贸易投资的重要壁垒。

四、中国代表团参会情况

中国代表团团长王受文在此次审议会议上做主旨发言，全面阐述了上次审议以来我国宏观经济体制和贸易政策最新进展，重点介绍了党的十八届三中全会关于全面深化改革的重大决定。王受文表示，中国新一届领导集体做出了全面深化改革的重大决定，核心是处理好政府和市场的关系。中国政府在行政审批、工商登记、财政金融体制等领域出台了一系列重大举措，积极扩大对外开放，通过设立中国（上海）自由贸易试验区，在外商投资管理体制改革、扩大服务业开放等方面探索新途径、新经验，还提出了“丝绸之路经济带”和“21 世纪海上丝绸之路”（“一带一路”）的重要倡议。

王受文强调，中国是多边贸易体制的积极参与者、坚定支持者和重要贡献者，坚决抵制贸易保护主义，确保各项贸易政策措施符合世贸组织规则，推动达成巴厘岛协议，全力支持“促贸援助”倡议，积极承担发展中大国应有的责任。作为今年亚太经合组织（APEC）东道主，中国推动 APEC 全力支持世贸组织实施巴厘岛协议。

审议期间，王受文还就成员普遍关注的问题做出了详细回应。他表示，中国政府正在落实全面深化改革的具体方案，不断完善社会主义市场经济体制，着力推动新一轮对外开放，为各类市场主体提供公开透明的法律环境、高效便利的行政环境和平等竞争的市场环境。

中国代表团在此次审议中向世贸组织成员释放了中国政府全面深化改革、主动扩大开放的积极信号，宣传了中国政府为促进世界经济贸易发展，特别是为援助发展中成员和最不发达成员所做的积极贡献，从而彰显了中国政府遵信守诺、率先垂范的负责任大国形象。

最后，此次审议会议主席在总结发言中表示，自上次审议以来，中国已经成为全球贸易大国，中国经济发展为全球贸易和世界经济复苏做出了重大贡献；中国代表团全面回应了各成员提出的大量关注，为本次审议取得圆满成功奠定了重要基础。

（商务部世界贸易组织司）

中国代表团团长、商务部王受文部长助理在世贸组织第五次中国贸易政策审议首日会议的发言

2014年7月1日

尊敬的主席 Mariam Md. Salleh 大使（女士），

尊敬的讨论人 Joakim Reiter 大使，

各位大使、各位代表：

很高兴出席世贸组织第五次中国贸易政策审议会议。首先，请允许我对主席女士和审议讨论人 Joakim Reiter 大使表示感谢！

我还要感谢世贸组织秘书处贸易政策审议司的同事们为此次审议会议所做的大量工作，以及他们准备的《秘书处报告》。尽管中国政府对秘书处报告的一些内容持不同看法，但仍然感谢秘书处为此次审议所付出的巨大努力。

中国政府高度重视这次贸易政策审议会议。过去几个星期，我的团队夜以继日地工作。昨天，我们又收到了3个成员的问题单。共有30个成员向中国提出了将近1600个书面问题。今天，我们尽最大努力，已经完成了26个成员1400多个问题的答复，包括一些在6月17日之后提交的问题。对于剩下的不到200个问题，我们将继续加紧工作，争取会后尽快向大家提交。

主席女士，改革开放是中国政府的一项基本国策。加入世贸组织以来，中国不断加快改革开放进程，深度融入全球价值链体系，经济社会实现了快速发展。新一届中国领导集体履职后，在十八届三中全会上做出了全面深化改革的重大决定。改革的核心是处理好政府与市场的关系，使市场在资源配置中起决定性作用，更好地发挥政府的作用。目前，各项工作已经全面展开。在中国提交的《政策声明》中，也有详细阐述。在此，我将就一些重要举措进行介绍。

——推进行政审批制度改革。2013年，中国政府共取消和下放416项行政审批事项，修订了《政府核准的投资项目目录》。企业投资《目录》以外的项目，仅需向政府备案，而无须报核准机关核准，需报国务院主管部门核准的项目数量减少了60%。

——推进工商登记制度改革。取消公司最低注册资本的限制，将注册资本实缴制改为认缴制。2013年新增私营企业233万家，同比增长30%。

——推进财税体制改革。重点推进部分服务业"营改增"试点，逐步扩大试点省份和试点行业。2013年8月，试点推广到全国。2014年1月1日起，铁路运输业务和邮政业纳入试点。

——推进金融体制改革。中国的利率和汇率市场化改革迈出了新的步伐。中国政府全面放开金融机构贷款利率管制，正式实行贷款基础利率集中报价和发布机制，扩大人民币汇率浮动幅度至2%。

——推动中小微企业发展。对部分小微企业减半征收企业所得税，暂免征收增值税和营业税。鼓励民间资本进入法律未明确禁止准入的金融、石油、电力、铁路、电信、资源开发、公用事业、服务业等行业和领域。2013年民间投资增长23%，占全部投资比重增至63%。

——强化知识产权执法保护。颁布一系列知识产权法律法规，提高侵权赔偿金额，加大对侵权的行政处罚和刑事处罚力度。

中国政府全面深化改革的一系列举措激发了市场活力，提升了居民消费能力。2013年，中国社会消费品零售总额近24万亿元，最终消费对经济增长的贡献率达到50%。同时，中国政府根据世贸组织倡导的公开、透明和可预见原则，努力营造公平竞争的营商环境。

主席女士，中国新一届领导集体在致力于全面深化改革的同时，积极主动扩大开放，加快完善开放型经济新体系，采取了一系列措施推进贸易投资自由化和便利化。

——简化进口管理程序。取消150多个10位海关编码商品的自动进口许可管理。许可证网上申领工作积极推进。

——推动通关便利化。推广海关通关作业无纸化，开展区域通关一体化和“单一窗口”试点。

——提高质检等边境程序便利化。从 2013 年 8 月 15 日起，1507 个 10 位海关编码项下的一般工业制成品不再实行出口商品法定检验。

——推进跨境人民币结算业务。所有进出口企业均可选择以人民币计价、结算和收付。2013 年跨境贸易人民币结算增长 57%。截至 2013 年 10 月，中国人民银行已与 23 个国家和地区的中央银行或货币当局签署了货币互换协议，总额度超过 2.5 万亿元人民币。

——继续鼓励外商投资。第三次修订《中西部地区外商投资优势产业目录》，鼓励外商投资中西部地区符合环保要求的劳动密集型产业。此次修订，新增 173 项。列入《目录》的外商投资项目，可视同鼓励类外商投资项目。

——扩大服务业开放。推进金融、教育、文化、医疗服务有序开放。例如，外资可在试点区域设立保理公司，合资证券公司境外股东持股比重可提高到 49%。

——开展资本项目外汇管理改革。大幅简化直接投资外汇管理，取消外汇账户开立核准等要求。加快 QFII 额度审批，提高特殊类型 QFII 机构投资额度上限，扩大 RQFII 机构和投资范围。

由于实施上述措施，中国贸易投资保持了持续较快增长。目前，中国已是 120 多个国家和地区的第一大贸易伙伴。2013 年货物贸易进出口近 4.2 万亿美元，成为世界第一货物贸易大国。其中，进口为 1.9 万亿美元，同比增长 7.3%，占全球比重升至 10.3%，比上年提高 0.5 个百分点。中国现已成为农产品净进口国。2013 年，中国进口粮食 1100 多万吨。

2013 年，服务贸易进出口达 5396 亿美元，服务贸易逆差由 2012 年的 897 亿美元增加到 1185 亿美元。中国已是全球第一大服务贸易逆差国。

中国是全球最具吸引力的投资东道国之一。2013 年实际使用外资 1100 多亿美元，连续 21 年居发展中国家首位。其中，服务业实际使用外资 614 多亿美元，同比增长 14.51%，首次占比过半。同时，中国对外投资范围扩大，增势强劲。2013 年，非金融类直接投资达 902 亿美元，成为全球对外投资的重要力量之一，也为南南合作做出了重要贡献。

主席女士，自上次审议以来，中国政府在对外开放方面，还有其他重大举措。例如，2013 年 9 月，中国宣布建立中国（上海）自由贸易试验区，主要试点内容包括加快政府职能转变、扩大投资领域开放、推进贸易便利化、深化金融领域的开放创新、推动政府管理由注重事前审批转为注重事中事后监管等。在推进外商投资管理体制改革方面，探索实施准入前国民待遇加负面清单的外商投资管理模式，为将来推广到全国探索新途径、积累新经验。

此外，中国政府还提出了“丝绸之路经济带”和“海上丝绸之路”重要倡议。

主席女士，中国是多边贸易体制的积极参与者、坚定支持者和重要贡献者。中国以自己的实际行动坚定不移地支持世贸组织，并积极承担发展中贸易大国应尽的责任。

——中国作为 APEC 成员，支持多边贸易体制。中国今年担任亚太经济合作组织（APEC）东道主，并于 5 月在青岛举行了 APEC 贸易部长会议。会议发表了《关于“支持多边贸易体制”的声明》，再次肯定多边贸易体制的价值及其核心和首要地位，呼吁忠实履行“巴厘一揽子”协议，承诺完成《贸易便利化协定》的目标和时间表，敦促世贸组织其他成员为多哈发展议程剩余议题制订明确的工作计划。

——中国一直避免采取贸易保护主义，坚持市场开放。中国对各种形式的削弱贸易和延缓经济复苏的贸易保护主义措施保持警惕。中国坚决反对贸易保护主义，继续致力于最大限度地克制适用可能符合世贸规则但却具有明显保护主义效果的措施。中国按期履行世贸组织金融危机监督机制下的通报义务，支持世贸组织在监督贸易投资壁垒方面开展的工作。

——认真参与贸易政策审议。中国政府对世贸组织成员在审议中反馈的建设性意见十分重视。2014 年，国务院办公厅下发了《关于进一步加强贸易政策合规工作的通知》（国办发［2014］29 号），要求国务院各部门、地方各级人民政府制定有关（或影响）货物贸易、服务贸易以及与贸易有关的知识产权的规章、规范性文件和其他政策措施时，需就是否符合世贸组织规则和中国加入承诺进一步做好把关工作。

——严格执行世贸组织裁决。中国是在执行世贸组织裁决方面做得最好的成员之一。中国尊重专家组和上诉机构的裁决，并保持良好的执行记录。到目前为止，中国在世贸组织被诉案件共19起，其中14起已有裁决。对于被裁决为违反世贸组织规则的措施，中国均在合理执行期结束前取消或进行了修改。

——推进实施《贸易便利化协定》。中国根据《巴厘岛部长宣言》所确定的时间表，加快推进《贸易便利化协定》的实施工作。6月30日，中国正式向世贸组织提交了A类措施通报。

主席女士，中国在坚持发挥多边贸易体制及规则的基础作用的同时，继续推进双边和区域经贸合作。今天，中国与冰岛、中国与瑞士的自贸协定正式生效。

尽管中国参与了一些双边和区域协定，但中国政府始终认为，以世贸组织为核心的多边贸易体制是推动全球贸易投资自由化与便利化的主渠道，双边和区域协定只是对多边贸易体制的有益补充，而不是替代。

主席女士，中国自加入以来，积极承担了发展中贸易大国应尽的责任。

中国关税总水平由15.3%降至9.8%，承诺不使用农产品出口补贴，取消了全部进口配额和特定招标管理，开放了100多个服务部门。中国已连续5年成为最不发达国家的第一大出口市场。自2010年7月1日中国对最不发达国家进口产品实施零关税待遇以来，截至2013年4月，中国从26个受惠国进口商品超过22亿美元，免除关税款13多亿元人民币。

中国积极支持世贸组织的促贸援助倡议，从2008年起开始向世贸组织多边框架下的促贸援助基金提供捐款。2011年，中国捐款设立了"中国支持最不发达国家及其加入项目"（"中国项目"）。2012年和2013年，中国又向"中国项目"捐款共80万美元，并在北京举办了"最不发达国家加入世贸组织圆桌会议"。2013年世贸组织第九届部长级会议期间，中国再次向该项目提供40万美元捐款。

主席女士，当前，中国经济发展形势总体是好的，但也面临不少困难。经济增长存在下行压力，内生动力不足，长期积累的深层次矛盾尚待缓解。

虽然中国的经济总量已居世界第二，但中国作为一个面临繁重发展任务的发展中国家的基本国情没有改变。目前，中国人均GDP不到7000美元，在全球排名第84位，还有1.28亿人口生活在贫困线以下。中国的城镇化发展还很滞后，还有6亿至7亿人居住在农村，1亿人在城市的棚户区里生活。中国的工业化任重道远，"中国制造"在全球价值链中总体处于低端位置。中国在继续致力于自身发展的同时，将在国际经贸事务中承担与自身发展水平相称的责任。

主席女士，未来，中国政府将继续致力于全面深化改革，加快推进行政、财税和金融体制改革，增强各类所有制经济活力。明年，中国政府将把"营改增"试点扩展到电信、金融、建筑、房地产等所有服务业。育幼养老、建筑设计、会计审计、商贸物流、电子商务将逐步放开。

中国政府将积极推动新一轮对外开放，坚持积极利用外资，推动服务业开放，打造内外资企业一视同仁、公平竞争的营商环境，扩大内陆沿边地区开放，推动出口升级和贸易平衡发展。中国将统一内外资法律法规，完善投资管理体制，进一步加大区域通关改革力度。

中国将继续支持和维护多边贸易体制，支持多哈回合谈判进程，推动多边贸易体制向更加均衡、普惠、共赢的方向发展。中国希望，处于不同发展水平和阶段的经济体能发扬同舟共济的精神，摒弃零和博弈的做法，携手应对共同挑战，塑造合作共赢的经济全球化新格局。

主席女士，我的发言到此结束。下面，我愿意倾听讨论引导人和其他成员的评论和问题。谢谢大家。

（商务部世界贸易组织司）

中国代表团团长、商务部王受文部长助理在世贸组织第五次中国贸易政策审议第二次会议的发言

2014 年 7 月 3 日

尊敬的主席 Mariam Md. Salleh 大使（女士），
尊敬的讨论人 Joakim Reiter 大使，
各位大使、各位代表：

在 7 月 1 日的会议上，与会成员和我们的讨论引导人，尊敬的 Reiter 大使就上次审议以来中国的经济贸易政策进行了评论，并提出了许多建设性的意见。我愿在此向成员和 Reiter 大使表示感谢！今天，我想就成员在发言中提及的一些问题进行回应。

关于政府与市场的关系，主席女士，中国新一届领导集体提出全面深化改革，核心就是要处理好政府与市场的关系，减少政府对市场的干预。我在 7 月 1 日的发言中介绍了中国政府大幅取消和下放审批权的情况，就是政府减少对市场直接干预的具体体现。目前，中国的劳动力成本完全取决于市场，土地使用权通过拍卖方式转让，贷款利率已经放开，而且随着改革的落实，利率市场化也将加快推进。市场已经是资本、劳动力和土地要素价格的决定性因素。

关于成员比较关心的发展规划和产业政策以及有关国有企业的问题，发展规划和产业政策实际上是就经济社会和产业发展提出的总体蓝图，其中的目标是预期性的，意见是指导性的，在实施中对各类市场主体都是公平、公正、公开的，不存在对国有企业的支持和补贴。中国政府早在 20 世纪 90 年代就通过财税改革等相关措施取消了专门针对国有企业的补贴。目前实践中出现的企业贷款额度和利率的不同，实际上并不是因为对国有企业有特殊政策，而是商业银行基于对市场的判断做出的自主行为。秘书处报告中提到，中国国有企业在出口总额中占三分之二。这个数字不准确。2011 年至 2013 年，中国国有企业进出口额占进出口总额的比重在持续下降，分别为 20.88%，19.44%和 17.98%。我们对由此给成员造成的误解表示遗憾。

关于一些成员提到的国有企业是否受《反垄断法》管辖的问题，我想举一个具体案例。2011 年，中国国家发展改革委员会对中国电信以过高价格变相拒绝与中国铁通交易进行了调查，对在中国互联网基础网络上处于垄断地位的中国电信和中国联通对互联网服务提供商实行价格歧视进行了调查。调查发现，两大公司没有实现充分互联互通，导致相关市场缺乏竞争。中国电信和中国联通 2011 年底分别向发展改革委提交了中止调查申请，承诺进行整改。目前，对两公司是否完全履行整改承诺、相关整改措施是否消除涉嫌垄断行为后果等情况，正在进行评估之中。这说明，中国的《反垄断法》执法并没有区分所有制类型。

关于补贴政策的通报，主席女士，2012 年，中国政府提交了 2005—2008 年补贴政策通报。目前，我们正在积极准备 2009 年以来的补贴政策的通报。由于补贴政策涉及多个政府部门和政府层级，收集政策信息、厘清政策之间的关系、对照（SCM）协定对补贴政策进行分析的工作量很大，因此补贴通报可以说是中国在履行世贸组织各个具体协定的通报义务中最为困难的一个。但是，这些困难不会成为我们不通报的理由。农业国内支持的通报也是一样，我们正在为确保数据的准确性等技术问题开展工作。我们将会同有关部门加快工作进程，尽可能早地提交通报。

主席女士，关于中国进一步开放市场的问题，正如我在 7 月 1 日发言中向成员介绍的，根据十八届三中全会深化改革、扩大开放的重大决定，中国政府一直不遗余力地推进重点服务业领域扩大开放，放宽外资准入限制。

在服务业开放方面，2014 年初，中国政府发布《外商投资道路运输业管理规定》，将外商投资道路运输业的立项审批权限全部下放到省级交通运输主管部门。中国政府将于 2014 年 7 月上旬发布

《关于开展外商独资医院设置试点工作的通知》，在北京、上海等7省市设立试点，将投资主体扩大为所有境外投资者。中国政府正在研究将已施行的有关自贸区放宽与电子商务有关的增值电信市场准入限制的政策扩大适用范围，逐步取消电子商务领域外资股比限制。

在投资领域，正如我在7月1日发言中提到的，中国政府大力推进投资管理体制改革，大幅缩小核准范围，下放核准权限。在上海自贸区探索实施准入前国民待遇加负面清单的投资管理模式，并在中美、中欧投资保护协定中引入这一模式。7月1日，中国政府公布了上海自由贸易试验区新的外商投资准入特别管理措施（负面清单）。修订后，特别管理措施由原先的190条调整为139条，减少51条，调整率达26.8%。

中国政府通过建立上海自由贸易试验区，为全面深化改革和扩大开放探索新途径、积累新经验，形成可复制可推广的体制机制。上海所取得的相关经验将适时向全国推广，一些具体措施如证明行之有效，可立即向全国推广。

此外，中国政府提出了建设“丝绸之路经济带”和“海上丝绸之路”战略构想，促进内陆沿边地区开放和区域协调发展。

关于成员关心的透明度，包括法规规章和有关政策措施的翻译问题，由商务部负责编辑和发行的《中国对外经济贸易文告》，是中国国政府指定的汇集刊登已按现行规定公布的所有有关或影响货物贸易、服务贸易、与贸易有关的知识产权或外汇管制的法规、规章及其他措施的官方刊物。自2002年发行至2014年5月底，《文告》已出版发行923期，刊登文件共5266件（含公开征求意见草案196件）。

目前，法律法规和其他措施的翻译工作已有专门的制度安排并逐步推进。全国人大法工委定期公布《中华人民共和国法律（英文版）》，国务院法制办定期公布《中华人民共和国涉外法规汇编（中英文对照）》。2003年2月24日，国务院办公厅下发了《关于做好行政法规英文正式译文翻译审定工作的通知》（国办发［2003］10号文），要求各地方和各部门按照通知的精神，做好地方政府规章和部门规章的翻译和审定工作。

我们注意到成员的意见和建议，并将按照加入世贸组织承诺，努力完善《文告》和法律法规的翻译工作，不断提高透明度。

关于成员质疑中国发起的几起贸易救济案件属于报复性措施的问题，我们认为这种质疑是没有根据的。中国所有的反倾销和反补贴调查均建立在申请人有足够正当理由的基础上。同其他世贸成员一样，中国的调查机关应当在有足够的初步证据的基础上受理申请，并以客观公正的方式发起调查。

中国一直审慎克制地使用贸易救济措施。以反倾销为例，根据世贸组织统计，自中国加入世贸组织到2013年底，中国共发起不到200起反倾销调查和7起反补贴调查，而同期其他成员对中国的反倾销立案调查超过700起、反补贴76起。从上述统计数字可以看出，如果中国确实采取了报复性制裁，发起案件数量不会这么少。

关于成员提出中国存在不符世贸规则的出口限制措施的问题，中方必须澄清的是，中国确实对一些产品维持着出口管理措施，但是这些措施符合世贸组织规则。

世贸组织规则既强调贸易自由，也允许成员采取必要手段实现保护资源、环境的政策目标。对高污染、高耗能和不可再生自然资源产品实施出口管理，是中国政府在面临日趋严峻的资源和环境压力下，为实现可持续发展而进一步强化的生态环境保护综合措施的一个组成部分，而且目前不得不采取。这一政策目标是符合世贸组织规则的。

关于海关程序的统一问题，需要澄清的是，中国海关依据《海关法》及有关法律法规实施海关监管程序，海关程序的立法和执法在全国关境内是统一的。实践中，个别地区海关因经济发展条件、地理环境、执法人员法律认知程度不同，难免对立法存在不同的理解，进而导致执法差异。在推行海关通关改革过程中，先行选择部分区域海关试点，也可能暂时引起与非试点区域的执法不平衡。

为统一规范海关执法，我们采取了多种有效措施，如建立执法不统一问题发现、解决、反馈机制，区域海关执法统一协作机制，实施海关业务标准化制度、行政解释制度等。加大了对海关自由裁量权的规范，并通过行政复议、对关员进行法制培训等方式，纠正执法偏差。

我们将继续致力于统一规范执法，为企业创造公平、公正、安全、便捷的通关环境。

关于知识产权保护问题，中国政府高度重视知识产权保护方面的立法、执法工作和长效机制建设，颁布了一系列知识产权领域的法律法规，提高了侵犯知识产权的赔偿金额，加大对侵犯知识产权的行政处罚和刑事处罚的力度。中国新一届政府保留了由国务院副总理担任组长的打击侵犯知识产权和制售假冒伪劣商品工作领导小组，推动将打击侵犯知识产权和制售假冒伪劣商品工作逐级纳入政府绩效考核体系。如果成员发现侵权案件，可随时向中国有关部门反映。

另外我想解释一下，个别成员关注中国出口商品的质量问题，首先我要明确的是中国出口商品质量不存在问题，但不排除一些不法进出口商相互勾结，趁机出口一些质量较差的产品。对此，中国政府愿意和进口国保持合作，共同打击假冒侵权产品。例如，双方可以共同建立一个不法贸易商名录，把这些不讲信用的人从市场上赶出去。

一些成员在发言中指出，中国现在已经是全球第一大货物贸易国，经济总量居世界第二，因此希望中国在多边贸易体制中发挥领导作用。然而，上述数字丝毫不能隐瞒一个事实，那就是中国依然是一个发展中国家。我注意到引导人 Reiter 大使在发言中引述了世行排名，根据 UNDP 人类发展指数，中国在 178 个国家中仅排名第 101 位。安提瓜和瓜布达大使也在发言中指出，虽然中国块头较大，但在经济可持续发展方面依然面临严峻的挑战。

我们将根据自己的发展水平、产业水平和收入水平，积极参加谈判，在多边贸易体制中发挥与我们身份相符的责任。

主席女士，我注意到一些成员在周一的发言中提到，希望中国前往投资。中国的对外投资虽然处于起步阶段，但发展很快。2013 年中国非金融类对外直接投资达到 902 亿美元，同比增长 16.8%，涉及全球 156 个国家和地区。发展中成员已经成为中国对外投资的重要目的地。未来 5 年，中国对外投资总额预计将超过 5000 亿美元。

中国政府鼓励企业开展对外投资，也希望成员为中国企业前往投资提供良好的环境和便利。我们欢迎成员，特别是发展中成员来中国开展招商引资工作。我想借此机会向大家推荐每年 9 月 8 日和 9 日在中国福建厦门经济特区举办的中国国际贸易投资洽谈会。这是一个中外投资者云集、充满合作商机的展会。建议大家充分利用这一平台，向投资者介绍自己的投资合作环境和政策，相信中国企业会很感兴趣。

主席女士，我对周一会议上大家提出的主要关注问题的回应就到这里了。谢谢大家。

（商务部世界贸易组织司）

王受文部长助理就 WTO 对华贸易政策审议接受采访

2014 年 7 月 4 日，商务部部长助理王受文就世贸组织第五次对华贸易政策审议的有关问题接受了记者联合采访。

问：中国在这次审议中向国际社会传递了什么重要信息？

答：这次审议应该说受到各方关注。我们利用这次审议，主要传递了三个方面的重要信息：第一，重点介绍了中国新一届领导集体执政以后，在改革开放方面采取的新举措，特别是十八届三中全会做出的全面深化改革的重大决定；第二，中国在过去两年推进贸易投资自由化和便利化方面采取的措施；第三，中国作为第一货物贸易大国，对以世贸组织为代表的多边贸易体制做出的重大贡献。

问：作为世界第一货物贸易大国和第二大经济体，国际社会怎样看待中国过去两年的表现？

答：世贸组织成员都给予了很高的评价。

具体来说，大家对中国在转变经济增长方式方面取得的成绩给予了肯定。以前，中国的经济发展对出口的依赖比较多，最近两年，出口依赖相对减少，比如说我们的贸易顺差占 GDP 的比重有所下降。

第二，他们非常看重中国的经济发展，特别是扩大对进口的需求给他们带来的机会。中国现在已经是 120 多个成员的最大贸易伙伴，中国的经济增长给他们带来了很多机会。

第三，他们特别赞赏中国在国际金融危机之后，在采取贸易保护措施方面非常克制，坚决反对贸易保护主义，对其他成员到了示范作用。中国作为贸易大国，以身作则，给世界发出了积极信号。

第四，成员对中国积极参与多边贸易体制，特别是对多哈谈判的支持表示高度赞赏。《贸易便利化协定》是世贸组织成立近 20 年以来达成的首个协议。这个协定的谈判过程可谓一波三折，中国在谈判的关键时刻发挥了重要作用，为达成协定做出了重要贡献。中国在世贸框架下积极参与促贸援助，专门成立了一个“中国项目”，每年给予捐助，帮助最不发达国家加入世贸组织及参与有关谈判。对于与中国建立外交关系的最不发达国家，中国给予他们 95%的产品零关税零配额待遇。现在中国已经是最不发达国家最大的市场。成员对这些举措非常赞赏。

此外，一些与中国签订有自贸协定的国家和地区也对中国的表现高度赞赏，比如说东盟、瑞士、冰岛和巴基斯坦，他们与中国签署了双边自贸协定，从与中国的贸易投资关系发展中得到或期待很多实惠。

问：此次审议中，中国收到多少个成员的书面提问？现场共有多少问题？集中在哪些领域？反映了对经贸领域的哪些关注？

答：中国现在是第一货物贸易大国。中国贸易政策的变化和采取的新措施，都会对其他世贸成员产生影响，因此成员对此次审议给予高度关注重视，共提出了 1700 多个书面问题，这些书面问题涉及中国经贸体制的方方面面。

审议期间，共有 47 个成员进行发言和评论，会议主席告诉我此次发言成员数量在历次审议中是非常靠前的，这说明成员非常重视和关注中国的贸易体制对他们的影响。他们关心的领域包括：(1) 中国经贸政策的透明度。作为第一货物贸易大国和第二大经济体，中国采取的措施可能对成员的贸易和投资产生重大的影响，希望中国统一公布影响贸易的政策和措施，并将这些文件翻译成英语，贸易政策执行时要有一致性；(2) 上海自贸区的建设。大家都非常欢迎上海自贸试验区的建设，因为上海自贸区的建设能探索中国进一步改革和扩大开放的新途径和新经验。成员关心上海自贸区积累的经验和好的做法能否在自贸区之外得以推广；(3) 知识产权保护。比如说中国现在的专利申请数量很大，保护专利等知识产权，有利于新的发明，有利于企业投入更多研发资金。外资企业在华知识产权利益较多，成员关注中国能否进一步提高知识产权保护力度。(4) 中国在海关程序、贸易便利化方面能否进一步完善。有的成员认为，中国幅员辽阔，不同口岸关税征收、进口产品的海关估价、进出口产品的检验检疫，这些均涉及成员的切身利益。所以希望中国在海关程序、动植物检验检疫、商品技术标准方面能更加透明统一。

问：审议中，WTO成员对中国有哪些积极评价？

答：一是大家对十八届三中全会做出的全面深化改革的决定给予高度赞赏。这次我们同事都有同样感受，与两年前的审议相比有很大不同。两年前，成员不知道中国下一步怎么走，这次审议成员知道了中国改革开放的政策走向和蓝图，他们希望中国政府能尽快落实改革开放的具体举措，并想了解具体的时间表。

二是中国经济增长给其他成员带来很多机会。中国2013年的GDP增速为7.7%，虽然不比以前两位数的增长，但还是为世界经济复苏和双边贸易投资带来了机会。韩国代表认为，中国经济的健康相当于世界经济的健康。

三是中国对多边贸易体制的支持。成员赞赏中国对巴厘岛一揽子协议的达成所做出的贡献，特别对贸易便利化协定，中国在关键时候所起的作用；赞赏中国抵制贸易保护主义，以身作则，不滥用贸易救济措施。

四是中国重视南南合作，尤其是对最不发达国家开放市场，中国现在是最不发达国家的最大市场。我们每年给予最不发达国家免关税待遇，免税额一年达到4亿元到5亿元人民币。这些国家把中国当作他们未来经济增长的重要机会。

问：对世贸成员提出的关注，中方将如何看待和处理？

答：贸易政策审议对中国意义重大。作为最大货物贸易国，我们出口最多，如大家都不遵守贸易政策，吃亏的是中国，受害的是中国企业。因此我们要把中国的贸易政策执行好，起表率作用。大家都遵守世贸规则，符合中国的利益，有利于世贸组织所有成员和世界经济的发展。

我们认为，成员提出关切是出于对自己利益的考虑，是可以理解的。有些关切不太准确，是出于误解，我们在会上给予解释和澄清。还有一部分关切是有道理的，如如何加强知识产权保护，如何加强透明度工作，对于这些，我们下一步要认真采取措施进一步完善。

参加这次审议会议的国务院部门有9个，但实际参与回答书面问题的有60多个部门。会后我们会对这些问题进行整理分类，并会同各部门根据其职责分工，研究如何处理和答复。

问：自去年12月WTO成员达成“巴厘一揽子协定”以来，中国在落实《贸易便利化》协定方面有何计划？

答：贸易便利化协定是世贸组织成立近20年来达成的首个协议，恢复了成员对世贸组织谈判功能的信心。协定谈判过程一波三折，中国与其他成员一起促成了贸易便利化协定，发挥了重要作用。

协定达成后，世贸组织成立贸易便利化的筹备委员会，中国也积极参与该委员会的工作。经国务院批准，我们对协定的实施进行通报。6月30日，我们已经通报了A类措施，得到世贸组织秘书处和成员的赞赏。下一步，协议需在完成法律程序、交成员进行批准之后予以实施。我们期待明年7月31日之前协定可以实施。贸易便利化协定的执行有利于降低贸易成本，减少交易费用，有利于全球贸易的发展。当然，对中国这样一个贸易大国的意义不言而喻。

问：近年来，中国在服务业开放方面取得了哪些突破和进展？下一步有何目标？

答：服务业发展对中国来说非常重要。现在中国服务业占中国经济发展的比重只有46%左右，发达国家则有70%左右，即便是很多发展中国家，服务业占GDP的比重也超过了中国。就服务业出口占总出口的比重来说，中国占比只有10%；全球平均而言，服务出口占总出口就有20%。因此，服务业出口方面，中国还有很多路要走。虽然中国的贸易发展很快，货物贸易总额已超过美国，但服务贸易总额只有美国的一半。十八届三中全会提出了进一步扩大服务业开放，最近一些具体措施正在落实。

比如独资医院，我们现在考虑在北京、上海等7个省市开展试点，允许设立外资独资医院。又如电信领域扩大开放。目前，在上海自贸试验区和CEPA、ECFA框架下已允许设立合资企业的基础上，从事经营性电子商务的在线数据处理与交易业务，外资上限扩大为55%。今后我们将研究在以上机制之外能否再进一步放开电子商务外商市场准入。此外，我们还将研究进一步放开广告业务。

7月1日上海颁布新的负面清单，对服务业放开了14条限制。商务部正和有关部门研究如何进一步开放服务业。

问：中国在WTO框架下如何与发展中国家及最不发达国家合作，实现共同发展？

答：现在中国对外贸易总额中55%左右的贸易是与发展中国家进行的，发展中国家经济增长速度快于其他国家，对外贸易新的潜力所在应该是发展中国家。我们继续保持对发达国家市场开拓的同时，非常重视与发展中国家的贸易关系。

(1) 我们推动自贸区战略来扩大与发展中国家的合作。RECP（10+6）谈判有很多发展中国家，我们推动东盟自贸区升级版，结束了与斯里兰卡自贸协定的可行性研究，与哥伦比亚探讨建立自贸区的可能性。

(2) “一带一路”倡议。丝绸之路经济带沿线有很多发展中国家，21世纪海上丝绸之路经济带也涉及很多发展中国家。这一倡议的实施有助于推动中国与发展中国家的经贸关系。

(3) 鼓励企业走出去，拓展对发展中国家的投资。2013年，中国非金融类对外直接投资达到900多亿美元，已是世界第三大投资输出国。很多发展中国家也表示欢迎中国去发展中国家投资。

(4) 与最不发达国家的关系。中国在WTO框架下，开展支持最不发达国家及加入WTO的项目，即中国项目。通过召开会议、做介绍、提供培训等方式帮助最不发达国家提升其加入世贸组织能力建设。

问：在您的发言中提到了一个文件，也就是《国务院办公厅关于进一步加强贸易政策合规工作的通知》，请您进一步介绍有关内容以及出台该文件的意义？

答：中国加入世贸已经13年了，我们执行世贸规则，促进了中国对外贸易发展，经济质量和效益明显提高。其他国家对中国政策是否符合世贸规则非常关心。如果中国政策不符合世贸规则，就会影响成员的利益。国务院对此非常重视，出台了《国务院办公厅关于进一步加强贸易政策合规工作的通知》。通知主要内容有两条，国务院各部门制定的政策，如认为必要，应征求商务部意见；地方政府制定的政策在其认为必要时也要征求商务部意见，使得国务院各部门和地方制定的政策符合世贸规则和我国加入世贸组织承诺。这项工作有利于减少贸易摩擦和成员的质疑，树立中国遵守世贸规则的良好形象。同时，中国遵守世贸规则，可以带动其他世贸组织成员遵循世贸组织规则，这也符合中国的利益。

（商务部世界贸易组织司）

世贸组织对中国台北第三次贸易政策审议我方代表团团长的发言

2014 年 9 月 16 日

主席先生：

中国对出席审议会议的中国台北代表团表示欢迎。

中国台北是全球重要的经济和贸易实体之一。自上次审议以来，随着外部需求的增加，其经济实现了较为平稳的增长。中国台北在信息技术等制造业方面具有竞争优势，但其经济严重依赖出口，经济波动风险大。对此，中国台北正在努力推进结构性改革，寻求经济增长新的引擎，以期实现经济多元化。我们高兴地看到中国台北正在推动自由经济示范区建设，加大对外开放力度，同时选取了包括旅游在内的关键服务行业重点推动经济发展，我们期待着这些改革措施和政策取得成效。

自上次审议以来，中国大陆和中国台北两岸经贸往来日益密切，经贸交流合作规模进一步扩大。据中国海关统计，两岸贸易额已从 2010 年的 1453.7 亿美元增长到 2013 年的 1972.8 亿美元，年均增长率高于 10%。目前，中国台北是我们的第七大贸易伙伴，我们是中国台北最大的贸易伙伴、最大的出口市场和最大的贸易顺差来源地。截至目前，经批准的台商在大陆投资项目累计达 9 万多个，金额累计达 1100 多亿美元，在中国累计吸收海外投资中列第二位。共有 530 多家大陆企业赴台投资，投资金额 10 多亿美元。

更值得一提的是，我们和中国台北之间的经贸合作水平提升迅速。自 2010 年 6 月签署《海峡两岸经济合作框架协议》（简称 ECFA）以来，双方业界充分享受了 ECFA 早期收获计划带来的红利。短短三年半时间，在货物贸易方面，双方合计受惠产品金额达 347 亿美元；在服务贸易方面，两岸共有 420 多个服务类企业和项目从中受惠。2013 年，双方陆续商谈并签署了《海峡两岸投资保护和促进协议》《海峡两岸服务贸易协议》等 ECFA 后续协议。这将会促进两岸经济融合，实现互利双赢。正如秘书处报告所述，ECFA 能推动服务行业的增长，促进就业，成为岛上经济增长的主要动力。

与此同时，我们也注意到，双方在贸易投资领域的合作还存在不平衡性。中国对中国台北的贸易逆差 2013 年高达 1160 亿美元，双方之间的相互投资也存在巨大差距。其中一个很重要原因，就是中国台北还没有给予我们与其他 WTO 成员相同的待遇，中国台北对中国大陆投资者的开放水平远不及对其他 WTO 成员的开放程度，在贸易和投资领域均还存在歧视性措施。如在贸易领域，秘书处报告指出“根据 2014 年 4 月 10 日最新限制进口清单显示，目前台湾仍对 2186 项（HS10 位编码）原产于中国大陆的货物禁止进口”，其中包括 1200 多项工业品和 900 多项农产品。在投资领域，中国台北对中国大陆投资者仅开放了 51%的服务业项目和 51%的公共建设项目，在已开放的领域也存在市场准入门槛高、审批手续烦琐以及所谓的安全审查等限制性措施。这些因素影响了两岸经贸合作潜力的进一步发挥，也不利于中国台北自身经济的发展。

我们期待中国台北全面履行其加入承诺，纠正其与 WTO 公平贸易原则尚存差距的贸易政策与做法，取消对大陆歧视性措施并保障大陆享有与其他成员相同的待遇，推动两岸平等、开放、共赢的贸易交流与合作。

主席先生，今天会后我们还将提交一些后续问题单，我们期待中国台北按时提供答复。

最后，我祝此次中国台北贸易政策审议成功！

谢谢。

（商务部世界贸易组织司）

世贸组织对美国第十二次贸易政策审议中国常驻世贸组织代表团俞建华大使的发言

2014 年 12 月 16 日

感谢主席女士。

我愿和此前发言的同事们一道，对庞克大使率领的美国代表团表示欢迎，对秘书处和美国政府准备的两份文件表示感谢，对讨论引导人的引导表示感谢。

在宏观经济及政策方面，我们高兴地看到美国经济已基本走出危机，GDP、财政收支、对外贸易、就业等各项指标均有改善，金融体系趋于稳健。但与此同时，中方对美国“量宽”实施与退出、债务问题，以及促进制造业回归和出口增长的一系列财税、信贷政策表示关切。我们希望美国充分考虑其政策溢出效应及对全球经济的潜在影响，尽可能减少相关政策对其他经济体可能形成的风险和挑战。

在维护多边贸易体制、推动多哈回合谈判方面，美国作为世界第一经济大国和多边贸易体制的主要创建者之一，长期致力于多边贸易体制，曾为以往多边谈判的成功发挥过十分关键的作用。世贸组织成员始终对美国的责任寄予厚望，期望美国能够继续承担推动多哈进程的重任。秘书处报告也认为美国“在世贸组织中发挥了积极领导作用”。但我们关切地注意到，此次美国政府贸易政策声明第一部分的标题由过去的“多边贸易体系中的美国”变为“全球贸易体系中的美国”，“多边”一词甚至在第一部分的正文中也未见踪影。其背后原因是什么？我们期待美方的澄清。

在 TPP、TTIP、TISA 等诸边大型自贸区谈判上，我们要求美方遵守透明度、包容性、开放性的原则，及时向各成员通报情况，打消发展中国家顾虑，与各方一道，采取实质行动，保证诸边谈判为多边贸易体制做贡献。与此同时，在制订“后巴厘工作计划”和推进多哈回合谈判的关键时刻，我们期待美方能坚定支持多边贸易体制，继续发挥领导作用，带领所有世贸组织成员尽早结束多哈回合谈判。

主席女士，

在贸易投资体制与政策方面，中方赞赏美国贸易投资环境总体开放，便利化水平较高，位于世界前列。但是，美国在贸易投资体制政策方面，仍存在着一系列亟待解决的新问题和老问题。

一方面，近年来美国一些带有保护主义色彩的新政策和新做法，严重影响中方在内的世贸组织成员的经贸利益，中方对此高度关注。

比如，美国的新《农业法》使未来 5 年内相关政府支出高达 4890 亿美元，较此前水平降幅微乎其微。美国农业国内支持由直接支付向差额补足支付的转变，以及新方式在价格设定和基期更新等方面的规定是否如秘书处报告所指，可能增加对农业生产和贸易的扭曲，中方将就此进一步研究。此外，美国一方面对本国农产品实施高额补贴，另一方面却对进口农产品大量设置关税高峰，这相当于提供了双重保护，对国际贸易造成扭曲。

再如，近年来美国贸易救济措施数量激增，2013 年美国正在执行的反倾销、反补贴措施达 294 项，较 2010 年增长 18%；仅 2013 年一年美国就启动 39 项反倾销和 19 项反补贴调查，均远高于历史水平，其中针对包括中国在内的发展中成员的调查占了很大比重；2013—2014 年美国进行的日落复审中，裁定继续执行贸易救济措施的比例高达 90%。特别需要指出的是，世贸组织争端解决机构做出的某些裁决一直未获得美方充分的尊重与全面的执行。争端解决机构在 DS379、DS437 和 DS449 等案件中均裁定美对华双反调查违反世贸规则，但美方在 DS379 上迄今未予完全纠正。

另一方面，中美双边经贸往来中，中方高度关注的一些老问题依然没有解决，中方借此机会愿意再次重申。

第一，美国频繁对华发起包括违反世贸规则的双反调查在内的贸易救济措施，在调查中滥用不合理的“替代国价格”；美继续实施对华高科技产品出口管制，不利于实现双边贸易的平衡；美方部分针对中国产鮰鱼、熟制禽肉、部分热带水果的检验检疫措施缺乏必要科学依据；美国众议院拨款委员会通过的有关修正案，美国政府拒绝采取实际行动，使中国禽肉目前无法进入美国学校早午餐计划。

第二，近年来由美国外国投资委员会针对中国发起的外资国家安全审查数量激增，由 2010 年的 6 起增加至 2012 年的 23 起。审查程序缺乏透明度且无须提供做出决定的理由，打击了中国企业在美投资的意愿。

第三，知识产权方面，337 调查多被美国专利经营公司滥用，背离了该条款加强知识产权保护的初衷，对企业在美经营造成了困难。此外，美国对有关标准的必要专利缺少统一的处理规则，增加了整个程序的不确定性和成本，并可能造成事实上的市场垄断。美国各州在技术标准、行政收费等方面存在立法与执法不统一的情况，也给企业经营带来了困扰。

我们真诚希望美方对上述新、老问题予以充分关注，并采取切实措施予以解决。

主席女士，

中美互为重要的经贸伙伴，近年来双边经贸合作不断深化。上个月，两国元首在北京成功会晤，确认经济关系作为双边关系核心的重要性。

今年是中美两国建交 35 周年，今天是中美建交公报发表 36 周年纪念日，此时此刻，中美双边商贸联委会正在美国芝加哥举行。我们相信，通过多双边互动与交流，中美双方能取得更多共识，促进双边经贸关系进一步发展，维护多边贸易体制的稳定。

最后，感谢美国代表团对中方问题单所做的答复，我们将认真研究。祝愿世贸组织对美国第 12 次贸易政策审议圆满成功。

再次感谢主席女士。

（商务部世界贸易组织司）

● WTO/TBT 与 SPS

2014 年 WTO/TBT、SPS 工作情况

一、TBT 通报总体情况

（一）通报数量

2014 年，成员共提交了 1535 件技术法规和合格评定程序的新通报（包含 29 个修订），还有 619 件通报补遗和 56 件通报的勘误。自 1995 年协定实施以来至 2014 年 12 月 31 日，共有 126 个成员提交了 18886 件通报和 4379 件补遗和 148 件勘误（参见图 1）。

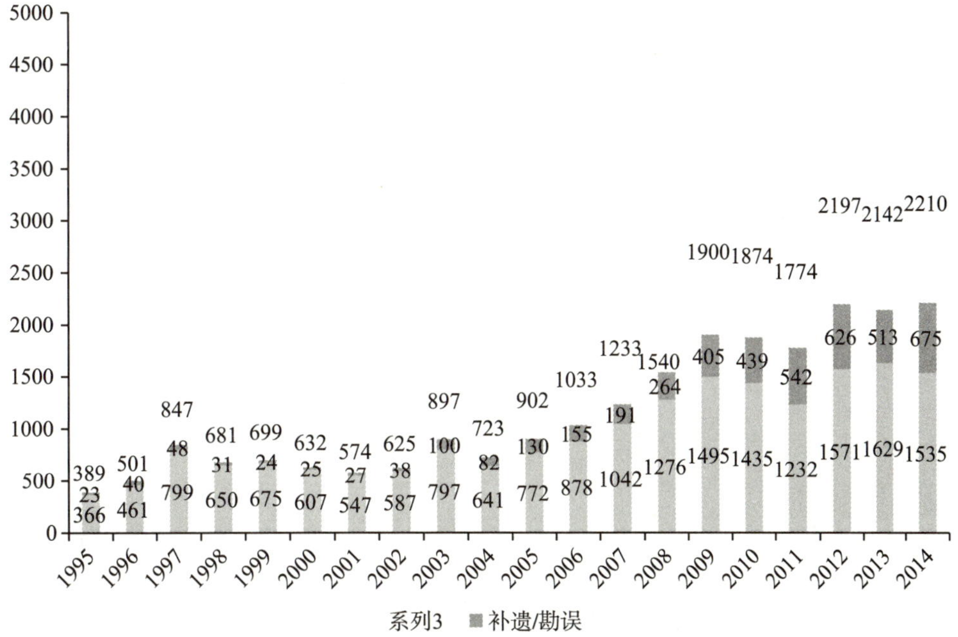

图 1 1995—2014 年 TBT 通报总数

2014 年，共有 75 个成员提交了 TBT 通报。

提交新通报数量位列前十位的成员依次是：厄瓜多尔、美国、巴西、沙特阿拉伯、以色列、欧盟、韩国、加拿大、阿拉伯联合酋长国、中国台北和科威特（中国台北和科威特均通报了 62 项措施）。

（二）制定通报文件的目标和理由

在 2014 年收到的 1535 件通报中，各成员提到了下述目标和理由：保护人类健康安全，防止欺诈行为，保护环境，质量要求，消费者信息，降低或去除贸易壁垒，接收国法，协调，保护动物或植物健康和安全，贸易便利，节约成本和提高生产力，国家安全等（参见图 2）。

表 1　　2014 年通报数量居前 10 位的成员通报情况

位次	成员	2014 年通报数量
1	厄瓜多尔	420
2	美国	181
3	巴西	130
4	沙特阿拉伯	117
5	以色列	97
6	欧盟	88
7	韩国	85
8	加拿大	66
9	阿拉伯联合酋长国	65
10	中国台北/科威特	62

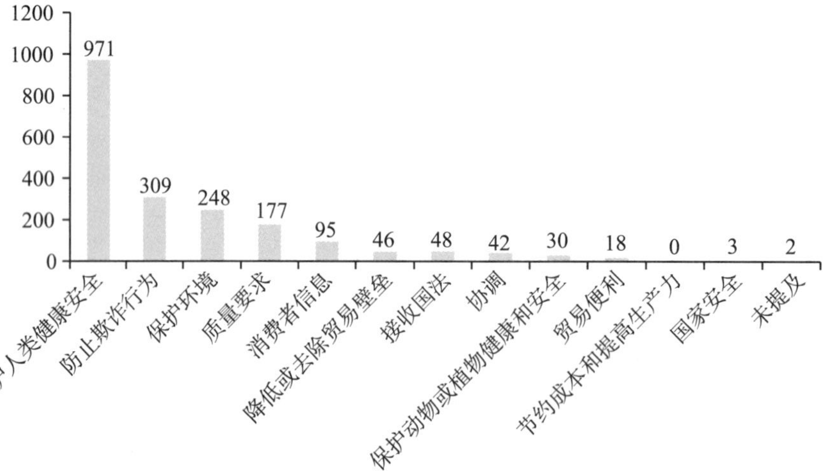

图 2　2014 年陈述各种理由的 TBT 通报数量

（三）通报涉及的类型和领域

通报中涉及最多的产品领域仍是食品及相关产品，计 580 件次①，占总通报件次的 32.79%。这说明在各国的技术法规中与食品相关的内容占很大比重，食品始终是各国政府重点管理的产品。其次为电气、电子、电器工程以及家用和商用设备、文娱、体育，这两个领域也一直是通报的热点，连续几年都位于通报领域的前 5 位（参见图 3）。

（四）中国 TBT 通报和外方评议

2014 年，中国通过 WTO 向各成员通报 TBT 措施 49 件，通报数量在所有 WTO 成员中列第 15 位。在 49 件 TBT 措施中，强制性国家标准 19 件。截至 2014 年 12 月 31 日，中国的 TBT 通报编号已编至 1064 号。

通报发出后，中国 TBT 国家通报咨询中心收到来自美国、欧盟、日本、韩国、印度、瑞士以及境外企业、行业协会的评议意见 47 件（次），涉及 19 件通报措施。中国政府有关部门对这些评议意见进行了认真研究考虑，并给予了回复。

① 部分通报涉及多种产品，有些覆盖多个不同领域，因此对于同一通报，在统计时可能多次计入相应“通报领域”，以“件次”表述。

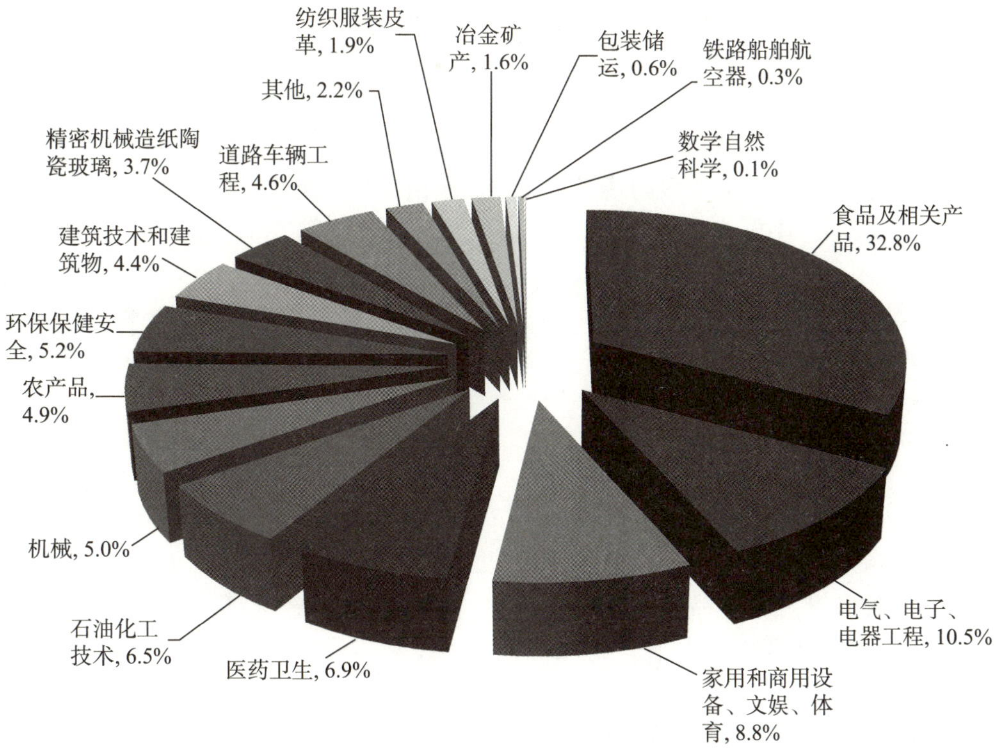

图 3　2014 年 TBT 通报涉及的产品类别

二、SPS 概况

（一）SPS 通报数量

2014 年，有 53 个成员向 WTO 提交了 1633 件 SPS 通报。排在前 10 位的成员分别是：加拿大 251 件，美国 156 件，巴西 152 件，秘鲁 114 件，欧盟 91 件，俄罗斯 71 件，中国 68 件，中国台北 67 件，日本 64 件，沙特阿拉伯、墨西哥各 52 件。前 10 位成员的通报数量（1138 件）占全部通报的 69.7%。2014 年，发展中成员通报的数量（1026 件）超出发达成员的通报数量（607 件）约 69.0%（参见图 4）。

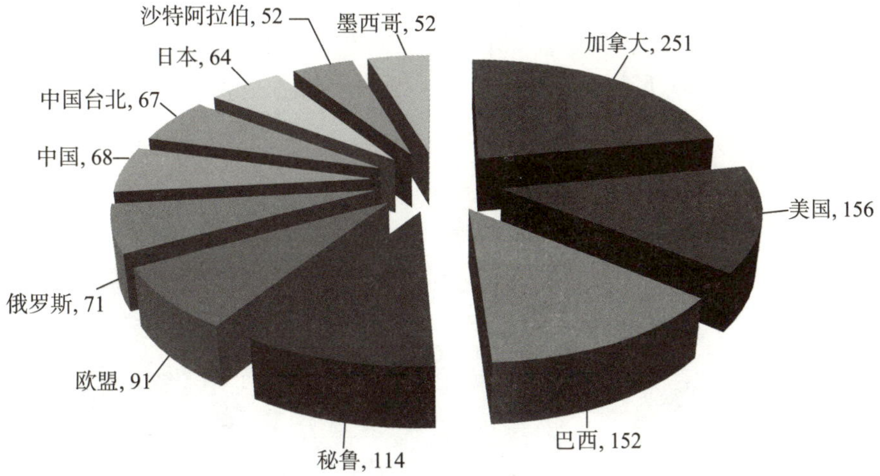

图 4　各成员通报情况

（二）SPS 通报目标和内容

通过对 1056 件常规通报（包括修订）中“涉及产品”和“内容摘要”栏目的分析发现，2014 年各成员的通报措施中：

(1) 涉及食品安全方面，农兽药残留限量354件，发布数量较多的成员有加拿大90，巴西86，美国74，日本42，欧盟17，澳大利亚12，中国台北8，韩国、新西兰、沙特阿拉伯各3件。食品的产品标准128件，发布数量较多的成员有沙特阿拉伯32，巴林25，中国22，土耳其10，卡塔尔5，菲律宾4，阿曼3件。食品添加剂安全标准125件，发布数量较多的成员有中国38，印度尼西亚24，加拿大21，欧盟11，日本8，美国、印度各4，沙特3件。食品中污染物限量16件，发布数量较多的成员有韩国5，中国台北3，印度、日本各2件。食品标签9件，发布成员有加拿大、巴西各2件，巴林、巴西、美国、南非、泰国各1件。饮用水安全标准8件，发布成员有阿曼、沙特阿拉伯各2件，食品接触材料安全标准6件，发布成员有中国台北2，韩国、巴林、欧盟、土耳其各1件。

(2) 涉及动物健康方面，活动物进口检疫要求23件，发布数量较多的成员有阿拉伯联合酋长国8，智利4，俄罗斯3，越南2件，防止动物疫病传入的卫生措施的21件，发布数量较多的成员有美国7，乌克兰6，巴西、加拿大各2。饲料和饲料添加剂的批准使用21件，发布数量较多的成员有欧盟14，乌拉圭4，巴西2件。兽药的批准和控制5件，发布成员有乌拉圭3，美国、越南各1件。

(3) 涉及植物保护方面，植物繁殖材料的进口卫生要求89件，发布数量较多的成员有秘鲁38，厄瓜多尔18，智利14，墨西哥13，尼加拉瓜3件。水果进口要求30件，发布数量较多的成员有美国、秘鲁各11件，墨西哥、智利、巴西各2件。植物保护法规或修订案14件，发布成员有中国台北、印度各3，几内亚2，加拿大、布隆迪、多米尼加、越南、马来西亚、尼泊尔各1件。有害生物的控制13件，发布成员有美国、加拿大各2件，墨西哥、欧盟、危地马拉、约旦、智利等各1件。有害生物名单12件，发布成员有秘鲁4件，哥伦比亚、哥斯达黎加、几内亚、中国澳门、挪威、尼泊尔、越南、智利等各1件。花卉进口要求12件，发布成员有秘鲁3，智利、墨西哥、哥斯达黎加各2，美国、中国台北、厄瓜多尔各1件。有害生物风险分析11件，发布成员有智利7，澳大利亚3，越南1件。植物疫病的预防7件，发布成员有加拿大2，多米尼加、墨西哥、中国台北、智利、巴西各1件。

（三）SPS 通报类型和领域

2014年发布的1633件通报中，常规措施通报为1056件，约占通报总数的64.8%（其中修订通报13件）；紧急措施通报112件，约占通报总数的6.7%（其中修订通报1件）；补遗通报455件，约占通报总数的27.8%；勘误通报10件，约占通报总数的0.6%（参见图5）。

就通报措施在SPS几大领域的分布情况而言，对可统计通报中“目的和理由”一栏的分析表明，2014年，涉及食品安全的通报数量789件，涉及动物健康185件，植物保护229件，保护人类免受动/植物有害生物的危害56件，保护国家免受有害生物的其他危害112件（参见图6）。

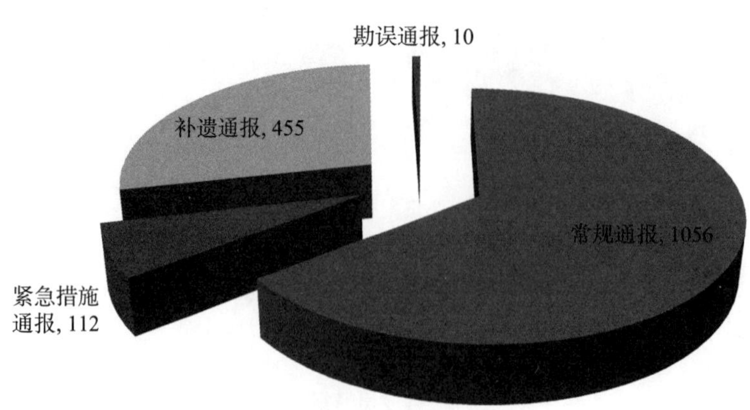

图5 通报类型（单位：件）

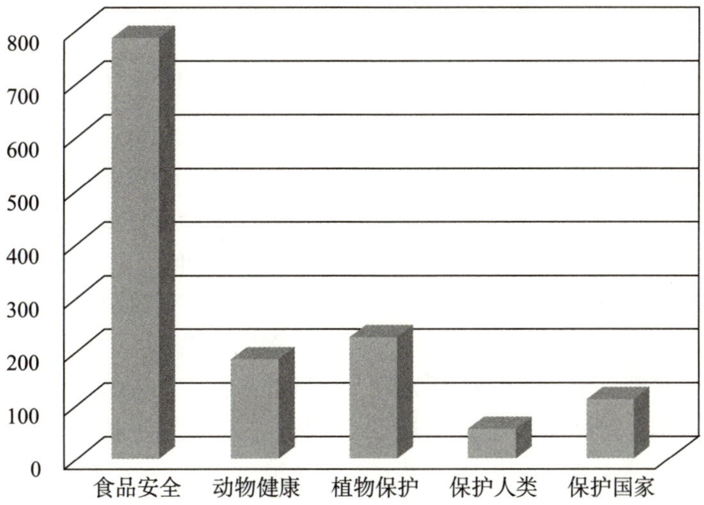

图6　通报领域（单位：件）

（四）中国SPS通报和外方评议

2014年，中国通过WTO向各成员通报SPS措施68件，通报数量在所有WTO成员中列第7位。截至2014年12月31日，中国的SPS通报编号已编至702号。

通报发出后，收到美国、欧盟、阿根廷等成员以及国际口香糖协会（ICGA）等行业协会的评议意见17件（次），涉及15项件通报措施。中国政府有关部门对这些评议意见进行了认真研究考虑。

（五）中国对其他成员SPS通报的评议

2014年，在其他WTO成员中，欧盟、土耳其、厄瓜多尔、阿尔巴尼亚、秘鲁、菲律宾发布了12件针对中国的SPS通报，其中厄瓜多尔4件，秘鲁3件，欧盟2件。涉及植物产品的8件，有厄瓜多尔、秘鲁进口中国榕属等植物以及马铃薯试管苗等的卫生要求，土耳其禁止从已知存在栗瘿蜂的国家进口栗属植物。涉及食品的2件，其中欧盟从提高对非官方控制标准的名单中撤销了中国的干切面。阿尔巴尼亚、菲律宾因禽流感、口蹄疫等对中国部分地区产品采取了限制措施。

（国家质量监督检验检疫总局国际合作司）

2014 年我国参加 WTO/TBT、SPS 例会简况

第一，主动应对，加强对国外技术性贸易措施的交涉力度。

2014 年，中国参加世贸组织技术性贸易壁垒委员会（WTO/TBT）和卫生与植物卫生措施委员会（WTO/SPS）共 6 次例会。中国共向其他成员“欧盟安全芯片领域通用准则认证（CC 认证）”“美国变更鲶鱼进口监管机构”等 7 项措施提出具体贸易关注。为提升部分议题关注度，中国联合其他成员共同应对、合力施压，要求实施措施的成员对不合理的措施进行修订和完善，取得一定成效。

第二，就其他成员对中国技术性贸易措施的关注做好增信释疑工作。

2014 年我有关部门就 WTO 其他成员关注我《信息安全等级保护管理办法》《医疗器械监督管理条例》《因疯牛病对牛肉及其产品进口禁令》等 11 项技术性贸易措施进行解释澄清，极力消除外方误解，防止贸易摩擦激化，努力创造良好的外部营商环境。

（商务部世界贸易组织司）

2014年世贸组织有关《TBT协定》和《SPS协定》的争端解决案件综述

1995年1月1日世贸组织成立以来，截至2015年11月30日，世贸成员诉诸争端解决机制的案件共500件。其中，涉及《技术性贸易壁垒协定》（《TBT协定》）案件共51件，占案件总数的10.2%；涉及《卫生和植物卫生措施协定》（《SPS协定》）案件共43件，占案件总数的8.6%。总体而言，世贸组织有关《TBT协定》和《SPS协定》的争端解决案件数量不多，但具有重要地位和影响。

2014年，世贸成员提起的涉及《TBT协定》的争端有1件，为巴西诉印度尼西亚鸡肉及鸡类产品进口限制措施案（DS484），该争端同时也涉及《SPS协定》。2014年，世贸组织成员提起的涉及《SPS协定》的争端有2件，除DS484案外，另一件为欧盟诉俄罗斯生猪、猪肉和其他猪类产品进口限制措施案（DS475）。上述案件中，DS484案争端方正在磋商中，DS475案目前在诉讼程序中，预计专家组将在2016年2月做出裁决。

2014年世贸组织共散发涉及《TBT协定》及《SPS协定》的2份专家组报告和1份上诉机构报告。5月22日，世贸组织上诉机构发布了加拿大和挪威诉欧盟海豹案（DS400/DS401）上诉机构报告。10月14日，世贸组织专家组发布了印度诉美国农产品进口限制措施案（DS430）专家组报告。10月20日，世贸组织专家组发布了加拿大和墨西哥诉美国肉类产品原产地标签案（DS384/DS386）执行之诉专家组报告。与此同时，世贸组织专家组和上诉机构还在审理其他多起涉及《TBT协定》和《SPS协定》的案件。现就有关案件进展情况介绍如下：

一、加拿大和挪威诉欧盟海豹案（DS400/DS401）

（一）磋商请求

2009年11月2日和5日，加拿大和挪威分别就欧盟影响海豹产品销售的某些措施，向欧盟提出磋商请求。涉案措施为：2009年9月16日通过的调整海豹产品贸易的《欧洲议会和欧盟委员会第1007/2009号条例》（简称“基本条例”），以及于2010年8月10日通过的基本条例的实施细则《欧盟委员会第737/2010号条例》（简称“实施细则”）（此为补充磋商请求中涉及的措施），上述两项条例统称为欧盟海豹制度（EU Seal Regime）。起诉方主张，欧盟海豹制度禁止所有海豹产品在欧盟市场上的进口和销售。而且，欧盟海豹制度中的例外条款带有歧视性，使起诉方国内的海豹产品无法与原产于欧盟或某些特定国家的海豹产品进行公平竞争，且该制度包含的证明海豹产品符合欧盟规定的进口、销售条件的规定，存在歧视和贸易限制的嫌疑。同时针对这项证明要求，欧盟海豹制度中并未规定足够详细的评估程序。加拿大和挪威指称，欧盟的上述措施不符合欧盟承担的WTO协定义务，包括：《TBT协定》第2.1条（DS400案）、第2.2条、第5.1.2条、第5.2.1条；以及《农业协定》第4.2条（DS401案）；《1994年关税总协定》第1.1条、第3.4条、第11.1条、第20条（a）项（b）项、第23.1条（b）项［加拿大附条件地提起该项诉求，仅当欧盟的被诉措施被判定并未违反《TBT协定》或《1994年关税与贸易总协定》（《1994年关税总协定》）时，才提起该项诉求，但是最终专家组在该项诉求的审理中行使了司法经济原则］。

（二）专家组审理

2011年2月11日和3月14日，加拿大和挪威先后请求设立专家组。2011年3月25日，WTO争端解决机构决定设立专家组，审理加拿大提起的争端。4月21日，WTO争端解决机构决定设立专家组，审理挪威提起的争端。根据DSU第9.1条的规定，在存在多个起诉方的情况下，WTO争端解决机构同意2011年3月25日设立的专家组亦对挪威提起的争端进行审理。阿根廷、加拿大（DS401案中）、中国、哥伦比亚、厄瓜多尔、冰岛、日本、墨西哥、纳米比亚（DS401案中）、美国、俄罗斯联邦和挪威（DS400 案中）保留作为第三方参与案件的权利。2012 年 10 月 4 日，WTO 总干事组成了专家组。在与争端方协商后，专家组制定了工作时间表。2013 年 11 月 25 日，专家组报告向成员散发。

本案主要涉及欧盟的海豹制度。该制度规定，欧盟禁止在其市场上销售海豹产品，除非该产品满足以下任意一项例外规定的要求：（1）海豹产品是由因纽特人或土著人猎杀的（IC 例外）；（2）海豹产品的取得源自基于海洋资源管理目的而猎杀的海豹（MRM 例外）；（3）在特定情况下，旅行者可以携带海豹产品进入欧盟（旅行者例外）。加拿大和挪威主要指称欧盟海豹制度禁止了所有海豹产品在欧盟市场上的进口和销售，且其例外规定带有歧视性。专家组首先判断欧盟海豹制度是否构成《TBT 协定》下的“技术法规”。在此方面，专家组做出肯定性结论，专家组对《TBT 协定》附件 1 第 1 段中列明的三个标准进行分析后（专家组着重分析了第二个标准，这也是当事方在此问题上的争议焦点），认为欧盟海豹制度是一项“技术法规”。专家组接下来起诉方根据《TBT 协定》第 2.1 条、第 2.2 条、附件第 1.3 条、第 5.1.2 条和第 5.2.1 条提起的诉讼请求。

关于《TBT 协定》第 2.1 条，专家组认为欧盟海豹制度，特别是其中的 IC 例外和 MRM 例外，违反了《TBT 协定》第 2.1 条的规定。专家组认为，被欧盟海豹制度禁止进口的海豹产品与符合其例外规定而可以进口和销售的海豹产品属于同类产品。确定为同类产品之后，专家组进一步判欧盟海豹制度是否给进口产品的竞争条件带来了有害影响，且该制度是否属于一种合理的差别规定。对于前者，专家组给予了肯定性回答。对于后者，由于欧盟无法证明 IC 例外和 MRM 例外给加拿大海豹产品带来的歧视性影响源于一种合理的差别对待，因此 IC 例外和 MRM 例外并未给予进口海豹产品不低于国内同类产品或来自任何其他国家同类产品的待遇，违反了第 2.1 条。

关于《TBT 协定》第 2.2 条，专家组认为欧盟海豹制度并未违反《TBT 协定》第 2.2 条，因为加拿大和挪威未能证明欧盟海豹制度对贸易的限制超过了为实现合法目标所必需的限度。考虑到替代方案是否存在及其无法落实的风险，欧盟关于海豹福利这一公共道德的合法目标并不能被其他对贸易限制更小的方案所替代。

关于《TBT 协定》附件第 1.3 条，专家组认为，如上所述，欧盟海豹制度属于一项“技术法规”，而且，欧盟海豹制度中“实施细则”第 3 条、第 5 条、第 6 条的规定，确立了判定某一海豹产品是否符合欧盟海豹制度中具体要求的程序，因此这些规定构成了满足《TBT 协定》要求的“合规评定程序”。

关于《TBT 协定》第 5.1.2 条，专家组认为欧盟海豹制度违反了第 5.1.2 条的规定。专家组认为，欧盟海豹制度中的“合格评定程序”具有对国际贸易产生非必要障碍的效果，因此违反了第 5.1.2 条中第一句话的规定。而专家组驳回了加拿大和挪威根据该条第二句话的规定而提出的主张，因为起诉方并未能证明存在替代的“合规评定程序”，得以在同等水平上保证合规性评定的可信度。

关于《TBT 协定》第 5.2.1 条，专家组驳回了起诉方的指称。专家组认为，没有足够的理由证明欧盟海豹制度中的“合规评定程序”没有做到尽快进行并完成评定。

此外，专家组拒绝就挪威根据《农业协定》第 4.2 条提出的诉讼请求做出裁决。专家组还判定，IC 例外和 MRM 例外分别违反了《1994 年关贸总协定》第 1.1 条和第 3.4 条的规定。而且，尽管欧盟海豹制度中的例外规定符合《1994 年关贸总协定》第 20 条（a）款的规定，但是它们并不满足第 20 条前言的要求。

（三）上诉机构审理

2014 年 1 月 24 日，加拿大和挪威提起上诉。2014 年 1 月 29 日，欧盟提起上诉。2014 年 5 月 22 日，上诉机构报告向成员散发。

加拿大和挪威的上诉涉及专家组就《TBT 协定》第 2.1 条和第 2.2 条，以及《1994 年关税总协定》第 20 条做出的裁决。欧盟就《TBT 协定》附件第 1.1 条、《TBT 协定》第 2.1 条和《1994 年关税总协定》第 20 条提起上诉。而且，争端当事方也对专家组审查时存在的与 DSU 第 11 条规定不符的问题，提出了上诉。

上诉机构首先推翻了专家组认定欧盟海豹制度规定了产品特征的裁决。上诉机构认为，欧盟海豹制度中关键性和整体方面均未规定产品特征。上诉机构认为，应该将欧盟海豹措施中的“禁止性条款”和“允许性条款”结合起来审查。本案被诉措施并非意在禁止在欧盟市场上销售海豹产品，而在于为在欧盟市场上销售海豹产品的活动设定条件，这些条件主要是根据猎人身份或海豹产品的捕猎类型、捕猎目的相关的标准来确定的。这才是该措施的主要性质。上诉机构并不认为整体上的欧盟海豹制度规定了产品特征。

由于专家组对于欧盟海豹制度属于《TBT 协定》第 1.1 条规定的“技术法规”的认定，主要是基于其中间裁定，即欧盟海豹制度规定了产品特征，上诉机构基于上述分析最终从整体上推翻了欧盟海豹制度构成“技术法规”的专家组裁决。但是上诉机构拒绝完成该项法律分析，因此其并未对欧盟海豹制度是否规定了“相关工艺和生产方法”做出判定。据此，上诉机构裁定专家组报告涉及《TBT 协定》第 2.2 条、第 5.1.2 条、第 5.2.1 条的相关裁决均没有法律效力。

此外，上诉机构维持了专家组根据《1994 年关贸总协定》第 1.1 条和第 3.4 条做出的裁决。

针对《1994 年关贸总协定》第 20 条，上诉机构首先维持了专家组对于欧盟海豹制度所涉及的公共道德的合理目标的认定。接着，上诉机构维持了专家组认定欧盟海豹制度满足《1994 年关贸总协定》第 20 条（a）款中“必需”要求的裁决。最后，上诉机构推翻了专家组涉及第 20 条前言的裁决，因为后者错误地将其适用在《TBT 协定》第 2.1 条的同样的法律标准，适用在对《1994 年关贸总协定》第 20 条前言的审查上，而并未对欧盟海豹制度是否满足第 20 条前言的具体条款和要求进行独立的分析。随后，上诉机构完成了该法律分析，但其最终结论与专家组裁决相同，即欧盟并未证明其海豹制度满足第 20 条前言的要求。

WTO 争端解决机构在 2014 年 6 月 18 日例会上正式通过了本案上诉机构报告和经上诉机构报告修改的专家组报告。

二、印度诉美国农产品进口限制措施案（DS430）

（一）磋商请求

2012 年 3 月 6 日，美国就印度对于美国各种农业产品采取的进口禁令，向印度提出磋商请求，据称该措施是为保护国内禽肉生产商免受禽流感影响而遭受损失。本案被诉措施为：《印度家畜进口法案（1898）》；若干由印度政府农业部（畜牧、制酪、渔业司）根据上述法案发布的命令，其中最新发布的命令为 S. O. 1663（E）；和任何修正案、相关措施或其实施条例。美国指称，印度的措施不符合印度承担的 WTO 协定义务，包括：《SPS 协定》第 2.2 条、第 2.3 条、第 3.1 条、第 5.1 条、第 5.2 条、第 5.5 条、第 5.6 条、第 5.7 条、第 6.1 条、第 6.2 条、第 7 条和附件 B 第 2 款、第 5 款、第 6 款，以及《1994 年关贸总协定》第 1 条和第 9 条。

2012 年 5 月 11 日，美国请求设立专家组。2012 年 5 月 24 日，WTO 争端解决机构宣布推迟设立专家组。

（二）专家组审理

2012 年 6 月 25 日，WTO 争端解决机构正式设立专家组。中国、哥伦比亚、厄瓜多尔、欧盟、危地马拉、日本、越南、阿根廷、澳大利亚和巴西保留作为第三方参与案件的权利。2013 年 2 月 18 日，WTO 总干事组成了专家组。2014 年 10 月 14 日，专家组向当事方散发最终报告。

本案主要涉及印度制定的针对从需要向世界动物卫生组织报告禽流感疫情的国家进口有关农产品的限制措施，包括：《印度家畜进口法案（1898）》；若干由印度政府农业部（畜牧、制酪、渔业司）根据上述法案发布的命令，其中最新发布的命令为 S. O. 1663（E）；以及任何修正案、相关措施或其实施条例。美国主要认为印度的措施不是根据相关国际标准制定，也不是在进行科学风险评估的基础上制定。

在专家组报告中，专家组裁定印度涉案农产品进口限制措施违反《SPS 协定》第 3.1 条，因为其既不是依据（based on）相关国际标准（即世界动物卫生组织所制定的陆生动物卫生法典第 10.4 条）制定的，也不是《SPS 协定》第 3.2 条规定的符合（conform to）相关国际标准的 SPS 措施。

专家组裁定印度涉案农产品进口限制措施违反《SPS 协定》第 5.1 条、第 5.2 条和第 2.2 条，因为其没有以风险评估为基础来进行指定。

专家组裁定印度涉案农产品进口限制措施违反《SPS 协定》第 2.3 条，因为该措施的实施在情形相同或相似的成员之间构成了任意或不合理的歧视，构成了对国际贸易的变相限制。

专家组裁定印度涉案农产品进口限制措施违反《SPS 协定》第 5.6 条和第 2.2 条，认为该措施对贸易的限制超过了陆生动物卫生法典第 10.4 条规定的适当保护水平，必然超过了保护人类和动物生命和健康所必需的限度。

专家组裁定印度涉案农产品进口限制措施违反《SPS 协定》第 6.2 条和 6.1 条，因为印度未认识到非疫区和低度流行区的概念，且没有使其措施适应这些不同区域的卫生特点。

专家组裁定印度违反《SPS 协定》第 7 条、附件 B（2）及附件 B（5）（a）（b）（c）项，因为其未履行一系列的通知和公布义务。

因专家组已认定印度措施违反《SPS 协定》的上述条款，对于美国的关于《SPS 协定》第 5.5 条和 GATT1994 第 11 条的诉请，专家组适用了司法经济。专家组同时裁定美国没有初步证明涉案措施违反《SPS 协定》附件 B（5）（c）项。

（三）上诉机构审理

2015 年 1 月 26 日，印度提出上诉。2015 年 6 月 4 日，上诉机构散发上诉机构报告，上诉机构做出了如下裁定：

关于《SPS 协定》第 2.2 条、第 5.1 条及第 5.2 条，上诉机构支持了专家组关于印度相关措施违反第 5.1 条和第 5.2 条的裁定，但是上诉机构认为，由于专家组没有考虑印度提出的关于从低致病禽流感区域进口新鲜猪肉和蛋的科学依据，所以专家组错误地裁定了印度禁止从低致病禽流感区域进口相关产品的措施违反《SPS 协定》第 2.2 条，但是上诉机构对此不能完成法律分析。

关于《SPS 协定》第 3.1 条及第 3.2 条，上诉机构认为专家组就陆生动物法典的含义咨询世界动物卫生组织并未违反《SPS 协定》第 11.2 条及《关于争端解决规则与程序的谅解》（DSU）第 13.2 条，驳回了印度关于认定专家组未尽 DSU 第 11 条进行客观全面审查义务的请求，并支持了专家组有关《SPS 协定》第 3.1 条及第 3.2 条的裁决，即认定印度相关措施既不是基于国际标准制定，也与国际标准不符。

关于《SPS 协定》第 6 条，上诉机构认定专家组没有错误地解释第 6.1 条和第 6.3 条的关系，同时认可了专家组将《家畜进口法案》和 S.O.1663（E）同时进行考虑。因印度措施排除了从非疫区进口相关产品的可能性，上诉机构支持了专家组对印度相关措施违反第 6.1 条和第 6.2 条的裁定。同时，驳回了印度基于 DSU 第 11 条所提出的请求。

关于《SPS 协定》第 5.6 条和第 2.2 条，上诉机构认为专家组对美国已指明有其他替代措施达到同样的保护水平的认定没有错误，支持了专家组关于印度措施违反第 5.6 条的裁定，同时，认为没有必要再考察专家组关于第 2.2 条的裁决。

关于《SPS 协定》第 2.3 条，上诉机构认定印度没有证明专家组就低致病禽流感是否对印度有害咨询有关专家或要求印度提供证据违反 DSU 第 11 条。同时，上诉机构认为印度相关措施的实施在情形相同或相似的成员之间造成了任意或不合理的歧视，支持了专家组关于印度有关措施违反《SPS 协定》第 2.3 条第一句的裁决。

WTO 争端解决机构在 2015 年 6 月 19 日例会上，正式通过了本案上诉机构报告和经上诉机构报告修改的专家组报告。

三、加拿大和墨西哥诉美国肉类产品原产地标签（COOL）案（DS384/DS386）执行之诉

（一）原审和执行阶段情况

加拿大、墨西哥分别于 2008 年 12 月 1 日和 2008 年 12 月 17 日请求与美国就美国原产地标签措施进行磋商（DS384/386）。

在磋商未果的情况下，加拿大、墨西哥于 2009 年 10 月 9 日向 DSB 请求设立专家组审理此案。阿根廷、澳大利亚、巴西、中国、哥伦比亚、欧盟、危地马拉、印度、韩国、共和国、新西兰、秘鲁、中国台北作为争端第三方参与了专家组程序的审理。

2011 年 11 月 18 日，世贸组织专家组就该案做出裁决，认为 COOL 措施给予进口牲畜的待遇低于国内同类牲畜的待遇，因而违反了《TBT 协定》第 2.1 条；同时，COOL 措施未满足美国为消费者提供肉品原产地信息的合法目标，违反《TBT 协定》第 2.2 条。

2012 年 3 月 23 日，美国向 DSB 提出上诉请求，3 月 28 日，加拿大和墨西哥也提出上诉请求，2012 年 6 月 29 日，上诉机构向成员国散发了其报

告，维持了专家组关于COOL措施违反《TBT协定》第2.1条的裁决，但采取的理由有所变化；推翻了专家组做出的该措施违反《TBT协定》第2.2条的裁决。

世贸组织争端解决机构在2012年7月23日的例会上，正式通过了本案上诉机构报告和经上诉机构报告修订的专家组报告。

在报告通过后，加拿大和墨西哥要求根据DSU第21.3（c）条确定合理执行期，仲裁人最后确定的合理执行期为10个月，截止日为2013年5月23日。

为了执行裁决，2013年5月23日，美国农业部（以下简称“USDA”）发布了《关于牛肉、猪肉、羊肉、鸡肉、山羊肉、野生和饲养鱼类和贝类、易腐农产品、花生、山核桃、人参和澳大利亚坚果强制性原产国标签的最终规则》（以下简称“《2013最终规则》”），作为新COOL措施的一部分。因此，新COOL措施包括：（1）COOL法案——经《2002年农场安全与农村投资法》和《2008年食物、环境保育与能源法》修订的《1946年农业销售法》；（2）《2009最终规则（AMS）》——《关于牛肉、猪肉、羊肉、鸡肉、山羊肉、野生和饲养鱼类和贝类、易腐农产品、花生、山核桃、人参和澳大利亚坚果强制性原产国标签的最终规则》；（3）《2013最终规则》——《关于牛肉、猪肉、羊肉、鸡肉、山羊肉、野生和饲养鱼类和贝类、易腐农产品、花生、山核桃、人参和澳大利亚坚果强制性原产国标签的最终规则》；（4）上述法规的修订或修正案。根据新COOL措施，对于在美国境内屠宰的动物肉块产品，必须标明其每一生产工序发生地，即出生、饲养和屠宰。并且，该最终规则不再允许对来源地不同的肉块产品进行混装，产品所有的原产地信息都必须注明。

在2013年5月24日的世贸组织争端解决机构会议上，美国通知DSB其已在5月23日通过了修改COOL标签要求的最终规则，其认为该最终规则已经符合裁决和建议，但是加拿大和墨西哥认为美国并未完全执行裁决。

（二）执行之诉专家组审理

2013年6月10日，美国分别与加拿大和墨西哥达成《DSU第21条和第22条程序约定》，根据约定，加拿大和墨西哥在要求设立第21.5条程序项下的专家组前无须与美国进行磋商。

2013年8月19日，加拿大和墨西哥提出根据DSU第21.5条程序设立专家组的请求。

2013年9月25日DSB会议上，专家组设立，DSB要求在可能的情况下由原审专家组进行审查。澳大利亚、巴西、加拿大（DS386）、中国、哥伦比亚、欧盟、危地马拉、印度、日本、韩国、墨西哥（DS384）和新西兰作为第三方参与了专家组程序。

2014年10月20日，专家组向全体成员散发了其报告。专家组主要裁定新COOL措施依然不符合GATT 1994第3.4条和《TBT协定》第2.1条的规定，但是驳回了加拿大和墨西哥在《TBT协定》第2.2条项下提出的主张，具体如下：

关于《TBT协定》第2.1条，首先，专家组认定涉案措施属于《TBT协定》附件第1.1条定义的“技术法规”，同时认定加拿大牛和美国牛、墨西哥牛和美国牛属于“同类产品”，并且加拿大猪和美国猪也属于第2.1条意义上的“同类产品”。并且由于新COOL措施增加了实践中的区分和记录需要，并且增加了使用国产牲畜的动机，因此，新COOL措施增加了美国企业选择国产牲畜而不是进口牲畜的实际需要，并加重了对进口牲畜在美国市场上竞争机会方面的不利影响。构成了违反第2.1条所需要确定的三个因素。但是由于在美国—丁香烟案中，上诉机构认为《TBT协定》第2.1条项下的低国民待遇分析，需要审查对进口产品竞争机会的不利影响是否仅仅是由合法的管理区分所造成的，若是由合法的管理区分造成，则不构成对第2.1条的违反。专家组认为，新COOL措施加重了记录负担但提供的信息仍然可能是不准确的，并且其继续豁免很大一部分的肉块产品，因此新COOL措施仍然存在任意性和不合理性。因此，新COOL措施所造成的不利影响并不仅仅是由合理的管理区分所造成的。综上，专家组认为，新COOL措施加重了原COOL措施对进口牲畜的竞争机会所造成的不利影响，并且这种不利影响不仅仅是由合理的管理上的区分所造成的，导致新COOL措施向进口牲畜提供的待遇低于美国牲畜的待遇，因此，新COOL措施违反了《TBT协定》第2.1条的规定。

关于《TBT协定》第2.2条，第2.2条项下的分析首先应当考虑以下几个因素：涉案措施可实现的合法目标的程度；措施对贸易的限制；以及相关风险的性质以及不实现相关目标的后果。并且，除上述三个要素外，在多数情况下第 2.2 条项下的分析还需要与替代措施进行比较。根据分析，专家组认为新 COOL 措施追求的目标合法，并且能够在很大程度上但是部分地实现其追求的目标。并且，新 COOL 措施在很大程度上加重了对贸易的限制；此外，专家组也确定了目标无法实现将造成的风险的性质以及后果，但是其无法确认后果的严重程度。之后专家组进行了比较分析，但是起诉方未能初步证明，存在任何替代措施，能够证明新 COOL 措施对贸易的限制超过了必要的限度。因此专家组认为，起诉方未能初步证明新 COOL 措施违反了《TBT 协定》第 2.2 条的规定。

关于《1994 年关贸总协定》第 3.4 条，专家组认为起诉方已经初步证明涉案措施满足了《1994 年关贸总协定》第 3.4 条法律分析的三项要素，即进口产品和国产品属于“同类产品”；涉案措施是一项影响涉案产品“国内销售、标价出售、购买、运输、分销或使用的……法律、法规和规定”；以及进口产品享受的待遇低于国内同类产品的待遇。因此，新 COOL 措施违反了《1994 年关贸总协定》第 3.4 条的规定。

专家组裁定其关于美国执行措施违反了《1994 年关贸总协定》第 3.4 条的认定；同时对于起诉方基于《1994 年关贸总协定》第 23.1 条（b）项提出的非违反之诉的诉请适用司法经济。

（三）执行之诉上诉机构审理

对于执行之诉专家组裁决，美国于 2014 年 11 月 28 日提出了上诉；2014 年 12 月 12 日，加拿大和墨西哥提出了交叉上诉。2015 年 5 月 18 日，上诉机构公布了执行之诉上诉机构报告。上诉机构对于大多数主张都维持了专家组的认定，依然认定新 COOL 措施违反了《TBT 协定》第 2.1 条和《1994 年关贸总协定》第 3.4 条。关于《TBT 协定》第 2.2 条，虽然上诉机构认定专家组在该条项做出的总体结论存在错误，但是上诉机构认为其并没有足够的事实就原告提出的第一项和第二项替代措施完成第 2.2 条项下的分析，具体如下：

关于《TBT 协定》第 2.1 条，上诉机构驳回了美国关于《TBT 协定》第 2.1 条的上诉请求，上诉机构维持了专家组关于新 COOL 案措施加重了记录负担的认定，驳回了美国关于专家组的结论是基于“不正确的假设”做出的观点。上诉机构维持了专家组关于新 COOL 措施可能造成记录不准确，并且其继续豁免很大一部分的肉块产品的认定，维持了专家组关于第 2.1 条的裁决，即新 COOL 措施加重了原 COOL 措施对进口牲畜的竞争机会所造成的不利影响，并且这种不利影响不仅仅是由合理的管理上的区分所造成的，导致新 COOL 措施向进口牲畜提供的待遇低于美国牲畜的待遇。

关于《TBT 协定》第 2.2 条，上诉机构认为，在审查实现目标的程度是否相同时还需要考虑涉案技术法规的性质、追求的目标的性质以及可获得的证据的性质、数量和质量。上诉机构认为，替代措施可以通过不同于涉案技术法规的方式来实现与其相同程度的目标。为了审查实现目标的程度是否相同，需要关注的是技术法规实现目标的整体程度，而不是某一单独的方面或因素。同时，由于专家组在认定其无法确定新 COOL 措施的目标无法实现时后果的严重性存在错误，而专家组又以此为理由认定其无法确定第一项和第二项替代措施实现目标的程度是否达到了新 COOL 措施的水平，因此，上诉机构认为专家组在做出原告未能初步证明新 COOL 措施违反了《TBT 协定》第 2.2 条的总体结论时存在错误，推翻了专家组做出的加拿大和墨西哥未能初步证明新 COOL 措施违反了《TBT 协定》第 2.2 条的结论。

上诉机构也维持了专家组有关《1994 年关贸总协定》第 3.4 条的分析。

WTO 争端解决机构在 2015 年 5 月 29 日的例会上，正式通过了本案执行之诉上诉机构报告和经上诉机构报告修改后的专家组报告。

四、阿根廷诉美国牛肉及其他肉类产品进口限制措施案（DS447）

（一）磋商请求

2012 年 8 月 30 日，阿根廷就美国对进口阿根廷动物、肉类及其他肉类产品实施的限制措施，向美国提出磋商请求。本案被诉措施为：

1. 美国动物卫生检查局（APHIS）做出的临时或最终裁决，决定对阿根廷新鲜牛肉（冷藏或冷冻）采取进口禁令，修改了美国联邦法规的规定；

2. 美国未承认阿根廷的某些领土为非口蹄疫疫区；

3. 认为美国在确定一个地区内的动物健康水平方面存在不正当的迟延，或在批准上述地区所产的动物或动物产品的出口方面存在不正当的迟延，而这两种迟延类型均是在美国联邦法规（CFR）规定的程序下产生的；而且阿根廷认为2009年美国《综合法案》第737条规定了进口附加条件。阿根廷指称，美国的措施不符合美国承担的WTO协定义务，包括：《1994年关贸总协定》第1.1条、第3.4条和第11.1条；《SPS协定》第1.1条、第2.2条、第2.3条、第3.1条、第3.3条、第5.1条、第5.2条、第5.6条、第6.1条、第6.2条、第8条、附件C.1和第10.1条；以及《WTO协定》第16.4条。

（二）专家组审理

2013年1月28日，WTO争端解决机构正式设立专家组。澳大利亚、中国、欧盟、印度和韩国保留作为第三方参与案件的权利。2013年8月8日，WTO总干事组成了专家组。2015年7月24日，专家组报告散发给各成员。专家组主要裁定如下：

美国涉案措施违反《SPS协定》第3.1条，因为美国的进口禁令并非基于世界动物卫生组织的国际标准。

因美国在审查阿根廷的牛肉进口申请以及将巴塔哥尼亚地区认可为非口蹄疫区的申请时存在不当迟延，也没有通知阿根廷程序所进行的阶段或解释迟延发生的原因，因此违反了《SPS协定》第8条及附件C（1）（a）、（b）项。

由于进口禁令的维持未能基于风险评估，因此其不符合《SPS协定》第5.1条和第2.2条；

因进口禁令超出了实现适当的卫生与植物卫生保护水平的需要，因此其不符合《SPS协定》第5.6条；

美国允许从乌拉圭进口牛肉、允许从智利进口动物产品，却禁止从阿根廷进口，构成任意或不合理的歧视，因此美国涉案措施不符合《SPS协定》第2.3条；

因进口禁令未能适应巴塔哥尼亚地区的卫生特点，因此美国涉案措施不符合《SPS协定》第6.1条等。

因美国没有在合理期限内寻求获得更加客观地进行风险评估所必需的额外信息来审议其采取的措施，因此其措施不属于《SPS协定》第5.7条的豁免范围。

因《SPS协定》第5.4条中规定的“在确定适当的卫生与植物卫生保护水平时，应考虑将对贸易的消极影响减少到最低程度的目标”中不包含有强制义务，因此美国涉案措施并未构成对该条的违反。

阿根廷没有提出初步证据证明美国未考虑作为发展中成员的阿根廷的特殊需要而制定该涉案措施，因此美国未违反《SPS协定》第10.1条。

因为上述分析，美国涉案措施违反《SPS协定》第1条和第3.3条。

同时，因专家组已裁定美国涉案措施违反《SPS协定》的上述条款，专家组对阿根廷基于《1994年关贸总协定》第1.1条（最惠国待遇）和第11.1条（数量限制）所提出的请求及美国基于《1994年关贸总协定》第20条（b）项提出的抗辩采用了司法经济。

WTO争端解决机构在2015年8月31日的例会上，正式通过了本案专家组报告。

五、其他涉及《TBT协定》争端解决案件进展情况

（一）乌克兰、洪都拉斯、多米尼加、古巴、印度尼西亚诉澳大利亚平装烟草措施案（DS434/435/441/458/467）

乌克兰、洪都拉斯、多米尼加、古巴、印度尼西亚分别在2012年3月13日、2012年4月4日、2012年7月18日、2013年5月3日和2013年9月20日，就澳大利亚在烟草产品及其包装上限制使用商标以及其他平装要求的相关法律法规，向澳大利亚提出磋商请求。

涉案措施为澳大利亚的《烟草平装法案（2011）》和其实施条例《烟草平装实施条例（2011）》；《商标法修正案（烟草平装）2011》；以及任何澳大利亚为了实施前述两项关键措施而进一步通过的法规、相关法案、政策或实践，指称澳大利亚的上述措施，尤其是从澳大利亚整体烟草监管制度的背景下看，不符合澳大利亚承担的WTO协

定义务，包括：《与贸易有关的知识产权协定》（《TRIPS 协定》）第 1 条、第 1.1 条、第 2.1 条、第 3.1 条、第 15 条、第 16 条、第 20 条和第 27 条；《TBT 协定》第 2.1 条、第 2.2 条；以及《1994 年关贸总协定》第 3.4 款。近 40 个成员作为第三方参与上述案件。

乌克兰、洪都拉斯、多米尼加、古巴、印度尼西亚分别在 2012 年 8 月 14 日、2012 年 10 月 15 日、2012 年 11 月 9 日、2014 年 4 月 4 日、2014 年 3 月 3 日请求设立专家组。2014 年 5 月 5 日，WTO 总干事指定由同一专家组审理上述案件。本案目前在专家组审理阶段。

（二）墨西哥诉阿根廷进口限制措施案（DS446）

2012 年 8 月 24 日，墨西哥就阿根廷针对进口货物实施的限制措施，向阿根廷提出磋商请求。认为阿根廷实行的外贸限制措施损害其出口贸易。涉案措施主要为：

（1）阿根廷要求批准一项非自动进口许可证：DJAI；

（2）进口某些产品需要取得非自动许可证，该许可证的形式为 CIs 或 CLCs；

（3）对进口商施加的承担某些贸易限制承诺的要求；

（4）在批准进口许可证或拒绝批准这类许可证，或批准进口许可证方面的制度性迟延；

（5）阿根廷为进口产品规定的合格评定程序，包含一项技术法规，涉及对进口产品的含铅和其他重金属量的检查。

墨西哥指称阿根廷的上述措施不符合其承担的 WTO 协定义务，包括：《TBT 协定》第 2.1 条、第 2.2 条；《1994 年关贸总协定》第 3.4 条、第 8 条、第 10.1 条、第 10.2 条、第 10.3 条和第 11.1 条；《与贸易有关的投资措施协定》（《TRIMs 协定》）第 2 条和第 6 条；《进口许可程序协定》第 1.2 条、第 1.3 条、第 1.4 条、第 1.5 条、第 1.6 条、第 1.7 条、第 2.2 条、第 3.2 条、第 3.3 条、第 3.4 条、第 3.5 条、第 5.1 条第 5.2 条第 5.3 条和第 5.4 条；《农业协定》第 4.2 条；《保障措施协定》第 11 条。

2012 年 11 月 21 日，墨西哥请求设立专家组。2012 年 12 月 17 日，墨西哥撤回了设立专家组的请求。

（三）阿根廷诉欧盟生物柴油进口和销售措施案（DS459）

2013 年 5 月 15 日，阿根廷就影响生物柴油进口、销售以及支持其生物柴油产业的相关措施，向欧盟及其成员国提出磋商请求，涉案措施为：欧盟为推广对可再生能源的利用、引进控制和减少温室气体排放机制的相关措施；欧盟对其生物柴油产业出台的支持计划。阿根廷指称，欧盟的措施不符合其承担的 WTO 协定义务，包括：《TBT 协定》第 2.1 条、第 2.2 条、第 5.1 条和第 5.2 条；《1994 年关贸总协定》第 1.1 条、第 3.1 条、第 3.2 条、第 3.4 条和第 3.5 条；《SCM 协定》第 1.1 条、第 2.3 条、第 3.1（b）条、第 3.2 条、第 5（b）条、第 5（c）条和第 6.3 条（a）；《TRIMs 协定》第 2.1 条、第 2.2 条；《马拉喀什建立世界贸易组织协定》（《WTO 协定》）第 16.4 条。本案目前仍在磋商阶段。

（四）日本诉俄罗斯关于机动车辆“回收费用”措施案（DS463）

2013 年 7 月 24 日，印度尼西亚就俄罗斯联邦关于机动车辆的“回收费用”措施，向俄罗斯提出磋商请求。日本认为，俄罗斯对进口和国内机动车辆征收回收费用，但规定了两种征税例外：（1）在俄罗斯登记的企业生产的车辆；（2）承诺在俄罗斯进行车辆生产的企业生产的车辆，包括在俄罗斯、白俄罗斯和哈萨克斯坦领土范围内存在的某些具体生产制造业务。日本指称俄罗斯的涉案措施不符合其承担的 WTO 协定义务，包括：《1994 年关贸总协定》第 1.1 条、第 2.1（a）条、第 2.1（b）条、第 3.2 条、和第 3.4 条；《TRIMs 协定》第 2.1 条、第 2.2 条；以及《TBT 协定》第 2.1 条、第 2.2 条。本案目前仍在磋商阶段。

六、其他涉及《SPS 协定》争端解决案件进展情况

（一）阿根廷诉美国柠檬进口措施案（DS448）

2012 年 9 月 3 日，阿根廷就美国对阿根廷西北部地区的新鲜柠檬实施的进口限制措施，向美国提出磋商请求。本案被诉措施为：

（1）美国过去 11 年维持的一系列措施，阿根廷认为这构成了对柑橘类水果的一项进口禁令，影

响了原产于阿根廷西北部地区的新鲜柠檬的进口；

(2) 美国未批准从阿根廷西北部地区进口新鲜柠檬；

(3) 美国针对阿根廷西北部地区的新鲜柠檬实施的进口批准程序存在不正当的迟延。

阿根廷指称，美国的措施不符合美国承担的WTO协定义务，包括：《1994年关贸总协定》第1.1条、第3.4条、第10.1条、第10.3条和第11.1条；《SPS协定》第1.1条、第2.2条、第2.3条、第3.1条、第3.3条、第5.1条、第5.2条、第5.4条、第5.6条、第7条、附件B、第8条、附件C和第10.1条；以及《WTO协定》第16.4条。

2012年12月6日，阿根廷请求设立专家组。2012年12月17日，WTO争端解决机构宣布推迟设立专家组。

（二）欧盟诉俄罗斯联邦生猪及其遗传物质、猪肉、猪肉产品以及部分其他产品进口限制措施案（DS475）

2014年4月8日，欧盟就俄罗斯影响生猪及其遗传物质、猪肉、猪肉产品以及部分其他产品从欧盟进口的相关措施，向俄罗斯提出磋商请求。欧盟指称，俄罗斯的措施不符合俄罗斯承担的WTO协定义务，包括：《SPS协定》第2.2条、第2.3条、第3.1条、第3.2条、第3.3条、第5.1条、第5.2条、第5.3条、第5.4条、第5.5条、第5.6条、第5.7条、第6.1条、第6.2条、第6.3条、第7条、第8条、附件B和附件C。本案目前仍处于磋商阶段。

（三）巴西诉印度尼西亚鸡肉及鸡类产品进口限制措施案（DS484）

2014年10月16日，巴西就印度尼西亚从对于特定家禽肉及其制品采取的进口限制措施，向印度尼西亚提出磋商请求。巴西指称印度尼西亚的涉案措施不符合其承担的WTO协定义务，包括：《SPS协定》第2.2条、第2.3条、第3.1条、第5.1条、第5.2条、第5.5条、第5.6条、第8条及附件C；《TBT协定》第2.1条、第2.2条、第2.4条、第5.1条及第5.2条；《农业协定》第4.2条及第14条；《进口许可程序协定》第1.3条、第3.2条及第3.3条；《装运前检验协定》第2.1条及第2.15条；GATT1994第3.4条、第10.1条、第10.3条及第11.1条。

2015年10月15日，巴西提交了设立专家组请求。在2015年10月28日WTO争端解决机构例会上，争端解决机构推迟了专家组的设立。

（商务部条约法律司）

第四篇　中国大陆与港、澳、台

与香港、澳门 WTO 事务

1995 年 1 月 1 日，世界贸易组织成立。香港、澳门作为关贸总协定缔约方，成为其创始成员。2001 年 12 月，中国内地以国家主体身份加入了世界贸易组织。从多边层面看，在世界贸易组织框架下，内地与港澳是平等的成员；从国内层面看，内地与港澳地区之间的经贸关系是国家主体与其单独关税区之间的关系。

2001 年底，在内地正式成为世界贸易组织成员之初，香港特区政府即提出，希望在内地与香港之间建立自由贸易区，以便香港能够充分借助中国内地“入世”后的过渡期，先行进入内地市场。2002 年 1 月，内地与香港就建立内地香港自由贸易区在北京进行了首次磋商，将两地未来的合作模式定位为更紧密经贸关系安排。

2003 年 6 月 29 日，《内地与香港关于建立更紧密经贸关系的安排》（CEPA，以下简称《安排》）及其 6 个附件在香港签署。同年 10 月，内地与澳门也签署了《安排》。2004 年 1 月 1 日，《安排》正式实施。此后的 2004—2013 年，内地分别与香港、澳门又相继签署了十个《安排》补充协议。内地与香港、澳门《关于建立更紧密经贸关系的安排》的内容主要包括货物贸易自由化、服务贸易自由化和贸易投资便利化三方面。在货物贸易领域，自 2006 年 1 月 1 日起，内地与港澳已经全面实现了自由化，即内地对原产于港澳的产品全部实行零关税。在服务贸易领域，内地与港澳《〈关于建立更紧密经贸关系的安排〉补充协议十》将内地对香港、澳门开放的服务贸易领域均增至 48 个，开放措施分别达 403 和 383 项。

2014 年 12 月 18 日，内地与香港、澳门分别签署《〈安排〉关于内地在广东与香港基本实现服务贸易自由化的协议》和《〈安排〉关于内地在广东与澳门基本实现服务贸易自由化的协议》（以下简称《协议》）。这次签署的《协议》是内地首次以准入前国民待遇加负面清单的方式签署的自由贸易协议，由以往完全的正面清单转变为以负面清单为主、以正面清单为辅的开放模式，有了根本性的改变。按照世界贸易组织服务贸易 160 个部门的分类标准，《协议》在广东对港澳的开放部门均达到 153 个，涉及 160 个部门的 95.6%，其中 58 个部门实现国民待遇；对港澳承诺的负面清单中保留的限制性措施均为 132 项；采用正面清单扩大开放的部门对港澳分别新增 27 项和 24 项开放措施，其中个体工商户对港澳新增开放行业均为 84 个，累计开放行业均达到 130 个。此外，《协议》将内地给予香港的最惠待遇以协议的方式进一步明确下来，即今后内地与其他国家和地区签署的自由贸易协定中，优于《安排》的开放措施均将适用于香港。按照一视同仁的原则，上述最惠待遇条款同样适用于澳门。内地通过《协议》在 CEPA 框架下进一步对香港、澳门扩大开放，将香港、澳门经济纳入国家发展全局中谋划。广东省对香港、澳门探索建立健全与负面清单管理模式相适应的相关配套制度，在落实好广东对香港、澳门基本实现服务贸易自由化的同时，也为内地进一步深化改革、通过开放促进自身体制机制改革探路。

《安排》是中国国家主体与其单独关税区之间建立的具有自由贸易区性质的经贸安排，也是内地对外签署、全面实施并接受世界贸易组织审议的最早的自由贸易协议之一。既遵循“一国两制”方针，也符合世界贸易组织规则。《安排》的实施，逐步减少了内地与港澳在经贸交流中的体制性障碍，加速了相互间资本、货物、人员等要素的便捷流动，对内地的改革开放、港澳经济的复苏和发展以及内地与港澳的经贸交流起到了积极促进作用；推动了内地经济建设和现代服务业发展，促进了内地与港澳经济互动；有利于充分发挥“两制”的优势，推动内地与港澳共同开拓国际市场。《安排》还为内地商签其他自由贸易协议起到了示范和借鉴作用。

（商务部台港澳司）

与中国台北 WTO 事务

2001 年 12 月 11 日，中国大陆正式加入世界贸易组织，成为其第 143 个成员。2002 年 1 月 1 日，台湾地区以“台澎金马单独关税区”（简称“中国台北”）的名义加入世界贸易组织。两岸由此在世贸组织框架下开启了相关问题的协商与互动，台先后三次参与了世贸组织对我贸易政策审议，我参与了两次世贸组织对台贸易政策审议。

2010 年 6 月 29 日，海峡两岸关系协会与台湾海峡交流基金会在重庆签署了《海峡两岸经济合作框架协议》（ECFA，以下简称框架协议）。框架协议包括序言和 5 章 16 条及 5 个附件，基本涵盖了两岸间的主要经济活动，是遵循世界贸易组织规则和平等互惠原则，并结合两岸经济发展的实际状况和特点，签署的综合性、具有两岸特色的经济合作协议。

2011 年 1 月 1 日，框架协议早期收获全面实施，大陆对 539 项原产于台湾的产品逐步降低或取消关税，在 11 个服务行业对台实施更加开放的政策措施；台对 267 项原产于大陆的产品实施降税，就 9 个服务行业对大陆进一步放开。2011 年 5 月 6 日，中国大陆和台湾分别致函世贸组织秘书处，就框架协议向世贸组织进行了早期通告。

框架协议签署后，两岸陆续启动了货物贸易、服务贸易、投资保障、争端解决四个后续协议的磋商工作。2012 年 8 月 9 日，海协会与海基会在台北签署了《海峡两岸投资保护和促进协议》（简称“投保协议”）。从实体权益看，两岸投保协议规定了一般投保协议通常包括的重要实体条款，包括投资定义、投资待遇、征收、损失补偿、代位、转移等，同时还就投资者人身安全保护和第三地转投资做了专门规定。从程序权利看，两岸投保协议为两岸投资者设计了一套行之有效的争端解决体系，这也是该协议的最大亮点之一。具体体现在如下方面：一是特别纳入了投资商事争议仲裁条款；二是为投资者与投资所在地一方的争端解决设计了多层次、多渠道的五种争端解决方式，包括争端双方友好协商解决、协调机制协调解决、投资争端协处机制协助解决、提交两岸投资争端解决机构通过调解方式解决、通过行政复议或司法程序解决。投保协议有利于保护两岸投资者权益，逐步减少投资限制，创造公平的投资环境，促进两岸双向投资。作为框架协议生效后第一个完成商谈并成功签署的后续协议，它对两岸经贸领域制度化合作具有承前启后的重要作用。

2013 年 6 月 21 日，海协会与海基会在上海签署《海峡两岸服务贸易协议》（以下简称服贸协议），这也是框架协议生效后第二个完成商谈并成功签署的后续协议。服贸协议旨在逐步减少或消除两岸间的服务贸易限制性措施，促进两岸间服务贸易自由化，扩大两岸民众的受惠面，是两岸间签署的首个服务贸易自由化协议。服贸协议中，陆方对台方开放涵盖 40 多个行业，共 80 条措施，其中 78 条（占总出价条数的 97.5%）超出我入世承诺水平。台湾对大陆开放共 64 条措施，其中 20 条（占 31%）超出其入世承诺水平，实现了自由化；23 条（占总出价条数的 36%）达到其入世承诺水平，实现了正常化；21 条（占 33%）低于其入世承诺水平，未实现正常化。

今后，商务部将按照世贸组织规则，结合《十二五规划纲要》中“关于建立健全两岸经济合作机制、全面深化两岸经济合作”的要求，加速推动框架协议后续协议的商谈工作，为两岸经济繁荣做出更大贡献。

（商务部台港澳司）

与港、澳、台经贸关系

（一）内地与港、澳经贸关系

1. 内地与港、澳经贸交流情况

2014年，内地与香港贸易额为3760.9亿美元，同比减少6.2%；其中，内地对香港出口为3631.9亿美元，同比减少5.5%；自香港进口为129亿美元，同比减少20.7%。

2014年，内地与澳门贸易额为38.2亿美元，同比增长7.1%。其中，内地对澳门出口为36.1亿美元，同比增长13.4%；自澳门进口为2.1亿美元，同比减少45.1%。

从相互投资看，截至2014年底，内地累计批准港资项目373067个，实际利用港资7469.4亿美元。按实际使用外资统计，港资在内地累计吸收境外投资中占49.3%。内地累计批准澳资项目13832个，实际利用澳资119亿美元，澳资在内地累计吸收境外投资中占0.8%。

与此同时，内地赴港澳投资也不断增加。截至2014年底，内地对香港非金融类累计直接投资为3474.9亿美元，占内地对外非金融类累计直接投资存量总额的53.8%。内地累计对澳门非金融类直接投资15亿美元。

2. 对港、澳经贸领域成就

成功签署内地与香港、澳门《安排》及十个补充协议，在广东省对港澳率先基本实现服务贸易自由化，取得积极成果。

2003年，内地与香港、澳门特区政府分别签署了内地与港、澳《安排》，开启了两地经贸往来的新篇章。此后的2004—2013年，两地又陆续签署了十个《安排》补充协议，形成了对港澳较为系统的开放体系，并于2014年12月签署了《内地与香港（澳门）CEPA关于内地在广东与香港（澳门）基本实现服务贸易自由化的协议》。

在货物贸易领域，据中国海关统计，2014年，《安排》项下内地进口香港零关税货物货值为13.1亿美元，关税优惠额6.8亿元人民币。截至2014年底，内地累计进口香港《安排》项下受惠货物84.7亿美元，关税优惠额46.7亿元人民币。据香港统计，截至2014年底，香港发证机构共签发121027份原产地证书，货物离岸价总值为669.7亿港元。

据中国海关统计，2014年，《安排》项下内地进口澳门零关税货物货值为1738.2万美元，关税优惠额713.5万元人民币。截至2014年底，内地累计进口澳门《安排》项下受惠货物8279.9万美元，关税优惠额4418.3万元人民币。据澳门统计，截至2014年底，澳门经济局共发出3375张“零关税原产地证书”，总出口额5.66亿澳门元。

在服务贸易领域，截至2014年底，香港工贸署共签发香港服务提供者证明书2879份。其中运输服务及物流服务共签发证明书1354份，占核发总数的47%。

截至2014年底，澳门经济局核发444张“澳门服务提供者证明书”，主要涉及货代、物流、运输、仓储、会议及展览等领域。

在金融领域，截至2014年底，香港共有215家银行开办人民币业务，人民币存款总额10035.6亿元。

截至2014年底，澳门共有23家银行开办人民币业务；澳门人民币存款总额1034.1亿元。

在个体工商户方面，截至2014年底，内地共注册香港个体工商户6920户，从业人员1.9万人，资金数额5.2亿元。

截至2014年底，内地共注册澳门个体工商户1084户，从业人员2684人，资金数额8268.9万元。

在个人游方面，据香港旅游局统计，2014年，内地赴港“个人游”旅客为3133.5万人次，占内地赴港旅客66.3%。2003年7月至2013年底，内地赴港“个人游”旅客累计达1.6亿人次，占内地赴港旅客的61.5%（同期内地赴港旅客为2.6亿人次）。

据澳门统计局统计，2014年，内地赴澳“个人游”旅客956.5万人次，占内地游客总数的45%。2003年7月至2014年底，内地赴澳“个人游”旅客累计达7257.1万人次，占内地游客总数的42.7%（同期内地赴澳旅客为1.7亿人次）。

（二）大陆与台湾经贸关系

1. 大陆与台湾经贸交流情况

据大陆统计，2014年两岸贸易额达1983.1亿美元，同比增长0.5%。其中，大陆对台湾出口462.8亿美元，同比增长13.9%；自台湾进口1520.3亿美元，同比下降2.9%。大陆对台贸易逆差1057.5亿美元。台湾是我第七大贸易伙伴，第九大出口市场和第五大进口来源地。大陆是台湾最大的贸易伙伴和贸易顺差来源地。

截至2014年底，按投资者注册地统计，大陆累计批准台资项目9.2万个，台资金额611.5亿美元。若加上台商经第三地的转投资，大陆累计实际使用台资约1100多亿美元，占我实际使用境外投资的8.3%，在我外资来源地中排第二。

自台湾2009年6月30日开放陆资入岛起计算，截至2014年底，经商务主管部门批准，大陆已有228家非金融企业赴台设立了公司或代表机构，陆资投资金额5.9亿美元。

2. 对台经贸领域的成就

ECFA早期收获于2011年1月1日全面实施。早期收获实施的覆盖面广、效果明显，普遍惠及两岸民众。

货物贸易领域，截至2014年底，自台进口方面，大陆对台累计减免关税约131.2亿人民币；对台出口方面，大陆对台出口享受的减免关税2.2亿美元。我对台减免关税与台对我之比为9.5∶1。

服务贸易领域，截至2014年底，共有45家台湾金融企业和301家台湾非金融企业利用早期收获优惠政策在大陆提供服务。大陆核准引进21部台湾电影片。

（商务部台港澳司）

第五篇　与 WTO 主要成员经贸关系

中国与美国的经济贸易关系

2014年是中美建交35周年。中美经贸合作继续深化和发展，双边贸易和投资保持稳定增长，高层经贸对话机制不断完善，取得丰硕成果。双边经贸关系沿着平等互利、合作共赢的方向前进。

一、元首会晤和高层经贸对话为中美经贸合作引领方向并创造有利条件

2014年11月，奥巴马总统来华出席亚太经合组织领导人非正式会议并对中国进行国事访问。习近平主席与奥巴马总统在北京成功举行会晤，双方就继续致力于构建中美新型大国关系达成重要共识，并确认经济关系作为双边关系核心的重要性，为两国深化和扩大经贸合作指明了方向。7月，第六轮中美战略与经济对话在北京成功举行，双方在加强宏观经济政策协调与合作、深化贸易与投资合作、国际合作与全球治理改革、促进金融稳定和改革等领域达成积极务实成果。12月，第25届中美商贸联委会在美国芝加哥召开，双方就各自关注的重点经贸议题深入交流，进一步增进了解，达成多项共识和成果。在本届联委会期间，双方首次举办一系列合作性活动，邀请企业界代表参与，充分发挥了联委会促进两国间经贸合作的平台作用。

二、双边贸易突破5500亿美元，规模不断扩大

据中方统计，2014年，中美贸易额达5551亿美元，同比上升6.6%。其中，中国自美进口1590亿美元，同比上升4.2%；对美出口3961亿美元，同比上升7.5%；中方顺差2371亿美元，同比上升9.8%。美国是中国第二大贸易伙伴、第一大出口市场和第五大进口来源地。

据美方统计，2014年美中货物贸易额[①]达6103亿美元，同比上升5%。其中，美自华进口额4863亿美元，同比上升5.9%；对华出口额1240亿美元，同比上升1.9%。美对华贸易逆差额3623亿美元，同比上升7.3%。中国是美国第二大贸易伙伴、第三大出口市场和第一大进口来源地。

三、美对华实际投资出现下降，中国对美投资保持快速增长

2014年，中国实际使用美资金额23.7亿美元，同比下降15.9%。截至2014年底，美国对中国投资实际投入达753.8亿美元，是中国第四大外资来源地。同时，中国对美国投资继续呈现快速增长势头。2014年在美非金融类直接投资52.4亿美元，同比增长23.9%。截至2014年底，中国企业在美累计非金融类直接投资205.1亿美元。2014年当年，美国是中国对外直接投资的第四大目的地。

四、中美省州和城市间经贸合作继续深化

2014年，中美省州和城市间经贸合作继续深入发展。中国相关省、市已与美国州、市建立了4个贸易投资合作工作组。2013年4月，中国六个省与美国加州建立起第一个省州间的贸易投资工作组。2014年6月，商务部推动河北、吉林、辽宁和黑龙江四省与美国艾奥瓦州签署谅解备忘录，成立“中国省与美国艾奥瓦州贸易投资合作联合工作组”；9月，商务部推动江苏、山东、福建、四川和天津五个省（市）与得克萨斯州签署谅解备忘录，成立“中国省与美国得克萨斯州贸易投资合作联合工作组”。在第25届中美商贸联委会期间，北京、上海、天津、沈阳、武汉、杭州、青岛、成都八个市的代表在“中国市与芝加哥市贸易投资合作工作组”的框架下组团访问芝加哥市，举办了中美城市间经贸合作主题午餐会及相关商务洽谈活动。

---

① 出口按离岸价（FAS）、进口按到岸价（CIF）统计。

五、经贸摩擦依然存在，但合作共赢仍是中美经贸关系的主旋律

2014 年，中美双方都采取了贸易救济措施，特别是在光伏产品领域的贸易纠纷较为突出。美方仍然实施对华高技术产品出口管制，并炒作网络窃密等问题。美国会在《2014 财年综合拨款法案》中纳入限制美国政府部门采购中国信息技术设备和限制对华科技合作等歧视性涉华内容。中方在世贸组织成功挑战美方滥用贸易救济措施的做法，取得阶段性成果。总体看，中美两国在发展阶段和经济结构上的互补性，决定了双边经贸合作互利共赢的本质。双方应相向而行，共同努力妥善处理分歧，扩大共同利益，促进双边经贸关系稳定健康发展，推动“不冲突、不对抗、相互尊重、合作共赢”的新型大国关系不断取得新的进展。

（商务部美大司）

中国与加拿大的经济贸易关系

2014年，中加经贸关系保持稳定发展。双方高层互访频繁，各层级交流增多。特别是2014年11月加拿大总理哈珀访华，两国领导人在经贸领域达成了一系列重要共识。

一、双边贸易稳步增长

据中国海关统计，2014年，中加双边贸易额552.4亿美元，同比增长1.5%。其中，中国对加出口300.1亿美元，自加进口252.3亿美元，同比分别增长2.7%和0.03%。中国对加出口的主要商品为：机械设备、电器及电子产品、计算机及通信技术产品、服装、家具、电话机、纺织品、农产品；中国自加进口的主要商品为：农产品、机电产品、纸浆、锯材、电子产品、铁矿砂、铜矿砂。

据加方统计，2014年，加中贸易额780亿加元，同比增长6.5%，占同期加拿大对外贸易总额的7.5%。其中，加从中国进口586.4亿加元，同比增长11.2%。加向中国出口193.6亿加元，同比下降5.5%。中国是加拿大的第二大贸易伙伴、第二大进口来源地和第二大出口市场。

二、双向投资持续发展

加拿大是中国外资的重要来源地之一。2014年，加拿大在华投资新设立企业399家，实际使用外资金额3.5亿美元。截至2014年底，加拿大在华投资设立企业累计约1.3万家，实际使用外资金额累计96.6亿美元。加拿大在华投资项目在沿海发达地区、中部地区和西部地区均有分布。投资的行业主要有：旅游、通信、电力、矿业和房地产等。

2014年，中国企业对加拿大非金融类直接投资4.9亿美元。截至2014年底，中国企业对加拿大直接投资累计66.8亿美元。涉及的行业主要有采矿业、金融业、租赁和商务服务业、制造业、批发和零售业等。

（商务部美大司）

中国与澳大利亚的经济贸易关系

2014年11月习近平主席访问澳大利亚，双方宣布实质性结束中澳自贸协定谈判，并将中澳关系提升为全面战略伙伴关系。2014年中澳经贸关系发展良好，澳大利亚继续成为中国重要的贸易投资伙伴。

一、双边贸易持续增长

据中国海关统计，2014年中澳双边贸易额达1369.5亿美元，同比增长0.4%。其中，中国对澳出口391.2亿美元，同比增长4.1%；自澳进口978.3亿美元，同比下降1%。澳是中国第八大贸易伙伴、第九大出口市场和第七大进口来源地。中国对澳出口主要产品有：计算机、服装、家具、纺织纱线、电话机等；自澳进口主要产品有：铁矿石、农产品、煤炭、粮食、液化天然气等。

据澳方统计，2014年澳中货物贸易额为1421.6亿澳元，同比增长0.5%，占澳货物贸易总额的27%。其中，澳对中国出口901.9亿澳元，同比下降4.4%；澳从中国进口519.8亿澳元，同比增长10.2%。中国是澳第一大货物贸易伙伴，第一大进口来源地和第一大出口目的地。

二、双向投资稳步增加

澳大利亚是我国重要的外资来源地。截至2014年底，澳大利亚在华设立外商投资项目累计10639个，实际对华投资累计77.5亿美元。

中国对澳投资近年来增长较快，澳已成为中国重要的海外投资目的国。据中方统计，截至2014年底，中国企业对澳非金融类投资累计为199亿美元。据澳统计局统计，截至2014年底，中国对澳投资存量为645亿澳元，占澳吸收外资存量的2.3%。按年度外国投资流量计算，2014年中国对澳投资133亿澳元，占澳当年外资流量的3%，是澳第三大外资来源地。

（商务部美大司）

中国与新西兰的经济贸易关系

2014年中国和新西兰经贸关系快速发展。

据中方统计，2014年中国和新西兰双边贸易额达142.5亿美元，同比增长15%。其中，中国自新西兰进口95.1亿美元，同比增长15.2%；中国对新西兰出口47.4亿美元，同比增长14.7%。

据新方统计，2014年，中国继续保持新西兰第一大货物贸易伙伴和第一大出口市场地位。中国连续四年为新西兰第一大进口来源地。2014年，新中贸易额186.7亿新元，同比增长2.5%。新西兰自中国进口主要商品为电子类产品、服装、机械设备和电子设备等。新西兰对中国主要出口商品为奶制品、木材和羊毛。

据中方统计，2014年，新西兰在华投资新设企业62家，同比增长63%，实际使用外资金额4748万美元，同比下降30%。截至2014年底，新西兰在华投资设立企业累计1791家，实际使用外资金额累计13.6亿美元。2014年，中国企业对新西兰非金融类投资为1.4亿美元。截至2014年底，中国企业对新西兰非金融类直接投资存量4.8亿美元。

（商务部美大司）

中国与拉美国家的经济贸易关系

中国和拉美地区国家经贸往来历史悠久。20 世纪 70～80 年代，随着中国同该地区大多数国家建立起外交关系，双边经贸往来逐渐增多。进入 21 世纪，特别是中国加入世界贸易组织以来，中拉经贸关系迎来了一个全方位快速发展的阶段。

近年来，中拉经贸合作规模持续扩大，领域不断拓宽，利益交汇点和契合点日益增多，形成了相互倚重、共同发展的经贸关系格局。截至目前，中国与智利、秘鲁和哥斯达黎加均实施了自由贸易协定。

一、双边贸易

改革开放初期的 1979 年，中拉贸易额仅为 12.6 亿美元；2000 年达到 126 亿美元，首次突破 100 亿美元；2007 年双边贸易额首次超过 1000 亿美元；2011 年突破 2000 亿美元。2014 年，中拉贸易额达到 2636.4 亿美元，同比增长 0.8%，占中国对外贸易份额从 2000 年的 2.7%上升到 2014 年的 6.1%，占拉美对外贸易总额的比重则从 2000 年的 1.7%上升到目前的约 12%。

目前，中国已成为大多数拉美国家第一或第二大贸易伙伴。中国对拉美的出口以机电产品和高新技术产品为主，进口主要是能矿和农产品。目前，拉美是中国大豆、豆油、花生油、食糖、鱼粉、毛条和铜矿产品进口的最大来源地。

二、投资合作

2005 年末，中国在拉美地区直接投资存量首次超过 100 亿美元（约 115 亿美元），到 2013 年底约为 861 亿美元，2014 年中国对拉非金融类直接投资流量为 128.5 亿美元。

近年来，中国在拉美地区投资领域从能矿领域逐步向制造业、电力、农业和金融等领域延伸，投资方式日趋多样化。

三、工程承包合作

拉美是中国重要的工程承包市场之一。截至 2014 年，中国累计在拉美新签工程承包合同额超过 1100 亿美元，实际完成营业额 676 亿美元。相关业务涉及天然气管道、电站、公路、港口疏浚、住房、通信设施等多个领域。

（商务部美大司）

中国与智利的经济贸易关系

一、双边贸易

自2006年中智自贸协定实施以来，双边贸易持续增长。目前，智利是中国在拉美的第三大贸易伙伴，中国则是智利第一大贸易伙伴、第一大进口来源国和第一大出口目的地国。据中国海关统计，2014年中智双边贸易总额341亿美元，同比增长0.9%。其中，中方出口130.2亿美元，同比增长1.9%；中方进口210.8亿美元，同比下降0.7%。

中国对智利主要出口机电产品、纺织品、鞋类、钢材和汽车等商品，主要进口铜矿砂、铁矿砂、纸浆、鱼粉、水果和葡萄酒等商品。

二、相互投资

据商务部业务统计，截至2014年底，智利在华投资项目165个，实际投入1.4亿美元，主要集中在航运、服装、化工、建材、食品和金属加工等领域。

据中国对外直接投资统计公报，截至2013年底，中国对智利直接投资存量1.79亿美元，主要涉及矿产资源勘探开发、农业、加工制造和渔业等领域。据商务部统计，2014年，中国对智非金融类直接投资882万美元。

三、承包工程

据商务部统计，截至2014年底，中国企业在智利累计签订承包工程合同额11.9亿美元，完成营业额8.6亿美元，主要涉及码头修建、水电、光伏电站等项目建设。

四、中国—智利自由贸易协定

《中国—智利自由贸易协定》（货物贸易及合作部分）于2005年11月签署，并于2006年10月开始实施。《中智自贸协定关于服务贸易的补充协定》于2008年4月13日签署，并于2010年8月正式实施。《中智自贸协定关于投资的补充协定》于2012年9月签署，并于2014年2月开始实施。

（商务部美大司）

中国与秘鲁的经济贸易关系

一、双边贸易

（一）总体情况

2014年，秘鲁是中国在拉美的第六大贸易伙伴，中国则是秘鲁第一大贸易伙伴、第一大出口目的地国和第一大进口来源国。据中国海关统计，2014年中秘双边贸易总额143.2亿美元，同比下降2.1%。其中，中方出口61亿美元，同比下降1.4%；中方进口82.2亿美元，同比下降2.6%。

中国向秘鲁主要出口机电产品、高新技术产品、钢铁板材、汽车、纺织品等，主要进口铜矿砂及其精矿、原油、鱼粉和铁矿砂及其精矿等。

（二）反倾销及保障措施

截至2014年底，秘鲁共对中国产品发起26起贸易救济调查，其中反倾销23起，保障措施2起，特保1起。目前，秘鲁正在征税的中国产品有鞋、拉链、不锈钢餐具、棉纺和混纺织物、滑水板、涤棉府绸、棉机织物和牛仔布等。

二、双向投资

据中国对外直接投资统计公报，截至2013年底，中国对秘直接投资存量8.68亿美元，主要涉及能矿资源开发、批发和零售业、建筑业等领域。据商务部业务统计，2014年中国对秘鲁非金融类直接投资6151万美元。

据商务部业务统计，截至2014年底，秘鲁在华投资项目173个，实际投资4348万美元，涉及电子、房地产、汽车零部件等行业。

三、承包工程

中国企业在秘鲁开展承包工程业务始于1986年。据商务部业务统计，截至2014年底，中国企业在秘鲁累计签订承包工程合同总额19.1亿美元，完成营业额21.2亿美元，主要涉及水电、交通基础设施建设、住房、城市排水、通信等项目。

四、中国—秘鲁自由贸易协定

《中国—秘鲁自由贸易协定》于2010年3月1日起实施，是中国在拉美继《中国—智利自由贸易协定》后开始实施的第二个自贸协定。

（商务部美大司）

中国与俄罗斯的经济贸易关系

一、中俄经贸关系总体评价

2014 年乌克兰危机爆发后，俄遭遇西方全面经济制裁，面临外交和经济双重困境，结构性问题日益凸显。加之国际市场油价持续暴跌，引发卢布暴跌，资本外流，全年 GDP 仅增长 0.6%，对中俄贸易造成较大冲击。尽管全年双边贸易额总体保持增长势头，但增幅较前有所回落。

（一）贸易规模逆势增长

在俄经济陷入衰退困境的背景下，2014 年中俄贸易仍实现逆势增长。全年中俄贸易额为 952.8 亿美元，同比增长 6.8%。其中，对俄出口 536.8 亿美元，同比增长 8.2%；自俄进口 416 亿美元，同比增长 4.9%。中俄贸易增速均超过两国各自对外贸易总体水平。

（二）投资合作稳中求进

受卢布大幅贬值，俄经济加速下滑等因素影响，双向投资合作步伐有所放缓。全年我对俄非金融类直接投资为 7.9 亿美元，同比下降 80.6%；俄对华直接投资 4088 万美元，同比增长 85.1%。但双方投资合作领域不断拓宽，形式趋于多元。中石油参股亚马尔 LNG 项目完成股权交割；中石油参股万科尔油田、中石化参股西布尔公司等项目正在稳步推进；长城汽车、力帆汽车分别在俄投资设厂；中俄投资基金积极开展工作，为推动同江铁路桥等项目取得进展发挥了作用。

（三）大项目合作取得突破

当前，俄加快战略重心东移，两国战略性大项目合作取得多项突破：双方签署了东线天然气合作“世纪大单”和西线天然气合作框架协议；远程宽体客机项目建议书进入审批程序，俄方确定以“技术入股”参与重型直升机研制合作；同江铁路桥项目启动融资谈判及招标工作，黑河公路桥政府间协定修订工作基本完成；高铁合作全面启动，将优先实施莫斯科—喀山高铁项目；双方在利用俄跨欧亚铁路运输潜力和实施“丝绸之路经济带”战略中找到新的契合点。

（四）金融合作步伐加快

西方制裁导致俄国际融资和结算渠道受阻，俄对人民币业务需求陡增，莫斯科外汇交易所人民币交易额迅猛增长。双边贸易中本币结算规模稳步扩大，双方积极探讨在大宗商品及农产品、高科技产品贸易中使用本币结算；两国央行签署了规模为 1500 亿元人民币/8150 亿卢布的双边本币互换协议；两国银行积极在对方国家境内设立机构，深入探讨开展人民币融资合作，开发多种新型金融产品；双方还积极探讨支付卡系统和信用评级等领域的合作。

（五）地方间合作势头良好

边境贸易稳步增长。全年中俄边境贸易额为 106.3 亿美元，同比增长 3.1%。双方建立了多个地方间合作机制和平台，地方间合作的地域范围不断拓宽，取得丰硕成果。年内，莫斯科州、鞑靼斯坦共和国、车里雅宾斯克州、伊尔库茨克州等地方政府代表团在中国各地访问推介，达吉斯坦共和国与广东省、巴什科尔托斯坦共和国与江西省、斯维尔德洛夫斯克州与山西省正在商谈有关合作协议。俄 38 个联邦主体组团参加首届中俄博览会，参会规模前所未有。双方积极推动开展俄远东地区开发合作，包括参与俄远东“跨越式发展区”的建设等。

2014 年，中俄两国领导人互访频繁，习近平主席与普京总统在索契冬奥会开幕式、上合组织和金砖国家元首峰会、APEC 领导人非正式会议等多个场合先后举行 6 次会晤，就深化双边经贸关系达成重要共识。2014 年 5 月，普京总统对中国进行国事访问，并出席在上海举行的“亚洲相互协作与信任措施会议”第四次峰会；10 月，李克强总理与梅德韦杰夫总理在莫斯科举行中俄总理第 19 次定期会晤，汪洋副总理与罗戈津副总理在索契共同主持召开中俄总理定期会晤委员会第 18 次会议。下一步，双方将继续发挥顶层设计和高层引领作用，确定双边关系发展主脉，推动务实合作取得突破：一是推动战略性大项目取得突破，包括能源、核能、航空、航天、装备制造、互联互通等领域战略性大项目合作取得积极进展，使其成为发展双边经贸关系的“压舱石”和“推进器”；二是维护双边经贸合作发展势头。在当前国际和地区形势复杂演变的背景下，中俄贸易面临严峻挑战，实现既定贸易目标任务艰巨。应采取积极措施，加大贸易融资和保险支持力度，对重点行业、重点企业和重点大宗商品交易给予集中扶持。三是拓展两国边境和地方间合作，利用中俄博览会等平台，加强两国省州间的交流，积极参与俄远东地区开发合作。

二、中俄双边贸易简况

中俄自1992年建交以来，双边贸易总体保持平稳较快增长态势，贸易额由1992年的58.6亿美元，增长到2014年的952.8亿美元，增幅逾15倍。中俄已互为主要的贸易伙伴，在对方国家的外贸关系中占有举足轻重的地位。

2014年，受俄经济发展的外部环境恶化等因素影响，中俄贸易遭遇较大冲击，总体来看，双方结构互补性强、合作领域宽的基本格局并未改变，企业合作意愿并未降低，中俄贸易实现可持续增长依然具备坚实基础，全年双边贸易仍实现微增。据中国海关统计，2014年，中俄贸易额为952.8亿美元，同比增长6.8%。其中，对俄出口536.8亿美元，同比增长8.2%；自俄进口416亿美元，同比增长4.9%。对俄贸易顺差120.8亿美元。俄在中国主要贸易伙伴中列第九位。据俄罗斯海关统计，2014年，俄中贸易额为888亿美元，同比下降0.5%，中国仍保持俄第一大贸易伙伴地位。

贸易结构方面，2014年，中国对俄主要出口机械设备、电子产品、轻纺产品（服装、鞋、纱线等）、农产品、钢材等，机电和高新技术产品在出口中的比重达到46%和13.8%，出口商品结构持续优化。自俄进口中，能源资源产品（原油、成品油、煤、铁矿砂、原木等）所占比重超过70%，机电和高新技术产品占比2.1%，商品结构失衡问题略有好转。

三、中俄投资合作简况

（一）中国对俄投资

截至2014年底，中国对俄累计非金融类直接投资92.9亿美元。其中2014年，中国对俄非金融类直接投资为7.9亿美元，同比下降80.6%。投资主要分布在能源资源、农林开发、建筑和建材生产、贸易、轻纺、家电、通信、服务等领域。

据俄方统计，截至2013年底，中国已对俄累计投资（含对俄提供贷款）321.3亿美元，占俄累计吸引外资总额的8.4%，中国是俄第四大外资来源地。

（二）俄对华投资

截至2014年底，中国累计实际使用俄直接投资9.1亿美元。其中，2014年中国实际使用俄直接投资4088万美元，同比增长85.1%。俄对华投资集中在制造业、建筑、交通运输等领域。

四、中俄劳务及工程承包合作简况

截至2014年底，中俄双方累计签署工程承包合同金额176.6亿美元，完成营业额115.6亿美元。其中，2014年中俄签署工程承包合同金额19.6亿美元，同比下降9.7%，完成营业额11.6亿美元，同比下降15.3%，期末在外人数20968人。中国对俄劳务合作集中在俄远东、西伯利亚地区，主要从事农业种植、建筑、森林采伐、木材加工、制衣、医疗及其他服务行业。

五、中俄边境贸易简况

2014年，中俄边境贸易额为106.3亿美元，同比增长3.1%，其中对俄出口51.6亿美元，同比增长6.5%，自俄进口54.7亿美元，同比增长0.2%。中国对俄边贸出口商品主要是轻纺、农产品和小家电等；进口以原木、原油、化肥、钢材、纸浆等初级产品为主。

（商务部欧亚司）

中国与欧洲联盟的经济贸易关系

中国与欧盟互为重要的贸易伙伴。1975年中欧正式建交，2003年建立全面战略伙伴关系。2014年是中欧互利共赢的全面战略伙伴关系新十年的开端，也是落实《中欧合作2020战略规划》的开局之年。这一年中欧双边关系升温，政治互信增强，高层互访频繁，有力地推动了中欧经贸合作。

一、双边贸易

（一）货物贸易

据中方统计，欧盟连续多年保持为中国第一大货物贸易伙伴、第一大进口来源地。2014年，中欧双边贸易额6151.4亿美元，同比增长9.9%。其中中国对欧出口3708.8亿美元，增长9.4%；自欧进口2442.5亿美元，增长10.7%。中国顺差1266.3亿美元，扩大6.5%。2014年中国出口欧盟的主要货物为机电产品、高新技术产品、服装和衣着附件、自动数据处理设备、电话机等商品，中国自欧盟进口的主要货物为机电产品、高新技术产品、汽车、汽车零配件、医药等商品。

据欧方统计，中国是欧盟第二大贸易伙伴，仅次于美国。2014年，中欧双边货物贸易额4671.9亿欧元，同比增长9.1%，占欧盟对外贸易总额的14%。其中，中国对欧出口3024.6亿欧元，增长8%；自欧进口1647.4亿欧元，增长11.2%。中国顺差1377.2亿欧元，扩大4.4%。中欧货物以工业制成品为主，制成品占中国自欧进口货物总额的86%，占中国向欧出口货物总额的97%。

（二）服务贸易

据中方统计，欧盟为中国第二大服务贸易伙伴。2014年，中欧服务贸易额749.9亿美元，同比增长7.1%。其中，中国对欧出口313.3亿美元，增长24.3%；自欧进口436.6亿美元，下降2.5%；中国逆差123.3亿美元。

据欧方统计，2014年中欧服务贸易额543亿欧元，同比增长8.8%。其中，中国对欧出口225.7亿欧元，同比增长8%；自欧进口317.3亿欧元，同比增长9.4%；中国逆差91.6亿欧元。

二、双向投资

欧盟连续多年保持为中国累计第四大实际投资来源地。据中方统计，截至2014年底，欧盟对华累计投资项目39598项，实际投资966.3亿美元。2014年，欧盟28国对华投资项目1499个，同比增长3.7%，实际投资62.3亿美元，下降4.5%。从国别来看，2014年德国、英国、法国、荷兰、爱尔兰为欧盟在华投资的主要国家。

近年来，中国企业对欧投资日渐活跃。据中方统计，截至2014年底，中国对欧累计直接投资498.6亿美元。2014年，中国对欧非金融类直接投资98.48亿美元，增长172.1%，当年中国对欧投资占中国对外投资流量总额的9.6%。从国别看，中国对欧投资主要分布在荷兰、德国、卢森堡、法国、英国等国。

据欧方统计，2014年，欧盟对华投资91.4亿欧元，同比下降46.6%，中国对欧盟投资121亿欧元，增长118.1%。

三、技术引进

欧盟长期保持为中国累计最大技术引进来源地。据中方统计，截至2014年，中国累计自欧引进技术48421项，合同金额1812.2亿美元。其中，2014年，中国自欧引进技术2665项，合同金额86.6亿美元。

四、重要经贸往来

2014年3月，习近平主席访问欧盟总部，实现了中国国家元首对欧盟总部的首访。访问期间，习主席提出共同打造中欧和平、增长、改革、文明四大伙伴关系，中欧双方发表《关于深化互利共赢的中欧全面战略伙伴关系的联合声明》。

2014年3月，第二轮中欧投资协定谈判在比利时布鲁塞尔举行。

2014 年 4 月，第 17 次中欧经贸工作组会议在比利时布鲁塞尔举行，双方就货物贸易、服务贸易、技术性贸易壁垒、卫生与植物卫生措施等议题进行了讨论。

2014 年 6 月，第 14 次中欧知识产权工作组会议在北京召开。

2014 年 6 月，第三轮中欧投资协定谈判在北京举行。

2014 年 10 月，第 8 次中欧钢铁非正式对话在布鲁塞尔举行。

2014 年 10 月，第 28 届中欧经贸混委会在布鲁塞尔召开。双方在会上就无线通信设备争端案达成一致，并讨论了中欧双边投资协定谈判、《信息技术协定》扩围谈判等多双边重点议题。

2014 年 11 月，习近平主席在澳大利亚布里斯班会见新任欧盟委员会主席容克。

2014 年 12 月，习近平主席与新任欧盟理事会主席图斯克通电话。

2014 年 12 月，中欧高技术贸易工作组第三次对话在布鲁塞尔举行。

2014 年 12 月，中欧知识产权工作组第 15 次会议在北京举行。

五、对话机制

中欧经贸对话机制健全，交流渠道畅通。1979 年中欧成立正部级经贸混委会，迄今已举行 28 次会议。2007 年，双方领导人达成共识，建立副总理级中欧经贸高层对话机制，迄今已成功举行 4 次对话，2013 年中欧双方共同制订的《中欧合作 2020 战略规划》将该对话确立为中欧合作三大支柱之一。中欧双方建立的经贸对话机制还包括中欧贸易与投资政策对话、竞争政策对话、知识产权对话、钢铁非正式对话、经贸工作组、高技术贸易工作组、贸易救济措施工作组等。多层次、宽领域的对话和磋商机制为双方协调立场、处理分歧、促进合作提供了重要平台。

（商务部欧洲司）

中国与英国的经济贸易关系

据中国海关统计，2014年中英双边贸易额为808.7亿美元，同比增长15.3%，其中中国出口571.4亿美元，增长12.2%，中国进口237.3亿美元，增长23.5%。主要进口产品有汽车、医药品、原油、计量检测分析自控仪器及器具、废金属、农产品、废纸、汽车零配件、航空器零件、阀门等；主要出口产品有服装及衣着附件、自动数据处理设备及其部件、家具及其零件、电话机、鞋类、纺织纱线、织物及制品、塑料制品、灯具、照明装置及类似品、箱包及类似容器、农产品等。

据中国商务部统计，截至2014年底，英国在华投资项目7477个，实际投入184.7亿美元，中国对英国累计实际投资123.7亿美元。2013年，英国在华新增投资项目236个，同比下降4.07%，实际投入3.92亿美元，同比下降4.31%。

截至2014年底，中国自英国技术引进累计合同金额达110.3亿美元。2014年，中国自英国技术引进合同金额为4.8亿美元。

截至2014年底，中国在英国承包工程合作项目累计合同额42.5亿美元，完成营业额32.8亿美元。2014年，中国在英国新签项目合同额5.5亿美元，完成营业额4.8亿美元。

截至2014年底，中英经贸联委会已举行了11次会议。2014年5月，商务部部长高虎城与英国商业、技能和创新部大臣坎布尔在北京共同主持了第11次会议。

2014年中国与英国的高层互访主要有：6月，李克强总理访英；9月，马凯副总理访英，与英国财政大臣奥斯本共同主持召开了中英经济财金对话第六次会议。

中国与英国经贸合作中的主要问题是：推动中欧自由贸易区可行性研究，放宽欧盟对华高技术产品出口限制，促进对英投资便利化，加强服务贸易和知识产权保护领域合作，加强中英核电、高铁合作。

（商务部欧洲司）

中国与德国的经济贸易关系

近年来，中德双边关系发展进入加速期，两国高层交往密度前所未有。2014 年 3 月，习近平主席成功访德，两国建立全方位战略伙伴关系；10 月，李克强总理与默克尔总理共同主持第三轮中德政府磋商，并发布以“共塑创新”为主题的《中德合作行动纲要》；2015 年 3 月，马凯副总理赴德主持首次中德高级别财金对话并就中德智能制造合作开展专题调研。在此背景下，中德经贸合作达到了新的高度，全方位、宽领域和多层次的合作格局不断凸显，中德经贸关系作为中欧经贸关系“领头羊”和“排头兵”的角色亦不断强化。

一、双边贸易

1972 年中德建交时，双边贸易额仅为 2.7 亿美元。2001 年中国加入世贸组织时，双边贸易额为 235.3 亿美元。2008 年，双边贸易额突破 1000 亿美元大关。目前，德国是中国在欧洲最大和全球第六大贸易伙伴。2014 年，中德贸易额为 1777.5 亿美元，同比增长 10.1%。其中，中方出口 727.1 亿美元，增长 8.0%；进口 1050.4 亿美元，增长 11.5%。

中国对德出口商品主要包括自动数据处理设备及其部件、服装及衣着附件、纺织纱线及织物制品、鞋类、农产品、电话机、家具及其零件等；自德进口商品主要包括汽车、汽车零件、计量检测分析自控仪器及器具、医药品、通断保护电路装置及零件、飞机、金属加工机床、集成电路、医疗仪器及器械等。

据德方统计，2014 年德中贸易额为 1538 亿欧元，增长 8.8%。其中，德对华出口 745 亿欧元，增长 11.3%；自华进口 793 亿欧元，增长 6.4%；德方逆差 48 亿欧元。中国继续保持德第三大贸易伙伴（仅次于法国、荷兰）、第四大出口目的国和第二大进口来源国（仅次于荷兰）地位。

二、双向投资

（一）德国对华投资

德国累计对华实际投资额居欧盟国家之首。据商务部统计，截至 2014 年底，中国累计批准德企业在华投资项目 8577 个，德方实际投入 239 亿美元。2014 年，中国新批德对华投资项目 384 个，增长 3%；德方实际投入 20.7 亿美元，下降 0.4%。德对华投资项目主要集中在化工、汽车、金融、电子电气、制药和零售等领域。

（二）中国对德投资

近年来，中国企业以并购、参股等形式在德实施“走出去”战略成效显著。据商务部统计，截至 2014 年底，中国累计在德非金融类投资额为 48.2 亿美元。2014 年，中国对德非金融类投资额为 8.4 亿美元。中国对德投资集中在机械制造、运输、汽车零配件、新能源、电信和贸易等领域。主要项目包括：潍柴动力 11.61 亿欧元入股凯傲集团；联想 6.29 亿欧元收购麦迪龙；三一重工 3.24 亿欧元收购普茨迈斯特等。

据德国联邦外贸与投资署统计，2014 年中国是对德投资项目数最多的国家，达 190 个，较上年增加 37%，远超第二名美国（168 个）和第三名瑞士（130 个），投资领域主要集中在半导体（16%）、机械设备（14%）、金融服务（9%）及信息通信和软件（7%）等。

三、技术合作

德国是中国自欧洲引进技术最多的国家。据商务部统计，截至 2014 年底，中国共批准自德技术引进合同 20970 项，合同金额 680.8 亿美元。2014 年，中国新批自德技术引进合同 1249 项，合同金额 43.5 亿美元，增长 2%。项目主要涉及交通运输、通信、电子电气、机械制造、金属加工和化工制药等领域。

四、中德经济合作联委会

1979 年 10 月，中德两国政府在波恩签署经济合作协定，并据此成立中德经济合作联合委员会（正部级）。1980 年 8 月，联委会在京举行首次会议，迄今共召开了 15 次会议。2012 年 8 月，联委会第15次会议在北京召开，时任商务部国际贸易谈判代表高虎城和时任德国副总理兼经济和技术部部长罗斯勒共同主持了会议。目前，联委会下设标准化委员会及煤炭、法律、服务领域合作和生态园4个工作组。

五、中德经济顾问委员会

中德经济顾问委员会（以下简称顾委会）是中国与世界主要经济体建立的首个双边经济合作顾问机制，旨在建立领导人与经济界直接对话的渠道，为中德企业、商协会、智库等建言献策、共谋合作提供平台。2013年5月李克强总理访德期间，顾委会正式成立，并被李总理称为与中德政府磋商并行、旨在推动两国经贸合作的“第二轨道”。2014年7月德国总理默克尔访华期间，顾委会召开首次会议，并与两国总理座谈。

附表　　中国入世以来中德贸易数据（中方统计）　　单位：亿美元

年度	总额	中方对德出口	中方自德进口	中方顺/逆差
2001	235.3（+19.5%）	97.5（+5.1%）	137.7（+32.3%）	−40.2
2002	278.0（+18.2%）	113.7（+16.6%）	164.3（+19.3%）	−50.6
2003	418.8（+50.7%）	175.4（+54.2%）	243.4（+48.3%）	−68.0
2004	541.2（+29.7%）	237.5（+36.2%）	303.7（+25%）	−66.1
2005	632.5（+16.9%）	325.3（+36.9%）	307.2（+1.2%）	+18.1
2006	782.0（+23.6%）	403.2（+23.9%）	378.8（+23.3%）	+24.4
2007	941.1（+20.4%）	487.2（+20.8%）	453.9（+19.8%）	+33.3
2008	1 150.1（+22.2%）	591.7（+21.5%）	558.4（+23.0%）	+33.3
2009	1 057.3（−8.1%）	499.2（−15.7%）	558.1（0%）	−58.9
2010	1 423.9（+34.8%）	680.5（+36.3）	743.4（+33.4%）	−62.9
2011	1 691.5（+18.9%）	764.3（+12.3%）	927.2（+24.9%）	−162.9
2012	1 611.3（−4.7%）	692.2（−9.4%）	919.1（−0.9%）	−226.9
2013	1 615.6（+0.3%）	673.6（−2.7%）	942（+2.5%）	−269
2014	1 777.5（+10.1%）	727.1（+8.0%）	1 050.4（+11.5%）	−323.3

（商务部欧洲司）

中国与法国的经济贸易关系

据中国海关统计，2014 年中法双边贸易额为 557.9 亿美元，同比增长 10.9%。其中中国出口 287.1 亿美元，同比增长 7.5%；中国进口 270.9 亿美元，同比增长 14.8%。中国对法国出口主要商品：服装及衣着附件、自动数据处理设备、家具及其零件、鞋类、电话机、纺织纱线及织物、箱包、灯具、塑料制品、农产品等。中国自法国进口主要商品：飞机、农产品、医药品、酒类、汽车零件、计量检测分析自控仪、美容化妆品及护肤品、通断保护电路装置及零件、乳品、钢材等。

据商务部统计，截至 2014 年底，法在华投资项目 4789 个，实际投资 136.4 亿美元。2014 年，法在华新增项目 159 个，同比下降 5.4%，实际投资 7.1 亿美元，同比下降 5.3%。法在华投资涵盖电力、汽车、航空、通信、化工、水务、医药等各大领域。

截至 2014 年底，中国对法国实际投资额为 86.5 亿美元。2014 年，中国对法国实际投资额为 14.2 亿美元，其中直接投资 3.2 亿美元，占 22.3%；境外再投资为 11 亿美元，占 77.3%。中国对法投资主要分布在化工、电子信息、电信、物流、贸易、金融、农产品加工、旅游等领域。

截至 2014 年底，中国自法国引进技术 5677 个，合同金额达 235.3 亿美元。2014 年，中国自法国引进技术 305 项，合同金额 7.7 亿美元。

截至 2014 年，中国在法国承包工程累计签订合同额 77.4 亿美元，完成营业额 70.4 亿美元。2014 年中国在法国新签工程承包合同额 19.5 亿美元，完成营业额 14.8 亿美元。

2014 年 2 月 24 日，中法经贸混委会第 22 次会议在巴黎举行，高虎城部长与时任法国外贸部长布里克共同主持。

2014 年中国与法国的高层互访主要有：3 月下旬，习近平主席访法；9 月下旬，马凯副总理访法并主持召开中法高级别经济财金对话第二次会议。

中国与法国经贸合作中的主要关注是：放宽欧盟对华高技术产品出口限制、促进对法投资便利化、共同反对贸易保护主义、进一步落实中法生态园合作、促进中法农产品贸易等。

（商务部欧洲司）

中国与东盟的经济贸易关系

近年来，中国—东盟友好合作持续稳定发展，经贸合作成效显著，贸易投资合作进一步发展，中国—东盟自贸区升级谈判、区域经济全面经济伙伴关系（RCEP）谈判稳步推进，区域经济一体化不断加深。中国—东盟战略伙伴关系经历了“黄金十年”，正步入起点更高、内涵更广、合作更深的“钻石十年”。

一、双边贸易增速稳居中国主要贸易伙伴前列

2014年，我与东盟进出口总额4803.9亿美元，占我国对外贸易总额的11.2%，同比增长8.3%，高于全国外贸增速4.9个百分点，增速稳居我主要贸易伙伴前列。其中，中国出口2720.7亿美元，进口2083.2亿美元，同比分别增长11.5%和4.4%，中方顺差637.5亿美元，同比增长43.2%。东盟已连续4年成为中国第三大贸易伙伴，东盟是中国第四大出口市场和第二大进口来源地。

2015年1—6月中国东盟双边贸易额为2242.7亿美元，同比增长1.6%，占中国对外贸易份额提高至11.9%。其中，中国出口1346.9亿美元，同比增长9.6%，进口895.8亿美元，下降8.4%。

二、双向投资突破1350亿美元

中方统计，截至2015年6月底，中国与东盟双向投资额累计达1355亿美元。中国企业累计在东盟国家非金融投资总额404.7亿美元，其中2014年新增直接投资58.8亿美元，增长2.5%，2015年1—6月，新增直接投资52.6亿美元；东盟国家来华累计实际投资950亿美元，占中国吸引外资的6%，其中2014年新增实际投资63亿美元，下降24.5%，2015年1—6月，新增实际投资32.6亿美元。

三、工程承包合作蓬勃发展

东盟国家是中国重要的海外承包工程市场和劳务合作市场。截至2015年6月底，中国企业累计在东盟国家签订承包工程合同总金额2134.1亿美元，完成营业额1515.8亿美元。其中，2014年新签合同额270.2亿美元，增长11.4%，完成营业额224.1亿美元，增长6.3%；2015年1—6月，新签合同额142.8亿美元，完成营业额110.2亿美元。2015年6月末，我在东盟国家各类技术劳务人员共约16.4万人。

四、中国—东盟自贸区升级谈判稳步推进

中国—东盟自贸区是我国对外建立的第一个自贸区，中国与东盟十国先后签署《中国—东盟全面经济合作框架协议》（2002年11月）、《货物贸易协议》（2004年11月）、《服务贸易协议》（2007年1月）。2010年，中国—东盟自贸区建成为世界上最大的发展中国家自贸区。2013年10月在第16次中国—东盟领导人会议上，李克强总理倡议打造自贸区升级版。2014年8月，中国—东盟经贸部长会议正式宣布启动升级谈判。中方与东盟方力争于2015年底前完成自贸区升级谈判。

（商务部亚洲司）

中国与新加坡的经济贸易关系

2015年是中新建交25周年，也是新加坡建国50周年。新加坡是世界上重要的金融、航运和贸易中心，具有人才、技术和管理优势，中国正在加快转变经济发展方式，着力提高经济增长的质量和效益，内需市场潜力巨大，双方开展经贸合作具有很多利益会合点，合作前景广阔。中新经贸合作是两国友好合作的重要组成部分，也是深化两国友好关系的重要推动力。中新经贸关系的不断发展不仅给两国和两国人民带来实实在在的利益，也有利于本地区的稳定与繁荣。

近年来，中新双边贸易发展顺畅。双边贸易额由2002年的140.2亿美元增长至2014年的797.4亿美元，年均增长14.3%。2014年，在东盟国家中，新加坡是我第三大贸易伙伴（仅次于马来西亚、越南），双边贸易额为797.4亿美元，增长5%，其中中国出口489.1亿美元，进口308.3亿美元，同比分别增长6.7%和2.4%。2015年1—6月，双边贸易额389.8亿美元，其中中国出口248.3亿美元，同比增长15.7%；进口141.4亿美元，同比下降7%。

中新两国相互投资势头良好。新加坡地理位置优越，基础设施完善，投资环境优良，是中国在东盟第一大投资目的地，新加坡连续两年成为中国最大的外资来源国（按外资来源地划分，2013、2014年新加坡为第三大外资来源地，仅次于香港和英属维尔京群岛）。中方统计，截至2015年6月，中国企业累计对新加坡的非金融类直接投资金额为190.3亿美元。其中，2015年1—6月，中国新增投资31.9亿美元，同比增长365%。中国对新加坡的投资主要集中在能源、矿业、房地产和建筑业、水上运输业。同期，新加坡在中国累计直接投资额752亿美元。新加坡在中国投资主要集中在制造业，主要投资地区为江苏、广东、上海、山东和天津等地区。开发区及园区建设合作是中新经贸合作的一大亮点。苏州工业园和天津生态城进展顺利，已成为中新合作的示范项目。

中新两国经济合作稳步发展。据中方统计，截至2015年6月，中国企业在新加坡累计签订承包工程合同金额292亿美元，完成营业额259亿美元。其中，2015年1—6月，中国在新加坡新签承包工程合同额为9.9亿美元，完成营业额14.8亿美元。新加坡是中国在海外第二大劳务派遣市场，目前在新加坡的各类劳务人员约有9万人。

（商务部亚洲司）

中国与日本的经济贸易关系

2014年世界经济继续缓慢复苏，但势头弱于预期，国际金融市场和大宗商品市场剧烈波动，地缘政治冲突此起彼伏，日元继续大幅贬值。中日关系因领土、历史问题持续低迷。11月，两国就处理和改善中日关系发表四点原则共识，习近平主席在亚太经合组织（APEC）会议期间应约会见日本首相安倍晋三。

一、双边贸易情况

（一）中日贸易统计

2014年中日贸易规模基本与上年持平。据中国海关统计，2014年中日贸易总额为3124.4亿美元，同比下降0.04%，占我国对外贸易总额的7.3%，较上年下降0.2个百分点。其中，我国对日本出口1494.4亿美元，同比下降0.5%，占我出口总额的6.4%；我国自日本进口1630.0亿美元，同比增长0.4%，占我进口总额8.3%；中方逆差135.6亿美元，同比增长13%。在我外贸国别排名中，日本位列美国之后为中国第二大贸易对象国，其中出口仅次于美国，进口仅次于韩国，均排第二位。

据日方统计，2014年日中贸易总额为3091.6亿美元，同比下降0.9%，占日本对外贸易总额的20.5%。其中，日本对中国出口1271.3亿美元，同比下降2.1%，占日本出口总额的18.3%；自中国进口1820.3亿美元，同比下降0.1%，占日本进口总额的22.3%；日方逆差549.0亿美元，同比下降5.0%。日本对华贸易额占日本对外贸易总额的比重较去年上升0.5个百分点。中国仍为日本第一大贸易伙伴和最大进口来源地，中国仅次于美国为日本第二大出口市场。

由于日元大幅贬值，本年度贸易统计受汇率影响较大。双方的美元统计贸易额均是下降，而同期的日元统计则是进出口均大幅增长，并创历史新高。按日方日元统计，2014年日中贸易总额为32.56万亿日元，同比增长7.5%。其中，日本自中国进口19.18万亿日元，同比增长8.6%；对中国出口13.38万亿日元，同比增长6.0%；日方逆差5.79万亿日元，同比增长15.1%。

再看同期中国公布的人民币统计。由于人民币汇率走势基本与美元一致，因此在贸易统计上与美元统计差别不大。按我方人民币统计，2014年中日贸易总额为19213.4亿元，同比下降1%。其中我对日出口9186.5亿元，同比下降1.4%；我自日进口10026.9亿元，同比下降0.5%。

（二）主要进出口商品情况

2014年，中国对日本货物贸易结构进一步优化。从出口商品看，机电产品对日出口805.5亿美元，同比增长2.0%，占我对日出口总额比重升至53.8%；高新技术产品出口398.3亿美元，同比增长2.8%，占比升至26.6%；传统大宗的农产品出口111.3亿美元，同比下降0.9%，占比降至7.4%。其中，主要对日出口商品有：服装及衣着附件出口197.1亿美元，同比下降10.9%，占比13.2%；自动数据处理设备及其部件出口113.3亿美元，同比下降0.2%，占比为7.6%；电话机出口63.3亿美元，同比下降2.0%，占比为4.2%；二极管及类似半导体器件出口53.6亿美元，同比增长50.6%，占比为3.6%；纺织纱线、织物及制品出口48.0亿美元，同比下降1.0%，占比为3.2%；太阳能电池出口44.0亿美元，同比增长57.2%，占比为2.9%；汽车零部件出口35.9亿美元，同比增长11.2%，占比为2.4%。

从进口商品看，机电产品自日进口827.4亿美元，同比下降3.3%，占中国自日本进口总额比重降至63.9%；高新技术产品进口363.7亿美元，同比下降6.5%，占比降至28.1%；贱金属及其制品进口154.5亿美元，同比微降0.1%，占比降至11.9%。其中，主要自日进口商品有：集成电路进口89.1亿美元，同比下降3.3%，占比为6.9%；汽车零配件进口79.7亿美元，同比增长0.4%，占比为6.2%；汽车进口63.9亿美元，同比增长12.2%，占比为4.9%；钢材60.2亿美元，同比增长1.6%，占比为4.7%；计量检测分析自控仪器及器具进口 45.7 亿美元，同比增长 10.4%，占比为 3.5%；液晶显示板进口 36.2 亿美元，同比增长 1.2%，占比为 2.8%；通断保护电路装置及零件 35.4 亿美元，同比增长 3.2%，占比为 2.7%；金属加工机床进口 30.7 亿美元，同比增长 23.5%，占比为 2.4%。

（三）中日技术贸易情况

2014 年，中国与日本签订技术引进合同 1980 份，同比下降 28.3%，合同总金额 53.5 亿美元，同比下降 26%，占我技术引进合同总金额 17%，较上年上升 0.3 个百分点，是我国第三大技术引进来源地，仅次于美国和欧盟。中国自日本引进技术主要集中在交通运输设备制造业、通信设备、计算机及其他电子设备制造业、通用设备制造业、专用设备制造业、电气机械及器材制造业、化学原料及化学制品制造业等。中国自日本技术引进方式主要包括技术咨询和技术服务、专有技术的许可或转让、专利技术的许可或转让等。

二、中日资金合作情况

（一）日本企业对华直接投资

2014 年，日本对华投资出现下降。据中国商务部统计，2014 年日本对华投资项目数 653 个，同比下降 30.8%，实际到位资金 43.3 亿美元，同比下降 38.7%，在国家排名中在新加坡之后位居第二。截至 2014 年底，日本对华投资累计项目数为 49197 个，实际到位金额 986.3 亿美元，是我利用外资最大来源国。

从投资地区分布看，2014 年日本对我国东部、中部和西部地区实际投资额分别为 38.6 亿美元、2.7 亿美元和 1.9 亿美元，比重分别为 89.3%、6.3%、4.4%。从投资行业分布看，日本对华投资仍主要集中在制造业，实际到位金额为 23.4 亿美元，服务、金融等非制造业为 19.8 亿美元，农林牧渔业为 0.1 亿美元，比重分别为 54.2%、45.7%和 0.1%。

（二）中国企业对日直接投资

2014 年，中国企业对日投资大幅上升。据中国商务部统计，2014 年中国非金融类对日本直接投资实际到位金额 2.3 亿美元，同比增长 79.6%。截至 2014 年年底，中国对日本非金融类投资存量为 15.7 亿美元。

（三）中日政府资金合作

根据 2005 年中日双方达成的协议，日本对华提供的日元贷款和大规模无偿援助已于 2008 年基本结束。截至 2014 年底，我国与日本政府签署日元贷款协议金额 30623 亿日元，累计提款 29118 亿日元，累计还本 14391 亿日元，累计计息 8608 亿日元，债务余额 14728 亿日元。截至 2011 年底，中国累计接受日本无偿援助 1423.45 亿日元，用于 148 个项目建设，涉及环保、教育、扶贫、医疗等领域。自 2012 年起，唯一保留的人才培养奖学金项目也已不再使用政府无偿援助资金。

三、中日工程承包和技能实习生合作情况

2014 年中国对日承包工程合同额 2.9 亿美元，完成营业额 3.3 亿美元。截至 2014 年底，中国累计对日承包工程合同额 29.3 亿美元，完成营业额 30.8 亿美元。

日本是中国第一大海外劳务市场。2014 年，中国对日派遣技能实习生 4.8 万人，占当年中国对外劳务派出人员的 16.5%。截至 2014 年底，中国累计对日派出技能实习生 98.5 万人次，2014 年底实际在日技能实习生 15.9 万人，占中国实际在外劳务人员总数的 26.7%，主要分布在日本的中小企业，涉及制造业、农林牧渔和建筑业等。

四、中日主要经贸往来

4 月 14 日，高虎城部长会见了以河野洋平会长为团长的日本国际贸易促进协会访华团。双方就当前形势下的中日经贸合作、中国（上海）自贸试验区等议题交换了意见。

4 月 15 日，高燕副部长陪同汪洋副总理会见以河野洋平会长为团长的日本国际贸易促进协会访华团，双方就中日关系、中日经贸合作等交换了意见。

5 月 17 日，在青岛亚太经合组织贸易部长会议期间，高虎城部长与日本经济产业大臣茂木敏充举行了双边会谈。双方就中日经贸关系以及在多边领域的合作等交换了意见。中国驻世贸组织大使俞建华参加会谈。

7 月 16 日高燕副部长会见了以东海日中贸易中心深谷纮一会长为团长的日本中部经济界代表团，就中日经贸合作等交换意见。

9月23日，高虎城部长出席了商务部以日中经济协会会长张富士夫为团长、日本经济团体联合会会长榊原定征为最高顾问的2014年度日中经济协会访华团座谈会并作主旨演讲。双方分别就推动中日韩自贸区谈判、服务业利用外资发展方向、中国（上海）自由贸易试验区、对外资实行负面清单管理模式、扩大中国对日投资、反垄断执法等各自关心的问题交换了意见。

9月24日，高虎城部长陪同汪洋副总理会见以日中经济协会会长张富士夫为团长、日本经济团体联合会会长榊原定征为最高顾问的2014年度日中经济协会访华团。

11月8日，高虎城部长会见了来华出席亚太经合组织第26届外交和贸易双部长会议的日本经济产业大臣宫泽洋一。双方就中日关系、双边经贸合作、本次会议及区域和多边领域经贸合作等交换了意见。中国驻世贸组织大使俞建华、部长助理王受文参加了会谈。

12月28日，高燕副部长出席第八届中日节能环保综合论坛并致辞，期间会见了来华出席该论坛的日本经济产业省高木阳介经济产业副大臣，双方就中日经贸合作、两部门合作等交换了意见。

（商务部亚洲司）

中国与韩国的经济贸易关系

韩国是东北亚新兴经济体，是中国的重要经贸伙伴。1992年8月，中韩两国正式建立外交关系。建交20多年来，双边经贸关系迅速发展，2014年双边贸易额达2900亿美元，双向投资累计近600亿美元，分别是建交之初的59倍和130倍。2014年7月，习近平主席对韩国进行国事访问。其间，习近平主席与韩国总统朴槿惠举行会晤，就进一步提升双边经贸合作关系进行了深入沟通，达成了广泛共识，取得丰硕成果。

一、中韩双边贸易

据中国海关统计，2014年中韩双边贸易额为2904.9亿美元，同比增长5.9%。其中，中国对韩国出口1003.4亿美元，自韩国进口1901.5亿美元，同比分别增长10.1%和3.9%。中国是韩国第一大贸易伙伴国和第一大出口、进口市场，韩国是中国第三大贸易伙伴国。据韩方统计，2014年，双边贸易额为2354亿美元，同比增长2.8%。其中，韩国对华出口1453.3亿美元，自华进口900.7亿美元，同比分别下降0.4%和增长8.5%。

二、韩国对中国投资

2014年，韩国对中国投资1558个项目，同比增长13.6%；中国实际使用韩资39.7亿美元，同比增长29.8%。截至2014年底，韩国累计对华投资项目数为57782个，实际投资额为599.1亿美元。韩国是中国第三大外资来源国，中国是韩国第二大投资对象国。

三、中国对韩投资

2014年，中国对韩国非金融类直接投资4.94亿美元，同比增长100%。截至2014年，中国累计对韩国非金融类直接投资17.4亿美元。据韩方统计，2014年，中国对韩国投资申报额11.9亿美元，同比增长147%。

四、中韩自贸区谈判进展情况

2010年5月，中韩正式完成历时6年的双边自贸区官产学联合研究，2012年5月双方正式宣布启动谈判。经过14轮谈判，2014年11月，习近平主席与韩国总统朴槿惠在北京共同宣布结束中韩自贸区实质性谈判。2015年6月，双方正式签署中韩自贸协定。协定涵盖货物贸易、服务贸易、投资和规则共17个领域22个章节，包含电子商务、竞争政策、政府采购、环境等“21世纪经贸议题”。

五、中韩雇佣许可制劳务合作

2010年5月，中国商务部和韩国劳动部在首尔签署了《关于启动雇佣许可制劳务合作的谅解备忘录》，就实质性启动中韩雇佣制劳务合作达成共识。2011年10月，中国商务部与韩国劳动部在首尔正式签署了《关于雇佣许可制下输韩劳务人员的谅解备忘录》，为新形势下中韩劳务合作发展奠定了基础。据中国商务部统计，2014年，中国对韩派出各类劳务人员3783名。截至2014年底，中国累计完成对韩工程承包营业额28.2亿美元，在韩劳务人员1.5万名。

（商务部亚洲司）

中国与印度的经济贸易关系

2014年是中印友好年，习近平主席对印度进行了历史性访问，推动中印战略合作伙伴关系进入新的发展阶段。双方工商界积极落实两国领导人达成共识，推动中印在贸易、投资等领域的互利合作取得积极进展。印度已成为中国在南亚地区的第一大贸易伙伴、第一大出口市场、第二大投资目的地和海外主要工程承包市场，中国是印度第一大贸易伙伴、最大的进口来源和第四大出口市场。目前，中印两国在基础设施、信息技术、产业园区等领域的合作不断推进。

一、双边贸易

货物贸易：印度是中国在南亚最大的贸易伙伴。据中国海关统计，2014年，中印贸易额706.1亿美元，同比增长7.8%；其中中国出口542.3亿美元，同比增长11.9%；进口163.8亿美元，同比下降3.8%，中国方顺差378.5亿美元，同比增长20.5%。印度为中国在全球的第六大出口市场。

据印方统计，2014年，印中贸易额716亿美元，同比增长8.5%；其中，印度对中国出口133.2亿美元，同比下降8.3%，自中国进口582.8亿美元，同比增长13.3%。中印贸易额占印外贸总额的9.2%。

中国对印度主要出口商品是钢材、纺织纱线、无线电话、自动数据处理设备、肥料、抗菌素等；自印度主要进口商品是铁矿石、农产品、棉花、铜材、钻石等。

服务贸易：据中方统计，2014年，中印服务进出口总额达29.2亿美元，同比增长4.7%。其中，中国对印服务出口13.6亿美元，同比增长13.6%；进口15.6亿美元，同比下降2.4%；中方服务贸易逆差2亿美元，主要来自运输和其他商业服务。旅游是中国对印度服务顺差最大的类别，顺差4.7亿美元。

二、工程承包

据中国商务部统计，2014年中国企业在印新签工程承包合同额15.7亿美元，同比下降30.9%；完成营业额25.4亿美元，同比下降52%。截至2014年底，中国在印度累计签订承包工程合同额639.7亿美元，完成营业额413.3亿美元，签约项目主要集中于火力发电和通信领域。2006至2011年，印度曾连续六年居中国海外工程承包市场之首。此后，由于印度经济增长放缓、融资难度增大等因素，中国企业在印度工程承包合作大幅下滑，2012年印度在中国海外工程承包市场排名降至第二，2013年后已跌到前十名之外。

三、中国对印度投资

印度是中国在南亚第二大投资对象国，仅次于巴基斯坦。据中国商务部统计，2014年，中国对印度非金融类直接投资流量2.43亿美元，同比增长12.5%；截至2014年底，中国在印度累计直接投资接近27亿美元。

另据印度商工部统计，自2000年4月至2014年底，中国累计对印度直接投资4.54亿美元，占印度利用外资总额的0.2%，在所有国家和地区中排名第28位。

中国对印度投资集中在重型机械、通信、汽车、电子等领域，重点分布在泰米尔纳德邦金奈、马哈拉施特拉邦浦那、安得拉邦海德拉巴、卡纳塔克邦班加罗尔、古吉拉特邦艾哈迈德巴德和巴罗达等地。投资规模较大的企业有北汽福田、徐州工程机械集团、中兴通讯和华为技术有限公司等。

四、印度对中国投资

据中国商务部统计，2014年，印度在中国投资新设企业86家，同比增长30.3%，外资实际到位金额为5075万美元，同比增长87.6%。截至2014年底，印度累计对中国直接投资项目952个，实际投资5.6亿美元，投资领域覆盖金融、软件、高等教育、制药、贸易、钢铁、化工、清洁能源等。代表性企业包括塔塔咨询、印孚瑟斯、马恒达多用途车辆等。此外，迄今共有10家印资银行在中国设立了 4 家分行和 9 个代表处，在华资产总额 27.5 亿元人民币。

五、中印边境贸易

1991 年 12 月、1993 年 9 月和 2006 年 7 月，中印分别开通强拉（利普勒克）山口（中方在西藏的普兰开辟边境贸易市场）、什布奇拉山口和乃堆拉山口边境贸易通道（中方在西藏的亚东县仁青岗，实际在洞青岗开辟边境贸易市场），其中以乃堆拉边贸通道最为重要。但印方于 2006 年单方面宣布了印中边境贸易进出口商品清单，对边贸市场的进出口商品品种做出限制，严重阻碍和限制了边民互市贸易的健康发展，也影响了边贸市场贸易功能的充分发挥。

六、孟中印缅经济走廊

自 1999 年以来，中、印、缅、孟四国在“孟中印缅地区经济合作论坛（BCIM）”框架下开展次区域合作，并于 2011 年 BCIM 第九次会议上就推动构建“昆明—曼德勒—达卡—加尔各答经济走廊”达成共识。2013 年 5 月李克强总理访问印度期间，中印双方共同倡议建设孟中印缅经济走廊。四方于 2013 年建立孟中印缅走廊四国联合工作组，迄今已举行两次会议。

根据设想，该走廊以中国昆明为东端，印度加尔各答为西端，以缅甸曼德勒、孟加拉国达卡为中间节点，连接中国西部和西南部地区、印度东部和东北部地区、缅甸和孟加拉国全境，形成促进沿线及周边地区发展的经济带，实现互利合作、共同发展。该走廊的建设拟主要包括基础设施互联互通、经贸合作、人文交流和地方政府合作等。

（商务部亚洲司）

中国与巴基斯坦的经济贸易关系

巴基斯坦是中国在南亚地区最大的投资目的地、第二大贸易伙伴和海外主要工程承包市场，中国是巴基斯坦第二大贸易伙伴、第二大进口来源地和第四大出口目的地。目前，中巴两国在基础设施建设、能源、水利、农业、矿产、电信等领域的合作不断推进。2014 年 2 月，巴基斯坦总统侯赛因访华，双方发表了两国《关于深化中巴战略与经济合作的联合声明》；4 月，巴基斯坦总理谢里夫来华出席博鳌亚洲论坛 2014 年年会；5 月，侯赛因总统来华出席亚信上海峰会；11 月，谢里夫总理来华出席加强互联互通伙伴关系对话会。

2014 年，双方在贸易、投资等领域的互利合作取得积极进展。

一、双边贸易

据中国海关统计，2014 年中巴双边贸易额为 160.1 亿美元，同比增长 12.6%；其中中国出口 132.5 亿美元，同比增长 20.2%，进口 27.6 亿美元，同比减少 13.8%。中国对巴出口主要商品为电器及电子产品、纺织品、钢材、化工产品、计算机与通信技术等，自巴进口主要商品为棉花、谷物、铜及其制品、矿砂等。

据巴方统计，2013/2014 财年（2013 年 7 月至 2014 年 6 月），中巴双边贸易额 87.1 亿美元，其中巴基斯坦出口 26.9 亿美元，进口 60.2 亿美元。

二、对巴投资

根据商务部投资台账报告，截至 2014 年底，中国对巴基斯坦各类投资存量 60.8 亿美元，其中直接投资 33.5 亿美元（占 55.1%），通过第三地转移投资和境外融资等方式实现的再投资 27.3 亿美元（占 44.9%）。对巴基斯坦投资主要分布在信息传输，软件和信息技术服务业（26.6 亿美元，占 43.8%），采矿业（22.6 亿美元，占 37.2%），建筑业（5.1 亿美元，占 8.4%），电力/热力/燃气及水的生产和供应（1.6 亿美元，占 2.6%）等行业。迄今中国在巴共设立中资企业 109 家，其中中央企业 52 家，地方企业 54 家，金融企业 2 家，个人投资 1 家；年末从业人员 34607 人，其中外籍员工 28514 人（占 82.4%）。

另据巴中央银行 2014 年 7 月发布的 2013/14 财年统计，该财年来自中国的直接投资流量为 7.46 亿美元，无存量统计。

三、工程承包

截至 2014 年底，中国企业在巴累计签订工程承包合同额 332.7 亿美元，完成营业额 279.2 亿美元。2014 年，中国企业在巴新签承包工程合同额 25.5 亿美元，同比减少 53.3%，完成营业额 42.5 亿美元，同比增长 14.7%。中国企业在巴完成的工程项目主要有恰希玛核电站一期和二期、喀喇昆仑公路、瓜达尔港等，在建的主要项目包括恰希玛核电站三期和四期、尼勒姆·杰勒姆电站等。

四、中巴经济走廊

2013 年 5 月李克强总理访问巴基斯坦期间，中巴双方发表联合声明，同意由中国国家发展改革委和巴基斯坦计划委员会就中巴经济走廊成立联合委员会，共同研究制订远景规划。该走廊北起中国新疆喀什，南至巴基斯坦瓜达尔港，覆盖以沿线主要城市和周边地区为关键节点的广大区域。双方将通过加快交通、能源和通信等多种方式的互联互通和产业园区建设，推动相互投资和贸易往来，扩大人文交流，以形成促进沿线地区发展的充满活力的经济带。2013 年 8 月，中巴双方召开了中巴经济走廊联合合作委员会第一次会议。随后，双方又分别召开了交通基础设施、能源、综合规划和瓜达尔港工作组会议。迄今，中巴经济走廊联合合作委员会共召开四次会议。

（商务部亚洲司）

中国与非洲国家的经济贸易关系

2014年，在全球经济增长乏力、大宗商品价格下跌的背景下，中非经贸合作继续表现出良好的发展势头，贸易、投融资、承包工程和互联互通合作不断向前推进，为中非各自的经济发展提供了有力支持。

一、高层互访引领合作升级

2014年，李克强总理成功访问埃塞俄比亚等非洲四国和非盟总部，提出对非合作“六大工程”，打造中非合作升级版。此访正值周恩来总理访非50周年，既是对习主席提出的“真、实、亲、诚”对非工作方针的具体实践，又与周总理对非关系五项立场和对外援助八项原则的一脉相承，指明了未来一个时期对非经贸合作的重点发展方向。年内，俞正声、李源潮等党和国家领导人也相继访非。南非总统祖马、埃及总统塞西等11个非洲国家领导人陆续访华或来华出席活动。通过互访，中非传统友谊不断巩固发展，战略互信进一步增强，为中非经贸合作全面、快速、持续发展夯实了基础。

二、中非合作论坛举措加快落实

2014年是中非合作论坛第五届部长级会议经贸举措落实的关键一年。在中非双方的密切配合和共同努力下，举措落实工作稳步推进。在扩大投融资合作方面，中方承诺的200亿美元融资额度已提前完成，主要用于支持非洲基础设施、农业、制造业和中小企业发展等领域，进一步增强了非洲的自身“造血”能力。在扩大发展援助方面，中国对非援助逐年扩大，援非农业技术中心、“光明行”活动和职业技术培训设施等项目进展顺利，为改善非洲国家民生做出了积极贡献。在支持非洲一体化建设方面，中非跨国跨区域基础设施合作蓬勃开展，推动区域内贸易便利化的合作项目稳步推进，促进了非洲的区域内相互联通融合。

三、政府间合作机制更趋丰富

双边层面，2014年中国与埃塞俄比亚、布隆迪、津巴布韦、刚果（布）、塞内加尔、埃及六国分别召开了新一届经贸联委会，卓有成效地协调推动了双边经贸合作中的重大事项；中国与南非举行了中南联合工作组首次会议，推动两国多双边大项目合作。多边层面，中国还与非盟委员会召开了中非跨国跨区域基础设施建设联合工作组首次会议，双方就开展中非互联互通基础设施合作深入交换了意见，为中国企业参与非洲经济一体化进程搭建了新的平台。

四、对非出口突破千亿美元

2014年中非双边贸易继续保持平稳健康发展，贸易质量日益提高，结构更趋合理。2014年，中非贸易额已到2220亿美元，同比增长5.6%，再创历史新高。其中，中国对非出口首次突破千亿美元大关，达到1062亿美元，同比增长14.4%，高于中国同期外贸出口增速9.5个百分点。技术装备对非出口实现重大突破，中国企业与南非签订机车供货合同，合计将向南非出口总额30亿美元的电力机车，创下了中国高端轨道交通装备整车出口的订单记录。

五、对非投资规模持续扩大

近年来，非洲已成为中国企业海外投资的新兴目的地之一。2014年，中国对非洲非金融类直接投资流量40亿美元，同比增长14%。在非洲兴业的中国企业已超过2500家，涉及金融、电信、能源、制造、农业等诸多领域，为当地直接创造了十余万个就业岗位。制造业和服务业是近年中非投资合作的新亮点，中国企业在工业、金融、科技、电力供应等领域积极开展投资合作，将中国优势产能与非洲实际需要有机对接，积极回应了非洲国家加快工业化进程的迫切诉求，为中非各自经济结构调整和转型做出了积极贡献。

六、承包工程合作增势强劲

非洲是中国企业的第二大海外承包工程市场。

2014 年，中国企业在非洲新签承包工程合同额 755 亿美元，完成营业额 530 亿美元，同比分别增长 11.3%和 10.6%，合作项目涉及公路、铁路、桥梁、港口、水利和电力建设等众多领域。在巩固传统优势的基础上，中国企业积极拓展合作领域，探索和尝试开展项目运营管理，并在参与非洲跨国跨区域基础设施合作方面取得了积极进展。由中国企业承建的肯尼亚蒙巴萨—内罗毕铁路、埃塞俄比亚的斯亚贝巴—吉布提铁路等重大项目已陆续开工建设，有力促进了中国的大型装备、技术和标准走进非洲。

七、区域航空合作拉开帷幕

2014 年 5 月，李克强总理在访非时倡议实施“中非区域航空合作”计划，鼓励和支持有实力的中国航空企业和金融机构，按照市场原则积极参与非洲区域航空业发展，同非方建立合资航空公司，出口民用支线客机，转让成熟适用技术，培训专业航空人才，建设机场、航校、维修中心、客服中心等配套基础设施，共同促进非方航空全产业链的建设和发展。

回顾 2014 年，中非经贸合作规模不断扩大，领域日益广泛，成绩引人注目。随着中非之间的相互需求日益增多，共同利益不断扩大，中非经贸合作正迎来加快发展的战略窗口期。我们应牢牢把握机遇，在习近平主席提出的“真、实、亲、诚”对非工作方针和李克强总理提出的对非合作六大工程的引领下，不断开拓创新，努力推动中非经贸合作不断向更深层次和更高水平发展。

（商务部西亚非洲司）

第六篇　与 WTO 有关的政策与管理措施（2014）

● 贸易政策与管理措施

中国行政审批制度改革

自2013年以来，国务院高度重视行政审批制度改革，将简政放权、放管结合作为“先手棋”，采取了一系列重大举措，推进行政审批制度改革向纵深发展。

一、加大精简行政审批力度，严格控制新设行政许可

（一）加大取消和调整国务院部门行政审批事项力度，彻底废止非行政许可审批

两年多来，国务院决定取消或下放了586项（大项）国务院部门实施的行政审批事项，提前完成了本届政府承诺减少三分之一的目标。工商登记实行“先照后证”，将152项工商登记前置审批改为后置审批。同时，下大决心清理资质资格许可认定和评比达标表彰事项，分四批取消职业资质资格认定211项，取消评比达标项目118项。探索实行工商营业执照、组织机构代码证和税务登记证“三证合一”改革，2015年6月公布了《国务院办公厅关于加快推进“三证合一”登记制度改革的意见》（国办发〔2015〕50号）。

2014年4月发布的《国务院关于清理国务院部门非行政许可审批事项的通知》（国发〔2014〕16号），决定对各部门现有非行政许可审批事项进行清理，不再保留“非行政许可审批”这一审批类别。国务院部门共有非行政许可审批项目453项，2013年和2014年取消了209项。2015年5月，国务院常务会议审议通过了对剩余244项非行政许可审批事项的处理意见，国务院颁布了《关于取消非行政许可审批事项的决定》，决定再取消49项，将84项调整为政府内部管理事项，新设行政许可20项，对于确有工作需要且符合行政许可法规定条件的，依照法定的程序履行新设行政许可程序；将91项调整为需要进一步改革和规范的其他权力。

（二）对中央指定地方实施的行政审批事项进行清理

地方政府实施的行政审批事项中，有些是法律、行政法规或国务院决定设定的，地方无权自行取消。2014年，国务院决定对中央指定地方实施的行政许可项目进行清理。2015年10月公布了《国务院关于第一批取消62项中央指定地方实施行政审批事项的决定》（国发〔2015〕57号），决定取消62项，要求年底前全部取消以部门规章、规范性文件等形式设定的具有行政许可性质的审批事项。

（三）严格控制新设行政许可，防止边减边增

坚决贯彻落实中央关于简政放权、放管结合的改革精神，按照《行政许可法》和《国务院关于严格控制新设行政许可的通知》要求，国务院法制办在起草或者审查法律、法规草案时，对现有和新设行政许可，加强合法性、必要性和合理性审查论证，注重征求各方面的意见，对可以用其他行政管理方式解决的，取消审批；对经过充分论证认为确需保留的审批项目，尽可能限制实施范围，并在立法中明确相关的审批条件和程序。

（四）清理和规范中介服务，防止明减暗增

2015年4月发布的《国务院办公厅关于清理规范国务院部门行政审批中介服务的通知》（国办发〔2015〕31号）决定，对国务院部门行政审批

涉及的中介服务事项进行清理和规范，审批部门所属事业单位、主管的社会组织及其举办的企业，不得开展与本部门行政审批相关的中介服务，审批部门不得以任何形式指定中介服务机构。经过清理，2015 年 10 月，国务院发布《关于第一批清理规范 89 项国务院部门行政审批中介服务事项的决定》（国发〔2015〕58 号），决定第一批清理规范 89 项国务院部门行政审批中介服务事项，不再作为行政审批的受理条件。

二、创新政府管理方式，加强事中事后监督

两年多来，在大力精简行政审批事项的基础上，各地区各部门坚持放管结合，积极创新政府管理方式。

·是在取消、调整行政审批事项时，提出事中报告、事后备案、制定行业从业标准、定期不定期抽查和加大行政问责等事中事后监管措施。

二是完善信用管理体系、建立透明诚信的市场秩序。2014 年 8 月国务院制定《企业信息公示暂行条例》，规定企业注册登记等信息自产生 20 日内必须公示，企业每年报送年度报告并公示，企业未如期公示年度报告或信息不实的将列入“黑名单”。2015 年 10 月国务院发布《国务院关于“先照后证”改革后加强事中事后监管的意见》（国发〔2015〕62 号），明确要求谁审批、谁监管，谁主管、谁监管，按照法律、行政法规、国务院决定，厘清各部门市场监管职责，推进市场监管法治化、制度化、规范化、程序化。

三是实行综合监管和执法，建立统一的监管平台。开展综合执法试点，清理整合各类行政执法队伍，推进跨部门、跨行业综合执法，让几个“大盖帽”合成一个“大盖帽”，形成监管和执法合力。另外，2015 年 6 月《国务院办公厅关于运用大数据加强对市场主体服务和监管的若干意见》（国办发〔2015〕51 号）要求以国家统一的信用信息共享交换平台为基础，运用大数据推动社会信用体系建设，建立跨地区、多部门的信用联动奖惩机制，构建公平诚信的市场环境。

三、及时清理修改有关法律法规

坚持积极稳妥依法推进行政审批制度改革和政府职能转变，按照简政放权、放管结合、优化服务的要求，及时对有关法律、行政法规进行清理修改。

2013 年 3 月以来，全国人大常委会审议修改了 39 部法律，国务院修改了 63 部行政法规、废止 3 部行政法规。督促部门废止或修改相关规章 116 部。清理修改法律法规过程中，坚持职权法定、放管结合、公开透明、法制统一的法治原则。既考虑改革的迫切性，及时破除法律障碍，又维护法律的稳定性和严肃性，尽量避免频繁修法。能合并修改的，尽可能合并修改；可以分步修改的，另行安排修改；对已列入当年立法计划且正在进行全面修改的法律、行政法规，不列入一揽子修改，在全面修改时一并修改；对同一部法律、行政法规设定的审批项目今后还将分批次取消和下放的，待取消和下放工作完成后再统一修改。

（国务院法制办公室　徐志群）

中国海关管理制度

伴随着我国向全球第二大经济体、世界第一货物贸易大国和最大出口国的发展，中国海关管理模式持续更新。2001年，中国海关以现代化为主线，不断推进管理创新，实施建设现代海关制度“两步走”发展战略。第一步发展战略以通关作业改革为突破口，大力推进海关信息化建设，对通关模式、作业流程、资源配置等进行了全面改革，基本实现了中国海关通关管理的“四肢协调”，基本上适应了中国入世和经济全球化带来的挑战和需求。第二步发展战略以建立健全风险管理机制为中心环节，全面协调地推进海关管理的各项改革和建设，基本建立起与社会主义市场经济体制相配套，与国际通行规则相衔接，严密监管与高效运作相结合的现代海关制度，“耳聪目明”的智能型海关初现雏形。2009年，中国海关启动海关大监管体系建设，重点推进实施“三查合一”，将企业稽查、保税中后期核查和减免税核查统一归口管理；发布新修订的《企业分类管理办法》；调整三级海关审批权限等。海关风险式管理思想进一步确立，综合监管模式逐渐形成，海关整体功能得到加强。2011年，中国海关认真贯彻落实国家“十二五”规划，围绕主题主线，提出“把好国门、做好服务、防好风险、带好队伍”的海关工作总体要求。2012年，中国海关深入学习贯彻党的十八大精神，提质增效，稳中求进，建设“学习型、服务型、法治型、创新型、廉洁型”海关。2013年，中国海关以上海自由贸易试验区建设和区域通关一体化等为重点，改革创新，优化机制，强化准军事化海关纪律部队建设。2014年，中国海关主动把握和积极适应新常态，坚决贯彻落实中央决策部署，全面深化改革创新，自觉践行“三严三实”，坚持抓好协同治理，在提高海关管理水平方面主要做了如下工作：

一、全面落实十八届三中全会《决定》部署的改革任务

（一）完成《落实“三互”推进大通关建设改革方案》起草，口岸大通关管理体制机制不断优化

海关总署会同国家发改委、交通运输部、商务部、质检总局等部门，在综合吸纳各方意见和建议的基础上，完成了改革方案的研究起草工作。2014年12月，国务院印发《落实“三互”推进大通关建设改革方案》（国发〔2014〕68号文，以下简称《大通关方案》）。改革方案从强化协作机制入手，通过推进国际贸易“单一窗口”建设、建立健全信息共享共用机制等，解决部门之间信息孤岛问题，实现“信息互换”；通过推行“一站式作业”、推动一体化通关管理、打造高效的口岸通关模式等，提升口岸通关效能，实现“监管互认”；通过整合监管设施资源、建立安全联合防控机制等，发挥监管合力，实现“执法互助”。对机制优化难以解决的问题，探索行政执法权相对集中行使和跨部门联合执法，开展综合执法试点。《大通关方案》从强化跨部门合作、跨地区协作、国际合作三个维度入手，实现全方位、立体化、网络化的互联互通，推进大通关、畅通大通道，真正做到“关通天下”，力争到2020年，形成既符合中国国情又具有国际竞争力的大通关管理体制机制。2014年，海关总署协同有关部门，先后实施了上海洋山保税港区国际贸易“单一窗口”试点、全面推广关检合作“三个一”等改革项目，在落实“三互”推动大通关建设方面取得了先行先试的改革成效。

（二）制定《海关全面深化改革总体方案》，不断提高海关治理体系和治理能力现代化水平

在深入开展内外部调研、广泛征求意见的基础上，2014年11月6日，海关总署党组印发《海关全面深化改革总体方案》（署党发〔2014〕35号）。总体目标是：建设中国特色社会主义海关，以构建一体化通关管理格局为抓手，转变职能实现方式，创新组织管理，打造在国际上最具竞争力的、先进的海关监管机制，促进贸易安全与便利，推进海关治理体系和治理能力现代化。构建一体化通关管理格局的具体路径是通关流程再造和机构重组，结构支撑是“两个中心、三项制度”。“两个中心”是风险防控中心和税收征管中心，风险防控中心侧重安

全准入风险防控、税收征管中心侧重税收风险防控。“三项制度”是指：(1) 实施货物通关“一次申报、分步处置”，实现安全准入风险甄别和税收征管作业相对分离；(2) 改革税收征管方式，推动税收要素审查由集中在进出口通关环节向全过程转变，由逐票审查确定向抽查审核转变，实行企业自报、自缴税款，缴税后自行打印税单；(3) 建设功能型海关，优化口岸海关和属地海关专业分工，强化通关监管、稽查、缉私三支执行力量，各有侧重地做好现场实际监管、后续监管和合规管理、打击走私违法活动等工作，切实增强协同监管合力。为确保各项改革扎实推进，以 2015 年、2017 年、2020 年为时间节点，对 45 大类改革任务，制定并下发了任务分解表。2014 年，开展区域通关一体化（京津冀、长三角和广东地区海关）改革，为构建一体化通关管理格局探索经验；海关监控指挥中心开始建设并在部分海关投入使用，为“两个中心”的建设提供了有力支撑；试点集中汇总征税，在保证税收安全的前提下，帮助企业降低贸易成本，在改革税收征管方式方面取得先行先试。同时，加快先期已开展的通关无纸化、完善海关企业信用管理制度、创新加工贸易和保税监管模式、改革统计监测预警体系、建设海关情报系统等各项改革，逐步推进建立集约化、信息化、职能化海关监管管理体制。

（三）完成《加快海关特殊监管区域整合优化改革方案》初步设计，海关特殊监管区域整合优化全面提速

海关总署会同国家发展改革委、财政部、国土资源部等 11 部委，研究形成了《加快海关特殊监管区域整合优化改革方案（征求意见稿）》的初步设计，提出推进海关特殊监管区域类型、存量、政策、管理“四个整合”及产业结构、贸易形式、业务功能、监管模式“四个优化”。通过推行“创新制度、统一类型、拓展功能、规范管理”四大改革，破除影响海关特殊监管区域向高端制造、销售、结算、物流、研发、维修转型的政策障碍，推动对内对外开放相互促进、货物贸易服务贸易融合发展、内陆沿海开放同步推进。2014 年 8 月，召开全国加快海关特殊监管区域整合优化推进工作会议，对达成共识的改革事项，先行启动实施。截至 2014 年底，先后启动了昆明等 7 个出口加工区转型升级为综合保税区工作；在北京、南京、成都等 8 个海关先行试点了区区、区港间保税货物流转“分送集报、自行运输”；开展企业自产产品返区维修、利用已解除海关监管的设备承接境内外委托加工等改革试点。这一系列改革措施有力提升了海关特殊监管区域发展内生动力，充分发挥了海关特殊监管区域在对外开放中的引擎作用，海关特殊监管区域正在成为进一步扩大开放、经济结构的战略性调整以及区域协调发展战略的重要载体。

此外，对参与的“推进丝绸之路经济带、海上丝绸之路建设”“建立健全社会征信体系，褒扬诚信，惩戒失信”等 9 项改革任务，海关总署通过制定完善相关管理办法、参与相关研究研提意见、积极参与各类自贸协定谈判等方式，配合做好相关改革任务的落实，助力其他部门各项管理制度不断优化。

二、扎实推进重点改革项目，海关管理制度建设迈出新步伐

（一）深化区域通关一体化改革，大力支持国家战略实施

大力支持“一带一路”、京津冀协同发展、长江经济带等国家战略实施，按照“试点先行、逐步推广”的原则，主动打破关际藩篱，再造通关管理流程，先后推进实施了京津冀、长江经济带、广东地区海关的区域通关一体化改革。7 月 1 日京津冀海关区域通关一体化改革在京津地区启动，成为率先落实京津冀区域协同发展重要国家战略的举措。长三角、广东地区海关于 9 月 22 日正式启动区域通关一体化改革，当日石家庄海关亦加入京津冀海关区域通关一体化。此项改革，通过建立区域通关中心，打造统一的申报平台、风险防控平台、专业审单平台、现场作业平台（简称“一中心、四平台”），形成监管更加严密、通关更加便捷、流程更加科学、运转更加高效，覆盖区域通关全流程的一体化管理机制和运作模式。目前，全国 80%以上进出口贸易可享受区域通关一体化的改革成果，区域海关间互联互通，企业可以自主选择申报、纳税、验放地点，让跨关区通关更便捷、物流顺畅，实现了“多地通关，如同一关”。

（二）持续创新上海自贸试验区海关监管制度，全面部署复制推广工作

以上海自贸试验区为海关监管创新的试验田，

先后实施了先进区后报关、保税展示交易、期货保税交割、融资租赁、内销选择性征税、集中汇总纳税等23项制度创新。2014年，上海自贸试验区内进口平均通关时间较区外减少41.3%，出口平均通关时间较区外减少36.8%。全年自贸区进出口货值7623.8亿元，增长8.3%，增速高于全国平均3.7个百分点；累计征税入库695.95亿元，增长7.99%，实现了贸易量、税收、监管质量、通关效率的同步增长。同时，按照中央"形成可复制可推广经验"的要求，坚持"试在上海，意在全国"，"成熟一批、推广一批"，全面部署复制推广工作。目前，17项制度创新已在全国复制推广，其他项目已经在长江经济带51个海关特殊监管区域复制。近期，由多家政府部门、专业机构、企业共同参与推荐评审的"中国（上海）自由贸易试验区企业创新案例"，海关监管服务制度创新案例有9个，占总数的45%。

（三）建立口岸工作部际联席会议机制，口岸管理制度改革取得新突破

2014年召开了全国口岸工作座谈会，汪洋副总理出席会议做重要指示，明确了未来一段时期口岸工作的思路和任务。海关总署牵头口岸有关部门共同研究，形成了加强口岸工作的若干意见报国务院审批。建立了口岸工作部际联席会议机制，国家口岸办牵头协调作用进一步发挥，和谐口岸建设迈出新步伐。口岸布局逐步优化，年内批准对外开放或扩大开放17个口岸。口岸基础设施建设得到改善，口岸通行能力稳步提升。口岸国际合作交流不断深化。截至2014年年底，与毗邻的11个国家和地区签署、修订了双边政府间边境口岸开放及其管理制度协定，与俄罗斯、哈萨克斯坦等国建立了口岸协作和交流机制，开通了中哈巴克图口岸农产品快速通关"绿色通道"，中欧海关"安智贸"，AEO国际互认等项目有序推进。国际贸易"单一窗口"试点稳步推广，2014年6月选择上海洋山保税港区，启动国际贸易"单一窗口"试点，传统的"串联式"口岸通关流程变为一次性、同步化的"并联式"流程，改革后的申报业务归类成103项，其中涉及海关35项、检验检疫36项，双方共有的32项，减少了三分之一的重复录入，最大限度地减少了企业多头申报，促进贸易便利，提升通关效率。

（四）反走私综合治理体制机制逐步完善，始终保持打私高压态势

服务国家整体安全战略，构建海关风险防控体系，加强对进出境活动安全态势的前瞻性研究和风险研判，统一实施全国进出境领域安全风险整体防控和监控指挥。充分发挥海关关境保护作用，严厉打击重点商品涉税走私，规范进出口贸易秩序；有力应对毒品、枪支弹药、"洋垃圾"等走私，侵权商品跨境流动，以及进出境环节暴力恐怖主义等方面的非传统安全威胁。充分发挥地方政府和打私办在打击走私中的基础作用和协调能力，反走私综合治理体制机制逐步完善，协作配合长效机制进一步健全。集中力量针对北部湾等重点地区和农产品等重点商品开展专项打击，主要办案指标再创历史新高。全年立案侦办走私犯罪案件2275起，案值668.94亿元，涉嫌偷逃税额124.58亿元，分别增长10.4%、65.5%和61.4%。破获涉嫌偷逃税额千万元以上重特大走私犯罪案件170起，增长1.1倍。严厉打击毒品、武器弹药、有害废物、濒危物种等走私违法活动，查获毒品4.4吨，查扣进境"洋垃圾"19.2万吨，是2013年的3.3倍。

三、加大简政放权力度，加快职能实现方式转变，为企业减负增效

（一）进一步加大行政审批制度改革力度

2014年，海关总署进一步加大了行政审批制度改革力度，大力推进"管、减、简、便"（有效监管、减少审批、简化手续、通关便利），将原定于2015年取消、下放的行政审批事项调整至2014年执行，共调整13项行政审批事项，其中拟取消7项、拟调整为政府内部审批事项3项、下放2项、拟调整为新设行政许可事项1项。截至2014年底，共取消、下放行政审批事项数量达16项，占审批事项总数的76%，超额完成了国务院设定的重点部门50%的清理目标。海关的简政放权激发了市场主体活力，取得了突出成效。例如，取消"报关员资格核准"审批事项，降低了就业门槛；取消加工贸易"外发加工"审批，跨关区外发加工不再收取保证金，减轻了企业负担。同时，积极开展取消、下放行政审批事项对应法律法规的修改工作，协助全国人大常委会和国务院法制办修改《海关法》和《进出口关税条例》，对行政审批制度改

革所涉23部海关规章进行集中修订。在此基础上，自我加压，认真开展了简化海关内部核批手续等相关工作，重点简化行政审批管理事项对应的海关内部核批，精简管理层级，实现“权力清单”管理，公布海关28类377个执法行为，出台自由裁量权规制办法，提高贸易政策透明度，最大限度消除审批“灰色地带”。坚持放管并重，通过强化和完善海关监管措施，加强事中事后监管。

（二）多措并举支持外贸稳定增长

一是公布了《关于支持外贸稳定增长的若干措施》，从抓改革、减负担、促升级、优环境4个方面，将国务院支持外贸稳定增长的若干意见中涉及海关工作的政策举措进行细化。二是全面推进关检合作“三个一”。在原有试点扩大到天津、上海等8个省区市17个直属海关56个现场的基础上，年内将“三个一”全面推行到全国所有直属海关和检验检疫部门、所有通关现场、所有依法需要报关报检的货物和物品。通过实施“三个一”，企业可减少30%的重复申报项目，节省25%～30%的申报时间，查验时间及费用均节省近半。三是深化通关无纸化改革。将通关无纸化范围扩大至全国所有通关现场和海关业务领域，使企业足不出户就可以完成报关。2014年无纸通关报关单占同期报关单总数的82.99%。四是降低查验率，提高海关查验效能。在有效监管的前提下，将出口货物查验率从5.5%调整为4%，对诚信守法企业适用较低查验率，同时增配大型集装箱检查设备（H986），提高非侵入式查验比例，增强查验的针对性，节约企业通关时间和费用。五是完善海关企业信用管理制度。取消信用评定的规模门槛，让更多诚信守法的中小微企业享受通关便利。六是促进跨境贸易电子商务健康发展。加快海关与电子商务信息平台对接，支持跨境电子商务进出境商品集中报关、纳税等。七是围绕我国外贸形势加强分析研究和统计监测，及时反映外贸发展变化，发布人民币计价统计数据和中国外贸先导指数。八是对现有涉及海关事业单位及其经济实体和社会团体的经营服务性收费项目开展全面清理，重点清理贴着海关执法的强制性收费和披着市场外衣的垄断性收费。

（三）围绕提升全面履职能力，加快配套改革

一是加强内部控制和管理。整合“瘦身”内控节点，结合行政审批项目取消下放等改革措施及通关流程优化的需要，精简、优化海关内部多层级审批的节点77个。梳理公布《海关行政职权目录表》，向社会公开海关85项执法权的具体内容和法律依据，推动阳光执法。规范自由裁量权，坚持惩治腐败“零容忍”，强化“一案双查”。二是加大科技投入和应用。加快推进金关工程（二期）建设，大力推动全国海关监控指挥、进出口领域企业诚信管理系统等重点改革项目建设，加强大数据、云计算、物联网、移动互联网等新技术应用。三是推进“瘦上强下”，优化资源配置。从总署机关选派占总数7%的人员到基层，从各直属海关机关调剂1000余人到一线，实行动态综合理编，探索综合保障一体化，建立人力资源跨关区调配和对口支援机制。四是继续实施“人才强关”战略，加强队伍业务知识技能培训与实践，推进海关专家制度扩大试点，拓宽人才成长渠道。完善干部考核评价机制，加大从基层一线提拔领导干部的力度。

（海关总署）

中国关税政策

中国关税政策包括进出口征税政策和减免税政策。2014年，中国海关共征收进出口关税2843.4亿元，进口环节税14425.3亿元，分别增长8.1%和3%。

进口关税设置最惠国税率、协定税率、特惠税率、普通税率、关税配额税率等税率。出口关税设置出口税率。对进出口货物在一定期限内可以实行暂定税率。

对进口货物需采取反倾销、反补贴、保障措施的，按照有关法律、行政法规的规定适用其税率。另外，对国家决定征收报复性关税的进口货物，适用报复性关税税率。

有关关税政策如下：

（1）履行入世承诺，约束性降税已完成。

2001年中国入世后，为履行降税承诺，经过几年的约束性降税，我国进口关税水平（最惠国税率算术平均税率）大幅降低，全部完成了入世承诺的降税义务。目前进口关税依据《中华人民共和国进出口税则》征收，税则共分为21类97章，共计8277个税号。2014年我国关税总水平为9.8%，其中农产品平均税率为15.1%，工业品平均税率为8.9%。如考虑到进口商品结构，进口征税货物关税加权平均税率约为3.25%。

（2）发挥税收调节作用，自主实施暂定税率。

暂定税率是国家对部分进出口货物实行的一种临时性进出口关税税率。一般根据国民经济发展的实际需要和进出口关税税率的总体调整情况，对部分进出口货物实行暂定税率，以更有效地发挥关税在提高国内竞争能力、促进企业技术进步、保障经济运行等方面的作用。2014年对767个8位税号商品实行进口暂定税率。

（3）发挥关税保护作用，抵制不正当竞争，主动实施特保措施。

反倾销税、反补贴税、保障措施关税、报复性关税等贸易救济措施是进口国在遭遇贸易冲击时或遭受歧视性贸易待遇时所采取的世界贸易组织允许的贸易保护手段。2014年我国共发布涉及反倾销和反补贴的公告共18个，主要涉及化工、造纸、光伏、钢铁等行业。

（4）促进对外经济、外交关系发展，开展多边贸易合作，实行协定税率和特惠税率。

我国目前已与23个国家（地区）签署了贸易或关税优惠协定，对有关国家或地区实施协定税率。同时，主动对老挝等东南亚3国，苏丹等非洲30国，也门等7国，共40个联合国认定的最不发达国家，实施特惠税率。

（海关总署）

中国关税政策

2014年，中国关税政策坚持稳中求进工作总基调，统筹国内国际两个大局，落实积极的财政政策，充分发挥关税职能作用，以科学发展、公平统一为目标，完善关税税收制度，优化进口税收政策体系，推动建设公平竞争的市场体系，促进经济转型升级；坚持互利共赢、互联互通，积极稳妥地做好关税谈判工作，推动自由贸易区建设取得新成果，增强国际经贸领域话语权，促进国际经贸合作；果断实施贸易救济措施，维护公平的贸易环境。一年来，关税工作有序开展、成效显著，为推动对外贸易平衡发展、加快转变经济发展方式、促进经济社会持续健康发展做出了积极贡献。2014年，全国海关征收关税和进口环节税17267.6亿元，同比增长3.8%，比全年17740亿元预算额短收472.4亿元。其中，征收关税2843.2亿元，增长8.1%；征收进口环节税14424.4亿元，增长3.0%。进出口税收约占中央一般公共财政收入的26.8%。

一、完善进出口税则体系，支持国内经济社会发展

（一）积极发挥进口关税的导向信号作用

1. 继续对部分产品实施较低的进口暂定税率

为满足国内生产和人民群众生活需要，继续通过暂定税率的方式，积极鼓励先进技术设备、关键零部件和能源原材料进口，适度支持一般消费品进口，2015年1月1日起，共对740多项商品实施低于最惠国税率的进口暂定税率。其中，新增和进一步降低税率水平的商品主要包括：光通信用激光器等有关先进技术设备、关键零部件以及基础性原材料，电动汽车用电子控制制动器等有利于节能减排的环保技术和设备，乙烯等国内生产所需的能源资源性产品，降脂原料药等与百姓生活密切相关的药品、日用品等。

2. 视市场变化提高部分产品税率水平

根据产业发展和市场供需变化情况，对部分国内已能生产，且数量、质量可以满足需求或市场价格已发生较大变化的产品进行反向调整，即提高税率水平。一是对汽车收音机等产品不再执行暂定税率，恢复实施最惠国税率；二是在原暂定税率基础上，对柴油发动机等产品适当提高暂定税率水平。

（二）主动调整出口关税政策

1. 取消部分具有一定加工深度产品的出口关税

随着我国产业结构不断调整，产品升级逐步推进，目前加征出口关税的产品中有部分已通过技术进步提升了附加值，为此，2015年将取消10项具有一定加工深度产品的出口关税，如钢铁颗粒粉末、个别无机化合物等。

2. 研究调整化肥出口关税

随着国内化肥产业的扩张发展，近年来氮磷肥市场由供需平衡转为产能严重过剩，而目前实施的季节性出口关税存在淡季外商压低我国出口价格，旺季国内供过于求，客观上刺激化肥过度使用，加剧土地面源污染等问题。对此，我国坚持实事求是原则，兼顾农业生产需要和化肥行业利益，协调上下游行业意见，对化肥出口关税进行了较大调整。2015年1月1日起，继续对化肥征收出口关税，但对尿素、磷酸铵等品种不再采取季节性措施，比照其他氮磷肥统一按5%税率征收出口关税。其中，鉴于尿素、磷酸铵出口量较大，为便于操作，经折算分别按80元/吨和100元/吨从量计征。

（三）研究调整重点产品进出口关税

1. 研究调整煤炭进出口关税

在国内煤炭市场供需关系发生逆转的情况下，为支持煤炭行业脱困、促进煤炭行业健康发展，研究提出了调整煤炭进出口关税的方案。经国务院批准，2014年10月15日起，取消了无烟煤、炼焦煤等5个煤炭品种的零进口暂定税率，分别恢复实施3%到6%不等的最惠国税率；2015年1月1日起，将煤炭产品的出口关税由10%统一降至3%。

2. 适当上调天然橡胶进口关税

受国际市场天然橡胶供过于求、国内外市场需求放缓影响，天然橡胶价格持续走低，国内橡胶生

产困难。为保护国内橡胶产业，同时兼顾轮胎等用胶行业利益，在多次协调部门意见、测算评估政策调整对上下游行业影响的基础上，适当上调了天然橡胶进口关税。

二、落实完善进口税收政策，支持经济结构调整

（一）支持科技创新和产业结构调整

1. 适时调整完善重大技术装备进口税收政策

为提高我国装备制造业核心竞争力和自主创新能力，会同有关部门对重大技术装备进口税收政策有关规定和目录进行了调整。自2014年3月1日起，将国家支持发展的页岩气钻探设备、湿式电除尘器等环保装备纳入重大技术装备进口税收政策支持范围，剔除了工程机械、轨道交通装备等国内已能生产的零部件及原材料。此外，将国家支持发展的民用飞机及发动机、机载设备纳入政策支持范围，支持我国航空制造业的发展。2014年，共计200多家企业享受了重大技术装备进口税收政策，有力地促进了国内装备制造业的发展。

2. 调整完善新型显示器件进口税收政策

为鼓励新型显示器件产业的发展，提高国内企业的自主创新能力，根据国内产业发展需要，及时调整了偏光片生产企业进口原材料免税清单；完成了新型显示器件新申请企业的免税资格认定工作；向国务院上报了重庆和江苏两个新型显示器件项目进口设备享受分期纳税政策的请示，并已获国务院批准。

3. 出台租赁企业进口飞机有关税收政策

为贯彻《国务院办公厅关于加快飞机租赁业发展的意见》（国办发〔2013〕108号）要求，促进飞机租赁业健康发展，提升航空服务能力，自2014年1月1日起，国内租赁企业一般贸易项下进口飞机并租给国内航空公司使用的，享受与国内航空公司进口飞机同等税收优惠政策，即进口空载重量在25吨以上的飞机减按5%征收进口环节增值税。

（二）积极支持农业农村发展

1. 落实支持农业发展的进口税收优惠政策

为支持发展优质高产农林业，会同有关部门制定了农业部、国家林业局2014年进口种子种源免征进口环节增值税政策；为支持地方发展特色农业，提高农民收入，会同有关部门制定了云南省2014年进口花卉种球种苗种籽免税政策；为巩固禁毒成果，会同商务部拟订了2014年度罂粟替代种植项下返销产品进口税收优惠政策，下发了两批免税品种和免税数量，并研究确定了替代种植项下免征出口关税的化肥数量，以促进边疆民族地区经济合作和社会稳定。

2. 研究加强大米进口管理

目前，我国稻谷和大米国家标准对籼米和粳米缺乏量化区分指标，海关在进口报验环节难以辨别。为加强大米进口管理，打击大米非法走私，在研究大米国际标准的基础上，提出了适合海关操作的籼米、粳米区分建议。

（三）丰富国内能源供应

1. 研究完善天然气进口税收政策

为鼓励使用清洁能源，促进节能减排，2014年继续对国家准许项目进口天然气实施按比例返还进口环节增值税的优惠政策，同时对政策进行了完善：根据发展改革委对天然气销售定价的调整情况，研究提出了政策调整思路，将全国天然气价格总体涨幅视为“西气东输”天然气价格涨幅，并据此调整了政策规定的国家天然气销售定价，从而较好地解决了天然气价格调整与现有政策的衔接问题。根据我国天然气进口快速增长的情况，对享受政策的具体项目、相应企业名单和部分项目进口规模进行了调整。

2. 落实自俄进口电力税收优惠政策

中俄能源合作是中俄战略协作伙伴关系中的重要组成部分，国家电网公司自俄进口电力项目已纳入两国政府能源合作框架。2014年，继续实施对自俄进口电力实施按比例返还进口环节增值税的税收政策。该政策落实了中俄两国达成的能源合作的共识，将进一步促进自俄进口电力。

3. 恢复执行石油（天然气）进口物资税收政策

为支持海上油气资源特别是深海资源开发，自2014年1月1日起，恢复执行中石油、中石化、中海油等三大石油公司勘探开发特殊地区石油（天然气）进口物资免税政策，但对国内已能自主生产但性能不能满足要求的勘探开发物资免税进口从紧控制。

（四）支持教科文等社会事业发展

1. 研究调整科教用品和科技开发用品进口税收政策

为满足科研和科技开发工作的现实需要，建议取消对非医药类院校、专业和非医药类科学研究、科技开发机构免税进口医疗检测、分析仪器及其附件的限制，并提出在适当放宽“事前”准入条件的同时，加强“事中、事后”监管，建立备案核查制度。有关建议已获国务院批准。

2. 全面落实重大科技专项进口税收政策

组织完成了 7 个进口科技重大专项 2014—2016 年免税进口物资需求清单评审，并印发了 2014—2016 年度的进口物资清单和执行方案。

3. 研究出台政策支持鲁甸地震灾后恢复重建

自 2014 年 8 月 3 日起，对受灾地区企业、单位或支援受灾地区重建的企业、单位，在 3 年内进口国内不能满足供应并直接用于灾后恢复重建的大宗物资、设备等，给予进口税收优惠。此外，支持设立政府间国际组织，研究办理了在我国境内设立政府间国际组织有关关税豁免事项。

三、调整规范区域税收政策，支持深化改革、扩大开放

（一）制定落实自贸试验区税收政策

1. 认真做好中国（上海）自由贸易试验区相关工作

围绕制度创新，总结评估中国（上海）自由贸易试验区（以下简称上海自贸试验区）政策执行情况，为全面深化改革和扩大开放探索可复制、可推广的经验，促进投资和贸易便利化。同时，对上海自贸试验区进一步深化改革开放所涉及的货物状态分类监管、国际船舶登记制度创新等问题进行了认真研究。此外，还参与研究了上海自贸试验区扩展区域相关问题。

2. 参与制订广东、天津、福建三地自由贸易试验区具体方案

按照符合税制改革方向和国际惯例，不形成“税收洼地”，成本和风险可控，可复制可推广等原则，对广东、天津、福建三地自由贸易试验区具体方案中涉及的税收政策问题进行了研究，并就试验区内不同区块的税收政策问题提出了原则性意见。

（二）推进海关特殊监管区域整合优化

1. 牵头研究规范海关特殊监管区域税收政策

对现行政策进行了梳理，对存在的主要问题进行了分析，撰写了《我国海关特殊监管区域发展情况及有关政策建议》。参与《加快海关特殊监管区域整合优化改革方案》和《海关特殊监管区域设立审核工作若干规范》的具体制定工作，就增强海关特殊监管区域设立审核的科学性和可操作性等问题研究提出了意见。

2. 开展调整相关税收规定促进贸易多元化的试点

牵头会同相关部门对促进海关特殊监管区域贸易多元化的问题进行了深入研究，并经国务院批准，印发了在苏州工业园综合保税区、重庆两路寸滩保税港区开展调整相关税收规定促进贸易多元化试点有关政策问题的通知。

3. 规范船舶、飞机进口有关税收政策

为维护税收政策的权威性和严肃性，增强行业政策之间的协调性，对船舶、飞机进口有关税收政策进行了规范，明确海关特殊监管区域的进口保税政策不适用于并不能实际入区、直接服务于海关特殊监管区域内经营活动的进境船舶，海关特殊监管区域内租赁企业从境外购买并租给国内航空公司使用的、空载重量在 25 吨以上、不能实际入区的飞机，不实施进口保税政策，减按 5%征收进口环节增值税。

（三）取消加工贸易项下进口钢材保税政策

为落实公平税赋政策，会同有关部门首批对国内完全能够生产、质量能够满足下游加工企业需要的 78 个税号的钢材产品，取消加工贸易项下进口钢材保税政策，自 2015 年 1 月 1 日起征收关税和进口环节税。

四、有效落实关税优惠协定，促进双边和区域经贸合作

依据我国与有关国家或地区签署的自由贸易协定或关税优惠协定，2014 年 1 月 1 日起，继续对原产于东盟各国、智利、巴基斯坦、新西兰、秘鲁、哥斯达黎加、韩国、印度、斯里兰卡、孟加拉等国家的部分进口产品实施协定税率，产品范围进一步扩大，部分税率水平进一步降低；在内地与香港、澳门更紧密经贸关系安排框架（CEPA）下，

对原产于港澳地区且已制定优惠原产地标准的产品实施零关税。根据海峡两岸经济合作框架协议（ECFA）早期收获计划的安排，对原产于台湾地区的部分产品实施零关税；继续对原产于老挝、苏丹等40个最不发达国家的部分产品实施特惠税率，并扩大对塞拉利昂等5个国家的特惠税率商品范围。2014年7月1日起，正式实施《中国—瑞士自由贸易协定》和《中国—冰岛自由贸易协定》关税减让方案。

五、妥善应对贸易摩擦，维护公平贸易环境

一是决定对原产于美国、韩国和欧盟的进口多晶硅，原产于美国、加拿大和巴西的进口浆粕，原产于印度的进口特丁基对苯二酚，原产于印度的进口单模光纤，原产于欧盟和美国的进口高温承压用合金钢无缝钢管以及原产于欧盟和美国的进口四氯乙烯等6项产品征收反倾销税。二是决定对原产于美国和欧盟的进口多晶硅征收反补贴税。三是决定对原产于日本、新加坡、韩国和台湾地区的进口丙酮在反倾销措施期终复审后继续征税。四是决定对原产于美国、意大利、英国、法国和台湾地区的进口聚酰胺—6，6切片，原产于美国、韩国、日本、俄罗斯和台湾地区的进口聚氯乙烯，以及原产于韩国、欧盟和美国的进口己二酸等3项产品在反倾销期终复审期间继续征收反倾销税。五是调整了原产于美国的进口白羽肉鸡适用的反倾销税税率。

（财政部关税司）

中国海关估价制度

中国于 2001 年 12 月 11 日正式成为世界贸易组织（WTO）的第 143 个成员。中国“入世”给海关带来的最直接影响就是《WTO 估价协定》的全面实施。2001 年以来，中国海关根据《WTO 估价协定》要求，从估价理念到估价方法、程序等方面进行了全方位深层次的改革，已实现了与国际惯例的接轨。

一、海关估价法律体系

中国目前的审价立法可以划分为三个层次：

第一个层次是《中华人民共和国海关法》第 55 条，“进出口货物的完税价格，由海关以该货物的成交价格为基础审查确定。成交价格不能确定时，完税价格由海关依法估定。”在法律层次上已经实现了和《WTO 估价协定》的衔接。

第二个层次是《中华人民共和国关税条例》（以下简称《关税条例》）。2004 年开始实施的新《关税条例》作为《海关法》的配套法规，对估价定义、估价方法、估价程序等均根据《WTO 估价协定》要求进行了修订。

第三个层次是《中华人民共和国海关审定进出口货物完税价格办法》（以下简称《审价办法》）。《审价办法》是《WTO 估价协定》在中国估价法律体系中最直接的体现，完整准确地体现了《WTO 估价协定》的有关规定。

二、海关估价原则

（一）以货物的成交价格为估价准则

货物的成交价格是中国海关估价的基本准则。进口货物的成交价格估价方法是《WTO 估价协定》所规定的六种估价方法的第一种，也是最重要和最基本的一种估价方法。它是建立在进口货物实际交易价格基础上的一种估价方法，也是在估价实践中使用率最高的一种估价方法。

确定进口货物成交价格的步骤依次是：审查构成成交价格的各种要素是否成立（销售、实付应付、该货物），审查进口货物是否符合 4 项条件（限制、不确定因素、转售收益、特殊关系），审查是否有必要根据销售情况对有关价格因素进行合理调整。

（二）其他估价方法

中国海关的估价方法与《WTO 估价协定》一致，除成交价格方法外，其他依次适用的估价方法有：

1. 相同或类似货物成交价格方法

相同货物成交价格方法是指海关无法按成交价格方法确定进口货物完税价格时，将以被估货物同时或大约同时向中华人民共和国境内销售的相同货物的成交价格为基础确定该进口货物完税价格的估价方法。这是按顺序使用的第二种估价方法。

类似货物成交价格方法是指海关无法按成交价格方法和相同货物成交价格方法确定进口货物完税价格时，将以被估货物同时或大约同时向中华人民共和国境内销售的类似货物的成交价格为基础确定该进口货物完税价格的估价方法。这是按顺序使用的第三种估价方法。

2. 倒扣方法

倒扣方法是以进口货物、相同或类似进口货物在被估货物进口时或大约同时，按进口时的状态在境内第一销售环节，以最大总量单位售予境内无特殊关系方的单价为基础估定完税价格，是第四种估价方法。采用倒扣方法估价通常的步骤是：一是确定倒扣方法的基础价格，即确定转售价格；二是扣除有关的税费。

3. 计算方法

计算方法是指在普遍接受的会计原则下利用有关资料，将进口货物生产商的生产成本加上从出口国出口销售到进口国通常发生的利润及一般费用，并在此基础上计算得到的价格作为对货物估价的方法。它是第五种估价方法，其计算基础不是货物的成交价格或转售价格，而是生产成本。

4. 合理方法

合理方法是第六种估价方法。所谓合理方法，实际上不是一种具体估价方法，而是规定了使用方法的范围和原则。也就是说，海关在使用合理方法时，应当根据公平、统一、客观的估价原则，且不得使用6种禁止使用的价格估价。

三、海关和进出口商的权利与义务

中国海关估价法律法规体系不但规定了海关审定货物完税价格的程序，还赋予了海关和进出口商在估价过程中的权利与义务。

海关权利包括：

查阅复制权：查阅、复制与进出口有关的书面资料和电子数据；

询问权：向进出口商及相关企业调查与进出口货物价格有关的问题；

查验、送验权：对进出口货物进行检验和化验；

检查权：检查进出口货物相关的场所；

查询权：查询进出口货物相关付汇或缴纳国内税情况。

海关义务包括：

保密义务：保守进出口商的商业秘密；

举证责任：海关履行估价程序必须向进口商举证；

书面告知的义务：据进出口商申请就如何确定进出口货物完税价格做出书面说明；

具保放行货物的义务：未做出估价决定前，进出口商提供担保后先放行进出口货物。

进出口商的权利包括：

要求具保放行货物的权利；

估价方法的选择权：选择倒扣价格方法和计算价格方法的适用次序；

知情权：要求海关估价透明公开；

申诉权：对海关估价决定不服的，可以向上一级海关申报复议和向法院提起诉讼的权利。

进出口商的义务包括：

如实申报的义务：向海关如实申报进出口货物的成交价格，提供相关的资料和电子数据；

举证责任：举证证明申报价格的真实性和准确性或举证交易价格没有受到买卖双方特殊关系影响。

四、海关审价工作流程

进出口货物向海关申报后，对其成交价格的审查从程序上通常可以分为：区域审单中心审价、通关现场验估、关税价格职能部门专业认定等。

（一）区域审单中心电子审核申报价格

进出口货物报关单电子数据首先经过区域审单中心对其申报价格进行电子审核，区域审单中心的审价主要是以价格信息资料为基础并结合企业信息等其他部门所掌握的相关的信息对企业的申报价格真实性进行初步判断。经审核认为申报价格合理的给予审结放行，对于判断风险值高的申报则转由其他审价环节通过更丰富的资料和手段进行判断。

（二）现场海关书面审核

现场海关要在区域审单中心电子审核申报价格的基础上，对区域审单中心提示重点作进一步审核的报关单或者现场海关分析认为存在风险需重点审核的，通过对书面报关数据与随附单证及相关信息的核对和审核，以及对货物的实际验估，确定进出口货物的完税价格。

（三）职能部门专业认定

当区域审单中心和现场海关经过电子审核和书面审核，仍无法确定进出口货的完税价格时，可以向上级关税职能部门提交估价专业认定申请。专业认定就是要发挥职能部门的专业优势，在掌握充分价格资料的基础上，通过企业进一步提供的更加充分的贸易单证对企业申报价格的进行验证，从而对企业申报价格的真实性和完整性做出判断。

从对具体货物的估价程序看，分为价格质疑、价格磋商以及价格核查等。

价格质疑：是指海关对进出口货物的申报价格的真实性和准确性有疑问时，应当书面将怀疑的理由告知进出口商，要求进出口商做进一步说明，提供相关资料或其他证据，证明其申报价格是真实准确的。

价格磋商：是指海关采用相同、类似货物成交价格资料或者采用倒扣价格方法、计算价格方法确定进口货物完税价格时，由海关与进出口商交流与进口货物有关的贸易状况、交易情况，相同或类似进口货物的成交价格，市场价格行情、成交数量、商业水平、运输方式、运输距离等信息，以及使用倒扣价格方法、计算价格方法估价时所需资料的过程。

价格核查：价格核查是海关审定完税价格的一种手段，是海关经过必要的审价程序后仍无法确定其完税价格时，依法通过审查单证、核实数据、核对实物及相关账册等方法，对进口货物申报成交价格的真实性、准确性进行的审查。

（海关总署）

中国海关原产地管理制度

一、中国海关原产地管理制度概述

我国对进出口货物原产地的管理分为非优惠原产地管理和优惠原产地管理。经过多年实践，初步形成了我国非优惠和优惠原产地管理体系。截至2014年底，海关总署颁布实施原产地相关署令23个、公告近80个。2014年，制定下发“海关总署关于公布《中华人民共和国海关〈中华人民共和国和瑞士联邦自由贸易协定〉项下进出口货物原产地管理办法》的令”等2个署令和11个公告。

二、中国非优惠原产地管理

（一）法制框架

中国非优惠原产地管理是以《中华人民共和国进出口货物原产地条例》和《关于非优惠原产地规则中实质性改变标准的规定》为基本法制框架，连同海关总署颁布的各项原产地管理规章和进出口原产地管理操作规程，形成了我国的非优惠原产地管理体系。

1.《原产地条例》

2004年9月，国务院颁布了《原产地条例》（国务院令第415号），自2005年1月1日起施行。《原产地条例》共27条，分别就立法宗旨、适用范围、原产地规则、原产地证书签发、海关监管及核查、法律责任等做了明确规定。该条例适用于进口税率的适用、贸易统计、最惠国待遇、反倾销和反补贴、保障措施、原产地标记管理、国别数量限制、关税配额等非优惠性贸易措施的实施，以及政府采购时对进出口货物原产地的确定。

《原产地条例》建立了判定进出口货物原产地的共同标准，实现进出口货物原产地规则的统一，明确了海关在进出口货物原产地管理上的主导地位，对进出口收发货人的权利和义务做出规范，对签证机构和签证程序提出要求，是我国实施非优惠原产地管理的根本法律依据。

2.《实质性改变标准规定》

依照《原产地条例》的有关规定，海关总署会同商务部、国家质检总局于2004年12月发布了《关于非优惠原产地规则中实质性改变标准的规定》，与《原产地条例》同时实施。《实质性改变标准规定》共9条，主要包含了实质性改变标准条款和产品特定原产地标准清单两部分。

（二）进出口货物原产地管理

1. 进口货物原产地管理

货物申报进口时，进口货物收货人应当按照海关的申报规定，填制进口货物报关单，申明进口货物的原产地，并随附有关单证。海关对进口报关单进行审核。

为确定货物原产地是否与进口货物收发货人提交的原产地证书及其他申报单证相符，海关可以对进口货物进行查验。

海关对进口货物收货人或者其代理人提交的原产地证书的真实性、货物原产地的准确性存在怀疑时，可请求出口方原产地主管机构对进口货物的原产地进行核查，或对进口货物收货人或者其代理人及其进口货物进行核查。

2. 出口货物原产地管理

出口货物发货人可以向签证机构申请领取出口货物原产地证书。出口货物发货人办理申请手续时，应当如实申报出口货物的原产地，并提供出口货物的原产地相关资料。

货物申报出口时，出口货物发货人或者其代理人应当按照海关的申报规定填制出口货物报关单，申明出口货物的原产地。

为确定出口货物的原产地是否与申报相符，海关可以对出口货物进行查验。

海关对出口货物发货人或者其代理人提交的原产地证书的真实性、货物原产地的准确性存在怀疑时，也可根据有关规定，对出口货物发货人或者其代理人及其出口货物进行核查。

3. 原产地行政裁定与预确定

2001年12月7日，海关总署发布《中华人民共和国海关行政裁定管理暂行办法》（海关总署令第92号）。在海关注册登记的进出口货物经营单位可在货物拟做进口或出口的3个月前提出书面申请，请求海关对有关货物预先做出原产地的行政裁定。海关做出的原产地行政裁定具有海关规章的同等效力，对与实际进出口原产地相关事务具有普遍约束力，自公布之日起在中华人民共和国关境内统一适用。

为规范进口货物原产地预确定管理，便利合法进口，提高通关效率，海关总署制定下发了《进口货物原产地预确定暂行规定》，于2012年4月1日起实施。进口货物的收货人及与进口货物直接相关的其他人，在有正当理由的情况下，可以在货物实际进口前提出书面申请，请求货物进口地直属海关对有关货物的原产地进行预确定。

三、中国优惠原产地管理

（一）法律框架

《原产地条例》第2条明确规定，实施优惠性贸易措施的进出口货物原产地规则及其管理办法，依照我国缔结或者参加的国际条约、协定的有关规定另行制定。

截至2014年底，我国已对外签署并实施了13个优惠贸易协定，分别是《亚太贸易协定》、中国—东盟自由贸易协定（FTA）、中国—巴基斯坦FTA、中国—智利FTA、中国—新西兰FTA、中国—新加坡FTA、中国—秘鲁FTA、中国—哥斯达黎加FTA、中国—冰岛FTA、中国—瑞士FTA、《内地与香港关于建立更紧密经贸关系安排（CEPA）》、内地与澳门CEPA、《海峡两岸经济合作框架协议》（ECFA），以及对台农产品优惠措施和对最不发达国家特惠措施等2个优惠贸易安排。原产地规则作为这些协定的组成部分，对确保各项优惠政策的有效实施起着不可或缺的重要作用。中国海关依据上述协定项下的原产地规则，分别制定相应的优惠原产地管理办法，并以海关总署令的形式对外发布，完成从国际法向国内法的转换，作为优惠贸易项下进出口货物原产地管理的法律依据。

为加强我国进出口货物优惠原产地的统一管理，海关总署制定了《中华人民共和国海关进出口货物优惠原产地管理规定》（海关总署令第181号），自2009年3月1日起施行。该《优惠原产地管理规定》共31条，就优惠贸易项下普遍适用的原产地规则、签证机构及签证程序、进出口申报规范、货物查验及原产地标记、原产地核查等做了统领性规定。

《优惠原产地管理规定》连同各项优惠贸易协定项下的原产地管理办法，形成了我国优惠原产地管理的基本法律框架。

（二）优惠原产地规则

由于各个优惠贸易协定的对象国（地区）不同，谈判条件和结果各异，所达成的各项条款互有差异。总体来说包括以下内容：

1. 原产地标准

对于完全在一国（地区）获得或者生产的货物，适用完全获得标准；对于非完全在一国（地区）获得或者生产的货物，适用实质性改变标准。

2. 完全获得

对于符合完全获得标准的动物产品、植物产品、渔获产品、废碎料等产品范围进行界定。

3. 实质性改变

非完全在一国（地区）获得或者生产的货物，按照相应的自贸协定或优惠贸易协定规定的税则归类改变标准、区域价值成分标准、制造加工工序标准或者其他标准确定其原产地。

4. 累积规则

原产于优惠贸易协定缔约一方的货物或者材料，在另一方境内用于生产另一货物，并构成另一货物组成部分的，该货物或者材料应当视为原产于另一方境内。

5. 微小加工

为便于装载、运输、储存、销售而进行的加工、包装、展示等微小加工或者处理，不影响货物原产地确定。

6. 包装

运输期间用于保护货物的包装材料及容器不影响货物原产地的确定。

7. 中性成分

在货物生产过程中使用，本身不构成货物物质成分，也不成为货物组成部件的材料或者物品，其原产地不影响货物原产地的确定。

8. 直接运输

优惠贸易项下进口货物，应当从缔约一方直接运输至我国境内；经过第三方境内运输至我国境内的，不论在运输途中是否转换运输工具或者做临时储存，只要同时符合各协定规定的条件，可以视为“直接运输”。

（三）签证程序

依照国家法律、行政法规规定有权签发出口货物原产地证书的机构，可以签发优惠贸易协定项下出口货物原产地证书。签证机构应依据相应优惠贸易协定项下的原产地规则签发出口货物原产地证书。

出口商或生产商应向签证机构提出书面申请，由签证机构对其出口货物的原产地资格进行核实。出口货物的发货人及其代理人应向签证机构书面申领原产地证书，并提交相关证明文件。签证机构有权在货物出口前采取任何适当的措施审核产品是否具有原产地资格。

（四）通关管理措施

1. 进口申报要求

货物申报进口时，进口货物收货人或者其代理人应当按照海关的申报规定，填制进口货物报关单，申明适用协定税率或者特惠税率，同时提交货物的有效原产地证书正本或相关优惠贸易协定规定的原产地声明，以及货物的商业发票正本、运输单证等其他商业单证。货物经过第三方境内运输或临时储存的，应当提交证明符合直运规则的证明文件。一份报关单对应一份原产地证书；一份原产地证书或原产地声明对应同一批次的进口货物。

货物申报进口时，进口货物收货人虽已申明适用有关优惠贸易安排的协定税率，但未能提供有效原产地证书正本以及相关文件的，海关应当按照规定收取保证金后放行货物。海关可以申请在保证金收取的期限内，根据进口货物收货人按规定提供的材料退还保证金。

2. 出口申报规范

出口货物申报时，出口货物发货人应当按照海关的申报规定填制出口货物报关单，并向海关提交原产地证书电子数据或者原产地证书正本的复印件。货物出口后，出口货物发货人向签证机构申请补发优惠原产地证书的，出口货物发货人应向原出口地海关补交原产地证书正本复印件。

3. 货物查验及原产地标记

为确定货物原产地是否与进出口货物收发货人提交的原产地证书及其他申报单证相符，海关可以对进出口货物进行查验。优惠贸易协定项下进出口货物及其包装上标有原产地标记的，其原产地标记所标明的原产地应当与海关按照有关规定确定的货物原产地相一致。

4. 原产地核查

海关对进口货物收货人或者其代理人提交的原产地证书的真实性、货物原产地的准确性存在怀疑时，可以请求出口方原产地主管机构对自贸协定或优惠贸易协定项下进口货物原产地进行核查。必要时，海关可以进行跨境核查访问。

应优惠贸易协定缔约一方的请求，或者海关认为必要时，可以对有关出口货物原产地进行核查，以确定其原产地。

在核查期间，海关可以按照该货物适用的其他种类税率征收相当于应缴税款的等值保证金后放行货物。核查结束后，海关应当根据核查结果，立即办理退还保证金手续或者办理保证金转为进口税款手续。

5. 原产地预确定与行政裁定

进出口货物收发货人可以依照《中华人民共和国海关行政裁定管理暂行办法》的有关规定，向海关申请原产地行政裁定；进口货物的收货人可以依照《进口货物原产地预确定暂行规定》，向海关申请原产地预确定。

（海关总署）

中国海关商品归类制度

一、中国海关与《协调制度》

（一）《协调制度》介绍

《商品名称及编码协调制度》（简称《协调制度》，又称“HS”），是指世界海关组织（WCO）主持制定的商品分类目录体系，是顺应国际贸易实践需要而产生的一种国际公约性质的商品分类标准，被称为国际贸易商品分类的一种“标准语言”。《协调制度》是《中华人民共和国进出口税则》制定的基础。

1983年中国成为海关合作理事会的成员国。中国海关于1987年将《协调制度》译成了中文，并开始着手对原中国海关的税则目录根据《协调制度》进行转换。1992年1月1日，中国海关加入了《协调制度》公约。同年，正式采用《协调制度》，使商品归类工作成为中国海关最早实现与国际接轨的执法项目之一。20多年来，中国海关作为协调制度目录的主管部门，为目录在我国的推广应用做了大量工作。

（二）《协调制度》在中国的应用

1.《协调制度》目录应用

《协调制度》公约第三条“缔约方的义务”第三款规定“本条规定不影响缔约各国在本国的税则目录或统计目录中，增列比《协调制度》目录更为详细的货品分类细目，但这些细目必须在本公约附件所规定的六位数级目录项下增列和编号。”因此，中国海关采用的《协调制度》分类目录，前6位数是协调制度国际标准编码，第7、8两位是根据我国关税、统计和贸易管理的需要加列的本国子目，同时，还根据代征税、暂定税率和贸易管制的需要对部分税号增设了第9、10位附加代码。随着进出口贸易的不断发展和商品种类的日益繁多，我国海关商品编号的数量也从1992年采用《协调制度》之初的6250个增加到了2015年的13154个。

此外，世界海关组织为使各缔约国能够统一理解和执行《协调制度》，编制了《商品名称及编码协调制度注释》，我国也将其完全翻译过来并据此制定了《进出口税则商品及品目注释》；在此基础上，我国还针对本国增列的子目逐步编制《中华人民共和国海关进出口税则—统计目录本国子目注释》，二者共同构成了对《税则》的有效补充。

2.《协调制度》目录转版

为了适应国际贸易和现代科技发展的需要，协调制度每4～6年都要做一次大的转版升级。到目前为止，我国海关先后组织完成了1992年版、1996年版、2002年版、2007年版、2012年版《协调制度》的翻译，并组织完成了我国《进出口税则》的修订转换以及1992年版、1996年版、2002年版、2007年版、2012年版《协调制度注释》的翻译工作，有力地推动了协调制度在我国的普及和应用。

现行2012年版的《协调制度》不仅成为海关征收关税和编制海关统计的基本工具，同样也成为国家发展改革委、财政部、商务部、科技部、税务总局等部门制定相关经济和贸易政策时的一项基本政策工具。

二、中国海关商品归类依据

（一）中华人民共和国进出口税则

中国海关完全采用《协调制度》的分类方式和6位数编码，并在此基础上根据本国贸易特点，增列了第7、8位本国子目，形成了8位数的编码体系，形成《中华人民共和国进出口税则》。

根据国际和国内贸易发展情况，出于技术的发展、贸易方式的改变、公共安全及环境保护的需要、贸易统计、国内行业的需求等原因，本国《税则》中的子目每年修订一次，经国务院批准，修订的《税则》在下一年度实施。中国海关是中国国务院关税税则委员会成员单位，每年向税委会提出修订意见。

（二）中国海关归类主要依据

中国海关归类主要依据《海关法》、《关税条例》以及《归类管理规定》开展。归类的法律依据主要包括《税则》《协调制度注释》《本国子目注释》以及以公告形式对外公布的归类决定。

归类工作的战略目标是建立一个守法便利的通关环境，减少通关环节归类原因造成的延误。以此为目标，中国海关加强自身建设，加强信息化与法制化建设，取得了较好的成效。中国海关不断公开归类决定，通过网络公开归类信息，全国海关化验结论实现联网，努力营造良好贸易环境。目前中国海关对外公布作为归类依据的本国子目注释共320项，以公告形式对外公布的归类决定3333项，其中对外公布的世界海关组织归类决定1007项，公布我国归类决定2326项，为归类业务的开展奠定了法律基础。

三、中国海关商品归类组织框架

中国海关归类工作是以世界海关组织协调制度为基础的进出口商品属性的认定工作，其目标就是在《协调制度》的框架下，确保进出口商品归类的准确性与一致性，保证税收及贸易管制等海关执法的进行，保证国际贸易便利化的有效开展，确保海关统计的准确性。

（一）中国海关商品归类组织结构

中国海关商品归类职能部门为海关总署关税征管司，负责规划、指导、税则立法建议、协调、数据库维护、争议解决、组织培训等工作。1998年机构改革后成立归类处，主管海关进出口商品的归类工作。经过近几年的发展，归类工作已经有较大的发展。目前，全国海关归类由关税司归类处主管，设有北京归类办，天津、大连、上海、广州归类分中心和化验中心，青岛、重庆化验中心。

北京海关商品归类办公室，上海、广州、天津、大连的4个商品归类分中心，为总署归类职能的外设机构，各负责部分全国海关的归类职能管理。同时在上海、广州、天津、大连、重庆、青岛设有海关化验中心。

各个直属海关的关税部门负责本关区的具体归类管理，如遇到归类问题，可按照分管商品向商品归类分中心提交归类申请。

（二）中国海关商品归类委员会制度

目前中国海关成立了两个商品归类委员会，分别是协调制度商品归类技术委员会和协调制度管理委员会。

协调制度商品归类技术委员会成立于1999年，主要由海关归类业务专家组成，研究和解决具体的商品归类疑难问题。归类技术委员会参照世界海关组织模式，下设一个顾问组，四个分委会（分别为审议分委会、政策分委会、科学分委会、数据分委会），四个专业组（分别为商品组、国际业务组、法规组、网络组）。其中，审议分委会负责税则和国家政策的研究，提出税则的修订和调整建议；政策分委会主要对商品归类工作的制度体系和业务规划进行系统性和前瞻性的研究；科学分委会主要由海关化验专家组成，为归类技术委员会提供技术支持和科学保障；数据分委会是归类化验数据的管理机构，负责对归类化验数据进行维护。各专业小组根据工作安排，完成总署分配的任务。归类技术委员会一年召开两次，研究海关面临的具体归类问题以及讨论涉及的法律、法规方面的问题，寻求解决途径。

协调制度管理委员会成立于2006年6月，由海关总署牵头其他十四个部委和二十余个行业协会组成，为海关与这些机构在归类事务上的沟通搭建了平台。协调制度管理委员会一年召开一次，由海关总署组织召开，各成员单位参与，主要是通报海关的重大措施以及征求相关意见等。

四、中国海关商品归类管理

（一）中国海关商品归类工作模式

归类业务具有专业性强、业务链条长、涉及领域广的特点，受到中国海关的重视。中国海关归类业务实行垂直、三级管理，即海关总署（归类分中心）——直属海关——隶属海关。遇到问题逐级请示，各层级有不同的处理权限。

归类业务涉及通关前、通关中及通关后三个阶段。

通关前：收发货人或者其代理人依据海关发布的归类依据和原则确定进出口商品归类。收发货人或者其代理人有义务按照上述归类规定如实正确确定进出口商品的海关商品编码。

通关中：海关依据风险管理模式，依靠技术平台，依法对收发货人或者其代理人申报的进出口货物商品的归类进行审核。

通关后：海关通过后续数据核查、风险评估进行后续监控以及维护风险数据，维护归类一致性和准确性。

（二）中国海关化验

中国海关分别在大连、天津、上海、广州、青岛和重庆设立了海关化验室，承接各直属海关报送的进出口商品化验任务。

1999 年 3 月，广州海关化验中心成为全国海关第一家通过国家认证的实验室，也是亚洲海关实验室中最早通过国际认证的实验室。2002 年 10 月，上海海关化验中心通过国家实验室认可委评审。上海海关化验中心首次将非标方法纳入认证项目并通过国家认可委评审。2002 年 12 月，大连海关化验中心通过国家实验室认可委评审，成为全国首家以电子化的质量管理体系通过评审的单位。2003 年 6 月，天津海关化验中心通过国家实验室认可委评审，并建立了全国唯一一个纸张检测专业实验室。各实验室通过 LIMS 系统实现联网，以方便化验结果的查询。2014 年 4 月，重庆海关化验中心通过国家实验室认可委评审。2014 年 6 月，青岛海关化验中心正式投入使用。

中国海关化验于 2014 年 11 月首次正式对外公布第一批 69 项海关化验标准，并利用中国海关化验信息管理系统（LIMS）成功实现海关化验数据全国联网，实现海关化验标准化和信息化。

海关化验中心自 1991 年陆续成立以来，共受理送检样品近 23 万宗，补税及罚没近 13 亿元。查获涉嫌逃避进出口许可证管制货物近 3000 批，查获毒品约 160 批共计 9300 多公斤，取得了显著的经济效益和社会效益。

（三）中国海关商品预归类制度

根据《中华人民共和国海关进出口货物商品归类管理规定》，在海关注册登记的进出口货物经营单位，可以在货物实际进出口的 45 日前，向直属海关申请就其拟进出口的货物预先进行商品归类。该规定在海关预归类的申请、受理、制发决定书等各个环节，从制度上给予保障，实现了海关预归类工作的有法可依。同时为了缓解日益增大的海关预归类需求压力，中国海关正在北京、天津、大连、上海、南京、厦门、青岛、广州、深圳、黄埔 10 个地区进行预归类服务的有益尝试，以更大程度地提高通关速度，提供贸易便利。

（海关总署）

中国进出口许可证制度

一、进出口许可证制度和国际通行做法

进出口许可证制度是世界各国管理对外贸易所普遍采用的一种重要的行政手段，是世贸组织规则允许在一定条件下使用的非关税措施。它包括有关许可证的申请、审查、颁发、使用、效力、撤销和废止等各方面的法律制度，具有严格、简便易行、效果显著等特点。进出口许可证制度对于贯彻一国经济贸易政策、进出口贸易统计和监测、维护正常的贸易秩序等具有重要作用。

进口许可证制度是指一国为加强对外贸易管制，规定某些商品的进口需由进口商向进口国有关部门提出申请并获得许可证的一种制度。进口许可证，是指对列入进口许可证管理的商品，进口商必须向有关部门提出申请，经审核批准后发给的许可证。

出口许可证制度是指一国出于国家安全、环境保护、维护出口秩序、履行国际协议等目的，对商品出口实现管制的一项措施。出口许可证，是根据一国出口商品管理的法令规定，由有关当局签发的准许出口的证件。

二、我国进出口许可证制度

加入世贸组织以来，为适应经济全球化和我国外贸发展的新要求，我国修订了相关法律法规，按照世贸组织的透明度要求，形成了一整套统一、规范、透明的进出口许可证管理体系。目前，我国进出口许可证制度以《对外贸易法》《行政许可法》为上位法依据，确立了许可证制度的法律地位；《货物进出口管理条例》《货物进口许可证管理办法》《货物出口许可证管理办法》等法规部门规章明确了许可证管理的体制框架和具体程序。

（一）进口许可证制度

为保护环境、人身健康安全，依据《对外贸易法》及相关国际公约，对消耗臭氧层物质、化工设备等重点旧机电产品实行进口许可证管理。为维护国家安全和社会公共利益，对监控化学品、易制毒化学品和放射性物质等实施两用物项和技术进口许可证管理。

根据《2014 年进口许可证管理货物目录》，目前我对化工设备、金属冶炼设备、工程机械等 12 类货物实行进口许可证管理。

（二）出口许可证制度

根据《2014 年出口许可证管理货物目录》，2014 年实行出口许可证管理的共有 48 种货物，分别实行出口配额许可证、出口配额招标和出口许可证管理。

实行出口配额许可证管理的货物是：玉米、大米、小麦、玉米粉、大米粉、小麦粉、棉花、锯材、活牛（对港澳）、活猪（对港澳）、活鸡（对港澳）、煤炭、原油、成品油、稀土、锑及锑制品、钨及钨制品、锡及锡制品、白银、铟及铟制品、钼、磷矿石。

实行出口配额招标的货物是：蔺草及蔺草制品、滑石块（粉）、镁砂、甘草及甘草制品。

实行出口许可证管理的货物是：活牛（对港澳以外市场）、活猪（对港澳以外市场）、活鸡（对港澳以外市场）、冰鲜牛肉、冻牛肉、冰鲜猪肉、冻猪肉、冰鲜鸡肉、冻鸡肉、消耗臭氧层物质、石蜡、部分金属及制品、铂金（以加工贸易方式出口）、汽车（包括成套散件）及其底盘、摩托车（含全地形车）及其发动机和车架、天然砂（含标准砂）、钼制品、柠檬酸、维生素 C、青霉素工业盐、硫酸二钠、焦炭、碳化硅、矾土、氟石。

（三）进出口许可证签发管理

根据《进出口许可证证书管理规定》，商务部配额许可证事务局受商务部委托，管理各类许可证书，并监督检查地方商务主管部门和商务部驻各地特派员办事处所属进出口许可证签发机构的执行情况。许可证书是指由商务部监制完成且尚未发放的各类具有许可进出口性质的证明、文件、原产地证书等。根据《货物进出口管理条例》和每年的出口许可证管理货物目录、进口许可证管理货物目录，商务部每年发布出口许可证管理货物分级发证目录和进口许可证管理货物分级发证目录。

在出口许可证发证方面，由商务部配额许可证事务局、商务部驻各地特派员办事处及地方商务主管部门签发出口许可证。其中，商务部配额许可证事务局负责签发玉米、小麦、棉花等货物的出口许可证；商务部驻各特派员办事处负责签发大米、锯材、稀土等货物的出口许可证；地方发证机构负责签发冰鲜牛肉、冰鲜猪肉、石蜡等货物的出口许可证；在京中央企业的出口许可证由商务部配额许可证事务局签发。

在进口许可证签发方面，目前商务部配额许可证事务局负责签发重点旧机电产品的进口许可证；地方发证机构负责签发消耗臭氧层物质的进口许可证；在京中央企业的进口许可证由商务部配额许可证事务局签发。

三、我国进出口许可证制度的作用和发展趋势

（一）我国进出口许可证制度对外贸发展的作用

1. 进出口许可证数据是反映外贸运行动态的先行指标。许可证数据领先于海关数据，是企业在国际国内两个市场中开展生产经营决策的提前反映，许可证发放数量、金额、价格和国别等数据信息的变动趋势，是研判对外贸易和宏观经济运行的重要视角，是政府实施对外贸易和宏观调控的重要依据。

2. 进出口许可证管理是保护资源环境和产业安全的重要手段。我国实行进出口许可证管理的商品，既有石油等重要能源资源性产品，粮食等关系国计民生的大宗商品，也有部分重点机电产品、两用物项和技术、消耗臭氧层物质等。对这些商品实施许可证管理，有利于保障国内能源资源安全和有效利用，有利于提前发现进口异动，保护产业安全。

3. 进出口许可证管理是应对国际贸易摩擦的重要环节。我国已连续多年成为遭遇贸易摩擦最多的国家，通过进出口许可证管理，可以收集掌握受监控商品的进出口动态，为政府部门、行业协会及相关企业提供重要信息；可以规范贸易秩序，预防和减少贸易摩擦。

（二）发展趋势

进出口许可证制度是对外贸易管理政策体系的重要组成部分，加强和完善进出口许可证制度和管理，对于转变外贸发展方式、培育外贸竞争优势、推动我国外贸强国进程具有重要意义。下一步，要继续发挥进出口许可证现有作用的基础上，学习和借鉴国外先进的管理经验和理念，同时结合我国实际、入世承诺、自由贸易协定和外贸新形势对许可证制度的要求，推动许可证制度创新；充分发挥和完善许可证监测预警功能，为有效应对贸易摩擦和提高外贸宏观调控质量提供参考和依据，推动许可证管理创新；建立统一规范的许可证签发平台，健全快速有效的许可证签发管理服务体系，利用互联网和计算机技术推动无纸化通关，推进相关部门数据互联互通，着力提高贸易便利化水平，为外贸企业提供优质高效的服务，推动许可证服务创新。

（商务部对外贸易司）

中国关税配额制度

一、关于关税配额的定义

关税配额是指进口国对商品进口在一定时期内总的数量不加限制，但设定一个数量界限，对该数量界限以内的进口产品适用较低的关税税率，对超过数量界限的进口产品适用较高的关税税率。这一设定的数量界限即称为关税配额。关税配额准入量是市场准入机会，而不是最低购买义务。按进口商品的来源，关税配额可分为全球关税配额和国别关税配额。

二、我国加入世贸组织时关于关税配额管理的承诺

（一）实施进口关税配额管理的商品

根据《中国加入世贸组织议定书》，我国对小麦、玉米、大米（包括中短粒米和长粒米，下同）、豆油、棕榈油、菜籽油、食糖、棉花、羊毛、毛条、化肥（包括磷酸氢二铵、尿素和氮磷钾复合肥，下同）的进口实施关税配额管理。其中，对小麦、玉米、大米、豆油、棕榈油、菜籽油、食糖、棉花和化肥进口实行国营贸易管理。

按照加入世贸组织承诺，自2006年1月1日起，我国取消了对豆油、棕榈油和菜籽油进口的关税配额和国营贸易管理。

（二）基本管理原则

1. 关税配额数量、配额内税率、国营贸易比例和实施期限按照中国入世议定书减让表的有关规定执行。

2. 任何配额持有者可通过国营贸易企业和/或通过国营贸易企业以外的其他拥有贸易权的企业进口，拥有贸易权的配额持有者也可自行进口。

3. 每一产品的关税配额将在每年1月1日启用。除非另有规定，关税配额分配量在该日历年度内有效。

4. 配额按如下要求分配：(1) 申请关税配额的具体条件将于申请期前1个月在官方刊物上公布，申请期为每年10月15日至10月30日（先来先领分配方式除外）。(2) 全部关税配额量应在每年1月1日前分配给最终用户（先来先领分配方式除外）。(3) 配额持有者获得的配额量不得少于上一年获得并实际完成的关税配额量（先来先领分配方式除外）。(4) 配额分配量应按商业上可行的装运量确定，并允许关税配额分配量分船装运。贸易条款，包括产品规格、定价、包装等，仅由进出口商决定，同时充分考虑最终用户的需求。(5) 关于关税配额分配情况的质询，管理机关应在10个工作日内提供有关信息。

配额持有者在每年9月15日前交还的未使用完的关税配额数量将进行再分配。

5. 应任何WTO成员请求，中国应就关税配额的管理与该成员磋商，以保证关税配额以透明、公平和非歧视的方式进行分配，并保证配额得到充分使用。

6. 实施期结束后的配额量将有待进一步磋商。除非议定新的配额量，否则实施期末的配额量将继续适用。

7. 2006年1月1日以后，向一种实行关税配额管理的化肥产品提供的关税配额量增长率，应向所有实行关税配额管理的其他化肥产品提供。

三、我国现行关税配额管理政策

（一）进口关税配额管理暂行办法

为有效实施进口关税配额管理，根据加入世贸组织承诺以及《中华人民共和国对外贸易法》《中华人民共和国海关法》《中华人民共和国货物进出口管理条例》《中华人民共和国进出口关税条例》，我国分别于2002年和2003年制定并颁布了《化肥进口关税配额管理暂行办法》（国家经贸委、海关总署2002年27号令）和《农产品进口关税配额管理暂行办法》（商务部、发展改革委2003年4号令）。根据上述办法，我国按以下规定对进口关税配额实施管理：

1. 管理口径

我国进口关税配额为全球配额。相关商品所有贸易方式的进口均纳入关税配额管理范围。《农产

品进口关税配额证》和《化肥进口关税配额证明》（以下统称“配额证明”）适用于一般贸易、加工贸易、易货贸易、边境小额贸易、援助、捐赠等贸易方式进口。由境外进入保税仓库、保税区、出口加工区的产品，免于领取配额证明。

2. 管理部门

小麦、玉米、大米和棉花进口关税配额由发展改革委会同商务部分配，并通过其授权机构受理企业申请和接受咨询，向经过批准的申请者发放《农产品进口关税配额证》。食糖、羊毛、毛条、化肥进口关税配额由商务部分配，并通过其授权机构受理企业申请和接受咨询，向经过批准的申请者发放配额证明。

3. 配额申请、分配和调整

（1）进口关税配额申请期为每年 10 月 15 日至 30 日（先来先领分配方式除外）。（2）商务部、发展改革委分别于申请期前 1 个月在官方刊物和各自网站上公布每种商品下一年度进口关税配额总量、关税配额申请条件等情况。（3）商务部、发展改革委各自授权机构根据公布的条件，受理申请者提交的申请及有关资料，并于 11 月 30 日前将申请转报商务部、发展改革委（先来先领分配方式除外）。（4）每年 1 月 1 日前，商务部、发展改革委通过各自授权机构向用户发放相应的进口关税配额。（5）持有进口关税配额的最终用户当年无法将已申领到的全部配额量签订进口合同或已签订进口合同无法完成，须在当年 9 月 15 日前将无法完成的配额量交还原发证机构。（6）进口关税配额再分配量的申请期为每年 9 月 1 日至 15 日（先来先领分配方式除外）。商务部、发展改革委分别于申请期前 1 个月在官方刊物和各自网站上公布再分配量的申请条件，并由各自授权机构受理申请者的申请。（7）每年 9 月 30 日前，商务部、发展改革委将进口关税配额再分配量分配到最终用户。

4. 配额执行

（1）小麦、玉米、大米、食糖、棉花、化肥进口关税配额分为国营贸易配额和非国营贸易配额。国营贸易配额须通过国营贸易企业进口；非国营贸易配额可通过完成对外贸易经营者备案的任何企业进口。（2）国营贸易配额需在相应的配额证明上注明。（3）配额证明实行一证多批制，即最终用户需分多批进口的，凭配额证明可多次办理通关手续。最终用户须如实填写配额证明上的“最终用户进口填写栏”，填满后，需持该证到原发证机构换领未办理通关部分的配额证明。（4）最终用户完成配额证明上标注配额量最后一批次进口报关后，于 20 个工作日内将海关签章的配额证明第一联（收货人办理海关手续联）原件交原发证机构。

5. 执行期限

（1）年度进口关税配额于每年 1 月 1 日开始实施，并在公历年度内有效。《农产品进口关税配额证》自每年 1 月 1 日起至当年 12 月 31 日有效，实行先来先领分配方式的《农产品进口关税配额证》《化肥进口关税配额证明》的有效期，按公布的实施细则执行。（2）当年 12 月 31 日前从始发港出运，需在下一年到货的进口关税配额产品，最终用户需持配额证明及有关证明单证到原发证机构申请延期。原发证机构审核情况属实后可予以办理延期，但延期最迟不得超过下一年的 2 月底。

6. 罚则

（1）最终用户于当年未能完成分配其的全部进口关税配额量进口，截至 9 月 15 日又未将当年不能实现进口的配额量交还原发证机构的，其下年度分配的关税配额量将按未完成的比例相应扣减，且不能参与当年的再分配。（2）最终用户连续两年未能完成分配其的全部进口关税配额量进口，并在该两年内每年 9 月 15 日前将当年不能使用的关税配额量交还原发证授权机构的，其下年度分配的关税配额量将按其最近一年未完成的比例相应扣减。（3）最终用户未在规定时间将海关签章的配额证明第一联（收货人办理海关手续联）原件交原发证机构的，视同未完成进口，相应扣减其下年度关税配额量。

（二）2014 年进口关税配额实施细则

2014 年，各商品进口关税配额申请条件如下：

1. 基本条件

企业需在申请前完成在国家工商管理部门登记注册；近年无在海关、外汇、工商、税务、质检、社保和环保等方面的违规记录；没有违反关税配额管理规定。

2. 对不同商品企业需满足如下具体条件

（1）小麦。国营贸易企业；具有国家储备职能的中央企业；2013年有进口实绩的企业；日加工小麦400吨以上的生产企业；2013年无进口实绩，但具有进出口经营权并由所在地外经贸主管部门出具加工贸易生产能力证明、以小麦为原料从事加工贸易的企业。

（2）玉米。国营贸易企业；具有国家储备职能的中央企业；2013年有进口实绩的企业；以玉米为原料，年需要玉米5万吨以上的配合饲料生产企业；以玉米为原料，年需要玉米10万吨以上的其他生产企业；2013年无进口实绩，但具有进出口经营权并由所在地外经贸主管部门出具加工贸易生产能力证明、以玉米为原料从事加工贸易的企业。

（3）稻谷和大米。国营贸易企业；具有国家储备职能的中央企业；2013年有进口实绩的企业；具有粮食批发零售资格，年销售额1亿元人民币以上的粮食企业；粮食年进出口额2500万美元以上的贸易企业；2013年无进口实绩，但具有进出口经营权并由所在地外经贸主管部门出具加工贸易生产能力证明、以稻谷和大米为原料从事加工贸易的企业。

（4）棉花。国营贸易企业；2013年有进口实绩的企业；纺纱设备5万锭以上的棉纺企业。

（5）食糖。国营贸易企业；具有国家储备职能的中央企业；持有2013年食糖关税配额且有进口实绩的企业；日加工原糖600吨以上（含600吨）、注册资金1000万以上（含1000万）、食糖年销售额4.5亿元以上（含4.5亿元）的制糖企业；以食糖为原料从事加工贸易的企业。

（6）羊毛和毛条。2013年有羊毛、毛条进口实绩者或新建成投产且羊毛、毛条年加工能力在5000吨以上的企业。

（7）化肥。2013年化肥进口关税配额实行凭合同先来先领的分配方式。凡是在工商行政管理部门登记注册的企业，在其经营范围内均可申请化肥进口关税配额。

2014年关税配额管理商品有关情况表

单位：万吨

品种	关税配额数量	关税配额税率	国营贸易比重
小麦	963.6	1%～10%不等	90%
玉米	720	1%～10%不等	60%
稻谷和大米	532	1%～9%不等	50%
食糖	194.5	15%	70%
棉花	89.4	1%	33%
羊毛	28.7	1%	—
毛条	8	3%	—
磷酸氢二铵	690	1%	55%
尿素	330	1%	90%
氮磷钾复合肥	345	1%	51%

四、进口关税配额政策实施效果

（一）充分体现了统一、透明、可预见、公平和非歧视的原则

我国在入世承诺中已明确了年度关税配额数量、关税配额申请条件和分配程序等。加入世界组织以来，我国依据国内的法律法规，先后制定并公布了《化肥进口关税配额管理暂行办法》和《农产品进口关税配额管理暂行办法》，建立起了统一、公开、透明、公平的关税配额管理政策体系和制度框架。在关税配额管理执行中，我国严格履行入世承诺，每年按时公布关税配额管理商品的年度进口实施细则，如期完成进口关税配额分配。我国现行的农产品进口关税配额分配和管理制度，与入世承诺和多哈早期收获农业谈判并不矛盾。

（二）提高了贸易便利化水平

按现行规定和做法，企业凭进口关税配额证明即可直接报关进口，不需再申领进口许可证，大大简化了原来凭进口配额证明和许可证双证报关的程

序，减少了通关环节，降低了企业成本，更加便利企业进口。

（三）接受 WTO 年度审议

按照 WTO 规定和要求，我国认真履行成员义务，主动接受 WTO 年度审议，及时提供年度进口关税配额等有关情况，向成员国提供咨询并就共同关注的有关问题加强多双边领域的交流与磋商。

（商务部对外贸易司）

中国与进出口有关的其他税收制度

2014 年，为了发展对外贸易，促进国内经济，中国在与进出口有关的其他税收制度方面采取了一系列的积极措施，取得了良好的效果。这里所说的与进出口有关的其他税收制度，主要包括进口环节征收的增值税、消费税（简称进口环节税），出口环节退还的增值税、消费税（简称出口退税），以及与进出口有关的增值税、营业税、企业所得税等税收和税收管理制度。

一、宏观决策和重大改革

1 月 2 日，中共中央、国务院发布《关于全面深化农村改革 加快推进农业现代化的若干意见》，其中提出了下列税收措施：

1. 加快实施农业“走出去”战略，制定和完善财税、金融等配套政策，平等支持国有企业、民营企业采取多种形式到中国境外直接投资农产品仓储物流设施、参股并购国际农产品加工和贸易企业，扶持培育具有国际竞争力的粮棉油等大型企业。

2. 拓宽“三农”投入资金渠道，充分发挥财政资金引导作用，通过贴息、奖励、风险补偿、税费减免等措施，带动金融和社会资金更多投入农业、农村。

3. 落实、完善相关税收优惠政策，支持农民合作社发展农产品加工流通。

4. 采取财政扶持、税费优惠和信贷支持等措施，大力发展主体多元、形式多样和竞争充分的社会化服务，推行合作式、订单式和托管式等服务模式，扩大农业生产全程社会化服务试点范围。

3 月 5 日，国务院总理李克强在第十二届全国人民代表大会第二次会议上所做的《政府工作报告》中提出：继续实施积极的财政政策和稳健的货币政策。推进税收制度改革，把营业税改征增值税（以下简称“营改增”）试点扩大到铁路运输、邮政服务和电信等行业，清费立税，推动消费税、资源税改革，做好房地产税、环境保护税立法相关工作。进一步扩展小微企业税收优惠范围，减轻企业负担。

同日，财政部部长楼继伟在上述会议上所做的《关于 2013 年中央和地方预算执行情况与 2014 年中央和地方预算草案的报告》中提出：继续实施积极的财政政策，深化财税体制改革，推动相关领域改革，发挥财税体制改革在整体改革中的基础性和支撑性作用；促进税收依法征管。全面清理规范财税优惠政策；税收优惠政策统一由专门税收法律、法规规定，各类发展规划不得另行规定财税优惠政策。

关于税制改革，楼继伟提出了七项任务：一是继续推进“营改增”，在全国范围内实施铁路运输和邮政服务业“营改增”试点，抓紧研究将电信业纳入试点的政策，力争 4 月 1 日实施；二是实施鼓励企业年金和职业年金发展的个人所得税递延纳税优惠政策；三是实施煤炭资源税从价计征改革；四是进一步扩展小型微利企业税收优惠政策；五是改革完善消费税制度，调整消费税征收范围、环节和税率；六是加快房地产税立法进程；七是加快推动环境保护税立法工作。

关于税收政策，楼继伟提出，要完善有利于结构调整的税收政策，促进经济提质增效升级；结合税收制度改革，进一步扩展小型微利企业税收优惠政策；完善促进养老、健康、信息和文化等服务消费发展的财税政策；对于先进技术设备、关键零部件和能源原材料等 767 种商品实施较低的进口暂定关税，对于 300 种资源、能源和高耗能产品实施税率为 2％至 40％的出口关税；完善促进企业创新的税收政策，研究完善加速设备折旧政策，落实好扩大企业研发费用加计扣除范围的政策。

上述会议批准了以上两个报告。

4 月 24 日，第十二届全国人民代表大会常务委员会第八次会议通过修订以后的《中华人民共和国环境保护法》，当日中华人民共和国主席令公布，自 2015 年 1 月 1 日起施行。该法中做出了下列有关税收的规定：

第二十一条　国家采取财政、税收、价格、政府采购等方面的政策和措施，鼓励和支持环境保护技术装备、资源综合利用和环境服务等环境保护产业的发展。

第二十二条　企业事业单位和其他生产经营者，在污染物排放符合法定要求的基础上，进一步减少污染物排放的，人民政府应当依法采取财政、税收、价格、政府采购等方面的政策和措施予以鼓励和支持。

第四十三条　排放污染物的企业事业单位和其他生产经营者，应当按照国家有关规定缴纳排污费。排污费应当全部专项用于环境污染防治，任何单位和个人不得截留、挤占或者挪作他用。

依照法律规定征收环境保护税的，不再征收排污费。

4 月 30 日，国务院批转国家发改委报送的《关于 2014 年深化经济体制改革重点任务的意见》。关于税制改革问题，该意见中提出：继续扩大"营改增"试点范围，促进服务业发展和产业结构优化升级；改革完善消费税制度，抑制高耗能、高污染产品消费，合理引导高档消费品、高端服务消费，鼓励居民基本生活消费；坚持正税清费，推进煤炭资源税改革和房地产税、环境保护税立法相关工作。

关于分税制，意见中提出：结合税制改革，厘清税种属性，进一步理顺中央和地方收入划分，保持现有中央和地方财力格局总体稳定。

6 月 6 日，中共中央总书记、国家主席、中央军委主席、中央全面深化改革领导小组组长习近平主持召开中央全面深化改革领导小组第三次会议，审议《深化财税体制改革总体方案》。习近平在上述会议中指出：财税体制改革不是解一时之弊，而是着眼长远机制的系统性重构。主要目的是明确事权，改革税制，稳定税负，透明预算，提高效率，加快形成有利于转变经济发展方式、有利于建立公平统一市场、有利于推进基本公共服务均等化的现代财政制度，形成中央和地方财力与事权相匹配的财税体制，更好发挥中央和地方两个积极性。深化财税体制改革，涉及面广，政策性强，利益调整难度大，落实工作任务艰巨而繁重。要充分认识深化财税体制改革的重要性、紧迫性、复杂性和艰巨性，树立全国一盘棋思想，加强组织领导，周密安排部署，正确引导舆论，凝聚各方共识，积极稳妥推进改革。

6 月 30 日，中共中央总书记习近平主持召开中共中央政治局会议，审议通过《深化财税体制改革总体方案》。

会议指出，财政是国家治理的基础和重要支柱，财税体制在治国安邦中始终发挥着基础性、制度性、保障性作用。我们党历来高度重视财政工作与财税改革，在建立适应中国特色社会主义发展要求的财政制度方面进行了不懈探索。新一轮财税体制改革是一场关系国家治理体系和治理能力现代化的深刻变革，是立足全局、着眼长远的制度创新。

会议认为，深化财税体制改革的目标是建立统一完整、法治规范、公开透明、运行高效，有利于优化资源配置、维护市场统一、促进社会公平、实现国家长治久安的可持续的现代财政制度。要重点推进三个方面的改革：改进预算管理制度，强化预算约束、规范政府行为、实现有效监督，加快建立全面规范、公开透明的现代预算制度；深化税收制度改革，优化税制结构，完善税收功能，稳定宏观税负，推进依法治税，建立有利于科学发展、社会公平和市场统一的税收制度体系，充分发挥税收筹集财政收入、调节分配和促进结构优化的职能作用；调整中央和地方政府间财政关系，在保持中央和地方收入格局大体稳定的前提下，进一步理顺中央和地方收入划分，合理划分政府间事权和支出责任，促进权力和责任、办事和花钱相统一，建立事权和支出责任相适应的制度。新一轮财税体制改革 2016 年基本完成重点工作和任务，2020 年基本建立现代财政制度。

会议强调，深化财税体制改革涉及中央和地方、政府和企业以及部门间权利调整，是一场牵一发而动全身的硬仗。各级党委和政府要全面贯彻党中央决策部署和要求，增强大局意识，以高度的政治责任感和历史使命感，加强组织领导，周密安排部署，注重统筹协调，把握力度节奏，精心组织实施，确保改革取得成功。

7 月 28 日，国务院发布《关于加快发展生产性服务业促进产业结构调整升级的指导意见》。意见中提出：尽快将"营改增"试点扩大到服务业全领域；根据生产性服务业产业融合度高的特点，完善促进生产性服务业的税收政策；研发设计、检验检测认证、节能环保等科技型和创新型生产性服务业企业，可以申请认定为高新技术企业，享受

15%的企业所得税优惠税率；研究适时扩大生产性服务业服务产品出口退税政策范围，制定产品退税目录和具体管理办法。

10月23日，中国共产党第十八届中央委员会第四次全体会议通过《中共中央关于全面推进依法治国若干重大问题的决定》。决定中提出：加强重点领域立法，完善社会主义市场经济法律制度，加强市场法律制度建设，编纂民法典，制定和完善发展规划、投资管理、土地管理、能源和矿产资源、农业、财政税收、金融等方面的法律法规，促进商品和要素自由流动、公平交易、平等使用。

12月9日至11日，中共中央、国务院在北京召开中央经济工作会议。会议提出：继续实施积极的财政政策，积极的财政政策要有力度。要加快推进改革开放。要敢于啃硬骨头，敢于涉险滩，敢于过深水区，加快推进经济体制改革。要围绕解决发展面临的突出问题推进改革，推出既具有年度特点、又有利于长远制度安排的改革举措，继续抓好各项改革方案制订。要尊重和发挥地方、基层、群众首创精神，从实践中寻找最佳方案。要抓好改革措施落地，狠抓落实，强化责任，加大协调力度。要强化督促评估，落实督办责任制和评估机制，让群众来评价改革成效。中共中央总书记、国家主席习近平和中共中央政治局常委、国务院总理李克强在会议上的讲话中就有关税收问题发表了重要的意见。

二、重要税收政策和税收措施

自1月1日起，根据2013年12月12日财政部、国家税务总局发出的《关于将铁路运输和邮政业纳入营业税改征增值税试点的通知》，铁路运输和邮政业纳入营业税改征增值税试点，铁路运输和邮政业的增值税税率均为11%。

1月21日，国务院发布《国家集成电路产业发展推进纲要》，其中提出了下列税收措施：

（1）进一步加大力度，贯彻落实国务院先后于2000年、2011年发出的《关于印发鼓励软件产业和集成电路产业发展若干政策的通知》和《关于印发进一步鼓励软件产业和集成电路产业发展若干政策的通知》，加快制定和完善相关实施细则和配套措施，保持政策稳定性，落实集成电路封装、测试、专用材料和设备企业所得税优惠政策。

（2）落实并完善支持集成电路企业兼并重组的企业所得税、增值税和营业税等税收政策。

（3）继续实施集成电路重大技术装备、产品关键零部件和原材料进口免税政策，有关科技重大专项所需国内不能生产的关键设备、零部件和原材料进口免税政策，适时调整免税进口商品清单或者目录。

1月22日，经国务院批准，国务院办公厅发布《关于促进地理信息产业发展的意见》，其中提出了下列税收措施：

（1）地理信息企业销售自主开发、生产和出版的地理信息产品，符合软件产品范围和认定条件的，可以申请享受国家鼓励软件产业发展的增值税优惠。

（2）地理信息企业符合软件企业认定条件的，认定以后可以申请享受有关软件企业所得税优惠。

（3）地理信息企业投资国家鼓励类项目，除了《国内投资项目不予免税的进口商品目录》所列商品以外，在投资总额以内所需进口自用设备和按照合同随设备进口的技术及配套件、备件，可以免征关税。

2月26日，国务院发布《关于推进文化创意和设计服务与相关产业融合发展的若干意见》，其中提出了下列税收措施：

（1）在文化创意和设计服务领域开展高新技术企业认定管理办法试点，将文化创意和设计服务内容纳入文化产业支撑技术等领域，认定为高新技术企业的文化创意和设计服务企业，减按15%的税率征收企业所得税。

（2）文化创意和设计服务企业发生的职工教育经费支出，不超过工资薪金总额8%的部分，可以在计算应纳税所得额时扣除。

（3）企业发生的符合条件的创意和设计费用，执行税前加计扣除政策。

（4）国家重点鼓励的文化创意和设计服务出口免征营业税。

（5）落实“营改增”试点有关政策，对纳入增值税征收范围的国家重点鼓励的文化创意和设计服务出口实行增值税零税率或者免税，对国家重点鼓励的创意和设计产品出口实行增值税零税率。

3月7日，国务院发布《关于进一步优化企业兼并重组市场环境的意见》，其中提出了下列税收措施：

（1）修订完善兼并重组企业所得税特殊性税务处理的政策，降低收购股权（资产）占被收购企业全部股权（资产）的比例限制，扩大特殊性税务处理政策的适用范围。

（2）抓紧研究完善非货币性资产投资交易的企业所得税、企业改制重组涉及的土地增值税等相关政策。

（3）企业通过合并、分立、出售和置换等方式，转让全部或者部分实物资产以及与其相关联的债权、债务和劳动力，不属于增值税和营业税征收范围，不应当视同销售征收增值税和营业税。

（4）税务部门要加强跟踪管理，企业兼并重组工作牵头部门要积极协助财税部门做好相关税收政策的落实。

据此，根据企业所得税法及其实施条例，财政部、国家税务总局于12月25日发出《关于促进企业重组有关企业所得税处理问题的通知》，12月31日发出《关于非货币性资产投资企业所得税政策问题的通知》。

4月2日，经国务院批准，国务院办公厅发布中共中央宣传部会同中共中央对外宣传办公室、财政部、国家税务总局等有关部门和单位拟订的《进一步支持文化企业发展的规定》，其中规定了下列税收措施，执行期限为2014年至2018年：

（1）电影制片企业销售电影拷贝、转让版权取得的收入，电影发行企业取得的电影发行收入，电影放映企业在农村的电影放映收入，免征增值税。

（2）一般纳税人提供的城市电影放映服务，可以按照现行政策规定，选择按照简易计税办法计算缴纳增值税。

（3）对于国家重点鼓励的文化产品出口实行增值税零税率。国家重点鼓励的文化服务出口，免征营业税。结合“营改增”试点，逐步将文化服务行业纳入试点范围。对于纳入增值税征收范围的上述文化服务出口，实行增值税零税率或者免税。

（4）为承担国家鼓励类文化产业项目进口国内不能生产的自用设备及配套件、备件，在政策规定范围以内免征关税。

（5）在国务院批准的中国服务外包示范城市从事服务外包业务的文化企业，符合现行税收优惠政策规定的技术先进型服务企业相关条件的，经过认定，可以享受有关税收优惠政策。

（6）从事文化产业支撑技术等领域的文化企业，按照规定认定为高新技术企业的，减按15%的税率征收企业所得税；开发新技术、新产品和新工艺发生的研究开发费用，可以依法在计算应纳税所得额时加计扣除。

（7）经过认定并符合软件企业相关条件的动漫企业，可以申请享受国家现行鼓励软件产业发展的所得税优惠政策；经认定的动漫企业自主开发、生产动漫直接产品确需进口的商品，按照现行规定免征关税和进口环节增值税。

（8）在国家许可范围以内，鼓励和引导社会资本以多种形式投资文化产业，参与国有经营性文化事业单位转企改制，参与重大文化产业项目实施和文化产业园区建设，在投资核准、银行贷款、土地使用、税收优惠、上市融资、发行债券、对外贸易和申请专项资金等方面给予支持。

（9）出版和发行单位处置库存呆滞出版物形成的损失，可以在企业所得税前扣除。

根据国务院办公厅发布的上述文件，11月27日，财政部、海关总署和国家税务总局发出《关于继续实施支持文化企业发展若干税收政策的通知》。

4月14日，经国务院批准，国务院办公厅转发国家发展和改革委员会报送的《关于建立保障天然气稳定供应长效机制的若干意见》。该文件中提出：落实鼓励开发低品位、老气田和进口天然气的税收政策。

4月29日，经国务院批准，财政部、国家税务总局发出《关于将电信业纳入营业税改征增值税试点的通知》，自6月1日起执行。通知中规定：提供基础电信服务，税率为11%；提供增值电信服务，税率为6%。

5月13日，经国务院批准，财政部、海关总署和国家税务总局发出《关于租赁企业进口飞机有关税收政策的通知》。通知中规定：自当年1月1日起，租赁企业一般贸易项下进口飞机并租给国内航空公司使用的，享受与国内航空公司进口飞机同等的税收优惠，即进口空载重量在25吨以上的飞机，减按5%征收进口环节增值税。

6月7日，经国务院批准，国务院办公厅发布《能源发展战略行动计划（2014—2020年）》。该计划中提出：加快资源税费改革，积极推进清费立税，逐步扩大资源税从价计征范围；研究调整能源消费税征税环节和税率，将部分高耗能、高污染产品纳入征收范围；完善节能减排税收政策，建立和完善生态补偿机制，加快推进环境保护税立法工作，探索建立绿色税收体系。

8月15日，国务院发布《关于促进海运业健康发展的若干意见》。该文件中提出：借鉴海运业发达国家经验，研究完善涉及国际海运的财税政策；加大现行财税政策执行力度，确保落实到位。

9月12日，国务院发布《物流业发展中长期规划（2014—2020年）》，该规划中提出：认真落实物流业相关税收优惠政策。

9月17日，国务院原则批准国家发改委报送的《国家应对气候变化规划（2014—2020年）》。该规划中提出：综合运用免税、减税和税收抵扣等多种税收优惠政策，促进低碳技术研发应用；研究对低碳产品（企业）的增值税（所得税）优惠政策；企业购进和自制低碳设备发生的进项税额，符合相关规定的，可以从销项税额中抵扣；实行鼓励先进节能低碳技术设备进口的税收优惠政策；落实促进新能源和可再生能源发展的税收优惠政策；在资源税、环境税、消费税和进出口税等税制改革中，积极考虑应对气候变化需要；研究符合中国国情的碳税制度。

10月20日，根据国务院关于完善固定资产加速折旧政策的决定，财政部、国家税务总局发出《关于完善固定资产加速折旧企业所得税政策的通知》，自当年1月1日起执行。通知中规定：

（1）生物药品制造业，专用设备制造业，铁路、船舶、航空航天和其他运输设备制造业，计算机、通信和其他电子设备制造业，仪器仪表制造业，信息传输、软件和信息技术服务业六个行业的企业2014年以后购进的固定资产，可以缩短折旧年限，或者采取加速折旧的方法。

上述六个行业的小型微利企业2014年以后购进的研发和生产、经营共用仪器、设备，单位价值不超过100万元的，可以一次性计入当期成本、费用，在计算应纳税所得额的时候扣除；单位价值超过100万元的，可以缩短折旧年限，或者采取加速折旧的方法。

（2）所有行业企业2014年以后购进的专门用于研发的仪器、设备，单位价值不超过100万元的，可以一次性计入当期成本、费用，在计算应纳税所得额的时候扣除；单位价值超过100万元的，可以缩短折旧年限，或者采取加速折旧的方法。

（3）所有行业企业持有的单位价值不超过5000元的固定资产，可以一次性计入当期成本、费用，在计算应纳税所得额的时候扣除。

11月16日，国务院发布《关于创新重点领域投融资机制鼓励社会投资的指导意见》。意见中提出：深化林业管理体制改革，减免林权流转税费，有效降低流转成本；进一步完善落实非营利性教育、医疗、养老、体育健身、文化机构税收优惠政策。

11月25日，经国务院批准，财政部、国家税务总局发出《关于调整消费税政策的通知》。通知中规定：自12月1日起，取消气缸容量不足250毫升的小排量摩托车消费税；取消汽车轮胎税目；取消车用含铅汽油消费税，汽油统一按照无铅汽油征收消费税；取消酒精消费税，“酒及酒精”税目相应改为“酒”。

11月28日，经国务院批准，财政部、国家税务总局发出《关于提高成品油消费税的通知》。通知中规定：自11月29日起，将汽油、石脑油、溶剂油和润滑油的消费税税额标准每升提高0.12元；将柴油、航空煤油和燃料油的消费税税额标准每升提高0.14元，航空煤油继续暂缓征税。

12月12日，财政部、国家税务总局发出《关于进一步提高成品油消费税的通知》。通知中规定：自12月13日起，将汽油、石脑油、溶剂油和润滑油的消费税税额标准从每升1.12元提高到每升1.4元；将柴油、航空煤油和燃料油的消费税税额标准从每升0.94元提高到每升1.1元，航空煤油继续暂缓征税。

三、进出口税收、跨国投资税收和国际税收关系

自1月1日起，2013年12月30日财政部、国家税务总局发出的《关于跨境电子商务零售出口税收政策的通知》开始执行：电子商务出口企业出口货物，符合规定条件的，适用增值税、消费税退（免）税或者免税规定。

1月13日，国家税务总局就新的中国政府和英国政府关于避免对所得和财产收益双重征税和防止偷漏税协定及议定书生效、执行发布公告：上述

协定和议定书自 2013 年 12 月 13 日起生效，适用于中国 2014 年以后纳税年度的所得和财产收益；英国 2014 年 4 月 6 日以后申报年度的所得税、财产收益税和 2014 年 4 月 1 日以后财政年度的公司税。

1 月 21 日，国家税务总局就新的中国政府和比利时共和国政府关于避免对所得双重征税和防止偷漏税协定及议定书生效、执行发布公告：上述协定和议定书自 2013 年 12 月 29 日起生效，自 2014 年 1 月 1 日起执行。

2 月 16 日，国务院发出《关于完善出口退税负担机制有关问题的通知》。通知中规定：自当年 1 月 1 日起，出口退税（包括出口货物退增值税和营业税改征增值税出口退税）全部由中央财政负担。

2 月 17 日，国务院发布《关于进一步做好境外投资工作的若干意见》。该文件中提出：加快与有关国家商签避免双重征税协定，扩大和完善避免双重征税协定网络，增强中国企业境外税收权益保障；落实企业境外所得税收抵免政策，改进避免国际重复征税方式，创造有利的税务环境。

2 月 18 日，财政部、国家发展改革委、工业和信息化部、海关总署、国家税务总局和国家能源局发出《关于调整重大技术装备进口税收政策的通知》。通知中规定：

（1）《重大技术装备进口税收政策规定》自 3 月 1 日起执行。符合规定条件的国内企业为生产国家支持发展的重大技术装备、产品确有必要进口部分关键零部件、原材料，免征关税和进口环节增值税。

（2）《国家支持发展的重大技术装备和产品目录（2014 年修订）》和《重大技术装备和产品进口关键零部件及原材料商品目录（2014 年修订）》自 3 月 1 日起执行，符合规定条件的国内企业为生产本通知附件 2 所列装备和产品确有必要进口本通知附件 3 所列商品，免征关税和进口环节增值税。

（3）《进口不予免税的重大技术装备和产品目录（2014 年修订）》自 3 月 1 日起执行。3 月 1 日以后批准的按照和比照《国务院关于调整进口设备税收政策的通知》（国发〔1997〕37 号）规定享受进口税收优惠政策的下列项目和企业，进口本通知附件 4 所列自用设备和按照合同随上述设备进口的技术及配套件、备件，一律照章征收进口税收：国家鼓励发展的国内投资项目和外商投资项目、外国政府贷款和国际金融组织贷款项目、由外商提供不作价进口设备的加工贸易企业、中西部地区外商投资优势产业项目、《海关总署关于进一步鼓励外商投资有关进口税收政策的通知》（署税〔1999〕791 号）规定的外商投资企业和外商投资设立的研究中心利用自有资金进行技术改造项目。

3 月 3 日，国务院发布《关于加快发展对外文化贸易的意见》，其中提出了下列税收的措施：

（1）国家重点鼓励的文化产品出口，适用增值税零税率。国家重点鼓励的文化服务出口，免征营业税。结合“营改增”试点，逐步将文化服务行业纳入试点范围，对纳入增值税征收范围的文化服务出口实行增值税零税率或者免税。享受税收优惠政策的国家重点鼓励的文化产品和服务的具体范围，由财政部、国家税务总局会同有关部门确定。12 月 30 日，财政部、国家税务总局据此发出《关于支持文化服务出口等营业税政策的通知》。通知中规定：纳税人为中国境外单位、个人在中国境外提供文物、遗址等的修复保护服务，纳入国家级非物质文化遗产名录的传统医药诊疗保健服务，免征营业税。上述规定自 2015 年起执行，此前没有处理的事项，按照上述规定执行。

（2）在国务院批准的服务外包示范城市从事服务外包业务的文化企业，符合现行税收优惠政策规定的技术先进型服务企业相关条件的，经过认定，减按 15%的税率征收企业所得税，职工教育经费不超过工资、薪金总额 8%的部分可以税前扣除。

3 月 10 日，国家税务总局就中国政府和厄瓜多尔共和国政府关于避免所得双重征税和防止偷漏税的协定和议定书生效、执行发布公告，上述协定和议定书自 2014 年 3 月 6 日起生效，并适用于 2015 年 1 月 1 日以后取得的所得。

3 月 25 日，经国务院批准，财政部、国家税务总局发出《关于广东横琴新区、福建平潭综合实验区、深圳前海深港现代化服务业合作区企业所得税优惠政策及优惠目录的通知》。通知中规定：设在横琴新区、平潭综合实验区和前海深港现代服务业合作区的鼓励类产业企业，可以减按 15%的税率征收企业所得税。企业既符合通知规定的减按 15%税率征收企业所得税优惠条件，又符合企业所得税法及其实施条例和国务院规定的其他各项税收优惠条件的，可以同时享受；其中符合其他税率优惠条件的，可以选择最优惠的税率执行；涉及定期减免税的减半优惠的，应当按照25%法定税率计算的应纳税额减半征收企业所得税。上述规定的执行期限为2014年至2020年。

3月26日，中国和法国在巴黎发表《中法关系中长期规划》。规划中提出：推进税务部门之间密切合作，落实2013年11月26日签署的谅解备忘录。

3月28日，中国政府与德国政府在柏林签订新的关于避免对所得和财产双重征税和防止偷漏税的协定，中国国家主席习近平和德国政府总理安格拉·默克尔出席该协定的签字仪式。

5月4日，经国务院批准，国务院办公厅发布《关于支持外贸稳定增长的若干意见》。该文件中提出：结合“营改增”范围扩大，对服务出口实行零税率或者免税；加大中央财政对出口退税负担较重地区的补助力度，进一步加快出口退税进度，确保及时足额退税；适时扩大融资租赁货物出口退税试点范围。同时，加大打击骗退税力度。9月1日，财政部、海关总署和国家税务总局据此发出《关于在全国开展融资租赁货物出口退税政策试点的通知》，决定自10月1日起将在天津东疆保税港区试点的融资租赁货物出口退税政策扩大到全国统一实施。

5月18日，中国国家税务总局与吉尔吉斯共和国国家税务总局签署合作备忘录，中国国家主席习近平、吉尔吉斯共和国总统阿尔马兹别克·阿坦巴耶夫总统出席该合作备忘录的签字仪式。

6月9日，经国务院批准，国务院办公厅发出《关于进一步加强贸易政策合规工作的通知》。通知中提及的直接影响进口的政策措施包括海关程序、估价和原产地规则，关税，影响进口的间接税等；直接影响出口的政策措施包括出口税、出口退税和加工贸易税收减让等；其他影响贸易的政策措施包括税收优惠政策等。

6月11日，经国务院批准，财政部、海关总署和国家税务总局发出《关于横琴、平潭开发有关增值税和消费税政策的通知》。通知中规定：内地销往横琴、平潭与生产有关的货物，视同出口，实行增值税和消费税退税；横琴、平潭各自的区内企业之间销售其在本区内的货物，免征增值税和消费税另有规定者除外。横琴、平潭已经享受免税、保税和退税的货物销往内地，除了在“一线”已经完税的生活消费类等货物以外，按照规定征收进口税收；在“一线”已经完税的生活消费类等货物销往内地的，按照规定征收增值税和消费税。

7月15日，中国国家主席习近平与巴西、俄罗斯、印度、南非领导人在巴西福塔莱萨举行金砖国家领导人第六次会晤，发表《金砖国家领导人第六次会晤福塔莱萨宣言》。宣言第十七条如下：“我们认为，对经济活动发生地辖区进行征税有利于实现可持续发展和经济增长。我们对逃税、跨国税务欺诈和恶意税收筹划给世界经济造成的危害表示关切。我们认识到恶意避税和非合规行为带来的挑战。因此，我们强调在税收征管方面合作的承诺，并将在打击税基侵蚀和税收情报交换全球论坛中加强合作。我们指示有关部门探讨在该领域加强合作，并指示相关部门在海关领域加强合作。”

8月1日，国家税务总局就新的《中国政府和荷兰政府关于避免对所得避免双重征税和防止偷漏税的协定及议定书》生效、执行发布公告，上述协定和议定书自2014年8月31日起生效，并适用于2015年1月1日以后取得的所得。

8月9日，国务院发布《关于促进旅游业改革发展的若干意见》。该文件中提出：在具备条件的口岸可以按照规定设立出境免税店；研究完善境外旅客购物离境退税政策，将实施范围扩大至全国符合条件的地区；在切实落实进出境游客行李物品监管的前提下，研究新增进境口岸免税店的可行性。

9月20日至21日，二十国集团（G20）财政部部长和中央银行行长会议在澳大利亚举行，讨论当前全球经济形势、G20全面增长战略、长期投资、金融监管改革和国际税收合作等议题，财政部部长楼继伟和中国人民银行行长周小川率领中国代表团参加会议。会议承诺2015年完成G20/OECD为期2年的应对税基侵蚀和利润转移行动计划；核准了基于互惠原则的税收情报自动交换全球标准；并明确将在2017年或者2018年底前，根据本国立法程序完成情况，在G20成员之间及与其他国家之间启动实施税收情报自动交换。

10月13日，中国政府与俄罗斯政府在莫斯科签订新的关于避免对所得双重征税和防止偷漏税的协定及议定书，中国国务院总理李克强和俄罗斯联邦政府总理德米特里·阿纳托利耶维奇·梅德韦杰夫出席上述协定及议定书的签字仪式。

11月15日至16日，中国国家主席习近平出席G20领导人第九次峰会并两次发言。他在谈及创新发展方式时提出："我们必须创新发展理念、政策、方式，更加重视增长质量和效益，特别是通过财税、金融、投资、竞争、贸易、就业等领域的结构改革，通过宏观经济政策和社会政策的结合，让创造财富的活力竞相迸发，让市场力量充分释放，推动经济从周期性复苏走向可持续性增长。"他在讨论增强世界经济抗风险能力议题时提出：加强全球税收合作，打击国际逃避税，帮助发展中国家和低收入国家提高税收征管能力。

峰会发表的公报中提出："我们正在采取措施，确保国际税收体系公平，保障各国税基。对经济利润课税时，应当在创造利润的经济活动发生地或价值创造地进行。我们欢迎G20/经合组织提出的税基侵蚀和利润转移行动计划在推动国际税收规则现代化方面取得的重大进展，承诺在2015年完成有关工作。我们欢迎在专利税方面取得的进展。为防止跨境逃税，我们核准在对等基础上开展的税收情报自动交换全球统一报告标准。根据各国完成必要立法程序情况，我们将于2017年或2018年底同各成员国和其他国家开展税收情报自动交换。我们欢迎金融中心承诺采取相同行动，并呼吁所有相关方加入。我们欢迎发展中国家深化参与税基侵蚀和利润转移项目，以解决其关切。我们将同他们一道，建设其税收征管能力，并落实税收情报自动交换全球标准。我们欢迎各国税收当局就跨境合规行为开展进一步合作。"

12月24日，国务院发布《关于促进服务外包产业加快发展的意见》。意见中提出：从区域和领域上扩大对技术先进型服务企业减按15%税率缴纳企业所得税和职工教育经费不超过工资总额8%部分税前扣除的税收优惠政策实施范围。实行国际服务外包增值税零税率和免税政策。

12月26日，经国务院批准，国务院办公厅发出《关于进一步规范同外国缔结贸易和投资条约有关问题的通知》。通知中规定：贸易和投资条约涉及法律规定的税率调整的，应当提请全国人民代表大会常务委员会决定批准；涉及行政法规规定的税率调整的，应当报请国务院核准。缔结其他国际经贸条约，具有上述情形的，国务院有关主管部门可以会商外交部以后建议国务院参照上述规定办理。

12月31日，经国务院批准，财政部、国家税务总局发出《关于调整部分产品出口退税率的通知》。通知中规定：自2015年1月1日起提高部分高附加值产品、玉米加工产品和纺织品服装的出口退税率，取消含硼钢的出口退税。

据财政部统计，2014年，随着中国进出口贸易的增长，增值税、消费税进口环节的征税额从2013年的14004.6亿元增加到14425.3亿元，增长了3.0%；出口退税额从2013年的10518.9亿元增加到11356.5亿元，增长了8.0%。

四、税收法制和税收管理

1月28日，国务院发布《关于取消和下放一批行政审批项目的决定》，其中涉及扣缴税款登记核准等四个税收方面的项目。

2月13日，经国务院批准，国务院办公厅发布《国务院2014年立法计划》。计划中将税收征管法（修订）和环境保护税法列为预备项目，将消费税暂行条例（修订）和资源税暂行条例（修订）列为研究项目。

同日，国家税务总局发布《关于公开行政审批事项等相关工作的公告》，公开现行行政审批事项清单，接受社会监督，并听取社会各界对进一步取消和下放行政审批事项的意见。本次公开的行政审批事项，包括国家税务总局审批事项、国家税务局审批事项和既可以由国家税务局审批、也可以由地方税务局审批的事项。

4月17日，全国人大常委会公布2013年12月16日第十二届全国人民代表大会常务委员会第十四次委员长会议原则通过、2014年4月14日第十二届全国人民代表大会常务委员会第二十一次委员长会议修改的《全国人大常委会2014年立法工作计划》。其中，预算法（修改）列为继续审议的法律案，将根据情况适时安排审议；单行税法列为预备项目。

6月6日，国务院发出《关于对稳增长促改革调结构惠民生政策措施落实情况开展全面督查的通知》，其中规定的重点督查内容包括扩大"营改增"试点、减轻和公平企业税负的政策措施落实情况。

6月14日，国务院发布《社会信用体系建设规划纲要（2014—2020年）》，其中提出了下列有关税收的措施：

（1）税务领域信用建设。建立跨部门信用信息共享机制。开展纳税人基础信息、各类交易信息、财产保有和转让信息以及纳税记录等涉税信息的交换、比对和应用工作。进一步完善纳税信用等级评定和发布制度，加强税务领域信用分类管理，发挥信用评定差异对纳税人的奖惩作用。建立税收违法黑名单制度。推进纳税信用与其他社会信用联动管理，提升纳税人税法遵从度。

（2）加强重点领域信用记录建设。以工商、纳税、价格、进出口、安全生产、产品质量、环境保护、食品药品、医疗卫生、知识产权、流通服务、工程建设、电子商务、交通运输、合同履约、人力资源和社会保障、教育科研等领域为重点，完善行业信用记录和从业人员信用档案。

（3）加强对守信主体的奖励和激励。加大对守信行为的表彰和宣传力度。按规定对诚信企业和模范个人给予表彰，通过新闻媒体广泛宣传，营造守信光荣的舆论氛围。发展改革、财政、金融、环境保护、住房城乡建设、交通运输、商务、工商、税务、质检、安全监管、海关和知识产权等部门，在市场监管和公共服务过程中，要深化信用信息和信用产品的应用，对诚实守信者实行优先办理、简化程序等“绿色通道”支持激励政策。

6月16日，经国务院批准，国务院办公厅发出《关于进一步加强涉企收费管理减轻企业负担的通知》。通知中规定：按照“正税清费”原则，进一步清理取消、整合规范现行涉企行政事业性收费和政府性基金项目，依法将具有税收性质的收费基金项目并入相应的税种。

7月4日，根据税收征管法及其实施细则和国务院的有关规定，国家税务总局公布《纳税信用管理办法（试行）》，自10月1日起施行。8月25日，国家税务总局据此公布《纳税信用评价指标和评价方式（试行）》，自10月1日起施行。

同日，根据税收征管法及其实施细则和国家税务总局的有关规定，国家税务总局公布《重大税收违法案件信息公布办法（试行）》，自10月1日起施行。

7月22日，国务院发布《关于取消和调整一批行政审批项目等事项的决定》。决定中规定取消的行政审批项目中，包括国家税务总局规定的享受小型微利企业所得税优惠的核准，国家税务总局、财政部等4个部门规定的吸纳下岗失业人员达到规定条件的服务型、商贸企业和下岗失业人员从事个体经营减免税的审批；取消的职业资格许可项目中，包括人力资源和社会保障部、国家税务总局规定的注册税务师。

8月7日，国务院公布《企业信息公示暂行条例》。条例中规定：企业应当按照规定向工商行政管理部门报送上一年度年度报告，其中包括纳税总额等信息；纳税总额由企业选择是否向社会公示；经企业同意，公民、法人和其他组织可以查询企业的纳税总额。

8月12日，最高人民法院、最高人民检察院公布《关于办理走私刑事案件适用法律若干问题的解释》，自9月10日起施行。解释中规定：走私普通货物、物品，偷逃应缴税额在10万元以上不满50万元的，应当认定为刑法第一百五十三条第一款规定的“偷逃应缴税额较大”；偷逃应缴税额在50万元以上不满250万元的，应当认定为“偷逃应缴税额巨大”；偷逃应缴税额在250万元以上的，应当认定为“偷逃应缴税额特别巨大”。

8月28日，国家税务总局发布《全国县级税务机关纳税服务规范（1.0版）》，自当年10月1日起试运行。12月23日，国家税务总局发布《全国税务机关纳税服务规范》，自2015年3月1日起施行。

8月31日，第十二届全国人民代表大会常务委员会第十次会议通过《全国人民代表大会常务委员会关于修改〈中华人民共和国预算法〉的决定》。修改以后的预算法第五十五条规定：“预算收入征收部门和单位，必须依照法律、行政法规的规定，及时、足额征收应征的预算收入。不得违反法律、行政法规规定，多征、提前征收或者减征、免征、缓征应征的预算收入，不得截留、占用或者挪用预算收入。”“各级政府不得向预算收入征收部门和单位下达收入指标。”第五十六条中规定：“政府的全部收入应当上缴国家金库（以下简称国库），任何部门、单位和个人不得截留、占用、挪用或者拖欠。”

9月26日，国务院发布《关于深化预算管理制度改革的决定》，其中做出了下列有关税收的规定：

（1）加强税收征管。各级税收征管部门要依照法律、法规及时足额组织税收收入，并建立与相关经济指标变化情况相衔接的考核体系。切实加强税收征管，做到依法征收、应收尽收，不收过头税。严格减免税管理，不得违反法律、法规的规定和超越权限多征、提前征收或者减征、免征、缓征应征税款。加强执法监督，强化税收入库管理。

（2）全面规范税收优惠政策。除了专门的税收法律、法规和国务院规定以外，各部门起草其他法律、法规、发展规划和区域政策都不得突破国家统一财税制度、规定税收优惠政策。未经国务院批准，各地区、各部门不能对企业规定财政优惠政策。各地区、各部门要规范已经出台的税收优惠政策，违反法律、法规和国务院规定的一律停止执行；没有法律、法规障碍且具有推广价值的，尽快在全国实施；有明确时限的到期停止执行，未明确时限的应当设定优惠政策实施时限。建立税收优惠政策备案审查、定期评估和退出机制，加强考核问责，严惩各类违法违规行为。

10月23日，国务院发布《关于取消和调整一批行政审批项目等事项的决定》，其中涉及销货退回的消费税退税审批等7个税收方面的项目。

11月24日，国务院公布《不动产登记暂行条例》，自2015年3月1日起施行。条例第二十五条规定："国土资源、公安、民政、财政、税务、工商、金融、审计、统计等部门应当加强不动产登记有关信息互通共享。"

11月27日，国务院发出《关于清理规范税收等优惠政策的通知》。通知中要求各地区、各部门充分认识清理规范税收等优惠政策的重大意义，明确指导思想和主要原则，切实规范各类税收等优惠政策，全面清理已有的各类税收等优惠政策，建立健全长效机制，健全保障措施。

12月2日，根据行政处罚法、税收征管法，国家税务总局公布修订以后的《重大税务案件审理办法》，自2015年2月1日起施行。

同日，根据税收征管法及其实施细则、车辆购置税暂行条例和有关法律、法规，国家税务总局公布修订以后的《车辆购置税征收管理办法》，自2015年2月1日起施行。

同日，根据企业所得税法及其实施条例、税收征管法及其实施细则，国家税务总局公布《一般反避税管理办法（试行）》，自2015年2月1日起施行。

12月17日，国家发改委、国家税务总局、中央文明办、最高人民法院、公安部、财政部、国土资源部、交通运输部、商务部和人民银行等21个单位签署《关于对重大税收违法案件当事人实施联合惩戒措施的合作备忘录》，对税务机关公布的重大税收违法案件当事人实施18项联合惩戒措施。

12月26日，国务院发布《落实"三互"推进大通关建设改革方案》（指"三互"口岸管理相关部门信息互换、监管互认和执法互助）。方案中提出：完善口岸监管执法互助机制，强化口岸管理相关部门在防控暴恐、应对突发事件、打击走私、打击骗退税、查处逃避检验检疫、反偷渡和制止不安全产品及假冒伪劣商品进出境等方面的全方位合作。优化出口退税服务。

12月27日，国务院发布《关于改革和完善中央对地方转移支付制度的意见》。意见中提出：结合税费制度改革，完善相关法律、法规，逐步取消城市维护建设税、排污费、探矿权和采矿权价款、矿产资源补偿费等专款专用的规定，统筹安排这些领域的经费。加强竞争性领域专项与税收优惠政策的协调，可以通过税收优惠政策取得类似或者更好政策效果的，应当尽量采用税收优惠政策，相应取消竞争性领域专项。税收优惠政策应当由专门税收法律、法规或者国务院规定。

同日，根据国务院关于取消有关行政审批项目的决定，国家税务总局公布《关于修改〈税务登记管理办法〉的决定》和《关于修改〈中华人民共和国发票管理办法实施细则〉的决定》。

据财政部统计，2014年全国税收收入119175.3亿元，比上年增长了7.8%；税收收入占财政收入的比重为84.9%，比上年下降了0.6个百分点。按照国家统计局初步统计的当年全年生产总值计算，税收收入占国内生产总值的比重为18.7%，比上年下降了0.1个百分点。

（中国税务报社　刘佐）

中国出入境检验检疫制度

中华人民共和国国家质量监督检验检疫总局（以下简称国家质检总局）是国务院主管全国质量、计量、出入境商品检验、出入境卫生检疫、出入境动植物检疫和认证认可、标准化等工作，并行使行政执法职能的正部级直属机构。

与国家质检总局职能关系密切的有两个协定，即世界贸易组织的《技术性贸易壁垒协定》（TBT协定）和《实施卫生与植物卫生措施协定》（SPS协定）。中国自加入世界贸易组织以来，积极遵循WTO相关规则的规定，制定修订并实施出入境检验检疫法律法规、规章、标准，形成了比较完善的出入境检验检疫制度，在保护人类健康和安全、保护动物或者植物的生命和健康、保护环境、防止欺诈行为、维护国家安全等方面发挥了积极作用。

一、中国检验检疫发展历程

1949 年中华人民共和国成立，我国依照国际惯例设立相应的检验检疫机构。1953 年，中央政府在贸易部内设立商检总局，并在各地设立检疫机构。1960 年开始，检验检疫机构实行以地方领导为主的双重领导体制，由各级外贸和卫生部门主管。1965 年对外植物检疫工作从商品检验部门移交给各地农业部门，一些重要的国境口岸设立了动植物检疫所。

改革开放以后，各级检验检疫机构又陆续划归中央垂直领导，逐渐形成了国家进出口商品检验局、国家动植物检疫局和国家卫生检疫局“三检”共同把关、各负其责的检验检疫体制。

1998 年 3 月，全国人大九届一次会议批准通过的国务院机构改革方案确定，国家进出口商品检验局、国家动植物检疫局和国家卫生检疫局合并组建国家出入境检验检疫局，将原由卫生部承担的国境卫生检疫、进口食品卫生监督检验的职能，交给国家出入境检验检疫局；将原由农业部承担的进出境动植物检疫的职能，交给国家出入境检验检疫局；将原国家进出口商品检验局承担的进出口商品检验、鉴定和监管的职能，交给国家出入境检验检疫局。国家出入境检验检疫局主管全国出入境卫生检疫、动植物检疫和商品检验工作，其职责更加明确，法律地位更加清晰，机构和人员更加精简。

2001 年 4 月，国务院决定将国家质量技术监督局、国家出入境检验检疫局合并，组建中华人民共和国国家质量监督检验检疫总局，同时成立国家认证认可监督管理委员会和国家标准化管理委员会，分别统一管理全国质量认证、认可和标准化工作。国家质检总局的成立，是实行政府职能转变、适应社会主义市场经济体制的需要，有利于制定统一的质量技术标准、防止和打击质量违法行为，有利于把好出入境检验检疫关、保护企业和消费者合法权益，有利于充分发挥检验检疫和质量监督的整体优势、进一步加强质量监督和出入境检验检疫工作，有利于引导企业提高产品和服务质量，有利于我国在 WTO 规则内更好地开展国际合作和竞争。

二、中国的口岸检验检疫制度

口岸是国家设立的供人员、物资、交通工具等进出境的关口，被形象地称为国门。国家在口岸负责监督人员、货物、交通工具等进出境的行政执法部门共三个，即“一关二检”——海关、边检、检验检疫。其中边检负责人员进出的管理，海关负责进出商品的税收征管，检验检疫负责对进出境人员、动植物、商品检验和检疫。对出入的动植物和商品，海关与检验检疫有交叉，二者的关系为：对国家规定的有关物品施行“先报检后报关”，即对纳入《出入境检验检疫机构实施检验检疫的进出境商品目录》的商品，进出口企业必须先报检，经检验检疫后，由检验检疫机构出具证明，海关予以放行。由于进出境动植物、商品的品质性状的可变性，在产地和口岸的检验检疫机构之间又形成了较为明确的分工，即产地检验，口岸查验、换证放行。

三、中国出入境检验检疫法律法规依据

中国现行出入境检验检疫方面的法律法规主要

是“四法三条例”，具体是：

（一）商检法及其实施条例

1989 年 2 月 21 日，第七届全国人民代表大会常务委员会第六次会议通过《中华人民共和国进出口商品检验法》，2002 年 4 月 28 日第九届全国人民代表大会常务委员会第二十七次会议修订，共 6 章 41 条。

商检法明确，为了加强进出口商品检验，保证商品质量，维护对外贸易有关各方的合法权益，促进对外经济贸易关系顺利发展，对进出口商品实施品质等检验。商检法是进出口商品检验和监督管理的法律依据，规定国家商检部门根据保护人类健康和安全、保护动物或者植物的生命和健康、保护环境、防止欺诈行为、维护国家安全的原则，制定、调整并公布实施必须实施检验的进出口商品目录，列入目录的进口商品未经检验不准销售、使用；列入目录的出口商品未经检验合格的不准出口。对必须经商检机构检验的进出口商品以外的进出口商品，商检法规定商检机构根据国家规定实施抽查检验。

（二）动植物检疫法及其实施条例

1991 年 10 月 30 日，第七届全国人民代表大会常务委员会第二十二次会议通过《中华人民共和国进出境动植物检疫法》，共 8 章 50 条。

动植物检疫法是进出境动植物检疫和监督管理的法律依据，明确了进出境的动植物、动植物产品和其他检疫物，装载动植物、动植物产品和其他检疫物的装载容器、包装物，以及来自动植物疫区的运输工具，应接受动植物检疫机关的检疫和监管。输入动物、动物产品、植物种子、种苗及其他繁殖材料的，必须事先办理检疫审批手续，并在进境时接受检疫，检疫合格的准予入境。输出动植物、动植物产品和其他检疫物，由动植物检疫机关实施检疫，经检疫合格或者经除害处理合格的准予出境。来自动植物疫区的船舶、飞机、火车抵达口岸时，由动植物检疫机关实施检疫。

（三）卫生检疫法及其实施细则

1986 年 12 月 2 日，第六届全国人民代表大会常务委员会第十八次会议通过《中华人民共和国国境卫生检疫法》，2007 年 12 月 29 日第十届全国人民代表大会常务委员会第三十一次会议修订，共 6 章 28 条。

卫生检疫法是国境卫生检疫和监督管理的法律依据，明确了出入境的人员、交通工具、运输设备以及可能传播检疫传染病的行李、货物、邮包等物品，都应当接受检疫，经国境卫生检疫机关许可，方准入境或者出境。入境的交通工具和人员，必须在最先到达的国境口岸的指定地点接受检疫；出境的交通工具和人员，必须在最后离开的国境口岸接受检疫。国境卫生检疫机关对入境、出境的人员实施传染病监测，并且采取必要的预防、控制措施，对国境口岸的卫生状况和停留在国境口岸的入境、出境的交通工具的卫生状况实施卫生监督。

（四）食品安全法

2009 年 2 月 28 日，第十一届全国人大常委会第七次会议通过《中华人民共和国食品安全法》，共 10 章 104 条。2009 年 7 月 20 日，国务院颁布食品安全法实施条例，共 10 章 64 条。2015 年 4 月 24 日，《中华人民共和国食品安全法》经第十二届全国人民代表大会常务委员会第十四次会议修订通过，自 2015 年 10 月 1 日起施行。

食品安全法规定出入境检验检疫机构在食品进出口环节的职责。进口食品应当经出入境检验检疫机构检验合格，出口食品由出入境检验检疫机构进行监督、抽检。向我国境内出口食品的出口商或者代理商应当向国家出入境检验检疫部门备案。向我国境内出口食品的境外食品生产企业应当经国家出入境检验检疫部门注册，出口食品生产企业和出口食品原料种植、养殖场应当向国家出入境检验检疫部门备案。国家出入境检验检疫部门收集、汇总进出口食品安全信息，并及时通报相关部门、机构和企业。国家出入境检验检疫部门建立进出口食品的进口商、出口商和出口食品生产企业的信誉记录，并予以公布。对有不良记录的进口商、出口商和出口食品生产企业，加强对其进出口食品的检验检疫。

新修订的《食品安全法》围绕最严谨的标准、最严格的监管、最严格的处罚和最严肃的问责这几项要求，突出了五大特点，一是更加突出预防为主；二是建立最严格的全过程的过程控制；三是创新食品安全的监管制度；四是建立最严格的法律责任制度；五是突出食品安全制度共治体系。在严格法律责任方面，首先是强化了企业主体责任的落实，明确提出食品生产经营者是食品安全第一责任人，对其生产经营的食品安全负责。规定了食品生产经营者应当建立食品追溯体系。另外应当对召回的食品采取无害化的处理，包括销毁，防止再次流入市场。

其他与出入境检验检疫相关的法律法规还有《中华人民共和国认证认可条例》《中华人民共和国农产品质量安全法》等，以上的法律法规共同构成了我国出入境检验检疫的法律体系。

四、国家质检总局检验检疫方面的职责和机构设置

质检总局在出入境检验检疫方面的职责主要是：组织起草有关检验检疫方面的法律、法规草案，研究拟定检验检疫工作的方针政策，制定和发布有关规章、制度；组织实施与检验检疫相关的法律、法规，指导、监督检验检疫的行政执法工作。

拟订出入境检验检疫综合业务规章、制度；负责口岸出入境检验检疫业务管理；负责商品普惠制原产地证和一般原产地证的签证管理。

组织实施出入境卫生检疫、传染病监测、卫生监督工作；管理国外疫情的收集、分析、整理，提供信息指导和咨询服务。

组织实施出入境动植物检疫和监督管理；管理国外重大动植物疫情的收集、分析、整理，提供信息指导和咨询服务；依法负责出入境转基因生物及其产品的检验检疫工作。

组织实施进出口食品和化妆品的安全、卫生、质量监督检验和监督管理；管理进出口食品和化妆品生产、加工单位的卫生注册登记和备案，管理出口企业对外卫生注册工作。

组织实施进出口商品法定检验和监督管理；监督管理进出口商品鉴定和外商投资财产价值鉴定；管理国家实行进口许可制度的民用商品的入境验证工作；审批法定检验商品免验和组织办理复验；组织进出口商品检验检疫的前期监督和后续管理；管理出入境检验检疫标志（标识）、进口安全质量许可、出口质量许可，并负责监督管理。依法审批并监督管理涉外检验、鉴定机构（含中外合资和合作的检验、鉴定机构）。

管理与协调质量监督检验检疫方面的国际合作与交流；代表国家参加与质量监督检验检疫有关的国际组织或区域性组织，签署并负责执行有关国际合作协定、协议和议定书，审批与实施有关国际合作与交流项目；按规定承担技术性贸易壁垒协议和卫生与植物卫生措施协定的实施、通报和咨询工作。

为履行出入境检验检疫职能，国家质检总局在全国31省（自治区、直辖市）共设有35个直属出入境检验检疫局，海陆空口岸和货物集散地设有近300个分支局和200多个办事处，共有检验检疫人员5万余人。质检总局对出入境检验检疫机构实施垂直管理。

五、中国出入境检验检疫工作的主要内容

出入境检验检疫工作的基本原则，是保护人类健康和安全、保护动物或者植物的生命和健康、保护环境、防止欺诈行为、维护国家安全。国家质检总局依法制定《出入境检验检疫机构实施检验检疫的进出境商品目录》（以下简称《目录》），对出入境货物、交通工具和人员实施检验检疫通关管理，在口岸对出入境货物实行“先报检，后报关”的检验检疫货物通关管理模式。在非口岸，实施产地检验，口岸查验、换证放行通关管理模式。

（一）防止疫病疫情传入传出

通过对出入境人员、货物、交通工具等实施检验检疫，防止各种严重传染病及其传播媒介的传播。其中对出境人员实行健康体检，预防接种，确保出境人员健康；对入境人员查验健康证书，实施健康监测，及时发现染疫人员，采取相应措施。经过多年的实践，特别是经过抗击非典、高致病性禽流感、登革热以及甲型H1N1流感等严重疫病疫情，出入境检验检疫机构形成了查验体温、疑似病例报告、染疫人员应急处理以及口岸值班制度、紧急情况报告制度等口岸卫生查验体系，完善突发事件紧急处置机制，形成了设施齐全、功能齐备、运转高效、反应灵敏、应对有力的口岸突发事件防御体系。

（二）防止有害生物传入传出

通过对出入境动植物及其产品和运输工具、集装箱、木制包装物等的检验检疫，防止有害生物和动植物疫病疫情传入传出。其中对出入境的动植物及其产品需经过风险分析、双边市场准入、强制隔离检疫、检疫处理，对来自疫区的入境运输工具和

集装箱进行消杀灭处理，对查出疫情的产品予以退回、销毁或无害化处理。我国基本建立了严格科学的防止有害生物入侵体系，并在全国进行了大范围的疫情监测，以切实保证农业生产、生态安全和经济安全。

（三）防止有毒有害物质传入传出

针对入境货物携带有毒有害物质，特别是前些年进口废物原料夹带生活垃圾和废钢铁放射超标，国外废旧淘汰机电产品大量进境等情况，检验检疫部门加强了对有毒有害物质的防范，加强了对进口废物原料供货企业的管理，全面实施了装运前检验和到岸查验制度，对不符合我国环保要求的废物原料一律实行退运处理。与有关部门联合对废旧机电产品进口加强了管理，实施了废旧机电产品到岸逐一检查制度，对未经审批和不符合规定的废旧机电产品禁止入境，严厉打击非法入境行为。

（四）防止不合格商品传入传出

实施出入境检验检疫制度，一方面确保出口商品的质量，维护国家利益和国家形象；另一方面防止不合格商品进入我国，保护消费者健康安全。为了提高进出口商品质量，特别是保证高风险的农产品、食品质量安全，保证大宗原料质量和保证我国急需的重要设备质量，分别实行了强制性认证、卫生注册、生产过程监管、口岸查验、境外预检、风险预警、驻厂检验检疫等措施。各级检验检疫机构还帮助企业完善质量管理，提高生产工艺，积极采用先进标准，建立健全企业自检体系。同时积极向企业提供国外有关规定和国际市场信息，促使企业严格按照国外标准进行生产，提高质量。

（国家质量监督检验检疫总局通关司）

中国出口退税情况

2014年中国出口退（免）税额为11329.31亿元，比上年增长7.7%，其中出口货物退增值税7939.31亿元，免抵调减增值税3375.26亿元，出口消费品退消费税14.74亿元。出口退（免）税额前三位的广东省（含深圳）3123.97亿元，浙江省（含宁波）1854.61亿元，江苏省1842.5亿元，占全国出口退税额总量的60%，突破百亿退税额的省市达到20个。在世界经济缓慢复苏、国内经济下行压力较大的形势下，中国采取的一系列出口退税政策有力地支持了外贸出口平稳健康增长。

一、落实完善出口税收政策，支持外贸出口发展

（一）率先落实国务院支持跨境电子商务发展的政策

2013年12月30日，财政部、国家税务总局发布《财政部 国家税务总局关于跨境电子商务零售出口税收政策的通知》（财税〔2013〕96号），对电子商务出口企业出口货物适用的具体税收政策和配套管理办法予以明确，率先落实了国务院支持电子商务发展政策。

（二）明确集装箱出口退税的政策

2014年10月21日，国家税务总局发布《国家税务总局关于企业出口集装箱有关退（免）税问题的公告》（国家税务总局公告2014年第59号），进一步明确企业出口集装箱的退（免）税政策，公平不同类型企业税负。

（三）修订《启运港退（免）税管理办法》，深化启运港退税政策试点工作

2014年7月30日，财政部、海关总署、国家税务总局发布《关于扩大启运港退税政策试点范围的通知》（财税〔2014〕53号），自2014年9月1日起将启运港退税政策的启运地口岸从青岛市前湾港、武汉市阳逻港扩大到南京市龙潭港、苏州市太仓港、连云港市连云港港、芜湖市朱家桥港、九江市城西港、岳阳市城陵矶港。2014年8月28日，发布《国家税务总局关于发布〈启运港退（免）税管理办法〉的公告》（国家税务总局公告2014年第52号），明确了出口企业适用启运港退（免）税政策的适用条件和具体管理办法。

（四）义乌“市场采购”贸易方式正式执行

2014年10月16日，义乌市场采购贸易方式改革试点顺利通过商务部、国家税务总局等八部委的验收，市场采购贸易方式正式落地。11月1日起，义乌国际贸易综合管理服务平台免税管理系统上线运行，市场采购贸易方式出口货物免税政策正式执行。市场采购贸易方式出口免税政策及管理办法，明确了出口货物免税主体、申报主体以及相应的法律责任，极大地简化了外贸出口税收管理流程，激发了外贸企业代理出口的积极性，为外贸出口增长提供了重要政策支持。

二、探索完善出口退税管理办法，优化退税服务

（一）出台外贸综合服务企业退（免）税办法，支持外贸综合服务企业发展

根据《国务院办公厅关于促进进出口稳增长、调结构的若干意见》（国办发〔2013〕83号）关于支持外贸综合服务企业健康发展的精神，2014年2月27日发布《国家税务总局关于外贸综合服务企业出口货物退（免）税有关问题的公告》（国家税务总局公告2014年第13号），规定自2014年4月1日起，外贸综合服务企业以自营方式出口国内生产企业与境外单位或个人签约的出口货物，可由外贸综合服务企业按自营出口的规定申报退（免）税。

（二）落实“便民办税春风行动”，便利出口企业

一是2014年4月4日发布《国家税务总局关于逾期未办理出口退（免）税可延期办理有关问题的公告》（国家税务总局公告2014年第20号），规定出口企业或其他单位在2013年12月31日前出口的货物，未在出口退（免）税申报期限截止之日前申报，符合规定情形的，可在2014年6月30日

前向主管税务机关提出延期申报申请，减少了出口企业因非主观原因未能及时办理退（免）税申报而造成的损失，支持出口企业发展。二是 2014 年 8 月 28 日发布《国家税务总局关于出口货物劳务退（免）税管理有关问题的公告》（国家税务总局公告 2014 年第 51 号），解决部分出口企业和基层税务机关反映出口企业申报出口货物退（免）税提供收汇资料有关问题、对外提供增值税零税率应税服务申报退（免）税的收款凭证问题和开具《中标证明通知书》提供资料问题，进一步方便了出口企业办理出口退（免）税。

（三）完善增值税零税率应税服务退（免）税管理办法

根据《财政部 国家税务总局关于将铁路运输和邮政业纳入营业税改征增值税试点的通知》（财税〔2013〕106 号），2014 年 2 月 8 日发布《国家税务总局关于发布〈适用增值税零税率应税服务退（免）税管理办法〉的公告》（国家税务总局公告 2014 年第 11 号），对《增值税零税率应税服务退（免）税管理办法（暂行）》（国家税务总局公告 2013 年第 47 号）进行了修改和补充：增加了以铁路运输方式提供国际运输服务、港澳台运输服务适用增值税零税率的管理规定；增加了从事航天运输服务适用增值税零税率的管理规定；明确了以期租、湿租等方式租赁交通工具提供国际运输、港澳台运输服务适用增值税零税率的管理规定；补充了外贸企业从事对外提供研发服务或设计服务申请适用增值税零税率的管理规定。

2014 年 6 月 13 日，针对部分水路国际运输服务因资质凭证问题不能享受零税率政策的情况，会同财政部发布《关于国际水路运输增值税零税率政策的补充通知》（财税〔2014〕50 号），规定境内的单位和个人取得交通部门颁发的《国际班轮运输经营资格登记证》或加注国际客货运输的《水路运输许可证》并以水路运输方式提供国际运输服务的，适用增值税零税率政策。

为落实将在天津东疆保税港区试点的融资租赁货物出口退税政策扩大到全国统一实施，2014 年 10 月 8 日发布《国家税务总局关于发布〈融资租赁货物出口退税管理办法〉的公告》（国家税务总局公告 2014 年第 56 号），对融资租赁货物出口退税税务登记、退（免）税资格认定管理、退税申报、审核管理等做了具体规定。

（四）制定《横琴、平潭有关增值税和消费税退税管理办法（试行）》

2014 年 12 月 19 日，出台了《国家税务总局关于〈横琴、平潭开发有关增值税和消费税退税管理办法（试行）〉的公告》（国家税务总局公告 2014 年第 79 号），明确销往横琴、平潭（以下简称区内）适用增值税和消费税退税政策的货物（包括水、蒸汽、电力、燃气），视同出口，由区内购买货物的企业或区内水电气企业向主管国税机关申报增值税和消费税退税，并对退税企业资格、税务认定、申报审核方法予以明确。

（五）推行出口退税管理工作规范，优化退税流程

按照国务院关于转变职能、简政放权的要求，国家税务总局利用近 3 年时间梳理了散见于 600 多份文件中有关税务机关办理出口退税的规定，2014 年 12 月 28 日发布《关于印发〈全国税务机关出口退（免）税管理工作规范（1.0）版〉的通知》（税总发〔2014〕155 号）。出口退税管理工作规范自 2015 年 2 月 1 日起开始在全国税务机关实施，通过规范税务机关对出口退税的管理，明确执行政策的流程和要求，加强政策执行的规范性和统一性，更好地服务纳税人。

出口退税管理工作规范共 20 章 93 条 32 个附件，主要包括三个方面的内容：一是便利企业与加强监管，主要内容为明确实施出口退税分类管理；下放审批权限，省国家税务局可以将出口退（免）税审批权限下放至符合条件的县（区）国家税务局；简化人工审核，原则上凡是能通过计算机进行信息比对的，都不再需要人工审核；明确审批出口退税的时限，对出口企业申报的符合规定的退（免）税，主管国税机关应在 20 个工作日内完成审批并办结相关退（免）税手续；进一步优化退税服务；实施出口退税“无纸化”管理；规范出口退税管理；优化进料加工核销。二是加强税务系统内部控制，主要内容为首次明确岗位及其职责；固化了退税审核流程；加强检查和监督；强化退税办理情况的监控，确定了 17 项监控出口税收管理的内容。三是防范出口骗税风险，主要内容为完善了关注信息办法和函调办法；规范实地核查，明确 6 种实地核查情形；完善出口退税预警、评估；构建内控外防的防骗体系。

三、进一步防范打击骗取出口退税行为，营造健康外贸环境

（一）从改革体制机制入手，开展防范骗税工作

为营造竞争公平、秩序规范的外贸出口环境，有效防范和打击骗取出口退税行为，保护纳税人的合法权益，支持守法企业的正常经营与健康发展，国家税务总局积极开展防范骗税工作，建立了科学、严密、操作性强的防范出口退税风险体系，研究并初步形成了《改革出口退税管理机制的初步方案》。按照“规范管理、简化流程、突出重点、明晰责任、提升站位”的原则，以风险管理为导向，以信息化手段为依托，以充分发挥出口退税支持外贸出口的职能作用为出发点和落脚点，通过构建责任明晰的合力体系、严密有效的管理体系、强大有效的风控体系、便捷高效的服务体系、规范系统的法律体系，改革出口退税管理的内外部机制，全力推进出口退税管理现代化。

（二）加强出口退税预警分析，对出口异常的商品和企业发布预警

通过丰富出口退税预警指标，进一步提高发现涉嫌骗税线索的针对性，对发现的出口较为异常的木制家具，布置各地开展了核查工作。

（三）集中开展打击骗取出口退税专项行动

国家税务总局会同有关部门集中开展打击骗取出口退税专项行动，要求各地国税机关从重点领域和重点地区着手，对下发的涉嫌骗税疑点企业加大检查力度；在全国范围内开展重点出口企业的出口退税业务检查；严厉查处典型骗税案件，对骗税行为严肃处理；加大打击骗税宣传力度，更好地发挥警示和震慑作用。

四、持续做好出口退税信息化建设，不断提高出口退税管理质效

（一）对现行出口退税审核系统进行了升级完善

增加了出口货物退（免）税情况月报表统计及《适用增值税零税率应税服务退（免）税管理办法》相关功能。

（二）进一步规范出口退税审核系统数据

明确了出口退税相关业务规范化操作处理的工作要求，对部分地区存在问题的数据进行纠正，为国家税务总局加强出口退税数据统计分析工作，提供可靠的数据支持。

（三）试点上线财税库银横向联网电子退库、更正、免抵调业务

2014年2月13日，国家税务总局下发《关于财税库银横向联网电子退库、更正、免抵调业务正式试点上线的通知》（税总函〔2014〕66号），将北京、江苏、浙江、陕西省（市）国家税务局作为财税库银横向联网电子退库、更正、免抵调业务试点单位。财税库银横向联网工作对提高部门工作效率、进一步优化纳税服务、缩短税款退付在途时间、创优发展环境意义重大。

附表1　2014年中国出口退税额超百亿元地区统计表

单位：亿元，%

序号	地区	出口退税额（含免抵税额）	出口退税额占全国出口退税总量的百分比
1	广东省（不含深圳）	2 024	17.87
2	江苏省	1 842.5	16.26
3	浙江省（不含宁波）	1 350.54	11.92
4	深圳市	1 099.97	9.71
5	上海市	881.24	7.78
6	山东省（不含青岛）	515.98	4.55
7	宁波市	504.07	4.45
8	福建省	375.44	3.31
9	厦门市	351.6	3.10
10	天津市	275.15	2.43

续 表

序号	地区	出口退税额（含免抵税额）	出口退税额占全国出口退税总量的百分比
11	青岛市	269.34	2.38
12	北京市	258.79	2.28
13	河北省	240.58	2.12
14	安徽省	145.21	1.28
15	辽宁省（不含大连）	133.55	1.18
16	大连市	122.5	1.08
17	湖北省	121.8	1.08
18	河南省	114.91	1.01
19	四川省	107.1	0.95
20	江西省	101.53	0.90

（国家税务总局　胡先明　崔巍）

中国进出口信贷制度

2014年，在国际金融危机后续影响下，世界经济总体增长乏力，世界经济复苏依旧艰难曲折，在世界贸易低速增长、国际市场需求低迷、国际经济金融形势依然复杂多变的情况下，我国对外贸易和投资仍保持了较高水平和较快增长。

2014年，我国进出口增速比全球贸易增速高出2.7个百分点，高于美国、欧盟、日本、印度、巴西等主要经济体增速，全球第一货物贸易大国地位进一步巩固。面对错综复杂的国内外经济金融形势发展，中国的银行业金融机构紧紧围绕科学发展这个主题和加快转变经济发展方式这条主线，加大进出口信贷制度建设力度，积极支持进出口融资和“走出去”融资，为进出口业务发展、促进经济平稳较快发展、构建开放型经济新体制提供了有力保障。

一、进出口信贷业务蓬勃开展

2014年，面对复杂严峻的国际经济形势，中国的进出口信贷坚持稳中求进的工作总基调，服务于对外经济合作和经济发展大局，为实体经济的发展提供了强有力的支持。

（一）出口信贷

出口信贷包括出口卖方信贷和出口买方信贷。其中，出口卖方信贷是我国银行为了支持我国资本性货物和服务的出口，给予出口商的中长期融资便利。出口买方信贷是我国银行为了支持我国机电产品、成套设备、对外工程承包等资本性货物和服务的出口，给予进口商或进口商银行的中长期融资便利。出口卖方信贷的借款人是出口国的国内出口商；出口买方信贷的借款人通常为贷款行认可的进口商、进口方银行或进口国主权级借款人（如财政部、中央银行等）。在出口信贷中，贷款行根据借款人的资信状况、借款金额、期限、担保方式等因素，自主确定贷款利率，并按照一定的费率征收管理费、承担费等费用。

出口卖方信贷方面，中国进出口银行2014年全年新签约贷款1842.98亿元，放款1785.98亿元，年末贷款余额4104.12亿元，比年初增加108.53亿元。

出口卖方信贷
实际发放贷款发展示意图

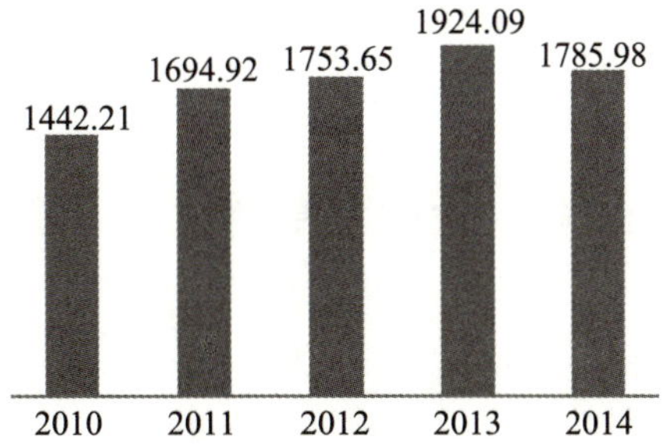

单位：亿元人民币

出口卖方信贷
实际发放贷款投向比例示意图

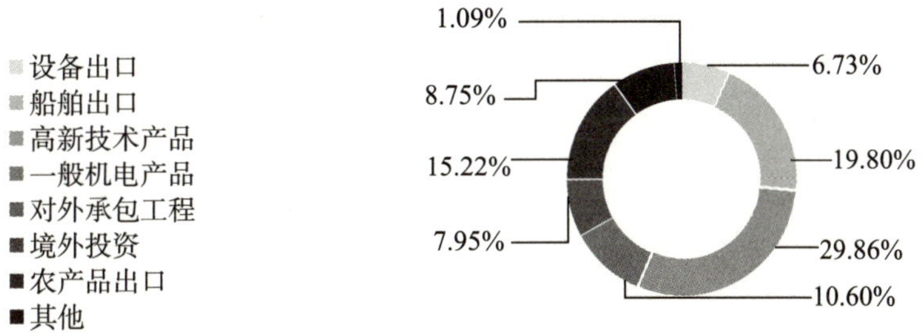

出口买方信贷方面，中国进出口银行2014年全年新签出口买方信贷项目金额536.12亿元，放款594.43亿元。年末贷款余额2222.95亿元，比年初增加325.27亿元。

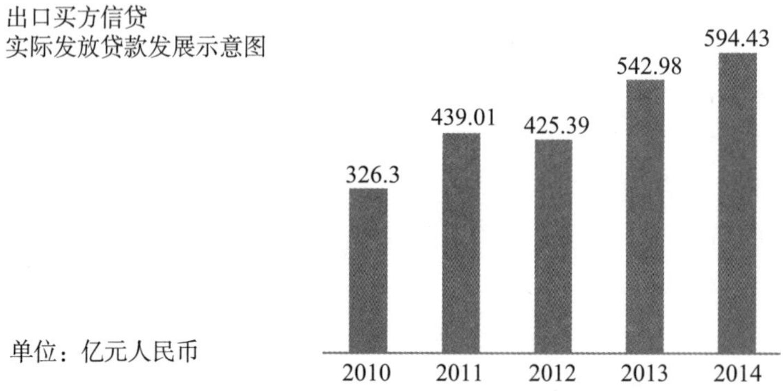

（二）进口信贷

进口信贷是指我国银行为我国企业从境外进口资本性货物以及相关配套建设、资源和能源以及企业生产经营所需产品的贷款。随着我国经济的快速发展，部分企业积极向供应链上游延伸，从国际市场进口先进的设备、技术、服务以及原材料等，以降低企业生产成本，提高企业的市场竞争能力，为进口信贷的发展拓宽了空间。

2014年，中国进出口银行在进口信贷业务方面全年新签约贷款2073.43亿元，放款1949.04亿元。年末贷款余额3888.2亿元，比年初增加581.14亿元。

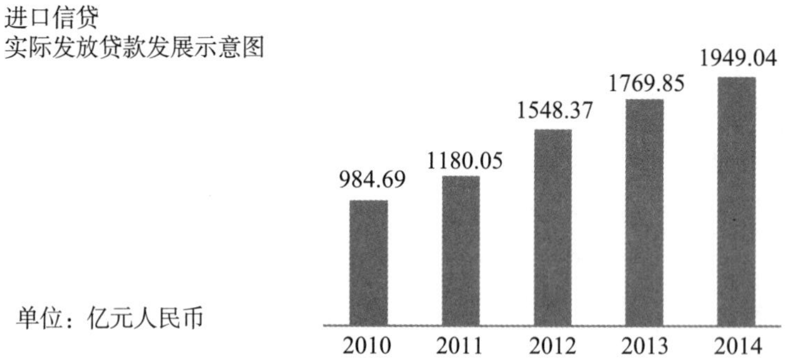

二、遵守世界贸易组织（WTO）有关出口信贷的制度规则

中国的进出口信贷，是按照市场化原则确定信贷条件，开展信贷业务，坚持项目长期财务可持续发展的原则，在全面履行加入世界贸易组织承诺的同时，中国银行业自身的业务水平和竞争能力也得到了显著提高。在办理出口信贷业务时，中国的银行业金融机构除遵守国家有关的法律法规和监管部门的管理规定外，还在我国承诺的基础上，遵守WTO框架下的有关规定；此外，对于官方出口信用机构，其出口买方信贷业务还遵照经济合作与发展组织（Organization for Economic Co-operation and Development，以下简称OECD）的《官方支持出口信贷的安排》（Arrangement on Officially Supported Export Credits，即通常所说的“君子协定”）等国际惯例的规定。

（一）《补贴与反补贴措施协定》

世界贸易组织（WTO）《补贴与反补贴措施协定》（Agreement on Subsides and Counter-vailing Measures，以下简称SCM协定）中对出口信贷的补贴问题做出了明确规定。根据SCM协定，满足以下三个条件的出口信贷构成WTO所禁止的补贴行为：（1）由政府或公共机构提供；（2）具有法律专向性或事实专向性；（3）授予了利益。但是，如果出口信贷是由经济合作与发展组织（OECD）《官方支持出口信贷的安排》（“君子协定”）的成员方所提供，或者出口信贷实施了“君子协定”规定的利率条款，则此等出口信贷不构成禁止性补贴（以下简称“安全港”条款）。

（二）《官方支持出口信贷的安排》（“君子协定”）

《官方支持出口信贷的安排》（“君子协定”）由于在官方支持的出口信贷领域的重要影响，已经成为一项国际惯例，为许多国家或出口信贷机构所遵从。同时，由于SCM协定中纳入“君子协定”的有关内容，因此“君子协定”在国际补贴与反补贴领域也起着重要的作用。“君子协定”旨在鼓励出口商之间以出口货物和服务的质量和价格，而不是以最优惠的融资条件进行竞争，为有序使用官方支持的出口信贷提供基本框架。从性质上看，“君子协定”只是参加国之间道义上的协议安排，不属于国际条约的范畴，没有国际法约束力。

“君子协定”适用于由政府或代表政府为货物和/或服务出口（包括融资租赁）提供的还款期在2年或2年以上的所有官方支持以及约束性援助贷款（其中第四章中规定的程序也适用于与贸易有关的非约束性援助贷款），不适用于军用设备和农产品。2015年1月，OECD发布了最新一版的《官方支持出口信贷的安排》（以下简称《安排》），在第二章规定了出口信贷的融资条款，包括官方支持的最大限度、最长还款期、本息偿还、利率和费用等，其中，以商业参考利率CIRR为基准的官方融资支持下的最低固定利率，是SCM协定“安全港”条款关注的核心内容。

《安排》的附件是对《安排》主体协议的重要补充，与主体协议构成了一个有机联系的整体。《安排》的几个重要附件主要对一些比较特殊的资本货物出口信贷，如船舶出口信贷、核电站出口信贷、民用航空器出口信贷等做出了规定。2015年1月版的《安排》对航空部门谅解（Aircraft Sector Understanding）、铁路部门谅解（Climate Change Sector Understanding）和气候变化部门谅解（Railway Sector Understanding）分别进行了小幅修订。

三、进一步加强对绿色信贷的支持力度

银行业践行绿色信贷，既是落实科学发展观、主动履行社会责任的具体体现，也是防范信贷风险、加快转型发展的必由之路。2014年，中国的银行业金融机构在进出口信贷中秉承“可持续发展”的理念，从战略高度推进绿色信贷工作，根据《赤道原则》等国际准则，进一步完善了绿色信贷制度，加大对节能环保项目的信贷支持力度，严控“两高一剩”行业和落后产能项目，将绿色信贷要求贯彻于整个信贷流程。

2014年3月，银监会印发《中国银监会办公厅关于支持产业结构调整和化解产能过剩的指导意见》（银监办发〔2014〕55号），督促银行业金融机构进一步完善差别化信贷政策，优化信贷结构，大力发展绿色信贷。中国银行业协会发布的《2014年度中国银行业社会责任报告》显示，截至2014年末，银行业机构绿色信贷余额7.59万亿元，其中，21家主要银行绿色信贷余额较年初增长15.67%，达6.01万亿元。

在监管机构的引导下，2014年各银行业金融机构进一步加强绿色信贷理念，并将其作为自身经营战略的重要组成部分，进一步完善了绿色信贷制度，特别是对“两高一剩”行业的授信政策、授信指导意见及实施细则等，细化了信贷审批条件，明确了准入和退出制度。将节能环保等绿色信贷要求嵌入业务全流程，在客户准入、贷前调查、授信审批、合同签订、贷款支付及贷后管理等方面均细化落实绿色信贷相关要求，将节能、环保、安全与社会风险纳入客户及项目风险的重要评价内容，确保项目节能环保方面的合规性、完整性和相关程序的合法性。在提升对节能环保领域信贷支持力度的同时，还加大了对“两高一剩”、落后产能企业和项目贷款的控制和管理力度。各机构从严制定“两高一剩”等高风险行业的准入标准和授信条件，实施名单制管理和限额管理，逐步压缩和退出国家产业政策明令限制、淘汰的落后产能项目，禁止介入不符合国家政策、环保不达标、审批手续不齐全的项目。

四、开展出口信贷规则的国际谈判，积极应对出口信贷面临的挑战

近年来，特别是金融危机以来，美国经济复苏乏力，欧洲主权债务危机加深，而中国经济在世界经济中的地位进一步突出，现已经成为世界第一货物贸易大国。美欧对我国出口信贷的关注和质疑不断加深，指责我国依靠提供低成本贷款，为中国企业提供补贴，借以占领国际市场份额，反补贴调查逐渐成为美欧等国家打击和遏制我国出口信贷和产

品出口的重要武器，甚至个别发展中国家也针对我国展开了反补贴调查。2015 年 5 月，土耳其对原产自中国的无缝钢管发起反补贴调查，这是发展中国家针对中国发起的第一例反补贴调查。在反补贴调查中相当一部分内容涉及出口信贷，相关银行业金融机构对有关问卷内容做出了回答。随着我国应对国际反补贴调查经验的积累，我国企业在调查中的被动局面也有所改善。自 2014 年 5 月起，历时一年多的美国对华集装箱双反案出现“大逆转”，美国国际贸易委员会于 2015 年 5 月 19 日最终否决了之前美国商务部对中国 53 英尺内陆干货集装箱征收高额反倾销和反补贴关税的决定，认定中国输美产品未对美国国内产业的建立造成实质阻碍。这是近年来为数不多的中资企业作为抗辩主体取得案件胜诉的成功案例。

WTO 规则是一个跨学科、跨领域的庞大的法律规则体系，在出口信贷与反补贴方面，利益的争夺与博弈正在越来越多地转化为规则和法律的争执。我们必须基于 WTO 及其规则本身，深刻了解和合理利用这些规则，积极参与规则谈判与制定，争取规则利益。目前，我国正在与美国、欧盟、金砖国家以及一些发展中国家进行出口信贷规则的国际谈判，力争制定一套参与国均可接受的、照顾不同的国家利益和国情、与国际最佳实践一致的新的出口信贷国际规则，使规则为我所用，努力从国际经贸规则的“参与者”向“制定者”转变，积极应对挑战，保护我国发展的重要战略机遇期。

（中国进出口银行　高小吉）

中国政府采购制度

2014年，我国继续全面深化政府采购制度改革，积极稳妥推进政府采购市场开放。

一、不断推进政府采购制度改革

2014年，政府采购制度改革围绕贯彻落实全国财政工作会议和全国政府采购工作会议精神，加快完善政府采购法规和政策，积极推进政府购买服务工作，全面加强监督管理，逐步推动政府采购管理从程序导向型向结果导向型转变。2014年全国政府采购规模为17305.34亿元，比上年增长5.6%，占全国财政支出和GDP的比重分别为11.4%和2.7%。

（一）着力推进政府采购制度建设

2014年围绕推动《政府采购法实施条例》出台，制定一系列制度办法推进相关政策和现行规章制度的执行，着力构建有利于结果导向的政府采购管理体制机制。配合国务院法制办完成《政府采购实施条例（草案）》起草工作，并报请国务院常务会议审议。推进政府与社会资本合作（PPP）模式顶层设计，研究制定《PPP项目政府采购管理暂行办法》和《竞争性磋商采购方式管理暂行办法》。

（二）开展政府采购制度改革创新试点

完善服务项目政府采购政策，按照“方式灵活、程序简便、竞争有效、结果评价”的原则，制定服务项目采购的有关宽免措施。规范公共资源交易平台建设，强调各级财政部门应依法履行监管职责。实施中央单位公务机票购买管理改革，对公务出行机票实行“双折扣”。取消政府采购社会代理机构资格认定行政许可，按照“自愿、免费、一地登记、全国通用”的原则，将资格审批制改为登记制，并进一步加强事中事后监管。

（三）积极发挥政府采购政策功能

不断延展政府采购政策功能，更好地发挥政府采购制度在实现经济社会发展目标、提高政府治理能力等方面的积极作用。研究制定支持监狱企业政策措施，与司法部联合印发《关于政府采购支持监狱企业发展有关问题的通知》（财库〔2014〕68号）。完善绿色采购制度体系，扩展节能环保产品政府采购清单范围，新增加服务器、商用开水器、扫描仪、照明光源、水泥等5种优先采购类产品。不断提高节能环保产品采购比例，2014年全国采购节能、环保产品金额分别占同类产品的81.7%和75.3%。加强落实支持中小企业发展相关政策，2014年政府采购合同授予中小企业的总采购额占全国政府采购规模的76.2%。

（四）强化政府采购监督检查

2014年，在处理政府采购投诉举报案件方面，进一步优化办案流程，提高办案效率。建立专项检查指标体系，统一行政处理处罚口径及尺度，对7省市42家甲级代理机构执行情况开展检查，有效规范代理机构的执业行为。研究建立政府采购严重违法失信行为记录名单，配合开展失信行为联合惩戒，启动失信行为信息发布平台建设。

（五）加快政府采购信息化建设

启动项目评审全流程全电子化试点，选择部分政府采购代理机构运用系统，对政府采购项目从委托采购到招投标、评标及合同的签订实行全电子化管理。完善政府采购信息统计指标体系和报表体系，组织开展政府采购信息统计数据收集、整理、汇总分析和评比工作。

二、积极稳妥推进政府采购各项谈判工作

我国从2007年启动加入WTO《政府采购协定》（GPA）谈判已历时7年。2014年，财政部根据谈判形势和国内改革情况，以加入GPA谈判为主线，积极稳妥推进多边和双边框架下的政府采购有关议题谈判工作，取得了明显进展。

（一）圆满完成我国加入GPA第六份出价工作

我国在第24届中美商贸联委会期间承诺，在2014年提交一份范围与参加方大体相当的出价。按照国务院GPA谈判工作领导小组（以下简称领导小组）的部署，财政部以确定“大体相当”衡量标准为核心，以国企出价实现零的突破为重点，全

面组织开展出价工作，研究起草与参加方出价范围大体相当的第六份出价清单草案，经国务院批准于12月22日提交WTO，圆满履行了我国承诺。

同时，我国积极与参加方开展谈判。多次组团赴日内瓦与美国、欧盟、加拿大、瑞士、韩国、日本、新加坡等7个参加方开展了10多场双边谈判，并参加WTO政府采购委员会多边谈判，表明我国加入GPA的积极立场，妥善回应参加方关注。为增进与主要谈判对手的互相理解，分别赴美、欧等参加方开展GPA工作谈判，就我国加入GPA以及政府采购政策开展深入磋商。

（二）妥善应对高层双边机制谈判

在第6届中美战略与经济对话期间，与美方就我国修改出价如何体现大体相当的具体要求和法律调整时间表进行了深入磋商。在第26届中美商贸联委会上，与美方就我国政府采购本国产品管理办法公开征求意见达成共识。在中欧财金对话等框架下，我国与欧盟就我国加入GPA有关问题开展密集磋商。财政部楼继伟部长专题就我国加入GPA进展，会见欧盟内部市场与服务委员巴尼耶，并交换了意见。在中欧政府采购对话期间，中欧双方进一步围绕我国加入GPA和政府与社会资本合作项目有关情况进行了深入探讨。

（三）统筹开展自贸区等相关谈判

统筹中韩、中日韩、中澳和区域全面经济伙伴关系（RCEP）四个自贸区框架下政府采购议题谈判。参加中美投资协定谈判，就政府采购领域有关问题与美方开展磋商。积极参加亚太经济合作组织（APEC）政府采购议题谈判和研讨，就APEC参加国提案和领导人声明提出应对措施和修改建议。积极应对WTO贸易政策审议，澄清了其他成员国对我国政府采购法律政策的误解，并对其他成员国的政府采购歧视性做法提出评论。

（四）利用国际舞台展示我国政府采购改革成果

与WTO秘书处联合召开政府采购国际研讨会，就政府采购政策功能实施及法律修改问题进行专题研讨。同时，接待欧洲议会、世界银行、经合组织等国际机构和组织来访，介绍中国政府采购最新进展，宣传我国政府采购制度改革成果。配合经合组织（OECD），参与起草加强政府采购诚信实践纲要，宣传中国政府采购最佳实践经验。

（财政部国库司）

中国的自由贸易区建设

一、2014年中国自贸区谈判新进展

2014年，按照党的十八大和十八届三中全会确定的加快实施自由贸易区战略的要求，抓住全球自贸区发展潮流和机遇，适应经济全球化的新要求和国际经贸规则的新变化，坚持互利共赢，推进更高水平的对外开放，积极开展自贸区谈判工作。截至2014年，已经签署并实施的自贸协定有12个，涉及20个国家和地区；实质性结束谈判的自贸区2个，涉及2个国家；正在谈判的自贸区有5个，涉及23个国家。

（一）亚太地区双边自贸区谈判取得突破

1. 实质性结束中韩自贸区谈判

2014年，中韩双方密集举行了6轮自贸区谈判。2014年11月10日，国家主席习近平与韩国总统朴槿惠在北京共同宣布中韩自贸区结束实质性谈判。在两国领导人共同见证下，商务部部长高虎城和韩国通商产业资源部部长尹相直，分别代表两国政府签署了结束中韩自贸区实质性谈判的会议纪要。中韩自贸区是我国迄今为止对外商谈的覆盖领域最广、涉及国别贸易额最大的自贸区。

2. 实质性结束中澳自贸区谈判

2014年11月17日，国家主席习近平与澳大利亚总理阿博特在澳大利亚首都堪培拉共同宣布实质性结束中澳自由贸易协定谈判。在两国领导人见证下，商务部部长高虎城和澳大利亚贸易与投资部长安德鲁·罗布，分别代表两国政府签署了实质性结束中澳自由贸易协定谈判的意向声明。中澳自由贸易协定是我国与亚太地区重要经济体完成的一个全面的高水平的自贸区谈判。

（二）全方位参与周边区域贸易安排谈判

1. 启动并推进中国—东盟升级谈判

2014年8月26日，商务部部长高虎城和东盟10国经贸部长在第13次中国—东盟经贸部长会议上，共同宣布启动中国—东盟自贸区升级谈判。9月，双方举行了第一轮升级谈判，重点讨论了升级谈判的工作安排，并就具体领域深入交换了意见。打造中国—东盟自贸区升级版是李克强总理于2013年10月在中国—东盟领导人峰会上提出的重要倡议。升级谈判的启动充分展示了我国与东盟深化并拓展经贸关系的共同愿望和推进区域一体化的决心。

2. 推动《区域全面经济伙伴关系协定》（RCEP）谈判

2014年，《区域全面经济伙伴关系协定》密集举行了4轮谈判。RCEP谈判已从程序磋商进入实质性磋商阶段。各方在货物关税减让模式和服务、投资的开放模式等方面进行了广泛而深入的磋商。

3. 推动中日韩自贸区谈判

2014年，中、日、韩三方共同举行了2轮自贸区谈判和1次会间会。三方主要就货物贸易的降税模式、服务贸易和投资的开放方式等议题展开磋商，并就协定的范围和领域深入交换了意见。

（三）推进“一带一路”沿线自贸区建设

中斯自贸区完成联合可研并启动谈判。在双方的共同努力下，中斯自贸区联合可研于2014年3月顺利完成。2014年9月16日，在国家主席习近平和斯里兰卡总统拉贾帕克萨的见证下，商务部部长高虎城与斯里兰卡经济发展部部长巴西尔·拉贾帕克萨在科伦坡共同签署关于启动中斯自贸区谈判的谅解备忘录，宣布正式启动中斯自贸区谈判。随后，双方在年内举行了2轮谈判，就谈判工作机制、覆盖范围、推进方式、路线图和时间表、货物贸易降税模式等多项议题进行了深入磋商。

我国还积极推进中国—海合会自贸区等自贸区谈判和中国—巴基斯坦自贸区第二阶段降税谈判，推动《亚太贸易协定》第四轮关税减让谈判。

（四）与欧洲国家自贸区正式开始实施

1. 中国—瑞士自贸协定正式生效

2014年4月29日，中国和瑞士双方在京互换了自贸协定生效照会，中国—瑞士自贸协定于2014年7月1日正式生效。中国—瑞士自贸协定是近年来我国对外达成的水平最高、最为全面的自贸协定之一，不仅货物贸易零关税比例高，还涉及环境、知识产权等许多新规则，将进一步提升中瑞

双边经贸合作水平，深化中欧经贸合作。

2. 中国—冰岛自贸协定正式生效

2014 年 5 月 20 日，中国和冰岛双方在京互换了自贸协定生效照会，中国—冰岛自贸协定于 2014 年 7 月 1 日正式生效。中国—冰岛自贸协定是我国与欧洲国家签署的第一个自由贸易协定，涵盖货物贸易、服务贸易、投资等诸多领域。

二、自贸协定实施成效显著

（一）自贸区深化了与自贸伙伴之间的经贸关系

通过自贸协定提供的制度性保障，参与各方的货物、服务、投资和人员流动等政策更加透明、更有预见性，有力地提升了自贸协定参与方的经贸关系和经济融合，促进各国经济互利共赢、共同发展。随着有关自贸协定的进一步实施，关税将不断降低或取消，自贸协定将进一步促进我国与有关国家和地区贸易、投资和经济合作的发展。

（二）自贸区提升了企业的国际竞争力

自贸区建成后，我国和自贸伙伴国之间的市场准入条件将进一步改善，贸易和投资环境也将更加规范透明。一方面，自贸区的优惠安排可以使企业获得更大的外部市场，创造更多贸易投资机会；另一方面，在全球价值链日益紧密的条件下，自贸区零关税将降低相关企业的生产成本，提高生产效率，提升国际竞争力。例如，中韩自贸协定实施后，我国在钢铁制品、电子、机械产品等领域可以进一步提升产业竞争力，巩固和提升在全球价值链中的地位。

（三）自贸区增加了消费者的实际利益

通过自由贸易互通有无，消费者可以更低的价格购买世界各地更多更丰富的商品，提高消费水平和生活质量。例如，实施中国—智利自贸协定后，我国消费者能享受到智利品质优良、价格合理的葡萄酒和提子。得益于中国—东盟自贸区，我国市场上的热带水果越来越多，价格也越来越实惠，榴梿、山竹、火龙果等热带水果成为我国广大消费者日常享用的水果。

下一步，我们将深入贯彻党的十八大、十八届三中、四中全会精神，坚持使市场在资源配置中起决定性作用和更好发挥政府作用，统筹考虑和综合运用国际国内两个市场、两种资源、两类规则，并与共建“一带一路”和实施国家外交战略紧密衔接，逐步构筑起立足周边、辐射“一带一路”、面向全球的高标准自由贸易区网络。

（商务部国际司）

●投资政策与管理措施

中国利用外资情况

一、2014年中国吸收外商直接投资概况

2014年，世界经济复苏依旧缓慢，国际引资竞争日趋激烈，国内经济下行压力较大，吸收外资形势十分严峻。通过进一步扩大对外开放，加快推进各项改革措施，我国2014年吸收外资规模稳中求进，利用外资质量进一步提升。2014年全年，全国新设立外商投资企业23778家，同比增长4.4%；实际使用外资金额1195.6亿美元，同比增长1.7%。其中，以并购方式设立外商投资企业1281家，同比增长2.2%；实际使用外资金额75亿美元，同比增长21%。截至2014年12月底，全国累计设立外商投资企业809829家，实际使用外资金额15160.5亿美元（不含银行、证券、保险领域数据，下同）。

（一）各领域吸收外商直接投资情况

在实际使用外资金额中，农、林、牧、渔业占1.3%，制造业占33.4%，服务业占55.4%。

1. 农、林、牧、渔业吸收外资简况

农、林、牧、渔业新设立外商投资企业719家，同比下降5%；实际使用外资金额15.2亿美元，同比下降15.4%，占全国总量的比重由上年同期的1.5%进一步降至1.3%。其中，农业实际使用外资金额仍占最大比重，实际使用外资金额8.5亿美元；而林业实际使用外资金额同比增长最快，2014年林业实际使用外资金额0.9亿美元，同比增长38.9%。

2. 制造业吸收外资简况

制造业新设立外商投资企业5178家，同比下降20.4%；实际使用外资金额399.4亿美元，同比下降12.3%，占全国总量的比重进一步降至33.4%。在制造业领域吸收外资较多的主要行业中，通信设备、计算机及其他电子设备制造业实际使用外资金额61.5亿美元，同比下降4.0%；交通运输设备制造业实际使用外资金额38.2亿美元，同比下降13.4%；电气机械及器材制造业实际使用外资金额33.5亿美元，同比下降38.8%；化学原料及化学制品制造业实际使用外资金额31.8亿美元，同比下降19.1%；通用设备制造业实际使用外资29.2亿美元，同比下降17.3%。上述五个行业占到制造业吸收外商直接投资总量的48.5%。

3. 服务业吸收外资简况

服务业新设立外商投资企业15766家，同比增长14.8%；实际使用外资金额662.3亿美元，同比增长7.8%，占全国总量的比重上升至55.4%。其中，外商投资房地产业实际使用外资金额346.3亿美元，同比增长20.2%，高于服务业增幅12.4个百分点，占服务业实际使用外资金额的52.3%。其他服务业领域吸收外资较多的主要行业中，分销服务业实际使用外资金额77.1亿美元，同比下降20.8%；运输服务业实际使用外资金额44.6亿美元，同比增长5.6%；金融服务业实际使用外资金额41.8亿美元，同比增长79.5%；能源、材料和机械电子设备批发业实际使用外资金额35.2亿美元，同比下降11.1%；仓储业实际使用外资金额27.5亿美元，同比上升0.5%；计算机应用服务业25.3亿美元，同比下降0.5%。（参见附表1）

（二）主要国别（地区）对华直接投资简况

2014年实际投入外资金额排名前十位的国家/

地区依次为：香港（857.4亿美元）、新加坡（59.3亿美元）、台湾（51.8亿美元）、日本（43.3亿美元）、韩国（39.7亿美元）、美国（26.6亿美元）、德国（20.7亿美元）、英国（13.5亿美元）、法国（7.1亿美元）和荷兰（6.4亿美元），前十位国家（地区）实际投入外资金额合计1125.9亿美元，占全国实际使用外资金额的94.2%，同比增长2.7%。其中，韩国和英国对华投资增长较快，实际投入金额分别为39.7亿美元和13.5亿美元，同比增长29.8%和28.0%。[①]（参见附表2）

（三）各区域吸收外商直接投资情况

2014年，我国东部地区实际使用外资金额979.2亿美元，同比增长1.1%；中部地区实际使用外资金额108.6亿美元，同比增长7.5%；西部地区实际使用外资金额107.8亿美元，同比增长1.6%。2014年，东、中、西部地区占全国吸收外资总量的比重分别为81.9%、9.1%和9.0%，其中中部地区所占比重相比去年提高了0.5个百分点。（参见附表3）

（四）外商投资企业主要经济指标

2014年，外商投资企业进出口总额19840.0亿美元，同比增长3.4%，占全国进出口总值的46.1%，其中出口10747.0亿美元，同比增长2.9%，占全国出口总值的45.9%；进口9 093.0亿美元，同比增长3.9%，占全国进口总值的46.4%。根据国家统计局和税务总局数据，2014年，规模以上外商投资工业企业实现利润总额1.6万亿元，增长9.5%，高于全国平均增幅6.2个百分点。2014年，外商投资企业缴纳税收2.5万亿元，增长10.4%，比2013年税收增幅高6.7个百分点，占全国税收收入的比重为19.2%。

二、2014年中国出台的主要外资政策及管理措施

（一）推进外商投资管理体制改革

一是落实外商投资企业注册资本实缴改认缴制度，出台《商务部关于改进外资审核管理工作的通知》，提高投资便利化。二是会同中编办开展规范和优化外商投资审批事项试点工作，缩短审批时限、简化申报程序及申报文件。三是进一步简政放权，取消外商投资鼓励类项目确认审批事项，简化外商投资宏观调控行业和房地产业备案程序。四是指导上海自贸试验区深化与负面清单相结合的“备案为主、审批为辅”的外商投资管理模式改革。五是推进广东对港澳基本实现服务贸易自由化，除涉及《内地与香港CEPA关于内地在广东与香港基本实现服务贸易自由化的协议》和《内地与澳门CEPA关于内地在广东与澳门基本实现服务贸易自由化的协议》保留的限制性措施，港澳服务提供者在广东投资，公司设立及变更的合同、章程审批改为备案管理。

（二）继续推动各领域扩大开放

一是会同发展改革委修订《外商投资产业指导目录》，进一步放开外资股比限制，大幅减少限制类条目并增加透明度。二是积极推进CEPA框架下服务业开放，内地在广东省对港澳基本实现服务贸易自由化。三是指导上海自贸试验区进一步缩短负面清单长度，由2013版的190条减少到139条。三是会同相关部门在医疗、养老、电子商务、教育、商贸物流等领域研究出台有关扩大开放文件，切实提高开放程度。例如，推动台商在平潭综合实验区开展海运业务试点，与民政部联合发布《关于外商投资设立营利性养老机构有关事项的公告》。

（三）推进区域协调发展

一是按照“一带一路”战略部署，做好跨境经济合作区的规划与建设。二是研究鼓励产业转移政策措施，引导外商投资中西部地区，探索建设中西部地区承接产业转移平台。三是促进国家级经济技术开发区转型升级创新发展。推动出台《国务院办公厅关于促进国家级经济技术开发区转型升级创新发展的若干意见》；修订完善国家级经开区综合发展水平评价办法和统计制度；创建生态工业示范园，推动节能环保国际合作。

---

① 上述国家（地区）对华投资数据包括这些国家（地区）通过英属维尔京群岛、开曼群岛、萨摩亚、毛里求斯和巴巴多斯等自由港对华投资。

附表 1　　**2014 年外商直接投资分行业简况**　　单位：亿美元

	新设企业数			实际使用外资金额		
行业	个数	同比%	比重%	金额	同比%	比重%
总计	23 778	4.4	100.0	1 195.6	1.7	100.0
农林牧渔业	719	−5.0	3.0	15.2	−15.4	1.3
制造业	5 178	−20.4	21.8	399.4	−12.3	33.4
服务业	15 766	14.8	66.3	662.3	7.8	55.4
其他	2 115	19.2	8.9	118.7	35.1	9.9

附表 2　　**2014 年对华投资前 15 位资金来源地简况**　　单位：亿美元

	企业数		实际使用外资金额	
	本年数	同比%	本年数	同比%
总计	23 778	4.4	1 195.6	1.7
香港	12 530	1.1	857.4	9.4
新加坡	770	3.4	59.3	−19.1
台湾省	2 660	10.8	51.8	−2.1
日本	655	−30.5	43.3	−38.8
韩国	1 560	13.7	39.7	29.8
美国	1 223	9.9	26.6	−20.6
德国	384	2.7	20.7	−1.1
英国	369	19.0	13.5	28.0
法国	159	−7.0	7.1	−6.5
荷兰	122	19.6	6.4	−50.1
澳门	381	22.9	5.9	24.3
百慕大	10	−16.7	5.3	−26.5
爱尔兰	18	−18.2	4.0	786.2
意大利	206	3.0	3.7	17.4
瑞典	52	23.8	3.6	73.6
其他	2 679	18.4	47.2	−23.2

附表 3　　**2014 年外商直接投资分区域简况**　　单位：亿美元

	新设企业数			实际使用外资金额		
行业	个数	同比%	比重%	金额	同比%	比重%
总计	23 778	4.4	100.0	1 195.6	1.7	100.0
东部地区	20 466	6.3	86.1	979.2	1.1	81.9
中部地区	2 208	−8.0	9.3	108.6	7.5	9.1
西部地区	1 104	−1.6	4.6	107.8	1.6	9.0

（商务部外国投资管理司）

中国外汇管理制度

2014年，外汇管理部门紧密围绕党中央、国务院各项部署，始终把改革作为重中之重，坚持以外汇管理“五个转变”为方向，坚持简政放权和转变政府职能，坚持推进人民币资本项目可兑换，坚持加强事中事后监测和管理，坚持创新完善外汇储备运用与管理，不断提高服务经济结构调整和转型升级的能力。

一、服务实体经济发展，推进简政放权和便利化取得新成效

（1）大幅减少行政审批项目。2014年取消5项行政审批项目，行政审批项目减至17项。开展法规清理，共废止外汇管理法规88件。通过简政放权，增强企业的内生动力。

（2）支持外贸平稳发展措施不断深化。继续深化贸易外汇管理改革，推进边贸和个人贸易便利化，取消边贸账户行政许可，加快企业资金周转，简化个人贸易单证要求，促进外贸多元化发展。

（3）稳步推进跨境电子商务外汇支付业务试点，支持电子商务等新型服务业发展。

二、积极推动改革试点，资本项目可兑换程度不断提高

（1）通过试点探索创新驱动的外汇管理改革措施。将跨国公司外汇资金集中运营试点推广到全国，允许集中收付、轧差结算、共享外债和对外放款额度；开展资本金意愿结汇改革，大幅简化资本金结汇手续，允许企业根据实际需要自行安排资本金结汇时间；开展企业跨境并购资金汇出便利化试点，企业境外并购平均节约120天以上，大幅提升境外投资效率，促进企业“走出去”。

（2）改革跨境投融资外汇管理体制。大幅简化返程投资外汇管理，取消全部跨境担保事前审批，统一中外资企业外保内贷政策，放宽境外直接投资前期费用管理，便利境内企业境外放款，提升跨境投融资便利化程度。

（3）资本市场双向开放不断扩大。简化人民币合格境外机构投资者额度管理，研究合格境外机构投资者外汇管理改革方案。

三、大力发展外汇市场，人民币汇率形成的市场化基础日益夯实

（1）取消了银行对客户美元挂牌买卖价差限制，银行可根据市场供求自主定价。

（2）修订发布《银行办理结售汇业务管理办法》和实施细则，简化市场准入门槛，支持非银行金融机构进入银行间外汇市场，提高银行头寸管理灵活性。

（3）以外汇期权为重点，丰富汇率避险工具；将业务监管原则和银行展业原则相结合，规范外汇衍生产品发展。

四、完善跨境资金流动监测分析管理体系，跨境资金流动风险防范能力有所提升

（1）提高对外汇资金流动的监测预警与管理水平。加强对跨境资金流动和国际金融市场的监测，提高分析判断的科学性和精准度。进一步完善应急管理预案，总结经验，摸索规律，丰富政策工具储备。

（2）通过优化系统建设、加强外汇监管信息数据共享，为强化事后监测分析和非现场监管能力奠定基础。

（3）加大对外汇违法违规行为的查处。加大对虚假转口贸易、违规远期结汇等行为的打击力度，2014年共查处外汇违规案件1903起。

（4）落实金融监管改革措施和稳健标准。完善对外金融资产负债存量及流量统计，提高数据采集频率。

（5）提高数据信息透明度。通过季度新闻发布会加强形势解读和市场预期引导。

五、创新完善外汇储备经营管理与运用，服务国家战略取得新成果

认真贯彻落实国务院有关要求，创新外汇储备

运用，加强共同投融资和多双边国际合作，服务好国家战略；坚持多元化投资，优化货币资产摆布，灵活调整资产配置，在确保外汇储备安全、流动的前提下，业绩不断提高；进一步完善风险管理框架，加强风险预警判断，健全预案，提高防范危机冲击的能力。

（国家外汇管理局综合司）

国有企业改革发展与国有资产监管

2014年，各级国资委、中央企业和地方国有企业认真贯彻落实党中央、国务院各项决策部署，积极面对复杂多变的国内外形势和艰巨繁重的改革发展稳定任务，攻坚克难保增长，坚定不移促转型，积极稳妥推改革，凝心聚力抓党建，保持了国有经济总体平稳运行。2014年，全国国资委系统监管企业累计实现营业收入44.6万亿元，同比增长4.8%；实现利润2.2万亿元，同比增长4.9%；上缴税金3.1万亿元，同比增长4.8%。国务院国资委监管的中央企业（以下简称中央企业）累计实现营业收入25.12万亿元，同比增长3.8%；实现利润1.37万亿元，同比增长4.2%；上缴税金2.1万亿元，同比增长4.4%。

一、加快转方式调结构，国有企业改革发展持续平稳推进

（一）企业实现平稳健康发展

国务院国资委根据经济形势及企业实际，在年初提出保增长目标，通过抓两头带中间、强化考核激励、加强运行监测等方式，不断加强对企业的指导和服务。中央企业紧紧咬住经济效益增长目标，制订工作方案，突出工作重点，健全工作机制，形成强大的保增长合力，有力保证了措施落地。各企业加强市场开拓，精耕细作主业，优化产品结构，完善营销网络，效益水平稳步提升。电力、汽车、轨道交通装备、建筑、建材等行业企业利润保持快速增长，67家中央企业效益增幅超过8%，困难企业总体实现减亏增利。各企业眼睛向内，深挖潜力，大力推进销售费用压降，加强管理费用管控，可控费用同比大幅下降；根据市场变化，科学组织生产运行，及时调减边际贡献低的项目；加强全员全业务全过程成本管控，推广应用标准成本体系，降本节支效果明显。2014年，中央企业成本费用增幅同比收窄4.7个百分点，管理费用、销售费用分别收窄3.2和11.4个百分点。各级国资委加大对所出资企业的指导帮扶力度，17个地方效益增幅超过8%。在全力以赴保增长的同时，国有企业积极履行社会责任，带头落实国家宏观调控政策，全力支持民生工程建设，积极参与援疆援藏援青扶贫工作，勇于承担急难险重任务，为经济社会发展做出了重要贡献。

（二）企业改革进一步深化

认真落实深化改革重点任务。逐项落实中央全面深化改革领导小组部署的涉及国务院国资委的重点改革任务，加强对国有企业改革重点难点问题的研究，认真研究起草深化国有企业改革相关文件。“四项改革”试点取得积极进展。先后选择8家企业分别开展改组国有资本投资公司试点、发展混合所有制经济试点、董事会行使高级管理人员选聘、业绩考核及薪酬管理职权试点等，坚持顶层设计与先行先试相结合，市场化方向与问题导向相结合，整体推进与重点突破相结合，通过试点，总结经验，完善措施，努力推出可推广可复制的有效做法和典型经验，为全面深化国企国资改革提供强有力的实践支撑。紧紧围绕“健全协调运转、有效制衡的公司法人治理结构”，着力推进中央企业规范董事会建设，董事会试点中央企业总数达到74家；加快剥离国有企业办社会职能和解决历史遗留问题，驻黑龙江省中央企业分离移交“三供一业”试点工作全面推进，河南、湖南、重庆三地中央企业分离移交试点正式启动。同时，积极指导推进国有企业棚户区改造，指导国有企业所办医院参与医改，配合卫生计生委研究国有企业所办医院改制试点意见。各国有企业在完善治理结构、健全激励约束机制、深化三项制度改革等方面做了大量工作，取得了积极成效。各级国资委因地制宜推进各项重点改革，在对所监管国有企业功能分类、改组或组建国有资本投资公司或运营公司、完善国有企业公司治理等方面进行了积极探索。

（三）企业转型升级成效进一步显现

产业升级步伐进一步加快。加大亏损业务清理和低效无效资产处置力度，资源更多向优势区域、优势企业和优势项目集中；加大技术改造力度，先

进产能比重逐步提高；主动配合国家化解过剩产能，粗钢和电解铝产能均没有增加；大力推动节能减排，提前完成国家“十二五”减排任务。并购重组和资源整合力度进一步加大。成立铁塔公司推动电信基础设施共建共享，招商局集团和中国外运长航集团组建了全球最大的油轮船队，中粮集团整合华孚集团进一步完善产业链，有关企业重组及项目转让工作稳步推进；央地战略合作、企业间合作继续加强。科技创新取得新突破。持续加大科技投入，不断加大高端人才引进和培养力度，专利申请和授权量快速增长，科技成果不断涌现。“北斗”正式成为第三个全球卫星导航系统，具备完整自主知识产权的第三代核电技术获得全面认可落地。国际化经营取得新成效。加大国际合作和市场开拓力度，加快海外资源整合，国际化经营的领域、区域、规模不断扩大，“走出去”层次和质量不断提升。高铁、核电、智能电网“走出去”取得积极进展。

（四）企业管理水平进一步提高

各级国资委和中央企业进一步巩固和扩大管理提升成果，加强内部管理、整合管理资源、补齐管理短板，管理基础进一步夯实。着力解决管理瓶颈问题。各企业着眼经营管理关键环节，通过全面对标查找问题，狠抓专项提升补齐差距，集中攻关、破解了一大批长期制约企业发展的难题，企业发展基础更加牢固。管理现代化水平不断提高。主动适应外部环境变化，找准市场定位，优化发展方向和目标，动态调整业务布局、发展节奏、资金投向和实施路径。加强企业战略管理，完善相关工作制度，建立战略管理考评体系，不断提高战略执行力。大力推行精益管理，积极运用先进的管理方法与信息化手段，推进信息化与业务深度融合，推动了管理制度化、制度流程化、流程信息化。风险管控能力进一步增强。各企业健全相关规章制度，严格经营决策程序，内控体系不断完善。加强投资全过程管控，把握投资方向，努力提高投资收益。继续加强法律风险防范机制建设，企业总法律顾问制度作用得到发挥，法律审核把关工作进一步规范，因企业自身违法违规引发的重大法律纠纷案件大幅减少。普遍开展清应收、去库存、减债务等工作，努力提高经营活动创现能力，进一步加强财务风险管控，中央企业平均资产负债率自2008年以来首次出现下降。

二、按照以管资本为主的要求加强监管，国有资产监管针对性有效性进一步增强

（一）大力加强依法监管

十八届四中全会闭幕后，国务院国资委立即组织召开直属机关和中央企业干部大会、中央企业法制工作会议，围绕推动国务院国资委依法监管、中央企业依法经营提出16条具体措施。大力打造国资监管法治机构，大力推进国资监管制度建设。截至2014年年底，国务院国资委出台的现行有效规章规范性文件达353件，国资监管各项工作进一步纳入法治化、制度化轨道；不断健全规章、规范性文件和重大决策合法性审查机制，2014年共开展了近30次合法性审核。全面推进法治央企建设，中央企业全部建立总法律顾问制度、设立法律事务机构，集团和重要子企业总法律顾问专职率接近80%，法律顾问队伍超过2万人，规章制度、经济合同、重要决策三项法律审核率均接近100%，中央企业法制工作第三个三年目标全面完成。

（二）持续改进监管方式

加大简政放权力度，努力把该管的管好、不该管和可管可不管的坚决不管，主动取消下放了一批监管事项，积极探索建立出资人监管事项清单制度；坚持放管结合，着力加强制度建设和公司章程管理。各级国资委突出企业市场属性，根据股权结构、产权特征、发展阶段，逐步实现差异化管理。按照监管企业功能定位和业务属性，探索分类深化董事会建设、分类完善业绩考核办法、工资总额分类管理办法，探索对企业负责人薪酬实施差异化管理。完善监事会监督方式，一企一策确定监督重点。

（三）进一步加大监管力度

加强产权管理，充分发挥资本市场在产权配置中的重要作用，引导企业积极处置低效无效资产，止住出血点。扎实推进产权登记、资产评估、进场交易监管等基础工作，筑牢防止国有资产流失的防线。加强财务监督，以提高质量和效益为中心强化全面预算管理和财务动态监测，实现中央企业负责人经济责任审计全覆盖，加强对企业的风险管理，组织开展资产损失责任追究工作。加强收入分配和劳动用工管理，在中央企业全面实行工资总额预算

管理，启动备案制试点，同时扩大工资总额周期管理试点范围。进一步增强监事会监督的针对性和有效性，全年累计揭示企业各类问题、风险和违纪违规线索 2100 余项；对 31 家企业 207 个境外项目进行了实地检查，揭示各类问题和风险 279 项；加强企业国有资产监督协同，向中央巡视组通报问题和风险线索 120 余项；着力推进监督成果运用，首次向社会公开监事会对中央企业 2013 年度监督检查情况。进一步加强和改进巡视工作，全面贯彻中央巡视工作新方针，聚焦中心任务，突出监督重点，着力发现问题，强化成果运用，加强对整改落实情况的监督检查，推动巡视工作取得新进展，全年完成对 12 家中央企业的常规巡视和 6 家中央企业的巡视回访，发现问题 325 个，向企业提出整改意见 61 条。

三、进一步加强党建工作，企业党组织政治优势得到有效发挥

（一）教育实践活动取得积极成效

按照中央统一部署，巩固第一批教育实践活动成果，认真开展了第二批教育实践活动，坚持聚焦问题、以上率下，通过铁面问责、刚性约束、严格执纪，层层传导压力，扎实有效地推进各项整改和专项整治工作，打通了服务联系职工群众的“最后一公里”，扎实有效地推进各项整改和专项整治工作，解决了一批社会关注度高、群众反映强烈的突出问题，广大党员干部党性修养和群众观点明显提升，践行群众路线的长效机制初步形成。

（二）领导班子建设和基层党组织建设进一步加强

紧密结合国资国企改革发展实际，不断加强领导班子的思想政治建设，提高干部考察质量，完善干部选拔任用方式，优化领导班子结构，增强了领导班子整体功能。创新企业党建工作的内容和方式，始终把企业改革发展稳定中的难点作为党建工作的重点，及时选树党内先进典型，充分发挥了基层党组织的战斗堡垒作用和党员的先锋模范作用。

（三）党风廉政建设和反腐败工作扎实推进

认真学习贯彻十八届中央纪委第三次、第四次全会和国务院第二次廉政工作会议精神，强化党对党风廉政建设和反腐败工作的统一领导，创新反腐败体制机制，认真落实主体责任，领导和推动纪检监察机构转职能、转方式、转作风，聚焦主业，强化监督执纪问责。把党风廉政建设和反腐败工作与中心工作同部署、同实施、同检查，积极推进国有企业反腐败体制机制创新，严明党的纪律，坚决克服组织涣散、纪律松弛现象，持之以恒贯彻落实中央八项规定精神，坚决纠正“四风”，扎实开展巡视工作，不断强化对权力运行的制约和监督，加大案件查办力度，腐败蔓延势头得到遏制。

（四）正面宣传工作力度不断加大

坚持总体谋划、系统设计，将习近平总书记关于加强国有企业宣传的重要指示精神贯彻落实到位。通过整合宣传资源、打造多种平台、加强媒体战略合作，形成了立体发声格局，正面宣传和舆论引导力度不断加大，培育践行社会主义核心价值观和企业文化建设效果明显，为国资国企改革发展营造了良好的环境和氛围。

（国务院国有资产监督管理委员会研究局
吴哲　牛聪）

对外投资合作发展情况及相关政策措施

2014年，商务部按照党中央、国务院的统一部署，深入落实中央关于深化经济体制改革的决定，扎实有序推进"走出去"各项工作，取得了新的成效。

一、2014年对外投资合作发展特点

2014年，面对复杂多变的国内外形势，我国对外投资合作仍保持了平稳较快增长，在众多领域取得新的突破，成为对外经贸合作的亮点。

（一）对外投资首次接近吸引外资规模

2014年，我国实现全行业对外直接投资1160亿美元，同比增长15.5%，对外直接投资接近同期吸引外资（1195.6亿美元）规模，双向投资更趋平衡。一是农业、信息服务等领域并购亮点突出。中粮集团收购新加坡来宝公司股权和荷兰尼德拉公司股权，是迄今我农业领域对外投资最大的两个并购项目；联想集团收购美国摩托罗拉手机业务，中国移动通信集团收购泰国True公司股权以及购买巴基斯坦3G和4G牌照业务，带动信息服务领域对外投资大幅增长。二是对发达国家和地区投资增长创新高。2014年中国对发达国家投资186.72亿美元，同比增长54.6%，其中对欧盟和美国投资同比分别增长172.1%和23.9%。三是地方投资占比首超四成。2014年地方企业对外直接投资451.14亿美元，同比增长36.8%，占对外直接投资总额的43.8%，较上年增加7.2个百分点。

（二）对外承包工程业务稳中求进

2014年，我国对外承包工程业务完成营业额1424.1亿美元，同比增长3.8%；新签合同额1917.6亿美元，同比增长11.7%。一是大项目带动作用明显。2014年对外承包工程新签合同额再创历史最高值，其中中铁建公司签订的尼日利亚沿海铁路项目119.7亿美元，创下我国对外承包工程单项合同金额之最。二是通过本土化加大对美等发达国家市场开拓力度。2014年我在美国承包工程新签合同额29.2亿美元，同比增长243.5%。其中合同金额在5000万美元以上的项目共14个，中建总公司等企业在美投资设立本土化企业积极承揽项目，实现对外投资与承包工程业务有机结合。三是房屋建筑、水利建设、交通运输领域增势强劲。2014年对外承包工程新签合同额5000万美元以上项目中，房建、电站和铁路项目分别达到184个、79个和12个，交通运输建设、水利建设、房屋建筑领域新签合同额同比分别增长55.6%、39%、11.2%。

（三）境外经贸合作区建设初显规模

"走出去"企业利用合作区抱团出海，形成大企业带动小企业、主导产业带动配套产业的聚集式发展模式。截至2014年年底，在建的16家合作区企业已完成总投资额58.5亿美元，入区企业共计404家，创造总产值176.4亿美元，上缴东道国政府税费7.3亿美元，为当地创造就业岗位4.2万个。

（四）对外劳务合作业务健康发展

2014年，我国对外劳务合作派出各类劳务人员56.2万人，较上年同期增加3.5万人，同比增长6.6%。年末在外各类劳务人员100.6万人，较上年同期增加15.3万人。

二、2014年出台的相关措施

2014年，商务部会同有关部门，按照"政府引导、企业为主、市场运作"的原则，引导并规范对外投资合作健康发展。

在深化管理体制改革方面，进一步简政放权、放宽审批，修订出台《境外投资管理办法》，确立了"备案为主、核准为辅"的管理模式，推进境外投资便利化，释放企业对外投资活力。新办法实施以来，99.85%的企业仅需办理境外投资备案，需要核准的不足0.2%。修订《对外直接投资统计制度》，进一步调整完善相关统计指标。

在加大政策支持力度方面，综合运用各类信贷、基金及中长期出口信用保险等各种手段，对企业境外投资加大融资支持。完善人民币跨境贸易和

跨境融资政策，通过委托贷款等方式有效利用外汇储备支持“走出去”，进一步放宽境内企业境外投资外汇管理。加强双边税收协商，进一步提高“走出去”企业人员出入境和进出口贸易便利化水平。

在推动双边务实合作开展方面，推动企业实施一批高铁、电力、通信等装备制造业“走出去”项目，引导钢铁、纺织、家电等优势制造业到有市场需求的国家或地区投资兴业，推动农、林业对外直接投资，与非洲开展跨国跨区域基础设施合作，稳步推进周边互联互通重点项目。

在强化政府公共服务方面，编制“走出去”有关规划，发布《对外投资合作国别（地区）指南》《中国对外投资合作发展报告》《国别投资经营障碍报告汇编》，汇编《“走出去”典型案例》，加强对企业开展对外投资合作的国别和产业指导。其中发布在商务部网站上的《指南》的访问量累计已接近4亿次，成为企业了解世界各国投资合作环境的权威信息渠道。发布《中国对外直接投资统计公报》。借助厦门“九八”投洽会、中国—东盟博览会等投资促进平台，加大“走出去”政策的宣讲和服务力度。

在保护对外投资合法权益方面，完善多双边投资促进机制，加强政府间磋商合作。加强国别风险评估和安全预警，发布了50多期安全预警信息，开展了境外重大经济合作项目风险排查，编制了境外企业项目外源性风险管控评价软件并向企业免费发放。妥善处置了发生在越南、利比亚、伊拉克和西非等国家和地区的30余起涉我重大境外突发事件，有效保障了在外企业和人员安全权益。

三、当前对外投资合作发展面临的总体形势

今后一段时期，我国经济将面临平稳发展的“新常态”，“走出去”也处于较快增长阶段、初级发展阶段、转型升级阶段的“三段交汇”期，机遇与风险并存。一方面，世界经济增长缓慢复苏，我国加快构建开放型经济新体制，经济政治影响力不断增加，大型装备和产能优势进一步体现，企业国际竞争力明显增强等将为“走出去”带来新的发展机遇和空间。另一方面，国际市场竞争加剧，新兴国家经济增速回落，能源资源价格下降，地缘争端和境外风险加大，“走出去”企业在全球价值链中的地位有待进一步提高，市场秩序有待进一步规范等不利因素也日益凸现。但总体来看，随着我国经济平稳增长，经济体制改革加快推进，以及各项支持和促进政策的效果进一步发挥，我国对外投资合作平稳较快发展的长期趋势不会改变。

四、2015年主要工作

2015年，商务部将继续深入贯彻党的十八大，十八届三中、四中全会和中央经济工作会议精神，坚持以提高发展质量和效益为中心，加快培育参与国际经济合作竞争新优势，推动“走出去”业务转型升级和平稳健康增长。

一是重点围绕“一带一路”加快战略布局。抓住实施“一带一路”、周边互联互通、非洲“三网一化”等重大战略的历史性机遇，推动我国与相关地区和国家基础设施建设领域合作。积极推进“中非工业化伙伴”行动计划，落实对非务实合作新举措。筹划境外经贸合作区建设新布局，构建跨境产业链。

二是大力推进装备制造业和优势产能“走出去”。发挥高铁、通信、电力等装备制造业以及钢铁、冶金、光伏等优势产业的竞争优势，通过对外投资合作促进国内设备、技术、标准和服务一体化“走出去”。贯彻落实好《国务院关于推进国际产能和装备制造合作的指导意见》，会同有关部门制定务实措施。支持并指导东北、河北等地开展国际产能和装备制造合作。

三是积极引导企业开展售后运营维护管理。推动对外承包工程向高附加值领域拓展，推动制造服务业“走出去”，探索开展投资和建设相结合的建营一体化项目。

四是深化境外投资管理体制改革。贯彻落实好《境外投资管理办法》，进一步提高境外投资便利化水平。加强境外中资企业商协会建设。加强对企业境外投资的指导。完善相关信息监测管理系统，加强深层次统计分析和事中事后监管。加大对境外重大项目合作的协调，大力规范对外承包工程和大型成套设备出口项目的竞争秩序。

五是不断加强政策和规划的导向作用。制订对外投资合作领域“十三五”发展规划，编制和落实重点国别、重点行业对外投资合作规划。完善有关信贷政策工具，保持政策的连续性和稳定性，提升

资金使用效益，优先支持国际产能和装备制造合作、“建营一体化”项目以及技术标准“走出去”。

六是进一步完善服务保障。加强对“走出去”企业的政策宣传和业务培训，支持企业间开展沟通合作。更新发布对外投资合作发展报告、国别地区指南，加强对企业境外投资的指导。完善境外安全风险管理体制，加强境外安全管理与突发事件应急处置，切实保障我在外企业和人员安全。

（商务部对外投资和经济合作司）

中国行政管理体制

行政管理是指政府运用行政权力执行法律、推行政务、管理（治理）公共事务的各项活动。行政管理体制是指行政管理主体和各主体之间制度化的关系模式。据此，行政管理体制的构成要素主要有二，一是行政管理主体（政府）的架构，二是由制度规制的不同行政管理主体之间的关系。自现行宪法颁布以来，为了适应改革开放和经济社会的发展变化，中国已经进行了七个轮次的政府机构改革。2013 年 3 月 14 日，十二届全国人大一次会议通过了《国务院机构改革和职能转变方案》，开启了新一轮国务院机构改革的序幕。由于不断推进行政管理体制改革，中国逐步形成了符合国情和市场经济发展需要的行政管理体制，为中国现代化建设和中国梦的实现提供了有力的体制保障。

一、中国政府系统的架构

在中国，政府系统是国家权力机关的执行系统，是行使行政权力、管理行政事务的国家机关。中国政府系统的架构在纵向上由不同层级的政府组成，在横向上由不同分工的政府部门组成。

（一）政府的纵向层级和横向部门

1. 政府的纵向层级

政府的纵向层级与行政区域密切相关。根据《宪法》第三十一条的规定，中国的行政区域全国分为省、自治区、直辖市；省、自治区分为自治州、县、自治县、市；县、自治县分为乡、民族乡、镇；直辖市和较大的市分为区、县；自治州分为县、自治县、市。自治区、自治州、自治县都是民族自治地方。国家在必要时，设立特别行政区。（参见表 1）

表 1　　2014 年全国行政区划统计表（截至 2014 年 12 月 31 日）

省级		地级		县级		乡级	
合计	行政区划单位	合计	行政区划单位	合计	行政区划单位	合计	行政区划单位
34	4 直辖市 23 省 5 自治区 2 特别行政区	333	288 地级市 12 地区 30 自治州 3 盟	2 854	897 市辖区 361 县级市 1425 县 117 自治县 49 旗 3 自治旗 1 特区 1 林区	40 381	2 区公所 20401 镇 11111 乡 151 苏木 1019 民族乡 1 民族苏木 7696 街道
北京市				16	14 市辖区 2 县	329	144 镇 33 乡 5 民族乡 147 街道
天津市				16	13 市辖区 3 县	240	121 镇 5 乡 1 民族乡 113 街道

续　表

省级		地级		县级		乡级	
合计	行政区划单位	合计	行政区划单位	合计	行政区划单位	合计	行政区划单位
	河北省	11	11 地级市	171	39 市辖区 20 县级市 106 县 6 自治县	2 246	1 区公所 1050 镇 857 乡 50 民族乡 288 街道
	山西省	11	11 地级市	119	23 市辖区 11 县级市 85 县	1 398	564 镇 632 乡 202 街道
	内蒙古自治区	12	9 地级市 3 盟	102	22 市辖区 11 县级市 17 县 49 旗 3 自治旗	1 010	495 镇 106 乡 151 苏木 17 民族乡 1 民族苏木 240 街道
	辽宁省	14	14 地级市	100	56 市辖区 17 县级市 19 县 8 自治县	1 530	645 镇 161 乡 56 民族乡 668 街道
	吉林省	9	8 地级市 1 自治州	60	21 市辖区 20 县级市 16 县 3 自治县	900	434 镇 156 乡 28 民族乡 282 街道
	黑龙江省	13	12 地级市 1 地区	128	65 市辖区 17 县级市 45 县 1 自治县	1 231	513 镇 327 乡 53 民族乡 338 街道
	上海市			17	16 市辖区 1 县	209	107 镇 2 乡 100 街道
	江苏省	13	13 地级市	99	55 市辖区 23 县级市 21 县	1 274	780 镇 78 乡 1 民族乡 415 街道
	浙江省	11	11 地级市	90	35 市辖区 20 县级市 34 县 1 自治县	1 321	629 镇 244 乡 14 民族乡 434 街道
	安徽省	16	16 地级市	105	43 市辖区 6 县级市 56 县	1 505	938 镇 306 乡 9 民族乡 252 街道

续 表

省级		地级		县级		乡级	
合计	行政区划单位	合计	行政区划单位	合计	行政区划单位	合计	行政区划单位
福建省		9	9 地级市	85	28 市辖区 13 县级市 44 县	1 104	628 镇 282 乡 19 民族乡 175 街道
江西省		11	11 地级市	100	20 市辖区 10 县级市 70 县	1 548	816 镇 579 乡 8 民族乡 145 街道
山东省		17	17 地级市	137	51 市辖区 28 县级市 58 县	1 826	1114 镇 81 乡 631 街道
河南省		17	17 地级市	158	50 市辖区 21 县级市 87 县	2 420	1103 镇 706 乡 12 民族乡 599 街道
湖北省		13	12 地级市 1 自治州	103	39 市辖区 24 县级市 37 县 2 自治县 1 林区	1 233	761 镇 160 乡 10 民族乡 302 街道
湖南省		14	13 地级市 1 自治州	122	35 市辖区 16 县级市 64 县 7 自治县	2 414	1153 镇 805 乡 97 民族乡 359 街道
广东省		21	21 地级市	119	61 市辖区 21 县级市 34 县 3 自治县	1 587	1128 镇 4 乡 7 民族乡 448 街道
广西壮族自治区		14	14 地级市	110	36 市辖区 7 县级市 55 县 12 自治县	1 243	773 镇 291 乡 59 民族乡 120 街道
海南省		3	3 地级市	24	8 市辖区 6 县级市 4 县 6 自治县	218	176 镇 21 乡 21 街道
重庆市				38	21 市辖区 13 县 4 自治县	1 023	610 镇 193 乡 14 民族乡 206 街道

续 表

省级		地级		县级		乡级	
合计	行政区划单位	合计	行政区划单位	合计	行政区划单位	合计	行政区划单位
四川省		21	18 地级市 3 自治州	183	49 市辖区 14 县级市 116 县 4 自治县	4 648	1937 镇 2284 乡 98 民族乡 329 街道
贵州省		9	6 地级市 3 自治州	88	14 市辖区 7 县级市 55 县 11 自治县 1 特区	1 396	762 镇 292 乡 208 民族乡 134 街道
云南省		16	8 地级市 8 自治州	129	13 市辖区 13 县级市 74 县 29 自治县	1 389	665 镇 421 乡 140 民族乡 163 街道
西藏自治区		7	3 地级市 4 地区	74	3 市辖区 71 县	694	140 镇 535 乡 9 民族乡 10 街道
陕西省		10	10 地级市	107	25 市辖区 3 县级市 79 县	1 420	1142 镇 74 乡 204 街道
甘肃省		14	12 地级市 2 自治州	86	17 市辖区 4 县级市 58 县 7 自治县	1 351	526 镇 668 乡 34 民族乡 123 街道
青海省		8	2 地级市 6 自治州	43	5 市辖区 3 县级市 28 县 7 自治县	399	140 镇 197 乡 28 民族乡 34 街道
宁夏回族自治区		5	5 地级市	22	9 市辖区 2 县级市 11 县	237	102 镇 91 乡 44 街道
新疆 维吾尔自治区		14	2 地级市 7 地区 5 自治州	103	11 市辖区 24 县级市 62 县 6 自治县	1 038	1 区公所 305 镇 520 乡 42 民族乡 170 街道
香港特别行政区							
澳门特别行政区							
* 台湾省							

注： * 台湾省的行政区划资料暂缺。

资料来源： 中华人民共和国民政部编：《中华人民共和国行政区划简册 2015》，中国地图出版社 2015 年，第 1～8 页。

与行政区域的划分相适应，从中央到地方，中国政府在纵向上分为五级政府和四级政府两种情况。第一种情况：省（自治区）分为五级政府。在设自治州的地方，政府在纵向上分为中央政府、省（自治区）政府、自治州政府、县（不设区的市）政府、乡（镇）政府；在设“设区的市”[①] 的地方，政府在纵向上分为中央政府、省（自治区）政府、市政府、区（县、不设区的市）政府、乡（镇）政府。第二种情况：直辖市分为四级政府，即中央政府、直辖市政府、区（县）政府、乡（镇）政府。

2. 政府的横向部门

除乡（镇）政府外，中国各级政府根据经济社会发展的需要，适应社会主义市场经济体制的要求，按照精简、统一、效能的原则设置政府部门，分工管理政治、经济、文化、社会等各项行政事务。根据政府部门在行政系统中的地位，可以将政府的横向部门划分为中央政府部门和地方政府部门。

（二）中央政府和地方政府

1. 中央政府

根据现行宪法的规定，国务院是最高国家权力机关的执行机关，是最高国家行政机关，对外是中国政府，对内是中央政府，统一领导所属部门和全国地方各级政府，一切国家行政机关都必须服从国务院的决定和命令。《宪法》和《国务院组织法》对国务院的组织和职权等做了明确规定。

（1）国务院的组成

国务院由总理、副总理、国务委员、各部部长、各委员会主任、审计长、秘书长组成。总理根据国家主席提名，由全国人大决定；副总理、国务委员、各部部长、各委员会主任、审计长、秘书长根据总理提名，由全国人大决定。在全国人大闭会期间，根据总理提名，由全国人大常委会决定部长、委员会主任、审计长和秘书长的任免。国务院总理领导国务院工作，副总理、国务委员协助总理工作，国务院秘书长在总理领导下，处理国务院日常工作，领导国务院办公厅。国务院的任期与全国人大任期相同，均为五年。总理、副总理、国务委员连续任职不得超过两届。

（2）国务院的职权

国务院行使《宪法》第八十九条规定的职权。这些职权有：①根据宪法和法律，规定行政措施，制定行政法规，发布决定和命令；②向全国人民代表大会或者全国人民代表大会常务委员会提出议案；③规定各部和各委员会的任务和职责，统一领导各部和各委员会的工作，并且领导不属于各部和各委员会的全国性的行政工作；④统一领导全国地方各级国家行政机关的工作，规定中央和省、自治区、直辖市的国家行政机关的职权的具体划分；⑤编制和执行国民经济和社会发展计划和国家预算；⑥领导和管理经济工作和城乡建设；⑦领导和管理教育、科学、文化、卫生、体育和计划生育工作；⑧领导和管理民政、公安、司法行政和监察等工作；⑨管理对外事务，同外国缔结条约和协定；⑩领导和管理国防建设事业；⑪领导和管理民族事务，保障少数民族的平等权利和民族自治地方的自治权利；⑫保护华侨的正当的权利和利益，保护归侨和侨眷的合法的权利和利益；⑬改变或者撤销各部、各委员会发布的不适当的命令、指示和规章；⑭改变或者撤销地方各级国家行政机关的不适当的决定和命令；⑮批准省、自治区、直辖市的区域划分，批准自治州、县、自治县、市的建置和区域划分；⑯依照法律规定决定省、自治区、直辖市的范围内部分地区进入紧急状态；⑰审定行政机构的编制，依照法律规定任免、培训、考核和奖惩行政人员；⑱全国人民代表大会和全国人民代表大会常务委员会授予的其他职权。

（3）国务院的工作制度

国务院的工作制度主要有总理负责制和会议制。

总理负责制。国务院总理领导国务院工作，对国务院工作负全部责任。国务院总理有权：①召集和主持国务院全体会议和常务会议；②签署国务院发布的决定、命令、行政法规；③签署向全国人大或者全国人大常委会提出的议案，例如国务院各部、各委员会的设立、撤销或者合并的议案；④签署任免人员等。国务院实行总理负责制是由国务院的性质和职能所决定的。国务院的性质是最高国家行政机关，职能是执行最高国家权力机关的决定，权力集中有利于高效、及时、果断地处理各种纷繁复杂的行政事务和突发事件。总理负责制符合现代社会对中央政府高效行政的要求。

---

① 根据《立法法》第七十二条的规定，在我国，设区的市包括四种城市，即省（自治区）政府所在地的市、经济特区所在地的市、国务院批准的较大的市和其他设区的市（地级市）。

会议制。国务院会议分为国务院全体会议和国务院常务会议。国务院全体会议由国务院全体成员组成；国务院常务会议由总理、副总理、国务委员、秘书长组成。根据《国务院组织法》第四条的规定，国务院工作中的重大问题必须经国务院常务会议或者国务院全体会议讨论决定。

（4）国务院部门

根据《国务院行政机构设置和编制管理条例》《国务院关于机构设置的通知》（国发〔2013〕14号），中国国务院部门分为以下八类（参见图1）：

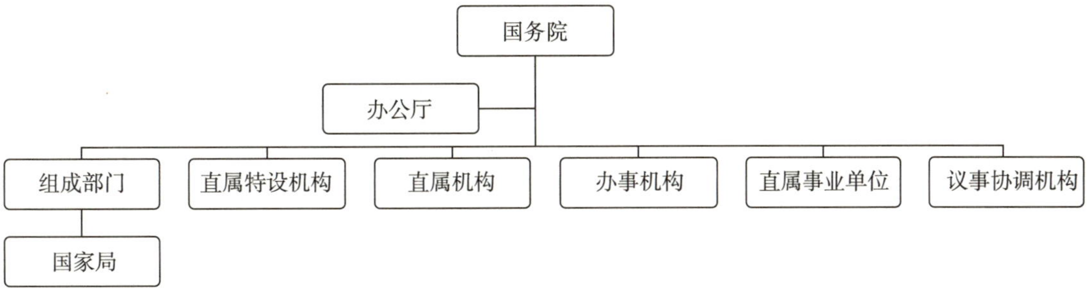

图1 国务院组织结构

• 国务院办公厅。国务院办公厅是协助国务院领导处理国务院日常工作的机构，由秘书长领导，并设副秘书长若干人协助秘书长的工作。

• 国务院组成部门。国务院组成部门是依法分别履行国务院基本行政管理职能的部门，包括各部、各委员会、中国人民银行和审计署。国务院组成部门具有行政主体资格，能够以自己的名义做出行政行为，并独立承担法律责任，即可以成为行政复议的被申请人、行政诉讼的被告和行政赔偿义务人，且可以依据上位法，在本部门的职责权限范围内发布命令、指示和制定规章。

• 国务院直属特设机构。国务院直属特设机构是指国务院国有资产监督管理委员会。该委员会代表国家履行出资人职责，对所监管企业国有资产的保值增值进行监督，监管范围是中央所属企业（不含金融类企业）的国有资产。

• 国务院直属机构。国务院直属机构主管国务院的某项专门业务，职能相对单一，专业性较强。国务院直属机构具有行政主体资格，能够以自己的名义做出行政行为，并独立承担法律责任，即可以成为行政复议的被申请人、行政诉讼的被告和行政赔偿义务人，且可以依据上位法，在本部门的职责权限范围内发布命令、指示和制定规章。

• 国务院办事机构。国务院办事机构是协助总理办理专门事项的机构，不具有行政主体资格，不能直接对外运用行政权，也无规章制定权。

• 国务院直属事业单位。国务院直属事业单位是指由国务院直接领导的事业单位。其中，有些事业单位承担行政职能，对某一行业实施集中统一监管，以维护市场经济秩序，例如中国证监会、中国保监会、中国银监会等；有些事业单位承担社会职能，以满足社会文化、教育、科学研究等方面的需要，例如新华通讯社、国家行政学院、中国科学院等。后一种直属事业单位不以营利为目的，其工作成果和价值不直接表现为物质或者货币形态。

• 国务院部委管理的国家局。部委管理的国家局是指受部委一级国务院机构的管理，有行政主体资格和法律规定的自治权，专司特定业务执行的国家行政机构。部委管理的国家局有四个特点：第一，受部委一级国务院机构管理。“部委一级”的提法意味着，不局限于部委，国务院办公厅、中国人民银行、国家安监总局等都可以是部委管理的国家局的主管部门。第二，是行政主体，有一定的自治权。部委管理的国家局相对独立于主管部门，不是主管部门的内设机构，其组织、运行、自治等遵循相关行政组织法。第三，专司特定业务执行。部委管理的国家局不对特定业务实行全程管理，其主要职责是执行法律和政策。第四，是国家行政机构。“国家行政机构”的提法意味着，部委管理的国家局属于国务院机构组成部分，法律地位低于主管部门但高于主管部门内设机构。

• 国务院议事协调机构。议事协调机构是指对跨国务院部门的重要业务工作进行组织协调工作的部门。议事协调机构一般不单设办事机构，少数根据工作需要单设办事机构，例如国务院扶贫开发领导小组办公室、全国老龄工作委员会办公室等。

根据《国务院关于机构设置的通知》（国发〔2013〕14号）、《国务院关于部委管理的国家局设置的通知》（国发〔2013〕15号）和《国务院关于议事协调机构设置的通知》（国发〔2008〕13号），国务院机构包括：国务院办公厅、国务院组成部门（25个）、国务院直属特设机构（1个）、国务院直属机构（16个）、国务院办事机构（4个）、国务院直属事业单位（13个）、国务院部委管理的国家局（16个）、国务院议事协调机构（29个，其中单设的办事机构4个）。（参见表2）

表2 **国务院机构设置**

机构类型	机构名称
办公机构	国务院办公厅
国务院组成部门	01. 外交部；02. 国防部；03. 国家发展和改革委员会；04. 教育部；05. 科技部；06. 工业和信息化部；07. 公安部；08. 国家安全部；09. 民族事务委员会；10. 监察部；11. 民政部；12. 司法部；13. 财政部；14. 人力资源和社会保障部；15. 国土资源部；16. 环境保护部；17. 住房和城乡建设部；18. 交通运输部；19. 水利部；20. 农业部；21. 商务部；22. 文化部；23. 国家卫生和计划生育委员会；24. 中国人民银行；25. 审计署
国务院直属特设机构	国有资产监督管理委员会
国务院直属机构	01. 海关总署；02. 税务总局；03. 工商行政管理总局；04. 质量监督检验检疫总局；05. 新闻出版广电总局；06. 体育总局；07. 安全生产监督管理总局；08. 食品药品监督管理总局；09. 统计局；10. 林业局；11. 知识产权局；12. 旅游局；13. 宗教事务局；14. 参事室；15. 机关事务管理局；16. 预防腐败局
国务院办事机构	01. 国务院侨务办公室；02. 国务院港澳事务办公室；03. 国务院法制办公室；04. 国务院研究室
国务院直属事业单位	01. 新华通讯社；02. 中国科学院；03. 中国社会科学院；04. 中国工程院；05. 国务院发展研究中心；06. 国家行政学院；07. 中国地震局；08. 中国气象局；09. 中国银行业监督管理委员会；10. 中国证券监督管理委员会；11. 中国保险监督管理委员会；12. 全国社会保障基金理事会；13. 国家自然科学基金委员会
国务院部委管理的国家局	01. 国家信访局（国务院办公厅）；02. 国家粮食局（国家发展和改革委员会）；03. 国家能源局（国家发展和改革委员会）；04. 国家国防科技工业局（工业和信息化部）；05. 国家烟草专卖局（工业和信息化部）；06. 国家外国专家局（人力资源和社会保障部）；07. 国家公务员局（人力资源和社会保障部）；08. 国家海洋局（国土资源部）；09. 国家测绘地理信息局（国土资源部）；10. 国家铁路局（交通运输部）；11. 中国民用航空局（交通运输部）；12. 国家邮政局（交通运输部）；13. 国家文物局（文化部）；14. 国家中医药管理局（国家卫生和计划生育委员会）；15. 国家外汇管理局（中国人民银行）；16. 国家煤矿安全监察局（国家安全生产监督管理总局）
国务院议事协调机构	01. 国家国防动员委员会；02. 国务院中央军委专门委员会；03. 国家边海防委员会；04. 国务院中央军委空中交通管制委员会；05. 全国爱国卫生运动委员会；06. 全国绿化委员会；07. 国务院学位委员会；08. 国家防汛抗旱总指挥部；09. 国务院妇女儿童工作委员会；10. 全国拥军优属拥政爱民工作领导小组；11. 国务院残疾人工作委员会；12. 国务院扶贫开发领导小组（单设办事机构）；13. 国务院关税税则委员会；14. 国家减灾委员会；15. 国家科技教育领导小组；16. 国务院军队转业干部安置工作小组；17. 国家禁毒委员会；18. 全国老龄工作委员会（单设办事机构）；19. 国务院西部地区开发领导小组；20. 国务院振兴东北地区等老工业基地领导小组；21. 国务院抗震救灾指挥部；22. 国家信息化领导小组；23. 国家应对气候变化及节能减排工作领导小组；24. 国家能源委员会；25. 国务院安全生产委员会；26. 国务院防治艾滋病工作委员会；27. 国家森林防火指挥部；28. 国务院三峡工程建设委员会（单设办事机构）；29. 国务院南水北调工程建设委员会（单设办事机构）。

注：

* 监察部与中共中央纪律检查委员会机关合署办公，机构列入国务院序列，编制列入中共中央直属机构。

* 国家预防腐败局列入国务院直属机构序列，在监察部加挂牌子。

* 国务院台湾事务办公室与中共中央台湾工作办公室、国务院新闻办公室与中共中央对外宣传办公室，一个机构两块牌子，列入中共中央直属机构序列。国家档案局与中央档案馆，一个机构两块牌子，列入中共中央直属机关的下属机构。

* 国家保密局与中央保密委员会办公室、国家密码管理局与中央密码工作领导小组办公室，一个机构两块牌子，列入中共中央直属机关的下属机构。工业和信息化部对外保留国家航天局、国家原子能机构牌子。教育部对外保留国家语言文字工作委员会牌子。环境保护部对外保留国家核安全局牌子。

2. 地方政府

中国的地方政府包括：省、自治区、直辖市、自治州、设区的市、县、自治县、不设区的市、市辖区、乡、镇政府。根据《宪法》第一百零五条、《地方各级人民代表大会和地方各级人民政府组织法》第五十四和五十五条的规定，地方各级政府是地方各级国家权力机关的执行机关，是地方各级国家行政机关，对本级人大和上一级行政机关负责并报告工作；县级以上地方各级政府在本级人大闭会期间，对本级人大常委会负责并报告工作。

(1) 地方政府的组成

根据《地方各级人民代表大会和地方各级人民政府组织法》第五十六条的规定，省、自治区、直辖市、自治州、设区的市的政府分别由省长、副省长，自治区主席、副主席，市长、副市长，州长、副州长和秘书长、厅长、局长、委员会主任等组成。县、自治县、不设区的市、市辖区的政府分别由县长、副县长，市长、副市长，区长、副区长和局长、科长等组成。乡、民族乡、镇的政府只设乡长、副乡长、镇长、副镇长，不设职能部门。民族乡的乡长由建立民族乡的少数民族公民担任。

(2) 地方政府的职权

• 县级以上地方政府的职权。根据《地方各级人民代表大会和地方各级人民政府组织法》第五十九条的规定，县级以上地方政府行使下列职权：①执行本级人民代表大会及其常务委员会的决议，以及上级国家行政机关的决定和命令，规定行政措施，发布决定和命令；②领导所属各工作部门和下级人民政府的工作；③改变或者撤销所属各工作部门的不适当的命令、指示和下级人民政府的不适当的决定、命令；④依照法律的规定任免、培训、考核和奖惩国家行政机关工作人员；⑤执行国民经济和社会发展计划、预算，管理本行政区域内的经济、教育、科学、文化、卫生、体育事业、环境和资源保护、城乡建设事业和财政、民政、公安、民族事务、司法行政、监察、计划生育等行政工作；⑥保护社会主义的全民所有的财产和劳动群众集体所有的财产，保护公民私人所有的合法财产，维护社会秩序，保障公民的人身权利、民主权利和其他权利；⑦保护各种经济组织的合法权益；⑧保障少数民族的权利和尊重少数民族的风俗习惯，帮助本行政区域内各少数民族聚居的地方依照宪法和法律实行区域自治，帮助各少数民族发展政治、经济和文化的建设事业；⑨保障宪法和法律赋予妇女的男女平等、同工同酬和婚姻自由等各项权利；⑩办理上级国家行政机关交办的其他事项。

• 乡（镇）政府的职权。根据《地方各级人民代表大会和地方各级人民政府组织法》第六十一条的规定，乡（镇）政府行使下列职权：①执行本级人民代表大会的决议和上级国家行政机关的决定和命令，发布决定和命令；②执行本行政区域内的经济和社会发展计划、预算，管理本行政区域内的经济、教育、科学、文化、卫生、体育事业和财政、民政、公安、司法行政、计划生育等行政工作；③保护社会主义的全民所有的财产和劳动群众集体所有的财产，保护公民私人所有的合法财产，维护社会秩序，保障公民的人身权利、民主权利和其他权利；④保护各种经济组织的合法权益；⑤保障少数民族的权利和尊重少数民族的风俗习惯；⑥保障宪法和法律赋予妇女的男女平等、同工同酬和婚姻自由等各项权利；⑦办理上级人民政府交办的其他事项。

(3) 地方政府的工作制度

与国务院的工作制度相同，地方政府同样实行行政首长负责制和会议制。

地方政府的行政首长负责制是指省长、自治区主席、直辖市市长、自治州州长、设区的市市长、县长、区长、乡长、镇长负责制。行政首长主持地方各级政府的工作，对上级政府和本级人民代表大会负责。实行首长负责制是由行政工作的性质和行政管理的客观需要决定的。行政首长负责制的突出特点是行政首长享有重大事项的决定权，但行政首长运用此项权力必须依法依规，依民主集中制的原则，同时也必须遵守相应的程序，在充分论证、听取意见、集体讨论的基础上做出决定。

县级以上地方政府的会议分为全体会议和常务会议。全体会议由本级政府的全体成员组成；省、自治区、直辖市、自治州、设区的市政府常务会议，分别由省长、副省长，自治区主席、副主席，市长、副市长，州长、副州长和秘书长组成。县、自治县、不设区的市、市辖区政府常务会议，分别由县长、副县长，市长、副市长，区长、副区长组成。省长、自治区主席、市长、州长、县长、区长召集和主持本级政府全体会议和常务会议。政府工作中的重大问题，须经政府常务会议或者全体会议讨论决定。

（4）地方政府部门的设置

县级以上地方政府根据工作需要和精干原则，设立必要的工作部门，负责本行政区域某一方面的行政事务。省级政府部门一般称为厅、委、办、局；设区的市政府部门一般称为委、办、局；县级政府工作机构一般称为局。乡（镇）政府不设政府部门，一般设几个综合办公室，规模较小的乡政府设若干助理员，例如民政助理员、司法助理员等。

改革开放前，受计划经济体制的制约，中国地方政府部门的设置与中央政府部门的设置保持一致。这种上下同构的政府结构便于上对下的控制、指挥和政令下达，但容易忽略地方特色。改革开放后，经过多轮次的政府机构改革，尤其是市场经济体制的建立，中国地方政府部门的设置有了一定的自主权，地方可以根据本行政区域的具体情况和实际需要因地制宜设置政府部门。例如，在资源型城市或者少数民族地方，适当设置资源利用与管理、民族发展等部门，不拘泥于中央政府部门设置的框架。一般而言，省级政府部门的设置与中央政府部门的设置基本对应，而省以下的州、市、县政府部门的设置较为灵活，可以不与中央或者省级政府部门的设置保持一致。中国广东省近些年来一直致力于推进大部制改革，出现了深圳模式、顺德模式、濠江模式、云安模式等不同改革模式，大幅精简了政府部门的数量，使政府部门的设立、调整与政府职能的新变化以及市场经济的新发展相适应。

（5）地方政府的派出机关

按照《地方各级人民代表大会和地方各级人民政府组织法》第六十八条的规定，省、自治区政府在必要时，经国务院批准，可以设立若干派出机关。县、自治县政府在必要时，经省、自治区、直辖市政府批准，可以设立若干区公所，作为其派出机关。市辖区、不设区的市政府，经上一级政府批准，可以设立若干街道办事处，作为其派出机关。这些政府派出机关虽然不是一级政府，但却拥有行政主体资格，能够以自己的名义做出行政行为，并独立承担法律责任，即可以成为行政复议的被申请人、行政诉讼的被告和行政赔偿义务人，因而可以被视为中国地方政府的一个管理层级。

二、政府和政府部门之间制度化的府际关系

府际关系泛指政府和政府部门之间的关系，这些关系包括上级政府和下级政府之间、上级政府部门和下级政府部门之间、不同行政区域政府之间、本级政府与政府部门之间、本级政府部门之间的关系等。根据关系的性质（内容），府际关系大体可以分为三种，即领导与被领导关系、跨区域合作关系、部门分工合作关系。所谓制度化的府际关系是指被法律制度、政府文件所规制的府际关系。在中国，制度化的府际关系主要有：

（一）政府的领导体制

中国是实行单一制国家结构形式的国家，中国政府系统实行中央政府统一领导、地方政府服从中央政府、地方下一级政府服从上一级政府的领导体制。《宪法》第八十九条第四项规定：国务院“统一领导全国地方各级国家行政机关的工作，规定中央和省、自治区、直辖市的国家行政机关的职权的具体划分”；《地方各级人民代表大会和地方各级人民政府组织法》第五十五条规定：“地方各级人民政府对本级人民代表大会和上一级国家行政机关负责并报告工作……全国地方各级人民政府都是国务院统一领导下的国家行政机关，都服从国务院。”具体到县级以上地方政府，既要接受上级政府的领导，同时也要领导下级政府，对此《宪法》第一百零八条规定：“县级以上的地方各级人民政府领导所属各工作部门和下级人民政府的工作，有权改变或者撤销所属各工作部门和下级人民政府的不适当的决定。”

（二）政府部门的领导体制

中央政府部门直接受国务院领导，地方政府部

门少数实行“垂直领导”[①]，大多数实行“条块结合”的双重领导体制，即大多数地方政府部门既受本级政府的统一领导，也受上一级主管部门的领导和业务指导。对此《地方各级人民代表大会和地方各级人民政府组织法》第六十六条规定：“省、自治区、直辖市的人民政府的各工作部门受人民政府统一领导，并且依照法律或者行政法规的规定受国务院主管部门的业务指导或者领导。自治州、县、自治县、市、市辖区的人民政府的各工作部门受人民政府统一领导，并且依照法律或者行政法规的规定受上级人民政府主管部门的业务指导或者领导。”

（三）跨行政区域的政府合作制度

跨行政区域的政府合作是指不同区域的同级政府之间在实现共同发展、争端解决、突发事件应对等方面实施的合作，合作的依据是法律规定、国务院文件规定等。

例如，2015年3月26日，国务院对国家发改委《关于报送长江中游城市群发展规划（送审稿）的请示》做出批复。《国务院关于长江中游城市群发展规划的批复》（国函〔2015〕62号），原则同意《长江中游城市群发展规划》，要求江西、湖北、湖南省政府加强组织领导，密切协调配合，完善定期会商机制和工作推进机制，抓紧制定实施方案和专项规划，依法落实该规划主要目标和重点任务。根据该规划提出的重点任务，湖北、湖南两省于2015年5月签署《长江中游城市群战略合作协议》，就深化交流合作达成共识。两省将在城镇发展、交通建设、产业发展、现代农业、水利建设、商贸市场、生态环保、文化旅游、教育医疗卫生等重点领域加强合作。

又如，《行政区域边界争议处理条例》第三条规定：“处理因行政区域界线不明确而发生的边界争议，应当按照有利于各族人民的团结，有利于国家的统一管理，有利于保护、开发和利用自然资源的原则，由争议双方人民政府从实际情况出发，兼顾当地双方群众的生产和生活，实事求是，互谅互让地协商解决，经争议双方协商未达成协议的，由争议双方的上级人民政府决定。必要时，可以按照行政区划管理的权限，通过变更行政区域的方法解决。”此条规定所提“协商协议”是处理行政区域边界争议的府际合作制度。

再如，《突发事件应对法》第五十二条规定：“履行统一领导职责或者组织处置突发事件的人民政府，必要时可以……请求其他地方人民政府提供人力、物力、财力或者技术支援”，此条规定所提“请求其他地方政府”是突发事件处置过程中的府际合作制度。

（四）政府部门的分工合作制度

政府部门分工管理是一种客观存在的行政现象，这种现象有利有弊。其利在于建立有限政府、权力相互制约和提高管理的专业化程度，其弊在于容易导致部门职责交叉和重复管理，降低管理效率。为了兴利除弊，建立政府部门间良好的公务合作制度势在必行。政府部门的公务合作有多种制度，例如信息共享、规划合议、联合执法、行政协调、行政协助等制度，这些制度都能在中国法律中找到出处。例如，《水法》第十七条规定：“国家确定的重要江河、湖泊的流域综合规划，由国务院水行政主管部门会同国务院有关部门和有关省、自治区、直辖市人民政府编制，报国务院批准”，这是对规划合议制度的规定；《海洋环境保护法》第十九条规定：“依照本法规定行使海洋环境监督管理权的部门可以在海上实行联合执法，在巡航监视中发现海上污染事故或者违反本法规定的行为时，应当予以制止并调查取证，必要时有权采取有效措施，防止污染事态的扩大，并报告有关主管部门处理”，这是对联合执法制度的规定；《行政监察法》第二十二条规定：“监察机关在办理违反行政纪律案件中，可以提请有关行政部门、机构予以协助。被提请协助的行政部门、机构应当根据监察机关提请协助办理的事项和要求，在职权范围内予以协助”，这是对行政协助制度的规定。

（五）政府部门工作流程衔接（制约）制度

部门分工管理的利处之一是形成权力间的相互制约。在中国，这种制约通过法律规定的部门工作流程衔接制度得以实现。按照这一制度，某部门履行某项职责必须以其他部门相关职责的履行为前提，其他部门的相关职责未履行，则某部门不能履

---

① 在中国，实行垂直领导的政府部门主要有海关、金融、国税、外汇管理、国家安全机关等部门。有些政府部门实行省以下垂直管理，例如土地、工商、质监、食品药品监督等部门。

行该项职责。例如，《环境影响评价法》第二十五条规定："建设项目的环境影响评价文件未经法律规定的审批部门审查或者审查后未予批准的，该项目审批部门不得批准其建设，建设单位不得开工建设。"《水污染防治法》第十七条规定：新建、改建、扩建直接或者间接向水体排放污染物的建设项目和其他水上设施，应当依法进行环境影响评价；建设单位在江河、湖泊新建、改建、扩建排污口的，应当取得水行政主管部门或者流域管理机构同意；涉及通航、渔业水域的，环境保护主管部门在审批环境影响评价文件时，应当征求交通、渔业主管部门的意见。部门工作流程衔接制度和该制度的监督功能，使行政权力的运用更加科学合理，更有利于社会的可持续发展。

（中国政法大学教授　郎佩娟

中国政法大学在读硕士研究生　林庆龙）

● 产业开放与管理措施

中国农业对外开放情况

一、中国农产品贸易环境变化情况

（一）世界农产品市场

2014 年，全球经济低迷抑制了农产品需求的增长，特别是作为生物能源原料的粮食和油脂以及作为工业原料的棉花受到的不利影响较大。与此同时，农产品供给则受益于正常气候条件而有所增加。在两方面因素作用下，全球农产品供求平衡格局有所改善，大宗农产品价格普遍呈现下降态势。据联合国粮农组织（FAO）发布的数据，2014/2015 年度，全球谷物产量上升至 25.48 亿吨的历史最高水平，比上年增长 0.9%；消费量 24.96 亿吨，增长 2.6%；出口量 3.51 亿吨，下降 1.8%；期末库存 6.46 亿吨，增长 5.9%。库存消费比上升到 25.6%，是进入 21 世纪以来的最高水平。

表 1　　2012—2015 年世界谷物生产、消费、库存和贸易情况　　单位：百万吨、%

年份		2012/2013	2013/2014	2014/2015	2014/2015 年度比上年度增长	年份		2012/2013	2013/2014	2014/2015	2014/2015 年度比上年度增长
生产	谷物	2 299.8	2 526.1	2 548.3	0.9	出口	谷物	314.1	357.8	351.4	－1.8
	小麦	660.0	717.2	729.5	1.7		小麦	141.6	156.7	153.0	－2.4
	大米	490.1	496.6	494.4	－0.5		大米	37.2	42.4	41.4	－2.3
	粗粮	1 149.7	1 312.3	1 324.4	0.9		粗粮	135.4	158.7	157.0	－1.1
使用	谷物	2 322.9	2 433.8	2 496.0	2.6	期末库存	谷物	549.4	609.4	645.6	5.9
	小麦	684.6	695.2	711.7	2.4		小麦	176.6	189.4	199.9	5.5
	大米	476.4	491.2	499.9	1.8		大米	176.8	181.1	176.2	－2.7
	粗粮	1 161.9	1 247.4	1 284.5	3.0		粗粮	196.0	238.9	269.5	12.8

数据来源：联合国粮农组织谷物供求概况，2015 年 5 月。

据世界银行发布的数据，2014 年国际农产品价格比上年下跌了 3.4%，食物价格下跌 7.1%，其中谷物价格大幅下跌 19%，油料油脂价格下跌 5.9%，工业原料农产品价格下跌 11.2%。能源价格下跌 7.2%，化肥价格下跌 11.6%。

除肉类产品以外的主要农产品价格普遍走低。美国 1 号硬粒红小麦海湾离岸价波动下滑，由年初的每吨 276 美元先上升至 5 月的 335 美元，随后从这一全年最高位下滑到 9 月 244 美元的最低位，年底回升到 270 美元。美国 2 号黄玉米海湾离岸价上半年处于每吨 200 美元以上的高位，7 月份下滑，8 月跌至 163 美元的年内最低位，四季度略有回升，12 月为 179 美元。泰国 5%碎米率大米曼谷离岸价年内波动起伏，2 月处于每吨 459 美元的年内最高位，5 月降至 388 美元的年内最低位，9 月回升到 445 美元后回落，12 月为 418 美元。美国大豆鹿特丹港到岸价 2 月处于每吨 591 美元的年内最高位，3 月跌至 500 美元，其后波动下滑，12 月为 446 美元。荷兰豆油出厂价 3 月处于每吨 1002 美元的年内最高位，其后持续下滑，12 月降到 820 美元。

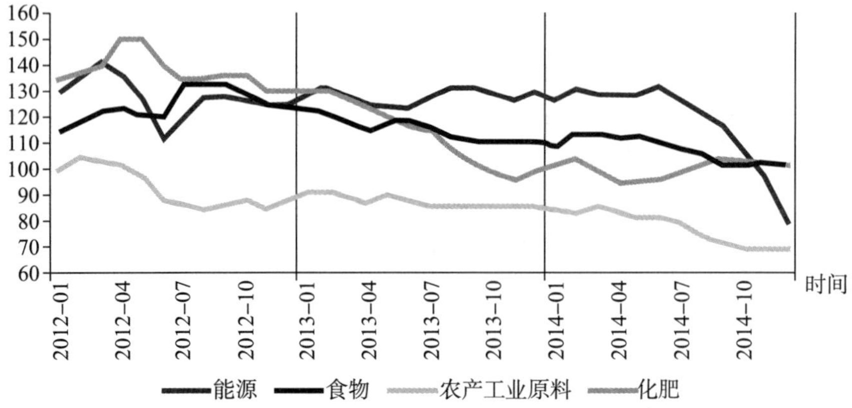

图 1 2012—2014 年国际市场初级产品价格指数变化

数据来源：世界银行（2015）。价格指数以 2011 年为 100。

棉花波动下滑。反映国际棉花市场现货价格水平的棉价指标 Cotlook A 远东指数价格上半年持续高于每吨 2000 美元，7 月开始下滑，11 月处于 1489 美元的年内最低位。国际食糖价格呈现倒 U 形变化，1 月为每吨 345 美元，5 月上升到年内最高的 403 美元，12 月降至最低的 338 美元。牛肉价格也呈现倒 U 形变化，由 1 月的每吨 4139 美元上升到 9 月的 5999 美元后回落，12 月为 5372 美元。鸡肉价格稳定上升，最低为 1 月的每吨 2302 美元，最高为 11 月的 2512 美元。

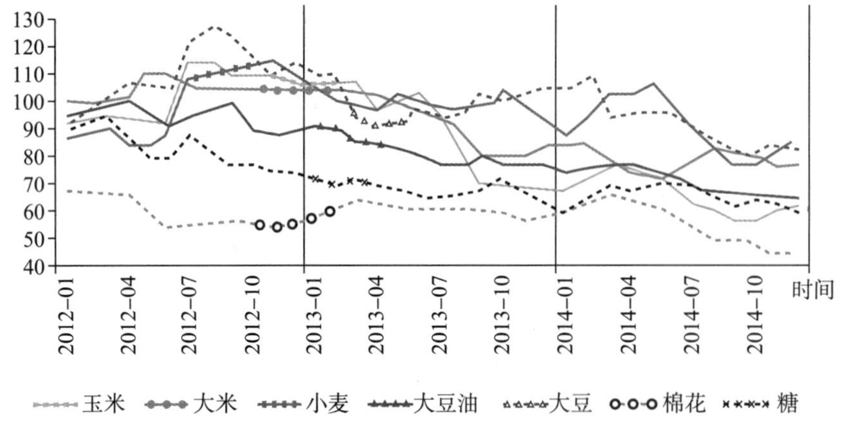

图 2 2012—2014 年国际市场主要农产品价格指数变化

数据来源：世界银行（2015）。价格指数以 2011 年为 100。

（二）中国农业和农村经济

2014 年，中国农业特别是粮食生产面临国际市场农产品价格继续下跌、国内劳动力成本上升、资源环境压力加大以及自然灾害频发等严峻挑战，中国政府采取了积极措施全面深化农村改革，加快推进农业现代化，农业生产和农村社会经济发展继续保持了良好势头。

全国粮食再获丰收，总产量 60703 万吨，比上年增产 0.8%，主要粮食作物中，稻谷产量 20651 万吨，比上年增产 1.4%；小麦产量 12621 万吨，增产 3.5%；玉米产量 21565 万吨，减产 1.3%。其他重要农产品生产也普遍保持较好的发展势头。其中经济作物中，棉花产量 618 万吨，减产 1.9%；油料产量 3507 万吨，减产 0.3%；糖料产量 13361 万吨，减产 2.8%；茶叶产量 210 万吨，增产 8.9%。肉类产量 8707 万吨，增长 2%，其中猪肉产量 5671 万吨，增长 3.2%；牛肉产量 689 万吨，增长 2.4%；羊肉产量428万吨，增长4.9%；禽肉产量1751万吨，下降2.7%。禽蛋产量2894万吨，增长0.6%。牛奶产量3725万吨，增长5.5%。水产品产量6462万吨，增长4.7%。

农村居民收入继续得到较快的提高，生活水平持续改善。全年农村居民人均可支配收入为10489元，扣除价格因素后，实际增长9.2%；人均消费支出8383元，扣除价格因素后，实际增长10%。农村劳动力非农业就业继续增加，全国农民工总量27395万人，比上年增长1.9%，其中外出农民工16821万人，增长1.3%；本地农民工10574万人，增长2.8%。以农村扶贫标准2010年不变价年人均纯收入2300元计算，年末农村贫困人口7017万人，比上年减少1232万人。

（三）中国农业贸易政策环境

1. 调整和强化农业国内支持措施

2014年，中国政府坚持把解决好“三农”问题作为全部工作的重中之重，以保障国家粮食安全和促进农民增收为核心推进农业现代化和农村改革，培育新型农业经营主体，发展多种形式适度规模经营。

中央财政全年安排农林水支出6474亿元，比上年增长8.4%，主要用于农业四补贴、金融保险支农、农田水利和江河湖库治理、农业综合开发、现代农业发展、农业资源生态保护、技术推广、动物防疫、农业生产救灾以及村级公益事业建设“一事一议”奖补等。

根据中央和国务院2015年1号文件精神，年内分别在东北和内蒙古启动了大豆目标价格的改革试点以及在新疆启动了棉花目标价格的改革试点，取代之前的临时收储政策。实行目标价格政策后，生产者按照市场价格出售产品，当市场价格低于目标价格时，国家根据目标价格与市场价格的差价对试点地区生产者给予补贴。此项改革的目标是探索推进农产品价格形成机制与政府补贴脱钩，在保障农民基本权益的前提下充分发挥市场在资源配置中的决定性作用，促进上下游产业的协调发展。从实践看，大豆和棉花价格开始与国际价格接轨，但政策的执行也遇到一些复杂情况，有待进一步探索。

2. 支持外贸稳定发展

5月4日，国务院办公厅针对国内外贸下行压力加大的情况，发布了《关于支持外贸稳定增长的若干意见》，就优化外贸结构、改善外贸环境、强化政策保障和增强外贸企业竞争力提出了指导意见。有关部委随后出台了相关具体措施。

9月29日，国务院常务会议讨论确定了加强进口的政策措施，其中提出合理增加与群众生活密切相关的牛羊肉、水产品等一般消费品的进口。10月23日，国务院办公厅下发《关于加强进口的若干意见》，要求加快与相关国家就水产品、水果以及牛羊肉等产品签订双边检验检疫协议并积极推动合格的加工企业和产品备案注册。

海关总署针对国内农产品走私活动处于高发阶段以致影响国家粮食安全和食品卫生安全的情况，布置展开了为期一年的打击农产品走私“绿风”专项行动，全力遏制农产品走私。

3. 利用贸易法规维护中国利益

海关总署针对自新西兰部分乳制品进口数量超过年度触发水平的情况于1月3日对原产于新西兰的12个税号的未浓缩乳及奶油实施了特殊保障措施，2月27日决定对原产于新西兰的乳酪实施特殊保障措施。商务部3月24日发布公告，根据国内中国酒业协会代表葡萄酒业提出的撤销案件申请，终止了对原产于欧盟的进口葡萄酒的反倾销调查和反补贴调查。商务部在对原产于美国的进口白羽肉鸡产品倾销和补贴情况做再调查之后于7月8日裁定美国相关产品存在倾销和补贴，从而使中国国内的白羽肉鸡产业受到实质损害。国务院关税税则委员会根据商务部的建议做出决定，自7月9日起对原产于美国的进口白羽肉鸡产品按照调整后的税率征收反倾销税。

农业部和国家质量监督检验检疫总局针对波兰发生的非洲猪瘟情况、美国加利福尼亚州农场发生H5亚型低致病性禽流感情况和加拿大发生的高致病性禽流感情况，为防止动物疫病传入国内，保护国内畜牧业安全和人体健康，分别于1月24日、5月20日和12月24日发布公告，禁止从疫区直接或间接输入相关产品。国家质量监督检验检疫总局还针对多批次从美国进口玉米检出未经农业部批准的MIR162转基因成分情况，对相关产品依法做出退运处理。农业部和国家质量监督检验检疫总局根据相关法律法规和世界卫生组织《国际陆生动物卫生法典》建议及风险评估结果，于6月25日发布公告，解除对疯牛病疫区进口牛血液制品的禁令。

二、2014 年中国农产品贸易情况

（一）进出口规模和贸易收支平衡

2014 年，中国农产品出口贸易发展面临多种不利因素影响，突出的有，主要出口市场经济低迷导致需求不振；地缘政治冲突导致贸易环境恶化；国际市场农产品价格下跌和人民币升值削弱了中国农产品在主要出口市场上的价格竞争力；中国经济增速放缓抑制了对进口农产品特别是加工原料的需求；农业支持政策调整减少了前几年在棉花等部分农产品进口上出现的扭曲；国际市场大宗农产品价格大幅下跌产生“量增额减”效应。在上述因素综合作用下，全国农产品贸易总额继续增长，全年出口额 719.6 亿美元，比上年增长 6.1%；进口额 1225.4 亿美元，增长 3.1%；农产品贸易逆差 505.8 亿美元，减少 4.8 亿美元。

年内各月农产品出口额除 2 月外均比上年同期有不同程度的增长，增幅在 1.2%～12.8%之间。各月农产品进口额呈前 7 个月增长、后 5 个月下降局面。

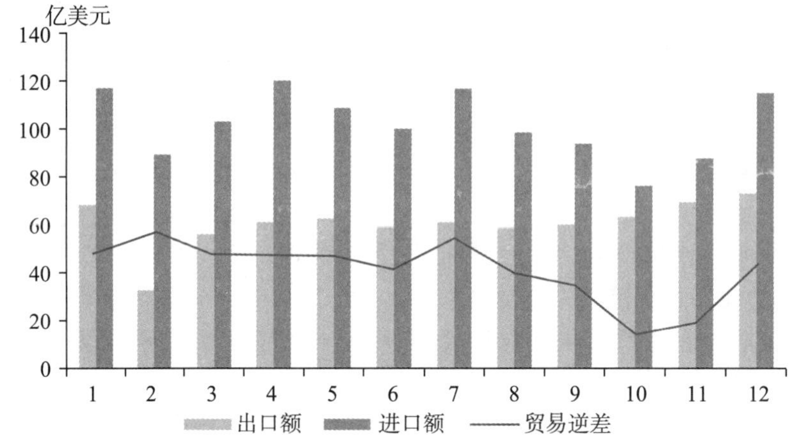

图 3　2014 年中国农产品对外贸易月度变化情况

数据来源：中国海关数据库。

（二）商品结构

农产品出口额居前五位的产品依次为水产品、蔬菜、畜产品、水果和饮品类；进口额居前五位的产品依次为油籽、畜产品、水产品、植物油和谷物。

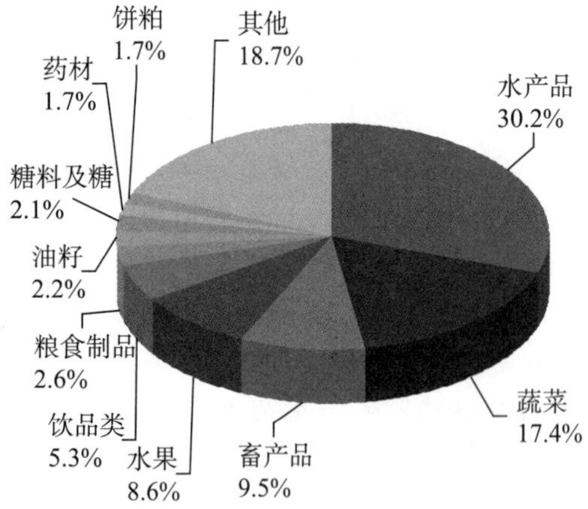

出口

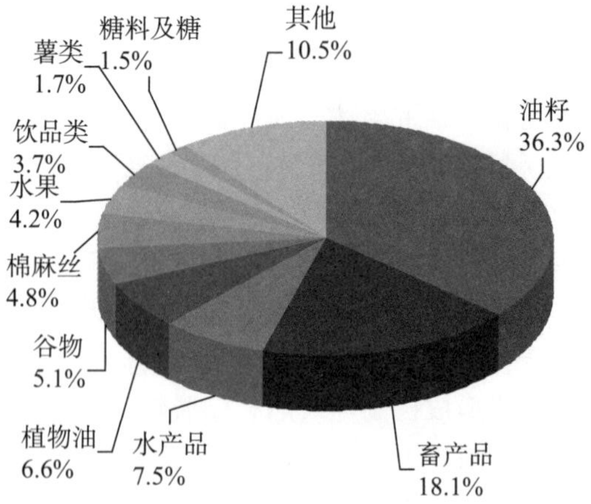

进口

图 4　2014 年中国农产品进出口结构

数据来源：中国海关数据库。

谷物贸易在国内谷物丰收和国内外价差拉大的背景下出现出口量大幅下降、进口量大幅增加的局

面。全年谷物出口76.9万吨，同比下降23.1%；主要谷物品种出口量均下降，其中稻谷产品和小麦产品分别下降12.4%和31.9%。进口1951.6万吨，增长33.8%，进口规模仅次于1995年；净进口1874.6万吨，比上年增加516万吨；贸易逆差56.2亿美元。谷物进口结构呈现不同的变化态势，传统大量进口的小麦产品和玉米产品进口下降，稻谷产品进口增加，各种杂粮产品进口急剧增长，其中高粱产品和大麦产品进口量均超过500万吨，分别比上年增加4.4倍和1.3倍。

食用油籽进口因国内价格下跌而明显增长。全年进口7751.8万吨，增长14.3%；出口87.2万吨，与上年基本持平。食用植物油则因食用油籽进口增加产生替代效应而呈现出口增加及进口下降局面，出口13.5万吨，增长16%；进口787.3万吨，下降14.6%。食用油籽和食用植物油贸易逆差分别为430.8亿美元和68.4亿美元。

棉花受全球经济低迷、国际市场棉制品需求不振以及前期超量库存未消化等因素影响，市场供过于求。此前国内棉花临时收储政策造成国产棉入库、进口棉入市的扭曲局面，导致棉花出口显著增加，出口量1.4万吨，比上年增长77.1%；进口量大幅萎缩，为266.9万吨，下降40.7%。

食糖国内市场上也存在政策导致的超量库存，因而尽管国际市场糖价下跌，食糖进口也仍减少，全年进口348.6万吨，比上年下降23.3%；进口额14.9亿美元，下降27.8%。

园艺产品贸易中的蔬菜类出口额为125亿美元，比上年增长7.9%；进口额5.1亿美元，增长21.7%；贸易顺差119.8亿美元，在农产品大类商品中居第二位。水果类出口61.8亿美元，下降2.3%；进口51.2亿美元，增长23.1%。坚果出口12.4亿美元，增长11.9%；进口5.2亿美元，增长37.7%。

畜产品随着国内市场对高品质产品需求的持续增加而使得贸易规模和结构受到影响，全年出口额为68.4亿美元，增长5%；进口额221.7亿美元，增长13.6%；贸易逆差153.2亿美元，居农产品大类商品贸易逆差的第二位。进口增长较快的产品主要是肉类和乳制品。

水产品出口217亿美元，增长7.1%；进口91.9亿美元，增长6.3%；贸易顺差125.1亿美元，在农产品大类商品中居首位。

（三）进出口市场结构

中国对各大洲农产品出口除南美洲外均为增长，且洲际间的增幅差异不大。其中对亚洲出口456.5亿美元，比上年增长8.4%，占农产品出口总额63.4%，比重提高1.3个百分点。对欧洲出口113亿美元，增长4.6%。对北美洲出口85.6亿美元，增长2.2%。对非洲出口28.6亿美元，增长1.3%。对大洋洲出口13.3亿美元，增长5.1%。对南美洲出口22.7亿美元，下降7.7%。

从各大洲农产品进口也除南美洲外均以相近幅度增长。其中从北美洲进口344.2亿美元，增长5.9%，再度回到各大洲进口总额的首位。从南美洲进口321.8亿美元，下降2.8%。从亚洲进口234.3亿美元，增长3.1%。从大洋洲进口150.3亿美元，增长5.1%。从欧洲进口142.4美元，增长8.6%。从非洲进口32.3亿美元，增长4%。

中国农产品贸易对亚洲继续保持顺差，对其他各大洲则均为逆差，其中对南美洲和北美洲的贸易逆差最大，分别为299.1亿美元和258.6亿美元。

表2　2014年中国农产品贸易区域分布　单位：亿美元、%

区域	贸易额				比上年增长		所占比重	
	进出口	出口额	进口额	差额	出口	进口	出口	进口
合计	1 945.0	719.6	1 225.4	−505.8	6.1	3.1	100.0	100.0
亚　洲	690.8	456.5	234.3	222.2	8.4	3.1	63.4	19.1
欧　洲	255.4	113.0	142.4	−29.4	4.6	8.6	15.7	11.6
北美洲	429.8	85.6	344.2	−258.6	2.2	5.9	11.9	28.1
非　洲	60.9	28.6	32.3	−3.7	1.3	4.0	4.0	2.6
南美洲	344.5	22.7	321.8	−299.1	−7.7	−2.8	3.2	26.3
大洋洲	163.5	13.3	150.3	−137.0	5.1	5.1	1.8	12.3

数据来源：中国海关数据库。

从国别（地区）贸易看，前五大农产品出口市场依序为日本、中国香港、美国、韩国和越南，合计占农产品出口总额的 49%。前五大农产品进口来源地依序为美国、巴西、澳大利亚、新西兰和加拿大，合计占农产品进口总额的 57.9%。农产品贸易顺差处于前五位的是对日本、中国香港、韩国、中国台湾和俄罗斯的贸易，顺差额分别为 105.6 亿美元、84.9 亿美元、41.1 亿美元、17.2 亿美元和 7.9 亿美元。农产品贸易逆差处于前五位的是对美国、巴西、澳大利亚、新西兰和加拿大的贸易，逆差额分别为 212.4 亿美元、209.2 亿美元、71.4 亿美元、66.3 亿美元和 45.6 亿美元。

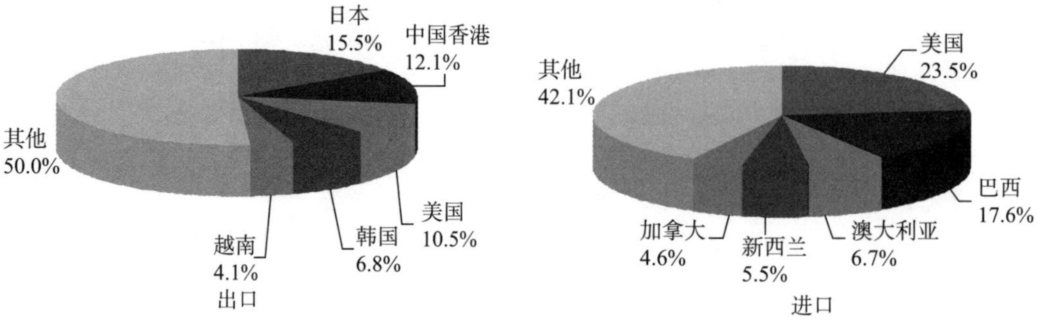

图 5　2014 年中国农产品出口市场和进口来源地结构

数据来源：中国海关数据库。

（四）贸易方式

2014 年，农产品一般贸易出口额 590 亿美元，占农产品出口总额的 82%；进料加工贸易出口额 78.8 亿美元，占农产品出口总额的 11%。农产品一般贸易进口额 987.6 亿美元，占农产品进口总额的 80.6%；保税区仓储转口货物 85.5 亿美元，占农产品进口总额的 7%；进料加工贸易进口额 79.9 亿美元，占农产品进口总额的 6.5%。

（五）国内进出口地区结构变化

农产品出口额排前五位的省（自治区、直辖市）依次为山东、广东、福建、浙江和辽宁，合计占农产品出口总额的 62.3%。出口额增幅超过全国平均值的有 16 个省（自治区、直辖市），其中青海、宁夏、湖南和云南等省（自治区、直辖市）增幅超过 20%；出口额下降的有 8 个省（自治区、直辖市），其中西藏、陕西、山西和黑龙江等省（自治区、直辖市）的降幅超过 10%。分区域看，东部地区农产品出口 535.9 亿美元，占农产品出口总额的 74.4%，增幅 16.6%；中部地区农产品出口额 99.4 亿美元，增幅 0.9%；西部地区农产品出口额 84.3 亿美元，增幅 9.7%。农产品进口额排前五位的省（自治区、直辖市）依次为广东、山东、江苏、上海和天津，合计占农产品进口总额的 65.9%。进口额增幅超过全国平均值的有 13 个省（自治区、直辖市），其中甘肃、山西、贵州、西藏、海南和黑龙江等省（自治区、直辖市）的增幅超过 20%；进口额下降的有 15 个省（自治区、直辖市），其中青海、陕西、宁夏和湖北等省（自治区、直辖市）的降幅超过 20%。分区域看，东部地区农产品进口额 1073.5 亿美元，占农产品进口总额的 87.6%，增幅 8.7%；中部地区农产品进口降幅 5.8%。

20 个省（自治区、直辖市）实现农产品贸易顺差，其中居前五位的省（自治区、直辖市）及顺差额分别为：福建 26.9 亿美元、云南 19.7 亿美元、湖北 14 亿美元、黑龙江 7.1 亿美元和江西 5.9 亿美元。逆差居前五位的省（自治区、直辖市）及逆差额分别为：江苏 143.6 亿美元、广东 134.5 亿美元、上海 85.8 亿美元、天津 78.9 亿美元和山东 44.9 亿美元。

（六）农产品贸易地位

2014 年，农产品进出口额分别占全国商品进出口额的 3.1%和 6.3%，均与上年基本持平。农产品进出口额与第一产业增加值比值分别为 13%和 7.6%，与上年相比，出口额上升 0.2 个百分点，进口额上升 0.1 个百分点。

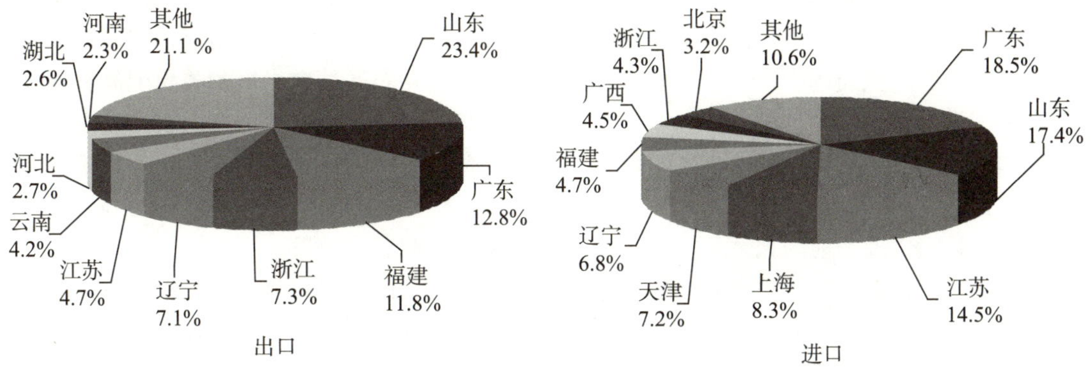

图 6　2014 年中国各省（自治区、直辖市）农产品进出口所占比重

数据来源：中国海关数据库。

三、中国参与国际粮食和农业事务情况

2014 年，中国农业多边外交丰富多彩，农业日益成为中国优势的外交资源，对国际粮农事务的影响力不断增强。在联合国粮农组织（FAO）、世界动物卫生组织（OIE）、国际农业研究磋商组织（CGIAR）、亚太经合组织（APEC）、二十国集团（G20）及世界粮食计划署（WFP）等重要平台上发挥着越来越重要的作用，在几大涉农国际组织中扮演着核心成员的角色，并深入参与了世界粮食安全委员会的改革，对国际粮食安全事务享有更高知情权和话语权，在国际粮农治理体系中的地位更加突出。在区域合作和新兴经济体合作中，中国也发挥了主导作用，加大了参与国际农业标准制度制定的力度，为构建公平的农业贸易环境逐渐发挥起关键作用。

中国政府致力于解决欠发达国家粮食不安全和饥饿问题。2008 年中国政府在联合国粮农组织设立了 3000 万美元信托基金支持联合国粮农组织在粮食安全特别计划框架之下开展农业多边“南南合作”项目，成效显著，过去几年里，粮农组织与中国已在 10 多个发展中国家实施了 11 个南南合作项目，选送了近 400 名专家，引进了 268 个作物品种，开展了 237 项示范活动与 1300 场培训，近 20000 名当地农民接受了培训，65000 农民从项目中受益。

中国与联合国粮农组织及全球环境基金合作的“全球重要农业文化遗产系统的保护和适应性管理（GIAHS）”项目在提供粮食安全、农业生物多样性保护和独特的本土知识方面也取得了积极成就，中国深入参与了粮农组织全球重要农业文化遗产工作，促进了中国及发展中国家生态文明建设与农业可持续发展。

四、中国农业利用外资情况

2014 年，中国农业紧密围绕国内现代农业产业发展需要，不断优化农业利用外资结构。结合农业结构调整方向，鼓励外资投向农业高新技术产业、新能源和节能环保产业，引导外资向中西部地区转移，鼓励外商在中西部地区发展符合环保要求的劳动密集型产业，鼓励东部地区与中西部地区以市场为导向强化农业招商引资，促进农业利用外资方式多元化，提高农业利用外资质量和水平。据商务部统计，2014 年全国农业实际利用外资额 15.2 亿美元，比上年下降 15.4 %，占同期全国实际利用外资总额 1.3%。农业“引进来”项目的实施对引进国外先进农业技术和管理理念，促进现代农业发展，提升农业粮食安全水平等具有积极作用。

五、中国农产品贸易发展前景展望

2015 年，国际市场大宗农产品供需宽松，价格持续低迷。上半年联合国粮农组织食品价格指数同比降幅由 11%逐月扩大至 21%。世界银行 2015 年 4 月预测，本年度国际农产品价格预期下跌 10%，其中谷物价格下跌 7%，油料油脂价格下跌 15%，棉花价格下跌 13%，糖价格下跌 11%。尽管能源、化肥等农业生产资料价格也处于低位，但农产品价格持续低迷势必将会引起生产者和消费者做出调整，进而影响全球农产品的供求格局。世界经济增长疲软，特别是新兴经济和发展中国家经济形势的恶化将成为影响全球农产品贸易发展的突出因素，如巴西等一些重要农产品出口国会因价格下跌和国内社会经济形势恶化而减少出口，一些重要进口国可能会因需求不振而减少进口。

近年来中国农业虽然保持了增粮增收的好势头，但数量与质量、总量与结构、投入与产出、成本与效益、生产与环境以及当前与长远等方面矛盾上升。中国农业农村工作将按照稳粮增收、提质增效、创新驱动的总要求继续全面深化农村改革，全面推进农村法治建设，推动新型工业化、信息化、城镇化、农业现代化和绿色化协调发展，努力在粮食生产能力上挖掘新潜力，在优化农业结构上开辟新途径，在转变农业发展方式上寻求新突破，在促进农民增收上获得新成效，在建设新农村上迈出新步伐。国家将调整完善农业相关补贴政策，增强农业补贴的指向性、精准性和实效性，加大对粮食适度规模经营的支持力度。

农业对外经贸合作方面，近年农业生产持续增长对维持国内市场稳定发挥了主要的作用，但在供给充裕的同时库存增加，产品价格竞争力在全球供应链上仍处于弱势。中国主要农产品面临着出口市场经济不景气、国内经济增速下滑和国际市场农产品价格继续走低等影响因素，中国在全球经济贸易中的地位迅速提升在带来农业国际合作机遇的同时，也增大了实际运作的复杂性。国家预计将会继续积极支持优势农产品出口，完善粮食、棉花、食糖等重要农产品进出口和关税配额管理，严格执行棉花滑准税政策，严厉打击农产品走私行为，加快培育具有国际竞争力的农业企业集团，加强农产品加工、储运以及贸易等环节的对外合作，支持开展境外农业合作开发。

从农产品贸易趋势看，中国农产品价格竞争力明显削弱，部分农产品库存压力需要释放，农产品贸易可能出现进出口额均缓慢增长甚至小幅下降局面，大宗农产品进口压力将进一步增强，进口价格的天花板效应将会增强，贸易逆差可能继续增大。从区域看，中美双边农产品贸易发展面临一些有利条件，如美国经济复苏有利于中国对其扩大出口，美国对中国出口则会受益于中国需求量的较快增长及消费者质量安全要求提高等趋势性变化。中国对日本和欧盟出口农产品的前景不容乐观，除经济低迷会抑制需求增长外，日元和欧元贬值也是不利因素。中国与发展中国家特别是与东盟、智利、秘鲁等自贸区伙伴间的双向贸易整体可望继续稳定发展，与巴西等个别国家间的贸易可能会由于其经济低迷及汇率波动而受到不利影响。

（农业部农业贸易促进中心　张晓婉）

中国纺织业对外开放情况

一、2014 年中国纺织工业发展概况

2014 年以来，我国纺织工业①坚持深入推进转型升级，积极适应经济发展新常态，努力克服了棉花价格大幅波动、市场需求增长放缓、综合成本持续上升等一系列复杂因素影响，总体上保持了平稳发展态势，经济运行基本处于合理区间，发展结构与质量逐步改善。行业发展主要呈现出以下特点：

（一）经济运行情况基本正常

2014 年，纺织行业主要运行指标均实现增长，但受到原料价格波动、市场需求放缓以及自身发展阶段转换等内外因素影响，延续了“十二五”以来的总量增速逐年放缓态势，各项指标增速较 2013 年均有不同程度下降。根据国家统计局和中国海关数据，全国 3.8 万户规模以上纺织企业②工业增加值同比增长 7 %，低于 2013 年 1.3 个百分点；主营业务收入为 67220.1 亿元，同比增长 6.8%，增速低于 2013 年 4.7 个百分点；利润总额为 3662.7 亿元，同比增长 6.1%，低于 2013 年 9.7 个百分点。全国纺织品服装出口总额③为 3069.6 亿美元，同比增长 5.1%，增速低于 2013 年 6.1 个百分点；全行业 500 万元以上项目固定资产投资完成额④为 10362.5 亿元，同比增长 13.4%，增速低于 2013 年 3.9 个百分点。

（二）转型升级取得进展

纺织行业转型升级在 2014 年继续取得新进展，成为行业实现平稳运行的主要支撑因素。全年规模以上产业用纺织品行业工业增加值和利润总额同比分别增长 11.7%和 13.8%，分别高于全行业增速 4.7 和 7.7 个百分点，产业链新增长点作用仍然突出。服装、家纺行业效益稳定，规模以上企业利润率分别达 6.0%和 5.7%，电子商务成交额达到约 6700 亿元，同比增长 37%，反映品牌附加价值与市场适应性提升。中西部地区规模以上纺织企业主营业务收入占全行业的比重达 22.5%，较 2013 年提高 0.8 个百分点；固定资产投资完成额占比为 40.2%，同比提高 1.2 个百分点，产业区域布局调整继续深入。规模以上纺织企业产成品周转率为 20.6 次/年，同比加快 0.8%；资产负债率为 53.4%，同比下降 1.8 个百分点；销售利润率为 5.45%，与 2013 年基本持平，经济运行质量总体稳中趋好。

（三）发展压力仍然突出

尽管运行基本平稳，但纺织行业发展压力仍较为突出，特别是 2014 年下半年以来，多数运行指标增速环比均呈下行走势。行业面临的突出问题：一是国内棉花市场形势较为复杂，种植直补新政实施效果尚不确定，内外棉价差仍维持在 3000 元/吨以上。二是综合成本持续上升，人均工资同比增加约 10%，染料价格自去年以来累计上涨 150%，加上融资、渠道等费用过高，中小微企业不堪成本重负。三是国际竞争更趋激烈，我国纺织行业由于成本高企，2014 年在美国、日本、欧盟进口市场所占份额同比分别降低 0.9、1.3 和 0.4 个百分点。四是环保形势严峻，行业污染物排放标准要求提高，总量减排任务较重，中小微企业应对能力普遍不足。

---

① 本文中纺织工业、纺织行业是广义概念，涵盖化学纤维制造、纺纱、织造、非织造、针织、染整、家用和产业用制成品、服装制造及纺织机械制造整个纺织产业链条。本文来源于国家统计局的纺织工业统计数据包括国家统计局标准分类中的纺织业、化学纤维制造业、纺织服装服饰业以及机械制造业中的纺织机械制造业。

② 规模以上企业指年主营业务收入达到 2000 万元及以上的工业企业。

③ 纺织品服装进出口统计数据包括中国海关商品分类第 50～63 章中的纺织纱线、织物、制成品、服装和第 94 章中的寝具。

④ 纺织行业固定资产投资统计包括 500 万元以上的城镇和农村固定资产投资项目，但不含农户投资项目。

表 1　　2014 年纺织工业主要运行指标

指标名称	单位	2014 年累计	同比（%）
主要经济指标（规模以上企业）			
主营业务收入	亿元	67 220.1	6.8
主营业务成本	亿元	59 189.8	7.2
利润总额	亿元	3 662.7	6.1
应交增值税	亿元	1 715.1	8.6
资产合计	亿元	4 3331.3	8.8
主要产品产量			
化学纤维（全社会）	万吨	4 390	5.5
纱（全社会）	万吨	3 379	5.6
布（全社会）	亿米	703.7	−0.5
印染布（规模以上企业）	亿米	536.7	−2.5
无纺布（规模以上企业）	万吨	361.4	10.7
服装（规模以上企业）	亿件	299.2	1.6
固定资产投资指标（500 万元以上项目）			
实际完成投资额	亿元	10 362.5	13.4
新开工项目数	个	13 646	−0.5
纺织品服装贸易指标（全社会口径）			
出口总额	亿美元	3 069.6	5.1
进口总额	亿美元	273.8	−0.6
贸易差额	亿美元	2 795.8	5.7

数据来源：中国国家统计局、中国海关。

二、2014 年中国纺织工业出口贸易情况

2014 年，我国纺织品服装出口总体实现平稳增长，但受需求增长缓慢、市场竞争加剧、出口价格走低等因素影响，增速较 2013 年有所放缓，出口结构呈现出新的特点。

（一）出口总额保持平稳增长

根据中国海关数据，2014 年我国纺织品服装出口总额达 3069.6 亿美元，同比增长 5.1%，与 2013 年相比增速放缓了 6.1 个百分点。从全年走势看，出口总额总体呈现逐渐回升态势，全年 5.1%的增速较一季度和上半年分别回升 4.6 和 0.9 个百分点。与全国出口总额 6.1%增速相比较，纺织行业出口总额增速偏低 1 个百分点，但占全国的比重仍稳定在 13.1%，较 2013 年略下降 0.1 个百分点。

表 2　　我国纺织品服装出口额及占全国的比重情况

年　份	纺织品服装出口		其中：纺织品出口额（亿美元）	服装出口额（亿美元）
	出口额（亿美元）	占全国（%）		
2010 年	2 120.0	13.4	825.2	1 294.8
2011 年	2 541.2	13.4	1 009.0	1 532.2
2012 年	2 625.6	12.8	1 024.1	1 601.5
2013 年	2 920.8	13.2	1 188.6	1 782.2
2014 年	3 069.6	13.1	1 191.4	1 878.2

数据来源：中国海关。

（二）数量增长发挥根本拉动作用

2014 年，受国内停止棉花收储及国际油价走低等因素影响，纺织原料价格进入下行通道，带动纺织品服装出口价格有所下降，2014 年同比略降低 0.5%，价格低位也成为纺织品服装出口总额增速较上年放缓的重要原因之一。即使剔除价格因素，纺织品服装出口数量增长仍相对平稳，全年同比增加 5.2%，仅低于 2013 年 1.5 个百分点，对出口总额的增长贡献率达到 101%，发挥了根本性的支撑作用。

表 3　我国纺织品服装出口价格、出口数量指数　上年同期＝100

年　份	出口价格指数			出口数量指数		
	纺织品服装	纺织品	服装	纺织品服装	纺织品	服装
2010 年	108.0	108.8	107.6	114.6	118.1	112.4
2011 年	119.3	120.3	118.6	100.5	101.6	99.8
2012 年	103.9	99.8	106.9	99.4	101.7	97.8
2013 年	104.3	105.0	103.8	106.7	105.9	107.2
2014 年	100.0	99.9	100.0	105.2	104.7	105.4

数据来源：中国纺织工业联合会统计中心根据中国海关统计数据整理。

（三）终端产品增长相对平稳

主要出口产品中，纺织产业链终端产品出口增长相对平稳，2014 年服装出口额同比增长 5.4%，家用和产业用制成品出口额分别增长 6.4%。服装中，梭织服装及附件出口额同比增长 19.3%，较 2013 年加快 7.8 个百分点，但针织服装及附件出口额同比减少 5%，增速较 2013 年大幅下滑 16.2 个百分点，除价格因素外，国际采购商及我国纺织企业将附加值相对较低的针织服装采购订单和制造产能转移至成本低廉的东南亚国家，也是影响出口的重要原因。

纺织产业链上游产品受到原料价格波动因素影响，出口增长缓慢，全年纱线出口额同比下降 1.3%，织物出口额仅增长 3.3%。其中，棉纱线和棉织物受国内棉价持续高于国际市场因素影响，出口竞争力削弱，出口额同比分别下降 18%和 5.4%。

表 4　2014 年我国主要纺织服装产品出口情况

主要出口产品	出口额（亿美元）	同比（%）	增速比 2013 年增减（百分点）
纺织品服装	3 069.6	5.1	−6.1
纺织品	1 191.4	4.7	−6.5
纺织纱线	112.7	−1.3	−8.0
纺织织物	270.6	3.3	−11.3
纺织制成品	708.1	6.4	−3.8
服　装	1 878.2	5.4	−5.9
针织服装及附件	920.0	−5.0	−16.2
梭织服装及附件	814.5	19.3	7.8

数据来源：中国海关。

（四）出口市场多元化水平有所提升

主要出口市场中，美、欧市场随经济稳步复苏实现平稳增长，2014 年我国对其纺织品服装出口额同比分别增长 7%和 13.4%，且增速分别与上年持平和加快 4.5 个百分点。日本市场受经济低迷及日元贬值影响，我国纺织行业对其出口规模继续萎缩，出口额同比减少 8.9%。东盟市场受经济景气下行影响，出现波动较大，我国纺织行业出口额同比仅增长 5.9%，较 2013 年大幅下滑 22.4 个百分点；但对越南出口额同比仍增长 19.8%，增速虽然较 2013 年明显放缓，但在主要出口市场中仍属较高水平。此外，非洲和韩国市场也实现较好增长，出口额同比分别增加17.3%和21%，均高于行业平均水平，我国纺织行业出口市场日益多元化的特征明显。

表5　　2014年我国对主要市场出口纺织品服装情况

国家和地区	出口额（亿美元）	同比（%）	增速比2013年增减（百分点）
欧　盟	599.3	13.4	4.5
美　国	470.4	7.0	0.0
东　盟	367.4	5.9	−22.4
越　南	158.3	19.8	−25.1
日　本	255.7	−8.9	−7.9
非　洲	202.0	17.3	10.8
中国香港	166.2	−15.6	−35.5
俄罗斯	132.6	6.2	−29.5
韩　国	85.0	21.0	4.2

数据来源：中国海关。

三、2014年中国纺织工业进口贸易情况

2014年，受人民币汇率高位及原料价格下行等因素影响，我国纺织品服装进口规模未能实现增长，进口总额为273.8亿美元，同比减少0.6%。纺织产业链配套产品受到行业生产增速放缓因素影响，进口规模也有所缩减，进口额为513亿美元，同比下降13.1%。

（一）服装进口保持较快增长

2014年，我国内需消费基本保持平稳增长，全国限额以上服装鞋帽针纺织品零售额同比增长10.9%，服装网上零售额同比增长41.5%，带动服装进口稳步扩大。我国服装进口额为69.3亿美元，同比增长19.3%，增速较2013年略放缓1.1个百分点。但剔除价格因素后，服装进口数量同比增加40.5%，增速较2013年加快14.7个百分点。主要进口来源国中，意大利仍位居首位，进口额为11亿美元，同比增长9.9%，表明我国高端消费稳步扩大；自日本进口额受日元贬值影响实现高增，同比增速达到68.7%；自朝鲜和越南进口则随订单及产能转移保持稳定增长，同比增速分别为26.2%和35.6%。

（二）纺织品进口规模有所缩减

2014年，我国纺织品进口额为204.5亿美元，同比下降5.9%；剔除价格因素后，进口数量同比下降5.1%，进口规模有所缩减。主要产品中，纱线进口额同比下降7.8%，增速较2013年大幅回落33.8个百分点点，原因主要是国内棉价随直补政策实施有所回落，棉花及棉纱供给能力有所提升。织物进口额同比下降9.3%，反映出我国面料自给自足能力的进一步提升。家纺、产业用纺织品大类产品进口基本保持增长，但针织物进口额同比下滑12.1%，带动纺织制成品进口总额同比减少3.1%。主要进口来源地中，印度和台湾地区受我国棉纱进口需求下降影响，进口额同比有所下滑，日本、韩国进口规模缩减则主要受织物进口需求下降影响。

表6　　我国纺织品服装进口额及占全国的比重情况

年　份	纺织品服装进口		其中：纺织品进口额（亿美元）	服装进口额（亿美元）
	进口额（亿美元）	占全国（%）		
2010年	203.2	1.5	178.1	25.2
2011年	231.6	1.3	91.5	40.1
2012年	248.0	1.4	199.8	48.2
2013年	275.4	1.4	217.3	58.1
2014年	273.8	1.4	204.5	69.3

数据来源：中国海关。

表7　　2014年我国主要纺织服装产品进口情况

主要出口产品	进口额（亿美元）	同比（%）	增速比2013年增减（百分点）
纺织品服装	273.8	−0.6	−11.7
纺织品	204.5	−5.9	−14.7
纺织纱线	86.2	−7.8	−33.8
纺织织物	45.1	−9.3	−3.7
纺织制成品	73.1	−1.4	−3.1
服　装	69.3	19.3	−1.1

数据来源：中国海关。

表8　　2014年我国纺织品服装主要进口来源地情况

纺织品				服装			
排序	国家和地区	进口额（亿美元）	同比（%）	排序	国家	进口额（亿美元）	同比（%）
	全　球	204.5	−5.9		全　球	69.3	19.3
1	中国台湾	30.1	−5.0	1	意大利	11.0	9.9
2	日　本	27.2	−6.7	2	朝　鲜	7.4	26.2
3	韩　国	21.2	−7.1	3	日　本	6.9	68.7
4	印　度	17.6	−17.4	4	越　南	5.6	35.6

数据来源：中国海关。

表9　　我国纺织品服装进口价格指数　　上年同期=100

年份	进口价格指数		
	纺织品服装	纺织品	服　装
2010年	109.5	109.4	110.5
2011年	116.7	116.3	118.7
2012年	99.5	99.3	100.4
2013年	100.0	101.2	95.7
2014年	95.9	99.2	84.9

数据来源：中国纺织工业联合会统计中心根据中国海关统计数据整理。

（三）天然纤维原料进口下降明显

2014年，我国停止实施棉花临时收储措施，为配套该政策执行，当年棉花进口配额发放减少，加上国储库停止轮入，以及企业因棉价回落停止全额清关，全年棉花进口总量仅为243.8万吨，较2013年减少41.2%。受此影响，2014年天然纤维进口额仅为85.1万吨，同比减少30.2%。化纤原料进口情况基本平稳，其中纤维素纤维进口额同比增长6.4%，合成纤维原料进口额随我国原料配套能力上升同比略下降4.2%。

（四）装备及染料进口需求有所减少

2014年，我国染料及助剂进口额保持增长，进口额为35亿美元，同比增加6.7%，其中染料进口额为7.7亿美元，同比增长9%，助剂进口额为27.3亿美元，同比增长6.3%。助剂进口呈现量、价齐升态势，表明需求有所增加，但染料进口额增长主要受到供应商高位垄断价格影响，进口价格同比上涨21.1%，进口数量则同比下降10%。纺织机械进口额为39.1亿美元，同比减少7.7%，化纤、织造、针织等主要品类进口数量均有所下降，其原因一方面是我国国产装备竞争力提升，另一方面也与我国纺织工业生产增速放缓、企业投资需求下降有关。

表 10　　2014 年我国纺织工业进口相关产品情况①

产品名称	进口量		进口额	
	全年累计（万吨）	同比（%）	全年累计（亿美元）	同比（%）
天然纤维	371.4	−32.1	85.1	−30.2
纤维素纤维原料	1808.8	6.4	121.2	6.0
合成纤维单体	2034.7	−4.2	232.6	−16.7
有机染料及助剂	81.4	2.9	35.0	6.7
纺织机械	—	—	39.1	−7.7
合　计	—	—	513.0	−13.1

数据来源：中国海关。

四、2014 年中国纺织工业利用外资情况

2014 年，我国纺织行业中的港澳台投资企业和外商投资企业运行压力有所增加，各项运行指标增速较 2013 年有所放缓，且均低于全行业平均水平，资本存量、流量及经济总量在纺织行业中的占比进一步下降。

（一）三资企业经济运行压力有所增加

根据国家统计局数据，2014 年，我国规模以上纺织企业中共有港澳台和外商控股企业 6005 户，实现主营业务收入 11325.6 亿元，同比增长 4.8%，增速较 2013 年放缓 3.3 个百分点，低于纺织全行业增速 2 个百分点；实现利润总额 583.7 亿元，同比增长 3.6%，增速较 2013 年放缓 4.9 个百分点，低于纺织全行业增速 2.5 个百分点。根据海关统计数据，全国三资企业纺织品服装出口额为 702.5 亿美元，同比下降 1.4%，增速低于 2013 年 2.9 个百分点，低于全国纺织品服装出口增速 6.5 个百分点。三资企业主营业务收入、利润总额和出口总额占纺织全行业的比重分别为 16.8%、15.9% 和 22.9%，较 2013 年分别下降 0.7、0.8 和 1.5 个百分点。

港澳台控股企业运行情况明显好于外商控股企业，特别是效益情况增长较为平稳。2014 年，规模以上港澳台控股纺织企业利润总额同比增长 7.6%，较 2013 年较快了 2.7 个百分点，高于纺织全行业增速 1.5 个百分点；销售利润率为 5.2%，同比提高了 0.1 个百分点。

表 11　　2014 年港澳台及外商控股纺织企业主要指标

主要经济指标（规模以上企业）							
指标名称	单位	港澳台控股			外商控股		
		累计	同比（%）	占全行业比重（%）	累计	同比（%）	占全行业比重（%）
企业户数	户	3 688	—	9.6	2 317	—	6.0
主营业务收入	亿元	7 415.3	5.7	11.0	3 910.3	3.3	5.8
利润总额	亿元	388.6	7.6	10.6	195.1	−3.4	5.3
应缴增值税	亿元	190.0	10.1	11.1	93.6	8.4	5.5
资产合计	亿元	6 161.2	5.1	14.2	2 716.8	3.3	6.3

纺织品服装贸易指标（全社会口径）				
指标名称	单位	三资企业		
		累计	同比（%）	占全行业比重（%）
出口总额	亿美元	702.5	−1.4	22.9
进口总额	亿美元	166.7	−2.0	60.9
贸易差额	亿美元	535.8	−1.3	19.2

数据来源：中国国家统计局、中国海关。

① 本表格中天然纤维包括各种棉、麻、丝和毛纤维；纤维素纤维原料包括用于制造再生纤维素纤维的棉短绒、化学木浆等；合成纤维单体指用于制造合成纤维的对苯二甲酸、乙二醇、己内酰胺等单体原料。

（二）三资企业投资规模继续下降

2014年，港澳台及外商企业投资信心仍然低迷，新增投资规模进一步下降。全年港澳台及外商企业500万元以上项目固定资产投资完成额为532.3亿元，同比减少9.1%，降幅较2013年扩大2.1个百分点；投资额占纺织全行业的比重为6.1%，较2013年降低0.2个百分点。其中，港澳台企业投资下降更为明显，同比降幅达到10.2%，较2013年降低4.5个百分点。

表12　2014年纺织行业固定资产投资情况（按企业注册类型，500万元以上项目）

指标名称	累计（亿元）	同比（%）	占全行业比重（%）
全行业投资合计	10 362.5	13.4	100.0
其中：内资	9 788.2	15.0	94.5
港澳台投资	294.9	−10.2	2.8
外商投资	237.4	−7.7	3.3
个体经营	42.0	0.3	0.4

数据来源：中国国家统计局。

（三）外资在纺织行业资本结构中占比持续下降

受新增投资持续减少影响，2013年，港澳台及外商企业在我国纺织行业资本结构中的占比继续下降。根据全国第三次经济普查数据，2013年①，我国规模以上纺织企业中，港澳台和外商资本为2300.9亿元，在全行业中占比为28.7%，较2012年下降1.2个百分点。其中，外商资本占比降幅更为突出，2013年占比为11.7%，较2012年下降0.8个百分点；港澳台资本占比为17%，较2012年下降0.4个百分点。

表13　2013年我国纺织工业实收资本及其结构（规模以上企业）

实收资本类别	实收资本额（亿元）	2013年占比（%）	占比较2012年增减（百分点）
实收资本总额	8 258.2	100.0	—
其中：国家资本	191.3	2.3	0.1
集体资本	85.8	1.0	−0.3
法人资本	2 552.1	30.9	−1.4
个人资本	3 031.8	36.7	2.5
港澳台资本	1 400.6	17.0	−0.4
外商资本	966.3	11.7	−0.8

数据来源：中国国家统计局。

（中国纺织工业联合会产业部　赵明霞）

① 实收资本数据来源于国家统计局年报，国家统计局每年四季度方发布上年度年报，故本部分内容使用2013年数据。本部分数据来源为全国第三次经济普查数据，纺织行业实收资本为纺织业、服装服饰制造业和化纤纤维制造业三大行业加总数据，不包括纺织机械制造业数据，故与本年鉴上历年数据口径略有区别。

中国汽车业对外开放情况

2014 年，中国汽车产销量分别超过 2300 万辆，再创新高的同时也连续第六年蝉联全球第一大汽车市场。从国内形势来看，行业总体发展特点如下：市场整体增速有所降低，乘强商弱的格局依旧未变，SUV、MPV 继续保持高速增长，商用车降幅较大；全行业经济效益增速提高；市场集中度进一步提高，产业结构进一步优化，新能源汽车呈现高速发展态势。

一、2014 年国内汽车行业运行情况

2014 年汽车行业坚持国家稳中求进的工作总基调，着力科学创新，优化产品结构、保证了全行业经济稳定增长。据 2014 年全国汽车行业 13714 家规模以上行业主要经济指标显示，汽车行业经济运行平稳，主要指标增速比 2013 年有所减缓。主要指标如下：

全国汽车行业规模以上企业累计实现主营业务收入 69649.67 亿元，同比增长 12.08%，增幅同比下降 6.27 个百分点。累计实现利润总额 6180.42 亿元，同比增长 17.90%，增幅同比下降 7.16 个百分点。

从全国汽车行业规模以上企业不同经济类型企业实现主营业务收入情况来看，2014 年外商投资企业（含中外合资企业）累计实现主营业务收入 29659.21 亿元，同比增长 11.57%，增幅同比下降 0.94 个百分点；内资企业累计实现主营业务收入 37424.90 亿元，同比增长 12.55%，增幅同比下降 4.67 个百分点。

从全国汽车行业规模以上企业小行业实现主营业务收入来看，5 个小行业主营业务收入均高于 2013 年。汽车制造业、汽车零部件制造业和摩托车零部件制造业增长率较高，均超过了 10%，分别为 12.10%、13.06%、11.76%；改装车制造业和摩托车整车制造业增长率分别为 7.57%和 3.72%。除主要经济指标外，2014 年国内汽车市场整体特点如下：

（一）全年汽车销量保持平稳增长，但增速低于年初预期

全年汽车销量达到 2349 万辆，再创历史新高，继续保持世界第一。但由于受到增长基数高、国内宏观经济形势下行压力增大及商用车市场下降等原因影响，使 2014 年国内汽车销量增速有较大回落。

（二）行业前十企业继续保持较快增速

汽车销量排名前十位的企业集团销量合计为 2107.7 万辆，比上年同期增长 8.9%，高于全行业增速 2 个百分点。占汽车销售总量的 89.7%，比上年同期提高 1.7 个百分点。

（三）乘用车销售增速平稳，SUV、MPV 继续高速增长

2014 年乘用车销售 1970 万辆，比上年同期增长 9.89%。其中轿车增速放缓，SUV、MPV 依旧保持高速增长，交叉型乘用车则继续下降。乘用车分车型看：轿车销售 1238 万辆，同比增长 3.1%；SUV 销量为 408 万辆，同比增长 36.4%；MPV 销量为 191 万辆，同比增长 46.8%；交叉型乘用车销量为 133 万辆，同比下降 18.1%。市场结构上，轿车占乘用车比重 62.8%，比去年下降 4.2 个百分点；SUV 占比 20.7%，比去年提高 4 个百分点，MPV 占比 9.7%，比去年提高 3 个百分点；交叉型乘用车占比为 6.8%，比去年下降 2.4 个百分点。

（四）商用车销量降幅较大

受宏观经济和相关政策法规影响，2014 年的商用车市场销量降幅较大。全年商用车销售完成 379 万辆，同比下降 6.5%，分车型看，其中货车销售 318 万辆，同比下降 8.9%，客车销售 61 万辆，同比增长 8.4%。货车车型中，受国四排放标准执行后带来成本上升和厂家生产准备不足等原因的影响，轻型货车出现了大幅下降，全年降幅达到了 12.9%。由于轻型货车占货车比重较高，导致货车整体降幅较高。客车方面受到城市公交（含新能源车）、校车增长及轻型客车带动，使客车市场继续保持平稳增长。

（五）新能源汽车呈现高速发展态势

随着政府全面出台支持发展新能源汽车的政策，企业对产品的升级改进和社会对新能源汽车认

可度的提升，2014年新能源汽车有了较快的发展，全年新能源汽车销量为7.5万辆，同比增长324%，其中纯电动汽车销售4.5万辆，同比增长208%，插电式电动车销售3万辆，同比增长878%。

（六）中国品牌汽车市场份额继续下降

受到合资企业生产的外国品牌汽车在新车推出数量和推出速度上的加快、中小型车推出力度的加大以及产品价格下探等因素影响，中国品牌市场份额持续下降，形势较为严峻，但中国品牌SUV市场份额上升，成为亮点。

中国品牌乘用车销售757万辆，同比增长4.1%，占有率为38.4%，比去年下降2.1个百分点。其中，中国品牌轿车销售277万辆，同比下降17.4%，占有率为22.4%，比去年下降5.6个百分点。中国品牌SUV销售55万辆，同比增长50.36%，占SUV市场份额为44.76%，比去年增长4.14个百分点。德、日、美、韩、法各系乘用车分别占到今年乘用车销量的20%、16%、13%、9%、4%，其中日系车占有率下降了0.34%，其余系别都有不同程度上升。

二、2014年汽车商品进出口情况分析

据海关总署汽车商品进出口数据显示，2014年中国汽车商品进出口总额首次超过1800亿美元，达到1829.13亿美元，同比增长13.65%，增幅高于2013年8.23个百分点，其中进口表现更为突出。具体情况如下：

（一）汽车商品进口情况分析

1. 进口总额接近千亿美元，整车进口贡献度明显提高

2014年，汽车商品进口表现好于上年，累计进口金额接近千亿美元，达到985.99亿美元，同比增长19.46%，增幅高于上年同期13.96个百分点。

在七大类汽车进口商品中，汽车整车增长贡献度较上年明显提高，进口金额增长贡献度达到74.29%，高于上年41.24个百分点。

2014年，汽车零部件进口金额也呈较快增长，累计进口金额375.51亿美元，同比增长12.12%。增幅高于上年同期2.78个百分点。在四大类汽车零部件品种中，发动机总体表现不佳，进口量及金额均结束上年增长，有所下降。共进口81.05万台，同比下降0.94%，进口金额22.46亿美元，同比下降5.47%。汽车零件、附件及车身进口金额315.11亿美元，同比增长12.98%，增幅较上年提升4.02个百分点。汽车摩托车轮胎进口金额7.07亿美元，同比增长4.13%，增幅较上年有所减缓。其他汽车相关商品进口金额30.87亿美元，同比增长21.18%，增幅略高于2013年。

2. 整车进口增幅明显高于上年，进口总量连续四年超过百万

2014年，进口车市场需求总体保持了两位数增长，自2011年以来，进口量连续四年超过百万。共进口142.60万辆，同比增长19.29%，增幅较上年提升13.72个百分点；进口金额609.17亿美元，同比增长24.39%，增幅较上年提升21.40个百分点。

2014年，在汽车主要进口品种中，乘用车占比依然最高，共进口140.27万辆，占汽车进口总量的98.37%。在三大类乘用车主要品种中，越野车进口量保持最多，共进口58.89万辆，同比增长16.54%，占汽车进口总量的41.30%。在越野车细分进口品种中，3升以下各系列品种进口量呈不同程度增长，3升及以上大排量品种有所下降。轿车进口结束上年下降，也呈一定增长。轿车共进口46.96万辆，同比增长10.91%。在轿车主要进口品种中，3.0升至4.0升系列进口量有所下降，其他系列品种各有增长，其中2.5升至3.0升排量升速较明显。小型客车继续保持较快增长，共进口34.42万辆，同比增长49.05%，增幅较上年提升20.41个百分点。在小型客车细分品种中，1.5升至4.0升各系列品种均呈较快增长。

2014年，按汽车整车进口来源国统计，与上年相比，欧美等发达国家仍然稳居进口市场主导，其中日本超过德国位居进口量第一，葡萄牙取代瑞典也进入前10。2014年，汽车进口量位居前10位的国家依次是：日本、美国、德国、英国、韩国、墨西哥、比利时、斯洛伐克、加拿大和葡萄牙，分别进口29.26万辆、29.17万辆、28.77万辆，15.63万辆、9.54万辆、7.96万辆、4.69万辆、4.24万辆、2.72万辆和2.27万辆。与上年相比，比利时和斯洛伐克进口量小幅下降，其他国家呈一定增长，其中葡萄牙和美国增速均超过30%，表

现更为突出。2014 年，我国从上述 10 国共进口汽车 134.25 万辆，占汽车进口总量的 94.14%。

3. 主要进口来源国保持较高占有率，德、日、美继续稳居三甲

2014 年，据海关统计，汽车商品进口金额排名前 50 位的国家（含地区）累计进口 985.71 亿美元，占汽车商品进口总额的 99.97%。其中进口金额排名前 10 位的国家（地区）依次是：德国、日本、美国、英国、韩国、斯洛伐克、墨西哥、比利时、意大利和法国，分别进口 301.63 亿美元、179.23 亿美元、147.83 亿美元、108.12 亿美元、67.05 亿美元、28.01 亿美元、26.24 亿美元、15.95 亿美元、13.81 亿美元、13.19 亿美元。与上年相比，斯洛伐克和比利时进口小幅下降，日本韩国增速都略低，其他国家增速均超过两位数，表现较为突出。2014 年上述 10 国累计进口金额 901.06 亿美元，占汽车商品进口总额的 91.39%。

（二）汽车商品出口情况分析

1. 出口金额保持小幅增长，零部件出口增幅稳中趋缓

2014 年，全球经济形势较上年有所好转，但局部不稳定因素依然存在，尤其是乌克兰危机爆发后，我国对俄罗斯及乌克兰出口下滑十分明显；受汇率波动影响，国际主要货币对美元贬值也在一定程度上削弱了我国汽车产品出口竞争力。此外，我国汽车出口企业总体实力依旧不强，出口品种多数集中在 1.0 升至 1.5 升的小排量市场，在中高端市场竞争力明显不足，出口在价值链竞争上基本处于劣势。更为重要的是，我国出口企业海外拓展能力亟须加强。目前，我国汽车出口在产品适应性、新产品研发等方面还有很大差距，如针对国外一些高寒地带、多山路地形等，中国汽车出口产品的及时改进能力较弱、反应缓慢。总体来看，中国汽车企业对于海外市场开拓能力存在诸多瓶颈问题，在人力、资金和综合能力方面都有待提高，目前的状况难以支撑出口的稳定增长。受此影响，2014 年汽车整车出口仍在低位徘徊，但在中东一些地区如伊朗、沙特等国呈现快速增长，委内瑞拉和哥伦比亚等南美国家以及越南等东南亚国家也呈一定增长，在一定程度上弥补了一些主要出口国下滑的压力。

2014 年，汽车商品出口金额继续保持小幅增长，累计出口金额 843.14 亿美元，同比增长 7.08%，贸易逆差为 142.85 亿美元，与上年相比，增加了 101.80 亿美元，逆差明显加大。

2014 年，从七大类汽车商品出口金额增长贡献度来看，摩托车贡献度最低，汽车整车贡献度较上年有所提升。汽车零部件出口表现略好于整车，累计出口金额 646.17 亿美元，同比增长 8.02%，增幅较上年略有减缓；占汽车商品出口总额的 76.64%，占有率较上年提升 0.36 个百分点。出口顺差达到 270.66 亿美元，比上年增加 7.38 亿美元。四大类汽车零部件品种出口金额较上年均呈增长，其中发动机共出口 366.2 万台，同比增长 10.56%；出口金额 16.80 亿美元，同比增长 6.69%；汽车零件、附件及车身出口金额 353.59 亿美元，同比增长 11.96%；汽车、摩托车轮胎出口金额 151.51 亿美元，同比增长 1.83%；其他汽车相关商品出口金额 124.27 亿美元，同比增长 5.43%。

2014 年，汽车商品出口金额排名前 50 位国家（含地区）累计出口 751.05 亿美元，占汽车商品出口总额的 89.08%。在出口金额排名前 10 位的目的国中，伊朗和越南取代巴西和加拿大进入前 10，其他国家排名变化不大。2014 年，出口金额排名前 10 位的国家依次是：美国、日本、俄罗斯、韩国、德国、伊朗、墨西哥、英国、越南和尼日利亚，出口金额分别为 177.33 亿美元、64.48 亿美元、31.99 亿美元、31.16 亿美元、23.74 亿美元、23.20 亿美元、22.81 亿美元、19.59 亿美元、17.62 亿美元、16.25 亿美元。与上年相比，俄罗斯出口金额下降明显，其他国家呈不同程度增长，其中伊朗和越南增速更快。2014 年上述 10 国共出口金额 428.17 亿美元，占汽车商品出口总额的 50.78%。

2. 汽车整车出口量降幅趋缓，中东主要出口目的国增势明显

2014 年汽车整车出口量降幅较上年有所趋缓，出口金额结束下降，呈小幅增长。共出口 94.73 万辆，同比下降 0.08%，增幅较上年减缓 6.51 个百分点；出口金额 138.06 亿美元，同比增长 6.95%。

在汽车整车出口主要品种中，轿车下降依旧明显，载货车结束下降，呈小幅增长，客车增幅有所减缓。

2014 年，轿车共出口 37.09 万辆，同比下降 12.61%。在轿车细分品种中，2 升及以上品种同比增速较明显，共出口 1.93 万辆，同比增长 5.66 倍；1.5 升及以下品种降幅依然明显，共出口 23.39 万辆，同比下降 22.40%，降幅较上年加大 14.07 个百分点。

载货车出口 29.65 万辆，同比增长 3.84%。在载货车细分品种中，5 吨以下汽油车和柴油车均呈小幅下降，分别出口 8.24 万辆和 11.72 万辆，同比下降 0.08%和 1.37%，降幅较上年分别减缓 11.01 百分点和 14.23 个百分点。2014 年，上述两个品种共出口 19.96 万辆，占载货车出口总量的 67.32%。此外，5～20 吨各系列柴油载货车总体呈较快增长，表现好于上年。

客车共出口 18.74 万辆，同比增长 12.78%，增幅较上年减缓 19.47 个百分点。在客车主要品种中，小型客车（9 座以下）出口量保持最大，出口增势明显减弱，共出口 9.93 万辆，同比增长 3.63%；大客车（30 座以上）和中轻型客车(10～29 座）增幅均高于上年，出口表现明显好于小型客车。

2014 年，轿车、载货车和客车等三大类整车品种共出口 85.48 万辆，占汽车出口总量的 90.24%，占比较上年有所下降。

2014 年，从出口主要国家来看，与 2013 年相比，伊朗和埃及需求增长较快，沙特阿拉伯也进入前 10 位，增势同样明显；哥伦比亚和委内瑞拉等拉美国家增速呈两位数快速增长，智利市场需求下降较快；作为非洲地区的主要市场，阿尔及利亚汽车出口量连续两年大幅下滑；在欧洲地区乌克兰和俄罗斯下降较为明显，乌克兰不仅退出前 10，出口量降幅超过 70%，表现更为低迷，越南等东南亚国家需求有所恢复，其中越南再度进入前 10。2014 年出口量排名前 10 位目的国分别为：伊朗、阿尔及利亚、俄罗斯、埃及、哥伦比亚、智利、越南、委内瑞拉、沙特阿拉伯和伊拉克，分别出口 11.41 万辆、8.27 万辆、6.21 万辆、5.31 万辆、4.67 万辆、4.01 万辆、3.75 万辆、3.13 万辆、3.11 万辆、2.78 万辆。与上年相比，伊朗和越南增速最为显著，埃及、委内瑞拉、沙特阿拉伯和哥伦比亚增速也超过 20%，其他国家有所下降，其中智利、阿尔及利亚和俄罗斯下降更快。2014 年，上述 10 国共出口 52.65 万辆，占汽车出口总量的 55.58%。

3. 摩托车出口表现不佳，五大系列主导品种出口量均呈下降

2014 年，摩托车出口表现不如 2013 年，共出口 927.59 万辆，同比下降 6.09%；出口金额 49.86 亿元，同比下降 5.36%。

2014 年，100ml 至 125ml 系列出口量继续稳居第一，共出口 515.91 万辆，同比下降 0.30%；125ml 至 150ml 系列居其次，共出口 194.99 万辆，同比下降 13.37%；排量小于 50ml 系列出口量位居第三，共出口 99.89 万辆，同比下降 15.08%；150ml 至 200ml 系列居第四，共出口 50.65 万辆，同比下降 11.40%；50ml～100ml 排量系列出口量位居第五，共出口 47.41 万辆，同比下降 8.64%。2014 年，上述五大系列共出口 908.85 万辆，占摩托车出口总量的 97.98%。

（中国汽车工业协会　王松岩）

中国电信业对外开放情况

一、2014年电信业发展情况

2014年，我国电信业务实现了持续健康发展，主要表现在：宽带中国战略进入全面落地实施阶段，信息通信基础设施水平进一步提升，TD－LTE引领全球发展，移动宽带用户发展成效明显，深化电信改革取得突破性成果，新兴信息消费快速增长，基础电信企业转型成效显著，互联网行业持续蓬勃发展，市场竞争格局进一步优化，互联网网络架构得到优化完善，通信村村通2014年度任务超额完成，市场监管能力稳步增强，网络与信息安全能力进一步提升，行业发展活力持续增强，加速推动了两化融合和信息化水平的提升。2014年，信息通信业基础战略性地位更加突出，经济社会贡献进一步加大，服务支撑经济社会发展的能力显著提升。

（一）行业整体增势平稳，对国民经济的贡献持续增强

2014年，全国电信业务总量累计完成18150亿元，同比增长16.1%。其中，固定话音业务总量563亿元，同比下降17.4%；固定数据及互联网业务总量2410亿元，同比增长11.1%；固定增值及其他业务总量656亿元，同比增长6.9%；移动话音业务总量6776亿元，同比增长1.2%；移动数据及互联网业务总量4888亿元，同比增长85.6%；移动增值及其他业务总量2863亿元，同比增长0.8%。面临国内经济结构转型升级，信息通信业服务和支撑经济社会发展的战略性、基础性和先导性作用更加突出，对国民经济的间接贡献持续增强。2014年基础电信业完成增加值6530亿元，同比增长9.1%，对GDP的直接贡献为1.0%，占第三产业GDP的比重为2.1%。其中，信息消费在稳增长、调结构、转方式等方面发挥的作用尤其突出。2014年，我国信息消费总体规模达到2.8万亿元，同比增长25%，增速为同期GDP的3倍以上。2014年基础电信业固定资产投资完成3993亿元，同比增长6.3%。由于4G的拉动作用，移动通信领域投资增速最快，同比增长20.2%，达到1618亿元。

（二）“宽带中国”战略落地，网络提速升级步伐加快

宽带中国战略进入全面落实实施阶段，各级政府大力推动宽带网络基础设施建设。光纤通信网络快速发展，截至2014年年底，新增FTTH覆盖家庭8859万户，光纤入户网络覆盖家庭达到2.56亿户。全国光缆总长度达到2046万公里，同比增长17.2%。新建小区基本上实现光纤到户网络建设，老旧小区光纤化改造进程加快，随着光纤接入网络的快速发展，全国接入光缆长度达到958万公里，同比增长16.6%。互联网数据流量爆炸式增长，传输网络向更高容量系统演进，100G波分复用设备开始在省际干线规模部署，并逐步向省内干线延伸，城域网内大容量波分系统开始普及，大容量灵活调度的城域传输网基本建成。固定互联网宽带接入端口超过4亿个，其中FTTH端口达到1.63亿个。

（三）基础电信企业加速构建4G网络，TD－LTE全球规模化发展

2014年，工业和信息化部分三次批准中国电信、中国联通TD－LTE/LTE FDD混合组网试验累计达到56个城市。全行业移动通信网络建设重点大幅向4G转移。4G基站规模达到73.3万个，网络覆盖超过300个城市，基本实现县级以上城市和发达乡镇覆盖，人口覆盖率超过25%，建成全球最大规模4G网络。2014年全球LTE网络发展取得巨大成绩。截至2014年底，全球新增LTE网络96张，商用网络总量达到360张。其中，TD－LTE商用网络达到51张，占比4G网络总量的14.2%。基站方面，全球LTE基站累计出货达到201.5万个，TD－LTE基站出货量超过98.5万个，占比达到48.9%。用户方面，2014年全球LTE用户新增2.65亿，总数突破4.7亿，较2013年增长128.82%。

（四）基础企业转型加快，步入互联网为主导的发展阶段

2014年，非话音业务实现收入6713.6亿元，

同比增长 8.0%，比话音业务收入增速高 19.6 个百分点，在电信业务收入中占比 58.2%，比 2013 年提高 5 个百分点，对电信业务收入的贡献达到 179.7%，同比提高 83 个百分点。其中，移动数据及互联网业务收入实现 2707.2 亿元，按可比口径测算同比增长 41.8%，对行业收入增长的贡献持续提升，全年贡献率达到 200.5%，比 2013 年贡献率提高 124.8 个百分点，移动数据及互联网业务成为电信业务发展的第一动力。2014 年，互联网接入流量仍为全部业务量中增长最快的领域，户均突破 200M，同比增长 53.5%；其中来自 4G 网络的接入流量占比超过 19%，4G 用户平均消费流量超过 700M。其中固定互联网宽带接入流量达到 1296.2 亿 G，同比增长 131.7%，移动互联网接入流量达到 20.6 亿 G，同比增长 62.9%。2014 年手机电视点播视频数达到 1.7 亿次。

（五）网民数量不断增加，互联网产业持续壮大

我国网民规模达 6.6 亿人，全年共计新增网民 4135 万人。互联网普及率为 48.4%，较 2013 年底提升 2.6 个百分点。手机网民规模达 5.7 亿，较 2013 年底增加 7015 万人，网民中使用手机上网的人群占比提升至 86.5%，较 2013 年年底提升 5.5 个百分点。2014 年，我国互联网服务业收入接近 9000 亿元，同比增长 35%。互联网上市企业营收全年累计达到近 4900 亿元，同比增长 48%。全国电子商务交易额超过 12 万亿元，同比增长 20%；天猫“双十一”当天的总销售额超过 571 亿元；国内网络零售总额达到 2.63 万亿元，同比增长 42.2%。搜索引擎、网络视频、网络广告市场规模同比增长分别为 43.1%、44.2%、55.1%。

二、当前我国电信业开放情况

自 2001 年加入 WTO 以来，我国根据在 WTO 中承诺开放的业务和条件，严格履行 WTO 承诺，积极应对 WTO 挑战，逐步建设完善相关法律法规。有关情况如下：

根据我国 WTO 承诺及 2003 版《电信业务分类目录》，我国对外资开放蜂窝移动通信业务、固定网本地电话业务、固定网长途电话业务、固定网国内数据传送业务、无线数据传送业务、国内通信服务设施业务、固定网国际长途电话业务、因特网数据传送业务、国际数据通信业务等基础电信业务，外资股比不超过 49%；开放基础电信业务中的无线寻呼业务以及增值电信业务中的信息服务业务、在线数据处理与交易处理业务、存储转发类业务，外资股比不超过 50%。

根据国务院《关于鼓励服务外包产业加快发展的复函》，我国在 21 个试点城市试点离岸呼叫中心业务，外资股权比例不设限制。同时，对外资离岸呼叫中心业务试点审批程序进行了简化。

根据《内地与香港（澳门）更紧密经贸关系（CEPA）安排》，在 WTO 承诺的基础上，向港澳资本增加了开放因特网数据中心业务、因特网接入服务、呼叫中心业务、国内因特网虚拟专用网业务等四项增值电信业务，港澳资本股比不超过 50%；允许港澳服务提供者在东莞和珠海两个试点城市设立独资或合资企业提供离岸呼叫中心业务；允许港澳服务提供者在广东省设立合资企业提供在线数据处理与交易处理业务（仅限于经营性电子商务网站），港澳资本股权占比不超过 55%。

根据《工业和信息化部 上海市人民政府关于中国（上海）自由贸易试验区进一步对外开放增值电信业务的意见》和《中国（上海）自由贸易试验区外商投资经营增值电信业务试点管理办法》，在 WTO 承诺的基础上试点进一步开放增值电信业务：一是放宽了已在 WTO 承诺开放的三项业务的外资股比限制，其中信息服务业务中的应用商店业务、存储转发类业务不设外资股比限制，在线数据处理与交易处理业务中的经营类电子商务业务外资股比放宽至 55%；二是新增试点开放呼叫中心业务、国内多方通信服务业务、为上网用户提供的因特网接入服务业务、国内因特网虚拟专用网业务等四项业务，其中前三项业务不设外资股比限制，国内因特网虚拟专用网业务外资股比不超过 50%。

截至目前，在增值电信领域，共有 34 家中外合资企业获得《电信业务经营许可证》，4 家上海自贸区企业获得自贸区试点批文并已开展相关业务，12 家外商独资企业获得服务外包示范城市批复后经营离岸呼叫中心业务。

（工业和信息化部信息通信发展司）

中国钢铁工业对外开放情况

一、2014 年中国钢铁工业发展概况

（一）粗钢产量小幅增长，增幅大幅下降

根据国家统计局统计，2014 年 1—12 月份累计生产粗钢 82269.78 万吨。随着我国经济结构性改革迈出新步伐，经济增长对钢材的需求强度持续下降，钢材消费增长乏力，粗钢表观消费量同比下降 3.4%，即使考虑钢材贸易商以及下游用户库存下降，粗钢实际消费量持平或略有下降，钢材消费进入平台区的特征十分明显。2014 年粗钢产量比去年同期增加 728.73 万吨，同比增长 0.89%，粗钢产量同比增幅大幅下降，10 月和 11 月产量同比出现负增长。（详见图 1、图 2）

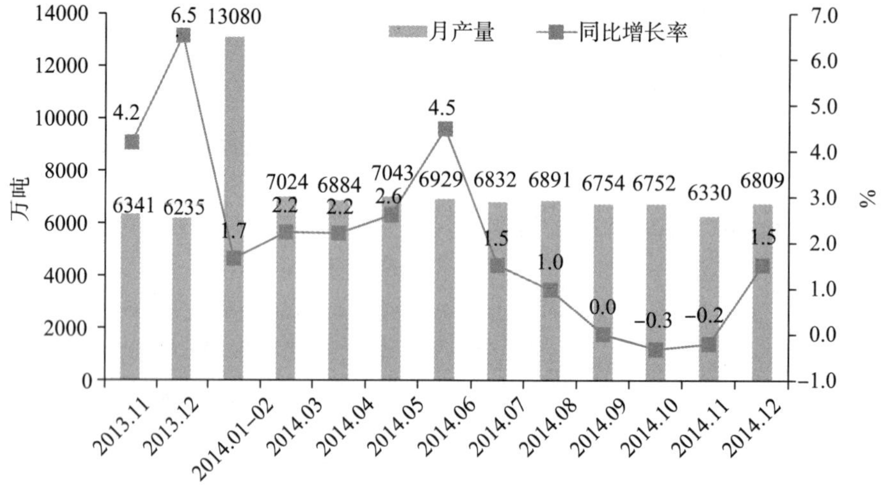

图 1　全国粗钢月产量及同比

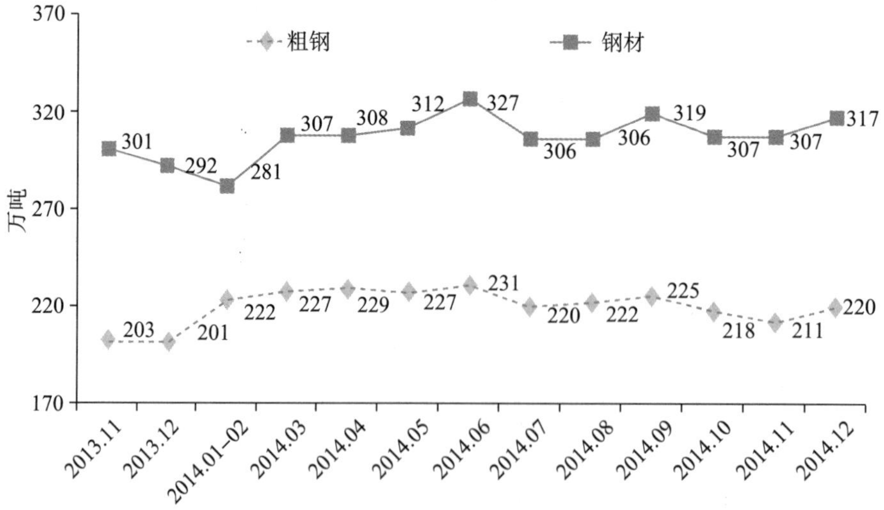

图 2　全国粗钢及钢材日产水平

（二）全球粗钢产量对比

根据国际钢铁协会统计，2014 年全球 65 个纳入国际钢铁协会统计国家的粗钢总产量达 16.62 亿吨，同比增长 1.2%。2014 年，亚洲全年粗钢产量

达到 11.32 亿吨，同比增长 1.4%；欧盟粗钢产量 1.69 亿吨，同比增长 1.8%；北美粗钢产量 1.21 亿吨，同比增长 2.0%（详见表 1）。

2014 年，全球粗钢产量前 10 名的国家粗钢总产量为 13.84 亿吨，同比增长 0.9%，占全球粗钢总产量的 83.27%。其中，中国的粗钢产量为 8.23 亿吨，同比增长 0.9%。中国粗钢产量占全球粗钢产量的份额，由 2013 年的 49.7%下降到 2014 年 49.5%。10 个国家中除巴西、土耳其和乌克兰产量下降外，其他国家粗钢产量均有所增长（详见表 2）。

表 1　2014 年全球粗钢产量　单位：万吨，%

	2014 年	2013 年	变化率%
欧盟（28）合计	16 924.3	16 631.1	1.8
欧洲其他国家合计	3 619.4	3 647.7	−0.8
独联体合计	10 508.9	10 808.3	−2.8
北美合计	12 124.7	11 887.6	2.0
南美合计	4 520.1	4 582.2	−1.4
非洲合计	1 557.9	1 569.4	−0.7
中东合计	2 805.9	2 600.7	7.9
亚洲合计	111 086.0	109 559.8	1.4
大洋洲合计	548.8	558.8	−1.8
全球 65 国/地区总计	163 696.0	161 845.6	1.1

表 2　2014 年世界粗钢产量前 10 位国家情况　单位：万吨，%

国家	2014 年 1—12 月累计	2013 年 1—12 月累计	累计同比
中国	82 270	81 540	0.9
日本	11 070	11 060	0.1
美国	8 830	8 690	1.7
印度	8 320	8 130	2.3
韩国	7 100	6 610	7.5
俄罗斯	7 070	6 890	2.6
德国	4 290	4 260	0.7
土耳其	3 400	3 470	−1.8
巴西	3 390	3 420	−0.7
乌克兰	2 720	3 280	−17.1
以上合计	138 460	137 350	0.8

（三）品种结构继续调整，长材占比明显下降

随着国民经济结构转型调整，消费逐渐取得推动国民经济发展的主导地位。新的消费潮流不断出现，引导着钢铁产品朝个性化、定制化需求转变。2014 年传统的长材占比明显下降，板带材、管材产量占比小幅下降，而其他钢材占比有所上升，品种结构继续朝着满足市场需求方向调整。

专用钢材结构也有所变化：造船板、集装箱板、汽车板产量增幅较大，管线钢、锅炉和压力容器用钢板、家电板产量下降较多。

（四）固定资产投资下降，化解产能过剩矛盾初见成效

2014 年，我国钢铁行业固定资产投资 6479 亿元，同比下降 3.8%。其中黑色金属冶炼及压延业投资 4789 亿元，下降 5.9%；黑色金属矿采选业投资 1690 亿元，增长 2.6%。从工序投资增长情况看，炼铁、炼钢和钢压延加工完成投资分别下降 40.4%、10.5%和 4.8%。从新开工项目情况看，2014 年新开工项目 2037 个，同比减少 215 个。其中炼铁项目 169 个，减少 51 个；项目 287 个，减

少 71 个；钢加工项目 1581 个，减少 93 个。

2014 年，纳入中国钢铁工业协会统计的会员钢铁企业累计完成投资 811.14 亿元，较去年同期降低 19.43％。

（五）原燃料价格大幅下降，行业利润有所好转，整体盈利水平仍较低

2014 年以来，铁矿石、炼焦煤等主要原燃料价格大幅下降，加上钢铁企业深入开展降本增效活动，钢铁生产成本相应下降，钢铁企业经济效益有所好转。1—12 月，销售收入同比略有下降，利税、利润同比均保持增长，亏损面及亏损额相应减少。但是，行业整体盈利水平仍然较低，“融资难、融资贵”的问题仍然突出。（详见表 3）

根据中国钢铁工业协会统计数据，2014 年协会会员企业产业利润增长率为：（304.44/216.9－1）×100％＝40.36％。

表 3　　2014 年行业主要经济效益指标　　单位：万元

指标	2014 年	上年同期	累计同比％
产品销售收入	358 820 666	369 827 091	－2.98
期间费用	25 021 946	23 689 871	5.62
实现利税	10 909 165	9 726 997	12.15
利润总额	3 044 439	2 169 046	40.36
亏损企业亏损额	－1 174 728	－1 277 177	－8.02
资产总额	464 729 845	445 066 892	4.42
负债总额	317 583 941	307 721 622	3.20

二、2014 年中国钢铁工业对外贸易情况

（一）钢材出口大幅增长，进口保持稳定

受国内市场钢材价格偏低、市场竞争激烈以及国际市场需求增长等因素影响，2014 年我国钢材出口大幅增长。全年累计出口钢材 9378 万吨，同比增加 3145 万吨，增长 50.5％，折合粗钢出口约 9977 万吨。进口钢材 1443 万吨，同比增加 35 万吨，增长 2.5％；钢坯 29.32 万吨，钢锭 5.38 万吨，坯锭合计 34.71 万吨，折合粗钢进口约 1570 万吨。钢材进出口数量趋势见图 3。

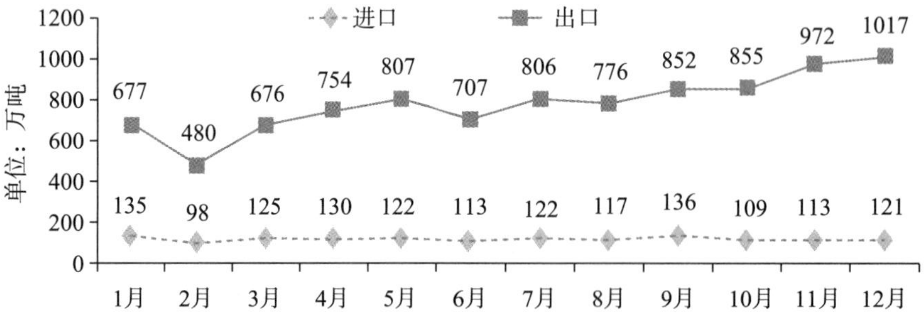

图 3　2014 年 1—12 月钢材进出口数量趋势图

（二）进出口品种结构

2014 年，我国进口钢材仍以板材为主，全年共进口板材 1208.06 万吨，同比增长 1.64％；进口金额 123.80 亿美元，同比增长 3.25％；进口板材占我国进口钢材总量的 83.71％，总金额的 69.11％（详见表 4）。

我国出口钢材以长材和板材为主，全年共出口长材 3086.28 万吨，同比增长 80.42％；出口金额 162.54 亿美元，同比增长 56.95％；出口长材占我国出口钢材总量的 32.91％，总金额的 22.95％。全年共出口板材 4367.04 万吨，同比增长 57.99％；出口金额 327.89 亿美元，同比增长 46.98％；出口板材占我国出口钢材总量的 46.56％，总金额的 46.30％（详见表 5）。

表 4　　**2014 年冶金产品进口品种**　　单位：吨，美元/吨

产品名称	2014 年累计		2013 年累计		累计同比%	
	数量	金额	数量	金额	数量	金额
1 棒线材	1 203 189.15	172 372.46	1 026 835.95	155 047.06	17.17	11.17
2 角型材	380 835.12	39 942.37	386 938.55	38 358.78	−1.58	4.13
3 板材	12 080 602.10	1 238 016.05	11 886 125.72	1 199 102.86	1.64	3.25
4 管材	476 491.50	199 218.11	424 691.74	170 269.79	12.20	17.00
5 铁道用材	46 041.28	5 166.91	110 903.87	7 783.42	−58.49	−33.62
6 其他钢材	244 927.62	136 726.57	242 061.70	134 349.67	1.18	1.77

表 5　　**2014 年冶金产品出口品种**　　单位：吨，美元/吨

产品名称	本年累计		去年累计		累计同比%	
	数量	金额	数量	金额	数量	金额
1 棒线材	30 862 820.67	1 625 408.17	17105858.17	1 035 592.89	80.42	56.95
2 角型材	4 598 790.60	274 546.17	4 104 796.65	254 695.88	12.03	7.79
3 板材	43 670 371.54	3 278 910.28	27 640 810.07	2 230 791.22	57.99	46.98
4 管材	10 057 815.32	1 140 154.22	9 570 842.86	1 140 204.21	5.09	0.00
5 铁道用材	593 813.88	55 479.82	378 473.88	38 249.61	56.90	45.05
6 其他钢材	4 000 188.97	708 128.46	3 536 753.40	623 975.66	13.10	13.49

（三）进出口市场结构

2014 年，进口钢材主要来自于日本、韩国、中国台湾和欧盟。从上述四个来源地共进口钢材 1378.96 万吨，占进口钢材总量的 95.55%，比 2013 年增长 1.04 个百分点；进口金额 164.38 亿美元，占进口钢材总金额的 91.76%，同比增长 0.03 个百分点（详见表 6）。

2014 年，我国钢材出口市场进一步拓展，全年共向 216 个国家和地区出口钢铁产品，比 2013 年增加了 3 个国家和地区。东盟、韩国和中东地区仍是我国钢材最主要的出口市场，中东地区首次超过韩国成为我国第二大钢材出口目的地（详见表 7）。

表 6　　**2014 年中国进口钢材主要来源国/地区**　　单位：吨，万美元，美元/吨

序号	区域组织	本年累计		去年累计		累计同比%	
		数量	金额	数量	金额	数量	金额
进口总量		14 432 086.77	1 791 442.48	14 077 557.52	1 704 911.56	2.52	5.08
其中：							
1	日本	6 002 916.02	664 504.64	6 016 911.37	659 710.00	−0.23	0.73
2	韩国	4 578 167.32	446 877.46	4 246 380.11	419 363.45	7.81	6.56
3	中国台湾	1 892 464.85	184 333.65	1 899 156.73	185 776.17	−0.35	−0.78
4	欧盟 28 国	1 316 035.79	348 104.36	1 141 766.05	299 131.61	15.26	16.37
	以上合计	13 789 583.98	1 643 820.11	13 304 214.26	1 563 981.23	3.65	5.10
	占进口总量比例	95.55	91.76	94.51	91.73		

表 7　　2014 年中国出口钢材主要目的国/地区　　单位：吨，美元/吨

序号	区域组织	2014 年累计		2013 年累计		累计同比%	
		数量	金额	数量	金额	数量	金额
世界合计		93 783 800.98	7 082 627.12	62 337 535.04	5 323 509.47	50.45	33.04
1	东盟	26 309 063.31	1 690 732.00	17 425 291.70	1 257 372.06	50.98	34.47
2	韩国	12 967 084.82	877 397.02	9 724 284.19	694 761.36	33.35	26.29
3	中东地区	12 587 889.96	931 300.70	7 185 577.48	645 045.62	75.18	44.38
4	亚洲其他	7 378 633.39	600 041.34	4 499 142.72	461 054.13	64.00	30.15
5	南美洲	6 869 755.24	489 896.90	4 971 866.90	399 743.34	38.17	22.55
6	非洲	6 586 970.47	472 764.74	4 561 005.05	383 527.24	44.42	23.27
7	欧盟 28 国	6 270 799.98	599 858.18	3 653 273.44	394 710.65	71.65	51.97
8	美国	3 400 750.08	401 825.18	2 207 962.17	273 946.70	54.02	46.68
9	中国台湾	2 822 968.52	308 441.50	1 561 031.74	224 353.89	80.84	37.48
10	中国香港	2 605 097.49	156 664.80	2 054 596.61	142 464.98	26.79	9.97
11	北美自由贸易区（除美国）	2 073 724.42	173 238.14	1 048 685.62	102 672.37	97.75	68.73
12	中美洲	1 651 405.70	102 827.73	1 038 530.01	71 466.04	59.01	43.88
13	日本	1 566 303.20	134 541.18	771 553.42	89 219.71	103.01	50.80
14	欧洲其他国家	1 295 244.25	147 253.41	1 443 711.43	162 519.13	−10.28	−9.39
15	大洋洲国家	793 703.74	88 353.30	651 320.07	69 279.36	21.86	27.53
16	澳门	128 074.40	13 165.36	196 789.68	13 683.94	−34.92	−3.79

三、中国钢铁工业贸易政策调整及贸易摩擦情况

2014 年，我国钢材出口量大幅增长。随着钢铁产品出口增长，钢铁产品进出口税收政策、国际贸易摩擦等问题成为困扰我国钢铁行业的重点和难点问题。为减少和化解国际贸易摩擦，我国钢铁行业适时对进出口关税进行了一些调整。同时，在加强与国外产业沟通和交流的基础上，积极应对贸易救济调查。

（一）取消加工贸易项下进口钢材保税政策

为贯彻落实《国务院关于化解产能严重过剩矛盾的指导意见》中“落实公平税赋政策，取消加工贸易项下进口钢材保税政策”的精神，财政部于 2014 年 7 月发布通知，决定首批对国内完全能够生产、质量能够满足下游加工企业需要的进口热轧板、冷轧板、窄带钢、棒线材、型材、钢铁丝、电工钢等 78 个税号的钢材产品，取消加工贸易项下进口钢材保税政策。自 2015 年 1 月 1 日起，对加工贸易项下进口上述 78 个税号钢材产品征收关税和进口环节税；对 2014 年 12 月 31 日前签订的合同，且在 2015 年 6 月 30 日前实际进口的，允许在合同有效期内继续以保税的方式开展加工贸易。

（二）取消含硼钢出口退税

2014 年，含硼钢出口问题受到广泛关注。由于普碳热轧产品与合金钢产品在出口关税和出口退税上存在较大差异，因此钢材出口企业在出口产品中添加微量合金元素。

为解决含硼钢出口问题，财政部和国家税务总局于 2014 年 12 月 31 日发布通知，于 2015 年 1 月 1 日起取消含硼钢出口退税。取消含硼钢出口退税，有利于调整钢铁行业出口秩序，使钢材出口退税和关税体系更为协调。

（三）国外对我国钢铁产品发起贸易救济调查情况

随着钢铁产品出口增长，贸易摩擦也成为困扰我国钢铁行业的重点和难点问题。自 2007 年以来，每年对中国钢铁产品的贸易救济调查均超过 10 起，2014 年以来针对主要钢铁产品的贸易救济调查已

超过30起，发起贸易救济调查的国家和地区增多，受贸易救济调查的产品范围也不断扩大。

1. 韩国对我国H型钢进行反倾销调查

2014年7月24日，韩国产业通商资源部下属的贸易委员会决定对从中国进口的H型钢进行为期三个月的反倾销调查。如果贸易委员会最终裁定从中国进口的H型钢存有倾销事实，并因此对韩国国内钢铁行业造成损害，委员会将对原产于中国的H型钢征收一定幅度的反倾销税。

H型钢被广泛应用于基础设施建设的各个领域，包括桥梁、地铁、高楼大厦等。此次反倾销调查是由现代制铁和东国制钢向韩国调查机关提出申请。申诉方指出，由于中国钢铁的价格优势，逐渐在韩国市场拓开了销路，市场占有率也在逐年递增。这令韩国本土钢铁企业遭受重创，销售额呈现下跌趋势。

2. 印尼对我国冷轧不锈钢进行反倾销调查

2014年12月22日，印尼反倾销委员会发布立案公告，称应其国内产业的申请，决定对自中国、泰国、马来西亚、韩国、新加坡和中国台湾进口的冷轧不锈钢发起反倾销调查。涉案产品在印尼的海关税则号为7219.32.00.00、7219.33.00.00、7219.34.00.00、7219.35.00.00、7219.90.00.00、7220.20.10.00、7220.20.90.00、7220.90.10.00、7220.90.90.00。

3. 欧盟对我国冷轧不锈钢发起“双反”调查

2014年6月26日，应欧洲钢铁工业联盟(Eurofer)的申请，欧盟对原产于中国和中国台湾的冷轧不锈钢板进行反倾销立案调查。涉案产品海关编码为7219.31.00、7219.32.10、7219.32.90、7219.33.10、7219.33.90、7219.34.10、7219.34 90、7219.35.10、7219.35.90、7220.20.21、7220.20.29、7220.20.41、7220.20.49、7220.20.81、7220.20.89。8月14日，欧盟对同一产品进行反补贴立案调查。

4. 欧盟对我国取向硅钢发起反倾销调查

2014年8月14日，应欧洲钢铁工业联盟(The European Steel Association)的申请，欧盟对原产于中国、日本、韩国、俄罗斯和美国的取向硅电钢进行反倾销立案调查。涉案产品在欧盟合并关税编码ex72251100、ex72261100项下。

5. 美国对我国盘条发起“双反”调查

2014年2月21日，美国商务部宣布，应赛洛米塔尔钢铁集团美国分公司（ArcelorMittal USA LLC)、纽柯钢铁公司（Nucor Corporation）、Charter Steel（WI)，Evraz Pueblo（前身为Evraz Rocky Mountain Steel)、Gerdau Ameristeel US Inc.(FL)、Keystone Consolidated Industries，Inc.六家公司的申请，对从中国进口的碳钢合金盘条进行反倾销和反补贴立案调查。涉案产品海关编码为：7213.91.3011、7213.91.3015、7213.91.3020等。

11月13日，美国商务部对华碳钢合金盘条做出反倾销和反补贴终裁。反倾销终裁税率为106.19%～110.25%。反补贴终裁中补贴率为：178.46%～193.31%；12月15日，美国国际贸易委员会发布公告，对原产于中国的碳钢合金盘条反倾销和反补贴案做出产业损害终裁，裁定自中国进口的涉案产品对美国国内产业造成了实质性损害。

除上述案件外，美国还先后对我国取向电工钢、冷轧钢板发起双反调查；欧亚经济委员会对我国油井管发起反倾销调查；泰国对我国低碳盘条发起反倾销调查；墨西哥对我国冷轧钢板发起反倾销调查；印尼对H型钢和条杆、马来西亚对热轧钢板发起保障措施调查。

近年来，部分国家利用现有规则的模糊性和调查机关的自由裁量权，在调查过程中对答卷和企业配合情况设置超出合理范围的高要求，从而限制我国产品出口。一些国家直接采用违反世贸规则的做法，如将国有企业认定为公共机构，把从国有企业采购的原材料认定为补贴；提高国有企业获得单独税率的门槛，通过追溯最终层级股权等方式将我国国有企业视为关联企业等。

钢铁产品贸易救济连锁效益明显，钢管、取向电工钢、不锈钢冷轧薄板、盘条、冷轧板等多个钢铁产品接连在不同国家和地区遭遇贸易摩擦，不断丢失出口市场份额。

（四）美国对中国取向电工钢WTO裁决执行提出执行异议

2014年1月13日，美国贸易代表迈克尔·弗罗曼表示，针对中国关于完全履行了WTO争端解决机构就中国对美国取向电工钢征收反倾销税和反补贴税案（DS414）建议和裁决的声明提出质疑，并要求根据《关于争端解决规则与程序的谅解》第21.5条就中国对该案的执行问题与中国展开磋商。这也是中国入世以来首次遭遇执行异议问题的诉讼。

（中国钢铁工业协会　蒋璇芳　臧若愚）

中国建筑业对外开放情况

一、2014 年建筑业发展

（一）建筑业发展情况

2014 年，建筑业深入贯彻落实党的十八大和十八届三中、四中全会精神，主动适应经济发展新常态，全面深化改革，加快转型升级，积极推进建筑产业现代化，整体发展稳中有进，发展质量不断提升。全国建筑业企业（指具有资质等级的总承包和专业承包建筑业企业，不含劳务分包建筑业企业，下同）完成建筑业总产值 176713.40 亿元，增长 10.2%；完成竣工产值 100719.51 亿元，增长 7.5%；房屋施工面积达到 125.02 亿平方米，增长 10.4%；房屋竣工面积达到 42.31 亿平方米，增长 5.4%；签订合同额 323613.77 亿元，增长 11.8%；实现利润 6913 亿元，增长 13.7%。截至 2014 年底，全国有施工活动的建筑业企业 81141 个，增长 2.8%；年末从业人数 4960.58 万人，增长 10.25%。2014，建筑业增加值占国内生产总值比重持续稳步上升，达到 7.03%，比上年增加 0.17 个百分点，进一步巩固了建筑业的国民经济支柱产业地位。

（二）对外工程承包情况

2014 年，我国对外工程承包营业收入保持良好增长态势，业务规模稳中有升，对外承包工程业务完成营业额 1424 亿美元，同比增长 3.9%，签订合同额 1917.6 亿美元，同比增长 11.7%。企业在亚、非传统市场业务规模保持稳定增长，欧洲、美洲的市场开拓取得新进展。企业承揽工程项目形式更加丰富，从承揽单一工程项目转向集区域规划、勘察设计、施工承包、管理咨询、运营维护于一体的综合性项目承包服务。在高铁、电信、风电、核电等领域的承包优势展现。

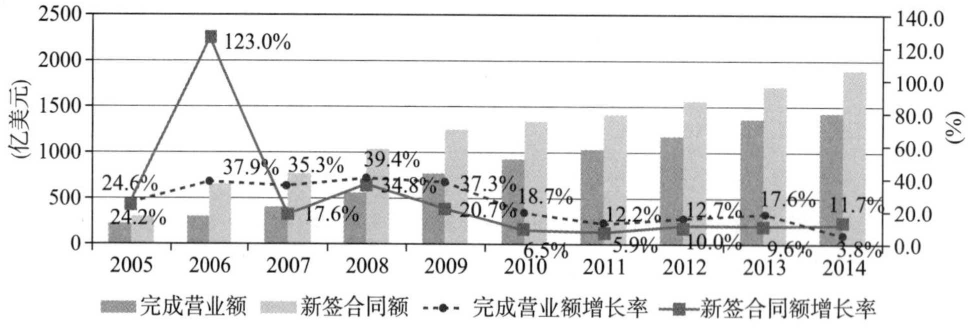

图 1　2005—2014 年我国对外承包工程业务情况

2014 年，我国对外劳务合作派出各类劳务人员 56.2 万人，较上年同期增加 3.5 万人，增长 6.6%。其中承包工程项目派出 26.9 万人，劳务合作项目派出 29.3 万人。2014 年年末在外各类劳务人员 100.6 万人，较上年同期增加 15.3 万人。

2014 年，我国 62 家内地企业入选 2014 年度 ENR 全球最大 250 家国际承包商榜单，共完成海外工程营业额 791.35 亿美元，比去年增加 17.8%。平均营业额为 12.76 亿美元，相比去年增长 4.59%；入选的中国企业最高海外营业额 131.62 亿美元，排名第 9 位；最低海外营业额 1.31 亿美元，排名第 244 位。2014 年我国内地 22 家企业入选 ENR 全球工程设计企业 150 强；19 家内地企业入选国际（海外）工程设计 225 强。

（三）重要法规及规范性文件

一是印发《住房城乡建设部关于推进建筑业发展和改革的若干意见》（建市［2014］92 号）。《若干意见》提出了推进建筑业发展和改革的目标：简政放权，开放市场，坚持放管并重，消除市场壁垒，构建统一开放、竞争有序、诚信守法、监管有力的全国建筑市场体系；创新和改进政府对建筑市场、质量安全的监督管理机制，加强事中事后监管，强化市场和现场联动，落实各方主体责任，确保工程质量安全；转变建筑业发展方式，推进建筑产业现代化，促进建筑业健康协调可持续发展。《若干意见》提出，建立统一开放的建筑市场体系。要进一步放开建筑市场，推进行政审批制度改革，改革招标投标监管方式，推进建筑市场监管信息化与诚信体系建设，进一步完善工程监理制度，强化建设单位行为监管，建立与市场经济相适应的工程造价体系。《若干意见》要求，强化工程质量安全管理。要加强勘察设计质量监管，落实各方主体的工程质量责任，完善工程质量检测制度，推进质量安全标准化建设，推动建筑施工安全专项治理，强化施工安全监督。《若干意见》还要求，促进建筑业发展方式转变。要推动建筑产业现代化，构建有利于形成建筑产业工人队伍的长效机制，提升建筑设计水平，加大工程总承包推行力度，提升建筑业技术能力。

二是印发《工程质量治理两年行动方案》（建市[2014] 130号）。工程质量治理两年行动的目标是：通过两年治理行动，规范建筑市场秩序，落实工程建设五方主体项目负责人质量终身责任，遏制建筑施工违法发包、转包、违法分包及挂靠等违法行为多发势头，进一步发挥工程监理作用，促进建筑产业现代化快速发展，提高建筑从业人员素质，建立健全建筑市场诚信体系，使全国工程质量总体水平得到明显提升。《方案》确定了重点工作任务：全面落实五方主体项目负责人质量终身责任，严厉打击建筑施工转包违法分包行为，健全工程质量监督、监理机制，大力推动建筑产业现代化，加快建筑市场诚信体系建设，切实提高从业人员素质。

三是颁布《建筑业企业资质管理规定》（住房和城乡建设部令第22号）。《规定》明确，企业应当按照其拥有的资产、主要人员、已完成的工程业绩和技术装备等条件申请建筑业企业资质，经审查合格，取得建筑业企业资质证书后，方可在资质许可的范围内从事建筑施工活动。建筑业企业资质分为施工总承包资质、专业承包资质、施工劳务资质三个序列。施工总承包资质、专业承包资质按照工程性质和技术特点分别划分为若干资质类别，各资质类别按照规定的条件划分为若干资质等级。施工劳务资质不分类别与等级。《规定》自2015年3月1日起施行。

四是印发《建筑业企业资质标准》（建市[2014] 159号）。《标准》将建筑业企业资质分为施工总承包、专业承包和施工劳务三个序列。其中，施工总承包序列设有12个类别，一般分为4个等级（特级、一级、二级、三级）；专业承包序列设有36个类别，一般分为3个等级（一级、二级、三级）；施工劳务序列不分类别和等级。《标准》包括建筑业企业资质各个序列、类别和等级的资质标准。《标准》自2015年1月1日起施行。

五是印发《住房城乡建设部关于印发〈全国建筑市场监管与诚信信息系统基础数据库数据标准（试行）〉和〈全国建筑市场监管与诚信信息系统基础数据库管理办法（试行）〉的通知》（建市[2014] 108号）。要求各省级住房城乡建设行政主管部门要进一步提高对建筑市场监管与诚信信息系统建设重要性、紧迫性的认识，按照该数据标准、管理办法的总体要求，结合本地实际，切实加强组织领导，将建筑市场监管信息化建设作为转变监管思路、完善监管手段的重要工作，在2015年底前完成本地区工程建设企业、注册人员、工程项目、诚信信息等基础数据库建设，建立建筑市场和工程质量安全监管一体化工作平台，动态记录工程项目各方主体市场和现场行为，有效实现建筑市场和施工现场监管的联动，全面实现全国建筑市场“数据一个库、监管一张网、管理一条线”的信息化监管目标。

二、建筑市场开放情况

（一）2014年6月28日，国务院批准《中国（上海）自由贸易试验区进一步扩大开放的措施》，建筑市场开放措施如下：

1. 对试验区内为上海市提供服务的外资工程设计（不包括工程勘察）企业，取消首次申请资质时对投资者的工程设计业绩要求；

2. 对试验区内的外商独资建筑业企业承揽上海市的中外联合建设项目时，不受建设项目的中外方投资比例限制。

2014年12月，将上述开放措施扩大至上海市浦东新区。

（二）配合商务部与韩国、澳大利亚开展自由贸易协定谈判，研究制定建筑业领域出价清单。

（住房和城乡建设部建筑市场监管司 陈波 胡楠）

中国服务贸易发展情况

2014 年，面对复杂多变的国际环境和艰巨繁重的商务改革发展任务，商务部积极完善政策支持体系，着力构建公平竞争的市场环境，服务贸易各项工作取得新突破。2014 年，我国服务贸易和服务外包在对外贸易中的比重稳步提升，成为我国对外贸易的新亮点和重要增长点，为稳增长、调结构做出了积极贡献。

一、2014 年我国服务贸易首次跃居世界第二位

（一）服务贸易保持较快增长速度

2014 年，我国服务贸易继续保持较快增长势头，服务进出口总额达 6043.4 亿美元，同比增长 12.6%，自 2010 年以来连续五年保持两位数增长，并首次超越德国跃居世界第二位，仅次于美国，服务贸易占对外贸易总额的比重达到 12.3%。其中，出口 2222.1 亿美元，同比增长 7.6%；进口 3821.3 亿美元，同比增长 15.8%。

高附加值服务进出口快速增长。2014 年，我国服务贸易结构持续优化，高附加值服务增长迅速。金融服务、通信服务、计算机和信息服务等高附加值服务进出口总额分别为 101 亿美元、41.2 亿美元和 268.6 亿美元，分别比上年增长 59.5%、24.6%、25.4%。随着电子商务服务业的崛起和商业模式的成熟，新的增长动力加速孕育，我国高附加值服务进出口还将继续保持快速发展态势。

国内区域发展差距逐渐缩小。我国服务贸易发展区域聚集度高，但区域差距逐渐缩小。2014 年，我国 85%的服务贸易集中在东部 11 个省份，其中北京、上海和广东三省（市）的服务进出口总额占全国的 66%；中部和西部地区的合计占比仅为 15%，但中西部占比较 2010 年提升 6 个百分点。

服务贸易国际市场格局相对稳定。中国香港、美国、日本、新加坡、德国仍为我国前五大服务贸易伙伴，2014 年双边服务进出口总额达 2487 亿美元，占我国服务贸易比重超过四成。香港地区仍为内地最大的服务出口目的地、进口来源地和顺差来源地，但占比下降较为明显，内地与香港双边服务进出口额占我国服务进出口总额的 19%，同比下降 7 个百分点。

服务贸易逆差规模有所扩大。2014 年，我国服务贸易逆差由上年的 1235 亿美元扩大至 1599 亿美元，同比增长 29.5%。服务贸易逆差主要集中于旅游、运输服务、专有权利使用和特许费、保险服务等领域，其中旅游和运输贸易逆差额合计达 1658 亿美元。加工服务、咨询、建筑服务则实现较大数额贸易顺差，顺差额合计达 483.6 亿美元。

（二）服务外包保持高速增长

2014 年，我国企业承接服务外包合同额首次超过 1000 亿美元，达到 1072.1 亿美元，执行金额 813.4 亿美元，同比分别增长 12.2%和 27.4%。其中，承接国际服务外包合同金额和执行金额分别为 718.3 亿美元和 559.2 亿美元，同比分别增长 15.1%和 23.1%。

产业发展向量质并举转型。创新成为服务外包企业发展的核心动力。2014 年，我国承接以知识和研发为主要特征的知识流程外包业务 186.7 亿美元，占离岸执行总额的 33.4%，服务外包产业稳步向价值链高端延伸。

外包成为吸纳大学生就业容纳器。2014 年，我国服务外包企业新增从业人员 71.1 万人，其中，大学毕业生 48.8 万人。截至 2014 年底，我国服务外包产业吸纳就业 607.2 万人，其中大学（含大专）以上学历 404.7 万人，占从业人员的 2/3。

多元化市场格局初步形成。离岸服务外包业务拓展至近 200 个国家，承接“一带一路”沿线国家外包合同金额和执行金额分别为 125 亿美元和 98.4 亿美元，分别增长 25.2%和 36.3%，美国、欧盟、中国香港和日本四个主要发包市场占比较去年同期下降 2.9 个百分点。

二、2014 年服务贸易各项工作取得新突破

商务部党组高度重视服务贸易工作。2013 年

12月底，高虎城部长在全国商务工作会议报告中，明确指出要“加快发展服务贸易”，并提出了具体落实要求。2014年3月11日，房爱卿副部长主持召开全国服务贸易和商贸服务业电视电话会，进一步明确服务贸易发展思路和工作重点，研究部署政策措施落实工作。一年来，我们主要做了四个方面的工作：

（一）注重顶层设计，营造发展环境

国务院第71次常务会议专题研究部署服务外包工作，推动出台了《国务院关于加快发展对外文化贸易的意见》（国发［2014］13号）和《国务院关于促进服务外包产业加快发展的意见》（国发［2014］67号）；牵头起草了《国务院关于加快发展服务贸易的若干意见》（国发［2015］8号），2015年2月也已正式印发，成为服务贸易领域的第一个纲领性文件。将服务贸易纳入《国务院办公厅关于支持外贸稳定增长的若干意见》（国办发［2014］19号）和《国务院办公厅关于加强进口的若干意见》（国办发［2014］49号）等两个国办文件。系列文件的印发和实施，使服务贸易发展思路日益清晰，发展环境日趋优化。

（二）完善支持政策，发展重点领域

一是大力发展服务外包产业。贯彻落实《国务院办公厅关于进一步促进服务外包产业发展的复函》（国办函［2013］33号），会同财政部等部门出台了利用出口信贷促进服务外包发展的有关政策；会同财政部等5部门出台《关于完善技术先进型服务企业有关企业所得税政策问题的通知》（财税［2014］59号），将苏州工业园区试点政策推广至21个示范城市；联合教育部出台《关于创新服务外包人才培养机制 提升服务外包产业发展能力的意见》（教高［2014］2号）。

二是推动中华文化“走出去”。贯彻落实《国务院关于加快发展对外文化贸易的意见》（国发［2014］13号），牵头完善配套支持政策。会同有关部门发布了2013—2014年度《国家文化出口重点企业目录》和《国家文化出口重点项目目录》；与中宣部共同牵头拟定了文化产品和服务出口增值税免税或零税率的重点支持范围，推动将28种文化产品出口退税率提高至17%；加强对外文化贸易促进，编制完成《对外文化贸易实务指南》（2014版），启动编制对外文化贸易国际市场开拓计划和《对外文化贸易和投资合作主要国别（地区）指南》。

三是加强技术贸易促进工作。发挥政策引导作用，完善技术贸易支持政策，鼓励引进先进技术，推动成熟的产业化技术出口。

四是推动中医药服务贸易载体建设。与国家中医药管理局共同研究确定中医药服务贸易先行先试重点区域和重点企业。参与京交会中医药服务贸易主题日活动，发布重点区域和重点企业目录。

五是完善国际货代物流业支持政策。推动出台《关于国际货物运输代理服务有关增值税问题的公告》。配合做好上合组织成员国经贸部长会议机制项下发展过境潜力工作组的日常协调工作。

（三）坚持改革创新，夯实发展基础

加强服务贸易法规建设，启动服务进出口法规的立法研究工作；启动编制《重点服务出口领域指导目录》；完善服务贸易统计体系，首次将服务贸易统计数据纳入《中华人民共和国统计公报》和《中国统计年鉴》，会同统计局联合修订并发布《国际服务贸易统计制度》；完成并公示《2011年和2012年中国服务外包示范城市综合评价结果》，开展了2013年度综合评价工作；成立了对外文化贸易部际联系机制并召开第一次会议；修订《文化产品和服务进出口统计目录》；发挥创新驱动作用，在服务外包支持资金中增加鼓励研发的方向，支持企业获得开发能力成熟度模型集成等13项国际资质认证；进一步完善技术先进型企业的认定条件，将从事离岸服务外包业务取得的收入调整为不低于企业当年总收入的35%；创新高校、培训机构和有关企业服务外包人才培养机制，提高人才培养质量，引导大学生创新创业。

（四）打造促进平台，开展务实合作

成功举办第三届中国（北京）国际服务贸易交易会（以下简称京交会）和第二届中国（上海）国际技术进出口交易会，初步形成以京交会为龙头，以各专业展会为支撑的服务贸易展会格局。召开中新服务贸易工作组会议，与美国就开展中美服务贸易对话达成一致，列入中美商贸联委会成果；积极筹备第二次中印服务贸易工作组会议。组织企业赴北欧开展中欧技术贸易交流与合作活动，与芬兰经济与就业部签署了《关于开展技术贸易交流与合作活动的谅解备忘录》。

（商务部服务贸易和商贸服务业司司长　邱丽新）

中国银行业对外开放情况

2014年，银监会积极贯彻国家深化改革、扩大开放精神，坚定不移地推进银行业对外开放，促进在华外资银行稳健发展。

截至2014年年末，共有15个国家和地区的银行在华设立了38家外商独资银行（下设分行296家）、2家合资银行（下设分行3家）和1家外商独资财务公司；26个国家和地区的66家外国银行，在华设立了97家分行。另有47个国家和地区的158家银行，在华设立了182家代表处。外资银行在我国27个省（市、区）的69个城市设立了机构，形成具有一定覆盖面和市场深度的总行、分行、支行服务网络，营业网点达1000家。35家外资法人银行、62家外国银行分行获准经营人民币业务；31家外资法人银行、28家外国银行分行获准从事金融衍生产品交易业务；6家外资法人银行获准发行人民币金融债；4家外资法人银行获准发行信用卡；3家外资法人银行获准开办信贷资产证券化项目。

表1　在华外资银行业金融机构情况（截至2014年年底）

	外国银行	独资银行	合资银行	独资财务公司	合计
法人机构总行		38	2	1	41
法人机构分行		296	3		299
外国银行分行	97				97
支行	16	537	10		563
总计	113	871	15	1	1 000

在华外资银行整体经营稳健。截至2014年年底，在华外资银行营业性机构资产总额2.79万亿元，同比增长9.16%；各项贷款1.19万亿元，同比增长7.22%；各项存款1.55万亿元，同比增长3.74%；平均不良贷款率0.81%，低于全国商业银行平均水平；拨备覆盖率231.63%，对预期损失的风险抵补能力较强；实现税后利润197.23亿元；流动性比例71.62%；外资法人银行资本充足率17.08%，一级资本充足率及核心一级资本充足率均为16.43%，资本质量较高。

2014年11月27日，国务院总理李克强签署国务院令，12月20日公布《国务院关于修改〈中华人民共和国外资银行管理条例〉的决定》。根据新修改的《外资银行管理条例》，从2015年1月1日起对外资银行实施三项扩大开放的措施：一是取消外资法人银行境内分行营运资金的最低数量要求；二是取消设立营业性机构前须设立代表处的要求；三是将外资银行申请经营人民币业务的开业年限要求从3年降至1年，并相应取消须连续2年盈利的要求。2014年12月，《〈内地与香港关于建立更紧密经贸关系的安排〉关于内地在广东与香港基本实现服务贸易自由化的协议》和《〈内地与澳门关于建立更紧密经贸关系的安排〉关于内地在广东与澳门基本实现服务贸易自由化的协议》签署。内地银行部门首次在商业存在模式下以负面清单方式做出承诺。

（中国银行业监督管理委员会）

中国保险业对外开放情况

2014 年是中国保险业具有历史意义的一年。国务院发布了《关于加快发展现代保险服务业的若干意见》，对新时期保险业改革、发展和监管进行了全面部署，提出了加快建设世界保险强国的战略目标，并明确要求提升保险业对外开放水平，推动保险市场进一步对内对外开放，实现“引进来”和“走出去”更好结合，以开放促改革促发展。鼓励中资保险公司尝试多形式多渠道“走出去”，为我国海外企业提供风险保障。支持中资保险公司通过国际资本市场筹集资金，多种渠道进入海外市场。努力扩大保险服务出口，引导外资保险公司将先进经验和技术植入中国市场。这个文件的出台翻开了中国保险业加速发展的新篇章，对中国保险业发展具有里程碑意义。

一、中国保险业总体发展情况

2014 年，在党中央、国务院的正确领导下，中国保险业面对增长速度换档期、结构调整阵痛期和前期刺激政策消化期“三期叠加”的挑战，继续深化改革，扎实推进各项工作，最终实现了重大跨域，驶入了发展的快车道，中国保险业已经站在新的发展起点上。

2014 年全国实现保费收入 20233.6 亿元，同比增长 17.5%，是国际金融危机以来增长速度最高的一年；保险深度为 3.18%，保险密度为 1479.3 元；赔款给付金额达 7194.4 亿元，同比增长 15.9%；保险公司总资产突破 10 万亿元。从经营效益来看，保险公司实现利润总额 1934.2 亿元，保险资金运用实现收益 5358.8 亿元，创历史新高。保险资金投资收益率达 6.3%，创五年来最好水平。

二、中国保险业对外开放的总体形势

自改革开放以来，短短 30 多年的时间，中国保险业经历了从小到大、从封闭到开放的发展历程，取得了辉煌的成就。总的来说，保险业是我国金融业开放时间最早、开放力度最大的行业。从“引进来”的角度看，外资的引入和发展使保险业发生了深刻变化，形成了中外保险公司良性互动、共同发展的良性局面，为推动行业深化改革发挥了显著的积极作用。

（一）完善了市场主体结构

截至 2014 年年底，共有 15 个国家和地区的境外保险公司在我国设立了 56 家外资保险法人机构和代表处 140 家，设立各级分支机构近 2000 家。目前，在华外资保险机构业务平稳发展。2014 年，外资保险公司实现保费收入 901.9 亿元，同比增长 32.6%，占全国保费收入的 4.5%，较上年提高 0.5 个百分点。各类赔款与给付支出 472 亿元。外资保险公司总资产 6646.7 亿元，较年初增加 2231.4 亿元，增长 50.5%，占保险业总资产的 6.5%，自 2008 年国际金融危机之后保持稳定。外资保险公司在参与推进中国保险市场发展的同时，也分享了行业改革发展的显著成果。总的来说，国内保险市场上多元化市场主体共同发展、中外资保险机构合作共赢的市场格局逐步形成。

（二）增强了行业资本实力

保险市场开放带来了大量资金。截至目前，共有近 700 亿元人民币的境外资金通过设立外资保险机构和参股中资保险公司进入我国保险业，有力促进了行业的发展。中资保险公司通过引进境外战略投资者、境外上市等方式，吸收境外资本超过千亿元人民币。引进外资有效解决了保险业资本实力较弱的问题，夯实了行业发展和抵抗风险的基础。

（三）提升了保险业创新和服务能力

外资保险公司带来的先进经验和理念促进了保险业产品、服务和营销模式的创新，填补了部分国内市场空白，促使保险产品从单一化向多元化过渡，保险功能得到充分发挥，保险服务更加贴近经济社会发展和人民需求。

（四）推动了中资保险机构改革发展

在与外资的竞争和合作中，中资保险公司的经营观念和经营机制有了明显转变，经营管理和发展模式从简单粗放向可持续发展转变，企业内部活力和市场竞争力不断增强。

（五）未对国家金融安全稳定产生负面影响

保险业开放以来，在引进外资的同时有效防范了金融风险传递；国际金融危机和欧洲债务危机期间，保险业没有发生外资集中撤资和消费者恐慌导致的群体性事件，在华外资公司保持了平稳的发展态势。

从“走出去”的角度看，随着近年来自身实力发展，中资保险机构在拓展海外市场的意愿逐步增强。截至 2014 年年末，共有 12 家境内保险机构在境外设立了 32 家营业机构，其中包括 10 家资产管理公司。共有 4 家境内保险机构在境外设立了 7 家代表处。另外，中国保监会积极推动中资保险机构在“一带一路”沿线国家设立营业机构，为我国在当地投资项目提供保险保障。

三、保险监管的国际交流与合作

中国保险业的对外开放过程，也是保险业不断改革发展的过程。保险市场开放带来了大量资金，有力促进了行业的发展。与外国资本相伴随进入我国的还有先进的保险经营模式、风险管理技术和保险监管理念，推动了我国保险业的改革创新。在三十多年的对外开放进程中，保险业充分利用了国内外两个市场、两种资源，加快发展，推进改革，在经济社会建设中的作用和地位不断提高。从 2014 年来看，全国保费收入首次突破 2 万亿元大关，总资产首次突破 10 万亿元。中国保险业的世界排名从 2012 年的第六位迅速上升至 2014 年的第三位，国际地位与影响力大幅提升，中国已经成为保险新兴市场的一面旗帜与国际保险业关注的焦点。随着国际影响力的提升与国际金融改革的不断深入，中国保险业监管层面的对外交流与合作也呈现出了新的态势。

（一）不断提高参与国际规则制定的深度与广度

为进一步增强我国保险监管在国际保险业的领导力和话语权，在国际规则制定中发出更多中国声音、注入更多中国元素，反映包括我国在内的亚洲地区及新兴市场的现实需要和发展诉求，维护我国保险业实际利益，中国保监会一直致力于提高参与国际规则制定的深度与光度。

作为国际保险监督官协会（IAIS）执行委员会和金融稳定委员会等核心委员会的成员以及首批全球系统重要性保险机构（G－SII）的全集团监管机构，中国保监会参加了 IAIS 资本开发工作组、实地测试工作组、G－SII 分析工作组及 G－SII 评估方法工作组等，积极参与并密切关注了更高损失吸收能力要求（HLA）草案的制定工作，就 HLA 草案制定中的重大战略问题和技术问题反馈了意见，获得了国际同行的肯定。同时，中国保监会继续参与了 G－SII 认定工作以及针对国际活跃保险集团（IAIG）的共同框架、以风险为基础的全球保险资本标准（ICS）和 HLA 的实地测试工作。接下来，中国保监会将全面参加 IAIS 各级机构，为进一步参与国际规则制定打下良好基础。

（二）继续加强与国际组织和重点国家的多双边合作

2014 年，中国保监会不断加强与国际保险监督官协会（IAIS）、国际养老金协会（IOPS）、亚洲开发银行（ADB）、扩大保险服务计划（A2ii）等国际组织的交流与合作，积极参与亚洲保险监督官论坛（AFIR）活动并担任轮值主席，继续巩固与重点国家（地区）的双边协作，探索开展跨境监管、养老保险、健康险、偿付能力和资金运用监管等专题合作。建立与美国、欧盟、加拿大、英国、法国、澳大利亚、泰国、马恩岛等国家（地区）保险监管机构合作机制，继续大力支持港澳台地区金融业发展。广泛参与国际保险交流活动和区域性平台建设，加强了与国外监管机构间的信息共享和技术交流，有效地防范了风险跨境传递、跨领域传递，为扩大中国保险业国际影响力，促进中国保险业持续健康稳定发展发挥了积极作用。

（三）配合国家整体对外经济战略，积极参与应对多个谈判机制

2014 年，中国保监会参与了中美投资协定、中欧投资协定、政府采购协定、中韩自贸区谈判、中新自贸区谈判、中澳自贸区谈判，以及 CEPA 磋商等多个开放谈判磋商，并认真协调落实好相关法规的修订和执行；积极稳妥地应对中美战略与经济对话、中英经济财金对话、中法财经对话、中日韩经济磋商、中加金融政策对话、中德高级别财金对话等十几个磋商机制，积极利用对话磋商加强对外沟通交流和政策协调，扩大保险业对外影响，为保险业对外开放和健康发展创造有利环境。

（四）积极拓展国际合作项目

中国保监会围绕偿付能力、养老保险、集团监管等监管重点工作，利用国际合作项目，整合各渠道资源，加快推动保险监管能力建设，完善保险监管体系。相继开展了中欧世贸项目、中美保险工作组研究、中德天气指数保险项目、与GIZ（德国政府授权的国际技术合作公司）及ADB（亚洲开发银行）小额保险国别研究、中英繁荣基金项目等多个保险监管国际合作项目，并积极与欧盟在偿付能力监管等效评估等方面开展合作。

四、我国保险业对外开放的主要经验

入世以来，中国保险业严格履行入世承诺，积极推动保险市场的对外开放，不断优化产业结构，促进了保险业协调均衡发展。保险业的对外开放不仅取得了显著成绩，同时也积累了一些重要经验，为保险业自身未来的发展及其他金融行业的发展提供了有益的借鉴：一是以我为主、安全可控的开放策略使保险市场准入的节奏得到了控制，避免了外资对国内市场带来过多的负面冲击；二是在对外开放的过程中，积极进行行政审批制度、条款费率制度等方面的改革，由此激发了保险企业的经营、创新活力，这些都为中资保险公司利用开放机遇、尽快发展壮大自己创造了良好的外部环境；三是注重引进外资公司的专长经营领域，有效提升了资源配置效率，促进了我国保险业产品结构的优化。

五、中国保险市场发展展望

当前我国经济结构、发展动力、市场机制和面临的国际环境都发生了深刻变化，宏观经济步入新的发展阶段。随着中国保险业发展政策红利的逐步释放，特别是“新国十条”的出台，标志着发展现代保险服务业已经从行业意愿上升到了国家意志。同时“一带一路”、新型城镇化等一系列创新发展战略为我国保险业的发展创造了美好前景。中国保险业将以此为契机，继续认真履行开放承诺，不断提高对外开放水平，维护保险业对外开放的良好形象，发挥全面开放对保险业改革发展的促进作用。通过不断拓宽对外开放的深度和广度，加快与国际接轨的步伐，增强我国保险业的综合竞争力，提高发展的质量和水平，提高保险业服务经济社会发展和构建社会主义和谐社会的能力。

外资寿险公司明细表

序号	公司名称	境外股东所在国家/地区	开业时间	注册地
1	中宏人寿保险有限公司	加拿大	1996.11.08	上海
2	中德安联人寿保险有限公司	德国	1998.10.20	上海
3	工银安盛人寿保险有限公司	法国	1999.04.07	上海
4	信诚人寿保险有限公司	英国	2000.09.18	北京
5	交银康联人寿保险有限公司	澳大利亚	2000.06.14	上海
6	中意人寿保险有限公司	意大利	2002.01.10	北京
7	中荷人寿保险有限公司	荷兰	2002.11.01	大连
8	同方全球人寿保险有限公司	荷兰	2003.04.03	上海
9	中法人寿保险有限责任公司	法国	2004.12.06	北京
10	中英人寿保险有限公司	英国	2002.12.04	北京
11	中美联泰大都会人寿保险有限公司	美国	2011.03.17	上海
12	北大方正人寿保险有限公司	日本	2002.11.15	上海
13	长生人寿保险有限公司	日本	2003.09.02	上海
14	招商信诺人寿保险有限公司	美国	2003.07.25	深圳
15	恒安标准人寿保险有限公司	英国	2003.11.25	天津
16	瑞泰人寿保险有限公司	南非	2003.12.08	北京

续 表

序号	公司名称	境外股东所在国家/地区	开业时间	注册地
17	陆家嘴国泰人寿保险有限责任公司	台湾	2004.12.24	上海
18	华泰人寿保险股份有限公司	美国	2005.03.01	北京
19	中银三星人寿保险有限公司	韩国	2005.05.18	北京
20	平安健康保险股份有限公司	南非	2005.06.13	上海
21	中新大东方人寿保险有限公司	新加坡	2006.05.08	重庆
22	汇丰人寿保险有限公司	香港	2009.06.03	上海
23	新光海航人寿保险有限责任公司	台湾	2008.09.03	北京
24	君龙人寿保险有限公司	台湾	2008.09.28	厦门
25	复星保德信人寿保险有限公司	美国	2012.09.13	上海
26	中韩人寿保险有限公司	韩国	2012.10.29	杭州
27	德华安顾人寿保险有限公司	德国	2013.05.29	济南
28	友邦保险有限公司	香港	1992.9.25	5个省（市）

外资再保险公司明细表

序号	公司名称	境外股东所在国家/地区	开业时间	注册地
1	慕尼黑再保险公司北京分公司	德国	2003.06.27	北京
2	通用再保险公司上海分公司	德国	2004.05.25	上海
3	汉诺威再保险股份公司上海分公司	德国	2008.03.31	上海
4	瑞士再保险公司北京分公司	瑞士	2003.09.11	北京
5	法国再保险公司北京分公司	法国	2008.02.03	北京
6	RGA 美国再保险公司上海分公司	美国	2014.9	上海

外资产险公司明细表

序号	公司名称	境外股东所在国家/地区	开业时间	注册地
1	美亚财产保险有限公司	美国	1992.09.25	北京
2	东京海上日动火灾保险（中国）有限公司	日本	1994.07.03	上海
3	安盛天平财产保险股份有限公司	瑞士	1996.11.08	上海
4	瑞再企商保险（中国）有限公司	卢森堡	1998.09.18	上海
5	丘博保险（中国）有限公司	美国	2000.09.27	上海
6	三井住友海上火灾保险（中国）有限公司	日本	2001.04.24	上海
7	三星财产保险（中国）有限公司	韩国	2001.04.24	上海
8	苏黎世财产保险（中国）有限公司	瑞士	2006.05.08	北京
9	安联财产保险（中国）有限公司	德国	2002.12.18	广州
10	利宝保险有限公司	美国	2003.11.07	重庆
11	日本财产保险（中国）有限公司	日本	2003.05.15	大连
12	中航安盟财产保险有限公司	法国	2004.08.30	北京

续　表

序号	公司名称	境外股东所在国家/地区	开业时间	注册地
13	劳合社保险（中国）有限公司	英国	2007.03.09	上海
14	中意财产保险有限公司	意大利	2007.04.06	北京
15	现代财产保险（中国）有限公司	韩国	2007.02.08	北京
16	爱和谊日生同和财产保险（中国）有限公司	日本	2007.05.17	天津
17	国泰财产保险有限责任公司	台湾	2008.08.26	上海
18	乐爱金财产保险（中国）有限公司	韩国	2009.09.18	南京
19	日本兴亚财产保险（中国）有限责任公司	日本	2009.06.11	深圳
20	信利保险（中国）有限公司	美国	2010.12.13	上海
21	富邦财产保险有限公司	台湾	2010.09.17	厦门
22	史带财产保险股份有限公司	美国	1995.01.25	上海

（中国保险监督管理委员会国际部）

中国资本市场对外开放情况

2014 年，中国证监会顺利开通沪港股票市场交易互联互通机制（以下简称沪港通）试点，支持境内企业境外上市，推动境内企业境外发行优先股、人民币股票和 B 股转 H 股，大力推进合格境外机构投资者（QFII）和人民币合格境外机构投资者（RQFII）发展，加大证券期货行业双向开放的力度，大力支持中国（上海）自由贸易实验区（以下简称上海自贸区）建设，推进国际化原油期货平台建设，强化与港澳台地区的合作与联系，加强国际监管合作与交流，中国资本市场对外开放取得丰硕成果。

一、顺利启动沪港通试点

2014 年 4 月，中国证监会与香港证券及期货事务监察委员会（以下简称香港证监会）发布联合公告，原则批准上交所、香港联合交易所有限公司（以下简称香港联交所）、中国结算、香港中央结算有限公司（以下简称香港结算）开展沪港通试点。2014 年 11 月，中国证监会与香港证监会发布联合公告，批准上交所、香港联交所、中国结算、香港结算正式启动沪港通试点。沪港通开创了操作便利、风险可控的跨境证券投资新模式，是境内资本市场双向开放的重大制度创新。同年 11 月 17 日沪港通正式开通以来，总体运行平稳有序，交易结算、额度控制、换汇等各个环节运作正常，沪港通下的制度安排、运作机制及技术系统经受了市场的检验，实现了预期目标。截至 2014 年年底，累计成交 1880.75 亿元人民币，其中沪股通 1675.12 亿元、港股通 205.63 亿元。

（一）全面构建沪港通规则体系

中国证监会发布实施《沪港股票市场交易互联互通机制试点若干规定》，作为市场参与者开展沪港通相关业务活动的重要依据。会同财政部、税务总局发布《关于沪港股票市场交易互联互通机制试点有关税收政策的通知》，明确了沪港通下有关税收政策。会同人民银行发布《关于沪港股票市场交易互联互通机制试点有关问题的通知》，明确了沪港通下账户开立及资金划转有关事项。批准发布《上海证券交易所沪港通试点办法》和《沪港股票市场交易互联互通机制试点登记、存管、结算业务实施细则》等有关规则。

（二）建立跨境监管和执法合作机制

中国证监会与香港证监会签订了《沪港通项目下中国证监会与香港证监会加强监管执法合作备忘录》，在线索与调查信息通报、协助调查和联合调查、送达、协助执行等方面进行全方位合作。

（三）做好投资者教育和保护工作

中国证监会与香港证监会、香港投资者教育中心就沪港通投资者诉求处理和投资者教育合作做了相应安排，强化投资风险教育，确保两地投诉渠道的开放和诉求的有效便捷处理。以“沪港通微讲堂”的形式，对投资者普遍关心的问题做出解答。

二、推动境内企业境外上市

（一）支持境内企业境外发行上市

取消境外上市申请的财务审核，促进境内企业到境外上市融资。截至 2014 年年底，共有 205 家境内股份有限公司到境外上市，融资总额 2444.43 亿美元。其中，在香港交易所主板上市 178 家（含香港地区、纽约同时上市 10 家，香港地区、伦敦同时上市 4 家，香港地区、纽约、伦敦同时上市 1 家），在香港交易所创业板上市 24 家，在新加坡交易所上市 3 家。境外上市公司中有 86 家已发行 A 股，1 家发行 A、B 股，1 家发行 B 股。

（二）支持境内企业境外发行优先股

中国证监会明确境外上市的境内企业在境外发行优先股的有关规定，要求其符合境外募集股份及上市的标准。核准中国银行、工商银行境外发行优先股，分别融资 65 亿美元和 56.4 亿美元。

（三）支持境内企业境外发行人民币股票

2014 年，核准工商银行在境外发行人民币计价优先股，融资人民币 120 亿元，进一步推动人民币国际化进程，扩大跨境金融合作的深度和广度，有利于境内企业拓宽直接融资的渠道，提高利用国际资本市场的效率。

(四) 推进B股转H股试点工作

中国证监会积极推动B股市场改革，核准丽珠医药和万科股份以介绍方式在香港联交所上市。

三、扩大证券期货行业双向开放

(一) 支持境内证券期货经营机构“引进来”和“走出去”

落实《关于建立更紧密经贸关系的安排》(CEPA) 承诺，拟进一步放开港澳金融机构参股内地证券公司、基金管理公司、证券投资咨询机构的股权比例和业务范围。研究推动证券公司、基金管理公司开展外汇业务，国泰君安证券和嘉实基金已正式获批结售汇业务资格。支持证券期货经营机构设立境外子公司，开展跨境投资业务。

(二) 大力推进QFII和RQFII发展

进一步扩大RQFII试点范围至英国、法国、韩国、德国，增加香港地区RQFII总额度，批准额度已达8200亿元。推动完善QFII、RQFII税收政策工作取得重要突破，会同财政部、税务总局发布《关于QFII和RQFII取得中国境内的股票等权益性投资资产转让所得暂免征收企业所得税问题的通知》，暂免征收QFII、RQFII对股票等权益投资差价所得的企业所得税。

四、支持上海自贸区建设

(一) 支持上海自贸区内证券期货经营机构发展

积极支持证券期货经营机构在上海自贸区内注册设立专业子公司和分支机构。截至2014年年底，华泰证券已在上海自贸区设立资产管理子公司；国泰君安、海通证券、中金公司、中信证券、中信建投5家证券公司已在上海自贸区设立分公司；银河证券、齐鲁证券和东方证券设立营业部；国金证券设立另类投资子公司；华安、浦银安盛、申万菱信、华泰柏瑞4家基金管理公司设立专业子公司；13家期货公司设立风险管理服务子公司；5家期货公司设立营业部。

(二) 大力推进原油期货上市工作

原油期货市场建设取得重大突破。2014年12月，中国证监会批准上海期货交易所（以下简称上期所）在其国际能源交易中心开展原油期货交易，同时建设国际化交易结算平台，积极引入境外交易者和经纪机构，逐步积累市场运作和监管经验，为稳步推进期货市场对外开放进行了积极探索。

五、稳步扩大对港澳台开放

根据CEPA及其补充协议，中国证监会推出了一系列促进内地证券期货业向港澳地区开放的政策措施，不断加强与港澳地区的合作与联系。积极研究内地与香港基金产品互认；允许符合设立外资参股证券公司条件的港资金融机构按照内地有关规定在上海、广东、深圳各设立1家两地合资的全牌照证券公司，港资合并持股比例最高可达51%，内地股东不限于证券公司；在“金融改革方面先行先试”的若干改革试验区内，允许港资证券公司在合资证券投资咨询公司中的持股比例达50%以上。中国证监会积极参与《内地与香港CEPA关于内地在广东与香港基本实现服务贸易自由化的协议》《内地与澳门CEPA关于内地在广东与澳门基本实现服务贸易自由化的协议》的签署，在内地证券期货领域首次以准入前国民待遇加负面清单的模式推进与港澳地区开放合作。2014年12月，两岸举行第二次证券及期货监管合作会议，就两岸资本市场的发展与合作进行了有益沟通，包括内地方面研究进一步降低QFII资格门槛、允许QFII投资国债期货，及台湾方面研究放宽内地证券期货机构参股的有关限制等。截至2014年年底，已批准3家香港地区中介机构参股内地期货公司。内地分别有23家证券公司、6家期货公司、22家基金管理公司在香港地区设立分支机构。批准了29家台资金融机构的QFII资格，批准了4家台资金融机构在内地设立合资基金管理公司。

六、推进战略对话和投资谈判

(一) 通过国际谈判探索双向开放新模式

2014年，中国证监会继续参与中美、中英、中法、中欧、中新等政府间双边对话机制，达成相关政策成果26项，拓展了RQFII的试点区域，启动了双边基金互认的研究。积极参与中美、中欧双边投资协定谈判及中韩、中澳、中日韩等双多边自贸区谈判，取得重要进展。

（二）推动 A 股纳入 MSCI 明晟等全球基准指数

2014 年，中国证监会积极与 MSCI 明晟公司等进行接触和磋商，系统梳理 A 股纳入相关基准指数面临的障碍，加强与相关部委协调沟通，推动解决相关的境外投资者税收政策等问题。

七、加强国际监管和执法合作

（一）继续积极参与 IOSCO 各项工作

2014 年 9 月，中国证监会在国际证监会组织（IOSCO）第 39 届年会期间当选新一届理事会常任理事，当选多边备忘录监督小组副主席，并再次当选投资管理委员会副主席。积极参与了 IOSCO《中小企业和基础设施长期融资可持续解决方案》和《证券市场风险展望 2014—2015》等重点报告的撰写工作，在国际组织中发挥了更重要的作用。

（二）积极开展跨境执法协助

自 2007 年签署 IOSCO 多边备忘录以来，中国证监会一直积极履行多边备忘录项下的跨境执法合作义务。2014 年，中国证监会共收到境外协查请求 97 件，办结 69 件；对外提出协查请求 13 件。中国证监会会同财政部与包括美国、加拿大在内的境外审计监管机构进行磋商，推动跨境审计监管合作。

（三）签署双边监管合作谅解备忘录

2014 年，中国证监会与白俄罗斯共和国财政部、文莱金融管理局、泽西金融服务委员会及马恩岛金融监督管理委员会 4 家境外监管机构签署了证券期货监管合作谅解备忘录。截至 2014 年年底，中国证监会共与 55 个国家（或地区）的证券期货监管机构签署了 59 个监管合作谅解备忘录。

（四）参与金融市场基础设施原则相关工作

中国证监会积极参与国际清算银行支付与市场基础设施委员会（CPMI）和 IOSCO 关于组织《金融市场基础设施原则》（以下简称 FMI 原则）实施的各项工作。中国证监会对内已按照 CPMI－IOSCO 要求，将 FMI 原则纳入对金融市场基础设施的监管框架，组织基础设施机构开展 FMI 原则评估；对外积极履行国际义务，参与制定 FMI 原则相关配套规则，指导与监督 FMI 原则全球落实工作。

八、促进与国际组织的合作与交流

2014 年，中国证监会继续配合相关部门，积极参与在二十国集团（G20）、金融稳定理事会（FSB）、国际货币基金组织（IMF）、世界贸易组织（WTO）、经济合作与发展组织（OECD）、亚太经合组织（APEC）、亚洲开发银行（ADB）等多边框架下的合作，进一步加深对外交流，增进了解与互信。

积极参与 FSB 中国国家同行评估工作，在宏观审慎监管、非银行信贷中介等方面加强积极正面的对外沟通。积极应对 WTO 第五次对华贸易政策审议。

继续推进“中国—欧盟世贸项目（二期）”框架下的项目执行合作，组织代表团赴欧洲研讨交流股票发行监管及信息披露规则，举办“中欧期货市场监管专题研讨会”和“中欧衍生品市场发展与监管专题研讨会”等。

（中国证券监督管理委员会国际合作部　姜沫）

中国交通运输业对外开放情况

（一）交通运输行业发展情况

2014 年，全国完成铁路公路水路固定资产投资 25259.5 亿元，同比增长 12.6%，占全社会固定资产投资的 4.9%。其中，铁路建设投资 6623 亿元，比上年增长 12.6%，公路建设投资 15460.9 亿元，比上年增长 12.9%，内河及沿海建设完成投资 1460.0 亿元，比上年下降 4.5%。

1. 公路

2014 年年底，中国公路总里程达 446.4 万公里，比上年年末增加 10.8 万公里，其中，高速公路达到 11.2 万公里，比上年末增加 0.75 万公里。公路密度继续增加，路网密度达到 46.5 公里/百平方公里，提高 1.12 公路/百平方公里，通达水平进一步提高。

全国通公路的乡（镇）占全国乡（镇）总数的 99.98%，比上年年末提高 0.01 个百分点，通公路的建制村占全国建制村总数的 99.82%，比上年年末提高 0.12 个百分点。其中，通硬化路面的乡（镇）占全国乡（镇）总数的 98.08%，通硬化路面的建制村占全国建制村总数的 91.76%，比上年年末分别提高 0.28 个和 2.76 个百分点。

2014 年，公路货运量、货物周转量、客运量、旅客周转量分别完成 333.3 亿吨、61016.6 亿吨公里、190.8 亿人、12084.1 亿人公里，按可比口径比上年分别增长 8.3%、9.5%、3.0%、7.4%。

2. 水路

截至 2014 年年底，全国港口拥有万吨级及以上泊位 2110 个，比上年年末增加 109 个，其中，沿海港口万吨级及以上泊位 1704 个，比上年末增加 97 个，内河港口万吨级及以上泊位 406 个，增加 12 个。全国内河航道通航里程 12.63 万公里，比上年年末增加 427 公里，其中三级及以上航道 10854 公里，占航道总里程的 8.6%，比上年提高 0.5 个百分点。

水路客货运输量继续保持平稳增长，港口生产总体良好。2014 年，全国完成货运量 59.8 亿吨、货物周转量 92774.6 亿吨公里，比上年分别增长 6.9%和 16.8%；完成客运量 2.6 亿人、旅客周转量 74.3 亿人公里，比上年分别增长 11.7% 和 8.8%。全国港口完成货物吞吐量 124.5 亿吨，比上年增长 5.8%，其中，完成外贸货物吞吐量 35.9 亿吨，比上年增长 6.9%。全国港口完成集装箱吞吐量 2.0 亿 TEU，比上年增长 6.4%。

全国港口完成液体散货吞吐量 9.97 亿吨，比上年增长 5.1%；干散货吞吐量 72.5 亿吨，增长 4.9%；件杂货吞吐量 12.5 亿吨，增长 7.3%；集装箱吞吐量（按重量计算）23.5 亿吨，增长 7.5%；滚装汽车吞吐量（按重量计算）6.1 亿吨，增长 9.4%。

货物吞吐量超过亿吨的港口由上年的 32 个增加到 33 个，集装箱吞吐量超过 100 万 TEU 的港口由上年的 24 个增加到 27 个。上海港集装箱吞吐量连续五年居全球第一。

2014 年底，全国拥有水上运输船舶 17.2 万艘，比上年末减少 0.3%；净载重量 25785.2 万吨，增长 5.7%；平均净载重量 1499.3 吨/艘，增长 6.0%；集装箱箱位 231.9 万 TEU，增长 36.3%。在集装箱箱位拥有量居世界前 20 位的世界集装箱班轮公司中，中国中远集运、中海集运分别排名第六和第七位。

（二）交通运输业最新开放情况

1. 海峡两岸海上直航

2014 年，台湾海峡两岸海上客货运输继续保持增长态势，共完成货运量 5459 万吨、客运量 177.9 万人次，同比分别增长 3.5%、13.8%。其中，大陆至台湾货运量 3448 万吨，同比增长 4.3%，客运量 90.7 万人次，同比增长 14%；台湾至大陆货运量 2011 万吨，同比增长 2.3%，客运量 87.2 万人次，同比增长 13.7%。

受两岸旅游热的影响，大陆与台湾本岛客运量继续大幅增长，全年完成 16.7 万人次，同比增长 16.3%。福建沿海与台湾金门、马祖、澎湖客运量止跌回升，完成 157 万人次，同比增长 13.5%；两岸间邮轮运输完成 4.2 万人次，同比增长 15.9%。

两岸货运结构调整取得阶段性成果，普通散杂货物运量 4 年来第一次出现增长，完成 2086 万吨，同比增长 1%；液体化工品、液化气运量继续保持增长，分别完成 563 万吨、88 万吨，同比增长 1.6%、29%。集装箱运量保持快速增长，完成 225 万标箱，同比增长 9.4%；在交通运输部有关促进两岸航运中心发展的政策作用下，两岸中转集装箱运量已连续 15 个月保持增长，2014 年完成 89 万标箱，同比增长 20%。

两岸“三通”6 年来，海上直航港口从 73 个增加到了 85 个，参与的公司和船舶从 43 家、122 艘增加到了 121 家、300 艘，6 年累计完成货运量 3.6 亿吨，集装箱运量 1100 万标箱，客运量 942 万人次。

2. 港航服务业

2014 年，交通运输部围绕行业发展的形势和要求，积极推进海运业上升为国家战略以及上海自贸区建设，贯彻落实中央关于进一步简政放权的要求，强化航运市场管理。

推动出台了《国务院关于促进海运业健康发展的若干意见》，提出到 2020 年基本建成安全、便捷、高效、绿色、具有国际竞争力的现代海运体系，适应国民经济安全运行和对外贸易发展需要的总体发展目标。发布了《交通运输部关于加快现代航运服务业发展的意见》，为下一步培育和发展现代航运服务业明确了目标、任务。按照上海自贸区总体方案要求，发布了《关于中国（上海）自由贸易试验区试行扩大国际船舶运输和国际船舶管理业务外商投资比例实施办法的公告》。试点允许设立不受股比限制的中外合资、合作企业开展国际船舶运输业务；试点允许设立中外合资、合作企业经营公共国际船舶代理业务，外资股比放宽至 51%；试点允许设立外商独资企业经营国际船舶管理、国际海运货物装卸、国际集装箱站和堆场业务；开展中资非五星旗国际航行船舶沿海捎带在上海的试点工作。实施国际集装箱班轮运价精细化报备制度，完成了 P3 经营者集中审查工作，对 G6 和 CKYHE 联盟联营协议报备工作进行了调查处理，开展了中日班轮航线运价备案执行情况检查。取消国际航行船舶转关运输备案、内外贸同船运输备案等许可事项。

截至 2014 年年底，我国持有国际船舶经营许可证的公司 246 家。外商在华设立独资船务公司 40 家，较上年减少 2 家；独资船务公司设立分公司 239 家，比上年增加 14 家。外商在华设立外商独资集装箱运输服务公司 7 家，分公司 73 家，较上年均没有变化。在华开展班轮运输业务的中外公司共 146 家，比上年减少 7 家。

3. 对外合作

2014 年，中国与保加利亚正式签署双边海运协定，与丹麦、加拿大、韩国、欧盟举行年度海运会谈，结合国际航运形势，主要围绕市场竞争秩序监管、节能环保技术交流、参与国际海运事务、航运安全发展等方面进行磋商及政策交流，同时，积极反映我方企业在国外经营诉求，为企业在海外经营营造良好环境，进一步密切了与相关国家和地区的海运交流与合作。在南京召开第十五届东北亚港湾局长会议，中日韩三方围绕着“港口转型升级发展”主题，就各国港口发展最新情况及共同关心的问题进行了相互通报和交流。

（三）运输服务贸易

2014 年，中国运输服务贸易进出口总额为 1344 亿美元，同比增长 1.8%，在中国服务贸易进出口总额中的占比为 21.9%。2014 年，中国运输服务贸易逆差为 579 亿美元，比 2012 年的 567 亿美元增长 2.2%。2014 年运输服务贸易逆差占中国服务贸易总逆差的 38.3%，比重比 2013 年下降 7.5 个百分点；运输服务贸易在中国服务贸易逆差行业中，属于第二大逆差行业，旅游服务贸易从 2012 年开始，成为中国服务贸易的第一大逆差行业，2014 年其逆差为 1079 亿美元。

（交通运输部规划研究院）

中国航空运输业对外开放情况

一、2014年中国民用航空行业发展情况

民航业深入贯彻党的十八大，十八届三中、四中全会和中央经济工作会议精神，认真落实中央领导批示精神和《国务院关于促进民航业发展的若干意见》，坚持安全第一，稳中求进，深化改革，各项工作取得较大成绩。在世界经济复苏缓慢，国内经济下行压力较大的情况下，2014年民航主要运输指标继续保持平稳较快增长。

全行业完成运输总周转量748.12亿吨公里，比上年增加76.39亿吨公里，增长11.4%，其中旅客周转量560.34亿吨公里，比上年增加58.91亿吨公里，增长11.7%；货邮周转量187.77亿吨公里，比上年增加17.48亿吨公里，增长10.3%。

国内航线完成运输周转量508.00亿吨公里，比上年增加46.96亿吨公里，增长10.2%，其中港澳台航线完成16.17亿吨公里，比上年增加1.95亿吨公里，增长13.7%；国际航线完成运输周转量240.11亿吨公里，比上年增长29.44亿吨公里，增长14.0%。

全行业完成旅客运输量39195万人次，比上年增加3798万人次，增长10.7%。国内航线完成旅客运输量36040万人次，比上年增加3298万人次，增长10.1%，其中港澳台航线完成1005万人次，比上年增加101万人次，增长11.2%；国际航线完成旅客运输量3155万人次，比上年增加500万人次，增长18.8%。全行业完成货邮运输量594.1万吨，比上年增长5.9%。国内航线完成货邮运输量425.7万吨，比上年增长4.7%，其中港澳台航线完成22.3万吨，比上年增长12.5%；国际航线完成货邮运输量168.4万吨，比上年增长9.0%。

在通航城市方面，截至2014年年底，定期航班国内通航城市198个（不含香港、澳门、台湾）。我国航空公司国际定期航班通航48个国家的123个城市，国内航空公司定期航班从37个内地城市通航香港，从11个内地城市通航澳门，大陆航空公司从43个大陆城市通航台湾地区。

表1　　2013、2014年中国运输统计数据

年度	运输总周转量（亿吨公里）	客运量（万人）	旅客周转量（亿吨公里）	货运量（万吨）	货邮周转量（亿吨公里）
2013年	671.72	35 397	501.43	561	170.29
2014年	748.12	39 195	560.34	594.1	187.77
同比增长	11.4%	10.7%	11.7%	5.9%	10.3%
年度	国际航线（条）*	国际客运量（万人）	国际货运量（万吨）	运输飞机（架）	旅客吞吐量（亿人次）
2013年	534	2 655	154.5	2 145	7.54
2014年	604	3 155	168.4	2 370	8.32
同比增长	13.1%	18.8%	9%	10.5%	10.2%

注：* 含港澳台航线。

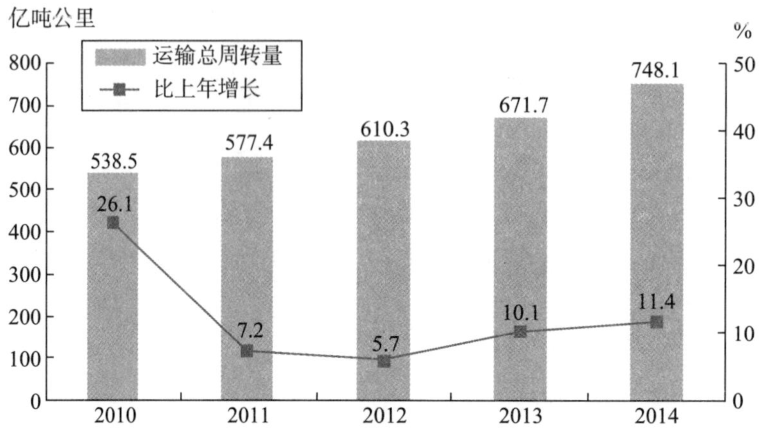

图 1　2010—2014 年民航运输总周转量

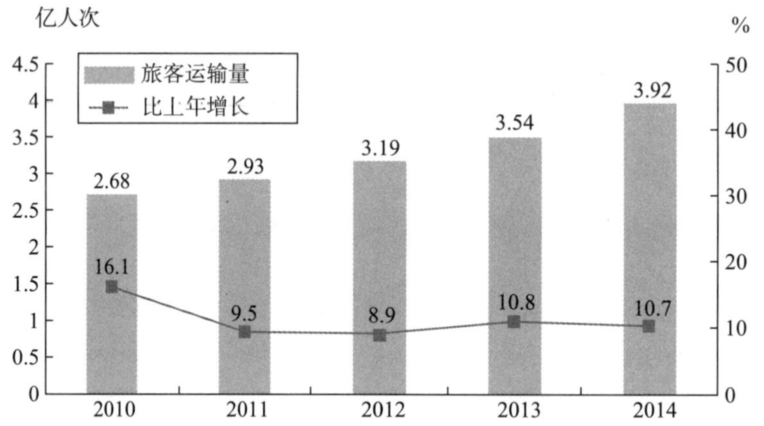

图 2　2010—2014 年民航旅客运输量

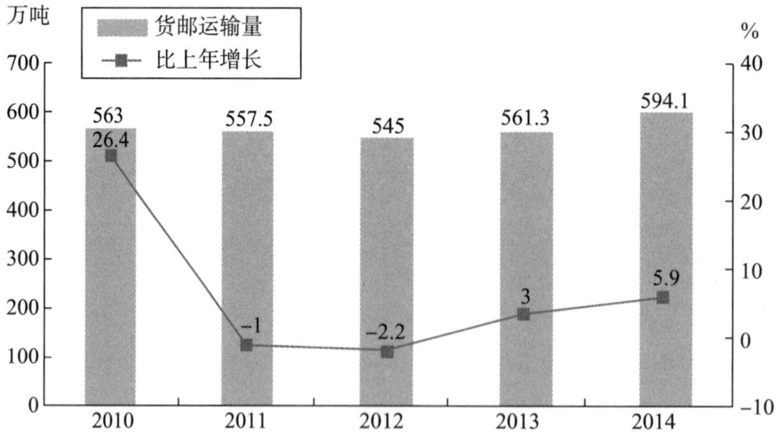

图 3　2010—2014 年民航货邮运输量

二、2014 年中国民航的对外开放情况

截至 2014 年年底，我国与其他国家或地区签订双边航空运输协定 116 个，比 2013 年底增加 1 个。其中：亚洲 43 个国家以及中国—东盟航空运输协定，非洲 23 个国家，欧洲 36 个国家，美洲 9 个国家，大洋洲 4 个国家。

2014 年，民航局积极参与中国—澳大利亚、中国—韩国等自贸区涉及民航领域开放措施谈判工作，并就地面服务、航空器维修以及计算机订座系统（CRS）等领域的内容完成了实质性谈判，进一步推动民航业对外有序开放。其中，中国—澳大利亚自贸区方面，澳方采用了负面清单的服务贸易开放模式，在航空器维修、空运服务的销售与营销、CRS、机场地面服务、通用航空服务领域对中国服务提供者完全开放，中方在入世承诺的基础上在航空器维修、空运服务的销售与营销、CRS 和机场地面服务等领域对澳大利亚服务提供者扩大了开放（取消澳大利亚服务提供者从事航空器维修服务承揽国际市场业务义务的要求，允许澳大利亚根据双边航空运输协定有权从事经营的企业在中国设立办事处，允许澳大利亚服务提供者与中国 CRS 服务提供者以合资形式在中国提供 CRS 服务，且中方应在合资企业中控股或处于支配地位，允许澳大利亚服务提供者设立合资企业提供部分地面服务）；中国—韩国自贸区方面，韩方在航空器维修、空运服务的销售与营销、CRS 服务领域对中国服务提供者完全开放，中方在入世承诺基础上在 CRS 服务领域对韩国服务提供者扩大了开放（允许韩国服务提供者与中国 CRS 服务提供者以合资形式在中国提供 CRS 服务，且中方应在合资企业中控股或处于支配地位）①。

2014 年，民航配合商务部完成 CEPA 框架下广东省对港澳服务贸易自由化工作，在港澳地区继续稳妥推进民航领域开放②。在新达成的协议中，首次采用了服务贸易负面清单的开放模式，大大推动了内地与港澳贸易自由化进程，也为 ECFA 和其他自贸区建设积累了经验。

（中国民用航空局政策法规司　陈婧丹）

① 《中华人民共和国政府和澳大利亚政府自由贸易协定》及《中华人民共和国政府和大韩民国政府自由贸易协定》已分别于 2015 年 6 月 17 日、2015 年 6 月 1 日正式签订。

② 《〈内地与香港关于建立更紧密经贸关系的安排〉关于在广东与香港基本实现服务贸易自由化的协议》。

中国房地产业基本情况

一、房地产市场调控政策及市场运行基本情况

（一）房地产市场调控工作情况

2014年以来，党中央、国务院高度重视房地产市场出现的新情况新变化，多次做出重要批示指示，召开专题会议，研究部署房地产市场调控工作，要求密切关注市场走势，妥善采取有效措施，促进房地产市场平稳健康发展。

按照党中央、国务院统一部署和2014年“两会”《政府工作报告》提出的“分类调控”要求，住房城乡建设部采取多种形式开展深入调研，加强市场分析和研判，做好调控政策储备，适时采取有关措施。指导地方政府承担调控主体权责，因地因时施策，主动科学合理地进行调控，促进市场平稳运行。配合人民银行、银监会下发《关于进一步做好住房金融服务工作的通知》，加大对居民家庭自住和改善性购房的信贷支持力度，放开对第三套及以上住房的限贷政策；同时，扩大市场化融资渠道，支持房地产企业利用银行间债券市场直接融资。配合财税主管部门加快研究完善差别化住房税收等政策，合理降低住房交易环节税负。配合国土资源部研究加强土地供应分类调控政策措施，严把供地总闸门。加强舆论引导，稳定市场预期。

各地结合当地实际，陆续采取了一些针对性措施。目前，多数城市适时暂停了限价、限签等行政性措施；实施住房限购措施的城市中，大多数城市调整或取消了住房限购措施；一些地方还出台了稳定房地产市场的综合性政策措施。这些举措对稳定市场预期、促进市场平稳运行起到了一定的积极作用。

（二）房地产市场运行基本情况

2014年，全国房地产市场进入调整期，市场呈现下行态势，但运行总体尚属平稳。

1. 房地产开发投资平稳增长

据国家统计局数据，2014年，全国房地产开发投资9.5万亿元，同比增长10.5%，增速比城镇固定资产投资增速低5.2个百分点，比2013年增速回落9.3个百分点。分区域看，东、中、西部房地产开发投资额分别为5.29万亿、2.07万亿和2.14万亿元，同比增速分别为10.4%、8.5%和12.8%。全年商品房新开工面积18亿平方米，同比下降10.7%；房地产开发企业土地购置面积3.3亿平方米，同比下降14%。

2. 商品房交易量同比下降

据国家统计局数据，2014年，全国新建商品房销售12.1亿平方米，同比下降7.6%。其中，新建住宅销售10.5亿平方米，同比下降9.1%。新建商品房销售额7.6万亿元，同比下降6.3%。分区域看，东、中、西部新建商品房销售面积同比分别下降13.7%、3.9%和增长0.6%。

3. 商品房待售面积有所增加

据国家统计局数据，2014年末，全国已竣工商品房待售面积6.2亿平方米，比2013年年末增加1.3亿平方米，同比增长26.1%。其中，已竣工住宅待售面积4.1亿平方米，比2013年年末增加8281万平方米，同比增长25.6%。

二、房屋交易与权属管理基本情况

（一）大力发展住房租赁市场

会同有关部门研究有关政策措施，鼓励基金或民间资金成立专营房屋租赁的机构，开展房屋租赁专业化规模化经营；鼓励房地产开发企业对其开发的项目进行长期租赁经营；鼓励大型房地产经纪机构开展房屋租赁托管业务。选取北京、上海、广州、深圳4个城市作为房地产投资信托基金（REITs）试点城市，研究制定试点方案。指导各地贯彻落实《商品房屋租赁管理办法》，稳定租赁关系，规范租赁行为，落实房屋租赁登记备案制度。

（二）加强房屋交易管理

指导各地以商品房预售资金监管为核心，加强预售许可的事中、事后监管，提高商品房预售门槛。指导各地搭建存量房交易服务平台，为群众、

中介机构提供房源发布、房源核验服务。会同国家工商总局出台《商品房买卖合同示范文本》，强化合同网上备案管理和交易资金监管等制度，保护买受人权利，有效杜绝一房多卖，防止市场交易风险。研究起草《关于加强房地产交易与产权管理的通知》(目前正在征求地方意见)。

(三) 规范房屋登记管理

认真落实国务院机构改革和职能转变工作要求，配合有关部门做好《不动产登记暂行条例》的制定工作。建立健全房屋登记制度，指导地方落实《房地产登记技术规程》，严格实行房屋登记官制度，积极开展房屋登记审核人员确认与培训考核工作。

(四) 加强房地产中介监管

指导各地规范市场准入，建立经纪人协理制度，引导房地产中介机构依法备案。完善行业诚信体系建设，健全机构和人员信用档案，加大对存在违法违规的机构、游离在政府部门监管之外的“黑中介”的查处和公示力度。发挥行业组织的作用，强化行业自律，鼓励地方积极组建行业协会。

三、物业管理发展基本情况

(一) 推动物业管理行业健康发展

贯彻落实服务业发展“十二五”规划，监督指导各地建立健全地方性政策法规，引导支持地方制定促进物业管理发展的扶持政策。对36个大中城市物业服务收费基本情况和一二三线代表性城市高中低档楼盘物业服务收费标准进行了调研，并针对物业服务收费存在的突出问题，会同发展改革委价格司研究完善物业服务收费政策。会同商务部和香港方面就香港物业服务提供者申请内地物业服务企业资质相关问题进行了协商并达成一致。协助国家机关事务管理局制定关于在京中央和国家机关职工住宅区物业管理改革意见和规范维修资金使用管理文件。配合国家质检总局研究维修资金用于电梯应急维修等问题。

(二) 加强和改进物业管理市场监管

贯彻落实国务院行政审批制度改革要求，提出物业服务企业一级资质核定和物业管理师执业资格注册认定的改革建议。印发《物业管理师继续教育暂行办法》，逐步规范物业管理师注册。督促山东、湖北、广东等地依法查处物业管理过程中的违法违规行为，撤销不合格物业服务企业的资质证书。

(三) 认真做好房屋使用安全和白蚁防治工作

研究城镇危旧房屋使用安全问题，提出政策措施建议报部领导。配合工程质量安全监管司，监督指导各地开展老楼危楼安全排查工作，并对部分省市进行了实地督查。监督检查全国白蚁防治中心重点工作完成情况和科研实验室建设情况，开展白蚁防治工程质量管理体系建设等课题研究。

四、城市房屋征收基本情况

(一) 建立健全房屋征收配套法规政策

各地相继制定了贯彻《条例》的规范性文件。其中，浙江、四川、山东等省制定了地方性法规，上海、湖南、河北、甘肃、云南、新疆、宁夏、福建、江西等省份出台了地方政府规章；青岛、吉林等城市制定了地方性法规，深圳、长沙、武汉、石家庄、西安、济南、长春等城市出台了地方政府规章。

(二) 稳步推进房屋征收与补偿信息系统建设

为进一步规范房屋征收与补偿行为，促进房屋征收与补偿活动公开、公平、公正，2014年6月，印发了《关于推进国有土地上房屋征收与补偿信息系统建设的指导意见》(建房［2014］95号)，要求各地明确任务分工、统一建设标准、确定进度安排，认真落实相关保障措施，大力推进房屋征收与补偿信息系统建设，提高房屋征收与补偿工作信息化水平。各地也都按要求积极推进房屋征收与补偿系统建设。

(三) 努力破解房屋征收强制执行难题

2014年8月，组织召开了房屋征收强制执行工作座谈会，研究讨论当前房屋征收过程中强制执行面临的问题及原因；9月，与最高人民法院行政审判庭在长春联合召开了国有土地上房屋征收工作经验交流会，总结交流法院、行政机关共同推动房屋征收工作好的经验和做法，努力解决强制执行问题。10月，将吉林等地在完善法规政策、健全工作机构、推进司法与行政之间的良性互动方面好的经验和做法以简报形式印发，供各地参考借鉴。

(四) 继续落实房屋征收与补偿信息公开工作

按照国务院办公厅要求，继续贯彻落实《关于推进国有土地上房屋征收与补偿信息公开工作的意见》（建房［2012］84 号）、《关于进一步加强国有土地上房屋征收与补偿信息公开工作的通知》（建房［2013］133 号），督促地方认真开展房屋征收与补偿信息公开工作。各地按照有关规定和要求，对房屋征收与补偿信息公开工作，进行了统一部署和安排，大力推进房屋征收信息公开。

（住房和城乡建设部房地产市场监管司）

中国教育业基本情况

一、教育行业发展概况

（一）国际发展概况

2014年度，全球经济进入国际金融危机后期调整阶段，复苏态势疲软，教育服务市场总体平稳。2014年，美国接受了886052名外国留学生，比上年增长8.2%，继续保持全球接受留学生第一大国地位。由此创造经济净收益267.92亿美元，比上年增长11.85%。2014年，中国新增出国留学人数突破45万，达到45.98万人，在外学习人员达108.89万人，由此而形成的教育服务进口贸易额约1628.01亿元人民币（约合259.01亿美元），继续保持全球输出留学生第一大国地位。

据世界贸易组织（WTO）资料，截至2014年底，160个成员中，共有70个经济体承诺开放了教育服务市场。根据经济合作与发展组织（OECD）统计数据测算，2014年全球高等教育阶段国际学生总数接近500万人。另外，作为教育服务贸易之商业存在模式的海外办学继续稳步发展，继欧美教育发达国家之后，部分发展中地区大国纷纷加入此行列。

（二）国内发展概况

1. 义务教育方面

义务教育阶段，小学在校生规模出现反弹，初中在校生规模继续下降。截至2014年年底，全国共有小学20.14万所，比上年减少1.22万所；在校生9451.07万人，比上年增加90.52万人。共有初中学校5.26万所（其中职业初中26所），比上年减少181所；在校学生4384.63万人，比上年减少55.5万人。①

2. 学前教育与特殊教育方面

学前教育规模继续较快发展。截至2014年年底，全国共有幼儿园20.99万所，比上年增加1.13万所，在园幼儿（包括附设班）4050.71万人，比上年增加156.02万人。幼儿园园长和教师共208.03万人，比上年增加19.52万人。学前教育毛入园率达到70.5%，比上年提高3个百分点。特殊教育学校数量和在校生数量均有所增加。全国共有特殊教育学校2000所，比上年增加67所；在校生39.49万人，比上年增加2.68万人。

3. 高中阶段教育方面

高中阶段教育总规模继续呈萎缩态势。截至2014年年底，全国高中阶段教育（包括普通高中、成人高中、中等职业教育）共有学校2.57万所，比上年减少548所；在校学生4170.65万人，比上年减少199.27万人。高中阶段毛入学率86.5%，比上年提高0.5个百分点。其中中等职业教育在校学生1755.28万人，比上年减少167.69万人，占高中阶段教育在校生总数的42.09%，比上年下降2个百分点。

4. 高等教育方面

高等教育保持稳步发展趋势。截至2014年年底，全国各类高等教育总规模达到3559万人，比上年增加99万人，高等教育毛入学率达到37.5%，比上年提高3个百分点。全国共有普通高等学校和成人高等学校2824所，比上年增加36所。其中，普通高等学校2529所（含独立学院283所），比上年增加36所；成人高等学校295所，比上年减少2所。普通高校中本科院校1202所，比上年增加32所；高职（专科）院校1327所，比上年增加6所。全国共有培养研究生的单位788个，比上年减少42个；其中高等学校571个，科研机构217个。

普通高等教育本专科在校生2547.7万人，比上年增加79.63万人，增长3.23%。成人高等教育本专科在校生653.12万人，比上年增加26.71万人。全国高等教育自学考试学历教育报考703.37万人次。

5. 成人培训与扫盲教育方面

全国接受各种非学历高等教育的学生736.66万人次，比上年增长8.56%；当年已结业920.28

① 数据来源：《2014年全国教育事业发展统计公报》。

万人次。接受各种非学历中等教育的学生达4613.67万人次，当年已结业5084.48万人次。全国职业技术培训机构10.51万所，比上年减少0.72万所。成人初等学校1.967万所，在校生162.69万人。

6. 民办教育方面

民办教育稳步发展。全国共有各级各类民办学校（教育机构）15.52万所，比上年增加6300所；在校生达4301.91万人，比上年增加223.6万人。另外，还有其他民办培训机构2万所，867.94万人次接受了培训。

二、最新开放情况

2014年新建的中法人文交流机制，与中俄人文交流机制（2001年）、中美人文交流机制（2010年）、中英人文交流机制（2012年）、中国欧盟人文交流机制（2012年）一起，成为我国对外关系的重要支柱之一，推动与有关国家的教育交流合作全面发展。

截至2014年年底，我国与近200个国家和地区以及联合国教科文组织等建立了教育交流合作关系，与俄罗斯、美国、欧盟、英国等国家和地区建立了人文交流高层磋商机制。同时，与德国、英国、法国、加拿大、澳大利亚、意大利、爱尔兰、瑞典、丹麦等39个国家和地区签署了学历学位互认协议，与澳大利亚、印度、韩国、俄罗斯等20个国家签署了亚洲和太平洋地区承认高等教育学历、文凭和学位的地区公约。目前，我国已与有关国家和地区建立了46个部级、司局级磋商机制或联合工作组。

截至2014年年底，我国与20个国家和地区签署了12个自贸协定，其中大部分协定包括相互开放教育服务的具体承诺。

三、重要政策与措施

2014年，是全面贯彻落实党的十八大和十八届二中、三中、四中全会精神，全面深化教育领域改革的起跑之年。有关部门将扩大教育开放作为教育综合改革的重要突破口，着力推动体制机制改革，转变政府职能。

2014年，我国召开了新中国成立以来的首次全国留学工作会议，统筹部署出国留学和来华留学工作。习近平总书记、李克强总理分别为留学工作会议做出了重要批示。会议明确提出了“支持留学、鼓励回国、来去自由、发挥作用”新16字出国留学工作方针，做出了坚持“五个并重”（即人才培养和发挥作用并重、出国留学和来华留学并重、公费留学与自费留学并重、扩大规模和提高质量并重、依法管理和完善服务并重），实现“安全留学、健康留学、文明留学、成功留学”的工作部署，并提出加大外语非通用语种人才、国际组织人才、国别区域研究人才、拔尖创新人才和来华青年杰出人才五类紧缺人才的培养力度。

2014年，积极配合中美投资协定谈判，推动教育领域不断深入开放。在国务院统一部署下，教育部与发改委、商务部反复磋商，做好教育领域政策法规梳理，研究制订教育领域负面清单，为推动中美投资协定谈判顺利进行做好了充分准备。同时，充分发挥自贸区在探索推进简政放权、放管结合及负面清单管理等方面的独特优势，为教育领域推进综合改革、健全监管机制、进一步扩大对外开放积累了宝贵经验。大力推动上海自贸区中外合作经营性培训机构试点工作，制定《中国（上海）自由贸易试验区中外合作经营性培训机构暂行管理办法》及与之配套的《申请指南》。稳步推进综合改革试验区工作，在宁波市、湖南省、上海市三个教育国际合作交流综合改革试验区和苏州独墅湖国际化示范区基础上，推进深圳教育国际合作交流综合改革试验区工作，并取得初步成效。

2014年，有关部门加强了中外合作办学质量保障工作，加强了处罚和引退机制建设。按照《中外合作办学评估方案（2014年）》要求，确认77个项目、15个机构参加年度评估。要求2013年评估工作中的64个违规招生的项目和机构限期进行整改，对其中的严重超规模招生项目进行全国通报批评，不合格项目一律停止相关办学活动，对已停止办学活动的252个本科以下层次办学机构和项目进行了办学信息公示。

四、教育服务贸易分析

2014年，中国教育服务保持稳步发展势头。新增出国留学生45.98万人，来华留学生达37万人，分别比上年有所增长。截至2014年年底，全国共举办合作办学项目和机构达1782个，在校生规模55万人，毕业生超过150万人。

（一）中国跨境服务贸易

1. 出国留学继续快速发展

2014年，出国留学生人数保持稳步增长。新增出国留学人数达到45.98万人，比上年增加4.59万人，增长了11.1%，增速较上年度有所加快。其中国家公派2.13万人，单位公派1.55万人，自费留学42.3万人；自费留学生占92.0%，比上年降低0.8个百分点。截至2014年年底，共有108.89万名中国学生在国外进行相关阶段的学习和研究，比上年增加1.38万人。

2014年各类留学回国人员总数达36.48万人，比上年增加1.13万人，同比增长3.2%；其中，国家公派1.61万人，单位公派1.26万人，自费留学33.61万人。①

据初步测算，108.89万名中国学生在外学习，直接带动了约1628.01亿元人民币（合259.01亿美元）的教育服务进口贸易，为相关国家带来数量可观的经济收益。其中，在美中国留学生274439名，由此而自美国进口教育服务约82.98亿美元，美国继续保持我教育服务第一大进口国地位。

2. 来华留学保持稳步发展

2014年，全年在华学习的外国留学人员总数突破37万人，共有来自203个国家和地区的377054名各类来华留学人员，分布在全国31个省、自治区、直辖市（不含台湾省、香港特别行政区和澳门特别行政区）的775所高等院校、科研院所和其他教学机构中学习。来华留学生总数、生源国家和地区数、我国接受留学生单位数及中国政府奖学金生人数等连续刷新历史纪录。

与2013年相比，2014年来华留学生总数增加了20555名，同比增长5.77%。其中中国政府奖学金生36943名，同比增长10.87%；自费生340111名，同比增长5.2%。

按留学生类别统计，学历生164394名，占来华留学生总数的43.6%，同比增长11.16%，增幅高于来华留学生总数增长速度约5个百分点，来华留学生结构进一步改善。

（二）商业存在

1. 境内的外国商业存在

截至2014年年底，经审批机关依法批准设立和举办的中外合作办学机构和项目共1782个，在校生规模55万人。2014年，批准新建了香港中文大学（深圳）和温州肯恩大学2所具有独立法人资质的中外合作办学机构，批准上海理工大学中德国际学院等非独立法人中外合作办学机构8个，批准西南交通大学等“985”“211”高校举办23个机构和项目，完成本科以下（包括非学历教育）中外合作办学机构项目备案编号33个。2014年，公告停办了252个本科以下层次办学机构和项目。

2. 境外的中国商业存在

2014年，新建孔子学院35所，新增孔子课堂205个。截至2014年年底，共建立孔子学院475所，孔子课堂851个，分布在126个国家（地区）。2014年，孔子学院和孔子课堂共有专兼职教职员工33745人，比上年增长17.7%；注册学员111万人，比上年增长30.6%。2014年，有1.55万名汉语教师和志愿者赴139个国家教授汉语，比上年增加1100人。②

各类汉语考试考生达542万人，比2013年增长8.0%。其中，参加HSK、HSKK、BCT、YCT等收费考试的考生达43万人，比2013年增长15.6%。全球考点886个，比上年增长11%。

截至2014年年底，我国教育机构共举办了98个境外教育机构和项目，其中办学机构4家，办学项目94个，分布在14个国家和地区。

五、教育行业发展展望

（一）全球教育服务大市场逐渐形成

随着全球化深入发展，教育要素跨境流动日趋便利和频繁，全球教育服务大市场正在逐渐形成③。与货物贸易和其他服务贸易相比较，教育服务的全球性更加明显，地区性尚不突出。无论发达

① 数据来源：教育部国际合作与交流司。

② 资料来源：国家汉办。

③ 朱兴德《发展教育，经略世界》，广西人民出版社，2013。

成员还是发展中成员，教育要素的跨境流动都将更加广泛地出现，较难出现排他性的地区性或双边性教育服务市场。鉴于教育服务广泛的人文影响，诸多排他性区域贸易安排很可能受到教育服务发展的冲击。特别是随着近期负面清单模式在诸多地区性贸易谈判中的广泛应用，预计全球教育服务市场将更加开放。教育服务市场走回封闭式发展已不再可能。

（二）国内教育国际化热情不减

国内新一轮教育国际化热潮持续升温，尚看不到减退的趋势。出国留学人数仍然在增加，热衷合作办学的院校依然很多，中外合作办学审批依然走俏，地方政府兴办国际学校、国际大学的热情依然很高。随着中国政府提出“一带一路”倡议，筹划开展境外办学的院校越来越多。在行政审批改革正式取消境外办学审批之后，预计不久的将来，会出现一波境外办学的新高潮。

（三）留学教育依然是教育服务发展主体

预计未来很长一段时期内，留学教育将继续担纲教育服务发展主体，继续担纲教育服务贸易主要模式。无论发达成员还是发展中成员，学生跨境流动将更加便利，选择将更加多样化，这有利于人类文明的交流与传播。短期内，美国作为全球接受留学生第一大国的地位不会改变，中国作为输出留学生第一大国的地位也不会改变。随着“一带一路”倡议的全面实施，预计赴“一带一路”沿线国家学习的中国学生会逐渐多起来，“一带一路”沿线地区也将继续作为来华留学生的主要来源地。

（上海市教科院 WTO 教育服务研究中心主任　朱兴德）

中国新闻出版业基本情况

2014 年，全国新闻出版系统紧紧围绕党和国家工作大局谋划和推进新闻出版工作，改革发展管理服务和自身建设各项工作取得新成绩。

一、深入学习宣传贯彻习近平总书记系列重要讲话精神，主题出版和精品生产取得新成果

坚持把主题出版作为唱响主旋律、传播正能量的首要任务，努力催生精品力作。

（一）全力抓好习近平总书记系列讲话精神重点读物出版发行

认真做好安排部署、编校印制、宣传发行各项工作，《习近平总书记系列重要讲话读本》《习近平谈治国理政》《摆脱贫困》《之江新语》《十八大以来重要文献选编》等重点出版物深受读者欢迎。截至 2015 年 3 月，《读本》发行超过 1700 万册，《习近平论治国理政》发行超过 366 万册，稳居畅销书排行榜前列。《全面深化改革书系》《中国能赢：只有去中国才能看到未来》《丰碑》《中国之最》等优秀出版物深受欢迎。报刊、网络、数字出版结合实际，积极宣传阐释系列重要讲话精神。

（二）精心做好重大主题出版

围绕培育和践行社会主义核心价值观、纪念邓小平同志诞辰 110 周年、庆祝新中国成立 65 周年、依法治国等重大主题和重要时间节点，推出了《爱国四章》《国家的儿子》《邓小平传（1904—1974）》《邓小平文集》《改革开放元勋画传丛书》《大美昆曲》等重点图书和《家风·家教·家训》《国旗的故事》《圆梦中国　德耀中华》等音像电子出版物。党的十八届四中全会文件及辅导读物出版发行工作成效显著，截至 2014 年 11 月月底，《会议公报》《决定》及有关辅导读物发行超过 800 万册，相关民族文字版本发行超过 20 万册。报刊、网络深入宣传社会主义核心价值观，做好禁毒防艾、航海日、证券期货信息、残疾人事业、打击拐卖妇女儿童、安全生产等公益主题宣传，积极传播正能量。

（三）积极抓好精品规划生产

继续推进精品出版战略，积极完善国家重点出版物中长期规划体系建设，形成了以“十二五”规划为主体，民文规划、古籍规划、辞书规划等专项规划为重要支撑的规划体系，“十二五”规划完成 65%，推出了一大批精品力作。认真学习贯彻文艺工作座谈会精神，召开出版界研讨会，提出文艺出版工作“抓好中心环节、推动两头发展、强化三项管理”的贯彻落实思路，原创精品出版机制进一步完善。完成《海外所藏中国古籍总目》项目总体规划和“散失海外中国古籍回归工程”总体实施方案及预算编制。实施“原动力”中国原创动漫出版扶持计划，推出一批优秀原创动漫作品。制定《关于推动网络文学健康发展的指导意见》，引导创作格调高雅健康向上的网络文学、网络游戏作品，涌现出一批网络文化精品。

二、认真贯彻落实党的十八届四中全会精神，新闻出版行政管理构建新格局

（一）治理非法出版

全国共收缴各类非法出版物 1600 余万件，查处各类“扫黄打非”案件 8300 余起，关闭近万个传播淫秽色情信息网站栏目，删除 300 余万条涉黄信息，对快播等网络企业传播淫秽色情信息行为予以严厉查处。

（二）治理报刊秩序

持续开展打击新闻敲诈和假新闻行动，查办并公开通报经济日报驻河南记者站等 4 批、27 家报刊单位违法违规典型案件。全国“扫黄打非”办督办假媒体、假记者站、假记者重点案件 17 起。强化报刊主管主办、属地管理、年度核验等基本制度，吊销《中国特产报》《商务时报》出版许可证，对《西部时报》《电子世界》杂志等 9 种报刊予以停业整顿，缓验 195 种报刊、210 家记者站，注销 75 家记者站。启动清理整顿中央媒体驻地方机构工作，计划关闭、停办、合并一批驻地方机构，清退一批违规聘用的驻地方机构人员。规范期刊出版

秩序，查办期刊刊发质量低劣论文案件 112 起。

(三) 治理出版质量

深入开展出版物质量专项年活动，深化少儿出版物市场整治专项行动，开展中小学教辅材料专项治理，重点查处群众反映强烈的教辅读物质量差和出版物低俗、跟风等问题，曝光 15 家出版单位 17 种不合格少儿出版物，查处 11 种少儿报刊违法违规案件，给予 7 种报刊警告处罚，处理 120 余家违规经营单位，收缴盗版或非法出版物 101221 余册（盘），没收盗版或非法出版教辅材料 191959 余册，取缔出版物市场和店档摊点 845 多个，对 18 家印刷企业和 12 家发行企业做出行政处罚。严格学术期刊出版资质，首次组织学术期刊认定，公布第一批认定的学术期刊名单共 5756 种，为实施期刊分类管理和开展学术期刊质量评估奠定了基础。严格学术期刊出版资质，扶持精品学术期刊发展，会同有关部门实施“中国科技期刊国际影响力提升计划”。加强网络文学出版引导管理，确定首批授予出版资质的网络文学出版企业，网络文学企业自我审核把关能力显著提高。

(四) 治理版权市场

积极开展打击侵犯知识产权和制售假冒伪劣商品专项行动，查办案件 532 件，其中行政处理 510 件，罚款 3321 万元，移送司法机关追究刑事责任 80 件，捣毁盗版窝点 188 个，公开案件信息 170 件。连续 10 年开展打击网络侵权盗版“剑网”行动，“剑网 2014”专项行动期间，各地版权行政执法部门共查处案件 440 起，移送司法机关 66 起，罚款人民币 352 万余元，关闭网站 750 家，全面深入打击网络侵权盗版，有力震慑了盗版侵权违法分子。开展国家版权监管平台升级改造及二期工程建设，启动对重点影视作品的版权预警保护。规范网络版权转载，组织 191 家各类网站签署联合倡议，推动完善网络转载许可付酬机制。推进政府机关和中央企业三级以上企业全部实现软件正版化，展示了中国政府保护知识产权的良好形象。充分发挥推进使用正版软件工作部际联席会议协调职能，通过改进软件正版化审计、软件采购、资产管理和督促检查等措施，巩固软件正版化工作成果，推进长效机制建设。

(五) 治理行业队伍

结合新版记者证统一换发，对全国 30 余万名新闻采编人员进行全员轮训和统一考核；印发《新闻从业人员职务行为信息管理办法》。严格执行《新闻采编人员不良从业记录登记办法》。首次将互联网出版专业技术人员纳入出版专业技术人员职业资格考试范围，全面推进新闻网站采编人员核发新闻记者证工作。开展马克思主义新闻出版观、文艺观培训。深入开展“好记者讲好故事”全国巡讲活动和“记录时代，记录你我”公益广告展播，推进新闻队伍正面建设。

三、全面贯彻落实党的十八届三中全会精神，改革发展取得新进展

坚持促改革、调结构、转方式相结合，抓住重要领域和关键环节攻坚克难，不断释放发展潜力，激发市场活力。

(一) 强化改革顶层设计

印发《深化新闻出版体制改革实施方案》，制订《贯彻实施党的十八届三中全会〈决定〉重要举措分工方案》，明确 23 项重点改革任务的时间表和路线图，通过 321 个新闻出版改革发展项目支持重点单位改革发展，以任务台账形式推进工作落实。

(二) 重点领域改革取得突破

取消下放新闻出版行政审批事项 14 项，提前完成本届政府减少行政审批事项 1/3 以上的目标。审批工作全程公开，实行“阳光审批”。精简并图示化许可申报材料，优化审批流程，平均审批时间缩短 1/3。印发《非公有制文化企业参与对外专项出版业务试点办法》，引导非公有制文化企业有序参与对外专项出版业务。做好中央和地方非时政类报刊出版单位转企改制收尾工作，重点推动不具有独立法人资格的报刊编辑部体制改革，报刊资源整合和结构调整有序推进。

(三) 市场主体进一步壮大

推动国有骨干出版企业兼并重组，组建中国水利水电出版传媒、辽宁北方期刊出版、陕西新华出版传媒等一批集团公司，中国教育出版传媒股份有限公司等引入战略投资者，东方航空传媒股份有限公司等企业上市融资。12 家新闻出版企业入选“文化企业 30 强”。15 家出版发行内地上市企业整体规模继续壮大，第三季度市值 2284.23 亿元，营业收入、资产总额同比增长 8.78%和 20.42%，跑赢沪深两市大盘。

（四）市场持续繁荣

继续加大实体书店扶持力度，财政奖励试点地区从12个城市扩大到12个省区市，55家特色品牌书店获奖励资助1.185亿元，鼓励社会资本设立小微出版服务企业的配套政策更加完善。图书批发零售环节免增值税政策全面落地，实现了全行业普惠。图书零售市场回暖，2014年前11个月实体书店零售额同比增长3.24%。大型书城和特色书店增势强劲，网上书店销售继续保持高速增长。书店连锁经营、“第三方”配送业务健康发展。加大展会市场化改革力度，全国图书交易博览会实现订货码洋13.26亿元、零售1200余万元，上海书展实现销售7029万元，显示出旺盛的市场需求。

（五）产业转型升级进程加快

主要经济指标平稳增长，规模继续扩大。新闻出版统计快报数据显示，2014年新闻出版业主要经济指标保持平稳增长，全国出版、印刷和发行服务实现营业收入1.95万亿元，较2013年增长7.0%；利润总额1542.13亿元，较2013年增长7.1%。出版结构进一步优化，截至12月5日，新书品种增速同比下降2.9%，再版品种同比增加31.9%，优质常销书所占比重显著增加。印刷业结构调整效果显著，逐步由环渤海、长三角、珠三角三足鼎立向东部、中部均衡发展过渡，中部地区产值已达珠三角地区85%，增量占全国增量25%；骨干特色企业综合实力继续壮大，全国规模以上重点印刷企业3075家，资产总额、印刷产值占全行业的比重50%以上；绿色印刷体系建设不断完善，继上年财政投入2.9亿元后再投入2.1亿元支持绿色印刷更新改造，撬动社会投资约150亿元。全国中小学教科书全部实现绿色印刷，三分之一出版社采用绿色印刷方式，超过700家企业通过绿色印刷认证。新闻出版产业基地（园区）建设蓬勃发展，管理工作纳入法制轨道，长三角地区、珠三角地区、环渤海地区以及西部地区新闻出版产业带已基本形成，集约化专业化水平明显提升。以文化创意为核心的版权产业蓬勃发展，第五届中国国际版权博览会交易金额超过20亿元，推出了一批代表性强的版权示范城市、单位、园区（基地）和版权贸易基地、版权交易中心。国家数字出版产业基地建设成效显著，产业集中度进一步提升。音乐产业基地建设积极推进，中国音乐产业市场总规模达2716.56亿元。开展新闻出版业“十二五”规划中期评估，启动“十三五”规划编制工作。

（六）融合发展全面提速

认真贯彻落实习近平总书记关于媒体融合发展重要讲话和中央有关文件精神，开展专题调研，召开出版传媒集团主要负责人座谈会，在出版融合发展“是什么”“怎么看”“怎么干”“怎么管”等基本问题上理清了思想，达成了共识。融合发展运营模式探索取得成功经验，平台建设大范围铺开，组织结构、传播体系、管理体制一体化步伐不断加快，一个内容多种创意、多次开发、多次增值的生产经营方式初现雏形。争取中央文化产业发展专项资金对新闻出版产业支持21.5亿元，占支持总数的40%。联合财政部出台《关于推动新闻出版业数字化转型升级的指导意见》，协调文化产业发展专项资金支持数字化转型升级项目99个、8.1亿元，国有资本金预算支持中央出版单位数字资源库建设项目1.5亿元。数字出版营业收入3168.4亿元，较上年增长24.7%。全国数字出版转型示范工作全面展开。科技进步取得新突破，新闻出版重大科技工程顺利推进，多媒体印刷读物（MPR）、中国出版物在线信息交换（CNONIX）国内标准应用取得实质性进展，数字化转型的技术支撑进一步强化。由我国专家任召集人的国际标准关联标识符（ISLI）标准获国际标准化组织高票通过，有利于打破发达国家信息资源标识管理垄断地位，在争夺互联网时代国际话语权方面取得实质性进展。

四、切实保障和改善文化民生，新闻出版公共服务迈上新台阶

加大政策投放、资金投入和工作创新力度，加快完善以重点工程项目为抓手的工作格局，公共服务标准化均等化水平进一步提高。

（一）全民阅读活动高潮迭起

“倡导全民阅读”首次进入总理政府工作报告，湖北、江苏、深圳等地颁布专门法规，《全民阅读促进条例》立法进程加速推进，越来越多的地区将全民阅读纳入经济社会发展规划，全民阅读正在上升为国家战略。“书香中国”系列活动形成热潮，全国400多个城市常设读书节、读书月活动，8亿多人深入参与。表彰首届全国“书香之家”，996个家庭入选。积极推进“2014全民数字阅读”活

动，经过评选的 20 个以弘扬社会主义核心价值观为主题的专题数字阅读活动反响强烈。深入开展“百社千校书香童年”阅读活动，城乡阅报栏（屏）建设范围进一步扩大。继续向全国青少年推荐百种优秀图书、50 种优秀音像电子出版物，向全国读者推荐“大众喜爱的 50 种图书”，首次向全国老年人推荐百种优秀出版物，受到广大读者欢迎。李克强总理就北京三联韬奋书店 24 小时书店开业专门致信，夜间售书成为城市文化新景，全国 11 家书店加入 24 小时书店联盟。“书香中国万里行”活动积极推进，集中投放全民阅读公益广告，取得良好效果。

（二）农家书屋建设提档升级

规范农家书屋补充资金使用、书目执行、采购配送管理，指导重点出版单位针对农村农民需求加强选题策划，完善以基层管理部门和农民为主体的选书机制。抓好农家书屋春节期间开放使用，会同教育部开展暑期农村少年儿童阅读实践活动。推进卫星数字农家书屋建设，已建成数字农家书屋 2.6 万家，其中卫星数字农家书屋 1.6 万家，有效解决了边远地区、网络未通达地区报刊投送难、信息获取难问题。支持西藏建设数字内容综合服务平台，安排 30 万专项资金开展数字阅读试点工作。

（三）少数民族出版工作扎实推进

贯彻落实中央民族工作会议、第二次中央新疆工作座谈会和对口支援西藏工作 20 周年电视电话会议精神。民族地区 155 个新建和改建县级新华书店已竣工 118 个，正在施工 26 个。中央财政投入民族文字出版专项资金 1.1 亿元，支持 13 个省区民族文字出版译制项目 69 个。新疆民族文字出版及数字新媒体基地建设、西藏民族文字出版基地建设项目完成前期工作。

（四）完善公共服务政策

参与制定加快构建现代公共文化服务体系和国家基本公共文化服务保障标准等重大政策措施，将公益性出版、全民阅读和出版物采购、配送等环节纳入公共文化服务政府采购和资助目录，将农家书屋、阅报栏（屏）等相关指标纳入《国家基本公共文化服务保障标准》。开展新闻出版“十三五”公共文化服务体系规划预研，按保障标准测算，2015—2020 年新闻出版基本公共文化服务项目投入财政资金将达 130 多亿元。

五、自觉服务党和国家外交工作，对外传播能力建设实现新突破

坚持以重大活动为核心、以重要书展为平台、以重点工程为支撑，积极推动新闻出版单位和产品走出去，努力讲好中国故事、传播中国声音。

（一）新闻出版工作在外交大局中的地位作用更加凸显

习近平总书记亲自为科伦坡国际书展中国主宾国活动揭幕，并向斯里兰卡政府赠送《大中华文库》。这是国家最高领导第一次为国际书展主宾国活动揭幕。习总书记访印期间，见证了总局与印方签署新德里书展中国主宾国活动合作备忘录，亲自宣布中国将作为主宾国参加 2016 年印度新德里国际书展。李克强总理见证总局与科威特方面签署“中科经典和当代文学作品互译出版项目”，对外出版交流亮点纷呈。

（二）重要书展外宣平台功能进一步发挥

第 21 届北京国际图书博览会取得圆满成功，达成版权协议 4346 项，同比增长 18.5%；输出版权 2594 项，同比增长 24%，版权输出与引进比为 1.48∶1。北京国际图书博览会国际影响力进一步提升，跻身世界第二大国际书展。利用贝尔格莱德国际书展中国主宾国活动、巴黎图书沙龙上海主宾城市活动、东京国际书展、法兰克福书展、伦敦书展等平台，推出一批“中国梦”主题图书，《习近平论治国理政》海外发行超过 28 万册，引起国际社会广泛关注。

（三）重点工程建设扎实推进

贯彻落实习近平总书记“一丝一路”重要战略构想，启动实施“丝路书香工程”，并纳入国家战略规划重点工程立项。启动图书版权输出普遍奖励计划，充分调动了民营企业和社会个体走出去的积极性。拉加代尔全球门店销售外文版中国图书 20 万余册，全球百家华文书店中国图书联展活动销售 45 万多册图书，亚马逊“中国书店”上线图书达 31.44 万种，累计发货 17.7 万册，云南昆明新知集团等民营走出去取得积极进展。中国图书对外推广计划顺利开展，中国当代作品翻译工程有序推进，新疆、西藏、云南等边疆地区企业走出去扶持计划稳步实施，中外互译项目加快步伐。版权输出区域、品种等结构不断优化，越来越多的中国出版

物进入欧美主流市场。

（四）版权国际事务取得新进展

积极参与世界贸易组织（WTO）、世界知识产权组织（WIPO）、亚太经合组织（APEC）等对华版权事务。完成并向 WIPO 递交批准《视听表演北京条约》的政府声明。妥善处理中美、中英、中俄等双边版权关系，积极参与中澳、中韩、中日韩、东盟 10+6 自贸协定知识产权谈判，首次建立与阿拉伯国家及非洲国家版权双边关系，不断加强我国版权对外话语体系建设。

（五）两岸四地出版及版权交流合作不断扩大

第十届海峡两岸图书交易会参展图书近 10 万种 31 万册，现场销售 2653 万元。落实《海峡两岸知识产权保护合作协议》，成功举办第七届海峡两岸著作权保护研讨会暨两岸著作权主管部门工作组会议。

（国家新闻出版广电总局办公厅）

中国文化产业和对外文化贸易发展情况

2014 年，中国继续加大对发展文化产业和对外文化贸易的政策支持力度，文化产业内部各行业结构不断优化，并取得了不同程度的增长；我国文化产业和对外文化贸易发展思路逐步明确，重点更加清晰。

一、政策扶持激发活力

2014 年，推进文化创意与相关产业融合、加快发展对外文化贸易、深入推进文化金融合作、继续完善税收优惠、支持小微文化企业发展等多项文化产业支持政策密集出台，力度空前，构建了助力文化产业和对外文化贸易快速发展的强大支撑，极大地激发了文化产业和对外文化贸易发展活力。

文化产业具有的高知识性、高增值性对提升各个行业产品和服务品质，增加附加值、增强市场竞争力具有重要意义。2014 年 3 月，国务院出台《关于推进文化创意和设计服务与相关产业融合发展的若干意见》，提出建立文化创意和设计服务与相关产业全方位、深层次、宽领域的融合发展格局，是对文化产业推动经济社会发展作用的认可，也是新形势下推动产业结构转型升级的重要举措。

近年来，我国对外文化贸易规模不断扩大、结构逐步优化。统计数据显示，2003 年至 2013 年，我国文化产品进出口从 60.9 亿美元攀升至 274.1 亿美元，年均增长 16.2%；文化服务进出口从 10.5 亿美元增长到 95.6 亿美元，年均增长 24.7%①。但我国核心文化产品和服务贸易逆差仍存在，对外文化贸易占对外贸易总额比重仍然较低。在此背景下，2014 年 3 月，国务院出台了《关于加快发展对外文化贸易的意见》，从加大财税支持、强化金融服务、完善服务保障等方面对加快发展对外文化贸易、推动文化产品和服务出口做出全面部署。

文化金融合作是中国文化产业和对外文化贸易发展的重要突破点。2014 年 3 月，中国人民银行、财政部和文化部联合印发《关于深入推进文化金融合作的意见》，提出建立文化金融合作部际会商机制、完善文化金融中介服务体系、推动文化企业直接融资、创建文化金融合作试验区等举措，强调更好发挥金融政策、财政政策与文化产业政策的协同作用，鼓励金融机构大力开拓文化金融市场，推动金融机构和文化企业步入深度合作阶段。

税收优惠是支持和推动文化产业和对外文化贸易发展的重要手段。2014 年，税收优惠仍是各相关政策文件中明确提出的重点措施，且文化科技领域日益受到重视。2014 年 11 月，财政部、海关总署、国家税务总局联合发布《关于继续实施支持文化企业发展若干税收政策的通知》，规定对从事文化产业支撑技术等领域的文化企业，按规定认定为高新技术企业的，减按 15%的税率征收企业所得税。

2014 年也是小微文化企业的转折之年。7 月，文化部、工业和信息化部、财政部联合印发《关于大力支持小微文化企业发展的实施意见》，从增强创新发展能力、健全金融服务体系、完善财税支持政策等方面支持小微文化企业发展。《意见》还首次将支持小微文化企业发展与公共文化体系建设结合起来，鼓励小微文化企业参与公共文化服务和政府采购，为小微文化企业提供了更大的发展空间。

二、重点行业发展概况

（一）广播影视行业

2014 年，我国广播电视行业总收入达到 4226.27 亿元，同比增长 13.16%②，呈现出增长平稳、结构优化的良好态势。截至 2014 年年底，民营企业占广播电视节目制作机构总量约 85%的比重，成为广电产业主体生力军。各级电台电视台纷纷成立版权管理中心，优质节目价值在基于 IP 开发的基础上，不断向产业链上下游和相关产业渗透、拓展和延伸。

---

① 毛俊玉：2014 文化政策之年：文化兴国“时不我待”，载于中国文化报，2015 年 01 月 12 日。

② 牛春颖：总局发展研究中心发布蓝皮书 广播电视业 2014 年收入 4226.27 亿元，载于中国新闻出版广电报，2015 年 7 月 9 日。

2014 年我国电影票房达 296.39 亿元，同比增长 36.15%。其中国产电影票房收入 161.55 亿元，占总票房收入的 54.51%，继续保持过半份额，表明中国电影产业应对进口片挑战能力增强。同期全球票房达 375 亿美元，美国占 27%，中国占 13%，英、法、德、日、韩、印等国家票房占比均不超过 5%。在全球票房增长的 16 亿美元中，中国贡献增量的 75%，对全球电影票房增量起到了主引擎作用。

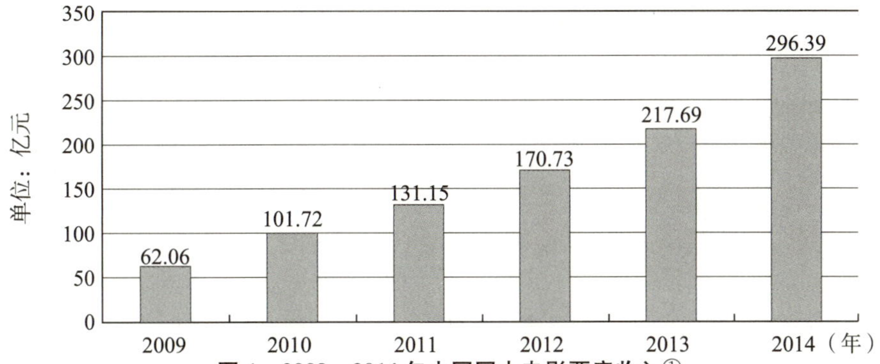

图 1　2009—2014 年中国国内电影票房收入①

近年来，进口片在中国电影市场总票房中占比呈稳定增长之势。2012 年“中美电影新政”后，3D/IMAX 等影片的增多推动了进口分账大片数量和票房的增幅。在出口方面，2013 年国产电影在海外销售数量为 45 部，累计海外票房和销售收入 14.14 亿元人民币，相较 2012 年的 10.63 亿元同比增长 33.02%，但与国内电影票房的快速增长相比，中国电影的国际认可度和市场份额仍有待提高。

随着知识产权保护意识地增强，中国电视台对模式节目逐渐认可。继引进欧美节目模式热潮后，《爸爸去哪儿》《我是歌手》等源于韩国的节目模式逐渐占据主导地位。在我国电视节目进口额逐年增长的基础上，2014 年电视节目进口额出现大幅增长，总额由 2013 年的 58658 万元攀升至 209024 万元；出口额也取得一定增长，由 2013 年的 18166 万元，增加至 27226 万元②，其中电视剧出口额始终占据我国电视节目出口的大部分份额。

（二）出版行业

2014 年全国出版、印刷和发行服务完成营业收入 19967.1 亿元，同比增长 9.4%；利润总额 1563.7 亿元，同比增长 8.6%。与往年相比，增速有所回落，但仍保持了较好的可持续发展能力。同时传统出版与新兴出版融合发展迅速，2014 年我国数字出版收入超过 3300 亿元，同比增长 33.4%，整体经济规模跃居行业第二③。

此外，我国版权贸易的结构也进一步优化，出版物版权输出实现持续增长。2014 年，全国共输出出版物版权 8733 种，较 2013 年增加 289 种，增长 3.4%；全国版权输出品种与引进品种比例由 2013 年的 1∶1.7 提高至 1∶1.6。其中，我国图书、期刊、报纸进出口金额发展趋势较为平稳（详见图 2），音像制品、电子出版物与数字出版物进口逐年增长，但出口存在一定波动（见图 3）。

（三）演艺行业

近年来，在政府利好产业政策和配套服务平台不断健全的影响下，我国演艺产业取得了规模性发展。2014 年，我国文艺表演团体总收入 193.87 亿元，比 2013 年同比上升 2.25%。其中国有文艺表演团体 1422 家，收入 78.77 亿元；民营文艺表演团体 8439 家，收入 115.10 亿元④。

2014 年，国家艺术基金正式成立，重点围绕艺术创作生产、宣传推广、征集收藏和人才培养四大方向进行资助，其中艺术创作是支持重点。基金改变了以往财政直接拨款的模式，通过间接赞助、专家评审、

① 根据国家统计局公布数据整理。
② 数据来源：《2015 文化及相关产业统计概览》，中国统计出版社。
③ 史竞男，2014 年我国数字出版高速增长 报刊业持续下滑，新华网，2015 年 7 月 16 日。
④ 数据来源：《2014 中国演出市场年度报告》，中国演出行业协会。

绩效考评等手段，充分发挥财政资金的导向作用，保证资金投入和使用的公平、透明，提高资金使用效率。基金的设立对于文化艺术发展具有重要意义，体现了文化部门创新艺术创作生产引导方式，也是激发全社会文化创造力、推进文化体制创新的重要举措。

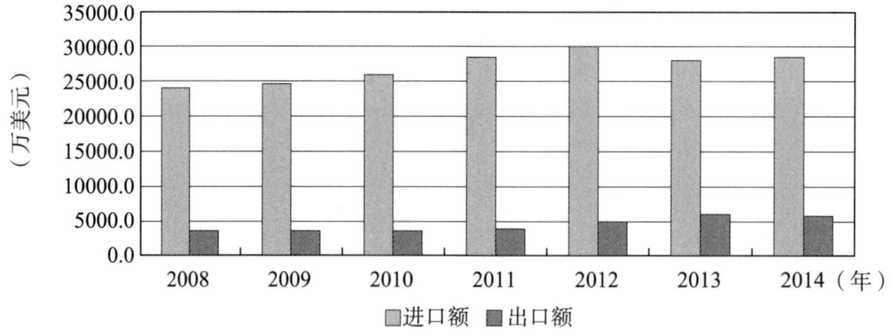

图 2　2008—2014 年中国图书、期刊、报纸进出口情况

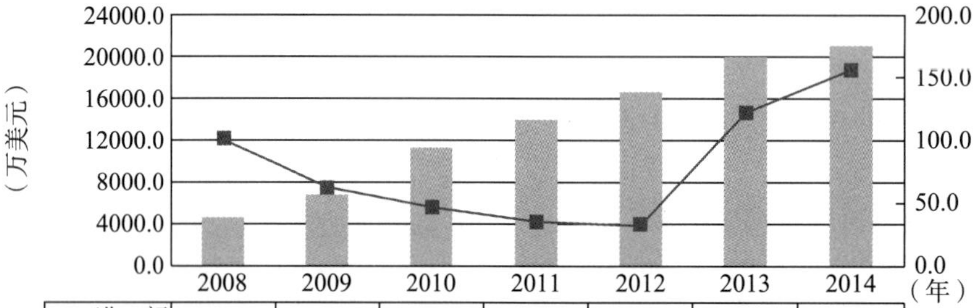

	2008	2009	2010	2011	2012	2013	2014
进口额	4556.8	6527.1	11382.7	14134.8	16686.0	20022.3	21000.1
出口额	101.3	61.1	47.2	35.2	33.5	122.4.0	156.5

图 3　2008—2014 年中国音像制品、电子出版物与数字出版物进出口情况①

注：上图数据仅包括全国有出版物进口经营许可的出版物进出口经营单位数据。

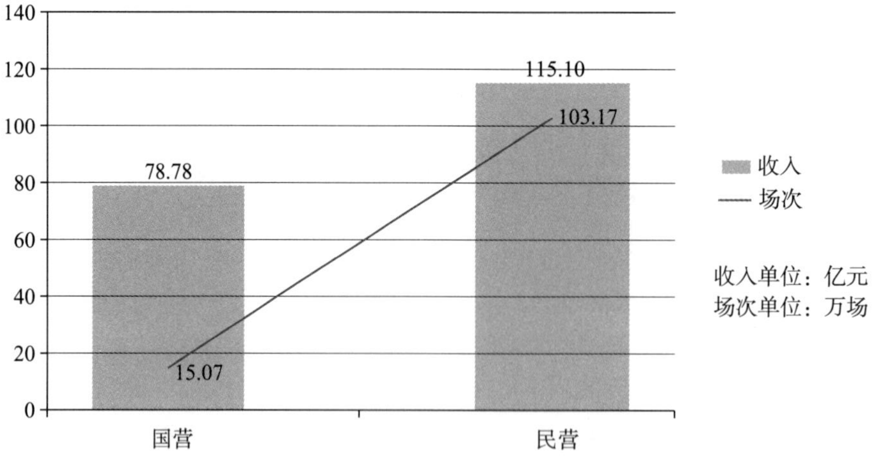

图 4　2014 年国有、民营院团演出收入、场次对比图

在国内演艺产业良性发展的基础上，我国对外演出在剧目数量、观演人次及演出贸易额等方

① 数据来源：《2015 文化及相关产业统计概览》，中国统计出版社。

面继续呈现出稳步增长的态势。国有、民营院团及其他演出经营主体参与对外演出积极性空前提高，演出贸易形式从传统单一型的剧目跨境演出向剧目版权贸易、院线联盟代理、中外合资制作等多元化方向过渡。优化我国演出对外贸易剧目结构、培育对外演出推介营销、法律咨询、融资贸易等服务平台将是提升我国演艺对外贸易竞争力面临的重要任务。

（四）艺术品行业

2014 年我国艺术品市场的整体发展较 2013 年有所增长，市场交易总额约为 2137 亿元，同比增长 6.67%。根据欧洲美术基金会发布的数据：2014 年中国占全球艺术品市场交易总额的 22%，在全球所有国家中排名第二位，可见中国艺术品市场的竞争力仍然较为强劲。2014 年艺术品行业各类市场的交易总额见表 1①。

表 1　2014 年中国艺术品市场数据表

序号	市场分类	金额（亿元人民币）
1	艺术品拍卖（原创艺术品）	451
2	画廊、艺术经纪、艺术博览会	500
3	艺术品出口	41
4	艺术品网上交易	45
5	现当代原创工艺美术品	850
6	艺术授权品、艺术复制品、艺术衍生品	250

中国是全球艺术品交易大国，但受较高的艺术品进口关税税率影响，中国艺术品市场基本以国内市场为主导，艺术品跨境间交易不够活跃，尚未成为全球艺术品贸易大国。2014 年，我国艺术品、收藏品及古董进出口额都出现小幅下降，进口总额由 2013 年的 7.7 亿美元降至 6.13 亿美元，出口总额由 2013 年的 10.41 亿美元降至 6.75 亿美元，进出口总额降至 12.89 亿美元，降幅约为 28.86%。长远来看，促进中国艺术品进出口贸易的增长，需要海关、文化、文物、工商、税务及行业协会等多部门协同，开展多方联动的监察体系，完善进出口艺术品备案制度，简化进出境报批手续，设定合理的艺术品进出口关税税率等。

（五）网络游戏行业

2014 年，我国网络游戏市场继续保持较好的发展势头，市场结构持续优化，移动游戏营收实现翻番，整体销售收入持续增长。2014 年中国网络游戏市场整体销售收入为 1062.1 亿元，同比增长 29.1%，首次突破千亿大关。网络游戏规模扩大主要得益于移动游戏的高速增长，中国移动游戏市场销售收入 268.6 亿元人民币，比 2013 年增长了 109.1%。

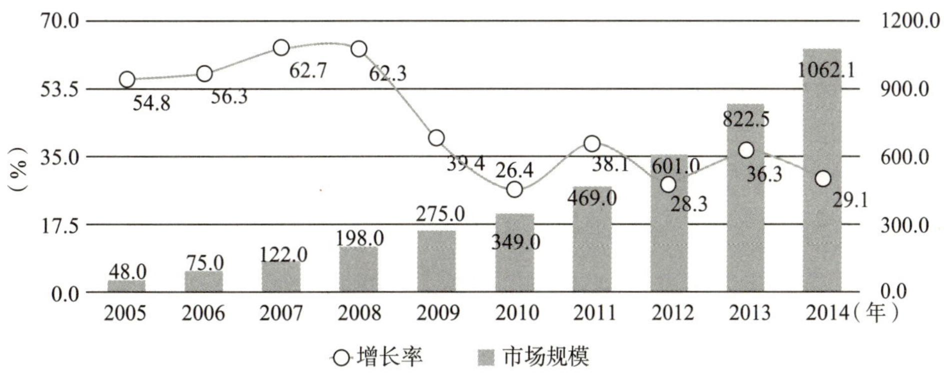

图 5　2005—2014 年我国网络游戏市场销售收入规模

① 数据来源：《2014 年中国艺术品市场年度报告》，文化部文化市场司，AMRC 艺术市场研究中心。

网络游戏与其他文化业态融合日益紧密，成为文学、音乐、影视、动漫等其他文化产品实现现金流的重要渠道。以 IP（知识产权）为核心横跨游戏、文学、音乐、影视、动漫等领域的数字文化娱乐内容逐渐增多。

2014 年文化部共通过了 78 款进口网络游戏（包括网络游戏资料片）的审批，较 2013 年增加 33 款。其中由韩国、日本公司开发的网络游戏各 21 款，占比达 53.8%；由美国公司开发的网络游戏共 12 款，占总数的 15.4%。此外，随着上海自贸区放开主机游戏的限制，部分知名主机游戏产品开始进入我国游戏市场。

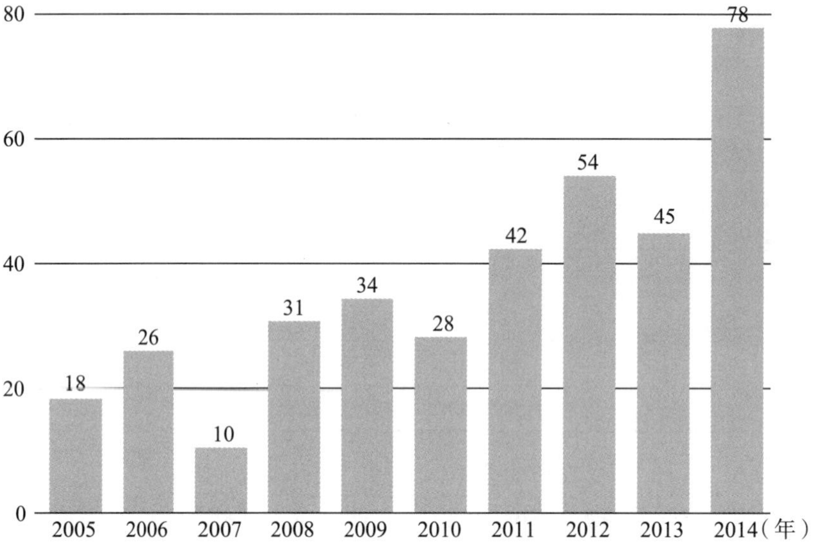

图 6　2005—2014 年中国进口网络游戏数量

网络游戏出口方面，2014 年国产游戏出口快速增长，收入达到 26.8 亿美元，比 2013 年增长 194.5%，增速较 2008 年增长近 37 倍。2010 年至今，国产网络游戏产品累计出口数量已经突破 500 款，参与出口的网络游戏企业接近 200 家，国产网络游戏海外出口收入稳步增长。

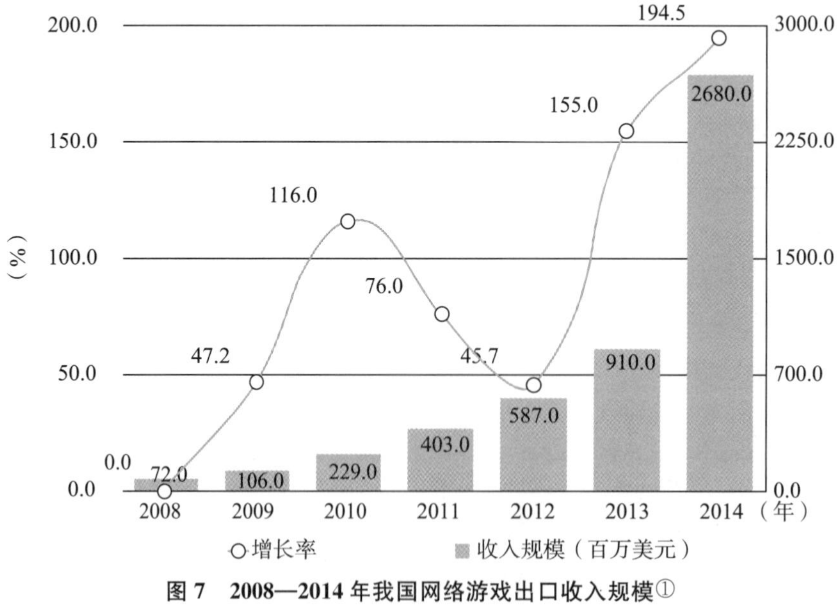

图 7　2008—2014 年我国网络游戏出口收入规模①

① 网络游戏行业相关数据均来源于《2014 网络游戏市场年度发展报告》，中华人民共和国文化部。

（六）网络音乐行业

2014 年网络音乐在我国网民中仍然拥有最多的用户，用户规模由 2013 年底的 4 .53 亿增长至 4. 78 亿，增长率为 5.5%，网络音乐在人们文化生活中占据重要地位。2014 年中国网络音乐市场呈现在线增，无线降的特点，总体规模达到 75.5 亿元人民币，其中无线音乐市场规模为 24.3 亿元，较 2013 年减少 20.4%；在线音乐市场规模为 51.2 亿元，较 2013 年增长了 17.4%①。

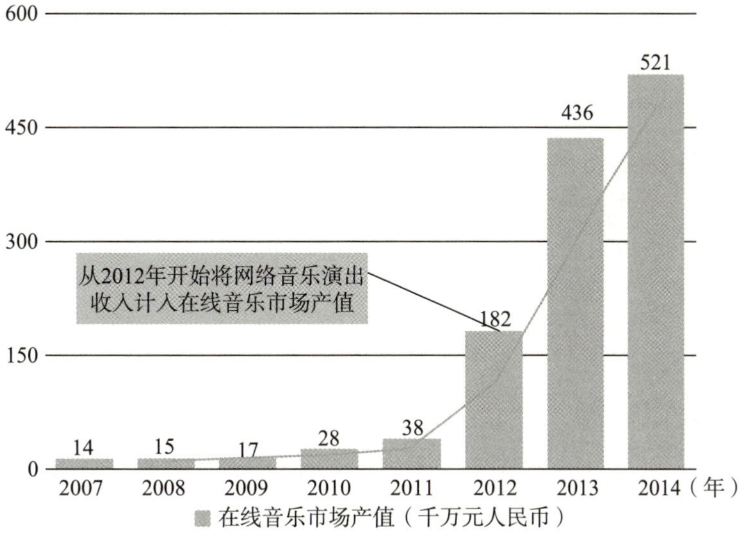

图 8　2007—2014 年我国在线音乐市场产值

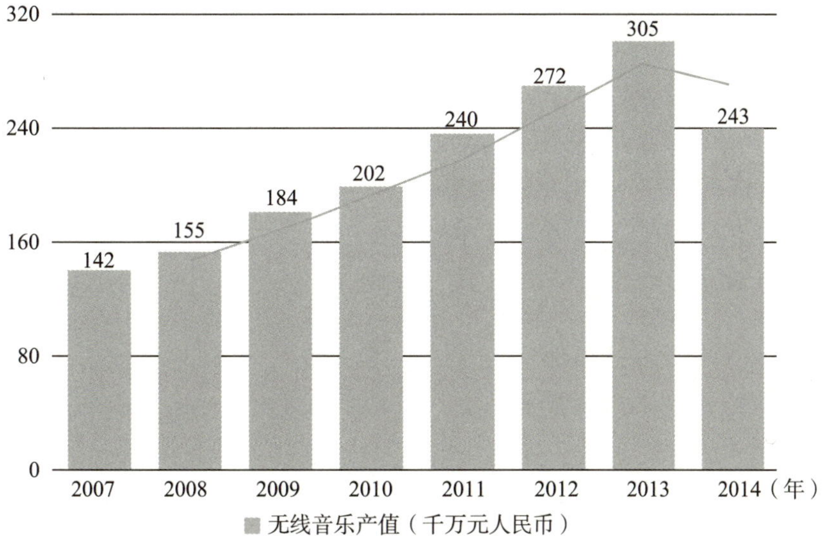

图 9　2007—2014 年我国无线音乐市场产值

网络音乐的概念以其应用创新、用户规模大等特点，依然备受资本市场的关注和青睐。随着移动网络的发展和智能终端的普及，PC 端的流量开始向移动端分散，用户消费音乐的方式正在向多场景多屏转移。在网络音乐收费模式未成熟的情况下，网络音乐的粉丝经济特点日益突出。

① 数据来源：《2014 年中国网络音乐市场年度发展报告》摘要，中国文化市场网。

三、未来发展思路及重点

2014年，在政府各项相关政策的大力支持下，我国文化产业和对外文化贸易均取得了良性发展，但依然存在销售渠道不畅、品牌影响力较弱和人才储备不足等现实问题。针对以上情况，未来我国文化产业和对外文化贸易的发展思路和重点将涵盖以下几个方面：

（一）推动政策贯彻落实

各项文化产业相关政策地密集出台，为我国文化产业和文化贸易发展提供了有力的政策保障，增强了文化企业的发展信心，也为文化产业和其他行业的深度融合带来重要机遇。深入落实政策各项内容，切实发挥相关政策引导和促进作用，是推动文化产业和文化贸易发展的重要前提。

（二）紧密结合国家重大发展战略

文化交流与合作是“一带一路”战略的重要内容之一，丝路沿线国家拥有丰富的文化资源，积极利用我国文化产业的资金和技术等优势，大力发展与沿线国家的文化贸易，是推动我国文化企业走出去，积极开拓国际文化市场和参与国际市场竞争的有利契机。

（三）搭建国际展会平台

利用国内深圳文博会、义乌文交会、香港授权展等国际性展会平台，举办政府政策对话会、开展文化企业产品和服务推介等活动。同时支持文化企业参加科隆游戏展、芝加哥艺博会等国际大型展会，面向国际同行，充分展示和推介我国文化精品，拓展我国优秀文化产品和服务销售渠道。

（四）积极推广民族品牌

以海外中国文化中心为平台，以创意设计为核心，继续打造“中国风格”等品牌活动，推介优秀民族品牌。利用米兰设计周、伦敦设计节、时装周、北京国际设计周等国际重要行业平台，打造中国设计师推广平台，提升中国创意设计的国际影响力。

（五）培育文化贸易人才

通过举办中国文化产品营销年会，邀请外国专家向国内文化企业介绍经验和国际最新行业趋势；与国外相关机构合作，在国内外举办文化贸易人才专题培训；举办中英文化贸易论坛、中国北京国际文化创意产业博览会—文化贸易人才推荐交流会等方式，加强文化贸易人才培养。

（文化部外联局　宋瑞雪）

中国旅游业对外开放情况

一、旅游发展环境更加完善

全国人大开展《旅游法》执法检查，推动了《旅游法》的贯彻落实。国务院出台《关于促进旅游业改革发展的若干意见》（国发〔2014〕31号），提出了新时期旅游业改革发展的方向和任务。各省区市深入贯彻落实国发〔2014〕31号文件，强化了旅游统筹协调机制，海南、北京、云南、江西、广西、西藏六个省区市先后成立旅游发展委员会。海南、云南、上海等地修订了旅游条例。山东、浙江、甘肃、安徽等省先后出台贯彻落实国发〔2014〕31号文件的政策文件。旅游综合改革深入推进，共有10个市县开展国家旅游综合改革试点。

二、旅游开放合作不断深化

举办第八届APEC旅游部长会议并发布《澳门宣言》。举办2014年中国国际旅游交易会和第14届世界旅游旅行大会。设立中国—中东欧旅游促进机构与旅游企业联合会协调中心。制订外国人入境旅游市场中长期发展规划。实施"美丽中国"全球统一品牌战略。推进大湄公河、大图们江次区域旅游合作。新增上海自贸试验区地中海邮轮旅行社作为试点经营出境游业务的外资社，广东省开放5家港澳独资旅行社经营内地居民赴境外团队旅游业务。开放太原等10个城市赴台个人游，增加第六批赴台游组团社。进一步简化赴台团队游手续，取消个人游城市赴台团队发票查验。大陆居民赴台旅游累计突破千万人次大关。以第十七届海峡两岸旅行业联谊会和第六届海峡两岸旅游交流圆桌会议为平台，深化两岸旅游合作，继续完善海旅会和台旅会磋商机制。到2014年年底，中国公民出境旅游目的地国家和地区达151个。

三、旅游市场有进一步发展

2014年，中国国内旅游人数36.11亿人次，增长10.67%；中国国内旅游收入达3.03万亿元，增长15.36%。中国出入境旅游总人数2.36亿人次，比上年增长7.73%，其中，入境旅游1.28亿人次，入境外国人2636万人次；出境旅游人数1.07亿人次。国际旅游收入569亿美元，比上年增长10.16%。

附表：

2014年入境外国游客人数

国籍	人数（万人次）	占总数比重（%）	比上年增长（%）
韩国	418.17	15.9	5.4
日本	271.76	10.3	−5.6
美国	209.32	7.9	0.4
俄罗斯	204.58	7.8	−6.4
越南	170.94	6.5	25.2
马来西亚	112.96	4.3	−6.4
蒙古	108.27	4.1	3.1
新加坡	97.14	3.7	0.5
菲律宾	96.79	3.7	−2.9
印度	70.99	2.7	4.9
澳大利亚	67.21	2.5	−7.1
加拿大	66.71	2.5	−2.5
德国	66.26	2.5	2.1
泰国	61.31	2.3	−5.9

续 表

国籍	人数（万人次）	占总数比重（%）	比上年增长（%）
英国	60.47	2.3	−3.2
印度尼西亚	56.69	2.2	−6.4
法国	51.70	2.0	−3.1
哈萨克斯坦	34.36	1.3	−12.7
意大利	25.31	1.0	0.8
朝鲜	18.44	0.7	−10.8
荷兰	18.04	0.7	−4.3
瑞典	14.20	0.5	−10.7
西班牙	14.10	0.5	6.5
缅甸	13.28	0.5	−1.4
新西兰	12.66	0.5	−1.5
乌克兰	11.81	0.4	−3.2
伊朗	11.37	0.4	27.9
巴基斯坦	10.89	0.4	2.2
土耳其	10.62	0.4	2.1
巴西	9.46	0.4	−1.2
埃及	8.39	0.3	12.7
瑞士	7.95	0.3	−1.3
以色列	7.85	0.3	−1.5
丹麦	7.76	0.3	−4.7
波兰	7.61	0.3	6.3
孟加拉国	6.98	0.3	18.5
南非	6.82	0.3	−0.6
比利时	6.74	0.3	−1.5
墨西哥	6.58	0.2	9.3
奥地利	6.48	0.2	−1.3
乌兹别克斯坦	6.30	0.2	9.2
芬兰	6.03	0.2	−8.2
尼日利亚	5.45	0.2	19.5
尼泊尔	5.36	0.2	−8.8
葡萄牙	5.23	0.2	5.9
吉尔吉斯斯坦	5.04	0.2	1.0
斯里兰卡	5.00	0.2	1.1
挪威	4.79	0.2	−7.0
爱尔兰	4.20	0.2	2.0
罗马尼亚	4.10	0.2	8.1

（国家旅游局政策法规司）

● 知识产权保护

中国知识产权发展状况

2014年，中国政府大力实施创新驱动发展战略，国家知识产权战略深入实施，知识产权工作与经济发展深度融合，明确提出“建设知识产权强国”的新目标，中国知识产权事业取得了新进展。

一、国家知识产权战略实施

国务院常务会议专题研究知识产权保护和运用问题，做出实施行动计划的重要决策，明确提出了建设知识产权强国的战略目标。国务院转发了联席会议成员单位共同制订的《深入实施国家知识产权战略行动计划（2014－2020年）》，在促进知识产权创造运用、加强知识产权保护、强化知识产权管理和拓展知识产权国际合作等方面部署四项主要行动，在知识产权信息服务、知识产权调查统计和知识产权人才队伍建设等方面实施三个工程，在组织实施、督促检查、财政支持和法律法规等方面提供四项保障。该文件是指导下一阶段战略实施工作开展的纲领性文件。

国家知识产权局组织联席会议成员单位制订发布《2014年国家知识产权战略实施推进计划》。会同教育部、科技部、工信部等制定印发《关于深入实施国家知识产权战略 加强和改进知识产权管理的若干意见》，推动政府、行业、企业、高校、科研机构和服务机构提高知识产权管理水平。文化部研究制定文化系统实施知识产权战略的指导性文件。

财政部、科技部、国家知识产权局联合印发通知，开展深化中央级事业单位科技成果使用权、处置权和收益权改革试点工作，教育部、工业和信息化部、中科院等积极推动清华大学等高校院所开展改革试点。科技部强化知识产权在科技计划管理、科技评价等工作中的战略导向，在国家科技计划管理办法中明确计划实施各环节的知识产权管理措施。文化部建立网络文化市场执法联席会议机制。工商总局探索建立地理标志工作部际联席协调机制。

二、知识产权法律法规

国务院法制办公室会同有关部门积极推进《著作权法》《专利法》《专利代理条例》等法律法规的修订工作。修改后的《商标法实施条例》于5月1日实施。总装备部、国防科工局启动《国防专利条例》修订工作。环境保护部推动《生物遗传资源获取管理条例》列入国家安全立法规划和国务院立法计划。

国家知识产权局开展《专利（修订草案）》的审议准备工作，就《职务发明条例（草案）》广泛征求意见，修改《专利审查指南》将图形用户界面纳入外观设计保护范围，修订《用于专利程序的微生物保藏办法》等。国家工商行政管理总局印发《关于执行修改后的〈中华人民共和国商标法〉有关问题的通知》，修订发布《商标评审规则》《驰名商标认定和保护规定》等配套措施；制定出台《网络交易平台经营者履行社会责任指引》《网络交易管理办法》等制度规范。国家版权局推进《著作权法》第三次修改及相关法规修订工作，颁布《使用文字作品支付报酬办法》《新闻出版（版权）行政执法部门公开制售假冒伪劣商品和侵犯知识产权行政处罚案件信息的实施细则（试行）》等制度规范。

农业部起草《农业植物新品种测试指南

2015—2020 研制规划》，印发《农产品地理标志登记审查若干问题的说明》。国家林业局印发《林业植物新品种保护行政执法办法》，制定《林业植物新品种申请审查规则》。

文化部制定《文化市场领域制售假冒伪劣商品和侵犯知识产权行政处罚案件信息公开实施办法(试行)》。海关总署出台《海关依法公开进出口侵犯知识产权货物行政处罚案件信息的实施办法》。

最高人民法院发布《关于审理商标案件有关管辖和法律适用范围问题的解释》，修改《关于审理专利纠纷案件适用法律问题的若干规定》，发布《关于北京、上海、广州知识产权法院案件管辖的规定》《关于知识产权法院案件管理等有关问题的通知》和《关于知识产权法院技术调查官参与诉讼活动若干问题的暂行规定》。最高人民检察院与最高人民法院联合颁布《关于输危害药品安全刑事案件适用法律若干问题的解释》。

三、知识产权审批登记

国家知识产权局全年受理发明、实用新型和外观设计三种专利申请 236.1 万件，与上年度基本持平。其中，发明专利申请 92.8 万件，同比增长 12.5%。全年累计完成发明专利实质审查 43.1 万件，同比增长 21.4%。全年授权发明专利 23.3 万件，同比增长 12.3%。截至 2014 年底，经授权并维持有效的发明专利为 119.6 万件；其中，国内拥有 70.8 万件，占 59.2%，同比增长 20.8%。受理依据《专利合作条约》(PCT) 提出的国际申请 26169 件，同比增长 14.2%。全年受理复审请求 24452 件，同比增长 29.9%；受理无效宣告请求 3422 件，同比减少 16.8%。全年收到集成电路布图设计登记申请 1838 件，予以公告并发出证书 1553 件。

国家工商行政管理总局全年受理商标注册申请 228.54 万件，同比增长 21.47%。全年审查商标注册申请 242.64 万件，同比增长 70.32%。截至 2014 年年底，商标有效注册量 839 万件。全年核准注册和初步审定地理标志证明商标、集体商标 507 件，同比增长 16.3%。全年国内申请人马德里商标国际申请 2140 件。全年受理商标评审案件 8.26 万件，同比减少 6.57%。

全国全年著作权登记量达 121.13 万件，同比增长 19.97%。其中，作品登记 992034 件，同比增长 17.39%；计算机软件著作权登记 218783 件，同比增长 33.12%。全年著作权质权登记 496 件，同比增长 121.4%。

农业部全年受理农业植物品种权申请 1772 件，同比增长 33%；授予品种权 827 件。累计受理植物新品种权申请 13483 件，授予品种权 4845 件。全年批准登记农产品地理标志 213 个，累计批准登记农产品地理标志 1588 个。林业局全年受理林业植物新品种申请 254 件、授予品种权 169 件，累计受理林业植物新品种申请 1515 件、授予林业品种权 827 件。

海关总署全年受理知识产权海关保护备案申请 7003 件，同比增长 10.3%。其中，核准备案 5306 件，同比增长 11%。

四、知识产权保护

2014 年，中国政府继续加大知识产权保护力度，全国打击侵犯知识产权和制售假冒伪劣商品工作领导小组研究部署全年重点工作，各成员单位认真贯彻工作部署，积极开展专项整治，严厉打击各类侵权假冒违法行为，取得显著成效。

商务部牵头推动国务院印发《关于依法公开制售假冒伪劣商品和侵犯知识产权行政处罚案件信息的意见》，推动行政处罚案件信息依法公开。国家发展改革委积极推动将恶意侵权行为纳入社会信用体系。最高人民检察院网上公开制售假冒伪劣商品和侵犯知识产权刑事案件相关信息。最高人民法院在北京、上海、广州建立知识产权法院，并制定相关司法解释及政策文件保障知识法院顺利运转。进一步调整和扩大具有一般知识产权案件管辖权的基层法院数量。

国家知识产权局加大专利行政执法力度，组织开展电子商务领域专利执法维权“护航”专项行动；出台《专利侵权判定和假冒专利行为认定指南(试行)》，规范和指导全国专利行政执法工作。国家工商行政管理总局加强商标专用权保护，组织开展“红盾护农”“红盾网剑”等专项行动。国家版权局大力打击侵权盗版行为，继续开展互联网侵权盗版专项治理；建成中央和省级各单位软件正版化责任人数据库，建立企业软件正版化信息报送制度，政府机关和中央企业三级以上企业已全部实现软件正版化。

农业部组织开展打击侵犯品种权和制售假劣种子专项行动。国家林业局组织开展打击侵犯林业植物新品种权专项行动。海关部署严厉打击侵权商品进出口违法活动，将与消费者健康安全密切相关的侵权药品、食品、汽配等列为重点打击对象，开展为期半年的邮递快件渠道知识产权海关保护重点执法活动。

全国行政执法机关立案查处案件 17.8 万件，捣毁制假售假窝点 3389 个；案件办结率 83%，同比提高了 17%。全国公安机关侦破涉嫌侵权假冒犯罪案件 28280 件。全国检察机关起诉侵权假冒案件 18789 件，同比增长 32%。全国审判机关审结侵权假冒刑事案件 18020 件，同比增长 52%。

全国地方法院共新收知识产权民事一审案件 95522 件，审结 94501 件，同比分别增长 7.83%和 7.04%。全年共审结涉外知识产权民事一审案件 1716 件，同比增长 0.11%。全年共审结涉及知识产权侵权的刑事案件 10803 件，判决发生法律效力 13904 人，其中有罪判决 13903 人。在审结案件中，以侵犯知识产权犯罪判决的案件 4180 件，生效判决人数 6959 人。全国检察机关全年批准逮捕涉及侵犯知识产权犯罪案件 2924 件、4859 人，起诉 5156 件、8834 人。

五、知识产权宣传

2014 年，全国打击侵犯知识产权和制售假冒伪劣商品工作领导小组办公室联合中央宣传部印发年度宣传方案，充分利用“中国打击侵权假冒工作网”平台，及时发布信息，组织专家访谈。围绕“两节”“两会”消费者权益保护日、全国法制宣传日、“4·26”全国知识产权宣传周等重要时间节点，组织集中报道，发布权威信息，回应社会关切。

国家知识产权局紧紧围绕经济社会发展大局，以宣传《国家知识产权战略纲要》实施为主线，以增强全社会知识产权意识为目标，探索改进宣传工作的方式和方法，全面展示我国知识产权事业的发展成就。联合中央宣传部等 24 个部门在全国范围内开展全国知识产权宣传周活动，期间参与报道的各类新闻媒体达 367 家，自主播发消息 965 条，网络转发总量达数百万次。

国家工商行政管理总局召开新修改的《商标法》实施新闻发布会，举办在线访谈，解读《商标法实施条例》及《驰名商标认定和保护规定》。国家版权局开通官方微信和微博，制作“软件正版化在中国”专刊，编制《中国的软件正版化工作进程》。农业部编辑出版《中国授权农业植物新品种(2013)》和《中国授权农业植物新品种保护发展报告》。国家林业局汇编出版《中国林业植物授权新品种（2013)》和《2013 中国林业知识产权年度报告》等。海关总署公布年度“中国海关保护知识产权十佳案例”，发布《中国海关保护知识产权状况》。

最高人民法院发布《中国法院知识产权司法保护状况（2013)》《2013 年中国法院十大知识产权案件、十大创新性知识产权案件和 50 件典型知识产权案例》《最高人民法院知识产权案件年度报告(2013)》，发行《中国知识产权司法保护年鉴(2013)》。最高人民检察院发布《2013 检察机关知识产权司法保护情况》和《2013 年中国检察机关保护知识产权十大典型案例》。

六、知识产权国际合作

2014 年，知识产权国际合作迈出新步伐。国家知识产权局继续深化与世界知识产权组织、各国和各地区知识产权机构的友好合作，不断拓展新的合作伙伴关系，新签订多边、双边合作协议 29 项。与相关部门密切配合，促成世界知识产权组织在北京设立中国办事处。与世界知识产权组织联合举办“PCT 高级巡回研讨会”和“有效利用《工业品外观设计国际注册海牙协定》国际研讨会”。牵头组织协调有关部门参加世界知识产权和国际植物新品种保护联框架下的各类会议。与美国、日本、韩国等国家或地区性组织开展知识产权高层交流。与捷克和斯洛伐克等国建立了双边合作关系，恢复与匈牙利知识产权局的合作关系。

国家工商行政管理总局继续开展多边及双边交流合作，作为正式成员参加中美日欧韩商标五方会谈。深化与美国、欧盟、英国、法国、非洲知识产权组织、非洲地区工业产权组织等的交流合作。举办中欧商业秘密研讨会。

国家版权局积极参与国际版权事务，完成世界贸易组织第五次对华贸易政策审议工作，向世界知识产权组织递交中国政府《视听表演北京条约》批准书，启动中国政府《关于为盲人、视障者和其他印刷品新闻记者障碍者获得已出版作品马拉喀什条约》的批准工作。首次建立与阿拉伯国家及非洲国家版权双边关系。与韩国文化体育观光部联合制作版权广告宣传片。

农业部积极参加国际植物新品种保护联盟系列会议和国际活动，参加国际植物新品种保护联盟理事会、咨询委员会、行政和法律委员会、技术委员会等会议。积极参与地理标志有关的国际谈判和合作研究，全程参与中欧、中美、中澳自贸区等地理标志及知识产权谈判对话，加快推进我国地理标志国际化合作进程。

国家林业局积极参加国际植物新品种保护联盟技术委员会第 50 次会议、理事会第 31 次特别会议等会议。积极参与遗传资源相关履约工作，参加名古屋议定书政府间委员会第三次会议。

海关总署加大国际合作力度，联合开展专项行动。中欧海关续签《中欧海关 2014—2017 年知识产权合作行动计划》。召开中欧海关知识产权工作组会议及风险管理专家组会议。与俄罗斯海关举行中俄总理定期会晤委员会海关合作分委会知识产权保护工作组会议，与美国移民海关执法局联合开展保护美国橄榄球职业联赛有关商标的联合执法行动。

公安部会同国际刑警组织联合开展打击侵权假冒犯罪“真实行动”，共破案 1544 起，抓获犯罪嫌疑人 2224 名，涉案总价值 2.1 亿元。联合美国开展打击假冒气囊案联合行动，联合英国打击跨国制售假冒注册商标标识案。

（国家知识产权局办公室综合信息处处长　沙开清）

中国专利制度

2014年，中国专利制度进一步健全完善，专利事业发展战略稳步推进，发明专利申请稳步增长，专利转化运用效益突出，专利保护进一步加强，各项工作取得新进展。

一、法律法规

圆满完成全国人大常委会专利法执法检查相关工作，着力推进执法检查报告和审议意见中一些关键问题的解决。配合国务院法制办开展《中华人民共和国专利法修订草案》审议准备工作，启动全面修改准备工作。开展《职务发明条例（草案）》征求意见工作。

国务院办公厅转发《深入实施国家知识产权战略行动计划（2014—2020年）》，明确下一阶段重点任务。会同教育部等部委制定印发《关于深入实施国家知识产权战略 加强和改进知识产权管理的若干意见》《关于深入实施知识产权战略 促进中原经济区经济社会发展的若干意见》。联合财政部等印发《关于开展深化中央级事业单位科技成果使用、处置和收益管理改革试点的通知》。制订发布《2014年国家知识产权战略实施推进计划》《2014年全国专利事业发展战略推进计划》等。

对《国家知识产权局规章制定程序的规定》《专利行政执法办法》《专利代理惩戒规则（试行）》等规范性文件进行评估。修改《专利审查指南》，将图形用户界面纳入外观设计保护范围。起草完成《专利费用减缴办法（修订草案）》《集成电路布图设计撤销审查办法草案》，修订《用于专利程序的微生物保藏办法》等。

二、申请与授权

全年受理发明、实用新型和外观设计三种专利申请236.1万件，与上年度基本持平。其中，发明专利申请92.8万件，同比增长12.5%；实用新型专利申请86.8万件，外观设计专利申请56.5万件，同比分别下降2.7%和14.4%。

国内发明专利申请（含港澳台地区，下同）为80.1万件，占总量的86.3%，同比增长13.6%。其中，职务申请64.8万件，占80.9%，同比增长13.5%；非职务申请15.3万件，占19.1%，同比增长14.4%。国内职务发明专利申请中，企业申请48.5万件，占74.8%，同比增长13.6%；高校申请11.2万件，占17.3%，同比增长13.7%；科研机构申请3.9万件，占6.0%，同比增长8.3%；机关团体申请1.2万件，占1.9%，同比增长23.5%。

全年授权发明专利23.3万件，同比增长12.3%。其中，国内发明专利授权16.3万件，占70.0%。授权实用新型专利70.8万件，同比增长2.2%。授权外观设计专利36.2万件，同比下降12.3%。

截至2014年年底，经国家知识产权局授权并维持有效的发明专利119.6万件，较2013年年底增长15.7%。其中，国内70.8万件，占59.2%，增长20.8%。我国每万人口发明专利拥有量（不含港澳台）达到4.9件。

国家知识产权局作为《专利合作条约》（PCT）受理局，全年受理PCT国际申请26169件，同比增长14.2%。自1994年起，累计受理国际申请132565件。

全年受理复审请求24452件，同比增长29.9%；复审请求结案20393件。全年受理无效宣告请求3422件，同比增长16.8%；无效宣告请求结案2742件。自1985年以来，共受理无效宣告请求37787件。全年当事人向北京市第一中级人民法院起诉和向北京市高级人民法院上诉的案件总计985件。

三、专利运用

深入实施专利导航试点工程，在8个实验区启动专利导航规划项目。制定专利导航平台建设指南、重点产业专利联盟建设指南等，完善专利导航业务指导体系。推动建立知识产权运营公共服务平台、运营机构和运营基金。

会同中国人民银行等部门联合印发《关于大力推进体制机制创新 扎实做好科技金融服务的意见》，与中国人民财产保险股份有限公司签订知识产权保险战略合作协议。组织13个省份开展知识产权质押融资和专利保险工作，推进知识产权质押融资保险业务试点，完成海外展会侵权责任保险产品开发备案工作。全年专利权质押金额489亿元，同比增长92.5%。全国有798家企业投保专利保险，共提供保障金额1.34亿元。

开展专利价值分析应用试点工作，支持和促进中科院、农科院等21家单位开展专利分级分类管理及促进转移转化工作，在全国13个地区高校专利分级分类动态管理工作。启动专利价值分析指标体系国家标准化工作。与世界知识产权组织共同完成第十六届中国专利奖评选工作，评出金奖25项，优秀奖472项。据不完全统计，自专利实施之日起至2013年底，25个金奖项目新增销售额1534亿元，新增利润203亿元。

四、专利保护

印发《电子商务领域专利执法维权专项行动工作方案》，推进电子商务领域及“护航”专利执法维权专项行动。全年专利行政执法办案总量24479件，同比增长50.9%。其中，办理专利纠纷案件8220件，同比增长62.6%；查处假冒专利案件16259件，同比增长45.5%。

实施专利行政执法能力提升工程，推动建立相对集中的省市级行政执法队伍，推动建立专利侵权判定咨询机制、专利纠纷快速调解机制、区域专利行政执法办案协作调度机制等。健全专利保护重点联系机制。专利行政执法案件报送系统正式运行，专利纠纷网上办案系统进入调试阶段。“12330”维权热线覆盖面进一步扩大，维权援助中心与快速维权中心建设不断加强，知识产权维权援助举报投诉系统试运行，全国知识产权维权援助工作体系初步形成。

印发《关于培育知识产权规范化市场的通知》，编制《全国知识产权保护重点专业市场名录》，制定《知识产权保护规范化市场培育指南》，选定65家专业市场开展培育工作。编制《2013年度知识产权保护社会满意度调查报告》和《2013年度专利保护满意度调查报告》。编制《地方满意度评价指标体系》，完善调查问卷，调整调查方式，完成2014年度知识产权保护社会满意度调查工作。在上海、江苏、江西等省市开展知识产权调解工作试点，成功调解知识产权纠纷案件近150件。编制发布《2013年中国知识产权保护状况》。

五、管理工作

组织召开知识产权促进京津冀协同发展工作启动会。在中新广州知识城启动建设国家知识产权运用和保护综合改革试验区。

与天津市人民政府建立新一轮合作会商制度，与广东省人民政府召开年度合作会商会议，与中国国际贸易促进会建立战略合作关系。截至2014年年底，已与15个省（区、市）人民政府及5家中央单位建立知识产权合作会商机制。印发《国家知识产权试点、示范城市评定和管理办法》，新批12个城市具备示范城市资格、试点城市16个，新批示范县（区）14个、试点县（区）64个。确定国家知识产权示范园区6家，试点园区10家。

协调科技部、工信部等部委推动实施《企业知识产权管理规范》。指导地方鼓励支持企业贯标，全国新增贯标企业3200多家，参与服务机构370多家，培训人数2万人。指导注册成立国内首个知识产权管理体系认证公司，166家企业通过认证审核。组织实施《知识产权管理规范试点企业认证工作方案》，推动知识产权认证国际化发展。筹建全国知识管理标准委员会。会同教育部和中科院开展高校和科研院所知识产权管理标准工作。

印发《关于知识产权支持小微企业发展的若干意见》，在天津、浙江全面深入开展中小企业托管工作，指导建立首个知识产权托管平台。联合工信部印发《关于开展中小企业知识产权战略推进工程总结验收工作的通知》。与贸促会合作，推动知识产权支撑企业“走出去”有关工作。

全面启动《专利代理行业中长期发展规划（2016—2025年）》制定工作。出台《关于促进专利代理行业发展的若干意见》。配合国务院审改办开展行政审批清理整顿工作，将专利代理机构设立审批由前置改为后置，简化审批手续和流程。取消专利代理机构年检，设立年度报告制度。发布《关于规范退休党政领导干部在专利代理机构执业等相关事宜的通知》，规范退休领导干部在专利代理机构执业等行为。

2014年全国专利代理人资格考试报名人数27542人，同比增长26.99%。通过考试人数4777人，同比增长25.3%。新批设立专利代理机构119家。截至2014年年底，全国共有22097人获得专利代理人资格，其中10459人在全国1103家专利代理机构执业。

六、宣传培训

2014年，宣传工作围绕国家经济社会发展大局，以宣传国家知识产权战略实施为主线，以增强全社会知识产权意识为目标，探索改进宣传工作的方式方法，全面展示我国知识产权事业的发展成就。配合专利法的修改，组织中央主要媒体围绕"加强专利行政执法"集中开展宣传报道活动。对全国局长会、2013年发明专利授权排行、世界知识产权组织成立中国办事处等十余项重要活动开展专项报道。

联合中宣部等24个部门在全国范围内开展知识产权宣传周活动，形成国家、省、地、县四级联动、全国一盘棋的宣传局面，引起社会广泛关注。编制完成《中学生知识产权教育读本》，编制出版普及读物《知识产权ABC》。推动广东、陕西等中小学校开展知识产权普及教育工作，支持山东、黑龙江推进知识产权文化建设。

创新全国知识产权人才工作政策，制定印发《关于加强国家知识产权培训基地工作的意见》《全国知识产权人才库与人才信息网络平台管理办法》《全国知识产权教育培训分类指导大纲》《2014年全国知识产权人才工作要点》等政策文件。推进专业技术人才知识产权更新工程，培养高层次、急需紧缺和骨干专业技术人才，完成面授培训班30余期，培训人员4000余人次。开展第二批全国知识产权领军人才和第四批高层次人才培养人选评选工作，从全国选拔出127名全国知识产权领军人才和120名百名高层次人才培养人选。

加强培训基地建设工作，批复国家知识产权培训基地2家，批复中小微企业知识产权培训基地2家。实施知识产权人才信息化工程，完善国家知识产权人才库和人才信息网络平台，形成初具规模的知识产权人才库。联合工信部和江苏省政府共建南京理工大学知识产权学院，联合同济大学开设"卓越专利代理人"法律硕士项目。全国共举办各级各类培训班6000余期，培训人次达60多万。

七、信息化和文献

2014年，电子审批（E）系统实施配套项目23个，完成专利事务服务系统建设，对专利代理管理系统进行升级改造。专利检索与服务（S）系统持续完善检索功能，丰富检索资源，优化系统性能，改进用户体验，提高检索效率。中国PCT申请国际阶段审查和流程管理（CEPCT）系统正式上线运行，实现了PCT国际阶段申请的受理、国际检索和初步审查业务的无纸化审查。

持续推进全国专利信息公共服务体系建设，优化国家专利数据中心数据申请流程，为区域和地方专利信息服务中心持续提供数据支持。制定《地方专利信息服务中心管理暂行办法》，加强和规范对地方专利信息服务中心的管理。完善公共服务信息化系统，积极推进专利基础数据资源开放，建设并开通专利数据服务试验系统，向社会公众免费提供最新国内外专利基础数据。

全年配置专利和非专利文献资源共计108种，包括专利资源13种和非专利资源95种，资源内容全面覆盖了与审查业务相关的主要技术与学科领域。与38个国家（地区）或组织建立并保持专利文献交换关系，向7个PCT国际检索与初审单位提供中国专利文献。与EPO建立文献传递合作途径，开创与国外知识产权局间的非专利文献交换新渠道。截至2014年年底，国家知识产权局累计拥有各类专利文献资源450余种，中国专利文献总量超过1200万件。全年出版发明、实用新型和外观设计专利公报文献共207.19万件，其中，发明公布777336件，发明授权29711件，实用新型700577件，外观设计364283件。

2014 年度各省、自治区、直辖市发明专利受理与授权统计表

	受理量（件）	授权量（件）	有效专利（件）
北 京	78 129	23 237	103 638
天 津	23 391	3 279	14 736
河 北	8 332	2 286	9 066
山 西	6 107	1 559	6 284
内蒙古	1 924	458	2 411
辽 宁	18 417	3 975	18 417
吉 林	5 288	1 434	6 305
黑龙江	13 468	2 454	9 816
上 海	39 133	11 614	56 515
江 苏	146 660	19 671	81 114
浙 江	52 406	13 372	52 418
安 徽	49 960	5 184	15 939
福 建	12 529	3 426	13 057
江 西	4 688	1 033	4 091
山 东	77 298	10 538	34 775
河 南	19 646	3 493	13 535
湖 北	22 536	4 855	18 825
湖 南	14 474	4 160	16 958
广 东	75 147	22 276	111 878
广 西	22 237	1 933	5 643
重 庆	19 418	2 321	10 010
四 川	29 926	5 682	21 209
贵 州	8 203	1 047	4 193
云 南	4 732	1 423	6 102
西 藏	92	50	261
陕 西	24 399	4 885	17 575
甘 肃	4 986	812	3 252
青 海	660	110	456
宁 夏	2 183	243	790
新 疆	2 360	605	2 353
海 南	969	380	1 792
香 港	909	466	3 437
澳 门	37	14	56
台 湾	10 491	4 405	41 783
合 计	801 135	162 680	708 690

（国家知识产权局办公室综合信息处处长　沙开清）

中国商标保护制度

2014年，国家工商行政管理总局深入贯彻落实新商标法，锐意进取，开拓创新，推进商标事业改革发展再上新台阶。

一、商标注册便利化水平不断提升

随着我国经济的转型升级，商事制度改革带来市场主体自主创新活力不断增强，2014年商标注册申请量继续保持快速增长态势，首次突破200万大关，达228.5万件，同比增长21.5%，再创历史新高，连续13年位居世界第一。国家工商总局积极应对商标申请量快速增长、三期系统上线和商标审查审理法定期限等多重压力，多措并举，大力推进商标注册便利化。

（一）不断提高商标注册审查效能

全年共完成商标审查242.6万件，审查能力首次突破200万件大关，同比增长70.3%；商标平均审查周期控制在法定9个月期限以内。全年审结商标评审案件共11.6万件，其中审结驳回复审案件8.6万件，审结复杂案件3万件。

（二）完善审查标准和制度

针对新商标法对审查工作的新要求，加强商标审查标准研究和制度建设。按照一标多类的要求修订了审查文书，建立了审查意见书制度，完善了新增药品等零售业服务商标受理及审查办法、声音商标受理及审查办法，完善了同日申请制度等，确保了审查工作高效、依法、有序开展。

（三）优化审查流程

根据新商标法的规定，及时调整优化了商标注册申请受理、异议形审等审查流程，修订了申请及发文书式，及时对外公布调整情况，耐心细致地做好讲解指导和解释说明工作。

（四）切实提升窗口服务水平

以落实"四难"问题专项整治、优化窗口服务为抓手，全面开展自查自纠，不断提高服务意识，加强软硬件建设，健全工作规范，严明工作纪律，商标注册大厅、驻中关村办事处窗口整体服务质量明显提高。2014年商标注册大厅共受理各类申请12.1万余件，接待咨询8.8万余人次；商标局驻中关村办事处共受理各类商标申请5.4万件。

（五）不断提高商标注册申请信息化水平

制定实施《商标注册网上申请暂行规定》，按时启用新版商标注册网上申请系统，商标注册网上申请继续保持同期申请总量的六成以上。

二、商标法治化水平不断提高

2014年是中国商标法治建设取得突破性进展的一年，国家工商总局积极配合国务院法制办，推动《商标法实施条例》修改工作圆满完成，于5月1日与新修改的商标法同步施行。我国商标法治建设水平进一步提升，为商标战略实施提供了有力法律保障。

（一）积极做好新商标法配套规章及规范性文件修订工作

国家工商总局圆满完成了《驰名商标认定和保护规定》《商标评审规则》的修订工作，并发布《工商总局关于商标代理机构备案有关问题的通知》。为确保新旧商标法有序衔接，制定发布《工商总局关于执行修改后的〈中华人民共和国商标法〉有关问题的通知》，规定了商标注册、商标评审、商标监督管理等在新旧法衔接过渡期间的适用问题。

（二）认真开展新商标法及其实施条例的宣传培训工作

国家工商总局以新商标法及其实施条例施行为契机，充分利用"4·26"知识产权宣传周、5月1日新商标法及其实施条例施行等时间节点，深入开展宣传活动。国家工商总局局长张茅接受新华社专访，副局长刘俊臣出席新商标法实施新闻发布会并回答记者提问。商标局及商评委有关负责同志参加人民网强国论坛在线访谈，解读《商标法实施条例》和《驰名商标认定和保护规定》。国家工商总局还举办了《商标法实施条例》暨第二届夏季青年奥林匹克运动会标志保护培训班。通过培训深化了广大干部对新商标法及其实施条例的认识和理解，提升了对新商标法及其实施条例的实践运用能力。各地工商行政管理和市场监管部门也结合“4·26”知识产权宣传周，积极组织开展新商标法的系列宣传培训活动，提升全社会商标法律意识。

（三）加强对新商标法实施工作的指导

商标局、商标评审委员会组织编撰《商标法理解与适用》一书，对立法背景和修改目的进行了介绍，解释了法律条文含义，并结合商标审查和审理工作实践，逐条讲解了商标法及其实施条例在商标注册管理工作中的具体适用。

三、商标监管执法不断强化

2014年，全国工商行政管理和市场监管部门按照国务院和国家工商总局统一部署，在新一轮地方政府市场监管机构改革和职能转变的新形势下，在扎实推进商事制度改革的过程中，坚持宽进严管相结合，加强事中事后监管，持续保持打击商标侵权假冒违法行为的高压态势，取得显著成效。

（一）商标专用权行政保护工作全面有序推进

国家工商总局商标局根据各地上报的案件线索，加强对地方商标行政执法工作的指导，先后对各地反映侵权较为普遍和严重的“维多利亚的秘密”“金城”“松板”“赣南脐橙”等商标侵权案件进行专项部署，督促地方工商和市场监管部门进行查处。各地工商和市场监管部门密切结合本地实际，针对市场上跨区域、大规模、社会公众反映强烈的商标侵权案件，加大打击力度，查办了一批大案要案。为做好青奥会标志保护工作，国家工商总局下发《保护第二届夏季青年奥林匹克运动会标志专项行动方案》，指导各地开展保护青奥会标志专项行动。各地工商和市场监管部门在商标执法中积极与公安、工信等部门协作，全年共查处商标一般违法案件5231件，查处商标侵权假冒案件37219件。

（二）打击侵犯知识产权和制售假冒伪劣商品工作成效显著

全国各级工商行政管理和市场监管部门按照工商总局统一部署，着力加强商标行政执法，全年共查处侵权假冒案件6.75万件，案值9.98亿元；依法向司法机关移送涉嫌犯罪案件355件，涉案金额4.8亿元。制定《工商总局关于依法公开制售假冒伪劣商品和侵犯知识产权行政处罚案件信息的意见（试行）》，组织各地做好案件信息的依法公开工作。

（三）积极推进商标专用权保护长效机制建设

加快推进建设商标行政执法信息共享平台，积极参与全国打击侵权假冒工作行政执法与刑事司法衔接工作信息共享平台建设，进一步做好商标行政执法与刑事司法衔接配合工作。着力加快打击侵权假冒工作信息共享平台的研究开发，拟实现总局全国范围内各级工商机关打击侵权假冒工作案件办理的统计分析、统一指挥、督办和协办功能，进一步增强全系统打击侵权假冒工作的协同性和统一性。

四、商标有效运用能力不断增强

全国各级工商行政管理和市场监管部门积极推进商标战略实施，以提升商标运用能力为目标，切实加强商标工作指导和服务。

（一）扎实做好地理标志和农产品商标的注册审查工作

加强对地理标志和农产品商标注册保护工作的指导、宣传和培训，引导农户和涉农企业增强商标品牌意识。截至2014年年底，累计注册农产品商标达168.9万件，累计注册和初步审定地理标志商标2697件，其中外国在我国注册和初步审定的地理标志商标达到81件。

（二）积极开展马德里商标国际注册宣传与培训工作

加大对国内企业进行商标国际注册的指导力度，大力支持国内企业商标海外维权。2014年，国内申请人提交马德里商标国际注册申请2140件（一标多类），位居马德里体系第七，累计达1.86万件；外国申请人指定我国的马德里商标国际注册申请2.03万件，继续位居马德里体系第一，累计达20.89万件。

（三）积极引导和支持企业运用商标权质权融资

全年共办理商标质权登记申请758件，质押商标8721件，帮助企业融资519亿元，同比增长29%。

（四）深入开展“商标与经济发展关系”课题研究

着力提升商标理论研究的前瞻性、政策性和实用性。举办了知识产权前沿问题研究高级研修班，加强政策研究和数据综合分析，推动研究成果的转化和运用。

五、国际及我国港澳台交流与合作不断加强

2014年，国家工商总局开展了一系列商标领域多边及双边交流合作项目，取得了显著成效。

（一）积极开展多边领域的交流与合作

继续与世界知识产权组织（以下简称“WIPO”）保持密切的交流与合作。国家工商总局局长张茅先后会见了世界知识产权组织总干事弗朗西斯·高锐先生和副总干事王彬颖女士。在会见世界知识产权组织总干事弗朗西斯·高锐先生时，张茅局长表示，世界知识产权组织中国办事处于7月10日正式揭牌，是双方合作史上的又一座里程碑，国家工商总局将与世界知识产权组织一道巩固已有合作成果，促进中国企业顺利走向国际市场，共同推动知识产权事业不断发展。派员参加世界知识产权组织的第54次成员国大会及各委员会工作会议。派员参加亚太经合组织（APEC）第39次知识产权专家组会议，认真研究并积极提出会议预案，与各国知识产权专家进行了深入交流。派员参加商标五方会谈2014年中期会议和年会，在京召开商标五方会谈分类专家技术会议。

（二）积极开展中美、中英、中欧等双边领域的交流与合作

与美国专利商标局在北京召开了中美地理标志保护研讨会。与欧洲内部市场协调局在北京共同举办了中欧商标最佳实践研讨会，并在辽宁省沈阳市、黑龙江省哈尔滨市分别举办了欧共体商标巡回研讨会。与英国知识产权局在北京召开了中英商标研讨会。在合作谅解备忘录框架下，与瑞士、韩国、法国、泰国、丹麦、非洲地区知识产权组织等加强合作与联系。

（三）积极开展与港、澳、台地区的交流与合作

国家工商总局副局长刘俊臣会见了来访的香港知识产权署署长梁家丽女士，就商标领域共同关心的问题进行了交流。积极派员参加2014海峡两岸商标研讨会论坛、2014年内地与香港、澳门知识产权研讨会。

（四）进一步加强与外国使馆及知识产权机构的工作联系

国家工商总局继续加强与美国、欧盟、韩国、法国、英国等国家或地区的商标主管机关、驻华使馆或知识产权机构的联系，了解各方工作最新进展，就商标法及其实施条例的实施等内容进行深入交流探讨，为加强对外宣传、树立我国保护知识产权的良好形象发挥了重要作用。

（国家工商行政管理总局商标局）

中国版权行政管理工作

2014 年国家版权局按照中央统一部署，创新方法、提高效能，突出网络版权执法和大案要案查办，认真履行了工作职责，全面完成了工作任务。

一、版权执法监管开创新局面

（一）打击侵权盗版行为

一是认真落实“双打”专项治理工作任务。按照国务院关于打击侵犯知识产权和制售假冒伪劣商品专项行动的工作部署，国家版权局把日常监管与“双打”专项行动相结合，标本兼治，整体推进。全年各地版权行政执法部门共查办案件 532 件，其中行政处理 510 件，罚款 3391 万元，移送司法机关追究刑事责任 80 件，捣毁盗版窝点 188 个。

二是继续开展互联网侵权盗版专项治理。自 6 月开始，联合国家互联网信息办公室、工业和信息化部、公安部启动了第十次打击网络侵权盗版“剑网 2014”专项行动。针对网络文学、音乐、影视、游戏、动漫、软件等重点领域以及图书、音像制品、电子出版物、网络出版物等重点产品，严厉打击各种侵权盗版行为。专项行动期间，全国各地版权行政执法部门共查处案件 440 起，移送司法机关 66 起，罚款人民币 352 万余元，关闭网站 750 家，网络侵权盗版高发势头得到遏制。

三是加大侵权盗版案件督办力度。为推动“剑网 2014”专项行动深入开展，国家版权局会同国家互联网信息办公室、工业和信息化部及公安部，于 8 月对北京、天津、河北等 12 个地区进行了督察，并自行及与全国“扫黄打非”办、公安部、最高人民法院和最高人民检察院等联合挂牌督办了安徽“DY161 电影网”侵犯著作权案等 33 起重大案件，有力促进版权行政执法工作。

四是严查“射手网”等以“网络字幕组”名目存在的典型网站，一批类似网站慑于压力自行关闭。

五是加大案件查办情况宣传力度。先后通报三批“剑网 2014”专项行动中典型案件的查处情况，营造了打击盗版、维护正版的良好舆论氛围，有效震慑了侵权盗版分子。

（二）强化版权重点监管

一是组建版权重点监管工作小组，利用国家版权监管平台，启动对重点影视作品的版权预警保护，公布了三批重点预警作品，逐步建立科学规范的工作制度、程序和措施。

二是继续推进国家版权监管平台升级改造及二期工程建设工作。完成平台一期恢复运行及升级改造工作，平台二期经过研究制定需求、公开招投标、确定承建单位等程序，已经进入开发阶段。通过监管平台建设，以技术手段，加强版权执法监管及社会服务。

三是规范网络版权转载。相继组织召开报刊社、重点互联网站版权座谈会，组织 191 家各类网站签署“守正创新，拒绝盗版、净化网络环境”联合倡议。指导各地积极探索“规范网络转载”管理手段，通过组织网站开展自查自纠、引导报刊社与大型商业网站开展版权合作、加强对网络转载的版权监管等方式，推动完善网络转载许可付酬机制，形成“先授权、后传播”的合法网络版权传播秩序。

（三）健全执法工作体系

一是加强执法队伍建设。2014 年，国家版权局对在 2013 年度查处侵权盗版案件的 215 家有功单位、179 名有功个人给予奖励，奖励金额达 600 余万元，有效激励了版权相关执法部门及人员的办案积极性。共举办 4 期版权执法培训班，对 31 个省（区、市）各级版权执法部门进行培训，提高了基层版权执法人员的版权执法能力。

二是加强案件信息公开。根据国务院及全国双打办工作部署，下发了《新闻出版（版权）行政执法部门依法公开制售假冒伪劣商品和侵犯知识产权行政处罚案件信息的实施细则（试行）》及《关于进一步做好版权行政处罚案件信息公开与信息报送工作的通知》，对全国版权行政处罚案件的信息公开和数据报送工作提出详细、具体要求。全年各地版权执法部门共公开版权案件信息 332 件。

二、软件正版化工作取得新进展

（一）完善长效机制，全面巩固政府机关软件正版化工作成果

推进政府机关和中央企业三级以上企业全部实现软件正版化，出台《关于贯彻落实〈政府机关使用正版软件管理办法〉的实施意见》，对《政府机关使用正版软件管理办法》的相关要求进行细化，指导各地区、各部门完善软件正版化工作相关制度，推进长效机制建设。建成中央和省级各单位软件正版化责任人数据库。其中，中央级数据库含129 个工作责任人信息，省级数据库含有全国 2327 个工作责任人信息。开展两轮政府机关软件正版化检查，通过改进软件正版化审计、软件采购、资产管理和督促检查等措施，巩固软件正版化工作成果，推进长效机制建设。

（二）加强协调指导，扎实推进企业软件正版化工作

印发了《关于做好企业软件正版化信息报送工作的通知》，建立了企业软件正版化信息报送制度。会同国资委组建联合工作组，共同研究制定中央企业软件正版化工作指南，并对 12 家中央企业进行督查。完善新闻出版行业企业软件正版化工作信息化平台，提高了软件正版化信息报送效率。推进新闻出版行业企业集团所属二级企业基本实现软件正版化。

（三）广泛培训宣传，积极营造使用正版软件良好氛围

举办 2 期政府机关软件正版化工作培训班。组织 128 家中央和国家机关，31 个省（区、市）政府办公厅、版权、工信、财政等部门参加培训，提高了相关软件正版化工作人员的业务水平。举办 1 期新闻出版行业、1 期勘察设计行业、3 期金融行业及国资委管理国有企业软件正版化工作培训班。同时，向社会公布了国务院通报的软件正版化上半年检查情况，制作“软件正版化在中国”专刊，编制《中国的软件正版化工作进程》白皮书，将在审核通过后发布。

三、版权产业发展迈上新台阶

（一）第五届中国国际版权博览会成功举办

9 月，在成都举办的第五届中国国际版权博览会取得圆满成功。博览会共举行了国际版权论坛、中国版权产业与金融创新高峰论坛、中国数字版权高峰论坛暨交易会等 12 项重要主题活动及影视剧本、纪录片交易洽谈会等 100 余项配套活动，现场达成 17 个重大版权项目签约，涉及音乐、出版、科技（软件）、影视、艺术设计、金融及版权服务等多个领域，交易金额超过 20 亿元人民币。

（二）全国版权示范建设工作成效显著

召开“全国版权社会服务工作交流会”，交流版权示范建设工作经验。经考察、评选，国家版权局授予厦门“全国版权示范城市”称号，北京出版集团有限责任公司等 18 家单位“全国版权示范单位”称号，山东鸿儒文化集团有限公司等 4 家园区（基地）“全国版权示范园区（基地）”称号；同意设立广州越秀区、上海自贸区“国家版权贸易基地”；西安、成都设立“国家版权交易中心”，促成版权贸易平台常态化，带动区域版权产业发展。

（三）版权产业相关研究工作不断深入

2014 年，国家版权局继续开展版权产业对国民经济贡献调研并对外公布了 2011 年度和 2012 年度相关数据。调查显示，2011 年我国版权产业行业增加值为 31528.98 亿元人民币，占全国 GDP 的 6.67%，比 2010 年增加 5158.72 亿元人民币，增长率为 19.56%。2012 年我国版权产业行业增加值为 35674.15 亿元人民币，占全国 GDP 的 6.87%，比 2008 年总量增加了 16105.75 亿元人民币，平均年增速达 16.20%。

四、版权社会服务得到新提升

（一）著作权登记工作有序进行

2 月，国家版权局上报《2013 年著作权登记量首破百万》的专报，引起中央领导高度重视和社会各界广泛关注。组织 6 家中央媒体对著作权登记工作集中开展宣传报道。召开“全国版权社会服务工作交流会”，交流各地著作权登记成功经验。下发《关于规范著作权合同备案申请表及证书的通知》，进一步规范有关登记事项。2014 年，我国著作权登记总量达 1211313 件，比 2013 年增加了 201656 件，增长 19.97%。其中，作品登记 992034 件，计算机软件著作权登记 218783 件，分别较 2013 年同期增长 17.39% 和 33.12%；著作权质权登记 496 件，涉及主债务金额 262543.1 万元。

（二）行业监管更加规范

一是加强对6家在我国常驻涉外著作权认证机构的监管。通过建立通气会制度、规范审批备案事项等，对其加强日常管理。二是加强对5家著作权集体管理组织的管理与服务，帮助其处理换届筹备及审核、年检、解决争议等方面的工作。三是清理涉外著作权认证及合同登记工作，进一步规范监管指导意见。重点梳理了1995年以来有关法律依据，召开相关省级版权管理部门及图书、音像出版单位座谈会，并与国家外汇管理局等部门沟通，为制定对涉外著作权认证及合同登记工作的规范性意见做必要准备。

（三）版权公共宣传广泛开展

按照创新方式、务求实效的方针，对版权工作广泛进行宣传。“4.26 全国知识产权宣传周”和“第五届中国国际版权博览会”期间，协调中央主要新闻媒体和各地版权相关部门共同参与，并利用平面、广电、网络、户外媒介等多种形式进行多维度宣传。在日常宣传中，以召开新闻发布会，组织媒体联合采访、人民网高端访谈、新浪微访谈，拍摄版权公益广告宣传片，设计版权宣传海报、制作官网宣传专区、开通国家版权局官方微信和官方微博（目前官方微博已发消息100多条，粉丝近43万），举办“版权相关热点问题媒体研修班”等形式，全面展示我国版权保护及产业发展。

五、版权国际事务取得新进步

（一）积极参与国际版权事务

2014年，积极参与世界贸易组织（WTO）、世界知识产权组织（WIPO）、亚太经合组织（APEC）等对华版权事务。完成WTO第五次对华贸易政策审议工作，完成并向WIPO递交批准《视听表演北京条约》的政府声明，参与《保护广播组织条约》《有关图书馆、档案馆和教育机构限制和例外国际文书》和《保护民间文艺条约》等国际条约的磋商。

（二）妥善处理版权涉外关系

在中美商贸联委会（JCCT）以及中美战略经济对话（SED）工作项下，积极做好中美版权应对工作，并着重做好中美商贸联委会项下知识产权工作组、第24届中美商贸联委会后续工作以及第25届中美商贸联委会的相关应对工作。参与中欧第12次知识产权对话和第13次知识产权工作组的相关工作。参与中澳、中韩、中日韩、东盟10加6自贸协定谈判及中俄、中巴知识产权工作组会议。与阿尔及利亚国家版权局签署《中阿版权交流合作备忘录》，首次建立与阿拉伯国家及非洲国家版权双边关系。与韩国文化体育观光部联合制作版权广告宣传片，同时在双方电视台和网络上播放，取得了良好效果。不断扩大两岸四地版权交流合作，落实《海峡两岸知识产权保护合作协议》，成功举办了第七届海峡两岸著作权保护研讨会暨两岸版权主管部门工作组会议。与香港海关就打击网络侵权盗版开展交流合作。与国际标准化组织（ISO）合作，推动成功查办“上海王某等利用互联网销售侵权盗版ISO标准案”，得到了国际标准化组织的高度赞赏。

（三）开展国际版权课题研究

依托国家版权局国际版权研究基地，有针对性地开展研究工作。组织编写《国际版权动态》，介绍国际版权发展信息；针对美国301报告、美国数字经济中版权政策创造与创新绿皮书等报告进行分析；完成对美国及欧盟与知识产权有关的贸易与外资准入壁垒调查报告；参与研究制定中韩和中澳自贸协定谈判对案。

（国家版权局综合处副处长　丁智勇）

中国地理标志产品保护工作情况

一、地理标志产品保护新规模

2014年，新受理170个产品申请（其含中国内169件、国际1件），新批准197个地理标志产品（含国内196件、国际1件），新核准地理标志产品专用标志使用企业646家。截至2014年年底，获保产品已达1806件，核准地理标志产品专用标志使用企业近10000家。

二、国家地理标志保护示范区建设

2014年新批准广西横县设立地理标志保护示范区。截至2014年年底，先后在北京市的平谷（大桃），江苏省的阳山（水蜜桃），四川省双流县、郫县、蒲江县，浙江省的衢州（椪柑），广西壮族自治区的横县设立了国家地理标志保护示范区，以挖掘地区特色产业潜力，有效带动产业升级发展，起到了良好的示范作用。

三、地理标志保护国际合作新局面

2014年，在中墨两国元首见证下，质检总局支树平局长向墨方颁发特其拉龙舌兰酒（Tequila）在华地理标志保护批准公告；经过中欧双方共同努力，双方共同许可中欧“10＋10”产品使用对方地理标志产品专用标志，积极推进中欧“10＋10”互认试点产品的国际化运用；在商务部的牵头下，积极推动中欧“100＋100”互认互保项目，顺利完成了第一阶段中欧地理标志质检清单和技术文件的筹备工作；参加中美第25届JCCT知识产权谈判，为中美知识产权地理标志早期收获奠定基础；参加了中欧地理标志谈判协定第9轮、第10轮谈判，举办2014年中欧地理标志保护研讨会，以利完善中欧双方的地理标志制度，深入开展国际合作，促进中国地理标志事业的健康持续发展。

四、地理标志服务民生新贡献

结合西藏地理标志产品申报实际，组织开展了2014年地理标志保护援藏活动，对“古荣糌粑”“尼木藏香”“林芝灵芝”“乃东泽贴尔”等11个西藏地理标志申报产品开展了专题技术审查活动，既结合实际对地理标志申报产品提出了具体改进意见，以提升西藏地理标志申报产品的声誉和产品附加值；又指导理清了西藏地理标志保护工作思路，发挥地理标志作为“富民强县”重要手段的作用，推动西藏特色产业的健康持续发展。积极推行地理标志保护促进欠发达地区经济发展，加强对欠发达地区的业务指导、技术培训、鼓励申报、加快流程、专项支持等服务措施。全年中西部申报量占总量50%以上，申报涨幅为历来之最，对欠发达地区的地理标志资源转化为现实生产力起到了重要的促进作用。

五、地理标志业务建设新进展

2014年组织召开《中国地理标志产品大典》编纂工作会议，推进《中国地理标志产品大典》编撰，向国内外媒体和公众集中展示质检系统保护的地理标志产品。开展2014年地理标志品牌价值评价工作，试评出茅台酒（贵州茅台酒）、南丰蜜橘、郫县豆瓣、四川泡菜、绍兴酒、武夷岩茶、西湖龙井、宣纸、云锦、烟台苹果、镇江香醋、章丘大葱等12个地理标志区域品牌，质检总局科技司武津生司长在中央电视台面向全国发布。

六、地理标志产品专项检查成效显著

质检总局每年开展地理标志保护产品专项监督检查工作，对存在假冒伪劣和质量安全事件的地理标志保护产品生产企业、地理标志保护示范区、业务工作规范化和工作责任风险开展专项监督检查，专项监督检查成果显著。

（国家质检总局科技司地理
标志管理处处长　姚泽华）

第七篇　中国地方 WTO 事务（2014）

辽宁省外贸及对外开放呈现新局面

一、外贸进出口总体平稳

（一）基本情况

2014年，辽宁省外贸工作面临前所未有的挑战，为实现外贸稳增长，省政府出台了《辽宁省关于支持外贸稳定增长的实施意见》，提出29项具体支持措施。全年全省进出口实现了1139.6亿美元，与上年同期基本持平。其中，出口587.6亿美元，同比下降8.9%；进口552亿美元，同比增长11%。

（二）进出口主要特点

1. 一般贸易进出口占全省的50%以上

2014年，全省一般贸易进出口635.46亿美元，占全省贸易总额的55.7%。其中出口322.95亿美元，下降11.55%；进口312.5亿美元，增长10.18%。

2. 国有企业进出口增长较快，民营企业进出口下降

全省国有企业出口149.06亿美元，增长14.63%；进口162.68亿美元，增长14.29%。外商投资企业出口217.32亿美元，下降0.87%；进口268.45亿美元，增长16.23%。民营企业出口221.21亿美元，下降25.3%；进口120.83亿美元，下降2.67%。

3. 对主要传统市场出口下降，从中东、欧美进口保持快速增长

全省对日本、韩国、东盟、欧盟、美国出口分别下降5.28%、0.35%、2.72%、13.08%和17.72%。从阿曼、卡塔尔、伊拉克等中东国家进口增长较快，从这三个国家增加进口36亿美元，从欧盟、美国进口增长20%以上。

4. 钢材、成品油出口保持较快增长，船舶和部分劳动密集型产品出口大幅下降

全省钢材出口76.46亿美元，增长41.68%；成品油出口51.4亿美元，增长11.33%。船舶出口17.98亿美元，比去年同期减少14.88亿美元，下降45.29%。海洋工程出口7.86亿美元，下降22.7%。鞋类、塑料制品、家具出口均下降35%以上。

5. 原油、天然气、机电产品进口快速增长

全省原油进口137.01亿美元，增长12.28%，天然气新增进口16亿美元，机电产品进口增长18.67%。医药品、钢材、成品油、水产品进口增长也较快。

（三）主要工作

1. 积极发展跨境电子商务

辽宁省外经贸厅与迈克集团签订了《关于开展全省跨境电子商务战略合作协议》，全年省内企业通过迈克集团“出口时代网”开展跨境电子商务出口近3000万美元。6月28日，海关总署同意葫芦岛市开展跨境电子商务出口试点，并参加首批总署跨境电子商务零售出口统一版系统联网试运行。11月11日，在葫芦岛市举行了跨境电子商务平台通关启动仪式。

2. 鼓励企业通过出口信用保险抢抓国际订单

针对辽宁省出口企业的特点，风险控制范围内的出口信用保险应保尽保。细化外贸出口企业为百强企业、成长型企业、小微企业三种类型，分别制定、出台并执行相关支持政策和差异化服务。全年共为1389家企业提供风险保障117.2亿美元，同比增长22.5%；参保企业出口总额达143.5亿美元，同比增长5.9%；为57户企业赔付资金1474.3万美元，为28户企业追回资金2991.3万美元，帮助企业实现融资170.5亿元人民币。

3. 创新方式全力开拓国际市场

制订了重点展会开拓计划，涵盖了轻工、纺织、建材、机电、农产品、化工行业的21个国际知名展和三个综合展。重点展会中有一半是针对新兴市场。全年共组织和协调省内380家企业1100余人次赴境外参展，现场成交及签订意向性贸易金额10.1亿美元。此外，在省内和境外还分别组织了采购洽谈会。

4. 出口基地建设取得重要成果

制定《辽宁省出口基地建设工作指导意见》和《辽宁省出口基地管理暂行办法》，初步建立了出口基地优胜劣汰的动态考核机制，规范了新的省级出

口基地评选认定的申报条件、申报材料和评定程序。全省 38 家省级出口基地中，22 家基地实现出口正增长。纳入基地管理的企业 2500 余家，其中有出口实绩的企业 1324 家。2014 年基地出口 265.5 亿美元，占全省出口额的 45.2%。

5. *积极探索内外贸结合市场建设工作*

重点推动鞍山西柳、沈阳五爱和辽阳佟二堡等地的内外贸结合市场建设，出台了《关于加快推进我省内外贸结合市场建设试点工作的实施意见》。同时，探索在境外特别是俄罗斯远东、伊尔库斯克地区建立商品市场，加强内外贸结合市场与境外市场的合作对接，拓展外贸出口渠道。

二、对外开放工作取得新进展

（一）大连金普新区获国务院批准

获批后的大连金普新区将为老工业基地转变发展方式、体制机制创新发挥示范作用，促进东北地区老工业基地全面振兴，推进面向东北亚区域的开放合作。

（二）海关特殊监管区建设取得成效

推进大连保税区新型业务开展、投资贸易便利化措施落地、园区体制机制创新等，力促大连保税区向自由贸易园区转变；积极指导和推进营口、丹东综合保税区的规划论证工作；研究并推进沈阳综合保税区资源整合工作；协调和组织了盘锦港、铁岭两个保税物流中心（B 型）申报工作，两个保税物流中心于 10 月份得到了海关总署的正式批复。

此外，大连自由贸易试验区先行先试全面展开，申办工作有序推进。丹东边合区区位调整得到国家住建部、国土资源部批准，沿边开放有了新进展。省级以上经济开发区保持了良好的发展态势，地区生产总值实现 9154 亿元，同比增长 4.6%；外贸出口 298.6 亿美元，实际利用外资 134.8 亿美元。

（辽宁省对外贸易经济合作厅）

江苏省对外经贸及公平贸易工作

2014 年，江苏省消费品市场增势平稳，外贸发展稳中有进，利用外资继续保持全国领先，服务外包发展势头良好，企业“走出去”保持了较快发展。

一、贸易及对外开放总体情况

（一）消费品市场增势平稳

2014 年，全省社会消费品零售总额 23209 亿元，同比名义增长 12.4%，高于全国平均水平 0.4 个百分点。城镇实现社零总额 20868.9 亿元，同比增长 12.4%，占全省比重 89.9%；乡村实现社零总额 2340.1 亿元，同比增长 11.9%，占全省比重 10.1%。

（二）货物贸易稳中有进

2014 年，全省进出口总额 5637.6 亿美元，同比增长 2.4%。其中，出口 3418.7 亿美元，同比增长 4%，进口 2218.9 亿美元，与 2013 年持平；进出口规模位居全国第二位，占全国比重 13.1%。

（三）利用外资规模继续保持全国领先

2014 年，全省实际使用外资 281.7 亿美元，占全国比重为 23.6%，同比下降 14.2%；新增项目 3031 个，同比下降 12.2%；协议外资 431.9 亿美元，同比下降 8.9%。

（四）服务外包发展势头良好

2014 年，服务外包合同总额为 372.8 亿美元，同比增长 26.0%，其中离岸合同金额为 208.5 亿美元，同比增长 25.0%。全省服务外包执行总额达到 311.3 亿美元，同比增长 30.3%，其中离岸执行金额为 174.7 亿美元，同比增长 26.9%。全省服务外包企业登记数近 8200 家，带动就业人数近 105 万。

（五）“走出去”保持较快发展

2014 年，全省共核准对外投资项目 736 个，同比增长 21.7%；中方协议投资额 72.2 亿美元，同比增长 17.5%。其中，核准境外分公司及办事处项目 38 个，核准境外企业项目 698 个。全省对外承包工程业务新签合同额 96.6 亿美元，同比增长 13.0%；对外劳务合作业务新签劳务人员合同工资总额 12.1 亿美元，同比增长 59.6%。

二、公平贸易简况

（一）以大案要案为工作重点，有效应对国际贸易摩擦

一是全力做好光伏产品贸易摩擦应对工作。组织我省 100 多家涉案企业积极应对美国、澳大利亚、加拿大先后对我国光伏产品发起的贸易摩擦调查，通过业内座谈、境外磋商、专业辅导等多种形式指导企业积极应诉；二是高效应对涉及江苏省的反补贴调查。2014 年，针对涉及江苏省的十几起反补贴调查案件，通过全省应对贸易摩擦联席会议机制，牵头组织省财政、环保、国土、科技、工商等十几个部门填答政府问卷；三是针对应诉企业进行重点辅导。召开应对工作会，并对相关企业进行一对一重点辅导。邀请律师介绍案件情况、法律程序以及企业应诉的注意事项，对企业的前、中、后期应诉工作提出相关建议，并解答企业对“双反”调查的疑问，推动企业积极有效应诉，同时积极配合商会指导企业应对贸易摩擦。四是加强贸易摩擦规律研究。联合南京理工大学国际贸易学院的科研团队，就如何有效提升江苏应对贸易摩擦综合能力这一课题开展了共同研究。

（二）加强产品监控，维护产业安全

2014 年江苏省设有 29 家进出口公平贸易预警点，涵盖了钢铁、化工、生物制药、光伏、纺织等省内重点行业，这些预警点主要承担产品的进出口监测、贸易摩擦应对、海外市场维护等职能，及时关注行业动态发展和进口国政策变化。预警点全年上报预警信息共计 2252 条。

截至 2014 年 12 月，江苏企业对进口产品累计发起反倾销原审案件 32 起（含支持企业提起），名列全国前茅，案件涉及化工、电子、冶金、轻工等 11 个行业的 28 种产品、38 家企业。目前已获得肯定性终裁案件 30 起，因倾销幅度小于 2%而终止调查 1 起，企业撤诉案件 1 起，正在调查 1 起，仍

在实施措施 22 起。省内企业提起期中复审 9 起，期终复审调查 19 起，反补贴案件 2 起，保障措施 1 起。

（三）积极维护省内产业安全

一是加强进口产品动态分析。加强产业安全数据收集和分析，跟踪多晶硅、吡啶等产品的进口情况，发现苗头即发出预警。二是支持龙头企业对影响产业安全的进口产品提出采取贸易救济措施申请，主动与商务部沟通，积极争取立案调查。三是积极深入企业分析评估贸易救济措施效果，提出进一步完善措施的建议。四是继续做好全省钢铁行业产业损害预警和产业安全数据库直报工作。

（江苏省商务厅）

浙江省 WTO 事务

一、公平贸易工作概况

2014 年，浙江省公平贸易工作紧紧围绕“拓市场、优服务”等商务中心工作，积极应对国际贸易摩擦案件，加强机制制度建设，努力维护企业合法权益，各项工作取得了新进展。

（一）积极应对贸易摩擦案件

2014 年浙江省共遭遇印度、土耳其、印尼、巴西、美国、欧盟等 21 个国家和地区提起的贸易救济调查案件 113 起（其中原审案件 68 起），同比增长 10.8%，涉案金额 16.2 亿美元，占全国的四分之一，同比上升了 65.7%。浙江省各级商务主管部门、企业和预警点行业协会积极应对，成效显著。

1. 加强欧美发达国家案件应对

主要围绕美国对华晶体硅光伏产品“双反”案、美国对华钢制搁架“双反”案、美国对华制冷剂“双反”案件、澳大利亚对华晶体硅光伏模块反倾销案、欧盟对华玻璃纤维反补贴案等重点案件开展应对工作。特别是针对美发起的四氟乙烷案不利的初裁形势，国企、央企、民企联合开展行业无损害抗辩，实现了无税结案，保住了近亿美元的出口市场。

2. 妥善应对发展中国家案件

分别就印度对华格列齐特反倾销、印度对华风力发电铸件反补贴、印度对华光伏反倾销、巴西对华树脂铅笔反倾销案、墨西哥对华门把手案等难点案件开展应对。在印度光伏反倾销案中，经过企业和行业的共同努力，印度最后做出了不征税的决定。2014 年前三季度浙江省光伏产品对印度出口 4307 万美元，同比增长 174.5%。在巴西对华尼龙长丝反倾销案中，浙江省企业获得了全球最低税率，2014 年前三季度涉案产品出口 2839 万美元，同比增长 80.58%。

3. 做好技术性贸易壁垒应对

《欧盟生物灭杀剂法规》涉及浙江省 9 大行业逾 200 亿美元出口。省商务厅联合质监局针对欧盟 F-Gas 法规积极召开应对协调会，共为省内 1500 余家企业开展了 11 场培训，邀请专家帮助企业研究制订应对策略，企业普遍反映良好。

（二）推动反倾销地方立法

2014 年 4 月 1 日，全国地方政府中出台的首个反倾销法规《浙江省出口产品及倾销应对办法》经省常务会议通过并正式实施。省商务厅向全省各级商务主管部门、预警点、行业协会和企业分发宣传海报及宣传手册，并在电视、报纸等主流媒体上进行了广泛宣传报道。

为更好地贯彻落实该《办法》，2014 年 10 月，省商务厅印发并实行了《浙江省出口产品反倾销应对办法》，从强化应对职能分工、注重宣传培训、建立预警信息快速反应机制、加强全程监督管理、做好后续跟踪及应对等方面做出了细化规定。

（三）推进进口贸易救济调查

省商务厅举行了“全省贸易救济与维护产业安全业务培训班”，邀请商务部领导、知名律师等向浙江省经信委、海关等部门及省商务系统、行业协会、律所、企业代表授课，并积极协助多家公司提起贸易救济调查，包括推进对印度单模光纤反倾销案调查，最终对印度进口单模光纤征收为期 5 年的反倾销税，此案减少了国内产业近三分之一进口量的冲击，维护了省内相关产业的安全发展。

（四）完善预警平台规范化管理

全省已设立 116 个对外贸易预警示范点。省商务厅下发了《浙江省对外贸易预警示范点暂行管理办法》，加强对预警点的规范化管理，完成了杭州、台州等三个预警点的承办主体确认变更，并对一批表现突出的预警点给予了通报表彰。

（五）着力打造法律服务品牌

省商务厅连续 5 年为各预警点行业举行法律服务月活动。2014 年以专题讲座、座谈、走访等方式为 550 多家企业提供了国际贸易救济调查、技术性贸易壁垒、国际贸易、知识产权等方面的法律咨询服务。针对美国贸易摩擦案件应对情况，举办了“对美贸易摩擦及其策略应对”专题法律讲座，为对美四氟乙烷案件的成功召开了总结培训会。

（六）提升为企业服务的水平

加强对涉案企业的后续跟踪服务和专题调研。与商务研究院联合完成了《国际贸易摩擦案件应对成功效应分析》，整理编写商务信息简报（专报）。与有关处室配合，鼓励企业参加对外投资说明活动，寻找走出去的良机。

（七）开展政策合规性审查工作

2014年，省商务厅公平贸易局对《关于支持外贸稳定增长的实施意见》《浙江省商务厅浙江省财政厅关于培育建设省级跨境电子商务园区的通知》等10多个政策性文件进行了政策合规性审查，提出了符合WTO规则的审查参考意见。

二、2014年全省贸易救济与维护产业安全工作概况

2014年，全省贸易救济工作建立了较为完善的"一体两翼"的产业损害预警工作长效机制和"四位一体"的产业预警监测体系，工作有序开展。

（一）继续夯实产业损害预警基础

印发了《浙江省产业损害预警体系建设考核评价暂行办法》，进一步明确了项目实施的主要内容和目标，以及项目资金使用的方向和要求。各市根据《办法》精神，结合当地实际制订了实施方案。

截至2014年12月底，产业安全数据库入库企业数已达906家，监测产品356个，涉及化工、轻工、纺织、机械、电子信息等12个行业。产业损害预警监测数据报送率达到95%左右，比年初提高了5个百分点。

在商务部产业安全管制局月度考核中，1—12月浙江省连续综合得分列全国第1名，产业安全预警工作走在全国前列，产业安全预警监测分析系统平稳运行，为政府决策和企业生产经营提供了帮助。

（二）做好"中国产业安全指南网浙江站"的信息维护以及《产业安全信息参考》和《产业损害预警监测报告》的发布工作

2014年1—12月上载产业损害预警、产业竞争力、工作动态等信息千余条；产业损害预警监测报告发布了5期，分析了产业安全形势和产业发展深层次矛盾，监测国际经济发展变化，揭示了进出口异常对我国产业及产业竞争力的影响。

（三）切实做好产业损害现场核查和效果跟踪分析

截至2014年12月底，全省有53家企业发起或参与发起了32起贸易救济案件（详见表1），其中原审案22起，复审案10起。在22起原审案中，除锦纶6、66长丝案因终裁倾销幅度小于2%不征收反倾销税，涂布白卡纸反倾销案延期以及光纤预制棒反倾销案正在调查外，商务部已做出肯定性终裁的有19起，其中初级形态二甲基环体硅氧烷、聚酯切片、涤纶短纤和聚酯薄膜4起案已到期终止。10起复审案，均已做出裁决。截至2014年12月底，省内仍在实施的贸易救济案件（包括原审案、复审案）共19起，涉及的行业有纺织、化工、造纸、机械、电子信息等。

表1　　浙江省贸易救济涉案基本情况

序号	被调查产品	涉案企业	涉案国家（地区）	立案时间	终裁时间	反倾销税	实施情况	行业
原审案								
1	聚酯薄膜	宁波五洲	韩国	1999年4月16日	2000年8月25日	13%～46%	到期终止	塑料
2	二氯甲烷	巨化股份	韩国、英国、美国、荷兰、法国、德国	2000年12月20日	2002年6月20日	4%～66%（法国除外）	到期终止	化工
3	聚酯切片	浙化联集团	韩国	2001年8月3日	2003年2月3日	5%～52%	到期终止	纺织
4	涤纶短纤	浙化联集团	韩国	2001年8月3日	2003年2月3日	2%～48%	到期终止	纺织
5	三氯甲烷	巨化股份	欧盟、韩国、美国、印度	2003年5月30日	2004年11月30日	32%～96%	复审后实施	化工
6	锦纶6、66长丝	华欧锦纶	台湾地区	2003年10月31日	2005年4月28日	<2%，忽略不计	终止	纺织

续 表

序号	被调查产品	涉案企业	涉案国家（地区）	立案时间	终裁时间	反倾销税	实施情况	行业
原审案								
7	初级形态二甲基环体硅氧烷	新安化工	日本、美国、英国、德国	2004年7月16日	2006年1月16日	13%～22%	到期终止	化工
8	氨纶	龙山氨纶、华峰氨纶等	日本、新加坡、韩国、美国、台湾地区	2005年4月13日	2006年10月13日	0～61%	复审后实施	纺织
9	电解电容器纸	凯恩股份	日本	2006年4月18日	2007年4月17日	15%～40.83%	复审调查	造纸
10	初级形态二甲基环体硅氧烷	新安化工	韩国、泰国	2008年5月28日	2009年5月27日	5.4%～25.1%	在实施	化工
11	碳钢紧固件	晋亿实业等30家企业	欧盟	2008年12月29日	2010年6月29日	6.1%～26.0%	在实施	机械
12	对苯二甲酸(PTA)	远东石化、逸盛石化	韩国、泰国	2009年2月12日	2010年8月12日	2%～20.1%	在实施	化工
13	锦纶6切片	舜龙锦纶、华建尼龙、宏福锦纶	美国、欧盟、俄罗斯、台湾地区	2009年4月29日	2010年4月21日	4%～96.5%	在实施	纺织
14	甲醇	晋巨化工	沙特阿拉伯、马来西亚、印度尼西亚、新西兰	2009年6月24日	2010年12月23日	8.90%～37.5%	在实施，但不征收反倾销税	化工
15	汽车	吉利	美国	2009年11月6日	2011年5月5日	反倾销税率2.0%～21.5% 反补贴税率0%～12.9%	在实施	机械
16	非色散位移单模光纤	富通集团	美国、欧盟	2010年4月22日	2011年11月18日	4.7%～21.0%	在实施	电子信息
17	高性能不锈无缝钢管	久立特材	欧盟、日本	2011年9月8日	2012年11月8日	9.2%～14.4%	在实施	钢铁
18	涂布白卡纸	宁波中华纸业 宁波浆纸业有限公司	美国	2011年11月18日	延期		初裁调查/终止审查	造纸
19	间苯二酚	浙江鸿盛化工股份有限公司	美国、日本	2012年3月23日	2013年3月22日	30.1%～40.05%	在实施	化工
20	四氯乙烯*	巨化*	欧盟和美国	2013年5月31日	2014年5月30日	27.6%～71.8%	在实施/配合调查	化工
21	单模光纤	富通集团	印度	2013年8月14日	2014年8月13日	7.4%～30.6%	在实施	电子信息

续 表

序号	被调查产品	涉案企业	涉案国家（地区）	立案时间	终裁时间	反倾销税	实施情况	行业
原审案								
22	光纤预制棒	富通集团	美国、日本	2014 年 3 月 19 日			正在调查	电子信息
复审案								
未发起原审，后参与复审								
1	丙烯酸酯	台塑丙烯酸酯（宁波）、卫星丙烯酸	韩国、马来西亚、新加坡、印度尼西亚	2008 年 4 月 9 日	2009 年 4 月 9 日	2%～49%	到期终止	化工
2	聚氯乙烯	巨化股份	美国、韩国、日本、俄罗斯、台湾地区	2008 年 9 月 29 日	2009 年 9 月 28 日	10%～115%	到期终止/日落复审止在调查	化工
3	乙醇胺	金燕化工	日本、美国、马来西亚、台湾地区	2009 年 11 月 13 日	2010 年 11 月 13 日	9%～74%	在实施	化工
4	非色散位移单模光纤	富通集团	韩国、日本	2009 年 12 月 31 日	2010 年 12 月 31 日	7%～46%	在实施	电子信息
5	三氯乙烯	巨化股份	俄罗斯、日本	2010 年 7 月 21 日	2011 年 7 月 21 日	5%～159%	在实施	化工
发起原审后继续复审								
1	聚酯薄膜	宁波五洲	韩国	2004 年 12 月 28 日	2005 年 12 月 27 日	13%～46%	到期终止	塑料
2	二氯甲烷	巨化股份	韩国、英国、美国、荷兰、法国、德国	2006 年 8 月 15 日	2007 年 8 月 14 日	4%～66%（法国除外）	到期终止	化工
3	三氯甲烷	巨化股份	欧盟、韩国、美国、印度	2009 年 11 月 29 日	2010 年 11 月 28 日	32%～96%	复审后实施	化工
4	氨纶	龙山氨纶、华峰氨纶等	日本、新加坡、韩国、美国、台湾地区	2011 年 11 月 14 日	2012 年 10 月 12 日	0～61%	复审后实施	纺织
5	电解电容器纸	凯恩股份	日本	2012 年 4 月 18 日	2013 年 4 月 17 日	15%～40.83%	复审后实施	造纸

续　表

序号	被调查产品	涉案企业	涉案国家（地区）	立案时间	终裁时间	反倾销税	实施情况	行业
发起原审后继续复审								
备注	截至 2014 年 12 月统计： 1. 浙江省企业发起或者参与发起的原审案共计 22 起（其中：汽车一案为反倾销和反补贴“双反”案计 2 起），复审案为 5 起，参与原审后复审案 5 起，共计 32 起。 解释：复审案中为浙江省企业在原审案时不参与发起，而在复审后参与发起的案件；参与发起原审案，而又参与复审的案件，同时计入原审案。 2. 浙江省目前正在实施的贸易救济案件共计 17 起，其中原审案 11 起、复审案 6 起（参与原审案后复审 3 起），汽车反倾销反补贴案算 2 起。 3. 正在调查产品 1 起（光纤预制棒，富通集团）；配合调查产品一起（四氯乙烯，巨化）；日落复审调查产品一起（聚氯乙烯，巨化）；期终复审调查产品一起（锦纶 6 切片，舜龙锦纶、华建尼龙、宏福锦纶）。 4. 如果按照世贸组织 1 个国家 1 种产品对应 1 起案件的统计方法，浙江省发起和参与发起的企业 53 家，贸易救济调查案为 60 起（包括原审案、复审案），其中反倾销案 59 起，反补贴案 1 起。 5. 下划线为“到期终止”和“终止实施”，* 为配合调查产品不做涉案统计。							

贸易救济措施的实施维护了公平竞争的市场环境，使企业经营和产业发展环境明显改善。如省内有机硅产业在贸易救济措施实施后，摆脱了困境，产能和生产技术水平大幅提升，反倾销案主要发起企业新安化工也跃居国内有机硅生产企业前列。氨纶、光纤产业通过实施贸易救济措施，在国内占据重要地位。又如恒逸集团进军技术含量较高的锦纶产业链上游——己内酰胺，富通集团掌握了光纤预制棒生产的核心技术，对泰国出口增长了 90 倍。

（四）开展工作思路研究

针对新经济常态下贸易救济工作的地位、作用和思路，开展了官、产、学、研各界的多次研讨交流，初步提出了省内“十三五”时期贸易救济和维护产业安全工作的思路并报送省委省政府。与省商务研究院合作完成了《开放型经济下加强浙江贸易救济工作研究》课题。

（浙江省商务厅）

广东省公平贸易与WTO事务工作

2014年，广东省商务厅主动适应经济发展新常态，力促内外贸稳定增长，积极调整外贸发展结构，扎实开展公平贸易与地方世贸组织事务工作。

一、公平贸易工作

（一）2014年广东遭遇贸易摩擦的相关情况

2014年以来，在新兴产业领域，美、欧、日甚至印度以保护知识产权和国家安全、国民和动植物健康、环境安全以及劳工权利等为名义打压我国新兴产业发展的势头更加明显。2014年，13个国家和地区对广东省出口产品发起救济调查43起，其中新立案件35起（含美国337调查8起），复审案件8起，涉案金额逾18亿美元，涉及广东省调查期内出口金额10万美元以上企业250多家，主要针对高新技术产业、新兴产业以及传统产业。

（二）2014年广东省公平贸易工作情况

1. 认真组织应对“两反两保”、337调查等贸易摩擦案件

针对贸易摩擦案件数量和涉案金额继续保持高位的特点，强化了三方面工作：一是加强应诉指导和协调。及时收集和通报案情，跟进案情进展，组织企业积极应诉。召开案件应诉辅导会7场，发布案件预警和立案信息29起。二是深入企业调研，加强重大案件的应诉组织和应诉效果跟踪，同时发挥广东省公平贸易工作站对行业的指导作用，引导工作站组织企业参加无损害抗辩活动；协调本省各级政府部门填答国外反补贴调查问卷；指导各涉案市召开应诉协调会议，落实价格承诺协议等，经积极协调应对，部分案件取得了较好结果。三是加强应对337调查及其他新型贸易壁垒。我省中兴、华为等龙头企业先后遭遇337调查，广东省商务厅除了及时通报案情外，还协助商务部贸易救济调查局领导赴华为、中兴等公司调研和指导工作。同时密切关注当前国外企业对省内企业专利侵权诉讼情况，指导企业积极应诉。

2. 建立健全广东省公平贸易工作站

加强对已成立的9个省公平贸易工作站的管理和考核。召开全省公平贸易工作站专题会议，分析形势，提出总体要求和具体部署。启动对第一批公平贸易工作站绩效评价工作，凡绩效评价不合格的，撤销工作站资格。

积极推动更多有行业代表性的行业协会和龙头企业建立公平贸易工作站，择优产生了15个成员单位，进一步加强工作站在贸易摩擦预警、协调、信息咨询服务等方面的功能。

3. 运用WTO规则维护产业安全

密切跟进广州泰邦食品科技有限公司代表我国产业对印度特丁基对苯二酚发起反倾销调查案，积极向商务部反映企业诉求。商务部于2013年8月22日立案，于2014年4月29日公告初裁，裁定自印度进口产品存在倾销，按相应倾销幅度37.6%～56.9%征收保证金，并在2014年8月21日终裁时，据实加大贸易救济力度，对所有印度进口产品都征收反倾销税49.8%，有效遏制了印度产品的倾销，维护了产业安全和企业权益。

4. 督促产业安全数据库重点监测企业报送数据，同时定期提供产业信息等公共服务

根据商务部《2014—2016年产业损害预警统计报表制度》等有关要求，加强与监测样本企业联系和沟通，组织和督促企业做好产业损害预警重点监测分产品企业报表和企业外贸出口订单调查问卷的报送工作。加强对企业上报数据的审核与分析，提高数据的连续性与准确性，同时及时整理行业分析、产业资讯和案件动向等相关情况，定期向各地市商务主管部门、广东省公平贸易工作站以及重点监测企业提供信息等公共服务。

5. 举办全省贸易摩擦应诉辅导会，提高外贸企业管理人员和公平贸易工作人员应对国际贸易摩擦的业务水平

2014年，分片分期举办四期全省贸易摩擦应诉辅导会，邀请商务部贸易救济调查局领导、资深

律师，就公平贸易工作形势，应对反倾销、反补贴和美国337调查做专题辅导。参训人员包括广东省各地市重点外贸企业的经管人员、有关行业商协会、省公平贸易工作站成员单位人员以及商务主管部门负责公平贸易相关工作人员，提升了广东省公平贸易工作人员的整体素质，提高了产业和企业运用国际规则维护权益的意识和能力。

二、WTO事务工作

广东省积极参与多边合作机制建设，扎实推进世贸组织研究与服务工作。

（一）开展贸易政策合规性工作，促进广东省涉外经济政策与国际接轨

一是在之前承接的“广东省建立涉外经济政策合规性长效机制的调查与评估”课题研究的基础上，按照国务院办公厅关于《进一步加强贸易政策合规工作的通知（代拟稿）》及商务部办公厅关于《贸易政策合规工作实施办法（试行）》征求意见的复函，结合广东实际提出了相关意见和建议。二是与深圳市经贸信息委联合主办“合规工作研讨会”，推进全省贸易政策合规性评估工作，推进规则层面与国际接轨，规范市场化建设。三是贯彻落实国务院办公厅和商务部要求，起草了《广东省贸易政策合规工作实施办法》（代拟稿），按程序上报省政府发文执行。

（二）开展WTO贸易政策审议，促进政策措施透明度提高

在商务部的指导下，先后对卡塔尔、巴林、阿曼、蒙古、巴拿马、美国等WTO成员进行贸易政策审议，收集了被审议成员在货物贸易、服务贸易、知识产权保护、信息安全保护和国际收支等领域违背WTO规则的歧视性或限制性做法和措施情况并上报，维护了企业在国际投资和贸易中的合法权益。

（三）关注和跟踪问题，加强WTO信息咨询与服务

及时收集整理最新资讯，对世贸组织《巴厘部长宣言及决定》贸易便利化条款进行释义，对WTO秘书处关于缅甸等WTO成员贸易政策审议报告进行翻译和整理，形成参阅材料，为省商务主管部门及有关单位、企业提供信息服务。

（四）开展自由贸易区协定优惠政策的解读工作

完成《中国—秘鲁自由贸易区协定解读与指引问答》《中国—瑞士自由贸易区协定解读与指引问答》《中国—哥斯达黎加自由贸易区协定解读与指引问答》等系列协定的解读与编印工作，为企业开拓多元化市场、开展国际化经营和解决国际贸易纠纷提供了操作指引。

（五）加强自贸区动态跟踪分析，提供及时信息参考

密切关注中日韩自贸区、服务贸易协定（TiSA）、信息技术协定（ITA）等谈判的最新进展，撰写《中日韩投资协定的主要特点及深化广东与日韩投资合作的思路》，跟进整编《服务贸易协定谈判（TiSA）进展情况》《内地在广东省向港澳开放服务贸易的具体承诺汇编手册》等参阅材料，及时为政府部门、企业提供了参阅信息。

（六）积极配合商务部有关司局开展相关工作

一是完成商务部世贸司涉外经济政策合规性长效机制调查和评估项目专项课题，参加相关座谈会并提出意见；二是参加商务部世贸司、中国世界贸易组织研究会举办的我国开放型经济体系新战略研讨会；三是派员参加政府采购协议（GPA）、世贸组织规则、产业损害调查等工作会议和培训。

（广东省商务厅公平贸易局
广东省世界贸易组织事务中心）

新疆生产建设兵团对外经贸工作与 WTO 事务简况

一、贸易及对外开放成绩

2014 年新疆生产建设兵团对外贸易增长稳定：外贸进出口总值 119.8 亿美元，同比增长 3.4%，其中出口 109.54 亿美元，进口 10.3 亿美元，自产品出口 20 亿美元，同比增长 20%，技术进出口涉及金额 460 万美元。利用外资实现预期，新设立外资企业 5 家，达到 2.28 亿美元，同比增长 5.4%，其中外商直接投资 6231.7 万美元，外资企业境内在投资 10.2 亿元人民币。对外经济合作取得新进展，对外承包工程 5.8 亿美元，同比增长 18%，新签对外承包工程合同额 2.9 亿美元，年末在外劳务人员 2200 人，对外投资 8604 万美元，同比增长 3.9 倍。

二、普及 WTO 知识规则、强化 WTO 咨询服务

切实开展 WTO 知识规则宣传，对原有网站增设了国别贸易、对外贸易、外经合作和贸易救济、涉外资讯等栏目，做好 WTO 知识的普及和宣传工作，并加强信息维护、及时更新。

三、公平贸易、应对贸易摩擦和产业预警工作

配合商务部通过 EDI 向各地商务主管部门和企业、单位免费推送有关信息，及时准确地采集了兵团主要行业 20 家龙头企业信息以及接收信息人员资料上报商务部并定期接收国别贸易投资环境信息。

及时与商务部职能调整之后的安全与管制局进行业务沟通，编制了产业预警方案上报。

跟踪指导兵团天业集团递交聚氯乙烯产品反倾销措施期终复审申请书工作。积极与有关企业沟通协商，督促企业按时填报产业预警数据库，指导企业做好应对工作。

及时督促和指导相关企业积极做好兵团产业安全数据报送工作。2014 年兵团产业安全数据报送正常有序，产业预警数据库兵团企业 89 家，产业安全月报数据直报率平均为 94%；外贸样本企业数据报送率平均为 73%。

（新疆生产建设兵团商务局）

深圳市经济贸易和 WTO 事务工作

2014 年，深圳牢牢把握“三化一平台”改革方向，坚持稳中求进工作总基调，突出质量引领、创新驱动，加快转型升级，主动适应和引领经济发展新常态，在攻坚克难中实现了全市经济有质量的稳定增长和可持续的全面发展。深圳市世贸组织事务中心紧紧围绕深圳“三化一平台”的战略部署，以深圳实现有质量的稳定增长、可持续的全面发展，加快开放型经济体系和国际化先进城市建设为出发点和落脚点，有序推进各项业务工作。

一、深圳市经济贸易发展概况

（一）主要经济指标表现良好

——经济增长稳中有升，逐季向好。经省统计局核定，2014 年全市生产总值（GDP）达 16001.98 亿元，按可比价计比上年（下同）增长 8.8%。经济规模继续居内地大中城市第四位；从增速看，经济增速逐季提高，全年增速比全国和全省分别高 1.4 和 1.0 个百分点；第一产业下降 19.4%，第二产业增长 7.7%，第三产业增长 9.8%。

——工业生产平稳增长。全年全市规模以上工业增加值 6501.06 亿元，增长 8.4%（联网直报平台数增长 9.4%），高于全国 0.1 个百分点，与全省持平。其中，占规模以上工业比重近六成的通信设备、计算机及其他电子设备制造业增长 14.0%，增速比上年提高 1.2 个百分点。

——固定资产投资增长较快。全年全市固定资产投资 2717.42 亿元，增长 13.6%。其中，第二产业投资增长 46.0%，占固定资产投资比重 19.2%；第三产业投资增长 8.1%，占固定资产投资比重 80.8%。城市更新改造投资增长 11.8%，占固定资产投资比重 14.7%。社会投资超过八成。原特区外投资达到 71.1%。

——消费市场平稳。全年全市社会消费品零售总额 4844.00 亿元，增长 9.3%；商品销售总额 21489.61 亿元，增长 10.8%。在主要类别商品销售中，家用电器和音响器材类增长 0.9%；服装鞋帽针织类增长 7.1%；汽车类增长 11.5%；食品饮料烟酒类增长 11.7%；日用品类增长 15.9%；体育娱乐用品类增长 19.3%；通信器材类增长 19.7%；文化办公用品类增长 20.9%；金银珠宝类增长 24.5%。

——外贸形势逐步好转。据海关统计，全市进出口总额 4877.65 亿美元，下降 9.2%，扣除融资性贸易因素后实际增长 9.8%，进出口规模连续三年蝉联全国内地大中城市首位。其中，出口总额 2844.03 亿美元，下降 7.0%，扣除融资性贸易因素后实际增长 9.7%，出口规模连续二十二年居全国内地城市首位；进口总额 2033.62 亿美元，下降 12.3%，扣除融资性贸易因素后实际增长 9.8%。

（二）产业结构持续升级

——第三产业比重持续提升。二三次产业结构持续调整，2014 年二三产业结构调整为 42.7:57.3，第三产业占比提高 0.7 个百分点。第三产业中现代服务业增加值增长 10.5%，占第三产业比重达 67.6%，比上年提高 0.6 个百分点。其中，金融业增长 13.8%，占 GDP 比重 14.0%，提高 0.2 个百分点；房地产业增长 6.7%，占 GDP 比重 9.0%，回落 0.2 个百分点。

——战略性新兴产业引擎作用更加凸显。预计全年战略性新兴产业增加值达 5645.33 亿元，增长 14.1%，约占全市 GDP 35.3%，比上年提高 0.8 个百分点。六大战略性新兴产业中，生物产业增长 8.7%；新能源产业增长 9.0%；新材料产业增长 10.1%；新一代信息技术产业增长 13.9%；互联网产业增长 15.3%；文化创意产业增长 17.4%。

——制造业高端化取得新的进展。据测算，全年全市先进制造业增加值 4823.98 亿元，增长 10.3%，增速高于全市规模以上工业 0.9 个百分点，占规模以上工业增加值比重 74.2%，在比重超过七成的情况下比上年提高 1.1 个百分点；高技术制造业增加值 4108.35 亿元，增长 13.2%，增速高于全市规模以上工业 3.8 个百分点，占全市规模以上工业增加值比重突破六成，达到 63.2%，比上年提高 4.0 个百分点。

（三）发展质量不断提高

——人均 GDP 实现较大攀升。全年全市人均 GDP 达到 14.95 万元，按平均汇率折算为 24336 美元，相当于 2013 年韩国水平，居内地副省级以上城市首位。

——公共财政预算收入增幅超过两成。全年全市一般公共预算收入突破 2000 亿元大关，达到 2082.44 亿元，增长 20.3%，高于 GDP 增速 11.5 个百分点，高于上年 3.5 个百分点，高于全省 6.4 个百分点。

——工业企业效益明显提高。全年全市规模以上工业企业利润总额增长 16.2%，高于规模以上工业增加值增速 7.8 个百分点，比全国和全省利润增速分别高 12.9 个和 3.8 个百分点。工业企业主营业务收入增长 5.1%，财务费用成本下降 8.4%，亏损企业亏损额下降 8.9%，工业经济效益综合指数达到 217.5%，提高 22.7 个百分点。

——单位能耗继续保持较低水平。初步统计，全年单位 GDP 能耗下降 4.35%，继续保持较低水平。

（四）发展动力不断增强

——科技创新动力持续增强。预计全年全社会研发投入占 GDP 比重约达 4.02%，占比相当韩国水平。全年全市高新技术产业增加值达 5173.49 亿元，增长 11.2%，高于规模以上工业增加值增速 2.8 个百分点。

——金融存贷款形势良好。2014 年末深圳金融机构（含外资）本外币各项存款余额 37350.50 亿元，比年初增长 10.0%；贷款余额 27922.13 亿元，比年初增长 12.5%。

——交通运输业务量全面回升。全年全市货运量、货运周转量、客运量、旅客周转量分别增长 6.8%、19.4%、24.8%、54.2%，分别比上年提高 3.3、13.3、15.8、28.0 个百分点。港口集装箱吞吐量达 2403.74 万标箱，增长 3.3%，比上年提高 1.8 个百分点；机场旅客吞吐量达 3627.25 万人次，增长 12.4%，比上年提高 3.3 个百分点。

——电子商务等新兴业态蓬勃发展。据有关部门预计，全年电子商务交易总额突破 1.5 万亿元，增长 50%。限额以上批发零售企业实现网上销售额增长 31.1%，高于商品销售额平均增速 20.3 个百分点。网购等电子商务发展带动邮政、快递业务量增长 31.4%。

——现代服务业发展势头良好。据调查，全市规模以上服务业营业收入增长 11.9%，营业利润增长 16.7%。其中，重点行业信息传输、软件和信息技术服务业分别增长 15.9%和 12.1%；租赁和商务服务业分别增长 18.1%和 35.5%。

二、深圳市 WTO 事务工作情况

（一）机构名称职能调整，服务外贸大局

为切实理顺与国家商务部、省商务厅的业务联系和工作衔接，更好地落实国务院、省市关于促进外贸稳定增长的若干措施，在经贸信息委的支持下，世贸组织事务中心向市编办申请更名为“深圳市公平贸易促进署”并保留“深圳市世贸组织事务中心”牌子，同时申请拟增加研究建立我市国际贸易质量评价体系和产业及贸易安全防范体系、建设我市走出去公共服务平台、开展 337 调查研究及反垄断调查等相关工作职能。2014 年底该申请已得到市编办的基本认可。

（二）做好我市主要出口市场的贸易监测和预警工作，推动贸易安全与产业损害预警系统建设

2014 年，世贸组织事务中心共发布了三个综合性预警监测报告：即《关注美国市场 促进我市开放型经济发展——2013 年美国市场进出口预警监测报告》《2013 年印度市场进出口预警监测报告》和《光伏产品案件情况分析与展望》。另外，世贸组织事务中心利用有关的国际贸易数据资源，发布了美国、欧盟等 14 国 2014 年度与 2014 年上半年进出口形势分析简报 28 份。在深圳市贸易安全与产业损害预警系统建设方面，系统软件的公开招投标和采购工作正积极推进。

（三）深入开展地方经贸政策及规范性文件合规工作，积极动员业界参与 WTO 贸易政策审议

从 2004 年起，世贸组织事务中心对我市拟出台的市级政策进行 WTO 规则一致性的审核。2012 年，我市以深府办【2012】42 号文颁布了《深圳市贸易政策符合世界贸易组织规则审查办法》，规范了我市贸易政策文件的审查制度，完善了工作机制。2014 年 9 月 11 日，在商务部世贸司指导下，由世贸组织事务中心联合广东省商务厅、深圳市经贸信息委等单位主办，中国世界贸易组织研究会、商务部驻深特派办合办的“落实《国务院办公厅关于进一步加强贸易政策合规工作的通知》宣贯及合规工作研讨会”在深圳召开，商务部世贸司主要负责人亲自到会做主旨演讲。这是全国首个落实国务院有关通知的宣贯会。2014 年，世贸组织事务中心应相关部门的请求，对市人大常委会办公厅交办的法规、市法制办、市科创委、市前海管理局、龙岗区人民政府办公室、罗湖区经促局、福田区企业发展服务中心等有关部门提交的规章、规范性文件草案共计 29 件中存在的与 WTO 规则不一致的条款，分别指出存在的问题和风险，并提出相应的评估和修改意见。

2014 年 WTO 对我国进行了第五次贸易政策审议。世贸组织事务中心密切关注并积极配合商务部开展此项工作，一方面及时向各 WTO 工作站、学会会员、企业行业协会等单位通报有关贸易政策审议工作的信息和动态，同时加强宣传贸易政策审议工作的重要性，让更多的企业、行业协会参与到贸易政策审议工作中，开展调研，向商务部提交有关报告，另一方面世贸组织事务中心分析 WTO 成员对我国尤其是对地方政府经贸政策等方面提出的问题，提出应对措施供有关部门借鉴。

（四）主动应对国际贸易摩擦，维护国际市场份额

2014 年，我市企业年内共遭遇贸易摩擦案件 13 起。其中，反倾销调查 4 起，反补贴调查 3 起，美国 337 调查 6 起。在美国 53 英寸集装箱双反调查案中，我市中集集团涉案。世贸组织事务中心按照“四体联动”应对工作机制的要求，及时向企业提供了法律咨询服务和应对工作意见；在美国光伏产品反补贴调查第一次行政复审案件中，世贸组织事务中心积极配合国家商务部有关部门和相关律师工作，组织我市市级、区级 8 个政府部门认真填写政府调查问卷，并及时反馈至商务部有关部门和律师事务所；世贸组织事务中心还及时通知我市涉案企业参加澳大利亚光伏产品、不锈钢拉制水槽双反、欧亚经委会不锈钢厨具刀具反倾销调查等多起案件预警会议和应诉辅导会。在与贸易有关的知识产权方面，2011 年以来，华为、中兴两家企业频繁遭受美国 337 调查。国家商务部和省、市领导对此高度重视，在各级领导的关怀下，世贸组织事务中心指导两家涉案企业积极应对，捷报频传。除 2 起案件与原告达成和解或原告撤诉外，其他已经取得初裁或终裁的案件全部取得了对两家企业有利的不侵权或专利无效裁决，应对成效非常显著。

为指导企业应诉美国 337 调查，提高应对效果，应国家商务部邀请，美国联邦巡回上诉法院首席法官雷德先生一行赴我市，世贸组织事务中心组织美国法官、专家与华为、中兴两家企业进行专门交流，并与我市相关政府部门和企业、律师代表围绕与贸易有关的知识产权相关议题进行了研讨。

另外，世贸组织事务中心积极与市财政委、市政府办公厅沟通，认真组织开展了对原《深圳市贸易救济研究资金管理办法》的延期和修订的相关工作，推进《深圳市进出口公平贸易研究专项资金管理办法》出台。

（五）强化跨部门联合工作机制建设，提高技术性贸易壁垒应对工作水平和能力

三年前，中心和国家质检总局标法中心、深圳出入境检验检疫局、深圳市市场监督管理局四方在深圳签署《关于技术性贸易措施工作战略框架合作协议》。2014 年 5 月，合作的四方联合召开技术性贸易措施工作座谈会，对此前签署的四方协议落实情况进行总结，就全面做好深化改革背景下技术性贸易措施工作，进一步深化在技术性贸易壁垒调查、通报评议、课题研究等方面的合作达成共识。与此同时，中心不断加强技术性贸易壁垒应对的理论探索，与多个机构合作开展技术性贸易壁垒课题研究，并积极组织申报市经贸信息委的课题，深入研究相关技术性贸易措施的发展趋势、对我市相关产业特别是电子信息产业的影响及应对措施。

（六）理论结合实际，努力发挥课题研究成果对业务工作的经验指导和智力支持作用

2014 年，中心在完成 2013 年深圳市委、市政府重大课题《加调整快贸易政策和产业政策构建开放型经济体系》的基础上，又针对近年来我市企业频繁遭遇美国 337 调查的问题，开展了《华为、中兴应对美国 337 调查案件评估》和《2014 年美国 337 调查发展研究报告》两项课题研究工作，总结国内及我市企业应对美国 337 调查案件的工作经验，为其他涉案企业提供经验参考；全面总结我市国际贸易摩擦的形势和应对工作情况，形成《2013 年深圳市进出口公平贸易报告》；与深圳市进出口商会合作开展《深圳市陶瓷反倾销案件应对总结》研究，总结深圳陶瓷反倾销情况，分析其发展趋势并提出相关政策建议；与天津大学深圳研究院合作开展《提高深圳市企业质量控制——应对国际能效标准研究》，跟踪和分析欧美能效标准出台的现状及其趋势，并为深圳企业的应对提出可操作性的意见和建议。中心还直接承担了两项市政府督察课题的研究，分别是《TPP、TTIP 对深圳外贸和投资发展的影响》《TISA 对深圳外贸和投资发展的影响》。世贸中心还参与了《深圳参与国家“海上丝绸之路”建设问题》等课题研究。

在博士后创新实践基地工作方面，按照 2014 年工作计划，3 月启动新一期博士后招聘工作，上半年先后赴对外经济贸易大学、中山大学、暨南大学等单位开展工作调研，就合作招收博士后、合作开展课题研究等深入交流，与三校博士后流动站建立起良好的交流合作关系，并组织完成了多名博士后的出入站工作。

（七）举办 WTO 事务培训、宣讲活动，加强体系建设

2014 年，重点开展了 WTO 热点问题培训，培训内容包括技术性贸易壁垒应对、企业低碳管理、知识产权保护、企业社会责任风险的防范与应对，2013 年欧美玩具召回案例分析以及应对方案、RoHS 指令最新进展及解析、REACH 法规最新进展及应对、消费类电子欧美能效标准法规最新动态解析、LED 照明产品性能要求及新兴市场准入要求、产品 360 度环保评估方案—绿色产品标识、企业社会责任管理体系建立与运行、企业能源管理成熟度测量、能效壁垒应对、国外技术性贸易措施通报评议及特别贸易关注工作及自贸区知识等方面，培训场次 20 场，培训人员约 2000 人次。另外，世贸中心继续密切联系各 WTO 事务联席单位、WTO 工作站、WTO 学会会员、科研院校、定点培训机构、企业行业协会等单位，继续加强 WTO 事务工作体系建设。

（八）配合商务部开展反垄断调查工作，配合全市做好外贸稳增长及自贸区申报等工作

4 月，中心配合商务部反垄断局及省商务厅，联系在 2012—2013 年度可能涉及实施经营者集中的深圳企业，汇总上报了企业的联系人及联系方式信息，并通知企业尽快与商务部反垄断局联系。9 月，配合省商务厅对深圳有代表性的企业和行业协会进行关于经营者集中反垄断专题调研；10 月，邀请参与调查的企业和行业协会参加由省商务厅组织的关于经营者集中反垄断调研的座谈会，现场对企业和行业协会进行了反垄断工作宣传并解答了企业和行业协会的疑问。11 月，参加商务部反垄断局在北京召开的全国商务系统反垄断工作会议，应邀介绍深圳几年来的反垄断工作并提出建议。

（九）举办 WTO 高级论坛、顾问委员会年会，搭建改革开放交流平台

12 月，召开了由深圳市人民政府主办，中国世界贸易组织研究会合办，深圳市经济贸易和信息化委员会、深圳市世贸组织事务中心承办的第十三届“WTO 与深圳”高级论坛，以及“深圳市世贸组织事务中心顾问委员会 2014 年会”，论坛主题是“后巴厘时代和中国的对外开放”。年会主题为“地方 WTO 事务工作与深圳‘三化一平台’建设”。

（深圳市世贸组织事务中心）

第八篇　WTO 学术成果

●专　　著

陈安. 国际经济法学刊（第20卷第3期）. 北京：北京大学出版社，2014

［作者简介］陈安，厦门大学法学院教授，国际经济法专业博士生导师，福建省福安市人。曾任厦门大学法学院院长、国际经济法研究所所长，兼任中国国际经济法学会会长、中国国际法学会顾问等。

［内容提要］本书设有“WTO法”“国际投资法”“国际知识产权法”“国际仲裁法”“国际发展法”“国际法学术动态”“附录”共七个专栏，收录了《论WTO争端解决机制程序设计缺陷的技术性修正》《WTO争端解决中的“中国现象”——中国涉案实证述评》《出口税应作为保护南非选矿业的法律策略》等。

陈德铭. 经济危机与规则重构. 北京：商务印书馆，2014

［作者简介］陈德铭，经济学硕士，管理学博士。现任海峡两岸关系协会会长；曾任十七届中央候补委员，商务部部长、党组书记；历任江苏省商业厅副厅长、党组成员，江苏省政府副秘书长、办公厅主任，江苏省苏州市委副书记、代市长、市长，苏州工业园区工委书记，苏州市委书记，江苏省委常委，陕西省委常委、副省长、省委副书记、代省长，陕西省委副书记、省长，国家发展和改革委员会副主任、党组副书记（正部长级），商务部党组书记、副部长。

［内容提要］本书立足世界多极化和经济全球化深入发展这一时代背景，从历史的、客观的、辩证的视角，着眼危机前后全球贸易规则的变迁，深入剖析规则调整背后映射出来的理念、利益、地缘等深层次问题，并对未来这些领域规则演进的趋势进行了分析。

陈辉庭. 世界贸易体制的改革——经济全球化背景下国际法与国内法的联结. 北京：社会科学文献出版社，2014

［作者简介］陈辉庭，男，副教授，1974年9月生，福建省惠安县人。1997年毕业于复旦大学国际政治系，获法学学士学位；2004年毕业于厦门大学法学院，获法学硕士学位；2007年毕业于厦门大学法学院，获法学博士学位。现任教于中共福建省委党校、福建行政学院。主要研究方向为国际经济法、涉外经济法和两岸关系法律问题等。

［内容提要］20世纪初以来，传统法律制度与观念面临着经济全球化浪潮的冲击。作为经济全球化的产物，世界贸易法律体制的演进反映了各国经济合作实践发展的客观需要和潜在规律。要全面深入地解释GATT/WTO实践及其规律，需要建立一种全新视角的分析语境，从而在长期割裂的国际法与国内法体系之间架起一座沟通的桥梁。本书揭示了经济全球化背景下国际法与国内法的互动联结及影响，深入辨析了近年在西方兴起的WTO新思潮。

高鸿钧. 清华法治论衡——全球化时代的中国与WTO（上）（第20辑）. 北京：清华大学出版社，2014

［作者简介］高鸿钧，清华大学法学院教授，全国外国法制史研究会理事（自1985），中国社科院法学所法社会学研究中心主任，1997年2月被中国社会科学院授予“中青年有突出贡献专家”，享受政府特殊津贴（1997）。

［内容提要］本辑《清华法治论衡》汇集了一批海内外专门从事WTO法律工作并对该领域有精深研究的专家学者，围绕法律全球化与WTO，

"入世"与中国法治改革，WTO 法律制度的功能、特点及问题，WTO 法对国际法的影响进行研究。

郭桂环. WTO 体制下的动物福利与贸易自由. 北京：中国政法大学出版社，2014

［作者简介］郭桂环，1972 年 10 月出生，河北邢台人。1996 年毕业于河北经贸大学计统系，2003 年毕业于河北师范大学法政学院，获得法学硕士学位。现为河北师范大学法政学院教师。研究方向为国际贸易法、国际投资法。

［内容提要］本书介绍了各国动物福利立法情况以及各国基于动物福利措施所采取的贸易限制措施；重点分析了这些动物福利措施在 WTO 体制下的合法性问题；提出在促进自由贸易目标的同时应注意动物福利保护的具体国际法建议。

国家知识产权培训（湖北）基地. 国际贸易中的知识产权保护. 北京：知识产权出版社，2014

［作者简介］国家知识产权培训（湖北）基地

［内容提要］本书从五个角度全方位论述了国际贸易中的知识产权问题。第一章论述了国际贸易与知识产权之间的关系；第二章和第三章全面介绍了 WIPO 和 WTO；第四章至第六章结合国际贸易的最新趋势对《自由贸易协定》《反假冒贸易协定》和《跨太平洋伙伴关系协定》中涉及的知识产权问题进行了论述，并分析了其对中国知识产权保护事业的影响；第七章至第九章对美、欧、日、韩在国际贸易中的知识产权政策和法律进行了介绍和研究；第十章对我国在国际贸易中面临的各种知识产权纠纷及其对我国国际贸易的影响做了介绍。

韩立余. 世贸规则与产业保护. 北京：北京大学出版社，2014

［作者简介］韩立余，中国人民大学法学院教授，博士生导师。中国人民大学法学博士，曾在香港大学法律学院普通法深造。兼任国务院关税税则委员会咨询专家委员会委员、世界贸易组织争端解决机构专家组成员、中国法学会世界贸易组织法研究会副秘书长。

［内容提要］本书通过有代表性的具体争端案件，分析论证了各国产业政策的成就与不足；最后结合对中国产业政策和相关争端的分析，指出了产业发展中应关注和避免的问题以及努力方向。

贺小勇. 中国产业政策与 WTO 规则协调研究. 北京：北京大学出版社，2014

［作者简介］贺小勇，男，1972 年生，华东政法大学国际法学院教授，国际法博士；英国华威大学发展法硕士；美国旧金山大学法学院客座教授；中国国际法学会理事；上海市优秀青年教师；2007 年上海曙光学者。在《中国法学》《比较法研究》《现代法学》《政法论坛》《法学评论》《法学》等杂志上发表学术论文 80 余篇。

［内容提要］本书首先对产业政策及其主权边界进行界定，然后阐述了产业政策应遵守的基本法律原则，在此基础上，重点分析讨论了补贴政策、汇率政策、知识产权保护政策、环境资源保障政策与 WTO 规则的协调问题等。

姜汉林. 世界贸易组织法. 北京：法律出版社，2014

［作者简介］姜双林，1967，男，浙江省江山市人，法学博士生，副教授，浙江农林大学环境法治与社会发展研究中心副主任，硕士研究生导师。研究方向为环境法学和国际法学。

［内容提要］本书系统介绍了世界贸易组织的基本原理，世界贸易组织协议（包括货物贸易、服务贸易、农产品贸易、与贸易相关的知识产权保护、与货物贸易相关的非关税壁垒措施），以及反补贴、反倾销和保障措施等贸易救济制度、争端解决机制，并概括介绍了贸易与环境、发展中国家与 WTO 等诸方面的理论与实践。

李冰洁. 跨国公司进入模式——基于反倾销壁垒下的选择. 北京：经济科学出版社，2014

［作者简介］李冰洁，女，1977 年出生于陕西省合阳县，现为西安财经学院教师。2003 年毕业于西北政法大学，获企业管理哲学硕士学位；2007 年毕业于西安交通大学，获应用经济学博士学位。主要研究方向为国际经济与贸易、跨国公司理论和政策等。

［内容提要］本书结合中国具体国情，研究进口反倾销和跨国公司进入模式的变动以及国内企业在出口反倾销壁垒下如何进行海外投资，具有重要的战略意义和学术价值。本书在对反倾销、国际贸易和投资理论综合分析的基础上，将反倾销壁垒下中外跨国公司进入模式分为一般模式和特殊模式来

进行研究，提出中国企业应对反倾销壁垒的海外进入模式和政策建议。

刘衡. 国际法之治：从国际法治到全球治理. 武汉：武汉大学出版社，2014

［作者简介］刘衡，法学博士，2011年毕业于武汉大学国际法研究所（国际公法专业），供职于中国社会科学院欧洲研究所。

［内容提要］本书从全球治理的理论语境入手，从法学角度分析全球治理的基本要素，并落脚于“国际法之治”，共分为5章。

刘华. 美欧社会倾销论实质研究. 北京：中国商务出版社，2014

［作者简介］刘华，中国政法大学外国语学院副教授，法学博士，中国政法大学中国国际反垄断和投资中心秘书长，曾在北京市环中律师事务所反倾销部兼职5年。主要研究方向：法律英语、外商投资法、美国公司法、反垄断法、国际经济法、欧盟法、贸易救济法。参编法律英语教材若干部，发表法学学术论文若干篇。

［内容提要］本书共分五章，第一章从历史角度介绍了倾销，第二章是对市场倾销的分析，第三章分析了社会倾销，第四章对比分析了市场倾销和社会倾销的区别与联系，第五章从中国的角度讨论有关市场倾销和社会倾销的几个重要问题。

刘敬东. WTO中的贸易与环境问题. 北京：社会科学文献出版社，2014

［作者简介］刘敬东，1968年生人，黑龙江省哈尔滨市人，中国社会科学院国际法研究所国际经济法室副主任、副研究员，兼任中国政法大学国际法研究中心研究员、北京市政法管理干部学院WTO法律实务研究所主任，国际法学博士，美国哥伦比亚大学、瑞士苏黎世大学访问学者。

［内容提要］本书共八章，主要内容包括：贸易与环境问题产生的法理根源、贸易与环境关系的历史回顾、与环境有关的贸易争端案件分析等。

刘维林. 区域产业全球价值链嵌入的绩效与升级路径研究. 北京：经济科学出版社，2014

［作者简介］刘维林，男，汉族，1979年生人，黑龙江省佳木斯市，博士。主讲课程：运输经济学。第一外语：英语，第二外语：日语、德语。

［内容提要］本书绪论部分剖析了全球价值链概念的演进脉络以及区域产业与全球价值链的关系，并对全球价值链的核心理论文献进行了梳理；第二章分析了区域产业嵌入全球价值链的动因、形式与特点；第三章提出基于功能架构与产品架构的双重视角及本土制造业的升级逻辑；第四章从贸易结构入手分析了中国区域产业的嵌入现状；第五章尝试运用非竞争型投入产出分析技术打开全球价值链的“黑箱”，对区域产业在全球价值链中的嵌入程度进行了初步的整体测度；第六章进一步区分二元贸易结构并按照双重嵌入架构对测度模型进行了优化，并得到更为精细化的价值分解结果；第七章运用计量模型验证了价值链嵌入对于区域产业绩效的动态影响；第八章提出了中国区域产业突破“低端锁定”的战略选择、政策设计与升级路径。

刘瑛. WTO视野下的中国自然资源产品贸易管理制度研究. 北京：中国社会科学出版社，2014

［作者简介］刘瑛，女，法学博士，武汉大学WTO学院副教授，珞珈青年学者，中国法学会世界贸易组织法研究会理事，牛津大学Queen's College访问学者。主要致力于国际经济法的研究，主要研究领域包括国际货物买卖法、WTO法和国际金融法。

［内容提要］WTO作为世界贸易组织，也管理自然资源产品贸易，但自然资源产品贸易因其与自然资源永久主权、可持续发展、资源与环境保护等价值的紧密联系而具有不同于其他产品贸易的特点。本书以WTO规则与争端解决实践为视角，研究中国的自然资源产品贸易管理制度。

刘勇. WTO框架下中国自然资源出口管制政策与法律问题研究. 北京：法律出版社，2014

［作者简介］刘勇，法学博士，浙江财经大学法学院副教授、硕士生导师。主要研究方向为国际贸易法与国际环境法。

［内容提要］本书主要围绕WTO框架下中国自然资源出口管制政策与法律问题的主题，通过背景介绍、理论分析和最新的“中国原材料案”的案例研究等多种方式，呈现出中国自然资源出口管制法律的主要状况，带有强烈的问题意识和鲜明的实践色彩。

吕微平．WTO 争端解决机制的正当程序研究——以专家组证据规则和评审标准为视角．北京：法律出版社，2014

［作者简介］吕微平，1975 年生人，福建漳州人。厦门大学法学院国际法博士，厦门大学马克思主义学院副教授。1993 年至 2000 年就读于南开大学法学院国际法专业，2000 年赴厦门大学工作，2005 年起就职厦门大学法学院，2011 年转任厦门大学马克思主义学院工作至今。主要研究方向为国际经济法、世界贸易组织法、国际关系和思想政治教育。

［内容提要］本书主要以 WTO 争端解决机制正当程序为研究对象，以专家组证据规则和评审标准为视角，探讨了正当程序的实体性保障和程序性保障在 WTO 争端解决机制中的发展。

孟夏．2014—亚太区域经济合作发展报告．北京：高等教育出版社，2014

［作者简介］孟夏，南开大学 APEC 研究中心（教育部首批人文社会科学重点研究基地）教授，长期从事亚太经济、国际区域经济合作、国际经济一体化理论与政策、APEC 问题、国际贸易与投资等领域的研究。

［内容提要］本研究报告将理论、实证与政策分析密切结合，既体现出学术研究的特点，同时也注重为我国参与区域经济合作提供直接的政策参考，得到了政府部门的高度评价。

乔慧娟．私人与国家间投资争端仲裁的法律适用问题研究．北京：法律出版社，2014

［作者简介］乔慧娟，女，1976 年生人，河南新郑人。北方工业大学文法学院法律系副教授，中南财经政法大学法学博士。现主要研究方向为国际私法、国际商事仲裁法。

［内容提要］私人与国家间投资争端问题是国际法司法实践中比较难处理的法律问题之一，作为一个吸引投资大国，我国在这方面的法律保护远远不够，关于投资者与东道国投资争端的法律适用，双边投资保护协定规定也各不相同。作者通过深入分析得出结论。

孙琬钟．2014—WTO 法与中国论坛年刊．北京：国家知识产权出版社，2014

［作者简介］孙琬钟，男，汉族，河北怀来县人，北京大学法学院兼职教授，中国法学会世界贸易组织法研究会的发起人之一。现任世界贸易组织法研究会会长，董必武法学思想研究会常务副会长，北京大学公法研究中心客座研究员，宪法、行政法博士生导师组成员，中国政法大学讲座教授，北京师范大学、中国人民大学兼职教授。

［内容提要］本书是“WTO 法与中国论坛暨中国法学会世界贸易组织法研究会 2013 年年会”论文集，以“WTO 的多边贸易机制：挑战与改革”为中心，研究了多边贸易体制的未来与挑战、WTO 决策机制面临的挑战与改革方向等内容。

孙玉红．多国博弈视角下 TPP 谈判引发的政策互动和中国的战略选择．北京：对外经济贸易大学出版社，2014

［作者简介］孙玉红，女，1965，辽宁本溪人，东北财经大学经济学博士，现任东北财经大学国际经济贸易学院副教授，硕士生导师，东北财经大学区域经济一体化与上海合作组织研究中心兼职研究员。

［内容提要］本书共包括十章内容。第一章为研究背景；第二章为理论依据；第三章为 TPP 谈判的启动；第四章为 TPP 谈判的主要内容；第五章到第七章为加入 TPP 的国家战略动机；第八章论述了被 TPP 排除在外的主要国家的政策互动；第九章分析了 TPP 引发的亚太区域一体化的双轨效应。第十章重点分析了 TPP 对中国的影响和中国的战略选择，并着重对中国应对 TPP 挑战而进行的改革进行了比较系统的分析。

王军．2011—2012 年——WTO 争端解决年度报告．北京：法律出版社，2014

［作者简介］王军，对外经济贸易大学法学院教授、博士生导师，曾任对外经济贸易大学法学院院长，兼任国务院学位委员会第六届学科评议组法学者成员、全国法律专业学位研究生教育指导委员会委员、中国法学会国际经济法研究会常务副会长、中国法学会民法学研究会常务理事、中国国际经济贸易仲裁委员会资深仲裁员，2004 年至 2005 年作为中美政府富布赖特项目访问学者在美国哈佛大学法学院东亚法律研究中心进修和讲学。

［内容提要］本书为 2011—2012 年度 WTO 争端解决法律报告，分为四个部分：发展概况、专家

评论、经典案例、国际交流。

王淼. WTO规则对低碳经济的约束与激励. 大连：东北大学出版社，2014

［作者简介］王淼，女，1983年生人，辽宁海城人，东北大学文法学院讲师，从事税法研究。

［内容提要］本书选取了五个方面的低碳经济措施（相同产品问题、GATT第20条一般例外、碳关税、所得税优惠与补贴以及碳标记）为研究对象，从制度、法律以及司法层面总结、梳理这些措施的运作机理，分析、探讨和展望它们在WTO法中如何运作，以及如何取得、发展其正当性，探讨WTO规则对低碳经济的约束与激励机制。

王茜. WTO服务贸易专题. 北京：法律出版社，2014

［作者简介］王茜，女，现任上海对外经贸大学WTO研究教育学院副教授、硕士生导师，上海高校智库国际经贸治理与中国改革开放联合研究中心研究员。2010年毕业于上海财经大学世界经济专业，获经济学博士学位。同年进入上海对外经贸大学任教至今，主要从事国际金融和国际贸易领域的教学与研究工作，主讲WTO经济学。

［内容提要］《WTO服务贸易专题》是世界贸易组织教席项目的阶段性成果，该项目旨在通过在全球范围内选拔院校设立WTO教席并与之长期合作，支持和促进发展中国家和欠发达国家内大学和研究机构与贸易相关的学术活动，通过课程设计、教学、培训科研和相关信息的普及、公开的学术讨论等方式，提高学生、研究人员、政策制定者和民众对于多边贸易体制的理解和认识。

王维然. 中亚区域经济一体化研究. 北京：知识产权出版社，2014

［作者简介］王维然，1971年生人，男，经济学博士，副教授。从事中亚经济及中亚区域经济一体化研究，先后主持国家社科基金项目、教育部社科项目、新疆维吾尔自治区哲社项目等课题九项，近年来在国内外学术刊物发表论文二十余篇。

［内容提要］本书分析中国与欧亚经济共同体成员国的贸易结构，研究双方可实现双赢的经济合作的领域，而不是仅局限于贸易领域。

熊建军.《TRIPs协议修正案》研究. 北京：知识产权出版社，2014

［作者简介］熊建军，男，1965年生人，汉族，湖北应城市人，中共党员，法学博士，副教授。现为福建工程学院法学院专任教师，民商法学学科带头人，法学研究所副所长，法学综合实践中心主任，福建省知识产权研究院骨干研究人员，福建省知识产权培训中心客座讲师。

［内容提要］本书旨在探讨《修正案》及其所涉强制许可制度如何发挥其旨在解决那些正在遭受艾滋病、肺结核、疟疾和其他传染病侵袭的国家廉价药品获取性危机的功能和作用问题。

许多. WTO规范特惠贸易协定问题研究. 南京：南京大学出版社，2014

［作者简介］许多，南京师范大学外国语学院讲师、博士。

［内容提要］本书作者通过梳理WTO现有关于特惠贸易协定的规则，了解机制的运行现状及WTO成员方已做的改革努力，结合特惠贸易协定近年来的发展变化，并以TPP协定为参照，提出一套多路径并行的规则改革方案，对相关领域的研究具有借鉴作用。

许立波. WTO贸易规则研究. 北京：中国商业出版社，2014

［作者简介］许立波，男，汉族，1965年生人，研究生学历，东北财经大学职业技术学院副教授。

［内容提要］本书全面系统地论述了世界贸易组织（WTO）贸易规则，主要包括WTO的基本原则、法律体系与组织结构、运行机制、贸易框架规则、非关税贸易规则、贸易救济规则、服务贸易规则、知识产权框架规则、诸边贸易协议等方面的内容。

徐昕. WTO货物贸易专题. 北京：法律出版社，2014

［作者简介］徐昕，2001、2004年分别获西北政法大学法学学士和法学硕士学位；2010年获厦门大学法学博士学位；2008—2009年赴法国马赛第三大学欧亚研究所参加中法博士生院项目；2013年赴美国乔治敦大学法学院做高级访问学者。现就职于上海对外经贸大学WTO研究教育学院，副教

授，硕士生导师。主要研究方向为 WTO 法律制度、区域贸易协定等。

［内容提要］本书分为六章，内容包括非歧视原则、市场准入原则、对不公正贸易的救济、与国内管制的协调、贸易自由化与其他社会价值和利益的冲突及调和。

殷敏. 新区域主义时代下中国区域贸易协定研究. 北京：中国政法大学出版社，2014

［作者简介］殷敏，女，上海对外经贸大学法学院副教授，苏州大学王健法学院博士后，华东政法大学国际法博士，美国奥尔巴尼法学院访问学者。

［内容提要］本书主要内容包括：新区域主义时代下区域贸易协定的基本法律问题、区域内区域贸易协定研究、跨区域贸易协定的特殊问题、中国区域贸易协定的现状、中国—巴西跨区域贸易协定研究、中国—南非跨区域贸易协定研究等。

于洋. 2012 年度 WTO 争端解决案例法理选析：DS406 与 DS414. 北京：法律出版社，2014

［作者简介］于洋，男，双硕士、法学博士(复旦大学)。现任上海对外经贸大学 WTO 研究教育学院教师，国际法学专业副教授。商务部企业知识产权海外维权援助中心专家。

［内容提要］本书主要分为三部分，第一部分首先对 2012WTO 争端解决的相关情况加以较详细地综述，第二部分择取了在该年度内裁决完毕的两起案件加以比较，深入分析，以期使读者能够“既见树木又见森林”。书的另一特色是在第三部分增加了对 WTO 争端解决条约解释的方法论方面的探讨。

于洋. WTO 争端解决涉华成案法理选析：DS397 与 DS399. 北京：法律出版社，2014

［作者简介］同前。

［内容提要］本书择取了近年来 WTO 争端解决实践中发生的两起以中国为申诉方而非应诉方的成案为研究对象，主要从国际法的视角有选择性地对其中涉及的法理问题进行较深入的研析，有助于我国今后对 WTO 争端解决机制的理解和运用。

张汉林. 2013——世界贸易组织发展报告. 北京：高等教育出版社，2014

［作者简介］对外经济贸易大学中国 WTO 研究院。

［内容提要］本书内容共分四篇：第一篇为总论，主要是世界经济发展回顾与展望，包括主要经济体的经济、贸易、投资和经贸政策发展情况，2012—2013 年以来 WTO 主要活动和多哈回合谈判进展情况，WTO 与中国；第二篇为主要议题分论，详细分析了农业、技术性贸易壁垒、投资、贸易救济措施、服务贸易、知识产权、争端解决、政府采购、区域贸易协议等 WTO 主要议题的发展演变情况；第三篇为主要成员经贸政策回顾与展望，包括美国、欧盟、日本、印度、巴西、俄罗斯和东盟；第四篇为专题，分别为中国（上海）自由贸易试验区制度创新研究和 2012—2013 年 WTO 相关问题研究综述。

张琪. 博弈双赢——论世界贸易组织争端解决机制中的磋商程序. 上海：上海人民出版社，2014

［作者简介］张琪，上海外国语大学法学院副教授、硕士生导师，从事国际（公）法和国际经济法的教学和研究工作。复旦大学法学学士、英国谢菲尔德大学法学硕士、瑞士伯尔尼大学法学博士。曾经担任德国海德堡马普比较法与国际公法研究所客座研究员、瑞士伯尔尼大学欧洲和国际法系与世界贸易学院研究员。

［内容提要］本书主要论述的是世界贸易组织争端解决机制中的第一个程序——磋商，从程序法的角度对这一很少有学者涉及的领域进行研究。本书内容的整体布局是从大到小来展开论述。

章辉. 中国政府采购市场开放风险与防范. 上海：上海三联书店，2014

［作者简介］章辉，男，1972 年生人，安徽太湖人，毕业于上海财经大学财政学专业，经济学博士。现为上海金融学院财税与公共管理学院教授。兼任财政部中央单位政府采购评审专家、上海市政府采购评审专家、上海市财政支出绩效评价评审专家，全国高校财政学教学研究会理事。

［内容提要］本书关注中国政府采购市场开放与 GPA 制度衔接及可能存在的风险冲击；2013 年，是中国政府采购法颁布十周年。

张晓京. WTO 与粮食安全——法律与政策问题. 湖北：湖北人民出版社，2014

［作者简介］张晓京，女法学博士，副研究员，

曾任中国人民大学教务处副处长、本科教学评估办公室副主任，现为中国人民大学党委学生工作部部长、学生处处长。主要研究领域：思想政治教育、高等教育管理、中国近现代历史人物研究。

［内容提要］本书为厘清贸易自由化与粮食安全之间的关系，从法律与政策的视角出发，分析论证农业贸易自由化进程对粮食安全的实际和潜在影响，并考察WTO对中国农业和粮食安全的影响与应对。

钟立国. 区域贸易协定争端解决机制：理论及其条约法实践. 上海：上海人民出版社，2014

［作者简介］钟立国，法学博士，教授，1964年生人，湖北仙桃人。现任教于广东财经大学法学院，主要从事国际贸易法与国际投资法的教学研究。

［内容提要］20世纪90年代以来，区域贸易协定数量在全球范围内急剧增加，作为区域贸易协定基本构成要素的争端解决机制，逐渐引起了学界的关注。本书主要采用条文分析与实证研究的方法，对区域贸易协定争端解决机制的理论及相关实践进行了研究。本书分为三大部分，第一章、第二章与第三章分析了区域贸易协定争端解决机制的价值功能、模式及民主化等理论性问题，第四章、第五章与第六章从争端解决机构的设置、管辖权的配置、争端解决的具体方法与程序三个方面，对区域贸易协定一般争端解决机制与投资争端解决机制进行具体分析，第七章则结合中国的区域贸易协定实践，分析中国签订的区域贸易协定争端机制的特点与未来可能的发展。

周灏. 中国遭受反倾销的影响因素及贸易救济体系研究. 北京：经济科学出版社，2014

［作者简介］周灏，武汉纺织大学经济学院。

［内容提要］本书实证研究与规范研究相结合(以实证研究为主)，总量研究与局部分析相结合等多种方法，综合应用多学科交叉展开研究，从不同的视角对中国遭受反倾销的影响因素进行了详细研究，同时也对影响效应进行了详细研究。

● 学术论文

➢ 中国与世界贸易组织

1. 全球经济制度深化下中国改革的突破. 张幼文，薛安伟. 探索与争鸣，2014

［作者简介］上海社会科学院世界经济研究所

［内容提要］摘要：20 世纪 80 年代起国际直接投资迅猛发展，全球市场不断深化，虽然多哈回合停滞，但是全球经济制度却发生着深刻变化。经济制度相对于市场具有滞后性，市场深化不断推动着经济制度深化。全球经济制度深化伴随着 BIT、TPP 和 TTIP 等双边合作与区域合作不断推进。当前，全球经济制度的新框架正处在形成期，全球化出现了新形势，发达国家正试图巩固其在全球经济制度中的地位。中国经济改革既要与全球经济制度兼容，又要在国内经济制度上积极突破，以开放倒逼改革实现新崛起。

2. 国际经贸规则发展的新趋势与中国的立场. 张晓君. 现代法学，2014

［作者简介］西南政法大学

［内容提要］随着多哈发展回合谈判陷入僵局，多边贸易体制面临严峻挑战。在此背景下，国际经贸规则发展呈现出新的趋势，区域化、拓展化和差异化现象在国际经贸规则发展中愈发凸显。经济全球化背景下国际经贸规则的发展动向已然深刻地影响到我国对外交往的策略选择。基于此，我国需要形成清晰系统的对外经贸战略思路和立场：以发展中国家利益为立足点，积极捍卫多边经贸体制的既有成果，并统筹发展具有重要战略意义和地缘优势的区域贸易安排，以制度来保障我国经济的可持续发展。

3. 地区架构制度性分裂：中国的自贸区战略与复兴 APEC. 张蕴岭. 亚太经济，2014

［作者简介］中国社会科学院国际研究学部

［内容提要］全球化与区域化是当今和未来世界经济发展的两大趋势。目前，多边体制推动的多哈回合进程成效甚微，区域化越来越受到各国的重视，成为各国的政策重点选择。在此背景下，中国要通过构建自贸区实现新时期发展的战略布局，必须抓住重点，即着眼于大市场，抓住“巨型自贸区”。值得注意的是，TPP 和 RCEP 两大区域自贸区架构使亚太地区陷入“制度性分裂的状态”。中国需要以 RCEP 为依托，在 2014 年中国举办 APEC 系列会议中做出切实的努力，力求使 APEC 重振活力，重新谈判亚太自贸协定的问题。

4. 巴厘岛会议后国际贸易规则的走向与我国的应对. 薛荣久，杨凤鸣. 中国财政，2014

［作者简介］中国 WTO 研究会；对外经济贸易大学

［内容提要］世界贸易组织第九届部长级会议 2013 年 12 月 7 日在印尼巴厘岛闭幕，发表了《巴厘部长宣言》，达成了“巴厘一揽子协定”。该协定对世贸组织本身，对涌起的地区性贸易集团，对中国加深对外开放，都具有积极的作用。

5. 我国加入 WTO《政府采购协议》信息安全研究. 孟晔. 中国财经，2014

［作者简介］国际关系学院

［内容提要］WTO《政府采购协议》（简称 GPA）是第一个有关政府采购贸易权利与义务的国际性法律框架，为政府采购在法律、规则、程序和措施方面设立了统一的国际标准。2007 年 12 月 28 日，我国正式启动加入 GPA 谈判，这是继加入 WTO 后，我国在对外经贸领域开展的又一项重大谈判，对经济社会发展将产生广泛和深远的影响。政府采购市场的开放是世界经济一体化的必然趋势，任何国家、政府都不可能回避这一现实。面对政府采购市场开放的紧迫形势，我国在政府采购贸易自

由化和政府采购透明化的过程中，如何采取有效措施保护信息安全成为当前亟须解决的严峻问题。

6. 加入WTO后我国商业银行发展战略探讨. 周巧彬. 财经问题研究，2014

［作者简介］中国农业银行厦门分行

［内容提要］本文立足于我国商业银行发展的现状，探讨商业银行面临的多方面竞争，提出加入WTO过渡期结束后我国商业银行必须制定符合自身定位的发展战略。

7. 中美双边投资协定对我国交通运输行业的影响及建议. 翁燕珍，王利彬，蒋桂芹. 经济问题探索，2014

［作者简介］交通运输部科学研究院；中国人民大学；交通运输部科学研究院

［内容提要］中美双边投资协定谈判已进入了实质性谈判阶段，该协定的签署意义堪比中国加入世贸组织。我国的交通运输行业是国民经济和社会发展的基础性、先导性产业和服务性行业，对外开放较早，协定的谈判及签署将对它带来积极影响，包括：有助于吸引外资、促进交通基础设施建设的提高；推动产业发展和升级，促进行业整体服务水平提升；带动国内企业主动提高创新意识和服务意识；推进企业更好地实施“走出去”战略，提高企业国际竞争力。为了做好下阶段交通运输领域应对谈判工作，建议应合理评价入世以来我国交通运输行业利用FDI绩效，全面分析中美两国交通企业竞争优劣势，听取国内交通企业利益诉求。

8. 入世以来主要发达经济体对中国直接投资下降影响因素分析. 庞明川，韩国高，刘婧. 财贸经济，2014

［作者简介］东北财经大学经济与社会发展研究院；东北财经大学投资工程管理学院；东北财经大学研究生院

［内容提要］改革开放初期，“引进来”战略的实施使得包括主要发达经济体在内的外资对中国直接投资流入高速增长。然而，在中国加入WTO以来，主要发达经济体对中国直接投资却呈现出持续下降的趋势。本文在对1996—2012年主要发达经济体对中国直接投资进行实证分析的基础上，认为中国市场需求的持续扩张、企业生产成本上升以及投资国经济发展水平是影响主要发达经济体对中国直接投资的主要决定因素，而中国外资政策红利的衰减、人民币汇率升值以及投资国对外投资政策的变化对于不同发达经济体对外投资的影响不尽一致。为进一步吸引主要发达经济体对中国的直接投资，东道国应在继续坚持扩大开放的基础上对外资政策进行适当的微调以及作为投资国的主要发达经济体消除投资保护主义以增进双边投资等，是中国与主要发达经济体互利共赢的重要策略。

9. 入世以来我国对外贸易结构的动态演化和升级路径选择. 路丽. 价格月刊，2014

［作者简介］首都经济贸易大学经济学院

［内容提要］加入WTO以来，我国的对外贸易不断取得历史性突破，对外贸易结构也在不断地变化过程中。本文基于入世以来我国对外贸易的数据，从贸易主体、方式、商品、区域结构4个方面分析了我国对外贸易结构的动态变化，指出以要素禀赋结构升级为基础的动态比较优势演进和我国现阶段发展水平是制约我国对外贸易结构升级的根本原因。在此基础上提出以要素禀赋升级和技术进步模式动态转型相结合的贸易结构升级路径。

10. WTO视角下中国（上海）自由贸易试验区知识产权保护问题探析. 孙益武. 上海对外经贸大学学报，2014

［作者简介］复旦大学法学院

［内容提要］中国（上海）自由贸易试验区（简称“上海自贸区”）不是世界贸易组织体制下的国际自由贸易区，而是根据《中国加入世界贸易组织议定书》所建立的国内特殊经济区。知识产权保护是世界贸易组织密切关注的重要议题，上海自贸区知识产权保护也是不可回避的焦点问题。“一线监管放开”的上海自贸区不是知识产权侵权的避风港，上海自贸区应当加强知识产权保护政策体系建设，严格知识产权海关执法；利用“先行先试”的优惠政策，在知识产权管理和执法体制方面为促进和完善国家知识产权政策体系提供示范效应，并为知识产权规则的国际协调提供实证支持。

11. 自贸区项下中国高新技术产品贸易现状、问题及对策. 崔卫杰. 国际贸易，2014

［作者简介］商务部研究院

［内容提要］贯彻党的十八大报告“加快实施自由贸易区战略”的总体要求，2013年以来，中

国先后与冰岛、瑞士签订了自由贸易协定，中韩、中澳（澳大利亚）、中日韩、RCEP（区域全面经济合作伙伴关系）等自贸区谈判也在加快推进，中国自贸区进入了加快发展阶段。自贸区成员在中国高新技术产品进出口贸易中一直占据重要地位。因此，把握中国与自贸区成员高新技术产品贸易现状与问题，并提出相应的对策建议，对推动我国高新技术产品贸易发展，加快对外开放非常有意义。

12. 中国WTO争端解决实践考察及反思. 沈木珠. 国际商务研究，2014

［作者简介］南京财经大学国际经济法研究所

［内容提要］中国“入世”十余载，在对外贸易迅猛发展的同时，WTO争端案件也呈上升态势，中国应对WTO争端解决的基本态度由谨慎向积极转变。考察中国WTO争端解决实践的基本事实，不难发现中国在“双反”问题、反倾销问题、SPS措施、特保措施、原材料出口措施等问题上既有胜诉，也有败诉，既取得了成绩，也存在着问题，值得总结与反思。

13. 加入WTO后中国食品出口贸易结构分析及展望. 李丹，王守伟，臧明伍，李响，程婧，董海芹. 世界农业，2014

［作者简介］北京食品科学研究院；中国人民大学；励德爱思唯尔信息技术有限公司

［内容提要］中国是食品贸易大国，了解中国加入WTO以后中国食品出口贸易的结构和变化，对深入了解中国食品出口的具体情况，判断未来食品贸易的趋势，具有重要意义。本文首先回顾了近年来国际食品出口情况和中国食品出口情况，然后介绍了中国加入WTO以后食品出口的种类结构，并分析了中国向美国、欧盟、日本、韩国、东盟等主要食品出口国家和地区的出口产品结构变化，最后对中国食品出口贸易的趋势进行了判断。结果表明，中国食品贸易逆差的情况将持续；中国食品出口结构仍将以水产品和蔬菜水果等劳动力密集型产品为主；食品出口市场主要集中在亚洲、欧洲和北美洲，出口呈现多元化倾向。

14. 中国电影生态系统中的后产业链发展战略——以入世以来的中国电影为例. 覃晓玲. 电影文学，2014

［作者简介］中华女子学院艺术学院

［内容提要］加入WTO后，中国电影在与好莱坞的竞争中逐渐摸索出了一套应对之道，完善了自己的生态系统，后产业链的开发也从无到有，从少到多。但是从非生物环境、生产者、消费者、分解者这四个方面来看，存在着版权保护不力、消费观念单薄、开发观念淡薄、与创作脱节等问题。为了保证中国电影生态系统良性循环，我们需要借鉴好莱坞的后产业链发展战略，依靠政府、电影制作企业、后产品生产企业和销售企业、消费者四方面集体发力，让中国电影产业处在一个良性发展的快速通道。

15. WTO视阈下跨区域贸易安排的发展动向与中国策略. 段辉艳. 学术界，2014

［作者简介］西南政法大学国际法学院

［内容提要］区域贸易安排（RTAs）自WTO多哈回合谈判陷入僵局后得以蓬勃发展，作为WTO明文规定的合理例外，跨区域贸易协定以其跨区域、开放性、高标准性对WTO多边体制造成冲击，进一步导致多边贸易体制碎片化。以TPP为代表的跨区域贸易安排对区域经济合作机制产生了重要影响，同时给中国的RTAs战略带来挑战。中国须在此基础上对RTAs战略做出合理调整，除战略重心仍保持在亚太地区外，应进一步升级现有的FTAs，以多样化的合作模式应对跨区域贸易安排带来的挑战。

16. 区域贸易协定与WTO多边贸易体制的对立统一及良性互动——兼论中国的战略选择. 肖雯. 商业时代，2014

［作者简介］西南政法大学

［内容提要］在WTO多边贸易谈判步履艰难、困难重重时，在区域贸易自由化蓬勃发展的趋势推动下，各国均致力于商签区域贸易协定来实现一定区域范围内贸易自由化和便利化程度的渐进提高。本文以区域贸易协定发展现状为基础，阐释在WTO多边框架下区域贸易协定生存的法律环境及其规制，进而揭示区域贸易协定与WTO多边贸易体制对立统一的互补性竞争关系，并基于对双方良性互动的发展愿景，对中国的战略选择提出切实建议。

17. WTO/SPS“特别贸易关注”对我国食品安全标准的影响. 周桂荣，程震. 对外经济实务，2014

［作者简介］天津商业大学

[内容提要]本文提出了要积极适应新的国际贸易特别关注的变化，整合我国食品安全标准不一的状况，构建与国际标准接轨的食品安全标准体系。

18. WTO多边贸易体制下成员谈判集团制度与中国的策略. 周跃雪. 中国科学研究，2014

[作者简介]西南政法大学国际法学院；西南科技大学法学院

[内容提要]发展中国家成员建立的各种类型的谈判集团其谈判模式仍为"主要供应国原则"的延续，谈判集团的实质在于纠正大国操纵，运用集体力量维护主权利益进而推进重构新的国际经济秩序。但是相关成员谈判集团制度在现行WTO多边贸易体制中并没有明确规定，因而面临制度障碍。中国应借助WTO决策过程的集团化趋势，与利益契合的其他成员合纵连横，共同发声。

19. 论WTO法"义务之法"的特性. 沈虹. 中国社会科学院研究生报，2014

[作者简介]厦门大学法学院；华南师范大学法学院

[内容提要]WTO法作为确立成员（WTO Member）之间权利义务的国际条约，存在权利义务不均衡的现象，成员承担的义务明显超过其所享有的权利。同时，有别于其他国际法对国家对外主权的限制，WTO法对成员的限制还体现在对成员内部行使主权的限制。WTO法的这一特征对国际条约的履行带来新挑战，潜移默化地侵蚀国家主权，尤其需要引起发展中国家的注意。

20. 贸易自由化与中国制造业企业出口行为："入世"是否促进了出口参与？毛其淋，盛斌. 经济学：季刊，2014

[作者简介]南开大学国际经济研究所、跨国公司研究中心；南开大学经济学院

[内容提要]基于异质性企业贸易的理论框架，本文使用中国工业企业微观数据全面深入地考察了贸易自由化对中国制造业企业出口行为的影响。研究表明：(1) 贸易自由化显著地促进了制造业企业的出口参与，本研究选取合适的工具变量克服内生性问题，并进行多角度的稳健性分析，结果均支持了这一结论；(2) 贸易自由化通过竞争效应与成本效应两个不同渠道促进了企业出口参与，其中成本效应对企业出口参与的影响程度相对更大；(3) 中国加入世界贸易组织显著地推动了企业的出口参与，其中对本土企业的推动作用更大，并且入世主要是通过集约边际的途径影响企业的出口行为。

21. 新型自由贸易协定的发展趋势及中国的因应策略. 姚新超，左宗文. 国际贸易，2014

[作者简介]对外经济贸易大学国际经贸学院；安徽财经大学商学院

[内容提要]近年来，随着WTO多哈谈判进展的停滞不前，各国为寻求新的经济发展动力，逐渐开始转向区域内的经济整合，其中以自由贸易协定（FTA）的发展最为活跃，最终使世界各国的经贸及投资活动更加自由化。但时至今日，FTA的发展不再仅局限于经贸及投资领域，在很大程度上FTA已被视为处理区域乃至世界问题的一种新型方式。本文拟对新型FTA的发展趋势予以分析，以期寻求中国的因应策略。

➢ 多边贸易体制、多哈回合与新议题

1. 加入WTO后我国参与国际分工变化及其影响因素研究. 杜运苏，余宇新. 世界经济研究，2014

[作者简介]南京财经大学国贸学院；上海外国语大学国际金融贸易学院

[内容提要]本文基于产业内贸易分析了加入WTO后我国参与国际分工的变化，并利用20个主要贸易伙伴国（地区）的双边面板数据，考察了影响加入WTO后我国参与国际分工的主要因素。结果显示：加入WTO后我国主要通过基于要素禀赋差异的产业间贸易参与国际分工，并且产业内贸易发展具有明显的"南北型"特点，低质量垂直型产业内贸易（LVIIT）占绝对主导地位；市场规模、贸易结构和地理距离是影响加入WTO后我国产业内贸易发展的重要因素，而FDI对垂直型产业内贸易的促进作用要明显大于水平型产业内贸易，亟须调整吸引外资和加工贸易政策。

2. 发展中国家粮食主权的思考——以WTO农产品自由贸易规则为视角. 江虹. 理论与改革，2014

[作者简介]湖南师范大学；湖南农业大学

[内容提要]20世纪90年代，在WTO首次

将农产品贸易纳入国际自由贸易体系的大背景下，粮食主权这一概念首次被提出。2001 年 WTO 多哈回合开启，旨在进一步推进国际贸易自由化，但进展并不顺利，每次会议都会招致发展中国家和不发达国家农民高喊“粮食主权”的口号而举行抗议与示威。因此非常有必要重新审视 WTO 农产品自由贸易规则对于发展中国家粮食主权所产生的影响。文章从粮食主权的含义与原则入手，阐述了 WTO 农产品自由贸易规则的内容，并分析其对发展中国家粮食主权实现带来的挑战，最后提出下一轮 WTO 农业谈判中对农产品自由贸易规则应做出必要的改革以更加有利于实现发展中国家的粮食主权。

3. 多哈回合谈判中的农产品特殊保障机制研究综述. 邓贤明，肖润华. 农业经济，2014

［作者简介］赣南师范学院政法学院；赣南师范学院商学院

［内容提要］随着国际贸易的进一步自由化，发展中国家农产品受到进口的发达国家农产品的损害越来越大。因此，发展中国家提出取消现有的有利于发达国家的农产品特殊保障机制，建立仅适用于发展中成员国家的新的特殊保障机制 SSM。本文综述了 WTO 各成员方在 SSM 的使用资格认定、产品范围、触发机制方面的分歧，以及我国在多哈回合农产品特殊保障机制谈判上的立场。

4.《贸易便利化协议》的主要内容及影响分析. 杨荣珍，王玮. 对外经贸实务，2014

［作者简介］对外经济贸易大学

［内容提要］2013 年 12 月 3 日至 7 日，世界贸易组织第九届部长级会议在印度尼西亚巴厘岛举行。会议发表了《巴厘部长宣言》，达成“巴厘一揽子协议”，是世界贸易组织成立 18 年以来首份全球贸易协议，打破多哈回合 12 年谈判僵局，成为完成多哈回合的重要基石。

5. 全球贸易便利化的评估研究与趋势分析. 王中美. 世界经济研究，2014

［作者简介］上海社会科学院世界经济研究所

［内容提要］对贸易便利化落实情况和效果的评估日益受到重视。这些评估不仅是一种总结，更是一种分析和建议。通过对包括 WTO、OECD、APEC、世界银行、世界海关组织、世界经济论坛以及美国、日本、欧盟等相关贸易便利化评估报告的比较研究和分析，本文试图探求全球贸易便利化的最新趋势和要求。

6. 服务贸易自由化的新选项：TISA 谈判的现状及其与中国的关系. 屠新泉，莫慧萍. 国际贸易，2014

［作者简介］对外经济贸易大学 WTO 研究院

［内容提要］本文将研究 TISA 谈判的发起背景、进展现状和未来前景，着重分析我国加入 TISA 谈判的难点和潜在影响，以利于我们更好地认识 TISA，制定更合理的谈判和应对策略。

7. 全球贸易治理中多边主义、诸边主义和大区域主义的比较与选择. 程大为. 经济纵横，2014

［作者简介］中国人民大学欧洲问题研究中心

［内容提要］在世界贸易组织多边谈判进展缓慢的背景下，全球贸易治理出现了大区域主义和诸边主义流行的趋势。大区域主义是欧美国家为占据新的“规则优势”、掌控全球贸易治理主导权而极力推行的，它并不是多边贸易体系的补充，而是消极的侵蚀。我国已成为世界贸易第一大国，维护 WTO 多边主义是我国的首要选择。但挽救 WTO 危机并建立和谐的全球贸易体系是一个长期过程。从目前的实际情况看，我国应在 WTO 体系内大力推进诸边主义，以实现挽救危机和推进规则制定的目的。

8. 服务贸易协定谈判基本特征分析. 王绍媛，张鑫. 国际贸易，2014

［作者简介］东北财经大学国际经济贸易学院

［内容提要］《服务贸易总协定》（GATS）作为基础性的多边贸易协定在一定程度上促进了成员服务业市场的开放，推动了全球服务贸易的快速发展。但是，随着国际经济形势的变化，在世界贸易组织（WTO）多边平台上推动成员继续开放服务市场的难度越来越大。

9. 中国环境产品的国际竞争优势评估. 龚清华. 对外经贸实务，2014

［作者简介］武汉工程大学法商学院

［内容提要］近些年来，一些国家及区域组织在世界范围大力发展环境产品贸易自由化，以期实现环境保护和经济发展双赢的目标。全面评估环境

产品贸易自由化的趋势下中国环境产品的国际竞争优势，将有利于中国认清所处的状况，并依此制定相应政策，实现预期的环境和贸易利益。本文以世界银行提出的43项与气候变化有关的环境产品作为研究对象，从环境产品的关税减让及环境产品贸易价值、数量和价格竞争力指数等方面，对中国环境产品的国际竞争优势进行综合评估，并提出了相应对策。

10. 环境产品贸易自由化对进口国的效应分析. 龚清华，张建民. 经济经纬，2014

［作者简介］中南财经政法大学工商管理学院；武汉工程大学法商学院

［内容提要］实施环境产品贸易自由化可以实现贸易与环境双赢，但一些国家出于顾虑使得环境产品贸易自由化进展缓慢。深入研究环境产品贸易自由化对进口国的效应十分必要。笔者试图通过建立环境产品贸易模型详细分析环境产品贸易自由化对进口国的效应，结果表明，削减环境产品关税会使进口国环境政策变宽松；会增加环境产品进口；但对环境质量的影响不确定。中国应积极谨慎地推动环境产品贸易自由化。

11. WTO补偿实践的动向及其改革启示. 李晓玲. 现代法学，2014

［作者简介］中国青年政治学院法学院

［内容提要］自WTO成立以来，补偿机制应用较少，甚至被视为“装饰品”。与WTO早期的补偿案相比，US-Section 110（5）Copyright Act、EC-Hormones、US-Upland Cotton、China-Publications案达成的补偿协议，在补偿原则、补偿形式、补偿程度的确定等方面，均有所发展，解决或缓解了敏感争端的执行僵局，并为多哈回合补偿机制改革提供了经验与启示。补偿机制的改革应关注如何为成员达成补偿提供规则基础和程序保障。改革的途径是多重的，在推进多哈谈判的同时，应充分利用现有的WTO制度，完善补偿机制。

12. WTO成员实施贸易报复的国内立法与实践研究. 李晓玲. 甘肃政法学院学报，2014

［作者简介］同前。

［内容提要］在WTO体系下，贸易报复是申诉方促使被诉方执行裁决的最后手段。在遵守DSU第22条的前提下，成员可根据个案案情和报复目的的不同，自由决定报复方案和国内实施程序。为有效实施贸易报复和执行WTO协定权利，美国、巴西、欧盟等已经或正在进行立法，规范实施DSB贸易报复授权的国内程序。我国作为WTO的重要成员和争端解决机制的主要参与方，应从其他成员的立法与实践经验中寻求启示，并着手立法。

13. WTO法律适用断层之探析及完善. 刘佳，王欣. 国际商务研究，2014

［作者简介］厦门大学法学院

［内容提要］乌拉圭回合长达8年艰苦谈判所达成的WTO规则堪称一部规范世界贸易秩序的宏大法典，为国际贸易活动的法治化和规范化做出了重要贡献。但基于WTO法律自身的模糊性、在各成员国的普遍非直接适用性、国际国内层面对WTO相关法律解释基本原则的不一致性等原因，WTO法律适用之国际、国内层面存在断层。现阶段包括贸易政策审议机制和争端解决机制在内的贸易政策监督机制不能有效监督WTO法律在各成员方内的贯彻实施，影响了WTO法律的一致性、有效性。如何对现阶段WTO争端解决机制进行改进，监督相关规则于各成员内之有效实施，更好地维护国际贸易私人主体之权利，促进贸易自由化目标之实现，为现在WTO工作者所面临的重要议题。

14. WTO多边体制再遭重击. 陆燕. 半月谈，2014

［作者简介］商务部国际贸易经济合作研究院

［内容提要］7月31日，由于印度等成员拒绝签署，世贸组织（WTO）极力推动的《贸易便利化协议》未能在最后期限获得通过，WTO再陷信誉危机。与此同时，全球自贸协定（FTA）谈判却相当活跃，与多边谈判步履维艰形成鲜明对照。面对全球贸易规则的重构，中国应当以更加积极、自信、负责的姿态，推动形成公正、合理、透明的国际经贸规则体系。

15. 自由贸易协定与多边贸易体系——基于美国贸易战略的洞察. 沈铭辉. 天津社会科学，2014

［作者简介］中国社会科学院亚太与全球战略研究院

［内容提要］20世纪80年代以前，美国基本主导了历次GATT谈判进程。20世纪末的欧盟一

体化和21世纪初的东亚合作对美国在多边贸易体系中的地位构成了挑战，使它不得不通过区域经济合作撬动多边贸易谈判，以推行美国版本的贸易规则，进而维持其影响国际经济规则的能力。在此过程中，作为美国力推的自由贸易协定，TPP对东亚合作、亚太经济一体化和多边贸易体系都产生了深远的影响。在新一轮的国际贸易规则转变期内，中国需要根据自身经济发展现状，适时调整贸易策略以应对挑战。

16. 国际贸易新规则：重构的关键期. 陆燕. 国际商务，2014

［作者简介］商务部国际贸易经济合作研究院

［内容提要］正随着经济全球化深入发展，国际贸易模式发生了深刻变化，并且随之出现了更为复杂的贸易关系。为应对国际贸易的结构性变革，许多新议题摆上贸易议程，预示着国际贸易规则正在酝酿重大变革。国际金融危机加快了全球经贸规则调整与重构的步伐。以美欧为代表的发达国家正在通过自贸协定、诸边协议等路径，全力主导新一代全球经贸规则的制定权，以引领未来国际经济新秩序的走向。

17. 迎接国际贸易与投资新规则的机遇与挑战. 盛斌. 国际贸易，2014

［作者简介］南开大学国际经济研究所和跨国公司研究中心；中国APEC研究院

［内容提要］党的十八届三中全会通过的《中共中央关于全面深化改革若干重大问题的决定》将“构建开放型经济新体制”作为新时期经济工作的一项重要任务，指出要适应经济全球化新形势，“促进国际国内要素有序自由流动、资源高效配置、市场深度融合，加快培育参与和引领国际经济合作竞争新优势，以开放促改革”。其中，“建立中国上海自由贸易试验区”、“加快同有关国家和地区商签投资协定”和“形成面向全球的高标准自由贸易区网络”成为深化全方位对外开放的关键举措。面对进展凸显与竞争激烈的下一代国际贸易与投资新规则，中国应充分利用上述举措迎接全球经济治理新的机遇与挑战。

18. 俄罗斯加入世贸组织对改善外资环境的影响. 宋艳梅. 东北亚论坛，2014

［作者简介］对外经济贸易大学外语学院

［内容提要］实现经济现代化是俄罗斯当务之急，为此俄罗斯必须大量吸引外资以弥补资金、技术和经济管理等方面的不足。然而长期以来投资环境不佳严重阻碍了外国资本进入俄罗斯。加入世贸组织对于俄罗斯改善投资环境无疑是有利的，但关键性问题是外国投资的软环境极度不佳，而软环境不会因为入世发生快速的实质性改变，而且在相当长的时期内继续阻碍外资进入俄罗斯。

➢ 区域贸易协定

1. 区域服务贸易协定、制度因素与服务贸易促进体系研究——基于49国之间双边服务贸易流量面板数据的实证分析. 陈丽丽，龚静. 国际贸易问题. 2014

［作者简介］西南财经大学国际商学院

［内容提要］WTO多哈回合谈判一再停滞，各种双边和区域自由贸易谈判风起云涌，这时大力发展服务贸易、优化服务贸易出口的区位结构、调整与服务贸易相关的制度安排就成为当务之急。本文从制度角度出发，结合区域服务贸易协定的法律视角，以49国之间共1526个经济体对2000—2011年的面板数据为样本，采用豪斯曼—泰勒估计方法对这些国家之间的双边服务贸易流量决定因素进行了实证研究。结果表明：(1) 区域服务贸易协定可以直接促进双边服务贸易发展，其提升幅度大致为5.77%～9.77%；(2) 进口国的制度质量可以有效促进双边服务贸易的发展，而两国间的制度距离将对双边服务贸易造成阻碍；(3) 区域服务贸易协定还具有间接的贸易促进作用，它不仅可以强化制度质量对于双边服务贸易流量的促进作用，还能反向调节制度距离对于双边服务贸易的负面影响程度。

2. 亚太经贸一体化的战略大趋势. 张茉楠. 瞭望，2014

［作者简介］国家信息中心经济预测部

［内容提要］2008年国际金融危机之后，世贸组织多哈回合谈判进展缓慢，甚至陷入僵局。而区域、次区域合作和自贸区谈判，正以前所未有的势头迅猛发展，然而贸易碎片化趋势越来越明显的不利于贸易全球化的进一步发展。区域自由贸易协定(FTA)盛行导致贸易碎片化。当前，区域性FTA

已经成为世界贸易自由化的风向标。由于WTO多哈回合谈判陷入僵局，多边贸易体系面临困境，区域性与跨区域性、双边与多边的贸易谈判逐渐成为全球新主流和新趋势，并正在从根本上改变世界经济、贸易和投资的版图。

3. 自由贸易区促进贸易了吗？——来自国家层面的经验考察. 罗来军，罗雨泽，刘畅. 世界经济研究，2014

［作者简介］中国人民大学经济学院；国务院发展研究中心对外经济研究部；宁波诺丁汉大学国际商学院

［内容提要］本文基于贸易引力模型，利用4个主要经济体与21个经济体之间的双边贸易样本分析评估了自由贸易区及相关变量对贸易总量和出口/进口流量的影响。分析发现，在样本考察期内，一国加入的自由贸易区数量以及贸易双方同属一个贸易区对贸易的影响虽然为正，但并不显著。本文认为这可能与WTO多边体系之下关税壁垒大幅降低、自由贸易区重合度增加以及跨国公司的全球布局有关，因此我国在新形势下制定自由贸易区建设策略时应注重多维度思考。

4. 东亚经济体参与区域服务贸易安排的"GATS－"特征研究. 周念利，朱慧慧. 亚太经济，2014

［作者简介］对外经济贸易大学WTO研究院

［内容提要］本文以东亚经济体参与缔结的25项区域服务贸易安排作为研究样本，对这些区域服务贸易安排中所包含的"GATS－"承诺表现进行了归纳梳理。本文指出，在区域服务贸易安排框架下，东亚经济体在对外做出或被动接受"GATS－"承诺时会呈现出四个典型特征：一是东亚经济体对外做出的"GATS－"承诺比率要普遍高于其接受的"GATS－"承诺比率；二是东亚经济体在市场准入方面所做"GATS－"承诺比率要普遍低于国民待遇方面的"GATS－"承诺比率；三是东亚经济体更易于对非东亚经济体做出"GATS－"承诺；四是跟"南南型"区域服务贸易安排比较而言，"GATS－"承诺更易于出现在东亚经济体对外缔结的"南北型"区域服务贸易安排中。通过对上述典型特征的分析，从中获取一系列可供中国借鉴的政策启示。

5. 发展中国家依WTO法调整其自由贸易区法的经验分析. 武轶尘. 姜作利. 东岳论丛，2014

［作者简介］山东社会科学院；山东大学法学院

［内容提要］近年来，许多发展中国家纷纷通过发展自由贸易区，并且为区内企业提供出口补贴来招商引资和增加出口。由于自由贸易区内企业获得的政府补贴与WTO规则相冲突，WTO为发展中国家提供的优惠期即将到期，不少发展中国家在严峻的形势下，开始依照WTO的相关规则对其自由贸易区进行调整，以达到既能促进出口，又能有效避免WTO成员指控的目的，例如通过法律取消出口补贴、发挥自由贸易区的综合作用、允许区内产品进口到东道国市场及鼓励私人设立和管理自由贸易区等。我国众多自由贸易区同其他发展中国家一样，正面临着WTO法制约的严峻挑战。因此，认真研究和借鉴发展中国家调整其自由贸易区法及政策的经验，有利于我国自由贸易区的顺利运行。

6. 经济增速放缓背景下强化金砖国家合作机制的对策. 蔡春林，丁畅. 国际商务研究，2014

［作者简介］广东工业大学金砖国家研究中心；广东工业大学经济与贸易学院

［内容提要］金砖国家经济放缓是多种因素叠加的结果，是一种主动的可控式的自我矫正。金砖国家政府不过分干预经济增速放缓实际上是为了更好地提升发展质量。"刮骨疗毒"式的增速放缓是解决经济增长深层次矛盾的重要环节。在经济增速放缓背景下更需要金砖国家强化合作激活长期增长潜力，以经济合作促进政治经济互动，采取以发展为导向的合作机制和运行模式，以金砖国家峰会带动其他实质性对话机制建设，联合制定加强金砖国家合作的路线图，尽快明确金砖国家开发银行设立细节，建立快速反应机制，防范金砖国家合作效应递减和凝聚力下降风险，强化金砖国家合作与经济社会发展之间的互动关系。

7. 中日韩FTA建设优势、问题及前景分析——基于与NAFTA比较的视角. 施锦芳. 国际贸易，2014

［作者简介］东北财经大学国际经济贸易学院

［内容提要］中日韩三国加快构建FTA是顺应世界经济潮流，推动本国经济发展，带动东亚经

济乃至世界经济腾飞的迫切需要。

8. 跨大西洋贸易与投资伙伴关系协定（TTIP）谈判及其对全球贸易格局的影响. 周茂荣. 国际经济评论，2014

［作者简介］武汉大学国际问题研究院

［内容提要］2013年2月，美国与欧盟决定就TTIP举行谈判，旨在通过扩大双边贸易和投资，以促进经济增长、创造就业，最终摆脱金融危机的影响；提高国际竞争力，应对新兴经济体的挑战；在世界贸易组织（WTO）之外解决“边境线后”的贸易壁垒问题。并为21世纪的国际商品、投资、服务贸易制定新的国际规则。这一协定一旦达成，将会强化以美国为首的发达国家在当今国际经济关系中的主导地位；新一轮区域主义浪潮的形成将对以WTO为核心的多边贸易体系带来严重冲击；围绕21世纪国际经济规则的竞争将变得更加激烈；很可能会在发达国家及与其有着紧密经贸联系的国家引发新一轮改革开放。

9. 新兴经济体参与新丝绸之路建设的策略研究. 蔡春林. 国际贸易，2014

［作者简介］广东工业大学金砖国家研究中心

［内容提要］中央领导提出“丝绸之路经济带和21世纪海上丝绸之路”（以下简称“一带一路”，或“新丝绸之路”）建设，相关部门全力配合强力推进，发展前景广阔。新兴经济体在新丝绸之路建设中具有独特地位，尤其是以金砖国家为代表的部分新兴经济体在新丝绸之路建设中具有得天独厚、无可比拟的优越条件和天然禀赋优势。这是新一轮发展的战略机遇期，是新兴经济体加强合作、提升经济发展质量和国际影响力的重要时间节点。

10. 区域服务贸易紧急保障机制的主要特征、争议焦点与中国对策. 周念利，蒋丽梅. 国际经贸探索，2014

［作者简介］对外经济贸易大学WTO研究院

［内容提要］服务贸易紧急保障机制的构建是区域服务贸易自由化进程中一个具备典型的“GATS＋”特征的制度创新因素。文章首先对区域服务贸易紧急保障机制的主要特征进行分析，然后重点论述在区域服务贸易紧急保障机制的构建过程中存在的三大焦点争议：紧急保障机制在立法模式上的“水平模式”或“部门模式”之争，“国内产业”界定的“地域”标准或“国籍”标准之争以及损害量化中的“标准选择”和“举证数据来源”之争。在此基础上，文章指出中国对外构建的区域服务贸易紧急保障机制呈现出“虚”“实”兼具但“实”而不详的问题并提出了政策建议。

11. 亚太地区自由贸易协定条款的比较及其对中国的启示. 盛斌，果婷. 亚太经济，2014

［作者简介］南开大学

［内容提要］本文在分析亚太地区FTAs发展现状和特点的基础上，对协定文本所涵盖的具体法律条款进行了深入的比较研究。从总体上看，亚太地区FTAs对于“第一代”贸易议题（WTO＋）的覆盖率和承诺率高于“第二代”贸易议题（WTO－X）。同时，以美国为代表的发达国家对于新一代贸易条款的覆盖率和约束力高于发展中国家。在具体议题条款上亚太国家FTAs的涵盖与法律实施水平也体现出较大的差异。中国应更加重视FTAs中“第二代”贸易政策的重大影响与作用，重新评估与制定新一代贸易和投资政策，通过认识、接纳，逐步推进国内深层次的规制改革，保证中国在全球经济治理中的核心利益和战略主导权。

12. APEC环境产品与服务合作进程、趋势及对策. 李丽平，张彬. 亚太经济，2014

［作者简介］环境保护部环境与经济政策研究中心

［内容提要］环境产品与服务合作是APEC最早开展，且具有重大成果的合作领域之一。APEC环境产品与服务合作进程可分为倡议初步提出期、实践期和合作措施密集出台期三个阶段，APEC环境产品与服务合作具有合作战略性、内容丰富、形式多样、广受国际社会关注等特点，中国在推动APEC环境产品与服务合作方面发挥了积极和重要作用。APEC环境产品与服务合作的原因是国际环境、环境产品与服务本身特性、发达成员贸易利益以及各成员最终博弈等各种因素综合作用的结果。未来，APEC环境产品与服务合作将进一步深化，将清单产品和成员“双扩”以及环境产品与服务贸易自由化平衡趋势明显，但仍将面临环境产品多用途和全生命周期评估等困难。

13. 欧盟在中欧投资协定谈判中的诉求简析及对策建议. 姚铃. 国际贸易，2014

［作者简介］商务部国际贸易经济合作研究院

［内容提要］自2014年1月以来，中国与欧盟的投资协定谈判已经进行了三轮。上半年，习近平主席和李克强总理分别访问欧洲，以及欧盟国家领导人相继访华，有力地推动了中欧投资协定谈判的进程。众所周知，欧盟是国际投资领域的先行者，研究其有关国际投资合作的政策诉求，对于进一步做好中欧投资协定谈判相关工作具有积极意义。

14. 巨型自由贸易协定：走向多边规则的垫脚石. 沈铭辉. 新视野，2014

［作者简介］中国社会科学院亚太与全球战略研究院

［内容提要］2008年国际金融危机以来，巨型自由贸易协定兴起成为区域经济合作的新特征。当今全球范围内正处于谈判阶段的巨型自由贸易协定包括跨太平洋伙伴关系协定、跨大西洋贸易与投资伙伴关系协定、区域全面经济伙伴关系协定以及服务贸易协定等。全面理解巨型自由贸易产生的根源、内涵及其影响对于下一阶段中国的对外经济政策至关重要。在未来一个时期的国际贸易规则重构阶段，中国需要统筹考虑多边贸易体系与区域经济合作的关系，对贸易协定的谈判顺序和时机做出策略性安排，以达到最佳政策配置。

15. APEC跨境隐私规则体系与我国的对策. 弓永钦，王健. 国际贸易，2014

［作者简介］对外经济贸易大学国际经济贸易学院

［内容提要］APEC电子商务指导组数据隐私分组历时十年，倡议并构建了跨境隐私规则体系(Cross-Border Privacy Rules，CBPR)，旨在建立跨境电子商务中的个人信息保护规则。CBPR体系于2012年正式启动，目前已有两个成员经济体成功加入，即美国（2012年7月）和墨西哥（2013年1月），澳大利亚和日本也提出了加入申请。随着更多APEC成员经济体加入到CBPR体系中，该体系将成为亚太区域规范跨境贸易和跨境投资的一个重要规则。作为亚太地区的贸易大国，中国应该及时了解CBPR体系，并做出相应的对策。

16. 中国自由贸易协定的出口效应——基于商品技术含量的分行业研究. 王开，靳玉英. 世界经济研究，2014

［作者简介］上海财经大学国际工商管理学院

［内容提要］自“多哈回合”多边贸易谈判陷入僵局以来，各国均积极寻求缔结双边或区域自由贸易协定（FTA）。作为全球贸易大国，中国也在积极推行FTA战略。本文旨在深入评估中国与贸易伙伴国缔结的FTA所产生的出口贸易效应。首先，基于联合国贸发委的出口贸易数据和产品分类标准，按照商品技术含量对出口产品进行分类。其次，在前人研究的基础上，本文构建了扩展的引力模型，就中国签订的FTA对贸易伙伴国的出口流量和结构所产生的影响进行分析。最终结果显示：中国签订的贸易自由化程度较高的FTA有助于中国产品的出口，而中国签订的贸易自由化程度较低的FTA减少了中国对这些国家初级产品、资源密集型商品和低技术劳动密集型商品的出口，但提高了中国中等技术商品的出口。

17. WTO“蓝箱”规则改革的新进展及我国的对策. 陈斌彬. 现代法学，2014

［作者简介］华侨大学法学院

［内容提要］“蓝箱”不仅是大国间贸易利益博弈的产物，而且由于其免于削减承诺，事实上已成为某些发达国家固有的特权，对农产品贸易的扭曲作用不可忽视。多哈回合“蓝箱”规则谈判的近期成果——2008年的“模式草案”虽严格限定了“蓝箱”使用纪律，为发展中国家提供了若干特殊与差别的待遇，但却从另一方面扩大了“蓝箱”的作用空间，使惯以使用“蓝箱”的发达国家继续从中获利。作为一个从未使用过“蓝箱”的农产品贸易大国，我国将会因之面临更加不利的竞争局面。故在即将重启的多哈回合农业谈判中，我国宏观上应继续恪守发展中国家的原则与立场，提高发达国家的“蓝箱”使用标准；微观上则应把握改革时机，采取更为灵活的谈判策略，促使发达国家对“蓝箱”支持进行实质性削减。与此同时，我国也应当对现行的国内农业补贴制度进行适时的调整与优化，以里外配合形成合力，为我国未来农业的长远健康发展创造一个良好的内外部规则环境。

18. 欧盟全球自贸战略对世界经贸格局的影响. 张晓兰. 宏观经济管理，2014

［作者简介］国家信息中心经济预测部

［内容提要］国际金融危机爆发以来，全球经贸格局明显改变，世界贸易增长乏力、贸易保护主义不断升温，多边贸易体制建设几近停滞。与此同时，以区域贸易安排 RTA 为主要形式的区域经济合作蓬勃发展，全球区域经济一体化进入了新一轮快速发展时期。在此背景下，欧盟为适应全球形势变化及实现经济复苏，调整并加速推进全球自贸战略。作为全球第一大自由贸易体，其自贸战略的实施对全球经贸格局的调整必将产生深刻影响。

➢ 争端解决

1. WTO 争端解决机制中的救济体系框架及改革问题实证研. 王军，粟撒. 当代法学，2014

［作者简介］对外经济贸易大学法学院

［内容提要］本文聚焦于 WTO 争端解决机制中的救济体系，从实证角度出发，通过对以往案件及 DSB 报告的深入考察，梳理出 WTO 争端解决机制中的救济体系法律框架。在研究 WTO 成员参与该体系的态度和行为的基础上，深入分析了 WTO 该如何利用该体系有效促使 DSB 裁决的履行。针对近年来 WTO 争端解决机制中的救济体系暴露出的不足与成员方争议的焦点问题，对该体系的未来改革趋势提出了思路和建议。

2. 中美轮胎特保案的法律争议及双方诉讼策略分析. 芦杰锋. 国际贸易问题，2014

［作者简介］对外经济贸易大学法学院

［内容提要］“中国诉美国轮胎特保措施案”始于 2009 年 9 月，2011 年 9 月完结。案件涉及美国对自中国进口的特定轮胎产品实施特别保障措施的合法性。中美双方主要围绕“421 条款”因果关系标准，“进口快速增长”的认定以及“进口快速增长”是否是造成实质损害的“一个重要原因”等方面展开争辩。通过本案的审理，WTO 争端解决机构首次就《入世议定书》第 16 条的含义和适用做出解释，并首次梳理了该条与 GATT1994 第 19 条以及 WTO《保障措施协定》之间的关系问题。WTO 专家组进行评估后裁定美方特保措施没有违反世贸组织相关规则。中方提出上诉。上诉机构则维持了专家组的裁定意见。

3. 多边贸易体制内知识产权争端解决机制研究. 史晓曦. 国际经济合作，2014

［作者简介］中国社会科学院国际法研究所

［内容提要］在多边贸易体制内，知识产权争端解决符合一般争端解决机制的运行规则，同时也具有其特殊性，如对非违约之诉的处理和知识产权协议条款的解释与实施。知识产权争端解决机制的运用，有助于规范知识产权争端解决的标准和程序，厘清知识产权贸易争端格局与发展动态。多边体制下知识产权争端解决机制也为我国应对知识产权摩擦提供了有益的经验和启示。

4. 国际投资争端解决机制的新挑战及其重构. 蒋德翠. 商业时代，2014

［作者简介］广西财经学院法学院

［内容提要］随着经济全球化的发展，国际投资流量与日俱增，随之引发的争端不断上升，当前国际投资争端解决机制面临着新挑战。本文介绍了这些新挑战，进而讨论了国际投资争端解决机制的发展趋势，并提出中国在新形势下所应采取的对策。

5. 论贸易救济措施裁决的逻辑性要求——以 WTO 争端解决机构取向电工钢案为视角. 刘彤. 国际贸易，2014

［作者简介］对外经济贸易大学法学院

［内容提要］以此案为契机，深入理解 WTO 相关协议对于贸易救济措施裁决的逻辑性要求和反思我国原有调查程序和具体行为中的不足，对于我国调查机关进一步完善相关法律、法规和调查程序、行为是非常必要和有益的。

6. WTO 争端解决裁决的国内效力问题研究——以国家主权为视角. 胡建国. 社会科学研究，2014

［作者简介］南开大学法学院

［内容提要］WTO 争端解决裁决的国内效力不同于 WTO 协定的国内效力。WTO 争端解决裁决与 WTO 协定的生成途径和国际法律地位有着显著差异。从其产生过程、自身品质和其他证据来看，WTO 争端解决裁决可能会对国家主权构成“软侵蚀”，各成员因此需要“看门人”，以防止

WTO争端解决裁决的国内不当影响。从实践看，欧盟和美国都明确拒绝了WTO争端解决裁决的直接效力，美国甚至还部分拒绝了WTO争端解决裁决的间接效力。我国应当借鉴欧盟和美国的立法与司法实践，一方面，不可一概承认WTO争端解决裁决的国内直接或间接效力，而是应该留有回旋余地，给予法院决定是否尊重WTO争端解决裁决的裁量权，确实维护我国国家主权；另一方面，可出于国际礼让、维持良好国际"守法"形象等考虑，给予WTO争端解决裁决适当尊重。

7. 试论WTO争端解决程序中适用盖然性优势证明标准的合理性. 姜作利. 比较法研究，2014

［作者简介］山东大学法学院

［内容提要］由于WTO协定中对证明标准没有做出明确具体的规定，专家组和上诉机构在审理实践中主要采用初步证据案件证明标准，以确定举证责任的转移。同时，又采用盖然性优势证明标准来评估当事方提交的证据，做出终结性的裁决。显然，采用初步证据证明标准不符合WTO争端解决的程序，既没有实际意义，又使专家组和上诉机构在审理实践中前后不统一，引起了不小的混乱。尤其是对不了解英美法的广大发展中国家来说，不公平地加重了他们在WT0争端中的举证难度。国际法庭和各国司法审判中普遍适用的盖然性优势证明标准，既适合WTO争端解决的程序，又有利于减轻发展中国家的证明标准和难度，增强他们胜诉的可能性。因此，WTO案件审理中尽快摒弃初步证据证明标准，直接采用盖然性优势证明标准已经成为必然的选择。

8. 世界贸易组织争端解决裁决执行之管辖权研究. 徐泉，钟英通. 法商研究，2014

［作者简介］西南政法大学国际法学院；中国—东盟法律研究中心

［内容提要］世界贸易组织争端解决裁决执行中的管辖权问题研究并未引起学界的广泛关注。世界贸易组织《关于争端解决规则与程序的谅解》第21. 3（c）条仲裁程序、第21. 5条专家组程序以及第22. 6条仲裁程序是世界贸易组织争端解决裁决执行中的争议解决程序，这三大程序中的管辖权问题对裁决的有效执行至关重要。三个程序中的裁判机构在实践中已就某些管辖权问题达成了共识，但囿于《关于争端解决规则与程序的谅解》的规定含糊不清，裁决执行中的管辖权规则仍有待完善。

9. 再论卡尔沃主义的复活——投资者—国家争端解决视角. 韩秀丽. 现代法学，2014

［作者简介］厦门大学法学院

［内容提要］晚近，一些国家为应对国际投资仲裁程序，修改宪法、法律和合同，限制或放弃国际投资协定中的投资者—国家争端解决条款，甚至终止双边投资条约和退出《解决国家与他国国民间投资争端公约》，这一系列现象是卡尔沃主义不同程度复活的表现。卡尔沃主义复活的原因在于经济危机引发的对新自由主义的质疑，解决投资争端国际中心为代表的国际投资仲裁制度本身的缺陷，以及各国对保留规制权的诉求。在这种国际潮流和背景下，中国应支持和提倡改革现行国际投资仲裁体制，在签订国际投资协定时，应审慎设计投资者—国家争端解决条款。

10. 从"中美家禽案"看WTO/SPS体制下中国利益的维护. 张超汉，张亮. 甘肃政法学院学报，2014

［作者简介］吉林大学；广西大学法学院

［内容提要］基于对中国在"中美家禽案"中诉讼表现的实证考察，结合现有判例对《实施卫生与植物卫生措施协定》第5条在案件审理中被解释适用的情况进行分析拆解与归纳整合，从SPS争端解决的侧面和SPS措施与成员内部制度互动角度探得WTO/SPS体制正反两面的意义与效用。中国应重视SPS通报制度并通过协调SPS措施制定权限、鼓励行业协会参与等途径积极参与国际标准制定，在处理此类争端时应立足不同的角色定位并紧扣DSB推理逻辑及审理思路设计攻防方案。

11. WTO视野中的可再生能源支持政策——兼评加拿大与日本、欧盟间FIT争端. 唐旗，仲谋. 国际贸易，2014

［作者简介］电子科技大学经济与管理学院；对外经济贸易大学国际经济贸易学院

［内容提要］在新能源贸易摩擦加剧之际，WTO适时扮演了一个积极的角色，不能不说是沉闷的多哈回合的一抹亮色。由于多边贸易体制的最初设计理念、能源牵扯的政治敏锐性等历史原因或现实障碍，WTO/GATT在传统能源贸易领域一向寂

寂无为。然而在新能源领域，WTO 成员已经自觉置身 WTO 规则框架之下来考虑政策取向问题，并不约而同地寻求在 WTO 框架内解决其贸易摩擦。

12. WTO 和多边环境协定的冲突与调和探析. 曾炜. 生态经济，2014

［作者简介］贵州民族大学法学院

［内容提要］随着国际贸易自由化和环境保护全球化趋势的不断增强，国际社会对环境与贸易的关系日益关注，各种环境保护公约不断频现，许多环境公约采取贸易措施作为实现环保目标的方法，从而可能与世界贸易组织产生冲突。对于同属多边环境公约和世界贸易组织成员方之间的矛盾，可以根据条约法公约关于条约之间冲突的解决方法来确定优先次序；若双方都属于世界贸易组织成员，而一方不是多边环境公约成员国，则只能使用 WTO 争端解决机制，但争端解决机构在解释 WTO 相关条文时，应尽可能采取与多边环境协定不相冲突的解释。

➢ 贸易摩擦

1. 澳大利亚对华反倾销中“特殊市场情况”的滥用. 赵海乐. 国际经贸探索，2014

［作者简介］吉林大学法学院

［内容提要］澳大利亚虽于 2005 年承认了中国的市场经济地位，但自 2010 年以来，仍然四次通过“特殊市场情况”的认定，持续采用替代国价格认定倾销幅度。中国同时也是 2010 年以来此种认定的唯一受害国。中国冶金产业占据澳大利亚市场的相当份额，是引发贸易救济的直接原因；而中国的“非市场经济”问题与澳大利亚反倾销调查机关广泛的行政裁量权，为贸易救济提供了可乘之机。中国的诉讼实践表明，此问题唯有通过国际法渠道寻求救济。一方面，澳大利亚对“特殊市场情况”的解释违反了 WTO 条约解释规则，因而可以通过诉讼澄清 WTO 条约间关系加以解决。另一方面，维护 WTO 法治环境的同时，中国还应通过 WTO 诉讼，寻求他国对中国特色经济体制合法性的认可。

2. 全球稀缺资源贸易限制措施及其影响. 陈文敬，赵玉敏. 国际贸易，2014

［作者简介］商务部研究院

［内容提要］近年来中国多种稀缺资源出口政策措施接连遭到美、欧、日等国家指控并上诉到世界贸易组织就是例证。因此，考察和借鉴世界主要资源性产品出口国的贸易政策实践，将有助于中国制定合规的出口贸易管理制度和实施措施，创造更好的国际贸易环境，进一步拓展国际市场空间。

3. 中国国际贸易争端的现状分析及对策探讨，李敏，刘丽影，卢秀茹. 世界农业，2014

［作者简介］河北农业大学经贸学院

［内容提要］中国加入 WTO 以来，中国市场进一步开放，对外经济贸易迅猛发展，国际竞争力明显增强。但与此同时也引发了众多以反倾销、反补贴、保障措施，以及以质量、技术、卫生、环保等标准对中国出口设限等为代表的国际贸易争端，形势不容乐观。基于此，本文将主要从贸易角度探讨中国国际贸易争端与摩擦问题，以中国面临的国际贸易争端现状为切入点，对中国对外贸易争端与摩擦形成的原因进行分析，并针对具体现状提出相应的对策建议，以提高中国贸易竞争力。

4. 美国农业补贴政策演变及对我国的启示. 李万君，李艳军. 农业现代化研究，2014

［作者简介］华中农业大学经济管理学院

［内容提要］美国农业补贴经历了孕育、诞生与发展、淡化、调整和新发展五个阶段，具有补贴投入数额巨大、以“黄箱”补贴为主；侧重主要农产品和大农场主；相关法律法规健全，辅助支持政策完善；充分做好前期工作，及时修正和调整以及着眼环境保护和食品安全等特点。因此具有有效应对农业生产风险，消除农民后顾之忧；提高农产品贸易竞争力，拓展国际市场以及发展现代农业，促进可持续发展的积极效应；同时农业补贴陷入恶性循环，导致政府财政负担增加，土地过度使用和环境遭到破坏，加剧了农户贫富差距，降低了农民“免疫”能力，容易引发国际贸易摩擦。上述总结为我国农业部门明确补贴目标、构建补贴体系、完善补贴机制、增强可持续发展能力、兼顾效率和公平，以及实现从“黄箱”到“绿箱”的转变等提供了有益的启示。

5. 从国际服务贸易摩擦透视自由化谈判的利益差异——兼论中国服务贸易发展的战略选择. 林峰，戴磊，林珊. 亚太经济，2014

［作者简介］华南理工大学经济与贸易学院；

浦发银行苏州分行；福建社会科学院

［内容提要］本文在对国际服务贸易摩擦的表征与内涵进行提炼的基础上，解析与透视服务贸易自由化谈判的利益差异。结论是：美国、欧盟等发达国家在服务业市场准入谈判中的利益趋同性更强，偏重于推动金融服务、信息服务等知识密集型服务业的市场准入，这种利益取向的差异正是造成国际服务贸易摩擦的重要成因；以中国为代表的发展中国家则偏向于紧急保障机制、自然人流动等议题的谈判，这些矛盾势必会造成服务贸易自由化谈判的僵化。针对以上论述，本文最后提出对中国服务贸易发展战略的政策性启示。

6. 中国对外贸易摩擦的特征、成因及应对策略. 边洁英. 价格月刊，2014

［作者简介］河南牧业经济学院外语系

［内容提要］目前，中国对外贸易摩擦数量越来越多，对外贸易发展难度加大。在分析中国对外贸易摩擦国际国内经济环境的基础上，研究了对外贸易摩擦的现状与特征及其产生的深层次原因，进而提出了相关应对策略。

7. 中美贸易摩擦的成因与对策. 姜团. 财经问题研究，2014

［作者简介］圣迪管理咨询（大连）有限公司

［内容提要］中美分别作为世界上最大的发展中国家和发达国家，两国在经济结构、产业结构、资源条件及消费水平等各方面存在着较大差异，两国发展贸易具有很强的互补性。然而近年来，美国持续的贸易逆差却使中美贸易摩擦愈演愈烈，在某种特定背景下，它可能会成为中美政治经济恶化的触媒。因此，分析中美贸易现状，探究贸易摩擦出现的原因，找出相应的解决对策并对以后可能出现的发展趋势加以预测，这对维持良好的中美政治经济关系、改善中国在全球政治经济中的地位有重要作用。

8. 互利共赢新内涵与我国应对贸易摩擦新思路. 戴翔，张二震. 天津社会科学，2014

［作者简介］安徽财经大学国际经济贸易学院；南京大学经济学院

［内容提要］从本质上看，贸易摩擦是国家间利益冲突激化的结果和表现。当前互利共赢的内涵已经从传统意义上依托比较优势获取贸易利益，演变为国家间利益呈现彼此相依的“共生性”和“包容性”特征，因此从互利共赢的思路探寻化解贸易摩擦的有效对策，不仅必要而且可行。以互利共赢的理念和思路指导开放型经济发展，通过加强贸易政策和产业政策的协调以及“走出去”融入全球价值链等途径，深度建立与全球各国的互利共赢竞合关系，是新形势下我国化解日益严峻贸易摩擦的有效举措。

9. 制度水平、出口潜力与稀土贸易摩擦——基于贸易引力模型的实证分析. 魏龙，潘安. 世界经济研究，2014

［作者简介］武汉理工大学经济学院；湖北省科技创新与经济发展研究中心

［内容提要］本文将制度水平变量加入贸易引力模型，并据此测算稀土出口潜力指数，试图解释稀土贸易摩擦的深层原因。研究发现，从进口国制度水平看，清廉程度和货币自由度是影响中国稀土出口的主要因素；“过度贸易型”国家如荷兰、日本、美国等与近年来中国稀有资源出口限制贸易案的发生显著相关；稀土产品的反向贸易政策是影响中国稀土贸易进而引起稀土贸易摩擦的直接原因，而中国与“过度贸易型”进口国的战略利益冲突是深层原因。

10. 我国对外贸易摩擦预警机制优化研究. 李娟. 管理世界，2014

［作者简介］华东政法大学国际法学院

［内容提要］中国的货物出口全球第一的地位，使得中国成为对外贸易摩擦的多发地。如何通过对贸易摩擦风险的提前预警，预防对外贸易摩擦的冲击，提升我国出口的国际竞争力，提高对外开放的质量，是我国企业和政府必须要重视的问题。

11. 欧盟对华贸易摩擦现状及对策探析——基于政府宏观视角. 王光丽. 广西财经学院学报，2014

［作者简介］山东广播电视大学经管学院

［内容提要］伴随着中欧经贸关系的发展，特别是在欧债危机的背景下，欧盟对华频繁使用反倾销、反补贴、技术性贸易壁垒的贸易救济措施，成为制约我国产品出口欧盟市场的羁绊。我国政府从宏观层面出发，通过开展经济外交、运用WTO争端解决机制等措施寻求贸易摩擦应对之道。

12. 探析贸易摩擦常态化的治理策略. 刘永平. 国际贸易，2014

［作者简介］北京交通大学经济管理学院

［内容提要］当前理论思考中，经济诸多层面并没有将经济新常态的讨论思潮贸易摩擦列为其一，习惯性地认为贸易摩擦只是给中国严重外向型的经济敲响了警钟；在赞叹习主席拉美之行掀起的中拉经济合作热潮时，也不无遗憾地指出贸易保护主义有所抬头，称其为中拉经贸合作中出现的不和谐音。诸多层面忽视贸易摩擦“常态化”的倾向，将会使之缺席当前对经济新常态的重新思考、重新设计、重新建设，错失从根本上改变长期被动局面的机遇。

13. 我国涉税贸易摩擦的新特征及应对策略. 程风雨. 经济纵横，2014

［作者简介］厦门大学经济学院

［内容提要］涉税国际贸易摩擦指由税制安排不同以及税收政策的运用最终引起的贸易当事国之间因贸易利害冲突而产生的意见对立或贸易争端等事态，其已成为我国贸易摩擦的主要形式，并在近些年表现出一些新特征。必须清醒地认识到我国涉税贸易摩擦存在的必然性、长期性与复杂性，重视特别关税的作用，构建我国贸易救济体系，并适时加快推动财税体制改革，提前部署服务贸易领域内涉税贸易摩擦的预警与防范工作。同时，推动企业“走出去”，不断提升涉税贸易摩擦解决的主动性与能动性。

14. 中美水产品贸易摩擦分析. 刘武兵，李婷. 世界农业，2014

［作者简介］农业部农业贸易促进中心

［内容提要］中美水产品贸易近年来在摩擦中持续发展，但美国对中国水产品发起的多起贸易救济调查，以及对中国输美水产品施加的多种非关税贸易壁垒，影响了中美水产品贸易的进一步发展。本文分析了中美水产品贸易摩擦情况，预计非关税贸易壁垒将成为未来美国限制从中国进口水产品的主要措施，并提出了相关应对建议。

15. 贸易保护政策对异质性企业影响的实证检验——兼论中美产业内贸易摩擦传导机制. 杨培强，张兴泉. 国际贸易问题，2014

［作者简介］浙江大学经济学院；嘉兴学院商学院

［内容提要］文章首先构建一个在产业内贸易条件下的异质性企业固定出口成本的理论模型，分析贸易保护政策对不同生产率企业的影响。针对中美产业内贸易摩擦现状，运用美国企业层面的面板数据，验证贸易保护政策对中国出口产品价格的影响和美国国内同一行业出口与非出口企业生产率的影响，并在此基础上探讨中美产业内贸易摩擦发生的动因。同时，结合贸易政治经济学理论，解析在“企业”路径下美国国内出口和非出口企业利益集团竞争对中美产业内贸易摩擦形成的传导机制，并提出相关对策建议。

16. 从税收制度看我国遭遇的反补贴争端. 胡若痴. 国际贸易，2014

［作者简介］对外经济贸易大学国际经济研究院

［内容提要］在全球化的背景下，税收优惠不再是单个国家内部的政策，而是涉及国际税收协调以及与国际贸易规则相符合的问题。在国际贸易争端日益复杂化的今天，经济体之间税收制度差异和税收优惠政策的使用也成为形成贸易纠纷的原因之一。从近年来我国所涉及的贸易摩擦来看，税收优惠政策的运用也成为越来越重要的影响因素。

17. 我国应对贸易救济调查中价格可比性问题研究. 刘永平. 价格理论与实践，2014

［作者简介］北京交通大学经济管理学院

［内容提要］近年来，我国越来越多的出口企业受到各国的反倾销、反补贴等贸易救济调查，由此造成很大的损失。贸易救济的本质就是公平比较，价格可比是实施贸易救济调查的前提。实践中，对一些客观不可比的情况需要进行主观调整。由于客观不可比情况的认定标准具有不精确性，加之主观调整的自由度很难进行严格约束，救济过度在所难免。本文探讨了价格可比性的法理基础，国际通行规则对价格比较的基本原则，以及在各国贸易救济实践中不进行严格比较对我国贸易救济的影响，并提出了积极应对贸易救济调查的对策和建议。

18. 中美贸易摩擦与日美贸易摩擦的比较分析. 徐梅. 日本学刊，2014

［作者简介］中国社会科学院日本研究所

［内容提要］2008年国际金融危机爆发以后，世界经济陷入低迷，贸易保护主义升温。正在崛起的中国日益成为全球经贸摩擦的中心，尤以中美贸易摩擦最受关注。与20世纪中后期愈演愈烈的日美贸易摩擦相比，中美贸易摩擦在经贸政策、进出口市场、汇率变动等方面存在一些相似之处，但在所处的时代环境、美国在摩擦中的表现及应对措施等方面又存在一些不同之处。中国不仅需要促进出口市场的多元化和内外需协调发展，尽快与国际通行规则接轨，强化自主研发能力，促进产业结构升级，而且需要深入了解贸易对象的相关法规、社会文化以及国际规则惯例等，以缓和、化解当前面对的摩擦，并以更加灵活多样的策略应对今后将会继续增多的摩擦。

19. 国际贸易中反垄断法壁垒及我国的对策研究. 刘彤. 价格理论与实践，2014

［作者简介］对外经济贸易大学法学院商事争议解决法律研究中心

［内容提要］反垄断域外适用的力度不断增强成为国际整体趋势。基于目标和效果原则的反垄断法域外适用，将外国出口商在本国的合法行为置于进口国反垄断法的管辖之下，并对其实施严厉的惩罚手段，逐渐成为威胁我国出口企业的新形式贸易壁垒。作为应对措施，我国应当通过完善国内立法限制外国反垄断法在我国境内的实施，并通过建立明确的出口卡特尔豁免制度，确立行业出口价格协调行为的合法性。在国际层面，我国应当充分的利用双边合作协议和国际礼让原则加强与其他国家的相互理解与合作；并通过积极参与国际统一反垄断法规则的制定抑制国际反垄断法的过度扩张。

20. 中国需要积极有效地应对国际经贸摩擦问题. 陆燕. 对外经贸实务，2014

［作者简介］商务部国际贸易经济合作研究院

［内容提要］在贸易大国向贸易强国的进程中，我国对外经贸发展面临诸多严峻挑战，其中之一便是国际经贸摩擦更加严峻和复杂。我国正面临更多的体制和规则层面的经贸摩擦。这些经贸摩擦，既是贸易利益的冲突，也是战略利益的博弈。如何有效应对各种经贸摩擦，维护国际市场的公平竞争环境，已经成为我国深化并稳定发展与其他国家经贸关系的一个十分关键的问题。

➢ 其他议题

1. 国际投资协定一般例外条款研究——与WTO共同但有区别的司法经验. 梁丹妮. 法学评论，2014

［作者简介］中山大学法学院

［内容提要］近年来，以条约为基础的投资仲裁案件不断涌现，过分倾向于投资者保护的国际投资仲裁制度饱受批评，发达国家积极推进国际投资协定制度改革，包括增加新条款以重新平衡外国投资者与东道国之间的权利义务。本文探讨国际投资协定是否有必要增设一般例外条款，如GATT第20条，允许东道国为实现保护如人类、动植物生命或健康等目标而豁免投资保护义务，以确保国际投资协定与国家公共政策之间的一致性。

2. 中国加入WTO政府采购协定谈判中的中小企业问题. 曹富国. 国家行政学院学报，2014

［作者简介］北京大学

［内容提要］新一轮WTO政府采购协定（GPA）谈判成果嵌入了有关中小企业的未来工作计划，其中包含了“最佳实践”。本文揭示其意义、可能内涵以及未来发展方向。中国中小企业政府采购政策最近有了实质性发展，中国加入WTO－GPA谈判出价方案也包含了对中小企业豁免。中国针对中小企业的政府采购优惠政策本身对国际贸易的影响微乎其微，在GPA谈判中中国应坚持既定出价立场；中国政府采购中的中小企业政策与GPA有关中小企业政策的未来发展方向有其一致性；即使在加入GPA之前，中国也能够积极参与GPA规则制定。基于谈判策略的需要，中国应促进采购国货条款的有效实施。

3. 国际投资体制改革及中国的对策. 詹晓宁，欧阳永福. 国际经济合作，2014

［作者简介］联合国贸发组织投资和企业司；联合国贸发组织

［内容提要］国际社会正在反思和重新评估当前的国际投资体制。改革和重塑国际投资体制将成为各方围绕建立新的全球经济治理结构进行角力的重点。

4. SPS措施对中国农产品出口贸易影响的实证分析——基于HMR法和极大似然法的比较. 秦臻，倪艳. 国际贸易问题，2014

[作者简介] 华中农业大学经济管理学院；湖北省社会科学院

[内容提要] SPS措施作为WTO多边贸易协定下的重要内容，一直对农产品贸易影响巨大，而且在短期内不会随着区域贸易协定的繁荣而削弱其贸易效应。本文采用前沿HMR法和极大似然法对中国农产品出口遭遇SPS措施的贸易效应进行比较研究。结论显示，在既定条件满足时，HMR模型可以很好地测算贸易广度和贸易深度。而基于拟极大似然法的ZINBPML模型能很好地解决过度散布问题。对于中国主要出口农产品，SPS措施既能增加贸易广度，也能提升贸易深度。其原因在于，SPS措施不仅能促进出口市场多元化，还能增加进口消费信心和安全感，反而可以扩大出口额。

5. 以“稀土案”为例试论中国环保如何融入国际贸易框架. 张彬，李丽平，柴琪. 环境保护，2014

[作者简介] 环境保护部环境与经济政策研究中心国际环境政策研究所；四川华成油气工程建设监理有限公司

[内容提要] 通过分析我国“稀土案”败诉的原因、存在的问题，针对中国环保如何融入国际贸易框架提出了取消资源类产品不符合WTO规则的出口关税、出口配额等贸易限制措施，充分利用WTO贸易政策审议等平台，阐释中国绿色贸易政策，防范与其相关纠纷于未然等对策建议。

6. 低碳经济对国际贸易规则的影响及中国的对策. 李丽. 财贸经济，2014

[作者简介] 对外经济贸易大学国际经济研究院

[内容提要] 全球应对气候变化和低碳发展正在对国际贸易规则产生影响，而国际贸易规则的制定将极大影响国际贸易的发展。目前，WTO已经将应对气候变化和低碳发展作为一项重要的内容给予高度肯定，并在贸易与环境谈判、农业谈判和非农谈判中都有涉及。越来越多的区域性贸易协定也把气候变化和低碳经济作为一项内容纳入进来，成为影响区域贸易的重要因素。此外，国际非政府组织、民间机构和企业也在通过一些非官方倡议和标准来进一步推动全球低碳贸易规则的形成。在此情况下，我国应了解低碳规则竞争现状，积极参与WTO多哈回合谈判，特别是环境产品清单的谈判，并关注区域及双边贸易协定中低碳规则的发展趋势，积极参与低碳领域国际标准及非官方标准的制定，为我国对外贸易发展创造良好的规则条件。

7. 多双边贸易协定中的国际核心劳工标准分析. 陈志阳. 国际贸易问题，2014

[作者简介] 武汉大学经济管理学院世界经济系；商务部国际经贸关系司

[内容提要] 国际贸易与国际核心劳工标准两者之间的关系近年来日益紧密，但对于是否应在贸易协定中纳入国际核心劳工标准，发达国家和发展中国立场相差较大。由于各成员难以达成一致，劳工标准未能纳入WTO多哈回合谈判范畴，目前WTO法律框架中仅有一些零散的规定与劳工问题有关。相比多边贸易体制在纳入劳工核心标准上的犹豫，美欧在区域自由贸易协定中积极纳入劳工问题，并形成了“NAFTA模式”和“欧盟模式”。正在谈判的超大型自贸区TPP和TTIP中也将纳入劳工标准问题。中国应参照国际标准，结合发展水平和国内改革进展，逐步同意将劳工标准与贸易问题适度挂钩，并在自贸协定谈判中先行先试。

8. 上海自贸试验区负面清单制定与中美BIT谈判联动性研究. 黄鹏，梅盛军. 国际商务研究，2014

[作者简介] 上海WTO事务咨询中心

[内容提要] 转变政府职能、推动管理模式创新和探索扩大开放新途径是上海自贸试验区建设的核心任务，而对于外商投资采取负面清单模式管理是其中最大的挑战。当前中美正在紧锣密鼓进行的双边投资保护协定谈判的最大难点同样是负面清单的谈判。作为为国家对外开放探索新途径的试验区，上海自贸试验区负面清单的制定必然要与中美BIT谈判中涉及的负面清单谈判进行联动，本文将对两者之间联动的必要性、负面清单模式的形成过程、核心内涵以及如何实现上海自贸试验区与中美BIT的联动等问题进行分析。

9. 美国对外贸易政策与 WTO 规则的关系分析与启示. 谢皓，杜莉. 世界经济研究，2014

[作者简介] 武汉大学商学院

[内容提要] 战后，以 GATT/WTO 原则为核心的国际贸易规则越来越多地影响着各国贸易政策的制定。可以说，这个多边贸易政策的框架是由美国倡导发起的。本文试从分析美国对外贸易政策入手，探讨它对 WTO 规则的历史性影响，同时研究在世界贸易体系建立之后，美国充分考虑到自身的经济利益，其贸易政策在同 WTO 保持一致的同时，也出现了同 WTO 规则的背离。

10. 数字时代国内文化规制与贸易自由化之间的互动——兼论我国文化规制的博弈空间. 彭光明. 法律适用，2014

[作者简介] 河北科技大学

[内容提要] 近年来，数字传播技术迅速发展，尤其是电子及视讯媒介的普及、人造卫星传输网络的建立，造就了文化的无边界化。许多国家担心民族文化被同化，倾向采取诸如限制市场准入等方式加强文化保护。但是，在世界贸易组织（WTO）推动的浓郁自由贸易氛围下，各成员可以在何种程度上保有自己的文化规制自主权，是考验各成员政府智慧的难题。本文在 WTO 框架下从争端实践和规则体系两个角度，剖析“文化因素”在 WTO 框架下的地位；探求面对数字科技的冲击，WTO 规则还能为文化规制留存多大空间，从而为我国提供文化规制政策的新思路。

11. 国际投资规则的演变及趋势. 聂平香. 国际经济合作，2014

[作者简介] 商务部国际贸易经济合作研究院

[内容提要] 进入 21 世纪以来，我国农业生产实现了从量的扩张到质、量并重转变，消费需求和国内外市场竞争都对农产品的质量安全水平提出了新要求。特别是随着我国进入 WTO 后过渡期，国际农产品对我国市场的冲击日益凸显，对国内农产品的质量结构、生产经营模式提出了挑战。农产品地理标志作为保护农业知识产权、促进农产品贸易的重要手段。

12. 我国探索负面清单管理模式宜关注五个问题. 吴频，吴伟华. 国际贸易，2014

[作者简介] 商务部政策研究室

[内容提要] 负面清单管理模式已在多个国家和地区实践。同时，我国探索负面清单管理模式取得了积极进展。我国推行负面清单模式符合改革开放要求，但需重点关注五大问题。发挥负面清单模式的试验效应，同时防控可能产生的风险，要准确把握和处理好国际与国内、开放与安全、试验与推广等几个方面的关系。需从两方面同时入手：一是要不断自我完善，及时修正完善负面清单，使清单的内容更加科学完整，既符合全面深化改革、扩大对外开放要求，又不超越现阶段国情；二是要加强风险管控，构建风险防御体系。

13. 国际贸易投资规则的新变化：竞争中立原则的应用与实践. 张琳，东艳. 国际贸易，2014

[作者简介] 中国社会科学院世界经济与政治研究所

[内容提要] 竞争中立规则从长期来看，有助于提高市场竞争效率，有助于资源在全球范围内更有效地配置，符合我国以开放促改革的发展要求，代表了更高标准的开放和更深层次的改革，从根本上符合我国的经济发展要求。但从短期来看，对于竞争中立框架和规则，我们仍存在几点担忧和疑虑。

14. 国际贸易投资规则发展趋势与中国的应对. 王金波. 国际问题研究，2014

[作者简介] 中国社会科学院亚太与全球战略研究院

[内容提要] 当前，亚太区域合作正进入一个新的“框架重构”阶段。由 TPP 所引发的东亚地区秩序或亚太区域合作格局的变化势必会对中国的东亚一体化战略和东盟为中心的渐进性一体化原则形成新的挑战。同时，以 TTIP 和 TISA 为代表的欧美新贸易投资协定正在成为影响中国未来发展的新的重大外部因素。因此，着眼于国际规则和全球治理的最新发展趋势，中国有必要在深化国内改革的基础上，加快完成更高标准的自贸区战略布局；在世界经济规则的重构中提出新的战略议程，以增强中国在国际经济治理中的话语权。

第九篇　与 WTO 有关的法规及政策（2014）

《进口饲料和饲料添加剂登记管理办法》

《进口饲料和饲料添加剂登记管理办法》业经2013年12月27日农业部第11次常务会议审议通过，现予公布，自2014年7月1日起施行。农业部2000年8月17日公布、2004年7月1日修订的《进口饲料和饲料添加剂登记管理办法》同时废止。

交通运输部、商务部《关于修改〈外商投资道路运输业管理规定〉的决定》

《关于修改〈外商投资道路运输业管理规定〉的决定》已于2013年12月16日经交通运输部第13次部务会议通过，现予公布，自2014年1月11日起施行。

交通运输部《国内水路运输管理规定》

《国内水路运输管理规定》已于2013年12月30日经第14次部务会议通过，现予公布，自2014年3月1日起施行。

银监会、国家发展改革委《商业银行服务价格管理办法》

为规范商业银行服务价格管理活动，保护商业银行服务对象的合法权益，促进商业银行健康可持续发展，中国银监会、国家发展改革委制定了《商业银行服务价格管理办法》，现予公布。

商务部《机电产品国际招标投标实施办法（试行）》

《机电产品国际招标投标实施办法（试行）》已于2013年12月9日经中华人民共和国商务部2013年第10次部务会议审议通过，现予公布，自2014年4月1日起施行。原《机电产品国际招标投标实施办法》（商务部2004年第13号令）同时废止。

商务部《关于经营者集中简易案件适用标准的暂行规定》

为了明确经营者集中简易案件的适用标准，根据《中华人民共和国反垄断法》，商务部制定了《关于经营者集中简易案件适用标准的暂行规定》。现予公布，自2014年2月12日起施行。

海关总署《中华人民共和国海关政府信息公开办法》

《中华人民共和国海关政府信息公开办法》已于2014年2月13日经海关总署署务会议审议通过，现予公布，自2014年4月1日起施行。

《海关总署关于废止部分规章的决定》

《海关总署关于废止部分规章的决定》已于2014年2月13日经海关总署署务会议审议通过，现予公布，自公布之日起施行。

海关总署《中华人民共和国海关进口货物直接退运管理办法》

《中华人民共和国海关进口货物直接退运管理办法》已于 2014 年 2 月 13 日经海关总署署务会议审议通过，现予公布，自公布之日起施行。2007 年 2 月 2 日以海关总署令第 156 号公布的《中华人民共和国海关进口货物直接退运管理办法》同时废止。

《国家知识产权局关于修改〈专利审查指南〉的决定》

《国家知识产权局关于修改〈专利审查指南〉的决定》已经局务会审议通过，现予公布，自 2014 年 5 月 1 日起施行。

《海关总署关于修改部分规章的决定》

《海关总署关于修改部分规章的决定》已于 2014 年 2 月 13 日经海关总署署务会议审议通过，现予公布，自公布之日起施行。

海关总署《中华人民共和国海关加工贸易货物监管办法》

《中华人民共和国海关加工贸易货物监管办法》已于 2014 年 2 月 13 日经海关总署署务会议审议通过，现予公布，自公布之日起施行。2004 年 2 月 26 日以海关总署令第 113 号发布，并以海关总署令第 168 号、195 号修改的《中华人民共和国海关对加工贸易货物监管办法》同时废止。

海关总署《中华人民共和国海关进出口货物报关单修改和撤销管理办法》

《中华人民共和国海关进出口货物报关单修改和撤销管理办法》已于 2014 年 2 月 13 日经海关总署署务会议审议通过，现予公布，自公布之日起施行。2005 年 12 月 30 日以海关总署令第 143 号公布的《中华人民共和国海关进出口货物报关单修改和撤销管理办法》同时废止。

国家发展和改革委员会《境外投资项目核准和备案管理办法》

《境外投资项目核准和备案管理办法》业经国家发展改革委主任办公会讨论通过，现予以发布，并于 2014 年 5 月 8 日起施行。我委 2004 年 10 月发布的《境外投资项目核准暂行管理办法》（国家发展改革委第 21 号令）同时废止。

商务部公布《饭店业碳排放管理规范》等 50 项国内贸易行业标准

《饭店业碳排放管理规范》等 50 项国内贸易行业标准已经商务部审核，现予公布。

中国人民银行业监督管理委员会《商业银行保理业务管理暂行办法》

《商业银行保理业务管理暂行办法》已经中国银监会2013年第21次主席会议通过。现予公布，自公布之日起施行。

国务院《中华人民共和国商标法实施条例》

现公布修订后的《中华人民共和国商标法实施条例》，自2014年5月1日起施行。

国家发展和改革委员会《外商投资项目核准和备案管理办法》

《外商投资项目核准和备案管理办法》已经国家发展和改革委员会主任办公会讨论通过，现予发布，自2014年6月17日起施行。国家发展和改革委员会2004年10月9日发布的《外商投资项目核准暂行管理办法》（国家发展和改革委员会令第22号）同时废止。

商务部、财政部《对外劳务合作风险处置备用金管理办法（试行）》

《对外劳务合作风险处置备用金管理办法（试行）》已经2014年1月21日商务部第13次部务会议审议通过，并经财政部同意，现予发布，自2014年8月17日起施行。

《中华人民共和国海关〈中华人民共和国和瑞士联邦自由贸易协定〉项下进出口货物原产地管理办法》

《中华人民共和国海关〈中华人民共和国和瑞士联邦自由贸易协定〉项下进出口货物原产地管理办法》已于2014年6月30日经海关总署署务会议审议通过，现予公布，自2014年7月1日起施行。

国家发展和改革委员会、环境保护部、商务部、海关总署、国家工商行政管理总局、国家质量监督检验检疫总局《商品煤质量管理暂行办法》

为提高商品煤质量，促进煤炭高效清洁利用，特制定《商品煤质量管理暂行办法》，现予发布，自2015年1月1日起施行。

国务院《国务院关于修改部分行政法规的决定》

《国务院关于修改部分行政法规的决定》已经2014年7月9日国务院第54次常务会议通过，现予公布，自公布之日起施行。

国家食品药品监督管理总局《医疗器械注册管理办法》

《医疗器械注册管理办法》已于2014年6月27日经国家食品药品监督管理总局局务会议审议通过，现予公布，自 2014 年 10 月 1 日起施行。

国家食品药品监督管理总局《体外诊断试剂注册管理办法》

《体外诊断试剂注册管理办法》已于 2014 年 6 月 27 日经国家食品药品监督管理总局局务会议审议通过，现予公布，自 2014 年 10 月 1 日起施行。

银监会《中国银监会外资银行行政许可事项实施办法》

《中国银监会外资银行行政许可事项实施办法》已经中国银监会主席会议通过。现予公布，自公布之日起施行。

商务部、国家发展和改革委员会《餐饮业经营管理办法（试行）》

《餐饮业经营管理办法（试行）》已经商务部部务会议审议通过，并经发展改革委同意，现予发布，自 2014 年 11 月 1 日起施行。

《海关总署关于修改中华人民共和国海关〈中华人民共和国与智利共和国政府自由贸易协定〉项下进口货物原产地管理办法的决定》

《海关总署关于修改〈中华人民共和国海关《中华人民共和国与智利共和国政府自由贸易协定》项下进口货物原产地管理办法〉的决定》已于 2014 年 9 月 30 日经海关总署署务会议审议通过，现予公布，自 2014 年 10 月 1 日起施行。

工业和信息化部《工业和信息化部关于废止和修改部分规章的决定》

现公布《工业和信息化部关于废止和修改部分规章的决定》，自公布之日起施行。

商务部《2015 年磷矿石出口配额申报条件、申报程序及分配原则》

根据《中华人民共和国对外贸易法》《中华人民共和国货物进出口管理条例》《货物出口许可证管理办法》的有关规定，我部制定了《2015 年磷矿石出口配额申报条件、申报程序及分配原则》，现予公布。

商务部《2015 年成品油（燃料油）非国营贸易进口允许量申领条件、分配原则及相关程序》

根据《中华人民共和国货物进出口管理条例》和《原油、成品油、化肥国营贸易进口经营管理试行办法》（原外经贸部令 2002 年第 27 号），商务部制定了《2015 年成品油（燃料油）非国营贸易进口允许量申领条件、分配原则及相关程序》，现予公布。

商务部《2015年化肥进口关税配额总量、分配原则及相关程序》

根据《中华人民共和国货物进出口管理条例》《化肥进口关税配额管理暂行办法》，我部制定了《2015年化肥进口关税配额总量、分配原则及相关程序》，现予以公布，请认真遵照执行。

海关总署《中华人民共和国海关企业信用管理暂行办法》

《中华人民共和国海关企业信用管理暂行办法》已于2014年9月4日经海关总署署务会议审议通过，现予公布，自2014年12月1日起施行。

国务院《国务院关于修改中华人民共和国外资银行管理条例的决定》

现公布《国务院关于修改中华人民共和国外资银行管理条例的决定》，自2015年1月1日起施行。

商务部《贸易政策合规工作实施办法（试行）》

根据国务院办公厅《关于进一步加强贸易政策合规工作的通知》（国办发〔2014〕29号）的有关规定，我部制定了《贸易政策合规工作实施办法（试行）》，现予公布。

商务部《网络零售第三方平台交易规则制定程序规定（试行）》

《网络零售第三方平台交易规则制定程序规定（试行）》已经2014年12月1日商务部第32次部务会议审议通过，现予发布，自2015年4月1日起施行。

国家质量监督检验检疫总局《进出境非食用动物产品检验检疫监督管理办法》

《进出境非食用动物产品检验检疫监督管理办法》已经2014年4月8日国家质量监督检验检疫总局局务会议审议通过，现予公布，自2015年2月1日起施行。

国家发展和改革委员会关于修改《境外投资项目核准和备案管理办法》和《外商投资项目核准和备案管理办法》有关条款的决定

根据国务院发布的《政府核准的投资项目目录》，特制定《国家发展改革委关于修改〈境外投资项目核准和备案管理办法〉和〈外商投资项目核准和备案管理办法〉有关条款的决定》，现予公布。

第十篇　贸易统计数据

●世界贸易统计

表 1

1950—2014 年世界货物出口、产量和 GDP　（指数，2005 年=100）

	总额				数量								GDP
	出口				出口				产量				
	总计 a	农产品	燃料和矿产品	制成品	总计 a	农产品	燃料和矿产品	制成品	总计	农业	矿业	制造业	
1950	1	3	1	0	4	15	10	2	13	26	22	9	13
1951	1	4	1	0	4	15	11	2	14	27	25	9	14
1952	1	4	1	0	4	15	12	2	14	28	25	10	14
1953	1	4	1	0	4	16	13	2	15	29	26	11	15
1954	1	4	1	1	5	16	14	3	15	29	26	11	16
1955	1	4	1	1	5	17	15	3	17	30	29	12	17
1956	1	4	1	1	6	18	16	3	17	31	31	13	17
1957	1	4	1	1	6	19	18	3	18	31	31	13	18
1958	1	4	1	1	6	20	17	3	18	34	31	13	18
1959	1	5	1	1	7	22	18	4	19	34	32	15	19
1960	1	5	1	1	8	24	22	4	21	35	35	16	20
1961	1	5	1	1	8	25	23	4	21	36	37	17	21
1962	1	5	1	1	8	25	24	5	23	37	40	19	22
1963	2	5	1	1	9	26	25	5	24	38	41	20	23
1964	2	6	2	1	11	27	27	6	27	40	45	22	25
1965	2	6	2	1	11	28	28	6	28	40	47	24	26
1966	2	6	2	2	12	29	30	7	30	41	49	26	28
1967	2	6	2	2	13	30	33	8	31	43	50	27	29
1968	2	6	2	2	14	32	37	9	33	44	54	29	30
1969	3	7	3	2	16	34	39	10	35	44	55	31	32
1970	3	8	3	3	17	35	44	11	37	45	59	33	34
1971	3	8	3	3	18	35	45	12	39	47	62	34	36
1972	4	10	4	4	20	38	48	13	41	47	63	37	38
1973	6	14	5	5	22	38	53	15	44	49	67	40	40
1974	8	17	12	6	24	36	52	17	45	50	69	42	41
1975	8	17	11	7	22	37	46	16	44	52	65	40	42
1976	10	19	13	8	24	40	49	18	47	52	70	43	44
1977	11	22	15	9	26	41	50	19	49	53	72	45	46
1978	13	25	15	11	27	44	53	20	51	55	73	47	48

续 表

	总额				数量								GDP
	出口				出口				产量				
	总计 a	农产品	燃料和矿产品	制成品	总计 a	农产品	燃料和矿产品	制成品	总计	农业	矿业	制造业	
1979	16	31	22	13	28	46	56	21	53	56	79	49	50
1980	20	35	32	15	29	49	52	22	53	56	77	50	51
1981	20	34	31	15	29	51	47	23	53	58	71	50	52
1982	18	32	27	14	28	50	44	23	52	60	66	49	52
1983	18	31	25	14	29	50	44	24	54	60	66	51	54
1984	19	33	25	16	31	52	46	26	57	63	68	54	56
1985	19	31	24	16	32	51	46	28	59	65	67	56	58
1986	21	35	18	19	33	50	50	29	60	66	69	58	60
1987	24	40	20	23	35	53	51	31	62	67	70	60	63
1988	28	45	21	27	38	55	53	34	65	68	74	64	66
1989	30	47	24	29	41	56	56	36	68	70	77	66	68
1990	34	49	28	33	42	57	59	38	69	72	78	67	70
1991	34	50	26	34	44	59	61	40	68	72	78	66	70
1992	36	53	26	37	46	62	63	41	68	74	78	66	71
1993	36	51	25	37	48	63	66	43	68	74	80	66	72
1994	41	59	26	42	52	68	70	48	70	76	81	68	73
1995	49	69	30	51	56	71	73	52	74	78	83	71	75
1996	52	71	34	53	59	74	75	55	76	81	85	74	77
1997	53	70	35	55	65	79	81	61	80	83	88	78	80
1998	52	67	28	56	68	80	83	64	82	85	89	80	82
1999	55	64	32	58	71	80	82	67	84	87	88	83	84
2000	62	65	47	64	79	83	83	76	88	89	91	88	88
2001	59	65	43	62	78	85	83	76	88	90	91	86	89
2002	62	69	44	65	81	87	86	79	89	91	91	88	91
2003	72	80	54	75	86	91	90	83	92	94	94	91	93
2004	88	92	72	91	94	94	97	93	97	98	98	96	97
2005	100	100	100	100	100	100	100	100	100	100	100	100	100
2006	116	111	128	113	109	106	104	111	104	102	101	105	104
2007	134	133	147	130	116	111	108	119	109	105	101	112	108
2008	154	158	195	143	118	113	109	122	109	109	103	111	110
2009	120	139	125	115	104	111	103	103	103	109	101	102	107
2010	146	160	167	137	119	119	109	122	110	109	103	112	111
2011	175	195	224	158	125	126	111	130	114	112	105	116	114
2012	175	194	228	157	128	129	114	133	116	113	107	119	116
2013	179	204	222	162	132	132	115	137	118	119	108	121	118
2014	180	207	209	168	135	136	116	142	121	121	110	124	121

a 包括未分类产品。

表 1（续表）

1950—2014 年世界货物出口、产量和 GDP （年度变化百分比）

	总额				数量								GDP
	出口				出口				产量				
	总计 a	农产品	燃料和矿产品	制成品	总计 a	农产品	燃料和矿产品	制成品	总计	农业	矿业	制造业	
1950—1963	7	4	8	10	8	4	7	9	5	3	5	7	5
1964	12	7	12	15	11	5	9	15	9	5	9	10	7
1965	8	4	7	11	7	5	3	7	6	0	4	9	4
1966	9	4	10	11	8	4	6	10	7	3	5	8	6
1967	5	0	6	8	6	2	10	5	5	3	2	5	4
1968	11	4	14	15	11	6	12	18	6	3	7	7	6
1969	14	7	9	16	12	5	6	16	6	0	2	8	7
1970	15	11	14	15	9	3	12	9	5	3	8	5	5
1971	12	7	11	14	7	2	1	9	5	3	4	5	4
1972	18	20	14	19	8	7	7	10	5	0	3	7	6
1973	38	46	47	34	12	1	10	14	8	5	7	10	7
1974	45	22	123	31	5	−5	−2	9	3	2	2	3	2
1975	4	1	−4	9	−7	1	−12	−4	−2	4	−6	−4	1
1976	13	11	16	13	12	8	7	13	7	1	8	8	5
1977	14	13	11	15	4	4	3	5	4	3	3	5	4
1978	16	13	4	22	5	7	5	6	5	3	1	5	5
1979	27	24	47	21	5	5	6	5	4	1	9	4	4
1980	22	14	42	16	2	7	−6	6	−1	1	−3	1	3
1981	−1	−2	−3	−1	0	5	−10	4	0	4	−8	0	2
1982	−6	−7	−11	−4	−2	−2	−6	−2	−1	3	−7	−1	1
1983	−2	−1	−8	1	2	0	−1	5	2	0	−1	3	3
1984	6	5	−1	8	8	3	5	11	7	5	4	7	5
1985	0	−6	−3	4	3	−1	−1	5	3	2	−1	3	4
1986	9	11	−24	20	4	−2	9	4	3	2	3	3	3
1987	17	15	11	20	6	6	2	6	3	1	1	4	4
1988	14	13	1	16	8	3	6	9	5	2	5	6	5
1989	8	4	15	7	6	3	4	8	3	3	4	3	4
1990	13	5	16	14	4	1	6	6	1	2	1	1	3
1991	1	1	−6	3	4	3	3	4	0	0	−1	−1	1
1992	7	7	−1	8	5	6	4	5	0	2	1	−1	1
1993	0	−4	−4	0	4	1	4	4	0	1	2	−1	1
1994	13	16	5	16	9	9	7	11	3	3	2	3	2
1995	19	18	15	20	7	5	4	9	5	2	2	6	2
1996	5	3	14	4	5	4	4	5	4	4	3	3	3
1997	3	−1	3	5	10	6	7	11	5	2	3	6	3
1998	−1	−5	−21	2	5	1	3	5	2	2	1	2	2
1999	4	−4	16	3	5	1	−1	5	3	3	−1	4	3
2000	13	1	46	10	11	4	4	14	5	2	4	6	4
2001	−4	0	−9	−4	0	2	0	−1	−1	2	0	−2	2
2002	5	6	1	5	4	3	3	4	1	1	0	2	2
2003	17	17	23	16	5	4	6	6	4	3	4	4	3
2004	22	15	35	20	10	4	7	11	5	5	4	6	4
2005	14	9	38	10	6	6	4	8	3	2	2	4	3
2006	16	11	28	13	9	6	4	11	4	2	1	5	4
2007	16	20	15	15	7	5	3	8	4	3	0	6	4
2008	15	19	33	10	2	2	1	2	1	4	2	0	1
2009	−23	−12	−36	−20	−12	−2	−5	−15	−5	1	−2	−8	−2
2010	22	15	33	19	14	7	6	18	7	0	2	9	4
2011	20	22	34	15	5	6	2	7	3	2	1	4	2
2012	0	−1	2	0	2	2	3	2	2	1	2	2	2
2013	2	5	−3	3	3	3	1	3	2	6	1	2	2
2014	0	2	−6	4	3	3	1	4	2	1	2	2	2

a 包括未分类产品。

表 2

2010—2014 年世界货物贸易流向（按地区）

单位：十亿美元

目的地		世界 a	北美洲		中、南美洲	欧洲			独联体	
原产地	年份		总计	美国		总计	欧盟（28）	欧洲其他地区	总计	俄罗斯
世界	2012	18 025.00	3 038.90	2 147.44	787.87	6 573.00	5 939.11	633.89	554.90	321.63
	2013	18 438.00	3 084.19	2 160.02	780.07	6 700.66	5 999.13	701.53	568.33	326.00
	2014	18 494.00	3 195.25	2 213.41	743.99	6 791.82	6 138.83	652.99	511.65	296.90
北美洲	2012	2 371.95	1 151.92	620.41	216.95	379.96	326.41	53.55	17.97	12.84
	2013	2 417.89	1 189.47	643.62	216.48	368.17	314.17	54.00	18.63	12.98
	2014	2 492.76	1 251.43	657.35	214.07	379.10	331.38	47.72	17.42	12.16
美国	2012	1 545.70	509.09	—	180.04	313.78	265.67	48.11	15.33	10.70
	2013	1 579.59	527.72	—	181.16	310.02	262.29	47.73	16.22	11.15
	2014	1 620.53	553.30	—	180.96	317.59	276.15	41.44	15.53	10.75
中、南美洲	2012	752.40	191.17	165.13	200.67	128.29	112.66	15.63	8.30	6.68
	2013	737.96	182.15	155.51	194.25	121.82	108.45	13.37	8.79	7.01
	2014	694.88	172.64	147.81	179.39	114.04	100.55	13.48	9.40	8.07
欧洲	2012	6 468.03	494.80	411.51	123.86	4 408.60	4 018.06	390.54	245.54	170.21
	2013	6 779.68	506.40	420.38	128.98	4 585.98	4 127.91	458.06	253.15	170.96
	2014	6 810.50	539.88	446.69	119.16	4 665.31	4 251.45	413.86	218.21	147.71
欧盟（28）	2012	5 812.56	447.62	373.05	113.53	4 020.67	3 648.67	372.00	220.92	157.75
	2013	6 081.35	457.44	381.17	118.51	4 210.53	3 775.01	435.52	225.99	157.82
	2014	6 162.24	488.20	404.77	109.21	4 293.03	3900.12	392.91	193.21	136.37
欧洲其他地区	2012	655.46	47.19	38.46	10.32	387.92	369.38	18.54	24.62	12.45
	2013	698.32	48.95	39.20	10.47	375.45	352.90	22.55	27.16	13.14
	2014	648.26	51.68	41.92	9.94	372.29	351.33	20.95	25.01	11.34
独联体	2012	799.81	36.84	30.08	9.15	416.75	359.12	57.62	154.93	50.38
	2013	780.43	33.39	27.72	9.23	406.17	352.60	53.57	152.09	48.73
	2014	735.10	28.36	24.59	6.96	384.88	337.08	47.81	131.22	40.30
俄罗斯	2012	529.26	29.16	27.12	6.49	301.22	260.43	40.79	77.42	—
	2013	523.28	26.86	24.96	7.35	295.55	258.28	37.28	78.13	—
	2014	497.76	24.06	22.05	5.45	276.75	244.71	32.04	68.83	—
非洲	2012	640.05	73.49	61.17	30.38	237.86	215.78	22.08	1.94	1.29
	2013	601.26	55.09	46.13	29.42	219.93	197.28	22.65	1.99	1.34
	2014	555.43	39.12	32.63	28.58	201.29	180.71	20.58	2.07	1.46
中东	2012	1 348.51	119.03	109.53	10.36	146.55	116.42	30.14	5.50	2.22
	2013	1 346.49	109.60	100.85	10.72	145.83	111.04	34.79	5.55	2.27
	2014	1 287.81	99.20	92.30	10.88	147.50	107.29	40.21	6.74	3.19
亚洲	2012	5644.24	971.65	749.61	196.50	855.00	790.66	64.33	120.73	78.01
	2013	5 774.10	1 008.08	765.80	191.00	852.75	787.67	65.08	128.13	82.71
	2014	5 917.25	1064.63	812.04	184.95	899.70	830.36	69.34	126.58	84.02
日本	2012	798.57	162.79	141.95	17.12	89.67	81.50	8.17	14.58	12.59
	2013	715.10	152.92	134.17	15.69	78.72	71.80	6.93	13.04	10.96
	2014	683.85	148.53	123.89	14.61	77.58	71.01	6.57	11.12	9.14
中国	2012	2048.71	504.90	345.00	104.37	436.13	412.74	23.39	75.65	44.06
	2013	2 209.00	537.93	358.22	103.03	447.64	422.44	25.20	83.52	49.59
	2014	2 342.31	568.54	389.70	101.86	479.03	452.40	26.62	85.74	53.68
澳大利亚和新西兰	2012	293.98	16.31	13.28	3.02	22.57	20.83	1.74	1.29	1.01
	2013	292.43	14.63	12.55	2.53	17.73	15.76	1.97	1.17	0.90
	2014	282.84	16.14	13.43	2.42	15.90	14.55	1.35	0.96	0.68
亚洲其他地区	2012	2 502.97	287.66	249.38	71.98	306.63	275.59	31.04	29.20	20.35
	2013	2 557.57	302.60	260.86	69.74	308.65	277.68	30.98	30.41	21.27
	2014	2 608.26	331.41	285.01	66.06	327.20	292.40	34.80	28.76	20.53

a 包括未分类产品。

单位：十亿美元

非洲			中东	亚洲						目的地	
总计	南非	非洲其他地区		总计	日本	澳大利亚/新西兰	亚洲其他地区			年份	原产地
							总计	中国	其他		
589.75	115.75	473.99	707.67	5392.08	817.34	267.47	4 307.27	1 341.33	2 965.93	2012	世界
618.41	115.63	502.77	745.87	5 554.54	795.09	258.08	4 501.38	1 416.52	3 084.86	2013	
638.51	108.80	529.71	780.02	5 485.30	760.71	255.17	4 469.41	1 407.98	3 061.43	2014	
37.66	8.44	29.22	75.02	488.31	82.94	38.00	367.37	135.61	231.77	2012	北美洲
40.43	7.99	32.44	78.25	501.59	77.84	32.46	391.30	148.18	243.11	2013	
43.36	7.02	36.35	79.17	503.91	79.14	33.91	390.86	147.08	243.78	2014	
33.13	7.55	25.58	69.58	422.37	69.97	34.39	318.01	110.50	207.51	2012	美国
35.75	7.30	28.45	73.35	432.32	65.27	29.37	337.69	121.81	215.88	2013	
38.37	6.37	32.00	73.74	438.70	66.83	30.84	341.03	123.67	217.36	2014	
21.02	3.31	17.70	17.68	171.25	22.48	3.01	145.76	85.36	60.40	2012	中、南美洲
19.22	2.88	16.34	17.75	176.38	21.58	2.80	152.00	93.34	58.66	2013	
17.67	2.20	15.47	16.80	170.36	18.72	2.87	148.77	85.79	62.98	2014	
209.43	33.46	175.97	212.51	690.56	80.10	52.05	558.41	199.92	358.49	2012	欧洲
221.98	33.73	188.25	229.37	763.14	79.47	51.52	632.15	223.40	408.75	2013	
221.47	32.07	189.40	228.95	738.44	79.00	48.56	610.89	242.45	368.44	2014	
190.55	32.14	158.41	158.90	580.29	70.48	47.56	462.25	184.44	277.81	2012	欧盟（27）
200.36	32.06	168.30	177.16	603.62	70.76	47.24	485.61	195.73	289.88	2013	
200.88	30.59	170.28	179.97	622.57	69.89	44.54	508.13	217.59	290.55	2014	
18.88	1.32	17.56	53.61	110.27	9.62	4.49	96.16	15.48	80.68	2012	欧洲其他地区
21.61	1.66	19.95	52.21	159.52	8.70	4.28	146.54	27.67	118.87	2013	
20.59	1.48	19.11	48.99	115.88	9.10	4.02	102.76	24.86	77.90	2014	
16.11	0.46	15.64	21.88	131.13	20.24	0.35	110.54	57.56	52.98	2012	独联体
13.22	0.47	12.75	18.96	138.56	22.53	0.76	115.27	58.36	56.91	2013	
15.58	0.43	15.15	22.43	133.88	23.84	0.69	109.35	55.44	53.91	2014	
9.66	0.28	9.38	7.72	94.26	18.72	0.12	75.43	35.77	39.66	2012	俄罗斯
7.22	0.29	6.93	7.89	99.90	21.29	0.40	78.21	35.63	42.58	2013	
9.44	0.29	9.16	10.34	101.39	22.82	0.55	78.02	37.49	40.52	2014	
93.53	21.21	72.32	16.32	158.41	18.79	6.50	133.12	68.76	64.36	2012	非洲
99.99	21.08	78.91	17.08	155.96	16.48	5.10	134.37	67.50	66.87	2013	
98.08	21.19	76.88	18.18	151.69	14.81	4.48	132.40	63.57	68.83	2014	
37.14	11.35	25.79	102.79	733.72	155.75	7.30	570.68	132.52	438.15	2012	中东
36.03	10.77	25.26	112.84	735.90	150.08	7.50	578.32	140.80	437.52	2013	
35.70	10.37	25.33	112.97	693.91	132.11	5.46	556.34	143.35	413.00	2014	
174.87	37.51	137.36	261.47	3 018.69	437.04	160.27	2 421.39	661.61	1759.78	2012	亚洲
187.55	38.73	148.82	271.62	3 083.01	427.12	157.94	2 497.96	684.92	1813.03	2013	
206.65	35.51	171.14	301.52	3 093.10	413.11	159.20	2 520.79	670.29	1850.50	2014	
10.61	4.06	6.55	28.33	459.59	—	20.38	439.21	144.21	295.00	2012	日本
9.65	3.46	6.18	25.39	408.78	—	19.16	389.61	129.40	260.21	2013	
9.34	3.19	6.15	28.05	386.81	—	16.54	370.27	124.99	245.28	2014	
82.79	15.32	67.46	85.62	754.30	189.48	50.92	513.90	—	513.90	2012	中国
91.17	16.83	74.34	97.01	845.89	193.11	51.67	601.12	—	601.12	2013	
105.01	15.70	89.31	117.57	882.70	188.45	53.56	640.69	—	640.69	2014	
5.08	1.78	3.30	8.58	233.90	52.28	15.69	165.93	81.39	84.54	2012	澳大利亚和新西兰
5.13	1.49	3.64	9.81	232.93	47.68	14.54	170.71	97.11	73.59	2013	
4.59	1.24	3.35	9.91	224.43	45.58	14.47	164.38	89.72	74.66	2014	
76.39	16.35	60.05	138.93	1 570.90	195.27	73.28	1 302.35	436.01	866.34	2012	亚洲其他地区
81.60	16.94	64.65	139.41	1 595.41	186.32	72.57	1 336.52	458.41	878.11	2013	
87.71	15.38	72.33	145.99	1 599.17	179.08	74.63	1 345.45	455.59	889.86	2014	

a 包括未分类产品。

表 3

2012—2014 年世界货物贸易流向（按产品类别和地区）

单位：十亿美元

目的地	世界 a			北美洲			中、南美洲			欧洲		
原产地	2012	2013	2014	2012	2013	2014	2012	2013	2014	2012	2013	2014
世界												
农产品	1 651.28	1 737.21	1 765.40	200.91	207.00	219.61	67.92	70.43	69.87	661.14	702.52	715.57
食品	1 371.10	1451.66	1 486.28	168.17	175.73	188.10	60.76	63.40	63.02	562.21	600.77	612.25
鱼产品	121.04	129.84	138.94	19.90	22.28	24.80	3.24	3.52	3.77	45.74	50.15	53.52
其他食品	1 250.06	1 321.82	1 347.34	148.27	153.45	163.30	57.52	59.88	59.25	516.47	550.62	558.73
原料	280.19	285.55	279.12	32.74	31.27	31.51	7.16	7.03	6.85	98.93	101.75	103.32
燃料和矿产品	4 144.88	4 023.02	3 788.94	577.33	541.18	504.68	178.54	169.51	168.99	1 388.66	1 339.88	1 232.31
矿石和其他矿物	392.41	387.80	366.19	24.97	24.37	25.40	6.72	6.65	6.45	110.56	102.09	99.77
燃料	3 384.50	3 289.84	3 068.47	497.17	466.42	427.57	163.51	154.90	154.60	1119.23	1093.11	982.37
有色金属	367.97	345.39	354.29	55.20	50.38	51.71	8.31	7.96	7.94	158.88	144.68	150.17
制成品	11 472.52	11 826.41	12 242.88	2 188.26	2 260.96	2 397.30	518.28	517.14	485.65	4 283.27	4 417.73	4 654.09
钢铁	484.87	449.48	471.65	68.31	61.09	75.46	21.39	20.01	19.62	181.98	173.27	179.64
化学品	1 958.87	1 993.99	2 053.85	280.61	280.49	295.28	107.68	108.77	107.51	877.14	896.72	938.60
药品	509.62	521.22	550.89	88.33	86.26	96.91	21.13	21.86	22.03	283.86	289.83	307.96
其他化学品	1 449.24	1472.77	1 502.96	192.29	194.23	198.37	86.55	86.92	85.47	593.28	606.89	630.64
其他半制成品	1 093.93	1 151.11	1 184.73	181.03	190.31	198.60	45.01	45.69	42.79	454.80	473.15	492.20
机械和运输设备	5 757.24	5 931.46	6 112.33	1 223.65	1 269.09	1 343.71	256.54	258.73	235.10	1 929.30	1 985.04	2 092.68
办公和电信设备	1 681.47	1 750.75	1 794.30	362.84	375.54	388.14	47.70	49.35	45.59	492.16	484.57	500.48
EDP 和办公设备	554.58	542.41	552.29	160.09	158.51	162.45	15.86	14.67	13.07	197.53	196.38	204.69
通信设备	640.45	671.78	700.26	162.73	172.99	182.05	25.48	27.47	26.17	215.89	222.49	231.31
集成电路	486.45	536.56	541.75	40.02	44.03	43.64	6.36	7.21	6.34	78.74	65.70	64.47
运输设备	1 969.69	2 031.33	2107.38	454.30	475.78	504.61	106.06	107.70	94.75	736.76	772.25	831.23
汽车	1 300.72	1 346.07	1 394.81	355.42	373.18	389.86	68.92	71.04	57.86	487.92	516.45	558.09
其他运输设备	668.98	685.26	712.57	98.88	102.60	114.75	37.14	36.66	36.89	248.84	255.79	273.14
其他机械	2 106.07	2 149.38	2 210.65	406.51	417.77	450.96	102.77	101.68	94.76	700.37	728.23	760.97
纺织品	283.57	304.09	314.08	39.23	41.48	42.91	18.15	17.75	17.84	89.44	95.02	99.70
服装	419.52	459.66	483.28	93.12	99.94	104.91	16.22	14.73	14.58	184.45	200.16	217.21
其他制成品	1 474.53	1 536.63	1 622.97	302.31	318.54	336.43	53.29	51.46	48.22	566.16	594.36	634.05
个人及家居用品	318.53	343.60	365.11	76.88	82.66	87.34	13.94	12.66	11.36	139.56	148.89	160.08
科学和控制仪器	390.05	394.77	402.71	76.55	77.90	82.11	14.07	14.32	13.29	121.85	125.53	132.43
杂项制成品	765.95	798.27	855.15	148.88	157.98	166.98	25.28	24.48	23.57	304.74	319.94	341.54
制成品出口总额 b	**18 025.00**	**18 438.00**	**18 494.00**	**3 038.90**	**3 084.19**	**3 195.25**	**787.87**	**780.07**	**743.99**	**6 573.00**	**6 700.66**	**6 791.82**
北美洲												
农产品	257.72	266.44	276.72	97.58	102.51	107.83	17.57	19.84	21.25	23.11	25.19	26.74
食品	205.92	212.76	223.71	83.56	87.41	91.78	15.05	17.46	18.91	16.79	18.82	20.27
鱼产品	10.20	10.65	11.14	4.10	4.54	4.73	0.20	0.17	0.18	1.70	1.65	1.87
其他食品	195.72	202.11	212.57	79.46	82.87	87.04	14.85	17.29	18.73	15.09	17.17	18.40
原料	51.80	53.68	53.02	14.02	15.10	16.05	2.51	2.38	2.34	6.32	6.37	6.47
燃料和矿产品	402.51	407.82	415.21	229.38	235.99	248.08	49.17	50.21	54.25	59.81	56.30	54.36
矿石和其他矿物	53.94	50.22	49.39	11.85	11.55	13.12	1.38	1.25	1.31	13.31	11.92	12.03
燃料	305.60	317.77	326.00	189.25	197.33	208.28	46.57	47.80	51.87	40.63	39.72	37.33
有色金属	42.97	39.83	39.82	28.28	27.11	26.68	1.23	1.16	1.07	5.87	4.66	5.00
制成品	1582.15	1617.27	1685.09	782.90	808.90	852.37	142.73	138.77	131.01	247.82	249.14	264.72
钢铁	33.17	32.20	32.79	24.17	23.15	24.81	3.22	3.22	2.59	2.08	1.90	1.87
化学品	259.02	261.98	265.40	92.19	94.67	97.62	33.26	34.11	32.35	63.40	63.95	66.22
药品	52.03	51.86	57.83	10.48	9.87	11.26	4.23	4.06	4.03	26.65	27.19	30.68
其他化学品	206.99	210.12	207.57	81.71	84.80	86.36	29.02	30.06	28.32	36.75	36.76	35.54
其他半制成品	127.59	133.58	139.14	69.40	71.49	73.96	9.62	9.95	9.42	18.11	18.63	20.02
机械和运输设备	947.55	967.18	1 015.41	497.87	516.07	546.54	79.26	74.28	69.67	120.17	119.10	127.31
办公和电信设备	214.05	213.45	219.19	111.59	112.05	114.67	21.72	21.03	19.11	21.85	21.21	22.46
EDP 和办公设备	74.71	71.96	76.09	44.62	43.92	47.39	8.88	7.75	7.05	8.51	8.24	8.94
通信设备	93.27	95.15	96.14	54.64	54.90	54.42	9.83	10.14	9.85	10.45	10.24	10.63
集成电路	46.07	46.35	46.96	12.32	13.23	12.86	3.01	3.15	2.21	2.89	2.73	2.90
运输设备	419.53	438.50	467.49	231.49	244.66	260.47	27.22	24.17	23.41	56.98	56.88	61.33
汽车	269.88	278.05	291.49	196.62	207.22	217.92	14.52	12.41	11.23	17.98	15.96	17.65
其他运输设备	149.66	160.45	176.00	34.87	37.44	42.55	12.70	11.76	12.18	39.00	40.92	43.67
其他机械	313.97	315.23	328.73	154.80	159.35	171.40	30.33	29.09	27.15	41.34	41.01	43.52
纺织品	17.73	18.28	18.75	9.92	10.34	10.66	3.92	3.83	3.91	1.43	1.49	1.57
服装	11.34	11.66	12.10	8.15	8.41	8.81	0.81	0.84	0.88	1.02	1.06	1.05
其他制成品	185.76	192.37	201.49	81.20	84.77	89.98	12.64	12.52	12.19	41.60	43.01	46.67
个人及家居用品	20.41	21.73	23.60	16.53	17.58	19.14	0.85	0.91	0.91	0.84	0.94	1.07
科学和控制仪器	75.15	77.38	79.68	24.84	26.05	27.75	5.10	5.12	5.02	18.66	19.44	20.64
杂项制成品	90.20	93.27	98.21	39.84	41.14	43.09	6.69	6.50	6.27	22.10	22.63	24.96
制成品出口总额 b	**2 371.95**	**2 417.89**	**2 492.76**	**1 151.92**	**1 189.47**	**1 251.43**	**216.95**	**216.48**	**214.07**	**379.96**	**368.17**	**379.10**

单位：十亿美元

独联体			非洲			中东			亚洲			目的地
2012	2013	2014	2012	2013	2014	2012	2013	2014	2012	2013	2014	原产地
												世界
66.61	71.28	61.59	95.51	97.69	99.84	87.36	94.53	94.79	462.40	482.11	492.82	农产品
60.30	64.84	55.91	87.61	89.80	91.49	81.79	88.99	88.97	342.89	360.06	378.15	食品
4.16	4.95	4.72	4.89	4.66	4.96	2.32	2.48	2.81	40.28	41.22	43.86	鱼产品
56.14	59.90	51.20	82.72	85.14	86.53	79.47	86.51	86.16	302.61	318.84	334.29	其他食品
6.31	6.44	5.67	7.90	7.89	8.34	5.57	5.54	5.82	119.51	122.05	114.67	原料
62.43	57.55	56.84	108.49	111.12	111.99	82.76	84.25	85.77	1 623.80	1 602.15	1 505.91	燃料和矿产品
7.34	7.42	7.21	6.73	6.64	6.17	8.06	7.66	7.65	226.00	230.26	210.93	矿石和其他矿物
50.54	46.03	45.15	95.32	97.93	98.76	64.99	67.98	69.29	1 276.72	1249.83	1172.18	燃料
4.56	4.10	4.48	6.44	6.55	7.06	9.71	8.60	8.84	121.09	122.07	122.80	有色金属
419.32	432.34	386.69	360.90	385.47	405.92	501.70	517.47	562.73	3 120.89	3 210.20	3 285.08	制成品
22.69	22.99	19.44	21.57	23.16	23.72	36.27	29.30	29.79	130.70	118.88	123.15	钢铁
63.06	66.76	62.47	57.20	61.25	63.05	55.07	57.20	59.95	508.08	511.12	514.65	化学品
19.10	20.81	19.63	14.77	16.22	16.95	12.83	14.89	15.15	66.12	66.66	68.73	药品
43.96	45.94	42.83	42.43	45.03	46.10	42.24	42.31	44.80	441.95	444.46	445.92	其他化学品
44.25	47.04	42.75	46.55	49.81	52.39	64.83	71.70	74.83	250.67	265.28	273.55	其他半制成品
211.88	208.89	176.31	168.87	180.67	188.31	243.74	251.17	275.96	1674.55	1733.63	1770.96	机械和运输设备
28.99	28.19	24.72	21.80	21.34	24.24	41.94	45.86	51.05	684.86	745.02	759.36	办公和电信设备
11.27	10.10	8.37	6.83	6.49	6.61	14.05	14.81	16.00	148.86	141.36	140.99	EDP和办公设备
16.09	16.48	14.87	13.46	12.73	15.74	24.61	28.20	32.22	181.14	190.67	197.34	通信设备
1.63	1.60	1.48	1.50	2.12	1.89	3.28	2.85	2.82	354.86	412.99	421.03	集成电路
87.05	82.64	65.10	68.74	73.16	74.85	100.99	105.58	118.48	371.94	374.26	392.60	运输设备
65.56	62.30	47.84	49.95	51.11	50.38	68.72	69.75	75.65	202.25	200.64	213.50	汽车
21.49	20.35	17.26	18.78	22.05	24.48	32.27	35.84	42.84	169.69	173.62	179.10	其他运输设备
95.84	98.06	86.48	78.34	86.17	89.21	100.81	99.73	106.43	617.75	614.35	619.00	其他机械
12.99	13.79	14.05	19.79	20.94	22.14	15.49	16.46	17.42	86.92	95.68	97.82	纺织品
21.14	25.99	25.29	10.31	10.84	13.19	16.92	19.51	21.99	69.35	77.39	77.19	服装
43.30	46.88	46.39	36.61	38.80	43.12	69.38	72.13	82.79	400.62	408.22	427.76	其他制成品
14.65	16.46	17.06	11.17	11.91	13.64	13.19	15.55	17.73	48.81	55.00	57.53	个人及家居用品
9.10	9.22	8.35	6.87	7.48	8.04	10.05	10.65	11.03	151.30	149.38	147.13	科学和控制仪器
19.55	21.20	20.98	18.57	19.42	21.44	46.14	45.93	54.03	200.51	203.84	223.10	杂项制成品
554.90	**568.33**	**511.65**	**589.75**	**618.41**	**638.51**	**707.67**	**745.87**	**780.02**	**5 392.08**	**5 554.54**	**5 485.30**	制成品出口总额 b
												北美洲
3.38	2.78	2.04	8.21	8.02	7.73	5.84	5.61	6.13	101.69	102.21	104.78	农产品
3.18	2.57	1.88	7.40	7.21	6.91	5.28	5.07	5.57	74.32	73.96	78.19	食品
0.28	0.36	0.20	0.03	0.05	0.03	0.03	0.03	0.03	3.85	3.85	4.07	鱼产品
2.90	2.21	1.68	7.37	7.16	6.87	5.25	5.04	5.54	70.47	70.10	74.12	其他食品
0.20	0.20	0.17	0.82	0.81	0.82	0.56	0.54	0.56	27.36	28.25	26.59	原料
0.75	0.73	0.61	3.95	6.70	7.24	2.13	2.48	2.23	56.35	54.17	47.54	燃料和矿产品
0.14	0.18	0.14	0.54	0.76	0.69	0.40	0.22	0.41	26.32	24.33	21.69	矿石和其他矿物
0.59	0.51	0.44	3.32	5.88	6.45	1.08	1.65	1.34	23.20	23.65	19.39	燃料
0.02	0.04	0.03	0.09	0.06	0.11	0.65	0.61	0.47	6.84	6.18	6.45	有色金属
13.61	14.91	14.54	23.74	23.55	27.23	62.08	63.81	65.62	308.12	316.74	328.49	制成品
0.13	0.14	0.16	0.53	0.63	0.58	0.68	0.87	0.68	2.36	2.29	2.10	钢铁
1.45	1.56	1.27	3.15	3.18	3.18	4.23	4.47	4.50	61.17	59.94	60.14	化学品
0.29	0.30	0.33	0.58	0.62	0.60	0.84	0.95	0.88	8.96	8.88	10.05	药品
1.16	1.26	0.94	2.57	2.57	2.59	3.39	3.52	3.61	52.21	51.06	50.10	其他化学品
0.54	0.55	0.53	1.40	1.76	2.18	7.82	8.39	9.40	20.56	22.63	23.47	其他半制成品
10.37	11.34	11.25	16.96	16.26	19.48	44.51	44.65	45.71	178.08	185.21	195.18	机械和运输设备
0.60	0.61	0.57	1.34	1.07	1.26	5.41	6.11	6.62	51.45	51.26	54.41	办公和电信设备
0.22	0.22	0.25	0.47	0.45	0.46	1.60	1.64	1.78	10.38	9.71	10.19	EDP和办公设备
0.29	0.32	0.25	0.82	0.56	0.72	2.31	3.44	3.64	14.86	15.50	16.59	通信设备
0.08	0.07	0.07	0.05	0.06	0.08	1.49	1.04	1.20	26.21	26.05	27.63	集成电路
4.77	6.28	6.52	8.40	7.23	9.73	26.95	26.55	26.93	63.58	72.64	79.02	运输设备
2.12	2.89	2.74	4.48	4.36	3.93	13.58	13.63	12.08	20.57	21.58	25.92	汽车
2.65	3.39	3.78	3.92	2.87	5.80	13.37	12.93	14.85	43.01	51.07	53.09	其他运输设备
5.00	4.45	4.16	7.23	7.96	8.49	12.15	11.99	12.16	63.05	61.31	61.76	其他机械
0.04	0.07	0.12	0.09	0.08	0.08	0.17	0.18	0.20	2.15	2.27	2.20	纺织品
0.05	0.05	0.05	0.05	0.05	0.06	0.26	0.27	0.29	0.98	0.96	0.94	服装
1.05	1.20	1.16	1.56	1.58	1.65	4.39	4.98	4.84	42.83	43.44	44.47	其他制成品
0.07	0.08	0.09	0.12	0.12	0.14	0.40	0.43	0.48	1.57	1.64	1.75	个人及家居用品
0.62	0.70	0.68	0.90	0.94	0.94	2.30	2.45	2.42	22.71	22.67	22.21	科学和控制仪器
0.36	0.41	0.38	0.54	0.52	0.57	1.69	2.10	1.95	18.55	19.13	20.51	杂项制成品
17.97	**18.63**	**17.42**	**37.66**	**40.43**	**43.36**	**75.02**	**78.25**	**79.17**	**488.31**	**501.59**	**503.91**	制成品出口总额 b

表 3（续 1）

单位：十亿美元

目的地	世界 a			北美洲			中、南美洲			欧洲		
原产地	2012	2013	2014	2012	2013	2014	2012	2013	2014	2012	2013	2014
中、南美洲												
农产品	205.83	216.08	212.32	27.71	28.69	30.18	35.73	35.53	33.62	48.80	48.80	48.61
食品	186.67	196.94	192.35	23.59	24.38	25.79	34.05	33.91	32.04	44.04	44.28	44.12
鱼产品	10.97	12.61	14.21	3.05	3.59	4.07	1.54	1.81	1.95	2.95	3.47	3.58
其他食品	175.70	184.34	178.14	20.53	20.79	21.71	32.50	32.09	30.09	41.09	40.81	40.53
原料	19.16	19.13	19.97	4.12	4.31	4.39	1.69	1.62	1.59	4.76	4.53	4.49
燃料和矿产品	319.76	297.77	277.47	97.64	87.83	77.37	72.44	66.53	65.30	44.08	41.18	36.61
矿石和其他矿物	83.41	82.22	74.61	6.12	5.60	5.71	4.14	4.41	4.19	17.87	17.58	14.98
燃料	200.40	182.45	172.13	84.92	75.52	66.34	63.54	57.64	57.31	18.94	17.75	16.07
有色金属	35.96	33.09	30.73	6.61	6.72	5.33	4.76	4.48	3.80	7.28	5.85	5.57
制成品	192.44	193.43	177.42	53.32	53.80	54.82	92.34	92.04	80.17	24.40	23.31	21.31
钢铁	19.38	16.12	17.22	5.68	4.97	5.75	5.92	5.12	4.48	3.00	2.31	3.28
化学品	48.34	46.12	43.82	14.50	14.03	12.62	22.39	22.07	21.15	7.03	5.69	5.65
药品	10.05	9.65	9.16	3.85	3.55	3.23	4.81	4.71	4.57	0.66	0.64	0.66
其他化学品	38.29	36.47	34.67	10.65	10.48	9.39	17.58	17.36	16.58	6.37	5.06	5.00
其他半制成品	24.33	24.64	24.90	5.43	5.81	6.15	11.80	11.44	10.71	3.74	3.73	3.92
机械和运输设备	66.57	74.06	59.33	13.42	14.59	15.30	36.00	38.43	29.75	8.67	9.63	6.51
办公和电信设备	5.48	5.68	5.27	1.35	1.42	1.39	2.15	1.97	1.70	0.63	0.60	0.57
EDP 和办公设备	0.76	0.80	0.68	0.25	0.23	0.22	0.37	0.45	0.36	0.05	0.05	0.05
通信设备	2.36	2.23	2.00	0.40	0.49	0.48	1.67	1.42	1.24	0.14	0.11	0.10
集成电路	2.36	2.65	2.58	0.70	0.70	0.70	0.11	0.10	0.10	0.44	0.44	0.43
运输设备	37.37	45.79	31.65	5.22	6.07	5.82	22.91	26.11	18.92	4.70	6.29	3.33
汽车	25.37	28.01	21.31	2.27	2.38	2.04	20.70	23.46	17.27	0.98	0.78	0.61
其他运输设备	12.00	17.78	10.35	2.95	3.69	3.77	2.20	2.65	1.66	3.72	5.51	2.71
其他机械	23.71	22.60	22.41	6.84	7.10	8.10	10.95	10.35	9.14	3.35	2.75	2.62
纺织品	4.11	4.07	3.94	0.57	0.58	0.59	3.23	3.20	3.07	0.15	0.16	0.16
服装	13.66	12.98	12.94	8.90	8.97	9.32	4.37	3.64	3.24	0.26	0.25	0.26
其他制成品	16.05	15.43	15.26	4.83	4.85	5.08	8.63	8.14	7.76	1.57	1.54	1.53
个人及家居用品	4.93	4.72	4.64	0.87	0.85	1.00	3.06	2.91	2.65	0.63	0.57	0.60
科学和控制仪器	3.29	3.45	3.49	1.94	2.09	2.17	0.82	0.76	0.70	0.36	0.39	0.40
杂项制成品	7.83	7.26	7.14	2.03	1.92	1.91	4.75	4.47	4.41	0.58	0.58	0.53
制成品出口总额 b	**752.40**	**737.96**	**694.88**	**191.17**	**182.15**	**172.64**	**200.67**	**194.25**	**179.39**	**128.29**	**121.82**	**114.04**
欧洲												
农产品	655.93	709.33	719.50	27.57	29.53	31.37	7.00	7.30	7.64	499.94	538.60	546.12
食品	563.19	611.45	621.69	25.21	26.98	28.56	6.17	6.43	6.76	432.53	467.39	473.77
鱼产品	38.50	42.51	44.79	1.06	1.25	1.49	0.55	0.52	0.51	29.97	33.30	35.43
其他食品	524.69	568.94	576.90	24.16	25.73	27.07	5.62	5.91	6.25	402.56	434.09	438.34
原料	92.74	97.88	97.81	2.36	2.55	2.81	0.83	0.87	0.88	67.42	71.20	72.35
燃料和矿产品	842.26	815.62	758.77	46.68	42.76	39.27	8.16	8.84	6.10	654.79	629.24	589.80
矿石和其他矿物	81.86	75.76	74.73	2.10	2.07	2.17	0.44	0.40	0.30	60.35	55.92	56.03
燃料	624.92	610.04	554.71	36.90	34.36	29.50	6.68	7.42	4.79	487.47	471.98	431.60
有色金属	135.48	129.83	129.32	7.68	6.33	7.59	1.03	1.02	1.00	106.97	101.34	102.18
制成品	4 728.51	4 916.21	5 095.95	412.98	425.66	461.19	106.00	110.67	103.32	3 131.68	3 265.55	3 422.90
钢铁	198.11	186.07	185.36	13.54	11.07	14.34	4.16	3.64	3.36	142.52	137.00	137.40
化学品	1040.50	1076.70	1112.15	114.00	112.48	121.38	26.16	27.01	27.02	702.89	731.23	758.08
药品	392.06	405.16	426.87	61.18	60.53	69.12	10.34	11.17	11.36	240.77	247.35	261.37
其他化学品	648.44	671.54	685.28	52.82	51.95	52.25	15.82	15.84	15.66	462.12	483.87	496.71
其他半制成品	484.99	510.50	521.81	26.78	28.71	30.27	8.74	9.43	8.81	349.98	366.63	378.08
机械和运输设备	2 216.59	2 305.85	2 391.58	197.18	207.36	223.83	56.27	59.67	53.47	1 386.02	1 447.39	1 529.18
办公和电信设备	358.95	351.68	359.35	14.96	14.87	15.69	2.96	2.98	2.98	273.08	269.27	279.50
EDP 和办公设备	130.34	129.68	133.75	4.78	4.80	5.09	0.81	0.81	0.74	104.34	104.33	109.22
通信设备	171.22	169.11	173.32	7.18	7.25	7.75	1.70	1.78	1.89	130.77	131.95	138.20
集成电路	57.39	52.88	52.28	3.00	2.82	2.85	0.45	0.38	0.35	37.97	32.98	32.08
运输设备	902.99	965.04	1020.48	82.84	90.28	97.00	20.98	23.58	20.51	583.78	627.58	677.84
汽车	635.88	677.86	718.19	58.62	64.18	68.81	10.93	12.91	9.65	426.38	457.55	494.50
其他运输设备	267.11	287.18	302.30	24.22	26.10	28.20	10.06	10.67	10.86	157.40	170.03	183.35
其他机械	954.65	989.13	1 011.74	99.38	102.20	111.14	32.33	33.11	29.98	529.16	550.54	571.84
纺织品	82.41	86.11	89.14	4.00	4.15	4.49	1.05	0.94	0.93	58.99	61.85	64.36
服装	127.26	137.31	146.62	4.55	4.83	5.37	0.69	0.71	0.70	103.01	110.69	118.69
其他制成品	578.66	613.67	649.30	52.94	57.05	61.53	8.93	9.26	9.02	388.27	410.77	437.10
个人及家居用品	123.89	134.55	143.98	6.77	7.63	8.61	0.75	0.80	0.80	95.26	102.55	110.53
科学和控制仪器	137.73	145.11	152.00	19.32	20.32	21.58	3.56	3.72	3.68	75.11	79.05	83.41
杂项制成品	317.05	334.01	353.33	26.85	29.11	31.34	4.62	4.75	4.54	217.89	229.17	243.16
制成品出口总额 b	**6 468.03**	**6 779.68**	**6 810.50**	**494.80**	**506.40**	**539.88**	**123.86**	**128.98**	**119.16**	**4 408.60**	**4 585.98**	**4 665.31**

单位：十亿美元

独联体			非洲			中东			亚洲			目的地
2012	2013	2014	2012	2013	2014	2012	2013	2014	2012	2013	2014	原产地
												中、南美洲
7.34	7.71	8.44	14.71	13.58	12.20	12.50	13.13	11.66	57.42	66.92	65.66	农产品
6.94	7.30	8.08	14.56	13.45	12.08	12.29	12.92	11.41	49.84	59.29	57.32	食品
0.23	0.48	0.55	0.34	0.28	0.29	0.06	0.07	0.10	2.72	2.84	3.60	鱼产品
6.72	6.82	7.53	14.22	13.17	11.79	12.24	12.85	11.31	47.13	56.45	53.72	其他食品
0.40	0.41	0.36	0.15	0.13	0.13	0.21	0.21	0.25	7.58	7.62	8.33	原料
0.23	0.33	0.44	1.88	1.49	1.74	3.07	2.56	2.78	97.47	94.62	88.99	燃料和矿产品
0.21	0.30	0.42	0.93	0.95	0.89	2.43	2.07	2.16	51.71	51.31	46.27	矿石和其他矿物
0.02	0.02	0.02	0.91	0.45	0.70	0.55	0.43	0.61	28.59	27.42	26.86	燃料
0.00	0.00	0.00	0.05	0.09	0.15	0.09	0.06	0.01	17.17	15.89	15.87	有色金属
0.73	0.74	0.52	4.15	3.82	3.64	1.34	1.22	1.56	15.69	14.05	14.89	制成品
0.05	0.06	0.06	0.50	0.51	0.51	0.25	0.31	0.40	3.97	2.83	2.74	钢铁
0.08	0.08	0.09	0.61	0.52	0.54	0.22	0.27	0.23	3.30	3.19	3.26	化学品
0.03	0.03	0.03	0.06	0.05	0.06	0.04	0.06	0.05	0.49	0.48	0.44	药品
0.04	0.05	0.06	0.55	0.47	0.48	0.18	0.22	0.18	2.81	2.71	2.82	其他化学品
0.05	0.05	0.04	0.43	0.41	0.40	0.14	0.14	0.18	2.69	3.03	3.46	其他半制成品
0.49	0.49	0.28	2.19	2.12	1.94	0.61	0.38	0.61	5.07	4.35	4.82	机械和运输设备
0.00	0.00	0.00	0.02	0.02	0.02	0.02	0.03	0.02	1.31	1.64	1.57	办公和电信设备
0.00	0.00	0.00	0.00	0.01	0.00	0.00	0.00	0.00	0.09	0.07	0.05	EDP 和办公设备
0.00	0.00	0.00	0.01	0.01	0.01	0.02	0.02	0.01	0.12	0.16	0.16	通信设备
0.00	0.00	0.00	0.00	0.00	0.00	0.00	0.00	0.00	1.10	1.41	1.36	集成电路
0.35	0.38	0.18	1.34	1.35	1.19	0.24	0.07	0.30	2.52	1.47	1.85	运输设备
0.13	0.05	0.05	0.73	0.69	0.73	0.03	0.01	0.14	0.54	0.64	0.46	汽车
0.23	0.33	0.13	0.61	0.67	0.46	0.22	0.06	0.16	1.98	0.83	1.39	其他运输设备
0.13	0.11	0.10	0.83	0.75	0.73	0.34	0.28	0.30	1.24	1.24	1.40	其他机械
0.00	0.00	0.01	0.03	0.02	0.02	0.00	0.00	0.01	0.11	0.08	0.07	纺织品
0.00	0.00	0.00	0.02	0.02	0.01	0.01	0.01	0.01	0.09	0.08	0.08	服装
0.05	0.05	0.04	0.38	0.22	0.23	0.10	0.11	0.13	0.46	0.48	0.45	其他制成品
0.03	0.04	0.02	0.14	0.14	0.15	0.06	0.06	0.08	0.14	0.15	0.14	个人及家居用品
0.01	0.01	0.00	0.03	0.03	0.03	0.01	0.01	0.02	0.13	0.16	0.14	科学和控制仪器
0.01	0.01	0.01	0.21	0.05	0.05	0.03	0.03	0.04	0.19	0.18	0.17	杂项制成品
8.30	**8.79**	**9.40**	**21.02**	**19.22**	**17.67**	**17.68**	**17.75**	**16.80**	**171.25**	**176.38**	**170.36**	制成品出口总额 b
												欧洲
24.89	26.96	22.28	25.89	28.59	30.44	21.52	24.44	25.36	47.75	52.50	54.67	农产品
22.47	24.51	20.19	22.13	24.72	26.27	19.71	22.62	23.36	34.12	37.78	41.55	食品
2.02	2.22	1.53	1.77	1.63	1.79	0.28	0.33	0.41	2.87	3.24	3.59	鱼产品
20.45	22.30	18.65	20.35	23.09	24.48	19.43	22.29	22.96	31.26	34.54	37.96	其他食品
2.42	2.45	2.09	3.76	3.87	4.17	1.81	1.82	2.00	13.63	14.72	13.13	原料
8.24	9.02	7.42	35.86	35.77	33.92	13.61	13.34	13.80	45.52	43.13	39.56	燃料和矿产品
0.89	0.95	0.70	1.96	1.57	1.55	1.26	1.16	1.30	14.75	13.50	12.50	矿石和其他矿物
6.06	6.83	5.61	31.29	31.58	29.47	10.42	10.23	10.32	17.10	14.69	15.07	燃料
1.29	1.25	1.11	2.62	2.63	2.90	1.93	1.95	2.18	13.67	14.95	11.99	有色金属
209.60	213.35	185.29	145.61	153.55	154.59	159.27	169.44	177.24	538.88	553.21	573.18	制成品
4.01	3.78	3.42	10.01	9.21	8.89	10.72	8.85	6.90	12.44	12.27	10.79	钢铁
39.95	42.70	39.88	25.95	27.71	28.60	25.51	27.18	28.02	99.23	100.90	102.84	化学品
16.14	17.84	16.25	9.75	10.54	10.85	10.24	11.89	12.07	40.41	41.61	42.50	药品
23.81	24.86	23.63	16.21	17.16	17.75	15.27	15.29	15.95	58.82	59.29	60.34	其他化学品
20.82	21.85	19.44	16.65	17.82	17.41	17.39	19.37	19.96	43.99	45.63	46.64	其他半制成品
110.87	109.25	90.32	73.94	78.13	78.43	77.98	82.86	87.64	299.07	306.44	319.36	机械和运输设备
14.04	13.07	10.21	9.03	8.13	8.00	11.36	11.32	11.25	32.74	31.71	31.36	办公和电信设备
6.38	5.63	4.15	3.80	3.47	3.46	4.09	4.43	4.81	6.13	6.19	6.25	EDP 和办公设备
6.88	6.64	5.24	4.33	3.70	3.72	6.43	6.08	5.86	13.16	11.40	10.33	通信设备
0.78	0.80	0.82	0.90	0.97	0.82	0.83	0.81	0.58	13.45	14.12	14.78	集成电路
40.66	38.29	28.38	26.30	26.96	26.82	23.17	26.87	31.72	112.58	118.69	130.86	运输设备
31.86	29.54	21.01	20.75	21.34	20.86	13.39	14.61	16.45	73.02	77.00	86.23	汽车
8.80	8.75	7.37	5.56	5.62	5.96	9.78	12.26	15.27	39.56	41.69	44.63	其他运输设备
56.17	57.90	51.74	38.61	43.04	43.60	43.45	44.67	44.67	153.75	156.05	157.14	其他机械
4.54	4.74	4.36	5.45	5.71	5.86	2.41	2.53	2.85	5.54	5.71	5.88	纺织品
6.69	7.45	6.78	1.63	1.71	1.91	3.34	3.84	4.28	7.16	7.87	8.76	服装
22.71	23.56	21.08	11.98	13.27	13.50	21.92	24.82	27.59	71.45	74.39	78.90	其他制成品
5.86	6.68	5.89	1.85	2.14	2.32	3.29	3.91	4.34	10.04	10.78	11.39	个人及家居用品
5.65	5.56	5.00	3.60	4.03	4.22	5.11	5.58	5.70	25.24	26.69	28.27	科学和控制仪器
11.20	11.32	10.19	6.53	7.10	6.96	13.52	15.33	17.54	36.17	36.91	39.24	杂项制成品
245.54	**253.15**	**218.21**	**209.43**	**221.98**	**221.47**	**212.51**	**229.37**	**228.95**	**690.56**	**763.14**	**738.44**	制成品出口总额 b

表 3（续 2）

单位：十亿美元

目的地	世界 a			北美洲			中、南美洲			欧洲		
原产地	2012	2013	2014	2012	2013	2014	2012	2013	2014	2012	2013	2014
独联体												
农产品	66.79	66.26	67.76	0.68	0.84	0.87	0.18	0.28	0.22	18.24	16.15	19.23
燃料和矿产品	520.00	519.39	486.24	27.15	24.00	17.12	1.81	2.36	2.06	330.43	337.22	304.68
制成品	185.92	170.07	164.52	8.40	7.67	9.42	5.55	4.74	4.67	54.82	44.45	53.98
制成品出口总额 b	**799.81**	**780.43**	**735.10**	**36.84**	**33.39**	**28.36**	**9.15**	**9.23**	**6.96**	**416.75**	**406.17**	**384.88**
非洲												
农产品	57.99	61.85	63.61	2.84	2.61	2.77	1.52	1.43	1.42	20.50	21.94	21.97
燃料和矿产品	437.99	396.49	349.19	61.23	43.58	27.11	26.05	25.20	24.39	167.03	149.44	130.45
制成品	108.60	116.07	118.29	8.71	7.93	7.93	2.79	2.78	2.75	41.71	42.60	42.01
制成品出口总额 b	**640.05**	**601.26**	**555.43**	**73.49**	**55.09**	**39.12**	**30.38**	**29.42**	**28.58**	**237.86**	**219.93**	**201.29**
中东												
农产品	26.99	29.76	29.82	0.53	0.54	0.58	0.06	0.07	0.06	3.05	3.19	3.32
燃料和矿产品	929.21	893.69	835.57	92.87	83.07	71.45	6.54	6.55	6.97	94.79	92.65	86.81
制成品	252.53	260.47	266.31	25.42	24.98	26.35	3.69	3.70	3.57	40.13	39.74	45.92
制成品出口总额 b	**1348.51**	**1346.49**	**1287.81**	**119.03**	**109.60**	**99.20**	**10.36**	**10.72**	**10.88**	**146.55**	**145.83**	**147.50**
亚洲												
农产品	380.02	387.50	395.67	44.00	42.28	46.01	5.86	5.98	5.65	47.50	48.65	49.59
食品	294.42	304.16	321.22	32.56	33.81	38.56	4.29	4.43	4.32	36.67	38.25	39.63
鱼产品	51.26	53.26	57.04	11.34	12.42	14.06	0.85	0.91	1.02	7.42	7.87	8.27
其他食品	243.16	250.90	264.18	21.22	21.39	24.50	3.44	3.51	3.30	29.25	30.38	31.36
原料	85.60	83.34	74.46	11.44	8.47	7.45	1.57	1.56	1.34	10.83	10.40	9.96
燃料和矿产品	693.15	692.25	666.50	22.38	23.95	24.28	14.36	9.82	9.93	37.72	33.85	29.60
矿石和其他矿物	113.95	120.89	111.42	3.06	3.19	2.25	0.21	0.22	0.19	4.90	3.98	3.59
燃料	491.68	484.45	465.07	11.27	14.20	13.77	13.29	8.61	8.57	23.47	21.93	18.14
有色金属	87.51	86.90	90.02	8.05	6.56	8.26	0.86	0.99	1.17	9.35	7.94	7.87
制成品	4 422.38	4 552.90	4 735.30	896.52	932.02	985.22	165.18	164.45	160.16	742.71	752.95	803.24
钢铁	167.11	157.79	177.71	20.50	18.28	24.65	7.38	7.45	8.66	15.29	15.18	19.21
化学品	447.34	455.96	473.76	47.69	48.38	53.23	18.41	19.27	19.87	60.21	58.11	62.61
药品	44.86	44.01	45.84	9.20	9.13	10.38	1.68	1.84	2.00	12.67	11.55	11.66
其他化学品	402.48	411.95	427.92	38.49	39.25	42.86	16.73	17.43	17.87	47.55	46.56	50.96
其他半制成品	351.96	371.68	381.10	70.00	74.25	77.33	14.32	14.36	13.47	57.80	59.02	63.15
机械和运输设备	2 385.41	2 439.69	2 510.06	505.39	521.93	549.12	82.15	83.02	79.64	384.70	381.24	399.15
办公和电信设备	1 081.29	1 155.58	1 185.74	233.36	245.52	254.55	20.30	22.53	21.17	193.09	190.48	194.72
EDP 和办公设备	343.98	334.90	336.28	110.03	109.17	109.34	5.76	5.61	4.88	83.97	83.17	85.81
通信设备	361.14	391.85	415.45	99.62	109.44	118.53	11.91	13.76	12.96	72.12	78.21	80.37
集成电路	376.17	428.83	434.02	23.71	26.90	26.68	2.63	3.16	3.33	36.99	29.10	28.55
运输设备	551.25	522.71	533.37	129.68	130.24	137.35	33.49	32.17	30.52	80.16	72.14	77.95
汽车	338.54	330.61	333.58	95.56	97.53	99.75	22.22	21.60	19.40	38.14	37.69	40.03
其他运输设备	212.71	192.10	199.78	34.12	32.71	37.61	11.27	10.57	11.12	42.03	34.44	37.93
其他机械	752.88	761.40	790.95	142.34	146.17	157.22	28.36	28.31	27.95	111.45	118.62	126.48
纺织品	167.35	181.86	187.59	23.77	25.43	26.18	9.84	9.66	9.81	25.74	28.27	30.12
服装	245.91	273.14	289.53	68.68	74.76	78.16	10.33	9.51	9.73	71.90	79.60	88.22
其他制成品	657.29	672.78	715.56	160.48	169.00	176.55	22.74	21.18	18.98	127.07	131.53	140.77
个人及家居用品	163.16	176.02	186.28	52.58	56.45	58.44	9.23	7.99	6.94	40.94	43.01	45.94
科学和控制仪器	167.05	161.52	160.82	29.28	28.32	29.39	4.40	4.52	3.78	26.17	25.02	26.42
杂项制成品	327.09	335.23	368.46	78.63	84.22	88.72	9.12	8.67	8.26	59.96	63.50	68.42
制成品出口总额 b	**5 644.24**	**5 774.10**	**5 917.25**	**971.65**	**1 008.08**	**1 064.63**	**196.50**	**191.00**	**184.95**	**855.00**	**852.75**	**899.70**

a 包括未分类的目的地。
b 包括未分类的产品。

单位：十亿美元

独联体			非洲			中东			亚洲			目的地
2012	2013	2014	2012	2013	2014	2012	2013	2014	2012	2013	2014	原产地
												独联体
20.73	23.24	18.54	6.52	4.66	5.36	6.62	5.28	5.98	12.04	14.29	15.58	农产品
51.20	45.38	46.16	3.15	2.79	3.50	6.55	5.92	7.66	93.38	97.94	100.46	燃料和矿产品
79.77	80.85	63.81	4.08	4.46	5.04	7.87	6.27	6.99	21.62	18.91	16.76	制成品
154.93	**152.09**	**131.22**	**16.11**	**13.22**	**15.58**	**21.88**	**18.96**	**22.43**	**131.13**	**138.56**	**133.88**	制成品出口总额 b
												非洲
1.06	1.15	1.25	15.59	17.12	17.14	4.47	4.98	4.69	11.48	12.04	14.15	农产品
0.41	0.41	0.43	30.19	29.64	29.58	3.88	3.48	3.30	133.36	129.19	121.70	燃料和矿产品
0.47	0.42	0.38	36.08	43.02	42.02	5.65	6.42	7.96	11.36	11.42	13.89	制成品
1.94	**1.99**	**2.07**	**93.53**	**99.99**	**98.08**	**16.32**	**17.08**	**18.18**	**158.41**	**155.96**	**151.69**	制成品出口总额 b
												中东
1.09	1.05	0.80	2.08	2.35	2.32	12.65	13.87	14.29	5.17	5.33	5.95	农产品
0.12	0.10	0.24	19.74	17.67	16.67	31.66	32.31	31.24	619.84	610.71	557.66	燃料和矿产品
4.23	4.31	5.58	14.24	14.88	15.23	55.24	55.35	57.85	91.93	92.48	92.19	制成品
5.50	**5.55**	**6.74**	**37.14**	**36.03**	**35.70**	**102.79**	**112.84**	**112.97**	**733.72**	**735.90**	**693.91**	制成品出口总额 b
												亚洲
8.12	8.38	8.23	22.51	23.37	24.65	23.76	27.22	26.67	226.85	228.83	232.04	农产品
7.36	7.72	7.65	21.18	21.96	23.17	22.25	25.69	25.21	168.70	171.14	180.40	食品
1.11	1.23	1.27	1.82	1.75	1.76	1.50	1.59	1.80	27.10	27.37	28.74	鱼产品
6.25	6.49	6.38	19.36	20.20	21.41	20.75	24.10	23.40	141.60	143.77	151.66	其他食品
0.76	0.66	0.58	1.33	1.41	1.48	1.51	1.53	1.47	58.15	57.69	51.64	原料
1.48	1.58	1.55	13.73	17.06	19.34	21.85	24.14	24.76	577.88	572.39	550.00	燃料和矿产品
0.30	0.26	0.16	0.19	0.19	0.22	0.90	1.34	1.44	104.39	111.69	103.56	矿石和其他矿物
0.70	0.76	0.84	11.70	15.03	17.35	18.24	20.35	20.60	409.27	394.14	378.78	燃料
0.48	0.56	0.54	1.84	1.84	1.77	2.72	2.45	2.72	64.21	66.56	67.67	有色金属
110.92	117.78	116.58	133.00	142.17	158.17	210.26	214.95	245.50	2 133.29	2 203.38	2 245.68	制成品
3.88	4.47	3.54	5.58	7.31	7.81	13.84	12.20	14.54	100.60	92.88	99.29	钢铁
6.94	7.42	7.35	13.99	15.49	16.96	13.43	13.64	15.27	286.52	293.24	298.37	化学品
1.06	1.17	1.05	3.42	3.80	4.29	0.94	1.03	1.13	15.84	15.30	15.33	药品
5.88	6.25	6.31	10.57	11.69	12.68	12.49	12.61	14.13	270.67	277.94	283.04	其他化学品
10.07	11.13	11.30	17.92	18.94	20.92	28.35	32.41	32.68	153.38	161.26	162.05	其他半制成品
56.42	54.85	51.83	57.00	60.61	65.74	98.04	99.84	116.53	1 173.18	1 217.26	1 232.05	机械和运输设备
11.76	11.49	11.96	9.21	9.86	12.31	20.72	22.88	26.46	592.80	652.61	664.47	办公和电信设备
4.14	3.67	3.17	1.91	1.95	2.03	6.45	6.50	7.05	131.69	124.80	123.97	EDP 和办公设备
7.04	7.30	8.54	6.81	6.88	9.35	13.63	15.71	18.74	149.98	160.36	166.91	通信设备
0.58	0.52	0.24	0.49	1.03	0.93	0.64	0.66	0.66	311.13	367.45	373.60	集成电路
25.59	23.46	20.70	23.84	24.93	25.49	41.99	42.76	49.88	188.06	176.44	175.70	运输设备
22.72	21.28	17.63	17.71	17.56	17.47	36.51	36.04	41.19	105.33	98.57	97.81	汽车
2.87	2.18	3.07	6.12	7.37	8.02	5.48	6.72	8.69	82.73	77.87	77.90	其他运输设备
19.07	19.89	19.18	23.95	25.82	27.94	35.33	34.20	40.19	392.33	388.21	391.87	其他机械
6.64	7.14	6.75	12.82	13.60	14.62	10.63	11.38	11.81	77.87	86.29	88.25	纺织品
12.94	16.95	17.14	7.56	7.81	9.96	12.08	14.08	15.96	60.96	68.30	67.23	服装
14.04	15.83	18.66	18.13	18.41	22.17	33.89	31.41	38.72	280.78	284.15	298.45	其他制成品
7.21	7.97	9.48	8.01	8.31	9.79	8.34	10.01	11.63	36.82	42.17	43.97	个人及家居用品
1.70	1.76	1.65	1.73	1.73	2.09	2.30	2.23	2.42	101.47	97.94	95.06	科学和控制仪器
5.13	6.10	7.53	8.39	8.37	10.29	23.25	19.17	24.67	142.49	144.04	159.42	杂项制成品
120.73	**128.13**	**126.58**	**174.87**	**187.55**	**206.65**	**261.47**	**271.62**	**301.52**	**3 018.69**	**3 083.01**	**3 093.10**	制成品出口总额 b

a 包括未分类的目的地。
b 包括未分类的产品。

表 4

2005—2014 年区域一体化协定的货物贸易

单位：十亿美元

	2005	2006	2007	2008	2009	2010	2011	2012	2013	2014
欧盟（28）										
总出口	4 082.7	4 606.1	5 366.0	5 954.9	4 613.5	5 183.9	6 092.3	5 812.6	6 081.4	6 162.2
内部出口	2 777.0	3 159.2	3 674.4	4 029.4	3 087.7	3 390.0	3 928.8	3 648.7	3 775.0	3 900.1
外部出口	1 305.7	1 446.9	1 691.6	1 925.5	1 525.9	1 793.9	2 163.5	2 164.1	2 306.6	2 262.2
总进口	4 249.7	4 870.3	5 655.2	6 358.4	4 809.2	5421.1	6 334.6	5 956.9	6 012.9	6 132.5
内部进口	2 776.7	3 156.9	3 672.3	4 026.8	3 085.7	3 390.0	3 928.8	3 648.7	3 775.0	3 900.1
外部进口	1 472.9	1 713.4	1 982.9	2 331.6	1 723.5	2 031.1	2 405.8	2 308.2	2 237.9	2 232.4
北美自由贸易区										
总出口	1 475.8	1 664.1	1 840.7	2 035.2	1 601.8	1 964.3	2 283.4	2 371.9	2 417.9	2 492.7
对内出口	824.5	901.0	950.0	1 012.5	767.9	956.7	1 102.2	1 151.2	1 188.9	1 250.7
对外出口	651.3	763.1	890.7	1 022.7	834.0	1 007.6	1 181.2	1 220.7	1 229.0	1 242.0
总进口	2283.4	2 540.6	2700.8	2 906.8	2 176.7	2 682.1	3 090.6	3 191.9	3194.3	3 299.1
内部进口	790.9	828.9	914.5	965.5	717.5	899.6	1 033.1	1 078.4	1 099.7	1 149.2
外部进口	1 492.5	1 711.6	1 786.4	1 941.3	1 459.2	1 782.5	2 057.5	2 113.6	2 094.7	2 149.9
东盟										
总出口 a	656.6	769.8	865.1	989.7	813.8	1 050.1	1 236.8	1 253.7	1 272.6	1 295.3
内部出口 a	164.9	191.3	217.9	251.4	201.1	264.8	312.9	324.9	330.8	330.6
外部出口	491.7	578.5	647.2	738.3	612.7	785.2	923.9	928.8	941.7	964.8
总进口 a	602.7	687.7	774.9	938.8	727.0	953.1	1 153.0	1 223.2	1 244.6	1 234.7
内部进口 a	150.6	173.8	194.3	228.1	175.5	230.7	267.0	278.8	279.3	277.8
外部进口	452.1	513.9	580.7	710.6	551.5	722.4	886.0	944.4	965.2	956.9
南方共同市场										
总出口	165.5	191.8	225.7	280.3	219.2	283.3	355.8	338.8	342.2	315.9
内部出口	22.6	27.3	34.1	43.1	34.0	44.6	54.2	48.5	51.3	44.0
外部出口	142.9	164.5	191.6	237.3	185.1	238.7	301.5	290.3	290.9	271.9
总进口	113.9	139.5	182.8	257.9	186.3	267.0	334.4	324.6	348.0	328.1
内部进口	22.5	25.9	33.4	43.7	32.8	44.7	53.8	47.7	48.7	42.7
外部进口	91.4	113.6	149.5	214.2	153.5	222.3	280.6	277.0	299.3	285.5
安第斯共同体										
总出口	51.5	64.9	76.9	94.0	78.6	99.4	134.0	142.6	137.8	132.1
内部出口	4.5	5.2	5.9	7.0	5.8	7.8	9.3	10.3	10.0	9.7
外部出口	46.9	59.7	71.0	87.0	72.8	91.6	124.7	132.3	127.8	122.4
总进口	46.4	56.5	70.7	93.6	74.3	96.7	124.3	135.4	139.2	144.5
内部进口	5.2	6.2	7.2	8.6	7.1	9.5	11.0	11.7	8.1	11.4
外部进口	41.2	50.3	63.6	85.0	67.3	87.2	113.3	123.6	131.1	133.1

表 5

2004—2014 年区域集团的货物贸易

单位：十亿美元

	2004	2002	2006	2007	2008	2009	2010	2011	2012	2012	2011
出口											
世界 a	**9 223.3**	**10 509.1**	**12 130.5**	**14 023.3**	**16 160.4**	**12 555.0**	**15 301.1**	**18 333.1**	**18 408.4**	**18 826.2**	**18 935.1**
北美洲和欧洲											
欧洲自由贸易联盟	208.2	237.8	273.5	313.2	377.9	293.3	330.9	400.6	392.0	388.5	386.7
欧盟（28）	3 771.6	4 082.7	4 606.1	5 366.0	5 954.9	4 613.5	5 183.9	6 092.2	5 812.6	6 081.4	6 162.2
北美自由贸易区	1 319.6	1 475.8	1 664.1	1 840.7	2 035.2	1 601.8	1 964.3	2 283.4	2 371.9	2 417.9	2 495.0
中、南美洲											
安第斯共同体	39.0	51.5	64.9	76.9	94.0	78.6	99.4	134.0	142.6	137.8	132.2
中美洲共同市场	20.5	22.5	25.1	28.2	30.6	27.1	31.9	38.2	39.7	39.7	40.4
加勒比共同体和共同市场	11.1	15.0	20.3	20.3	26.4	15.0	17.8	23.2	22.2	21.4	19.6
南方共同市场	137.1	165.5	191.8	225.7	280.3	219.2	283.3	355.8	338.8	342.2	315.9
非洲											
中部非洲经济与货币共同体	16.6	22.9	26.8	30.2	42.7	27.0	35.7	44.6	44.3	41.6	38.0
东南非共同市场	49.2	66.0	82.9	98.7	127.0	92.6	118.5	98.2	134.4	121.6	96.4
中部非洲国家经济共同体	32.1	49.6	61.6	78.0	111.3	71.7	92.0	119.1	122.4	116.9	107.9
西非国际经济共同体	53.7	67.1	78.1	87.5	111.9	83.4	114.8	153.0	155.4	146.5	139.8
南部非洲发展共同体	79.7	97.9	116.7	144.2	177.7	131.3	181.0	223.0	219.0	214.7	205.9
西非经济和货币同盟	11.6	12.7	14.2	15.0	18.5	19.3	20.7	23.9	23.8	25.8	25.2
中东和亚洲											
东盟	569.0	656.6	769.8	865.1	989.7	813.8	1 049.8	1 239.5	1 253.8	1 272.6	1 299.0
海湾（阿拉伯国家）合作委员会	285.2	397.6	480.7	555.0	762.5	525.9	661.7	950.0	1 061.2	1 084.2	1 024.6
南亚自由贸易区	105.2	132.6	158.9	190.0	240.8	206.3	277.3	364.9	357.6	381.0	385.6
备忘项：											
非洲、加勒比和太平洋国家集团	181.5	226.8	269.9	316.9	399.2	288.8	391.6	492.4	484.3	471.1	448.0
最不发达国家	60.4	82.4	103.4	128.2	167.8	127.7	162.4	202.1	204.6	214.4	211.1
WTO 成员（161）	9 032.5	10 248.4	11 794.7	13 615.5	15 612.6	12 199.8	14 845.6	17 765.4	17 908.7	18 426.1	18 509.3
进口											
世界	**9 574.5**	**10 870.5**	**12 461.5**	**14 330.5**	**16 572.3**	**12 781.6**	**15 510.7**	**18 507.7**	**18 615.1**	**18 903.8**	**19 023.7**
北美洲和欧洲											
欧洲自由贸易联盟	168.0	187.0	211.8	248.2	280.1	228.0	257.5	303.8	289.9	295.8	297.2
欧盟（28）	3 874.5	4 249.7	4 870.3	5 655.2	6 358.4	4 809.2	5421.1	6 330.1	5 956.9	6 012.9	6 132.5
北美自由贸易区	2 007.9	2 283.4	2 540.6	2 700.8	2 906.8	2 176.7	2 682.1	3 090.7	3191.9	3 194.3	3 295.9

续 表

	2004	2002	2006	2007	2008	2009	2010	2011	2012	2012	2011
中、南美洲											
安第斯共同体	36.9	46.4	56.5	70.7	93.6	74.3	96.7	124.8	135.4	139.2	144.5
中美洲共同市场	32.4	36.5	41.8	48.2	54.9	41.6	49.5	60.0	63.0	64.1	64.3
加勒比共同体和共同市场	17.0	20.2	23.0	26.3	31.7	23.6	24.9	30.3	30.9	30.7	30.0
南方共同市场	95.1	113.9	139.5	182.8	257.9	186.3	267.0	334.4	324.6	348.0	328.0
非洲											
中部非洲经济与货币共同体	6.9	7.9	10.5	14.2	17.4	17.3	20.0	25.0	26.4	26.2	26.0
东南非共同市场	51.0	65.1	76.0	93.7	119.4	114.7	134.9	140.5	172.8	172.5	180.1
中部非洲国家经济共同体	15.3	19.8	23.2	32.4	44.4	45.7	43.2	53.6	59.4	62.1	64.3
西非国际经济共同体	33.1	43.6	51.9	66.1	89.5	67.1	83.6	103.1	104.4	114.5	116.0
南部非洲发展共同体	85.3	99.7	119.6	140.4	171.3	140.6	165.2	208.7	221.8	227.3	226.1
西非经济和货币同盟	12.8	15.3	16.0	20.0	25.5	22.0	24.5	25.1	29.7	34.8	32.0
中东和亚洲											
东盟	513.6	602.7	687.7	774.9	938.8	727.0	953.5	1 154.3	1 224.1	1 244.6	1 235.5
海湾（阿拉伯国家）合作委员会	154.3	188.3	225.1	295.0	383.0	318.4	350.0	426.3	484.5	532.8	539.5
南亚自由贸易区	140.7	194.4	238.4	296.6	406.7	326.6	436.5	573.2	595.8	574.2	580.3
备忘项：											
非洲、加勒比和太平洋国家集团	176.3	216.5	260.0	309.5	388.2	314.0	369.9	454.8	478.6	498.9	504.4
最不发达国家	70.9	87.1	100.7	124.8	161.9	153.7	169.5	209.2	231.6	251.3	271.2
WTO 成员（161）a	9 390.1	10 657.8	12 228.2	14 047.2	16 205.3	12 453.6	15 139.7	18 094.3	18 275.6	18 579.2	18 656.0

a 包括重要的转口及因转口的进口。

表 6

2005—2014 年区域集团的服务贸易

单位：十亿美元

	2005	2006	2007	2008	2009	2010	2011	2012	2013	2014
出口										
世界	**2 614.2**	**2 959.7**	**3 543.6**	**3 981.8**	**3 549.8**	**3 864.8**	**4 325.8**	**4 466.4**	**4 709.0**	**4 939.6**
北美洲和欧洲										
欧洲自由贸易联盟	96.9	103.9	124.6	140.0	127.8	137.0	150.1	156.1	163.8	167.0
欧盟（28）	…	…	…	…	…	1 705.2	1 916.5	1 906.7	2 051.3	2 164.5
北美自由贸易区	431.6	477.7	553.0	604.3	573.3	633.4	702.7	735.3	771.5	793.6
中、南美洲										
安第斯共同体	6.7	7.8	8.7	10.1	9.9	10.6	12.1	13.9	15.5	16.1
中美洲共同市场	8.5	9.2	11.2	12.1	9.8	11.3	12.5	13.5	14.7	15.5
加勒比共同体和共同市场	9.2	9.6	10.3	10.6	9.7	10.1	10.3	10.5	10.6	11.0

续 表

	2005	2006	2007	2008	2009	2010	2011	2012	2013	2014
南方共同市场	22.1	26.3	34.9	43.1	39.5	46.6	55.9	57.1	55.9	56.7
非洲										
中部非洲经济与货币共同体	1.3	1.4	1.8	2.1	1.9	2.2	2.9	2.6	3.0	…
东南非共同市场	21.6	24.2	29.9	36.3	32.0	36.3	34.3	38.8	36.2	39.5
中部非洲国家经济共同体	1.7	2.0	2.6	3.2	3.4	3.6	4.3	4.0	5.0	…
西非国际经济共同体	5.3	6.3	6.6	7.9	7.2	8.1	9.0	10.3	9.7	…
南部非洲发展共同体	18.1	20.1	23.8	22.8	21.7	25.6	28.4	30.0	30.0	30.9
西非经济和货币同盟	2.2	2.3	3.0	3.5	3.0	3.4	3.6	3.6	3.9	…
中东和亚洲										
东盟	113.8	134.2	167.7	190.9	175.5	211.8	249.5	273.0	298.0	300.6
海湾（阿拉伯国家）合作委员会	26.0	36.0	41.2	37.5	37.3	38.8	44.0	48.6	50.7	55.8
南亚自由贸易区	56.7	74.6	93.0	113.3	100.1	125.7	148.8	156.4	161.4	170.3
备忘项：										
非洲、加勒比和太平洋国家集团	51.8	56.8	64.5	67.3	62.1	70.4	78.1	84.7	86.5	87.7
最不发达国家	9.6	11.4	14.3	18.2	18.9	22.4	27.1	30.3	34.4	37.1
WTO 成员（161）	2 573.5	2 913.5	3 487.8	3 913.6	3 483.1	3 790.5	4 247.6	4 387.5	4 628.8	4 855.3
进口										
世界	**2 507.3**	**2 812.7**	**3 332.2**	**3 800.3**	**3 378.5**	**3 704.6**	**4 139.4**	**4 290.0**	**4 545.1**	**4 782.4**
北美洲和欧洲										
欧洲自由贸易联盟	78.0	82.7	100.4	113.7	104.0	116.3	133.0	139.9	149.8	151.9
欧盟（28）	…	…	…	…	…	1 475.6	1 617.1	1 607.1	1 731.2	1 821.8
北美自由贸易区	363.7	409.1	449.7	493.6	460.1	496.8	536.5	560.7	577.2	589.4
中、南美洲										
安第斯共同体	11.0	12.3	14.3	17.3	16.1	19.2	21.8	24.3	25.8	27.3
中美洲共同市场	5.3	6.0	6.7	7.1	6.2	7.1	7.7	8.2	8.9	9.2
加勒比共同体和共同市场	5.9	6.4	6.7	6.9	5.9	6.2	6.8	7.4	7.4	7.8
南方共同市场	30.0	35.6	46.6	59.3	57.5	76.0	93.1	98.7	105.5	106.4
非洲										
中部非洲经济与货币共同体	6.4	8.1	9.6	11.4	10.4	12.3	13.3	13.7	14.8	—
东南非共同市场	20.8	23.3	29.2	36.0	31.8	36.0	37.3	42.9	44.5	49.1
中部非洲国家经济共同体	13.9	16.2	23.6	34.4	31.0	31.5	39.2	37.4	39.1	—
西非国际经济共同体	12.9	19.5	24.4	33.1	26.6	31.1	35.2	36.6	36.3	—
南部非洲发展共同体	25.5	28.4	37.9	48.3	43.9	48.3	58.8	56.6	57.2	56.3
西非经济和货币同盟	4.7	5.0	6.1	7.2	6.8	7.5	8.0	8.2	9.1	—
中东和亚洲										
东盟	139.8	159.8	185.6	218.0	191.3	228.8	266.2	288.6	310.7	312.1
海湾（阿拉伯国家）合作委员会	54.6	75.0	104.3	122.1	109.6	122.6	153.3	164.6	174.4	193.7
南亚自由贸易区	58.9	71.6	84.9	104.4	92.6	129.6	142.2	147.9	145.6	169.5
备忘项：										
非洲、加勒比和太平洋国家集团	60.3	74.3	92.5	116.1	102.0	117.2	135.8	138.1	139.3	142.0
最不发达国家	25.8	30.0	39.6	54.1	50.6	55.5	68.0	72.1	74.8	78.7
WTO 成员（161）	2 449.4	2 748.1	3 253.4	3 704.1	3 282.8	3 600.5	4 032.9	4 177.3	4 426.5	4 655.4

表 7

2004—2014 年世界货物出口（按地区和国家）

单位：百万美元

	2004	2005	2006	2007	2008	2009	2010	2011	2012	2013	2014
世界 a	9 223 297	10 509 146	12 130 534	14 023 293	16 160 364	12 554 999	15 301 115	18 338 014	18 495 525	18 953 501	19 002 190
北美洲	1 319 698	1 475 820	1 664 141	1 840 749	2 035 212	1 601 883	1 964 302	2 283 428	2 371 950	2 417 886	2 492 761
百慕大	73	49	27	27	24	29	15	13	11	12	12
加拿大	316 762	360 475	388 178	420 693	456 471	316 094	387 481	451 335	455 592	458 318	474 709
墨西哥	187 980	214 207	249 961	271 821	291 265	229 712	298 305	349 569	370 643	379 961	397 506
美国	814 875	901 082	1 025 967	1 148 199	1 287 442	1 056 043	1 278 495	1 482 508	1 545 703	1 579 593	1 620 532
中、南美洲	292 603	371 456	448 945	514 118	617 101	474 211	591 869	761 380	752 402	737 955	694 880
安提瓜和巴布达	57	83	74	59	65	51	46	56	63	68	55
阿根廷	34 576	40 351	46 546	55 779	70 018	55 672	68 187	84 051	80 246	81 660	71 977
阿鲁巴（荷兰）	3 435	4 416	4 716	5 206	5 456	1 952	265	5 180	1 389	278	237
巴哈马	477	549	694	802	956	711	702	834	984	955	849
巴巴多斯	278	359	510	524	488	379	429	475	565	457	435
伯利兹	305	319	419	416	469	381	478	604	627	608	590
玻利维亚	2 166	2 827	3 952	4 504	6 525	4 960	6 402	8 358	11 254	11 657	12 266
巴西	96 678	118 529	137 807	160 649	197 942	152 995	201 915	256 040	242 578	242 034	225 101
智利	32 520	41 267	58 680	67 972	64 510	55 463	71 109	81 438	77 791	76 477	75 675
哥伦比亚	16 224	21 190	24 391	29 991	37 626	32 853	39 713	56 915	60 125	58 824	54 795
哥斯达黎加	6 301	7 026	8 200	9 337	9 504	8 784	9 448	10 408	11 433	11 603	11 252
古巴	2 332	2 319	3 159	3 981	3 957	3 092	4 914	6 440	5 900	5 566	5 187
库拉索岛	—	—	—	—	—	—	—	928	948	705	720
多米尼克	42	42	41	37	40	33	37	29	36	38	39
多米尼加	5 936	6 145	6 610	7 160	6 748	5 483	6 754	8 492	9 069	9 651	9 920
厄瓜多尔	7 753	10 100	12 728	14 321	18 818	13 863	17 490	22 322	23 765	24 848	25 732
萨尔瓦多	3 305	3 418	3 706	4 015	4 641	3 866	4 499	5 308	5 339	5 491	5 273
格林纳达	32	28	25	33	31	29	25	31	35	38	37
危地马拉	5 036	5 381	6 025	6 898	7 737	7 214	8 463	10 401	9 979	10 028	10 834
圭亚那	593	553	588	679	795	763	880	1 129	1 416	1 375	1 167
海地	391	470	509	522	480	576	579	767	815	885	917
洪都拉斯	4 534	5 048	5 277	5 784	6 199	4 827	6 264	7 977	8 359	7 805	8 072
牙买加	1 402	1 532	1 948	2 254	2 439	1 316	1 328	1 623	1 712	1 569	1 452
荷属安的列斯	521	608	695	676	1088	810	807	—	—	—	—
尼加拉瓜	1 369	1 654	1 932	2 186	2 531	2 391	3 251	4 133	4 686	4 794	5 126
巴拿马	944	7 050	8 034	8 821	9 817	10 717	10 987	14 555	16 215	14 755	13 184
巴拉圭	2 874	3 153	3 472	4 724	6 407	5 080	6 505	7 763	7 271	9 432	9 657
秘鲁	12 809	17 368	23 830	28 094	31 019	26 962	35 803	46 376	47 411	42 474	39 326
圣基茨和尼维斯	40	34	40	34	51	38	32	45	46	41	42
圣卢西亚	80	64	94	98	164	166	215	160	182	174	159
圣文森特和格林纳丁斯	37	40	38	48	52	49	42	38	43	49	48
圣马丁岛	—	—	—	—	—	—	—	127	131	177	130
苏里南	874	997	1 175	1 359	1 743	1 402	2 026	2 467	2 695	2 394	2 145
特立尼达和多巴哥	6 517	9 942	14 155	13 396	18 650	9 126	10 982	14 944	12 983	12 770	12 590
乌拉圭	2 931	3 422	3 989	4 518	5 942	5 405	6 724	7 912	8 709	9 067	9 163
委内瑞拉	39 668	55 716	65 578	69 980	95 021	57 603	65 745	92 811	97 340	88 962	80 470

续 表

	2004	2005	2006	2007	2008	2009	2010	2011	2012	2013	2014
欧洲	4 051 103	4 404 322	4 979 263	5 803 062	6 483 418	5 021 188	5 650 067	6 654 099	6 468 026	6 779 676	6 810 497
阿尔巴尼亚	605	658	798	1078	1 355	1 091	1 545	1 951	1 968	2 332	2 431
奥地利	118 376	125 182	136 751	163 620	181 289	136 989	152 560	177 428	166 611	175 156	177 961
比利时	306 866	334 400	366 745	430 952	471 840	370 125	407 692	475 672	445 939	468 760	471 384
波斯尼亚和黑塞哥维那	1 793	2 400	3 323	4 152	5 021	3 954	4 803	5 850	5 162	5 687	5 892
保加利亚	9 932	11 739	15 064	18 518	22 362	16 318	20 630	28 208	26 686	29 579	29 299
克罗地亚	8 028	8 795	10 361	12 340	14 112	10 403	11 806	13 338	12 371	12 659	13 858
塞浦路斯	948	1 465	1 333	1 394	1 633	1 257	1 402	1 818	1 740	2 019	1 806
捷克	68 986	78 110	94 929	122 498	146 799	112 955	132 982	162 939	157 041	162 274	173 873
丹麦	77 079	85 121	92 558	103 171	116 923	93 984	96 440	111 864	105 469	110 107	111 074
爱沙尼亚	5 932	7 716	9 692	11 010	12 458	9 048	11 591	16 709	16 087	16 328	16 062
法罗群岛	616	599	651	746	852	762	839	1 008	952	1 087	1 128
芬兰	61 520	65 498	77 206	90 025	96 455	62 854	69 518	79 142	73 077	74 437	74 303
法国	452 106	463 428	495 868	559 612	616 240	484 781	523 767	596 473	568 708	580 963	582 590
马其顿	1 676	2 041	2 401	3 398	3 991	2 708	3 351	4 478	4 015	4 299	4 934
德国	909 887	970 914	1 108 107	1 321 214	1 446 171	1 120 041	1 258 924	1 473 985	1 405 096	1 451 826	1 507 594
希腊	15 308	17 278	20 749	23 578	26 382	20 469	27 950	33 819	35 442	36 601	36 078
匈牙利	55 567	62 936	75 255	95 400	108 504	83 008	95 483	112 312	103 570	107 503	110 794
冰岛	2 839	3 091	3 453	4 783	5 382	4 057	4 604	5 347	5 064	4 998	5 053
爱尔兰	104 788	109 657	108 726	121 543	125 719	115 928	116 497	125 740	116 773	114 356	117 568
意大利	353 782	373 135	416 875	499 882	542 748	406 909	447 301	523 258	501 306	518 268	528 738
拉脱维亚	4 009	5 161	6 155	8 308	10 144	7 702	9 532	13 130	14 112	14 467	14 569
立陶宛	9 302	11 807	14 142	17 144	23 646	16 454	20 748	28 050	29 611	32 598	32 417
卢森堡	16 250	19 120	22 980	22 933	25 694	21 339	19 748	20 866	18 834	18 448	19 193
马耳他	2 517	2 399	2 796	3 437	3 481	2 857	3 586	4 386	4 250	3 637	2 813
黑山	—	—	556	626	617	388	437	628	469	494	446
荷兰	357 417	406 372	463 629	550 755	637 918	497 891	574 251	667 101	655 374	671 556	672 127
挪威	82 527	103 759	122 208	136 354	171 764	116 778	130 657	160 410	160 952	154 391	143 893
波兰	75 047	89 437	110 780	140 146	170 458	136 503	159 724	188 696	185 374	204 984	216 636
葡萄牙	35 787	38 738	44 750	52 482	57 137	442 11	494 06	59 617	58 090	62 823	64 003
罗马尼亚	23 553	27 688	32 458	40 488	49 535	40 567	49 579	63 035	57 841	65 835	69 739
塞尔维亚	—	—	6 428	8 825	10 972	8 345	9 795	11 779	11 229	14 611	14 843
塞尔维亚和黑山	3 979	5 065	—	—	—	—	—	—	—	—	—
斯洛伐克	27 745	31 889	41 862	58 516	71 142	56 082	64 664	79 830	80 612	85 750	86 560
斯洛文尼亚	16 361	19 248	23 230	30 102	34 128	26 177	29 200	34 682	32 163	34 019	36 123
西班牙	182 623	192 644	213 717	253 297	281 493	227 338	254 418	306 551	295 250	317 833	324 863
瑞典	123 267	130 962	147 793	168 817	183 327	130 781	158 549	186 963	172 345	167 550	164 374
瑞士	122 844	130 930	147 856	172 078	200 759	172 474	195 609	234 819	312 464	357 851	311 203
土耳其	63 167	73 476	85 535	107 272	132 027	102 143	113 883	134 907	152 462	151 803	157 617
英国	347 493	390 860	450 907	441 831	472 168	354 893	415 959	506 570	47 2792	541 019	505 841
欧盟（28）b	3 771 572	4 082 707	4 606 066	5 366 012	5 954 870	4 613 534	5 183 906	6 092 183	5 812 562	6 081 354	6 162 240
欧盟（28）对外出口	1 175 716	1 305 672	1 446 904	1 691 637	1 925 494	1 525 858	1 793 930	2 163 418	2 163 888	2 306 344	2 262 120
独联体	265 494	343 707	430 954	520 475	702 540	450 312	589 214	785 950	799 809	780 431	735 101
亚美尼亚	723	974	985	1 152	1 057	710	1 011	1 334	1 380	1 479	1 519
阿塞拜疆	3 615	7 649	13 015	21 269	30 586	21 097	26 476	34 495	32 634	31 703	28 260

续 表

	2004	2005	2006	2007	2008	2009	2010	2011	2012	2013	2014
白俄罗斯	13 774	15 979	19 734	24 275	32 571	21 304	25 284	41 419	46 060	37 203	36 392
格鲁吉亚	647	865	936	1 232	1 495	1 134	1 677	2 189	2 375	2 908	2 861
哈萨克斯坦	20 093	27 849	38 250	47 755	71 172	43 196	59 971	84 336	86 449	84 700	78 238
吉尔吉斯共和国	719	672	891	1 321	1 856	1 673	1 756	1 979	1 894	1 791	1 650
摩尔多瓦	985	1 091	1 052	1 342	1 591	1 283	1 541	2 217	2 162	2 428	2 340
俄罗斯	183 207	243 798	303 551	354 403	471 606	303 388	400 630	522 011	529 255	523 276	497 764
塔吉克斯坦	915	909	1 399	1 468	1 409	1 010	1 195	1 257	1 360	1 162	1 078
土库曼斯坦	3 870	4 944	7 156	8 932	11 945	5 000	6 500	13 000	16 500	16 800	17 500
乌克兰	32 666	34 228	38 368	49 296	66 954	39 782	51 478	68 460	68 530	64 338	54 199
乌兹别克斯坦	4 280	4 749	5 617	8 029	10 298	10 735	11 695	13 254	11 210	12 643	13 300
非洲	239 576	310 977	370 710	436 512	562 212	393 483	521 371	610 678	640 052	601 265	555 426
阿尔及利亚	31 304	46 002	54 613	60 163	79 298	45 174	57 053	73 489	71 866	64 974	62 956
安哥拉	13 475	24 109	31 862	44 396	63 914	40 828	50 595	67 310	71 093	68 247	62 400
贝宁	569	578	736	1 047	1 282	1 225	1 282	1 410	1 443	1 870	2 010
博茨瓦纳	3 513	4 425	4 529	5 174	4 951	3 456	4 693	5 882	5 971	7 608	7 800
布基纳法索	479	468	588	623	693	900	1 591	2 399	2 182	2 356	2 489
布隆迪	47	58	58	59	57	67	101	123	134	94	125
佛得角	15	18	21	19	32	35	44	69	53	69	81
喀麦隆	2 477	2 861	3 576	4 230	5 241	3 552	3 878	4 517	4 275	4 515	4 853
中非共和国	134	128	158	178	150	120	140	190	200	150	90
乍得	2 191	3 081	3 352	3 666	4 169	2 800	3 600	4 800	4 400	3 800	3 600
科摩罗	19	12	10	14	7	15	21	26	20	20	25
刚果	3 433	4 745	6 078	5 635	8 325	6 100	9 400	11 851	10 055	9 090	8 263
刚果（金）	1 917	2 403	2 705	3 100	4 400	3 500	5 300	6 600	6 300	6 200	6 900
科特迪瓦	6 919	7 697	8 477	8 669	10 390	11 327	11 410	12 635	12 124	13 247	12 783
吉布提	38	40	55	58	69	77	85	93	118	120	139
埃及	9 661	12 912	16 728	19 224	26 224	23 062	26 438	30 528	29 397	28 492	27 091
赤道几内亚	4 599	7 064	8 207	10 210	15 218	9 100	10 000	13 500	15 700	14 700	12 600
厄立特里亚	11	11	12	13	11	11	13	430	480	330	766
埃塞俄比亚	678	903	1 043	1 277	1 602	1 618	2 330	2 875	2 891	4 077	4 437
加蓬	3 728	5 065	5 450	6 309	9 566	5 356	8 686	9 766	9 661	9 524	8 926
冈比亚	2 450	2 802	3 727	4 195	5 270	5 840	7 960	12 785	13 552	13 752	13 216
加纳	744	853	1 033	1 203	1 342	1 050	1 471	1 433	1 300	1 300	1 400
几内亚	76	89	74	107	128	122	127	242	130	140	162
几内亚比绍	2 684	3 420	3 502	4 081	5 001	4 463	5 169	5 756	6 127	5 856	6 115
肯尼亚	708	651	718	830	884	734	878	1172	972	847	925
莱索托	104	131	158	200	242	149	222	367	460	559	583
利比里亚	20 410	31 358	40 260	46 970	62 100	36 951	48 673	18 996	60 946	43 500	21 000
利比亚	992	855	985	1 238	1 310	1 052	1 149	1 590	1 516	1 923	2 126
马达加斯加	483	509	668	869	879	1 188	1 066	1 425	1 183	1 208	1 374
马拉维	976	1 101	1 550	1 556	2 097	1 774	1 996	2 374	2 610	2 339	2 100
马里	440	625	1 367	1 454	1 788	1 364	2 074	2 749	2 641	2 652	1 946
毛里塔尼亚	1 993	2 143	2 329	2 238	2 384	1 939	2 261	2 565	2 649	2 869	3 107
毛里求斯	9 925	11 190	12 744	15 340	20 345	14 054	17 771	21 654	21 446	21 972	23 663
摩洛哥	1 504	1 783	2 381	2 412	2 653	2 147	3 000	3 604	3 856	4 024	4 725

续 表

	2004	2005	2006	2007	2008	2009	2010	2011	2012	2013	2014
莫桑比克	1 827	2 070	2 647	2 922	3 141	3 146	4 026	4 407	4 369	4 615	4 441
纳米比亚	437	489	508	663	910	1 000	1 150	1 250	1 450	1 600	1 500
尼日尔	38 631	50 467	58 726	66 606	86 274	56 742	84 000	116 000	116 000	104 000	97 000
尼日利亚	98	125	147	177	268	235	297	464	591	703	736
卢旺达	5	7	8	7	11	8	11	11	12	13	17
圣多美和普林西比	1 509	1 578	1 594	1 674	2 170	2 017	2 161	2 542	2 532	2 666	2 812
塞内加尔	291	340	380	360	430	395	400	483	497	578	539
塞舌尔	139	158	231	245	216	231	341	350	1 122	1 917	1 886
塞拉利昂	…	…	…	…	…	…	…	…	…	…	…
南非	46 146	51 626	58 175	69 784	80 782	61 677	91 347	108 815	99 606	95 938	91 047
苏丹	3 778	4 824	5 657	8 879	11 671	8 257	11 404	10 193	4 066	4 790	4 350
斯威士兰	1 949	1 640	1 660	1 740	1 570	1 660	1 800	1 910	1 926	1 895	1 918
坦桑尼亚	1 479	1 679	1 865	2 139	3 121	2 982	4 051	4 735	5 547	4 413	4 645
冈比亚	18	7	11	13	14	66	68	95	119	106	108
多哥	601	660	630	677	853	903	976	1 179	1 314	1 522	1 350
突尼斯	9 685	10 494	11 694	15 165	19 320	14 445	16 427	17 847	17 007	17 060	16 756
乌干达	654	813	962	1 337	1 724	1 568	1 619	2 159	2 357	2 408	2 274
赞比亚	1 576	1 810	3 770	4 617	5 099	4 312	7 200	9 001	9 365	10 594	9 696
津巴布韦	1 887	1 850	2 000	2 400	2 200	2 269	3 199	3 512	3 882	3 507	3 064
中东	400 834	541 236	659 499	766 232	1 034 138	722 224	906 815	1 267 385	1 348 514	1 346 491	1 287 806
巴林	7 558	10 242	12 200	13 634	17 316	11 874	14 971	19 650	19 768	20 927	20 470
伊朗	41 697	56 252	77 012	88 733	113 668	78 830	101 316	132 000	104 000	82 500	88 800
伊拉克	17 810	23 697	29 361	41 268	61 273	41 929	52 483	83 226	94 392	89 742	84 630
以色列	38 618	42 770	46 789	54 091	61 337	47 935	58 413	67 796	63 141	66 781	68 120
约旦	3 883	4 302	5 204	5 725	7 938	6 375	7 028	8 006	7 887	7 911	8 215
科威特	28 599	44 869	56 016	62 691	87 457	54 008	69 978	102 103	118 912	115 034	104 250
黎巴嫩	2 199	2 337	2 814	3 574	4 454	4 187	5 021	5 664	5 615	5 168	4 548
阿曼	13 342	18 692	21 585	24 692	37 719	27 651	36 601	47 092	52 138	56 429	53 221
卡塔尔	18 684	25 762	34 051	42 020	67 307	48 007	74 964	114 448	132 962	136 767	131 716
沙特阿拉伯	125 997	180 711	211 305	233 329	313 462	192 314	251 143	364 699	388 401	375 933	353 836
叙利亚	7 378	8 708	10 919	11 546	15 410	10 855	12 796	11 000	4 000	2 000	2 000
阿联酋	90 997	117 287	145 587	178 630	239 213	192 000	214 000	302 000	349 000	379 000	360 000
也门	4 072	5 608	6 654	6 299	7 584	6 259	8 100	9 700	8 300	8 300	8 000
亚洲 a	2 653 366	3 060 839	3 576 140	4 141 180	4 724 686	3 890 700	5 076 344	5 975 096	6 114 773	6 289 798	6 425 719
阿富汗	305	384	416	454	540	403	388	376	429	515	571
澳大利亚	86 565	106 097	123 437	141 358	187 257	154 331	212 634	271 733	256 675	252 981	241 222
孟加拉国	8 305	9 297	11 802	12 453	15 370	15 083	19 194	24 439	25 127	29 114	30 405
不丹	183	258	414	675	521	496	641	675	535	544	555
文莱达鲁萨兰	5 057	6 249	7 636	7 668	10 319	7 200	8 907	12 465	13 001	11 447	10 509
柬埔寨	2 798	3 092	3 692	4 088	4 708	4 196	5 143	6 704	7 838	9 248	10 800
中国	593 326	761 953	968 978	1 220 456	1 430 693	1 201 612	1 577 754	1 898 381	2 048 714	2 209 004	2 342 306
斐济	693	701	694	755	922	630	841	1 069	1 221	1 108	1 373
法属波利尼西亚	199	217	235	197	195	148	153	168	139	151	170
中国香港	265 543	292 119	322 669	349 386	370 242	329 422	400 692	455 573	492 907	535 187	524 065
国内出口	19 978	20 050	22 765	18 109	16 958	16 839	14 798	16 846	22 371	19 488	15 599

续 表

	2004	2005	2006	2007	2008	2009	2010	2011	2012	2013	2014
转口	245 565	272 069	299 904	331 276	353 284	312 583	385 894	438 727	470 537	515 699	508 466
印度	76 649	99 616	121 808	150 159	194 828	164 909	226 351	302 905	296 828	314 848	321 596
印度尼西亚	70 767	86 996	103 527	118 013	139 606	119 646	157 779	203 497	190 032	182 552	176 293
日本	565 675	594 941	646 725	714 327	781 412	580 719	769 774	823 184	798 568	715 097	683 846
基里巴斯	2	4	6	10	8	6	4	9	6	7	5
韩国	253 845	284 419	325 465	371 489	422 007	363 534	466 384	555 214	547 870	559 632	572 664
老挝	363	553	882	923	1 092	1 053	1 746	2 190	2 271	2 264	2 650
中国澳门	2 812	2 476	2 557	2 543	1 997	961	870	869	1 021	1 138	1 241
马来西亚	126 646	141 626	160 749	175 966	199 414	157 244	198 612	228 086	227 538	228 331	234 139
马尔代夫	181	162	225	228	331	169	198	346	314	331	326
蒙古	870	1 065	1 543	1 889	2 539	1 903	2 899	4 818	4 385	4 269	5 775
缅甸	2 355	3 776	4 539	6 253	6 882	6 662	8 661	9 238	8 877	11 233	11 031
尼泊尔	772	863	838	868	939	823	856	919	911	879	889
新喀里多尼亚	1 033	1 093	1 352	2 104	1 300	993	1 493	1 663	1 326	1 226	1 591
新西兰	20 344	21 730	22 409	26 943	30 580	24 933	31 396	37 669	37 305	39 445	41 622
北马里亚纳群岛	826	691	509	329	115	9	5	2	4	4	2
巴基斯坦	13 379	16 051	16 930	17 838	20 323	17 523	21 410	25 383	24 567	25 121	24 714
帕劳	6	13	14	11	10	6	6	6	9	7	6
巴布亚新几内亚	2 552	3 273	4 166	4 681	5 713	4 394	5 742	6 908	6 328	5 951	5 670
菲律宾	39 681	41 255	47 410	50 466	49 078	38 436	51 496	48 305	52 099	56 698	62 100
萨摩亚	85	87	65	97	72	46	70	66	76	62	72
新加坡	198 637	229 649	271 807	299 308	338 176	269 832	351 867	409 503	408 393	410 250	409 769
国内出口	106 663	124 546	143 176	156 038	175 702	138 064	182 726	223 913	228 160	219 107	216 044
转口	91 974	105 103	128 631	143 270	162 474	131 769	169 141	185 590	180 233	191 142	193 725
所罗门群岛	97	103	121	165	210	165	224	418	500	448	450
斯里兰卡	5 757	6 347	6 886	7 740	8 452	7 345	8 602	10 236	9 380	10 208	11 295
中国台北	182 432	198 432	224 017	246 677	255 629	203 675	274 601	308 257	301 181	305 441	313 696
泰国	96 248	110 936	129 722	153 867	177 778	152 422	193 306	222 576	229 106	228 505	227 574
东帝汶	7	8	8	8	13	8	16	13	31	16	20
汤加	15	10	10	8	9	8	8	14	16	17	20
图瓦卢	0	0	0	0	0	0	0	0	0	0	
瓦努阿图	37	38	49	50	57	57	49	67	55	39	63
越南	26 485	32 442	39 826	48 561	62 685	57 096	72 237	96 906	114 529	132 033	150 475
备忘项:											
世界 不含 a											
欧盟(28)对内出口	6 627 440	7 732 111	8 971 372	10 348 918	12 130 988	9 467 322	11 911 140	14 409 249	14 846 851	15 178 490	15 102 070
欧洲 不含											
欧盟(28)对内出口	1 455 246	1 627 287	1 820 101	2 128 687	2 454 042	1 933 511	2 260 091	2 725 334	2 819 352	3 004 665	2 910 376

a 含重要转口。

b 由于欧洲统计局对塞浦路斯、爱沙尼亚和立陶宛使用不同的统计方法,2004 年前,欧盟(28)总体数据并不是由单个成员国加总而来。

注:统计总额无连续性的国家和地区集团标示为"I",主要在于货物贸易统计数据收集和报告的方法不同。

注意世界和亚洲数据含重复计算的因素,源于其使用一般货物贸易统计体系,该方法含转口贸易。

一些国家和地区近几年的数据由秘书处统计。

表 8

2004—2014 年世界货物进口（按地区和国家）

单位：百万美元

	2004	2005	2006	2007	2008	2009	2010	2011	2012	2013	2014
世界 a	**9 574 488**	**10 870 483**	**12 461 492**	**14 330 484**	**16 572 298**	**12 781 621**	**15 510 669**	**18 503 484**	**18 713 181**	**19 025 527**	**19 091 010**
北美洲	2 008 933	2 284 427	2 541 720	2 702 089	2 908 063	2 177 865	2 683 150	3 091 742	3 192 943	3 195 459	3 300 222
百慕大	988	985	1 094	1 167	1 159	1 064	972	900	900	1 012	976
加拿大 b	279 931	322 411	359 000	390 188	419 011	329 907	402 690	463 640	474 940	474 300	475 000
墨西哥	202 260	228 240	263 476	290 246	318 304	241 515	310 205	361 068	380 477	390 965	411 581
美国	1 525 680	1 732 706	1 918 077	2 020 403	2 169 487	1 605 296	1 969 184	2 266 024	2 336 524	2 329 060	2 412 547
中、南美洲	246 234	308 822	374 046	467 798	608 591	451 766	584 680	735 618	755 528	774 599	739 332
安提瓜和巴布达	454	506	624	728	743	534	501	430	492	503	500
阿根廷	22 445	28 689	34 152	44 706	57 462	38 786	56 793	74 319	68 020	73 656	65 324
阿鲁巴（荷兰）	3 589	4 288	4 723	5 126	6 011	2 449	1 394	5 917	2 042	1 361	1 347
巴哈马	1 905	2 312	2 727	2 956	3 199	2 535	2 591	2 966	3 386	3 166	3 270
巴巴多斯	1 413	1 604	1 697	1 746	1 920	1 449	1 569	1 805	1 780	1 759	1 739
伯利兹	520	593	660	684	837	669	706	831	861	928	1 004
玻利维亚	1 877	2 431	2 916	3 586	5 081	4 545	5 590	7 927	8 578	9 338	10 421
巴西	66 433	77 628	95 838	126 645	182 377	133 677	191 537	236 964	233 398	250 559	239 150
智利	24 794	32 735	38 406	47 164	62 787	42 806	59 207	74 695	80 073	79 249	72 159
哥伦比亚	16 746	21 204	26 162	32 897	39 669	32 898	40 486	54 233	59 048	59 381	64 029
哥斯达黎加	8 268	9 824	11 548	12 952	15 372	11 395	13 570	16 220	17 591	18 014	17 186
古巴	5 615	8 084	10 258	10 886	15 373	9 619	11 496	14 243	13 869	14 773	13 114
库拉索岛	—	—	—	—	—	—	—	2 130	2 254	1 934	1 870
多米尼克	144	165	167	196	247	225	224	226	208	203	205
多米尼加 b	7 888	9 869	12 174	13 597	15 993	12 296	15 489	17 409	17 739	16 873	17 288
厄瓜多尔	8 226	10 287	12 114	13 893	18 852	15 090	20 591	24 438	25 477	27 146	27 739
萨尔瓦多	6 329	6 690	7 663	8 821	9 818	7 325	8 416	9 965	10 258	10 772	10 513
格林纳达	233	328	299	365	363	282	318	336	341	368	340
危地马拉	9 475	10 499	11 915	13 576	14 547	11 531	13 838	16 613	16 994	17 515	18 276
圭亚那	651	788	889	1 059	1 312	1 161	1 397	1 771	1 997	1 875	1 779
海地	1 306	1 454	1 619	1 682	2 315	2 124	3 146	3 020	3 170	3 403	3 600
洪都拉斯 b	5 827	6 545	7 303	8 888	10 453	7 372	8 907	11 126	11 371	10 953	11 070
牙买加	3 940	4 739	5 650	6 893	8 465	5 064	5 225	6 439	6 331	6 219	5 838
荷属安的列斯	1 723	1 950	2 209	2 549	3 079	2 607	2 622	—	—	—	—
尼加拉瓜	2 457	2 956	3 404	3 989	4 731	3 929	4 792	6 355	6 778	6 688	6 946
巴拿马	3 594	9 600	10 775	13 269	15 737	13 877	16 737	21 802	22 821	21 795	21 200
巴拉圭	3 097	3 715	4 744	5 859	9 033	6 940	10 033	12 366	11 555	12 142	12 169
秘鲁	10 101	12 502	15 312	20 368	29 953	21 814	30 030	37 747	42 274	43 357	42 346
圣基茨和尼维斯	183	210	250	272	325	296	270	247	226	249	274
圣卢西亚	422	486	592	614	656	520	662	697	644	598	593
圣文森特和格林纳丁斯	226	240	271	327	373	333	338	332	356	370	362
圣马丁岛	—	—	—	—	—	—	—	734	768	924	880
苏里南	742	1 050	1 013	1 044	1 304	1 390	1 398	1 638	1 994	2 174	2 012
特立尼达和多巴哥	4 858	5 694	6 484	7 663	9 591	6 955	6 480	9 511	9 065	8 871	7 490
乌拉圭	3 114	3 879	4 806	5 628	9 069	6 907	8 622	10 726	11 652	11 642	11 485
委内瑞拉	16 679	24 027	33 616	46 097	50 450	41 540	39 000	48 000	60 730	54 420	44 280

续 表

	2004	2005	2006	2007	2008	2009	2010	2011	2012	2013	2014
欧洲	4 164 677	4 579 875	5 252 937	6 117 235	6 895 464	5 217 038	5 904 385	6 923 232	6 626 795	6 728 284	6 794 021
阿尔巴尼亚	2 309	2 618	3 058	4 188	5 251	4 550	4 406	5 396	4 882	4 902	5 230
奥地利	119 905	127 327	137 212	163 037	184 293	143 063	159 009	191 417	178 513	183 278	181 851
比利时	285 621	318 700	351 635	411 558	466 307	353 364	391 177	466 943	439 129	451 677	452 479
波斯尼亚和黑塞哥维那	5 915	7 070	7 345	9 720	12 189	8 773	9 223	11 051	10 019	10 295	10 990
保加利亚	14 453	18 163	23 270	29 961	36 908	23 539	25 513	32 582	32 710	34 303	34 783
克罗地亚	16 612	18 599	21 477	25 617	30 728	21 123	20 067	22 663	20 832	22 022	22 790
塞浦路斯	5 502	6 316	6 928	8 615	10 644	7 835	8 569	8 678	7 296	6 314	6 742
捷克	69 967	76 512	93 191	118 169	142 038	105 048	126 652	152 125	141 412	144 259	152 462
丹麦	68 157	75 581	85 507	98 027	109 362	83 133	83 052	95 663	91 925	96 590	99 299
爱沙尼亚	8 336	10 238	13 449	15 677	16 026	10 140	12 287	17 459	18 086	18 446	18 261
法罗群岛	628	743	790	1 016	988	783	780	987	1 153	1 115	1 065
芬兰	51 443	58 766	69 375	81 704	91 781	60 889	68 803	84 264	76 468	77 570	76 662
法国	470 945	504 124	541 919	630 861	716 795	560 873	611 070	720 028	674 415	681 467	677 703
马其顿	2 932	3 228	3 763	5 281	6 883	5 073	5 474	7 027	6 522	6 620	7 277
德国	715 742	777 073	906 684	1 054 983	1 185 067	926 347	1 054 814	1 254 869	1 163 230	1 191 554	1 215 654
希腊	52 760	54 436	63 619	78 532	92 580	69 448	66 913	67 475	63 330	62 166	63 467
匈牙利	60 538	66 552	78 262	95 565	108 940	77 761	88 178	102 440	95 176	100 111	104 919
冰岛	3 643	4 979	6 137	6 738	6 205	3 604	3 920	4 841	4 772	5 020	5 375
爱尔兰	61 814	68 565	73 118	83 822	83 965	62 704	60 276	66 606	62 769	65 853	70 970
意大利	355 301	384 790	442 555	511 662	561 919	415 105	487 049	558 787	488 600	479 447	471 770
拉脱维亚	7 096	8 697	11 541	15 322	16 143	9 811	11 691	16 290	17 228	17 865	17 675
立陶宛	12 387	15 548	19 373	24 412	31 099	18 304	23 403	31 773	31 965	34 806	35 246
卢森堡	20 046	22 607	27 145	28 029	32 157	25 330	25 092	28 860	27 542	26 926	26 713
马耳他	3 641	3 681	4 307	4 801	5 300	4 478	5 062	6 293	6 598	6 142	6 487
黑山	—	—	1 842	2 867	3 731	2 313	2 182	2 544	2 336	2 349	2 360
荷兰	319 669	363 822	416 832	492 616	580 937	443 153	516 409	594 366	586 927	589 697	587 588
挪威	48 534	55 488	64 261	80 297	90 293	68 970	77 330	90 784	87 308	89 816	89 185
波兰	89 696	101 639	126 989	165 710	208 804	149 459	178 049	210 597	199 059	207 607	219 877
葡萄牙	54 948	63 921	70 684	82 129	94 416	71 663	77 749	82 896	72 429	75 719	78 187
罗马尼亚	32 691	40 518	51 160	70 314	84 053	54 324	62 109	76 480	70 207	73 417	77 773
塞尔维亚	—	—	13 172	19 164	24 331	16 047	16 735	19 862	18 925	20 551	20 609
塞尔维亚和黑山	11 752	11 635	—	—	—	—	—	—	—	—	—
斯洛伐克	29 862	34 649	44 986	60 616	73 912	55 650	65 026	79 842	77 398	81 735	82 150
斯洛文尼亚	17 759	20 337	24 141	31 559	37 034	26 507	30 094	35 531	32 035	33 373	34 084
西班牙	258 331	288 786	328 696	389 301	420 803	293 218	327 016	376 606	337 338	340 598	358 498
瑞典	100 433	111 697	127 547	153 226	168 503	119 876	148 946	177 026	164 436	160 609	162 584
瑞士	115 799	126 574	141 400	161 180	183 574	155 378	176 281	208 220	295 961	321 509	275 742
土耳其	97 540	116 774	139 576	170 063	201 964	140 928	185 544	240 842	236 545	251 661	242 177
英国	470 633	519 273	612 671	638 263	657 783	519 078	591 095	676 896	691 232	655 826	683 979
欧盟（28）	3 874 544	4 249 661	4 870 288	5 655 159	6 358 376	4 809 188	5 421 065	6 330 061	5 956 908	6 012 876	6 132 501
欧盟（28）自外进口	1 277 973	1 472 931	1 713 400	1 982 854	2 331 558	1 723 465	2 031 090	2 401 296	2 308 234	2 237 865	2 232 380
独联体	172 976	215 610	279 773	378 973	500 089	333 314	415 446	541 197	571 875	571 394	506 436
亚美尼亚	1 351	1 802	2 192	3 268	4 426	3 321	3 783	4 145	4 261	4 386	4 402
阿塞拜疆	3 516	4 350	5 269	6 045	7 574	6 514	6 746	10 166	10 417	10 321	9 332

续　表

	2004	2005	2006	2007	2008	2009	2010	2011	2012	2013	2014
白俄罗斯	16 491	16 708	22 351	28 693	39 381	28 569	34 884	45 759	46 404	43 023	40 788
格鲁吉亚	1 846	2 490	3 678	5 215	6 302	4 500	5 257	7 065	8 049	8 026	8 596
哈萨克斯坦	12 781	17 353	23 677	32 756	37 889	28 409	31 107	36 906	46 358	48 806	41 213
吉尔吉斯共和国	941	1 102	1 931	2 789	4 072	3 040	3 223	4 261	5 374	6 070	5 732
摩尔多瓦	1 769	2 292	2 693	3 690	4 899	3 278	3 855	5 191	5 213	5 492	5 317
俄罗斯 b	97 382	125 434	164 281	223 486	291 861	191 803	248 634	323 831	335 446	341 335	308 027
塔吉克斯坦	1 191	1 330	1 723	2 455	3 273	2 570	2 657	3 206	3 778	4 151	4 500
土库曼斯坦	3 320	2 947	2 560	3 619	5 600	6 800	5 700	7 600	9 900	10 000	10 300
乌克兰	28 997	36 136	45 039	60 618	85 535	45 487	60 911	82 594	84 639	76 787	54 330
乌兹别克斯坦	3 392	3 666	4 380	6 340	9 277	9 023	8 689	10 472	12 034	12 998	13 900
非洲	212 527	256 523	302 868	374 929	481 396	411 217	478 977	566 650	616 932	635 814	641 950
阿尔及利亚	18 169	20 357	21 456	27 631	39 479	39 294	40 473	47 247	50 378	55 028	58 330
安哥拉 b	5 832	8 353	8 778	13 661	20 982	22 660	16 667	20 228	23 717	26 344	28 320
贝宁	894	1 018	1 228	2 037	2 289	2 064	2 054	2 129	2 350	3 100	2 481
博茨瓦纳	3 231	3 161	3 086	4 067	5 211	4 728	5 657	7 272	8 025	7 544	7 750
布基纳法索	1 270	1 260	1 319	1 678	2 018	1 870	2 048	2 406	3 200	3 900	3 730
布隆迪	176	269	431	319	403	402	509	752	751	811	769
佛得角	431	438	542	750	825	709	742	947	765	726	770
喀麦隆	2 406	2 735	3 150	4 657	5 686	4 442	5 133	6 800	6 515	6 649	6 982
中非共和国	151	175	203	249	300	270	300	310	320	250	255
乍得	953	950	1 350	1 800	2 000	2 000	2 400	3 300	3 500	4 000	4 300
科摩罗	86	99	115	138	180	210	233	277	273	284	275
刚果 b	969	1 304	2 013	2 530	3 050	2 900	4 000	5 007	5 485	6 050	6 200
刚果（金）	2 051	2 690	2 892	3 400	4 300	3 900	4 500	5 500	6 100	6 300	6 600
科特迪瓦	4 715	5 865	5 820	6 683	7 884	6 960	7 849	6 720	9 770	12 483	10 863
吉布提 b	261	277	336	473	574	451	374	511	564	719	970
埃及	15 950	22 449	27 300	37 100	48 382	44 946	52 923	58 903	69 200	58 295	67 495
赤道几内亚	1 092	1 310	2 020	2 767	3 787	5 200	5 200	6 500	7 500	7 000	6 500
厄立特里亚	480	490	495	510	600	590	660	950	970	1030	1 127
埃塞俄比亚	2 874	4 095	5 207	5 809	8 277	7 668	8 602	8 896	11 913	14 899	18 987
加蓬	1 347	1 471	1 725	2 157	2 563	2 501	2 983	3 665	3 629	3 880	2 993
冈比亚	4 074	5 347	6 754	8 061	10 269	8 046	10 922	15 838	17 763	17 600	14 566
加纳	780	820	956	1 218	1 366	1 060	1 405	2 106	2 254	2 100	2 032
几内亚	83	106	127	168	199	202	196	240	180	180	228
几内亚比绍 b	4 553	5 846	7 233	8 989	11 128	10 202	12 093	14 782	16 290	16 358	18 396
肯尼亚	1 440	1 410	1 500	1 738	1 800	1 850	2 300	2 500	2 600	2 200	2 208
莱索托	337	310	467	499	813	551	710	1 044	1 005	1 150	1 046
利比里亚	6 326	6 079	6 041	6 733	9 150	12 859	17 674	8 000	22 000	27 000	19 000
利比亚	1 680	1 706	1 804	2 635	3 781	3 199	2 584	2 905	3 094	3 260	3 259
马达加斯加	933	1 165	1 207	1 378	2 204	2 022	2 173	2 428	2 360	2 845	2 973
马拉维	1 364	1 544	1 820	2 185	3 339	2 486	3 428	3 352	3 463	3 800	3 977
马里	923	1 428	1 167	1 432	1 941	1 498	1 935	2 467	3 129	3 044	2 666
毛里塔尼亚	2 771	3 157	3 627	3 894	4 651	3 733	4 386	5 149	5 354	5 397	5 610
毛里求斯	17 822	20 790	23 980	32 010	42 366	32 881	35 381	44 272	44 872	45 190	45 832
摩洛哥	2 035	2 408	2 869	3 050	4 008	3 764	4 600	6 312	8 688	10 099	8 747

续 表

	2004	2005	2006	2007	2008	2009	2010	2011	2012	2013	2014
莫桑比克	2 396	2 577	2 884	3 520	4 340	4 980	5 570	6 593	7 256	7 359	7 596
纳米比亚	750	943	949	1 149	1 696	2 200	2 476	2 190	1 900	2 020	2 250
尼日尔	14 164	20 754	26 523	34 830	49 951	33 906	44 235	56 000	51 000	560 00	60 000
尼日利亚	284	471	591	771	1 174	1 308	1 431	2 039	2 300	2 302	2 457
卢旺达	41	50	71	79	114	103	112	134	131	152	170
圣多美和普林西比	2 839	3 498	3 671	4 871	6 528	4 713	4 782	5 909	6 434	6 659	6 639
塞内加尔	497	675	757	859	1 087	794	984	1 049	1 071	1 083	1 143
塞舌尔	286	345	389	445	534	520	770	1 717	1 604	1 780	1 489
塞拉利昂	…	…	…	…	…	…	…	…	…	…	…
南非	53 466	62 304	78 715	88 450	101 640	74 054	96 835	124 430	127 154	126 350	121 940
苏丹	4 075	6 757	8 074	8 775	9 352	9 691	10 045	9 236	9 230	9 918	9 211
斯威士兰	1 925	1 890	1 910	1 840	1 580	1 780	1 960	1 950	1 848	1 693	1 579
坦桑尼亚	2 726	3 287	4 246	5 337	7 703	6 411	7 874	10 799	11 346	12 120	12 390
冈比亚	229	260	259	321	322	304	285	341	380	350	370
多哥	880	1 060	1 085	1 237	1 509	1 509	1 683	2 187	2 380	2 666	2 800
突尼斯	12 818	13 177	15 007	19 099	24 638	19 096	22 215	23 952	24 471	24 266	24 828
乌干达	1 726	2 054	2 557	3 493	4 526	4 247	4 664	5 631	6 044	5 818	5 874
赞比亚	2 152	2 558	3 074	4 007	5 060	3 832	5 321	7 178	8 805	10 162	9 545
津巴布韦	2 204	2 350	2 300	2 550	2 950	2 900	3 800	4 400	4 400	4 300	4 200
中东	280 600	335 424	375 848	469 613	603 448	512 323	581 379	679 446	736 505	780 771	784 409
巴林	7 385	9 393	10 515	11 488	14 980	10 100	12 260	12 730	12 830	14 360	13 910
伊朗	31 976	40 041	40 772	44 942	57 401	50 768	65 404	61 760	57 092	49 000	51 000
伊拉克	21 302	23 532	20 892	21 516	33 000	38 437	43 915	47 803	56 234	61 000	59 000
以色列	42 864	47 142	50 334	59 039	67 656	49 278	61 209	75 830	75 392	74 861	75 407
约旦	8 179	10 498	11 548	13 681	16 995	14 236	15 564	18 930	20 752	21 864	22 866
科威特	12 631	15 801	17 243	21 362	24 840	19 892	22 675	25 090	27 259	29 299	31 484
黎巴嫩	9 609	9 633	9 647	12 251	16 754	16 574	18 460	20 750	21 945	22 024	21 135
阿曼	8 796	8 971	11 039	16 025	23 137	17 936	19 973	24 019	28 636	35 577	30 367
卡塔尔	6 005	10 061	16 440	23 429	27 900	24 922	23 240	29 888	34 200	34 900	34 600
沙特阿拉伯	47 376	59 459	69 800	90 214	115 134	95 552	106 863	131 586	155 593	168 181	163 000
叙利亚	8 411	10 862	11 488	14 655	18 105	15 443	17 562	16 800	7 300	5 400	6 700
阿联酋	72 082	84 654	100 057	132 500	177 000	150 000	165 000	203 000	226 000	251 000	262 000
也门	3 986	5 378	6 074	8 511	10 546	9 185	9 255	11 260	13 273	13 305	12 940
亚洲 a	2 488 276	2 889 469	3 333 931	3 819 456	4 574 836	3 677 709	4 861 780	5 965 599	6 212 603	6 339 206	6 324 639
阿富汗	2 177	2 471	2 744	3 022	3 020	3 336	5 154	6 515	9 069	8 724	7 729
澳大利亚	109 384	125 281	139 253	165 336	200 273	165 471	201 639	243 701	260 940	242 140	236 919
孟加拉国	12 036	13 889	16 034	18 596	23 860	21 833	27 821	36 214	34 173	37 085	42 268
不丹	411	386	420	526	543	529	854	1 043	991	909	810
文莱达鲁萨兰	1 422	1 491	1 676	2 101	2 572	2 449	2 538	3 629	3 572	3 612	3 599
柬埔寨 b	3 193	3 927	4 771	5 439	6 508	5 830	6 791	9 300	11 350	12 800	13 500
中国	561 229	659 953	791 461	956 116	1 132 567	1 005 923	1 396 247	1 743 484	1 818 405	1 949 989	1 959 356
斐济	1 446	1 607	1 804	1 800	2 264	1 440	1 808	2 182	2 253	2 826	3 250
法属波利尼西亚	1 500	1 723	1 656	1 863	2 169	1 717	1 726	1 796	1 705	1 815	1 762
中国香港	272 893	300 160	335 754	370 132	392 962	352 241	441 369	510 855	553 486	621 417	600 613
留存进口	70 044	75 269	86 097	93 791	98 927	88 672	112 587	131 822	136 229	142 411	150 669

续 表

	2004	2005	2006	2007	2008	2009	2010	2011	2012	2013	2014
印度	99 775	142 870	178 410	229 370	321 032	257 202	350 233	464 462	489 694	465 397	463 033
印度尼西亚	54 877	75 725	80 650	93 101	127 538	93 786	135 663	177 436	191 691	186 629	178 179
日本	454 542	515 866	579 064	622 243	762 534	551 981	694 059	855 380	885 843	833 166	822 251
基里巴斯	59	74	62	70	75	67	73	92	109	97	95
韩国	224 463	261 238	309 383	356 846	435 275	323 085	425 212	524 413	519 585	515 584	525 514
老挝	713	882	1 060	1 067	1 403	1 461	2 060	2 404	3 055	3 020	3 300
中国澳门	4 094	4 514	5 236	6 045	5 880	4 751	5 629	7 927	8 982	10 250	11 396
马来西亚	105 166	114 324	130 441	146 170	156 348	123 757	164 622	187 473	196 393	205 897	208 864
马尔代夫	642	745	927	1 096	1 388	963	1 091	1 465	1 554	1 733	1 993
蒙古	1 021	1 184	1 486	2 117	3 616	2 131	3 278	6 598	6 738	6 358	5 237
缅甸	2 174	1 908	2 538	3 247	4 256	4 348	4 760	9 019	9 201	12 043	16 226
尼泊尔	1 938	2 283	2 492	3 122	3 590	4 384	5 133	5 774	6 066	6 571	7 561
新喀里多尼亚	1 636	1 774	2 117	2 809	3 233	2 574	3 312	3 698	3 245	3 240	3 323
新西兰	23 195	26 219	26 424	30 882	34 369	25 574	30 617	37 105	38 254	39 641	42 518
北马里亚纳群岛	664	591	489	300	160	70	90	90	90	100	125
巴基斯坦	17 949	25 357	29 825	32 590	42 329	31 668	37 807	44 012	44 157	44 647	47 636
帕劳	107	105	115	116	130	90	107	129	142	169	180
巴布亚新几内亚	1 680	1 729	2 260	2 945	3 510	3 210	3 950	4 760	5 330	6 080	4 000
菲律宾	46 102	49 487	54 078	57 996	60 420	45 878	58 468	63 693	65 350	65 097	67 546
萨摩亚	210	239	275	266	288	231	310	346	346	367	390
新加坡	173 599	200 047	238 710	263 155	319 780	245 785	310 791	365 770	379 723	373 016	366 247
留存进口	81 625	94 944	110 079	119 885	157 306	114 016	141 650	180 180	199 490	181 874	172 522
所罗门群岛	121	185	217	294	328	268	404	469	486	521	509
斯里兰卡	7 973	8 834	10 258	11 301	13 953	10 049	13 512	20 269	19 190	18 003	19 417
中国台北	169 250	182 614	202 698	219 252	240 448	174 371	251 236	281 438	270 473	269 897	274 026
泰国	94 410	118 178	128 773	139 966	179 225	133 709	182 921	228 787	249 115	250 407	227 952
东帝汶	146	109	101	183	269	295	246	319	664	843	940
汤加	105	121	116	143	168	145	159	193	199	198	200
图瓦卢	11	13	13	16	26	14	16	25	30	14	12
瓦努阿图	128	149	217	229	314	294	285	304	296	313	311
越南	31 969	36 761	45 015	62 682	80 714	69 949	84 839	106 750	113 780	132 033	149 261
备忘项：											
世界 不含 a											
欧盟（28）自内进口	6 977 917	8 093 754	9 304 605	10 658 179	12 545 480	9 695 897	12 120 694	14 574 719	15 064 508	15 250 516	15 190 889
欧洲 不含											
欧盟（28）自内进口	1 568 105	1 803 146	2 096 049	2 444 930	2 868 646	2 131 315	2 514 409	2 994 467	2 978 122	2 953 273	2 893 901

a 含重要转口。

b 进口以 f.o.b. 计。

注：统计总额无连续性的国家和地区集团标示为“I”，主要在于货物贸易统计数据收集和报告的方法不同。

注意世界和亚洲数据含重复计算的因素，源于其使用一般货物贸易统计体系，该方法含转口贸易。

一些国家和地区近几年的数据由秘书处统计。

表 9

2005—2014 年世界商务服务出口（按地区和国家） 单位：百万美元

	2005	2006	2007	2008	2009	2010	2011	2012	2013	2014
世界 a	2 614 200	2 959 700	3 543 600	3 981 800	3 549 800	3 864 800	4 325 800	4 466 400	4 709 000	4 939 600
北美洲	431 600	479 200	554 600	605 700	574 600	634 700	704 100	736 600	772 800	794 900
百慕大	…	1 500	1 600	1 400	1 300	1 300	1 400	1 300	1 300	1 300
加拿大	58 900	64 900	69 300	73 500	67 100	75 300	83 700	88 500	88 500	84 900
墨西哥	15 700	15 900	17 200	17 700	14 800	15 200	15 600	16 100	20 100	21 000
美国	357 000	397 000	466 500	513 200	491 400	542 900	603 400	630 600	662 900	687 600
中、南美洲	74 500	83 400	99 600	114 100	103 300	117 100	134 200	141 400	145 000	147 000
安奎拉	100	100	100	100	100	100	100	100	100	100
安提瓜和巴布达	500	500	500	500	500	500	500	500	500	500
阿根廷	6 300	7 700	10 000	11 700	10 500	13 300	15 300	14 800	14 400	13 500
阿鲁巴（荷兰）	1 300	1 300	1 500	1 600	1 500	1 500	1 700	1 700	1 900	2 000
巴哈马	2 500	2 400	2 600	2 500	2 300	2 500	2 400	2 600	2 600	2 700
巴巴多斯	1 400	1 600	1 700	1 800	1 500	1 600	1 600	1 400	1 500	1 400
伯利兹	300	300	400	400	300	300	300	400	400	500
玻利维亚	600	700	700	700	700	700	900	1 100	1 200	1 300
巴西	14 200	17 000	22 600	28 800	26 200	30 100	36 400	38 100	37 500	39 200
智利	7 200	7 900	9 000	10 700	8 500	11 100	13 100	12 500	12 800	11 200
哥伦比亚	2 900	3 700	3 900	4 500	4 500	5 000	5 500	6 300	6 800	6 900
哥斯达黎加	3 600	4 000	5 600	5 800	3 900	4 700	5 500	6 000	6 700	6 900
古巴	7 100	7 200	8 600	9 300	8 400	10 500	11 100	12 800	13 000	12 300
库拉索岛	—	—	—	—	—	—	1 300	1 500	1 600	1 700
多米尼克	100	100	100	100	100	100	100	100	100	100
多米尼加	6 100	6 600	6 800	6 800	6 200	5 200	5 400	5 800	6 200	6 800
厄瓜多尔	900	1 000	1 100	1 400	1 200	1 400	1 500	1 700	1 900	2 200
萨尔瓦多	1 400	1 500	1 500	1 500	1 300	1 500	1 600	1 800	2 000	2 200
格林纳达	100	100	200	200	200	200	200	200	200	200
危地马拉	1 200	1 400	1 600	2 000	2 000	2 200	2 100	2 300	2 400	2 600
圭亚那	100	100	200	200	200	200	300	300	200	100
海地	100	100	200	400	400	400	500	500	600	600
洪都拉斯	1 800	1 800	1 800	2 000	1 800	2 100	2 200	2 200	2 400	2 600
牙买加	2 300	2 600	2 700	2 800	2 600	2 600	2 600	2 700	2 600	2 800
蒙特塞拉特	0	0	0	0	0	0	0	0	0	0
荷属安的列斯	1 900	2 000	2 100	2 100	2 100	2 000	—	—	—	—
尼加拉瓜	500	500	600	800	800	800	1 000	1 200	1 200	1 300
巴拿马	3 100	3 900	4 800	5 600	5 500	6 300	8 000	9 200	9 700	10 700
巴拉圭	200	300	400	400	500	600	700	700	800	800
秘鲁	2 200	2 500	3 000	3 500	3 500	3 600	4 100	4 800	5 700	5 700
圣基茨和尼维斯	200	200	200	200	100	100	100	100	100	200
圣卢西亚	400	300	400	400	400	400	400	400	400	400
圣文森特和格林纳丁斯	200	200	200	200	100	100	100	100	100	100
圣马丁岛	—	—	—	—	—	—	900	1 000	1 100	1 100
苏里南	200	200	200	200	300	200	200	200	200	200
特立尼达和多巴哥	900	800	900	900	800	900	1 000	…	…	…

续 表

	2005	2006	2007	2008	2009	2010	2011	2012	2013	2014
乌拉圭	1 300	1 400	1 800	2 200	2 300	2 700	3 600	3 400	3 300	3 200
委内瑞拉	1 300	1 400	1 700	2 000	2 000	1 600	1 700	1 900	1 800	1 600
欧洲	1 405 600	1 570 300	1 884 400	2 101 600	1 840 800	1 899 900	2 128 800	2 119 100	2 272 500	2 401 700
阿尔巴尼亚	1 300	1 600	2 100	2 700	2 600	2 500	2 800	2 400	2 400	2 700
奥地利	…	45 100	53 900	62 500	53 300	52 200	58 600	57 300	63 500	66 300
比利时	…	…	…	94 800	90 400	96 500	103 200	104 900	111 700	122 100
波斯尼亚和黑塞哥维那	1 000	1 100	2 000	2 200	1 900	1 900	1 900	1 700	1 700	1 800
保加利亚	…	…	…	…	…	8 100	9 000	8 700	9 000	10 000
克罗地亚	10 300	11 200	13 000	15 800	12 600	11 900	13 100	12 400	13 000	13 500
塞浦路斯	…	…	…	…	…	…	…	…	10 000	10 000
捷克	13 100	15 500	19 000	23 700	20 600	22 400	24 700	24 300	24 400	25 600
丹麦	43 600	52 300	62 300	73 700	56 700	61 000	66 800	66 800	70 300	72 100
爱沙尼亚	3 400	3 800	4 600	5 600	4 600	4 700	5 600	5 700	6 300	6 800
法罗群岛	100	200	200	300	200	200	200	200	200	…
芬兰	18 100	19 500	25 100	33 300	29 100	28 900	31 100	29 700	27 600	25 700
法国	152 400	164 500	195 800	223 100	192 800	201 100	236 100	236 300	253 700	267 100
马其顿	700	700	1 000	1 200	1 100	1 000	1 400	1 400	1 500	1 700
德国	153 000	175 000	202 600	235 400	215 300	220 000	242 800	235 500	255 300	266 200
希腊	…	…	…	…	37 900	37 100	39 200	34 600	37 100	41 200
匈牙利	12 500	13 400	16 900	20 400	18 400	19 300	21 600	21 100	22 200	24 100
冰岛	2 200	2 200	3 000	2 700	2 600	3 000	3 400	3 500	4 000	4 300
爱尔兰	56 200	66 500	82 800	90 500	85 200	89 900	104 500	109 500	122 200	133 400
意大利	90 700	101 000	115 000	114 700	96 000	99 800	109 100	106 700	111 900	115 900
拉脱维亚	2 400	3 000	4 300	5 300	4 400	4 000	4 800	4 800	5 100	5 000
立陶宛	3 000	3 600	4 200	5 000	4 000	4 500	5 500	6 100	7 100	7 800
卢森堡	40 100	49 800	63 300	67 800	57 200	62 900	73 200	76 700	87 900	98 500
马耳他	…	…	…	9 800	9 800	10 000	11 200	11 000	11 600	11 900
黑山	—	…	900	1 200	1 100	1 100	1 300	1 200	1 300	1 400
荷兰	…	…	…	…	…	159 600	173 300	166 300	176 900	186 600
挪威	29 600	31 800	37 600	42 400	35 200	41 200	40 900	46 400	48 400	49 500
波兰	18 100	22 500	31 700	38 100	31 200	35 300	39 100	41 900	44 800	47 900
葡萄牙	14 900	18 200	23 000	25 800	22 400	22 600	26 600	25 300	28 800	30 000
罗马尼亚	9 600	12 200	13 000	16 300	11 800	10 300	12 000	12 600	17 600	19 700
塞尔维亚	—	…	3 100	4 000	3 500	3 500	4 200	4 000	4 500	5 000
塞尔维亚和黑山	…	—	—	—	—	—	—	—	—	—
斯洛伐克	…	…	…	9 400	6 600	6 400	7 300	7 800	9 600	8 700
斯洛文尼亚	4 000	4 300	5 400	7 400	6 100	6 200	6 800	6 600	7 000	7 300
西班牙	…	…	…	131 600	112 100	112 400	129 800	122 100	128 200	133 700
瑞典	37 600	43 200	53 200	58 700	49 900	52 800	61 500	61 500	74 700	76 700
瑞士	65 000	69 900	83 900	94 900	90 000	92 800	105 800	106 300	111 400	113 300
土耳其	27 500	25 800	29 600	36 600	35 400	36 100	40 900	42 900	46 400	49 800
英国	230 600	264 200	310 800	303 300	261 400	269 000	301 400	305 300	312 400	337 200
欧盟（28）	…	…	…	…	…	1 705 200	1 916 500	1 906 700	2 051 300	2 164 500
欧盟（28）对外出口	…	…	…	…	…	743 500	838 500	856 900	930 800	984 900
独联体	47 500	58 100	72 500	92 300	75 900	85 400	100 800	110 700	121 600	111 400

续 表

	2005	2006	2007	2008	2009	2010	2011	2012	2013	2014
亚美尼亚	400	500	600	600	600	800	1 000	1 000	1 100	1 600
阿塞拜疆	700	900	1 400	1 600	2 000	2 400	2 900	4 700	4 100	4 300
白俄罗斯	2 300	2 700	3 500	4 600	3 700	4 800	5 600	6 300	7 500	7 800
格鲁吉亚	700	800	1 000	1 200	1 200	1 600	1 900	2 500	2 900	3 000
哈萨克斯坦	2 000	2 600	3 300	4 000	3 800	3 900	4 100	4 600	5 100	6 300
吉尔吉斯共和国	200	400	700	800	600	600	800	1 000	1 000	900
摩尔多瓦	400	500	700	1 000	800	700	900	1 000	1 100	1 100
俄罗斯	28 600	35 500	43 600	56 500	45 400	48 600	57 300	61 500	69 100	64 900
塔吉克斯坦	100	100	100	100	100	400	500	700	700	500
土库曼斯坦	…	…	…	…	…	…	…	…	…	…
乌克兰	10 000	11 700	14 700	18 700	14 400	17 700	20 600	21 400	21 900	14 500
乌兹别克斯坦	700	800	1 000	1 200	1 000	1 300	1 800	2 300	2 500	…
非洲	57 700	65 400	77 700	87 300	80 200	89 900	91 500	98 200	94 800	100 000
阿尔及利亚	2 500	2 500	2 800	3 400	2 800	3 500	3 600	3 600	3 800	3 500
安哥拉	200	200	300	300	600	900	700	800	1 300	…
贝宁	200	200	300	300	200	300	400	400	500	…
博茨瓦纳	800	800	800	200	200	200	400	200	500	500
布基纳法索	100	100	100	100	100	300	400	400	500	…
布隆迪	0	0	0	0	0	0	0	0	0	…
喀麦隆	900	900	1 200	1 400	1 100	1 200	1 800	1 500	1 900	…
佛得角	300	400	500	600	500	500	600	600	700	600
中非共和国	0	0	0	0	0	0	0	0	0	…
乍得	100	100	100	100	200	300	300	300	300	…
科摩罗	0	0	100	100	100	100	100	100	100	100
刚果	200	300	300	400	400	400	500	500	600	…
刚果（金）	100	200	300	500	500	300	300	200	200	200
科特迪瓦	800	800	900	1 000	1 000	1 000	900	800	800	…
吉布提	100	100	100	100	100	100	100	100	200	…
埃及	14 400	15 800	19 700	24 700	21 300	23 600	19 000	21 300	17 900	20 300
赤道几内亚	0	0	0	0	0	0	0	0	0	…
厄立特里亚	…	…	…	…	…	…	…	…	…	…
埃塞俄比亚	800	900	1 100	1 600	1 500	1 900	2 500	2 500	2 900	2 700
加蓬	100	100	100	200	100	200	200	200	200	…
冈比亚	100	100	100	100	100	100	100	200	200	200
加纳	1 100	1 200	1 600	1 600	1 500	1 300	1 700	3 200	2 400	2 000
几内亚	0	0	0	100	100	100	100	200	100	…
几内亚比绍	0	0	0	0	0	0	0	0	0	…
肯尼亚	1 500	2 000	2 400	2 500	2 200	3 000	3 300	3 900	4 000	4 000
莱索托	0	0	0	0	0	0	0	100	100	…
利比里亚	100	100	200	200	100	0	400	…	…	…
利比亚	400	400	100	200	400	400	0	200	200	…
马达加斯加	400	600	800	1 100	700	1 000	1 200	1 300	1 300	…
马拉维	100	100	100	100	100	100	100	100	100	100
马里	300	300	400	400	300	400	400	300	400	…
毛里塔尼亚	100	100	100	100	100	100	200	100	200	…

续　表

	2005	2006	2007	2008	2009	2010	2011	2012	2013	2014
毛里求斯	1 600	1 700	2 200	2 500	2 200	2 700	3 200	3 400	3 300	3 300
摩洛哥	8 700	10 900	13 400	14 700	14 400	14 300	15 500	14 900	13 900	15 900
莫桑比克	300	400	400	400	500	600	600	1 000	1 000	1 200
纳米比亚	400	500	600	500	600	700	700	1 100	900	1 000
尼日尔	100	100	100	100	100	100	100	100	100	…
尼日利亚	1 400	2 100	1 100	1 800	1 800	2 600	2 300	2 100	1 900	1 500
卢旺达	100	200	200	400	300	300	400	400	400	500
圣多美和普林西比	0	0	0	0	0	0	0	0	0	100
塞内加尔	700	700	1 100	1 200	900	900	1 000	1 100	1 200	…
塞舌尔	300	400	500	500	400	400	500	400	500	500
塞拉利昂	100	0	0	100	100	100	200	200	200	…
索马里	…	…	…	…	…	…	…	…	…	…
南非	11 600	12 800	14 500	13 600	12 800	15 700	17 000	17 200	16 400	16 500
苏丹	100	200	500	400	300	200	300	900	1 000	1 500
斯威士兰	200	300	500	300	200	300	300	200	200	300
坦桑尼亚	1 200	1 500	1 800	2 000	1 800	2 000	2 300	2 800	3 200	3 400
多哥	100	200	200	300	300	300	500	400	400	…
突尼斯	3 800	4 000	4 600	5 600	5 100	5 300	4 300	4 800	4 600	4 600
乌干达	500	500	500	700	900	1 000	1 600	1 900	2 200	2 400
赞比亚	500	600	700	600	500	600	700	1 000	800	900
津巴布韦	300	300	200	200	300	300	400	400	…	…
中东	64 300	78 800	90 900	98 900	96 800	105 500	110 800	116 200	118 600	126 500
巴林	3 200	3 500	3 700	3 900	3 800	4 200	3 300	3 100	3 300	…
伊朗	4 900	5 500	6 800	7 600	7 900	8 700	8 000	6 500	6 400	8 600
伊拉克	300	400	800	1 200	1 700	2 200	2 200	2 700	2 400	…
以色列	16 800	19 000	21 400	25 000	22 500	25 400	27 400	31 200	33 700	34 600
约旦	2 200	2 900	3 400	4 400	4 200	5 200	5 200	6 000	6 000	6 600
科威特	3 800	7 500	9 100	11 400	11 000	8 400	9 500	8 200	5 600	5 700
黎巴嫩	10 800	11 700	12 700	17 600	16 900	16 000	19 600	16 400	14 700	13 500
阿曼	900	1 300	1 700	1 800	1 600	2 000	2 400	2 600	2 900	3 000
卡塔尔	2 600	3 500	3 100	2 300	1 900	2 800	5 600	8 900	10 300	12 800
沙特阿拉伯	11 200	14 000	16 200	9 100	9 400	10 400	11 100	10 600	11 300	11 700
叙利亚	2 600	2 600	3 600	4 100	4 600	7 000	2 400	…	…	…
阿联酋	4 300	6 300	7 400	9 000	9 500	11 000	12 100	15 300	17 300	19 800
也门	300	500	600	1 000	1 100	1 500	1 100	1 400	1 600	…
亚洲	533 000	624 400	763 900	881 900	778 200	932 300	1 055 500	1 144 100	1 183 800	
阿富汗	…	…	…	1 200	1 900	3 100	3 400	3 000	2 900	…
澳大利亚	30 000	32 500	39 700	42 400	39 200	45 800	51 700	53 000	52 600	53 400
孟加拉国	700	800	900	900	1 100	1 300	1 500	1 300	1 500	1 400
不丹	0	0	100	100	100	100	100	100	100	100
文莱达鲁萨兰	600	700	800	900	900	1 100	1 200	1 100	500	500

续 表

	2005	2006	2007	2008	2009	2010	2011	2012	2013	2014
柬埔寨	1 100	1 300	1 400	1 500	1 700	1 900	2 600	3 100	3 400	3 900
中国	88 700	113 300	147 000	165 300	143 200	170 500	184 000	215 200	206 800	232 500
斐济	900	800	900	1 100	800	900	1 100	1 100	1 100	1 200
法属波利尼西亚	900	900	1 000	1 000	800	700	900	900	900	…
中国香港	47 300	54 400	64 400	69 800	64 600	80 500	91 200	98 400	104 700	106 000
印度	51 900	69 200	86 200	105 700	92 500	116 600	137 900	145 000	148 200	155 600
印度尼西亚	13 200	11 200	12 100	14 900	12 700	16 300	21 300	23 100	22 300	22 900
日本	99 700	107 200	119 400	138 700	118 400	128 500	134 500	131 100	132 600	158 100
基里巴斯	0	0	0	0	0	0	0	0	…	…
朝鲜	…	…	…	…	…	…	…	…	…	…
韩国	49 300	55 700	70 000	90 100	71 600	82 200	89 700	102 300	102 500	105 800
老挝	200	200	300	400	400	500	500	600	800	…
中国澳门	8 700	10 600	14 300	18 000	19 000	29 000	39 800	45 400	53 600	53 100
马来西亚	19 600	21 000	29 000	30 700	28 200	31 900	36 100	37 800	39 700	39 400
马尔代夫	300	500	1 600	1 600	1 500	1 800	2 100	2 200	2 600	3 000
密克罗尼西亚联邦	0	0	0	0	0	0	0	0	0	…
蒙古	400	500	600	500	400	500	600	1 000	700	600
缅甸	300	300	300	300	300	300	700	1 200	2 200	…
尼泊尔	300	300	300	500	600	600	800	800	1 000	1 000
新喀里多尼亚	300	300	400	400	300	400	400	400	400	…
新西兰	10 000	9 700	11 500	11 700	10 100	11 400	13 100	13 000	13 300	14 400
巴基斯坦	2 000	2 200	2 200	2 500	2 500	2 900	3 400	3 200	3 300	3 500
巴布亚新几内亚	300	300	300	300	200	300	400	400	400	200
菲律宾	8 600	11 100	13 500	13 100	14 100	17 800	18 900	20 400	23 300	24 800
萨摩亚	100	100	200	200	200	200	200	200	200	200
新加坡	46 200	59 000	74 000	89 400	81 600	100 600	118 300	127 000	137 000	140 100
所罗门群岛	0	0	100	0	100	100	100	100	100	100
斯里兰卡	1 500	1 600	1 800	2 000	1 900	2 500	3 100	3 800	4 700	5 600
中国台北	25 600	28 900	33 000	36 600	31 400	40 100	45 700	48 800	51 000	56 900
泰国	19 800	24 400	29 900	32 800	29 900	34 100	41 300	49 300	58 300	54 900
东帝汶	…	0	0	0	0	0	0	0	0	100
汤加	0	0	0	0	0	0	0	100	100	0
图瓦卢	0	0	0	0	0	0	0	0	0	…
瓦努阿图	100	100	200	200	200	300	300	300	300	300
越南	4 200	5 100	6 400	7 000	5 700	7 400	8 600	9 500	10 600	10 800
备忘项：										
世界 不含										
欧盟（28）对内出口	…	…	…	…	…	2 903 100	3 247 800	3 416 600	3 588 600	3 760 000
欧洲 不含										
欧盟（28）对内出口	…	…	…	…	…	938 200	1 050 900	1 069 300	1 152 000	1 222 100

注：由于服务贸易数据的频繁修正，致使大量国家和地区的数据缺少连续性。参阅技术注释。

表 10

2005—2014 年世界商务服务进口（按地区和国家）

单位：百万美元

	2005	2006	2007	2008	2009	2010	2011	2012	2013	2014
世界	**2 507 300**	**2 812 700**	**3 332 200**	**3 800 300**	**3 378 500**	**3 704 600**	**4 139 400**	**4 290 000**	**4 545 100**	**4 782 400**
北美洲	363 700	410 000	450 800	494 600	461 000	497 800	537 400	561 600	578 000	590 300
百慕大	…	800	1 100	1 000	1 000	1 000	900	900	900	900
加拿大	64 500	72 200	81 400	88 300	81 900	97 000	106 000	111 400	111 100	106 000
墨西哥	22 300	23 100	24 100	25 100	22 800	22 500	26 100	26 800	29 300	31 700
美国	277 000	313 800	344 300	380 200	355 300	377 400	404 500	422 500	436 800	451 700
中、南美洲	71 000	80 900	101 700	123 600	115 300	143 500	171 900	182 000	194 300	194 000
安奎拉	100	100	100	100	100	100	100	100	100	100
安提瓜和巴布达	200	200	300	300	200	200	200	200	200	200
阿根廷	7 200	8 100	10 400	12 900	11 700	14 300	17 300	17 700	18 100	16 400
阿鲁巴（荷兰）	700	700	800	800	700	600	800	800	800	800
巴哈马	1 200	1 500	1 500	1 300	1 100	1 100	1 300	1 500	1 600	1 700
巴巴多斯	600	600	600	700	700	700	500	400	400	400
伯利兹	100	100	200	200	200	200	200	200	200	200
玻利维亚	700	800	900	1 000	1 000	1 100	1 600	1 900	2 300	3 000
巴西	21 500	26 200	34 700	44 400	44 100	59 500	73 000	77 800	83 200	85 800
智利	8 000	8 700	10 400	11 900	10 500	13 000	16 200	14 700	15 700	14 600
哥伦比亚	5 300	6 000	6 800	7 800	7 900	9 300	10 700	12 100	12 700	13 400
哥斯达黎加	1 400	1 500	1 700	1 800	1 500	1 800	1 800	2 100	2 100	2 100
古巴	1 000	1 300	1 300	2 100	1 700	1 900	2 500	2 400	2 300	2 500
库拉索岛	—	—	—	—	—	—	800	900	900	900
多米尼克	0	100	100	100	100	100	100	100	100	100
多米尼加	1 400	1 500	1 700	1 900	1 700	3 200	2 800	2 800	2 800	2 900
厄瓜多尔	2 100	2 300	2 500	2 900	2 600	2 900	3 000	3 100	3 400	3 400
萨尔瓦多	1 100	1 200	1 300	1 300	1 000	1 100	1 200	1 300	1 400	1 400
格林纳达	100	100	100	100	100	100	100	100	100	100
危地马拉	1 400	1 800	2 000	2 000	2 100	2 400	2 500	2 500	2 700	3 000
圭亚那	200	200	300	300	300	300	400	500	500	500
海地	500	600	500	600	600	700	800	800	800	800
洪都拉斯	900	1 000	1 100	1 200	900	1 100	1 400	1 500	1 600	1 700
牙买加	1 700	2 000	2 200	2 300	1 800	1 800	1 900	2 100	2 000	2 100
蒙特塞拉特	0	0	0	0	0	0	0	0	0	0
荷属安的列斯	700	800	800	900	900	900	—	—	—	—
尼加拉瓜	400	500	700	800	700	700	800	900	1 000	900
巴拿马	1 700	1 600	2 000	2 600	2 100	2 700	4 200	4 500	4 700	4 700
巴拉圭	300	400	400	600	500	700	900	900	1 000	1 100
秘鲁	3 000	3 300	4 200	5 600	4 700	5 900	6 400	7 200	7 500	7 500
圣基茨和尼维斯	100	100	100	100	100	100	100	100	100	100
圣卢西亚	200	200	200	200	200	200	200	200	200	200
圣文森特和格林纳丁斯	100	100	100	100	100	100	100	100	100	100
圣马丁岛	—	—	—	—	—	—	200	300	300	300
苏里南	300	300	300	400	200	200	600	600	600	800
特立尼达和多巴哥	500	300	300	300	300	400	500	…	…	…

续 表

	2005	2006	2007	2008	2009	2010	2011	2012	2013	2014
乌拉圭	900	900	1 100	1 500	1 200	1 500	2 000	2 300	3 200	3 200
委内瑞拉	5 200	5 800	10 300	12 700	11 800	12 600	15 100	17 100	19 200	16 600
欧洲	1 228 900	1 356 600	1 613 000	1 803 000	1 576 700	1 625 000	1 785 800	1 767 400	1 900 000	2 001 400
阿尔巴尼亚	1 300	1 500	1 900	2 400	2 200	2 000	2 200	1 900	2 200	2 300
奥地利	…	35 100	40 900	45 100	38 900	38 600	44 400	44 000	49 700	53 100
比利时	…	…	…	89 000	82 200	87 400	94 800	97 300	103 800	115 000
波斯尼亚和黑塞哥维那	400	500	500	600	600	500	500	500	500	500
保加利亚	…	…	…	…	…	4 600	5 000	5 400	5 600	6 200
克罗地亚	3 500	3 800	4 200	5 200	4 400	3 800	4 000	3 900	4 000	3 900
塞浦路斯	…	…	…	…	…	…	…	…	6 200	6 600
捷克	10 200	12 100	14 600	18 300	16 200	18 100	20 100	20 300	20 800	22 800
丹麦	38 300	47 000	56 400	66 000	54 200	54 400	61 300	61 200	63 100	64 000
爱沙尼亚	2 200	2 500	3 100	3 500	2 600	2 900	3 800	4 000	4 600	4 800
法罗群岛	200	300	400	400	300	400	400	400	400	…
芬兰	18 900	20 800	24 800	33 100	29 200	28 800	31 100	31 800	29 800	27 900
法国	133 600	145 500	168 500	193 800	175 200	180 900	203 100	202 600	230 000	247 900
马其顿	500	500	700	900	800	800	900	900	1 000	1 200
德国	208 100	223 300	257 600	287 000	248 800	262 100	293 600	286 900	323 100	326 400
希腊	…	…	…	…	19 800	19 800	19 100	15 700	14 600	15 100
匈牙利	11 400	11 900	15 500	18 300	16 800	15 800	17 200	16 100	16 800	17 400
冰岛	2 400	2 400	2 800	2 400	1 900	2 100	2 500	2 700	2 800	3 100
爱尔兰	71 700	80 900	95 600	112 300	104 700	107 900	116 100	118 800	122 200	141 800
意大利	92 700	104 000	125 100	129 600	107 700	110 900	116 500	106 100	107 900	113 200
拉脱维亚	1 600	2 000	2 800	3 300	2 400	2 300	2 800	2 700	2 800	2 800
立陶宛	2 000	2 500	3 300	4 100	3 000	2 900	3 700	4 200	5 200	5 600
卢森堡	27 400	34 400	44 100	46 500	39 600	41 800	48 700	50 900	59 200	66 800
马耳他	…	…	…	7 900	8 400	8 400	9 300	9 100	9 600	9 700
黑山	—	…	400	600	500	400	400	400	400	400
荷兰	…	…	…	…	…	135 600	149 900	142 500	151 200	156 200
挪威	29 000	31 600	41 100	47 600	36 800	44 900	47 600	52 300	55 600	56 300
波兰	15 400	19 500	24 000	30 300	23 900	30 800	32 200	33 600	34 000	35 600
葡萄牙	9 300	10 900	13 200	15 200	13 600	14 100	15 600	13 600	14 300	15 400
罗马尼亚	5 400	6 900	8 900	11 900	10 400	8 300	9 700	9 400	11 300	12 000
塞尔维亚	—	…	3 400	4 200	3 400	3 500	3 900	3 700	4 100	4 400
塞尔维亚和黑山	…	—	—	—	—	—	—	—	—	—
斯洛伐克	…	…	…	9 900	7 800	7 200	7 600	7 200	8 800	8 500
斯洛文尼亚	2 900	3 200	4 200	5 200	4 500	4 500	4 800	4 500	4 700	5 000
西班牙	…	…	…	87 800	71 100	68 000	71 100	65 100	64 500	69 600
瑞典	35 500	38 800	46 700	52 900	45 000	46 400	53 500	54 500	61 500	66 600
瑞士	46 600	48 700	56 400	63 700	65 300	69 200	82 800	84 900	91 500	92 600
土耳其	10 800	11 000	14 900	17 100	16 000	18 600	19 600	19 500	22 600	23 000
英国	165 900	181 700	203 100	204 700	171 000	172 400	181 800	184 500	189 500	196 900
欧盟（28）	…	…	…	…	…	1 475 600	1 617 100	1 607 100	1 731 200	1 821 800
欧盟（28）自外进口 a	…	…	…	…	…	597 700	647 500	652 900	697 600	744 300
独联体	62 300	71 900	93 500	116 600	94 900	111 100	131 400	156 100	179 300	171 900

续　表

	2005	2006	2007	2008	2009	2010	2011	2012	2013	2014
亚美尼亚	600	700	900	1 000	900	1 100	1 100	1 200	1 200	1 700
阿塞拜疆	2 600	2 900	3 300	3 900	3 600	3 800	5 700	7 300	8 200	10 200
白俄罗斯	1 100	1 700	2 100	2 700	2 200	3 000	3 300	4 000	5 200	5 600
格鲁吉亚	600	700	900	1 200	900	1 000	1 200	1 400	1 500	1 600
哈萨克斯坦	7 400	8 700	11 600	11 000	9 900	11 200	10 800	12 700	12 000	12 600
吉尔吉斯共和国	300	500	600	900	700	800	1 000	1 300	1 100	1 200
摩尔多瓦	400	500	600	800	700	700	800	900	900	1 000
俄罗斯	39 500	45 200	59 200	75 700	61 200	73 200	89 400	106 700	125 800	118 900
塔吉克斯坦	300	400	600	500	300	500	700	900	1 100	800
土库曼斯坦	…	…	…	…	…	…	…	…	…	…
乌克兰	7 000	8 600	11 100	15 800	11 100	12 200	12 800	14 000	15 500	11 800
乌兹别克斯坦	400	400	400	400	400	500	600	900	1 000	…
非洲	71 100	85 600	108 900	141 300	125 900	140 300	157 400	162 000	163 400	171 900
阿尔及利亚	4 500	4 500	6 400	10 500	11 200	11 500	12 000	10 500	10 200	11 200
安哥拉	6 200	6 900	12 000	20 500	18 200	16 000	22 400	21 200	21 300	…
贝宁	300	300	500	500	500	500	500	600	800	…
博茨瓦纳	600	600	700	400	500	600	700	500	500	500
布基纳法索	300	300	400	600	500	800	1 100	1 200	1 400	…
布隆迪	100	200	200	200	200	200	200	200	200	…
喀麦隆	1 400	1 400	1 700	2 600	1 900	1 700	2 000	2 100	2 600	…
佛得角	200	300	300	400	300	300	300	400	300	400
中非共和国	100	100	100	200	200	200	200	200	200	…
乍得	1 500	2 100	1 700	1 800	1 900	2 400	2 400	2 300	2 600	…
科摩罗	0	100	100	100	100	100	100	100	100	100
刚果	1 400	2 400	3 500	3 600	3 200	3 700	4 100	4 100	4 600	…
刚果（金）	1 000	800	1 400	1 900	1 700	2 500	2 600	1 900	2 300	2 700
科特迪瓦	2 100	2 200	2 400	2 700	2 600	2 700	2 600	2 700	2 800	…
吉布提	100	100	100	100	100	100	100	100	200	…
埃及	9 500	10 300	13 100	16 300	12 800	13 000	13 100	15 600	14 800	16 800
赤道几内亚	900	800	1 100	1 700	2 100	2 600	2 700	3 000	2 700	…
厄立特里亚	…	…	…	…	…	…	…	…	…	…
埃塞俄比亚	1 200	1 200	1 700	2 400	2 200	2 500	3 300	3 600	3 500	4 400
加蓬	1 000	1 200	1 400	1 600	1 300	1 800	2 000	2 000	2 200	…
冈比亚	0	100	100	100	100	100	100	100	100	100
加纳	1 100	1 400	1 800	2 000	2 400	2 400	3 100	3 800	4 400	3 800
几内亚	200	200	300	400	300	400	500	800	600	…
几内亚比绍	0	0	100	100	100	100	100	100	100	…
肯尼亚	1 000	1 300	1 500	1 700	1 700	1 900	2 000	2 300	2 200	2 700
莱索托	400	400	400	400	400	400	500	400	400	…
利比里亚	100	200	200	300	100	200	300	400	400	…
利比亚	2 100	2 300	2 500	3 600	4 300	5 300	3 600	6 300	7 400	…
马达加斯加	500	600	1 000	1 400	1 100	1 100	1 100	1 100	1 200	…
马拉维	100	100	100	100	100	100	200	200	200	…
马里	600	700	800	1 000	800	1 000	1 100	1 100	1 200	…
毛里塔尼亚	400	400	500	700	600	600	700	1 000	900	…

续 表

	2005	2006	2007	2008	2009	2010	2011	2012	2013	2014
毛里求斯	1 200	1 300	1 600	1 900	1 600	2 000	2 400	2 400	2 600	2 400
摩洛哥	3 100	3 600	4 500	5 600	5 300	5 700	6 700	6 600	6 400	8 000
莫桑比克	600	700	800	800	1 000	1 200	2 100	4 200	3 900	3 600
纳米比亚	400	400	500	600	600	700	800	700	900	1 100
尼日尔	300	300	400	600	700	800	900	800	1 000	…
尼日利亚	6 400	12 100	15 600	22 600	16 500	19 900	22 500	22 500	20 700	22 500
卢旺达	200	200	300	400	400	500	600	400	500	600
圣多美和普林西比	0	0	0	0	0	0	0	0	0	100
塞内加尔	800	800	1 200	1 400	1 100	1 100	1 200	1 300	1 400	…
塞舌尔	200	300	200	200	200	300	300	200	200	200
塞拉利昂	100	100	100	100	100	200	400	500	600	…
索马里	…	…	…	…	…	…	…	…	…	…
南非	11 900	13 800	15 900	16 600	15 000	19 200	20 400	18 400	17 600	16 600
苏丹	1 500	2 500	2 600	2 500	2 100	2 400	2 100	2 000	1 900	1 900
斯威士兰	400	400	500	600	500	700	900	800	700	800
坦桑尼亚	1 100	1 200	1 400	1 600	1 700	1 800	2 200	2 300	2 400	2 600
多哥	200	300	300	400	400	400	500	400	500	…
突尼斯	2 000	2 200	2 600	3 100	2 700	3 100	3 000	3 000	3 100	3 200
乌干达	600	800	1 000	1 200	1 400	1 800	2 400	2 400	2 600	3 000
赞比亚	400	500	800	800	600	800	1 100	1 300	1 800	1 600
津巴布韦	600	500	500	500	600	900	1 100	1 000	…	…
中东	98 300	122 600	160 100	189 500	175 300	192 500	223 800	233 500	245 500	268 800
巴林	1 400	1 600	1 700	2 000	1 700	1 900	1 800	1 500	1 600	…
伊朗	10 400	11 400	14 800	17 100	16 900	18 200	16 200	12 400	12 700	14 300
伊拉克	5 400	5 000	4 700	7 200	8 400	9 600	10 900	13 000	14 500	…
以色列	13 600	14 900	17 500	19 600	17 200	18 400	20 200	20 700	20 000	21 600
约旦	2 500	2 900	3 400	3 900	3 700	4 300	4 400	4 500	4 500	4 500
科威特	7 400	8 800	10 500	14 800	12 900	14 300	17 600	20 000	19 900	22 300
黎巴嫩	7 900	8 700	10 000	13 400	14 000	13 000	12 900	11 900	13 000	12 700
阿曼	3 100	3 900	5 100	5 900	5 500	6 400	7 700	8 700	10 000	10 400
卡塔尔	4 000	6 900	7 300	7 100	5 700	7 700	15 500	22 100	24 800	30 000
沙特阿拉伯	19 700	29 500	46 300	49 600	47 000	51 000	55 000	49 900	51 700	59 100
叙利亚	2 300	2 400	2 900	3 100	2 600	3 400	2 800	…	…	…
阿联酋	18 900	24 300	33 400	42 800	36 800	41 300	55 700	62 300	66 400	70 300
也门	1 200	1 800	1 800	2 300	2 000	2 100	2 100	2 300	2 200	…
亚洲	611 900	685 100	804 300	931 600	829 400	994 500	1 131 600	1 227 500	1 284 500	1 384 000
阿富汗	…	…	…	500	800	1 200	1 200	2 200	2 100	…
澳大利亚	30 500	32 700	41 300	48 300	41 600	50 800	61 700	65 700	67 100	62 400
孟加拉国	2 100	2 300	2 900	3 500	3 300	4 500	5 200	5 300	6 100	7 200
不丹	100	100	100	100	100	100	200	200	200	200
文莱达鲁萨兰	900	1 000	1 100	1 200	1 200	1 400	1 500	1 500	2 400	2 000

续 表

	2005	2006	2007	2008	2009	2010	2011	2012	2013	2014
柬埔寨	600	800	800	800	800	900	1 300	1 500	1 700	2 000
中国	83 600	100 500	129 400	158 100	158 400	192 900	237 800	281 000	330 400	381 600
斐济	500	500	500	600	500	400	500	600	600	600
法属波利尼西亚	700	500	600	700	700	600	600	500	500	…
中国香港	56 100	63 600	68 600	72 500	61 000	70 200	74 100	76 500	75 000	75 600
印度	46 700	58 000	69 800	87 200	79 600	114 000	124 200	129 000	125 200	146 900
印度尼西亚	22 500	23 800	25 900	29 800	24 100	26 000	31 200	33 600	34 400	33 100
日本	137 400	139 800	156 900	176 800	154 000	162 900	173 800	182 800	169 000	189 900
基里巴斯	0	0	0	0	0	0	100	100	…	…
朝鲜	…	…	…	…	…	…	…	…	…	…
韩国	59 100	69 600	83 900	96 900	81 600	96 500	102 000	107 800	109 200	114 000
老挝	0	0	0	100	100	300	300	300	500	…
中国澳门	2 500	3 100	4 700	5 900	5 000	7 500	10 500	11 400	11 800	10 500
马来西亚	21 800	23 400	28 500	30 100	27 300	32 200	37 900	42 200	44 400	44 700
马尔代夫	200	200	300	400	400	400	600	600	700	800
密克罗尼西亚联邦	100	100	100	100	100	100	100	100	100	…
蒙古	500	500	500	600	600	800	1 800	2 000	2 000	2 100
缅甸	500	500	600	600	600	800	1 100	1 400	1 500	…
尼泊尔	400	500	700	800	800	800	800	900	1 000	1 100
新喀里多尼亚	800	1 100	1 300	1 300	1 000	1 300	1 400	1 400	1 400	…
新西兰	8 300	8 000	9 500	10 400	8 600	10 100	12 000	12 300	12 400	12 900
巴基斯坦	7 300	8 200	8 600	9 400	6 000	6 600	7 300	7 600	7 200	7 700
巴布亚新几内亚	1 300	1 600	1 900	1 800	1 800	2 700	2 900	3 700	3 900	2 300
菲律宾	6 400	6 500	7 400	10 900	9 000	11 700	12 000	14 000	16 100	19 700
萨摩亚	100	100	100	100	100	100	100	100	100	0
新加坡	56 000	66 200	76 300	91 000	83 900	101 000	117 200	128 900	141 400	141 300
所罗门群岛	100	100	100	100	100	200	200	200	200	200
斯里兰卡	2 100	2 400	2 600	3 000	2 500	3 100	4 000	4 400	5 200	5 600
中国台北	31 400	31 800	34 100	34 200	29 100	37 100	41 300	41 900	41 900	45 200
泰国	26 700	32 400	37 800	45 800	36 300	44 800	52 000	52 800	54 600	52 900
东帝汶	…	0	100	100	300	400	700	500	300	300
汤加	0	0	0	0	0	0	100	100	100	100
图瓦卢	0	0	0	0	0	0	0	0	0	…
瓦努阿图	100	100	100	100	100	100	100	100	100	100
越南	4 400	5 100	7 100	7 900	8 000	9 800	11 700	12 400	13 600	14 300
备忘项：										
世界 不含										
欧盟（28）自内进口	…	…	…	…	…	2 826 800	3 169 800	3 335 800	3 511 500	3 704 900
欧洲 不含										
欧盟（28）自内进口	…	…	…	…	…	747 100	816 200	813 100	866 400	924 000

表 11

2010—2014 年世界货物出口量和产量增长　　单位：年度变化百分比

	2010—2014	2012	2013	2014
世界货物出口	3.5	2.5	3.0	2.5
农产品	3.5	1.5	3.0	2.5
燃料和矿产品	1.5	3.0	0.5	1.0
制成品	4.0	2.0	2.5	4.0
世界货物产量	2.5	2.0	2.0	2.0
农业	2.5	1.5	5.5	1.5
采掘业	1.5	2.5	0.5	2.5
制造业	2.5	2.5	1.5	2.5
世界 GDP	2.0	2.0	2.0	2.0

表 12

2010—2014 年世界主要地区和经济体货物贸易量增长　　单位：年度变化百分比

出口				进口		
2010—2014	2013	2014		2010—2014	2013	2014
3.5	3.0	2.5	**世界**	3.0	2.0	2.5
4.5	2.5	4.0	北美洲	3.5	1.0	4.5
4.0	2.0	5.5	加拿大	2.5	1.5	2.0
6.0	4.5	7.0	墨西哥	6.0	3.0	7.0
4.5	2.5	3.5	美国	3.0	1.0	4.5
2.0	2.0	−1.5	中、南美洲	3.5	3.5	−2.5
2.5	2.5	1.5	欧洲	1.0	0.0	2.5
2.5	2.0	2.0	欧盟（28）	1.0	−0.5	3.0
−1.5	−5.0	1.5	挪威	1.5	1.5	1.0
4.5	16.0	−6.0	瑞士	−2.5	2.0	−13.0
1.0	1.0	0.0	独联体	2.5	−1.0	−10.0
4.5	5.0	4.5	亚洲	4.5	5.0	3.5
3.5	6.0	6.0	澳大利亚	2.5	−2.5	2.0
7.5	7.5	7.0	中国	6.5	10.0	4.0
6.0	8.5	3.0	印度	4.5	−0.5	3.0
−1.0	−2.0	0.5	日本	3.0	0.5	2.5
3.5	3.0	4.0	六个东亚贸易方 a	3.0	3.5	3.0

a　中国香港，马来西亚，韩国，新加坡，台、澎、金、马单独关税区和泰国。

表 13

2010—2014 年世界货物和服务贸易（按地区和国家）

单位：年度变化百分比

出口				进口		
2010—2014	2013	2014		2010—2014	2013	2014
			货物贸易			
6	2	0	世界	5	1	1
6	2	3	北美洲	5	0	3
6	2	3	美国	5	0	4
5	1	4	加拿大	4	0	0
4	−2	−6	中、南美洲	6	3	−5
3	0	−7	巴西	6	7	−5
2	−2	−1	阿根廷	5	−1	−9
5	5	0	欧洲	4	2	1
4	5	1	欧盟（28）	3	1	2
—	15	−13	瑞士	—	9	−14
6	−2	−6	独联体	5	0	−11
6	−1	−5	俄罗斯	6	2	−10
7	−2	−8	乌克兰	7	5	−16
2	−6	−8	非洲	8	3	1
0	−4	−5	南非	6	−1	−3
4	−10	−7	尼日利亚 a	8	10	7
9	0	−4	中东	8	6	0
14	9	−5	阿联酋 a	12	11	4
9	−3	−6	沙特	11	8	−3
6	2	2	亚洲	7	1	0
10	8	6	中国	9	7	0
−3	−10	−4	日本	4	−6	−1
			服务贸易			
6	5	5	世界	7	6	5
6	5	3	北美洲	4	3	2
6	5	4	美国	5	3	3
3	0	−4	加拿大	2	0	−5
6	3	1	中、南美洲	8	7	0
7	−2	5	巴西	10	7	3
0	−3	−6	阿根廷	3	2	−10
6	7	6	欧洲	5	8	5
6	8	6	欧盟（28）	5	8	5
5	5	2	瑞士	8	8	1
7	10	−8	独联体	12	15	−4
7	12	−6	俄罗斯	13	18	−5
−5	2	−34	乌克兰	−1	11	−24
3	−3	6	非洲	5	1	5
−4	−16	13	埃及	7	−5	13
1	−5	0	南非	−3	−5	−6
5	2	7	中东	9	5	9
16	14	14	阿联酋	14	7	6
3	7	3	沙特阿拉伯	4	4	14
8	3	6	亚洲	9	5	8
8	−4	12	日本	19	18	15
5	1	19	中国	4	−8	12

a　秘书处估计。

表 14

2014 年世界货物出口（按产品类别）

单位：十亿美元，%

	总额	份额	年度变化百分比								
	2014	占世界货物贸易	1980—1985	1985—1990	1990—1995	1995—2000	2000—2005	2010—2014	2012	2013	2014
农产品	17 65	9.5	−2	9	7	−1	9	7	−1	5	2
燃料和矿产品	3 789	20.5	−5	3	2	10	16	6	2	−3	−6
燃料	3 068	16.6	−5	0	1	12	17	7	5	−3	−7
制成品	12 243	66.2	2	15	9	5	9	5	0	3	4
钢铁	472	2.6	−2	9	8	−2	17	3	−8	−7	5
化工产品	2 054	11.1	1	14	10	4	14	5	−2	2	3
办公和通信设备	1 794	9.7	9	18	15	10	6	3	0	4	2
汽车	1395	7.5	5	14	8	5	10	6	1	3	4
纺织品	314	1.7	−1	15	8	0	6	6	−4	7	3
服装	483	2.6	4	18	8	5	7	8	0	10	5
农产品（AoA）a	1 454	7.9	—	—	—	—	10	7	1	5	1
非农产品（NAMA）	16 850	91.1	—	—	—	—	10	5	0	2	1

a. 见（AoA）（第 5 章，第 2.1.2 节）的农产品定义。

表 15

2014 年世界货物出口（按产品类别和地区）

单位：十亿美元，%

	农产品	燃料和矿产品		制成品						
		总额	燃料	总额	钢铁	化工产品	办公和通信设备	汽车	纺织品	服装
世界	1 765	3 789	3 068	12 243	472	2 054	1 794	1 395	314	483
占所有出口比重	9.5	20.5	16.6	66.2	2.6	11.1	9.7	7.5	1.7	2.6
年度变化百分比										
2010—2014	20	20	20	14	10	17	9	11	12	15
2013	5	−3	−3	3	−7	2	4	3	7	10
2014	2	−6	−7	4	5	3	2	4	3	5
北美洲	277	415	326	1685	33	265	219	291	19	12
占所有出口比重	11.1	16.7	13.1	67.6	1.3	10.6	8.8	11.7	0.8	0.5
年度变化百分比										
2010—2014	19	23	26	11	12	14	6	11	2	−4
2013	3	1	4	2	−3	1	0	3	3	3
2014	4	2	3	4	2	1	3	5	3	4
中、南美洲	212	277	172	177	17	44	5	21	4	13
占所有出口比重	30.6	39.9	24.8	25.5	2.5	6.3	0.8	3.1	0.6	1.9
年度变化百分比										
2010—2014	24	18	16	8	2	17	−7	6	6	−3

续 表

	农产品	燃料和矿产品		制成品						
		总额	燃料	总额	钢铁	化工产品	办公和通信设备	汽车	纺织品	服装
2013	5	−7	−9	1	−17	−5	4	10	−1	−5
2014	−2	−7	−6	−8	7	−5	−7	−24	−3	0
欧洲	719	759	555	5 096	185	1 112	359	718	89	147
占所有出口比重	10.6	11.1	8.1	74.8	2.7	16.3	5.3	10.5	1.3	2.2
年度变化百分比										
2010—2014	16	16	17	10	5	14	−1	9	3	10
2013	8	−3	−2	4	−6	3	−2	7	4	8
2014	1	−7	−9	4	0	3	2	6	4	7
独联体	68	486	438	165	43	44	3	7	5	3
占所有出口比重	9.2	66.1	59.6	22.4	5.9	6.0	0.4	1.0	0.7	0.4
年度变化百分比										
2010—2014	28	22	23	16	6	23	35	14	30	13
2013	−1	0	2	−9	−16	−16	4	−2	18	12
2014	2	−6	−9	−3	2	4	−32	−24	37	−5
非洲	64	349	298	118	9	24	5	12	3	11
占所有出口比重	11.5	62.9	53.6	21.3	1.6	4.3	0.9	2.1	0.6	1.9
年度变化百分比										
2010—2014	22	14	12	17	3	25	25	21	16	4
2013	7	−9	−11	7	−2	5	3	6	8	5
2014	3	−12	−13	2	2	3	35	2	2	4
中东	30	836	815	266	6	91	17	11	6	9
占所有出口比重	2.3	64.9	63.3	20.7	0.5	7.1	1.3	0.9	0.5	0.7
年度变化百分比										
2010—2014	16	21	21	26	22	32	19	25	12	23
2013	10	−4	−4	3	−23	−4	17	0	17	27
2014	0	−7	−7	2	3	3	3	8	−9	−24
亚洲	396	666	465	4 735	178	474	1 186	334	188	290
占所有出口比重	6.7	11.3	7.9	80.0	3.0	8.0	20.0	5.6	3.2	4.9
年度变化百分比										
2010—2014	26	27	27	20	21	23	14	14	18	21
2013	2	0	−1	3	−6	2	7	−2	9	11
2014	2	−4	−4	4	13	4	3	1	3	6

表 16

2014 年世界商业服务贸易（按产品类别）

单位：十亿美元，%

	总额	份　额				
	2014 年	2005 年	2010 年	2012 年	2013 年	2014 年
出口						
所有服务	4940	100.0	100.0	100.0	100.0	100.0
运输服务	160	3.6	3.2	3.5	3.2	3.2
旅游服务	955	22.4	21.3	20.5	19.9	19.3
其他服务	1 240	26.4	24.7	24.8	25.2	25.1
进口	2 585	47.7	50.7	51.2	51.7	52.4
所有服务						
运输服务	4 780	100.0	100.0	100.0	100.0	100.0
旅游服务	105	2.5	2.1	2.1	2.2	2.1
其他服务	1 225	27.3	26.5	26.9	26.1	25.6

表 17

2005—2014 年世界商业服务出口增长（按产品类别和地区）

单位：年度变化百分比

		世界	北美洲	中、南美洲	欧洲	独联体	非洲	中东	亚洲
商业服务									
	2005—2010	8	8	9	6	12	9	…	12
	2013	5	5	3	7	10	−3	2	3
	2014	5	3	1	6	−8	6	7	6
与货物相关的服务									
	38626	6	12	−12	7	11	16	19	3
	2013	−2	7	7	15	−8	−31	−16	−27
	2014	4	19	9	4	−22	36	−13	2
运输服务									
	2005—2010	7	6	9	6	12	10	9	9
	2013	2	3	5	5	7	2	−10	−3
	2014	2	2	−4	3	−3	4	11	1
旅游服务									
	2005—2010	7	5	7	3	9	8	15	13
	2013	7	7	4	8	9	−8	4	9
	2014	4	3	5	5	−13	6	10	5
其他商业服务									
	2005—2010	9	10	17	8	16	11	…	14
	2013	6	4	0	7	17	0	9	6
	2014	6	2	0	7	−8	6	1	10

表 18

2014 年区域间和区域内货物贸易

单位：十亿美元，%

原产地	目的地							世界
	北美洲	中、南美洲	欧洲	独联体	非洲	中东	亚洲	
	贸易额							
世界	**3 195**	**744**	**6 792**	**512**	**639**	**780**	**5 485**	**18 494**
北美洲	1 251	214	379	17	43	79	504	2 493
中、南美洲	173	179	114	9	18	17	170	695
欧洲	540	119	4 665	218	221	229	738	6 810
独联体	28	7	385	131	16	22	134	735
非洲	39	29	201	2	98	18	152	555
中东	99	11	148	7	36	113	694	1 288
亚洲	1 065	185	900	127	207	302	3 093	5 917
区域内贸易流量占每一区域总货物贸易出口的份额								
世界	**17.3**	**4.0**	**36.7**	**2.8**	**3.5**	**4.2**	**29.7**	**100.0**
北美洲	50.2	8.6	15.2	0.7	1.7	3.2	20.2	100.0
中、南美洲	24.8	25.8	16.4	1.4	2.5	2.4	24.5	100.0
欧洲	7.9	1.7	68.5	3.2	3.3	3.4	10.8	100.0
独联体	3.9	0.9	52.4	17.8	2.1	3.1	18.2	100.0
非洲	7.0	5.1	36.2	0.4	17.7	3.3	27.3	100.0
中东	7.7	0.8	11.5	0.5	2.8	8.8	53.9	100.0
亚洲	18.0	3.1	15.2	2.1	3.5	5.1	52.3	100.0
每一区域的出口额占世界对此区域出口总额的份额								
世界	**100.0**	**100.0**	**100.0**	**100.0**	**100.0**	**100.0**	**100.0**	**100.0**
北美洲	39.2	28.8	5.6	3.4	6.8	10.1	9.2	13.5
中、南美洲	5.4	24.1	1.7	1.8	2.8	2.2	3.1	3.8
欧洲	16.9	16.0	68.7	42.6	34.7	29.4	13.5	36.8
独联体	0.9	0.9	5.7	25.6	2.4	2.9	2.4	4.0
非洲	1.2	3.8	3.0	0.4	15.4	2.3	2.8	3.0
中东	3.1	1.5	2.2	1.3	5.6	14.5	12.7	7.0
亚洲	33.3	24.9	13.2	24.7	32.4	38.7	56.4	32.0
区域内贸易流量占世界总货物贸易出口的份额								
世界	**17.3**	**4.0**	**36.7**	**2.8**	**3.5**	**4.2**	**29.7**	**100.0**
北美洲	6.8	1.2	2.0	0.1	0.2	0.4	2.7	13.5
中、南美洲	0.9	1.0	0.6	0.1	0.1	0.1	0.9	3.8
欧洲	2.9	0.6	25.2	1.2	1.2	1.2	4.0	36.8
独联体	0.2	0.0	2.1	0.7	0.1	0.1	0.7	4.0
非洲	0.2	0.2	1.1	0.0	0.5	0.1	0.8	3.0
中东	0.5	0.1	0.8	0.0	0.2	0.6	3.8	7.0
亚洲	5.8	1.0	4.9	0.7	1.1	1.6	16.7	32.0

表 19

1948，1953，1963，1973，1983，1993，2003 和 2014 年

世界货物出口（按地区和国家）

单位：十亿美元，%

	1948 年	1953 年	1963 年	1973 年	1983 年	1993 年	2003 年	2014 年
				总额				
世界	59	84	157	579	1 838	3 688	7 380	18 494
				份额				
世界	100.0	100.0	100.0	100.0	100.0	100.0	100.0	100.0
北美洲	28.1	24.8	19.9	17.3	16.8	17.9	15.8	13.5
美国	21.7	18.8	14.9	12.3	11.2	12.6	9.8	8.8
加拿大	5.5	5.2	4.3	4.6	4.2	3.9	3.7	2.6
墨西哥	0.9	0.7	0.6	0.4	1.4	1.4	2.2	2.1
中、南美洲	11.3	9.7	6.4	4.3	4.5	3.0	3.0	3.8
巴西	2.0	1.8	0.9	1.1	1.2	1.0	1.0	1.2
委内瑞拉	1.5	1.7	1.5	0.6	0.8	0.4	0.4	0.4
欧洲	35.1	39.4	47.8	50.9	43.5	45.3	45.9	36.8
德国 a	1.4	5.3	9.3	11.7	9.2	10.3	10.2	8.2
荷兰	2.0	3.0	3.6	4.7	3.5	3.8	4.0	3.6
法国	3.4	4.8	5.2	6.3	5.2	6.0	5.3	3.2
意大利	1.8	1.8	3.2	3.8	4.0	4.6	4.1	2.9
独联体 b	—	—	—	—	—	1.5	2.6	4.0
非洲	7.3	6.5	5.7	4.8	4.5	2.5	2.4	3.0
南非 c	2.0	1.6	1.5	1.0	1.0	0.7	0.5	0.5
中东	2.0	2.7	3.2	4.1	6.7	3.5	4.1	7.0
亚洲	14.0	13.4	12.5	14.9	19.1	26.0	26.1	32.0
中国	0.9	1.2	1.3	1.0	1.2	2.5	5.9	12.7
日本	0.4	1.5	3.5	6.4	8.0	9.8	6.4	3.7
印度	2.2	1.3	1.0	0.5	0.5	0.6	0.8	1.7
澳大利亚和新西兰	3.7	3.2	2.4	2.1	1.4	1.4	1.2	1.5
六个东亚贸易方	3.4	3.0	2.5	3.6	5.8	9.6	9.6	9.6
备忘项：								
欧盟 d	—	—	24.5	37.0	31.3	37.3	42.4	33.3
苏联	2.2	3.5	4.6	3.7	5.0	—	—	—
GATT/WTO 成员 e	63.4	69.6	75.0	84.1	77.0	89.0	94.3	97.3

a 联邦德国的数据参考 1948—1983 年。

b 数据受到显著影响，包括波罗的海国家和独联体 1993 和 2003 年的相互贸易。

c 自 1998 年，统计数据均来自南非，而不再是南部非洲关税同盟。

d 数据参考 EEC（6）1963 年、EC（9）1973 年、EC（10）1983 年、EU（12）1993 年、EU（25）2003 年和 EU（28）2013 年。

e 其成员以所提年份为准。

注：1973 年、1983 年和 1993—2003 年的出口份额受到石油价格的影响。

表 20

1948，1953，1963，1973，1983，1993，2003 和 2014 年

世界货物进口（按地区和国家）

单位：十亿美元，%

	1948 年	1953 年	1963 年	1973 年	1983 年	1993 年	2003 年	2014 年
				总额				
世界	62	85	164	594	1 883	3 805	7 696	18 641
				份额				
世界	100.0	100.0	100.0	100.0	100.0	100.0	100.0	100.0
北美洲	**18.5**	**20.5**	**16.1**	**17.2**	**18.5**	**21.3**	**22.4**	**17.7**
美国	13.0	13.9	11.4	12.3	14.3	15.9	16.9	12.9
加拿大	4.4	5.5	3.9	4.2	3.4	3.7	3.2	2.5
墨西哥	1.0	0.9	0.8	0.6	0.7	1.8	2.3	2.2
中、南美洲	**10.4**	**8.3**	**6.0**	**4.4**	**3.9**	**3.3**	**2.5**	**4.0**
巴西	1.8	1.6	0.9	1.2	0.9	0.7	0.7	1.3
智利	0.4	0.4	0.4	0.2	0.2	0.3	0.3	0.4
欧洲	**45.3**	**43.7**	**52.0**	**53.3**	**44.1**	**44.5**	**45.0**	**36.4**
德国 a	2.2	4.5	8.0	9.2	8.1	9.0	7.9	6.5
英国	13.4	11.0	8.5	6.5	5.3	5.5	5.2	3.7
法国	5.5	4.9	5.3	6.4	5.6	5.7	5.2	3.6
荷兰	3.4	3.3	4.4	4.8	3.3	3.3	3.4	3.2
独联体 b	—	—	—	—	—	**1.2**	**1.7**	**2.7**
非洲	**8.1**	**7.0**	**5.2**	**3.9**	**4.6**	**2.6**	**2.2**	**3.4**
南非 c	2.5	1.5	1.1	0.9	0.8	0.5	0.5	0.7
中东	**1.8**	**2.1**	**2.3**	**2.7**	**6.2**	**3.3**	**2.8**	**4.2**
亚洲	**13.9**	**15.1**	**14.1**	**14.9**	**18.5**	**23.5**	**23.5**	**31.5**
中国	0.6	1.6	0.9	0.9	1.1	2.7	5.4	10.5
日本	1.1	2.8	4.1	6.5	6.7	6.4	5.0	4.4
印度	2.3	1.4	1.5	0.5	0.7	0.6	0.9	2.5
澳大利亚和新西兰	2.9	2.3	2.2	1.6	1.4	1.5	1.4	1.5
六个东亚贸易方	3.5	3.7	3.2	3.9	6.1	10.2	8.6	9.4
备忘项：								
欧盟 d	—	—	25.5	37.1	31.4	36.2	41.3	32.9
苏联	1.9	3.3	4.3	3.6	4.3	—	—	—
GATT/WTO 成员 e	58.6	66.9	75.3	85.5	79.7	89.3	96.0	97.7

a 联邦德国的数据参考 1948—1983 年。

b 数据受到显著影响，包括波罗的海国家和独联体 1993 和 2003 年的相互贸易。

c 自 1998 年，统计数据均来自南非，而不再是南部非洲关税同盟。

d 数据参考 EEC（6）1963 年、EC（9）1973 年、EC（10）1983 年、EU（12）1993 年、EU（25）2003 年和 EU（28）2013 年。

e 其成员以所提年份为准。

注：1973 年、1983 年和 1993—2003 年的出口份额受到石油价格的影响。

表 21

2014 年世界货物贸易的主要进出口方

单位：十亿美元，%

排名	出口方	总额	份额	年度变化百分比	排名	进口方	总额	份额	年度变化百分比
1	中国	2 342	12.3	6	1	美国	2 413	12.6	4
2	美国	1 621	8.5	3	2	中国	1 959	10.3	0
3	德国	1 508	7.9	4	3	德国	1 216	6.4	2
4	日本	684	3.6	−4	4	日本	822	4.3	−1
5	荷兰	672	3.5	0	5	英国	684	3.6	4
6	法国	583	3.1	0	6	法国	678	3.5	−1
7	韩国	573	3.0	2	7	中国香港	601	3.1	−3
						留用进口	151	0.8	6
8	意大利	529	2.8	2	8	荷兰	588	3.1	0
9	中国香港	524	2.8	−2	9	韩国	526	2.8	2
	内部出口	16	0.1	−20					
	转口	508	2.7	−1					
10	英国	506	2.7	−7	10	加拿大 a	475	2.5	0
11	俄罗斯	498	2.6	−5	11	意大利	472	2.5	−2
12	加拿大	475	2.5	4	12	印度	463	2.4	−1
13	比利时	471	2.5	1	13	比利时	452	2.4	0
14	新加坡	410	2.2	0	14	墨西哥	412	2.2	5
	内部出口	216	1.1	−1					
	转口	194	1.0	1					
15	墨西哥	398	2.1	5	15	新加坡	366	1.9	−2
						留用进口	173	0.9	−5
16	阿联酋 b	360	1.9	−5	16	西班牙	358	1.9	5
17	沙特阿拉伯	354	1.9	−6	17	俄罗斯 a	308	1.6	−10
18	西班牙	325	1.7	2	18	瑞士	276	1.4	−14
19	印度	322	1.7	2	19	中国台北	274	1.4	2
20	中国台北	314	1.7	3	20	阿联酋 b	262	1.4	4
21	瑞士	311	1.6	−13	21	土耳其	242	1.3	−4
22	澳大利亚	241	1.3	−5	22	巴西	239	1.3	−5
23	马来西亚	234	1.2	3	23	澳大利亚	237	1.2	−2
24	泰国	228	1.2	0	24	泰国	228	1.2	−9
25	巴西	225	1.2	−7	25	波兰	220	1.2	6
26	波兰	217	1.1	6	26	马来西亚	209	1.1	1
27	奥地利	178	0.9	2	27	奥地利	182	1.0	−1
28	印度尼西亚	176	0.9	−3	28	印度尼西亚	178	0.9	−5
29	捷克	174	0.9	7	29	沙特阿拉伯	163	0.9	−3
30	瑞典	164	0.9	−2	30	瑞典	163	0.9	1
31	土耳其	158	0.8	4	31	捷克	152	0.8	6
32	越南	150	0.8	14	32	越南	149	0.8	13
33	挪威	144	0.8	−7	33	南非	122	0.6	−3
34	卡塔尔	132	0.7	−4	34	匈牙利	105	0.5	5
35	爱尔兰	118	0.6	3	35	丹麦	99	0.5	3
36	丹麦	111	0.6	1	36	挪威	89	0.5	−1
37	匈牙利	111	0.6	3	37	斯洛伐克	82	0.4	1

续 表

排名	出口方	总额	份额	年度变化百分比	排名	进口方	总额	份额	年度变化百分比
38	科威特	104	0.5	−9	38	葡萄牙	78	0.4	3
39	尼日利亚 b	97	0.5	−7	39	罗马尼亚	78	0.4	6
40	南非	91	0.5	−5	40	芬兰	77	0.4	−1
41	伊朗 b	89	0.5	8	41	以色列	75	0.4	1
42	斯洛伐克	87	0.5	1	42	智利	72	0.4	−9
43	伊拉克	85	0.4	−6	43	爱尔兰	71	0.4	8
44	委内瑞拉 b	80	0.4	−10	44	菲律宾	68	0.4	4
45	哈萨克斯坦	78	0.4	−8	45	埃及	67	0.4	16
46	智利	76	0.4	−1	46	阿根廷	65	0.3	−11
47	芬兰	74	0.4	0	47	哥伦比亚	64	0.3	8
48	阿根廷	72	0.4	−12	48	希腊	63	0.3	2
49	罗马尼亚	70	0.4	6	49	尼日利亚 b	60	0.3	7
50	以色列	68	0.4	2	50	伊拉克 b	59	0.3	−3
	以上总计 c	**17608**	**92.7**	—		以上总计 c	**17361**	**90.9**	—
	世界 c	**19002**	**100.0**	**0**		世界 c	**19091**	**100.0**	**0**

a 进口以 f.o.b. 计价。
b 秘书处估计。
c 包括转口以及为转口的进口。

表 22

2014 年世界货物贸易的主要进出口方［不包括 EU（28）内部贸易］ 单位：十亿美元，%

排名	出口方	总额	份额	年度变化百分比	排名	进口方	总额	份额	年度变化百分比
1	中国	2 342	15.5	6	1	美国	2 413	15.9	4
2	EU（28）对外出口	2 262	15.0	−2	2	EU（28）从外进口	2 232	14.7	0
3	美国	1 621	10.7	3	3	中国	1 959	12.9	0
4	日本	684	4.5	−4	4	日本	822	5.4	−1
5	韩国	573	3.8	2	5	中国香港	601	4.0	−3
						留用进口	151	1.0	6
6	中国香港	524	3.5	−2	6	韩国	526	3.5	2
	内部出口	16	0.1	−20					
	转口	508	3.4	−1					
7	俄罗斯	498	3.3	−5	7	加拿大 a	475	3.1	0
8	加拿大	475	3.1	4	8	印度	463	3.0	−1
9	新加坡	410	2.7	0	9	墨西哥	412	2.7	5
	内部出口	216	1.4	−1					
	转口	194	1.3	1					
10	墨西哥	398	2.6	5	10	新加坡	366	2.4	−2
						留用进口	173	1.1	−5
11	墨西哥	360	2.4	−5	11	俄罗斯 a	308	2.0	−10
12	阿联酋 b	354	2.3	−6	12	瑞士	276	1.8	−14
13	沙特阿拉伯	322	2.1	2	13	中国台北	274	1.8	2
14	印度	314	2.1	3	14	阿联酋 b	262	1.7	4

续 表

排名	出口方	总额	份额	年度变化百分比	排名	进口方	总额	份额	年度变化百分比
15	中国台北	311	2.1	－13	15	土耳其	242	1.6	－4
16	澳大利亚	241	1.6	－5	16	巴西	239	1.6	－5
17	马来西亚	234	1.6	3	17	澳大利亚	237	1.6	－2
18	泰国	228	1.5	0	18	泰国	228	1.5	－9
19	巴西	225	1.5	－7	19	马来西亚	209	1.4	1
20	印度尼西亚	176	1.2	－3	20	印度尼西亚	178	1.2	－5
21	土耳其	158	1.0	4	21	沙特阿拉伯	163	1.1	－3
22	越南	150	1.0	14	22	越南	149	1.0	13
23	挪威	144	1.0	－7	23	南非	122	0.8	－3
24	卡塔尔	132	0.9	－4	24	挪威	89	0.6	－1
25	科威特	104	0.7	－9	25	以色列	75	0.5	1
26	尼日利亚 b	97	0.6	－7	26	智利	72	0.5	－9
27	南非	91	0.6	－5	27	菲律宾	68	0.4	4
28	伊朗 b	89	0.6	8	28	埃及	67	0.4	16
29	伊拉克	85	0.6	－6	29	阿根廷	65	0.4	－11
30	委内瑞拉 b	80	0.5	－10	30	哥伦比亚	64	0.4	8
31	哈萨克斯坦	78	0.5	－8	31	尼日利亚 b	60	0.4	7
32	智利	76	0.5	－1	32	伊朗 b	59	0.4	－3
33	阿根廷	72	0.5	－12	33	阿尔及利亚	58	0.4	6
34	以色列	68	0.5	2	34	乌克兰	54	0.4	－29
35	阿尔及利亚	63	0.4	－3	35	伊朗 b	51	0.3	4
36	安哥拉	62	0.4	－9	36	巴基斯坦	48	0.3	7
37	菲律宾	62	0.4	10	37	摩洛哥	46	0.3	1
38	哥伦比亚	55	0.4	－7	38	委内瑞拉 b	44	0.3	－19
39	乌克兰	54	0.4	－16	39	新西兰	43	0.3	7
40	阿曼	53	0.4	－6	40	秘鲁	42	0.3	－2
41	新西兰	42	0.3	6	41	孟加拉国	42	0.3	14
42	秘鲁	39	0.3	－7	42	哈萨克斯坦	41	0.3	－16
43	白俄罗斯	36	0.2	－2	43	白俄罗斯	41	0.3	－5
44	孟加拉国	30	0.2	4	44	卡塔尔	35	0.2	－1
45	阿塞拜疆	28	0.2	－11	45	科威特	31	0.2	7
46	埃及	27	0.2	－5	46	阿曼	30	0.2	－15
47	厄瓜多尔	26	0.2	4	47	安哥拉 a	28	0.2	8
48	巴基斯坦	25	0.2	－2	48	厄瓜多尔	28	0.2	2
49	摩洛哥	24	0.2	8	49	突尼斯	25	0.2	2
50	利比亚 b	21	0.1	－52	50	约旦	23	0.2	5
	以上总计 c	**14 622**	**96.8**	**—**		**以上总计 c**	**14 487**	**95.4**	**—**
	世界［除 EU（27）］c	**15 102**	**100.0**	**－1**		**世界［除 EU（27）］c**	**15 191**	**100.0**	**0**

a 进口以 f. o. b. 计价。

b 秘书处估计。

c 包括转口以及为转口的进口。

表 23

2014 年世界商业服务贸易的主要进出口方

单位：十亿美元，%

排名	出口方	总额	份额	年度变化百分比	排名	进口方	总额	份额	年度变化百分比
1	美国	688	13.9	4	1	美国	452	9.4	3
2	英国	337	6.8	8	2	中国	382	8.0	15
3	法国	267	5.4	5	3	德国	326	6.8	1
4	德国	266	5.4	4	4	法国	248	5.2	8
5	中国	232	4.7	12	5	英国	197	4.1	4
6	荷兰	187	3.8	5	6	日本	190	4.0	12
7	日本	158	3.2	19	7	荷兰	156	3.3	3
8	印度	156	3.2	5	8	印度	147	3.1	17
9	新加坡	140	2.8	2	9	爱尔兰	142	3.0	16
10	西班牙	134	2.7	4	10	新加坡	141	3.0	0
11	爱尔兰	133	2.7	9	11	俄罗斯	119	2.5	−5
12	比利时	122	2.5	9	12	比利时	115	2.4	11
13	意大利	116	2.3	4	13	韩国	114	2.4	4
14	瑞士	113	2.3	2	14	意大利	113	2.4	5
15	中国香港	106	2.1	1	15	加拿大	106	2.2	−5
16	韩国	106	2.1	3	16	瑞士	93	1.9	1
17	卢森堡	98	2.0	12	17	巴西	86	1.8	3
18	加拿大	85	1.7	−4	18	中国香港	76	1.6	1
19	瑞典	77	1.6	3	19	阿联酋	70	1.5	6
20	丹麦	72	1.5	3	20	西班牙	70	1.5	8
21	奥地利	66	1.3	5	21	卢森堡	67	1.4	13
22	俄罗斯	65	1.3	−6	22	瑞典	67	1.4	8
23	中国台北	57	1.2	12	23	丹麦	64	1.3	1
24	泰国	55	1.1	−6	24	澳大利亚	62	1.3	−7
25	澳大利亚	53	1.1	1	25	沙特阿拉伯	59	1.2	14
26	中国澳门	53	1.1	−1	26	挪威	56	1.2	1
27	土耳其	50	1.0	7	27	奥地利	53	1.1	7
28	挪威	49	1.0	2	28	泰国	53	1.1	−3
29	波兰	48	1.0	7	29	中国台北	45	0.9	8
30	希腊	41	0.8	11	30	马来西亚	45	0.9	1
31	马来西亚	39	0.8	−1	31	波兰	36	0.7	5
32	巴西	39	0.8	5	32	印度尼西亚	33	0.7	−4
33	以色列	35	0.7	3	33	墨西哥	32	0.7	8
34	葡萄牙	30	0.6	4	34	卡塔尔	30	0.6	21
35	芬兰	26	0.5	−7	35	芬兰	28	0.6	−6
36	捷克	26	0.5	5	36	土耳其	23	0.5	2
37	菲律宾	25	0.5	6	37	捷克	23	0.5	10
38	匈牙利	24	0.5	8	38	尼日利亚	22	0.5	9
39	印度尼西亚	23	0.5	3	39	科威特	22	0.5	12
40	墨西哥	21	0.4	5	40	以色列	22	0.5	8
	以上总计	**4 420**	**89.5**	**—**		**以上总计**	**4 185**	**87.5**	**—**
	世界	**4 940**	**100.0**	**5**		**世界**	**4 780**	**100.0**	**5**

表24

2014年世界商业服务贸易的主要进出口方［不包括EU（28）内部贸易］ 单位：十亿美元，%

排名	出口方	总额	份额	年度变化百分比	排名	进口方	总额	份额	年度变化百分比
1	欧盟（28）对外出口	985	26.2	6	1	欧盟（28）从外出口	744	20.1	7
2	美国	688	18.3	4	2	美国	452	12.2	3
3	中国	232	6.2	12	3	中国	382	10.3	15
4	印度	158	4.2	19	4	日本	190	5.1	12
5	日本	156	4.1	5	5	印度	147	4.0	17
6	新加坡	140	3.7	2	6	新加坡	141	3.8	0
7	瑞士	113	3.0	2	7	俄罗斯	119	3.2	−5
8	中国香港	106	2.8	1	8	韩国	114	3.1	4
9	韩国	106	2.8	3	9	加拿大	106	2.9	−5
10	加拿大	85	2.3	−4	10	瑞士	93	2.5	1
11	俄罗斯	65	1.7	−6	11	巴西	86	2.3	3
12	中国台北	57	1.5	12	12	中国香港	76	2.0	1
13	泰国	55	1.5	−6	13	阿联酋	70	1.9	6
14	澳大利亚	53	1.4	1	14	澳大利亚	62	1.7	−7
15	中国澳门	53	1.4	−1	15	沙特阿拉伯	59	1.6	14
16	土耳其	50	1.3	7	16	挪威	56	1.5	1
17	挪威	49	1.3	2	17	泰国	53	1.4	−3
18	马来西亚	39	1.0	−1	18	中国台北	45	1.2	8
19	巴西	39	1.0	5	19	马来西亚	45	1.2	1
20	以色列	35	0.9	3	20	印度尼西亚	33	0.9	−4
21	菲律宾	25	0.7	6	21	墨西哥	32	0.9	8
22	印度尼西亚	23	0.6	3	22	卡塔尔	30	0.8	21
23	墨西哥	21	0.6	5	23	土耳其	23	0.6	2
24	埃及	20	0.5	13	24	尼日利亚	22	0.6	9
25	阿联酋	20	0.5	14	25	科威特	22	0.6	12
26	南非	16	0.4	0	26	以色列	22	0.6	8
27	摩洛哥	16	0.4	14	27	安哥拉 a	21	0.6	…
28	乌克兰	14	0.4	−34	28	菲律宾	20	0.5	23
29	新西兰	14	0.4	8	29	埃及	17	0.5	13
30	阿根廷	14	0.4	−6	30	南非	17	0.4	−6
31	黎巴嫩	14	0.4	−8	31	委内瑞拉	17	0.4	−13
32	卡塔尔	13	0.3	24	32	阿根廷	16	0.4	−10
33	古巴	12	0.3	−5	33	伊拉克 a	15	0.4	…
34	沙特阿拉伯	12	0.3	3	34	智利	15	0.4	−7
35	智利	11	0.3	−12	35	伊朗	14	0.4	12
36	越南	11	0.3	2	36	越南	14	0.4	5
37	巴拿马	11	0.3	10	37	哥伦比亚	13	0.4	6
38	伊朗	9	0.2	35	38	新西兰	13	0.3	4
39	白俄罗斯	8	0.2	4	39	黎巴嫩	13	0.3	−2
40	哥伦比亚	7	0.2	1	40	哈萨克斯坦	13	0.3	5
	以上总计	**3 555**	**94.5**	**—**		**以上总计**	**3 440**	**92.9**	**—**
	世界［除EU（28）］	**3 760**	**100.0**	**5**		**世界［除EU（28）］**	**3 705**	**100.0**	**6**

a 秘书处估计。

表 25

2004—2014 年美国的货物贸易（按地区和国家）

单位：十亿美元

	2004	2005	2006	2007	2008	2009	2010	2011	2012	2013	2014
出口											
世界	**814.9**	**901.1**	**1 026.0**	**1 148.2**	**1 287.4**	**1 056.0**	**1 278.5**	**1 482.5**	**1 545.7**	**1 579.6**	**1 620.5**
北美洲	301.0	332.6	364.9	385.4	413.2	334.3	413.5	480.2	509.1	527.7	553.3
加拿大	189.1	211.4	230.2	248.4	260.9	204.7	249.2	281.2	292.6	300.7	312.4
墨西哥	110.7	120.2	133.7	135.9	151.2	128.9	163.6	198.3	215.8	226.2	240.2
中、南美洲	60.7	71.5	87.3	105.4	135.0	108.0	137.1	166.5	180.0	181.2	181.0
巴西	13.9	15.4	18.9	24.2	32.3	26.1	35.4	43.0	43.8	44.1	42.4
其他中、南美洲国家	46.8	56.1	68.4	81.2	102.7	81.9	101.6	123.5	136.3	137.0	138.5
欧洲	187.0	204.0	235.8	272.5	311.1	249.9	276.3	316.5	313.8	310.0	317.6
欧盟（28）	171.9	186.0	212.7	244.2	271.8	220.6	239.6	269.6	265.7	262.3	276.2
欧洲其他地区	15.0	17.9	23.1	28.3	39.3	29.3	36.7	46.9	48.1	47.7	41.4
独联体	4.8	5.9	7.1	10.5	13.8	8.1	9.2	12.9	15.3	16.2	15.5
俄罗斯	3.0	4.0	4.7	7.3	9.3	5.3	6.0	8.3	10.7	11.2	10.8
其他独联体国家	1.8	1.9	2.4	3.2	4.5	2.8	3.2	4.6	4.6	5.1	4.8
非洲	13.4	15.5	18.8	24.1	28.8	24.7	28.7	33.2	33.1	35.8	38.4
南非	3.2	3.9	4.5	5.5	6.5	4.5	5.6	7.3	7.6	7.3	6.4
非洲其他地区	10.2	11.6	14.4	18.5	22.3	20.2	23.1	26.0	25.6	28.5	32.0
中东	23.5	31.5	37.2	45.1	55.0	44.8	48.7	58.5	69.6	73.3	73.7
亚洲	224.1	239.5	274.2	304.4	329.4	285.4	364.0	412.8	422.4	432.3	438.7
中国	34.4	41.2	53.7	62.9	69.7	69.5	91.9	104.1	110.5	121.8	123.7
日本	53.6	54.7	58.5	61.2	65.1	51.1	60.5	65.8	70.0	65.3	66.8
六个东亚贸易方	100.2	103.7	116.8	125.8	131.0	107.7	143.5	162.3	158.3	165.1	167.1
亚洲其他地区	35.9	40.0	45.3	54.6	63.6	57.1	68.1	80.6	83.6	80.2	81.1
进口											
世界	**1 525.7**	**1 732.7**	**1 918.1**	**2 020.4**	**2 169.5**	**1 605.3**	**1 969.2**	**2 265.9**	**2 336.5**	**2 329.1**	**2 412.5**
北美洲	417.7	464.6	507.9	531.6	559.0	407.1	512.2	584.5	607.6	619.8	649.2
加拿大	259.7	291.9	307.7	317.5	339.1	227.6	276.5	313.7	323.0	331.0	346.8
墨西哥	157.9	172.5	200.4	213.3	218.6	178.8	232.3	265.3	280.0	283.0	296.9
中、南美洲	105.2	129.9	140.4	141.8	167.4	113.5	136.4	178.5	177.3	163.9	155.9
巴西	22.7	26.2	28.0	27.2	32.1	21.1	25.0	32.5	33.2	28.6	31.4
其他中、南美洲国家	82.5	103.7	112.4	114.6	135.2	92.4	111.4	146.0	144.1	135.2	124.5
欧洲	317.5	346.8	369.9	393.5	409.6	314.5	359.2	415.5	429.8	439.0	472.9
欧盟（28）	292.7	320.1	341.5	365.2	378.2	288.0	327.4	376.0	389.5	396.3	426.6
欧洲其他地区	24.8	26.7	28.3	28.2	31.4	26.6	31.8	39.5	40.3	42.7	46.2
独联体	14.9	19.8	25.3	26.5	38.5	24.1	32.3	42.0	34.9	31.9	28.7
俄罗斯	12.6	16.2	20.7	20.2	27.9	19.0	26.5	35.5	30.1	27.7	24.5
其他独联体国家	2.3	3.6	4.6	6.3	10.5	5.1	5.7	6.5	4.8	4.2	4.2
非洲	48.3	67.9	83.8	95.2	117.3	64.6	87.5	94.8	68.5	51.3	35.5
南非	6.2	6.1	7.7	9.3	10.1	6.0	8.3	9.6	8.8	8.6	8.5
非洲其他地区	42.2	61.8	76.1	85.9	107.1	58.7	79.1	85.2	59.7	42.7	27.1
中东	54.2	65.7	74.7	80.3	115.3	61.0	76.9	106.2	119.6	109.5	105.8
亚洲	567.7	638.0	716.0	751.4	762.5	620.4	764.7	841.0	896.0	912.9	960.0
中国	210.5	259.8	305.7	340.3	356.6	309.7	383.1	417.3	444.4	460.0	486.2
日本	133.4	142.0	152.2	149.6	143.6	98.6	123.7	132.4	150.4	142.1	137.4
六个东亚贸易方	157.1	162.3	174.9	173.0	167.0	133.4	160.5	177.2	180.9	183.4	195.6
亚洲其他地区	66.7	73.9	83.2	88.5	95.3	78.7	97.5	114.0	120.3	127.4	140.8

表 26

2010—2014 年欧盟（28）的货物贸易（按地区和国家）

单位：十亿美元

	总额					年度变化百分比				
	2010	2011	2012	2013	2014	2010—2014	2011	2012	2013	2014
出口										
世界	**5 183.9**	**6 092.3**	**5 812.6**	**6 081.4**	**6 162.2**	**4**	**18**	**−5**	**5**	**1**
北美洲	378.6	434.9	447.6	457.4	488.2	7	15	3	2	7
美国	314.3	360.0	373.0	381.2	404.8	7	15	4	2	6
其他北美洲国家	64.3	74.8	74.6	76.3	83.4	7	16	0	2	9
中、南美洲	91.1	109.8	113.5	118.5	109.2	5	20	3	4	−8
巴西	41.0	48.9	49.5	51.5	48.2	4	19	1	4	−6
其他中、南美洲国家	50.2	60.8	64.0	67.0	61.0	5	21	5	5	−9
欧洲	3 705.1	4 333.4	4 020.7	4 210.5	4 293.0	4	17	−7	5	2
欧盟（28）	3 390.0	3 928.8	3 648.7	3 775.0	3 900.1	4	16	−7	3	3
欧洲其他地区	315.1	404.6	372.0	435.5	392.9	6	28	−8	17	−10
独联体	162.7	211.2	220.9	226.0	193.2	4	30	5	2	−15
俄罗斯	113.6	150.2	157.8	157.8	136.4	5	32	5	0	−14
其他独联体国家	49.1	61.0	63.2	68.2	56.8	4	24	4	8	−17
非洲	164.1	187.0	190.5	200.4	200.9	5	14	2	5	0
南非	28.1	35.5	32.1	32.1	30.6	2	26	−10	0	−5
非洲其他地区	136.0	151.5	158.4	168.3	170.3	6	11	5	6	1
中东	139.5	160.4	158.9	177.2	180.0	7	15	−1	11	2
亚洲	477.2	578.6	580.3	603.6	622.6	7	21	0	4	3
中国	149.5	188.9	184.4	195.7	217.6	5	17	5	0	−1
日本	57.4	67.4	70.5	70.8	69.9	5	17	5	0	−1
六个东亚贸易方	152.8	180.5	187.3	197.8	197.2	7	18	4	6	0
亚洲其他地区	267.0	330.8	322.5	335.0	355.5	7	24	−2	4	6
进口										
世界	**5 421.1**	**6 334.6**	**5 956.9**	**6 012.9**	**6 132.5**	**3**	**17**	**−6**	**1**	**2**
北美洲	275.6	331.0	326.1	316.7	328.1	4	20	−1	−3	4
美国	224.5	265.0	263.4	258.8	269.4	5	18	−1	−2	4
其他北美洲国家	51.0	66.0	62.7	57.9	58.7	4	29	−5	−8	1
中、南美洲	109.6	134.7	119.0	107.6	105.2	−1	23	−12	−10	−2
巴西	44.1	54.2	47.8	41.1	40.9	−2	23	−12	−14	−1
其他中、南美洲国家	65.5	80.5	71.2	66.5	64.3	0	23	−12	−7	−3
欧洲	3 663.7	4 254.1	3 967.6	4 085.8	4 217.8	4	16	−7	3	3
欧盟（28）	3 390.0	3 928.8	3 648.7	3 775.0	3 900.1	4	16	−7	3	3
欧洲其他地区	273.8	325.2	318.9	310.8	317.7	4	19	−2	−3	2
独联体	266.5	360.7	352.0	352.1	317.8	4	35	−2	0	−10
俄罗斯	211.2	277.6	274.7	275.3	242.6	4	31	−1	0	−12
其他独联体国家	55.4	83.1	77.2	76.8	75.2	8	50	−7	−1	−2
非洲	179.9	209.7	238.6	222.1	206.2	3	17	14	−7	−7
南非	26.5	29.8	25.6	19.9	24.1	−2	13	−14	−22	21
非洲其他地区	153.4	179.9	213.0	202.2	182.1	4	17	18	−5	−10
中东	95.7	141.0	119.8	108.5	100.5	1	47	−15	−9	−7
亚洲	766.7	843.8	770.1	756.8	797.3	1	10	−9	−2	5
中国	375.4	408.4	374.7	371.4	401.0	2	9	−8	−1	8
日本	89.0	98.0	82.9	75.0	72.1	−5	10	−15	−10	−4
六个东亚贸易方	178.6	179.9	164.5	160.4	168.3	−1	1	−9	−2	5
亚洲其他地区	123.7	157.4	148.1	150.0	155.9	6	27	−6	1	4

表 27

2004—2014 年日本的货物贸易（按地区和国家）

单位：十亿美元

	2004	2005	2006	2007	2008	2009	2010	2011	2012	2013	2014
出口											
世界	**565.7**	**594.9**	**646.7**	**714.3**	**781.4**	**580.7**	**769.8**	**823.2**	**798.6**	**715.1**	**683.8**
北美洲	142.5	151.7	164.7	164.5	159.4	109.9	139.3	146.8	162.8	152.9	148.5
美国	128.7	135.9	145.5	143.7	138.7	95.3	120.2	127.8	142.0	134.2	123.9
其他北美洲国家	13.8	15.8	19.3	20.8	20.7	14.6	19.0	19.0	20.8	18.8	24.6
中、南美洲	8.1	9.4	12.0	15.0	19.1	12.2	17.9	17.8	17.1	15.7	14.6
巴西	2.3	2.7	3.0	4.0	5.9	4.2	6.2	6.2	5.9	5.7	4.7
其他中、南美洲国家	5.8	6.6	9.0	11.0	13.2	7.9	11.7	11.6	11.2	10.0	9.9
欧洲	94.8	93.5	100.7	112.7	119.5	81.5	98.7	109.8	89.7	78.7	77.6
欧盟（28）	89.3	87.9	94.0	105.5	110.5	72.5	87.1	95.9	81.5	71.8	71.0
欧洲其他地区	5.4	5.6	6.6	7.2	9.0	9.1	11.6	13.8	8.2	6.9	6.6
独联体	3.8	5.2	8.3	12.5	19.3	4.1	9.1	13.8	14.6	13.0	11.1
俄罗斯	3.1	4.5	7.1	10.8	16.5	3.3	8.0	11.8	12.6	11.0	9.1
其他独联体国家	0.7	0.7	1.2	1.7	2.8	0.8	1.1	1.9	2.0	2.1	2.0
非洲	6.6	7.0	8.7	10.5	12.1	8.0	10.1	9.9	10.6	9.6	9.3
南非	2.9	3.3	4.1	4.6	4.6	2.6	3.8	4.3	4.1	3.5	3.2
非洲其他地区	3.7	3.7	4.6	5.9	7.5	5.4	6.2	5.6	6.6	6.2	6.1
中东	14.5	16.5	19.2	26.2	33.8	21.6	25.3	24.6	28.3	25.4	28.1
亚洲	288.7	303.5	322.2	361.0	406.5	329.5	452.5	482.9	459.6	408.8	386.8
中国	92.9	98.4	111.5	129.7	144.6	125.9	171.3	183.6	144.2	129.4	125.0
六个东亚贸易方	153.6	161.2	167.0	179.8	198.7	155.2	212.5	222.1	233.3	207.7	193.2
亚洲其他地区	42.3	43.8	43.6	51.5	63.2	48.4	68.7	77.2	82.0	71.7	68.6
进口											
世界	**454.5**	**515.9**	**579.1**	**622.2**	**762.5**	**552.0**	**694.1**	**855.4**	**885.8**	**833.2**	**822.3**
北美洲	74.2	76.9	80.4	84.1	95.5	72.6	83.4	93.2	95.3	88.2	90.2
美国	63.6	65.4	68.0	70.9	78.9	60.6	69.1	76.3	78.2	72.0	74.4
其他北美洲国家	10.6	11.5	12.4	13.1	16.6	12.0	14.4	16.9	17.1	16.2	15.9
中、南美洲	10.4	12.1	16.2	19.6	22.5	15.8	22.8	29.0	28.8	27.6	24.2
巴西	3.7	4.4	5.1	6.0	9.1	6.4	9.9	12.7	12.0	11.1	9.7
其他中、南美洲国家	6.8	7.7	11.1	13.6	13.4	9.4	13.0	16.3	16.8	16.4	14.5
欧洲	64.5	65.6	66.8	72.5	79.7	67.8	75.9	91.6	94.8	88.7	89.6
欧盟（28）	58.0	58.9	59.9	65.0	70.5	59.3	66.5	80.6	83.3	78.5	78.7
欧洲其他地区	6.5	6.7	6.9	7.5	9.2	8.6	9.4	11.0	11.5	10.3	10.9
独联体	6.2	6.8	7.4	11.5	14.9	9.6	17.2	20.1	22.1	24.9	26.7
俄罗斯	5.7	6.2	6.7	10.6	13.4	8.8	16.1	19.0	20.8	23.7	25.4
其他独联体国家	0.5	0.6	0.7	1.0	1.5	0.8	1.1	1.0	1.3	1.3	1.3
非洲	8.7	9.8	13.5	15.3	20.9	9.1	11.7	17.2	21.3	19.1	19.0
南非	4.6	5.5	6.6	7.7	9.0	5.0	7.2	8.5	6.4	6.8	7.8
非洲其他地区	4.1	4.3	6.9	7.6	11.9	4.1	4.5	8.7	14.8	12.4	11.2
中东	62.7	87.4	109.1	114.0	167.6	92.6	118.6	161.2	169.7	160.6	149.7
亚洲	227.8	257.2	283.3	303.2	361.3	284.3	362.7	443.1	453.6	423.8	422.8
中国	94.3	108.4	118.0	127.5	143.2	122.6	153.2	183.9	188.4	181.0	181.7
六个东亚贸易方	74.6	81.3	88.9	91.2	104.7	80.3	105.1	128.3	131.4	120.4	120.4
亚洲其他地区	59.0	67.5	76.3	84.5	113.4	81.5	104.5	130.9	133.8	122.5	120.6

表 28

2004—2014 年中国的货物贸易（按地区和国家）

单位：十亿美元

	2004	2005	2006	2007	2008	2009	2010	2011	2012	2013	2014
出口											
世界	**593.3**	**762.0**	**969.0**	**1 220.5**	**1 430.7**	**1 201.6**	**1 577.8**	**1 898.4**	**2 048.7**	**2 209.0**	**2 342.3**
北美洲	176.2	226.0	284.2	326.2	349.7	304.8	394.5	458.1	504.9	537.9	568.5
美国	159.7	204.9	255.0	289.4	308.0	269.3	346.7	398.9	345.0	358.2	389.7
其他北美洲国家	16.4	21.1	29.2	36.9	41.7	35.5	47.9	59.3	159.9	179.7	178.8
中、南美洲	13.0	17.7	26.6	39.5	56.9	42.9	69.9	94.0	104.4	103.0	101.9
巴西	3.7	4.8	7.4	11.4	18.8	14.1	24.5	31.8	33.4	35.9	34.9
其他中、南美洲国家	9.3	12.9	19.3	28.1	38.0	28.8	45.4	62.2	71.0	67.1	67.0
欧洲	140.5	186.8	244.3	317.8	371.5	301.5	396.5	460.0	436.1	447.6	479.0
欧盟（28）	134.8	178.9	232.2	300.8	353.4	287.0	377.9	435.8	412.7	422.4	452.4
欧洲其他地区	5.7	7.9	12.0	17.0	18.1	14.6	18.6	24.1	23.4	25.2	26.6
独联体	13.8	21.4	28.0	48.1	64.7	39.0	53.8	67.2	75.7	83.5	85.7
俄罗斯	9.1	13.2	15.8	28.5	33.1	17.5	29.6	38.9	44.1	49.6	53.7
其他独联体国家	4.7	8.2	12.2	19.6	31.6	21.5	24.2	28.3	31.6	33.9	32.1
非洲	13.6	18.5	26.2	36.8	50.5	46.3	56.1	69.1	82.8	91.2	105.0
南非	3.0	3.8	5.8	7.4	8.6	7.4	10.8	13.4	15.3	16.8	15.7
非洲其他地区	10.7	14.7	20.4	29.3	41.9	39.0	45.3	55.8	67.5	74.3	89.3
中东	16.9	22.2	29.6	44.3	58.8	51.1	62.6	79.7	85.6	97.0	117.6
亚洲	219.1	269.2	329.5	406.6	477.4	413.4	537.0	663.3	754.3	845.9	882.7
日本	89.6	102.4	112.0	124.9	138.7	118.1	148.4	182.8	189.5	193.1	188.4
六个东亚贸易方	86.5	111.7	145.8	181.1	212.0	175.2	223.3	270.9	335.4	394.1	400.3
亚洲其他地区	43.0	55.2	71.6	100.6	126.7	120.0	165.3	209.6	229.4	258.7	294.0
进口											
世界	**561.2**	**660.0**	**791.5**	**956.1**	**1 132.6**	**1 005.9**	**1 396.2**	**1 743.5**	**1 818.4**	**1 950.0**	**1 959.4**
北美洲	54.2	58.5	69.6	83.8	97.9	93.7	124.5	154.7	166.1	188.9	196.2
美国	44.8	48.7	59.3	69.6	81.6	77.8	102.7	123.1	133.8	153.4	159.8
其他北美洲国家	9.5	9.7	10.3	14.2	16.4	15.9	21.8	31.5	32.4	35.5	36.4
中、南美洲	19.5	24.4	31.5	47.7	67.7	60.2	84.2	109.3	116.0	116.1	114.9
巴西	8.7	10.0	12.9	18.3	29.9	28.3	38.1	52.4	52.3	54.3	51.7
其他中、南美洲国家	10.9	14.4	18.6	29.4	37.8	32.0	46.1	56.9	63.7	61.8	63.2
欧洲	76.2	79.9	97.2	120.0	144.4	139.8	192.3	245.9	242.2	284.9	292.7
欧盟（28）	70.6	74.1	90.8	111.3	132.9	128.1	168.5	211.2	212.1	219.9	243.5
欧洲其他地区	5.7	5.8	6.4	8.7	11.5	11.7	23.8	34.6	30.1	64.9	49.2
独联体	16.2	20.7	22.8	28.0	33.9	31.0	42.3	65.5	72.8	70.9	67.3
俄罗斯	12.1	15.9	17.6	19.7	23.8	21.3	25.9	40.4	44.1	39.7	41.6
其他独联体国家	4.1	4.8	5.2	8.3	10.1	9.8	16.4	25.2	28.6	31.3	25.7
非洲	15.6	21.1	28.8	36.4	56.0	43.3	67.1	93.2	113.2	117.5	115.7
南非	3.0	3.4	4.1	6.6	9.2	8.7	14.9	32.1	44.7	48.4	44.6
非洲其他地区	12.7	17.6	24.7	29.7	46.7	34.6	52.2	61.1	68.6	69.1	71.1
中东	21.6	31.0	40.8	47.9	79.9	56.2	86.7	134.1	145.2	155.5	161.2
亚洲	357.7	424.3	500.8	592.3	652.7	581.2	797.4	934.7	956.4	1011.6	1 008.4
中国	38.7	55.2	73.3	85.8	92.5	86.4	106.9	122.6	142.9	157.5	144.6
日本	94.3	100.4	115.7	133.9	150.6	130.9	176.7	194.6	177.8	162.2	162.8
六个东亚贸易方	182.5	214.3	246.8	286.5	306.3	272.0	374.7	432.4	444.2	484.4	479.6
亚洲其他地区	42.2	54.4	65.0	86.1	103.3	91.9	139.2	185.1	191.4	207.3	221.3

表 29

2014 年 NAFTA 成员的货物贸易（按产品和原产地/目的地）　　单位：十亿美元，%

目的地	世界					NAFTA					其他原产地/目的地				
	总额	份额		年度变化百分比		总额	份额		年度变化百分比		总额	份额		年度变化百分比	
	2014	2010	2014	2013	2014	2014	2010	2014	2013	2014	2014	2010	2014	2013	2014
出口															
加拿大															
农产品	68	13.5	14.3	4	4	37	9.3	10.0	8	6	31	26.4	29.3	1	1
燃料和矿产品	160	31.4	33.8	2	5	138	34.5	37.5	5	6	22	21.7	20.7	−13	−1
制成品	212	48.0	44.7	−2	2	174	50.8	47.3	−1	3	38	39.3	35.5	−5	2
总出口	475	100.0	100.0	1	4	368	100.0	100.0	2	5	107	100.0	100.0	−5	0
墨西哥															
农产品	26	6.3	6.6	10	5	21	6.0	6.2	12	6	6	7.8	8.6	5	3
燃料和矿产品	53	16.7	13.4	−9	−12	36	15.9	11.1	−10	−14	17	20.6	24.8	−4	−6
制成品	309	74.5	77.8	6	8	266	75.7	80.6	7	10	43	68.5	64.1	−1	−2
总出口	398	100.0	100.0	3	5	330	100.0	100.0	4	6	68	100.0	100.0	−3	−3
美国															
农产品	182	11.2	11.2	2	4	50	9.5	9.1	1	4	132	11.9	12.4	3	4
燃料和矿产品	202	10.1	12.4	4	3	73	9.6	13.3	9	15	128	10.3	12.0	2	−3
制成品	1164	73.8	71.8	2	3	412	77.7	74.5	3	4	752	72.0	70.4	2	3
总出口	1621	100.0	100.0	2	3	553	100.0	100.0	4	5	1 068	100.0	100.0	1	1
NAFTA															
农产品	277	10.9	11.1	3	4	108	8.5	8.6	5	5	169	13.1	13.6	2	3
燃料和矿产品	415	15.3	16.7	1	2	248	18.9	19.8	3	5	167	11.8	13.5	−1	−3
制成品	1 685	68.8	67.6	2	4	852	68.9	68.1	3	5	833	68.8	67.1	1	3
总出口	2 493	100.0	100.0	2	3	1251	100.0	100.0	3	5	1 242	100.0	100.0	1	1
进口															
加拿大															
农产品	41	8.2	8.7	2	4	26	8.9	9.1	4	3	15	7.1	8.1	0	5
燃料和矿产品	62	13.1	13.0	−3	−4	42	8.9	14.4	22	25	20	18.7	10.9	−21	−34
制成品	353	74.7	74.4	0	1	212	78.6	73.4	0	2	142	69.5	75.9	1	0
总出口	475	100.0	100.0	0	0	288	100.0	100.0	3	4	187	100.0	100.0	−4	−5
墨西哥															
农产品	31	7.8	7.5	8	3	24	12.2	11.5	7	4	7	3.3	3.3	11	1
燃料和矿产品	44	10.7	10.6	−3	2	34	14.6	16.2	−2	2	9	6.5	4.6	−7	2
制成品	326	79.5	79.2	4	5	149	72.0	70.3	2	5	177	87.4	88.6	5	6
总出口	412	100.0	100.0	3	5	212	100.0	100.0	1	5	200	100.0	100.0	5	6
美国															
农产品	157	5.9	6.5	3	7	57	8.0	8.8	9	8	100	5.2	5.7	0	7
燃料和矿产品	408	20.7	16.9	−10	−7	172	26.9	26.5	1	1	235	18.6	13.3	−15	−13
制成品	1752	69.5	72.6	2	6	390	59.8	60.1	2	6	1 362	73.0	77.2	2	6
总出口	2413	100.0	100.0	0	4	649	100.0	100.0	2	5	1 763	100.0	100.0	−1	3
NAFTA															
农产品	229	6.5	6.9	4	6	108	9.0	9.4	7	6	122	5.2	5.7	1	6
燃料和矿产品	513	18.4	15.6	−8	−6	248	20.1	21.6	3	5	265	17.5	12.3	−15	−14
制成品	2432	71.5	73.7	2	5	751	66.7	65.3	1	4	1 681	73.9	78.2	2	6
总出口	3 299	100.0	100.0	0	3	1149	100.0	100.0	2	5	2 150	100.0	100.0	−1	3

表 30

2014 年 MERCOSUR 成员的货物贸易（按产品和原产地/目的地）

单位：十亿美元，%

目的地	世界					MERCOSUR					其他原产地/目的地				
	总额	份额		年度变化百分比		总额	份额		年度变化百分比		总额	份额		年度变化百分比	
	2014	2010	2014	2013	2014	2014	2010	2014	2013	2014	2014	2010	2014	2013	2014
出口															
阿根廷															
农产品	40	50.8	55.4	4	−11	5	23.9	26.8	−7	−5	35	60.9	66.1	5	−12
燃料和矿产品	6	12.2	8.0	−23	−10	1	10.6	7.2	−28	−11	4	12.8	8.3	−21	−10
制成品	22	32.2	31.2	4	−15	13	65.4	66.0	12	−17	10	19.8	18.3	−6	−10
总出口	72	100.0	100.0	2	−12	20	100.0	100.0	3	−14	52	100.0	100.0	1	−11
巴西															
农产品	88	34.0	39.0	5	−3	4	12.6	17.3	14	11	84	37.2	41.8	5	−4
燃料和矿产品	55	27.9	24.4	−11	−6	4	9.6	14.3	0	28	51	30.6	25.6	−11	−8
制成品	75	34.9	33.3	4	−12	17	77.7	68.2	6	−25	58	28.4	28.9	3	−7
总出口	225	100.0	100.0	0	−7	25	100.0	100.0	6	−15	200	100.0	100.0	−1	−6
巴拉圭															
农产品	6	61.4	66.4	48	2	1	20.9	29.4	11	11	5	94.4	91.6	58	0
燃料和矿产品	2	31.1	23.8	0	−2	2	68.7	56.5	0	−3	0	0.5	1.7	1	31
制成品	1	7.4	9.4	20	19	1	10.4	14.1	18	20	0	4.9	6.2	22	19
总出口	10	100.0	100.0	30	2	4	100.0	100.0	5	4	6	100.0	100.0	54	1
乌拉圭															
农产品	7	71.8	75.0	6	1	1	47.1	46.7	0	−13	6	85.4	86.2	7	5
燃料和矿产品	0	3.3	1.4	−42	78	0	8.1	3.5	−59	159	0	0.7	0.6	−3	−1
制成品	2	23.7	22.8	5	−1	1	44.7	49.8	8	−6	1	12.0	12.2	1	9
总出口	9	100.0	100.0	4	1	3	100.0	100.0	2	−8	7	100.0	100.0	5	5
MERCOSUR															
农产品	141	32.1	35.6	6	−5	12	17.2	20.8	1	1	129	34.9	38.2	6	−5
燃料和矿产品	138	37.1	34.8	−10	−8	13	21.0	23.0	−9	0	125	40.1	36.8	−10	−9
制成品	104	27.6	26.3	3	−12	32	61.8	56.1	8	−21	72	21.1	21.3	1	−7
总出口	396	100.0	100.0	−1	−8	57	100.0	100.0	3	−13	339	100.0	100.0	−2	−7
进口															
阿根廷															
农产品	2	3.8	3.4	−2	−7	1	4.3	4.5	−7	−14	2	3.5	3.1	1	−4
燃料和矿产品	13	11.2	20.0	20	1	2	11.0	12.3	16	−8	11	11.2	22.3	21	3
制成品	49	84.3	75.5	7	−15	13	84.6	83.1	8	−28	37	84.1	73.1	6	−9
总出口	65	100.0	100.0	8	−11	15	100.0	100.0	8	−25	50	100.0	100.0	8	−6
巴西															
农产品	14	6.0	5.9	8	−5	5	25.6	25.9	−10	−7	9	3.8	4.2	22	−4
燃料和矿产品	54	20.0	22.5	11	−1	2	12.5	10.9	−5	−15	52	20.9	23.5	12	−1
制成品	171	74.0	71.6	6	−6	12	61.9	63.2	7	−11	159	75.3	72.3	6	−5
总出口	239	100.0	100.0	7	−5	19	100.0	100.0	1	−10	220	100.0	100.0	8	−4
巴拉圭															
农产品	1	8.1	9.0	5	5	1	13.7	14.5	5	1	0	3.7	4.8	5	15
燃料和矿产品	2	12.5	16.2	−5	8	1	25.1	24.9	−13	20	1	2.8	9.5	10	−9

续 表

目的地	世界					MERCOSUR					其他原产地/目的地				
	总额	份额		年度变化百分比		总额	份额		年度变化百分比		总额	份额		年度变化百分比	
	2014	2010	2014	2013	2014	2014	2010	2014	2013	2014	2014	2010	2014	2013	2014
制成品	9	79.3	74.6	8	−2	3	61.1	60.5	11	−1	6	93.4	85.5	6	−3
总出口	12	100.0	100.0	5	0	5	100.0	100.0	4	4	7	100.0	100.0	6	−3
乌拉圭															
农产品	1	12.0	12.9	19	−6	1	17.4	25.0	14	−1	0	7.8	6.3	30	−15
燃料和矿产品	2	20.7	17.0	−31	−13	1	22.8	20.2	−50	8	1	19.1	15.3	−15	−24
制成品	8	67.1	70.1	10	3	2	59.7	54.7	0	−6	6	72.7	78.4	16	7
总出口	11	100.0	100.0	0	−1	4	100.0	100.0	−13	−2	7	100.0	100.0	9	−1
MERCOSUR															
农产品	27	7.2	7.4	6	−9	11	18.1	21.1	−2	−10	17	4.9	5.2	12	−9
燃料和矿产品	72	15.9	19.2	9	−1	6	12.6	12.1	−11	−4	66	16.6	20.4	12	−1
制成品	269	76.7	72.2	3	−9	33	69.3	64.9	4	−18	236	78.3	73.3	2	−7
总出口	372	100.0	100.0	4	−7	51	100.0	100.0	2	−15	322	100.0	100.0	5	−6

表 31

2014 年安第斯共同体成员的货物贸易（按产品和原产地/目的地）

单位：十亿美元，%

目的地	世界					安第斯共同体					其他原产地/目的地				
	总额	份额		年度变化百分比		总额	份额		年度变化百分比		总额	份额		年度变化百分比	
	2014	2010	2014	2013	2014	2014	2010	2014	2013	2014	2014	2010	2014	2013	2014
出口															
玻利维亚															
农产品	2	16.1	14.7	25	−6	1	66.7	88.6	29	−3	1	10.6	6.4	19	−11
燃料和矿产品	9	76.2	71.5	8	0	0	28.3	8.2	−28	−50	9	81.4	78.7	9	1
制成品	0	6.3	3.2	−18	−12	0	5.1	3.2	14	−6	0	6.4	3.2	−21	−13
总出口	12	100.0	100.0	4	5	1	100.0	100.0	15	−10	11	100.0	100.0	2	7
哥伦比亚															
农产品	7	14.5	13.4	1	10	0	9.2	11.5	−11	10	7	14.9	13.5	2	10
燃料和矿产品	36	57.7	66.5	−1	−9	0	17.7	9.6	−33	−15	36	61.0	70.1	0	−9
制成品	9	22.0	16.8	0	−7	2	73.1	76.0	1	−9	7	17.7	0	13.1	−6
总出口	55	100.0	100.0	−2	−7	3	100.0	100.0	−6	−5	52	100.0	100.0	−2	−7
厄瓜多尔															
农产品	10	33.8	38.0	13	13	0	14.6	16.7	−3	−9	9	36.4	40.3	14	15
燃料和矿产品	14	55.9	53.1	3	−5	1	51.5	52.0	−10	−15	12	56.5	53.2	4	−3
制成品	1	9.5	5.6	−21	−4	1	33.8	31.3	−7	−1	1	6.1	2.8	−32	−7
总出口	26	100.0	100.0	5	4	3	100.0	100.0	−8	−10	23	100.0	100.0	6	5
秘鲁															
农产品	8	16.7	20.9	−7	15	1	16.8	18.8	−15	17	8	16.7	21.1	−6	15
燃料和矿产品	20	50.8	50.3	−7	−9	1	32.7	30.0	8	48	19	51.8	51.8	−7	−11
制成品	5	10.7	12.2	−7	−2	1	50.5	51.2	0	2	3	8.4	9.3	−9	−4
总出口	39	100.0	100.0	−10	−7	3	100.0	100.0	−1	15	37	100.0	100.0	−11	−9
安第斯共同体															

续 表

目的地	世界					安第斯共同体					其他原产地/目的地				
	总额	份额		年度变化百分比		总额	份额		年度变化百分比		总额	份额		年度变化百分比	
	2014	2010	2014	2013	2014	2014	2010	2014	2013	2014	2014	2010	2014	2013	2014
农产品	27	18.8	20.5	4	11	2	17.2	24.7	5	1	25	18.9	20.2	4	12
燃料和矿产品	79	56.1	59.6	−1	−7	3	31.6	26.2	−13	−4	76	58.2	62.2	−1	−7
制成品	16	14.7	12.0	−5	−6	5	51.1	48.1	−1	−5	11	11.6	9.1	−6	−6
总出口	132	100.0	100.0	−3	−4	10	100.0	100.0	−3	−2	122	100.0	100.0	−3	−4
进口															
玻利维亚															
农产品	1	8.4	8.1	11	14	0	12.3	13.6	9	6	1	7.9	7.6	11	16
燃料和矿产品	1	13.1	12.5	1	−4	0	6.5	10.8	36	48	1	13.7	12.6	−1	−7
制成品	8	78.1	78.9	11	14	1	80.8	75.5	6	3	8	77.8	79.2	11	16
总出口	10	100.0	100.0	9	12	1	100.0	100.0	9	6	10	100.0	100.0	9	12
哥伦比亚															
农产品	6	11.0	10.2	−3	2	1	23.4	27.7	20	−1	5	10.1	9.1	−6	3
燃料和矿产品	9	7.1	13.9	5	21	1	10.5	15.1	−9	124	8	6.9	13.8	5	17
制成品	48	80.4	75.0	7	2	0	66.0	57.0	−19	11	46	81.5	76.1	1	7
总出口	64	100.0	100.0	1	8	4	100.0	100.0	−9	16	60	100.0	100.0	1	7
厄瓜多尔															
农产品	2	9.4	8.5	0	8	1	14.8	20.9	−2	12	2	8.4	6.9	1	6
燃料和矿产品	7	20.2	25.5	12	6	0	19.1	9.6	53	−31	7	20.4	27.5	10	9
制成品	18	67.7	64.8	6	−1	2	66.1	69.4	−5	−5	16	68.0	64.2	8	0
总出口	28	100.0	100.0	7	2	3	100.0	100.0	0	−6	25	100.0	100.0	8	3
秘鲁															
农产品	5	11.9	11.7	0	3	1	14.9	23.1	3	4	4	11.6	10.6	0	3
燃料和矿产品	7	15.4	15.4	10	−9	2	50.6	47.1	−9	−10	5	11.4	12.4	18	−8
制成品	31	72.6	72.5	2	−2	1	34.5	29.9	4	−14	30	76.9	76.6	2	−2
总出口	42	100.0	100.0	3	−2	4	100.0	100.0	−3	−8	39	100.0	100.0	3	−2
安第斯共同体															
农产品	15	10.8	10.2	−1	4	3	17.2	23.3	8	4	12	10.1	9.0	−2	4
燃料和矿产品	24	12.8	16.4	8	6	3	26.0	23.4	−1	1	21	11.4	15.8	10	6
制成品	105	75.1	72.6	2	3	6	56.7	53.2	−8	−1	99	77.1	74.3	3	4
总出口	145	100.0	100.0	3	4	11	100.0	100.0	−3	0	133	100.0	100.0	3	4

表 32

2014 年 ASEAN 成员的货物贸易（按产品和原产地/目的地） 单位：十亿美元，%

目的地	世界					ASEAN					其他原产地/目的地				
	总额	份额		年度变化百分比		总额	份额		年度变化百分比		总额	份额		年度变化百分比	
	2014	2010	2014	2013	2014	2014	2010	2014	2013	2014	2014	2010	2014	2013	2014
出口															
印度尼西亚															
农产品	44	22.8	24.9	−5	3	6	18.8	16.1	−21	9	37	23.9	27.4	−2	2
燃料和矿产品	60	39.4	33.9	−7	−15	17	37.0	41.5	−2	−3	43	40.1	31.7	−8	−19
制成品	70	37.0	39.6	0	5	16	43.4	40.1	1	−4	54	35.3	39.4	0	8
总出口	176	100.0	100.0	−4	−3	40	100.0	100.0	−3	−2	136	100.0	100.0	−4	−4
马来西亚															
农产品	30	14.5	12.9	−11	0	7	10.2	10.5	−10	8	23	16.0	13.8	−12	−2
燃料和矿产品	58	17.8	25.0	13	0	18	20.5	28.3	16	4	40	16.9	23.7	11	−1
制成品	144	67.0	61.6	−1	4	40	68.4	60.8	3	1	104	66.5	61.9	−3	6
总出口	234	100.0	100.0	0	3	65	100.0	100.0	5	2	169	100.0	100.0	−1	3

续 表

目的地	世界					ASEAN					其他原产地/目的地				
	总额	份额		年度变化百分比		总额	份额		年度变化百分比		总额	份额		年度变化百分比	
	2014	2010	2014	2013	2014	2014	2010	2014	2013	2014	2014	2010	2014	2013	2014
菲律宾															
农产品	7	8.0	11.2	33	3	1	4.7	8.8	17	−11	6	8.9	11.6	36	5
燃料和矿产品	6	6.2	9.5	50	1	1	7.8	12.4	44	4	5	5.8	9.0	52	0
制成品	49	85.1	78.3	3	11	7	87.4	78.8	−15	3	41	84.4	78.2	7	13
总出口	62	100.0	100.0	9	10	9	100.0	100.0	−8	2	53	100.0	100.0	13	11
新加坡															
农产品	12	2.2	2.9	10	9	5	3.0	4.0	10	7	7	1.9	2.4	11	11
燃料和矿产品	73	17.2	17.8	−4	−4	40	25.9	31.4	−4	1	33	13.4	11.7	−4	−9
制成品	291	72.4	70.9	2	1	79	67.2	62.1	1	−3	211	74.7	74.9	2	2
总出口	410	100.0	100.0	0	0	128	100.0	100.0	−1	−1	282	100.0	100.0	1	0
泰国															
农产品	40	18.0	17.5	−4	−1	8	15.6	14.1	−5	3	31	18.7	18.7	−4	−3
燃料和矿产品	15	6.2	6.6	−2	−13	9	15.6	15.8	−2	−8	6	3.5	3.3	−2	−20
制成品	170	72.5	74.7	3	1	41	68.7	68.5	6	3	129	73.6	76.9	2	1
总出口	228	100.0	100.0	0	0	59	100.0	100.0	5	0	168	100.0	100.0	−2	−1
ASEAN															
农产品	164	12.6	12.6	−3	3	32	9.8	9.8	−8	6	131	13.5	13.6	−1	2
燃料和矿产品	239	18.6	18.4	−1	−6	96	25.4	29.1	2	0	142	16.3	14.8	−3	−10
制成品	850	65.2	65.7	4	4	197	63.0	59.5	3	−1	654	65.9	67.8	4	6
总出口	1 295	100.0	100.0	2	2	331	100.0	100.0	2	965	0.0	100.0	100.0	1	2
进口															
印度尼西亚															
农产品	22	11.5	12.5	3	3	3	6.2	5.6	−28	4	19	13.7	15.2	10	3
燃料和矿产品	50	23.8	27.9	5	−3	22	40.5	43.1	7	−11	28	17.0	21.9	4	3
制成品	105	63.2	58.7	−6	−6	26	53.1	51.0	−1	−2	79	67.3	61.8	−8	−8
总出口	178	100.0	100.0	−3	−5	51	100.0	100.0	0	−6	127	100.0	100.0	−4	−4
马来西亚															
农产品	20	9.8	9.7	−7	1	7	15.1	13.0	−18	−3	13	7.8	8.5	1	3
燃料和矿产品	47	15.1	22.5	21	3	17	24.0	32.3	8	−2	30	11.8	19.1	31	6
制成品	137	73.3	65.8	2	1	29	59.4	53.0	1	−1	109	78.5	70.2	2	2
总出口	209	100.0	100.0	5	1	54	100.0	100.0	0	−2	155	100.0	100.0	7	3
菲律宾															
农产品	9	11.7	12.8	−1	21	3	16.7	15.6	−10	46	6	9.7	12.0	2	13
燃料和矿产品	15	20.7	21.8	−5	−5	3	24.9	18.8	−9	4	12	19.1	22.7	−4	−7
制成品	44	66.8	65.0	2	4	11	57.9	65.2	−3	11	33	70.2	65.0	3	2
总出口	68	100.0	100.0	0	4	16	100.0	100.0	−5	14	51	100.0	100.0	1	1
新加坡															
农产品	15	3.5	4.0	3	2	5	5.8	7.2	−6	3	9	2.8	3.2	8	2
燃料和矿产品	120	27.6	32.8	−5	−2	25	22.1	33.5	1	−6	95	29.3	32.6	−7	−1
制成品	225	64.9	61.3	1	−2	43	64.3	57.3	−4	−2	181	65.1	62.4	2	−1
总出口	366	100.0	100.0	−2	−2	75	100.0	100.0	−2	−3	291	100.0	100.0	−2	−1
泰国															
农产品	16	6.6	7.1	−2	−2	3	6.2	6.8	−11	5	13	6.6	7.2	0	−4
燃料和矿产品	56	22.0	24.8	6	−7	14	27.3	31.3	5	0	43	20.8	23.2	7	−10
制成品	148	66.8	65.1	−4	−6	27	65.6	61.4	3	−3	122	67.0	66.0	−5	−7
总出口	228	100.0	100.0	1	−9	43	100.0	100.0	3	−2	185	100.0	100.0	0	−11
ASEAN															
农产品	103	7.7	8.3	1	5	27	9.6	9.7	−11	7	76	7.1	7.9	7	4
燃料和矿产品	311	22.0	25.2	2	−2	92	27.0	33.0	3	−4	219	20.4	22.9	2	−1
制成品	800	67.4	64.8	1	0	156	60.3	56.3	0	1	644	69.6	67.3	2	0
总出口	1 235	100.0	100.0	2	−1	278	100.0	100.0	0	−1	957	100.0	100.0	2	−1

表 33

2014 年最不发达国家货物贸易进出口

单位：百万美元，%

	出口					进口				
	总额	年度变化百分比				总额	年度变化百分比			
	2014	2010—2014	2012	2013	2014	2014	2010—2014	2012	2013	2014
LDCs	207236	6	1	4	−2	266134	12	11	9	5
石油出口方 a										
安哥拉	62 400	5	6	−4	−9	28 320	14	17	11	8
赤道几内亚	12 600	6	16	−6	−14	6 500	6	15	−7	−7
缅甸	11 031	6	−4	27	−2	16 226	36	2	31	35
也门	8 000	0	−14	0	−4	12 940	9	18	0	−3
苏丹	4 350	−21	−60	18	−9	9 211	−2	0	7	−7
乍得	3 600	0	−8	−14	−5	4 300	16	6	14	8
不丹	555	−4	−21	2	2	810	−1	−5	−8	−11
南苏丹	…	…	…	…	…	…	…	…	…	…
制成品出口方										
孟加拉国	30 405	12	3	16	4	42 268	11	−6	9	14
柬埔寨	10 800	20	17	18	17	13 500	19	22	13	5
马达加斯加	2 126	17	−5	27	11	3 259	6	6	5	0
莱索托	925	1	−17	−13	9	2 208	−1	4	−15	0
海地	917	12	6	9	4	3 600	3	5	7	6
尼泊尔	889	1	−1	−4	1	7 561	10	5	8	15
萨摩亚	72	1	15	−18	16	390	6	0	6	6
农产品出口方										
埃塞俄比亚	4 437	17	1	41	9	18 987	22	34	25	27
布基纳法索	2 489	12	−9	8	6	3 730	16	33	22	−4
乌干达	2 274	9	9	2	−6	5 874	6	7	−4	1
贝宁	2 010	12	2	30	8	2 481	5	10	32	−20
马拉维	1 374	7	−17	2	14	2 973	8	−3	21	5
多哥	1 350	8	11	16	−11	2 800	14	9	12	5
卢旺达	736	25	27	19	5	2 457	14	13	0	7
阿富汗	571	10	14	20	11	7 729	11	39	−4	−11
索马里	510	3	4	−4	−2	1 300	12	0	8	0
所罗门群岛	450	19	20	−10	0	509	6	4	7	−2
几内亚比绍	162	6	−46	8	16	228	4	−25	0	27
布隆迪	125	5	8	−30	33	769	11	0	8	−5
冈比亚	108	12	25	−11	2	370	7	12	−8	6
中非	90	−10	5	−25	−40	255	−4	3	−22	2
瓦努阿图	63	7	−19	−30	63	311	2	−3	6	−1
科摩罗	25	5	−24	1	29	275	4	−1	4	−3
圣多美和普林西比	17	12	10	6	33	170	11	−2	16	12
基里巴斯	5	9	−32	15	−19	95	7	18	−11	−2
非燃料产品出口方										
赞比亚	9 696	8	4	13	−8	9 545	16	23	15	−6
刚果（金）	6 900	7	−5	−2	11	6 600	10	11	3	5
莫桑比克	4 725	12	7	4	17	8 747	17	38	16	−13

续　表

	出　口					进　口				
	总额	年度变化百分比				总额	年度变化百分比			
	2014	2010—2014	2012	2013	2014	2014	2010—2014	2012	2013	2014
坦桑尼亚	4 645	3	17	−20	5	12 390	12	5	7	2
老挝	2 650	11	4	0	17	3 300	12	27	−1	9
马里	2 100	1	10	−10	−10	3 977	4	3	10	5
毛里塔尼亚	1 946	−2	−4	0	−27	2 666	8	27	−3	−12
塞拉利昂	1 886	53	221	71	−2	1 489	18	−7	11	−16
尼日尔	1 500	7	16	10	−6	2 250	−2	−13	6	11
几内亚	1 400	−1	−9	0	8	2 032	10	7	−7	−3
厄立特里亚	766	177	12	−31	132	1127	14	2	6	9
其他										
塞内加尔	2 812	7	0	5	5	6 639	9	9	3	0
黎巴嫩	583	27	25	22	4	1 046	10	−4	14	−9
吉布提	139	13	27	1	16	970	27	11	27	35
东帝汶	20	5	133	−48	25	940	40	108	27	12
图瓦卢	0	0	0	0	0	12	−7	20	−53	−14
备忘项：										
世界 b	19 002 190	6	1	2	0	19 091 075	5	1	2	0
世界 b	18 816 000	8	20	0	2	18 890 000	7	19	1	1

a　不丹的数据包括其出口的电流。
b　包括重要的复出口和为复出口的进口。
注：2014 的数据主要为估计值。

表 34

2004—2015 年初级产品的出口价格

（指数 2005 年＝100）

	2008	2008	2008	2008	2008	2009	2010	2011	2012	2013	2014	2014				2015	
												Q1	Q2	Q3	Q4	Q1	Q2
食品和饮料	98	100	110	127	157	136	153	182	175	175	171	176	181	168	160	150	145
食品	100	100	111	127	157	134	150	180	176	178	170	177	181	166	158	148	142
谷类	102	100	122	159	222	161	166	230	236	218	180	191	198	167	164	158	148
小麦	103	100	126	167	214	147	147	207	206	205	187	195	211	172	169	157	142
玉米	114	100	124	166	227	168	189	297	303	263	196	214	217	177	176	177	171
大米	85	100	106	116	243	205	181	192	202	180	148	153	142	151	146	141	133
大麦	104	100	123	181	211	135	167	218	251	217	154	171	176	140	128	139	135
植物油和蛋白粉、蛋白肉	111	100	103	143	193	154	170	209	216	206	191	203	212	180	169	162	157
肉类	100	100	95	99	103	98	117	134	132	136	159	143	156	174	165	141	140
牛肉	96	100	97	99	102	101	128	154	158	155	189	162	165	213	216	182	171
羊肉	103	100	96	101	106	91	91	93	63	66	81	77	84	83	81	76	70
猪肉	105	100	94	94	96	82	110	132	122	128	152	137	170	167	133	97	106
家禽	102	100	94	106	115	116	116	118	128	141	149	142	148	153	154	154	156
海产品	88	100	121	113	113	114	140	139	113	160	162	186	171	150	141	140	132
鱼类	82	100	125	112	119	121	151	146	117	166	163	191	171	146	142	137	126
虾类	105	100	105	116	91	85	98	115	97	136	160	166	172	165	138	151	152
糖	83	100	133	102	117	152	172	211	175	148	146	144	154	151	136	124	114
香蕉	91	100	118	117	146	147	153	169	171	161	162	164	161	163	158	169	170
柑橘	101	100	98	114	132	108	118	102	99	111	90	89	96	89	85	80	71

续 表

	2008	2008	2008	2008	2008	2009	2010	2011	2012	2013	2014	2014				2015	
												Q1	Q2	Q3	Q4	Q1	Q2
饮料	83	100	108	123	152	154	176	206	167	147	178	168	181	183	180	170	170
咖啡	70	100	112	129	150	132	165	231	180	147	185	168	193	188	192	168	156
可可豆	100	100	103	127	167	187	203	193	154	158	198	191	200	209	193	189	199
茶	92	100	112	98	125	145	146	160	161	123	110	115	103	108	114	135	148
农业原材料	98	100	109	114	113	94	124	153	133	136	139	141	142	138	134	129	126
木料	96	100	108	107	109	102	101	111	107	107	109	110	111	110	106	105	103
棉花	112	100	105	115	129	114	188	280	162	164	151	170	168	140	125	125	131
羊毛	105	100	104	144	138	115	153	234	215	196	178	186	182	177	167	155	171
橡胶	87	100	140	153	174	128	243	321	225	186	130	150	141	122	108	115	119
生皮	102	100	105	110	98	68	110	125	127	144	168	164	167	169	172	161	147
金属和有色金属（不含石油）	79	100	156	183	169	136	202	229	190	182	164	171	165	166	154	137	135
铜	78	100	183	194	189	141	205	240	217	199	187	191	185	190	180	159	165
铝	90	100	135	139	136	88	114	126	106	97	98	90	95	105	104	95	93
铁矿石	58	100	119	130	219	285	522	597	457	482	345	429	365	321	263	222	206
锡	115	100	119	196	250	184	276	353	286	302	297	307	313	297	269	249	211
镍	94	100	163	251	143	99	148	155	119	102	114	99	125	126	107	97	88
锌	76	100	237	235	137	120	157	159	141	138	157	147	150	167	162	151	159
铅	91	100	132	265	215	177	221	246	212	220	215	216	215	224	205	186	199
铀	65	100	171	355	230	167	165	201	175	138	120	126	107	111	135	135	132
以上总计	**91**	**100**	**123**	**140**	**151**	**127**	**161**	**190**	**171**	**169**	**162**	**167**	**168**	**161**	**153**	**142**	**138**
能源	72	100	119	132	185	117	147	201	203	196	180	195	197	185	143	105	115
天然气	70	100	115	117	174	110	113	154	171	165	160	169	165	153	154	137	102
原油	71	100	121	133	182	116	149	204	208	201	184	200	203	191	142	100	116
煤	113	100	104	138	266	149	206	254	202	177	149	163	155	144	134	130	125
所有初级产品	**77**	**100**	**121**	**135**	**172**	**121**	**152**	**197**	**191**	**186**	**173**	**184**	**186**	**176**	**146**	**119**	**123**

注：这些指数是美元价格的长期平均。季度数据未经过季节调整。

表 35

2014 年农产品占货物贸易和初级产品的份额（按地区）

单位：%

	出口	进口
	占货物贸易份额	
世界	9.5	9.5
北美洲	11.1	6.9
中、南美洲	30.6	9.4
欧洲	10.6	10.5
独联体	9.2	12.0
非洲	11.5	15.6
中东	2.3	12.2
亚洲	6.7	9.0
	占初级产品份额	
世界	31.8	31.8
北美洲	40.0	30.3
中、南美洲	43.3	29.3
欧洲	48.7	36.7
独联体	12.2	52.0
非洲	15.4	47.1
中东	3.4	52.5
亚洲	37.3	24.7

表 36

2014 年农产品出口（按目的地）

单位：十亿美元，%

地区 \ 年份	总额	占地区出口份额		占世界出口份额		年度变化百分比		
	2013	2005	2013	2005	2013	2005—2013	2012	2013
世界	**1 745**	**100.0**	**100.0**	**100.0**	**100.0**	**9**	**−1**	**6**
欧洲								
世界	**708**	**100.0**	**100.0**	**46.8**	**40.6**	**7**	**−2**	**8**
欧洲	537	80.9	75.9	37.9	30.8	7	−4	7
亚洲	52	5.3	7.4	2.5	3.0	12	2	9
北美洲	29	5.1	4.2	2.4	1.7	5	4	7
非洲	29	2.7	4.0	1.3	1.6	13	2	10
独联体	27	2.6	3.8	1.2	1.5	12	4	8
中东	24	2.2	3.4	1.0	1.4	14	10	13
中、南美洲	7	0.8	1.0	0.4	0.4	10	5	4
亚洲								
世界	**390**	**100.0**	**100.0**	**18.3**	**22.3**	**12**	**−1**	**3**
亚洲	230	58.0	59.1	10.6	13.2	12	0	2
欧洲	48	15.4	12.4	2.8	2.8	9	−10	2
北美洲	42	14.2	10.8	2.6	2.4	8	4	−4
中东	27	4.9	7.0	0.9	1.6	17	0	15
非洲	24	4.0	6.1	0.7	1.4	18	1	6
独联体	8	1.9	2.2	0.4	0.5	14	−4	4
中、南美洲	6	1.2	1.6	0.2	0.3	16	−9	4
北美洲								
世界	**266**	**100.0**	**100.0**	**16.0**	**15.3**	**9**	**3**	**3**
北美洲	102	29.9	38.4	4.8	5.9	12	6	0
亚洲	102	46.4	38.5	7.4	5.9	6	4	4
欧洲	25	12.1	9.4	1.9	1.4	5	−3	8
中、南美洲	20	5.8	7.4	0.9	1.1	12	1	13
非洲	8	2.7	3.0	0.4	0.5	10	−12	−3
中东	6	1.9	2.1	0.3	0.3	10	−18	−4
独联体	3	1.1	1.0	0.2	0.2	8	27	−18
中、南美洲								
世界	**217**	**100.0**	**100.0**	**10.6**	**12.4**	**12**	**−1**	**6**
欧洲	67	20.2	31.1	2.1	3.9	18	5	17
亚洲	49	31.7	22.4	3.4	2.8	7	−10	0

续 表

地区 \ 年份	总额	占地区出口份额		占世界出口份额		年度变化百分比		
	2013	2005	2013	2005	2013	2005—2013	2012	2013
中、南美洲	36	13.8	16.4	1.5	2.0	14	6	0
北美洲	29	18.7	13.3	2.0	1.6	7	−2	4
中东	14	5.5	6.4	0.6	0.8	14	−4	−6
非洲	13	4.7	6.1	0.5	0.8	15	−3	6
独联体	8	5.0	3.6	0.5	0.4	7	−8	5
非洲								
世界	**69**	**100.0**	**100.0**	**3.0**	**4.0**	**13**	**13**	**4**
欧洲	23	32.3	33.6	1.0	1.3	14	1	11
非洲	17	26.4	24.5	0.8	1.0	12	39	−10
亚洲	17	26.7	24.0	0.8	0.9	12	−17	49
北美洲	5	5.7	7.7	0.2	0.3	18	58	−19
中东	5	5.0	6.8	0.2	0.3	18	58	−28
独联体	1	2.4	1.1	0.1	0.0	2	5	8
中、南美洲	0	0.1	0.4	0.0	0.0	36	−16	58
独联体								
世界	**62**	**100.0**	**100.0**	**3.3**	**3.5**	**10**	**−2**	**5**
独联体	20	50.3	32.8	1.7	1.2	5	−13	3
欧洲	17	19.1	27.5	0.6	1.0	15	3	8
亚洲	13	16.8	21.5	0.6	0.8	14	18	5
非洲	5	4.9	8.2	0.2	0.3	18	−10	12
中东	2	5.8	4.0	0.2	0.1	5	−15	−15
北美洲	2	0.4	2.6	0.0	0.1	40	1	4
中、南美洲	1	1.7	1.9	0.1	0.1	12	−15	13
中东								
世界	**33**	**100.0**	**100.0**	**1.9**	**1.9**	**9**	**−4**	**18**
中东	18	32.9	54.2	0.6	1.0	16	6	30
亚洲	4	9.8	12.9	0.2	0.2	13	−7	−8
欧洲	3	13.0	10.4	0.2	0.2	6	4	14
非洲	3	4.7	7.7	0.1	0.1	16	10	24
独联体	1	2.6	3.8	0.0	0.1	15	11	−3
北美洲	1	2.0	1.8	0.0	0.0	8	9	10
中、南美洲	0	0.2	0.3	0.0	0.0	11	−6	7

表 37

2014 年农产品的主要进出口方

单位：十亿美元，%

地区＼年份	总额	占世界出口/进口份额				年度变化百分比			
	2013	1980	1990	2000	2014	2010—2014	2012	2013	2014
出口方									
欧盟（28）	670	—	—	41.9	38.0	6	−2	8	1
欧盟（28）对外出口	178	—	—	10.0	10.1	9	3	8	1
美国	182	17.0	14.3	13.0	10.3	6	2	2	4
巴西	88	3.4	2.4	2.8	5.0	6	0	5	−3
中国	74	1.5	2.4	3.0	4.2	10	2	6	6
加拿大	68	5.0	5.4	6.3	3.9	7	5	4	4
印度尼西亚	44	1.6	1.0	1.4	2.5	5	−6	−5	3
印度	43	1.0	0.8	1.1	2.5	17	21	7	−3
泰国	40	1.2	1.9	2.2	2.3	3	−12	−4	−2
澳大利亚	39	3.3	2.9	3.0	2.2	9	3	−2	3
阿根廷	38	1.9	1.8	2.2	2.1	2	−5	−3	−10
俄罗斯	31	—	—	1.4	1.7	10	3	−6	8
马来西亚	30	2.0	1.8	1.5	1.7	1	−13	−11	0
新西兰	29	1.3	1.4	1.4	1.6	10	0	12	8
越南 a	27	…	…	0.7	1.5	12	5	0	14
墨西哥	26	0.8	0.8	1.7	1.5	9	−1	10	5
以上 15 个经济体总计	**1 430**	—	—	**83.5**	**81.0**	—	—	—	—
进口方									
欧盟（28）	675	—	—	42.7	36.1	5	−5	6	2
欧盟（28）自外进口	183	—	—	13.2	9.8	4	−7	3	2
中国	170	2.1	1.8	3.3	9.1	12	8	6	3
美国	157	8.7	9.0	11.6	8.4	8	3	3	7
日本	82	9.6	11.5	10.4	4.4	1	−2	−8	−5
俄罗斯 b	41	—	—	1.3	2.2	3	−3	6	−8
加拿大 b	40	1.8	2.0	2.6	2.1	6	4	2	3
韩国	35	1.5	2.2	2.2	1.9	7	−5	1	5
墨西哥 b	30	1.2	1.2	1.8	1.6	6	−7	8	3
中国香港	29	—	—	—	—	9	3	11	5
留用进口 a	20	1.0	1.0	1.1	1.1	10	4	12	6
印度	27	0.5	0.4	0.7	1.5	11	14	−5	12
沙特阿拉伯	25	1.5	0.8	0.9	1.3	9	8	10	0
印度尼西亚	22	0.6	0.5	1.0	1.2	9	−7	3	3
马来西亚	20	0.5	0.5	0.8	1.1	6	1	−7	1
土耳其	18	0.1	0.6	0.7	1.0	9	−7	3	7
阿联酋 a	18	0.3	0.4	0.5	1.0	11	13	10	0
以上 15 个经济体总计	**1 381**	—	—	**81.5**	**73.7**	—	—	—	—

a 进口以 f.o.b. 计价。

b 包括秘书处估计。

表 38

1990—2014 年主要经济体的农产品出口

单位：百万美元，%

地区＼年份	总额					占经济体总货物出口的份额	
	1990	2000	2012	2013	2014	2010	2014 a
世界	414 723	550 808	1 651 285	1 737 207	1 765 405	9.2	9.5
阿根廷	7 482	11 954	43 151	41 994	37 890	50.8	52.6
澳大利亚	11 875	16 446	38 405	37 596	38 632	12.7	16.0
巴西	9 779	15 464	86 435	90 664	87 890	34.0	39.0
喀麦隆 b	695	438	1 403	1 457	1 641	39.2	33.8
加拿大	22 339	34 789	62 868	65 679	68 105	13.5	14.3
智利	2 779	6 399	18 842	20 776	22 080	22.2	29.2
中国	10 060	16 384	66 169	70 153	74 472	3.3	3.2
哥伦比亚	2 514	3 106	6 629	6 680	7 343	14.5	13.4
哥斯达黎加	927	1 812	4 083	4 189	4 372	35.7	38.9
科特迪瓦 b	2374	2 308	5 949	5 602	7 471	52.4	58.4
多米尼加 b	…	542	1 715	1 815	2 281	20.1	23.0
厄瓜多尔	1 236	1 948	7 618	8 614	9 770	34.1	38.0
埃及 b	669	610	4 738	5 154	5 066	19.4	18.7
埃塞俄比亚 b	260	406	2 445	3 319	3 629	81.2	81.8
欧盟（28）	—	230 985	613 643	662 533	670 417	10.3	10.9
欧盟（28）对外出口	—	55 286	162 030	175 765	177 781	7.1	7.9
欧盟（28）对内出口	—	175 699	451 613	486 768	492 636	12.0	12.6
加纳	…	621	2 890	2 642	3 087	15.9	23.4
危地马拉 b	849	1 618	4 840	4 811	4 941	46.3	45.6
洪都拉斯	680	782	2 736	2 393	2 449	25.4	30.3
中国香港	4 556	5 693	9 346	10 198	10 550	2.0	2.0
内部出口 b	821	453	1 043	1 049	1 085	5.7	7.0
转口 b	3 735	5 240	8 303	9 149	9 465	1.9	1.9
冰岛	1 274	1 257	2 298	2 395	2 250	41.9	44.5
印度	3 506	5 951	41 890	44 685	43 466	10.2	13.5
印度尼西亚	4 154	7 764	45 023	42 628	44 087	22.8	25.0
伊朗	601	932	5 973	5 661	5 992	4.9	6.7
以色列	1 327	1 182	2 433	2 588	2 519	3.9	3.7
日本	3 298	4 349	10 859	10 769	10 590	1.3	1.5
肯尼亚	559	1 062	3 227	3 157	3 105	55.3	50.8
韩国	2 985	4 298	12 628	11 805	11 915	2.0	2.1
马拉维 b	382	342	955	972	1 105	79.7	80.4

续 表

地区＼年份	总额					占经济体总货物出口的份额	
	1990	2000	2012	2013	2014	2010	2014 a
马来西亚	7 500	8 015	33 911	30 044	30 130	14.5	12.9
墨西哥	3 466	9 100	22 749	25 092	26 388	6.3	6.6
摩洛哥	1 228	1 746	3 928	4 334	4 611	20.6	19.5
缅甸 b	…	…	2 363	2 991	2 922	26.6	26.5
新西兰	5 966	7 665	24 088	26 894	28 985	62.3	69.6
尼加拉瓜	295	547	2 254	2 078	2 405	44.7	46.9
巴基斯坦	1 081	1 234	4 979	5 571	5 155	18.4	20.9
巴拿马 b	263	580	925	1 020	600	7.4	4.6
巴拉圭	863	699	4 255	6 299	6 420	61.4	66.5
秘鲁	789	1 911	7 696	7 161	8 231	16.6	20.9
菲律宾	1 683	2 026	5 075	6 425	6 948	8.0	11.2
俄罗斯	—	7 554	30 149	28 482	30 877	5.4	6.2
新加坡	4 095	3 723	9 860	10 882	11 891	2.2	2.9
内部出口	1 183	1 202	4 038	4 711	5 683	1.8	2.6
转口	2 912	2 521	5 457	5 608	5 600	2.5	2.9
南非	1 691	3 270	10 499	11 137	11 374	10.9	12.5
斯里兰卡 b	758	1 093	2 732	2 914	3 208	29.8	28.4
瑞士	2 244	2 502	8 975	9 672	10 040	4.0	3.2
叙利亚 b	767	621	908	403	403	20.1	20.1
中国台北	3 732	3 509	6 938	6 266	6 487	2.0	2.1
坦桑尼亚 b	…	432	1 729	1 499	1 506	29.0	32.4
泰国	7 786	12 220	42 030	40 357	39 742	18.2	17.5
突尼斯 b	418	548	1 672	1 734	1 675	8.2	10.0
土耳其	3 300	3 828	15 671	17 419	18 430	10.9	11.7
乌干达	…	292	1 236	1 439	1 359	60.2	59.8
乌克兰	—	1 585	18 456	17 763	17 505	20.3	32.3
阿联酋 b，c	501	1 185	6 544	7 763	8 045	2.3	2.2
美国	59 404	71 408	172 112	175 677	182 235	11.2	11.2
乌拉圭	1 025	1 278	6 422	6 794	6 878	71.8	75.1
越南 b	…	3 954	23 404	23 293	26 546	23.3	17.6

a 接近一年。
b 包括秘书处估计。
c 主要的转口。

表 39

1990—2014 年主要经济体农产品进口

单位：百万美元，%

地区 \ 年份	总额					占经济体总货物进口的份额	
	1990	2000	2012	2013	2014	2010	2014 a
阿尔及利亚	2 766	2 815	10 755	11 270	12 712	18.2	21.8
阿根廷	326	1 644	2 478	2 407	2 234	3.8	3.4
澳大利亚 b	2 735	4 234	14 109	14 611	15 631	5.9	6.9
孟加拉 c d	835	1 716	9 158	9 939	11 327	21.5	26.8
白俄罗斯	—	1 226	4 193	4 529	5 088	9.4	12.5
波斯尼亚和黑塞哥维那	…	…	1 988	1 999	2 012	19.7	18.3
巴西 e	2 690	4 762	13 109	14 174	13 528	6.0	5.9
加拿大 d	9 009	15 272	37 907	38 781	40 134	8.2	8.7
智利	461	1 421	6 386	6 568	6 601	7.8	9.1
中国	7 855	19 544	156 823	165 459	170 083	7.8	8.7
哥伦比亚	593	1 736	6 395	6 348	6 507	11.1	10.2
科特迪瓦	…	453	2 023	1 887	1 942	20.1	17.9
古巴	…	826	…	…	…	…	…
多米尼加 d f	413	964	2 588	2 624	2 858	14.3	16.5
厄瓜多尔	206	423	2 203	2 208	2 370	9.4	8.5
埃及 d	4 793	4 195	17 660	13 590	17 234	22.4	25.5
萨尔瓦多	158	692	1 868	1 832	1 915	17.7	18.2
欧盟（28）g	—	254 480	625 137	665 309	675 469	10.3	11.0
欧盟（28）自外进口	—	78 865	173 525	178 541	182 833	7.6	8.2
危地马拉	196	673	2 500	2 551	2 706	14.6	14.8
中国香港	8 325	11 728	25 003	27 816	29 195	4.7	4.9
留用进口 d	4 591	64 88	16 700	18 667	19 730	11.9	13.1
印度	1 721	3 993	25 668	24 417	27 314	5.1	5.9
印度尼西亚	2 126	5 727	20 906	21 512	22 220	11.5	12.5
伊朗 d	3 830	2 943	13 989	14 567	13 879	14.4	27.2
以色列	1 565	2 288	5 916	6 126	6 336	8.3	8.4
日本	50 762	62 150	93 724	85 994	81 868	11.2	10.0
约旦	709	942	3 838	3 929	4 307	17.2	18.8
哈萨克斯坦	—	506	4 442	4 727	4 433	7.8	10.8
韩国	9 531	12 837	33 076	33 386	35 001	6.3	6.7
科威特 d	589	1 312	3 849	4 591	5 105	13.5	16.2
黎巴嫩 d	…	1 210	3 436	3 567	3 423	16.2	16.2
马来西亚	2 404	4 610	21 429	19 963	20 162	9.8	9.7

续　表

地区＼年份	总额					占经济体总货物进口的份额	
	1990	2000	2012	2013	2014	2010	2014 a
墨西哥 b	5 374	10 989	27 076	29 202	30 027	7.8	7.5
摩洛哥 d	1 096	1 941	6 421	5 673	6 427	13.6	14.0
新西兰	756	1 204	4 307	4 508	4 922	11.0	11.6
尼日利亚 d	658	1 212	8 418	9 203	9 861	11.0	16.4
挪威	2 090	2 956	9 008	9 447	9 542	9.4	10.7
阿曼	506	1 158	3 066	3 298	3 766	12.6	12.4
巴基斯坦	1 568	1 882	6 524	6 332	7 435	17.8	15.6
秘鲁	668	998	4 800	4 811	4 960	12.0	11.7
菲律宾	1 665	3 104	7 240	7 157	8 668	11.7	12.8
俄罗斯 d	—	7 561	42 037	44 726	41 216	14.7	13.4
沙特阿拉伯 d	3 487	5 663	22 600	24 926	24 818	16.5	15.2
塞内加尔 d	372	394	1 652	1 685	1 578	23.9	23.8
新加坡	4 702	4 890	13 953	14 305	14 624	3.5	4.0
留用进口	1 789	2 369	8 496	8 697	9 023	4.7	5.2
南非	1 219	1 650	8 399	7 677	7 148	7.6	7.2
斯里兰卡 d	549	934	2 278	2 365	2 845	15.3	14.7
苏丹 d	…	376	1 030	1 078	1 001	31.5	10.9
瑞士	5 920	5 712	12 868	13 724	13 956	6.8	5.1
叙利亚 d	791	850	1 707	1 263	1 566	23.4	23.4
中国台北	6 203	7 899	14 990	12 324	15 446	5.2	5.6
泰国	3 230	4 484	16 844	16 645	16 246	6.6	7.1
突尼斯	819	968	2 698	3 010	2 908	11.5	11.7
土耳其	2 806	4 133	16 370	16 914	18 058	6.9	7.5
乌克兰	—	1 092	8 036	8 674	6 445	10.3	11.9
阿联酋 d	1 726	3 230	16 290	17 859	17 849	7.2	6.8
美国	39 966	69 115	141 849	146 482	156 885	5.9	6.5
委内瑞拉	986	1 970	9 858	8 657	8 868	13.8	20.0
越南 d	236	1 269	13 241	15 247	17 236	12.1	11.5
也门 d	…	…	3 714	3 917	3 809	31.6	29.4

a　或最近年份。
b　进口以 f. o. b. 计价。
c　财政年数字。
d　包括秘书处估计。
e　始自 2000 年，进口以 f. o. b. 计价。
f　直至 2010 年，进口以 f. o. b. 计价。
g　EU（28）内部数据见元数据。

表 40

1990—2014 主要经济体的食品出口

单位：百万美元，%

地区 \ 年份	总额					占经济体总货物出口的份额	
	1990	2000	2012	2013	2014	2010	2014 a
世界	315 559	431 088	1 371 099	1 451 660	1 486 281	7.5	8.0
阿根廷	6 949	11 491	42 407	41 306	37 172	49.6	51.6
澳大利亚	7 937	12 583	30 704	30 057	31 984	10.3	13.3
白俄罗斯	—	495	4 519	5 349	5 333	12.6	14.7
巴西	8 697	12 808	77 212	82 081	78 820	30.1	35.0
加拿大	10 898	17 630	46 355	47 106	49 490	9.6	10.4
智利	1 965	4 424	14 418	15 919	16 970	16.6	22.4
中国	7 868	13 559	56 312	59 978	63 491	2.8	2.7
哥伦比亚	2 222	2 502	5 251	5 187	5 815	11.2	10.6
哥斯达黎加	848	1 648	3 814	3 941	4 126	33.1	36.7
科特迪瓦	…	1 806	4 778	4 425	6 385	43.8	49.9
厄瓜多尔	1 198	1 758	6 702	7 627	8 785	29.9	34.1
埃及	251	375	4 038	4 576	4 492	16.5	16.6
埃塞俄比亚 b	186	321	2 229	2 696	2 925	73.1	65.9
欧盟（28）	—	189 781	523 606	567 599	575 693	8.7	9.3
欧盟（28）对外出口	—	45 921	132 711	144 906	148 331	5.8	6.6
欧盟（28）对内出口	—	143 860	390 896	422 693	427 362	10.3	11.0
加纳	…	513	2 628	2 326	2 681	14.2	20.3
危地马拉	778	1 518	4 464	4 409	4 612	42.0	42.6
洪都拉斯	649	730	2 691	2 341	2 394	24.8	29.7
中国香港	3 385	3 664	7 243	7 808	8 619	1.5	1.6
内部出口 b	742	362	787	837	924	4.1	5.9
转口 b	2 644	3 302	6 457	6 970	7 695	1.4	1.5
冰岛	1 266	1 240	2 257	2 347	2 214	41.3	43.8
印度	2 782	5 418	31 214	36 304	36 730	8.0	11.4
印度尼西亚	2 853	5 526	33 692	31 939	35 389	16.2	20.1
伊朗	…	818	5 600	5 223	5 564	4.7	6.3
以色列	1 022	824	2 050	2 171	2 116	3.1	3.1
日本	1 706	2 124	4 557	4 589	4 696	0.6	0.7
肯尼亚	502	927	2 599	2 531	2 407	44.9	39.4
韩国	2 162	2 665	6 398	6 202	6 597	1.1	1.2
马拉维 b	374	331	895	916	1 042	76.3	75.8
马来西亚	3 434	5 440	28 451	25 099	26 008	11.9	11.1

续　表

地区 \ 年份	总额					占经济体总货物出口的份额	
	1990	2000	2012	2013	2014	2010	2014 a
墨西哥	3 057	8 179	21 338	23 758	25 097	5.9	6.3
摩洛哥	1 105	1 596	3 692	4 143	4 402	18.8	18.6
缅甸 b	…	…	1 534	1 941	2 495	17.3	22.6
新西兰	4 272	5 819	20 108	22 170	24 350	52.2	58.5
尼加拉瓜	251	534	2 220	2 047	2 361	44.1	46.1
挪威	2 365	3 827	9 657	11 202	11 716	7.2	8.1
巴基斯坦	516	964	4 187	4 995	4 669	16.5	18.9
巴拿马 b	258	569	887	977	549	7.2	4.2
巴拉圭	502	564	4 099	6 140	6 267	59.4	64.9
秘鲁	703	1 736	7 274	6 726	7 753	15.5	19.7
菲律宾	1 532	1 815	4 638	5 843	6 308	7.3	10.2
俄罗斯	—	3 950	20 567	18 989	19 775	3.1	4.0
塞尔维亚	…	…	2 638	2 711	2 985	22.3	20.1
新加坡	2 747	3 091	8 807	9 644	10 554	2.0	2.6
内部出口	1 077	1 092	3 988	4 599	5 319	1.7	2.5
转口	1 671	1 999	4 804	5 031	5 223	2.2	2.7
南非	…	2 232	8 742	9 294	9 455	9.0	10.4
斯里兰卡	649	…	2 426	2 651	2 916	26.0	25.8
瑞士	1 756	2 021	8 414	9 119	9 435	3.7	3.0
叙利亚 b	577	408	841	373	373	18.6	18.6
中国台北	2 703	1 819	3 761	3 287	3 716	1.0	1.2
坦桑尼亚 b	…	359	1 413	1 295	1 263	23.6	27.2
泰国	6 611	9 924	30 704	29 368	30 848	12.9	13.6
突尼斯 b	384	510	1 588	1 657	1 596	7.7	9.5
土耳其	2 906	3 521	15 033	16 749	17 759	10.4	11.3
乌干达 b	…	241	1 092	1 335	1 261	54.8	55.4
乌克兰	—	1 339	17 778	16 962	16 553	19.2	30.5
阿联酋 b c	73	1 128	6 209	7 388	7 609	2.2	2.1
美国	42 422	54 341	138 237	141 901	149 122	8.8	9.2
乌拉圭	670	1 064	5 687	5 989	5 939	61.3	64.8
越南 b	…	3 666	19 521	19 072	21 735	19.3	14.4

a　接近一年。
b　包括秘书处估计。
c　主要的转口。

表 41

1990—2014 年主要经济体的食品进口

单位：百万美元，%

地区 \ 年份	总额					占经济体货物进口的份额	
	1990	2000	2012	2013	2014	2010	2014 a
阿尔及利亚	2 306	2 578	9 998	10 467	11 784	16.5	20.2
阿根廷	164	1 267	1 726	1 709	1 598	2.6	2.4
澳大利亚 b	1 943	3 245	12 643	13 199	14 067	5.2	6.2
孟加拉国 c，d	650	1 254	6 662	7 229	8 240	17.5	19.5
白俄罗斯	—	1 027	3 509	3 972	4 656	7.9	11.4
波斯尼亚和黑塞哥维纳	…	…	1 826	1 841	1 841	18.1	16.8
巴西 e	2112	3 665	10 626	11 713	11 224	4.6	4.9
加拿大 b	7 143	12 027	33 360	34 346	35 600	7.1	7.7
智利	308	1 228	5 911	6 076	6 114	7.1	8.5
中国	4 619	9 043	90 650	98 646	105 264	4.3	5.4
哥伦比亚	395	1 405	5 872	5 842	5 989	9.7	9.4
科特迪瓦	…	427	1 955	1 820	1 883	19.2	17.3
古巴	…	765	…	…	…	…	…
多米尼加 f	…	…	2 425	2 418	2 542	13.2	14.7
厄瓜多尔	156	310	1 959	1 977	2 133	8.3	7.7
埃及	2 903	3 519	15 666	11 674	14 898	19.2	22.1
萨尔瓦多	128	613	1 663	1 641	1 717	15.7	16.3
欧盟（28）g	—	200 685	533 491	570 660	579 958	8.7	9.5
欧盟（28）从外进口	—	57 224	142 595	147 968	152 596	6.1	6.8
危地马拉	169	592	2 255	2 320	2 478	13.3	13.6
中国香港	6 551	9 165	22 087	24 362	26 816	4.1	4.5
留用进口 d	3 908	5 863	15 631	17 392	19 121	11.1	12.7
印度	771	2 283	17 672	16 690	19 103	3.5	4.1
印度尼西亚	1 104	3 336	15 828	16 395	17 028	8.5	9.6
伊朗	…	2 585	12 442	13 140	12 695	12.5	24.9
以色列	1 197	1 923	5 196	5 388	5 589	7.1	7.4
日本	34 154	48 543	78 870	71 749	68 861	9.2	8.4
约旦	672	851	3 598	3 691	4 042	15.9	17.7
哈萨克斯坦	—	459	4 165	4 462	4 228	7.3	10.3
肯尼亚	199	403	1 961	1 820	1 895	11.6	10.3
韩国	3 912	7 722	24 879	25 285	27 014	4.5	5.1
科威特 d	561	1 249	3 676	4 435	4 917	13.0	15.6
黎巴嫩	…	1 107	3 229	3 360	3 224	15.2	15.3

续　表

地区＼年份	总　额					占经济体货物进口的份额	
	1990	2000	2012	2013	2014	2010	2014 a
马来西亚	2 021	3 526	16 518	15 610	16 537	7.8	7.9
墨西哥 b	4 326	8 485	22 859	25 113	25 811	6.5	6.5
摩洛哥	677	1 585	5 581	4 872	5 619	11.5	12.3
新西兰	643	1 074	4 059	4 238	4 629	10.4	10.9
尼日利亚 d	…	1 159	8 147	7 952	8 520	10.3	14.2
挪威	1 584	2 221	7 888	8 327	8 382	7.9	9.4
阿曼 d	486	1 122	2 913	3 159	3 612	12.0	11.9
巴基斯坦	1 276	1 524	4 846	4 467	5 565	12.9	11.7
秘鲁	621	864	4 221	4 268	4 437	10.3	10.5
菲律宾	1 348	2 598	6 819	6 723	8 243	11.0	12.2
俄罗斯 b	—	6 853	39 045	41 760	38 598	13.7	12.5
沙特阿拉伯 d	3 319	5 375	21 413	23 756	23 652	15.6	14.5
塞内加尔 d	350	362	1 554	1 588	1 481	22.4	22.3
新加坡	3 685	4 354	12 558	12 937	13 348	3.2	3.6
留用进口	2 014	2 354	7 754	7 906	8 125	4.3	4.7
南非	846	1 254	7 448	6 777	6 272	6.6	6.3
斯里兰卡	502	…	2 038	2 140	2 541	13.9	13.1
苏丹 d	…	360	992	1 038	964	30.6	10.5
瑞士	4371	4 549	11 194	12 012	12 235	5.8	4.4
叙利亚 d	745	726	1 536	1 136	1 410	21.0	21.0
中国台北	3 495	5 013	11 247	8 654	11 872	3.8	4.3
泰国	1 672	2 677	12 638	12 851	12 590	4.7	5.5
突尼斯 d	582	706	2 219	2 579	2 444	9.4	9.8
土耳其	1 856	2 128	10 420	10 830	12 047	4.0	5.0
乌克兰	—	882	7 225	7 912	5 850	9.2	10.8
阿联酋 d	1 627	3 026	15 572	17 012	17 024	6.8	6.5
美国	30 055	51 226	117 138	122 902	133 119	4.9	5.5
委内瑞拉	739	1 704	9 237	8 276	8 528	12.8	19.3
越南 d	…	814	9 473	10 903	12 325	8.6	8.3
也门 d	…	…	3 642	3 799	3 694	30.7	28.5

a　接近一年。
b　进口以 f. o. b. 计价。
c　财政年度的数据。
d　包括秘书处估计。
e　自 2000 年进口以 f. o. b. 计价。
f　参见欧盟（27）从外进口的详细数据。
g　欧盟（27）自内进口见元数据。

表 42

2014 年燃料和矿产品占货物贸易和初级产品的份额（按地区）

单位：%

地区＼份额	出　口	进　口
	占货物贸易份额	
世界	20.5	20.5
北美洲	16.7	15.8
中、南美洲	39.9	22.7
欧洲	11.1	18.1
独联体	66.1	11.1
非洲	62.9	17.5
中东	64.9	11.0
亚洲	11.3	27.5
占初级产品份额		
世界	68.2	68.2
北美洲	60.0	69.7
中、南美洲	56.7	70.7
欧洲	51.3	63.3
独联体	87.8	48.0
非洲	84.6	52.9
中东	96.6	47.5
亚洲	62.7	75.3

表 43

2014 年燃料占货物贸易和初级产品的份额（按地区）

单位：%

地区＼份额	出　口	进　口
	占货物贸易份额	
世界	16.6	16.6
北美洲	13.1	13.4
中、南美洲	24.8	20.8
欧洲	8.1	14.5
独联体	59.6	8.8
非洲	53.6	15.5
中东	63.3	8.9
亚洲	7.9	21.4
	占初级产品份额	
世界	55.2	55.2
北美洲	47.1	59.0
中、南美洲	35.1	64.7
欧洲	37.5	50.4
独联体	79.1	38.1
非洲	72.1	46.6
中东	94.2	38.4
亚洲	43.8	58.6

表 44

2014 年制成品占货物贸易的份额（按地区）

单位：%

地区 \ 份额	出 口	进 口
	占货物贸易份额	
世界	66.2	66.2
北美洲	67.6	75.0
中、南美洲	25.5	65.3
欧洲	74.8	68.5
独联体	22.4	75.6
非洲	21.3	63.6
中东	20.7	72.1
亚洲	80.0	59.9

表 45

2014 年各地区制成品的出口（按目的地）

单位：十亿美元，%

地区 \ 年份	总额	占地区出口份额		占世界出口份额		年度变化百分比		
	2014	2010	2014	2010	2014	2010—2014	2013	2014
世界	**12 243**	**100.0**	**100.0**	**100.0**	**100.0**	**5**	**3**	**4**
欧洲								
世界	**5 096**	**100.0**	**100.0**	**43.1**	**41.6**	**4**	**4**	**4**
欧洲	3 423	69.1	67.2	29.8	28.0	4	4	5
亚洲	573	10.5	11.2	4.5	4.7	6	3	4
北美洲	461	8.0	9.1	3.5	3.8	8	3	8
独联体	185	3.5	3.6	1.5	1.5	5	2	−13
中东	177	3.3	3.5	1.4	1.4	6	6	5
非洲	155	3.0	3.0	1.3	1.3	4	5	1
中、南美洲	103	2.0	2.0	0.9	0.8	5	4	−7
亚洲								
世界	**4 735**	**100.0**	**100.0**	**37.3**	**38.7**	**6**	**3**	**4**
亚洲	2 246	48.0	47.4	17.9	18.3	6	3	2
北美洲	985	19.8	20.8	7.4	8.0	8	4	6
欧洲	803	18.9	17.0	7.0	6.6	3	1	7
中东	246	4.4	5.2	1.6	2.0	11	2	14
中、南美洲	160	3.3	3.4	1.2	1.3	6	0	−3
非洲	158	2.7	3.3	1.0	1.3	12	7	11
独联体	117	2.1	2.5	0.8	1.0	11	6	−1
北美洲								
世界	**1 685**	**100.0**	**100.0**	**13.5**	**13.8**	**6**	**2**	**4**
北美洲	852	48.8	50.6	6.6	7.0	7	3	5
亚洲	328	20.2	19.5	2.7	2.7	5	3	4
欧洲	265	17.1	15.7	2.3	2.2	3	1	6

续 表

地区＼年份	总额	占地区出口份额		占世界出口份额		年度变化百分比		
	2014	2010	2014	2010	2014	2010—2014	2013	2014
中、南美洲	131	8.6	7.8	1.2	1.1	3	−3	−6
中东	66	3.1	3.9	0.4	0.5	11	3	3
非洲	27	1.5	1.6	0.2	0.2	8	−1	16
独联体	15	0.6	0.9	0.1	0.1	16	10	−2
中东								
世界	**266**	**100.0**	**100.0**	**2.0**	**2.2**	**7**	**3**	**2**
亚洲	92	33.9	34.6	0.7	0.8	8	1	0
中东	58	21.8	21.7	0.4	0.5	7	0	5
欧洲	46	16.8	17.2	0.3	0.4	8	−1	16
北美洲	26	11.5	9.9	0.2	0.2	3	−2	5
非洲	15	5.9	5.7	0.1	0.1	7	5	2
独联体	6	1.7	2.1	0.0	0.0	12	2	29
中、南美洲	4	1.6	1.3	0.0	0.0	3	0	−4
中、南美洲								
世界	**177**	**100.0**	**100.0**	**1.6**	**1.4**	**2**	**1**	**−8**
中、南美洲	80	48.4	45.2	0.8	0.7	0	0	−13
北美洲	55	27.5	30.9	0.5	0.4	5	1	2
欧洲	21	12.8	12.0	0.2	0.2	0	−4	−9
亚洲	15	7.7	8.4	0.1	0.1	4	−10	6
非洲	4	2.1	2.1	0.0	0.0	1	−8	−5
中东	2	0.9	0.9	0.0	0.0	2	−9	28
独联体	1	0.2	0.3	0.0	0.0	16	1	−29
独联体								
世界	**165**	**100.0**	**100.0**	**1.4**	**1.3**	**3**	**−9**	**−3**
独联体	64	40.3	38.8	0.6	0.5	2	1	−21
欧洲	54	27.9	32.8	0.4	0.4	8	−19	21
亚洲	17	13.3	10.2	0.2	0.1	−3	−13	−11
中东	9	4.8	5.7	0.1	0.1	8	−9	23
北美洲	7	5.7	4.3	0.1	0.1	−4	−20	12
中、南美洲	5	2.9	2.8	0.0	0.0	3	−15	−1
非洲	5	2.1	3.1	0.0	0.0	13	9	13
非洲								
世界	**118**	**100.0**	**100.0**	**1.0**	**1.0**	**4**	**7**	**2**
欧洲	42	39.2	35.5	0.4	0.3	2	2	−1
非洲	42	33.8	35.5	0.3	0.3	6	19	−2
亚洲	14	10.9	11.7	0.1	0.1	6	1	22
北美洲	8	7.9	6.7	0.1	0.1	0	−9	0
中东	8	5.0	6.7	0.0	0.1	12	14	24
中、南美洲	3	2.2	2.3	0.0	0.0	6	−1	−1
独联体	0	0.2	0.3	0.0	0.0	19	−11	−10

表 46

2014 年制成品的主要进出口方

单位：十亿美元，%

年份	总额	占世界出口/进口份额				年度变化百分比			
地区	2014	1980	1990	2000	2014	2010—2014	2012	2013	2014
出口方									
欧盟（28）	4718	—	—	43.0	38.5	4	−5	4	4
欧盟（28）对外出口	1787	—	—	14.1	14.6	6	0	4	1
中国 a	2202	0.8	1.9	4.7	18.0	11	9	8	6
美国	1 164	13.0	12.1	13.8	9.5	5	5	2	3
日本	598	11.2	11.5	9.6	4.9	−3	−2	−12	−5
韩国	495	1.4	2.5	3.3	4.0	5	−2	4	3
中国香港	454	—	—	—	—	5	4	4	3
内部出口 b	5	1.2	1.1	0.5	0.0	−11	−11	−6	3
转口 b	449	—	—	—	—	5	4	4	3
墨西哥 a	309	0.4	1.1	3.0	2.5	9	9	6	8
新加坡	291	0.8	1.6	2.5	2.4	3	1	2	1
内部出口	122	0.4	1.0	1.3	1.0	0	1	−7	−3
转口	172	0.3	0.6	1.2	1.4	6	1	10	3
中国台北	263	1.6	2.6	3.0	2.1	2	−3	1	0
加拿大	212	2.7	3.1	3.7	1.7	3	3	−2	2
瑞士	212	2.4	2.5	1.5	1.7	6	−4	3	5
印度	200	0.5	0.5	0.7	1.6	10	−4	6	7
泰国	170	0.1	0.6	1.1	1.4	5	2	3	1
马来西亚 a	144	0.2	0.7	1.7	1.2	2	−1	−1	4
土耳其	121	0.1	0.4	0.5	1.0	8	4	7	5
以上 15 个经济体总计	**11 103**	**—**	**—**	**92.5**	**90.7**	**—**	**—**	**—**	**—**
进口方									
欧盟（28）	4242	—	—	40.0	33.2	3	−8	3	5
欧盟（28）自外进口	1311	—	—	12.6	10.3	2	−7	1	5
美国	1 752	11.2	15.4	19.8	13.7	6	6	2	6
中国 a，c	1 178	1.1	1.7	3.5	9.2	7	3	7	4
中国香港	493	—	—	—	—	6	5	4	5
留用进口 b	43	1.1	0.9	0.6	0.4	21	18	1	22
日本	408	2.3	4.1	4.3	3.2	4	4	−4	2
加拿大 d	344	3.7	3.8	4.1	2.7	4	5	0	1
墨西哥 a，d	317	1.5	1.3	3.1	2.5	7	8	4	5
韩国	276	0.9	1.8	2.0	2.2	4	−4	2	5
俄罗斯 d	226	—	—	0.4	1.8	6	7	−1	−12
新加坡	225	1.2	1.8	2.2	1.8	3	3	1	−2
留用进口	52	0.8	1.2	1.1	0.4	−5	7	−19	−14
印度	186	0.5	0.5	0.5	1.5	4	−2	−4	3
瑞士	169	2.3	2.4	1.4	1.3	5	−5	4	4
中国台北	169	0.9	1.5	2.3	1.3	1	−8	0	4
巴西 d	164	0.9	0.5	0.8	1.3	5	0	6	−5
澳大利亚	161	1.3	1.3	1.2	1.3	4	10	−8	−2
以上 15 个经济体总计	**9 491**	**—**	**—**	**86.1**	**76.9**	**—**	**—**	**—**	**—**

注：a　包括重要的出口加工区的货物。
　　b　包括秘书处的估计。
　　c　2014 年，中国统计的制成品进口为 1442 亿美元。具体参阅元数据。
　　d　进口以 f.o.b. 计价。

表 47

2014 年美国、欧盟（28）和中国的制成品贸易（按原产地和目的地） 单位：十亿美元，%

出口							进口					
总额	份额		年度变化百分比				总额	份额		年度变化百分比		
2014	2010	2014	2010—2014	2013	2014		2014	2010	2014	2010—2014	2013	2014
						美国						
1 164	100.0	100.0	5	2	3	世界	1 752	100.0	100.0	6	2	6
412	34.0	35.4	6	3	4	北美洲	390	22.4	22.3	6	2	6
106	10.0	9.1	3	−3	−5	中、南美洲	47	2.7	2.7	6	−2	−2
32	3.1	2.8	2	0	−6	巴西	15	0.7	0.9	10	−7	7
239	21.9	20.5	4	2	7	欧洲	386	20.8	22.0	8	3	9
215	19.9	18.5	4	1	7	欧盟（28）	352	19.1	20.1	8	2	9
13	0.7	1.1	19	11	0	独联体	9	0.5	0.5	9	−8	27
10	0.5	0.8	20	9	0	俄罗斯	8	0.4	0.4	12	−4	35
25	1.9	2.1	8	−1	17	非洲	10	0.6	0.6	3	2	1
62	4.3	5.3	11	3	2	中东	28	1.7	1.6	4	3	3
306	27.2	26.3	4	3	4	亚洲	883	51.4	50.4	6	2	5
80	6.0	6.9	9	18	8	中国	470	27.0	26.8	6	4	6
45	4.2	3.8	3	−8	1	日本	131	8.6	7.5	3	−6	−3
123	11.6	10.6	3	2	4	六个东亚贸易方	142	10.3	8.1	0	0	7
						欧盟（28）						
4 718	100.0	100.0	4	4	4	世界	4 242	100.0	100.0	3	3	5
419	7.9	8.9	7	3	8	北美洲	244	5.6	5.7	4	−1	5
95	2.0	2.0	5	4	−6	中、南美洲	20	0.7	0.5	−6	−16	−6
43	0.9	0.9	4	7	−5	巴西	10	0.3	0.2	−4	−13	−4
3 216	70.0	68.2	3	4	5	欧洲	3 128	72.4	73.7	3	4	5
2 931	64.1	62.1	3	4	5	欧盟（28）	2 931	68.1	69.1	3	4	5
166	3.5	3.5	4	1	−14	独联体	36	0.8	0.8	4	1	2
121	2.4	2.6	5	−1	−12	俄罗斯	23	0.5	0.5	5	1	2
139	3.0	2.9	4	5	0	非洲	41	1.0	1.0	3	3	2
145	2.9	3.1	5	7	4	中东	27	0.6	0.6	3	8	−9
523	10.3	11.1	6	3	4	亚洲	726	18.2	17.1	1	−1	7
185	3.2	3.9	9	6	11	中国	387	9.6	9.1	2	−1	8
59	1.2	1.2	5	0	−2	日本	69	2.2	1.6	−5	−9	−4
150	3.9	3.2	−1	4	3	六个东亚贸易方	130	4.2	3.1	−5	−3	4
						中国 a						
2 202	100.0	100.0	11	8	6	世界	1 178	100.0	100.0	7	7	4
549	25.7	24.9	10	7	6	北美洲	121	8.7	10.3	12	24	7
97	4.4	4.4	10	−1	−1	中、南美洲	9	0.8	0.8	5	−13	−6
34	2.2	1.5	1	7	−2	巴西	3	0.3	0.3	7	−14	6
460	25.8	20.9	5	2	7	欧洲	228	17.6	19.3	10	4	12
434	24.6	19.7	5	2	7	欧盟（28）	213	16.4	18.1	10	4	12
82	3.5	3.7	13	10	3	独联体	6	0.8	0.5	−3	−4	−8
51	1.9	2.3	17	13	9	俄罗斯	3	0.4	0.2	−7	−19	−8
100	3.6	4.5	17	10	16	非洲	9	0.4	0.7	27	31	61
113	4.0	5.1	17	13	22	中东	23	1.6	1.9	12	7	2
800	32.6	36.3	14	12	4	亚洲	782	70.1	66.4	6	6	1
169	8.8	7.7	7	3	−2	日本	151	18.2	12.8	−2	−9	1
314	13.7	14.3	12	17	0	六个东亚贸易方	374	36.6	31.7	3	14	2

a 中国通报其 2014 年内部进口占制成品进口的 14%。具体参见元数据。

表 48

1990—2014 年主要经济体的制成品出口

单位：十亿美元，%

地区＼年份	总额					占经济体总货物出口的份额	
	1990	2000	2012	2013	2014	2010	2014 a
世界	2 391	4 690	11 473	11 826	12 243	67.0	66.2
阿根廷	4	9	25	25	21	32.2	29.6
澳大利亚	7	15	32	30	29	12.6	11.9
孟加拉国 b，c	1	6	23	27	28	93.3	92.3
白俄罗斯	—	5	22	17	17	52.8	45.7
博茨瓦纳 c	…	2	5	7	7	78.5	90.3
巴西	16	32	82	85	75	34.9	33.3
柬埔寨 b	…	1	7	9	10	95.8	92.8
加拿大	73	176	211	207	212	48.0	44.7
智利	1	3	10	10	10	11.9	13.6
中国 d	44	220	1 925	2 077	2 202	93.6	94.0
哥伦比亚	2	4	10	10	9	22.0	17.1
哥斯达黎加 d	0	4	7	7	7	58.1	59.2
多米尼加 d	2	5	5	5	5	60.8	52.2
埃及 c	1	2	13	14	13	41.5	49.6
萨尔瓦多 d	0	2	4	4	4	71.4	75.4
欧盟（28）	—	2 015	4 387	4 556	4 718	77.3	76.6
欧盟（28）对外出口	—	663	1 709	1 771	1 787	80.3	79.0
欧盟（28）对内出口	—	1 352	2 678	2 785	2 931	75.8	75.1
危地马拉	0	1	4	4	4	42.6	39.4
中国香港	76	192	423	440	454	93.1	86.7
内部出口 c	27	22	5	5	5	46.4	32.4
转口 c	48	170	418	435	449	94.9	88.4
印度 e	13	33	177	188	200	61.0	62.3
印度尼西亚 d	9	37	68	68	71	37.0	40.2
以色列 e	10	30	58	62	64	93.0	93.8
日本	275	450	710	626	598	88.4	87.4
约旦	1	1	5	6	6	72.6	73.8
哈萨克斯坦	—	1	12	8	8	11.2	9.6
韩国	61	155	463	481	495	88.2	86.4
马来西亚 d	16	79	140	138	144	67.1	61.6
墨西哥 d	25	139	269	285	309	74.5	77.8
摩洛哥 c，d	2	5	14	14	16	63.4	67.0
新西兰	2	4	8	8	8	22.6	19.9

续 表

地区 \ 年份	总额					占经济体总货物出口的份额	
	1990	2000	2012	2013	2014	2010	2014 a
挪威	11	13	24	25	25	18.2	17.5
巴基斯坦 c	4	8	19	18	18	74.4	74.7
菲律宾 c，d	6	35	43	42	49	85.1	78.3
俄罗斯	—	26	102	97	104	20.9	20.8
沙特阿拉伯 c	4	6	46	48	45	12.7	12.8
塞尔维亚	…	…	7	10	10	59.4	67.7
新加坡	37	118	283	288	291	72.2	70.9
内部出口	23	63	134	125	122	66.2	56.5
转口	14	54	152	167	172	82.1	88.9
南非 e	8	14	43	40	42	43.5	46.5
斯里兰卡 c	1	4	7	7	8	64.2	68.2
瑞士	60	70	195	201	212	86.3	68.1
中国台北	62	141	262	264	263	89.1	83.8
泰国	15	52	163	168	170	73.2	74.7
突尼斯 c	2	5	12	12	12	76.0	72.2
土耳其	9	22	108	115	121	77.7	76.8
乌克兰	—	10	41	36	29	63.6	53.3
阿联酋 c，f	3	7	69	83	85	24.7	23.6
美国	290	646	1 102	1 125	1 164	73.8	71.8
越南 c	…	6	79	98	111	64.0	73.9

a 接近一年。
b 财政年度的数据。
c 包括秘书处估计。
d 包括重要的自加工区的出口。
e 包括重要的钻石出口。最近几年，钻石占制成品出口的份额，印度为 12.1%，以色列是 32.1%，南非则是 5.7%。
f 重要的转口。

表 49

1990—2014 年主要经济体的制成品进口

单位：十亿美元，%

地区 \ 年份	总额					占经济体总货物进口的份额	
	1990	2000	2012	2013	2014	2010	2014 a
阿尔及利亚	7	6	34	39	42	77.5	71.9
阿根廷	3	22	55	58	49	84.3	75.5
澳大利亚 c	32	59	178	164	161	72.3	71.0
孟加拉国 b，d	2	5	22	23	27	66.0	63.3
白俄罗斯	—	4	22	23	21	47.4	50.3

续 表

地区 \ 年份	总额					占经济体总货物进口的份额	
	1990	2000	2012	2013	2014	2010	2014 a
巴西 e	13	41	163	173	164	74.0	71.6
加拿大 c	93	201	340	341	344	74.7	74.4
智利 b	5	12	54	54	49	68.5	67.8
中国 f	42	170	1 059	1 135	1 178	64.0	60.1
哥伦比亚	4	9	44	45	48	80.8	75.1
哥斯达黎加 b，f	1	5	13	13	12	74.8	71.0
科特迪瓦	…	1	5	7	6	54.6	56.8
多米尼加 b，f，g	2	7	10	9	10	58.2	59.2
厄瓜多尔	2	3	17	18	18	67.7	64.8
埃及 b	7	8	35	32	37	59.9	55.3
欧盟（28）h	—	1 960	3 915	4 029	4 242	69.6	69.2
欧盟（28）自外进口	—	615	1 237	1 244	1311	59.2	58.7
危地马拉 f	1	3	11	11	12	65.9	64.3
中国香港	71	193	453	471	493	88.2	82.0
留用进口 b	22	27	35	35	43	20.3	28.7
印度 i	12	22	188	181	186	45.0	40.2
印度尼西亚 b，f	17	30	119	112	105	63.2	58.8
伊朗 b	15	10	36	29	35	58.4	69.6
伊拉克 b	…	2	40	44	42	75.5	71.9
以色列 i	12	29	50	50	52	69.2	68.6
日本	100	213	418	400	408	50.0	49.6
约旦	1	3	9	11	11	55.2	47.6
哈萨克斯坦	—	4	34	38	34	60.8	81.6
肯尼亚	1	2	10	10	12	59.2	63.8
韩国	44	98	257	263	276	56.4	52.5
科威特 b	3	6	21	23	25	80.7	78.2
黎巴嫩 b	…	3	10	11	11	54.7	51.7
马来西亚 f	23	68	133	136	137	73.3	65.8
墨西哥 c，f	32	150	290	302	317	79.5	79.2
摩洛哥 b，f	4	7	24	26	26	58.8	57.7
新西兰	8	11	26	27	30	68.8	70.7
尼日利亚 b	5	4	26	26	27	86.5	45.6
挪威	21	27	66	68	69	74.8	77.0

续 表

地区 \ 年份	总额					占经济体总货物进口的份额	
	1990	2000	2012	2013	2014	2010	2014 a
阿曼 b	2	3	18	21	21	72.4	70.4
巴基斯坦	4	5	20	21	24	48.0	49.7
秘鲁	2	5	31	31	31	72.5	72.5
菲律宾	9	29	42	42	44	66.8	65.0
卡塔尔	1	3	20	22	25	83.0	71.9
俄罗斯 c	—	19	262	258	226	73.4	73.4
沙特阿拉伯 b	18	22	120	125	125	76.1	76.4
塞尔维亚	…	…	12	13	13	51.8	61.9
新加坡	44	110	227	228	225	64.9	61.3
留用进口	30	55	75	61	52	44.5	30.4
南非 b	13	18	64	65	61	64.6	60.7
斯里兰卡 b	2	5	11	11	12	58.6	60.3
瑞士	58	68	157	163	169	80.0	61.4
叙利亚 b	1	2	4	3	4	54.1	54.1
中国台北	37	110	163	163	169	65.1	61.7
泰国	25	47	163	158	148	66.8	65.1
特立尼达和多巴哥 b	1	2	5	5	4	49.8	49.8
突尼斯 b	4	6	16	16	16	72.3	66.2
土耳其	14	38	132	146	144	62.5	59.7
乌克兰	—	6	48	44	31	52.8	56.7
阿联酋 b	9	23	127	142	139	58.0	53.2
美国	376	968	1 618	1 651	1 752	69.5	72.6
委内瑞拉	5	12	45	32	27	67.0	60.9
越南 b	2	11	84	101	114	72.0	76.5

a 接近一年。
b 包括秘书处估计。
c 进口以 f. o. b. 计价。
d 财政年度的数据。
e 自 2000 年进口以 f. o. b. 计价。
f 包括重要的加工区进口。
g 2010 年前进口以 f. o. b. 计价。
h EU (28) 从内部的进口见元数据。
i 包括重要的钻石进口。最近几年，钻石占制成品进口的份额，印度为 11.6%，以色列是 18.0%。

表 50

2014 年钢铁的主要进出口方

单位：十亿美元，%

地区＼年份	总额	占世界出口/进口份额				年度变化百分比			
	2014	1980	1990	2000	2014	2010—2014	2012	2013	2014
出口方									
欧盟（28）	169	—	—	47.1	35.9	1	−13	−6	0
欧盟（28）对外出口	49	—	—	11.4	10.3	2	−5	−8	−2
中国 a	72	0.3	1.2	3.1	15.3	16	−3	2	32
日本	37	20.1	11.8	10.4	7.9	−3	−6	−11	−4
韩国	29	2.2	3.4	4.7	6.1	4	−5	−12	9
俄罗斯	25	—	—	5.0	5.3	1	−2	−18	19
美国	20	4.2	3.3	4.4	4.2	4	3	−4	0
乌克兰	14	—	—	3.6	2.9	−3	−15	−7	−14
中国台北	12	0.4	0.8	3.2	2.5	2	−11	−3	5
印度	12	0.1	0.2	0.9	2.4	2	5	6	−1
土耳其	11	0.0	1.4	1.3	2.3	1	2	−12	−7
巴西	11	1.1	3.4	2.5	2.3	5	−11	−19	19
加拿大	7	2.3	1.9	2.3	1.6	1	1	−9	8
南非	7	1.6	2.0	1.9	1.4	−4	−15	−7	10
墨西哥 a	5	0.1	0.7	1.2	1.1	4	−13	14	−1
新加坡	3	0.3	0.4	0.4	0.7	5	1	−5	2
内部出口	1	0.2	0.1	0.1	0.1	3	−8	−8	14
转口	3	0.1	0.3	0.3	0.6	3	5	−6	−9
以上 15 个经济体总计	**434**	**—**	**—**	**92.0**	**92.1**	**—**	**—**	**—**	**—**
进口方									
欧盟（28）	158	—	—	41.4	32.0	1	−19	−4	3
欧盟（28）自外进口	37	—	—	7.5	7.5	2	−27	−2	8
美国	49	10.1	9.5	12.7	10.0	12	10	−13	26
中国 a	22	2.7	2.5	6.4	4.6	−3	−16	−6	5
韩国	21	1.2	2.9	3.5	4.3	−2	−17	−10	10
泰国	13	0.6	2.4	1.8	2.7	3	10	1	−13
加拿大 b	13	1.6	2.0	3.5	2.6	5	3	−12	11
墨西哥	11	2.2	1.0	2.6	2.3	8	23	−11	9
土耳其	11	0.4	1.1	1.6	2.3	4	−4	10	−7
阿拉伯 c	10	2.3	0.7	0.7	2.0	10	26	−12	0
印度	10	1.0	1.0	0.5	2.0	0	−3	−24	17
阿联酋 c	10	0.7	0.4	0.6	1.9	13	13	6	4
印度尼西亚	9	1.2	1.1	1.1	1.9	6	28	−8	−14
日本	9	1.1	4.1	2.4	1.9	2	−15	−19	13
中国台北	9	1.4	2.5	3.1	1.9	0	−14	−5	7
越南 c	9	…	…	0.6	1.8	6	−4	10	13
以上 15 个经济体总计	**365**	**—**	**—**	**82.4**	**74.3**	**—**	**—**	**—**	**—**

a　包括主要的加工区的货物。
b　进口以 f. o. b. 计价。
c　包括秘书处估计。

表 51

1990—2014 年主要经济体的汽车出口

单位：百万美元，%

地区 \ 年份	总额					占经济体总货物出口份额	
	1990	2000	2012	2013	2014	2010	2014 a
世界	318 959	576 436	1 300 719	13 46 072	1 394 809	7.3	7.5
阿根廷	200	2 108	9 635	10 320	8 555	11.8	11.9
澳大利亚	726	2 151	3 246	3 104	2 713	1.3	1.1
白俄罗斯	—	739	2 959	2 182	1 755	6.3	4.8
巴西	2 034	4 683	13 038	14 409	9 991	6.2	4.4
加拿大	28 442	60 656	62 157	59 934	61 019	12.9	12.9
智利	18	203	927	763	871	1.1	1.2
中国 b	258	1 581	43 107	45 975	50 901	1.8	2.2
哥伦比亚	6	226	563	839	524	0.9	1.0
科特迪瓦	…	11	27	147	112	0.2	0.9
厄瓜多尔	1	60	490	138	121	2.0	0.5
欧盟（28）	—	287 225	617 418	655 770	695 259	10.5	11.3
欧盟（28）对外出口	—	70 233	238 473	251 630	254 957	9.8	11.3
欧盟（28）对内出口	—	216 991	378 946	404 140	440 302	10.9	11.3
格鲁吉亚	—	1	637	767	562	14.6	19.6
中国香港	354	764	1 340	1 397	1 625	0.4	0.3
内部出口 c	27	23	0	0	0	0.1	0.0
转口 c	328	741	1 340	1 397	1 624	0.4	0.3
印度	198	588	10 030	10 260	11 865	3.5	3.7
印度尼西亚	22	369	4 293	4 194	4 930	1.6	2.8
伊朗	…	61	412	198	181	0.5	0.2
以色列	31	31	167	160	204	0.7	0.3
日本	66 195	88 043	165 888	151 846	145 141	19.4	21.2
约旦	19	62	104	136	95	1.7	1.2
韩国	2 301	15 194	72 005	74 451	75 386	11.7	13.2
科威特 c	65	49	1 014	856	1 003	0.9	1.0
马来西亚 b	121	307	1 530	1 630	1 628	0.7	0.7
墨西哥 b	4 383	30 655	75 458	83 388	92 398	18.6	23.2
摩洛哥 b，c	28	24	996	1 660	2 445	1.4	10.3
挪威	305	459	772	801	789	0.5	0.5
菲律宾 b	23	583	1 626	1 568	1 762	3.5	2.8
卡塔尔 c	32	32	467	481	463	0.6	0.4
俄罗斯	—	1 156	4 340	5 095	3 799	0.6	0.8
沙特阿拉伯 c	229	59	883	1 098	1 035	0.4	0.3
新加坡	348	678	4 284	3 125	3 109	1.0	0.8
内部出口 c	82	90	521	349	259	0.3	0.1

续 表

年份 地区	总　额					占经济体总货物出口份额	
	1990	2000	2012	2013	2014	2010	2014 a
转口 c	266	588	3 513	3 713	3 499	1.7	1.8
南非	249	1 708	8 631	8 001	8 694	8.5	9.5
瑞士	591	777	2 111	2 152	2 291	0.9	0.7
中国台北	829	2 221	6 309	6 491	6 892	1.8	2.2
泰国	108	2 417	24 276	25 946	26 188	9.7	11.5
突尼斯 c	30	63	315	369	336	2.0	2.0
土耳其	153	1 517	14 837	16 765	17 497	12.1	11.1
乌克兰	—	145	520	337	242	1.0	0.4
阿联酋 c d	1	641	7 234	8 814	8 756	2.7	2.4
美国	32 547	67 195	132 262	134 726	138 070	7.8	8.5
委内瑞拉	73	223	1	4	22	0.1	0.0
越南 c	…	8	928	1 036	1 181	0.7	0.8

a　接近一年。
b　包括重要的出口加工区的出口。
c　包括秘书处估计。
d　主要的转口。

表 52

1990—2014 年主要经济体的汽车进口　　单位：百万美元，%

年份 地区	总　额					占经济体总货物进口的份额	
	1990	2000	2012	2013	2014	2010	2014 a
阿尔及利亚	658	615	7 565	7 506	6 642	9.8	11.4
阿根廷	183	2 805	12 566	14 743	9 190	18.7	14.1
澳大利亚 b	3 794	8 550	30 777	27 674	24 844	12.1	10.9
巴林	152	214	699	917	1 286	7.1	9.2
白俄罗斯	—	297	1 848	2 218	1 439	2.9	3.5
巴西 c	532	4 154	21 681	23 468	20 323	9.4	8.9
加拿大 b	24 640	46 276	71 355	71 634	70 554	15.2	15.3
智利	579	1 507	9 199	9 426	7 623	12.3	10.6
中国 d	1 796	3 798	73 973	78 035	93 479	3.8	4.8
哥伦比亚	416	590	6 176	5 154	5 834	9.8	9.1
多米尼加 d，e	…	…	792	811	927	5.7	5.4
厄瓜多尔	157	184	2 109	2 065	2 035	11.1	7.3
埃及	416	512	3 438	3 314	5 167	7.0	7.7
埃塞俄比亚	114	141	1 037	1 421	1 661	8.7	8.8
欧盟（28）g	—	246 075	442 404	468 517	506 856	7.9	8.3
欧盟（28）自外进口	—	32 199	63 459	64 378	66 553	2.9	3.0
加纳	…	331	2 228	2 043	1221	9.3	8.4
危地马拉 d	117	481	924	852	937	5.4	5.1
中国香港	994	2 195	3 731	3 822	4 576	0.8	0.8
留用进口 c g	666	1 455	2 391	2 426	2 951	1.8	2.0
印度	260	421	5 870	5 277	5 312	1.3	1.1

续 表

地区＼年份	总额					占经济体总货物进口的份额	
	1990	2000	2012	2013	2014	2010	2014 a
印度尼西亚	1 523	1 870	9 608	7 601	6 159	4.1	3.5
伊朗	…	770	2 305	2 141	3 714	4.1	7.3
以色列	871	2 298	4 078	4 773	5 307	7.0	7.0
日本	7 327	9 956	20 440	20 450	21 342	2.0	2.6
约旦	108	519	1 059	1 266	1 531	7.6	6.7
哈萨克斯坦	—	435	3 140	4 256	4 251	3.2	10.3
肯尼亚	255	156	966	1062	1 255	6.3	6.8
韩国	929	1 773	9 794	10 777	13 324	1.9	2.5
科威特 g	453	1 141	6 439	5 042	4 911	16.2	15.6
黎巴嫩 g	…	535	1 445	1 546	1 484	10.1	7.0
马来西亚 e	1 312	1 833	7 169	7 109	6 612	3.5	3.2
墨西哥 b，d	933	20 003	39 437	40 323	43 109	9.8	10.8
摩洛哥 d，g	317	471	3 307	3 607	3 358	6.7	7.3
新西兰	1 012	1 480	3 797	4 354	5 056	9.0	11.9
挪威	1 419	2 597	8 139	8 610	8 228	8.7	9.2
阿曼 g	429	1 109	4 445	5 870	6 400	24.4	21.1
巴基斯坦	390	324	1 451	1 112	1 181	2.9	2.5
巴拿马 g	111	332	1 317	1 257	1 217	5.8	5.7
秘鲁	176	510	4 585	4 611	3 725	9.8	8.8
菲律宾	537	974	3 104	3 102	3 179	4.4	4.7
卡塔尔	202	409	3 563	3 425	3 799	10.2	11.0
俄罗斯 b	—	1 044	46 122	42 204	33 208	9.5	10.8
沙特阿拉伯 g	2 839	3 815	22 802	23 390	23 289	14.6	14.3
新加坡	1 418	2 417	4 821	4 173	4 691	1.3	1.3
留用进口 g	1 152	1 829	1 308	460	1 193	0.8	0.7
南非	…	1 455	8 778	8 680	7 773	8.3	7.8
苏丹 g	…	155	475	497	461	13.2	5.0
瑞士	6 048	6 263	14 067	13 391	13 884	6.6	5.0
叙利亚 g	75	184	515	381	473	7.1	7.1
中国台北	2 565	2 676	5 399	5 718	6 518	1.7	2.4
泰国	2 651	2 084	13 439	12 531	8 908	4.7	3.9
突尼斯 g	306	595	1 718	1 717	1 750	7.3	7.0
土耳其	1 177	5 831	16 368	19 040	17 928	8.3	7.4
乌克兰	—	446	5 472	4 916	2 183	5.1	4.0
阿联酋 g	964	2 384	13 245	15 289	14 342	6.5	5.5
美国	79 320	170 195	250 375	260 065	274 431	9.6	11.4
委内瑞拉	426	1 451	1 993	852	751	2.5	1.7
越南 g	…	294	1 675	1 939	2 192	2.7	1.5

a 接近一年。
b 进口以 f. o. b. 计价。
c 自 2000 年，进口以 f. o. b. 计价。
d 包括重要的加工区的进口。
e 直到 2010 年进口以 f. o. b. 计价。
f EU（28）内部进口参见元数据。
g 包括秘书处的统计。

表 53

1990—2014 年主要经济体的纺织品出口

单位：百万美元，%

地区＼年份	总额					占经济体总货物出口的份额	
	1990	2000	2012	2013	2014	2010	2014 a
世界	104 354	154 784	283 569	304 086	314 075	1.7	1.7
阿根廷	158	258	222	205	200	0.4	0.3
澳大利亚	153	347	257	227	215	0.1	0.1
孟加拉国 b，c	343	393	1 634	2 261	2 361	6.6	7.8
白俄罗斯	—	410	729	738	673	2.4	1.8
巴西	769	895	996	949	883	0.5	0.4
加拿大	687	2 204	2 018	1 900	1 830	0.5	0.4
智利	33	114	193	170	175	0.3	0.2
中国 d	7 219	16 135	95 442	106 568	111 662	4.9	4.8
哥伦比亚	133	268	454	386	361	1.0	0.7
多米尼加 d	…	…	333	493	473	4.1	4.8
厄瓜多尔	3	40	119	122	115	1.1	0.4
埃及	554	411	1 365	1 489	1 548	4.9	5.7
萨尔瓦多 d	38	79	276	319	319	5.3	6.0
欧盟（28）	—	56 824	69 725	72 284	74 827	1.3	1.2
欧盟（28）对内出口	—	15 301	22 029	22 749	23 379	1.1	1.0
欧盟（28）向外出口	—	41 523	47 696	49 535	51 448	1.4	1.3
危地马拉	34	53	247	259	267	3.1	2.5
中国香港	8 213	13 441	10 546	10 714	9 785	2.8	1.9
内部出口 c	2 171	1 174	186	161	147	1.7	0.9
转口 c	6 042	12 267	10 360	10 554	9 638	2.9	1.9
印度	2 180	5 593	15 348	17 417	18 340	5.7	5.7
印度尼西亚	1241	3 505	4 541	4 632	4 725	2.6	2.7
伊朗	510	766	1 097	950	892	1.0	1.0
以色列	270	490	743	702	765	1.5	1.1
日本	5 871	6 994	7 819	6 841	6 385	0.9	0.9
约旦	31	43	96	111	92	1.0	1.1
肯尼亚	21	26	70	61	62	1.2	1.0
韩国	6 076	12 710	11 970	12 043	11 908	2.4	2.1
黎巴嫩	…	8	37	37	32	0.7	0.7
中国澳门	136	271	21	21	6	6.3	0.5
马来西亚 d	343	1 270	1 786	1 849	1 896	0.8	0.8

续 表

地区 \ 年份	总额					占经济体总货物出口的份额	
	1990	2000	2012	2013	2014	2010	2014 a
毛里求斯 c，d	35	81	97	114	120	3.3	3.9
墨西哥 d	713	2 571	2 236	2 446	2 549	0.6	0.6
摩洛哥 d	203	123	355	364	421	1.9	1.8
尼泊尔 c	82	182	267	259	262	31.1	29.5
新西兰	135	146	268	256	258	0.8	0.6
尼日利亚 C	…	10	291	168	180	0.3	0.2
挪威	163	173	207	201	206	0.1	0.1
巴基斯坦	2 663	4 532	8 705	9 341	9 077	36.7	36.7
秘鲁	221	128	489	465	491	0.8	1.2
菲律宾 d	132	297	170	172	253	0.3	0.4
俄罗斯	—	483	582	585	1 915	0.1	0.4
塞尔维亚	…	…	132	163	194	1.0	1.3
新加坡	903	907	801	891	878	0.2	0.2
内部出口	141	293	260	293	332	0.1	0.2
转口	762	614	553	609	553	0.3	0.3
南非 c	167	237	426	424	407	0.5	0.4
斯里兰卡 c	25	244	226	236	267	2.0	2.4
瑞士	2 557	1 278	1 166	1 164	1 246	0.6	0.4
叙利亚 c	555	158	236	105	105	5.2	5.2
中国台北	6 128	11 891	10 293	10 217	10 229	3.5	3.3
坦桑尼亚 c	…	11	106	103	97	2.9	2.1
泰国	928	1 958	3 521	3 874	3 891	1.9	1.7
突尼斯	112	154	424	413	411	2.7	2.5
土耳其	1 440	3 672	11 054	12 149	12 522	7.9	7.9
乌克兰	—	127	232	247	238	0.4	0.4
阿联酋 ce	6	1 289	2 218	2 736	2 724	0.8	0.8
美国	5 039	10 952	13 479	13 935	14 374	1.0	0.9
越南 c	…	299	3 894	4 612	5 256	4.2	3.5

a 接近一年。
b 财政年度的数据。
c 包括秘书处估计。
d 包括重要的出口加工区的出口。
e 主要的转口。

表 54

1990—2014 年主要经济体的纺织品进

单位：百万美元，%

地区 \ 年份	总额					占经济体总货物进口的份额	
	1990	2000	2012	2013	2014	2010	2014 a
阿根廷	53	653	1 133	1 136	1 054	1.9	1.6
澳大利亚 b	1 445	1 632	2 587	2617	2 720	1.2	1.2
孟加拉国 c，d	452	1 350	5 480	5 947	6 778	16.1	16.0
白俄罗斯	—	256	640	653	643	1.5	1.6
波斯尼亚和黑塞哥维那	…	…	297	361	435	3.2	4.0
巴西 e	252	1045	4300	4221	4 380	2.1	1.9
柬埔寨 b d	…	432	2 487	2 843	2 999	26.6	22.2
加拿大 b	2 325	4 126	4 584	4 561	4 580	1.1	1.0
智利	203	431	1 198	1 194	1 274	1.7	1.8
中国 f	5 292	12 832	19 810	21 563	20 248	1.3	1.0
哥伦比亚	75	558	1522	1461	1619	2.7	2.5
哥斯达黎加 f	83	184	343	284	262	2.1	1.5
多米尼加 f，g	…	1 173	862	865	933	4.3	5.4
埃及	211	206	2 278	2 390	2 389	3.8	3.5
萨尔瓦多 f	111	325	1 024	1 100	1 115	10.4	10.6
欧盟（28）h	—	57 671	75 027	78 734	83 181	1.4	1.4
欧盟（28）自外进口	—	16 189	27 330	29 199	31 733	1.3	1.4
马其顿	…	27	443	481	525	7.5	7.2
危地马拉 f	38	59	984	1 015	916	6.8	5.0
洪都拉斯 b，d	26	501	1647	1 566	1 700	17.7	15.4
中国香港	10182	13716	10 364	10 411	9 358	2.6	1.6
留用进口	…	…	…	…	…	0.2	…
印度	240	585	3 318	3 579	3 760	0.8	0.8
印度尼西亚	785	1 251	5 570	5 788	5 814	3.1	3.3
伊朗	…	298	654	745	814	0.9	1.6
以色列	474	759	706	710	771	1.2	1.0
日本	4 133	4 934	9 013	8 766	8 890	1.0	1.1
约旦	107	172	692	829	839	3.6	3.7
肯尼亚	17	47	324	346	405	2.3	2.2
韩国	1 947	3 359	4 882	5 218	5 367	1.1	1.0
科威特 d	168	212	548	371	390	1.6	1.2
黎巴嫩 d	…	178	265	293	282	1.5	1.3
中国澳门	619	906	66	33	43	1.8	0.4

续 表

年份 / 地区	总额					占经济体总货物进口的份额	
	1990	2000	2012	2013	2014	2010	2014 a
马达加斯加 d	20	200	269	330	330	10.1	10.1
马来西亚 f	951	1 114	1 368	1 452	1 476	0.7	0.7
毛里求斯 d	336	411	274	270	268	5.4	4.8
墨西哥 b, f	992	5 822	6 003	6 180	6 408	1.7	1.6
摩洛哥 f	361	1 364	2 413	2 479	2 702	5.7	5.9
新西兰	396	369	605	637	677	1.7	1.6
尼日利亚 d	…	38	370	438	469	2.5	0.8
挪威	554	509	906	934	948	1.1	1.1
巴基斯坦	126	130	1 077	1 245	1 545	2.5	3.2
秘鲁	17	165	974	965	1 030	2.4	2.4
菲律宾	910	1250	796	907	876	1.1	1.3
俄罗斯 b	—	714	4 663	4 365	4 098	1.4	1.3
沙特阿拉伯 d	1 312	986	1 939	1 864	1 856	1.4	1.1
新加坡	1 778	1 275	1 081	1 072	1 049	0.3	0.3
留用进口	1 016	661	528	463	496	0.4	0.3
南非	561	569	1 377	1 368	1 344	1.4	1.3
斯里兰卡 d	412	1 483	2 185	1 959	2 232	12.8	11.5
瑞士	1 849	1 300	1 994	2 055	2 253	1.1	0.8
叙利亚 d	168	399	207	153	190	2.8	2.8
中国台北	1 013	1 460	1 255	1 260	1 305	0.5	0.5
泰国	898	1 630	3 245	3 059	2 999	1.5	1.3
突尼斯 d	790	1 207	1 700	1 710	1 737	8.3	7.0
土耳其	567	2 124	6 441	6 789	7 117	3.5	2.9
乌克兰	—	450	1 280	1341	1 170	1.8	2.2
阿联酋 d	983	2 055	3 067	3 460	3 278	1.4	1.3
美国	6 730	15 985	25 956	27 056	28 275	1.2	1.2
委内瑞拉	112	286	1 029	673	629	1.6	1.4
越南 d	…	1 379	9 075	10 633	12 020	8.3	8.1

a 接近一年。
b 进口以 f. o. b. 计价。
c 财政年度的数据。
d 包括秘书处估计。
e 自 2000 年进口以 f. o. b. 计价。
f 包括重要的加工区的进口。
g 直到 2010 进口以 f. o. b. 计价。
h EU (28) 从内进口参看元数据。

表 55

2014 年服装的主要进出口方

单位：十亿美元，%

地区 \ 年份	总总额	占世界出口/进口份额				年度变化百分比			
	2014	1980	1990	2000	2014	2010—2014	2012	2013	2014
出口方									
中国 a	187	4.0	8.9	18.2	38.6	9	4	11	5
欧盟（28）	127	—	—	28.7	26.2	6	−6	8	7
欧盟（28）对外出口	32	—	—	6.4	6.6	10	2	8	5
孟加拉	25	0.0	0.6	2.6	5.1	13	3	19	5
中国香港	21	—	—	—	—	−4	−8	−3	−6
内部出口 b	0	11.5	8.6	5.0	0.0	−15	−29	−16	−6
转口 b	20	—	—	—	—	−2	−8	−3	−6
越南 b	20	…	…	0.9	4.0	17	10	19	14
印度	18	1.7	2.3	3.0	3.7	12	−5	12	14
土耳其	17	0	3	3.3	3.5	7	2	8	8
印度尼西亚	8	0.2	1.5	2.4	1.6	3	−6	2	0
美国	6	3.1	2.4	4.4	1.3	7	7	5	4
柬埔寨 b	6	…	…	0.5	1.2	18	8	17	17
巴基斯坦	5	0.3	0.9	1.1	1.0	6	−7	8	10
斯里兰卡 b	5	0.3	0.6	1.4	1.0	9	−5	13	9
马来西亚 a	5	0.4	1.2	1.1	1.0	5	0	0	4
墨西哥 a	5	0.0	0.5	4.4	1.0	1	−4	2	2
泰国	4	0.7	2.6	1.9	0.9	−1	−6	−4	1
以上 15 个经济体总计	**435**	**—**	**—**	**78.8**	**90.0**	**—**	**—**	**—**	**—**
进口方									
欧盟（28）	198	—	—	41.1	37.7	4	−9	5	8
欧盟（28）自外进口	104	—	—	19.6	19.7	4	−9	2	9
美国	93	16.4	24.0	33.0	17.7	3	−1	3	2
日本	31	3.6	7.8	9.7	5.9	4	3	−1	−7
中国香港	16	—	—	—	—	−1	−5	1	−2
留用进口	…	0.9	0.7	0.9	…	—	−13	−12	…
加拿大 c	10	1.7	2.1	1.8	1.9	5	−2	6	1
俄罗斯 c	9	—	—	0.1	1.6	3	0	−2	−6
韩国	8	0.0	0.1	0.6	1.6	18	3	20	12
澳大利亚 c	7	0.8	0.6	0.9	1.2	8	4	3	4
瑞士	6	3.4	3.1	1.6	1.2	4	−7	3	4
中国 a	6	0.1	0.0	0.6	1.2	25	13	18	15
阿联酋 b	4	0.6	0.5	0.4	0.7	11	13	10	−1
墨西哥 a c	4	0.3	0.5	1.8	0.7	12	8	9	11
土耳其	3	0.0	0.0	0.1	0.6	3	−18	17	3
沙特阿拉伯 b	3	1.6	0.7	0.4	0.6	9	5	6	0
智利	3	0.2	0.0	0.2	0.6	13	8	6	4
以上 15 个经济体总计 d	**385**	**—**	**—**	**93.3**	**73.3**	**—**	**—**	**—**	**—**

a 包括加工区的重要货物。
b 包括秘书处估计。
c 进口以 f.o.b. 计价。

表 56

1990—2014 年主要经济体的服装出口

单位：百万美元，%

地区 \ 年份	总额					占经济体总货物出口份额	
	1990	2000	2012	2013	2014	2010	2014 a
世界	108 129	197 930	419 518	459 662	483 280	2.4	2.6
阿尔巴尼亚 b	…	97	292	327	341	18.2	14.0
孟加拉国 c	643	5 067	19 788	23 501	24 584	77.4	80.9
白俄罗斯	—	262	577	575	535	1.7	1.5
波斯尼亚和黑塞哥维那	…	…	177	207	237	3.5	4.0
博茨瓦纳	…	30	57	19	20	3.1	0.3
巴西	247	282	167	163	159	0.1	0.1
柬埔寨 b	…	970	4 294	5 025	5 869	59.1	54.3
加拿大	328	2 077	1 280	1 270	1 371	0.3	0.3
中国 d	9 669	36 071	159 610	177 414	186 607	8.2	8.0
哥伦比亚	460	520	703	615	546	1.6	1.0
哥斯达黎加 d	54	660	193	129	103	1.7	0.9
多米尼加 d	782	2555	753	578	824	8.1	8.3
埃及	144	313	1 258	1 365	1 292	4.8	4.8
萨尔瓦多 d	184	1 673	1 912	2 067	2 076	37.7	39.4
欧盟（28）	—	56 709	109 853	118 639	126 587	1.9	2.1
欧盟（28）对内出口	—	12 753	28 268	30 579	31 977	1.2	1.4
欧盟（28）向外出口	—	43 956	81 585	88 060	94 610	2.3	2.4
马其顿	…	318	603	624	669	16.8	13.6
危地马拉	24	49	1 229	1 318	1 325	14.0	12.2
海地 b	63	245	738	811	836	90.2	91.1
洪都拉斯 b	64	2 275	3 093	3 085	3 182	46.5	39.4
中国香港	15 406	24 214	22 573	21 922	20 510	6.0	3.9
内部出口 b	9 266	9 933	256	214	200	2.8	1.3
转口 b	6 140	14 281	22 317	21 708	20 310	6.1	4.0
印度	2 530	5 965	13 928	15 542	17 742	5.0	5.5
印度尼西亚	1 646	4 734	7 524	7 692	7 670	4.3	4.4
以色列	482	729	161	155	159	0.3	0.2
日本	568	534	557	487	623	0.1	0.1
约旦	11	115	1 049	1 150	1 288	12.6	15.7
肯尼亚	9	9	241	279	325	3.7	5.3
韩国	7 879	5 027	1 910	2 100	2 248	0.3	0.4
吉尔吉斯斯坦 b	—	…	157	105	117	7.2	7.1

续 表

地区 \ 年份	总额					占经济体总货物出口份额	
	1990	2000	2012	2013	2014	2010	2014 a
莱索托 b	…	161	377	328	359	20.8	38.8
中国澳门	1 111	1 844	111	89	61	18.9	4.9
马达加斯加 b	11	309	304	397	439	32.5	20.7
马来西亚 d	1 315	2 257	4 560	4 581	4 766	2.0	2.0
毛里求斯 b，d	607	948	821	761	810	29.1	26.1
墨西哥 d	587	8 631	4 449	4 530	4 618	1.5	1.2
摩尔多瓦	—	76	254	260	278	15.1	11.9
摩洛哥 b d	722	2 401	3 225	3 155	3 278	16.9	13.9
缅甸 b	12	800	884	1 132	986	3.9	8.9
新西兰	67	116	187	228	262	0.6	0.6
巴基斯坦	1 014	2 144	4 214	4 549	4 991	18.4	20.2
秘鲁	120	504	1 619	1 392	1 201	3.3	3.1
菲律宾 d	1 733	2 536	1 612	1 558	1 843	3.4	3.0
俄罗斯	—	439	308	400	344	0.0	0.1
塞尔维亚	…	…	505	603	629	4.2	4.2
新加坡	1 588	1 825	1 335	1 272	1 346	0.3	0.3
内部出口	995	504	131	142	131	0.1	0.1
转口	593	1 321	1 204	1 129	1 214	0.6	0.6
南非	85	218	478	503	496	0.5	0.5
斯里兰卡 b	638	2 812	4 005	4 517	4 919	40.6	43.5
瑞士	686	611	1 409	1 389	1 386	0.7	0.4
叙利亚 b	330	129	135	60	60	3.0	3.0
中国台北	3 987	3 015	971	920	866	0.4	0.3
泰国	2 817	3 759	4 275	4 100	4 129	2.2	1.8
突尼斯 b	1 126	2 227	2 724	2 802	2 718	18.8	16.2
土耳其	3 331	6 533	14 290	15 393	16 680	11.2	10.6
乌克兰	—	417	573	585	568	1.1	1.0
阿联酋 b，e	146	464	1 223	1 599	1 501	0.5	0.4
美国	2 565	8 629	5 606	5 862	6 109	0.4	0.4
越南 b	…	1 821	14 443	17 148	19 544	14.4	13.0

a 接近一年。
b 包括秘书处估计。
c 财政年度的数据。
d 包括重要的出口加工区的出口。
e 主要的转口。

表 57

1990—2014 年主要经济体的服装进口

单位：百万美元，%

年份/地区	总额					占经济体总货物进口的份额	
	1990	2000	2012	2013	2014	2010	2014 a
阿尔巴尼亚 b	…	68	175	202	215	3.9	4.1
阿尔及利亚	4	38	289	329	407	0.5	0.7
阿根廷	6	333	460	405	369	0.7	0.6
澳大利亚 c	711	1 858	6 080	6 257	6 524	2.6	2.9
孟加拉国 b，d	14	174	559	607	692	0.6	1.6
白俄罗斯	—	50	249	320	380	0.4	0.9
波斯尼亚和黑塞哥维那	…	…	179	195	226	1.9	2.1
巴西 e	59	173	2 556	2 775	2 940	0.8	1.3
加拿大 c	2 388	3 690	9 371	9 950	10 076	2.1	2.2
智利	52	501	2 706	2 855	2 983	3.1	4.1
中国 f	48	1 192	4 522	5 335	6 124	0.2	0.3
哥伦比亚	19	80	802	856	901	1.0	1.4
哥斯达黎加 f	17	592	308	308	308	1.8	1.8
多米尼加 f，g	…	…	252	218	271	1.3	1.6
厄瓜多尔	1	23	253	319	329	0.7	1.2
埃及	9	11	452	530	917	1.1	1.4
萨尔瓦多 f	171	713	337	407	405	3.5	3.8
欧盟（28）h	—	83 459	174 526	183 192	198 256	3.1	3.2
欧盟（28）自外进口	—	39 729	92 942	95 132	103 646	4.4	4.6
危地马拉 f	5	33	181	193	203	1.2	1.1
洪都拉斯 b	25	1304	502	457	431	4	3.9
中国香港	6 913	16 008	16 338	16 448	16 173	3.8	2.7
留用进口	…	…	…	…	…	−6.2	…
冰岛	75	88	118	126	132	2.9	2.5
印度	2	22	403	522	608	0.1	0.1
印度尼西亚	16	39	481	570	540	0.3	0.3
以色列	61	471	1 450	1 555	1 689	1.8	2.2
日本	8 765	19 705	33 942	33 632	31 161	3.9	3.8
约旦	28	61	331	399	393	1.8	1.7
韩国	151	1 307	6 267	7 535	8 475	1.0	1.6
科威特 b	206	317	851	1 131	1 194	2.6	3.8
黎巴嫩 b	…	171	510	514	493	2.4	2.3

续 表

地区 \ 年份	总额					占经济体总货物进口的份额	
	1990	2000	2012	2013	2014	2010	2014 a
中国澳门 b	26	540	391	446	513	4.7	4.5
马来西亚 f	76	148	856	1 010	1 068	0.2	0.5
墨西哥 c，f	573	3 602	2 965	3 231	3 587	0.8	0.9
摩洛哥 b，f	8	232	383	343	397	0.8	0.9
新西兰	149	401	1 152	1 187	1 235	3.1	2.9
挪威	1 231	1 287	2 667	2 800	2 727	3.2	3.1
巴拿马 b	71	97	2 492	2 378	2 302	11.2	10.9
秘鲁	1	59	583	716	748	1.2	1.8
卡塔尔	29	54	413	482	588	1.4	1.7
俄罗斯 c	—	198	9 245	9 014	8 513	3.0	2.8
沙特阿拉伯 b	833	813	3 020	3 200	3 186	2.1	2.0
塞尔维亚	…	…	311	334	365	1.7	1.8
新加坡	920	1 881	2 389	2 916	2 584	0.6	0.7
留用进口	328	560	1 185	1 787	1 369	0.7	0.8
南非	108	223	1 813	1 900	1 866	2.0	1.9
瑞士	3437	3 181	5 721	5 904	6 131	3.0	2.2
中国台北	290	978	1 638	1 605	1 760	0.5	0.6
泰国	29	131	726	789	872	0.3	0.4
突尼斯 b	191	438	453	468	469	2.4	1.9
土耳其	16	264	2 677	3 140	3 229	1.5	1.3
乌克兰	—	60	1 157	974	614	1.2	1.1
阿联酋 b	514	832	3 569	3 921	3 885	1.6	1.5
美国	26 977	67 115	87 957	91 028	93 164	4.2	3.9
委内瑞拉	101	390	1 065	732	587	1.6	1.3
越南 b	…	450	619	716	809	0.5	0.5

a 接近一年。
b 包括秘书处估计。
c 进口以 f.o.b. 计价。
d 财政年度的数据。
e 自 2000 年进口以 f.o.b. 计价。
f 包括重要的加工区的进口。
g 直至 2010 进口以 f.o.b. 计价
h EU (28) 从内进口参看元数据库。

表 58

2014 年世界制造性服务贸易（按地区）

单位：十亿美元，%

地区 \ 年份	总额	份额		年度变化百分比			
	2014	2010	2014	2010—2014	2012	2013	2014
出口							
世界	160	100.0	100.0	6	14	−2	4
北美洲	21	12.3	13.3	8	6	7	19
中南美洲	4	2.3	2.5	9	1	7	9
欧洲	86	54.4	54.3	6	−4	15	4
欧盟（28）	83	52.8	52.6	6	−1	12	3
独联体	6	5.5	3.5	−5	7	−8	−22
非洲	2	2.0	1.2	−6	−2	−31	36
中东	0	0.3	0.2	−3	20	−16	−13
亚洲	39	23.3	24.9	8	61	−27	2
进口							
世界	105	100.0	100.0	7	2	12	1
北美洲	9	9.2	8.3	4	1	−3	0
中南美洲	0	0.2	0.5	30	25	−3	85
欧洲	52	40.9	51.0	13	2	38	−2
欧盟（28）	48	35.7	46.6	14	6	38	−2
独联体	2	1.5	2.4	20	27	14	1
非洲	1	0.5	0.7	17	6	30	34
中东	0	0.1	0.1	…	…	…	…
亚洲	38	47.6	36.9	0	1	−10	4

表 59

2014 年制造性服务的主要进出口方

单位：十亿美元，%

地区 \ 年份	总额	份额		年度变化百分比			
	2014	2010	2014	2010—2014	2012	2013	2014
出口方							
欧盟（28）	83.1	52.8	52.6	6	−1	12	3
欧盟（28）对外出口	45.5	25.0	28.8	10	1	12	16
中国 a	22.9	14.8	14.5	…	…	…	−6
美国	19.6	11.1	12.4	9	6	8	20
新加坡	8.0	5.1	5.1	6	−2	11	−1
瑞士	5.1	3.0	3.2	8	4	11	−1
韩国	3.5	1.8	2.2	11	15	6	18

续　表

地区 \ 年份	总额	份　额		年度变化百分比			
	2014	2010	2014	2010—2014	2012	2013	2014
俄罗斯	3.2	3.3	2.0	−6	0	5	−22
日本	2.3	0.5	1.5	40	10	32	168
摩洛哥	1.7	1.8	1.1	−6	−3	−34	39
乌克兰	1.6	1.4	1.0	−3	9	−14	−32
加拿大	1.5	1.1	0.9	1	7	−6	7
洪都拉斯	1.4	0.9	0.9	5	−3	8	7
挪威 a	0.8	0.6	0.5	…	−42	11	…
尼加拉瓜	0.6	0.3	0.4	15	13	14	5
哥斯达黎加	0.6	0.4	0.4	8	20	5	−12
以上 15 个经济体合计	**155.0**	**99.0**	**98.6**	—	—	—	—
进口方							
欧盟（28）	47.8	35.7	46.6	14	6	38	−2
欧盟（28）自外进口	16.1	11.6	15.7	15	13	41	−11
中国香港	13.9	24.4	13.5	−8	0	−16	−8
日本	12.0	10.8	11.7	9	0	−9	40
韩国	8.7	9.0	8.4	5	−2	−6	0
美国	7.6	8.8	7.4	2	−3	−4	0
瑞士	2.0	2.4	1.9	1	−4	27	−32
俄罗斯	1.8	1.2	1.8	19	25	18	−10
挪威 a	1.3	1.3	1.3	…	10	2	…
加拿大	0.8	0.3	0.8	38	103	15	12
中国 a	0.7	0.9	0.7	…	…	…	−34
新加坡	0.7	0.8	0.6	1	−3	1	−2
澳大利亚	0.5	0.3	0.5	17	20	38	−30
印度尼西亚	0.5	0.3	0.5	21	192	−35	27
土耳其	0.4	…	0.3	…	53	25	25
哈萨克斯坦	0.3	0.0	0.3	67	−8	9	488
以上 15 个经济体合计	**100.0**	…	**96.3**	—	—	—	—

a　秘书处估计。

表 60

2013 和 2014 年对他人拥有实物投入的制造性服务的主要进口方 单位：百万美元，%

地区＼年份	总额		占 10 个经济体的份额	年度变化百分比			
	2013	2014	2013	2010—2014	2012	2013	2014
出口方							
欧盟（28）	56 204	58 488	61.3	4	−2	6	4
欧盟（28）对外出口	27 854	32 838	30.4	4	−3	6	18
中国	23 257	21 421	25.4	…	…	…	−8
韩国	2 941	3 147	3.2	9	17	15	7
俄罗斯	2 325	1 531	2.5	0	−3	7	−34
乌克兰	1 951	1 275	2.1	14	15	−6	−35
洪都拉斯	1 289	1 374	1.4	4	−3	8	7
摩洛哥	1 236	1 505	1.3	−18	−3	−34	22
瑞士	1 120	1 276	1.2	13	35	1	14
日本	750	297	0.8	26	18	55	−60
哥斯达黎加	653	563	0.7	17	24	5	−14
以上 10 个经济体合计	**91 725**	**90 880**	**100.0**	—	—	—	—
进口方							
欧盟（28）	26 038	27 088	44.7	10	13	0	4
欧盟（28）自外进口	8 202	6 682	14.1	11	33	−11	−19
中国香港	14 956	13 746	25.6	−8	0	−16	−8
韩国	8 649	8 647	14.8	7	−2	−6	0
日本	8 009	4 933	13.7	0	−3	−8	−38
俄罗斯	324	220	0.6	17	−9	53	−32
多米尼加	97	…	0.2	12	−6	12	…
中国	79	116	0.1	…	…	…	46
中国澳门	70	…	0.1	6	27	17	…
白俄罗斯	47	26	0.1	89	15	213	−44
土耳其	45	60	0.1	…	57	16	33
以上 10 个经济体合计	**58 315**	…	**100.0**	—	—	—	—

表 61

2013 和 2014 年维护和维修服务的主要进出口方 单位：百万美元，%

地区＼年份	总额		占 10 个经济体的份额	年度变化百分比			
	2013	2014	2013	2010—2013	2012	2013	2014
出口方							
欧盟（28）	24 565	24 648	42.4	17	2	31	0
欧盟（28）对外出口	11 395	12 641	19.7	24	16	29	11
美国	16 295	19 563	28.1	6	6	8	20
新加坡	8 118	8 035	14.0	9	−2	11	−1
瑞士	4 014	3 797	6.9	10	−3	15	−5
俄罗斯	1 801	1 676	3.1	0	5	1	−7
加拿大	1 402	1 502	2.4	0	7	−6	7

续 表

地区 \ 年份	总额		占10个经济体的份额	年度变化百分比			
	2013	2014	2013	2010—2013	2012	2013	2014
挪威	772	…	1.3	1	−42	11	…
乌克兰	373	295	0.6	−7	−7	−39	−21
巴林	319	…	0.6	20	4	20	…
马来西亚	310	363	0.5	12	−10	17	17
以上10个经济体合计	**57 970**	…	**100.0**	—	—	—	—
进口方							
欧盟（28）	22747	20706	57.9	38	−10	145	−9
欧盟（28）自外进口	9 776	9 381	24.9	46	−20	175	−4
美国	7 620	7 602	19.4	3	−3	−4	0
瑞士	2 913	1 900	7.4	16	−6	30	−35
俄罗斯	1 725	1 625	4.4	33	31	13	−6
挪威	1 280	…	3.3	7	10	2	…
加拿大	709	791	1.8	49	103	15	12
澳大利亚	701	488	1.8	39	20	38	−30
新加坡	675	664	1.7	2	−3	1	−2
日本	541	7 075	1.4	5	51	−19	…
印度尼西亚	374	477	1.0	19	192	−35	27
以上10个经济体合计	**39 285**	…	**100.0**	—	—	—	—

表 62

2014年世界运输服务贸易（按地区）

单位：十亿美元，%

地区 \ 年份	总额	份额		年度变化百分比			
	2014	2010	2014	2010—2014	2012	2013	2014
出口							
世界	955	100.0	100.0	4	2	2	2
北美洲	104	10.3	10.9	5	4	3	2
中、南美洲	29	3.1	3.1	4	0	5	−4
欧洲	468	48.5	49.0	4	−1	5	3
欧盟（28）	414	43.4	43.3	4	−2	5	3
独联体	41	3.9	4.3	6	6	7	−3
非洲	29	3.0	3.1	5	6	2	4
中东	30	2.8	3.2	7	14	−10	11
亚洲	253	28.4	26.4	2	5	−3	1
进口							
世界	1 225	100.0	100.0	6	3	3	3
北美洲	132	10.9	10.7	5	3	5	4
中、南美洲	54	4.5	4.4	5	4	4	−6
欧洲	403	35.9	32.9	3	−3	6	2
欧盟（28）	366	32.5	29.9	3	−3	5	2
独联体	28	2.4	2.3	5	10	4	−12
非洲	71	5.7	5.8	6	11	1	5
中东	113	7.4	9.3	12	10	5	5
亚洲	423	33.2	34.6	7	6	−1	6

表 63

2014 年运输服务的主要进出口方

单位：十亿美元，%

地区 \ 年份	总额	份额		年度变化百分比			
	2014	2010	2014	2010—2014	2012	2013	2014
出口方							
欧盟（28）	413.7	43.4	43.3	4	−2	5	3
欧盟（28）对外出口	184.2	19.9	19.3	3	−1	4	−3
美国	89.9	8.7	9.4	6	5	4	3
新加坡	44.8	4.7	4.7	4	5	0	0
日本	39.5	4.7	4.1	0	5	−2	0
中国	38.2	4.2	4.0	3	9	−3	2
韩国	35.3	4.8	3.7	−3	12	−9	−6
中国香港	31.6	3.6	3.3	1	0	−2	1
挪威	22.1	2.2	2.3	5	4	4	5
俄罗斯	20.5	1.8	2.2	8	10	8	−1
印度	18.6	1.6	2.0	9	−1	−3	10
土耳其	14.3	1.1	1.5	11	15	4	9
瑞士	13.5	1.3	1.4	7	6	6	4
加拿大	13.3	1.5	1.4	2	2	−2	−4
中国台北	11.1	1.2	1.2	3	3	1	10
埃及	9.8	1.0	1.0	5	8	6	4
以上 15 个经济体总计	**815.0**	**85.8**	**85.5**	—	—	—	—
进口方							
欧盟（28）	366.3	32.5	29.9	3	−3	5	2
欧盟（28）自外进口	159.8	14.6	13.0	3	−3	6	−2
中国	96.2	6.4	7.8	11	7	10	2
美国	94.3	7.6	7.7	6	4	7	4
印度	77.3	4.7	6.3	14	4	−6	35
日本	45.8	4.7	3.7	0	12	−15	−2
阿联酋	45.5	2.6	3.7	15	11	7	5
新加坡	39.3	3.0	3.2	7	7	4	4
韩国	31.6	3.1	2.6	1	2	−3	4
泰国	26.7	2.3	2.2	4	7	−1	−6
加拿大	22.4	2.2	1.8	1	−1	−2	−4
沙特	19.9	1.3	1.6	12	16	8	4
中国香港	18.4	1.6	1.5	4	3	−1	2
俄罗斯	15.4	1.2	1.3	7	7	6	−12
澳大利亚	15.1	1.4	1.2	3	10	−4	−9
巴西	14.9	1.2	1.2	7	0	7	−2
以上 15 个经济体总计	**930.0**	**76.0**	**75.8**	—	—	—	—

表 64

2014 年世界旅游服务贸易（按地区）

单位：十亿美元，%

地区 \ 年份	总额	份额		年度变化百分比			
	2014	2010	2014	2010—2014	2012	2013	2014
出口							
世界	1 240	100.0	100.0	7	4	7	4
北美洲	212	17.3	17.1	6	7	7	3
中、南美洲	55	4.5	4.4	6	5	4	5
欧洲	483	40.8	39.0	6	−2	8	5
欧盟（28）	425	36.1	34.3	5	−3	8	4
独联体	23	1.8	1.8	8	10	9	−13
非洲	43	4.4	3.4	0	7	−8	6
中东	52	4.9	4.2	3	5	4	10
亚洲	372	26.3	30.0	10	10	9	5
进口							
世界	1 165	100.0	100.0	8	6	8	8
北美洲	155	14.5	13.3	6	10	4	4
中、南美洲	51	4.0	4.3	10	7	10	3
欧洲	422	41.8	36.2	4	−4	7	5
欧盟（28）	379	38.2	32.5	4	−5	7	6
独联体	65	4.1	5.6	17	28	22	−5
非洲	26	3.0	2.2	0	−5	−1	1
中东	87	7.6	7.5	8	6	6	20
亚洲	360	25.2	30.9	14	15	10	13

表 65

2014 年旅游服务的主要进出口方

单位：十亿美元，%

地区 \ 年份	总额	份额		年度变化百分比			
	2014	2010	2014	2010—2014	2012	2013	2014
出口方							
欧盟（28）	425.1	36.1	34.3	5	−3	8	4
欧盟（28）对外出口	142.1	11.2	11.5	7	4	11	4
美国	177.5	14.3	14.3	7	7	7	3
中国	56.9	4.8	4.6	6	3	3	10
中国澳门	50.9	2.9	4.1	16	14	18	−2
泰国	38.4	2.1	3.1	18	25	23	−8
中国香港	38.4	2.3	3.1	15	16	18	−1
澳大利亚	32.0	3.0	2.6	3	0	−2	2
土耳其	29.6	2.4	2.4	7	1	10	6
马来西亚	22.1	1.9	1.8	5	3	4	5
印度	19.7	1.5	1.6	8	1	2	7
新加坡	19.2	1.5	1.5	8	5	2	−1
日本	18.3	1.4	1.5	8	33	4	21
韩国	18.1	1.1	1.5	15	8	9	24
加拿大	17.5	1.7	1.4	3	4	2	−1
瑞士	17.5	1.5	1.4	4	−6	5	4
以上 15 个经济体总计	**980.0**	**78.5**	**79.1**	—	—	—	—

续 表

地区 \ 年份	总额	份额		年度变化百分比			
	2014	2010	2014	2010—2014	2012	2013	2014
进口方							
欧盟（28）	378.6	38.2	32.5	4	−5	7	6
欧盟（28）自外进口	126.6	13.2	10.9	3	−5	2	7
中国	164.9	6.4	14.1	32	40	26	28
美国	111.4	10.1	9.6	6	12	4	6
俄罗斯	50.4	3.1	4.3	17	30	25	−6
加拿大	33.8	3.5	2.9	3	5	0	−4
澳大利亚	26.3	2.6	2.3	4	3	2	−8
巴西	25.6	1.9	2.2	12	5	12	2
沙特阿拉伯	24.1	2.5	2.1	3	−1	4	37
新加坡	23.9	2.2	2.1	6	7	5	−1
韩国	23.5	2.2	2.0	6	4	5	8
中国香港	22.0	2.0	1.9	6	6	6	4
日本	19.4	3.3	1.7	−9	2	−22	−11
挪威	18.9	1.6	1.6	9	5	11	2
阿联酋	17.8	1.4	1.5	11	14	7	10
瑞士	16.6	1.3	1.4	10	10	6	4
以上 15 个经济体总计	**955.0**	**82.2**	**82.1**	—	—	—	—

表 66

2014 年世界其他服务贸易（按地区）

单位：十亿美元，%

地区 \ 年份	总额	份额		年度变化百分比			
	2014	2010	2014	2010—2014	2012	2013	2014
出口							
世界	**2 585**	**100.0**	**100.0**	**7**	**3**	**6**	**6**
北美洲	458	18.8	17.7	6	4	4	2
中、南美洲	58	2.3	2.3	6	8	0	0
欧洲	1 364	53.2	52.8	7	1	7	7
欧盟（28）	1 243	47.8	48.0	7	1	8	7
独联体	42	1.5	1.6	9	14	17	−8
非洲	26	1.0	1.0	6	11	0	6
中东	43	1.8	1.7	5	−1	9	1
亚洲	594	21.3	23.0	9	6	6	10
进口							
世界	**2 290**	**100.0**	**100.0**	**6**	**3**	**6**	**5**
北美洲	295	14.5	12.9	3	3	2	1
中、南美洲	89	3.6	3.9	8	7	7	1
欧洲	1 124	49.4	49.1	6	1	7	7
欧盟（28）	1 029	44.8	45.0	6	2	8	7
独联体	77	2.9	3.3	10	16	13	−1
非洲	74	3.3	3.2	6	−1	1	7
中东	68	3.1	3.0	6	−6	5	6
亚洲	562	23.2	24.6	8	8	7	6

表 67

2014 年其他服务的主要进出口方

单位：十亿美元，%

地区＼年份	总额	份额		年度变化百分比			
	2014	2010	2014	2010—2014	2012	2013	2014
出口方							
欧盟（28）	1 242.6	47.8	48.0	7	1	8	7
欧盟（28）对外出口	613.2	22.5	23.7	9	3	10	8
美国	400.7	16.3	15.5	6	3	4	4
印度	116.9	4.5	4.5	7	7	3	4
中国	114.4	3.7	4.4	12	7	8	23
日本	98.0	3.9	3.8	7	−11	2	27
瑞士	77.3	3.3	3.0	5	1	4	1
新加坡	68.1	2.1	2.6	13	12	15	5
加拿大	52.6	2.3	2.0	4	7	0	−5
韩国	48.8	1.6	1.9	13	18	6	3
中国香港	35.6	1.4	1.4	6	9	4	4
中国台北	31.1	1.1	1.2	10	9	6	9
俄罗斯	29.4	1.1	1.1	9	12	17	−9
巴西	26.2	1.0	1.0	8	8	−3	3
以色列	24.6	0.8	1.0	11	20	11	4
挪威	21.0	0.9	0.8	5	34	5	0
以上 15 个经济体总计	**2 385.0**	**91.7**	**92.3**	—	—	—	—
进口方							
欧盟（28）	1 029.2	44.8	45.0	6	2	8	7
欧盟（28）自外进口	441.8	18.6	19.3	7	4	8	11
美国	238.3	11.7	10.4	3	2	2	2
中国	119.9	4.1	5.2	13	10	15	13
日本	112.7	4.5	4.9	9	3	2	23
新加坡	77.4	2.9	3.4	11	13	14	−2
瑞士	61.7	2.6	2.7	7	0	8	3
印度	54.8	3.2	2.4	−1	7	1	−2
俄罗斯	51.3	1.9	2.2	11	15	15	−3
韩国	50.3	2.3	2.2	6	11	4	4
加拿大	49.0	2.5	2.1	2	7	0	−6
巴西	45.2	1.8	2.0	9	10	4	5
挪威	28.4	1.1	1.2	10	26	10	2
中国香港	21.3	1.0	0.9	4	4	3	3
澳大利亚	20.5	0.8	0.9	9	9	7	−3
中国台北	20.0	1.0	0.9	3	−1	−8	5
以上 15 个经济体总计	**1 980.0**	**86.1**	**86.5**	—	—	—	—

表 68

2013 和 2014 年世界建筑服务出口（按地区）

单位：十亿美元，%

地区＼年份	总额		份额		年度变化百分比		
	2013	2014	2010	2014	2010—2014	2013	2014
出口							
世界	**100**	**110**	**100.0**	**100.0**	**5**	**3**	**6**
北美洲	3	3	3.7	2.9	0	−17	−1
中、南美洲	0	1	0.2	0.5	29	37	221
欧洲	37	41	37.0	37.8	6	13	9
欧盟（28）	32	34	30.7	31.9	6	23	6
独联体	8	7	4.9	6.5	13	28	−15
非洲	2	2	2.2	1.8	0	12	−3
中东	3	3	2.8	2.7	5	1	17
亚洲	48	51	49.1	47.7	5	−5	7

表 69

2013 和 2014 年建筑服务的主要进出口方

单位：百万美元，%

地区＼年份	总额		占 10 个经济体的份额	年度变化百分比			
	2013	2014	2013	2010—2013	2012	2013	2014
出口方							
欧盟（28）	32 480	34 337	37.2	7	−3	23	6
欧盟（28）对外出口	19 577	19 294	22.4	16	−1	37	−1
韩国	20 375	17 103	23.3	19	27	3	−16
中国	10 663	15 355	12.2	−10	−17	−13	44
日本	9 666	11 548	11.1	−3	6	−17	19
俄罗斯	5 906	4 730	6.8	19	7	25	−20
美国	2 590	2 710	3.0	−3	2	−18	5
新加坡	1 757	1 786	2.0	19	4	9	2
瑞士	1 366	1 363	1.6	2	−11	2	0
伊朗	1 359	…	1.6	−5	0	−8	…
印度	1 219	1 613	1.4	32	10	32	32
以上 10 个经济体总计	**87 380**	…	**100.0**	—	—	—	—
进口方							
欧盟（28）	23 262	23 715	36.0	5	18	3	2
欧盟（28）自外进口	7 055	6 844	10.9	2	13	−5	−3
俄罗斯	9 362	7 532	14.5	27	36	23	−20
日本	7 504	10 304	11.6	−2	1	−3	37
安哥拉	5 049	…	7.8	3	−21	−19	…
韩国	4 852	3 258	7.5	28	−11	44	−33
中国	3 890	4 870	6.0	−8	−3	8	25
沙特阿拉伯	3 619	3 108	5.6	−2	6	33	−14
美国	2 651	2 541	4.1	2	11	−19	−4
马来西亚	2 524	2 624	3.9	29	74	8	4
科威特	1 992	2 686	3.1	−5	41	−4	35
以上 10 个经济体总计	**64 705**	…	**100.0**	—	—	—	—

表 70

2013 和 2014 年保险和养老服务的主要进出口方

单位：百万美元，%

地区＼年份	总额		占 10 个经济体的份额	年度变化百分比			
	2013	2014	2013	2010—2013	2012	2013	2014
出口方							
欧盟（28）	76 210	78 372	65.8	8	−4	8	3
欧盟（28）对外出口	41 960	46 045	36.2	8	−2	4	10
美国	16 096	16 435	13.9	4	9	−3	2
瑞士	6 846	7 215	5.9	8	5	5	5
中国	3 996	4 574	3.5	32	10	20	14
新加坡	3 768	3 939	3.3	2	2	9	5
墨西哥	2 793	3 554	2.4	15	−11	39	27
印度	2 144	2 285	1.9	6	−13	−5	7
加拿大	1 882	1 615	1.6	−1	−14	0	−14
中国香港	1 020	1 160	0.9	6	10	10	14
土耳其	1 000	1 162	0.9	11	4	16	16
以上 10 个经济体总计	**115 755**	**120 310**	**100.0**	—	—	—	—
进口方							
美国	50 454	47 316	35.0	−6	−4	−5	−6
欧盟（28）	38 384	45 018	26.6	0	−9	8	17
欧盟（28）自外进口	14 727	17 908	10.2	−3	−12	4	22
中国	22 093	22 454	15.3	12	4	7	2
日本	6 752	5 162	4.7	0	8	−9	−24
印度	5 935	7 921	4.1	6	4	−7	33
加拿大	5 357	4 614	3.7	4	20	−5	−14
墨西哥	4 835	4 220	3.4	23	−6	26	−13
新加坡	4 615	4 765	3.2	5	−1	3	3
泰国	2 976	2 705	2.1	11	11	−3	−9
伊拉克	2 685	…	1.9	15	24	12	…
以上 10 个经济体总计	**14 4085**	…	**100.0**	—	—	—	—

表 71

2013 和 2014 年金融服务的主要进出口方

单位：百万美元，%

年份 地区	总额		占 10 个经济体的份额	年度变化百分比			
	2013	2014	2013	2010—2013	2012	2013	2014
出口方							
欧盟（28）	213 851	224 853	56.0	6	−2	8	5
欧盟（28）对外出口	97 993	98 237	25.7	8	3	10	0
美国	84 066	87 264	22.0	5	−2	10	4
瑞士	24 121	22 123	6.3	1	−5	4	−8
新加坡	18 355	20 541	4.8	15	9	11	12
中国香港	16 475	17 096	4.3	8	8	6	4
加拿大	7 659	7 568	2.0	12	5	3	−1
印度	6 376	5 645	1.7	3	−14	19	−11
日本	4 561	7 204	1.2	8	13	−2	58
中国	3 185	4 531	0.8	34	122	69	42
挪威	3 135	3132	0.8	26	−7	51	0
以上 10 个经济体总计	**381 785**	**399 955**	**100.0**	—	—	—	—
进口方							
欧盟（28）	111 202	120 859	67.5	7	−3	12	9
欧盟（28）自外进口	40 290	44 047	24.5	9	0	10	9
美国	18 683	19 675	11.3	6	−2	10	5
印度	5 893	4 115	3.6	−5	−36	10	−30
瑞士	5 333	3 900	3.2	2	−11	8	−27
加拿大	4 845	4 663	2.9	−4	−5	−3	−4
中国香港	4 215	4 431	2.6	6	1	7	5
新加坡	3 758	4 347	2.3	14	4	16	16
中国	3 691	4 940	2.2	39	158	92	34
日本	3 613	5 300	2.2	5	−4	12	47
俄罗斯	3 391	2 400	2.1	8	14	22	−29
以上 10 个经济体总计	**164 625**	**174 630**	**100.0**	—	—	—	—

表 72

2013 和 2014 年世界对知识产权使用费收入 n. i. e.（按地区）

单位：十亿美元，%

地区＼年份	总额		份额		年度变化百分比		
	2013	2014	2010	2014	2010—2014	2013	2014
出口							
世界	285	300	100.0	100.0	6	4	5
北美洲	136	136	46.1	45.5	5	5	0
中南美洲	1	1	0.4	0.3	−3	8	−33
欧洲	103	110	38.6	37.0	5	2	7
欧盟（28）	83	91	31.1	30.3	5	2	9
独联体	1	1	0.2	0.3	12	15	−12
非洲	0	0	0.1	0.1	−3	6	−9
中东	1	1	0.2	0.2	10	9	−3
亚洲	43	50	14.3	16.7	10	3	15

表 73

2013 和 2014 年知识产权使用费的主要进出口方

单位：百万美元，%

地区＼年份	总额		占 10 个经济体的份额	年度变化百分比			
	2013	2014	2013	2010—2013	2012	2013	2014
出口方							
美国 a	129 178	131 636	46.9	6	2	3	2
欧盟（28）	83 279	90 541	30.2	4	−4	2	9
欧盟（28）对外出口	47 575	55 249	17.3	7	−5	2	16
日本	31 573	36 832	11.5	6	10	−1	17
瑞士	17 360	16 628	6.3	9	4	6	−4
韩国	4 328	5 151	1.6	11	−11	11	19
加拿大	4 066	3 973	1.5	13	19	2	−2
新加坡	3 109	3 151	1.1	47	11	69	1
中国台北	1 017	866	0.4	30	11	9	−15
中国	887	676	0.3	2	40	−15	−24
澳大利亚	812	894	0.3	−6	−9	−6	10
以上 10 个经济体总计	**275 610**	**290 350**	**100.0**	—	—	—	—
进口方							
欧盟（28）	123 924	143 478	46.0	6	−3	9	16
欧盟（28）自外进口	58 843	78 693	21.8	4	−2	4	34
美国 a	39 015	42 141	14.5	6	9	−1	8
新加坡	21 935	22 230	8.1	10	11	1	1
中国	21 033	22 614	7.8	17	21	19	8
日本	17820	20 916	6.6	−2	4	−10	17
瑞士	12217	12 351	4.5	15	8	6	1
加拿大	10 870	10 229	4.0	4	4	0	−6
韩国	9 837	10 369	3.6	2	16	14	5
俄罗斯	8 389	8 039	3.1	20	31	10	−4
泰国	4 586	3 971	1.7	14	16	27	−13
以上 10 个经济体总计	**269 625**	**296 340**	**100.0**	—	—	—	—

a 美国经济分析局将影视带分销服务记录在知识产权使用费中 n. i. e.（而不是视听和相关服务）。

表 74

2013 和 2014 年世界电信、计算机和信息服务出口（按地区）

单位：十亿美元，%

地区＼年份	总额		份额		年度变化百分比		
	2013	2014	2010	2014	2010—2014	2013	2014
出口							
世界	430	460	100.0	100.0	8	8	6
北美洲	44	44	10.2	9.5	7	2	0
中南美洲	9	9	2.2	2.0	6	0	2
欧洲	256	273	60.7	59.6	8	10	7
欧盟（28）	241	257	56.9	56.1	8	9	7
独联体	8	9	1.4	1.9	18	22	11
非洲	6	6	1.5	1.3	5	4	−2
中东	12	12	3.1	2.6	4	2	−1
亚洲	97	105	21.0	23.0	11	9	9

表 75

2013 和 2014 年电信、计算机和信息服务的主要进出口方

单位：百万美元，%

地区＼年份	总额		占 10 个经济体的份额	年度变化百分比			
	2013	2014	2013	2010—2013	2012	2013	2014
出口方							
欧盟（28）	240 794	256 765	62.7	8	4	9	7
欧盟（28）对外出口	107 044	116 724	27.9	8	4	10	9
印度	52 876	55 666	13.8	9	4	8	5
美国	33 409	34 221	8.7	10	10	4	2
中国	17 098	20 173	4.5	18	17	5	18
瑞士	11 191	11 897	2.9	11	12	9	6
加拿大	10 051	9 185	2.6	6	4	−4	−9
以色列	6 105	…	1.6	11	11	10	…
新加坡	4 889	5 290	1.3	11	8	16	8
俄罗斯	4 163	4 497	1.1	17	13	19	8
科威特	3 351	3 064	0.9	−2	−4	−3	−9
以上 10 个经济体总计	**383 930**	**…**	**100.0**	**—**	**—**	**—**	**—**
进口方							
欧盟（28）	156 603	160 997	64.2	6	3	10	3
欧盟（28）自外进口	62 204	63 750	25.5	6	3	12	2
美国	32 877	32 394	13.5	4	−2	2	−1
瑞士	12 753	13 422	5.2	8	−4	16	5
中国	7 624	10 748	3.1	23	9	39	41
新加坡	6 937	7 371	2.8	25	15	25	6
日本	6 349	11 341	2.6	11	9	12	79
俄罗斯	6 080	6 861	2.5	15	4	18	13
加拿大	5 828	6 148	2.4	7	7	−1	5
巴西	5 208	3 667	2.1	11	12	10	−30
印度	3 743	4 318	1.5	1	9	8	15
以上 10 个经济体总计	**244 005**	**257 270**	**100.0**	**—**	**—**	**—**	**—**

表 76

2013 和 2014 年电信服务的主要进出口方

单位：百万美元，%

年份 地区	总　额		占 10 个经济体的份额	年度变化百分比			
	2013	2014	2013	2010—2013	2012	2013	2014
出口方							
欧盟（28）	51 101	…	64.8	3	−2	3	…
欧盟（28）对外出口	23 951	…	30.4	4	2	3	…
美国	14 154	13 253	17.9	9	11	3	−6
科威特	3 351	3 064	4.2	−2	−4	−3	−9
加拿大	2 206	2 016	2.8	9	10	1	−9
印度	2 180	2 163	2.8	13	−1	34	−1
中国香港	1 599	…	2.0	19	12	14	…
俄罗斯	1 553	1732	2.0	7	4	10	12
挪威	984	983	1.2	4	−29	23	0
日本	916	1 389	1.2	8	27	−5	52
印度尼西亚	837	917	1.1	−9	−25	−23	10
以上 10 个经济体总计	**78 880**	…	**100.0**	—	—	—	—
进口方							
欧盟（28）	41 336	…	70.0	2	−4	4	…
欧盟（28）自外进口	17 265	…	29.2	4	−3	6	…
美国	7 298	6 610	12.4	−3	2	2	−9
俄罗斯	2 792	2 839	4.7	11	0	11	2
加拿大	1 732	1 827	2.9	3	−5	−5	5
日本	1 357	2 041	2.3	10	22	15	50
印度	1 095	1 053	1.9	0	−28	14	−4
韩国	1 049	829	1.8	6	3	10	−21
中国香港	957	…	1.6	20	24	8	…
挪威	777	792	1.3	−1	−11	−10	2
印度尼西亚	696	728	1.2	8	−11	−3	5
以上 10 个经济体总计	**59 090**	…	**100.0**	—	—	—	—

表 77

2013 和 2014 年计算机服务的主要进出口方

单位：百万美元，%

地区＼年份	总额		占 10 个经济体的份额	年度变化百分比			
	2013	2014	2013	2010—2013	2012	2013	2014
出口方							
欧盟（28）	179280	…	67.9	10	6	9	…
欧盟（28）对外出口	78039	…	29.6	10	4	10	…
印度	50520	53261	19.1	10	4	8	5
美国	12346	13718	4.7	11	6	2	11
加拿大	6429	5875	2.4	3	−2	−5	−9
以色列	5529	…	2.1	12	17	7	…
菲律宾	2835	3121	1.1	14	5	13	10
俄罗斯	2508	2644	1.0	25	20	26	5
阿根廷	1661	1219	0.6	8	−1	−3	−27
挪威	1499	1497	0.6	5	12	1	0
澳大利亚	1309	1322	0.5	4	−6	4	1
以上 10 个经济体总计	**263 915**	…	**100.0**	—	—	—	—
进口方							
欧盟（28）	107 515	…	72.0	8	6	12	…
欧盟（28）自外进口	41 671	…	27.9	7	6	14	…
美国	23 643	23 593	15.8	7	−3	2	0
巴西	4 804	3 013	3.2	12	10	11	−37
加拿大	3 146	3 319	2.1	14	17	0	5
俄罗斯	2 909	3 596	1.9	21	8	26	24
印度	2 280	2 882	1.5	2	68	8	26
挪威	1 869	1 904	1.3	15	24	−9	2
澳大利亚	1 632	1 880	1.1	11	0	14	15
印尼	852	892	0.6	13	2	17	5
以色列	749	…	0.5	9	17	−6	…
以上 10 个经济体总计	**149 400**	…	**100.0**	—	—	—	—

表 78

2013 和 2014 年其他专业服务的主要进出口方

单位：百万美元，%

地区＼年份	总额		占 10 个经济体的份额	年度变化百分比			
	2013	2014	2013	2010—2013	2012	2013	2014
出口方							
欧盟（28）	481 846	526 569	56.2	8	3	7	9
欧盟（28）对外出口	236 730	266 625	27.6	8	5	10	13
美国	120 143	127 676	14.0	7	7	4	6
中国	57 235	68 895	6.7	10	9	12	20
印度	46 318	47 305	5.4	10	22	−2	2
新加坡	32 382	32 803	3.8	18	17	16	1
加拿大	28 433	27 424	3.3	5	8	1	−4
日本	28 256	36 940	3.3	−4	−31	11	31
中国台北	23 833	25 862	2.8	8	8	4	9
巴西	20 509	21 515	2.4	9	8	−4	5
俄罗斯	18 449	16 736	2.2	14	11	12	−9
以上 10 个经济体总计	**857 405**	**931 725**	**100.0**	—	—	—	—
进口方							
欧盟（28）	484 172	504 913	57.4	7	4	6	4
欧盟（28）自外进口	202 234	216 483	24.0	8	9	7	7
美国	89 145	93 401	10.6	10	5	7	5
日本	48 568	58 837	5.8	9	1	8	21
中国	47 325	53 370	5.6	11	7	12	13
新加坡	40 322	37 471	4.8	19	18	23	−7
巴西	29 084	31 395	3.4	12	12	3	8
韩国	28 124	31 231	3.3	6	13	−3	11
印度	27 953	26 875	3.3	3	19	−7	−4
瑞士	26 552	29 221	3.1	9	0	6	10
俄罗斯	22 876	23 152	2.7	14	8	14	1
以上 10 个经济体总计	**844 120**	**889 865**	**100.0**	—	—	—	—

表 79

2013 年主要经济体的其他专业服务贸易（按类别）

单位：百万美元，%

地区	总额	份额									
			专业的管理咨询服务			技术与贸易及其他专业服务					
	其他专业服务总额	研发服务	总计	法律、会计、管理咨询和公共关系服务	广告、市场研究、民意调查服务	总计	建筑、工程、科学和其他技术服务	废物处理和去污染、农业和矿业服务	经营租赁服务	与贸易相关的服务	其他专业服务 n. i. e.
出口方											
欧盟（28）	481846	13.6	32.9	23.9	9.0	53.5	14.2	3.2	5.3	8.9	22.0
欧盟（28）对外出口	236 730	15.9	30.5	22.1	8.4	53.6	16.8	4.9	5.5	6.2	20.2
美国	120 143	25.0	46.4	39.2	7.2	28.6	10.7	…	7.1	0.8	2.0
中国	57 235	…	…	…	…	…	…	…	…	…	…
印度	46 318	2.2	64.6	…	…	33.2	…	…	…	…	…
新加坡	32 382	2.8	59.9	…	…	37.3	…	…	…	…	…
加拿大	28 433	15.2	43.1	38.1	4.9	41.7	22.1	…	3.2	7.1	9.4
日本	28 256	13.6	…	…	…	…	…	…	…	…	…
中国台北	23 833	…	…	…	…	…	…	…	…	…	…
巴西	20 509	2.4	19.0	…	…	78.6	…	…	…	…	…
俄罗斯	18 449	2.0	44.4	…	25.9	53.7	23.6	7.8	7.5	…	14.7
韩国	17 660	3.5	10.5	7.6	2.9	86.0	15.8	0.4	3.8	13.6	52.4
瑞士	15 030	15.7	37.0	…	…	47.3	…	…	…	…	…
挪威	13 859	3.3	15.5	…	…	81.3	…	…	…	…	…
菲律宾	13 208	0.1	0.3	…	…	99.6	…	…	…	…	…
中国香港	12 834	0.9	…	…	6.5	…	3.8	…	0.1	41.4	11.0
以色列	12 725	65.1	10.5	4.5	6.1	24.3	10.8	…	0.5	7.1	5.9
马来西亚	8 785	…	…	…	…	…	…	…	…	…	…
澳大利亚	8 717	7.9	50.7	41.7	9.0	41.4	19.1	3.9	2.9	7.1	8.4
泰国	7 995	…	…	…	…	100.0	…	…	…	…	…
印度尼西亚	6 641	…	…	…	…	…	…	…	…	…	…
进口方											
欧盟（28）	484 172	15.8	32.8	22.6	10.2	51.3	8.4	1.4	4.5	12.2	24.7
欧盟（28）自外进口	202 234	18.2	29.4	20.2	9.2	52.4	7.1	1.4	4.7	15.0	24.2
美国	89 145	36.1	38.7	35.2	3.5	25.3	5.9	…	3.9	1.7	6.4
日本	48 568	25.0	…	…	…	…	…	…	…	…	…
中国	47 325	…	…	…	…	…	…	…	…	…	…
新加坡	40 322	18.5	37.3	…	…	44.2	…	…	…	…	…
巴西	29 084	0.2	6.9	…	…	92.9	…	…	…	…	…
韩国	28 124	7.6	25.2	9.1	16.1	67.2	3.6	0.1	4.3	9.2	50.0
印度	27 953	0.9	37.6	…	…	61.5	…	…	…	…	…
瑞士	26 552	23.5	54.3	…	…	22.2	…	…	…	…	…
俄罗斯	22 876	0.8	28.3	…	9.5	70.9	24.2	15.7	18.5	…	12.5
加拿大	22 049	6.6	48.5	44.8	3.7	44.9	20.7	…	4.2	4.8	15.2
挪威	14 913	3.0	12.4	…	…	84.7	…	…	…	…	…
中国台北	11 949	…	…	…	…	…	…	…	…	…	…
澳大利亚	11 221	2.6	44.5	41.6	2.9	52.9	30.2	2.1	5.6	2.7	12.3
中国香港	10 965	1.3	…	…	5.2	…	3.0	…	16.4	38.6	7.7
泰国	10 529	…	…	…	…	100.0	…	…	…	…	…
安哥拉	9 453	…	0.1	…	…	99.9	…	…	…	…	…
马来西亚	8 656	…	…	…	…	…	…	…	…	…	…
中国澳门	8 513	0.0	1.6	…	…	98.4	…	…	…	…	…
印度尼西亚	7 672	…	…	…	…	…	…	…	…	…	…

表 80

2013 和 2014 年个人、文化及娱乐服务的主要进出口方　　单位：百万美元，%

地区 \ 年份	总额		占 10 个经济体的份额	年度变化百分比			
	2013	2014	2013	2010—2013	2012	2013	2014
出口方							
欧盟（28）	29 838	28 989	75.8	12	2	19	−3
欧盟（28）对外出口	12 018	10 413	30.5	14	12	23	−13
加拿大	2 927	2 448	7.4	9	19	1	−16
土耳其	1 286	1 796	3.3	12	−4	5	40
印度	1 232	1 266	3.1	8	123	61	3
俄罗斯	770	681	2.0	18	13	39	−12
韩国	731	955	1.9	23	30	8	31
澳大利亚	722	882	1.8	1	4	−20	22
美国 a	714	747	1.8	−11	9	−20	5
瑞士	606	770	1.5	19	−5	56	27
新加坡	543	550	1.4	2	3	2	1
以上 10 个经济体总计	**39 370**	**39 085**	**100.0**	—	—	—	—
进口方							
欧盟（28）	26 936	28 757	61.4	5	−2	11	7
欧盟（28）自外进口	12 763	13 643	29.1	6	−2	13	7
委内瑞拉	3 791	2 961	8.6	5	3	1	−22
加拿大	2 646	2 437	6.0	8	14	1	−8
卡塔尔	2 115	1 480	4.8	…	−2	51	−30
巴西	1 671	1 719	3.8	18	−8	62	3
澳大利亚	1 633	1 563	3.7	9	3	−6	−4
挪威	1 584	1 613	3.6	43	16	−13	2
俄罗斯	1 264	1 611	2.9	8	6	13	28
日本	1 130	849	2.6	7	23	−6	−25
瑞士	1 128	818	2.6	8	0	6	−27
以上 10 个经济体总计	**43 900**	**43 810**	**100.0**	—	—	—	—

a 美国经济分析局将影视带分销服务记录在知识产权使用费中 n. i. e.（而不是视听和相关服务）。

表 81

2013 和 2014 年视听及相关服务的主要进出口方

单位：百万美元，%

地区 \ 年份	总额		占 10 个经济体的份额	年度变化百分比			
	2013	2014	2013	2010—2013	2012	2013	2014
出口方							
欧盟（28）	19 009	…	80.8	10	－4	27	…
欧盟（28）对外出口	8 040	…	34.2	13	3	41	…
加拿大	2 428	…	10.3	7	15	0	…
印度	505	406	2.1	30	117	66	－20
韩国	441	536	1.9	25	43	13	22
阿根廷	336	306	1.4	4	－12	9	－9
俄罗斯	289	216	1.2	－7	1	－8	－25
中国	147	175	0.6	6	2	17	19
澳大利亚	142	214	0.6	3	－5	－25	51
南非	127	129	0.5	6	3	2	1
厄瓜多尔	110	99	0.5	18	22	10	－9
以上 10 个经济体总计	**23 535**	…	**100.0**	—	—	—	—
进口方							
欧盟（28）	14 637	…	62.3	1	－3	－2	…
欧盟（28）自外进口	6 060	…	25.8	2	－2	0	…
加拿大	2 339	…	10.0	6	11	2	…
澳大利亚	1 325	1 292	5.6	9	4	－6	－2
巴西	1 229	1 274	5.2	9	－8	27	4
日本	873	697	3.7	6	20	－9	－20
俄罗斯	865	846	3.7	1	－7	6	－2
中国	783	874	3.3	28	41	39	12
挪威	514	524	2.2	6	9	－16	2
阿根廷	484	463	2.1	9	7	6	－4
韩国	445	487	1.9	15	30	32	9
以上 10 个经济体总计	**23 495**	…	**100.0**	—	—	—	—

表 82

2014 年中间品的主要进出口方

单位：十亿美元，

地区 \ 年份	总额	占世界进出口的份额		年度变化百分比			
	2014	2010	2014	2010—2014	2012	2013	2014
出口方							
欧盟（28）	2 784	35.9	34.8	4	−6	7	0
欧盟（28）对外出口	1 023	12.6	12.8	6	−1	12	−4
中国 a	963	9.6	12.1	11	6	11	6
美国	771	10.2	9.6	4	1	0	1
日本	368	6.5	4.6	−3	−3	−10	−7
韩国	323	3.8	4.0	7	1	5	5
中国台北	282	2.9	3.5	11	−3	1	37
新加坡	226	3.1	2.8	3	0	3	1
加拿大	201	2.7	2.5	3	−2	−1	1
瑞士	177	1.4	2.2	19	−4	3	72
巴西	148	2.0	1.9	4	−7	2	−6
印度	140	1.7	1.8	6	−2	16	−10
澳大利亚	135	1.7	1.7	5	−7	4	−8
马来西亚	128	1.8	1.6	3	−5	−1	3
泰国	112	1.5	1.4	3	−7	0	−1
俄罗斯	111	1.2	1.4	8	19	−4	−3
以上 15 个经济体总计	**6 868**	**86.0**	**86.0**	**5**	**−3**	**4**	**2**
进口方							
欧盟（28）	2 602	33.9	32.4	3	−10	3	3
欧盟（28）自外进口	898	12.1	11.2	2	−10	1	3
中国 a	1 147	13.2	14.3	7	1	8	0
美国	833	9.4	10.4	7	4	0	6
日本	290	4.0	3.6	2	−5	−6	4
墨西哥 a	237	2.7	3.0	7	5	2	5
印度	213	2.7	2.7	4	−4	−7	0
韩国	200	3.1	2.5	−1	−5	0	−14
加拿大 b	198	2.5	2.5	4	3	−2	1
新加坡	173	2.3	2.2	3	2	2	0
瑞士	159	1.1	2.0	21	−8	5	88
中国台北	124	2.1	1.5	−3	−10	−4	−9
马来西亚	123	1.6	1.5	3	−2	3	2
土耳其	123	1.4	1.5	7	−3	11	−5
泰国	121	1.6	1.5	2	2	0	−11
巴西	118	1.4	1.5	6	−1	7	−4
以上 15 个经济体总计	**6 661**	**83.1**	**83.0**	**4**	**−4**	**2**	**2**

a　包括出口加工区。

b　进口以 f. o. b. 计价。

表 83

2011 年主要经济体总出口的增值含量

单位：%

地 区	出口的增值含量 a					
	国 内				国外	总计
	直接出口	出口至第三方	复进口	总计		
阿根廷	69.4	16.5	0.0	85.9	14.1	100.0
澳大利亚	56.1	29.7	0.1	85.9	14.1	100.0
奥地利	47.0	25.0	0.2	72.2	27.8	100.0
比利时	41.5	23.8	0.2	65.5	34.5	100.0
巴西	64.6	24.6	0.1	89.2	10.8	100.0
保加利亚	43.1	16.9	0.0	60.0	40.0	100.0
加拿大	57.0	19.1	0.4	76.5	23.5	100.0
智利	47.7	32.1	0.0	79.8	20.2	100.0
中国	51.2	15.7	1.0	67.8	32.2	100.0
哥伦比亚	62.1	30.2	0.0	92.4	7.6	100.0
哥斯达黎加	55.3	16.9	0.0	72.2	27.8	100.0
克罗地亚	65.9	14.0	0.0	79.8	20.2	100.0
捷克	34.7	19.8	0.3	54.7	45.3	100.0
丹麦	42.5	24.6	0.2	67.4	32.6	100.0
爱沙尼亚	44.2	20.5	0.1	64.8	35.2	100.0
芬兰	42.3	22.9	0.1	65.3	34.7	100.0
法国	52.4	22.1	0.4	74.9	25.1	100.0
德国	49.2	24.3	1.0	74.5	25.5	100.0
希腊	56.5	18.5	0.0	75.0	25.0	100.0
中国香港	55.6	23.9	0.1	79.6	20.4	100.0
匈牙利	34.4	16.8	0.1	51.3	48.7	100.0
印度	56.5	19.3	0.1	75.9	24.1	100.0
印度尼西亚	56.3	31.6	0.1	88.0	12.0	100.0
爱尔兰	40.3	16.0	0.1	56.4	43.6	100.0
以色列	55.1	19.6	0.0	74.7	25.3	100.0
意大利	52.0	21.3	0.3	73.5	26.5	100.0
日本	52.0	33.0	0.4	85.3	14.7	100.0
韩国	37.4	20.6	0.4	58.3	41.7	100.0
拉脱维亚	46.9	24.3	0.1	71.3	28.7	100.0
立陶宛	53.5	22.7	0.1	76.3	23.7	100.0
卢森堡	28.4	12.5	0.1	41.0	59.0	100.0

续 表

地 区	出口的增值含量 a					
	国 内				国外	总计
	直接出口	出口至第三方	复进口	总计		
马来西亚	39.2	19.9	0.3	59.4	40.6	100.0
墨西哥	52.9	15.1	0.3	68.3	31.7	100.0
荷兰	51.9	27.9	0.1	80.0	20.0	100.0
新西兰	66.6	16.7	0.0	83.3	16.7	100.0
挪威	41.7	40.9	0.3	82.8	17.2	100.0
菲律宾	48.5	27.9	0.0	76.4	23.6	100.0
波兰	43.9	23.5	0.2	67.6	32.4	100.0
葡萄牙	49.1	18.0	0.1	67.2	32.8	100.0
罗马尼亚	50.9	24.7	0.1	75.6	24.4	100.0
俄罗斯	47.6	38.4	0.3	86.3	13.7	100.0
沙特阿拉伯	54.6	42.0	0.0	96.7	3.3	100.0
新加坡	37.8	20.2	0.1	58.2	41.8	100.0
斯洛伐克	32.3	20.7	0.2	53.2	46.8	100.0
斯洛文尼亚	41.1	22.7	0.0	63.8	36.2	100.0
南非	54.0	26.5	0.0	80.5	19.5	100.0
西班牙	53.0	19.9	0.3	73.1	26.9	100.0
瑞典	45.6	24.9	0.3	70.8	29.2	100.0
瑞士	52.0	26.0	0.2	78.2	21.8	100.0
中国台湾	31.9	24.2	0.3	56.4	43.6	100.0
泰国	45.4	15.5	0.1	61.0	39.0	100.0
突尼斯	49.1	18.4	0.0	67.6	32.4	100.0
土耳其	58.9	15.3	0.1	74.3	25.7	100.0
英国	51.7	24.9	0.4	77.0	23.0	100.0
美国	59.2	25.0	0.7	85.0	15.0	100.0
越南	47.7	16.0	0.1	63.7	36.3	100.0
欧盟（28）b，d	**48.3**	**22.7**	**0.4**	**71.3**	**28.7**	**100.0**
其他 c	**55.6**	**33.4**	**0.4**	**89.4**	**10.6**	**100.0**
世界 d	**51.0**	**24.3**	**0.4**	**75.8**	**24.2**	**100.0**

a 细节可见元数据第 V 节第 2.4 部分。
b 包括欧盟对内出口。
c 除表中所列的所有国家。
d 所有经济体的平均值。

表 84

2011 年主要经济体国内外对总出口的贡献度

单位：%

地　区	出口增值的来源 a						
	国　内			国　外			总　计
	初级产品	制成品	服务	初级产品	制成品	服务	
阿根廷	23.0	24.0	38.9	3.3	4.3	6.5	100.0
澳大利亚	33.5	10.8	41.6	4.9	3.3	5.9	100.0
奥地利	2.1	24.8	45.5	4.8	8.5	14.3	100.0
比利时	0.9	15.7	49.0	7.5	6.8	20.1	100.0
巴西	22.8	20.0	46.4	2.9	2.9	4.9	100.0
保加利亚	7.5	18.5	34.2	11.2	9.8	18.8	100.0
加拿大	20.4	19.6	36.6	4.3	8.7	10.4	100.0
智利	16.0	32.7	31.0	8.3	4.0	7.9	100.0
中国	8.1	30.7	29.1	6.1	11.3	14.7	100.0
哥伦比亚	53.2	15.3	23.8	1.3	2.8	3.5	100.0
哥斯达黎加	7.1	18.3	46.9	4.6	11.9	11.2	100.0
克罗地亚	3.5	16.1	60.2	5.3	4.8	10.0	100.0
捷克	2.2	23.5	29.2	6.0	16.8	22.3	100.0
丹麦	6.6	14.6	45.9	5.1	6.3	21.4	100.0
爱沙尼亚	3.4	17.8	43.7	3.7	11.1	20.3	100.0
芬兰	3.0	23.4	39.0	7.0	9.0	18.6	100.0
法国	2.6	20.3	52.0	4.4	8.5	12.1	100.0
德国	1.0	32.8	40.8	4.1	7.8	13.6	100.0
希腊	3.7	14.6	56.8	8.6	4.6	11.8	100.0
中国香港	0.0	2.1	77.5	2.6	4.7	13.2	100.0
匈牙利	2.7	19.9	28.9	5.3	18.0	25.2	100.0
印度	9.3	17.6	49.2	9.6	4.4	10.0	100.0
印度尼西亚	40.2	23.1	24.7	4.0	3.2	4.9	100.0
爱尔兰	1.1	20.6	34.8	3.2	6.4	33.9	100.0
以色列	2.3	23.2	49.5	5.5	7.1	12.4	100.0
意大利	1.8	27.3	44.4	5.9	7.8	12.7	100.0
日本	0.8	38.4	46.1	4.9	4.1	5.7	100.0
韩国	0.7	31.3	26.4	14.7	11.5	15.5	100.0
拉脱维亚	5.8	16.5	49.1	3.5	9.3	15.8	100.0
立陶宛	3.5	22.0	50.8	4.7	6.3	12.7	100.0
卢森堡	0.2	3.4	37.4	3.0	6.2	49.8	100.0
马来西亚	16.1	18.4	25.0	7.7	14.5	18.4	100.0
墨西哥	18.6	23.9	25.8	3.5	15.0	13.2	100.0
荷兰	7.7	15.9	56.5	3.6	3.0	13.4	100.0
新西兰	14.5	16.9	52.0	5.2	3.3	8.1	100.0
挪威	42.3	9.4	31.2	2.0	5.2	10.1	100.0
菲律宾	7.3	27.6	41.5	7.2	7.0	9.3	100.0
波兰	5.6	22.8	39.3	4.5	11.7	16.1	100.0
葡萄牙	2.7	19.4	45.3	8.3	9.1	15.2	100.0
罗马尼亚	5.7	36.1	33.8	4.5	7.9	11.9	100.0

续　表

地　区	出口增值的来源 a						
	国　内			国　外			总　计
	初级产品	制成品	服务	初级产品	制成品	服务	
俄罗斯	25.7	20.9	39.6	1.7	5.2	6.9	100.0
沙特阿拉伯	81.4	8.2	7.2	0.6	0.7	2.0	100.0
新加坡	0.2	15.7	42.3	9.0	7.5	25.2	100.0
斯洛伐克	2.7	21.9	28.7	8.7	17.0	21.0	100.0
斯洛文尼亚	1.9	23.9	38.1	5.5	11.6	19.0	100.0
南非	24.4	16.2	40.0	8.0	4.1	7.3	100.0
西班牙	3.0	21.0	49.2	6.6	7.2	13.0	100.0
瑞典	2.9	22.6	45.4	4.9	8.0	16.2	100.0
瑞士	0.6	24.9	52.8	2.4	7.0	12.3	100.0
中国台湾	0.6	24.9	31.0	11.8	14.5	17.3	100.0
泰国	9.9	23.5	27.7	9.2	12.3	17.5	100.0
突尼斯	14.0	18.1	35.5	5.1	10.7	16.6	100.0
土耳其	7.2	22.3	44.8	5.2	9.1	11.4	100.0
英国	5.3	18.7	53.1	4.2	6.9	11.8	100.0
美国	5.8	28.7	50.5	4.1	4.8	6.1	100.0
越南	23.0	15.7	25.0	7.9	12.7	15.7	100.0
欧盟（28）b d	**2.8**	**23.4**	**45.2**	**5.0**	**8.0**	**15.6**	**100.0**
其他 c	**50.8**	**13.1**	**25.5**	**1.8**	**3.8**	**5.1**	**100.0**
世界 d	**13.2**	**23.4**	**39.2**	**5.1**	**7.3**	**11.7**	**100.0**

a　细节可见元数据第 V 节第 2.4 部分。
b　包括欧盟对内出口。
c　除表中所列的所有国家。
d　单个经济体的平均。

表 85

2012 年美国海外子公司提供的货物和服务　单位：十亿美元，%

	总　额	占总供应的份额
海外子公司的总供应	**1 739.0**	**30.3**
给母公司	471.0	8.2
给其他当地分支机构 a	349.0	6.1
给非当地的分支机构 b	919.0	16.0
无关联公司的总供应	**3 999.0**	**69.7**
给美国的无关联机构	111.0	1.9
给非关联的本地公司 a	3 063.0	53.4
给非关联的非本地公司 b	825.0	14.4
分支机构与无关联公司的总供应	**5 738.0**	**100.0**

a　在同一个经济体内。
b　公司设在第三方国家。

中国商务统计

表 1

1981—2014 年全国进出口总值

单位：亿美元，%

年　度	进出口	出　口	进　口	同　　比		
				进出口	出　口	进　口
1981	440.2	220.1	220.2	—	—	—
1982	416.1	223.2	192.9	−5.5	1.4	−12.4
1983	436.2	222.3	213.9	4.8	−0.4	10.9
1984	535.5	261.4	274.1	22.8	17.6	28.1
1985	696.0	273.5	422.5	30.0	4.6	54.1
1986	738.5	309.4	429.0	6.1	13.1	1.5
1987	826.5	394.4	432.2	11.9	27.5	0.7
1988	1 027.8	475.2	552.7	24.4	20.5	27.9
1989	1 116.8	525.4	591.4	8.7	10.6	7.0
1990	1 154.4	620.9	533.5	3.4	18.2	−9.8
1991	1 357.0	719.1	637.9	17.6	15.8	19.6
1992	1 655.3	849.4	805.9	22.0	18.1	26.3
1993	1 957.0	917.4	1 039.6	18.2	8.0	29.0
1994	2 366.2	1 210.1	1 156.2	20.9	31.9	11.2
1995	2 808.6	1 487.8	1 320.8	18.7	23.0	14.2
1996	2 898.8	1 510.5	1 388.3	3.2	1.5	5.1
1997	3 251.6	1 827.9	1 423.7	12.2	21.0	2.5
1998	3 239.5	1 837.1	1 402.4	−0.4	0.5	−1.5
1999	3 606.3	1 949.3	1 657.0	11.3	6.1	18.2
2000	4 743.0	2 492.0	2 250.9	31.5	27.8	35.8
2001	5 096.5	2 661.0	2 435.5	7.5	6.8	8.2
2002	6 207.7	3 256.0	2 951.7	21.8	22.4	21.2
2003	8 509.9	4 382.3	4 127.6	37.1	34.6	39.8
2004	11 545.5	5 933.3	5 612.3	35.7	35.4	36.0
2005	14 219.1	7 619.5	6 599.5	23.2	28.4	17.6
2006	17 604.4	9 689.8	7 914.6	23.8	27.2	19.9
2007	21 765.7	12 204.6	9 561.2	23.6	26.0	20.8
2008	25 632.6	14 306.9	11 325.7	17.8	17.3	18.5
2009	22 072.7	12 016.6	10 056	−13.9	−16	−11.2
2010	29 792.6	15 779.3	13 948.3	34.7	31.3	38.7
2011	36 420.6	18 986.0	17 434.6	22.5	20.3	24.9
2012	38 667.6	20 489.3	18 178.3	6.2	7.9	4.3
2013	41 596.9	22 093.7	19 503.2	7.6	7.9	7.3
2014	43 030.4	23 427.5	19 602.9	3.4	6.1	47.7

表 2

2014 年全国进出口简要情况

单位：亿美元，%

项 目	12 月份		1～12 月累计	
	绝对值	同比	绝对值	同比
进出口总值	4 054.1	4.0	43 030.4	3.4
出口总值	2 275.1	9.7	23 427.5	6.1
进口总值	1 779.0	−2.4	19 602.9	0.4
进出口差额	496.1	96.7	3 824.6	47.7

表 3

2014 年全国进出口主要国别/地区总值

单位：千美元，%

进口原产国（地）	进 出 口		出 口		进 口		累计同比（±%）		
出口最终目的国（地）	12 月份	1～12 月累计	12 月份	1～12 月累计	12 月份	1～12 月累计	进出口	出口	进口
总值	405 414 601	4 303 038 237	227 513 932	2 342 747 940	177 900 669	1 960 290 297	3.4	6.1	0.4
其中：中国香港	42 855 228	376 094 148	41 540 049	363 191 444	1 315 179	12 902 704	−6.2	−5.5	−20.7
印度	6 240 548	70 593 572	4 869 824	54 222 132	1 370 723	16 371 439	7.9	12.0	−3.5
日本	27 464 758	312 438 377	12 509 087	149 441 787	14 955 671	162 996 589	0.0	−0.5	0.4
韩国	26 307 230	290 492 439	9 220 136	100 340 329	17 087 094	190 152 110	5.9	10.1	3.9
中国台湾	18 812 038	198 314 347	3 943 529	46 284 835	14 868 508	152 029 512	0.6	13.9	−2.8
东南亚国家联盟	47 717 257	480 394 105	28 584 087	272 072 412	19 133 170	208 321 693	8.3	11.5	4.4
其中：印度尼西亚	5 802 650	63 580 941	3 754 814	39 059 495	2 047 835	24 521 446	−7.0	5.8	−22.0
马来西亚	10 451 095	102 020 546	4 739 480	46 359 122	5 711 615	55 661 424	−3.8	0.9	−7.5
菲律宾	3 913 864	44 456 657	2 012 805	23 474 425	1 901 059	20 982 232	16.8	18.2	15.4
新加坡	8 452 155	79 740 866	5 549 283	48 914 504	2 902 872	30 826 362	5.0	6.7	2.4
泰国	7 247 833	72 673 161	3 556 288	34 296 258	3 691 544	38 376 903	2.0	4.8	0.4
越南	9 629 801	83 639 763	7 490 144	63 736 325	2 139 658	19 903 437	27.7	31.2	17.8
欧洲联盟	57 718 830	615 139 195	34 584 570	370 884 340	23 134 260	244 254 855	9.9	9.4	10.7
其中：英国	7 543 026	80 872 434	5 306 870	57 143 434	2 236 156	23 729 000	15.3	12.2	23.5
德国	16 520 589	177 752 629	6 809 025	72 712 277	9 711 565	105 040 352	10.1	8.0	11.5
法国	5 627 707	55 796 801	2 720 654	28 708 154	2 907 053	27 088 647	10.9	7.5	14.8
意大利	4 643 755	48 044 808	2 810 581	28 758 443	1 833 175	19 286 365	10.7	11.7	9.2
荷兰	6 960 366	74 282 588	5 949 636	64 931 392	1 010 731	9 351 196	5.9	7.7	−4.9
俄罗斯联邦	8 567 272	95 284 981	4 892 514	53 677 572	3 674 758	41 607 409	6.8	8.2	4.9
南非	6 346 228	60 291 914	1 301 794	15 700 923	5 044 434	44 590 991	−7.6	−6.7	−7.8
巴西	6 133 085	86 579 143	3 209 275	34 893 565	2 923 810	51 685 578	−4.0	−2.8	−4.8
加拿大	5 511 193	55 219 267	2 902 924	30 005 760	2 608 269	25 213 507	1.4	2.7	−0.1
美国	52 609 274	555 118 075	36 634 771	396 082 119	15 974 503	159 035 957	6.6	7.5	4.2
澳大利亚	10 933 117	136 904 716	3 425 577	39 153 639	7 507 539	97 751 077	0.3	4.3	−1.2
新西兰	1 006 346	14 247 216	461 328	4 740 612	545 017	9 506 604	15.0	14.7	15.2

表 4

2014 年全国进口重点商品量值

单位：千美元

商品名称	计量单位	12 月份		1～12 月累计		2013 年同期累计		累计比去年同期±%	
		数量	金额	数量	金额	数量	金额	数量	金额
鲜、干水果及坚果	万吨	45	572 387	384	5 023 342	312	3 983 217	23.0	26.1
谷物及谷物粉	万吨	237	727 645	1 951	6 217 150	1 458	5 100 598	33.8	21.9
大豆	万吨	853	4 190 044	7 140	40 285 043	6 338	38 009 435	12.7	6.0
食用植物油	万吨	59	461 664	650	5 931 783	810	8 075 021	−19.7	−26.5
铁矿砂及其精矿	万吨	8 685	6 566 908	93 251	93 642 293	81 910	106 175 378	13.8	−11.8
铜矿砂及其精矿	万吨	117	2 173 610	1 181	21 645 117	1 007	19 508 977	17.3	11.0
煤及褐煤	万吨	2 722	1 900 289	29 122	22 249 979	32 702	29 066 367	−10.9	−23.5
原油	万吨	3 037	17 263 321	30 838	228 311 556	28 174	219 660 366	9.5	3.9
成品油	万吨	320	1 952 361	3 000	23 434 886	3 959	32 025 729	−24.2	−26.8
5－7 号燃料油	万吨	190	891 812	1 771	10 804 273	2 257	14 576 146	−21.5	−25.9
液化石油气及其他烃类气	万吨	275	1 736 817	2 726	18 578 179	2 252	14 811 431	21.1	25.4
医药品	吨	11 971	1 977 695	112 356	19 094 211	97 584	16 216 230	15.1	17.7
矿物肥料及化肥	万吨	89	292 426	955	3 347 522	789	3 371 078	21.1	−0.7
初级形状的塑料	万吨	224	4 375 425	2 535	51 573 108	2 462	49 095 516	3.0	5.0
天然及合成橡胶（包括胶乳）	万吨	41	776 002	409	8 929 984	400	10 820 936	2.4	−17.5
原木及锯材	万立方米	671	1 625 608	7 685	19 863 155	6 918	16 146 433	11.1	23.0
纸浆	万吨	162	1 047 700	1 796	12 065 069	1 685	11 375 263	6.6	6.1
纺织纱线、织物及制品	—	—	1 816 471	—	20 375 418	—	21 677 048	—	−6.0
陶瓷产品	万吨	1	67 022	16	777 592	17	688 559	−6.7	12.9
钢材	万吨	121	1 465 608	1 443	17 912 750	1 408	17 052 458	2.5	5.0
未锻轧铜及铜材	万吨	42	2 975 230	483	35 647 229	449	34 993 013	7.4	1.9
固体废物（废塑料、废纸、废金属）	万吨	417	2 499 643	4 455	27 511 590	4 850	32 293 162	−8.1	−14.8
金属加工机床	台	8 121	867 280	106 118	10 825 672	75 490	10 065 937	40.6	7.5
自动数据处理设备及部件	万台	7 715	3 025 561	76 508	30 541 240	74 743	30 824 426	2.4	−0.9
二极管及类似半导体器件	百万个	53 894	2 419 717	528 086	23 550 776	374 001	21 355 914	41.2	10.3
集成电路	百万个	27 699	21 972 797	285 663	217 615 518	266 277	231 221 901	7.3	−5.9
汽车及汽车底盘	万辆	13	5 581 597	142	60 776 880	119	48 852 614	19.3	24.4
汽车零配件	—	—	2 793 726	—	32 152 483	—	28 702 224		12.0
＊飞机及其他航空器	架	477	3 191 991	10 773	26 012 981	741	20 904 037	1 353.8	24.4
液晶显示板	万个	26 492	3 795 062	297 834	43 775 286	339 898	49 580 450	−12.4	−11.7
＊农产品	—	—	11 403 491	—	121 571 077	—	118 664 255	—	2.5
＊机电产品	—	—	83 510 852	—	854 338 462	—	839 835 982	—	1.7
＊高新技术产品	—	—	55 502 527	—	551 411 083	—	557 945 037	—	−1.2

注：1. ＊“农产品”、“机电产品”和“高新技术产品”包括本表中已列名的有关商品，请数据使用者注意。

2. 为准确表达商品包含范围，原用名称“飞机”变更为“飞机及其他航空器”，参数范围不变。

表 5

2014 年全国出口重点商品量值

单位：千美元

商品名称	计量单位	12 月份		1～12 月累计		2013 年同期累计		累计比去年同期±%	
		数量	金额	数量	金额	数量	金额	数量	金额
水、海产品	万吨	42	2 110 432	403	20 864 746	384	19 429 234	4.9	7.4
大米	吨	73 703	68 533	419 071	378 283	478 404	416 665	−12.4	−9.2
中药材及中式成药	吨	20 891	174 889	203 227	1 527 507	211 710	1 466 691	−4.0	4.1
稀土	吨	2 902	33 408	27 769	374 691	22 493	576 165	23.5	−35.0
煤及褐煤	万吨	43	48 779	574	695 433	751	1 061 883	−23.5	−34.5
焦炭及半焦炭	万吨	102	187 731	851	1 709 153	467	1 134 078	82.1	50.7
原油	万吨	24	206 846	60	490 435	162	1 456 209	−62.9	−66.3
成品油	万吨	282	2 204 200	2 967	25 783 636	2 851	24 504 963	4.1	5.2
矿物肥料及化肥	万吨	365	1 164 039	2 904	8 909 164	1 901	6 227 833	52.8	43.1
塑料制品	万吨	86	3 557 797	951	37 088 937	896	35 293 161	6.1	5.1
箱包及类似容器	万吨	25	2 540 104	300	27 124 574	302	27 586 303	−0.6	−1.7
纺织纱线、织物及制品	—	—	9 753 874	—	112 141 507	—	106 931 907	—	4.9
服装及衣着附件	—	—	15 920 373	—	186 284 805	—	177 030 978	—	5.2
鞋类	万吨	42	5 135 359	488	56 249 733	467	50 761 328	4.5	10.8
陶瓷产品	万吨	242	2 720 294	2 598	22 073 688	2 541	19 162 590	2.2	15.2
贵金属或包贵金属的首饰	千克	125 971	5 207 472	963 577	48 512 552	897 337	28 898 758	7.4	67.9
钢材	万吨	1 017	6 888 017	9 378	70 823 201	6 233	53 212 510	50.5	33.1
未锻轧铝及铝材	万吨	54	1 750 019	434	13 380 771	364	11 685 795	19.2	14.5
手持无线电话机及其零件	—	—	19 362 097	—	146 407 876	—	130 608 147	—	12.1
彩色电视机	万台	520	970 552	7 405	13 553 270	5 959	11 052 503	24.3	22.6
集成电路	百万个	15 635	5 250 942	153 519	60 865 570	142 655	87 563 878	7.6	−30.5
自动数据处理设备及其部件	万台	18 800	18 205 178	191 836	181 717 420	187 040	182 169 188	2.6	−0.2
电动机及发电机	万台	26 482	989 403	297 005	10 729 068	308 576	9 862 453	−3.8	8.8
汽车及汽车底盘	万辆	9	1 550 647	90	12 621 191	93	12 058 687	−2.7	4.7
汽车零配件	—	—	4 313 064	—	49 182 473	—	45 343 567	—	8.5
船舶	万艘	27	1 817 348	331	23 022 171	305	25 927 075	8.9	−11.2
液晶显示板	百万个	227	2 567 310	2 451	31 785 395	3 266	35 868 564	−25.0	−11.4
家具及其零件	—	—	5 504 832	—	52 022 013	—	51 822 828	—	0.4
灯具、照明装置及零件	—	—	3 053 306	—	31 099 307	—	24 658 724	—	26.1
玩具	—	—	1 060 092	—	14 136 692	—	12 378 883	—	14.2
*农产品	—	—	7 158 247	—	71 339 881	—	67 092 563	—	6.3
*机电产品	—	—	131 272 498	—	1 310 904 238	—	1 264 662 462	—	3.7
*高新技术产品	—	—	69 021 237	—	660 533 921	—	660 081 300	—	0.1

注：* “机电产品”和“高新技术产品”包括本表中已列名的有关商品，请数据使用者注意。

表 6

2014 年进出口商品贸易方式总值表

单位：千美元，%

贸易方式	累计			累计同比（±%）		
	进出口	出口	进口	进出口	出口	进口
总值	4 303 038 237	2 342 747 940	1 960 290 297	3.4	6.1	0.4
一般贸易	2 313 194 934	1 203 681 777	1 109 513 157	5.3	10.7	0.0
国家间、国际组织无偿援助和赠送的物资	516 676	478 329	38 347	8.3	4.9	81.8
其他捐赠物资	15 784	6 068	9 717	−16.9	−25.7	−10.3
补偿贸易	224	224	—	—	—	—
来料加工装配贸易	188 229 269	90 691 798	97 537 471	4.6	−1.9	11.5
进料加工贸易	1 220 511 674	793 668 112	426 843 562	3.7	3.4	4.3
寄售代销贸易	118	—	118	−81.9	—	—
边境小额贸易	47 063 980	37 207 616	9 856 364	4.6	20.3	−29.9
加工贸易进口设备	686 530	—	686 530	−29.2	—	−29.2
对外承包工程出口货物	16 326 085	16 326 085	—	2.1	2.1	—
租赁贸易	10 538 857	327 158	10 211 699	17.5	7.6	17.9
外商投资企业作为投资进口的设备、物品	9 059 376	—	9 059 376	−7.0	—	−7.0
出料加工贸易	542 397	235 213	307 185	20.2	18.0	21.9
易货贸易	6 319	3 418	2 901	107.7	66.3	194.0
免税外汇商品	19 923	—	19 923	−27.5	—	−27.5
免税品	1 561 367	—	1 561 367	−3.6	—	−3.6
保税监管场所进出境货物	153 158 285	53 288 347	99 869 938	16.6	14.6	17.7
海关特殊监管区域物流货物	297 084 812	110 395 489	186 689 322	−17.6	−22.2	−14.5
海关特殊监管区域进口设备其他	5 133 206	—	5 133 206	28.8	—	28.8
其他	39 388 420	36 438 306	2 950 114	42.1	44.2	20.0

注：自 2014 年起，免税品列入海关统计。

表 7

2014 年出口商品企业性质贸易方式总值表

单位：千美元，%

	合计	国有企业	外商投资企业				私营企业	其他
			小计	中外合作	中外合资	外商独资		
	金额/±%	金额/±%	金额/±%	金额/±%	金额/±%	金额/±%	金额/±%	金额/±%
总值	2 342 746 552	256 493 682	1 074 734 924	13 646 375	305 527 745	755 560 804	954 671 022	56 846 924
	6.1	3.1	3	−13	1.7	3.9	10.6	6.4
一般贸易	1 203 680 388	151 137 101	289 925 280	6 071 041	114 596 759	169 257 480	717 626 740	44 991 268
	10.7	4.3	7	−6.2	3.3	10.3	13.8	9.4
国家间、国际组织无偿援助和赠送的物资	478 329	391 523	5 494	—	5 494	—	32 757	48 556
	4.9	11.8	−36.1	—	−36.1	—	27.5	−32

续 表

	合 计	国有企业	外商投资企业				私营企业	其 他
			小 计	中外合作	中外合资	外商独资		
	金额/±%	金额/±%	金额/±%	金额/±%	金额/±%	金额/±%	金额/±%	金额/±%
补偿贸易	224	—	—	—	—	—	224	—
	—	—	—	—	—	—	—	—
来料加工装配贸易	90 691 798	16 868 762	58 454 096	2 906 755	13 352 482	42 194 860	13 444 608	1 924 333
	−1.9	−4.1	−3.8	−31.8	−0.8	−1.9	12.5	−13.1
进料加工贸易	793 668 112	33 947 260	662 100 860	4 291 689	154 861 368	502 947 803	89 549 942	8 070 050
	3.4	2.1	1.5	−2.6	1	1.7	20.7	−0.1
寄售代销贸易	—	—	—	—	—	—	—	—
	—	—	—	—	—	—	—	—
边境小额贸易	37 207 616	1 725 255	—	—	—	—	35 293 479	188 882
	20.3	−17.1	—	—	—	—	22.9	41.8
对外承包工程出口货物	16 326 085	15 306 263	144 001	10 266	57 390	76 345	749 591	126 231
	2.1	4.8	−46.6	−20	−64.4	−20.1	−27.3	65
租赁贸易	327 158	51 327	18 961		7 736	11 226	251 416	5 453
	7.6	9.6	227.2	—	105.4	1 574.8	0.6	308.1
出料加工贸易	235 213	121 482	110 704	405	83 107	27 192	2 869	157
	18	−1.4	58.5	−95	146.5	−3.1	−50.1	−74.8
易货贸易	3 418	—	—	—	—	—	3 418	—
	66.3	—	—	—	—	—	67.5	—
保税监管场所进出境货物	53 288 347	20 225 001	14 198 184	353 976	10 265 187	3 579 021	17 563 672	1 301 4 90
	14.6	−6.1	20.9	−27.7	17.3	43.1	48.1	−4.7
海关特殊监管区域物渣货物	110 395 489	16 083 657	49 464 417	10 511	12 193 352	37 260 554	44 691 518	155 898
	−22.2	19	3.6	−66.6	−11. 1	9.6	−44.5	−25.2
其他	36 438 306	634 817	312 927	1 732	104 872	206 323	35 458 006	32 557
	44.2	−28.8	61.8	22.5	8.8	115.8	47.6	−78.6

注：①深色区域内数字为去年累计同期比±%。

②自 2013 年起，“集体企业”不再单列，“私营企业”单独列出，“其他”范围比同比相应调整。

表 8

2014 年进口商品企业性质贸易方式总值表

单位：千美元，%

	合 计	国有企业	外商投资企业				私营企业	其 他
			小 计	中外合作	中外合资	外商独资		
	金额/±%	金额/±%	金额/±%	金额/±%	金额/±%	金额/±%	金额/±%	金额/±%
总值	1 960 290 297	491 054 473	909 310 578	8 651 740	285 793 177	614 865 662	447 530 641	112 394 605
	0.4	−1.9	3.9	4.4	0.5	5.5	2.6	−19.6
一般贸易	1 109 513 157	385 390 940	372 442 068	4 753 697	140 350 612	227 337 759	275 989 415	75 690 735
	0	−4.1	6	−3.6	−0.9	10.9	5.6	−20.5
国家间、国际组织无偿援助和赠送的物资	38 347	32 182	—	—	—	—	4 169	1 997
	81.8	81	—	—	—	—	65.1	152.9
其他捐赠物资	9 717	979	—	—	—	—	847	7 890
	−10.3	56.2	—	—	—	—	−75.2	16.2

续 表

	合 计	国有企业	外商投资企业				私营企业	其 他
			小 计	中外合作	中外合资	外商独资		
	金额/±%	金额/±%	金额/±%	金额/±%	金额/±%	金额/±%	金额/±%	金额/±%
补偿贸易	—	—	—	—	—	—	—	—
	—	—	—	—	—	—	—	—
来料加工装配贸易	97 537 471	26 091 513	57 926 880	1 211 603	13 553 940	43 161 336	7 559 449	5 959 629
	11.5	22.7	7.1	−3.9	10.5	6.4	5.8	18.4
进料加工贸易	426 843 562	15 136 262	338 694 432	1 759 161	89 801 243	247 134 027	46 163 661	26 849 207
	4.3	14.7	1.7	−10.6	2.7	1.4	71.6	−25.2
寄售代销贸易	118	—	118	—	—	118	—	—
	—	—	—	—	—	—	—	—
边境小额贸易	9 856 364	2 272 721	—	—	—	—	7 498 151	85 492
	−29.9	−58	—	—	—	—	−11.4	−55.8
加工贸易进口设备	686 530	38 321	600 294	8 758	90 157	501 379	32 704	15 212
	−29.2	−37.8	−29.3	−30.1	296.6	−38.4	−21.8	−5.7
租赁贸易	10 211 699	4 926 403	3 811 288		3 751 776	59 512	1 472 208	1 800
	17.9	−0.1	38.1	—	42.1	−49.1	66.4	−98
外商投资企业作为投资进口的设备、物品	9 059 376		9 059 376	14 324	3 411 984	5 633 067	—	—
	−7	—	−7	−37.3	−14.5	−1.8	—	—
出料加工贸易	307 185	170 608	133 861	1 126	105 449	27 286	2 715	—
	21.9	2.8	65.9	−83.1	119.6	4.8	−47.9	—
易货贸易	2 901	188	—	—	—	—	2 713	—
	194	442.1	—	—	—	—	184.9	—
免税外汇商品	19 923	19 923	—	—	—	—	—	—
	−27.5	−27.5	—	—	—	—	—	—
免税品	1 561 367	1 086 876	474 490		284 503	189 987	—	—
	−3.6	7	−21.5	—	13.1	−46.2	—	—
保税监管场所进出境货物	99 869 938	34 142 568	26 386 672	870 018	17 437 864	8 078 789	37 122 250	2 218 448
	17.7	10.1	5.1	3 010.2	0.3	5.1	37.8	24.8
海关特殊监管区域进口货物	186 689 322	21 373 501	93 237 132	21 780	14 331 453	78 883 899	70 590 946	1 487 743
	−14.5	1.8	1.2	−44.4	−10.8	3.8	−32	3.7
海关特殊监管区域进口设备	5 133 206	8 590	4 933 287	1 184	2 146 925	2 785 178	190 972	356
	28.8	−85	28.1	−21.1	−5.4	76.1	149.7	64
其他	2 950 114	362 898	1 610 681	10 088	527 269	1 073 324	900 441	76 095
	20	17.4	18.5	−13.9	39.8	10.6	24.7	11.3

注：①深色区域内数字为去年累计同期比±%。
②自 2013 年起，“集体企业”不再单列，“私营企业”单独列出，“其他”范围比同比相应调整。
③自 2014 年起，免税品列入海关统计。

表 9

2014 年全国月度出口和进口统计

单位：亿美元，%

出口	当月		1月至当月累计	
	金额	同比	金额	同比
2014.01	2 071.3	10.6	2 071.3	10.6
2014.02	1 140.9	−18.1	3 212.3	−1.6
2014.03	1 701.1	−6.6	4 913.1	−3.4
2014.04	1 885.4	0.9	6 797.8	−2.3
2014.05	1 954.7	7.0	8 752.0	−0.4
2014.06	1 867.9	7.2	10 618.6	0.9
2014.07	2 128.9	14.5	12 751.1	3.0
2014.08	2 084.6	9.4	14 834.6	3.8
2014.09	2 136.9	15.3	16 970.9	5.1
2014.10	2 068.7	11.6	19 038.4	5.8
2014.11	2 116.6	4.7	21 153.6	5.7
2014.12	2 275.1	9.7	23 427.5	6.1
进口	当月		1月至当月累计	
	金额	同比	金额	同比
2014.01	1 752.6	10.0	1 752.6	10.0
2014.02	1 370.8	10.1	3 123.5	10.0
2014.03	1 624.0	−11.3	4 745.7	1.6
2014.04	1 700.9	0.8	6 445.4	1.4
2014.05	1 595.5	−1.6	8 039.0	0.8
2014.06	1 552.2	5.5	9 590.0	1.5
2014.07	1 655.9	−1.6	11 245.5	1.0
2014.08	1 586.3	−2.4	12 829.3	0.6
2014.09	1 827.4	7.0	14 655.1	1.3
2014.10	1 614.6	4.6	16 267.3	1.6
2014.11	1 571.9	−6.7	17 828.9	0.8
2014.12	1 779.0	−2.4	19 602.9	0.4

表 10

2014 年月度进出口总值统计

单位：亿美元，%

月份	当月		1月至当月累计	
	进出口	同比	进出口	同比
2014.01	3 823.9	10.3	3 823.9	10.3
2014.02	2 511.8	−4.8	6 335.7	3.8
2014.03	3 325.1	−9.0	9 658.8	−1.0
2014.04	3 586.3	0.8	13 243.2	−0.5
2014.05	3 550.2	3.0	16 791.0	0.2
2014.06	3 420.1	6.4	20 208.6	1.2
2014.07	3 784.8	6.9	23 996.6	2.0
2014.08	3 670.9	4.0	27 663.9	2.3
2014.09	3 964.3	11.3	31 626.0	3.3
2014.10	3 683.3	8.4	35 305.7	3.8
2014.11	3 688.5	−0.5	38 982.5	3.4
2014.12	4 054.1	4.0	43 030.4	3.4

表 11

1982—2013 年全国年度服务进出口

单位：亿美元，%

年份	中国进出口额			中国出口额			中国进口额		
	金额	同比	占世界比重	金额	同比	占世界比重	金额	同比	占世界比重
1982	44	—	0.6	25	—	0.7	19	—	0.5
1983	43	−2.3	0.6	25	0.0	0.7	18	−5.3	0.5
1984	54	25.6	0.7	28	12.0	0.8	26	44.4	0.7
1985	52	−3.7	0.7	29	3.6	0.8	23	−11.5	0.6
1986	56	7.7	0.6	36	24.1	0.8	20	−13.0	0.4
1987	65	16.1	0.6	42	16.7	0.8	23	15.0	0.4
1988	80	23.1	0.7	47	11.9	0.8	33	43.5	0.5
1989	81	1.3	0.6	45	−4.3	0.7	36	9.1	0.5
1990	98	21.0	0.6	57	26.7	0.7	41	13.9	0.5
1991	108	10.2	0.6	69	21.1	0.8	39	−4.9	0.5
1992	183	69.4	1.0	91	31.9	1.0	92	135.9	1.0
1993	226	23.5	1.2	110	20.9	1.2	116	26.1	1.2
1994	322	42.5	1.6	164	49.1	1.6	158	36.2	1.5
1995	430	33.5	1.8	184	12.2	1.6	246	55.7	2.1
1996	430	0.0	1.7	206	12.0	1.6	224	−8.9	1.8
1997	522	21.4	2.0	245	19.0	1.9	277	23.8	2.2
1998	504	−3.4	1.9	239	−2.5	1.8	265	−4.5	2.0
1999	572	13.5	2.1	262	9.6	1.9	310	17.0	2.3
2000	660	15.4	2.2	301	15.2	2.0	359	15.8	2.5
2001	719	9.0	2.4	329	9.1	2.2	390	8.8	2.6
2002	855	18.9	2.7	394	19.7	2.5	461	18.1	3.0
2003	1 013	18.5	2.8	464	17.8	2.5	549	19.0	3.1
2004	1 337	32.0	3.1	621	33.8	2.8	716	30.5	3.4
2005	1 571	17.5	3.2	739	19.1	3.0	832	16.2	3.5
2006	1 917	22.0	3.5	914	23.7	3.2	1 003	20.6	3.8
2007	2 509	30.9	3.9	1 217	33.1	3.6	1 293	28.8	4.1
2008	3 045	21.4	4.1	1 464	20.4	3.9	1 580	22.2	4.5
2009	2 867	−5.8	4.5	1 286	−12.2	3.9	1 581	0.1	5.1
2010	3 624	26.4	5.1	1 702	32.4	4.6	1 922	21.5	5.5
2011	4 191	15.6	5.2	1 821	7.0	4.4	2 370	23.3	6.1
2012	4 706	12.3	5.6	1 904	4.6	4.4	2 801	18.2	6.8
2013	5 396	14.7	6.0	2 106	10.6	4.6	3 290	17.5	7.6

注：根据 WTO 有关服务贸易的定义，中国服务进出口数据不含政府服务。

数据来源：WTO 国际贸易统计数据库（International Trade Statistics Database）；中国商务部和国家外汇管理局。

表 12

1997—2013 年全国服务进出口差额

单位：亿美元

年份	1997	1998	1999	2000	2001	2002	2003	2004	2005	2006	2007	2008	2009	2010	2011	2012	2013
总计	−32.2	−25.9	−48.0	−57.1	−61.3	−67.0	−84.8	−95.5	−92.6	−89.1	−76.0	−115.6	−295.1	−219.3	−549.2	−897.0	−1 184.6
运输服务	−69.9	−44.6	−54.8	−67.3	−66.9	−78.9	−103.3	−124.8	−130.2	−133.5	−119.5	−119.1	−230.1	−290.5	−448.7	−469.5	−566.8
旅游	39.4	34.0	32.3	31.2	38.8	49.9	22.2	65.9	75.4	96.3	74.5	46.9	−40.3	−90.7	−241.2	−519.5	−769.2
通信服务	−0.2	6.1	4.0	11.0	−0.5	0.8	2.1	−0.3	−1.2	−0.3	0.9	0.6	−0.1	0.8	5.4	1.4	0.3
建筑服务	−6.2	−5.3	−5.5	−3.9	−0.2	2.8	1.1	1.3	9.7	7.0	24.7	59.7	36.0	94.2	110.0	86.3	67.7
保险服务	−8.7	−13.7	−17.2	−23.6	−24.8	−30.4	−42.5	−57.4	−66.5	−82.8	−97.6	−113.6	−97.1	−140.3	−167.2	−172.7	−181.0
金融服务	−3.0	−1.4	−0.6	−0.2	0.2	−0.4	−0.8	−0.4	−0.1	−7.5	−3.3	−2.5	−2.9	−0.6	1.0	−0.4	−5.0
计算机和信息服务	−1.5	−2.0	0.4	0.9	1.2	−4.9	0.7	3.8	2.2	12.2	21.4	30.9	32.8	62.9	83.4	106.1	94.5
专有权利使用费和特许费	−4.9	−3.6	−7.2	−12.0	−18.3	−29.8	−34.4	−42.6	−51.6	−64.3	−78.5	−97.5	−106.4	−122.1	−139.6	−167.1	−201.5
咨询	−1.2	−2.4	−2.4	−2.8	−6.1	−13.5	−15.6	−15.8	−8.6	−5.6	7.2	46.1	52.1	76.8	98.1	134.3	169.5
广告、宣传	0.0	−0.5	0.0	0.2	0.2	−0.2	0.3	1.5	3.6	4.9	5.8	2.6	3.6	8.4	12.4	19.8	17.7
电影、音像	−0.3	−0.2	−0.3	−0.3	−0.2	−0.7	−0.4	−1.3	−0.2	0.2	1.6	1.6	−1.8	−2.5	−2.8	−4.3	−6.4
其他商业服务	24.3	7.8	3.2	9.7	15.4	38.3	85.9	74.7	75.0	84.3	86.8	28.9	59.2	184.1	140.1	88.6	195.5

数据来源：中国商务部、国家外汇管理局。

表 13

1997—2013 年全国服务贸易出口（分项目）

单位：亿美元，%

年份		总计	运输服务	旅游	通信服务	建筑服务	保险服务	金融服务
1997	金额（亿美元）	245.0	29.5	120.7	2.7	5.9	1.7	0.3
	占比（%）	100.0	12.1	49.3	1.1	2.4	0.7	0.1
1998	金额（亿美元）	238.8	23.0	126.0	8.2	5.9	3.8	0.3
	比上年增长（%）	−2.5	−22.1	4.4	201.4	0.7	120.5	−1.3
	占比（%）	100.0	9.6	52.8	3.4	2.5	1.6	0.1
1999	金额（亿美元）	261.6	24.2	141.0	5.9	9.9	2.0	1.1
	比上年增长（%）	9.6	5.2	11.9	−28.0	65.8	−47.0	310.8
	占比（%）	100.0	9.2	53.9	2.3	3.8	0.8	0.4
2000	金额（亿美元）	301.5	36.7	162.3	13.5	6.0	1.1	0.8
	比上年增长（%）	15.2	51.7	15.1	128.2	−38.9	−47.1	−29.7
	占比（%）	100.0	12.2	53.8	4.5	2.0	0.4	0.3
2001	金额（亿美元）	329.0	46.4	177.9	2.7	8.3	2.3	1.0
	比上年增长（%）	9.1	26.3	9.6	−79.8	37.8	110.9	27.3
	占比（%）	100.0	14.1	54.1	0.8	2.5	0.7	0.3
2002	金额（亿美元）	393.8	57.2	203.9	5.5	12.5	2.1	0.5
	比上年增长（%）	19.7	23.4	14.6	102.9	50.1	−8.1	−48.5
	占比（%）	100.0	14.5	51.8	1.4	3.2	0.5	0.1
2003	金额（亿美元）	463.7	79.1	174.1	6.4	12.9	3.1	1.5
	比上年增长（%）	17.8	38.2	−14.6	16.1	3.5	49.7	197.9
	占比（%）	100.0	17.0	37.5	1.4	2.8	0.7	0.3
2004	金额（亿美元）	620.6	120.7	257.4	4.4	14.7	3.8	0.9
	比上年增长（%）	33.8	52.6	47.9	−31.0	13.8	21.7	−38.2
	占比（%）	100.0	19.4	41.5	0.7	2.4	0.6	0.2
2005	金额（亿美元）	739.1	154.3	293.0	4.9	25.9	5.5	1.5
	比上年增长（%）	19.1	27.8	13.8	10.2	76.7	44.3	54.6
	占比（%）	100.0	20.9	39.6	0.7	3.5	0.7	0.2
2006	金额（亿美元）	914.2	210.2	339.5	7.4	27.5	5.5	1.5
	比上年增长（%）	23.7	36.2	15.9	52.1	6.2	−0.3	−0.2
	占比（%）	100.0	23.0	37.1	0.8	3.0	0.6	0.2
2007	金额（亿美元）	1216.5	313.2	372.3	11.7	53.8	9.0	2.3
	比上年增长（%）	33.1	49.1	9.7	59.2	95.3	64.9	59.0
	占比（%）	100.0	25.7	30.6	1.0	4.4	0.7	0.2
2008	金额（亿美元）	1464.5	384.2	408.4	15.7	103.3	13.8	3.2
	比上年增长（%）	20.4	22.6	9.7	33.7	92.1	53.0	36.7
	占比（%）	100.0	26.2	27.9	1.1	7.1	0.9	0.2
2009	金额（亿美元）	1286.0	235.7	396.8	12.0	94.6	16.0	4.4
	比上年增长（%）	−12.2	−38.7	−2.9	−23.7	−8.4	15.4	38.7
	占比（%）	100.0	18.3	30.9	0.9	7.4	1.2	0.3
2010	金额（亿美元）	1702.5	342.1	458.1	12.2	144.9	17.3	13.3
	比上年增长（%）	32.4	45.2	15.5	1.8	53.2	8.2	204.6
	占比（%）	100.0	20.1	26.9	0.7	8.5	1.0	0.8
2011	金额（亿美元）	1820.9	355.7	484.6	17.3	147.2	30.2	8.5
	比上年增长（%）	7.0	4.0	5.8	41.5	1.6	74.7	−36.2
	占比（%）	100.0	19.5	26.6	0.9	8.1	1.7	0.5
2012	金额（亿美元）	1904.4	389.1	500.3	17.9	122.5	33.3	18.9
	比上年增长（%）	4.6	9.4	3.2	3.7	−16.8	10.3	122.5
	占比（%）	100.0	20.4	26.3	0.9	6.4	1.7	1.0
2013	金额（亿美元）	2105.9	376.5	516.6	16.7	106.6	40.0	29.2
	比上年增长（%）	10.6	−3.2	3.3	−6.9	−13.0	20.0	54.2
	占比（%）	100.0	17.9	24.5	0.8	5.1	1.9	1.4

数据来源：中国商务部、国家外汇管理局。

单位：亿美元，%

计算机和信息服务	专有权利使用费和特许费	咨询	广告、宣传	电影、音像	其他商业服务	年　份	
0.8	0.5	3.5	2.4	0.1	76.8	金额（亿美元）	1997
0.3	0.2	1.4	1.0	0.0	31.3	占比（%）	
1.3	0.6	5.2	2.1	0.2	62.1	金额（亿美元）	1998
59.7	14.3	49.5	-11.4	53.0	-19.1	比上年增长（%）	
0.6	0.3	2.2	0.9	0.1	26.0	占比（%）	
2.7	0.7	2.8	2.2	0.1	69.1	金额（亿美元）	1999
98.8	18.9	-45.9	4.6	-56.7	11.2	比上年增长（%）	
1.0	0.3	1.1	0.8	0.0	26.4	占比（%）	
3.6	0.8	3.6	2.2	0.1	70.8	金额（亿美元）	2000
34.1	7.8	26.9	1.3	69.8	2.5	比上年增长（%）	
1.2	0.3	1.2	0.7	0.0	23.5	占比（%）	
4.6	1.1	8.9	2.8	0.3	72.8	金额（亿美元）	2001
29.6	37.0	150.0	24.1	146.8	2.8	比上年增长（%）	
1.4	0.3	2.7	0.8	0.1	22.1	占比（%）	
6.4	1.3	12.8	3.7	0.3	87.6	金额（亿美元）	2002
38.3	20.6	44.5	34.5	6.4	20.3	比上年增长（%）	
1.6	0.3	3.3	0.9	0.1	22.2	占比（%）	
11.0	1.1	18.8	4.9	0.3	150.6	金额（亿美元）	2003
72.7	-19.5	46.7	30.4	12.7	71.8	比上年增长（%）	
2.4	0.2	4.1	1.0	0.1	32.5	占比（%）	
16.4	2.4	31.5	8.5	0.4	159.5	金额（亿美元）	2004
48.5	120.9	67.2	74.5	22.6	5.9	比上年增长（%）	
2.6	0.4	5.1	1.4	0.1	25.7	占比（%）	
18.4	1.6	53.2	10.8	1.3	168.8	金额（亿美元）	2005
12.4	-33.4	68.8	26.8	226.5	5.9	比上年增长（%）	
2.5	0.2	7.2	1.5	0.2	22.8	占比（%）	
29.6	2.1	78.3	14.5	1.4	196.9	金额（亿美元）	2006
60.7	30.2	47.2	34.3	2.3	16.6	比上年增长（%）	
3.2	0.2	8.6	1.6	0.1	21.5	占比（%）	
43.4	3.4	115.8	19.1	3.2	269.1	金额（亿美元）	2007
46.9	67.1	47.8	32.3	130.9	36.7	比上年增长（%）	
3.6	0.3	9.5	1.6	0.3	22.1	占比（%）	
62.5	5.7	181.4	22.0	4.2	260.1	金额（亿美元）	2008
43.9	66.7	56.7	15.2	32.2	-3.4	比上年增长（%）	
4.3	0.4	12.4	1.5	0.3	17.8	占比（%）	
65.1	4.3	186.2	23.1	1.0	246.9	金额（亿美元）	2009
4.2	-24.8	2.7	5.0	-76.7	-5.1	比上年增长（%）	
5.1	0.3	14.5	1.8	0.1	19.2	占比（%）	
92.6	8.3	227.7	28.9	1.2	355.9	金额（亿美元）	2010
42.1	93.4	22.3	24.8	26.4	44.1	比上年增长（%）	
5.4	0.5	13.4	1.7	0.1	20.9	占比（%）	
121.8	7.4	283.9	40.2	1.2	322.8	金额（亿美元）	2011
31.6	-10.5	24.7	39.3	-0.1	-9.3	比上年增长（%）	
6.7	0.4	15.6	2.2	0.1	17.7	占比（%）	
144.5	10.4	334.5	47.5	1.3	284.2	金额（亿美元）	2012
18.6	40.1	17.8	18.2	5.9	-12.0	比上年增长（%）	
7.6	0.5	17.6	2.5	0.1	14.9	占比（%）	
154.3	8.9	405.4	49.1	1.5	401.4	金额（亿美元）	2013
6.8	-14.8	21.2	3.3	13.2	41.2	比上年增长（%）	
7.3	0.4	19.3	2.3	0.1	19.1	占比（%）	

表 14

1997—2013 年全国服务贸易进口（分项目）

单位：亿美元，%

年份		总计	运输服务	旅游	通信服务	建筑服务	保险服务	金融服务
1997	金额（亿美元）	277.2	99.4	81.3	2.9	12.1	10.5	3.2
	占比（%）	100.0	35.9	29.3	1.0	4.4	3.8	1.2
1998	金额（亿美元）	264.7	67.6	92.1	2.1	11.2	17.6	1.6
	比上年增长（%）	−4.5	−32.0	13.2	−28.3	−7.4	68.1	−49.7
	占比（%）	100.0	25.6	34.8	0.8	4.2	6.6	0.6
1999	金额（亿美元）	309.7	79.0	108.7	1.9	15.4	19.2	1.7
	比上年增长（%）	17.0	16.8	18.0	−7.0	37.5	9.3	2.1
	占比（%）	100.0	25.5	35.1	0.6	5.0	6.2	0.5
2000	金额（亿美元）	358.6	104.0	131.1	2.4	9.9	24.7	1.0
	比上年增长（%）	15.8	31.6	20.7	25.1	−35.4	28.6	−41.6
	占比（%）	100.0	29.0	36.6	0.7	2.8	6.9	0.3
2001	金额（亿美元）	390.3	113.2	139.1	3.3	8.5	27.1	0.8
	比上年增长（%）	8.8	8.9	6.1	34.7	−14.8	9.7	−20.6
	占比（%）	100.0	29.0	35.6	0.8	2.2	6.9	0.2
2002	金额（亿美元）	460.8	136.1	154.0	4.7	9.6	32.5	0.9
	比上年增长（%）	18.1	20.2	10.7	44.3	13.8	19.7	16.1
	占比（%）	100.0	29.5	33.4	1.0	2.1	7.0	0.2
2003	金额（亿美元）	548.5	182.3	151.9	4.3	11.8	45.6	2.3
	比上年增长（%）	19.0	33.9	−1.4	−9.1	22.8	40.6	158.8
	占比（%）	100.0	33.2	27.7	0.8	2.2	8.3	0.4
2004	金额（亿美元）	716.0	245.4	191.5	4.7	13.4	61.2	1.4
	比上年增长（%）	30.5	34.6	26.1	10.5	13.1	34.2	−40.6
	占比（%）	100.0	34.3	26.7	0.7	1.9	8.6	0.2
2005	金额（亿美元）	831.7	284.5	217.6	6.0	16.2	72.0	1.6
	比上年增长（%）	16.2	15.9	13.6	27.8	21.0	17.6	15.9
	占比（%）	100.0	34.2	26.2	0.7	1.9	8.7	0.2
2006	金额（亿美元）	1003.3	343.7	243.2	7.6	20.5	88.3	8.9
	比上年增长（%）	20.6	20.8	11.8	26.6	26.6	22.7	456.9
	占比（%）	100.0	34.3	24.2	0.8	2.0	8.8	0.9
2007	金额（亿美元）	1292.6	432.7	297.9	10.8	29.1	106.6	5.6
	比上年增长（%）	28.8	25.9	22.5	41.6	41.9	20.8	−37.5
	占比（%）	100.0	33.5	23.0	0.8	2.3	8.3	0.4
2008	金额（亿美元）	1580.0	503.3	361.6	15.1	43.6	127.4	5.7
	比上年增长（%）	22.2	16.3	21.4	39.6	49.9	19.5	1.6
	占比（%）	100.0	31.9	22.9	1.0	2.8	8.1	0.4
2009	金额（亿美元）	1581.1	465.7	437.0	12.1	58.7	113.1	7.3
	比上年增长（%）	0.1	−7.5	20.9	−19.9	34.5	−11.3	28.2
	占比（%）	100.0	29.5	27.6	0.8	3.7	7.2	0.5
2010	金额（亿美元）	1921.7	632.6	548.8	11.4	50.7	157.5	13.9
	比上年增长（%）	21.5	35.8	25.6	−6.0	−13.6	39.3	91.2
	占比（%）	100.0	32.9	28.6	0.6	2.6	8.2	0.7
2011	金额（亿美元）	2370.0	804.4	725.9	11.9	37.3	197.4	7.5
	比上年增长（%）	23.3	27.2	32.3	4.7	−26.5	25.3	−46.2
	占比（%）	100.0	33.9	30.6	0.5	1.6	8.3	0.3
2012	金额（亿美元）	2801.4	858.6	1019.8	16.5	36.2	206.0	19.3
	比上年增长（%）	18.2	6.7	40.5	38.6	−2.9	4.4	158.4
	占比（%）	100.0	30.6	36.4	0.6	1.3	7.4	0.7
2013	金额（亿美元）	3290.5	943.2	1285.8	16.4	38.9	220.9	34.2
	比上年增长（%）	17.5	9.9	26.1	−0.7	7.5	7.2	77.0
	占比（%）	100.0	28.7	39.1	0.5	1.2	6.7	1.0

单位：亿美元，%

计算机和信息服务	专有权利使用费和特许费	咨询	广告、宣传	电影、音像	其他商业服务	年份	
2.3	5.4	4.7	2.4	0.4	52.5	金额（亿美元）	1997
0.8	2.0	1.7	0.9	0.2	18.9	占比（%）	
3.3	4.2	7.6	2.7	0.4	54.4	金额（亿美元）	1998
44.0	−22.8	62.0	9.8	−11.1	3.5	比上年增长（%）	
1.3	1.6	2.9	1.0	0.1	20.5	占比（%）	
2.2	7.9	5.2	2.2	0.3	65.9	金额（亿美元）	1999
−32.8	88.6	−30.8	−17.4	−13.0	21.2	比上年增长（%）	
0.7	2.6	1.7	0.7	0.1	21.3	占比（%）	
2.7	12.8	6.4	2.0	0.4	61.2	金额（亿美元）	2000
18.5	61.8	22.0	−7.6	10.2	−7.2	比上年增长（%）	
0.7	3.6	1.8	0.6	0.1	17.1	占比（%）	
3.4	19.4	15.0	2.6	0.5	57.4	金额（亿美元）	2001
30.1	51.3	134.8	27.5	34.2	−6.1	比上年增长（%）	
0.9	5.0	3.8	0.7	0.1	14.7	占比（%）	
11.3	31.1	26.3	3.9	1.0	49.3	金额（亿美元）	2002
228.6	60.7	75.1	52.9	91.2	−14.1	比上年增长（%）	
2.5	6.8	5.7	0.9	0.2	10.7	占比（%）	
10.4	35.5	34.5	4.6	0.7	64.6	金额（亿美元）	2003
−8.6	13.9	31.1	16.1	−27.6	31.1	比上年增长（%）	
1.9	6.5	6.3	0.8	0.1	11.8	占比（%）	
12.5	45.0	47.3	7.0	1.8	84.8	金额（亿美元）	2004
20.9	26.7	37.2	52.5	152.9	31.2	比上年增长（%）	
1.7	6.3	6.6	1.0	0.2	11.8	占比（%）	
16.2	53.2	61.8	7.2	1.5	93.9	金额（亿美元）	2005
29.5	18.3	30.6	2.4	−12.4	10.7	比上年增长（%）	
2.0	6.4	7.4	0.9	0.2	11.3	占比（%）	
17.4	66.3	83.9	9.6	1.2	112.6	金额（亿美元）	2006
7.2	24.7	35.7	33.5	−21.4	20.0	比上年增长（%）	
1.7	6.6	8.4	1.0	0.1	11.2	占比（%）	
22.1	81.9	108.6	13.4	1.5	182.4	金额（亿美元）	2007
27.0	23.5	29.4	40.0	27.0	62.0	比上年增长（%）	
1.7	6.3	8.4	1.0	0.1	14.1	占比（%）	
31.7	103.2	135.4	19.4	2.6	231.2	金额（亿美元）	2008
43.3	26.0	24.7	45.2	65.9	26.8	比上年增长（%）	
2.0	6.5	8.6	1.2	0.2	14.6	占比（%）	
32.3	110.7	134.2	19.5	2.8	187.7	金额（亿美元）	2009
2.1	7.2	−0.9	0.7	9.2	−18.8	比上年增长（%）	
2.0	7.0	8.5	1.2	0.2	11.9	占比（%）	
29.7	130.4	150.9	20.4	3.7	171.8	金额（亿美元）	2010
−8.3	17.8	12.5	4.4	33.2	−8.5	比上年增长（%）	
1.5	6.8	7.9	1.1	0.2	8.9	占比（%）	
38.4	147.1	185.8	27.7	4.0	182.6	金额（亿美元）	2011
29.6	12.8	23.1	35.9	7.8	6.3	比上年增长（%）	
1.6	6.2	7.8	1.2	0.2	7.7	占比（%）	
38.4	177.5	200.2	27.7	5.6	195.6	金额（亿美元）	2012
−0.1	20.7	7.7	−0.3	40.2	7.1	比上年增长（%）	
1.4	6.3	7.1	1.0	0.2	7.0	占比（%）	
59.9	210.3	235.8	31.3	7.8	205.9	金额（亿美元）	2013
55.9	18.5	17.8	13.3	39.8	5.3	比上年增长（%）	
1.8	6.4	7.2	1.0	0.2	6.3	占比（%）	

表 15

2014 年全国派出各类劳务人员（省市区排名）

单位：人

序　号	省市区	累计派出各类劳务人员数量	期末在外各类劳务人员数量
1	北京市	17 031	29 457
2	天津市	15 648	18 403
3	河北省	9 239	11 280
4	山西省	1 511	4 232
5	内蒙古自治区	1 641	4 146
6	辽宁省	17 284	46 952
	其中：大连市	11 748	25 308
7	吉林省	9 215	35 338
8	黑龙江省	7 666	12 188
9	上海市	26 695	35 728
10	江苏省	44 239	96 402
11	浙江省	19 472	31 279
	其中：宁波市	327	867
12	安徽省	14 139	24 709
13	福建省	49 402	56 199
	其中：厦门市	12 631	15 202
14	江西省	5 965	14 883
15	山东省	59 941	115 328
	其中：青岛市	13 107	23 728
16	河南省	31 660	89 563
17	湖北省	31 957	32 250
18	湖南省	13 413	32 260
19	广东省	44 060	76 193
	其中：深圳市	2 118	1 838
20	广西壮族自治区	2 528	3 740
21	海南省	8	42
22	重庆市	2 738	5 655
23	四川省	7 956	18 414
24	贵州省	2 114	2 737
25	云南省	9 225	12 278
27	陕西省	9 218	14 945
28	甘肃省	4 095	4 833
29	青海省	728	712
30	宁夏回族自治区	371	623
31	新疆维吾尔自治区	5 079	3 377
32	新疆生产建设兵团	3 249	3 278

表 16

2014 年全国对外承包营业额（分省市区排序）

单位：万美元

序号	省市区	新签合同额	完成营业额
1	北京市	429 369	357 432
2	天津市	380 264	403 259
3	河北省	485 335	408 696
4	山西省	34 586	73 542
5	内蒙古自治区	0	1 653
6	辽宁省	180 618	236 557
	其中：大连市	44 803	72 650
7	吉林省	8 490	56 481
8	黑龙江省	56 079	89 805
9	上海市	1 088 940	740 168
10	江苏省	966 108	795 426
11	浙江省	387 930	517 582
	其中：宁波市	99 375	168 250
12	安徽省	266 764	322 693
13	福建省	35 842	71 559
14	江西省	264 781	285 147
15	山东省	1 060 559	925 011
	其中：青岛市	227 540	359 106
16	河南省	239 763	299 691
17	湖北省	1 269 954	579 636
18	湖南省	95 287	257 945
19	广东省	1 524 873	1 241 121
	其中：深圳市	1 267 534	1 027 377
20	广西壮族自治区	86 373	87 736
21	海南省	760	100
22	重庆市	78 090	103 210
23	四川省	335 552	706 295
24	贵州省	61 792	50 129
25	云南省	134 406	207 036
26	陕西省	116 867	178 759
27	甘肃省	29 040	33 939
28	青海省	0	15 477
29	宁夏回族自治区	9 494	5 243
30	新疆维吾尔自治区	177 071	159 077
31	新疆生产建设兵团	29 420	58 232

表 17

2014 年我国对外承包工程业务完成营业额前 100 家企业

单位：万美元

序号	企业名称	完成营业额
1	华为技术有限公司	971 546
2	中国建筑工程总公司	723 910
3	中国水电建设集团国际工程有限公司	628 182
4	中国港湾工程有限责任公司	396 051
5	中国路桥工程有限责任公司	279 954
6	中国土木工程集团有限公司	269 046
7	中国葛洲坝集团股份有限公司	256 825
8	中国机械设备工程股份有限公司	255 948
9	中信建设有限责任公司	205 472
10	中国石油工程建设公司	194 032
11	中国石油天然气管道局	170 283
12	中国石油集团长城钻探工程有限公司	169 098
13	上海振华重工（集团）股份有限公司	168 771
14	中国水利电力对外公司	152 035
15	中交第四航务工程局有限公司	140 284
16	青建集团股份公司	131 507
17	东方电气股份有限公司	131 310
18	中交第一公路工程局有限公司	130 914
19	中工国际工程股份有限公司	123 850
20	中国石油集团东方地球物理勘探有限责任公司	123 345
21	山东电力建设第三工程公司	117 153
22	中地海外集团有限公司	110 232
23	中国中铁股份有限公司	104 863
24	中铁二局集团有限公司	99 744
25	上海电气集团股份有限公司	97 321
26	中国交通建设股份有限公司	86 589
27	国家电网公司	81 259
28	特变电工股份有限公司	81 047
29	上海贝尔股份有限公司	76 493
30	中国电力技术装备有限公司	76 295
31	中国石油集团工程设计有限责任公司	71 562
32	中国成套设备进出口（集团）总公司	68 296
33	山东电力基本建设总公司	67 483
34	中国石油集团渤海钻探工程有限公司	65 790
35	中国技术进出口总公司	63 703
36	中国中原对外工程有限公司	63 431
37	江苏省建筑工程集团有限公司	62 303

续 表

序号	企业名称	完成营业额
38	中国江西国际经济技术合作公司	61 916
39	中国河南国际合作集团有限公司	61 523
40	中国地质工程集团公司	60 585
41	威海国际经济技术合作股份有限公司	59 516
42	中电投电力工程有限公司	59 000
43	大庆石油国际工程公司	58 960
44	中国铁建股份有限公司	57 642
45	中石化中原石油工程有限公司	54 942
46	上海福伊特水电设备有限公司	54 503
47	中钢设备有限公司	54 239
48	中国二十冶集团有限公司	53 755
49	北京建工集团有限责任公司	52 267
50	安徽建工集团有限公司	52 028
51	中铁四局集团有限公司	51 946
52	中国成达工程有限公司	51 562
53	中兴通讯股份有限公司	51 295
54	海尔集团电器产业有限公司	49 568
55	中成进出口股份有限公司	48 169
56	中材建设有限公司	47 726
57	中海油田服务股份有限公司	47 067
58	中国石油集团川庆钻探工程有限公司	46 987
59	中铁建工集团有限公司	46 945
60	中国能源建设集团天津电力建设公司	46 753
61	中交第二航务工程局有限公司	46 659
62	新疆生产建设兵团建设工程（集团）有限责任公司	45 387
63	中国建筑第五工程局有限公司	45 185
64	中国石油集团西部钻探工程有限公司	44 585
65	中鼎国际工程有限责任公司	44 143
66	中铁十四局集团有限公司	43 943
67	江西中煤建设集团有限公司	43 922
68	北方国际合作股份有限公司	43 772
69	中国能源建设集团广西水电工程局有限公司	43 445
70	中国中材国际工程股份有限公司	43 040
71	浙江省建设投资集团有限公司	42 227
72	沈阳远大铝业工程有限公司	40 976
73	中国大连国际经济技术合作集团有限公司	40 001
74	中铁七局集团有限公司	39 881
75	中铁十八局集团有限公司	39 470
76	江苏中信建设集团有限公司	39 003

续 表

序号	企业名称	完成营业额
77	湖北省电力建设第二工程公司	38 288
78	中交第二公路工程局有限公司	37 621
79	江苏南通三建集团有限公司	37 487
80	上海建工集团股份有限公司	37 092
81	安徽省外经建设（集团）有限公司	36 257
82	中铁十局集团第三建设有限公司	35 364
83	天津水泥工业设计研究院有限公司	35 050
84	中国十七冶集团有限公司	34 185
85	云南阳光基础建设有限公司	34 021
86	中国寰球工程公司	33 490
87	中国冶金科工集团有限公司	32 522
88	中国海外工程有限责任公司	32 081
89	中国电力工程有限公司	31 457
90	中国航空技术国际工程有限公司	31 365
91	中国有色金属建设股份有限公司	31 327
92	烟台国际经济技术合作集团有限公司	31 132
93	云南建工集团有限公司	30 011
94	中国华电工程（集团）有限公司	29 408
95	中铁五局（集团）有限公司	28 347
96	中国山东对外经济技术合作集团有限公司	27 577
97	上海建工（集团）总公司	27 343
98	中国天辰工程有限公司	27 289
99	天元建设集团有限公司	27 245
100	南通建工集团股份有限公司	27，108

表 18

2014 年我国对外承包工程业务新签合同额前 50 家企业

单位：万美元

序　号	企业名称	新签合同额
1	中国土木工程集团有限公司	1 603 409
2	中国水电建设集团国际工程有限公司	1 260 812
3	中国建筑工程总公司	1 233 790
4	华为技术有限公司	1 139 172
5	中国葛洲坝集团股份有限公司	1 044 787
6	中国路桥工程有限责任公司	686 330
7	中国港湾工程有限责任公司	655 885
8	中国石油工程建设公司	593 211
9	中国铁建股份有限公司	509 547
10	中工国际工程股份有限公司	384 651
11	山东电力基本建设总公司	372 943

续 表

序 号	企业名称	新签合同额
12	中国机械设备工程股份有限公司	275 261
13	中国交通建设股份有限公司	265 861
14	上海振华重工（集团）股份有限公司	251 711
15	中国机械进出口（集团）有限公司	236 100
16	中国石油天然气管道局	218 977
17	中国石油集团长城钻探工程有限公司	208 487
18	中国水利电力对外公司	204 150
19	中地海外集团有限公司	203 140
20	上海电气集团股份有限公司	172 433
21	中国寰球工程公司	165 944
22	中国石油集团东方地球物理勘探有限责任公司	162 797
23	中国能源建设集团广东省电力设计研究院有限公司	159 860
24	中铁大桥局股份有限公司	156 005
25	浙江省建设投资集团有限公司	146 465
26	中国电力技术装备有限公司	145 800
27	中国天辰工程有限公司	134 280
28	中兴通讯股份有限公司	123 545
29	中国江西国际经济技术合作公司	118 315
30	江苏省建筑工程集团有限公司	116 018
31	特变电工股份有限公司	111 896
32	上海贝尔股份有限公司	107 866
33	中交第一公路工程局有限公司	96 710
34	中国石油集团工程设计有限责任公司	91 867
35	云南路桥股份有限公司	88 001
36	中铁国际集团有限公司	86 143
37	海尔集团电器产业有限公司	81 642
38	中国地质工程集团公司	79 784
39	青建集团股份公司	78 077
40	中国石油集团渤海钻探工程有限公司	77 089
41	威海国际经济技术合作股份有限公司	73 792
42	中铁建工集团有限公司	72 975
43	中国电建集团成都勘测设计研究院有限公司	72 300
44	中国长城工业集团有限公司	70 748
45	苏州中材建设有限公司	70 731
46	上海电力建设有限责任公司	70 190
47	中国中材国际工程股份有限公司	69 291
48	安徽建工集团有限公司	66 003
49	中国技术进出口总公司	65 590
50	江西中煤建设集团有限公司	63 162

表 19

2014 年全国外商投资企业进出口情况

单位：亿美元

	全国		外商投资企业					
	金额	比去年%	金额		占全国比重%		比重+/-（百分点）	比去年
进出口总值	43 030	3.40%	19 840		46.10%		0	3.40%
出口总值	23 427	6.10%	10 747		45.90%		-1.4	2.90%
进口总值	19 603	0.40%	9 093		46.40%		1.6	3.9%
			投资进口设备	91	占三资企业进口比重	1.00%	-0.1	-7.50%

注：1～12 月份贸易顺差值为 1654 亿美元，扣除投资项下进口设备、物料，贸易净顺差值为 1745 亿美元。

表 20

2014 年我国非金融类对外直接投资（按省市区排序）

单位：万美元

序号	省市区	直接投资额
1	北京市	554 737
2	天津市	147 455
3	河北省	34 959
4	山西省	18 776
5	内蒙古自治区	21 200
6	辽宁省	142 081
	其中：大连市	58 949
7	吉林省	25 569
8	黑龙江省	58 586
9	上海市	344 773
10	江苏省	417 526
11	浙江省	359 113
	其中：宁波市	84 484
12	安徽省	46 877
13	福建省	137 686
	其中：厦门市	54 923
14	江西省	65 809
15	山东省	441 095
	其中：青岛市	108 036
16	河南省	62 614
17	湖北省	57 618
18	湖南省	75 955
19	广东省	960 066
	其中：深圳市	397 747
20	广西壮族自治区	28 934
21	海南省	72 291
22	重庆市	68 884
23	四川省	89 837
24	贵州省	10 093
25	云南省	105 228
26	西藏自治区	394
27	陕西省	45 372
28	甘肃省	22 568
29	青海省	2 039
30	宁夏回族自治区	34 471
31	新疆维吾尔自治区	50 280
32	新疆生产建设兵团	8 604

表 21

2000—2014 年两岸贸易统计

单位：亿美元，%

年 份	贸易总额		大陆对台出口额		大陆自台进口额		贸易差额
	金额	同比	金额	同比	金额	同比	
2000	305.3	30.1	50.4	27.6	254.9	30.6	－204.5
2001	323.4	5.9	50.0	－0.8	273.4	7.2	－223.4
2002	446.7	38.1	65.9	31.7	380.8	39.3	－314.9
2003	583.6	30.7	90.0	36.7	493.6	29.7	－403.6
2004	783.2	34.2	135.5	50.4	647.8	31.2	－512.3
2005	912.3	16.5	165.5	22.2	746.8	15.3	－581.3
2006	1 078.4	18.2	207.4	25.3	871.1	16.6	－663.7
2007	1 244.8	15.4	234.6	13.1	1 010.2	16.0	－775.6
2008	1 292.2	3.8	258.8	10.3	1 033.4	2.3	－774.6
2009	1 062.3	－17.8	205.1	－20.8	857.2	－17.0	－652.1
2010	1 453.7	36.9	296.8	44.8	1156.9	35.0	－860.1
2011	1 600.3	10.1	351.1	18.3	1 249.2	7.9	－898.1
2012	1 689.6	5.6	367.8	4.8	1 321.8	5.8	－954
2013	1 972.8	16.7	406.4	10.5	1 566.4	18.5	－1 160
2014	1 983.1	0.6	462.8	13.9	1 520.3	－2.8	－1 057.5

表 22

2000—2014 年台商投资大陆统计

单位：亿美元，%

年 份	项 目 数			实际使用台资金额		
	个数	同比	占当年总额比重	金额	同比	占当年总额比重
2000	3 108	24.4	13.9	23.0	－11.7	5.6
2001	4 214	35.6	16.1	29.8	29.8	6.4
2002	4 853	15.2	14.2	39.7	33.3	7.5
2003	4 495	－7.4	10.9	33.8	－14.9	6.3
2004	4 002	－11.0	9.2	31.2	－7.7	5.1
2005	3 907	－2.4	8.8	21.6	－31.0	3.6
2006	3 752	－4.0	9.1	21.4	－0.7	3.4
2007	3 299	－12.1	8.7	17.7	－20.4	2.4
2008	2 360	－28.5	8.6	19.0	7.0	2.1
2009	2 555	8.3	10.9	18.8	－1.0	2.1
2010	3 072	20.2	—	24.8	31.7	—
2011	2 639	－14.10	—	21.8	－11.81	—
2012	2 229	－15.5	—	28.5	20.4	3
2013	2 017	－9.5	—	20.9	－26.7	4.2
2014	2 318	14.9		20.2	－3.3	—

表 23

2000—2014 年内地与香港贸易统计

单位：亿美元，%

年　份	进　出　口		出　口		进　口	
	总额	同比	总额	同比	总额	同比
2000	539.5	23.3	445.2	20.8	94.3	36.8
2001	559.7	3.7	465.5	4.6	94.2	−0.1
2002	629.1	23.7	584.7	25.6	107.4	14
2003	847.1	26.3	762.9	30.5	111.2	3.7
2004	1 126.8	28.9	1 008.8	32.3	118	6.1
2005	1 367.1	21.3	1 244.8	23.4	122.3	3.6
2006	1 661.7	21.6	1 553.9	24.8	107.9	−11.8
2007	1 972.5	18.7	1 844.3	18.7	128.2	18.8
2008	2 036.7	3.3	1 907.4	3.4	129.2	0.9
2009	1 749.5	−14.1	1 662.3	−12.8	87.1	−32.6
2010	2 035.8	31.8	2 183.2	31.3	133.6	40.9
2011	2 835.2	23.0	2 680.3	22.8	155.0	26.4
2012	3 414.9	20.5	3 235.3	20.7	179.6	15.9
2013	4 010.1	17.5	3 847.9	19	162.2	−9.9
2014	3 760.9	−6.2	3 631.9	−5.5	129	−20.7

表 24

2000—2014 年香港对内地投资统计

单位：亿美元，%

年　份	项　目　数			实际使用港资金额		
	个数	同比	占比	金额	同比	占比
2000	7 199	22	32.21	155	−6.3	38.07
2001	8 008	11.2	30.64	167.1	7.8	35.66
2002	10 845	35.4	31.74	178.6	6.88	33.86
2003	13 633	25.7	33.19	177.0	−0.9	33.08
2004	14 719	7.97	33.71	189.9	7.29	31.08
2005	14 831	0.76	33.71	179.5	5.48	24.72
2006	15 496	4.5	37.36	202.3	12.7	32.11
2007	16 208	4.6	42.8	277.0	30.0	37.1
2008	12 857	−20.7	45.7	410.4	48.1	44.4
2009	10 701	−16.8	45.7	460.8	12.3	51.2
2010	13 070	22.1	—	605.7	31.5	—
2011	13 889	6.27	—	705.0	16.4	—
2012	12 604	−9.3	—	655.6	−7.0	58.7
2013	12 014	−4.8	—	733.9	11.9	—
2014	12 169	1.3	—	812.7	10.7	—

表 25

2000—2014 年内地对香港承包工程统计

单位：亿美元，%

年份	项目数		新签合同额		完成营业额		年末在港人数	
	份数	同比	金额	同比	金额	同比	人数	同比
1998	116	－36.30	18.30	－7.60	19.00	24.20	497	－21.40
1999	156	34.00	27.70	51.40	19.60	3.10	924	85.90
2000	162	3.80	25.50	－8.00	20.20	3.10	1037	12.20
2001	235	45.06	23.64	－7.25	16.99	－16.18	958	－7.62
2002	187	20.43	22.03	－6.79	21.38	25.76	907	－5.32
2003	284	51.87	23.34	5.94	26.37	23.38	850	－6.28
2004	649	128.52	17.74	－23.99	25.43	－3.58	839	－1.29
2005	209	67.80	14.46	－18.51	17.83	－29.89	991	18.12
2006	258	23.44	18.28	26.42	17.55	－18.11	1037	4.64
2007	263	1.94	16.27	－11.00	19.94	13.62	767	－26.04
2008	95	－63.88	16.1	－1.04	16.9	－15.25	375	－51.11
2009	94	－1.05	29.3	81.99	18.0	6.51	449	19.73
2010	1 632	—	35.1	—	19.0	—	21 052	—
2011	94	—	44.9	—	19.7	—	24 046	—
2012	120	—	54.0	—	27.9	—	35 098	—
2013	164	—	30.3	—	—	—	33 820	—
2014	235	—	31.2	—	37.3	—	51 540	—

注：2010—2014 年数据包括内地在香港承包工程、劳务合作合同数；年末在港劳务人数。

表 26

2000—2014 年内地与澳门贸易统计

单位：亿美元，%

年份	进出口		出口		进口	
	总额	同比	总额	同比	总额	同比
2000	8.05	9.6	7.10	11.3	0.95	－2.0
2001	8.63	7.2	7.43	4.7	1.19	25.4
2002	10.18	18.2	8.76	18.0	1.42	19.4
2003	14.67	44.1	12.81	46.3	1.86	30.6
2004	18.28	24.7	16.11	25.9	2.16	16.3
2005	18.70	2.0	16.05	－0.8	2.65	22.5
2006	24.41	30.5	21.84	36.1	2.56	－3.4
2007	29.2	19.7	26.4	20.9	2.8	9.7
2008	29.1	－0.5	26	－1.5	3.1	9.1
2009	21	－27.9	18.5	－28.8	2.5	－19.6
2010	22.6	8.0	21.4	15.7	1.2	－49.8
2011	25.2	11.2	23.6	10.0	1.6	31.3
2012	29.9	18.6	27.1	14.9	2.8	72
2013	35.7	19.4	31.8	17.4	3.9	38.7
2014	38.2	7.1	36.1	13.4	2.1	－45.1

表 27

2000—2014 年澳门对内地投资统计

单位：亿美元，%

年份	项目		实际利用澳资	
	个数	同比	金额	同比
2000	433	70.5	3.47	12.5
2001	458	5.8	3.21	−7.6
2002	518	13.1	4.68	45.9
2003	580	12	4.16	−11.1
2004	715	23.3	5.46	31.2
2005	707	−1.2	6.00	10
2006	868	22.8	6.00	0.41
2007	856	−1.4	6.4	−6.0
2008	435	−96.8	5.8	−9.4
2009	294	−32.4	8.1	40.1
2010	274	−6.8	6.6	−19.6
2011	283	3.28	6.8	3.84
2012	303	7.1	5.1	25.7
2013	310	2.3	4.6	−8.9
2014	380	22.6	5.5	19.6

表 28

1998—2014 年内地对澳门劳务合作统计

单位：亿美元，人

年份	劳务合作			承包工程		
	新签合同额	完成营业额	年末在外人数	新签合同额	完成营业额	年末在外人数
1998	1.34	1.12	27 066	1.30	1.45	436
1999	0.73	1.31	28 260	0.55	1.18	614
2000	0.98	1.23	28 253	0.62	0.98	451
2001	1.24	1.38	36 563	0.93	0.64	241
2002	1.23	1.09	21 033	1.25	0.79	611
2003	0.90	1.18	23 590	2.13	1.70	1024
2004	1.20	1.31	21 983	5.24	2.18	1 146
2005	2.74	1.38	27 063	5.79	3.73	219
2006	3.14	2.57	37 557	18.13	7.92	456
2007	4.04	2.63	44 510	11.03	11.72	578
2008	5.41	3.64	53 399	8.86	8.79	899
2009	1.1	3.3	47 908	2.8	5.3	2091

	新签合同额	完成营业额	年末在外人数
2010	15.6	14.5	48 951
2011	8.2	5.0	58 543
2012	7.5	4.7	68 216
2013	8.7	4.2	89 152
2014	19.1	7.9	114 883

注：2010—2014 年数据未单列。

表 29

2014 年中国对亚洲国家（地区）贸易统计

单位：亿美元，%

	进出口		出口		进口		贸易差额	
	金额	同比	金额	同比	金额	同比	当年	上年同期
总值	43 038.40	3.45	23 430.34	6.02	19 608.06	0.54	3 822.27	2 597.30
亚洲地区	22 745.67	2.23	11 888.83	4.78	10 856.84	−0.41	1 032.00	445.36
亚洲司主管国别	12 778.44	6.31	6 569.05	9.53	6 209.39	3.10	359.66	−25.60
占总值比（%）	29.69	0.79	28.04	0.94	31.67	0.77	—	—
东北亚 4 国	6 167.34	2.91	2 555.58	3.24	3 611.77	2.67	−1 056.19	−1 042.48
日本	3 124.84	−0.02	1 494.64	−0.54	1 630.20	0.46	−135.56	−120.03
韩国	2 905.63	5.95	1 003.56	10.07	1 902.08	3.90	−898.52	−918.97
朝鲜	63.88	−2.57	35.22	−3.05	28.67	−1.97	6.55	7.08
蒙古	72.99	22.55	22.16	−9.52	50.82	44.96	28.66	−10.56
东盟	4 801.25	8.23	2 717.92	11. 36	2 083 32	4.41	635.20	445.30
文莱	19.36	7.96	17.47	2.51	1.90	111.37	15. 57	16.14
缅甸	249.73	146.03	93.70	27.66	156.03	455.18	−62.33	45.29
柬埔寨	37.57	−0.39	32.7.5	−3.99	4.83	33.54	27.92	30.49
印度尼西亚	635.86	−6.98	390.62	5.77	245.25	−21.95	145.37	55.10
老挝	36.14	31.87	18.43	7.13	17.72	73.56	0.71	7.00
马来西亚	1 019.75	−3.87	462.79	0.75	556.97	−7.39	−94.18	−142.10
菲律宾	444.43	16.75	234.59	18.27	209.83	15.10	24.76	16.05
新加坡	796.48	4.92	488.46	6.50	308.02	2.50	180.45	158.14
泰国	726.75	1.98	343.02	4.78	383 73	−0.39	−40.72	−57.85
越南	835.16	27.54	636.11	30.91	199.05	17.86	437.05	317.03
东帝汶	0.60	26.50	0.60	27.35	0.00	−74.85	0.60	0.47
南亚 8 国	1060.56	10.10	858.44	14.07	202.13	−4.05	656.31	541.92
印度	706.05	7.84	542.26	11.94	163.79	−3.81	378.47	314.15
巴基斯坦	160.06	12.57	132.48	20.23	27.58	−13.81	104.90	78.19
孟加拉国	125.47	21.72	117.85	21.42	7.62	26.56	110.23	91.04
斯里兰卡	40.42	11.66	37.93	10.35	2.49	36.24	35.45	32.55
尼泊尔	23 .30	3.38	22.83	3.28	0.47	8.50	22.36	21.67
马尔代夫	1.04	6.72	1.04	6.86	0.00	−20.74	1.04	0.97
不丹	0.11	−35.57	0.11	−36.14	0.00	1 119.33	0.11	0.7
阿富汗	4.11	21.56	3.94	19.82	0 17	81.06	3.76	3.19
西亚 2 国	748.68	21.24	436.51	36.83	312.17	4.57	124.34	29.67
伊朗	518.50	31.13	243.44	72.07	275.06	8.32	−31.61	−112.46
土耳其	230.18	3.63	193.07	8.75	37.12	−16.76	155.95	132.94
西亚 12 国	2 162.12	75.95	855.82	138.53	1 306.31	−100.62	−450.49	−514.66
中国香港	3 765.77	−6.09	3 636.73	−5.49	129.04	−20.42	3 507.68	3 685.77
中国澳门	38.19	7.09	36.06	13.44	2.12	−45.13	33.94	27.92
中国台北	1 983.21	0.53	462.87	13.89	1 520.34	−2.94	−1 057.47	1 159.93
欧盟（28）	6 151.96	10.05	3 709.04	9.42	2 442.92	11.01	1 266.13	1 189.30
美国	5 551.16	6.55	3 960.93	7.51	1 590.22	4.23	2 370.71	2 158.51

注：①十大贸易伙伴：欧盟、美国、东盟、中国香港、日本、韩国、中国台北、澳大利亚、俄罗斯、巴西。

②十大出口市场：美国、欧盟、香港、东盟、日本、韩国、印度、俄罗斯、中国台北、澳大利亚。

③十大进口来源：欧盟、东盟、韩国、日本、美国、中国台北、澳大利亚、巴西、沙特阿拉伯、南非。

④占总值比中的“同比”为同比增减点数；亚洲司主管 25 个国别。

表 30

2014 年美国对中国出口主要商品构成（章）

单位：百万美元，%

HS 编码	商品类别	2014 年 1—12 月	上年同期	同比	占比
章	总值	124 024	121 736	1.9	100.0
12	油籽；子仁；工业或药用植物；饲料	15 260	13 701	11.4	12.3
88	航空器、航天器及其零件	13 924	12 587	10.6	11.2
87	车辆及其零附件，但铁道车辆除外	13 213	10 319	28.1	10.7
84	核反应堆、锅炉、机械器具及零件	12 451	12 201	2.1	10.0
85	电机、电气、音像设备及其零附件	12 047	11 375	5.9	9.7
90	光学、照相、医疗等设备及零附件	7 527	7 667	−1.8	6.1
39	塑料及其制品	5 075	4 742	7.0	4.1
47	木浆等纤维状纤维素浆；废纸及纸板	3 373	3 602	−6.4	2.7
74	铜及其制品	2 919	3 472	−15.9	2.4
44	木及木制品；木炭	2 677	2 352	13.9	2.2
29	有机化学品	2 373	3 102	−23.5	1.9
38	杂项化学产品	2 151	1 988	8.2	1.7
76	铝及其制品	2 118	2 627	−19.4	1.7
41	生皮（毛皮除外）及皮革	1 814	1 769	2.5	1.5
27	矿物燃料、矿物油及其产品；沥青等	1 791	2 809	−36.2	1.4
10	谷物	1 760	2 374	−25.9	1.4
23	食品工业的残渣及废料；配制的饲料	1 718	1 785	−3.7	1.4
30	药品	1 609	1 220	31.9	1.3
26	矿砂、矿渣及矿灰	1 488	1 476	0.8	1.2
52	棉花	1 224	2 366	−48.3	1.0
03	鱼及其他水生无脊椎动物	1 150	1 095	5.1	0.9
71	珠宝、贵金属及制品；仿首饰；硬币	1 094	1 156	−5.3	0.9
72	钢铁	1 024	1 399	−26.8	0.8
28	无机化学品；贵金属等的化合物	984	938	4.9	0.8
40	橡胶及其制品	884	949	−6.9	0.7
73	钢铁制品	869	751	15.7	0.7
48	纸及纸板；纸浆、纸或纸板制品	800	773	3.5	0.7
02	肉及食用杂碎	705	1 060	−33.5	0.6
34	洗涤剂、润滑剂、人造蜡、塑型膏等	626	568	10.2	0.5
37	照相及电影用品	607	601	1.0	0.5
	以上合计	115 257	112 826	2.2	92.9

表 31

2014 年美国自中国进口主要商品构成（章）

单位：百万美元，%

HS 编码	商品类别	2014 年 1—12 月	上年同期	同比	占比
章	总值	466 656	440 448	6.0	100.0
85	电机、电气、音像设备及其零附件	127 086	117 535	8.1	27.2
84	核反应堆、锅炉、机械器具及零件	105 255	100 450	4.8	22.6
94	家具；寝具等；灯具；活动房	25 528	24 134	5.8	5.5
95	玩具、游戏或运动用品及其零附件	22 597	21 686	4.2	4.8
64	鞋靴、护腿和类似品及其零件	17 066	17 016	0.3	3.7
61	针织或钩编的服装及衣着附件	16 104	15 577	3.4	3.5
62	非针织或非钩编的服装及衣着附件	14 380	14 905	−3.5	3.1
39	塑料及其制品	13 863	12 922	7.3	3.0
87	车辆及其零附件，但铁道车辆除外	11 451	9 824	16.6	2.5
90	光学、照相、医疗等设备及零附件	10 336	9 524	8.5	2.2
73	钢铁制品	9 795	8 925	9.8	2.1
42	皮革制品；旅行箱包；动物肠线制品	8 537	8 651	−1.3	1.8
63	其他纺织制品；成套物品；旧纺织品	7 092	6 797	4.3	1.5
29	有机化学品	6 714	6 714	0.0	1.4
40	橡胶及其制品	5 754	5 280	9.0	1.2
83	贱金属杂项制品	4 336	4 202	3.2	0.9
44	木及木制品；木炭	3 695	3 333	10.9	0.8
71	珠宝、贵金属及制品；仿首饰；硬币	3 616	3 672	−1.5	0.8
82	贱金属器具、利口器、餐具及零件	3 504	3 340	4.9	0.8
48	纸及纸板；纸浆、纸或纸板制品	2 764	2 608	6.0	0.6
96	杂项制品	2 621	2 484	5.5	0.6
72	钢铁	2 581	1 540	67.6	0.6
76	铝及其制品	2 548	2 345	8.7	0.6
70	玻璃及其制品	2 418	2 094	15.5	0.5
69	陶瓷产品	2 339	2 212	5.7	0.5
03	鱼及其他水生无脊椎动物	2 102	1 958	7.3	0.5
49	印刷品；手稿、打字稿及设计图纸	1 934	1 936	−0.1	0.4
28	无机化学品；贵金属等的化合物	1 615	1 481	9.0	0.4
65	头饰	1 419	1 300	9.2	0.3
67	加工羽毛及制品；人造花；人发制品	1 381	1 439	−4.0	0.3
	以上合计	440 429	415 884	5.9	94.4

表 32

2014 年美国对中国出口主要商品构成（类）

单位：百万美元，%

海关分类	HS 编码	商品类别	2014 年 1—12 月	上年同期	同比	占比
类	章	总值	124 024	121 736	1.9	100.0
第 17 类	86—89	运输设备	27 259	23 037	18.3	22.0
第 16 类	84—85	机电产品	24 498	23 576	3.9	19.8
第 2 类	06—14	植物产品	17 493	16 728	4.6	14.1
第 6 类	28—38	化工产品	9 678	9 754	−0.8	7.8
第 15 类	72—83	贱金属及制品	7 894	9 089	−13.2	6.4
第 18 类	90—92	光学、钟表、医疗设备	7 556	7 691	−1.8	6.1
第 7 类	39—40	塑料、橡胶	5 959	5 692	4.7	4.8
第 10 类	47—49	纤维素浆；纸张	4 356	4 525	−3.7	3.5
第 5 类	25—27	矿产品	3 520	4 485	−21.5	2.8
第 4 类	16—24	食品、饮料、烟草	2 734	2 815	−2.9	2.2
第 9 类	44—46	木及木制品	2 679	2 356	13.7	2.2
第 1 类	01—05	活动物；动物产品	2 620	2 944	−11.0	2.1
第 11 类	50—63	纺织品及原料	2 279	3 485	−34.6	1.8
第 8 类	41—43	皮革制品；箱包	1 921	1 987	−3.4	1.6
第 14 类	71	贵金属及制品	1 094	1 156	−5.3	0.9
		其他	2 484	2 418	2.8	2.0

表 33

2014 年美国自中国进口主要商品构成（类）

单位：百万美元，%

海关分类	HS 编码	商品类别	2014 年 1—12 月	上年同期	同比	占比
类	章	总值	466 656	440 448	6.0	100.0
第 16 类	84—85	机电产品	232 340	217 985	6.6	49.8
第 20 类	94—96	家具、玩具、杂项制品	50 746	48 304	5.1	10.9
第 11 类	50—63	纺织品及原料	41 183	40 680	1.2	8.8
第 15 类	72—83	贱金属及制品	24 234	21 696	11.7	5.2
第 12 类	64—67	鞋靴、伞等轻工产品	20 365	20 248	0.6	4.4
第 7 类	39—40	塑料、橡胶	19 617	18 202	7.8	4.2
第 6 类	28—38	化工产品	13 716	12 688	8.1	2.9
第 17 类	86—89	运输设备	12 847	10 836	18.6	2.8
第 18 类	90—92	光学、钟表、医疗设备	11 759	10 820	8.7	2.5
第 8 类	41—43	皮革制品；箱包	8 661	8 757	−1.1	1.9
第 13 类	68—70	陶瓷；玻璃	6 057	5 498	10.2	1.3
第 10 类	47—49	纤维素浆；纸张	4 702	4 549	3.4	1.0
第 9 类	44—46	木及制品	4 019	3 657	9.9	0.9
第 14 类	71	贵金属及制品	3 616	3 672	−1.5	0.8
第 4 类	16—24	食品、饮料、烟草	2 786	2 918	−4.5	0.6
		其他	10 007	9 938	0.7	2.1

表 34

2014 年美国自中国进口的十大类商品及其国别/地区构成

单位：百万美元，%

HS84－85：机电产品				HS39－40：塑料、橡胶			
国家和地区	金额	同比	占比	国家和地区	金额	同比	占比
中国	232 340	6.6	36.4	中国	19 617	7.8	26.0
墨西哥	103 235	3.2	16.2	加拿大	14 367	3.9	19.0
日本	48 262	－1.5	7.6	墨西哥	6 656	10.8	8.8
德国	32 013	8.4	5.0	日本	4 661	0.3	6.2
加拿大	28 903	4.1	4.5	德国	4 073	10.8	5.4
韩国	27 000	6.0	4.2	韩国	3 659	5.0	4.8
HS94－96：家具、玩具、杂项制品				HS28－38：化工产品			
国家和地区	金额	同比	占比	国家和地区	金额	同比	占比
中国	50 746	5.1	59.6	爱尔兰	24 299	9.2	13.2
墨西哥	11 351	12.7	13.3	德国	21 503	14.6	11.7
加拿大	5 223	2.9	6.1	加拿大	19 839	－0.3	10.8
越南	3 514	20.6	4.1	中国	13 716	8.1	7.5
中国台北	1 994	6.5	2.3	瑞士	11 804	10.2	6.4
意大利	1 194	11.9	1.4	英国	8 756	4.7	4.8
HS50－63：纺织品及原料				HS86－89：运输设备			
国家和地区	金额	同比	占比	国家和地区	金额	同比	占比
中国	41 183	1.2	37.2	墨西哥	69 386	14.3	23.2
越南	9 594	14.1	8.7	加拿大	64 486	2.4	21.6
印度	7 061	6.4	6.4	日本	50 350	－6.5	16.8
墨西哥	5 491	2.0	5.0	德国	37 456	5.2	12.5
印度尼西亚	5 108	－3.1	4.6	韩国	20 148	15.4	6.7
孟加拉国	4 907	－2.7	4.4	中国	12 847	18.6	4.3
HS72－83：贱金属及制品				HS90－92：光学、钟表、医疗设备			
国家和地区	金额	同比	占比	国家和地区	金额	同比	占比
加拿大	24 282	7.1	19.0	中国	11 759	8.7	14.4
中国	24 234	11.7	19.0	墨西哥	11 694	7.8	14.3
墨西哥	11 174	13.4	8.7	德国	9 328	3.4	11.4
韩国	6 891	34.1	5.4	日本	7 838	－0.7	9.6
德国	6 341	11.0	5.0	瑞士	6 125	7.4	7.5
日本	5 848	0.0	4.6	爱尔兰	5 774	0.2	7.1
HS64－67：鞋靴、伞等轻工产品				HS41－43：皮革制品；箱包			
国家和地区	金额	同比	占比	国家和地区	金额	同比	占比
中国	20 365	0.6	67.0	中国	8 661	－1.1	59.3
越南	3 792	23.4	12.5	意大利	1 347	11.1	9.2
意大利	1 477	7.8	4.9	越南	972	28.7	6.7
印度尼西亚	1 452	4.3	4.8	法国	645	10.7	4.4
墨西哥	576	－6.6	1.9	印度	458	13.0	3.1
印度	375	19.3	1.2	加拿大	337	14.0	2.3

表 35

2014 年日本对中国出口主要商品构成（章）

单位：百万美元，%

HS 编码	商品类别	2014 年 1—12 月	上年同期	同比%	占比%
章	总值	126 483	129 093	−2.0	100.0
85	电机、电气、音像设备及其零附件	25 456	25 659	−0.8	20.1
84	核反应堆、锅炉、机械器具及零件	24 276	25 191	−3.6	19.2
87	车辆及其零附件，但铁道车辆除外	12 871	12 554	2.5	10.2
90	光学、照相、医疗等设备及零附件	11 745	11 279	4.1	9.3
29	有机化学品	8 092	9 503	−14.8	6.4
39	塑料及其制品	7 248	7 461	−2.9	5.7
72	钢铁	6 650	7 055	−5.7	5.3
74	铜及其制品	3 223	3 398	−5.2	2.6
73	钢铁制品	1 835	1 906	−3.7	1.5
38	杂项化学产品	1 665	1 669	−0.3	1.3
27	矿物燃料、矿物油及其产品；沥青等	1 467	1 580	−7.2	1.2
40	橡胶及其制品	1 324	1 521	−12.9	1.1
70	玻璃及其制品	913	1 217	−25.0	0.7
32	鞣料；着色料；涂料；油灰；墨水等	852	797	6.9	0.7
96	杂项制品	822	588	39.8	0.7
34	洗涤剂、润滑剂、人造蜡、塑型膏等	785	733	7.0	0.6
82	贱金属器具、利口器、餐具及零件	723	651	11.1	0.6
47	木浆等纤维状纤维素浆；废纸及纸板	722	843	−14.4	0.6
54	化学纤维长丝	687	752	−8.6	0.5
76	铝及其制品	682	634	7.4	0.5
55	化学纤维短纤	643	741	−13.2	0.5
37	照相及电影用品	643	694	−7.4	0.5
28	无机化学品；贵金属等的化合物	559	548	2.0	0.4
71	珠宝、贵金属及制品；仿首饰；硬币	531	536	−0.9	0.4
30	药品	507	453	12.0	0.4
68	矿物材料的制品	504	467	7.8	0.4
48	纸及纸板；纸浆、纸或纸板制品	395	430	−8.2	0.3
60	针织物及钩编织物	325	359	−9.4	0.3
59	浸、包或层压织物；工业用纺织制品	295	313	−5.8	0.2
03	鱼及其他水生无脊椎动物	280	246	13.8	0.2
	以上合计	116 720	119 781	−2.6	92.3

表 36

2014年日本自中国进口主要商品构成（章）

单位：百万美元，%

HS编码	商品类别	2014年1—12月	上年同期	同比%	占比%
章	总值	180 996	180 841	0.1	100.0
85	电机、电气、音像设备及其零附件	50 500	48 578	4.0	27.9
84	核反应堆、锅炉、机械器具及零件	31 899	31 437	1.5	17.6
61	针织或钩编的服装及衣着附件	11 106	12 588	−11.8	6.1
62	非针织或非钩编的服装及衣着附件	9 921	11 484	−13.6	5.5
39	塑料及其制品	5 294	5 175	2.3	2.9
95	玩具、游戏或运动用品及其零附件	5 051	5 266	−4.1	2.8
94	家具；寝具等；灯具；活动房	4 975	4 976	0.0	2.8
90	光学、照相、医疗等设备及零附件	4 683	4 758	−1.6	2.6
87	车辆及其零附件，但铁道车辆除外	4 307	4 059	6.1	2.4
73	钢铁制品	3 903	3 705	5.3	2.2
64	鞋靴、护腿和类似品及其零件	3 614	3 872	−6.7	2.0
29	有机化学品	3 269	3 154	3.7	1.8
42	皮革制品；旅行箱包；动物肠线制品	3 018	3 260	−7.4	1.7
63	其他纺织制品；成套物品；旧纺织品	2 967	3 064	−3.2	1.6
16	肉、鱼及其他水生无脊椎动物的制品	2 670	2 836	−5.9	1.5
28	无机化学品；贵金属等的化合物	2 095	1 894	10.6	1.2
76	铝及其制品	1 821	1 539	18.3	1.0
44	木及木制品；木炭	1 747	1 826	−4.3	1.0
72	钢铁	1 704	1 155	47.5	0.9
20	蔬菜、水果等或植物其他部分的制品	1 501	1 610	−6.8	0.8
07	食用蔬菜、根及块茎	1 425	1 450	−1.7	0.8
48	纸及纸板；纸浆、纸或纸板制品	1 357	1 390	−2.4	0.8
38	杂项化学产品	1 147	1 097	4.5	0.6
27	矿物燃料、矿物油及其产品；沥青等	1 146	1 056	8.5	0.6
03	鱼及其他水生无脊椎动物	1 102	1 127	−2.2	0.6
68	矿物材料的制品	1 100	1 164	−5.5	0.6
91	钟表及其零件	958	915	4.8	0.5
23	食品工业的残渣及废料；配制的饲料	833	628	32.7	0.5
96	杂项制品	820	861	−4.8	0.5
40	橡胶及其制品	820	767	6.9	0.5
	以上合计	166 751	166 691	0.0	92.2

表 37

2014 年日本对中国出口主要商品构成（类）

单位：百万美元，%

海关分类	HS 编码	商品类别	2014 年 1—12 月	上年同期	同比%	占比%
类	章	总值	126 483	129 093	−2.0	100.0
第 16 类	84—85	机电产品	49 732	50 850	−2.2	39.3
第 15 类	72—83	贱金属及制品	13 745	14 282	−3.8	10.9
第 6 类	28—38	化工产品	13 658	14 930	−8.5	10.8
第 17 类	86—89	运输设备	13 123	12 727	3.1	10.4
第 18 类	90—92	光学、钟表、医疗设备	11 985	11 515	4.1	9.5
第 7 类	39—40	塑料、橡胶	8 572	8 982	−4.6	6.8
第 11 类	50—63	纺织品及原料	2 820	3 094	−8.9	2.2
第 5 类	25—27	矿产品	1 667	1 769	−5.8	1.3
第 13 类	68—70	陶瓷；玻璃	1 590	1 853	−14.2	1.3
第 10 类	47—49	纤维素浆；纸张	1 230	1 420	−13.4	1.0
第 20 类	94—96	家具、玩具、杂项制品	1 132	986	14.8	0.9
第 14 类	71	贵金属及制品	531	536	−0.9	0.4
第 1 类	01—05	活动物；动物产品	290	255	13.6	0.2
第 4 类	16—24	食品、饮料、烟草	115	110	4.0	0.1
第 2 类	06—14	植物产品	69	73	−6.1	0.1
		其他	6 225	5 709	9.0	4.9

表 38

2014 年日本自中国进口主要商品构成（类）

单位：百万美元，%

海关分类	HS 编码	商品类别	2014 年 1—12 月	上年同期	同比%	占比%
类	章	总值	180 996	180 841	0.1	100.0
第 16 类	84—85	机电产品	82 399	80 015	3.0	45.5
第 11 类	50—63	纺织品及原料	26 116	29 242	−10.7	14.4
第 20 类	94—96	家具、玩具、杂项制品	10 846	11 102	−2.3	6.0
第 15 类	72—83	贱金属及制品	9 891	8 719	13.4	5.5
第 6 类	28—38	化工产品	8 237	7 847	5.0	4.6
第 7 类	39—40	塑料、橡胶	6 113	5 942	2.9	3.4
第 18 类	90—92	光学、钟表、医疗设备	5 783	5 802	−0.3	3.2
第 4 类	16—24	食品、饮料、烟草	5 615	5 741	−2.2	3.1
第 12 类	64—67	鞋靴、伞等轻工产品	4 465	4 719	−5.4	2.5
第 17 类	86—89	运输设备	4 464	4 182	6.7	2.5
第 8 类	41—43	皮革制品；箱包	3 155	3 432	−8.1	1.7
第 2 类	06—14	植物产品	2 567	2 585	−0.7	1.4
第 13 类	68—70	陶瓷；玻璃	2 406	2 538	−5.2	1.3
第 9 类	44—46	木及制品	2 034	2 129	−4.4	1.1
第 5 类	25—27	矿产品	1 871	1 779	5.2	1.0
		其他	5 033	5 066	−0.7	2.8

表 39

2014 年日本自中国进口的十大类商品及其国别/地区构成 单位：百万美元，%

HS84－85：机电产品				HS39－40：塑料、橡胶			
国家和地区	金额	同比%	占比%	国家和地区	金额	同比%	占比%
中国	82 399	3.0	50.2	中国	6 113	2.9	29.9
美国	15 678	5.0	9.6	泰国	2 557	0.0	12.5
中国台北	13 221	4.7	8.1	美国	2 165	－0.3	10.6
韩国	9 891	－4.9	6.0	韩国	1 850	－1.6	9.1
泰国	7 347	3.5	4.5	印度尼西亚	1 497	－18.6	7.3
马来西亚	5 373	－0.3	3.3	中国台北	1 489	－6.4	7.3
HS50－63：纺织品及原料				HS90－92：光学、钟表、医疗设备			
国家和地区	金额	同比%	占比%	国家和地区	金额	同比%	占比%
中国	26 116	－10.7	67.6	美国	7 672	－0.7	26.8
越南	3 136	12.7	8.1	中国	5 783	－0.3	20.2
印度尼西亚	1 437	3.6	3.7	瑞士	2 641	7.2	9.2
意大利	1 023	－5.1	2.7	德国	2 373	5.3	8.3
泰国	867	6.0	2.2	爱尔兰	1 478	－5.5	5.2
孟加拉国	687	13.3	1.8	泰国	824	11.8	2.9
HS94－96：家具、玩具、杂项制品				HS16－24：食品、饮料、烟草			
国家和地区	金额	同比%	占比%	国家和地区	金额	同比%	占比%
中国	10 846	－2.3	68.4	中国	5 615	－2.2	22.4
越南	874	16.5	5.5	美国	3 584	－6.1	14.3
泰国	604	3.7	3.8	泰国	2 977	－7.2	11.9
中国台北	588	－3.0	3.7	荷兰	1 652	－25.6	6.6
美国	391	0.2	2.5	法国	1 452	0.4	5.8
马来西亚	354	0.6	2.2	韩国	1 195	7.4	4.8
HS72－83：贱金属及制品				HS64－67：鞋靴、伞等轻工产品			
国家和地区	金额	同比%	占比%	国家和地区	金额	同比%	占比%
中国	9 891	13.4	27.8	中国	4 465	－5.4	64.6
韩国	4 776	10.0	13.4	越南	685	26.6	9.9
美国	1 928	7.4	5.4	意大利	385	－0.2	5.6
中国台北	1 885	9.0	5.3	印度尼西亚	272	1.5	3.9
澳大利亚	1 731	25.8	4.9	柬埔寨	209	－2.7	3.0
俄罗斯	1 640	30.9	4.6	孟加拉国	108	－16.3	1.6
HS28－38：化工产品				HS86－89：运输设备			
国家和地区	金额	同比%	占比%	国家和地区	金额	同比%	占比%
美国	10 262	1.4	18.5	德国	6 920	－0.8	23.7
中国	8 237	5.0	14.9	美国	6 350	－3.1	21.8
德国	6 218	－2.0	11.2	中国	4 464	6.7	15.3
法国	3 697	－9.8	6.7	法国	1 717	5.9	5.9
瑞士	2 651	－6.7	4.8	泰国	1 202	－14.3	4.1
韩国	2 417	－2.9	4.4	韩国	1 004	18.8	3.4

附　录

附录一：多哈回合及中国参与谈判大事记（2014）

1月23—27日	世界经济论坛及世贸组织（WTO）小型部长会议在达沃斯举行，成员就“后巴厘”工作计划等问题交换了意见。王受文部长助理、俞建华大使出席会议。
1月24日	WTO小型部长会议期间，包括中国在内的14个成员宣布启动《环境产品协定》（EGA）诸边谈判的意愿。
2月6日	WTO贸易谈判委员会举行非正式会议，俞建华大使参会并阐述了中方立场。
3月14日	WTO总理事会举行会议，听取了阿泽维多总干事关于“后巴厘”工作计划和贸易便利化筹备委员会主席关于实施《贸易便利化协定》的工作报告，并选举了WTO各机构主席。俞建华大使参会。
4月7日	WTO贸易谈判委员会举行会议，俞建华大使参会并阐述中方立场。
5月7日	经合组织（OECD）举行小型部长会议，评估“巴厘一揽子”协议实施情况及“后巴厘”谈判问题。中国、美国、欧盟、印度、巴西等二十多个WTO成员的贸易部长或部长代表，以及阿泽维多总干事参会。王受文部长助理、俞建华大使出席会议。
5月12日	WTO总理事会举行会议，讨论“后巴厘”工作计划和《贸易便利化协定》实施问题，俞建华大使参会并阐述中方立场。
5月17—18日	高虎城部长主持2014年亚太经合组织（APEC）贸易部长会议，会议达成了一系列重要共识，并发表了《2014亚太经合组织贸易部长会议青岛声明》和《亚太经合组织贸易部长支持多边贸易体制的单独声明》，王受文部长助理、俞建华大使出席会议。
5月19日	汪洋副总理会见来华参加APEC贸易部长会议的阿泽维多总干事。汪副总理强调中国政府坚定维护多边贸易体制，一如既往地积极支持WTO开展工作。
6月25日	WTO贸易谈判委员会举行会议，俞建华大使参会并阐述中方立场。
7月1—3日	WTO举行第5次对华贸易政策审议。王受文部长助理率团参会，俞建华大使出席。中方在发言中重申了对多边贸易体制和多哈回合谈判的坚定支持。
7月8日	《环境产品协定》（EGA）诸边谈判启动首轮磋商，俞建华大使出席。
7月24—25日	WTO总理事会举行会议，讨论“后巴厘”工作计划和《贸易便利化协定》实施问题，俞建华大使参会并阐述中方立场。
10月16日	WTO贸易谈判委员会举行会议，俞建华大使参会，并在发言中呼吁成员尽早就《贸易便利化协定》的实施和粮食安全问题找到解决办法。
10月21日	WTO总理事会举行会议，讨论“后巴厘”工作计划和《贸易便利化协定》实施问题，俞建华大使参会并阐述中方立场。
11月7日	汪洋副总理会见了来华参加APEC部长级会议的阿泽维多总干事。汪副总理表示，中国将继续支持多边贸易体制，积极推动世贸成员全面落实“巴厘一揽子”协议、制订“后巴厘”工作计划、完成多哈回合谈判。
11月7—8日	外交部部长王毅、商务部部长高虎城联合主持第26届APEC部长级会议，会议重申了对多边贸易体制的坚定支持，一致同意尽快打破谈判僵局，全面落实“巴厘一揽子”协议，抓紧制订“后巴厘”工作计划。王受文部长助理出席会议并发言。

续 表

11月19—21日	WTO举行对中国香港第7次贸易政策审议，俞建华大使参会并发言。
11月27日	WTO举行总理事会特别会议及贸易便利化筹备委员会会议，通过了《贸易便利化协定》议定书、粮食安全和“后巴厘”工作等三项决定，全面恢复了“巴厘一揽子”协议实施和“后巴厘”工作计划制订。朱洪临时代办参会并阐述中方立场。
12月10—11日	WTO总理事会举行会议，俞建华大使参会并阐述中方立场。
12月16—18日	WTO举行对美国第12次贸易政策审议，俞建华大使参会，在发言中表达了中方对部分美国贸易政策问题的关注，呼吁美国积极承担多边责任，推动多哈谈判尽快结束。

（商务部世界贸易组织司）

附录二：中国自贸区建设总体情况

在2001年正式加入世贸组织后，为在新时期寻求对外开放的新平台，为改革发展提供新动力，我国顺应世界区域经济一体化快速发展的新特点，积极稳妥推进自贸区建设。经过十来年的发展，我国自贸区建设取得了积极进展，初步形成了周边自贸平台和全球自贸区网络。

截至2014年，我国已经签署和正在商谈的自贸区有19个，其中已经签署并实施的自贸协定12个，涉及20个国家和地区。这些协定分别是中国与东盟、新加坡、巴基斯坦、新西兰、智利、秘鲁、哥斯达黎加、冰岛、瑞士的自贸协定，内地与香港、澳门的更紧密经贸关系安排（CEPA），以及大陆与台湾的海峡两岸经济合作框架协议（ECFA）。实质性结束谈判的自贸区2个，分别为中国与韩国和澳大利亚的自贸谈判。正在谈判的自贸区有5个，涉及23个国家，包括区域全面经济合作伙伴关系协定（RCEP）、中国—海湾合作委员会自贸区、中国—挪威自贸区、中日韩自贸区、中国—斯里兰卡自贸区。我国还在推进中国—东盟自贸区升级谈判、中国—巴基斯坦自贸区第二阶段谈判和《海峡两岸经济合作框架协议》后续谈判。

此外，我国完成了与印度的区域贸易安排（RTA）联合研究，正与哥伦比亚等开展自贸区联合可行性研究，还加入了《亚太贸易协定》。

（商务部国际司）

附录三：WTO 年度大事记（2014）

◇ 2014 年 1 月

3 日

阿泽维多：巴厘仅仅是起点

总干事阿泽维多在 2014 年 1 月 6 日里斯本举行的外交研讨会上发言指出：“强化多边贸易体制和推进多哈发展回合是非常难的任务，但并非不可能。许多人有理由不相信我们能在巴厘部长级会议上取得成果，但是我们做到了，而且我们还可以做得更多。巴厘仅仅是起点。”

17 日

阿泽维多赞扬有关贸易融资的巴塞尔协议对发展中国家而言是“好信息”

2014 年 1 月 17 日，总干事阿泽维多对巴塞尔委员会就银行监管达成的协议表示欢迎，认为这“对发展中世界贸易融资的可获得性尤为重要”。

20 日

WTO 为发展中国家成员的官员举办了高级贸易政策课程

2014 年 1 月 20 日至 3 月 13 日，来自发展中国家成员、最不发达国家成员和观察员政府的 26 位官员参加了在日内瓦 WTO 秘书处举办的为期 2 个月的高级贸易政策课程。该课程是由赞助人美国大使 Michael Punke 以及培训和技术合作学院（ITTC）院长 Bridget Chilala 主持。

◇ 2014 年 2 月

6 日

阿泽维多督促成员在 2014 年实施巴厘一揽子协议并使多哈重回正轨

第九届部长级会议后的各成员驻 WTO 大使第一次会议于 2014 年 2 月 6 日召开。总干事阿泽维多告诉谈判委员会，“巴厘成果不仅仅代表巨大的成功，还代表着巨大的机遇。这是一个真正的政治势头，我们要抓住。”他说他已经跟各谈判组的主席“就可能推进的议题启动对话”。

11 日

阿泽维多强调学术界在发展中国家政策制定中的作用

总干事阿泽维多在 2014 年 2 月 11 日“联接全球市场”新书启动会上发言指出，“通过展示学术界对政策制定的贡献，这本书使世贸组织教席方案本身成为一个典型案例。它显示了构建发展中国家学术能力的价值，有时短期供应就可以解决这一问题。”

17 日

阿泽维多把脉全球贸易：增长恢复，但限制措施上升

总干事阿泽维多 2014 年 2 月 17 日向 WTO 成员展示其首份全球贸易监测报告时，指出今年的贸易增长预测“得到了极大改善，增长率约为 4%到 4.5%。”然而，他又指出“监测期间共有 407 项贸易限制措施”，影响了世界货物进口的 1.3%，总价值为 2400 亿美元。

“巴厘一揽子”成为 WTO 为最不发达国家开设课程的课程内容

2014 年 2 月 17—28 日，为最不发达国家成员在日内瓦开设首次 WTO 中级主题课程，法语讲授，共有 25 位政府官员参加。该课程由技术合作学院（ITTC）院长 Bridget Chilala 女士和 ITTC 的课程设计和训练科科长侯爵 Serafino 先生主持。

24 日

WTO 启动 2014 年青年经济学家学术论文奖征集活动

WTO 呼吁青年经济学家于 2014 年 6 月 1 日前提交论文，以便参与“2014WTO 青年经济学家学术论文奖”，目的是促进年轻经济学家高质量研究 WTO 及其相关的问题，并加强 WTO 与学术界的联系。

◇ **2014年3月**

6日

UNCTAD－EIF 报告：改善渔业部门的贸易政策可以解决性别不平等问题

一份新的 UNCTAD－EIF 报告发现，渔业部门的扩张有助于减少冈比亚的贫穷问题，尤其是女性贫穷问题，由此得出在贸易政策中考虑性别因素，是带来整体繁荣的有益的方式。案例研究警示大家，不考虑性别因素，促进冈比亚的鱼类出口在一些案例中将加大男女之间的不平等。

10日

WTO和WIPO为政策制定者启动了知识产权高级培训课程

2014年3月10日，为政府官员开设的知识产权高级培训课程启动，旨在加强发展中国家参与者监测和参与国际事态发展的能力，并更好地对知识产权政策问题做出明智的评估。

11日

修订版的WTO《政府采购协定》将于2014年4月6日生效

修订版的WTO《政府采购协定》将于2014年4月6日生效，该修订条款于2012年3月通过。总干事阿泽维多指出："这是一个非常受欢迎的成就。修订的WTO《政府采购协定》将会开放成员的市场并改善政府采购领域的监管。"

13日

WTO高级贸易政策课程结束

2014年1月20日至3月13日，在日内瓦WTO秘书处举办了为期2个月的高级贸易政策课程，该课程进行了概念重建。课程由培训和技术合作学院组织，共有来自世界范围内的26位政府官员参加。

17日

WTO在突尼斯为非洲法语国家开设区域课程

2014年3月17日至5月9日，在突尼斯的马努巴（Manouba）大学，WTO为非洲法语国家开设了区域贸易政策课程，共有来自发展中国家的27位政府官员参加。

◇ **2014年4月**

2日

WTO启动2014公共论坛建议收集工作

2014年公共论坛将于10月1—3日在WTO总部举办，论坛主题是"为何贸易与所有人息息相关"。现开始征集论坛提议，提议提交的截止期限为2014年5月30日。2014年公共论坛将致力于讲述贸易背后的人性故事，并借此展示贸易与人们日常生活之间千丝万缕的联系，同时展示贸易如何影响和改善全球（无论是发达成员还是发展中成员）公民的日常生活。

4日

阿泽维多在UNCTAD：贸易必须在2015年后的国际发展合作中发挥核心作用

2014年4月4日，联合国贸易与发展会议第二次日内瓦对话"2015年后的可持续发展议程：巴厘后的道路"上，总干事阿泽维多发言指出：贸易是2015年后议程中起核心作用的包容性和可持续发展的关键因素之一，这是一种新的紧迫性。

8日

新研究表明，巴厘贸易便利化协议挑战了传统的WTO智慧

《贸易便利化协议》简化海关程序，减少繁文缛节，于2013年12月在巴厘岛签署。这是日内瓦谈判的成果。根据2014年4月8日发布的报告看，此谈判有破冰之意义，且为其他议题的推进提供了范例。

9日

贸易援助流量反弹，并成为未来优先选项

贸易援助已经反弹，非洲成为最大的受益方，WTO成员于2014年4月9日召开听证会。会议中WTO成员讨论了未来两年相关倡议的优先安排。

11日

阿泽维多：全球贸易体制旨在改善儿童的生活水平和未来愿景

2014年4月11日，总干事阿泽维多在斯德哥

尔摩的全球儿童论坛上发言指出："通过支持经济增长和消除贫困，贸易是变革的重要引擎，因此也是儿童前景的重要变数。"

14 日

阿泽维多：贸易统计显示全球经济下行对最不发达国家的冲击最大

2014 年 4 月 14 日，总干事阿泽维多在最近的贸易统计新闻发布会上指出，最不发达国家 2012 年和 2013 年的增长低于前期的平均水平，但是将有可能因其对欧洲的出口而有所复苏，该出口份额占其总出口的比重又非常大，从而使经济增长呈上行趋势。

15 日

4 月 15 日是 WTO 协议签署二十周年

二十年前的今天，1994 年 4 月 15 日，WTO 协议在摩洛哥的马拉喀什签署。它是 1986—1994 年乌拉圭回合谈判的成果，是目前多边贸易体制建立的基础。

23 日

WTO 研究：区域主义的增长趋势可能逆转

WTO 一项新研究，旨在勾画出 2035 年的世界经济发展情况，结果表明未来主要区域贸易协定内的贸易份额将可能下降。

◇ ＊ 2014 年 5 月

5 日

阿泽维多强调贸易在未来可持续发展中的作用

2014 年 5 月 5 日，总干事阿泽维多在"日内瓦周"开幕式上对非常驻成员和观察员发言指出，"贸易已经在最近几年使数百万人民在脱离贫困上发挥了关键作用。"他说，他将在 2015 年后发展议程的讨论中努力"确保使大家认识到贸易对可持续发展的重要作用"。

关于贸易政策分析的 WTO 专题课程启动

2014 年 5 月 5—9 日，关于贸易政策分析的 WTO 主题课程开办，共有来自世界各地的 26 位政府官员参加。

7 日

新书探讨服务贸易的监管实践和世贸组织法律原则的作用

WTO 和剑桥大学出版社联合出版了一本新书，突出了服务贸易监管问题的关键挑战。新书发布会于 2014 年 5 月 7 日召开，"WTO 国内规制和服务贸易"讨论了国内法规对服务贸易的影响，以及良好的监管措施和 WTO 法律原则如何帮助解决这些问题。

12 日

成员期待海关估价软件决议的更新建议

海关估价委员会在 2014 年 5 月 12 日讨论了乌拉圭的建议，即更新一个 30 年决议，允许成员进行海关估价，在载体介质成本的基础上对软件和数据进行估价（如磁带、CD 和 DVD，它们是从一个国家运至其他国家）。

15 日

成员欢迎 WTO 增加有关数量限制的数据库

2014 年 5 月 15 日在市场准入会议上，各代表团欢迎 WTO 数据库通过 WTO 网站向公众发布数量限制信息，他们说将给商人和贸易商提供有用的信息，即产品在不同国家受到的配额限制。

16 日

新出版物解释了 WTO 规则如何帮助解决法规的使用

关于 WTO 技术性贸易壁垒（TBT）相关协议的一个小册子在 2014 年 5 月 16 日出版，它凸显了该协议的作用，TBT 委员会的工作旨在帮助政府解决法规和标准以免影响货物贸易。

19 日

阿泽维多列举了中国在贸易自由化上的"关键作用"

2014 年 5 月 19 日，总干事阿泽维多在对外经济贸易大学发表演讲，指出"中国自己的经验表明，开放和参与多边体制可以带来多么巨大和多么具有变革性的作用"。他希望中国支持推进巴厘一揽子成果。

22 日

马达加斯加总理希望借助 EIF 促进马达加斯加的未来贸易发展

2014 年 5 月 22 日举行的 WTO 会议上，马达加斯加总理 Christophe Roger Kolo 说，他们国家准备重新投入全球贸易体制，并借助 WTO、加强综合框架（EIF）和其他发展中伙伴的帮助来发展贸易。

27 日

也门成为 WTO 第 160 位成员

也门于 2014 年 5 月 27 日完成并提交了国内批准程序，WTO 总干事阿泽维多确认其满足成员资格。根据 WTO 规则，也门将于 2014 年 6 月 26 日正式成为 WTO 成员。

28 日

WTO 延长 2014 年公共论坛的建议收集时限至 6 月 20 日

WTO 将为 2014 年公共论坛提供建议的时限延长至 2014 年 6 月 20 日。2014 年公共论坛将于 10 月 1—3 日召开，论坛的主题是“为何贸易与每个人息息相关”。

WTO 教席项目增加了 7 所大学

WTO 宣布增加来自贝宁、巴西、印度尼西亚、阿曼、南非、突尼斯和土耳其的 7 家学术机构，列入 WTO 教席项目的学校名单。

◇ **2014 年 6 月**

2 日

西班牙语的高级贸易政策课程在日内瓦开办

2014 年 6 月 2 日至 7 月 24 日，将在 WTO 总部日内瓦开办为期 2 个月的西班牙语的高级贸易政策课程。共有来自发展中国家成员和最不发达国家成员的 20 名政府官员参加。

3 日

WTO 发布 2014 年年度报告

2014 年 WTO 年度报告于 2014 年 5 月 28 日出版，汇总了过去一年 WTO 的所有主要活动。该报告可以从 APP 上下载，有 PDF 版本和打印版本。

10 日

阿泽维多指出在《贸易便利化协议》实施中有效支持的“关键”作用

2014 年 6 月 10 日 WTO 贸易便利化工作组会议上，总干事阿泽维多发言指出，WTO 要确保在发展中国家实施《贸易便利化协议》时提供“及时、有效和有针对性的支持”。他说：“我们已经在搭桥上付出了艰苦的努力，现在是时候通车了。”

18 日

阿泽维多报告了贸易限制措施的减少，督促 G—20 领导人推进后巴厘议程

2014 年 6 月 18 日 G—20 贸易措施报告发布，指出“G—20 经济体在 2013 年 11 月中旬至 2014 年 5 月中旬共发布了 112 项新的贸易限制措施，比前一时期 2013 年 5 月中旬至 11 月中旬的 116 项措施略有减少。”总干事阿泽维多说，“很明显，在这一时期，贸易限制的外衣已经变得越来越厚，这将不利于我们支持世界各地的增长和发展的努力，因此我们必须保持警惕。”

20 日

阿泽维多承诺全面支持 WTO 对小经济体的工作

2014 年 6 月 20 日，总干事阿泽维多在日内瓦举行的小岛屿发展中国家圆桌讲话，在巴厘达成了一个工作方案，同意将重点放在小经济体融入货物贸易、服务贸易的全球价值链时所面对的挑战和机遇。

27 日

阿泽维多赞扬 WCO 对贸易便利化的支持

2014 年 5 月 27 日在世界海关组织委员会上，总干事阿泽维多称 WCO 和 WTO 在推进《贸易便利化协议》实施上是“天然的合作者”。总干事感谢了 WCO 的支持，包括共建贸易便利化工作组和启动墨卡托计划。

20 日

智利是最新向贫穷国家提供更好的出口机会的成员

越来越多的国家为来自最贫穷国家的产品放开了市场，增加资源以帮助它们强化贸易能力。2014

年6月20日WTO成员举行了最不发达国家分委员会听证会。

◇ **2014年7月**

1日

阿泽维多：贸易便利化将支持非洲的工业化和发展

2014年7月1日，在非洲举行的工业化和包容性增长非洲统一论坛上，阿泽维多指出《贸易便利化协议》“将开始移除一些阻碍全面融入全球价值链的贸易壁垒。因此，将为工业化和包容性可持续发展创造更多助力”。

8日

阿泽维多欢迎诸边环境产品谈判的启动

2014年7月8日，14位WTO成员启动了诸边的《环境产品协议》谈判。这些成员认为谈判将会促进绿色增长和可持续发展，同时为多哈回合谈判提供助力。

9日

委员会制定了调解食品安全、动植物卫生摩擦的步骤

2014年7月9—10日，WTO成员会议就解决成员在食品安全和动植物卫生措施上的分歧达成一致解决方案制定了新的程序，只要2014年9月5日前没有反对意见则生效。

15日

WTO启动“贸易故事”自拍竞赛

依据今年10月1—3日公共论坛的主题“为何贸易与每个人息息相关”，WTO启动了“自拍”照竞赛。所有人都可以参与此活动，通过一张你自己的照片讲述自己的贸易故事，并说明贸易如何影响你的日常生活。

22日

阿泽维多启动了新的WTO《贸易便利化协议》设施以帮助最不发达国家和发展中国家

2014年7月22日，WTO推出了一个新的倡议，该倡议将帮助发展中国家和最不发达国家从2013年12月达成的新的《贸易便利化协议》中获益。

24日

WTO高级贸易政策课程在日内瓦结束

为期2个月的密集培训课程于2014年7月24日结束，来自发展中国家和最不发达国家的20名政府官员参加了课程。

31日

阿泽维多：成员无法弥补贸易便利化的分歧

2014年7月31日，总干事阿泽维多向驻WTO大使报告，尽管经过了密集的磋商，在《贸易便利化协议》的实施问题上，“我们也没有找到一个足以弥补分歧的解决方案。”他督促成员“考虑这一挫折的长期的艰苦的后果”。

◇ **2014年8月**

6日

WTO教席项目：关于贸易和环境问题的上海暑期学校

大约80名来自不同大学的研究生参加了由上海对外经济贸易大学世界贸易组织研究教育学院举办的一个暑期学校，专门讨论贸易与环境的关系。

8日

WTO把就业、消费者保护和非洲问题纳入2014年公共论坛议程

2014年世界贸易组织公共论坛共有71个分论坛将举行。论坛主题为“为何贸易与每个人息息相关”，10月1—3日为期三天的论坛将重点讲述贸易背后的故事，给参与者机会，讨论贸易对就业、消费者保护和非洲贸易的影响。

11日

阿泽维多：支持私营部门是多边贸易体制未来的关键

2014年8月11日，总干事阿泽维多在墨西哥市的企业家周开幕致辞中提到：“通过锁定各国对贸易惯例的义务，WTO保障了重要的商业利益，增加了企业蓬勃发展需要的稳定性。”他感谢墨西哥对于WTO的大力支持，呼吁中小企业和企业家支持墨西哥对多边贸易体制的参与。

◇ 2014年9月

8日

记者和非政府组织在WTO曼谷工作组分享其贸易观点

2014年8月13—15日以及18—20日，WTO的信息和外部关系部与泰国的贸易和发展国际研究院共同举办了区域工作组会议，邀请东盟的记者和非政府组织参加，以分享其对贸易的观点。

亚太地区第4次区域贸易政策课程在新德里结束

2014年9月8日至10月31日，第4次WTO区域贸易政策课程在印度新德里开课。该课程由WTO研究中心（CWS）、印度对外贸易研究院（IIFT）和印度政府共同举办。

20日

调解食品安全、动植物卫生摩擦的步骤得到正式通过

帮助成员解决其在食品安全和动植物卫生问题上分歧的新的调解程序，因在2014年9月5日前没有反对意见，而获得正式通过。

11日

WTO宣布2014年青年经济学家学术论文奖获胜者

WTO宣布2014年青年经济学家学术论文奖获胜者为Jonathan Dingel和Claudia Steinwender，这是2014年9月11日在德国慕尼黑召开的欧洲贸易研究小组年度会议上宣布的。学术评选专家组赞扬了所提交论文的高质量，获奖论文强调了重要的贸易政策的影响。

15日

英语的高级贸易课程在日内瓦启动

2014年9月15日至11月6日，在日内瓦WTO总部召开为期2个月的英语的高级贸易课程，来自世界各地的22位参与者参加了课程。该课程由赞助人荷兰常驻WTO代表Roderick van Schreven阁下与技术合作学院（ITTC）院长Bridget Chilala女士共同组织。

17日

WTO 2014年将授予7个教席，从南非的西北大学开始

2014年9月17日，在南非的波切夫斯特鲁姆西北大学启动WTO教席项目，WTO副总干事Dave Shark发言指出，“学术机构帮助WTO提升了对贸易议题的认识，为决策制定的有效性储备了知识。”WTO今年将在贝宁、巴西、印度尼西亚、阿曼、突尼斯和土耳其的高校启动WTO教席项目。

19日

三大组织将在中等收入国家启动医疗技术联合活动

世界卫生组织（WHO）、世界知识产权组织（WIPO）和世界贸易组织（WTO）将于2014年11月5日在WTO总部日内瓦召开技术研讨会，讨论“创新和医疗技术的获得：中等收入国家的挑战和机遇”。

23日

WTO下调2014下半年的贸易增长预测

WTO经济学家已经将2014贸易增长预测下调至3.1%（4月时的预测为4.7%），同时将2015年的预期从此前的5.7%下调至4.0%。这一下调主要来自弱于预期的GDP增长，2014年上半年进口需求的沉寂，尤其是中南美洲自然资源出口区的需求。总干事阿泽维多说：“这是提醒我们贸易可以起到积极的作用。削减贸易成本，拓宽贸易机会是逆转这一下行趋势的重要因素。”

25日

阿泽维多：区域贸易协定“不能替代”多边贸易体制

2014年9月25日，在WTO区域贸易协定的交叉问题研讨会闭幕式上，总干事阿泽维多说，区域贸易协定“对于多边贸易体制是重要的，但是它们并不取代多边贸易体制”。他提出“重大议题”如贸易便利化、金融或电信规则、农业和渔业补贴“只能通过WTO在多边层面以有效的方式得到解决”。

26 日

阿泽维多：WTO 争端解决机制的成功提出了迫切挑战

2014 年 9 月 26 日，在争端解决机构会议上，总干事阿泽维多就 WTO 争端解决机制面临的挑战指出，“毋庸置疑，WTO 争端解决机制是成功的，”在二十年中，该机制已经收到了 482 份磋商请求，远远高于 GATT 过去 47 年所收到的 300 份磋商请求。同时他也指出，WTO 前十六年，WTO 所解决的争端涉及 1 万亿美元的贸易流量，“在受欢迎的同时，也创造了一些真正的挑战”，包括自 2012 年起秘书处处理的争端数量开始翻倍，上诉率也远高于预期。

WTO 为拉丁美洲开设的首次区域课程在厄瓜多尔基多开办

2014 年 8 月 4 日至 9 月 26 日，WTO 首次为拉丁美洲开设的区域贸易政策课程在基多的西蒙玻利瓦尔安第斯大学开课。共有来自发展中国家的 27 位政府官员参加。

土耳其为区域政府官员开办 WTO 贸易课程

2014 年 8 月 4 日至 9 月 26 日，WTO 区域贸易政策课程在伊斯坦布尔比尔基大学开办。共有来自中东欧、中亚和高加索地区（CEECAC）的发展中国家的 27 位政府官员参加。

29 日

WTO 成员对贸易便利化未来工作进行讨论以解决协议存在的僵局

2014 年 9 月 29 日，WTO 委员会就如何推进贸易便利化协议的实施所进行的准备工作仍未达成一致，触发该协议生效的僵局仍然存在。

30 日

WTO 任命新的上诉机构成员

2014 年 9 月 26 日，WTO 争端解决机构任命毛里求斯的 Shree Baboo Chekitan Servansing 先生为上诉机构七位成员之一，任期自 2014 年 10 月 1 日起，共 4 年。Servansing 先生将取代 David Unterhalter，后者第二届任期于 2013 年 12 月 11 日到期。

公共论坛调查显示贸易对公众生活的影响是复杂的

WTO 发起的最近的一项调查显示，约有 97% 的受访者认为，贸易对他们生活的影响是日复一日的；但是微小多数认为贸易将会损害其财富。调查的全部结果将在世贸组织的公共论坛上透露，该论坛将于 10 月 1 日召开。

◇ 2014 年 10 月

1 日

潘基文：贸易对于消除贫困非常重要，支持多哈回合

2014 年 10 月 1 日 WTO 公共论坛上，联合国秘书长潘基文在开幕致辞中指出，“国际贸易是消除贫困的完整努力中的关键部分，国际贸易可以确保食品安全，促进经济增长”，增加“一盎司的贸易可以得到一磅的援助”。他说“联合国充分支持 WTO 结束多哈回合的努力。这仍然是一个以公平、发展为导向的贸易体系的最佳途径。”

阿泽维多：我们希望倾听，并向你学习

2014 年 10 月 1 日 WTO 公共论坛上，总干事阿泽维多欢迎数百位与会者，他们来自非政府组织、学术界、私营部门、媒体、政府、国际组织和普通大众。这些与会者将参与为期 3 天的 68 个分论坛。提到今年论坛的主题，他说，“贸易与每个人息息相关，因为每一天无论是好是坏，它都会影响我们每一个人……影响最贫穷的人。”他指出一项研究表明对于贸易的看法正在改变，“贸易支持者大多在发展中国家”。

公共论坛第一天聚焦贸易如何影响人们的生活质量

公共论坛的开幕演讲聚焦于贸易对公众生活质量的影响，以及这些看法是如何转变的。联合国秘书长潘基文强调贸易是有尊严生活的动力。总干事阿泽维多指出贸易支持者大多在发展中国家。肯尼亚副总统 William Ruto 指出非洲已经从自由资源的仓库发展至世界贸易的积极参与者。

2 日

阿泽维多强调在认识非洲“巨大潜力”上贸易的作用

总干事阿泽维多在 WTO 公共论坛第二次全体会议“为何贸易与非洲息息相关”开幕致辞中指出，贸易在认识到非洲“巨大潜力”上发挥了重要作用。他认为全面实施《贸易便利化协议》“将助于整合非洲，并且极大地削减贸易成本”。

公共论坛第二天探求为何贸易与非洲息息相关

WTO 公共论坛第二次全体会议讨论了贸易便利化，区域一体化和中小企业的发展对于非洲公平、包容性增长的影响。利比里亚商业和工业部长阿克塞尔·阿迪（Axel Addy）说，非洲经济发展“只是时间问题”。

3 日

公共论坛第三天探求贸易对就业、消费者福利和发展的影响

WTO 公共论坛最后一天，几个分论坛上讨论了贸易对就业的可能影响，几个分论坛讨论了贸易和消费者福利的关系，还有论坛继续了第二天的讨论：贸易如何帮助非洲经济体的发展。

9 日

圣彼得堡 WTO 教席项目举办了国际贸易问题的研讨会

作为 WTO 教席项目的一员，圣彼得堡州立大学于 2014 年 10 月 9—10 日组织了学术研讨会，讨论国际贸易问题。该研讨会由 Sutyrin 教授主持 。

10 日

WTO 与世界银行联手为贸易便利化提供支持

WTO 与世界银行已经达成一致，加强合作以帮助发展中国家和最不发达国家更好地利用贸易便利化项目，从而促进这些国家的减贫和发展目标。

贸易援助会议强调将向小企业提供更大的支持

2014 年 10 月 10 日，贸易与发展委员会会议上，WTO 成员更新了最近的 ITC－WTO 工作组内容，呼吁向中小企业提供更大的支持，以帮助它们更好地融入全球贸易中。各成员还讨论了监管和评估实践，这些内容将在 2015 年 6 月的第五次全球贸易援助审议大会上讨论。

15 日

阿泽维多：联接贸易与投资网络将有助于快速增长

2015 年 10 月 15 日，WTO－UNCTAD 共同举办的贸易和投资圆桌论坛上，总干事阿泽维多在开题式上指出“通过与成熟的贸易、投资网络联接，发展中国家将有潜力步入快速增长转道。”

WTO 将印度尼西亚的 Pelita Harapan 大学纳入教席项目

印度尼西亚的 Pelita Harapan 大学被纳入 WTO 教席项目，WTO 副总干事易小准出席了 2014 年 10 月 15 日的庆祝典礼。

20 日

WTO 帮助发展中国家适应贸易环境的转变

2014 年 10 月 20 日 WTO 发布的旗舰出版物，表明 WTO 在帮助国家适应改变贸易和发展之间的关系的四个最近的趋势，发挥了关键作用。总干事阿泽维多在发布会上提到，“报告凸显了这一趋势，表明贸易将是 21 世纪发展的主要动力。”

上诉机构新成员宣誓就职

上诉机构新成员 Shree Baboo Chekitan Servansing 先生于 2014 年 10 月 20 日宣誓就职。

27 日

阿泽维多：WTO 强化与加强综合框架的伙伴关系，以帮助最贫穷的国家

2014 年 10 月 30 日，总干事阿泽维多在加强综合框架（EIF）委员会上发言指出，“我们希望 EIF 更加强大，更加高效，从而可以战胜过去的挑战，并在帮助最不发达国家实现其未来发展目标方面做得更多。”他进一步指出，“没有任何一个项目可以像 EIF 这样全面地支持最不发达国家以解决它们贸易能力的方方面面。”

WTO 教席项目在阿曼的苏丹卡布斯大学启动

2014 年 10 月 27 日，WTO 教席项目在阿曼的苏丹卡布斯大学启动，副总干事 David Shark 代表

总干事出席。同时还启动了首次针对阿拉伯和中东地区的 WTO 区域贸易政策课程，该课程由苏丹卡布斯大学和 WTO 秘书处共同组织。

28 日

WTO 发布年度的贸易和关税数据

2014 年 10 月 28 日，WTO 发布了新的统计数据：国际贸易统计、贸易概况、世界关税概况和服务概况。这四个统计数据详细地描述了最近的贸易发展情况。

29 日

黑山和新西兰加入 WTO《政府采购协定》

2014 年 10 月 29 日，黑山和新西兰的出价获得批准，它们将成为《政府采购协议》（GPA）的新成员。此举将有助于两国进入目前价值高达每年 1.7 万亿美元的采购市场。

30 日

WTO 将突尼斯大学商学院纳入教席项目

突尼斯大学商学院被纳入 WTO 教席项目。2014 年 10 月 30 日的庆祝典礼上，WTO 副总干事 Karl Brauner 出席。该学院是今年加入 WTO 教席项目的第四个机构，该项目旨在加强发展中国家学术界和政策制定者对多边贸易体制的了解。

◇ 2014 年 11 月

3 日

总干事在联合国会议发言：贫穷内陆国家对贸易便利化的贡献需要宣扬

2014 年 11 月 3 日在维也纳联合国就贫穷内陆国家问题召开的第二次会议上，总干事阿泽维多发言指出，内陆最不发达国家在削减海关和其他边境程序的繁文缛节方面的谈判有了声音——“贸易便利化”——它们将继续支持这一谈判，它们的贡献需要被大家了解，特别是现在协议实施陷入僵局的时刻。

6 日

WTO 报告揭示 G—20 国家的贸易限制措施继续增加

2014 年 11 月 6 日 WTO 发布了最近贸易发展问题的报告，该报告揭示自 2008 年起 G—20 国家引入的贸易限制措施一直在增加。考虑到全球经济的持续不确定性，报告强调了需要这些国家限制实施类似新措施，并逐步消除现存的贸易限制措施。

贫穷国家的出口 2013 年有所恢复，但贸易份额仍很低

2014 年 11 月 6 日，最不发达国家分委员会举行听证会。2013 年最不发达国家的货物和商务服务出口增长了 5.2%，但占全球贸易的份额仍然非常低。

8 日

阿泽维多寻求 APEC 对多边贸易体制的新支持

2014 年 11 月 8 日在北京召开的 APEC 部长级会议上，总干事阿泽维多呼吁 APEC 领导人支持多边贸易体制，帮助解决“关闭多边谈判”的僵局。阿泽维多指出他承诺寻找任何可能推进巴厘一揽子和后巴厘议程的方式，并将继续在这周的 G—20 峰会上与领导人继续探讨这一问题。

11 日

阿泽维多赞扬 WTO《信息技术产品协定》的突破

总干事阿泽维多赞扬了中国和美国的谈判者，认为他们达成谅解，从而为《信息技术产品协定》扩围谈判的迅速缔结扫清了道路。他说：“我非常欢迎这一突破性声明，这代表了 ITA 扩围谈判取得了关键进展。”

24 日

贝宁阿波美—卡拉维大学纳入 WTO 教席项目

2014 年 11 月 24 日，在贝宁科努托的阿波美—卡拉维大学启动了 WTO 教席项目。WTO 副总干事 Yonov Frederick Agah 到场致辞，他表达了对教席项目的信心，“教席项目将有助于培训出新的贸易政策方面的专家，并将最终从教席网络中受益。”

◇ 2014 年 12 月

5 日

WTO 教席项目被授予巴尔加斯基金会和圣保罗经济学院

2014 年 12 月 5 日，WTO 副总干事 David

Shark 在巴尔加斯基金会和圣保罗经济学院启动 WTO 教席项目。他指出“就贸易能力建设而言，WTO 教席项目不仅是 WTO 旗舰项目之一，而且这一项目是联接学术界的有效方式，还加强了学术界和政策界的联系。”

8 日

阿泽维多：贸易限制措施的增长“要引起关注”

2014 年 12 月 8 日在贸易政策审议机构会议上，总干事阿泽维多在做年度报告“国际贸易环境的发展”时，指出“自 2008 年以来 WTO 成员引入的贸易限制措施存量持续在增加”。他说“经济不确定性的氛围下贸易限制措施的持续累积构成了明确的风险”。

阿泽维多开启了针对非常驻成员和观察员的第 29 届“日内瓦周”

2014 年 12 月 8 日，总干事阿泽维多开启了第 29 届“日内瓦周”，此活动旨在为非常驻成员和观察员提供了解 WTO 的机会。总干事简述了 WTO 近来的发展，包括总理事会就巴厘议题的突破。“我们将在这里倾听他们，以任何我们可以采取的合适的方式支持你们。”

10 日

中国香港成为首个批准《贸易便利化协议》的 WTO 成员

中国香港成为首个批准《贸易便利化协议》的成员。香港政府于 2014 年 12 月 10 日通知 WTO 总理事会，香港已经于 12 月 8 日向 WTO 秘书处提交了批准文书。

阿泽维多：加入工作是 WTO 的重要工作

2014 年 12 月 10 日，总干事阿泽维多向总理事会就加入 WTO 做年度报告，指出通过入世谈判，WTO 已经将其涵盖的全球贸易由 1995 年的 91%扩展至 2013 年的 98%。他说，“有证据表明入世谈判已经强化了我们的多边体制，支持国内改革，为全球增长、发展和繁荣做出了贡献。”

总理事会批准了塞舌尔的成员资格，进入其国内批准程序

2014 年 12 月 10 日，总理事会批准了塞舌尔的入世条件。塞舌尔将在 2015 年 6 月 1 日前完成其国内批准程序，然后在通知 WTO 总干事后的 30 天内正式成为 WTO 成员。

肯尼亚的内罗毕将举行第 10 届部长级会议

2014 年 12 月 10 日，总理事会一致同意第 10 届部长级会议将在肯尼亚的内罗毕举行，举办时间为 2015 年 12 月 15—18 日。

18 日

旨在帮助最贫穷国家贸易的项目被延长

2014 年 12 月 18 日 EIF 指导委员会决定，一个旨在帮助最贫穷国家更积极地融入全球贸易的多边捐助项目“加强综合框架（EIF）”，其授权被扩展至新的阶段。总干事阿泽维多在委员会发言指出：“当合适的条件存在时，贸易是经济增长和消除贫困的有效工具。EIF 的构建就是帮助最不发达国家创造这些合适的条件。”

附录四：《世界贸易报告（2014）》内容摘要

A 引言

《世界贸易报告 2014》分析了过去十年的四个趋势：(1) 发展中国家的崛起，(2) 全球价值链的扩张，(3) 大宗商品出口数量和价格的上涨；(4) 宏观经济冲击的日益全球化。在分析这些趋势后，本报告探讨了这些因素在重塑贸易对促进发展的作用，同时也指出了全球经济发展面临的障碍。基于这些分析，报告阐述了多边贸易体制是如何通过允许发展中国家适应、利用这四个趋势并规避其带来的风险，来帮助发展中国家巩固其近年来的发展成就。

18 世纪末到 19 世纪初的工业革命以来，世界经历了几次经济发展浪潮。每次浪潮都伴随着同等幅度的全球贸易扩张，并且一浪高于一浪。最初的经济发展浪潮发生在 19 世纪下半叶，早期的工业化经济体欧洲和北美脱颖而出，不断扩展其贸易规模。经过战争期间的经济崩溃，第二次世界大战以后的经济发展浪潮体现为战后开放贸易的逐渐恢复，以及日本和其他新兴工业化经济体快速追赶西方，尽管西方国家的经济增速也在提高。当前最广泛的经济发展浪潮发生在 20 世纪 80 年代后，包括中国、印度等在内的部分国家，开启了对外开放、速度空前的工业化追赶进程。

国际经济体系必须适应全球经济更广泛、深入和不断加速的发展现实。19 世纪中叶，全球经济关系由以欧洲为中心的双边贸易协定网络和全球金本位体系，名义上由当时经济实力最强大的英国所主导。1945 年以后，全球经济关系首次回归到一系列多边规则体系主导下，包括关税与贸易总协定和布雷顿森林体系。这些类似机构的迅速扩张也巩固了全球经济进入新的发展阶段。

B 发展中国家在全球经济中的重要性不断增强

20 世纪 90 年代以来，由于发展中国家经济的快速增长和发达国家的经济增长放缓，发展中国家与发达国家的收入差距在不断缩小。发展中的 20 个成员的经济表现尤为强劲。

发展中国家爆发式的经济增长是引人注目的，从 20 世纪 90 年代年均增长只有 1.5%，到之后的 4.7%。与此同时，发达国家人均收入的年均增长由 2.8%下降到 0.9%。发展中的 20 个成员表现尤为出色，年均收入增长 5.2%，最不发达国家和其他发展中国家也达到年均 3.7%。考虑到经济规模，发展中的 20 个成员例如中国、印度和巴西，其工业化速度和贸易开放度远远高于其他发展中国家。21 世纪最初十年，对大宗商品需求的上升导致许多资源出口型国家收入快速增长，其中包括许多最不发达国家。现在，发展中经济体占到全球总产出和贸易的一半左右（2000 年分别为 39% 和 32%）。

这种发展模式改变了全球财富的分配格局。随着各国之间收入差异的缩小，全球财富分配变得更加公平。2000 年以前，这种分配格局的特点有两个高峰，一个是代表贫穷的发展中国家，与之相对应的是富裕的发达经济体。2000 年以后，发展中国家减少了穷国和富国的收入差距，分配格局出现了介于两个高峰之间更为显著的第三个高峰，反映了许多 G20 发展中经济体相比其他发展中国家更为高速的增长，如中国。

尽管缩短了与发达国家的收入差距，发展中国家仍将经历漫长的发展历程。最不发达国家仍然远远落后，其人均国民收入只有发达国家平均收入的 4%。

更高的人均 GDP 可以实现其他社会目标。假定更多的贸易在一定程度上意味着更快的经济增长，贸易可以更容易地实现这些目标。

贸易可以从许多方面增加一个国家的 GDP，

例如：通过发挥比较优势来进行专业化分工实现资源的优化配置，或者是利用生产的规模效应来实现经济发展。贸易可以促进投资、创新和制度改革，因此开放型经济体也能够更快增长。

然而，发展不只是更高水平的人均GDP，还有其他的一些十分重要的民生指标，包括出生率、婴儿死亡率、营养条件、识字率、性别不平等和就业。其中一些因素在人类发展指数（HDIs）中有所反映，这些因素只有与人口数量加权时才有显著的正向关联。

经济增长对诸如收入不平等及环境问题等其他发展要素的影响尚不明朗。

如果经济增长伴随着收入不平等的话，那么更高水平的人均GDP或许并不能使多数人受益。现有证据并不能表明人均GDP增长和收入不平等具有显著关系。库兹涅茨曲线假说表明，随着经济的发展，一国的收入不平等在其发展的初期会加剧，但一旦达到某一发展水平时，收入不平等的现象会有所改善。然而，经验证据并不能够强有力地支持这一发现。在特定国家的特定时期，技术变化和政府政策很可能对收入不平等发挥着更为重要的作用。

从温室气体排放到森林退化，许多环境指标可以在环境绩效指数（EPI）上得到体现，环境绩效指数反过来也能够与收入增长相比较。在过去的十年中，环境质量和经济增长有着正向的关联。这表明收入增长的国家可以在保护环境上付出更多的努力。在一定程度上，贸易和其他政策能够促进经济增长，也会间接地帮助改善自然环境。然而到目前为止，经验证据在这一问题上却有着许多不同的解答。

在过去几十年中，发展中国家整体上降低了最惠国关税水平。仅从最惠国关税的角度看，G20中的发展中国家的关税减让的程度更为明显。

发展中经济体主要的贸易开放阶段开始于20世纪80年代。过去十年，这一趋势加速发展。总体来讲，发展中国家降低了进口的最惠国关税水平。这些国家同时还增加了“约束”关税上限的产品种类，降低了这些约束关税的税率。

就其他贸易政策措施而言，G20中的发展中国家在降低最惠国关税上最为积极，其削减平均关税的幅度远远超过其他发展中国家和最不发达国家，其最惠国关税水平削减三分之一以上，从1996年的15.6%下降到2009—2011年的10.1%。它们还约束了80%以上的关税税目，同时削减了四分之一的约束关税，从1996年的39%下降到2009—2011年的29.2%。例如，中国的平均约束关税从1985年的40%下降到今天的低于10%。相关研究表明，中国2001年加入WTO有效推动了关税削减，对其经济发展产生了积极影响。

C 全球价值链的兴起

发展中国家越来越多地加入到国际化生产网络中，南南全球价值链正变得日益重要。

全球价值链并不是一个新生事物。然而，全球价值链对贸易的重要性却与日俱增。

尽管全球价值链通常被认为是发达国家与发展中国家之间的联系，但最近的数据显示，发展中国家更多地参与相互间的全球价值链贸易。尽管以南北形式为基础的全球价值链的贸易形势依然稳固，但是发展中国家之间的中间品贸易占贸易总量的比重从1988年的6%左右上升到2013年的25%。

量化国际化生产网络的重要性需要确定出口增加值，但是出口增加值的数据只在少数几个经济体可以获得。尽管有这样的限制，依然有数据表明将近半数的全球出口与全球价值链有关，而在1995—2008年，全球价值链分工地位提升最快的几个经济体分别是韩国、中国台北、菲律宾、印度和中国大陆。然而，最不发达国家参与全球价值链分工依然有限。

外国直接投资（FDI）流量通常是建立全球价值链联系的重要因素。它们的发展同样表明，发展中国家正在越来越多地参与全球价值链。2012年，发展中国家吸收全球超过一半的外国直接投资，而在2000年这一数字要小于20%。发展中国家正在成为投资的重要来源。尽管在20世纪80年代末，全球只有7%的外国直接投资来自发展中国家，但到2012年，发展中国家占全球外国直接投资的比重为34%。

已有数据表明，平均而言，发展中国家通过服务出口的方式参与全球价值链的比重正在上升。

在全球价值链内部，跨国服务贸易占发达国家出口的将近16%，占发展中国家出口的10%略多。但这些指标忽略了隐含在制成品中的服务增加值的间接出口。在增加值方面，全球价值链内的服务贸易出口仅略低于发展中国家制造业出口，甚至超过发达国家的制造业出口。

根据IT和商业离岸外包测算全球价值链，发展中国家在全球服务出口中的份额从2005年的25%上升到2012年的31%。而2013年，最不发达国家在全球出口中只有0.33%的份额，这一比重明显低于这些国家的商业服务（0.65%）和货物贸易（1.14%）在全球出口中的比重。

总体上看，服务贸易比货物贸易呈现相对更少的区域化特征。然而，市场邻近度或许与离岸服务的相关度较低，以语言、技术、商业环境或境内监管为形式的其他商业限制依然是决定发展中国家能够以何种程度融入全球价值链的主要因素。

全球价值链提供了一个低成本地融入世界经济的机会。然而，参与全球价值链并不一定自动地带来收益。

全球价值链为许多国家提供了以更好的中间品生产或工艺，而不是完整产品生产加入到全球贸易的可能。

并不是所有国家都愿设法加入全球价值链，如果加入全球价值链，一国需要充分达到产品生产的全球质量标准和效率水平。如果能够加入全球价值链，其他国家的知识和技术通常会通过外国直接投资转移到该国，一国可以迅速地跨越质量和效率门槛。这种最初层次的参与全球价值链，会使得农业部门的劳动力转移到高生产率的制造业和服务业，以此来获得发展的收益。

发展中国家最初是以低技术的生产环节参与全球价值链，例如发展中国家从事生产的加工制造环节可以比较容易地变成有竞争力的出口国家。相比较而言，全球价值链中的领导厂商主导研发、设计、品牌和营销等难以复制的环节，而加工制造环节的附加值往往较低且有下降的趋势。因此，为避免陷入中等收入陷阱，制造加工的功能升级（如从加工组装到产品设计）是获取更多发展收益的重要环节。技术转移可能帮助产品的功能升级并提高产品质量，但是功能升级往往很难实现。

当然，参与全球价值链也有许多风险。

第一，如果一国参与全球价值链，生产关键的中间投入，则该国会更多地受到商业周期和远距离市场供给中断的影响。

第二，融入全球价值链会使一个国家相对集中其生产能力，这意味着竞争优势变得更为短暂，产业重置的风险变得更高。

第三，吸引投资的竞争可能会使参与全球价值链的国家陷入国内监管“竞次”的情况。

第四，参与全球价值链可能会加大收入不平等，相对于低技术劳动力而言，高技术劳动力报酬增长较快。同时，产出利润的增加与劳动投入的增长有关，从而在许多国家形成寡头垄断。

发展中国家融入全球价值链的主要障碍是基础设施和关税壁垒。有关这些贸易目标的贸易援助依然是我们优先考虑的问题。

WTO和OECD最近的一份调查揭示了发展中国家参与全球价值链的主要障碍。发展中国家的供应商和领导厂商认为，运输成本和延误、海关手续是与贸易相关的主要障碍，而进口关税和许可证要求也构成贸易的重要障碍。这份调查同时强调，落后的基础设施、有限的贸易融资机会和标准一致性也是影响贸易的障碍。

证据表明基础设施和机构的质量水平高、关税壁垒越低的国家，全球价值链的参与度往往越高。

与贸易便利化相关的促贸援助十分重要，因为海关通关手续被认为是发展中国家参与全球价值链的主要障碍。WTO《贸易便利化协定》的实施将为消除这些阻碍，进而提高发展中国家参与全球价值链的能力起到重要作用。

随着中间品关税水平下降，许多国家日益参与到更深层的优惠贸易协定之中。

当产品的生产扩展到不同国家，而不是停留在单一地点，贸易成本的边际效应就会明显提高。平均而言，发展中国家大幅降低了零部件的关税，但各国情况大不相同。

优惠贸易协定数量的不断增加，一定程度上反映了各国深度融入全球价值链的需要。由于贸易性质的变化，这会产生一个新的跨境效应。事实上，这些优惠贸易协定越来越多地包含与边境非关税措施相关的内容，特别是与竞争政策、投资、标准和知识产权有关的条款占到了2012年优惠贸易协定的40%以上。然而，由于这些优惠贸易协定试图解决的问题本质上是全球性的，它们终将成为需要多边层面解决的议题。

融入全球价值链程度较深的国家通常在WTO《服务贸易总协定》(GATS）中有更多的承诺。

D 大宗商品在发展战略中的新角色

大宗商品的价格在2003—2008年之间有大幅的上升，使得许多专家提出了大宗商品“超周期”论。许多供给和需求的附带效应是这种超周期产生的原因。

能源、金属和矿物的价格在2003—2008年间翻了一倍以上。G20中的发展中国家对资源和能源需求的增长是推动矿产和能源大宗商品价格上涨的主要原因。在同一时期，农产品的实际价格指数也几乎翻了一番。农产品价格的上升开始于2003年，上升的原因有许多方面，包括极端天气、生物能源的推广政策、美元的贬值、几个大的发展中国家的长期经济增长等。投机和投资组合多样化、股票市场的低迷、贸易政策和大量储备大宗商品也使得商品期货交易的需求增加。

大宗商品的繁荣—萧条交替循环并非罕见。尽管大宗商品的价格在最近有所下降，其价格仍是十年前的两倍。许多原因可以使我们相信大宗商品的价格会继续保持高位，未来几年仍将取决于繁荣—萧条交替循环。

价格波动是自然资源的一个特征。分析显示，尽管价格波动没有到达20世纪70年代的峰值，过去5年的价格波动超过了过去20年的波动水平，价格波动将继续受到主要大宗商品进口国和出口国的关注。

商品供给的发展、技术变革、公共政策和消费者偏好的变化是难以预测的。然而，对于需求前景的展望清晰地表明，未来几年大宗商品价格仍将持续保持高位。联合国粮农组织认为，2050年全球农产品生产需要增加70%才能养活全球不断增长的人口以及消除营养不良和饥饿。农产品和粮食的价格可能继续保持高位的另一个原因是原油价格和粮食价格的联动效应，这种效应在2006年以后变得更为明显。

在许多发展中国家，农业的发展对于就业、生产和消费来说是十分重要的。农业生产率的提高对于消除贫困是至关重要的。农业发展也因此成为发展中国家最为重要的发展战略。

农业部门的劳动力占到发展中国家劳动力总量的一半左右。最不发达国家则占到70%以上。农业部门对于减少贫困格外重要，主要基于以下两个原因：首先，贫穷的家庭倾向于将收入的绝大部分用于食品购买；其次，在发展中国家四分之三的贫困人口生活在农村地区，而且绝大多数的贫困人口依靠农业收入来维持他们的生活。

证据表明，农业的增长对于减少贫困的作用超过其他部门。事实上，所有经济体在显著消除贫困的过程中都经历了农业生产率上升的阶段。通过融入全球价值链的方式增加农业生产率，对于消除贫困同样具有积极效应。

最近几十年农产品贸易的增长为经济增长和减少贫困做出了贡献。

从出口额看，2000—2012年间，农产品出口额几乎增长了两倍，同期出口数量增长了60%。农产品贸易作为国内农业产出和消费的一部分，在最近几十年中同样有所增加，体现了全球农产品市场的进一步融合。

高附加值产品需求的不断增加和国际食品市场价格居高不下，为发展中国家通过增加出口实现经济增长和消除贫困提供了良机，其主要途径是出口价值链中的就业增长。

农产品贸易性质的变化主要包括新的市场细分、新的最终市场和新的生产结构。

过去50年间，传统未加工的农产品出口在农产品总出口中的比重明显下降。目前，农产品制成品出口在总出口中占到最大的比重，其份额超过60%。新鲜水果和蔬菜出口的比重同样在过去几十年中有平稳的增加，目前占农产品出口总量的10%。农产品贸易方式同样发生变化：发展中国家间的贸易以及亚洲和非洲在全球所占比重显著上升。

近年来，农业部门吸引了包括外国直接投资在内的大量投资。随着食品加工链具有越来越多的“垂直协作分工”特点，即产品的生产、加工和营销被连续地搭配起来，食品安全和质量标准以很快的速度传播。农产品贸易的这些变化对发展中国家来说意义重大。最引人注目的是，这种变化可以给发展中国家在全球价值链中带来更多的技术转移。然而新的农产品生产结构在有些情况下会产生战利品，价值链中领导厂商利用他们的主导地位可以获得其中的绝大部分利益。

居高不下的价格和价格波动等农产品贸易变化特征引发的机会和挑战在不同国家之间有着显著的差异。

发展中国家最近不断增长的市场份额主要体现在，大型新兴经济体以及一定程度上除最不发达国家之外的其他发展中经济体，在全球经济中的重要性不断增加。最不发达国家在全球农产品出口中的份额持续下降。这表明其他发展中经济体比最不发达国家在农产品价格上涨中获益更多。

新兴经济体的比较优势越来越多地倾向于农产品加工。在过去二十年中，新鲜水果和蔬菜是最不发达国家出口份额增长的仅有产品。目前这两项产品约占最不发达国家农产品总出口的14%。

鉴于大多数最不发达国家是食品净进口国，食品安全问题对于最不发达国家来说也非常重要。这是因为食物在家庭支出中占有很高的份额，而且贫困家庭通常很难减少他们的食品消费数量，价格冲击对于贫困家庭来说尤为剧烈。2010年6月到12月的食品价格新增了4400万民众生活在日均1.25美元的贫困线以下，对其食物摄取产生了负面影响。

发展中国家在考虑农业发展战略时，面临着五个主要挑战。

第一，发展中国家的生产商面临生产率的差距。

刺激农业研发的私人投资对加强发展中国家农业出口地位十分重要。然而，由于农业领域的市场失灵，公共投资在农业领域的研发中继续扮演着至关重要的角色。在贸易政策领域，新技术准入壁垒的降低有利于促进农业领域研发中的私人投资。

第二，农业领域关税、补贴和其他价格措施的频繁使用，将继续影响发展中国家的出口商。

最不发达国家农产品出口到发达国家面临的关税最低，发展中国家从最不发达国家进口农产品的关税在2011年是12%以上。这一关税水平要远高于石油和矿产（几乎零关税）以及非农产品的关税（考虑到优惠措施的话，大约2%左右）。

补贴在农业部门十分常见，特别是在一些发达国家，对于农业的支持要高于非农业部门，但是在一些发展中国家情况相反。不同种类的农产品受到的支持程度也不一样，一些独特的出口品如糖类、大米和牛奶得到的补贴支持就十分明显。这些农产品补贴将继续影响发展中国家的出口商。

第三，贸易相关的固定成本在农产品贸易中有重要作用，尤其是与食品安全和涉及动植物健康的卫生与植物卫生相关的实施成本。

全球食品贸易有关的标准种类和复杂程度近几年有增无减。正如《世界贸易报告2012》中指出的，这些措施可能会严重地阻碍贸易，即使这些措施追求有效的政策目标。成本的增加可以从许多渠道体现，包括满足国外标准（包括私人部门的标准）或规制，以及为达到这些标准所需的认证成本。

边境产生的成本构成了另外一种固定成本，这会对贸易流量产生很明显的影响。与进出口贸易有关的行政和物流程序需要时间，它们也会严重阻碍贸易，对于新鲜水果、蔬菜或者鲜花等时令产品尤为如此。

第四，农业部门的价值链特征多由市场集中度决定，有时候产生在价值链的不同环节，从而对农业生产商尤其是发展中国家小农户造成困难。

食品加工链上规模经济的存在使得单个生产环节被少数的几个公司所支配，通常是大型的跨国农业企业。2004年，四家最大的农药企业占到全球市场份额的60%。同样的市场集中度也在农产品价值链的下游有所体现，例如四家最大的全球咖啡贸易商占全球市场份额的40%，而最大的四家咖啡烘焙企业占市场份额的45%。

第五，价格波动给资源受限消费者和生产者带来投资决策的困难。

当人们对食品安全的担心不断增加的时候，政府通常会直接干预市场以抑制国内市场价格和价格波动。证据表明，如果净出口商和净进口商同时采取逆周期措施，则将刺激价格的上涨。实际上，如果净出口国政府限制出口，同时净进口国政府对消费进行补贴，这将进一步造成全球对农产品的过度需求进而推动价格进一步高涨。

2003—2010 年自然资源贸易显著增长。

2003—2008 年间，化石能源和金属以及矿物的贸易额增加了两倍，贸易量增加了大约 50%。相较于化石能源，2008 年的贸易崩溃和 2009 年的贸易复苏对金属和矿物贸易的影响更为显著。

主要由于物价上涨（至少到 2008 年之前），全球能源和矿物产品在全球制造业出口中的比重从 2000 年的 13.2%上升到 2012 年的 22.7%。

对于撒哈拉以南的非洲、拉丁美洲及加勒比地区来说，过去十年中能源和矿物产品在这些国家制造业出口中的比重有显著增长。从全球范围来看，"资源驱动型" 国家的数量从 1995 年的 58 个（占全球 GDP 的 18%）上升到 2011 年的 81 个（占全球 GDP 的 26%）。

大宗商品价格上涨和对新资源探索的大量投资使资源富集的发展中国家人均 GDP 大幅增加，特别是撒哈拉以南的非洲国家和拉美国家。

在撒哈拉以南的非洲，自 2000 年以来，资源出口国经历了人均 GDP 高增长时期。研究表明，在 1980—1999 年间，自然资源的出口对人均 GDP 的增加有负面影响或不明显的关系，但是在 2000—2012 年间，考虑到其他因素，这一影响变为正向且具有显著的统计意义。

对于拉丁美洲国家来说，统计表明，2000 至 2010 年，世界大宗商品价格上涨拉动这些国家产出和出口三分之一到一半左右。

但是资源充裕并不是经济增长和发展的必要条件，更不用说是充分条件。

1995—2010 年间，撒哈拉以南非洲经济表现最好的六个国家中没有一个是资源富集的国家。这说明资源丰富并不是这一地区通往持续和良好经济发展的唯一途径。一些资源富集的国家已经设法将 GDP 增长转变为更广泛的繁荣。

资源富集国家在实施基于资源的发展战略时面临很多挑战。首先，面对居高且不稳定的自然资源价格，获得稳定收益同时避免繁荣—萧条周期是很重要的。

通常观点认为，不应立刻消费自然资源的巨额收益而是将其组成一个基金，一般来说是主权财富基金，以实现后代长期的收益同时可以避免其他负面效应，如荷兰病，当自然资源的收入增加时，由于实际汇率的增加会导致制造业部门的萎缩，这种现象被称作资源诅咒。古典经济理论的观点认为，最优政策应依赖于自然资源价格波动、一国经济发展水平及其经济面临的更广泛约束等因素。

建立一种国内投资基金投资本国基础设施、医疗和教育，以及通过流动性基金募集预防性储蓄应对价格波动，都被证实是行之有效的。

发展中国家财政政策的周期性直到 21 世纪初都很常见。之后，许多国家包括一些资源富集的国家开始采用反周期的财政政策。本报告估计，1960—1999 年和 2000—2009 年间，在政府支出数据可得的 45 个资源富集的发展中国家中，16 个（占 35%）发展中国家由顺周期财政政策转变为反周期财政政策。

第二，一定程度的经济多样性是可取的。

经济多样性有许多基本原理，尤其适用于那些主要依靠自然资源的经济体。这些原理包括：非资源部门对其他部门的正向外溢效应及其对环境可能造成的负面影响；技术冲击改变比较优势；以及自然资源实质性价格波动。

第三，自然资源部门的外国直接投资对发展有利，这一点是很重要的。

出于对大宗商品价格上涨及关键资源供给安全的担心，近些年来全球兴起了对自然资源领域的投资和开发。例如，全球最大的 70 个石油公司对石油的勘探开采支出从 2007 年的 3150 亿美元增长到 2011 年的 4800 亿美元。

毫无疑问，自然资源富集的国家资源领域会吸引更多的外国直接投资，但对其吸引的外国直接投资的总体影响并不显著，甚至有研究认为，以自然资源为目标的外国直接投资会挤占非自然资源的外国直接投资。一个潜在的风险是此类外国直接投资资本密集度很高，对东道国非自然资源部门的正向溢出效应很有限。

第四，社会和环境问题可能成为主要的担忧。

一国自然资源的丰富与社会不公平有着正向的关系，而与环境却有着负向的关系。然而，考虑到其他国别情况和全球商业周期，这两种关系在统计上并不显著。

与制成品贸易相比，自然资源领域通常关税较低，但出口限制更多。

目前，全球矿产和能源产品关税水平很低。发达国家的矿产品（不是能源部门）明显存在关税升级（对于半成品的进口关税要高于原材料的关税）。这些国家是发展中国家最大的出口市场。

数据显示，全球贸易大约有 5%被征收出口税，而 11%的自然资源产品被课以出口税。OECD 最新数据显示，2009—2012 年间，57 个国家采取的 5000 多项限制措施中，出口税措施占一半左右。

E 宏观经济冲击更加同步化和全球化

尽管 2008 年经历了从 20 世纪 30 年代以来最为严重的经济下滑，但是全球并没有重现当年大规模的贸易保护主义。除其他解释外，多边贸易规则在其中发挥了主要作用。

宏观经济波动不利于社会发展。一方面，经济波动导致经济增速下降，同时也会对收入分配产生不利影响。

总体来讲，发展中国家经历着比发达国家更加严重的经济波动。最主要但非唯一的解释是，经济波动使人力资源和物质资本的投资收益变得更为不确定，导致资本积累速度放慢。发展中国家经济波动的来源可以分为内部因素（经济结构体系，特别是供给方面）和外部因素（开放度和融入全球经济的程度）。

贸易既是经济波动的传感器，也是经济波动多样化的根源。

具有紧密贸易关系的国家在商业周期方面也会更加密切，这表明贸易是某一国家经济冲击的传导机制。在 2008—2009 年经济危机背景下，一些理论认为贸易是危机全球化的主要传导机制，其他理论强调了全球价值链在其中发挥的作用，以及所谓的“长鞭效应”，即最终需求发生的细小变化，都会对价值链中的中间品需求造成很大变化，包括库存调整产生的效应。

然而，贸易开放同样可以减少经济波动。如果经济冲击很大程度上是内部因素导致的话，那么贸易是经济冲击多样化的来源。同样地，当一个国家有多个贸易伙伴时，国内经济的衰退或者其中一个贸易伙伴国的经济衰退会对其经济产生较小的需求冲击。

许多更有利的证据解释了宏观经济波动与出口结构之间的关系。如果出口过分集中在较小范围的初级产品，通常会对该国总产出的波动造成很大的影响。

自 20 世纪 90 年代中期开始，“大稳健”现象延伸到发展中国家。

发展中国家的另一个宏观经济波动特征是自 20 世纪 90 年代以来的长期经济下滑，这一现象在全球经济危机中更加明显。这种模式与同一时期开始的 G7 国家的产出减少和通货膨胀波动相一致，也就是“大稳健”。事实证明，大稳健同样扩散到发展中国家，造成这种现象的一个并不出人意料的原因就是发达国家成为发展中国家主要的出口市场，同时也是发展中国家主要的融资来源。

全球经济危机突出表明了各国协作应对全球经济冲击的重要性

2008—2009 年贸易的下滑和复苏反映了新兴经济体和发展中国家对主要发达经济体周期性发展的依赖。全球经济同步下滑和上升，表明各国经济之间密切的贸易和金融关系，特别是供应链在传播冲击和贸易融资枯竭方面发挥着作用。

鉴于上述关联和发展中国家在全球产出及贸易中的比重，发展中国家应该成为任何全球协同政策的一部分，无论是财政政策、货币政策还是贸易政策。这仍然是 G20 国家领导应对危机的重要经验。

尽管对金融危机的起源几乎没有责任，很多低收入国家在全球经济冲击中一直处于受害者的地位。他们饱受金融危机的负面连锁反应，比如，随着全球贸易融资越来越困难，这种负面作用不仅体现为海外工人越来越少的汇款，也体现为对原材料和大宗商品需求的下降。然而，危机之前确立的宏观经济缓冲效应有助于低收入国家缓解这一冲击。

危机以来，发展中国家经济逐渐恢复增长，一定程度上得益于这些国家继续保持国际化进程。由于发展中国家自身需求旺盛，其出口恢复速度比发达国家快得多。但是低收入国家仍易受到商品周期逆转的影响，其国际化进程也由于受供应方面的严重限制而有所放慢。

经济危机中的贸易保护主义得到有效遏制。

贸易理论专家认为，保护措施应当与经济活动反其道而行。而在此次危机中，贸易保护主义的反周期行为，尤其是贸易救济的情况却并非如此。

2008—2009 年的经济危机中，发展中国家或发达国家并没有效仿20世纪30年代"大萧条"时期的类似做法，或基于早先对经济周期的反应进行预测，掀起贸易保护主义的浪潮，这是令人吃惊的。学术研究以及来自WTO的监测数据都表明，贸易保护主义并没有兴风作浪。此外，由于大多数发展中国家同一时间降低了贸易壁垒，贸易限制措施在此次危机中没有发挥很大作用。

贸易保护主义消失的原因：贸易规则的存在、WTO的有效监测、各国参与全球价值链而对贸易保护主义自我伤害的预料，以及宏观经济政策的国际合作协调。

关于保护主义为什么没有出现的第一个解释就是各国对风险与不确定性的厌恶态度。如果对贸易伙伴的行为不加束缚，这种不确定性在经济波动时期尤为明显。因而当经济面临波动时，政府更希望各方恪守贸易合约。

第二，包括WTO在内的对贸易限制的监督效果明显，虽然这有可能导致有意提高贸易壁垒的政府在某种程度上使用其他有类似效果的政策（政策替代）。

第三，并没有任何事后证据表明，采取更多贸易限制措施的经济体比那些较少采取限制措施的经济体表现更好。从某种程度上来说，决策者已经预见到了这种做法的后果，比如通过与股东对话得知在全球价值链中，一国的出口严重依赖于其进口，这更打消了贸易保护主义的念头。

最后但同样重要的是，各国用宏观经济政策管控（危机给）收入和就业带来的负面影响，限制了贸易政策使用的必要性。

国际宏观经济政策协同应对非常有效，还因为这种合作能调动更多资源。这也表明如果缺乏有利的初始条件，这场危机（以及潜在保护主义）的后果将会更加严重。

各个国家以史无前例的规模协同实施扩张性财政和货币政策以解决这场危机。财政政策的一大显著特点就是对于财政部门的大力支持。G20发达国家和发展中国家的财政支持力度大不相同，发达国家承诺其GDP的11%支持财政部门，而发展中国家承诺的财政支持措施都未达到其GDP的1%。

为避免金融崩溃，对财政部门的支持很有必要，但也可能导致贸易扭曲后果。

从某种程度而言，财政救助可以防止金融崩溃，维持社会总需求，帮助维持发达国家的进口需求，包括从发展中国家进口的需求。然而，有证据表明这也导致了跨国借贷的减少。此外，由于财政状况与出口密切相关，财政救助更能帮助发达国家保持出口，变相挤占发展中国家的出口。

F 世贸组织与发展中国家

世贸组织允许发展中国家利用、适应并规避报告所列四个趋势引发的风险取得经济发展，并通过约束承诺、灵活性、技术援助及制度性基础设施，巩固了许多发展中国家的这一进程。

许多发展中国家强劲的经济表现与其保护措施的减少相关，这也是它们履行世贸组织承诺的重要组成部分。这对那些正在加入世贸组织的国家而言尤为明显。世贸组织规则中的灵活性尤其是优惠准入，在提振最不发达国家经济中发挥了作用。

通过构建可预测的商业环境、降低贸易壁垒与贸易成本，发展中国家加入全球价值链是有可能的。这一过程通过履行世贸组织承诺得到保障，不仅是货物贸易，在服务贸易中更为重要，因为后者在全球价值链中作用更大。若第九届世贸组织部长级会议达成的《贸易便利化协定》生效的话，将进一步减少贸易成本，扩大发展中国家在全球价值链的参与度。通过指向性促贸援助来协助贸易便利化的实施，技术援助也是十分重要的。

高企的商品价格使很多发展中国家出口商获益。他们同时能对其他国家尤其是粮食净进口国构成挑战。世贸组织条约的机制可以帮助缓解这一问题，世贸成员目前正在就巴厘岛关于粮食安全公共储备的灵活性进行磋商。多哈发展议程取得进展有助于全面激发农业部门的潜能，从而促进整体发展。

最后，尽管遭受过去七十年来全球最大的经济危机，世贸组织维护了广大发展中国家的经济成果。世贸组织通过其贸易规则体系以及有效的监管机制，遏制了贸易保护主义的泛滥。

经济学文献已经表明，世贸组织下的承诺对促进发展中国家的贸易和发展有重要作用。与此同时，已有研究还解释了由于发展中国家的经济状况影响其履行义务的能力，因而需要灵活性。

承诺是国际贸易协定中的核心信条。就这一点而言，很多研究都表明关贸总协定与世贸组织的经验相关性，包括促进发展中国家经济增长方面。一项研究表明，在加入世贸组织中承诺实质性改革的国家，加入之后的经济增速通常可提高约2.5%。

与此同时，为了贸易协定的可行性，在特定情况下暂时中止某些承诺的可能性很有必要，事实上，所有申请加入的成员都需要灵活性。灵活性并不是出于自身利益考虑，而是为了让贸易协定各成员都能做出进一步承诺。

就发展中国家而言，经济理论一再表明，发展中经济体在市场长期失灵时，特殊和差别待遇是行之有效的。发展中国家的小规模经济是发达国家非互惠及优惠市场准入长期存在的依据。较高的不确定性、不完善的金融市场或不充足的政府资源可能是发展中国家快速实施开放贸易政策的其他约束。特殊和差别待遇旨在帮助发展中国家以一种反映其经济状况的方式和节奏来履行承诺，追求贸易机会。

发展中国家可以享受多种形式的特殊和差别待遇。

关贸总协定和世贸组织里，发展中国家获得特殊和差别待遇的主要方式是在市场准入谈判中的非完全互惠承诺，尤其是在关税减让谈判中。世贸组织协定中的许多条款都力图解决发展中国家在履行某些特定承诺时的资源限制，通过给予履行承诺的过渡期、呼吁增加技术援助条款等。当然，发展中国家也从那些适用于所有成员的普惠条款中受益。

世贸组织为发展中国家提供了特定的论坛和机构。

贸易与发展委员会是世贸组织解决发展关注的核心场所。在发展中国家、发展中国家特定团体（小型经济体、最不发达国家）提出的议题，促进优惠关税待遇和区域贸易协定的透明度，以及监督世贸组织实施相关技术援助等方面，贸易与发展委员会扮演着重要角色。对于最不发达国家而言，贸易政策审议机制在确定其贸易能力发展需要、提供政策体制透明度等方面发挥着重要作用。

G 结论

成功结束多哈发展议程将有助于世贸组织进一步实现其发展目标。在2013年12月巴厘岛部长级会议上达成的协议，是向这一目标迈出的积极一步，也向发展中国家提供了更多新的机会。

本报告表明，全球经济一体化与过去二十年的成功发展密切相关，它还表明全球价值链能促进全球经济一体化，阐述了大宗商品价格上涨是如何帮助商品出口国获得了更多出口收益，从而促进GDP增长的，同时也阐述了WTO在应对危机时期贸易保护主义、维护全球贸易体系中所发挥的作用。

从过去十年的四个趋势看，发展中国家进一步从全球贸易体系中获得利益面临重大障碍。这些障碍主要有技术缺乏、基础设施落后、满足标准的高额成本以及对发展中国家优势出口产品的贸易保护。报告还强调了促贸援助等倡议如何帮助发展中国家有效参与全球市场。

多哈回合旨在创造条件来帮助所有国家发展，特别是增加发展中国家从有效参与全球贸易体系中获取利益的机会。巴厘部长级会议做出的决定对多边贸易体制发展十分重要。

贸易和开放、以规则为导向的多边贸易体制在应对2015年后世界所面临的发展挑战中扮演主要角色。

过去十年的四个趋势和发展历史表明，贸易在发展中起着至关重要的作用。近年来，贸易在帮助数百万贫困人口脱离贫困、实现联合国千年发展目标中扮演着重要的角色。WTO及其贸易规则被认为是实现2015年后发展议程不可分割的一部分。

附录五：WTO成员一览表、WTO观察员一览表

WTO成员一览表

（截至2015年11月30日）

序　号	中文名称（简称）	英文名称（简称）	加入时间
1	阿尔巴尼亚	Albania	2000—09—08
2	安哥拉	Angola	1996—11—23
3	安提瓜和巴布达	Antigua and Barbuda	1995—01—01
4	阿根廷	Argentina	1995—01—01
5	亚美尼亚	Armenia	2003—02—05
6	澳大利亚	Australia	1995—01—01
7	奥地利	Austria	1995—01—01
8	巴林	Bahrain	1995—01—01
9	孟加拉国	Bangladesh	1995—01—01
10	巴巴多斯	Barbados	1995—01—01
11	比利时	Belgium	1995—01—01
12	伯利兹	Belize	1995—01—01
13	贝宁	Benin	1996—02—22
14	玻利维亚	Bolivia	1995—09—12
15	博茨瓦纳	Botswana	1995—05—31
16	巴西	Brazil	1995—01—01
17	文莱	Brunei Darussalam	1995—01—01
18	保加利亚	Bulgaria	1996—12—01
19	布基纳法索	Burkina Faso	1995—06—03
20	布隆迪	Burundi	1995—07—23
21	柬埔寨	Cambodia	2004—10—13
22	喀麦隆	Cameroon	1995—12—13
23	加拿大	Canada	1995—01—01
24	佛得角	Cape Verde	2008—07—23
25	中非	Central African Republic	1995—05—31
26	乍得	Chad	1996—10—19
27	智利	Chile	1995—01—01
28	中国	China	2001—12—11
29	中国台北	Chinese Taipei	2002—01—01
30	哥伦比亚	Colombia	1995—04—30

续 表

序　号	中文名称（简称）	英文名称（简称）	加入时间
31	刚果（布）	Congo	1997—03—27
32	哥斯达黎加	Costa Rica	1995—01—01
33	科特迪瓦	Côte d'Ivoire	1995—01—01
34	克罗地亚	Croatia	2000—11—30
35	古巴	Cuba	1995—04—20
36	塞浦路斯	Cyprus	1995—07—30
37	捷克	Czech Republic	1995—01—01
38	刚果（金）	Democratic Republic of the Congo	1997—01—01
39	丹麦	Denmark	1995—01—01
40	吉布提	Djibouti	1995—05—31
41	多米尼克	Dominica	1995—01—01
42	多米尼加	Dominican Republic	1995—03—09
43	厄瓜多尔	Ecuador	1996—01—21
44	埃及	Egypt	1995—06—30
45	萨尔瓦多	El Salvador	1995—05—07
46	爱沙尼亚	Estonia	1999—11—13
47	欧盟（前欧共体）	European Community	1995—01—01
48	斐济	Fiji	1996—01—14
49	芬兰	Finland	1995—01—01
50	法国	France	1995—01—01
51	加蓬	Gabon	1995—01—01
52	冈比亚	The Gambia	1996—10—23
53	格鲁吉亚	Georgia	2000—06—14
54	德国	Germany	1995—01—01
55	加纳	Ghana	1995—01—01
56	希腊	Greece	1995—01—01
57	格林纳达	Grenada	1996—02—22
58	危地马拉	Guatemala	1995—07—21
59	几内亚	Guinea	1995—10—25
60	几内亚比绍	Guinea-Bissau	1995—05—31
61	圭亚那	Guyana	1995—01—01
62	海地	Haiti	1996—01—30
63	洪都拉斯	Honduras	1995—01—01
64	中国香港	Hong Kong，China	1995—01—01
65	匈牙利	Hungary	1995—01—01
66	冰岛	Iceland	1995—01—01
67	印度	India	1995—01—01

续 表

序 号	中文名称（简称）	英文名称（简称）	加入时间
68	印度尼西亚	Indonesia	1995—01—01
69	爱尔兰	Ireland	1995—01—01
70	以色列	Israel	1995—04—21
71	意大利	Italy	1995—01—01
72	牙买加	Jamaica	1995—03—09
73	日本	Japan	1995—01—01
74	约旦	Jordan	2000—04—11
75	哈萨克斯坦	Kazakhstan	2015—11—30
76	肯尼亚	Kenya	1995—01—01
77	韩国	Korea，Republic of	1995—01—01
78	科威特	Kuwait	1995—01—01
79	吉尔吉斯斯坦	Kyrgyz Republic	1998—12—20
80	老挝	Lao People's Democratic Republic	2013—02—02
81	拉脱维亚	Latvia	1999—02—10
82	莱索托	Lesotho	1995—05—31
83	列支敦士登	Liechtenstein	1995—09—01
84	立陶宛	Lithuania	2001—05—31
85	卢森堡	Luxembourg	1995—01—01
86	中国澳门	Macau，China	1995—01—01
87	马达加斯加	Madagascar	1995—11—17
88	马拉维	Malawi	1995—05—31
89	马来西亚	Malaysia	1995—01—01
90	马尔代夫	Maldives	1995—05—31
91	马里	Mali	1995—05—31
92	马耳他	Malta	1995—01—01
93	毛里塔尼亚	Mauritania	1995—05—31
94	毛里求斯	Mauritius	1995—01—01
95	墨西哥	Mexico	1995—01—01
96	摩尔多瓦	Moldova	2001—07—26
97	蒙古	Mongolia	1997—01—29
98	黑山	Montenegro	2012—4—29
99	摩洛哥	Morocco	1995—01—01
100	莫桑比克	Mozambique	1995—08—26
101	缅甸	Myanmar	1995—01—01
102	纳米比亚	Namibia	1995—01—01
103	尼泊尔	Nepal	2004—04—23

续 表

序 号	中文名称（简称）	英文名称（简称）	加入时间
104	荷兰	Netherlands	1995—01—01
105	新西兰	New Zealand	1995—01—01
106	尼加拉瓜	Nicaragua	1995—09—03
107	尼日尔	Niger	1996—12—13
108	尼日利亚	Nigeria	1995—01—01
109	挪威	Norway	1995—01—01
110	阿曼	Oman, Sultanate of	2000—11—09
111	巴基斯坦	Pakistan	1995—01—01
112	巴拿马	Panama	1997—09—06
113	巴布亚新几内亚	Papua New Guinea	1996—06—09
114	巴拉圭	Paraguay	1995—01—01
115	秘鲁	Peru	1995—01—01
116	菲律宾	Philippines	1995—01—01
117	波兰	Poland	1995—07—01
118	葡萄牙	Portugal	1995—01—01
119	卡塔尔	Qatar	1996—01—13
120	罗马尼亚	Romania	1995—01—01
121	俄罗斯	Russian Federation	2012—08—22
122	卢旺达	Rwanda	1996—05—22
123	圣基茨和尼维斯	Saint Kitts and Nevis	1996—02—21
124	圣卢西亚	Saint Lucia	1995—01—01
125	圣文森特和格林纳丁斯	Saint Vincent and the Grenadines	1995—01—01
126	萨摩亚	Samoa	2012—05—10
127	沙特阿拉伯	Saudi Arabia	2005—12—11
128	塞内加尔	Senegal	1995—01—01
129	塞舌尔	Seychelles	2015—04—26
130	塞拉利昂	Sierra Leon	1995—07—23
131	新加坡	Singapore	1995—01—01
132	斯洛伐克	Slovakia Republic	1995—01—01
133	斯洛文尼亚	Slovenia	1995—07—30
134	所罗门群岛	Solomon Islands	1996—07—26
135	南非	South Africa	1995—01—01
136	西班牙	Spain	1995—01—01
137	斯里兰卡	Sri Lanka	1995—01—01
138	苏里南	Suriname	1995—01—01
139	斯威士兰	Swaziland	1995—01—01

续 表

序　号	中文名称（简称）	英文名称（简称）	加入时间
140	瑞典	Sweden	1995—01—01
141	瑞士	Switzerland	1995—07—01
142	塔吉克斯坦	Tajikistan	2013—03—02
143	坦桑尼亚	Tanzania	1995—01—01
144	泰国	Thailand	1995—01—01
145	马其顿	The former Yugoslav Republic of Macedonia	2003—04—04
146	多哥	Togo	1995—05—31
147	汤加	Tonga	2007—07—27
148	特立尼达和多巴哥	Trinidad and Tobago	1995—03—01
149	突尼斯	Tunisia	1995—03—29
150	土耳其	Turkey	1995—03—26
151	乌干达	Uganda	1995—01—01
152	乌克兰	Ukraine	2008—05—16
153	阿联酋	United Arab Emirates	1996—04—10
154	英国	United Kingdom	1995—01—01
155	美国	United States	1995—01—01
156	乌拉圭	Uruguay	1995—01—01
157	瓦努阿图	Vanuatu	2012—08—24
158	委内瑞拉	Venezuela，Bolivarian Republic of	1995—01—01
159	越南	Viet Nam	2007—01—11
160	也门	Yemen	2014—06—26
161	赞比亚	Zambia	1995—01—01
162	津巴布韦	Zimbabwe	1995—03—05

WTO 政府观察员一览表

（截至 2015 年 11 月 30 日）

序号	中文名称	英文名称
1	阿富汗	Afghanistan
2	阿尔及利亚	Algeria
3	安道尔	Andorra
4	阿塞拜疆	Azerbaijan
5	巴哈马群岛	Bahamas
6	白俄罗斯	Belarus
7	不丹	Bhutan
8	波斯尼亚和黑塞哥维那	Bosnia and Herzegovina
9	科摩罗	Comoros
10	赤道几内亚	Equatorial Guinea
11	埃塞俄比亚	Ethiopia
12	梵蒂冈	Holy See (Vatican)
13	伊朗	Iran
14	伊拉克	Iraq
15	黎巴嫩共和国	Lebanese Republic
16	利比里亚	Liberia, Republic of
17	利比亚	Libya
18	圣多美和普林西比	Sao Tone and Principe
19	塞尔维亚	Serbia
20	苏丹	Sudan
21	叙利亚	Syrian Arab Republic
22	乌兹别克斯坦	Uzbekistan

注：除了梵蒂冈，其他所有观察员必须在其成为观察员后五年内开始其加入 WTO 谈判。

附录六：中国世界贸易组织研究会年度大事记（2014）

1月

11日 中国世界贸易组织研究会主办的“第七届对外投资与经济合作形势展望2014年年会”在北京召开。

15日 孙振宇会长出席中国国际贸易学会举办的“学习三中全会精神构建开放型经济新体制”为主题的2014年新春座谈会并发表讲话。

16日 孙振宇会长会见深圳世贸组织事务中心高瞻主任一行4人并举行工作会谈，双方就落实《关于加强地方世贸组织事务工作合作机制合作备忘录》进行了深入的讨论。

21日 我会名誉会长、海峡两岸关系协会会长陈德铭在上海出席“国际投资促进（上海）高层论坛—上海自贸区：机遇与冲击”并发表演讲，孙振宇会长出席。该论坛由美中国际投资和贸易联盟主办，商务部投资促进局和我会为支持单位。

24日 孙振宇会长参加中国国际贸易学会组织的“对当前中美关系包括经贸关系基本态势和若干基本问题”的研讨会。

31日 我会编辑出版《中国世界贸易组织年鉴（2013）》。

2月

11日 孙振宇会长和陈鹏副会长兼秘书长会见中国洲际新资源集团董事长耿斌。

12日 孙振宇会长在北京参加新西兰外交贸易部副部长贝雷特的晚宴。

14日 中国世界贸易组织研究会外经贸咨询顾问委员会（外顾委）举办2014年度第一次例会，研讨“后巴厘”相关问题。

19日 上午，孙振宇会长应邀出席国家外专局举办的“对上海自贸区发展的建议”讨论会。下午，孙振宇会长会见WTO前总干事拉米，并主持拉米与企业家座谈会。

25日 孙振宇会长、陈鹏副会长兼秘书长、王成安副会长到中铁集团调研。

26日 上午，孙振宇会长应邀参加“美驻华大使骆家辉谈美中关系”讲座。晚上，孙振宇会长应邀出席美国驻华大使骆家辉离任招待会。

3月

3日 孙振宇会长宴请新加坡驻华大使罗家良并进行工作会谈，新加坡使馆经济参赞陈如海、一秘萧淑安参加。

10日 孙振宇会长同日本、新西兰和哥斯达黎加驻华大使在京会晤，就多哈回合、TISA、ITA、TPP、RCEP等多边和区域自贸区谈判及我国与各国经贸领域合作等议题交换意见。

13日 上午，孙振宇会长应邀出席中国国际贸易学会召开的“乌克兰危机对我国经贸发展的影响”座谈会，并就乌克兰危机对我国的影响提出看法和建议。我会副会长兼秘书长陈鹏也参加了会议。下午，孙振宇会长应邀到财政部国际司就“中国在多边贸易体系中的地位、作用和发展方向”等问题做报告。我会竞争政策与法律专业委员会（竞委会）召开《中国竞争法律与政策研究报告（2014年）》编撰工作会议。竞委会主席俞晓松出席并做总结，执行主席兼秘书长王成安主持会议。

14日 孙振宇会长会见国际贸易中心（ITC）执行主任阿兰查·冈萨雷斯·拉雅（Arancha Gozalez Laya）一行，并主持其与企业家的座谈会。

21日 我会竞委会召开“中国反垄断法执法研讨会”，研讨《关于经营者集中简易案件适用标准的暂行规定》有关问题。

28日 我会外顾委召开2014年度第二次例会，会议议题是“金砖国家在全球经济治理中的合作”。

4月

2日 孙振宇会长应邀出席由中国机电产品进出口商会和美国信息产业机构在京联合举办的信息技术与服务贸易及全球经济发展圆桌会并发表演讲。

8日 我会与美国驻华使馆共同主办的“美国

房地产市场投资圆桌会”在美国驻华使馆举行。我会副会长王成安主持会议，美国驻华使馆官员和中国20多家企业与会。

23日　上午，中国世界贸易组织研究会第三届理事会第三次会议在北京举行，我会常务理事、理事和商务部官员约120人出席大会。会议由孙振宇会长主持，商务部部长助理王受文和海峡两岸关系协会会长兼我会名誉会长陈德铭出席会议并发表重要讲话，我会副会长兼秘书长陈鹏向大会做工作报告。会议还增补王新奎为研究会副会长，并向其颁发聘书。

下午，我会在京主办召开“地方WTO事务圆桌会议”，孙振宇会长主持会议，北京、天津、重庆、广东、湖南、浙江、内蒙古和深圳等地的WTO事务机构代表，对外经济贸易大学、南开大学和武汉大学的学者以及研究会人员约20人出席会议。会议围绕“地方WTO事务机构如何在多边贸易体制框架下发挥作用”等议题展开讨论。

24日　孙振宇会长应邀出席第十八届中国国际投资贸易洽谈会北京推介会并讲话。

29日　孙振宇会长应邀出席在北京举行的中国机电产品进出口商会第六届会员代表大会并就如何利用多边贸易体制与区域经济合作扩大对外贸易做主旨演讲。

5月

5日　应“北京东盟委员会”轮值主席、菲律宾驻华大使巴西里奥女士的邀请，孙振宇会长出席在菲律宾驻华使馆举行的“北京东盟委员会”会议，并做了题为“多边贸易体系的未来”的主旨演讲。

9日　孙振宇会长会见世界贸易组织秘书处贸易政策审议司区域贸易协定处的Rohini Acharya女士。双方就“后巴厘”计划等话题交换意见。

12日　孙振宇会长在北京主持召开2014年中国国际投资论坛专家委员会选题会。

15日　孙振宇会长会见日本驻华使馆经济部公使尾池厚之先生。双方就当前的信息技术协定（ITA）、跨太平洋伙伴关系协议（TPP）、RCEP和中日韩自贸区协定等诸边、区域谈判交换意见。

16日　我会外顾委2014年第三次例会暨实施《贸易便利化协定》情况通报会在北京举行，来自政府部门、商协会和企业的代表、专家学者及外顾委委员近40人出席会议。商务部世贸司副司长洪晓东、处长丁为和我会副会长李恩恒在会上分别通报了《贸易便利化协定》、《服务贸易协定》和WTO后巴厘多哈回合工作方案谈判的进展情况，与会代表就《贸易便利化协定》的实施等问题展开了热烈讨论。

19日　我会与对外经济贸易大学共同举办世界贸易组织总干事阿泽维多报告会。会前商务部部长助理王受文、我驻世界贸易组织大使俞建华、我会孙振宇会长、外经贸大学施建军校长等与阿泽维多总干事会晤并出席报告会。阿泽维多夫人、世界贸易组织总干事办公室主任Timothy John Yeend、法律顾问Ae Gyoung Jung女士陪同。

28日　我会和北京市WTO事务中心联合主办的“WTO与中国：北京国际论坛”在北京国家会议中心召开。世界贸易组织副总干事易小准在会上发表主旨演讲，商务部部长助理童道驰、北京市商务委员会副主任宋建平到会并致辞。论坛由孙振宇会长主持。

29日　孙振宇会长在北京参加由我会、国际贸易和可持续发展中心（ICTSD）、对外经济贸易大学共同主办的“后巴厘进程与中国：中国在结束多哈回合谈判和重振WTO中的作用”研讨会，并发表主旨演讲。

30日　我会与北京市国际服务贸易事务中心在国家会议中心共同举办中非服务贸易：服务基础设施，提升贸易投资能力国际论坛。论坛共有政府部门负责人、专家、学者、企业和媒体等200余人参加。

6月

5—8日　孙振宇会长参加在昆明举办的第二届中国—南亚博览会暨第22届中国昆明进出口商品交易会。

9日　孙振宇会长应邀出席菲律宾驻华大使举办的菲律宾独立116周年国庆招待会

10日　我会外顾委召开2014年度第四次例会。会议邀请美国法律专家Gregory Shaffer教授和新加坡管理大学高树超教授介绍巴西和印度参与WTO争端解决的经验。

17日　民政部通过我会2013年年检。

18日　孙振宇会长会见英国驻华使馆公使兼副

馆长安勇（Andrew Key）和贸易政策与商业环境二等秘书安德鲁·麦肯锡（Andrew Mackenzie），双方就多双边贸易谈判、区域自由贸易协定、中英经贸领域合作等议题交换了意见，并就使馆与我会进一步加强联系及合作进行了交流。陈鹏副会长兼秘书长、王成安副会长等到中非工业发展论坛考察。

19日　我会竞委会召开工作会议，竞委会主席俞晓松出席。

23日　我会在京举行“中欧文化贸易高端研讨会”，陈鹏副会长兼秘书长出席开幕式并致辞。

30日　王成安副会长出席在清华大学法学院召开的研讨会。

7月

1日　孙振宇会长出席首届中国—俄罗斯博览会：欧亚经济一体化潜力推介会暨中俄经贸合作研讨会，并在研讨会上发表《中俄全面战略合作前景广阔》的讲话。

3日　国际投资专家委员会投资沙龙在北京举办，国际投资专家委员会主任委员、我会孙振宇会长出席会议并致辞。

8日　孙振宇会长会见中国美国商会前会长麦健陆（James McGregor）先生。双方就中美经贸关系、双边投资环境以及商会与我会合作等事宜进行了交流。

9日　我会竞委会举办法律咨询会议。竞委会主席俞晓松出席会议并讲话。晚上孙振宇会长应邀会见美国副国务卿凯瑟琳·诺维利（Catherine Novelli）。参加会见的还有北京大学卢锋教授、社科院张斌研究员。

21日　上午，孙振宇会长会见印度驻世界贸易组织前大使吉加大·达斯古朴塔先生、世界贸易组织前副总干事哈沙·辛格、印度世界贸易组织事务中心主任阿比吉·达斯，双方就中国和印度的WTO政策、WTO相关的培训、WTO法律咨询中心（ACWL）起到的作用、跨太平洋伙伴关系协议（TPP）目前遇到的问题及未来的展望以及中国与印度加强WTO方面的合作的意义几个话题深入交换了意见。

下午，由中国世界贸易组织研究会、国际可持续发展研究院、国际贸易和可持续发展中心联合在对外经济贸易大学举办“跨太平洋伙伴关系协议对中国和印度的影响”研讨会暨中国世界贸易组织研究会外经贸咨询顾问委员会2014年第五次例会，探讨跨太平洋伙伴关系协议（TPP）对中国和印度的影响。中印两国知名专家、世贸组织研究会外经贸咨询顾问委员会的委员等65人出席会议。

30日　由商务部世贸司和我会共同组织的首次“世界贸易组织工作产业通气会”在北京召开。商务部部长助理王受文出席会议并做主旨演讲，孙振宇会长宣布通气会正式启动并主持会议。世贸司通报了多哈回合“后巴厘”和环境产品谈判情况、技术性贸易措施工作情况等。

8月

4日　孙振宇会长应邀出席新加坡驻华使馆举行的四十九周年国庆招待会。

7日　孙振宇会长会见深圳WTO事务中心主任高瞻等一行五人。高主任汇报了深圳上半年外贸经济形势和深圳WTO事务中心下半年的工作安排，并就有关工作征询孙会长的意见。双方就下一步合作进行了深入讨论。

11日　陈鹏副会长兼秘书长会见澳大利亚商会会长Tracy Colgan女士等一行四人。双方回顾了2013年4月澳大利亚总理亚吉拉德阁下访华时双方签订的战略合作协议，并就下一步在文化、教育、金融及进出口贸易的合作进行了深入的讨论。

15日　王成安副会长会见美国驻华使馆经济官员戴贝琦女士，双方回顾了我会与美国驻华使馆合作共同举办的多场美国投资环境介绍会，并一致认为取得了较好效果。双方就下一步合作等事宜进行了深入交谈。

19日　我会竞委会召开秘书处全体会议，竞委会执行主席兼秘书长王成安主持会议。会议研究了如何贯彻“关于加强当前竞委会工作的建议”等事项。我会与中非工业合作发展论坛签订合作协议。

21日　我会外顾委召开2014年度第六次例会。会议专项讨论了中国的对外援助和国际发展援助问题，重点研讨中国促贸援助和中国支持国际多边机构发展援助问题。

25日　孙振宇会长会见湖南省商务厅徐湘平厅长一行。副会长兼秘书长陈鹏、商务部中国国际经济技术交流中心主任姚申洪、中国联合国采购促进会会长王粤和副会长王成安等也一同参加了会见。

9月

1日　孙振宇会长会见瑞士驻世贸组织前大使瓦塞沙，并同瓦塞沙大使一同参加了由对外经济贸易大学赵忠秀副校长主持的座谈会。瓦塞沙大使在座谈会上就“WTO 前景”做了专题发言，并与参会人员进行互动，回答了相关问题。

4日　王成安副会长会见荷兰外交部战略司 Wiers 先生一行。双方就当前热议的后巴厘议题以及多边发展前景，区域和诸边议题，中欧、美欧的双边发展前景及展望做了深入的探讨和交流。

5日　我会竞委会召开“当前垄断案件发展趋势与执法情况解析”研讨会，俞晓松主席主持会议。

8日　孙振宇会长、陈鹏副会长兼秘书长、王成安副会长出席第十八届中国国际投资贸易洽谈会。

9日　我会与厦门市会议展览事务局共同举办“国际投资论坛·投资沙龙”。

11日　由商务部世界贸易组织司指导，深圳市经济贸易和信息化委员会和深圳市世贸组织事务中心主办，中国世界贸易组织研究会、商务部驻深圳特派员办事处及广东省商务厅合办的“落实《国务院办公厅关于进一步加强贸易政策合规性工作的通知》宣传贯彻会议和合规工作研讨会”在深圳举行，孙振宇会长、陈鹏副会长兼秘书长、王成安副会长出席。

15日　王成安副会长参加由部世贸司与欧盟驻华代表团联合主办的“环境产品研讨会”。

17日　孙振宇会长参加中国国际贸易学会召开的关于外商对我反垄断和投资环境反映的分析和建议会。

22日　我会召开对非工作会议，王成安副会长主持会议，会议就如何加强对非工作各抒己见。

26日　我会外顾委召开 2014 年度第七次例会。会议就外商投资环境进行了深入研讨。

29日　“中国世界贸易组织研究会庆国庆 65 周年暨中国世贸组织研究会成立 12 周年联谊会”在对外经济贸易大学举行。

10月

8日　孙振宇会长会见巴西淡水河谷矿产品（中国）有限公司首席代表爱杰龙先生（AJ Nichols）。

10日　孙振宇会长会见厦门市会展局王琼文局长、杨少菁副局长等一行 6 人，双方就进一步发挥各自优势、加强合作进行了深入探讨。

11日　我会竞委会召开秘书处工作会议，对当前各项工作进行了讨论研究，并对下一步工作进行了部署。

12日　由我会与南开大学联合发起，南开大学中国国际发展研究中心承办的“中国参与全球经济治理复合人才高级研修项目”－“2014 国际谈判与国际经济谈判”专题研修班在南开大学举办。孙振宇会长出席开幕式并致辞，陈鹏副会长兼秘书长也出席了开幕式。

15日　陈鹏副会长兼秘书长会见中国宏泰产业市镇发展有限公司潘锋高级副总裁一行。双方就中国城镇化发展、京津冀一体化建设、海外投资促进等方面进行了探讨，对下一步双方合作达成初步共识。

17日　陈鹏副会长兼秘书长参加商务部召开的“2014 年第四次党风廉情通气会”。

21日　陈鹏副会长兼秘书长会见广东省经济科技发展研究会邢正猛副会长。

22日　孙振宇会长会见深圳市世贸组织事务中心曾建中副主任一行 4 人。

23日　孙振宇会长应邀出席由农业部农业贸易促进中心和经济发展与合作组织（OECD）举办的“后巴厘农业与贸易政策选择”2014 年农业贸易政策国际会议并发表演讲。陈鹏副会长兼秘书长会见中国食品工业协会花卉（果蔬）食品专业委员会执行会长王加伟。

25—26日　由我会主办的“海外市场项目融资、保函信贷与外账财务管理专题说明会”在北京举行。

29日　孙振宇会长应邀出席“2014 年中国国际投资洽谈会”开幕式暨高峰论坛“国际投资，政策与服务”，并发表演讲。

31日　孙振宇会长主持召开参加中美市场准入谈判部分人员座谈会。

30—31日　上海财经大学举办“2014 现金管理与支付创新论坛”，王成安副会长代表我会作为支持单位出席。

11月

3—5日　孙振宇会长应邀出席上海 WTO 事

务咨询中心年会。

14 日 王成安副会长应邀参加中国国际扶贫中心与经济合作组织发展援助委员会举办的“中国发展援助委员会研究小组”促进发展领域的企业伦理与公私伙伴关系国际研讨会。

19 日 我会与美中国际投资和贸易联盟共同主办的“海外并购的机遇与挑战圆桌会”在对外经济贸易大学召开。

22 日 陈鹏副会长兼秘书长代表孙振宇会长出席对外经贸大学国际经贸学院建院六十周年庆典大会，并代表我会致信表示祝贺。我会终身荣誉顾问沈觉人、谷永江部级老领导也应邀出席并致辞祝贺。

24 日 孙振宇会长应邀出席国家外国专家局召开的外国专家建言工作会议并发言。

25 日 陈鹏副会长兼秘书长与对外经贸大学赵忠秀副校长共同研究“WTO 20 年与中国”活动事项。确定开展“一书一会一展一气”系列活动，即校会联合主编《WTO 20 年与中国》一书及召开“WTO 20 年与中国国际研讨会”、“WTO 20 年与中国图片展”、2015 年世界贸易组织工作产业通气会。

26 日 我会外顾委召开 2014 年度第八次例会——“非洲投资环境及发展趋势”。

12 月

3 日 上午孙振宇会长会见日本驻世界贸易组织前大使大岛正太郎（Shotaro Oshima）和日本国际经济研究所大辻纯夫（Sumio Ohtsuji）所长。下午孙振宇会长会见青岛贸促会会长冯文青。

4 日 我会与厦门会展局共同举办“2015 年国际投资专家委员会投资沙龙·北京”。

5 日 王成安副会长代表我会出席中国出入境检验检疫协会中国国际旅游卫生保健协会第二次理事会。

11—12 日 孙振宇会长、陈鹏副会长兼秘书长、王成安副会长出席第十三届“WTO 与深圳”高级论坛暨深圳市世贸组织事务中心顾问委员会 2014 年年会。

13—14 日 我会举办“外账财务、保函风险与信贷融资业务”说明会。

15 日 我会召开年终工作总结会。

18 日 我会与国际贸易和可持续发展中心、对外经贸大学 WTO 研究院共同召开“2014 年第十三届 WTO 与中国学术年会”。

19 日 我会与国度投资控股集团有限公司签订合作协议。

27 日 我会与对外经贸大学联合举办“后巴厘”谈判报告会，邀请中国驻世界贸易组织大使俞建华做报告。

30 日 我会与中国食品工业协会花卉食品专业委员会及北京食安健食品科技有限公司签订合作协议。

附录七：对外经济贸易大学年度大事记（2014）

1. 全面深化体制机制改革方案出台　深化改革为学校发展注入新活力

2014年7月7日，校党委召开第十一届委员会第四次全体（扩大）会议，审议并通过了《对外经济贸易大学关于全面深化教育体制机制改革若干问题的实施意见》（简称“贸大综合改革方案”）。“贸大综合改革方案”共9大部分49条，系统设计了学校人才培养、人力资源管理、科学研究与社会服务、学科建设、开放办学和国际化办学、内部治理结构和体制、资源配置和后勤保障、贸大文化与和谐校园、加强党的领导等重点领域和关键环节深化改革的指导思想、基本原则和目标任务，是当前和今后一段时间学校科学发展的根本指导和重要依据。

2. 首部“贸大章程”诞生　学校依法治校踏上新征程

2014年11月4日，校党委召开第十一届委员会第五次全体（扩大）会议，审议并通过了《对外经济贸易大学学术委员会章程（修订）》（简称“贸大章程”），获教育部核准后正式生效，成为对外经济贸易大学建校以来的首部章程。

“贸大章程”共10章74条，以中国特色社会主义理论体系为指导，以宪法、法律法规为依据，坚持社会主义办学方向，遵循高等教育规律，推进高等学校科学发展；促进改革创新，围绕人才培养、科学研究、服务社会、推进文化传承创新的任务，依法完善内部法人治理结构，体现和保护学校改革创新的成功经验与制度成果；着重完善学校自主管理、自我约束的体制机制，是我校完善治理结构、科学发展，加快建设现代大学制度，促进依法治校的重要举措，标志着贸大依法治校踏上了新征程。

3. 科研成果再创新高　连续两年荣获国家自科重点项目

2014年，学校共获各类纵向课题108项，连续第二年获得国家自然科学基金重点项目支持。其中，国家社会科学基金项目30项（重点项目5项，一般和青年项目24项，特别委托项目1项）；国家自然科学基金项目29项（重点项目1项，面上项目12项，青年项目16项）；教育部人文社会科学各类研究项目28项；司法部研究项目1项；北京市各类科研项目20项（重点项目3项，基地项目4项，一般和青年项目11项，教委共建项目2项）。2014年度学校共获各级各类科研课题经费达4350余万元。

2014年，学校产出各类科研成果1769项，发表各类论文1519篇，其中，SSCI收录89篇；SCI收录31篇。共获各级各类省部级奖项14项：其中获北京市第十三届哲学社会科学优秀成果奖9项，在北京财经外语类高校中居第一；5项成果获第十八届“安子介国际贸易研究奖”。

4. 国际商学院通过EQUIS国际认证　贸大成为中国财经类院校EQUIS认证领头雁

2014年10月7日，欧洲管理发展基金会（European Foundation for Management Development，EFMD）官方通报对外经济贸易大学国际商学院正式通过EQUIS国际认证，成为中国大陆地区第12家获得此认证的院校，第一所获得EQUIS认证的财经类院校，标志着我校办学质量得到国际教育界认可。

5. 生源质量继续稳居全国领先地位　本科文科生招生跻身北京前四强

2014年，我校在全国录取分数继续保持领先地位，录取分数全线上扬，部分省市分数再创新高。本科文科录取分数在全国25个省市超出一本线50分以上，理科录取分数在全国25个省市超过一本线100分以上，在全国绝大多数省份的录取分数排名在前十名以内。在北京地区高校招生中，我校文科排名第四，理科排名第五。

研究生录取总规模达到2093人，创历史新高，研究生与本科生录取人数持平，其中，来自“211工程”或“985工程”高校的生源占比近60%，生源结构进一步优化。

6. 毕业生就业创业实现新突破　首次荣膺“全国高校百家网站”

2014 年，我校本科生毕业就业率为 98.54%，研究生毕业就业率为 99.22%。超过 50%的毕业生到金融、外贸、会计审计类行业就业，毕业生去向与专业的契合度超过 73%。2 月，对外经济贸易大学新闻网首次荣获第六届“全国高校百佳网站”称号；12 月，贸大就业信息网荣膺第七届“全国高校百佳网站”。

2014 年以“经纬杯”创业大赛为依托，成立创业导师团，筹建“大学生创新创业俱乐部”，开展学生创新创业教育，取得了一系列成果。3 个学生创业项目入选“北京市高校百支优秀创业团队”，免费入驻大学生创业园；20 个学生创业团队获北京市“2015 年高校大学生创业团队支持项目”；我校入选首批北京市“示范性创业中心重点建设高校”。

7. 教育教学改革务实创新　人才培养质量明显提升

2014 年，学校获北京市教委学分制改革试点项目，正式启动本科生培养方案重构工作。推出《对外经济贸易大学本科人才培养体系框架》，推出小班教学方法试验改革，扩大新生研讨课范围，加大 MOOC 课程建设步伐，2014 国际化暑期学校完美收官，近百名外教开课，2700 余名中外学子参加学习。11 种 20 册教材入选教育部第二批“十二五”普通高等教育本科国家级规划教材；4 项获 2014 年北京高校教育教学改革立项；2 门课程通过教育部 2014 视频公开课第一阶段评审遴选。研究生教育教学推出综合改革方案，建立全过程的研究生质量保障体系，出台《关于在博士研究生普通招考中推行两段制考试的实施方案》、《对外经济贸易大学“硕博一体化”培养模式实施方案（试行）》等十余项管理制度，全力培养助推高层次人才。

在 2014 年美国数学建模竞赛、2014 全国大学生数学建模竞赛、2014 年全国大学生数学竞赛中，我校多人荣膺特等奖、一等奖、二等奖，参赛队伍和获奖层次均创历史新高。在 2014 年全国大学生英语竞赛中，3 人获特等奖，3 人获一等奖。在“贸大高远杯”全国首届商务外语技能大赛、2014 欧莱雅校园市场策划大赛中国赛区、“外经贸杯”2014 未来国际商务英语谈判精英赛、2014 年北京市大学生创业设计竞赛、2014“创青春”创业大赛国家级主体赛事中，我校学子均表现突出，多次获奖。“新丝路，重新开始的征程”主题社会实践 6 支团队跻身国家级重点团队，10 支团队获评北京市优秀团队，10 篇报告入选北京市优秀实践成果，我校获全国社会实践先进单位，校志愿服务中心首获北京市“青年文明号”，二三课堂获团中央“学校共青团重点创新试点项目”。

8. 国际化特色日益彰显　孔子学院建设获表彰

2014 年，学校国际化工程深入推进，国际化特色日益彰显。WTO 总干事罗伯托·阿泽维多、联合国副秘书长盖图、美国联邦贸易委员会主席伊迪丝·拉米雷斯、沙特阿拉伯亲王费塞尔、哈佛大学教授 Elhanan Helpman 等多位国际著名学者来校访问并做精彩演讲；成功举办“文化传统与绿色经济——技术创新、产业增长与绿色流动”2014 年北京洪堡论坛、全面深化中泰战略合作国际研讨会等高端学术会议；与国外多所高校签署合作协议；成功举办中俄经济类大学联盟两国四地青年精英夏令营等活动；新增俄罗斯联邦、沙特阿拉伯和南部非洲三个国际校友分会。我校中外学生之比位居中国两岸四地大学前列。来华留学教育取得新成绩，学校国际影响力不断提升。

2014 年，学校 8 所孔子学院活动有声有色，以孔子学院为平台的全球商务汉语、经贸合作进一步加强。成功举办庆祝孔子学院成立十周年和首个全球“孔子学院日”系列活动，受到孔子学院总部肯定。在第九届孔子学院大会上，我校英国利兹大学孔子学院中方院长王波获“先进个人奖”，专职教师郭广伟获“全球最美汉语教师奖”。

9. 红天体育馆落成　学校综合实力取得新提升

10 月 26 日，作为对外经济贸易大学历史上第一个综合体育馆——红天体育馆正式落成开馆。红天体育馆造型酷似“金元宝”，总建筑面积为 17165 平方米，地上 4 层，地下 2 层。地下设有 50 米标准泳池，人防层平时作为大学生活动及多媒体教学用房；地上是集篮球场、排球、羽毛球、乒乓球等为一体的综合馆，兼做可容纳 4000 人的会堂，也可做大型演出场所。红天体育馆建设得到了教育部的投资及校友陈红天博士的捐款资助。

2014 年，学校财务状况持续向好，青年教师住房难问题得到有效缓解，智能化校园和平安校园建设取得新进展，学校综合实力取得了新提升。

10. 基金会成立满五岁　五年间筹资近 3 亿

学校教育基金会自 2009 年 11 月注册成立，迄今已满五年。2014 年 12 月，学校隆重召开对外经济贸易大学教育基金会成立五周年庆祝大会。我校基金会依托全校师生、广大校友、校董及社会各界关心支持我校发展的热心人士，发扬艰苦创业精神，积极开拓，努力进取，共接受各类货币捐赠达 260 项，筹资总额近 3 亿元，为学校事业发展提供了有力支持。

附录八：北京市国际服务贸易事务中心年度大事记（2014）

北京市国际服务贸易事务中心是北京市商务委员会所属的全额拨款事业单位，是中国（北京）国际服务贸易交易会（简称京交会）组委会执行机构，主要负责京交会总体策划、整体形象设计和宣传推介；负责京交会主办方、协办方和支持单位的联络与协调，落实重要来宾的邀请工作；负责京交会招商招展和展览会务工作，以及对相关情况进行统计、汇总和分析；负责京交会经费预算、支出、审计等财务管理工作。

除围绕京交会开展的工作外，北京市国际服务贸易事务中心保留原北京 WTO 事务中心的部分国际事务职能，主要负责“WTO 与中国：北京国际论坛”的组织筹备工作，开展与 WTO 有关的国际交往活动等。

1. 举办第三届京交会

京交会是经国务院批准，由商务部与北京市人民政府共同主办的国际展会，也是世界上第一个专门为服务贸易搭建的国际交流平台。京交会定位于国家级、国际性、综合型的服务贸易交易平台，世界贸易组织、联合国贸易和发展会议、经济合作与发展组织是其永久支持机构。京交会涵盖商业服务、通信服务、销售服务、教育服务等世界贸易组织界定的服务贸易全部 12 类领域，致力于成为中国服务业“引进来”和“走出去”的重要渠道、权威服务贸易政策和信息的发布窗口、各国服务贸易企业的交流合作桥梁，成为具有持续发展力和国际影响力的国际盛会。

第三届京交会于 2014 年 5 月 28 日至 6 月 1 日在北京国家会议中心举办。本届京交会以扩大服务业开放为主线，举办了展览展示、论坛活动、洽谈交易三种形式共 133 场活动；洽谈展览区域总面积 5 万平方米；共有 2524 家参展企业注册参会，比第二届增长 33%；来自 117 个国家和地区的 15.3 万人次参展参会，其中专业客商 14.5 万人次，比第二届增长 20.8%，境外专业买家达 210 家，增加 17 家；首次实现全球服务贸易 20 强国家和地区均有客商参会；达成签约项目 236 个，意向签约额累计 818.3 亿美元，其中国际项目意向签约额占比 43.4%，比第二届提高了 29.6 个百分点。

本届京交会取得了以下四项成果。

（1）传递了中国坚定不移扩大服务业开放的决心

京交会组委会、经济合作与发展组织共同主办了主题为“服务贸易在全球价值链中的作用”的高峰会。国务院副总理汪洋在发来的书面致辞中，向国际社会清晰传递了中国政府坚定不移地扩大服务业开放的信心和决心。全国人大常委会副委员长张宝文强调，中国将通过服务业开放，更大程度地嵌入到以服务为主导的全球价值链。高峰会及系列专业大会的成功举办，传递了中国坚定不移地扩大服务业开放的态度，增强了外界对中国扩大服务业开放、推动经济可持续发展的信心。

（2）拓展了服务贸易国际合作的广度和深度

本届京交会进一步深化了世界各国、国际组织、行业商协会之间的交流与合作。91 位国内外政要、政府部长、驻华大使、国际组织和行业协会负责人及跨国公司全球负责人出席了第三届京交会。继续举办了“WTO 与中国：北京国际论坛”和联合国服务采购说明会。世界贸易网点联盟、国际贸易中心、日内瓦国际贸易与可持续发展中心有关负责人出席了京交会活动。国际设计联合会、国际展览业协会、欧盟电子商务协会、巴西服务业联合会等国际行业协会和境外商协会组团参展参会。英国、德国、新加坡、韩国、印度等 17 个境外国家和地区组团参展，全球服务贸易 10 强中有 6 个组团参展；12 个境外国家和地区举办了国别主题日及专场活动，在文化创意、信息技术、旅游服务等领域开展交流合作。

（3）推动了各行业跨界融合和服务业转型发展

京交会重点展示了服务贸易领域的创新成果，探讨了国际服务业发展趋势，不仅为不同服务行业间融合发展创造了机会，也为服务业与其他行业的跨界融合搭建了桥梁。故事驱动大会通过讲故事、卖故事，把故事这一核心内容通过图书、游戏、电影、动漫、电子出版等多种形式展现出来，促进文化跨媒体、跨文化、跨地域的交流。电子商务大会以“跨界融合·创新发展”为主题，邀请中外电商企业领袖探讨电子商务如何实现跨界融合。体育服务专题围绕体育与新媒体和资本市场对接合作开展了研讨和推介活动，以助力体育服务贸易新发展。

（4）促进了企业务实合作和交易对接

京交会期间，共有来自科技服务、环境服务、会展服务、体育服务、中医药服务、文化贸易等领域的4000余人次专业客商进行了面对面深入沟通洽谈。5月29日，数字内容商务大会接待了2000多人次专业观众，开展一对一洽谈350轮次，达成合作意向金额20.6亿元。快递服务板块有近400家企业参加线上线下电子商务模式（OTO）洽谈会，实现意向签约额500亿元。国际体育服务贸易发展大会促成包括“2014法国超级杯”“2014红牛飞行世锦赛”“乐视购买NBA转播权”等体育服务领域签约项目33项。

2. 举办“WTO与中国：北京国际论坛（2013）”

5月28日下午，“WTO与中国：北京国际论坛（2014）”在北京国家会议中心成功举办。论坛以“服务贸易创新与产业结构升级”为主题，分为“加快政府职能转变，提高服务贸易开放水平”和“发挥市场决定性作用，促进服务产业结构升级与创新”两大专题，是京交会最具亮点和影响力的重要专业大会之一。

论坛以嘉宾演讲和互动交流形式为主，“服务贸易创新与产业结构升级”为研讨主题，既契合当前世界经济发展形势，也对应中国服务经济发展战略。国际组织负责人、驻华使节、知名专家、企业高管等与会嘉宾齐聚一堂，以促进国内外服务业和服务贸易发展为宗旨，围绕两大专题内容发表演讲并展开讨论，对促进中国服务业扩大开放和服务贸易进一步发展积极建言献策，提出许多前瞻性见解，对中国服务贸易发展具有重要指导意义。

论坛得到了世界贸易组织（WTO）和我国商务部的大力支持，WTO总干事阿泽维多特意发信祝贺。WTO副总干事易小准、WTO服务贸易司司长阿卜杜勒·哈米德·马姆杜等代表WTO出席并演讲。商务部部长助理童道驰、服贸司司长周柳军、世贸司副司长洪晓东等嘉宾出席了论坛并演讲，还为参会代表进行详细政策解读。日内瓦国际贸易和可持续发展中心总裁梅林德、中国美国商会主席葛国瑞、对外经济贸易大学副校长赵忠秀、国务院发展研究中心副主任卢中原和中国国际贸易学会副会长李永等出席并演讲。会议规模达350多人。

3. 举办2014年北京台湾名品博览会

11月13日至16日，由北京市人民政府主办，市商务委、市台办和台湾贸易中心共同承办的2014年北京台湾名品博览会，在全国农业展览馆新馆成功举办。

此次博览会展出规模13000平方米，严选250家有出口业绩或得奖记录的厂商参展，展出万余种商品。其中，11项全球领先产品亮相台湾精品馆，特别规划了“高新科技”、“精致生活”、“运动休闲”、“居家医疗”与“行动空拍”五大主题，涉及近百个台湾品牌。

博览会采用展销结合、展洽结合的方式，客流量达12万人次，现场销售额超过千万元。通过组织数十场厂商对接活动，达成明确采购意向突破12亿元人民币，较上届博览会增长22%。

附录九：上海WTO事务咨询中心年度大事记（2014）

2014年3月15日至21日，龚柏华总监、罗海蓉赴巴西里约热内卢参加了第五届“金砖国家贸易和经济研究网络会议”和第六届“金砖国家学术论坛”，就TTP和TTIP可能带来的规则改变影响及贸易转移的流量影响做了专题研讨。

2014年4月21日，“经济全球化新形势下我国对外开放战略”专题研究成果报告会在北京举行。该课题是商务部与上海市政府合作建设的“全球贸易投资研究咨询中心”国家级平台的首个部市合作决策咨询研究项目，分为货物贸易、服务贸易、投资规则、区域开放格局、自贸区建设等8个子课题，分别由上海社科院、复旦大学、上海交通大学、华东政法大学、上海对外经贸大学和市政府发展研究中心的专家学者承担研究任务，上海市决策咨询委员会和上海WTO事务咨询中心承担了专题研究的组织管理工作。

2014年6月17日，中国商务部与英国商业、创新和技能部在伦敦举办“欧盟—中国贸易前景展望：欧盟—中国自由贸易协定和中国自由贸易园区”学术研讨会，就世界贸易近期发展和前景展望、欧中自由贸易协定前景展望、中国自由贸易园区对中国未来贸易和投资协定的支持作用等议题进行了交流讨论，黄鹏副总裁出席并发言。

2014年6月20日，王新奎总裁、梁庆副总裁接待欧盟驻华代表团来访，就中国（上海）自由贸易试验区及外商直接投资管理体制改革的进程与前景进行座谈。

2014年7月15日，龚柏华总监、冯军总监赴北京参加商务部世贸司召开的“《贸易政策合规工作实施办法》专家研讨会”，商讨建立专门的专家咨询机制。

2014年8月13日，上海WTO事务咨询中心承办在北京举行的APEC全球价值链贸易增加值核算专家工作会议，为落实青岛贸易部长会议批准的《亚太经合组织促进全球价值链发展与合作战略蓝图》与《全球价值链中的APEC贸易增加值核算（数据库）战略框架》倡议，对亚太地区贸易增加值核算工作方案进行讨论。

2014年9月12日，上海WTO事务咨询中心与上海社科院联合举办了“开放战略升级与贸易便利化”理论研讨会。

2014年10月2日，上海WTO事务咨询中心在世界贸易组织秘书处2014WTO公众论坛中主办的第6分场在日内瓦举行。主题是“贸易与就业机会——中国的进程”，探讨全球贸易的不断融合对中国就业机会的影响，专家们通过数据分析等手段尽可能真实全面地展现出中国社会不同阶层的就业状况。会议由王新奎总裁主持，并邀请国际贸易中心（ITC）、法国经济社会研究院（IRES）以及上海复旦大学的专家学者就他们的研究成果进行演讲和讨论。

2014年11月3日，上海WTO事务咨询中心与美中贸易全国委员会共同举办“中美推进多哈发展议程谈判商学界对话会”，中美两国企业界和学术界的行家和学者就世界贸易组织框架下的服务贸易协定谈判、多哈发展议程非农产品市场准入谈判、信息技术协定扩围谈判和环境产品协定谈判等议题进行深入探讨，为推进多哈发展议程谈判进程、共同发展世界经济建言献策。

2014年11月5日，2014中国国际工业博览会发展论坛“全球价值链框架下中国制造业的比较优势和劳动分工变化趋势研讨会”暨上海WTO事务咨询中心顾问委员会年会在上海举行，会议主题为“全球价值链框架下中国制造业的比较优势和劳动分工变化趋势”，议题包括全球价值链贸易增加值的核算方法、全球价值链理论的政策应用，以及全球价值链框架下中国制造业的比较优势和劳动分工。会议以全球价值链视野理清了全球价值链框架下中国制造业的比较优势和劳动分工变化趋势。

附录十：深圳市世贸组织事务中心年度大事记（2014）

2月21日，深圳市世贸组织事务中心召开“深圳市WTO事务工作联络员工作会议”。市WTO事务联席会议成员单位、市WTO事务工作站、市WTO学会、市WTO事务定点培训机构等全市的WTO事务工作联络员共计60余人参加了会议。

3月12日，为加强全省贸易摩擦预警监测平台建设，进一步提高全省应对国际贸易摩擦水平，省商务厅公平贸易局产业损害调查处、贸易救济处、省WTO事务中心联合调研组来深调研。

4月16—18日，在国家商务部贸易救济调查局刘丹阳副局长的陪同下，美国联邦巡回上诉法院首席法官雷德（Randall Rader）、美国国际贸易委员会行政法官埃塞克斯（Theodore Essex）及数名美国资深律所的律师一行来深就应对美国337调查进行调研和技术交流。

7月10日，为庆祝中国共产党成立93周年，深入贯彻落实党的十八届三中全会精神，积极响应省委、省政府“扶贫济困，雪中送炭”的号召，进一步发挥党员的先锋模范作用和党支部的战斗堡垒作用，促进我市扶贫济困工作和公益慈善事业的发展，中心主任高瞻同志和党支部书记曾建中同志带领中心党员干部赴汕尾开展“扶贫济困”和党建革命传统教育活动。

8月28日，深圳市陶瓷行业协会向我中心发来感谢函，感谢我中心对该协会“2014年秋季广交会业务咨询座谈会”给予的支持和帮助。

9月11日，深圳市在全国率先召开落实《国务院办公厅关于进一步加强贸易政策合规工作的通知》宣贯及合规工作研讨会。

11月26日，中心在深圳组织召开了深圳市WTO法律服务体系工作会议，全面总结2014年贸易摩擦应对工作，并对2015年国际贸易摩擦形势和我市开展进出口公平贸易工作新思路进行了探讨。

12月11日，第十三届“WTO与深圳”高级论坛召开，论坛主题是“后巴厘谈判与中国的进一步对外开放”和“贸易便利化与深圳外贸稳增长”。

中国世界贸易组织研究会
China Society for World Trade Organization Studies

CWTO

名誉会长
Honorary Chairman

徐匡迪
Xu Kuangdi

陈德铭
Chen Deming

终身荣誉顾问
Lifelong Honorary Advisors

沈觉人
Shen Jueren

佟志广
Tong Zhiguang

谷永江
Gu Yongjiang

龙永图
Long Yongtu

会长
Chairman

孙振宇
Sun Zhenyu

副会长
Vice Chairmen

廖晓淇
Liao Xiaoqi

霍建国
Huo Jianguo

王新奎
Wang Xinkui

施建军
Shi Jianjun

陈 鹏
Chen Peng

薛荣久
Xue Rongjiu

王成安
Wang Chengan

中国世界贸易组织研究会是中华人民共和国商务部直属管理的从事世贸组织（WTO）及相关经济和贸易问题研究的全国性社团组织。由全国长期致力于世贸组织相关事务的政府官员、权威专家学者和机构自愿组成，是国内进行世贸组织有关事务研究、咨询、培训、编辑、出版、国际交流与合作的权威机构之一。

China Society for World Trade Organization Studies (CWTO) is the sole nation-wide non-governmental organization of studying WTO and relevant economic and trade issues based in Beijing,China. Formed voluntarily by government officials, experts, scholars, and institutions all over the country engaged in WTO-related affairs, CWTO is one of the authoritative institutions in the country carrying out research, consulting, training, compilation, publication, international exchange and cooperation activities in connection with WTO.

国务院前副总理李岚清会见中国世界贸易组织研究会领导。（左起：廖晓淇、俞晓松、佟志广、李岚清、谷永江、徐秉金、刘光溪）

Former Vice Premier Li Lanqing met with CWTO leaders. (From left: Liao Xiaoqi, Yu Xiaosong, Tong Zhiguang, Li Lanqing, Gu Yongjiang, Xu Bingjin, Liu Guangxi)

2009年3月20日，徐匡迪院士、陈德铭部长出席中国世界贸易组织研究会第二届理事会第三次会议并发表重要讲话。（左起：郑志海、孙振宇、俞晓松、徐匡迪、陈德铭、谷永江、易小准、徐秉金、吴家煌、刘光溪）

On March 20, 2009, Academician Xu Kuangdi and Minister Chen Deming attended and gave speech at the third session of the Second CWTO Council Meeting. (From left: Zheng Zhihai, Sun Zhenyu, Yu Xiaosong, Xu Kuangdi, Chen Deming, Gu Yongjiang, Yi Xiaozhun, Xu Bingjin, Wu Jiahuang and Liu Guangxi)

宗旨：服务国家，面向企业，依托智库院校，开展国际合作。

Our mission

To serve the country, support enterprises, rely on think tanks and universities and carry out international cooperation.

主要职能

- 研究世界贸易组织相关理论和实际问题；
- 组织国内外学术成果、工作经验和信息交流；
- 向我国政府部门、企业提供培训、咨询和法律服务；
- 国内外信息采编，编辑出版书籍、报刊、音像资料，宣传普及世界贸易组织知识；
- 促进我国与包括广大发展中国家在内的所有世贸组织成员的自由、公平贸易和经济技术合作；
- 推动我国企业参与国际竞争；
- 促进和推动我国与其他国家和地区包括自贸区在内的区域性经济合作；
- 协助我国政府部门在完善多边贸易体制进程中发挥积极和建设性作用。

Main functions

- Study WTO-related theories and practical issues;
- Organize domestic and international exchanges of academic research, work experiences and information;
- Provide relevant training, consultancy and legal services to China's government agencies, industries and enterprises;
- Collect information, edit and publish books, newspapers, audio and video materials, and periodicals to popularize WTO knowledge;
- Promote free-and-fair trade, and economic and technological cooperation between China and other WTO members, including developing countries;
- Encourage Chinese enterprises to participate in global competition;
- Enhance regional economic cooperation between China and other economies including FTAs;
- Assist the Chinese government to play an active and constructive role in improving the world trading system.

2013年9月30日,我会主办的“两岸经贸问题研讨会”在对外经贸大学召开。我会名誉会长、海峡两岸关系协会会长陈德铭和有关专家学者及商务部相关司局参加了本次研讨会。会议由孙振宇会长主持。

On September 30, 2013, a seminar on "Economic Issues Across the Taiwan Straits" was held in UIBE. Mr. Chen Deming, Honorary Chairman of CWTO and President of ARATS attended the seminar with scholars and relevant officials from Ministry of Commerce. The seminar was presided over by Mr. Sun Zhenyu, Chairman of CWTO.

2013年8月23日，世界贸易组织副总干事易小准视察我会并座谈。（左起：王琴华、王成安、薛荣久、易小准、孙振宇、陈鹏、霍建国、吴家煌、林桂军）

On August 23, 2013, Deputy Director-general of WTO Yi Xiaozhun visited CWTO. (From left: Wang Qinhua, Wang Chengan, Xue Rongjiu, Yi Xiaozhun, Sun Zhenyu, Chen Peng, Huo Jianguo, Wu Jiahuang, Lin Guijun)

2013年12月20日，我国驻世界贸易组织大使俞建华莅临我会并合影。

On December 20, 2013, Ambassador of China to WTO YU Jianhua visited CWTO.

地 址：对外经济贸易大学逸夫科研楼608 朝阳区惠新东街10号　邮编：100029
Add： Suite 608, Yifu Research Bldg., No. 10, Huixin Dongjie, Chaoyang District, Beijing 100029, China
电话（Tel）：64493232　传 真(Fax)：84255122
Email：cwto2015@126.com

上海WTO事务咨询中心

Shanghai WTO Affairs Consultation Center

SCC / WTO

理事长兼总裁
王新奎
Council Chairman & President
Mr. Wang Xinkui

上海WTO事务咨询中心是上海市人民政府主办的非营利性WTO事务专业咨询服务机构和国际交流沟通平台，建于中国加入世界贸易组织前夕的2000年10月。

上海WTO事务咨询中心设理事会，理事会成员由上海地区与WTO事务相关的主要政府部门的代表组成。

上海WTO事务咨询中心设顾问委员会，顾问委员会成员由经中华人民共和国国务院批准的国外WTO事务资深专家和经上海市人民政府批准的国内WTO事务权威人士组成。

上海WTO事务咨询中心业务团队成员的知识结构覆盖经济学、政治学、法学、管理学、系统工程、信息工程等专业领域，并具有从事WTO事务研究和咨询工作的长期经验。经中华人民共和国人力资源和社会保障部批准，中心设有以全球多边贸易体制为主要研究方向的博士后科研工作站。

作为WTO事务的专业咨询服务机构和国际交流沟通平台，上海WTO事务咨询中心向政府、企业和社会公众提供下列与WTO事务相关咨询服务：

1 与WTO有关的各类贸易谈判与磋商的数据分析或决策咨询服务；
2 与WTO争端解决有关的法律、法规和其他措施的合规性咨询服务；
3 针对各主要贸易伙伴的贸易环境和贸易壁垒调查服务；
4 按具体产品的反倾销、反补贴和保障措施的预警及监控服务；
5 反映贸易政策、贸易流量和产业产出相关关系的贸易运行监控服务；
6 与全球多边贸易体制有关的各国中长期宏观贸易政策趋势的研究服务；
7 通过电子网络发布或纸质文献资料查讯的WTO信息服务；
8 与WTO 事务有关的专题和热点培训服务；

The Shanghai WTO Affairs Consultation Center (SCC/WTO), funded by the Shanghai Municipal Government and established in October 2000 just prior to China's accession to the World Trade Organization, is a nonprofit think tank dedicated to professional consulting services and international exchanges on WTO affairs.

The SCC/WTO Board of Trustees consists of representatives from Shanghai's leading government departments related to WTO affairs.

The SCC/WTO also has a high-level Advisory Committee with members from home (accredited by the Shanghai Municipal Government) and abroad (accredited by China's State Council).

The SCC/WTO boasts a strong contingent of experienced researchers and veteran consultants in WTO affairs with expertise in multidisciplinary and interdisciplinary areas such as economics, political science, law, public administration, systems engineering, and information engineering. Upon approval from China's Ministry of Human Resources and Social Security, the SCC/WTO runs a postdoctoral program with a research focus on the global multilateral trading system.

As a professional institute specializing in WTO affairs consultancy and communication, the SCC/WTO provides the government, business, academia, and public with a broad range of services:

1 Statistical analysis and policy advice on trade negotiations under WTO;
2 Compliance consulting on laws, regulations and other measures related to the settlement of disputes under WTO;
3 Survey of trade environment and trade barriers in China's major trading partners;
4 Early-warning and monitoring of anti-dumping, countervailing, and safeguard measures against selected products;
5 Tracking and monitoring trade operations based on the interrelationship between trade policies, trade flows and industrial output;
6 Identifying trends in medium- and long-term macroeconomic policies of WTO members within the framework of multilateral trading system;
7 Distributing WTO-related information in print and electronic formats;
8 Training programs on hot topics and current issues related to WTO affairs.

地址：上海市古北路620号院内WTO中心办公楼
邮编：200336
电话：021-62591080

WTO Building,620, Gu Bei Road, Shanghai, China
Zip: 200336
Tel: 86-21-62591080

武汉大学WTO学院

简介

武汉大学WTO学院是武汉大学直属学院之一，是按照国际国内开放办学的模式和高效管理机制运行的新型学院。学院旨在以实现学生的国际就业为目标，提供高质量的教学计划和培养方案，使学生在学习的基础上，树立敢于面向国际职业市场的观念，提高就业竞争能力。

学院与多个国家的多所名校建立了联合培养机制，为高中毕业生开创了更新更好的就读机会，学生因此改变了自己的人生轨迹，拥有更好的学习机会、更大的发展空间、更高的就业层次。学院教学以严谨著称，学生管理以严格闻名，教学成效异常显著，学院因此获得了国外高校的高度肯定，吸引了多所世界名校前来我院寻求合作。

国内第二学位教育项目

武汉大学WTO双学位实验班至今已成功举办7届，是面向武汉地区十八所普通高校在校大学生开发的双学位教育（学生在大一时申请）。WTO双学位班将“培养具有国际交流能力的法律、经济、管理学的综合性人才”作为武汉大学特色人才培养目标之一；强调学生在继续学习原本科专业的同时，不转学籍参加本班学习，学生可以用原专业的学位或武大授予的学位进行就业、深造和申请出国，真正使学生获得综合优势。

网　　址：www.whuwto.com

地　　址：武汉大学桂园WTO学院

电　　话：027－68753872

　　　　　027－68754413

传　　真：027－68754690

安庆经济技术开发区

【概况】安庆经济技术开发区始建于1992年8月，1993年经安徽省政府批准为省级开发区，2010年3月升格为国家级。2015年，按照安庆市委、市政府的部署和要求，紧盯年初目标，认真践行“三严三实”，迎难而上、开拓创新、扎实工作，经济发展态势逐步向好，实现规上工业产值470.2亿，规上工业增加值99.3亿，固定资产投资153.7亿，限额上社会消费品零售总额23.6亿，进出口总额42120万美元，一般预算收入11.46亿。

【项目建设】通过招商引资、做大做强现有企业等方式，谋划了富士康安庆自动化生产制造及系列研发量产、新能源汽车零部件产业园、赛富环新汽车零部件产业园、安庆（皖西南）保税物流中心（B型）、安庆经济技术开发区22.24平方公里拓区基础设施建设（两区共建）等重大项目，中航工业健康环保设备产业园、华霆动力年产2万台套的新三元电池成组等项目成功签约，赛富环新粉末冶金项目和动力锂电池冷却系统项目厂房主体完工，富士康安庆自动化铆压机、高光机、三轴数控加工中心3个产品投入生产，节能高速薄件全电注塑机、五轴车铣复合加工机、高精密伺服马达3个研发项目进展顺利， 100公斤级蓝宝石长晶项目开始试生产。新能源汽车项目取得重大进展，产业园主厂区主体工程结束，设备陆续进场安装，资金保障、工程进度达到预期进度。

【平台建设】依据安庆城市总体规划，“两区共建”项目控规编制有条不紊地进行。有效实施“两区共建”项目一期、新能源汽车起步区二期、外环北路等重点工程项目，完成征地1.031万亩，拆迁房屋59.86万平米，完成棚户区改造18.4万平米。正式启动实施老城改造，对中兴大道、迎宾西路、同安路等主干道路进行了白加黑改造，完成一期园区内道路绿化提升，市政基础设施和老旧小区改造改造进展顺利，市容市貌有了新改观。

【融资上市】融资取得突破，全年金融机构授信48.31亿，增幅137.6%，筹集到位资金19.51亿，增幅45.9%，有力保障了建设发展需要。全国第一单农发行老峰片“两区共建”项目授信100亿，首期放贷30亿。二期10个亿的城投债国家发改委已审核批复，10个亿的私募债已报银行间交易商协会审核，5个亿的城镇化一号基金徽商银行总行已批复。经开区建投公司获联合资信AA主体评级，拿到了资本市场直接融资入场券。企业上市有进展，拟IPO辅导备案企业6家，申报新三板企业2家，1家企业报备IPO。

【科技创新】积极创建“安徽省首批省知识产权示范培育园区”，各项考核指标基本完成。在第一批国家高企申报中，经开区全年申报企业11家，通过认定企业8家。全年专利申请量1386件，其中：发明专利729件，比上年增长187.01%，专利授权411件。区内环新集团、安庆电厂申报了安徽省百强企业；恒昌、长谷川公司申报了省级工业设计中心，安簧公司、联动属具、天润机械、虹宇化工、爱唯科、三维等申报了市级工业设计中心；新增18件产品进入安徽省高新技术产品目录；22家企业列入安庆市首批“小智专”企业名单。

开发区全貌

青岛保税港区

青岛保税港区进口汽车停放场地

青保国际汽车城和进口商品总部基地

进口商品展示交易区

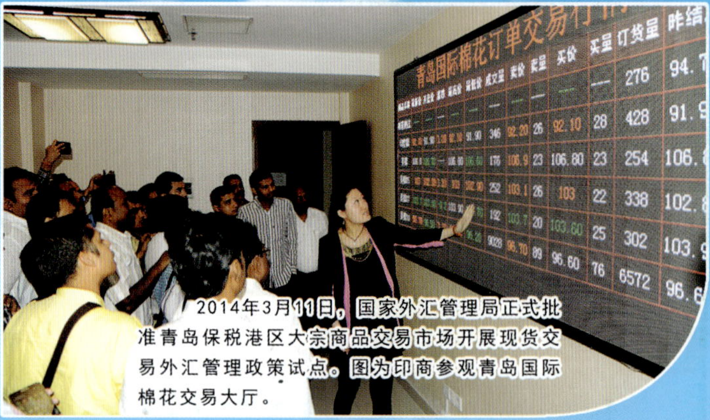

2014年3月11日，国家外汇管理局正式批准青岛保税港区大宗商品交易市场开展现货交易外汇管理政策试点。图为印商参观青岛国际棉花交易大厅。

青岛保税港区设立于2008年9月7日，由青岛保税区、青岛保税物流园区整合临近港口转型升级而成，规划面积9.72平方公里，码头泊位21个，具有“保税、免税、免证”和“境内关外”等特殊政策，拥有国际物流、国际贸易、交易市场、保税加工、码头作业、航运服务、研发及企业总部、检测和售后服务维修等功能。根据山东省和青岛市规划建设部署，目前青岛保税港区形成了保税区、保税港区、出口加工区、汽车物流园区和功能拓展区“四种政策、五个区域”联动发展格局，规划总面积达到65.73平方公里。

近年来，青岛保税港区已建成全国第一家“美元挂牌、保税交易”的国际橡胶交易市场，并发展成为全球第三大进口胶交易定价中心；建成全国第一家矿权、矿产品交易所；建成全国第一家棉花交易市场；培育出全国第一家境外烟叶国际采购中心；培育了三个国家重点实验室和两个国家企业技术中心；培育出山东省第一家民营上市企业青岛软控并在深圳挂牌，被授予“国际科技合作基地”称号；获批汽车整车进口口岸，建设酒水基地，力争建成东北亚地区独具特色的进口汽车贸易中心、酒水贸易中心、奢侈品贸易中心和航运服务贸易中心；与胶州、董家口等地探索互利共赢发展机制，在德州、临沂、潍坊、济宁、菏泽等地辟建50多平方公里功能园区，并通过开建内陆无水港、功能政策推介，为中西部对外开放打开大进大出、快进快出的物流通道。

青岛保税港区将以深化改革为动力，以扩大开放为引领，进一步解放思想，开拓创新，锐意进取，扎实推进各项开放改革试点工作，努力建设投资贸易便利、高端产业集聚、航运服务完善、金融功能健全、辐射联动效益突出、监管高效便捷、法制环境规范的国际一流自由贸易港区，打造深耕东北亚、面向世界的国际贸易中心、国际航运中心、国际物流中心、大宗商品定价中心，为全国的对外开放事业做出新的贡献！

肇庆国家高新区

Zhaoqing National High-tech Industry Development Zone

园区一角

肇庆高新区是国家高新区、广东省吸收外资重点工业园区、广东省山区吸收外资示范区、广东省首批示范性产业转移园，享有地市一级经济管理和相关行政审批权限，所在地大旺总面积 98 平方公里，全部为国有土地。

该区位于珠三角中心区西部、肇庆市最东端，距广州市区 50 公里，属广佛半小时经济生活圈，到广州白云机场仅需 40 多分钟车程。铁路、公路、高速公路、城际轨道交通、水路交通均四通八达。

近年来，该区经济社会实现了超常规、跨越式发展。2014 年，全区实现 GDP201. 76 亿元，实现工业总产值 778. 86 亿元，实现地方公共财政预算收入 11. 4 亿元。目前，全区已投产企业 250 多家，吸引了一大批国内外知名企业落户，初步形成了金属新材料、电子信息、生物医药、先进装备制造四大主导产业。

下阶段，该区将按照现代科技工业城的发展定位，全力以赴谋招商，聚精会神抓工业，大力发展四大主导产业，努力实现“二次创业”新辉煌，引领全市新型工业化。

大旺中学高中部

省、市领导会见美国威蒙汽车公司高层

肇庆高新区行政服务中心为区内企业提供“一站式”便捷服务

安居工程三期

Zhaoqing National High-tech industry development Zone has three provincial titles: the key foreign investment-attracting industrial zone, the foreign investment-attracting demonstration zone of mountainous area, the first industrial-transfer demonstration zone. It enjoys prefecture-level economical management right, and prefecture-level administrative approval. It lies in Dawang district, which consists of 98 square kilometers state-owned land.

Zhaoqing National High-tech industry development Zone located in the west of the Pearl River Delta’ s centre the east of Zhaoqing city. It lies within the “economy and life half hour circle of Guangzhou and Foshan”. There is only 50 kilometers from Dawang to Guangzhou, and 40-minutes’ drive from Dawang to Guangzhou Baiyun Airport. There are railways, highways, intercity railways, and waterway transportation leading in all directions.

In recent years, the economy of this area has grown by leaps and bounds extraordinarily. In 2014, the GDP of this region was 20.18 billion Yuan, the industrial output was 77.87 billion Yuan and the public budget revenues was 1.14 billion Yuan. With more than 250 enterprises in production now, it attracts a large number of well-known domestic and foreign enterprises and enjoys four leading industries--the new metal materials，electronic information, biomedicine and advanced equipment manufacturing .

In accordance with the development orientation of modern science and technology industrial city, the people in the district will go all out to seek investment, focus on industry production, make efforts on developing the four leading industries, strive for creating “Second Startup” and hold the lead in Zhaoqing’ s new industrialization.

2014年10月14日，澳雪国际新生产基地暨公司成立20周年庆典

中国轻纺城传统市场区

中国柯桥国际纺织品纺博会

中国轻纺城国际物流中心

中国轻纺城国际贸易区

中国轻纺城

China Textile City

始建于20世纪80年代的中国轻纺城坐落于浙江省绍兴市柯桥区，是全国首家冠名“中国”的专业市场。近年来，中国轻纺城坚持市场与产业、城市联动发展，大力推进“三次创业”，市场的集群化、现代化、国际化水平不断提升。

目前，中国轻纺城以“轻纺城+”核心，在实体市场基础上，大力发展时尚创意、电子商务、现代物流、会展经济、现代金融、文化体育等产业，着力打造国际化、时尚化、智慧型、复合型的国际时尚纺织之都。市场面积已扩展到365万平方米，经营品种4万余种，经营户2.8万，国（境）外常驻代表机构及商业企业1200余家，常驻国（境）外采购商近6000人。市场日客流量10万人次，年成交额突破1200亿元，年出口额近40亿美元，年货运量400余万吨，“网上轻纺城”成交额突破100亿元，销售网络涉及世界187个国家和地区，已成为全球最大的纺织品集散中心。

China Textile City is located in Keqiao District of Shaoxing City, founded in the 1980s, is the first national professional market with “China” as part of its name. In recent years, Keqiao District has insisted on the interactive development of market, industry and city, and vigorously pushed to start a new undertaking, which continuously enhances the level of clustering, modernization and internationalization of the market.

At present, China Textile City to "Textile City+" in the core, on the basis of the real market, vigorously develop the creative fashion, electronic business, modern logistics, convention and exhibition economy, modern finance, culture, sports and other industry, and strive to build internationalization, fashion, smart composite type international fashion and textile. China Textile City covers a market area of over 3.6 million square meters and over 28,000 companies managing over 50,000 kinds of products. There are over 1,200 permanent overseas representative agencies and commercial enterprises and nearly 6,000 overseas permanent purchasers, creating an annual turnover of more than RMB 120 billion and an annual export of nearly USD 4 billion. The turnover of Online China Textile City has reached nearly RMB 10 billion and the annual volume of freight is over 4 million tons. With 100,000 visits to the markets every day, the sales network has covered 187 countries and regions, which has made China Textile City the world’s largest textile distributing center.

中国轻纺城俯瞰图

天津子牙循环经济产业区

天津子牙循环经济产业区是目前中国北方最大的循环经济园区，是国家级经济技术开发区，是中日循环型城市合作项目，先后被批准为“国家循环经济试点园区”、“国家‘城市矿产’示范基地”、“国家循环经济教育示范基地”、“国家新型工业化产业示范基地”、“国家废旧电子信息产品回收拆解处理示范基地”、“国家进口废物‘圈区管理’园区”、“中国国际青少年活动中心（天津）”和“国家循环经济标准化试点园区”。

园区地理位置优越，区位优势明显。园区位于天津市静海县西南部，与河北省大城县、文安县接壤。距天津市区60公里，距北京市区150公里，距天津滨海国际机场60公里，距天津新港90公里，与京沪、京九、京广、天津机场、天津新港形成了立体式、综合化、现代化交通运输网络。

园区产业基础雄厚，“城市矿山”初现。园区现有企业302家，年吞吐能力为150万吨。每年可向市场提供原材料铜45万吨、铝25万吨、钢铁30万吨、橡塑材料30万吨、其他材料20万吨，形成了覆盖全国各地的较大的有色金属原材料市场。

园区基础设施完善，环保设施齐全。水、电、路、通讯等基础设施达到了“九通一平”标准。区内建有大型公用工程岛，统一建设集污水处理、中水回用、雨水收集、废弃物处理等为一体的综合节能环保系统。水资源循环利用率、废弃物无害化处理率、绿色建筑普及率等均达国内先进水平。产业区以“厂在林下、林在厂中”为理念，形成绿林碧水蓝天的园区生态景观。

园区科研体制完善，行业技术领先。园区建有再生资源研究所、院士专家服务中心和循环经济教育培训基地等。围绕发展循环经济、生态环境建设、清洁生产技术、资源综合利用等课题开展科技研发和教育培训，逐步形成了产学研结合一体化、产业管理信息化和规模经济科技化。

园区服务功能高效，投资程序快捷。建有综合管理服务大厦，对各类建设项目实行集中审批、限时办理、一条龙服务，并设有工商、公安、税务、海关、检验检疫等派驻机构，形成了海关、检验检疫、环保、园区“四位一体”的联合监管体制。

园区现代物流畅通，经营环境优良。园区建有“无水港”，专门用于进出口运输的监管车队及再生资源交易所；建有“智慧子牙”信息化中心，以信息化管理、市场化运作，形成了辐射滨海新区乃至环渤海地区的现代化物流网络。

园区总体规划科学，产业布局合理。总体规划面积135平方公里，近期开发建设50平方公里。设有工业区、林下农业循环经济示范区和科研服务居住区。重点发展废旧机电产品拆解加工、废弃电器电子产品处理加工、报废汽车拆解加工、废橡塑再生利用、精深加工再制造和节能环保新能源产业六大产业。现已形成了“静脉串联”、“动脉衔接”、产业间“动态循环”的循环经济发展模式——“子牙模式”。

2014年--韩国世源集团签约仪式

长寿经济技术开发区

长寿经开区地处中国最年轻的直辖市重庆市城市发展新区，比邻长江黄金水道，渝怀、渝利、渝万铁路穿境而过。利用良好的区位优势和资源禀赋，重点发展天然气化工、石油化工、新材料新能源、钢铁冶金、装备制造五大产业。累计引进了德国巴斯夫、英国BP、韩国浦项等世界500强企业在内的知名企业246家，协议引资2483亿元，实际到位资金1280亿元。拥有院士工作站、博士后工作站等科技创新平台。荣获全国循环经济示范园区、国家新型化工业示范基地等多项国家荣誉称号。2014年，实现工业产值700亿元，税收20亿元，到位外资4.04亿美元，进出口额12.4亿美元。

装备制造产业--重庆小康汽车公司

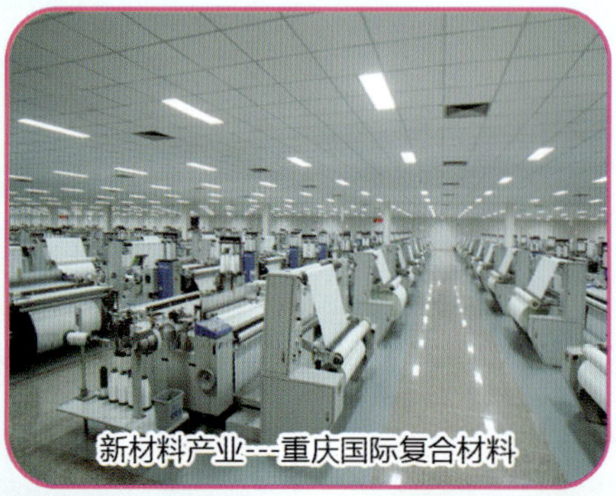

新材料产业---重庆国际复合材料

钢铁冶金产业--重钢集团

2014年--株式会社LG化学签约仪式

化工产业--四川维尼纶厂

团结进取　奋勇拼搏

力争率先成为超千亿元工业园区

—安宁工业园区概况

安宁工业园区是省级重点工业园区，已先后被评为“中国50家投资环境诚信安全区”和“国家级新型工业化（磷、盐化工）产业示范基地”，经济总量连续多年居全省三十个重点工业园区前列，被省委、省政府列为重点打造的“千亿元工业园区”和“国家产业园区”之一。园区规划面积395.26平方公里，建设用地69.78平方公里，已成功引进中石油云南1000万吨/年炼油项目、武钢集团草铺390万吨钢铁项目以及云天化石化项目等一批百亿元以上项目落地，按照“一点一带多组团”规划，形成了以石化、钢铁、磷化工三大支柱产业为主，以装备制造、新材料、新能源、电子信息、生物医药等为重点发展方向的产业规划布局，已发展成为全国少见的集石油、钢铁、磷盐三大产业于一身的园区。

园区紧密结合“桥头堡”建设、滇中产业新区、现代新昆明建设等重大战略部署，紧紧围绕安宁在全省实现“两个率先”的全市目标和　“到十二五末，实现在全省率先建成工业销售收入超千亿元园区”的园区目标，按照“236”工作思路，全力推进招商引资、产业发展和投资环境建设工作，全面实现了园区经济平稳持续健康发展。

园区经济发展呈现出总量不断提升、结构不断优化、环境不断改善的良好态势。2014年，园区内规模以上企业共有87户，新增6户；规模以上工业增加值完成81.25亿元；规模以上工业主营业务收入完成496亿元；工业固定资产投资完成113.49亿元，排名居全省工业园区第一。随着园区招商引资快速推进，将在全省率先成为工业销售收入超千亿元园区。

北京兴谷经济开发区

XIDZ Beijing xing valley economic development zone

北京兴谷经济开发区是北京市政府批准，并通过国家发改委审核的16家市级开发区之一，规划面积10.26平方公里，地处京津冀的交汇处，位于平谷区城区北侧，是城区规划的一部分。京平高速路从开发区南侧经过，距开发区5公里，可以方便到达天津、北京乃至东北、华东等地区，平谷到首都机场40公里、到天津港140公里。

主要产业被定位为汽车零部件、食品、高端设备制造，被列为“全国农产品加工示范基地”、“北京汽车及配套零部件生产基地”，“北京市总部经济发展新区”，2012年底，纳入中关村国家自主创新示范区，成为中关村国家自主创新示范区平谷园的主要区域，享受北京市总部经济各项政策、中关村各项优惠政策及配套政策措施。

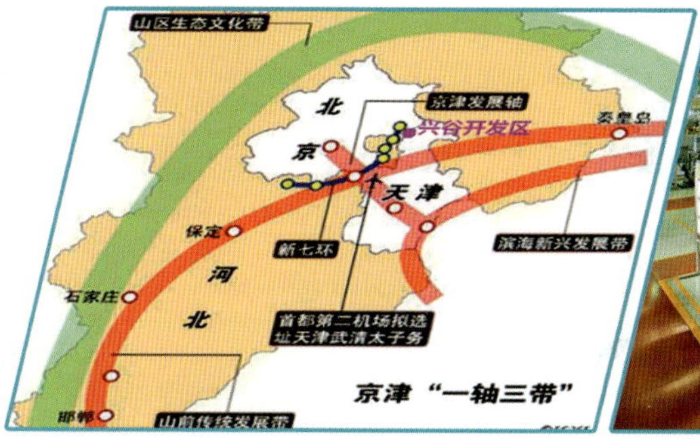

兴谷开发区以打造“华北最大的饮食品工业基地”和“北京现代汽车配件基地”为招商方向，规划建设韩资企业园和食品工业园，已形成产业集群，吸引了星宇车、日进、和信、旺旺集团、千喜鹤、老才臣等一批知名企业入区，投资60多亿元。2014年兴谷开发区完成产值180亿元，占平谷区工业产值的72%，预计到2020年，将成为年销售收入300亿、人口规模10万人的现代化工业新城。2014年经济总量在全市16个市级开发区中名列前茅。

北京兴谷经济开发区具有以下比较优势：

一、平谷设有海关，方便企业办理各种通关手续，降低货物进出口的成本。平谷海关分管顺义、密云等区县的进出口业务。

二、平谷建有公共保税仓库和物流中心，可以提高通关效率，加快进出口速度。

三、平谷有丰富地下水资源，可充分满足企业的生产建设需要。

四、有专为饮食品企业配套的“饮食品工业园”，政策优惠、服务周到。

五、土地、厂房等资源丰富且价格较低，发展空间大。

老才臣 LAOCAICHEN

QIANXIHE 千喜鹤

北京市平谷区平谷北街15号　邮政编码：101200

电话：（010）69959702　69959703

传真：（010）69959702　69959703

网址：www .xidz.com　E- mail：xidz@xidz.com

西安国际港务区
获批国家电子商务示范基地

根据《关于确认第二批国家电子商务示范基地的通知》，西安国际港务区获批国家电子商务示范基地。西安国际港务区将以创建国家电子商务示范基地为契机，大力推进电子商务产业发展，打造特色鲜明、企业云集、环境优越的电子商务产业高地。

西安国际港务区是陕西省委省政府、西安市委市政府为发展外向型经济，调整产业结构，打造内陆改革开放新高地而设立的开放型经济先导区，被写入国家“一带一路”战略规划。在有效利用园区现有的港口、物流、通道及信息等平台功能的基础上，西安国际港务区积极运用互联网思维打造区域性商贸物流集散中心，明确将电子商务产业作为园区未来发展的主导产业。

依据西安综合保税区、西安铁路集装箱中心站及“长安号”、“西安港”、一类口岸等立体物流平台和通道，西安国际港务区为电商企业构建完善的物流贸易链条、拓展国际国内市场提供了极大的便利，为园区打造电商产业高地奠定了基础，并已吸引了一大批龙头电商企业入驻，成为“丝路经济带”上电商产业聚集新高地。截至 2014 年底，西安国际港务区已入驻电子商务及配套类企业 260 多家，其中电子商务交易及技术服务类企业 42家，从业人员5000余人；网络技术服务商20家，从业人员800余人；物流配送企业50家，从业人员1000余人；配套企业 131 家，从业人员 2500 余人。

西安铁路集装箱中心站

内陆崛起“西安港”

西安跨境电商平台——洋货码头

作为电商发展的标志性平台，西安国际港务区开展的跨境贸易电子商务服务试点“洋货码头”已经实现了常态化运营，日进出口业务量突破 10000 单；阿里巴巴、京东、国美、卡行天下、百利威、新加坡辉联集团和本地企业陕西利安等二十多家国内外知名电商及配套企业入驻园区；积极引导企业建设中小电商创业孵化平台，新丝路电商产业园已经开园，中西部大宗商品电子商务平台正式落户园区。同时，西安国际港务区还鼓励已经入驻的传统服务业企业大力发展电子商务，与实体经济高度融合发展，西安华南城、陕西医药控股集团派昂医药有限责任公司、西安爱菊粮油集团等入区企业均已开展了电子商务的有效实践。

西安国际港务区将紧抓获批国家电子商务示范基地的契机，充分发挥国家电子商务示范基地和跨境贸易电子商务试点的作用，促进传统产业与电子商务深度融合，通过模式创新、管理创新和技术创新，形成平台齐全、运行高效、领域广泛、重点突出的电子商务产业发展格局，形成完整的电子商务产业发展链条。到 2017 年末，力争实现电子商务年交易额突破 1000 亿元，其中西安跨境电子商务交易额超过 1 亿元，电子商务企业达到 2000 家，推动西安乃至陕西逐步成为西部以至全国领先的电子商务产业高地。

中国（青海）藏毯国际展览会

China (Qinghai) International Carpet Exhibition

“中国（青海）藏毯国际展览会”由商务部、青海省人民政府共同主办。“2015中国（青海）藏毯国际展览会”得到了国家相关部委、兄弟省市区商务部门和相关企业的大力支持，中国纺织工业联合会副会长兼秘书长高勇、中国食品土畜进出口商会会长边振瑚、中国家用纺织品行业协会杨兆华等国家商协会领导来青参会。“一带一路”沿线国家土库曼斯坦、白俄罗斯的驻华大使，吉尔吉斯坦国家议员，巴基斯坦旁遮普省商工投资部长，塔吉克斯坦驻华使馆参赞等驻华使节和政府官员出席了展会相关活动。

“2015中国（青海）藏毯国际展览会”在青海国际会展中心进行，总面积30000平方米，共设国际标准展位957个。展示交易展品为国内外各类手工地毯、机织地毯、艺术挂毯、有机地毯、原辅材料，国内外参展货物总量达230吨，创历届之最。

来自伊朗、尼泊尔、土耳其、德国等十三个国家的128家地毯生产企业参展，来自德国、瑞典、法国等五个国家的22家采购商、经销商到会采购。国内有新疆山东、江苏、广东等十三个省区市的137家企业参展。参展和参会的国内外客商总数超过6100人。

展会现货交易合同订单和意向签约额近1.5亿美元，现货交易总额达到7900万美元。通过电子商务平台运行的“网上藏毯展”，网上交易额达60.5万元，实现了零的突破。

在“2014藏毯展”荣获年度“中国会展行业十佳优秀特色展会”大奖的基础上，“2015藏毯展”积极申报争取国际UFI认证（世界展览业质量品牌唯一全球认证），着力在开拓创新上再下工夫，在拓展展会功能上再求延伸，充分发挥自身区域特色优势和国际专业展会本质特性，积极争创国际展览业知名品牌。

The “China (Qinghai) International Carpet Exhibition” is cosponsored by Chinese Ministry of Commerce and the People's Government of Qinghai Province. The “2015 China (Qinghai) International Carpet Exhibition” has received strong support from relevant national ministries and commissions, commercial departments and relevant enterprises, Mr. Gao Yong, the Vice Chairman and Deputy Secretary General of China National Textile and Apparel Council, Mr. Bian Zhenhu, Chairman of China Chamber of Commerce of Foodstuffs and Native Produce, Mr. Yang Zhaohua, Chairman of China Home Textile Association and some other leaders of national associations has come to Qinghai to attend the Exhibition. Ambassadors and government officials of countries along the “Belt and Road” including Turkmenistan Ambassador to China, Belorussian Ambassador to China, Kyrgyzstan Senator, Pakistan Punjab provincial Minister of commerce and investment and Counselor of Tajikistan Embassy in China has attended relevant activities of the Exhibition.

The “2015 China (Qinghai) International Carpet Exhibition” was held in Qinghai International Conference and Exhibition Center, a total area of 30,000 square meters, 957 international standard booths. Exhibits include various domestic and foreign hand-made and machine-made carpets, artistic tapestries, organic carpets and raw & auxiliary materials, domestic and foreign exhibits totaled 230 tons, which is the greatest in the history.

13 countries (including Iran, Nepal, Turkey and Germany), 128 carpet manufacturers participated in the Exhibition. 22 dealers and purchasers from 5 countries including Germany, Sweden and France came to the Exhibition to purchase. 137 domestic enterprises from 13 provinces such as Xinjiang, Shandong, Jiangsu, Guangdong, etc., took part in the Exhibition. More than 6,100 merchants attended the Exhibition.

The Exhibition spot trading contract orders and intention contracts amounted to nearly 150 million US dollars, spot transactions totaled 79 million US dollars, The “Online Carpet Exhibition” running on the E-commerce platform has achieved online transactions of 605000 Chinese Yuan, fulfilled the zero breakthrough.

On the basis of The “2014 China (Qinghai) International Carpet Exhibition” won the “Top Ten Outstanding Characteristic Exhibition of China Convention and Exhibition Industry”, The “2015 China (Qinghai) International Carpet Exhibition” is active in applying for the only global exhibition industry quality brand authentification--UFI Authentification, putting forth effort on exploration and innovation, extending the exhibition function, giving full play to regional characteristic advantage and essential properties of international professional exhibition, actively strive for international exhibition industries well-known brand.

CHINA SOUTH ASIA EXPO
KUNMING IMPORT&EXPORT FAIR

3rd CHINA-SOUTH ASIA EXPO
第 3 届 中 国 - 南 亚 博 览 会

23rd CHINA KUNMING IMPORT & EXPORT FAIR
第23届中国昆明进出口商品交易会

中国—南亚博览会（简称“南博会”）是一个综合性国际博览会，由中国商务部和云南省人民政府主办，并邀请南亚各国商务部门联合举办。南博会的前身是业已举办5届的南亚国家商品展。为适应形势发展，进一步加强中国与南亚国家互利合作，2012年10月被批准升格为中国—南亚博览会，自2013年起在中国昆明举办。

2015年6月12日，第3届中国—南亚博览会暨第23届中国昆明进出口商品交易会开幕。来自31个国家2个地区的70位正副部长、省市长，2个国际组织的代表，8位驻华大使，17位总领事，以及国家相关部委和27个省市区领导，18家央企、100余家民企、10余个金融机构负责人共2000多名贵宾出席了开幕式。

第3届南博会和第23届昆交会累计成交251.9亿美元，同比增长19.8%；外贸签约和成交完成126.1亿美元，同比增长8.6%（出口70.9亿美元，进口55.2亿美元）；利用外资95.8亿美元，同比增长5.5%；外经签约项目12个，合同金额26.97亿美元，同比增长569.2%；签订外来投资项目903个，签约金额7850亿元人民币，同比增长10.8%（内资项目815个，签约金额7256亿元人民币，外资项目88个，协议外资95.8亿美元）。签约项目涵盖旅游、能源开发、基础设施、商贸、教育、环保、现代物流等领域。

China-South Asia Exposition (“China-South Asia Expo” in short), which features a comprehensive international exposition authorized by the State Council of China, is jointly hosted by the Ministry of Commerce of China and the People’s Government of Yunnan Province, while commercial administrations of the South Asian countries are invited to serve as co-hosts. The former body of China-South Asia Expo was the Commodities Exhibition of the South Asian Countries that had been held for 5 sessions. To adapt to development of the times and further deepen the mutually beneficial cooperation among China and the South Asian countries, the State Council of China approved in October 2012 to upgrade the Commodities Exhibition of the South Asian Countries to China-South Asia Exposition, which would be held in Kunming of China from 2013 onwards.

On June 12, 2015, over 2,000 distinguished guests attended the opening ceremony, including 70 ministerial officials from 31 countries and 2 regions, representatives of 2 international organizations, 8 Ambassadors of foreign countries to China, 17 Consuls-General, leaders of related Chinese ministries, commissions and China’s 27 provinces and municipalities, domestic leaders of 18 centrally-administered SOEs, 100-plus private enterprises and 10-plus banking institutions.

The 3rd China-South Asia Expo and the 23rd China Kunming Import and Export Commodities Fair yielded turnover of foreign trade totaling USD 25.19 billion, a 19.8% increase on year-on-year basis. The gross volume of contractual trade and turnover reached USD 12.61 billion, an 8.6% year-on-year increase, which included USD 7.09 billion in exports and USD 5.52 billion in imports. The gross volume of utilized foreign investment amounted to USD 9.58 billion, a 5.5% year-on-year increase. 12 foreign economic cooperation projects were signed, with contractual value of USD 2.697 billion, a 569.2% year-on-year increase. 903 exterior-investment projects were signed, which yielded gross contractual value of RMB 785 billion and a 10.8% year-on-year increase, including 815 domestic-investment projects with total contractual value of RMB 725.6 billion and 88 foreign-investment projects with total contractual value of USD 9.58 billion. The contracted projects involved extensive fields such as tourism, energy, infrastructure facilities, trade, education, environmental protection, modern logistics and so on.

云南国际博览事务局
YUNNAN INTERNATIONAL EXPOSITIONS BUREAU

南京
农副产品物流配送中心

南京农副产品物流配送中心是省市重点打造的国家级特大型“菜篮子”工程。中心按照“南京唯一、全国一流”定位，以及“业态先进、管理规范、产品安全、运行高效”标准规划设计，占地3000亩，总建筑面积 150 多万平方米，分设农产品交易展示、冷藏物流配送、综合商务三大功能区。项目于2007年11月开工建设，2009年5月，建筑面积52万平方米的一期项目建成运营，内设蔬菜、果品、水产、肉类、副食品、粮油六大专业市场。2010年，实现交易额158亿，2015年交易额达420.7亿元，连续三年位居全国前列，实现了经济效益和社会效益双提升。作为华东地区有影响的大型农副产品综合市场，南京农副产品物流配送中心已发展成为覆盖南京、辐射周边农产品唯一的源头集散市场，中小超市、宾馆酒店、集团购买的配货配载中心，引领全国农副产品批发市场整合改造、提档升级和打造公益市场的示范工程。被列入国家农副产品批发市场重点扶持项目、国家双百市场、全国“三绿工程”示范市场、农业部定点市场、国家农业产业化重点龙头企业、全国十强市场、全国最具竞争力市场和国家级公益性农产品批发市场建设试点单位，并荣获省农业产业化重点龙头企业、省重点物流基地、省农业龙头企业“五个一”先进企业、省现代服务业集聚区等荣誉。

在建设发展中，中心按照“稳定、平衡、发展”的工作思路，以“建设智慧众彩、发展平台经济”为核心，积极探索新型交易方式，加快市场信息网络建设，充分利用子信息平台，加大无形市场培育力度，大力发展物流配送和电子商务，其自主研发的O2O宜鲜美城市生鲜配送平台和B2B“众彩行”电子商务平台，在行业内起到了引领作用，受到国家商务部高度关注并在全国进行推广，被列入“全省农产品社区直配点建设示范工程”、“南京市为民办实事十大民生工程”。同时，积极探索发展期货贸易等新型业态，进一步推动交易方式的转型升级，努力实现管理一流、规模一流、队伍一流、效益一流，加快建设“长三角”地区菜篮子中心、华东地区业态先进的农副产品集散中心、中国乃至亚洲有影响的物流配送中心。

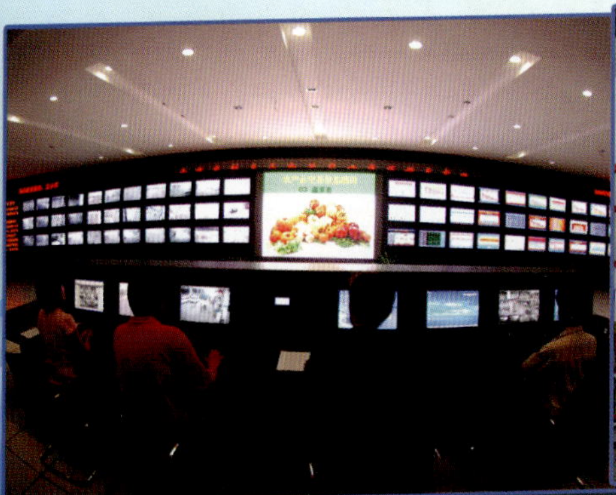

富士康淮安科技城

创业新高地

辉映软件园

鸟瞰台玻

综合保税区

淮安经济技术开发区

淮安经济技术开发区成立于1992年，1993年获批为省级开发区，2010年获批为国家经济技术开发区，常住人口30万人，管辖面积166平方公里。近年来，淮安经济技术开发区始终坚持走产业兴区之路，吸引了日韩、港台、欧美等近30个国家和地区的客商来区投资兴业，先后引进了富士康、台玻、明基达方、膳魔师、华达利、敏实汽车零部件项目等一批世界500强企业或品牌项目，累计进区企业达6000余家，其中台资企业400多家，成为江苏长江以北知名台资高地，综合排名跃居江苏省开发区第一板块。同时，区内还拥有国家综合保税区、国家淮安留学人员创业园、国家科技企业孵化器淮安软件园、国家大学科技园、空港产业园等一批特色功能区，以及日资、欧美、韩资三大国别工业园区，功能园区数量苏北领先。

当前，淮安经济技术开发区正按照“勇当跨越发展标兵，建好对外开放门户”的目标定位，致力于打造优势产业、完善载体功能、提升国际化水平，全面构建最具发展活力、发展潜力和发展竞争力的开发区。

Huaian Economic and Technological Development Zone was established in 1992, 1993 approved as a provincial level development zone, approved in 2010 for the state-level economic and Technological Development Zone, the resident population of 30 million people, the area under the jurisdiction of 166 square kilometers. In recent years, Huaian Economic and Technological Development Zone always adhere to the industry Hing Road, attract the South Korea, Hong Kong and Taiwan, Europe and the United States nearly 30 countries and regions of the businessmen to invest here, has been the introduction of Foxconn, Taibo, BenQ of party, thermos, HTL, minth Auto parts project etc. a number of world top 500 enterprise or brand project, a total of enterprises in the area of more than 6,000, of which more than 400 Taiwan funded enterprises, become Jiangsu Yangtze River to the north of the famous Taiwan funded high, ranking leapt to the first plate of development zones in Jiangsu Province. At the same time, the district also has national comprehensive bonded zone, national Huaian study abroad personnel business park, national level science and technology business incubator Huaian Software Park, national level university science and Technology Park, Airport Industrial Park a number of features and functions of the District, and Japanese, Europe and the United States, South Korea three countries industrial park, the park features a number of Northern Jiangsu lead.

At present, Huaian Economic and Technological Development Zone is in accordance with the “Yong when span development pacesetter, built the target of door opening to the outside world”, dominant industry is committed to creating, vector function to improve and upgrade the level of internationalization, to build a comprehensive the most vitality and development potential and competitiveness of the development zone.

企业服务中心

发挥“两沿三区”优势

打造广西“两个建成”先行区

中国西部第一大港

防城港市市区航拍

中国第三大陆路口岸
东兴口岸

防城港市是中国仅有的两个沿边与沿海交汇的城市之一，总面积6222平方公里，总人口约100万人。作为21世纪“海上丝绸之路”的重要始发港、中国—东盟自贸区的主门户、广西北部湾经济区的核心城市，防城港市在国家建设“一带一路”等重大战略中具有特殊的地位。

——中国唯一与东盟海陆相连的门户城市。防城港市拥有4个国家级口岸，其中东兴口岸是我国陆路边境第一大口岸、沿海主要出入境口岸之一；拥有西部第一大港，与170多个国家和地区的250多个港口通航贸易，是西南、中南地区最便捷的出海通道，2012年跨入亿吨大港行列，即将打造成为中国—东盟区域性国际航运枢纽和港口物流中心。

——中国最具潜力的沿边经济特区。目前，正加快建设东兴国家重点开发开放试验区、中越东兴—芒街跨境经济合作区、沿边金融改革试验区，实施个人跨境贸易人民币结算、进境种苗（景观树）指定口岸、全国首批入境粮食指定口岸、边境旅游异地办证等多项先行先试政策，建有全国规模最大、功能最全的互市贸易区，2015年互市贸易进出口成交额达220亿元。

——北部湾经济区的新兴港口工业城市。拥有580公里海岸线，腹地广阔，环境容量大，是发展大型临港产业的理想之地。已形成钢铁、有色金属、粮油食品、能源、石化、装备制造等一批千百亿元产业，建成中国第一大植物油籽加工基地和磷酸出口加工基地，并有望成为世界最大镍产品加工基地。

——北部湾畔唯一的全海景生态海湾城市。拥有世界唯一的金花茶自然保护区，是世界三大海湾红树林示范区之一，也是中国沿海最干净的海域之一。广西最大的半岛——江山半岛，可同时供20万人滨海活动，有“东方夏威夷”美誉；有氧都之称的十万山森林地区原始热带雨林，负氧离子含量高达每立方厘米8.9万个，是休闲养生的理想之地，已形成“上山下海又出国”的独特旅游品牌。

“十二五”期间，全市经济保持了平稳较快增长。2015年GDP达620亿元，人均GDP广西第一。五年累计完成规上工业总产值4799.8亿元，年均增长22.4%；完成港口建设投入124.2亿元，成为中国西部首个亿吨大港。南防高铁开通，高速公路县县通，全市形成了一小时经济圈。城镇化水平达到55%，环境空气质量优良率达94.2%，政府治理能力广西第一，先后获得全国宜居城市竞争力50强、中国避寒旅游城市等称号。对外开放合作取得新突破。一批先行先试政策落地，东兴试验区、跨境合作区等开放平台也在加快推进。

“城在海中、海在城中”的防城港市

张家口经济开发区

Zhangjiakou Economic Development Area

张家口经济开发区设立于1992年，是张家口市第一个由设区市直接管理的省级经济技术开发区。区域面积125平方公里，辖三镇两街，共34个行政村、1个农场、14个社区居委会，人口22万。

张家口经济开发区位于京、冀、晋、蒙四省市交界区域中心区，地处北京上风上水。交通发达，区位优越。距首都北京180公里，京张高铁已经批复动工，到北京的车程将由2小时缩短至40分钟；京包、京张、大秦铁路和京张、张石等高速公路穿境而过，19条国省干道交汇，机场已通航上海、深圳、沈阳、石家庄等特大城市。生态优美，环境宜人。打造了5000亩湿地森林公园和13.8公里的滨河绿廊，全面扩张“城市绿肺”，城市绿化覆盖率达49.41%，人均公共绿地15.39平方米，在长江以北空气质量综合指数排名第一。功能完善，配套齐全。海关、商检、金融、学校、医院、酒店、市场、商住和楼宇等配套完善，形成了“一刻钟公共服务圈”，现代化新城区建设步伐和城市化进程进一步加快。产业勃兴、发展强劲。培育的“新型工业、金融服务、商贸物流、电子信息、总部经济、文化旅游”六大主导产业初显成效。重点打造了洋河高科园、现代产业园、流平寺新型工业园等多个产业园区，形成“一区多园”的产业城市联动发展新格局。机遇叠加、潜力无限。京张联合申奥已经有了实质性进展，经开区作为京张高铁站的坐落点，将成为联接北京与崇礼的中转站和交通枢纽，将是各类配套服务项目的首选地。在京津冀一体化协同发展中，经开区处于张家口对外开放最前沿，承接北京产业转移近水楼台、得天独厚，将是直接受益、借力提升的重要战略据点。

财富中心

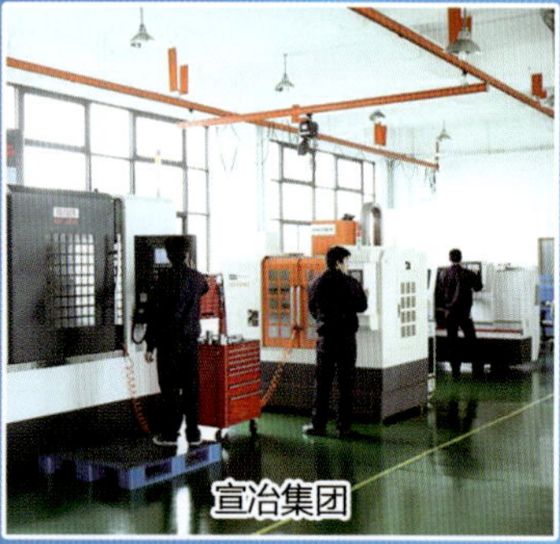
宣冶集团

智慧云谷

图书馆、档案馆、城市博物馆

Zhangjiakou Economic Development Area, which was established by the provincial government in 1992 and managed directly by the city government, is the first provincial-level economic and technological development zone in Zhangjiakou. There is 125 square kilometers in the Economic Development Area, which is divided into 3 towns and 2 streets, 34 administrative villages, 1 farm and 14 communities. The population is 220,000.

Zhangjiakou Economic Development Area, with its developed traffic condition and superior site, is located at the junction of city centers in four provinces/cities--Beijing, Hebei, Shanxi and Mongolia. Distance to the capital city--Beijing is 180 kilometers. It takes two hours' drive, which will shorten to 40 minutes because the Beijing-Zhangjiakou express railway has been approved to construct; Both Beijing-Baotou, Beijing-Zhangjiakou, Datong-Qinhuangdao railways and Beijing-Zhangjiakou, Zhangjiakou-Shijiazhuang and other highways cross through the territory, while 19 national and provincial roads converge here. Because airport has come into use, directly accessing to Shanghai, Shenzhen, Shenyang, Shijiazhuang and other large cities are actualized. Besides, the ecology and environment condition is pleasant. Specifically, in order to achieve goal of full expansion of "City's Green Lung" scheme, 5000 acres of wetland forest park and 13.8 km long riverfront green corridor are built, thus the urban green coverage rate has reached 49.41% and the per capita